MARKETING

MARKETING
CONCEPTS AND STRATEGIES

Third European Edition

Sally Dibb
University of Warwick

Lyndon Simkin
University of Warwick

William M. Pride
Texas A & M University

O. C. Ferrell
University of Memphis

HOUGHTON MIFFLIN   BOSTON   NEW YORK

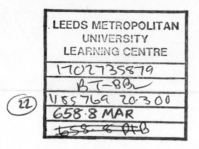
Sponsoring Editor: Jennifer B. Speer
Senior Associate Editor: Susan M. Kahn
Senior Project Editor: Margaret M. Kearney
Senior Production/Design Coordinator: Jill Haber
Senior Manufacturing Coordinator: Florence Cadran
Marketing Manager: Michael B. Mercier

Cover Design: Chroma Design

Credits for chapter-opening photos: Ch. 1, p. 4, Bob Crandall/Stock Boston. Ch. 2, p. 32, Tony Freeman/Photo Edit. Ch. 3, p. 66, S. Ruet/Sygma. Ch. 5, p. 134, Courtesy of SKF Limited. Ch. 6, p. 164, Christopher Bissell/Tony Stone Images. Ch. 8, p. 241, Barbara Alper/Stock Boston. Ch. 9, p. 263, Tony Freeman/Photo Edit. Ch. 10, p. 288, Crawford/Gamma Liaison. Ch. 12, p. 341, Courtesy of BP and Mobil. Ch. 14, p. 391, Jeff Greenberg/The Picture Cube. Ch. 15, p. 429, David Stimson/Stock Boston. Ch. 16, p. 456, David Stimson/Stock Boston. Ch. 17, p. 482, Gamma Liaison. Ch. 18, p. 522, Courtesy of Tesco. Ch. 19, p. 560, R. Lucas/The Image Works. Ch. 20, p. 582, Farnsworth/The Image Works. Ch. 22, p. 648, Steve Benbow/Stock Boston. Ch. 23, p. 678, Rhoda Sidney/Stock Boston. Ch. 25, p. 739, Courtesy of Schotts.

ISBN: 0-395-79005-0

23456789-DOW-01 00 99 98

BRIEF CONTENTS

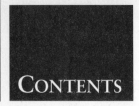

CONTENTS

Note: Each contains a Summary, a list of Important Terms, Discussion and Review Questions, and Recommended Readings.

Marketing affects everyone: we are all consumers. Most businesses depend on marketing to provide an understanding of the marketplace and to ensure that their products and services satisfy the needs of customers. There is little doubt that marketing is an important facet of today's society and commerce. In the majority of business schools and colleges in the UK, Eire, Benelux and Scandinavia, *Marketing: Concepts and Strategies* is used to introduce students to the nature and scope of marketing. The first edition of *Marketing: Concepts and Strategies* appeared in 1991. Since then, this text has become the leader in its market. Whether for undergraduates seeking a comprehensive introduction to marketing, MBA candidates requiring a grounding in marketing analysis or marketing management, or students in colleges wishing to pass degrees and diplomas, *Marketing: Concepts and Strategies* is used by lecturers and teaching staff to provide an accessible, topical and enlightening insight into the world of marketing. *Marketing: Concepts and Strategies* is also recommended by the Chartered Institute of Marketing and the Irish Marketing Institute.

The Authors

Sally Dibb and Lyndon Simkin have been at the UK's top ranked university management centre, Warwick Business School, since the mid-1980s, teaching undergraduates, MBA candidates—full time, part time and distance learning—and executives the basics of marketing, advanced strategic marketing, buyer behaviour, marketing communications and marketing research. Sally's and Lyndon's research focuses on services marketing, market segmentation, marketing planning, retail modelling, marketing communications and teaching methods—areas in which they have published extensively in the academic journals in the UK and USA. In addition to being joint authors of *Marketing: Concepts and Strategies*, Sally and Lyndon produced the innovative *Marketing Casebook: Cases and Concepts* (Routledge) in 1994, which mixes real-world cases with overviews of theory, and *The Market Segmentation Workbook* and *The Marketing Planning Workbook* (both International Thomson Business Press) in 1996, which help marketing practitioners re-assess their target markets and understand the complexities of marketing planning. These workbooks are based on the authors' consultancy experiences with organisations as diverse as Andersen Consulting, DRA (MoD), Forte, ICI, JCB, McDonald's, Standard Chartered, Tesco and Zeneca.

Bill Pride and O.C. Ferrell first teamed up to produce *Marketing* for Houghton Mifflin in 1977. Since then, the American sister of *Marketing: Concepts and Strategies*, now in its tenth edition, has been used by more than one million students and has become one of the principal marketing texts in the United States. O.C. is Distinguished Professor of Marketing and Business Ethics at the University of Memphis, where he has also been dean, and in 1997 he is the president of the Academic Council for the prestigious American Marketing Association (AMA). O.C. chaired committees that developed the AMA Code of Ethics and AMA Code for Marketing on the Internet. He is the author of many texts, including *Management: Comprehension, Analysis and Application* (Austen Press), *Strategic Marketing Management* (South-Western), *Business Ethics* (Houghton Mifflin) and *Business: A Changing World* (Irwin). Bill Pride is Professor of Marketing at Texas A&M University, where he specialises in marketing communications, strategic marketing planning and business marketing education. As with O.C., Bill has published articles in many journals and is widely recognised in the marketing field. Bill is also co-author of *Business* (Houghton Mifflin).

Changes for the Third Edition

Marketing is a quickly evolving discipline in a rapidly changing world. A while ago, peace in Ireland seemed a real possibility, and businesses previously deterred by acts of violence sought to establish operations in a newly emerging marketplace. A market once perceived as unattractive by many organisations was seen in a new light. Such "external" forces affecting the attractiveness of markets are not unusual to marketers, and they do not result only from the violence in the former Yugoslavia or the Gulf. Only a decade ago, the Berlin Wall stood as a very real barrier to trade between Western and Eastern Europe: today, the markets in the former Eastern Bloc are a major opportunity for many businesses. A few years ago, German households sorting their rubbish into separate containers depending on the recyclability of their trash seemed quirky to many observers. Now, with the "greening" consumer, most businesses must be environmentally aware. The Internet is no longer the preserve only of computer buffs, with increasing numbers of households using the "net" to purchase goods. In such a fast-moving world, it is essential to keep abreast of developments. This is particularly true in marketing. After all, in most businesses, it is the responsibility of the marketers to make their colleagues aware of trends in the marketplace, the actions of competitors and perpetually changing customer requirements.

The third edition of *Marketing: Concepts and Strategies* strives to explain the nature of marketing and the importance of understanding the complexities of the marketplace. In so doing, the intention as ever is for the text to be easy to read, informative, interesting and topical. To this end, there has been a restructuring of the twenty-five chapters into eight parts. Each part has improved scene-setting and postscripts to explain the interrelationships of the many concepts and strategies introduced. The parts, described below, follow a logical structure based on the premise that for effective marketing there must first be analysis of the marketplace, then the recommendation of a marketing strategy and finally the production of marketing mix programmes with control processes that facilitate implementation of the desired strategy.

Part I: Marketing Defined—An introduction to the nature and scope of marketing, the composition of the marketing environment and the importance of global marketing

Part II: Understanding and Targeting Markets—Consumer and business-to-business buying behaviour, marketing research and the principal task in developing a marketing strategy: target market selection

Part III: Product, Branding, Packaging and Service Decisions—The first ingredients of the marketing mix, product and people decisions

Part IV: Place (Distribution and Channel) Decisions—The nature of marketing channels in the marketing mix and the key participating players

Part V: Promotion Decisions—The use of advertising, publicity and public relations, sponsorship, personal selling, sales promotion and direct mail in marketing communications

Part VI: Pricing Decisions—The concepts of price and value, setting price and determining pricing policies

Part VII: Manipulating the Marketing Mix—Adapting the marketing mix for business-to-business, services and global markets

Part VIII: Marketing Management—Strategic marketing and competitive strategy, marketing planning and sales forecasting, implementing strategies and measuring performance, ethics and social responsibility in modern marketing.

In addition, every chapter has been up-dated in terms of the current research and thinking in the area as well as in terms of the latest statistics and industry figures, where relevant. Each chapter has also been up-dated to reflect the views of leading academics and practitioners who have kindly reviewed the chapters, provided thought-provoking quotes and suggested the key readings in their area of expertise as additional references. The principal aim of *Marketing: Concepts and Strategies* has always been to provide a book that students find easy to use and that reflects accurately the current thinking in the world of marketing. There have been extensive changes to the third edition, but they are to reflect students' needs, suggestions by peers and the current developments in marketing as identified by practitioners, the journals and at conferences. In summary, the improvements for the third edition include:

- more extensive cross-referencing between chapters and parts, with more thorough part openers and new part postscripts, utilising schematics to indicate progress.
- the inclusion in each chapter of the views of leading "gurus" and recommended additional readings.
- new chapter opening vignettes, Marketing Insights illustrating current developments and end-of-chapter cases for discussion.
- a new appendix that presents longer strategic marketing cases and guidance on using cases for studying.
- concepts of internal marketing, total quality management (TQM), relationship marketing and implementation of marketing strategies.
- more balanced coverage of the issues relating to marketing in consumer, services and business-to-business markets.
- a new chapter that examines how the marketing mix must be manipulated differently for consumer, business-to-business, services and global markets.
- a stronger explanation of marketing strategy and the role of competition.
- current industry/market statistics and figures for the EU as it now stands.
- appendices covering revision tips for examinations and an overview of career opportunities in marketing.

As ever, *Marketing: Concepts and Strategies* is supported by comprehensive indexing, a running glossary of key terms—that now appears in the margins of the relevant chapters—questions for discussion and a full listing of the key terms and jargon detailed chapter by chapter. For tutors, there is a full ancillary pack including transparencies, software, a tutor's manual and videos.

The views of student users and fellow academics have guided changes for this third edition. These modifications have been made to improve *Marketing: Concepts and Strategies*, to up-rate its usability and to reflect how the discipline of marketing is evolving. Current adopters of *Marketing: Concepts and Strategies* should find little difficulty in incorporating the new look of this text in their teaching. New readers should find that *Marketing: Concepts and Strategies* is even more accessible and topical.

Acknowledgments

This text would not have happened without the comments and enthusiasm of past and current students, support from colleagues, and specifically the advice from:

Colin Egan, *Leicester De Montfort University*
Peter Jackson, *Adsearch, Richmond-Upon-Thames*
Hans Kasper, *Rijksuniversiteit Limburg, Maastricht*
John Wringe, *Cogent, Meriden*

And also to Pat Ibbotson and Miriam Catterall, both of *University of Ulster,* for their assistance with the support package.

We are also indebted to those who generously contributed chapter opening quotes and recommended readings in their areas of expertise:

Michael Baker, *University of Strathclyde*

Elaine O'Brien, *University of Strathclyde*

Colin Egan, *Leicester De Montfort University*

Gordon Foxall, *University of Birmingham*

David Ford, *University of Bath*

David Birks, *University of Bath*

Susan Hart, *University of Stirling*

Peter Doyle, *Warwick Business School*

Michael Thomas, *University of Strathclyde*

Hans Kasper, *Rijksuniversiteit Limburg, Maastricht*

David Shipley, *Trinity College/University of Dublin*

John Fernie, *University of Abertay, Dundee*

Peter J. McGoldrick, *Manchester Business School*

Martin Christopher, *Cranfield University School of Management*

Peter De Pelsmacker, *University of Antwerp*

Norman Hart, *CIM/Hart, Inc.*

Antonis Simintiras, *The Open University*

Peter Leeflang, *Rijksuniveriteit Groningen*

Eric Waarts, *Erasmus University, Rotterdam*

Constantine Katsikeas, *Cardiff Business School*

Robin Wensley, *Warwick Business School*

Malcolm McDonald, *Cranfield University School of Management*

Nigel Piercy, *Cardiff Business School*

O.C. Ferrell, *University of Memphis*

A number of individuals have made many helpful comments and recommendations in their reviews of this edition. We appreciate the inestimable help of these reviewers:

David Arnott, *Warwick Business School*

Stewart Arnold, *University of Hull*

Derrick Chong, *Royal Holloway University of London*

David Crick, *University of Leicester*

Leslie de Chernatony, *The Open University*

Aidan Daly, *University of Galway*

Deane Ford, *American University of Cairo*

Andrea Frame, *University of Central England*

Audrey Gilmore, *University of Ulster at Jordanstown*

Phil Harris, *Manchester Metropolitan University*

Andrew Inglis, *London Guildhall University*

Colin Jenkins, *Nene College*

David Jobber, *University of Bradford Management Centre*

David Marshall, *University of Edinburgh*

Vincent W. Mitchell, *UMIST*

Sandra Mohabir-Collins, *University of Paisley*

Elaine O'Brien, *University of Strathclyde*

Daragh O'Reilly, *University of Bradford*

John Saunders, *University of Loughborough Business School*

Viv Shaw, *Warwick Business School*

Antonis Simintiras, *The Open University*

Robert Grafton Small, *University of St. Andrews*

Dominic Wilson, *UMIST*

Sally Dibb
Lyndon Simkin
William M. Pride
O. C. Ferrell

I MARKETING DEFINED

Marketing consists of individual and organisational activities that facilitate and expedite satisfying exchange relationships in a dynamic environment through the creation, distribution, promotion and pricing of goods, services and ideas. The simple premise of marketing is that to be successful, any organisation must understand its customers' requirements and satisfy them in a manner that gives the organisation an edge over its competitors. This involves offering the "right" mix of product, people, service, pricing, promotion and distribution channel. Marketing also depends on constant up-dating of ideas. Customers are often surprisingly fickle and modify their needs and wants, rivals alter their strategies and forces in the marketplace regularly change.

Part I of Marketing: Concepts and Strategies introduces the concept of marketing and explores its nature and scope.

Chapter 1, "An Overview of the Marketing Concept", defines marketing; establishes its importance to business organisations and to consumers; outlines the major components of marketing strategy—notably marketing opportunity analysis, target market selection and the development of marketing mix programmes that implement the marketing strategy. The chapter also establishes the ethos of *Marketing: Concepts and Strategies* and describes the structure of the text. Important concepts presented in Chapter 1 are deliberately repeated throughout the text. It is important for the reader to understand and accept them before progressing to the following chapters.

Chapter 2, "The Marketing Environment", examines the many forces at work in a market over which consumers and businesses have little or no control but which tangibly affect the nature of the products and services marketed. These forces of what is termed "the marketing environment" include economic and competitive, political, legal, regulatory, societal and technological impacts. The chapter also examines the concept of environmental scanning, the process many businesses use to address the marketing environment.

Chapter 3, "Marketing in International Markets", acknowledges that today many businesses operate across national borders and modify their marketing practices accordingly. The chapter defines the nature of marketing internationally, establishes why the concept is so important and explains the need for international marketing intelligence. The discussion then focuses on how forces of the marketing environment differ between territories and how regional trade alliances create the need to treat non-domestic markets differently. The chapter concludes with an examination of alternative market entry strategies for companies wishing to become involved in international marketing activities.

By the conclusion of Part I of *Marketing: Concepts and Strategies,* readers should understand what is meant by the term *marketing* and be able to grasp its nature and scope. The essential themes in Part I are developed further as the text continues.

1 AN OVERVIEW OF THE MARKETING CONCEPT

"Marketing is concerned with the establishment and maintenance of mutually satisfying exchange relationships."

Michael Baker
University of Strathclyde

OBJECTIVES

- To understand the definition of marketing
- To understand the importance of marketing
- To gain insight into the basic elements of the marketing concept and its implementation
- To understand the major components of a marketing strategy and the marketing mix
- To gain a sense of general strategic marketing issues, such as market opportunity analysis, target market selection and marketing mix development
- To grasp the ethos and structure of this text

Being fashion-conscious in the 1990s means more than simply owning a pair of Levi 501s. In 1995 Italian jeans company Diesel set up a stand-alone UK division. Just twelve months later, with sales in excess of a quarter of a million pairs of jeans, availability from over 350 outlets and a flagship Covent Garden store, the brand is well established as one of the UK's most fashionable jeans choices. Diesel UK managing director Don Henshall has a clear image of the ethos behind the brand. "Diesel's about being an individual, it's about having a laugh, not taking yourself too seriously". This interpretation, consistent with Diesel's positioning as a fun, lifestyle clothing brand, is also carried through the company's TV, cinema and press advertising. The marketing strategy, Levi's is now planning to open 300 branches of Dockers & Co across Europe. The outlets will sell the casual clothing label Dockers, Levi's up-market sister brand. With shops in Amsterdam, Nice, Paris and Milan already open, a full roll out into the rest of Europe is imminent, and 15 outlets are already planned in the UK.

As it gears up its marketing campaign to promote Dockers, Levi's is keenly aware that this new label must be positioned away from the Levi's brand. The initial impetus for the brand was the concern that the Levi's brand in Europe had achieved virtual saturation of its core 15 to 24 year old market. The Dockers range, deliberately smarter than traditional Levi's clothing, encompasses chino trousers and casual shirts and is positioned somewhere between comfortable jeans and formal suits. Ultimately, Levi's hopes that Dockers will enjoy some of the success already experienced in the US and will allow Levi's to increase its coverage of the casual clothing market. For all Levi's experience in the fashion business, managers know that customers will be the ones to judge the acceptability of the new brand. ■

company is currently the fastest-growing jeans brand in Europe and has grown globally to a £300m business in just 10 years.

In the overall market for jeans, Diesel remains a relatively small player. Perhaps not surprisingly, the business has not attempted to compete head-on with firms such as Levi's, Wrangler and Lee. Instead Diesel has looked for a broader interpretation of casual wear than the blue jeans look. However, the attractions of the area of the market that Diesel has captured are generating interest from these larger players. Even a classic brand like Levi's, with a massive one quarter share of the world market, must work hard to maintain its rapport with the marketplace, staying in tune with changes in street culture. As part of its current

SOURCES: Julian Lee, "Diesel power: Don Hensall, Managing Director, Diesel UK", *Marketing*, 9 May 1996, p. 17; Julian Lee, "Jeans genie: Roy Edmondson, Marketing Director, Levi Strauss UK," *Marketing*, 7 March 1996, p. 23; Claire Murphy, "Levi's Dockers take on Europe", *Marketing*, 30 May 1996, p. 1.

As explained in the preceding chapter opener, Levi's has noted Diesel's success in identifying a customer need and is developing its own retail chain to compete with the quickly expanding Italian company.

This first chapter of *Marketing: Concepts and Strategies* provides an overview of the concepts and decisions covered in this text. This chapter first develops a definition of marketing and explains each element of the definition. It next focuses on some of the reasons people should study marketing and on why marketing is important. The text then introduces the marketing concept and examines several issues associated with successful implementation. The chapter goes on to define and discuss the major tasks associated with marketing strategy: market opportunity analysis, target market selection, marketing mix development and the management of marketing activities. It concludes by discussing the organisation and running order of this text. Like all the chapters in *Marketing: Concepts and Strategies*, this one contains detailed illustrative examples in the Marketing Insight boxes, presents cases for discussion at its conclusion, lists all the key terms presented in the chapter and provides discussion and review questions to emphasise the key themes. In addition, as the principal definitions are introduced in the text, they are repeated in the margins for ease of understanding.

• •

Marketing Defined

Asking members of the public to define marketing is an illuminating experience. They will respond with a variety of descriptions, including "advertising", "selling", "hype", "conning people", "targeting", "packaging". In reality, marketing encompasses many more activities than most people realise and depends on a wealth of formal concepts, processes and models not implied by the sound-bites just listed. Since it is practised and studied for many different reasons, marketing has been, and continues to be, defined in many different ways, whether for academic, research or applied business purposes. This chapter begins with an examination of what is meant by the term **marketing**.

Marketing Individual and organisational activities that facilitate and expedite satisfying exchange relationships in a dynamic environment through the creation, distribution, promotion and pricing of goods, services and ideas

> Marketing consists of individual and organisational activities that facilitate and expedite satisfying exchange relationships in a dynamic environment through the creation, distribution, promotion and pricing of goods, services and ideas.
>
> *Dibb, Simkin, Pride and Ferrell*

The basic rationale of marketing is that to succeed, a business requires satisfied and happy customers who return to the business to provide additional custom. In exchange for something of value, typically payment or a donation, the customers receive a product or service that satisfies their needs. Such a product has an acceptable level of quality, reliability, customer service and support, is available at places convenient for the customer at the "right" price and is promoted effectively by means of a clear message that is readily comprehended by the customers in question. For example, in return for quenching thirst at affordable prices with a reliable product that is widely available in easy to use containers, Coca-Cola receives a great deal of money from customers. Unfortunately for companies and their marketers, customers' requirements change as their needs alter, marketing messages infiltrate their thinking, friends and colleagues discuss purchases and competing products are pushed by rival businesses. In the dynamic world of marketing, an effective solution to satisfying customer needs does not have longevity. High specification turntables no longer satisfy the majority of music lovers' needs: compact disc players, therefore, have taken over the dominant share of Sony's range. Marketers must constantly assess their customers' requirements and be prepared to modify their marketing activity accordingly. An assessment of marketing opportunities is an ever evolving process requiring regular revision and up-dating.

> Marketing is the management process responsible for identifying, anticipating and satisfying customer requirements profitably.
>
> *Chartered Institute of Marketing*

Understanding customers and anticipating their requirements is a core theme of effective marketing.[1] So, too, is understanding general market trends and developments that may affect both customers' views and the activities of businesses operating in a particular market. These factors may include social trends, technological enhancements, economic patterns and changes in the legal and regulatory arena, as well as political influences. These forces are often termed "the marketing environment." Compared with five years ago, for example, look at how many companies now produce products in "environmentally friendly" packaging in line with the social trend of the "greening consumer". A business does not have a marketplace to itself. There are direct competitors, new entrant rivals, substitute products with alternative solutions to a customer's specific need. Construction equipment giant JCB markets trench digging equipment to utilities and local authorities. The growth of subterranean tunnelling robotic "moles" for pipe laying, requiring no trench digging, is a substitute for the traditional JCB backhoe loader and a major competitive threat. The competitive context is of fundamental importance to marketers of any good or service. So, too, is the internal resource base and the strengths and weaknesses within the business that will determine which market opportunities are in fact viable for the business to pursue. Marketing, therefore, depends on the successful analysis of customers, the marketing environment, competition and internal capabilities.

> The aim of marketing is to make selling superfluous. The aim is to know and to understand the customer so well that the product or service fits him/her and sells itself!
>
> *US management guru Peter Drucker*

With an understanding of these aspects of the marketplace, a business must then develop a marketing strategy. Even the mighty global organisations such as GM/Vauxhall or ICI choose not to offer a product for every type of consumer or customer need. Instead, they attempt to identify groups of customers where each separate group, or *market segment,* has "similar" needs. Each group of customers may then be offered a specifically tailored product or service proposition and a *marketing mix* programme. The Vauxhall Frontera off-roader appeals to a separate group of customers than does the Vauxhall Corsa town car, and it is marketed totally differently. In developing unique marketing programmes for individual market segments—groups of customers—a business must prioritise which particular groups of customers it has the ability to serve and which will provide satisfactory returns. Resources will not permit all segments in a market to be targeted. In deciding on which segments to target, a business must be clear about the message—or *positioning*—it intends to offer to each group of customers. The business should endeavour to serve those customers it targets in a manner that gives it an edge over its competitors. Knowing how to group customers sensibly into homogeneous market segments, determining which to ultimately target, selecting a suitable positioning platform and seeking superiority over rivals are the core elements of marketing strategy.

> The marketing concept holds that the key to achieving organisational goals lies in determining the needs and wants of target markets and delivering the desired satisfaction more efficiently and effectively than the competition.
>
> *US marketer Philip Kotler*

Once a company has devised a marketing strategy, its attention must switch to marketing mix programmes.[2] As consumers of food brands, audio products or banking services, all readers of this text will have experienced the marketing mix programmes of major companies such as Kellogg's, Aiwa or Barclays. These are the tactical actions of marketing departments, which are designed to implement the desired marketing strategy. The product or offer must be clearly defined in line with target customer needs, service levels and guarantees must be determined, pricing and payment issues decided, channels of distribution established to make the product or service available and promotional strategies devised and executed to communicate with the targeted customers. These tactical aspects of marketing—the marketing mix—must be supported with carefully managed control programmes in a business to ensure their effective execution and the monitoring of their effectiveness.

It is important to remember the following simple sequential process: analysis, strategy, programmes for implementation (ASP). The focus must be on providing customer satisfaction, but in a manner that leads to the business's successful performance. By addressing customers' needs and adopting a marketing culture incorporating clear controls, JCB has recently enjoyed the most successful financial returns in the company's history. The intention of this introductory marketing text is to explore these facets of marketing comprehensively and thus provide a sound conceptual basis with which to understand the nature and activities of marketing.

There are many definitions of marketing, since it is not a pure science. However, certain core ingredients of the various definitions collectively indicate the basic priorities of marketing:

- satisfying customers
- identifying/maximising marketing opportunities
- targeting the "right" customers
- facilitating exchange relationships
- staying ahead in dynamic environments
- endeavouring to beat or pre-empt competitors
- utilising resources/assets effectively
- increasing market share
- enhancing profitability

These aims form the objectives for many marketing directors and marketing departments. They are featured throughout this text, which adopts the following definition: *marketing consists of individual and organisational activities that facilitate and expedite satisfying exchange relationships in a dynamic environment through the creation, distribution, promotion and pricing of goods, services and ideas.* A definition of marketing must acknowledge that marketing relates to more than just tangible goods, that marketing activities occur in a dynamic environment and that such activities are performed by individuals as well as organisations.

• • • • • • • • • • • • • • • • • •

The Definition Explored

Marketing Consists of Activities

Marketing products or services effectively requires many activities. Some are performed by producers; some are accomplished by intermediaries, who purchase products from producers or from other intermediaries and re-sell them; and some are even performed by purchasers. Marketing does not include all human and

Marketing Mix Variables	Possible Decisions and Activities
Product	Develop and test market new products; modify existing products; eliminate products that do not satisfy customers' desires; formulate brand names and branding policies; create product guarantees and establish procedures for fulfilling guarantees; plan packages, including materials, sizes, shapes, colours and designs
Place Distribution	Analyse various types of distribution channels; design appropriate distribution channels; design an effective programme for dealer relations; establish distribution centres; formulate and implement procedures for efficient product handling; set up inventory controls; analyse transportation methods; minimise total distribution costs; analyse possible locations for plants and wholesale or retail outlets
Promotion	Set promotional objectives; determine major types of promotion to be used; select and schedule advertising media; develop advertising messages; measure the effectiveness of advertisements; recruit and train salespersons; formulate payment programmes for sales personnel; establish sales territories; plan and implement sales promotion efforts such as free samples, coupons, displays, competitions, sales contests and co-operative advertising programmes; prepare and disseminate publicity releases; evaluate sponsorships and provide direct mail
Price	Analyse competitors' prices; formulate pricing policies; determine method or methods used to set prices; set prices; determine discounts for various types of buyer; establish conditions and terms of sales; understand the consumers' notion of value.
People	Manipulate the marketing mix and establish service levels, guarantees, warranties, expertise, sales support, after sales back-up, customer handling requirements, personnel skills training and motivation (marketers); make products and services available (intermediaries); provide market for products (consumers)

Table 1.1 Possible decisions and activities associated with marketing mix variables

organisational activities, but only those aimed at facilitating and expediting exchanges. Table 1.1 lists several major categories and examples of marketing activities, as ultimately encountered by the consumer, who remains at the "sharp end" of such tactical decisions. Note that this list is not all-inclusive. Each activity could be subdivided into more specific activities.

Marketing Is Performed by Individuals and Organisations

All organisations perform marketing activities to facilitate exchanges. Businesses as well as not-for-profit and public sector organisations such as colleges and universities, charitable organisations, community theatres and hospitals perform marketing activities. For example, colleges and universities and their students engage in exchanges. To receive instruction, knowledge, entertainment, a degree, the use of facilities and sometimes room and board, students give up time, money and perhaps services in the form of labour; they may also give up opportunities to do other things. Many organisations engage in marketing activities. Various police forces have surveyed their communities in order to prioritise services and reassure the general public that people's concerns will be addressed. Even the sole owner of and worker in a small corner shop decides which products will sell, arranges

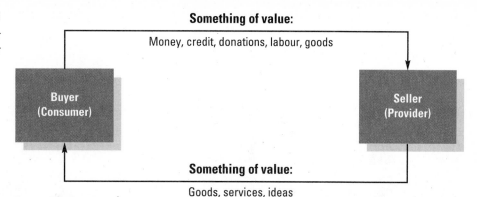

Figure 1.1

Exchange between buyer and seller

Something of value:

Money, credit, donations, labour, goods

Buyer (Consumer)

Seller (Provider)

Something of value:

Goods, services, ideas

deliveries to the shop, prices and displays products, advertises and serves customers.

Marketing Facilitates Satisfying Exchange Relationships

Exchange The provision or transfer of goods, services and ideas in return for something of value

For an **exchange** to take place, four conditions must exist. (1) Two or more individuals, groups or organisations must participate. (2) Each party must possess something of value that the other party desires. (3) Each party must be willing to give up its "something of value" to receive the "something of value" held by the other party. The objective of a marketing exchange is to receive something that is desired more than is given up to get it: that is, a reward in excess of costs. (4) The parties to the exchange must be able to communicate with each other to make their "somethings of value" available.[3]

Figure 1.1 illustrates the process of exchange. The arrows indicate that the parties communicate and that each has something of value available to exchange. Note, though, that an exchange will not necessarily take place just because these four conditions exist. Nevertheless, even if there is no exchange, marketing activities still have occurred. The "somethings of value" held by the two parties are most often products and/or financial resources, such as money or credit. When an exchange occurs, products are traded for other products or for financial resources.

Customer satisfaction A state that results when an exchange meets the needs and expectations of the buyer

An exchange should be *satisfying* to both the buyer and the seller. In fact, in a study of marketing managers, 32 per cent indicated that creating **customer satisfaction** was the most important concept in a definition of marketing.[4] Marketing activities, then, should be orientated towards creating and maintaining satisfying exchange relationships. To maintain an exchange relationship, the buyer must be satisfied with the goods, service or idea obtained in the exchange; the seller must be satisfied with the financial reward or something else of value received in the exchange.

Maintaining a positive relationship with buyers is an important goal for a seller, regardless of whether the seller is marketing cereal, financial services or a construction plant. Through buyer-seller interaction, the buyer develops expectations about the seller's future behaviour. To fulfil these expectations, the seller must deliver on promises made. Over time, a healthy buyer-seller relationship results in interdependencies between the two parties. The buyer depends on the seller to furnish information, parts and service; to be available; and to provide satisfying products in the future. Toys "R" Us's advertising emphasises the company's ample stock of goods to reassure existing and potential customers (see Figure 1.2).

Figure 1.2 Building satisfying customer relationships. To successfully implement the marketing concept, organisations must place a high priority on satisfying customers. By emphasising its impressive range coverage, Toys "R" Us tells its customers that it sells everything their children want.

Source: Courtesy of Bill Mayer.

Marketing Occurs in a Dynamic Environment

Marketing environment
External changing forces within the trading environment: laws, regulations, political activities, societal pressures, changing economic conditions and technological advances

The **marketing environment** consists of many external changing forces within the trading environment: laws, regulations, political activities, societal pressures, changing economic conditions and technological advances. Each of these dynamic forces has an impact on how effectively marketing activities can facilitate and expedite exchanges. For example, the development and acceptance of facsimile (fax) machines has given businesses another vehicle through which to promote their products. Some office suppliers and restaurants send advertisements about their goods and services to businesses and individuals through their fax machines. The Internet is similarly altering how companies communicate with consumers. Another example is the impact EU regulations have had on reducing distribution headaches within much of Europe.

Marketing Focuses on Goods, Services and Ideas

Marketing means more than simply advertising or selling a product; it involves developing and managing a product that will satisfy certain needs. It focuses on making the product available at the right place, at the right time, at a price that is acceptable to customers and with the right people. It also requires transmitting the kind of information that will help customers determine whether the product will in fact be able to satisfy their needs. Marketing Insight 1.1 discusses the successful use of marketing in the airline wars.

Marketing Involves Products, Distribution, Promotion, Pricing and People

Product A good, service or idea

Good A physical entity that can be touched

Service The application of human or mechanical efforts to people or objects in order to provide intangible benefits to customers

Idea A concept, philosophy, image or issue

The word *product* has been used a number of times in this chapter. For purposes of discussion in this text, a **product** is viewed as being a good, a service or an idea. A **good** is a physical entity that can be touched. A Ford Escort, a Sony compact disc player, Kellogg's Frosties, a bar of Lux soap and a kitten in a pet shop are examples of goods. A **service** is the application of human and mechanical efforts to people or objects in order to provide intangible benefits to customers. Services such as air travel, dry cleaning, hairdressing, banking, medical care and child care are just as real as goods, but an individual cannot actually touch them. **Ideas** include concepts, philosophies, images and issues. For instance, a marriage counsellor gives couples ideas and advice to help improve their relationships. Other marketers of ideas include political parties, churches, schools and marketing lecturers.

• • • • • • • • • • • • • • • • • • •

The Importance of Marketing

Marketing Activities Are Used in Many Organisations

The commercial importance of marketing and its relevance as a topic worth studying are apparent from the definition of marketing just presented. This section discusses several less obvious reasons why marketing should be studied.

In Europe and the United States between 25 and 33 per cent of all civilian workers perform marketing activities. The marketing field offers a variety of interesting and challenging career opportunities, such as personal selling, advertising, packaging, transport, storage, marketing research, product development, wholesaling, retailing, strategic planning and consultancy. In addition, many individuals who work for not-for-profit organisations engage in marketing activities. Marketing skills are used to promote political, cultural, church, civic and charitable activities. The advertisement in Figure 1.3 encourages support of the British Heart Foundation, a non-profit organisation. Whether a person earns a living through marketing activities or performs them without compensation in non-business settings, marketing knowledge and skills are valuable assets.

Marketing Activities Are Important to Businesses and the Economy

A business organisation must sell products to survive and to grow. Directly or indirectly, marketing activities help sell an organisation's products. By doing so, they generate financial resources that can be used to develop innovative products. New products allow a firm to better satisfy customers' changing needs, which in turn enables the firm to generate more profits. Charities and other not-for-profit organisations use marketing to generate revenues and funds, as described in Marketing Insight 1.2.

Europe's highly complex economy depends heavily on marketing activities. They help produce the profits that are essential not only to the survival of individual businesses but also to the health and ultimate survival of the economy as a whole. Profits are essential to economic growth because without them businesses

Changing Times for Air Travellers

The newly forged links between British Airways and American Airlines look set to revolutionise transatlantic air travel. Although the relationship could potentially reduce competition in the short term, causing prices to rise, industry experts believe that over time an increase in marketing activity may ultimately work in the consumer's favour. The link-up may also allow consumers to fly with one operator from the US to Australia via London.

Competitor Virgin is not so sure about the relationship, arguing that the size of the BA-AA market share goes against the interests of competition. The company's concerns are understandable. On current figures the combined transatlantic market share of BA and AA already exceeds 60 per cent. If the links between the two airlines are to be accepted by the US and UK governments, the UK will have to reduce its current restrictions on foreign airlines flying into the UK. The resulting so called open skies policy will open the UK market to a host of American and other operators. Virgin already has to compete in an increasingly crowded market because of the recent rise in the number of small companies offering cheap, no-frills flights.

The likes of new entrants easyJet, World Airlines and Denim are all seeking to take advantage of deregulation in 1997, which will allow much freer access to routes than existed previously. Many of these airlines operate the concept of cut-price air travel on selected routes. For example, easyJet offers customers the benefit of cutting out the travel agent through "ticketless" travel, a method by which seats can be booked directly with the airline simply by quoting a personal identification number as confirmation on arrival at the airport.

For the consumer, the new operators look set to drive air travel prices down further as larger airlines respond to the new threat. For example, Virgin's response to the changing market has been to launch Virgin Express, its own version of the no-frills air travel service. This follows Virgin's purchase of Belgian airline EBA, which gives the company instant access to EBA's "slots" at major airports. Alitalia, Lufthansa and BA are also responding with discount economy fares. In the longer term, it remains to be seen how well the new operators will be able to sustain their efforts as the market changes become more established, or what will be the impact of the BA-AA relationship. In the meantime, customers continue to enjoy a wider choice of cut-price air travel than ever before.

SOURCES: Claire Murphy, "Why airlines face revolution in the skies", *Marketing,* 20 June 1996, pp. 16–17; Alistair Osbourne, "Voyage of discovery", *Marketing,* 6 June 1996, pp. 22–24; Jon Rees, "Wings of desire", *Marketing Week,* 17 May 1996, pp. 36–37.

Transatlantic High-Fliers

Airline	Market Share	Share of Take-off Slots
British Airways	43.8%	40.1%
American Airlines	17.7%	24.4%
Virgin Atlantic Airways	13.2%	10.0%
United Airlines	10.9%	12.2%
Delta Airlines	4.7%	5.3%
Delta on Virgin	1.5%	—
Northwest Airlines	3.9%	3.3%
Continental Airlines	3.1%	3.3%
Trans World Airlines	1.3%	1.3%

SOURCE: Claire Murphy, "Why airlines face revolution in the skies", *Marketing*, 20 June 1996, pp. 16–17.

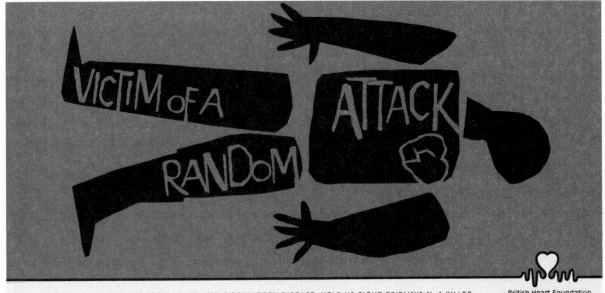

HALF OF ALL DEATHS ARE FROM HEART AND CIRCULATORY DISEASE. HELP US FIGHT BRITAIN'S No 1 KILLER.

British Heart Foundation
The heart research charity

Figure 1.3 Promotion of a non-profit organisation The British Heart Foundation uses marketing to communicate its message.

SOURCE: Courtesy of the British Heart Foundation.

find it difficult, if not impossible, to buy more raw materials, hire more employees, attract more capital and create the additional products that in turn lead to more profits.

Marketing Knowledge Enhances Consumer Awareness

Besides contributing to a country's economic well-being, marketing activities permeate everyone's lives. In fact, they help to improve the quality of life. Studying marketing activities enables the costs, benefits and flaws of marketing to be evaluated. The need for improvement and ways to accomplish changes can be determined. For example, an unsatisfactory experience with a guarantee may lead consumers to demand that laws be enforced more strictly to make sellers fulfil their promises. Similarly, there may be the desire for more information about a product—or more accurate information—before purchase. Understanding marketing leads to the evaluation of the corrective measures (such as laws, regulations and industry guidelines) that may be required to stop unfair, misleading or unethical marketing practices. The results of the survey presented in Table 1.2 indicate that there is a considerable lack of knowledge about marketing activities, as reflected by the sizeable proportion of respondents who agree with the myths in the table.

Marketing Costs Consume a Sizeable Portion of Buyers' Incomes

The study of marketing emphasises that many marketing a[...] to provide people with satisfying goods and services. Obvi[...] activities cost money. A family with a monthly income of £[...] goes on taxes and savings, spends about £700 on good[...] amount, typically £350 goes for marketing activities. [...] expenses consume that much income, it is necessary to [...] is used.

14

PART I

Charities Turn to Marketing: Promoting the Children's Society

FMCGs (fast moving consumer goods) used to be the domain of marketing managers. The need to identify customers' needs and satisfy them no longer applies only to the likes of Heinz and Kellogg's. Irrespective of their products or markets, some of the most successful organisations in the world are experts in marketing, be they American Express, British Airways, JCB, Nestlé or Unilever. It is no longer just the manufacturers of baked beans or cornflakes that worry about keeping their customers happy, staying abreast of market trends and endeavouring to remain ahead of their rivals. The service sector, especially banking and financial services, leisure and tourism, has in recent years been a major employer of marketing graduates. There are few areas of commercial activity in which the concepts and strategies of marketing are not employed. One area that is currently adopting the ethos of marketing and engaging in the practices once left only to the FMCG companies is the charity sector.

The increasing use of marketing by charities is both a response to the strategies of other businesses seeking alliances and an ever important foundation for the charities' own fund raising initiatives. Some businesses perceive that by allying with "good causes", not only will these causes benefit but so too will the businesses, as their own customers see them in a better light. For example, Midland Bank has invested over £1 million in bolstering its position as a community bank, signing support deals with Shelter, Age Concern and the National Deaf Children's Society. Charity involvement at business events is growing too. Companies organising conferences are benefiting from having charities on board, making presentations or exhibiting in the foyer. The event's patrons gain a "feel good" factor, while the charity benefits from much needed exposure and goodwill.

The charities themselves are increasingly exploiting marketing. By identifying why members of the public or businesses donate to good causes and targeting those who do so regularly, Oxfam's marketers help the charity maximise use of scare publicity and promotional resources to generate the maximum income for the charity. The Children's Society has recently embarked on a major advertising campaign. While cynics will say it is a waste of £500,000, the charity on the other hand knows that many potential donors have been deterred by uncertainty over who benefits from its fund raising: the 360,000 children with a disability, the 43,000 runaways, the 160,000 homeless families or the two million children living with asthma. The campaign aims to explain to the public that there are significant issues that need tackling and many thousands of youngsters who require financial or material support. Having determined that these issues were not being raised in the media or being adequately linked to the charity's own fund raising, the Children's Society confidently expects not only to cover the costs of the campaign by increasing the level of donations being received but also to awaken people's desire to improve conditions for the children and families it supports.

Sources: Andy Fry, "When justice is child's play", *Marketing*, 4 July 1996, p. 31; Pat Anderson, "Cause and effect", *Marketing Week*, 21 October 1994, pp. 66–67; Harriot Lane Fox, "Good cause better effect", *Marketing*, 11 January 1996, pp. 25–27; "Midland ties in with charity trio", *Marketing*, 11 January 1996, p. 8.

Myths	Strongly Agree	Somewhat Agree	Neither Agree nor Disagree	Somewhat Disagree	Strongly Disagree
Marketing is selling	14%	34%	26%	18%	8%
Marketers persuade	21%	25%	20%	11%	23%
Dealers' profits significantly increase prices consumers pay	21%	32%	12%	8%	27%
Marketing depends on advertising	17%	44%	12%	9%	18%
Strategic planning is nothing to do with marketing	19%	19%	21%	17%	24%

SOURCES: Student surveys.

Table 1.2 Popular marketing myths

Business Performance

Marketing puts an emphasis on satisfying customers. Marketing analyses should lead a business to develop a marketing strategy that takes account of market trends, aims to satisfy customers, is aware of competitive activity and targets the right customers with a clear positioning message. In so doing, a business should benefit from customer loyalty and advantages over its rivals, while making the most efficient use of resources to effectively address the specific requirements of those markets it chooses to target. Hence, marketing should provide both a financial benefit and a greater sense of well-being for the organisation.

● ● ● ● ● ● ● ● ● ● ● ● ● ● ● ● ● ● ●

The Marketing Concept

Some organisations have tried to be successful by buying land, building a factory, equipping it with people and machines, and then making a product that they believe consumers need. However, these organisations frequently fail to attract buyers with what they have to offer because they defined their business as "making a product" rather than as "helping potential customers satisfy their needs and wants". Such organisations have failed to implement the marketing concept. It is not enough to be "product led", no matter how good the product. An organisation must be in tune with consumer requirements.

Marketing concept The philosophy that an organisation should try to provide products that satisfy customers' needs through a co-ordinated set of activities that also allows the organisation to achieve its goals

According to the **marketing concept,** an organisation should try to provide products that satisfy customers' needs through a co-ordinated set of activities that also allows the organisation to achieve its goals. Customer satisfaction is the major aim of the marketing concept. First, an organisation must find out what will satisfy customers. With this information, it then attempts to create satisfying products. But the process does not end there. The organisation must continue to alter, adapt and develop products to keep pace with customers' changing desires and preferences. The marketing concept stresses the importance of customers and emphasises that marketing activities begin and end with them.

In attempting to satisfy customers, businesses must consider not only short run, immediate needs but also broad, long term desires. Trying to satisfy customers' current needs by sacrificing their long term desires will only create future dissatisfaction. For instance, people want efficient, low cost energy to power their homes and cars, yet they react adversely to energy producers who pollute the air and water, kill wildlife or cause disease or birth defects. To meet these short and long run needs and desires, a firm must co-ordinate all its activities. Production, finance, accounting, personnel and marketing departments must work together.

The marketing concept is not a second definition of marketing. It is a way of thinking—a management philosophy guiding an organisation's overall activities. This philosophy affects all the efforts of the organisation, not just marketing activities. However, the marketing concept is by no means a philanthropic philosophy aimed at helping customers at the expense of the organisation. A firm that adopts the marketing concept must not only satisfy its customers' objectives but also achieve its own goals, or it will not stay in business long. The overall goals of a business might be directed towards increasing profits, market share, sales or a combination of all three. The marketing concept stresses that an organisation can best achieve its goals by providing customer satisfaction. Thus, implementing the marketing concept should benefit the organisation as well as its customers.

Evolution of the Marketing Concept

The marketing concept may seem an obvious and sensible approach to running a business. However, businesspeople have not always believed that the best way to make sales and profits is to satisfy customers. A famous example is the marketing philosophy for cars widely attributed to Henry Ford in the early 1900s: "The customers can have any colour car they want as long as it is black." The philosophy of the marketing concept emerged in the third major era in the history of business, preceded by the **production era** and the **sales era**. Surprisingly, nearly forty years after the **marketing era** began, many businesses are only just now adopting the marketing concept.

Production era The period of mass production following industrialisation

Sales era The period from the mid-1920s to the early 1950s when competitive forces and the desire for high sales volume led business to emphasise selling and the salesperson in its business strategy

Marketing era The current period, in which product and aggressive selling no longer suffice if customers either do not desire a product or prefer a rival brand, and in which customer needs must be identified and satisfied

The Production Era During the second half of the nineteenth century, the Industrial Revolution was in full swing in Europe and the United States. Electricity, railways, the division of labour, the assembly line and mass production made it possible to manufacture products more efficiently. With new technology and new ways of using labour, products poured into the marketplace, where consumer demand for manufactured goods was strong. This production orientation continued into the early part of this century, encouraged by the scientific management movement that championed rigidly structured jobs and pay based on output.

The Sales Era In the 1920s, the strong consumer demand for products subsided. Businesses realised that products, which by this time could be made quite efficiently, would have to be "sold" to consumers. From the mid-1920s to the early 1950s, businesses viewed sales as the major means of increasing profits. As a result, this period came to have a sales orientation. Businesspeople believed that the most important marketing activities were personal selling and advertising.

The Marketing Era By the early 1950s, some businesspeople began to recognise that efficient production and extensive promotion of products did not guarantee that customers would buy them. These businesses, and many others since then, found that they must first determine what customers want and then produce it, rather than simply make products first and then try to change customers' needs to correspond to what was being produced. As more organisations have realised the importance of knowing customers' needs, businesses have entered into the marketing era—the era of customer orientation.

Implementing the Marketing Concept

A philosophy may sound reasonable and look good on paper, but that does not mean it can be put into practice easily. The marketing concept is a case in point. To implement it, an organisation must focus on some general conditions and recognise several problems. Because of these conditions and problems, the marketing concept has yet to be fully accepted by many businesses.

Because the marketing concept affects all types of business activities, not just marketing activities, the top management of an organisation must adopt it wholeheartedly. High level executives must incorporate the marketing concept into their philosophies of business management so completely that it becomes the basis for all the goals and decisions that they set for their firms. They must also convince other members of the organisation to accept the changes in policies and operations that flow from their acceptance of the marketing concept. Costs and budgetary controls are important, products and manufacturing essential, and personnel management necessary; but all are to no avail if the organisation's products or services are not desired by the targeted customers.

As the first step, management must establish an information system that enables it to discover customers' real needs and to use the information to create satisfying products. Because such a system is usually expensive, management must be willing to commit money and time for development and maintenance. Without an adequate information system, an organisation cannot be customer orientated.

Management's second major task is to restructure the organisation. If a company is to satisfy customers' objectives as well as its own, it must co-ordinate all its activities. To achieve this, the internal operations and the overall objectives of one or more departments may need restructuring. If the head of the marketing unit is not a member of the organisation's top level management, he or she should be. Some departments may have to be abolished and new ones created. Implementing the marketing concept demands the support not only of top management but also of managers and staff at all levels within the organisation.

Even when the basic conditions of establishing an information system and reorganising the company are met, the firm's new marketing approach may not work perfectly. (1) There is a limit to a firm's ability to satisfy customers' needs for a particular product. In a mass production economy, most business organisations cannot tailor products to fit the exact needs of each customer. (2) Although a company may attempt to learn what customers want, it may be unable to do so, and when the organisation does correctly identify customers' needs, it often has a difficult time developing a product that satisfies those needs. Many companies spend considerable time and money to research customers' needs and yet still create some products that do not sell well. (3) By striving to satisfy one particular segment of society, a firm sometimes dissatisfies other segments. Certainly, government and non-business organisations also experience this problem. (4) A business organisation may have difficulty maintaining employee morale during any restructuring needed to co-ordinate the activities of various departments. Management must clearly explain the reasons for the various changes and communicate its own enthusiasm for the marketing concept. Adoption of the marketing philosophy takes time, resources, endurance and commitment.

Marketing Strategy

Marketing strategy One that encompasses the selection and analysis of a target market and the creation and maintenance of an appropriate marketing mix that will satisfy those people in the target market

Marketing mix The tactical "tool kit" of product, distribution, promotion, price and people that an organisation can control in order to facilitate satisfying exchange

To achieve the broad goal of expediting desirable exchanges, an organisation's marketing managers are responsible for developing and managing marketing strategies. Specifically, a **marketing strategy** encompasses selecting and analysing a target market (the group of people whom the organisation wants to reach) and creating and maintaining an appropriate **marketing mix** (the tactical "tool kit" of product, distribution, promotion, price and people) that will satisfy those people in the target market. A marketing strategy articulates a plan for the best use of the organisation's resources and tactics to meet its objectives.

When marketing managers attempt to develop and manage marketing activities, they must deal with two broad sets of variables: those relating to the marketing mix and those that make up the marketing environment. The marketing mix decision variables—product, distribution, promotion, price and people—are factors over which an organisation has control. As Figure 1.4 shows, these variables are constructed around the buyer or consumer. The marketing environment variables are political, legal, regulatory, societal/green, technological, and eco-

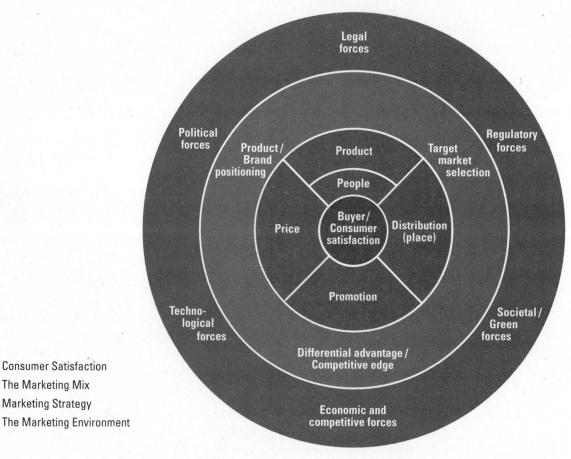

■ Consumer Satisfaction
■ The Marketing Mix
■ Marketing Strategy
■ The Marketing Environment

Figure 1.4 The Marketing environment, marketing strategy, the marketing mix and customer satisfaction. Consumers and businesses are affected by the forces of the marketing environment. Businesses must determine a marketing strategy, implemented through the ingredients of the marketing mix, which aims to satisfy targeted customers.

nomic and competitive forces. These factors are subject to less control by an organisation, but they affect buyers' needs as well as marketing managers' decisions regarding marketing mix variables.

To develop and manage marketing strategies, marketers must focus on several marketing tasks: marketing opportunity analysis (the marketing analyses), target market selection (determination of the marketing strategy), marketing mix development and effective marketing management (the programmes that facilitate implementation of the marketing strategy). Figure 1.5 lists these tasks, along with the chapters of this book in which they are discussed.

Figure 1.5
Marketing tasks: analysis, strategy and programmes for implementation and control

Marketing Opportunity Analysis	Chapters
• The marketing environment	2
• Marketing in international markets	3
• Consumer markets and buyer behaviour	4
• Business-to-business markets and buyer behaviour	5
• Marketing research and information systems	6

Target Market Selection	Chapters
• Market segmentation and prioritisation	7, 22
• Product and brand positioning	7, 22
• Competitive advantage	7, 22

Marketing Mix Development	Chapters
• Product, branding, packaging and service decisions	8–11
• Distribution (place and channel) decisions	12–15
• Promotion decisions	16–18
• Pricing decisions	19, 20
• Supplementary decisions	3, 21, 24, 25

Marketing Management	Chapters
• Strategic marketing and competitive strategy	22, 23
• Marketing planning and sales forecasting	23
• Implementing strategies and measuring performance	24
• Marketing ethics and social responsibility	25

Marketing Strategy: Marketing Opportunity Analysis

Marketing opportunity One that exists when circumstances allow an organisation to take action towards reaching a particular group of customers

A **marketing opportunity** exists when circumstances allow an organisation to take action towards reaching a particular group of customers. An opportunity provides a favourable chance or opening for the firm to generate sales from identifiable markets. For example, during a heat wave, marketers of electric fans have a marketing opportunity—an opportunity to reach customers who need electric fans.

Marketers should be capable of recognising and analysing marketing opportunities. An organisation's long term survival depends on developing products that satisfy its customers. Few organisations can assume that products popular today will interest buyers ten years from now. A marketing organisation can choose among several alternatives for continued product development through which it can achieve its objectives and satisfy buyers. It can modify existing products (for example, by removing preservatives from jams and sauces to address increasing health consciousness among customers) introduce new products (such as Hooper's Hooch or Mars Miniatures) and delete some that customers no longer want (such as disc cameras or turntables). A company may also try to market its products to a greater number of customers, persuade current customers to use more of a product or perhaps expand marketing activities into additional countries. Diversification into new product offerings through internal efforts or through acquisitions of other organisations may be viable options for a firm. For example, BSN Groupe, a French consumer goods marketer of pasta, bakery goods and other products, bought RJR Nabisco's European consumer goods division, gaining the rights to market a number of highly successful Nabisco products in Europe, and Grand Metropolitan's purchase of Pillsbury led to the European appearance of Häagen-Dazs premium adult ice creams. An organisation's ability to pursue any of these alternatives successfully depends on its internal characteristics and the forces within the marketing environment.

Internal Organisational Factors

The primary factors inside an organisation that should be considered when analysing marketing opportunities are organisational objectives, financial resources, managerial skills, organisational strengths and weaknesses, and cost structures. Most organisations have overall organisational objectives. Some marketing opportunities may be consistent with these objectives; others are not, and to pursue them is hazardous. Frequently, the pursuit of such opportunities ends in failure or forces the company to alter its long term objectives.

Obviously, a firm's financial resources constrain the type of marketing opportunities it can pursue. Typically, an organisation does not develop projects that can bring economic catastrophe. In some situations, however, a firm must invest in a high risk opportunity, because the costs of not pursuing the project are so high. Thus, despite an economic recession and reduced house and road building, construction equipment manufacturer JCB continues to launch new ranges and enter new markets. It developed and launched its Compact Division, at a cost of millions, to respond to changing market requirements.

The skills and experience of management also limit the types of opportunities that an organisation can pursue. A company must be particularly cautious when exploring the possibility of entering unfamiliar markets with new products. If it lacks appropriate managerial skills and experience, the firm can sometimes acquire them by hiring additional managerial personnel.

Like people, most organisations have strengths and weaknesses. Because of the types of operations in which a company is engaged, it normally has employees with specialised skills and technological information. Such characteristics are a strength when launching marketing strategies that require them. However, they may be a weakness if the company tries to compete in new, unrelated product areas.

An organisation's cost structure may be an advantage if the company pursues certain marketing opportunities and a disadvantage if it pursues others. Such factors as geographic location, employee skills, access to raw materials and type of equipment and facilities all can affect the cost structure.

Marketing Environment Forces

The marketing environment, which consists of political, legal, regulatory, societal/green, technological, and economic and competitive forces, surrounds the buyer (consumer) and the marketing mix (see Figure 1.4). Each major environmental force is explored in considerable depth in Chapter 2. Marketers know that they cannot predict changes in the marketing environment with certainty. Even so, over the years marketers have become more systematic in taking these forces into account when planning their competitive actions.[5]

Marketing environment forces affect a marketer's ability to facilitate and expedite exchanges in three general ways. (1) They influence customers by affecting their lifestyles, standards of living, preferences and needs for products. Because a marketing manager tries to develop and adjust the marketing mix to satisfy consumers, the effects of environmental forces on customers also have an indirect impact on the marketing mix components. (2) Marketing environment forces help determine whether and how a marketing manager can perform certain marketing activities. (3) The environmental forces may affect a marketing manager's decisions and actions by influencing buyers' reactions to the firm's marketing mix.

Although forces in the marketing environment are sometimes viewed as "uncontrollables", a marketing manager may be able to influence one or more of them. However, marketing environment forces fluctuate quickly and dramatically, which is one reason marketing is so interesting and challenging. Because these forces are highly interrelated, a change in one may cause others to change. For example, from Freons in fridges to additives in foods, most consumers have become increasingly aware of health and environmental issues. Manufacturers have altered product specifications and production methods. Legislators and regulatory bodies have also responded to expert and consumer opinions with new regulations and informal agreements, forcing companies to re-think their manufacturing and marketing policies.

Even though changes in the marketing environment produce uncertainty for marketers and at times hurt marketing efforts, they can also create opportunities. After the 1989 oil spills, for example, more companies began developing and marketing products designed to contain or dissipate spilled oil. The BSE beef crisis gave producers of other meats significant opportunities. Thus a marketer must be aware of changes in environmental forces not only to adjust to and influence them but also to capitalise on the opportunities they provide.

Marketing Strategy: Target Market Selection

Target market A group of people for whom a firm creates and maintains a marketing mix that specifically fits the needs and preferences of that group

A **target market** is a group of people for whom a firm creates and maintains a marketing mix that specifically fits the needs and preferences of that group.[6] When choosing a target market, marketing managers try to evaluate possible markets to see how entering them would affect the company's sales, costs and profits. Marketers also attempt to determine whether the organisation has the resources to produce a marketing mix that meets the needs of a particular target market and whether satisfying those needs is consistent with the firm's overall objective. The size and number of competitors already marketing products in possible markets are also of concern.

Marketing managers may define a target market as a vast number of people or as a relatively small group. For example, Ford produces cars suitable for much of the population (although specific models are quite narrowly targeted, such as the family runaround Fiesta or the executive Scorpio). Porsche focuses its marketing effort on a small proportion of the population, believing that it can compete more effectively by concentrating on an affluent target market. Although a business may concentrate its efforts on one target market through a single marketing mix, businesses often focus on several target markets by developing and employing multiple marketing mixes. Reebok, for example, markets different types of shoes to meet the specific needs of joggers, walkers, aerobics enthusiasts and other groups.

Target market selection is crucial to generating productive marketing efforts. At times, products and organisations fail because marketers do not identify the appropriate customer groups at which to aim their efforts. Organisations that try to be all things to all people typically end up not satisfying the needs of any customer group very well. It is important for an organisation's management to designate which customer groups the firm is trying to serve and to have adequate information about these customers. The identification and analysis of a target market provide a foundation on which a marketing mix can be developed.

Marketing Strategy: Marketing Mix Development

As mentioned, the marketing mix consists of four major components: product, distribution, promotion and price. Increasingly, people are becoming the fifth component. These components are called marketing mix decision variables because a marketing manager decides what type of each component to use and in what amounts. A primary goal of a marketing manager is to create and maintain a marketing mix that satisfies consumers' needs for a general product type. Notice in Figure 1.4 that the marketing mix is built around the buyer (as is stressed by the marketing concept). Bear in mind, too, that the forces of the marketing environment affect the marketing mix variables in many ways.

Marketing mix variables often are viewed as controllable variables because they can be changed. However, there are limits to how much these variables can be altered. For example, because of economic conditions or government regulations, a manager may not be free to adjust prices daily. Changes in sizes, colours, shapes and designs of most tangible goods are expensive; therefore, such product features cannot be altered very often. In addition, promotional campaigns and the methods used to distribute products ordinarily cannot be changed overnight. People, too, require training and motivating, and cannot be recruited or sacked overnight.

Marketing managers must develop a marketing mix that precisely matches the needs of the people in the target market. Before they can do so, they have to collect in-depth, up to date information about those needs. The information might include data about the age, income, ethnic origin, sex and educational level of people in the target market; their preferences for product features; their attitudes towards competitors' products; and the frequency and intensity with which they use the product. Armed with these kinds of data, marketing managers are better able to develop a product, distribution system, promotion programme and price that satisfy the people in the target market.

This section looks more closely at the decisions and activities related to each marketing mix variable (product, distribution, promotion, price and people). Table 1.1 on page 8 contains a list of the decisions and activities associated with each marketing mix variable.

Product variable The aspect of the marketing mix that deals with researching consumers' product wants and designing a product with the desired characteristics

The Product Variable As noted earlier, a product can be a good, a service or an idea. The **product variable** is the aspect of the marketing mix that deals with researching consumers' product wants and designing a product with the desired characteristics. It also involves the creation or alteration of packages and brand names and may include decisions about guarantees and repair services. The actual manufacturing of products is not a marketing activity.

Product variable decisions and related activities are important because they directly involve creating products and services that satisfy consumers' needs and wants. To maintain a satisfying set of products that will help an organisation achieve its goals, a marketer must be able to develop new products, modify existing ones and eliminate those that no longer satisfy buyers or yield acceptable profits. For example, after realising that competitors were capturing large shares of the low calorie market, Heinz introduced new product items under its Weight Watchers name.

Distribution (place) variable The aspect of the marketing mix that deals with making products available in the quantities desired to as many customers as possible and keeping the total inventory, transportation and storage costs as low as possible

The Distribution (Place) Variable To satisfy consumers, products must be available at the right time and in a convenient location. In dealing with the **distribution (place) variable,** a marketing manager seeks to make products available in the quantities desired to as many customers as possible and to keep the total inventory, transport and storage costs as low as possible. A marketing manager may become involved in selecting and motivating intermediaries (wholesalers, retailers and dealers), establishing and maintaining inventory control procedures, and developing and managing transport and storage systems.

Promotion variable The aspect of the marketing mix that relates to activities used to inform one or more groups of people about an organisation and its products

The Promotion Variable The **promotion variable** relates to activities used to inform one or more groups of people about an organisation and its products—communication. Promotion can be aimed at increasing public awareness of an organisation and of new or existing products. In addition, promotion can serve to educate consumers about product features or to urge people to take a particular stance on a political or social issue. It may also be used to keep interest strong in an established product that has been available for decades. The advertisement in Figure 1.6 is an example.

Price variable The aspect of the marketing mix that relates to activities associated with establishing pricing policies and determining product prices

The Price Variable The **price variable** relates to activities associated with establishing pricing policies and determining product prices. Price is a critical component of the marketing mix because consumers are concerned about the value obtained in an exchange. Price often is used as a competitive tool; in fact, extremely intense price competition sometimes leads to price wars. For example, airlines like United, British Airways and Virgin Atlantic Airways are engaged in ruthless price cutting in the battle for transatlantic routes. Price can also help to establish a product's image. For instance, if Chanel tried to sell Chanel No. 5 in a two litre bottle for £3, consumers probably would not buy it because the low price would destroy the prestigious image of Chanel's de luxe brand.

The People Variable *Product, distribution, promotion* and *price* are the principal elements of the marketing mix. Marketers of services include *people* as a core element. Writers such as Kotler include people as part of the augmented product element. Whether part of the product element or a separate element of the marketing mix, there is no doubt that people are important. As marketers they manipulate the rest of the marketing mix. As intermediaries in the marketing channel they help make products and services available to the marketplace. As consumers

Figure 1.6 Promoting an established brand. Champagne house Moët & Chandon uses its heritage in its advertising to reinforce its brand appeal.

SOURCE: Courtesy of Olivia Beasley.

People variable The aspect of the marketing mix that reflects the level of customer service, advice, sales support and after market back-up required, involving recruitment policies and training, retention and motivation of key personnel

or buyers they create the need for the field of marketing. In the marketing mix, the **people variable** reflects the level of customer service, advice, sales support and after market back-up required, involving recruitment policies, training, retention and motivation of key personnel. For many products and most services, personnel interface directly with the intended purchaser and are often perceived by such consumers as being part and parcel of the product offering.

Developing and maintaining an effective marketing mix is a major requirement for a strong marketing strategy. Thus, as indicated in Figure 1.5, a large portion of this text (Chapters 8 through 21) focuses on the concepts, decisions and activities associated with the components of the marketing mix. It is the marketing mix that readers, as consumers, will most frequently have experienced. It is important to remember, however, that analysis must precede the development of a marketing strategy before the marketing mix is formulated for a product or a service.

Marketing Strategy: Marketing Management

Marketing management is a process of planning, organising, implementing and controlling marketing activities to facilitate and expedite exchanges effectively and efficiently. Effectiveness and efficiency are important dimensions of this definition. Effectiveness is the degree to which an exchange helps achieve an organisation's objectives. Efficiency is the minimisation of resources an organisation must spend to achieve a specific level of desired exchanges. Thus the overall goal of marketing management is to facilitate highly desirable exchanges and to min-imise as much as possible the costs of doing so.

Marketing planning is a systematic process of assessing opportunities and resources, determining marketing objectives, developing a marketing strategy and developing plans for implementation and control. Planning determines when and how marketing activities will be performed and who is to perform them. It forces marketing managers to think ahead, to establish objectives and to consider future marketing activities. Effective marketing planning also reduces or elimi-nates daily crises.

Organising marketing activities refers to developing the internal structure of the marketing unit. The structure is the key to directing marketing activities. The marketing unit can be organised by function, product, region, type of customer or a combination of all four.

Proper implementation of marketing plans hinges on co-ordination of market-ing activities, motivation of marketing personnel and effective communication within the unit. Marketing managers must motivate marketing personnel, co-ordinate their activities and integrate their activities both with those in other areas of the company and with the marketing efforts of personnel in external organisa-tions, such as advertising agencies and marketing research firms. An organisa-tion's communication system must allow the marketing manager to stay in contact with high level management, with managers of other functional areas within the firm and with personnel involved in marketing activities both inside and outside the organisation.

The marketing control process consists of establishing performance standards, evaluating actual performance by comparing it with established standards and reducing the difference between desired and actual performance. An effective con-trol process has four requirements. (1) It should ensure a rate of information flow that allows the marketing manager to quickly detect differences between actual and planned levels of performance. (2) It must accurately monitor different kinds of activities and be flexible enough to accommodate changes. (3) The control process must be economical so that its costs are low relative to the costs that would arise if there were no controls. (4) Finally, the control process should be designed so that both managers and subordinates can understand it. To maintain effective marketing control, an organisation needs to develop a comprehensive control process that evaluates marketing operations at regular intervals. Chapters 23 and 24 examine the planning, organising, implementing and controlling of marketing activities in greater detail.

● ● ● ● ● ● ● ● ● ● ● ● ● ● ● ● ●

The Organisation of This Book

The structure of this book adheres to the principle that is important to ana-lyse marketing opportunities, then develop strategies and finally construct programmes that implement the desired marketing strategy—the ASP process. Marketing analyses develop a thorough understanding of the marketplace—par-ticularly customers, competitors and market trends. This knowledge of the mar-ketplace provides a sound basis on which to devise marketing strategies. These should identify attractive target market segments, with a clear positioning and awareness of the competitive situation. Finally, to implement the recommended marketing strategy, marketing programmes must be designed with marketing mix combinations and control processes to ensure effective implementation. This analysis-strategy-programmes process is fundamental to sound marketing practice and is the sentiment behind Figure 1.5.

The first two parts of *Marketing: Concepts and Strategies*, therefore, address marketing opportunity analysis and target market selection:

- Part I: Marketing Defined
- Part II: Understanding and Targeting Markets

The next five parts examine in detail the core ingredients of the marketing mix. These are the tactical marketing activities at the heart of marketing programmes that take a product or service to the targeted consumers:

- Part III: Product, Branding, Packaging and Service Decisions
- Part IV: Place (Distribution and Channel) Decisions
- Part V: Promotion Decisions
- Part VI: Pricing Decisions
- Part VII: Manipulating the Marketing Mix

Finally, the implementation issues of effective marketing management are discussed in the last part of the book. This set of chapters returns to the core issues of marketing strategy and additionally discusses marketing planning, implementing strategies and the important consideration of ethical and social responsibility concerns in marketing:

- Part VIII: Marketing Management

Marketing: Concepts and Strategies also includes:

- a glossary of key terms
- full subject and name indexing
- a section of extended cases to enhance readers' understanding of key topics, supported with extensive guidance on how to tackle cases
- an appendix providing a summary of career choices and opportunities in marketing
- an appendix presenting revision hints and tips for readers about to take marketing examinations

• • • • • • • • • • • • • • • • • • •

Summary

● *Marketing* consists of individual and organisational activities that facilitate and expedite satisfying exchange relationships in a dynamic environment through the creation, distribution, promotion and pricing of goods, services and ideas. An *exchange* is the provision or transfer of goods, services and ideas in return for something of value. Four conditions must exist for an exchange to occur: (1) two or more individuals, groups or organisations must participate; (2) each party must have something of value desired by the other; (3) each party must be willing to give up what it has in order to receive the value held by the other; and (4) the parties to the exchange must be able to communicate with each other to make their "somethings of value" available. In an exchange, products are traded either for other products or for financial resources, such as cash or credit. *Products* can be *goods, services* or *ideas*. Through the exchange, the recipient (the customer) and the provider (the business) must be *satisfied*.

● It is important to study marketing because it permeates society. Marketing activities are performed in both business and non-business organisations. Moreover, marketing activities help business organisations generate profits and income, the life-blood of an economy. The study of marketing enhances consumer awareness. Marketing practised well improves business performance. Finally, marketing costs absorb about half of what the consumer spends.

● The *marketing concept* is a management philosophy that prompts a business organisation to try to satisfy customers' needs through a co-ordinated set of activities that also allows the organisation to achieve its goals. Customer satisfaction is the major objective of the marketing concept. The philosophy of the marketing concept emerged during the 1950s, as the *marketing era* succeeded the *production* and the *sales eras*. To make the marketing concept work, top management must accept it as an overall management philosophy. Implementing the marketing concept requires an efficient information system and sometimes the restructuring of the organisation.

● *Marketing strategy* involves selecting and analysing a target market (the group of people whom the organisation wants to reach) and creating and maintaining an appropriate *marketing mix* (product, distribution, promotion, price and people) to satisfy this market. Marketing strategy requires that managers focus on four tasks to achieve set objectives: (1) marketing opportunity analysis, (2) target market selection, (3) marketing mix development and (4) marketing management.

● Marketers should be able to recognise and analyse *marketing opportunities,* which are circumstances that allow an organisation to take action towards reaching a particular group of customers. Marketing opportunity analysis involves reviewing both internal factors (organisational objectives, financial resources, managerial skills, organisational strengths, organisational weaknesses and cost structures) and external ones in the *marketing environment* (the political, legal, regulatory, societal/green, technological, and economic and competitive forces).

● A *target market* is a group of people for whom a firm creates and maintains a marketing mix that specifically fits the needs and preferences of that group. It is important for an organisation's management to designate which customer groups the firm is trying to serve and to have some information about these customers. The identification and analysis of a target market provide a foundation on which a marketing mix can be developed.

● The five principal variables that make up the marketing mix product, distribution, promotion, price and people. The *product variable* is the aspect of the marketing mix that deals with researching consumers' wants and designing a product with the desired characteristics. A marketing manager tries to make products available in the quantities desired to as many customers as possible and to keep the total inventory, transport and storage costs as low as possible—the *distribution (place) variable*. The *promotion variable* relates to activities used to inform one or more groups of people about an organisation and its products. The *price variable* refers to establishing pricing policies and determining product prices. The *people variable* controls the marketing mix, facilitates the product's distribution and sale, and—as consumers or buyers—gives marketing its rationale. Marketing exists to encourage consumer satisfaction.

● *Marketing management* is a process of planning, organising, implementing and controlling marketing activities to facilitate and expedite exchanges effectively and efficiently. Marketing planning is a systematic process of assessing opportunities and resources, determining marketing objectives, developing a marketing strategy and developing plans for implementation and control. Organising marketing activities refers to developing the internal structure of the marketing unit. Properly implementing marketing plans depends on co-ordinating marketing activities, motivating marketing personnel and effectively communicating within the unit. The marketing control process consists of establishing performance standards, evaluating actual performance by comparing it with established standards and reducing the difference between desired and actual performance.

Important Terms

Marketing

Exchange

Customer satisfaction

Marketing environment

Product

Good

Service

Idea

Marketing concept

Production era

Sales era

Marketing era

Marketing strategy

Marketing mix

Marketing opportunity

Target market

Product variable

Distribution (place) variable

Promotion variable

Price variable

People variable

Marketing management

Discussion and Review Questions

1. What is marketing? How did you define marketing before you read this chapter?
2. Why should someone study marketing?
3. Discuss the basic elements of the marketing concept. Which businesses use this concept? Have these businesses adopted the marketing concept? Explain.
4. Identify several business organisations that obviously have not adopted the marketing concept. What characteristics of these organisations indicate non-acceptance of the marketing concept?
5. Describe the major components of a marketing strategy. How are the components related?
6. Identify the tasks involved in developing a marketing strategy.

7. What are the primary issues that marketing managers consider when conducting a market opportunity analysis?
8. What are the variables in the marketing environment? How much control does a marketing manager have over environmental variables?
9. Why is the selection of a target market such an important issue?
10. Why are the elements of the marketing mix known as variables? What are these variables?
11. What type of management activities are involved in the marketing management process?
12. Why is it important to adhere to the principle of analyses first, then marketing strategy development, followed ultimately by programmes for implementing the recommended strategy?

Recommended Readings

M. Baker, "The nature and scope of marketing", in the *Companion Encyclopaedia of Marketing*, M. Baker, ed. (London: Routledge, 1995).

M. Baker, "What is marketing?" in *The Marketing Book*, M. Baker, ed. (Oxford: Butterworth-Heinemann, 1994).

J. Lynch, "What is marketing?" in *Effective Industrial Marketing*, N. Hart, ed. (London: Kogan Page, 1994).

T. Levitt, "Marketing myopia", *Harvard Business Review*, 1960, vol. 38, no. 4, pp. 45–56.

Cases

1.1   Sweden's IKEA Marches On

When Swedish home furnishings retailer IKEA opened its first store in the UK, a retail shed near the M6 at Warrington, curious shoppers found queues jamming nearby roads, parking spaces at a premium and retailing analysts by the score. With just one store, IKEA had the UK furniture industry on its toes: large retail groups and manufacturers alike feared large market share losses. With its acquisition of the UK's Habitat, IKEA has conquered yet another territory.

IKEA has grown from one store in 1958 to 131 stores in 27 countries, 22,000 employees and sales of over £3 billion. Close to 80 per cent of sales are from within Europe, but recent expansion in North America, South East Asia and Australasia is now increasing *rest of the world* sales—despite some initial franchising difficulties in certain territories. IKEA's distinctive catalogue is produced in-house and now printed in 14 languages. IKEA is perhaps one of the world's most successful retailers with a brand name that is known, recognised and discussed; a retail concept that stands for value, style and quality; everything for the home under one roof, with easy parking, children's play areas and cafés—"a day out"! As the company succinctly states in its advertising:

IKEA: the furnishings store from Sweden
More for your money

IKEA's huge volumes, cheap out-of-town sites and dedication to keeping costs low through self-assembly packs mean that unlike many competitors, the company coped with the recession of the early 1990s. Low prices have been the key to IKEA's success, but price alone cannot create an internationally long term marketing success story. Products are updated consistently to match consumers' expectations and lifestyles. In-store service and staff training are integral to the IKEA shopping experience. Sites are chosen to maximise catchment areas, to make access easy for shoppers and to bring the brand name to the attention of the whole community. Logistics give IKEA an edge, with carefully managed ordering and delivery reducing both stock-holdings and stock-outs. Promotion emphasises the "style without expense" philosophy and the IKEA name. The result has been a country by country revolution as staid furniture markets have been rejuvenated with the entry of IKEA. Shoppers intending to buy just a sofa return home with a sofa, a chair, some lamps and a general excitement about a new store where they can buy home furnishings at unbelievable prices.

The latest strategic developments for IKEA include entering eastern European markets, developing a new IKEA format and expanding its mail order/electronic ordering. Eastern Europe has been the recent target for expansion, with IKEA stores opening in Poland, the Czech Republic and Hungary. The company is also sourcing furniture from eastern European manufacturers, which now supply 15 per cent of its range. The standard "big box" IKEA concept has been brought to a smaller stage with the New York opening in Manhattan of the first IKEA *Marketing Outpost,* a 720 square metre (7,500 square foot) "boutique", significantly smaller than the normal 19,000 square metre (200,000 square foot) IKEA superstore. Even more unusual is the decision to offer only a selected, themed, reduced range at any moment in time. For example, *IKEA Cook* showcases the company's kitchen-related merchandise. Every 8 to 12 weeks the store closes completely, to re-open with a new look, different merchandise, signage, lighting and staff uniforms. If successful, the *Marketing Outpost* concept will be rolled out into other cities and countries. IKEA is also recognising the growing use of the Internet and is developing sales tools to utilise this new technology.

IKEA has its ideals and operating philosophies: standards matter. IKEA has a forceful, well directed marketing strategy actioned through two tightly developed marketing mixes: one for the core super-stores, and another for the new *Marketing Outpost* operation. The result is a successful, expanding company, satisfied target customers and unhappy competitors.

SOURCES: Helen Jones, "IKEA's global strategy is a winning formula", *Marketing Week,* 15 March 1996, p. 22; Jennifer Pellet, "IKEA takes Manhattan!", *Discount Merchandiser,* October 1995, pp. 22–23; "IKEA", *Retail Business,* March 1995, pp. 78–81; Jonathan Pell, "IKEA successfully penetrates east European consumer markets", *Central European,* June 1994, pp. 13–14; *IKEA Facts,* 1990 and 1992; B. Solomon, "A Swedish company corners the business: worldwide", *Management Review,* 80(4), 1991, pp. 10–13.

Questions for Discussion

1. Explain why IKEA is successful.
2. To whom does the *Marketing Outpost* concept appeal? Why has IKEA developed this novel format?
3. In what ways does IKEA deploy the marketing concept?

1.2 Le Shuttle: P&O Fights Back

For decades, the majority of tourists leaving the UK for France or Benelux travelled with their cars on the cross-Channel ferries. For German, Dutch and French tourists wishing to explore Britain and Eire, the car ferries were a popular option. Flights were used more for business and longer haul visitors, were costly and required car hire or a thorough knowledge of public transport networks in a foreign land. Car ferry operators fought initially on price or availability of routes, but as the 1980s drew to a close, service levels, duty free shopping and on-board entertainment became the focus.

Now the strategies have changed. The big ferry operators—P&O European Ferries, Sealink-Stena Line and Hoverspeed—are engaged in fierce competition both with each other and with the airlines of Europe. In addition, now there is the Channel Tunnel. Motorists can drive themselves and their vehicles on purpose built rail wagons and be transported under the Channel between France and England for less than the price of a cross-Channel ferry and with considerable time savings. The journey is now only three hours from London's Waterloo Station to central Paris. Eurotunnel first advertised its service—Le Shuttle—through agency BMP DDB Needham in 1992, aiming at the freight market. During 1993, public relations activities brought Le Shuttle rail service to the attention of consumers throughout Europe. Le Shuttle takes freight lorries, cars and coaches from Folkestone to Calais. Eurostar is a city-to-city rail passenger service with schedules connecting most major UK cities with continental Europe.

Fully operational in 1996, Eurotunnel intends to attract half of the annual 12 million car ferry passengers onto its tracks beneath the Channel, plus an additional one million passengers who previously were deterred from travelling by sea or air. Car ferry brand leader P&O, previously with 54 per cent of the market, has responded aggressively to the attack from the Channel Tunnel. P&O has invested £500 million in new, larger, faster, more comfortable ferries, with a further £5 million for a reservation system for travel agents. Each year, £3.5 million is spent on advertising, reinforcing P&O's brand name, routes and reputation. The advertising also stresses the spacious, comfortable ferries with a wide choice of bars and restaurants, duty free shopping and on-board entertainment—the implication being that a car ferry journey may take longer but is less claustrophobic, more comfortable and less boring than Le Shuttle's service.

All the ferry companies are emphasising what were once secondary aspects of their service—the additional amenities and facilities on board the new generation of super ferries:

> On board you'll be eased effortlessly into the holiday spirit as you wander from the pool to a movie or from the bar to the cabaret.

The main operators have changed their advertising agencies in order to gain fresh ideas for the battle with a debt-ridden but highly professional and aggressive Eurotunnel and operators Le Shuttle and Eurostar. In addition, several ferry operators are diversifying into other leisure or transport activities, into new markets and with new car ferry routes to Iberia and Scandinavia (not served by the new Channel Tunnel).

The marketing environment has altered dramatically with the launch of Le Shuttle. Ferry operators' product offerings have been redefined, branding strengthened and promotional strategy significantly re-thought over the past two years. Strategies and tactics have altered as a new mode of transport and competitor has entered the marketplace. Inevitably, however, the tunnel is going to gain the dominant market share.

SOURCES: Penny Kiernan, "Gale warning for the ferry firms", *Marketing Week*, 16 November 1992, pp. 15–16; Todd Pruzan, "Chunnel surfing with Eurostar", *Advertising Age*, 12 June 1995, p. 30; James Bredin, "Tunnel vision!", *Industry Week*, 5 December 1994, pp. 50–52; Emma Hall, "Fight at the end of the tunnel", *Marketing Week*, 28 October 1994, pp. 38–41.

Questions for Discussion

1. How has P&O modified its marketing mix?
2. Why has the competitive environment forced the ferry companies to re-think their marketing strategies?
3. In the face of competition from Le Shuttle and Eurostar, why is the role of marketing increasingly important for P&O?

2

THE MARKETING ENVIRONMENT

"All businesses operate within an environment, which directly or indirectly affects the way in which they function, just as we as consumers live within a cultural and social environment which to a greater or lesser degree determines the way in which we behave as individuals."

Elaine O'Brien
University of Strathclyde

OBJECTIVES

- To understand the concept of the marketing environment and the importance of environmental scanning and analysis
- To identify the types of political forces in the marketing environment
- To understand how laws and their interpretation influence marketing practices
- To determine how government regulations and self-regulatory agencies affect marketing activities
- To identify societal issues that marketers must deal with as they make decisions
- To explore the effects of new technology on society and on marketing activities
- To understand how economic and competitive factors affect organisations' ability to compete and customers' willingness and ability to buy products

In 1947 the launching of the Marshall Plan presented a blueprint for the economic reconstruction of a Europe devastated by the Second World War. This led in 1948 to the creation of the Organisation for European Economic Co-operation (OEEC), the precursor of today's Economic Union. In March 1957 the Treaty of Rome was signed to establish the European Economic Community (EEC). By 1973, with the arrival of Denmark, Ireland and the UK, the EEC had grown to nine member states. Greece joined in 1981 and Portugal and Spain in 1986 to create the "Euro 12". The momentous signing of the Maastricht Treaty in 1992 established the European Union (EU) and by 1 January 1993 the European single market was at last a reality. The single market is defined by the EU as "*an economic area within which persons, goods, services and*

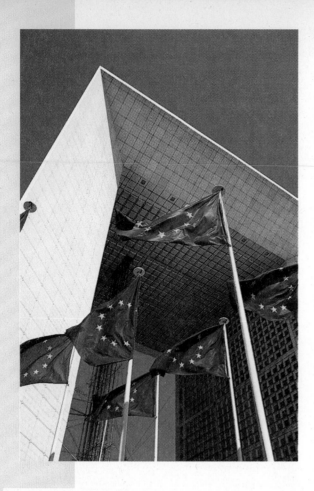

ing states, as well as on marketers representing their companies. With the removal of so many bureaucratic barriers on 1 January 1993, professionally qualified personnel could seek employment without retraining in other member states; companies could tender for government contracts throughout the EU; imports and exports became subject to far fewer restrictions, less red tape, reduced customs controls and much freer movement within and between EU states. Immigration and travel have become much quicker and simpler than before. Health and safety working regulations have been harmonised, as have air travel regulations and even standards for mobile phone networks and VAT collection.

The EU has many critics, not least due to its Common Agricultural Policy (CAP), which is a significant drain on the resources of the richer member states; the often top-heavy bureaucracy of European government in Brussels; and the inevitable formalisation of so many working practices when so many countries' rules and regulations are combined to form a single, cohesive approach. However, there are few marketers who would claim that in the years since the harmonisation of Europe in 1993, doing business across Europe has not been simplified, opening up significant marketing opportunities for many businesses and presenting new competitive threats.

For businesses that are located in or trading with the EU's latest batch of recruits—Austria, Finland and Sweden—the EU continues to present new challenges and a reason to re-think marketing strategies. There is little doubt that the EU is an external factor in the marketing environment of most businesses and consumers that cannot be ignored. ∎

capital have unrestricted freedom of movement, which entails not only the elimination of customs barriers, but also of technical, tax and legislative obstacles". Many more countries now wish to join the EU, notably former eastern bloc communist states, but until they offer an open economy capable of standing up to competition from western Europe and democratic institutions attentive to human rights, the EU will block further moves by these states to join.

The single market has a significant impact on the populations of member and non-member trad-

SOURCES: EU policy documents, 1990–1996; *Europe in Figures*, Eurostat, Luxembourg, 1995; *Europe on the Move, From Single Market to European Union, Internal Market*: all EU, Brussels, publications.

The formation of the EU will have a tremendous impact on the decisions and activities of marketers. This chapter explores the political, legal, regulatory, societal, technological, and economic and competitive forces that make up what is termed the marketing environment. The first section defines the marketing environment and considers why it is critical to scan and analyse it, before exploring the major elements of the marketing environment. The chapter then goes on to discuss the political forces that generate government actions affecting marketing activities, the effects of laws and regulatory agencies on these activities, the desires and expectations of society and the major dimensions of the technological forces in the environment. The final section in Chapter 2 considers the effects of general economic conditions—prosperity, recession, depression and recovery—and also examines several types of economic forces that influence the ability of companies to compete and consumers' willingness and ability to buy. These are all factors that companies cannot ignore and that also influence what consumers are offered.

● ●

Examining and Responding to the Marketing Environment

Marketing environment The external forces that directly or indirectly influence an organisation's acquisition of inputs and generation of outputs, comprising six categories of forces: political, legal, regulatory, societal/green, technological, and economic and competitive

The **marketing environment** consists of external forces that directly or indirectly influence an organisation's acquisition of inputs and generation of outputs. Inputs might include personnel, financial resources, raw materials and information. Outputs could be information (such as advertisements), packages, goods, services or ideas. As indicated in Chapter 1 and as shown in Figure 1.4 on page 18, the marketing environment consists of six categories of forces: political, legal, regulatory, societal/green, technological, and economic and competitive. Although there are numerous environmental factors, most fall into one of these six categories.

Whether they fluctuate rapidly or slowly, environmental forces are always dynamic. Changes in the marketing environment can create uncertainty, threats and opportunities for marketers. Although the future is not very predictable, marketers can estimate what will happen, although some fail to do so, thus negatively affecting the performance of their businesses. It can be stated with certainty that marketers will continue to modify their marketing strategies in response to the dynamic environment. Furthermore, marketing managers who fail to recognise changes in environmental forces leave their firms unprepared to capitalise on marketing opportunities or to cope with threats created by changes in the environment.

Organisations that cannot deal with an unfavourable environment are at risk of going under. For example, on Merseyside and Tyneside during the OPEC led recession of the mid-1970s many manufacturers cut back on their workforces, causing unemployment rates of over 40 per cent in many suburbs. Many local retailers and small shopkeepers, restaurants, take-aways and garages had anticipated neither the extent of the unemployment nor its effect on their businesses. Dozens of small, local businesses closed down. The 1990 Persian Gulf crisis caused huge increases in the price of petrol. The car buying public became even more concerned about fuel consumption, with a resultant decline in the sales of high horsepower sports cars and executive saloons. The Gulf crisis also hit business travel and tourism, affecting the fortunes of many airlines and hotel operators. Civil war in what was once Yugoslavia has had tragic implications for the peoples of that region and an economic impact on the tour operators who specialised in holidays to the Yugoslavian coastline. Yet another example is the BSE beef crisis, which has affected farmers, meat producers and supermarkets. Thus monitoring the environment is crucial to an organisation's survival and to the long term achievement of its goals.

Environmental Scanning and Analysis

Environmental scanning The process of collecting information about the forces in the marketing environment

Environmental analysis The process of assessing and interpreting the information gathered through environmental scanning

To monitor changes in the marketing environment effectively, marketers must engage in environmental scanning and analysis. **Environmental scanning** is the process of collecting information about the forces in the marketing environment. Scanning involves observation; keeping "an ear to the ground"; perusal of secondary sources, such as business, trade, government and general interest publications; and marketing research. However, managers must be careful not to gather so much information that sheer volume makes analysis impossible.

Environmental analysis is the process of assessing and interpreting the information gathered through environmental scanning. A manager evaluates the information for accuracy, tries to resolve inconsistencies in the data and, if warranted, assigns significance to the findings. Through analysis, a marketing manager seeks to describe current environmental changes and to predict future changes. By evaluating these changes, the manager should be able to determine possible threats and opportunities linked to environmental fluctuations. Understanding the current state of the marketing environment and recognising the threats and opportunities arising from changes within it help marketing managers assess the performance of current marketing efforts and develop marketing strategies for the future.

JCB, the construction equipment producer, allocates to individual managers the task of monitoring aspects of the marketing environment: political, legal, regulatory, societal—particularly the green movement—technological, and economic and competitive. A small committee meets to prepare short papers and presentations to interested colleagues. When the laws relating to roadworks altered, making contractors responsible for the safety of their sites and the long term quality of the re-laid road surface, JCB recognised that many of its customers would have to alter their working practices as a result. So the company produced guides to assist these contractors in responding to the new legislation. In so doing, JCB was able to enhance its image and at the same time promote its products.

Responding to Environmental Forces

In responding to environmental forces, marketing managers can take two general approaches: to accept environmental forces as uncontrollable or to confront and mould them. If environmental forces are viewed as uncontrollable, the organisation remains passive and reactive towards the environment. Instead of trying to influence forces in the environment, its marketing managers tend to adjust current marketing strategies to environmental changes. They approach marketing opportunities discovered through environmental scanning and analysis with caution. On the other hand, marketing managers who believe that environmental forces can be shaped adopt a proactive approach. For example, if a market is blocked by traditional environmental constraints, marketing managers may apply economic, psychological, political and promotional skills to gain access to it or operate within it. Once they identify what blocks a marketing opportunity, marketers can assess the power of the various parties involved and develop strategies to try to overcome environmental forces.[1]

In trying to influence environmental forces, marketing management may seek to create market opportunities or to extract greater benefits relative to costs from existing market opportunities. For instance, a firm losing sales to competitors with lower priced products may strive to develop technology that would make its production processes more efficient; greater efficiency would allow it to lower the prices of its own products.

Political action is another way of affecting environmental forces. UK retailers, for example, are lobbying government to permit longer Sunday trading and legal opening of retail outlets all day. A proactive approach can be constructive and bring desired results. However, managers must recognise that there are limits on how much an environmental force can be shaped and that these limits vary across environmental forces. Although an organisation may be able to influence the enactment of laws through lobbying, it is unlikely that a single organisation can significantly increase the national birthrate or move the economy from recession to prosperity.

Generalisations are not possible. It cannot be stated that either of these approaches to environmental response is better than the other. For some organisations, the passive, reactive approach is more appropriate, but for other firms, the aggressive approach leads to better performance. The selection of a particular approach depends on an organisation's managerial philosophies, objectives, financial resources, customers and human skills, and on the composition of the set of environmental forces within which the organisation operates.

The rest of this chapter explores in detail each of the six environmental forces—political, legal, regulatory, societal/green, technological, and economic and competitive.

• • • • • • • • • • • • • • • • • • • •

Political Forces

The political, legal and regulatory forces of the marketing environment are closely interrelated. Legislation is enacted, legal decisions are interpreted by the courts and regulatory agencies are created and operated, for the most part, by persons elected or appointed to political offices or by civil servants. Legislation and regulations (or the lack of them) reflect the current political outlook. Consequently, the political force of the marketing environment has the potential to influence marketing decisions and strategies.

Marketing organisations need to maintain good relations with elected political officials for several reasons. When political officials are well disposed towards particular firms or industries, they are less likely to create or enforce laws and regulations unfavourable to these companies. For example, political officials who believe that oil companies are making honest efforts to control pollution are unlikely to create and enforce highly restrictive pollution control laws. In addition, governments are big buyers, and political officials can influence how much a government agency purchases and from whom. Finally, political officials can play key roles in helping organisations secure foreign markets.

Many marketers view political forces as beyond their control; they simply try to adjust to conditions that arise from those forces. Some firms, however, seek to influence political events by helping to elect to political office individuals who regard them positively. Much of this help is in the form of contributions to political parties. A sizeable contribution to a campaign fund may carry with it an implicit understanding that the party, if elected, will perform political favours for the contributing firm. There are, though, strict laws governing donations and lobbying in most countries.

Legal Forces

A number of laws influence marketing decisions and activities. This discussion focuses on procompetitive and consumer protection laws and their interpretation.

Procompetitive legislation is enacted to preserve competition and to end various practices deemed unacceptable by society. Some of the most important of these are discussed next in greater detail.

Monopolies and Mergers   In the UK the President of the Board of Trade and the Director General of the **Office of Fair Trading** can refer monopolies for investigation by the **Monopolies and Mergers Commission,** an independent body whose members are drawn from a variety of backgrounds, including lawyers, economists, industrialists and trade unionists. The legislation defines a monopoly as a situation where at least a quarter of a particular kind of good or service is supplied by a single person or a group of connected companies, or by two or more people acting in a way that prevents, restricts or distorts competition. Local monopolies can also be referred to the commission.

If the commission finds that a monopoly operates against the public interest, the President of the Board of Trade has power to take action to remedy or prevent the harm that the commission considers may exist. Alternatively, the Director General may be asked to negotiate undertakings to remedy the adverse effects identified by the commission. The government believes that the market is a better judge than itself of the advantages and disadvantages of mergers, so most take-overs and proposed mergers are allowed to be decided by the companies' shareholders. However, when too much power would be placed in the hands of one organisation, company or person, the government will insist on a Monopolies and Mergers Commission appraisal. If the commission believes it is against the public interest for a take-over or merger to proceed, then it will prohibit any agreement between the companies or organisations involved. For example, generator PowerGen was prevented from taking over regional electricity company Midlands Electricity.

The EU has a minister responsible for competition. In recent years, that minister has ruled on anti-competitive practices in many industries, from airlines to financial services, forcing companies to alter their trading practices and encouraging competition from a broader base of organisations.

Financial Services Act 1986   The Director General of the Office of Fair Trading is required to consider the implications for competition of rules, regulations, guidance and other arrangements and practices of the regulatory bodies, investment exchanges and clearing houses. The Director General must report to the President of the Board of Trade whenever a significant or potentially significant effect on competition has been identified. This legislation is for the protection of investors, and the Secretary of State may refuse or revoke recognition of the organisation or require it to make alterations to its activities.

Anti-competitive Practices   The Director General of the Office of Fair Trading can investigate any business practice, whether in the public or private sector, that may restrict, distort or prevent competition in the production, supply or acquisition of goods or services in Britain. The Secretary of State has power to take remedial action.

Restrictive Trade Practices Act 1976 If two or more people who are party to the supply of goods or services in Britain accept some limitation on their freedom to make their own decisions about matters such as prices or conditions of sale, the Office of Fair Trading must be notified and such an agreement must be registered. Once an agreement has been registered, the Director General is under a general duty to refer it to the Restrictive Practices Court, and the court must declare the restrictions in it contrary to the public interest unless the parties can satisfy the court that the public interest is not an issue. The vast majority of agreements never reach the court because parties elect to give up the restrictions rather than go through such a procedure.

European Union The objective of the European Union's competition policy is to ensure that there is free and fair competition in trade among member states and that the government trade barriers the Treaty of Rome seeks to dismantle are not replaced by private barriers that fragment the Common Market. The EU has powers to investigate and terminate alleged infringements and impose fines. The Treaty of Rome prohibits agreements or concertive practices that may affect trade among member states and aims to prevent restriction or distortion of competition within the Common Market.[2]

Most countries have similar procompetitive legislation. For example, in the United States the Sherman Antitrust Act prevents monopolistic situations; the Clayton Antitrust Act specifically prohibits price discrimination; and the Federal Trade Commission Act broadly prohibits unfair methods of competition and empowers the Federal Trade Commission to work with the Department of Justice to enforce the provisions of the Clayton Antitrust Act. The Wheeler-Lea Act essentially makes unfair and deceptive acts or practices unlawful, regardless of whether they incur competition. The Robinson-Patman Act deals with discriminatory price differentials.[3]

Consumer Protection Legislation

The second category of regulatory laws, *consumer protection legislation,* is not a recent development. However, consumer protection laws mushroomed in the mid-1960s and early 1970s. A number of them deal with consumer safety, while others relate to the sale of various hazardous products such as flammable fabrics and toys that might injure children. In the UK, the Fair Trading Act (1973) provides a machinery—headed by the Director General of the Office of Fair Trading—for continuous review of consumer affairs, for actions dealing with trading practices that unfairly affect consumers' interests, for action against persistent offenders under existing law and for the negotiation of self-regulatory codes of practice to raise trading standards.

Consumers' interests with regard to the purity of food, the description and performance of goods and services, and pricing information are safeguarded by the Food Act (1984), the Medicines Act (1968), the Misrepresentations Act (1967), the Trade Descriptions Act (1968), the Prices Act (1974), the Unfair Contract Terms Act (1977), the Sale of Goods Act (1979), the Supply of Goods and Services Act (1982) and the Consumer Protection Act (1987). The marking and accuracy of quantities are regulated by the Weights and Measures Act (1985). The Consumer Credit Act of 1974 provides comprehensive protection for consumers who enter into credit or hire transactions. The Consumer Protection Act of 1987 implements a harmonised European Union code of civil law covering product liability, creates a general criminal offence of supplying unsafe consumer goods, makes it an offence to give any misleading price indication and consolidates the powers provided under safety related acts. The Financial Services Act (1986) offers greater protection to investors by establishing a new regulatory framework for the industry.

In addition, consumer advice and information are provided to the general public at the local level by the Citizens' Advice Bureaux and the Trading Standards or Consumer Protection departments of local authorities, and in some areas by specialist consumer advice centres. The independent, non-statutory National Consumer Council, which receives government finance, ensures that consumers' views are made known to those in government and industry. Nationalised industries have consumer councils whose members investigate questions of concern to the consumer, and many trade associations in industry and commerce have established codes of practice. In addition, several private organisations work to further consumer interests, the largest of which is the **Consumers' Association,** funded by the subscriptions of its membership of over one million people. The association conducts an extensive programme of comparative testing of goods and investigation of services; its views and test reports are published in its monthly magazines and other publications.

Consumers' Association A private organisation, funded by members' subscriptions, that works to further consumer interests

Interpreting Laws

Laws certainly have the potential to influence marketing activities, but the actual effects of the laws are determined by how marketers and the courts interpret them. Laws seem to be quite specific because they contain many complex clauses and sub-clauses. In reality, however, many laws and regulations are stated in vague terms that force marketers to rely on legal advice rather than their own understanding and common sense. Because of this vagueness, some organisations attempt to gauge the limits of certain laws by operating in a legally questionable way to see how far they can go with certain practices before being prosecuted. Other marketers, however, interpret regulations and statutes very conservatively and strictly to avoid violating a vague law.

Although court rulings directly affect businesses accused of specific violations, they also have a broader, less direct impact on other businesses. When marketers try to interpret laws in relation to specific marketing practices, they often analyse recent court decisions, both to understand better what the law is intended to do and to gain a clearer sense of how the courts are likely to interpret it in the future.

• • • • • • • • • • • • • • • • • • •

Regulatory Forces

Interpretation alone does not determine the effectiveness of laws and regulations; the level of enforcement by regulatory agencies is also significant. Some regulatory agencies are created and administered by government units; others are sponsored by non-governmental sources.

UK Government

Ministry of Agriculture, Fisheries and Food This ministry develops and controls policies for agriculture, horticulture, fisheries and food; it also has responsibilities for environmental and rural issues and food policies.

Department of Employment This department controls the Employment Service, employment policy and legislation; training policy and legislation; health and safety at work; industrial relations; wages councils; equal opportunities; small firms and tourism; statistics on labour and industrial matters for the UK; the Careers Service; and international representation on employment matters.

Department of the Environment The DoE controls policies for planning and regional development, local government, new towns, housing, construction, inner city matters, environmental protection, water, the countryside, sports and recreation, conservation, historic buildings and ancient monuments.

Export Credit Guarantee Department This department is responsible for the provision of insurance for exporters against the risk of not being paid for goods and services, access to bank finance for exports and insurance cover for new investment overseas.

Central Statistical Office The office prepares and interprets statistics needed for central economic and social policies and management; it co-ordinates the statistical work of other departments.

Department for Trade and Industry/Board of Trade The DTI controls industrial and commercial policy, promotion of enterprise and competition in the UK and abroad, and investor and consumer protection. Specific responsibilities include industrial innovation policy; regional industrial policy; business development, management development and business/education links; international trade policy; commercial relations and export promotions; competition policy; company law; insolvency; consumer protection and safety; radio regulations; and intellectual property.

Department of Transport This department is responsible for land, sea and air transport; sponsorship of the nationalised transport authorities and the rail network regulation; domestic and international civil aviation; international transport agreements; shipping and ports industries; navigation issues, HM Coastguard and marine pollution; motorways and trunk roads; road safety; and overseeing local authority transport. For example, JCB's advertising of its compact equipment range shows how the company has responded to changing regulations in general, and the Streetworks Act in particular (Figure 2.1).

These examples of British government departments are not unusual. Similar administrative bodies exist in most countries. Increasingly in the EU, political, legal and regulatory forces are being harmonised to reflect common standards and enforcement.

Local Authorities The functions of the UK local authorities are far reaching; some are primary duties, whereas others are purely discretionary. Broadly speaking, functions are divided between county and district councils on the basis that the county council is responsible for matters requiring planning and administration over wide areas or requiring the support of substantial resources, whereas district councils on the whole administer functions of a more local significance. English county councils are generally responsible for strategic planning, transport planning, highways, traffic regulations, local education, consumer protection, refuse disposal, police, the fire service, libraries and personal social services. District councils are responsible for environmental health, housing decisions, most planning applications and refuse collection. They may also provide some museums, art galleries and parks. At both county and district council level, arrangements depend on local agreements.

Most countries in Europe have a similar structure: resource hungry issues with wide ranging social and political consequences are controlled centrally. Planning

WE'VE GOT THE WORKS FOR STREETWORKS.

THE BIGGEST NAME IN COMPACT EQUIPMENT.

Its never been tougher out on the streets. Thanks to the New Roads and Streetworks Act, working on our highways and by-ways has never been more demanding. But thanks to the JCB Compact Equipment range, its never been easier or safer. Each of our minis, backhoes, Robot skid steers and wheeled loaders combines a number of model variants and attachment options to give you the output, productivity and versatility you need. Call free for our Compact Equipment Guide. Because complying with the letter & the law is easier with the letters J. C. B. **FREEPHONE 0800 581761**

Figure 2.1   Responding to regulatory changes. JCB's compact equipment range advertising responds to changing regulations and the Streetworks Act.

SOURCE: Client: *John Bradley, JCB Sales Ltd.* Agency: *CB Brookes Advertising Ltd.*

and service provision within the community are viewed as being better controlled at the local level by the actual communities that will experience the advantages or problems resulting from such decision-making. The European Union aims to establish commonly accepted parameters for planning, service provision and regulation, and a framework to assist in inter- and intra-country disputes.

Non-governmental Regulatory Forces

In the absence of governmental regulatory forces and in an attempt to prevent government intervention, some businesses try to regulate themselves. For example, many newspapers have voluntarily banned advertisements for telephone chat services used for undesirable activities, even though technically not illegal. Trade associations in a number of industries have developed self-regulatory programmes. Even though these programmes are not a direct outgrowth of laws, many were established to stop or stall the development of laws and governmental regulatory groups that would regulate the associations' marketing practices. Sometimes trade associations establish codes of ethics by which their members must abide or risk censure by other members, or even exclusion from the programme. For example, many cigarette manufacturers have agreed, through a code of ethics, not to advertise their products to children and teenagers. The ITC Code of Advertising Standards and Practice aims to keep broadcast advertising "legal, decent, honest and truthful".[4]

Self-regulatory programmes have several advantages over governmental laws and regulatory agencies. They are usually less expensive to establish and implement, and their guidelines are generally more realistic and operational. In addition, effective industry self-regulatory programmes reduce the need to expand government bureaucracy. However, these programmes also have several limitations. When a trade association creates a set of industry guidelines for its members, non-member firms do not have to abide by them. In addition, many self-regulatory programmes lack the tools or the authority to enforce guidelines. Finally, guidelines in self-regulatory programmes are often less strict than those established by government agencies.

Deregulation Governments can drastically alter the environment for companies. In the UK the privatisation of the public utilities created new terms and conditions for their suppliers and sub-contractors. The state's sales of Jaguar and Rover in the car industry and of British Airways created commercially lean companies that suddenly had new impetus to become major competitors in their industries. Deregulation in the European Union has created opportunities across borders and also new threats. Car manufacturers were previously able to restrict certain models to specific countries. They placed rigorous controls on their dealers, forbidding them to retail cars produced by rival manufacturers in the same showroom or on the same site, many of which have been swept aside. Marketing Insight 2.1 highlights some of the changes instigated by EU deregulation in 1993.

• • • • • • • • • • • • • • • • • • • •

Societal/Green Forces

Societal/green forces
Individuals and groups and the issues engaging them that pressure marketers to provide high living standards and enjoyable lifestyles through socially responsible decisions and activities

Societal/green forces comprise the structure and dynamics of individuals and groups and the issues that engage them. Society becomes concerned about marketers' activities when those activities have questionable or negative consequences. For example, in recent times, well publicised incidents of unethical behaviour by marketers and others have perturbed and even angered consumers. Chapter 25 takes a detailed look at marketing ethics and social responsibility. When marketers do a good job of satisfying society, praise or positive evaluation rarely follows. Society expects marketers to provide a high standard of living and to protect the general quality of life. This section examines some of society's expectations, the means used to express those expectations, and the problems and opportunities that marketers experience as they try to deal with society's often contradictory wishes.

Living Standards and Quality of Life In society, most people want more than just the bare necessities; they want to achieve the highest standard of living possible. For example, there is a desire for homes that offer not only protection from the elements but also comfort and a satisfactory lifestyle. People want many varieties of safe and readily available food that is also easily prepared. Clothing protects bodies, but many consumers want a variety of clothing for adornment and to project a certain image to others. Consumers want vehicles that provide rapid, safe and efficient travel. They want communication systems that give information from around the globe—a desire apparent in the popularity of products such as facsimile machines and the 24 hour news coverage provided by cable and satellite television networks. In addition, there is a demand for sophisticated medical services that prolong life expectancy and improve physical appearance. Education is expected to help consumers acquire and enjoy a higher standard of living.

Regulatory Changes Impact on Business

The first of January 1993 heralded significant changes throughout Europe. As news broadcasts and press headlines explained, "the single Euro-market is here!". For over a decade bureaucrats in the EU had been steering member countries towards an agreement that would make trade and commerce within the European Union simpler to conduct and more uniform. The UK government's Department of Trade and Industry highlighted some of the changes in its press releases.

- *Duty.* No more quotas for duty paid goods brought back from holidays and business trips within the EU.
- *Professional permits.* Professionally qualified workers such as nurses or teachers can work in other EU countries without lengthy retraining.
- *Exports.* Businesses can tender for government contracts in other member states. Less red tape for companies importing or exporting in the EU.
- *Inward investment.* The enlarged single market is expected to be more attractive for investment by North American and Pacific Rim countries, particularly American and Japanese corporations.
- *Competition and choice.* Opportunities and threats as firms offer products and services across national borders, competing with domestic suppliers.
- Working practices. Increasing pressure for member states to agree on working conditions, pay, hours and legislation.
- *Safety.* Europe wide safety standards for products produced in and imported to the EU.

- *Airline deregulation.* The end of preferential treatment for national flag carriers, with greater competition and more flexible pricing.
- *Transport.* Uniform safety levels. Less bureaucratic entry into EU states for HGVs. Two way haulage loads. Fewer restrictive working practices.
- *VAT collection.* More uniform sales and purchase taxes. Simpler collection systems for companies trading across national borders.
- *Harmonisation.* Common operating and trading standards. Products such as mobile phones to work across Europe.
- *Immigration.* Fast tracking through customs for EU nationals. More opportunities to live and work in other EU countries.

Easier access between EU member countries and the removal of duty paid goods allowances had an immediate effect, but for working practices and product harmonisation it will still be several years before changes are really noticeable. In certain industries, such as airlines and car retailing, the new regulations may not be fully implemented until the end of the century. For consumers, companies and governments, practices from the 1980s are suddenly no longer relevant owing to these EU regulatory changes.

SOURCES: DTI press office, 1993; "Our single Euro-market is here", *Le Magazine*, January–February 1993, pp. A8–A9; EU press office, 1995.

Society's high material standard of living often is not enough. Many desire a high degree of quality in their lives. People do not want to spend all their waking hours working: they seek leisure time for hobbies, voluntary work, recreation and relaxation. The quality of life is enhanced by leisure time, clean air and water, an unlittered beach, conservation of wildlife and natural resources, and security from radiation and poisonous substances. A number of companies are expressing concerns about the quality of life. As illustrated in Figure 2.2, many companies have not been slow to latch onto the "greening concerns" and social concerns.

Figure 2.2

Environmently concerned customers

Many companies have not been slow to latch on to the "greening consumer". Here, ICI promotes "environmentally friendly" liquid soap crystals.

SOURCE: Courtesy of ICI Homecare.

Because of these desires, consumers have become increasingly concerned about environmental issues such as pollution, waste disposal and the so called greenhouse effect. Society's concerns have created both threats and opportunities for marketers. For example, one of society's biggest environmental problems is lack of space for refuse disposal, especially of plastic materials such as disposable nappies and Styrofoam packaging, which are not biodegradable. In the United States, several cities have passed laws banning the use of all plastic packaging in stores and restaurants, and governments around the world are considering similar legislation. This trend has created problems for McDonald's and other fast food restaurants, which have now developed packaging alternatives. Other firms, however, see such environmental problems as opportunities. Procter & Gamble, for example, markets cleaners in bottles made of recycled plastic.[5] Environmentally responsible, or green, marketing is increasingly extensive. For example, the German companies Audi, Volkswagen and BMW are manufacturing "cleaner" cars that do not pollute the atmosphere as much as traditional ones. Italian chemical companies are investing billions to reduce toxic wastes from their plants, and British industry is investing equally large sums to scrub acid emissions from power stations and to treat sewage more effectively.[6]

The **green movement** is concerned about these environmental issues. Several years ago few consumers were concerned about the well-being of their natural environment—their planet. Resources were not seen as scarce, pollution was

Green movement The trend arising from society's concern about pollution, waste disposal, manufacturing processes and the greenhouse effect

Social Awareness: BMW Recycling the Consumer

The European Recovery and Recycling Association (ERRA) is indicative of the growing concern for the environment and consumer awareness of this social issue. With members including Cadbury Schweppes, Coca-Cola, Heineken, Nestlé, L'Oréal, Petrofina and Tetra Pak, the Brussels based ERRA has developed a recycling scheme that could lead to the regular collection of discarded packaging—containers and bottles from housing estates, factories, schools, offices and shops—and their sorting and re-use. The scheme in many countries is far from becoming reality, requiring the significant commitment of government, local authorities and, of course, consumers. However, ERRA exists, supported by an extensive array of manufacturers and environmental pressure groups. The public's interest in the environment and in safeguarding the planet and its resources for generations to come has led companies to pay real attention to the green lobby.

BMW, the German de luxe car maker, has been stressing the "recyclability" of its vehicles in its television and press advertising for its 3 Series range. These cars are produced using more environmentally friendly production processes, with a greater proportion of components suitable for reworking. BMW's commitment to the future, however, goes further. In Landshut, Germany, it has a recycling factory. Two workers can strip all the re-usable parts from a 1970s car in under 45 minutes, including the careful draining of all fluids, at a cost of about £90.

Landshut's role is as a huge scrap merchant, but one that adheres to the strictest code of ethical working practices and the latest understanding of how to dispose of "dead" vehicles with the least harm to the environment. BMW executives support the notion of a European wide initiative, requiring an authorised recycler to issue a disposal certificate for every car at the end of its life. Until such a certificate is issued, the last registered owner would continue to be liable to pay road taxes. This initiative would eventually require legislation and the support of governments. Meanwhile, several leading car manufacturers have joined forces, adopting standardised colour coding for all re-usable parts.

The investment for BMW is significant, but anticipating eventual EU legislation to enforce recycling, the German manufacturer believes it is thinking strategically and is working towards maintaining its position as a major producer of vehicles. BMW has 30 partner recycling plants worldwide, with its first UK site in Sussex. By 1995, the company had an international network, with more than 5 sites in the UK. Simultaneously, BMW is striving to make more of its cars reclaimable; 40 per cent of the current 3 Series can be stripped down and re-used.

SOURCES: "The can and bottle story: environment", Coca-Cola & Schweppes Beverages Ltd, 1993; "Helping to solve the waste management puzzle", ERRA, Brussels, 1991; John Eisenhammer, "Where cars will go when they die", *The Independent on Sunday*, 21 February 1993, pp. 24–5; "Helping the earth begins at home", Central Office of Information, Department of the Environment, HMSO, 1992; BMW 3 Series promotional material, 1995.

poorly acknowledged and people had a short term—perhaps selfish—perspective. Now there is a growing awareness that is affecting everyone: consumers, manufacturers and legislators.

Supermarket shelves are rapidly filling with packaging that can be recycled or re-used and products for which manufacturing processes have altered. Children are now taught in the classroom to "re-educate" their parents to take a more responsible view of the earth's environment. The changes are not just in the supermarkets and schools, as highlighted by BMW in Marketing Insight 2.2. The rising importance and role of the green aspect of the societal forces must not be under-estimated.

As these examples illustrate, changes in the forces of the marketing environment require careful monitoring and often demand a clear and effective response. Since marketing activities are a vital part of the total business structure, marketers have a responsibility to help provide what members of society want and to minimise what they do not want.

Consumer Movement Forces

Consumer movement A diverse collection of independent individuals, groups and organisations seeking to protect the rights of consumers

The **consumer movement** is a diverse collection of independent individuals, groups and organisations seeking to protect the rights of consumers. The main issues pursued by the consumer movement fall into three categories: environmental protection, product performance safety and information disclosure. The movement's major forces are individual consumer advocates, consumer organisations and other interest groups, consumer education and consumer laws.

Consumer advocates, such as David Tench, take it upon themselves to protect the rights of consumers. They band together into consumer organisations, either voluntarily or under government sponsorship. Some organisations, such as the Consumers' Association, operate nationally, whereas others are active at local levels. They inform and organise other consumers, raise issues, help businesses develop consumer orientated programmes and pressure legislators to enact consumer protection laws. Some consumer advocates and organisations encourage consumers to boycott products and businesses to which they have objections.

Educating consumers to make wiser purchasing decisions is perhaps one of the farthest reaching aspects of the consumer movement. Increasingly, consumer education is becoming a part of school curricula and adult education courses. These courses cover many topics—for instance, what major factors should be considered when buying specific products, such as insurance, housing, cars, appliances and furnitures, clothes and food. The courses also cover the provisions of certain consumer protection laws and provide the sources of information that can help individuals become knowledgeable consumers.

● ● ● ● ● ● ● ● ● ● ● ● ● ● ● ●

Technological Forces

Technology The knowledge of how to accomplish tasks and goals

The word *technology* brings to mind creations of progress such as computers, super-conductors, lasers and heart transplants. Even though such items are outgrowths of technology, none of them *is* technology. **Technology** has been defined as the knowledge of how to accomplish tasks and goals.[7] Often this knowledge comes from scientific research. The effects of technology are broad in scope and today exert a tremendous influence on everyone's lives.

Technology grows out of research performed by businesses, universities and not-for-profit organisations. Much of this research is paid for by governments, which support investigations in a variety of areas, including health, defence, agriculture, energy and pollution. Because much centrally funded research requires the use of specialised machinery, personnel and facilities, a sizeable proportion of this research is conducted by large business organisations or research institutions that already possess the necessary specialised equipment and people.

The rapid technological growth of the last several decades is expected to continue through the 1990s. Areas that hold great technological promise include digital electronics, artificial intelligence, super-conductors, materials research and biotechnology. Current research is investigating new forms of memory chips and computers that are a hundred times faster and smaller than current models. Because these and other technological developments will clearly have an impact on buyers' and marketers' decisions, it is important to discuss here the effects of technology on society and marketers and to consider several factors that influence the adoption and use of technology.

The Impact of Technology

Marketers must be aware of new developments in technology and their possible effects because technology can and does affect marketing activities in many different ways. Consumers' technological knowledge influences their desires for goods and services. To provide marketing mixes that satisfy consumers, marketers must be aware of these influences.

The various ways in which technology affects marketing activities fall into two broad categories. It affects consumers and society in general, and it influences what, how, when and where products are marketed.

Effects of Technology on Society   Technology determines how consumers as members of society satisfy their physiological needs. In various ways and to varying degrees, eating and drinking habits, sleeping patterns, sexual activities and health care are all influenced both by existing technology and by changes in technology. Technological developments have improved standards of living, thus creating more leisure time; they have also enhanced information, entertainment and education.

Nevertheless, technology can detract from the quality of life through undesirable side effects, such as unemployment, polluted air and water, and other health hazards. Some people believe that further applications of technology can soften or eliminate these undesirable side effects. Others argue, however, that the best way to improve the quality of our lives is to decrease the use of technology.

Effects of Technology on Marketing   Technology also affects the types of products that marketers can offer. The introduction and general acceptance of cassette tapes and compact discs drove manufacturers of vinyl long playing (LP) albums out of business or forced them to invest in new technology. Yet this technology provided new marketing opportunities for recording artists and producers, record companies, retailers and those in related industries. The following items are only a few of the many thousands of existing products that were not available to consumers 20 years ago: disposable 35mm cameras, cellular telephones, ultralight laptop computers, high resolution televisions and hand-held video cameras.

Computer technology helps make warehouse storage and keeping track of stored products more efficient and, therefore, less expensive. Often these savings can be passed on to consumers in the form of lower prices. Because of technological changes in communications, marketers now can reach large masses of people through a variety of media more efficiently. The development and widespread use of facsimile machines and services, for example, allows marketers to send their advertisements or sales specifications directly to selected groups of customers who want their products.

Technological advances in transport enable consumers to travel farther and more often to shop at a larger number of stores. Changes in transport have also affected producers' ability to get products to retailers and wholesalers. The ability of present day manufacturers of relatively lightweight products to reach any of their dealers within 24 hours (via overnight express delivery services, such as TNT and Federal Express) would astound their counterparts of 50 years ago.

Adoption and Use of Technology

Technology assessment A procedure by which managers try to foresee the effects of new products and processes on their firm's operation, on other business organisations and on society in general

Through a procedure known as **technology assessment**, some managers try to foresee the effects of new products and processes on their firm's operation, on other business organisations and on society in general. With the information gained through a technology assessment, management tries to estimate whether the benefits of using a specific kind of technology outweigh the costs to the firm and to society at large. The degree to which a business is technologically based will also influence how its management responds to technology. Firms whose products and product changes grow out of recent technology strive to gather and use technological information.

Although available technology could radically improve their products (or other parts of the marketing mix), some companies may put off applying this technology as long as their competitors do not try to use it. The extent to which a firm can protect inventions stemming from research also influences its use of technology. The extent to which a product is secure from imitation depends on how easily others can copy it without violating its patent. If new products and processes cannot be protected through patents, a company is less likely to market them and make the benefits of its research available to competitors.

How a company uses (or does not use) technology is important for its long run survival. A firm that makes the wrong decisions may well lose out to the competition. Poor decisions may also affect its profits by requiring expensive corrective actions. Poor decisions about technological forces may even drive a firm out of business.

• • • • • • • • • • • • • • • • • • •

Economic and Competitive Forces

Economic and competitive forces Factors in the marketing environment—including the effects of general economic conditions, buying power, willingness to spend, spending patterns, types of competitive structures, competitive tools and competitive behaviour—that influence both marketers' and consumers' decisions and activities

The **economic and competitive forces** in the marketing environment influence both marketers' and customers' decisions and activities. This section first examines the effects of general economic conditions, also focusing on buying power, willingness to spend, spending patterns and competition. Then the discussion moves to competitive forces, including types of competitive structures, competitive tools and some methods for monitoring competitive behaviour. The strategic importance of competition is discussed in Chapter 22.

General Economic Conditions

The overall state of the economy fluctuates in all countries. Table 2.1 presents some economic measures of performance for the UK. These changes in general economic conditions affect (and are affected by) the forces of supply and demand, buying power, willingness to spend, consumer expenditure levels and the intensity of competitive behaviour. Therefore, current economic conditions and changes in the economy have a broad impact on the success of organisations' marketing strategies. Fluctuations in the economy follow a general pattern often referred to as the **business cycle**. In the traditional view, the business cycle consists of four stages: prosperity, recession, depression and recovery.

Business cycle Fluctuations in the economy that follow the general pattern of prosperity, recession, depression and recovery

Prosperity A period during which unemployment is low and total income is relatively high

During **prosperity**, unemployment is low and total income is relatively high. Assuming a low inflation rate, this combination causes buying power to be high. To the extent that the economic outlook remains prosperous, consumers generally are willing to buy. In the prosperity stage, marketers often expand their marketing mixes (product, distribution, promotion, price and people) to take advantage of the increased buying power. They sometimes capture a larger market share by intensifying distribution and promotion efforts.

Recession A period during which unemployment rises and total buying power declines

Because unemployment rises during a **recession,** total buying power declines. The pessimism that accompanies a recession often stifles both consumer and business spending. As buying power decreases, many consumers become more price and value-conscious; they look for products that are basic and functional. For instance, people ordinarily reduce their consumption of more expensive convenience foods and strive to save money by growing and preparing more of their own food. Individuals buy fewer durable goods and more repair and do-it-yourself products. During a recession, some firms make the mistake of drastically reducing their marketing efforts and thus damage their ability to survive. Obviously, marketers should consider some revision of their marketing activities during a recessionary period. Because consumers are more concerned about the functional value of products, a company must focus its marketing research on determining what product functions buyers want and then make sure that these functions become part of its products. Promotional efforts should emphasis value and utility.

Depression A period during which unemployment is extremely high, wages are very low, total disposable income is at a minimum and consumers lack confidence in the economy

A **depression** is a period in which unemployment is extremely high, wages are very low, total disposable income is at a minimum and consumers lack confidence in the economy. Governments have used both monetary and fiscal policies to offset the effects of recession and depression. Monetary policies are employed to control the money supply, which in turn affects spending, saving and investment by both individuals and businesses. Through the establishment of fiscal policies, the government is able to influence the amount of savings and expenditures by adjusting the tax structure and by changing the levels of government spending. Some economic experts believe that the effective use of monetary and fiscal policies can completely eliminate depressions from the business cycle.

		1989	1990	1991	1992	1993	1994	1995
Gross Domestic Product[1]								
at current prices	£ billion	516.0	551.1	575.3	597.2	630.7	668.5	702.2
	% change	+9.4	+6.8	+4.4	+3.8	+5.6	+6.0	+5.0
at 1990 prices	£billion	548.9	551.1	540.3	537.4	549.6	571.2	585.8
	% change	+2.2	+0.4	−2.0	−0.5	+2.3	+3.9	+2.6
Gross Domestic Product[1] per Capita								
at current prices	£	8,995	9,575	9,952	10,296	10,839	11,449	11,983
	% change	+9.1	+6.4	+3.9	+3.5	+5.3	+5.6	+4.7
at 1990 prices	£	9,570	9,575	9,347	9,265	9,445	9,782	9,997
	% change	+1.8	—	−2.4	−0.9	+1.9	+3.6	+2.2
Consumers' Expenditure								
at current prices	£billion	327.4	347.5	365.0	381.7	405.5	427.5	449.6
	% change	+9.3	+6.2	+5.0	+4.6	+6.2	+5.4	+5.2
at 1990 prices	£billion	345.4	347.5	339.9	339.5	348.4	358.2	367.0
	% change	+3.2	+0.6	−2.2	−0.1	+2.6	+2.8	+2.4
Retail Sales Volume	Index	99.3	100.0	98.6	99.4	102.4	106.2	107.5
	% change	+2.0	+0.8	−1.4	+0.8	+3.0	+3.7	+1.2
Retail Prices	Index	91.3	100.0	105.9	109.8	111.5	114.3	118.2
	% change	+7.8	+9.5	+5.9	+3.7	+1.6	+2.5	+3.4
Population (Mid-Year Est.)	Million	57.4	57.6	57.8	58.0	58.2	58.4	58.6

(Continues)

Table 2.1 UK main economic indicators, 1989–95

		1989	1990	1991	1992	1993	1994	1995
Average Earnings Index	Index	91.2	100.0	108.0	114.6	118.5	123.2	127.4
	% change	+9.1	+9.7	+8.0	+6.1	+3.4	+3.9	+3.4
Industrial Production (Total)	Index	100.3	100.0	96.1	95.9	98.1	103.1	105.4
	% change	+2.1	−0.3	−3.9	−0.2	+2.3	+5.1	+2.3
Unemployment (% of Labour Force)[2]		6.3	5.8	8.1	9.8	10.3	9.3	9.3
Vacancies at Job Centres[3]	Thousands	219.5	173.6	117.9	117.2	127.9	157.8	182.5
	% change	−11.7	−20.9	−32.1	−0.6	+9.1	+23.4	+15.7
Interest Rate (Bank Rate)[4]	%	13.85	14.77	11.70	9.56	6.01	5.46	6.71
Gross Domestic Fixed Capital Formation at 1990 prices	£billion	111.5	107.6	97.4	96.0	96.5	99.5	100.7
	% change	+6.0	−3.5	−9.5	−1.5	+0.6	+3.1	+1.2
Gross Fixed Investment by Manu. Industry at 1990 prices	£billion	15.0	14.2	12.8	11.8	11.1	11.8	—
	% change	+8.2	−5.1	−10.0	−7.6	−6.1	+6.5	—
Gross Trading Profits[5] North Sea Oil Companies at current prices	£billion	6.8	7.1	6.4	6.7	8.1	9.7	—
	% change	−3.1	+4.6	−9.6	+4.3	+20.9	+20.0	—
Other Companies at current prices	£billion	67.5	68.0	67.9	68.3	77.0	88.1	—
	% change	+8.5	+0.8	−0.1	+0.5	+12.7	+14.4	—
at 1990 prices	£billion	73.9	68.0	64.2	62.2	69.1	77.1	—
	% change	+0.6	−8.0	−5.7	−3.1	+11.0	+11.7	—
Balance of Payments at current prices	£billion	−22.4	−19.3	−8.5	−9.5	−11.0	−2.0	−4.6

NOTES: All indices 1990 = 100. [1]Gross Domestic Product is at market prices. [2]Unemployment percentage is the total number of unemployed (excluding school leavers) expressed as a percentage of the estimated total workforce (the sum of unemployed claimants, employees in employment, self-employed, HM forces and work related government training programmes). [3]Vacancies at Job Centres excluding Community Programme vacancies from 1980. [4]Selected Retail Banks' Base Rate. [5]Net of stock appreciation.
SOURCE: *Monthly Digest of Statistics and Financial Statistics*, 1996, British Crown Copyright 1996. Reproduced by permission of the Controller of HMSO and of the Office for National Statistics.

Table 2.1 UK main economic indicators, 1989–95 (cont.)

Recovery The stage of the business cycle in which the economy moves from depression or recession to prosperity

Recovery is the stage of the business cycle in which the economy moves from depression or recession to prosperity. During this period, the high unemployment rate begins to decline, total disposable income increases and the economic gloom that lessened consumers' willingness to buy subsides. Both the ability and the willingness to buy rise. Marketers face some problems during recovery—for example, the difficulty of ascertaining how quickly prosperity will return and of forecasting the level of prosperity that will be attained. During this stage, marketers should maintain as much flexibility in their marketing strategies as possible to be able to make the needed adjustments as the economy moves from recession to prosperity.

Consumer Demand and Spending Behaviour

Marketers must understand the factors that determine whether, what, where and when people buy. Chapters 4 and 7 look at behavioural factors underlying these choices, but here the focus is on the economic components: buying power, willingness to purchase and spending patterns.

Buying power Resources such as goods, services and financial holdings that can be traded in an exchange situation

Buying Power The strength of a person's **buying power** depends on the size of the resources that enable the individual to purchase and on the state of the economy. The resources that make up buying power are goods, services and financial holdings. Fluctuations of the business cycle affect buying power because they influence price levels and interest rates. For example, during inflationary periods, when prices are rising, buying power decreases because more pounds or ECUs are required to buy products. Table 2.2 indicates some trends in UK consumers' expenditure; Table 2.3 looks at EU consumers' expenditure.

The major financial sources of buying power are income, credit and wealth. From an individual's viewpoint, **income** is the amount of money received through wages, rents, investments, pensions and subsidy payments for a given period, such as a month or a year. Normally, this money is allocated among taxes, spending for goods and services, and savings. Tables 2.4 and 2.5 present statistics for wealth and income. However, because of the differences in people's educational levels, abilities, occupations and wealth, income is not equally distributed in any country.

Income The amount of money received through wages, rents, investments, pensions and subsidy payments for a given period

Disposable income After-tax income, which is used for spending or saving

Marketers are most interested in the amount of money that is left after payment of taxes. After-tax income is called **disposable income** and is used for spending or saving. Because disposable income is a ready source of buying power, the total amount available in a nation is important to marketers. Several factors affect the size of total disposable income. One, of course, is the total amount of income. Total national income is affected by wage levels, rate of unemployment, interest rates and dividend rates. These factors in turn affect the size of disposable income. Because disposable income is the income left after taxes are paid, the number of taxes and their amount directly affect the size of total disposable income. When taxes rise, disposable income declines; when taxes fall, disposable income increases.

Discretionary income Disposable income that is available for spending and saving after an individual has purchased the basic necessities of food, clothing and shelter

Disposable income that is available for spending and saving after an individual has purchased the basic necessities of food, clothing and shelter is called **discretionary income**. People use discretionary income to purchase entertainment, holidays, cars, education, pets and pet supplies, furniture, appliances and so on. Changes in total discretionary income affect the sales of these products—especially cars, furniture, large appliances and other costly durable goods.

Credit enables people to spend future income now or in the near future. However, credit increases current buying power at the expense of future buying power. Several factors determine whether consumers use or forgo credit. First, credit must be available to them. Interest rates, too, affect consumers' decisions to use credit, especially for expensive purchases such as homes, appliances and cars. When credit charges are high, consumers are more likely to delay buying expensive items. Use of credit is also affected by credit terms, such as the size of the down payment and the amount and number of monthly payments.

Wealth The accumulation of past income, natural resources and financial resources

A person can have a high income and very little wealth. It is also possible, but not likely, for a person to have great wealth but not much income. **Wealth** is the accumulation of past income, natural resources and financial resources. It may exist in many forms, including cash, securities, savings accounts, jewellery, antiques and property. Like income, wealth is unevenly distributed. The significance of wealth to marketers is that as people become wealthier they gain buying power in three ways: they can use their wealth to make current purchases, to generate income and to acquire large amounts of credit. Buying power information is available from government sources, trade associations and research agencies. One of the most current and comprehensive sources of buying power data is the Central Statistical Office's *National Income and Expenditure Survey*.

	Expenditure				Change Over Ten Years	Change in Share Over Ten years
	1985 £m	Share of Total %	1994 £m	Share of Total %	%	%
Housing	49,677	15.0	66,636	15.6	34.1	0.6
Rent of dwellings	19,628	5.9	35,115	8.2	78.9	2.3
Other rent	10,902	3.3	15,960	3.7	46.4	0.4
Rates, etc.	11,198	3.4	4,078	1.0	−63.6	−2.4
DIY goods	4,300	1.3	6,068	1.4	41.1	0.1
Contractors	3,650	1.1	5,415	1.3	48.4	0.2
Fuel, Light and Power	16,092	4.9	14,885	3.5	−7.5	−1.4
Electricity	7,482	2.3	8,082	1.9	8.0	−0.4
Gas	6,147	1.9	5,747	1.3	−6.5	−0.5
Coal and coke	1,548	0.5	595	0.1	−61.6	−0.3
Other fuel	914	0.3	461	0.1	−49.6	−0.2
Food	46,718	14.1	47,158	11.0	0.9	−3.1
Bread	2,350	0.7	1,991	0.5	−15.3	−0.2
Cakes and biscuits	2,164	0.7	2,181	0.5	0.8	−0.1
Other cereals	1,833	0.6	2,572	0.6	40.3	—
Meat and bacon	12,036	3.6	10,558	2.5	−12.3	−1.2
Fish	1,608	0.5	1,706	0.4	6.1	−0.1
Milk, cheese and eggs	6,682	2.0	6,082	1.4	−9.0	−0.6
Oils and fats	1,586	0.5	1,056	0.2	−33.4	−0.2
Fruit	2,539	0.8	3,021	0.7	19.0	−0.1
Potatoes	1,845	0.6	2,356	0.6	27.7	—
Vegetables	3,548	1.1	4,019	0.9	13.3	−0.1
Sugar	504	0.2	288	0.1	−42.9	−0.1
Confectionery	4,101	1.2	4,624	1.1	12.8	−0.2
Coffee, tea and cocoa	1,797	0.5	1,268	0.3	−29.4	−0.2
Soft drinks	2,586	0.8	3,316	0.8	28.2	—
Other manu. food	1,539	0.5	2,120	0.5	37.7	—
Alcohol	23,850	7.2	25,766	6.0	8.0	−1.2
Beer	12,825	3.9	13,810	3.2	7.7	−0.6
Spirits	5,838	1.8	5,945	1.4	1.8	−0.4
Wine, cider and perry	5,187	1.6	6,011	1.4	15.9	−0.2
Tobacco	10,676	3.2	11,017	2.6	3.2	−0.6
Cigarettes	9,314	2.8	10,028	2.3	7.7	−0.5
Other	1,362	0.4	989	0.2	−27.4	−0.2
Clothing	22,724	6.9	24,689	5.8	8.6	−1.1
Male clothing	6,260	1.9	6,596	1.5	5.4	−0.3
Female clothing	12,228	3.7	13,760	3.2	12.5	−0.5
Footwear	4,236	1.3	4,333	1.0	2.3	−0.3
Motoring	40,375	12.2	52,951	12.4	31.1	0.2
Car purchase, etc.	15,015	4.5	21,301	5.0	41.9	0.5
Petrol and oil	12,219	3.7	11,972	2.8	−2.0	−0.9
Vehicle excise duty	2,258	0.7	2,546	0.6	12.7	−0.1
Other running costs	10,884	3.3	17,132	4.0	57.4	0.7

(Continues)

Table 2.2 Trends in UK consumers' expenditure (constant 1994 prices)

	Expenditure				**Change Over Ten Years**	**Change in Share Over Ten years**
	1985 £m	**Share of Total %**	**1994 £m**	**Share of Total %**	**%**	**%**
Other Travel	11,400	3.4	14,211	3.3	24.7	−0.1
Rail fares	2,246	0.7	2,482	0.6	10.5	−0.1
Bus and coach fares	3,004	0.9	2,808	0.7	−6.5	−0.2
Air fares	4,243	1.3	5,887	1.4	38.8	0.1
Other travel	1,908	0.6	3,034	0.7	59.0	0.1
Household Goods	18,153	5.5	21,882	5.1	20.5	−0.4
Furniture, pictures, etc.	4,339	1.3	5,944	1.4	37.0	0.1
Floor coverings	2,051	0.6	1,985	0.5	−3.2	−0.2
Major appliances	4,846	1.5	5,437	1.3	12.2	−0.2
Soft furnishings	2,155	0.7	2,910	0.7	35.0	—
Hardware	2,868	0.9	3,338	0.8	16.4	−0.1
Cleaning goods, etc.	1,894	0.6	2,268	0.5	19.7	—
Household Services	9,416	2.8	13,159	3.1	39.7	0.2
Postal services	744	0.2	997	0.2	34.1	—
Telecommunications	5,326	1.6	6,790	1.6	27.5	—
Other services	3,346	1.0	5,372	1.3	60.5	0.2
Personal	27,395	8.3	45,403	10.6	65.7	2.4
Medicinal goods	1,813	0.5	3,186	0.7	75.7	0.2
NHS payments, etc.	2,175	0.7	3,496	0.8	60.8	0.2
Toiletries and perfume	3,791	1.1	5,788	1.4	52.7	0.2
Hairdressing and beauty	1,981	0.6	2,295	0.5	15.8	−0.1
Jewellery, watches, etc.	2,289	0.7	2,294	0.5	0.2	−0.2
Other personal goods	3,014	0.9	4,060	0.9	34.7	—
Life ass./pension admin.	5,800	1.8	10,058	2.4	73.4	0.6
Other personal services	6,531	2.0	14,226	3.3	117.8	1.4
Leisure Goods	17,487	5.3	23,504	5.5	34.4	0.2
Durable leisure goods	4,480	1.4	5,770	1.3	28.8	—
Sports and games goods	3,129	0.9	4,044	0.9	29.3	—
Books	1,151	0.3	1,680	0.4	46.0	—
Newspapers and mags.	3,519	1.1	3,720	0.9	5.7	−0.2
Other leisure goods	5,209	1.6	8,290	1.9	59.2	0.4
Leisure Services	13,189	4.0	19,152	4.5	45.2	0.5
TV/video hire and fees	3,886	1.2	3,472	0.8	−10.7	−0.4
Education	2,496	0.8	5,677	1.3	127.4	0.6
Betting and gaming	3,231	1.0	3,801	0.9	17.7	−0.1
Other services	3,577	1.1	6,202	1.5	73.4	0.4
Catering	21,144	6.4	36,662	8.6	73.4	2.2
Total	331,423	100.0	427,454	100.0	29.0	—

SOURCE: British Crown Copyright 1995. Reproduced by permission of the Controller of HMSO and of the Office for National Statistics.

Table 2.2 Trends in UK consumers' expenditure (cont.)

	Belgium	Denmark	Germany	Greece	Spain	France	Ireland	Italy	Luxembourg	The Netherlands	Portugal	United Kingdom
Reference year	1978/88	1991	1985	1988	1991	1993	1989	1989/90	1987	1985	1989/90	1993
Food	16.5	14.5	17.8	29.0	26.2	17.5	21.2	19.6	18.4	14.9	39.2	13.2
Beverages and tobacco	3.6	6.6	5.2	3.9	3.2	4.6	16	3.2[1]	2.1[2]	3.1	4.1	7.2
Clothing and footwear	8.6	5.7	7.0	14.3	11.5	7.4	6.8	10.8	13.1	7.2	9.4	5.8
Rent, fuel and power	19.4	28.5	25.0	11.4	10.3	10.9	13.1	7.6	13.7	26.1	11.8[3]	20.3
Household goods and services	7.9	6.5	7.2	8.0	6.7	8.4	6.2	10.6	10.1	8.0	7.7	7.7
Health expenses	4.9	1.8	4.1	7.8	3.1	9.1	2.6	6.7	8.2	0.6	3.0	1.8
Transport and communication	16.5	17.1	14.4	13.7	16.5	19.3	15.2	13.5	14.9	14.4	16.1	17.9
Leisure, education and culture	8.3	9.5	8.4	9.4	7.3	8.2	6.0	10.0	8.0	10.7	3.9	9.0
Miscellaneous goods and services	14.3	9.8	10.9	2.5	15.3	14.6	12.8	18.0	11.5	15.0	4.9	17.1

NOTES: [1]Excluding tobacco.
[2]Excluding alcoholic beverages and tobacco.
[3]Rents included but not published.
SOURCE: From Eurostat: *Europe in Figures*, 4th Edition, Office for Official Publications of the European Community, p. 367. Reprinted by permission.

Table 2.3 Share of consumer product categories in the general price index (%)

(i) Range of Net Wealth in £	Number of Owners		Marketable Wealth	
	'000s	%	£'000m	%
Nil– 4,999	11,706	26.1	19	1.1
5,000–14,999	7,757	17.3	60	3.3
15,000–24,999	6,210	13.8	114	6.3
25,000–49,999	8,871	19.8	347	19.2
50,000–99,999	7,118	15.8	503	27.8
100,000+	3,235	7.2	766	42.3
Total	44,897	100.0	1,809	100.0

(ii) Percentage of Wealth Owned By	Marketable Wealth		Marketable Wealth Incl. Occupational and State Pension Rights	
	1979	1993	1979	1993
Most wealthy 1% of population	20	17	12	10
" " 10% " "	50	48	36	33
" " 25% " "	72	72	58	56
" " 50% " "	92	92	80	82

NOTE: Marketable wealth includes cash, liquid assets, houses, land, shares and personal chattels but excludes occupational and State pension rights, unless otherwise indicated.
SOURCE: From *Marketing Pocket Book 1996*, p. 14. Reprinted by permission of NTC Publications, Ltd.

Table 2.4 Distribution of marketable wealth of individuals in the UK in 1993 (% of adult [18+] population)

Income, wealth and credit equip consumers to purchase goods and services. Marketing managers should be aware of current levels and expected changes in buying power in their own markets because buying power directly affects the types and quantities of goods and services that consumers purchase, as explained later in the discussion of spending patterns. Just because consumers have buying power, however, does not necessarily mean that they will buy. Consumers must also be willing to use their buying power.

Willingness to spend A disposition towards using buying power, influenced by the ability to buy, expected satisfaction from a product and numerous psychological and social forces

Consumers' Willingness to Spend People's **willingness to spend** is, to some degree, related to their ability to buy. That is, people are sometimes more willing to buy if they have the buying power. However, a number of other elements also influence willingness to spend. Some elements affect specific products; others influence spending in general. A product's absolute price and its price relative to the price of substitute products influence almost everyone. The amount of satisfaction currently received or expected in the future from a product already owned may also influence consumers' desire to buy other products. Satisfaction depends not only on the quality of the functional performance of the currently owned product, but also on numerous psychological and social forces.

| Range of Total Income, £ | Number | | | | Value |
| | Before Tax | | After Tax | | After Tax |
	'000s	%	'000s	%	%
3,445– 4,999	3,470	12.7	3,960	14.5	5.2
5,000– 7,499	4,830	17.7	5,810	21.3	11.2
7,500– 9,999	4,110	15.1	4,690	17.2	12.7
10,000–14,999	6,220	22.8	6,480	23.8	24.7
15,000–19,999	3,810	14.0	3,310	12.2	17.7
20,000–29,999	3,150	11.5	2,140	7.9	15.8
30,000–49,999	1,230	4.5	643	2.4	7.3
50,000–99,999	335	1.2	160	0.6	3.3
100,000+	95	0.3	41	0.2	2.2
All Ranges	27,200	100.0	27,200	100.0	100.0

NOTE: Total income is the sum of all income subject to tax.

SOURCE: From *Marketing Pocket Book 1996*, p. 14. Reprinted by permission of NTC Publications, Ltd.

Table 2.5 Distribution of total income of individuals before and after tax in the UK in 1992/93

Factors that affect consumers' general willingness to spend are expectations about future employment, income levels, prices, family size and general economic conditions. If people are unsure whether or how long they will be employed, willingness to buy ordinarily declines. Willingness to spend may increase if people are reasonably certain of higher incomes in the future. Expectations of rising prices in the near future may also increase willingness to spend in the present. For a given level of buying power, the larger the family, the greater the willingness to buy. One of the reasons for this relationship is that as the size of a family increases, a larger amount of money must be spent to provide the basic necessities of life to sustain the family members. Finally, perceptions of future economic conditions influence willingness to buy. For example, in the late 1980s, rising short term interest rates cooled consumers' willingness to spend.

Consumer Spending Patterns Marketers must be aware of the factors that influence consumers' ability and willingness to spend, but they should also analyse how consumers actually spend their disposable incomes. Marketers obtain this information by studying consumer spending patterns. **Consumer spending patterns** indicate the relative proportions of annual family expenditures or the actual amount of money spent on certain kinds of goods and services. Families are usually categorised by one of several characteristics, including family income, age of the household head, geographic area and family life cycle. There are two types of spending patterns: comprehensive and product specific.

The percentages of family income allotted to annual expenditures for general classes of goods and services constitute **comprehensive spending patterns.** Comprehensive spending patterns or the data to develop them are available in government publications and in reports produced by the major marketing research companies and by trade associations.

Consumer spending patterns Information indicating the relative proportions of annual family expenditures or the actual amount of money spent on certain kinds of goods and services

Comprehensive spending patterns The percentages of family income allotted to annual expenditures for general classes of goods and services

Product specific spending patterns indicate the annual monetary amounts families spend for specific products within a general product class. Information sources used to construct product specific spending patterns include government publications, trade publications and consumer surveys.

A marketer uses spending patterns to analyse general trends in the ways that families spend their incomes for various kinds of products. Analyses of spending patterns yield information that a marketer can use to gain perspective and background for decision-making. However, spending patterns reflect only general trends and thus should not be used as the sole basis for making specific decisions.

Assessment of Competitive Forces

Competition Those firms marketing products that are similar to, or can be substituted for, a given business's products in the same geographic area

Few firms, if any, operate free of competition. Broadly speaking, all firms compete with each other for consumers' money. From a more practical viewpoint, however, a business generally defines **competition** as those firms marketing products that are similar to, or can be substituted for, its products in the same geographic area. For example, a local Tesco or Aldi supermarket manager views all grocery stores in a town as competitors, but almost never thinks of other types of local or out-of-town stores (DIY or electrical, for example) as competitors. This section considers the types of competitive structure and the importance of monitoring competitors.

Types of Competitive Structure The number of firms that control the supply of a product may affect the strength of competition. When only one or a few firms control supply, competitive factors will exert a different sort of influence on marketing activities than when there are many competitors. Table 2.6 presents four general types of competitive structure: monopoly, oligopoly, monopolistic competition and perfect competition.

Monopoly A market structure that exists when a firm turns out a product that has no close substitutes

A **monopoly** exists when a firm turns out a product that has no close substitutes. Because the organisation has no competitors, it completely controls the supply of the product and, as a single seller, can erect barriers to potential competitors. In reality, the monopolies that survive today are some utilities, such as telephone, electricity (in many countries) and cable companies, which are heavily regulated. These monopolies are tolerated because of the tremendous financial resources needed to develop and operate them; few organisations can obtain the resources to mount any competition against a local electricity producer, for example.

Oligopoly A market structure that exists when a few sellers control the supply of a large proportion of a product

An **oligopoly** exists when a few sellers control the supply of a large proportion of a product. In this case, each seller must consider the reactions of other sellers to changes in marketing activities. Products facing oligopolistic competition may be homogeneous, such as aluminum, or differentiated, such as cigarettes and cars. Usually, barriers of some sort make it difficult to enter the market and compete with oligopolies. For example, because of the enormous financial outlay required, few companies or individuals could afford to enter the oil refining or steel producing industries. Moreover, some industries demand special technical or marketing skills that block the entry of many potential competitors.

Monopolistic competition A market structure that exists when a firm with many potential competitors attempts to develop a differential marketing strategy to establish its own market share

Monopolistic competition exists when a firm with many potential competitors attempts to develop a differential marketing strategy to establish its own market share. For example, Levi's has established a differential advantage for its blue jeans through a well known trade mark, design, advertising and a quality image. Although many competing brands of blue jeans are available, this firm has carved out its market share through use of a differential marketing strategy.

Type of Structure	Number of Competitors	Ease of Entry into Market	Product	Knowledge of Market	Examples
Monopoly	One	Many barriers	Almost no substitutes	Perfect	Non-privatised railways, many government departments
Oligopoly	Few	Some barriers	Homogeneous or differentiated (real or perceived differences)	Imperfect	Airlines, petroleum retailers, some utility providers
Monopolistic competition	Many	Few barriers	Product differentiation with many substitutes	More knowledge than oligopoly; less than monopoly	Jeans, fast food, audio-visual
Perfect competition	Unlimited	No barriers	Homogeneous products	Perfect	The London commodity markets, vegetable farms

Table 2.6 Selected characteristics of competitive structures

Perfect competition A market structure that entails a large number of sellers, not one of which could significantly influence price or supply

Perfect competition, if it existed at all, would entail a large number of sellers, not one of which could significantly influence price or supply. Products would be homogeneous, and there would be full knowledge of the market and easy entry into it. The closest thing to an example of perfect competition would be an unregulated agricultural market.

Few, if any, marketers operate in a structure of perfect competition. Perfect competition is an ideal at one end of the continuum, with monopoly at the other end. Most marketers function in a competitive environment that falls somewhere between these two extremes.

Competitive Tools Another set of factors that influences the level of competition is the number and types of competitive tools used by competitors. To survive, a firm uses one or several available competitive tools to deal with competitive economic forces. Once a company has analysed its particular competitive environment and decided which factors in that environment it can or must adapt to or influence, it can choose among the variables that it can control to strengthen its competitive position in the overall marketplace.

Probably the competitive tool that most organisations grasp is price. Bic, for example, markets disposable pens and lighters that are similar to competing products but less expensive. However, there is one major problem with using price as a competitive tool: competitors will often match or beat the price. This threat is one of the primary reasons for employing non–price competitive tools that are based on the differentiation of market segments, product offering, service, promotion, distribution or enterprise.[8]

By focusing on a specific market segment, a marketer sometimes gains a competitive advantage. For instance, Saab cars and Porsche sports coupés are narrowly targeted at specific groups of consumers. Most manufacturers try to gain a competitive edge by incorporating product features that make their brands distinctive to some extent. Firms use distinguishing promotional methods to compete, such as advertising and personal selling. Competing producers sometimes use different distribution channels to prevail over one another. Retailers may compete by placing their outlets in locations that are convenient for a large number of shoppers. Dealers and distributors offer wide ranges, advice and service.

Monitoring Competition Marketers in an organisation need to be aware of the actions of major competitors. They should monitor what competitors are currently doing and assess the changes occurring in the competitive environment. **Competitor monitoring** allows firms to determine what specific strategies competitors are following and how those strategies affect their own. It can also guide marketers as they try to develop competitive advantages and can aid them in adjusting current marketing strategies, as well as in planning new ones. Information may come from direct observation or from sources such as salespeople, customers, trade publications, syndicated marketing research services, distributors and marketing studies. As well as monitoring direct competitors, marketers should be aware of new entrants coming into a market with competing propositions and of the danger of substitute products or services being developed. This theme will be addressed later in *Marketing: Concepts and Strategies*.

An organisation needs information about competitors that will allow its marketing managers to assess the performance of its own marketing efforts. Comparing their company's performance with that of competitors helps marketing managers recognise strengths and weaknesses in their own marketing strategies. Data about market shares, product movement, sales volume and expenditure levels can be useful. However, accurate information on these matters is often difficult to obtain.

Competition exists in most markets and situations. Even charities compete with one another and with manufacturers for consumers' attention and financial commitment. Marketing places an emphasis on meeting consumers' needs and offering satisfaction. To be successful, however, competing organisations need to identify unique marketing mixes; otherwise all rival products and services will merely replicate each other. The search for a competitive edge—achieved through a differential advantage in a market over competitors—is central to effective marketing strategy. Competition is much more than an aspect of the marketing environment and is explored in Chapter 22.

Competitor monitoring The process by which a company studies the actions of its major competitors in order to determine what specific strategies they are following and how those strategies affect its own; also used by marketers as they try to develop competitive advantages, adjust current marketing strategies and plan new ones

• • • • • • • • • • • • • • • • • • • •

Summary

● The *marketing environment* consists of external forces that directly or indirectly influence an organisation's acquisition of inputs (personnel, financial resources, raw materials, information) and generation of outputs (information, packages, goods, services, ideas). The marketing environment comprises political, legal and regulatory forces; societal forces, including green concerns for the earth's natural environment; and technological forces. Along with economic forces and trends, these macro, broader aspects of the marketing environment have an impact on manufacturers and their customers. The more narrowly focused force of competition is also of fundamental importance.

● To monitor changes in these forces, marketers should practise environmental scanning and analysis. *Environmental scanning* is the process of collecting information about the forces in the marketing environment; *environmental analysis* is the process of assessing and interpreting the information obtained in scanning. This information helps marketing managers predict opportunities and threats associated with environmental fluctuation. Marketing management may assume either a passive, reactive approach or an active, aggressive approach in responding to these environmental fluctuations. The choice depends on an organisation's structure and needs and on the composition of the environmental forces that affect it.

● The political, legal and regulatory forces of the marketing environment are closely interrelated. The current political outlook is reflected in legislation and regulations or the lack of them. The political environment may determine what laws and regulations affecting specific marketers are enacted and how much the government purchases and from which suppliers; it can also be important in helping organisations secure foreign markets.

● Legislation affecting marketing activities can be divided into *procompetitive legislation*—laws designed to preserve and encourage competition— and consumer protection laws. The Restrictive Trade Practices Act and the Competition Act sought to prevent monopolies and activities that limit competition; legislation such as the Financial Services Act, the Sale of Goods Act and the Consumer Credit Act was directed towards more specific practices. Consumer protection laws generally relate to product safety and information disclosure. The actual effects of legislation are determined by how marketers and the courts interpret the laws.

● Regulatory agencies influence most marketing activities. For example, the *Monopolies and Mergers Commission* and the *Office of Fair Trading* usually have the power to enforce specific laws and some discretion in establishing operating rules and drawing up regulations to guide certain types of industry practices. Self-regulation by industry represents another regulatory force; marketers view this type of regulation more favourably than government action, because they have more opportunity to take part in creating the guidelines. Self-regulation may be less expensive than government regulation, and its guidelines are often more realistic. However, such regulation generally cannot assure compliance as effectively as government agencies.

● *Societal forces* refer to the structure and dynamics of individuals and groups and the issues that concern them. Many members of society want a high standard of living and a high quality of life, and they expect business to help them achieve these goals. Of growing concern is the well being of the earth, its resources, climate and peoples. The *green movement* is increasing general awareness of the natural environment and is altering product design, manufacture, packaging and use. The *consumer movement* is a diverse collection of independent individuals, groups and organisations that attempt to protect the rights of consumers. The major issues taken up by the consumer movement fall into three categories: environmental protection, product performance and safety, and information disclosure. Consumer rights organisations inform and organise other consumers, raise issues, help businesses develop consumer orientated programmes, and pressure legislators to enact consumer protection laws. Some are quite formally organised, such as the *Consumers' Association*.

● *Technology* is the knowledge of how to accomplish tasks and goals. Product development, packaging, promotion, prices and distribution systems are all influenced directly by technology. Several factors determine how much and in what way a particular business will make use of technology; these factors include the firm's ability to use technology, consumers' ability and willingness to buy technologically improved products, the firm's perception of the long run effects of applying technology, the extent to which the firm is technologically based, the degree to which technology is used as a competitive tool and the extent to which the business can protect technological applications through patents. Many businesses conduct a *technology assessment*.

● The *economic forces* that can strongly influence marketing decisions and activities are general economic conditions, buying power, willingness to spend, spending patterns and *competitive forces*. The overall state of the economy fluctuates in a general pattern known as a *business cycle*. The stages of the business cycle are *prosperity, recession, depression* and *recovery*.

● Consumers' goods, services and financial holdings make up their *buying power*—that is, their ability to purchase. The financial sources of buying power are *income,* credit and wealth. After-tax income used for spending or saving is called *disposable income*. Disposable income left after an individual has purchased the basic necessities of food, clothing and shelter is called *discretionary income*. It is important to identify levels of *wealth*. Two measures of buying power are effective buying income (which includes salaries, wages, dividends, interest, profits and rents, less taxes) and the buying power index (a weighted index consisting of population, effective buying income and retail sales data). The factors that affect consumers' *willingness to spend* are product price, the level of satisfaction obtained from currently used products, family size and expectations about future employment, income,

prices and general economic conditions. *Consumer spending patterns* indicate the relative proportions of annual family expenditures or the actual amount of money spent on certain kinds of goods and services. *Comprehensive spending patterns* specify the percentages of family income allotted to annual expenditures for general classes of goods and services. *Product specific spending patterns* indicate the annual amounts families spend for specific products within a general product class.

● *Competition* is a fundamental concern for all marketers. Although all businesses compete for consumers' spending, a company's direct competitors are usually the businesses in its geographic area marketing products that resemble its own or can be substituted for them. The number of firms that control the supply of a product may affect the strength of competition. There are four general types of competitive structure: *monopoly, oligopoly, monopolistic competition* and *perfect competition*. Marketers should *monitor* what competitors are currently doing and assess the changes occurring in the competitive environment.

Important Terms

Marketing environment
Environmental scanning
Environmental analysis
Procompetitive legislation
Office of Fair Trading
Monopolies and Mergers
    Commission
Consumers' Association
Societal/green forces
Green movement
Consumer movement
Technology
Technology assessment

Economic and competitive
    forces
Business cycle
Prosperity
Recession
Depression
Recovery
Buying power
Income
Disposable income
Discretionary income
Wealth
Willingness to spend

Consumer spending patterns
Comprehensive spending
    patterns
Product specific spending
    patterns
Competition
Monopoly
Oligopoly
Monopolistic competition
Perfect competition
Competitor monitoring

Discussion and Review Questions

1. Why are environmental scanning and analysis so important?
2. How are political forces related to legal and regulatory forces?
3. Describe marketers' attempts to influence political forces.
4. What types of procompetitive legislation directly affect marketing practices?

5. What is the major objective of most procompetitive laws? Do the laws generally accomplish this objective? Why or why not?

6. What types of problems do marketers experience as they interpret legislation?

7. What are the goals of the Monopolies and Mergers Commission? How does it affect marketing activities?

8. Name several non-governmental regulatory forces. Do you believe that self-regulation is more or less effective than governmental regulatory agencies? Why?

9. How is the so called green lobby altering the shape of business?

10. Describe the consumer movement. Analyse some active consumer forces in your area.

11. What does the term *technology* mean to you?

12. How does technology affect you as a member of society? Do the benefits of technology outweigh its costs and dangers?

13. Discuss the impact of technology on marketing activities.

14. What factors determine whether a business organisation adopts and uses technology?

15. In what ways can each of the business cycle stages affect consumers' reactions to marketing strategies?

16. What business cycle stage are we experiencing currently? How is this stage affecting business firms in your area?

17. Define income, disposable income and discretionary income. How does each type of income affect consumer buying power?

18. How is consumer buying power affected by wealth and consumer credit?

19. How is buying power measured? Why should it be evaluated?

20. What factors influence a consumer's willingness to spend?

21. What are the principal types of competition?

22. Why is it important for businesses to understand the nature of competitive forces?

• • • • • • • • • • • • • • • • •

Recommended Readings

A. Palmer and I. Worthington, *The Business and Marketing Environment* (Maidenhead: McGraw-Hill, 1992).

P. Drucker, *Management in Turbulent Times* (London: Butterworth-Heinemann/Pan, 1981).

M. E. Porter, "How competitive forces shape strategy", *Harvard Business Review*, March–April 1979, pp. 137–145.

K. Peattie, *Environmental Marketing Management* (London: Pitman, 1995).

P. S. H. Leeflang and W. F. van Raaij, "The changing consumer in the European Union: a meta-analysis", *International Journal of Research in Marketing*, 1995, vol. 12, no. 5, pp. 373–387.

• • • • • • • • • • • • • • • • •

Cases

2.1 Buying Heinz on a Sunday

For decades Sunday was a day of rest: churches were busy, bars and restaurants operated on restricted hours and very few shops opened their doors. Gradually this situation changed throughout the 1980s. New working practices presented more leisure time, and consumers expected greater choice and variety in pursuits away from work. To many, shopping is a social activity. Increased travel and tourism enabled many Britons to experience the more relaxed shopping and licensing hours typical in many Mediterranean countries, for example.

Some businesses were noting these trends and the potential profits to be made from trading on a Sunday. A major amendment to the licensing laws in the 1980s permitted pubs to open longer and many restaurants to open all day. Continental drinking customs were coming to the UK, so why not shopping habits too?

For retailers, though, doors remained closed. Seaside and holiday resorts allowed their shops to open seven days per week for the summer season. Throughout England and Wales, newsagents could open to distribute newspapers, forecourts could sell petrol, and off-licences could open for a couple of hours at lunchtime and in the evening. For the retailers of groceries and consumer durables, shop doors remained closed. Even garden centres, historically allowed to open, could not sell garden furniture or tools on Sundays, having to chain off those display areas.

In the 1990s, the pattern has changed. DIY giants Texas and B&Q risked hefty fines to breach the Sunday trading laws and to open their doors. Despite having to pay their volunteer staff bonuses for working, Sunday trading was financially worthwhile and apparently popular with a large proportion of the general public. MPs debated the issue, with support growing for an upheaval in the Sunday trading laws. Votes for amendments were only narrowly defeated in the House of Commons. Religious leaders and shop workers' unions were appalled by the moves to bring in seven day shopping. Campaigns were initiated to keep Sunday free from trading, with significant support from churches, unions, some of the media and one or two retail chains that opposed the extension to opening hours and did not wish to increase staff and operating costs.

The most significant development came in 1992, when Sunday opening was introduced by the large grocery groups: Sainsbury, Tesco, Safeway and Asda. Groceries are a necessity, more so than clothing or footwear; grocery shopping is also a regular, frequent expedition in most households. The higher wage bills and fines imposed on retailers by some local authorities and councils did not outweigh the popularity of the move with many consumers. There were good returns for the retailers. For many households, Sunday shopping became a welcome option in a busy week's schedule. For others, it provided another leisure pursuit!

Legally, the issue went right through the English courts. There were victories on both sides, but ultimately Parliament had to abide by the existing statute books: Sunday trading for most retailers was illegal. Some of the large retailers, led by Kingfisher—owner of DIY retailer B&Q, electrical chain Comet, as well as Woolworth and Superdrug—went to the European courts, believing that the Sunday trading laws were poorly configured, ambiguous and wrongly restrictive. Initial verdicts were in these retailers' favour. More chains started to open on Sundays. Local authorities resented wasting resources to enforce legislation that seemed flawed.

The UK government admitted that the existing legislation was unclear, difficult to enforce and not in line with current retailing practices. Kenneth Clarke, the then Home Secretary, believed he had three options to put before MPs:

- Total freedom for all shops to choose to open on Sundays
- A *Keeping Sunday Special* proposition, which would allow opening only for leisure pursuits
- A reform of shops' hours, which would allow some shops to open on Sundays

To many observers' surprise, in 1993 the European Court delivered its verdict on the appeals on behalf of the local authorities' right to uphold existing anti-opening laws, and against retailers' desires to open when they wished. The verdicts upheld the restricted Sunday opening laws already on the statute books and ruled against those DIY and grocery retailers that had extended their hours of operation.

The reaction was mixed. Journalists and MPs ridiculed the government's inability to act on the issue to establish up to date, enforceable working legislation in line with EU regulations. Some local authorities began once more to take retailers to court for opening, while other authorities decided to take no action and to await the central government's new legislation. A few retailers closed their doors, but most continued to trade.

For consumers, regulators and retailers there was confusion; often circumstances differed from town to town. If one local authority appeased the Keep Sunday Special lobby by enforcing the restrictions on Sunday trading, shoppers there might be able to travel a few miles to a neighbouring town where retailers opened on a Sunday without fear of prosecution. Retailers who wanted to open thus found consistency hard to attain, different circumstances from region to region and legal developments weekly. For those companies with objections to Sunday trading, there was loss of market share. John Lewis Partnership's department stores and Waitrose supermarkets, for example, saw healthy profits turn into losses as their doors remained locked on Sundays. Finally, common sense prevailed. New legislation permitted retailers to trade on Sundays, but for a maximum of six hours. The move pleased most retailers and consumers, but by no means all.

Changing social practices and legal, regulatory and competitive forces are all at work in the Sunday trading debate, with major implications for all those involved.

SOURCES: "Sunday trading verdict soon", *Marketing*, 12 November 1992, p. 8; John Lewis, "MP's threat to Sunday shopping", *Marketing*, 28 January 1993, p. 7; BBC TV news, November 1992–January 1993; John Lewis, "Limit to Sunday hours threatened", *Marketing*, 17 December 1992, p. 6.

Questions for Discussion

1. What changes are likely in trading practices as a result of the more lenient Sunday trading laws?
2. Which aspects of the marketing environment are at work here?
3. What competitive implications from the Sunday trading debate are there for companies such as John Lewis?

2.2 Ericsson Sights Global Markets

Sweden has many internationally known organisations, many of which are leaders in their respective fields: Saab Scania in aerospace and vehicles; Volvo in cars and trucks; Electrolux in domestic appliances and electrical goods; IKEA in home furnishings; Tetra Pak in packaging and Ericsson in electronics and telecommunications. These companies all succeed by having a global focus and the ability to exploit technological niches. In the early 1980s, Ericsson anticipated that mechanical switching in telecommunications would be replaced by the faster and more efficient electronic switching, with the total transformation of telephone exchanges worldwide. By taking the decision to accept this trend and become one of the instigators of such change, Ericsson created an enviable lead in the marketplace and achieved significant market share increases.

It is perhaps not too surprising, therefore, that in the rapidly growing cellular (mobile) phone market, the world leader should be Sweden's Ericsson. Globally, 9 million new subscribers to mobile telephones are currently being added every six months, making it the fastest growing sector within the rapidly growing telecommunications industry. It is estimated that 40 per cent of all mobile phones in the world are connected to cellular networks delivered by Sweden's Ericsson. In Sweden, which has the highest penetration of mobile phones—11 per cent of the population, compared with 8.5 per cent in the UK—there are no signs of saturation, and penetration of an incredible 90 per cent is expected by the year 2000.

While Ericsson has succeeded in this marketplace largely because of insightful business planning and product development, the external marketing environment acted in favour of this Swedish multinational. There are various technologies at work in the rival cellular networks. A regional initiative by the Swedish, Norwegian and Finnish authorities established the Nordic Mobile Telephone (NMT) standard. It is a fact of most industries that an organisation's view of the world and of global customer needs is heavily influenced and biased by what is happening in a business's domestic marketplace. In this instance, the NMT standard for Scandinavia was more homogeneous than that applied in other parts of the world. While this forced Ericsson and Nokia to invest in new and more expensive technologies initially, the result was a product capability and knowledge genuinely superior to that being developed elsewhere in the world. It is not surprising, therefore, that network operators throughout Europe turned to Ericsson to provide infrastructure and networks. By contrast, the US has significant regulatory inconsistencies and barriers, as a result of which domestic US manufacturers produce equipment not deemed desirable worldwide. Indeed, through a joint venture with GE, the large American electronics conglomerate, Ericsson has successfully entered the US market and has beaten Motorola in its own home market. As a result, Ericsson now has 80 per cent of the joint venture with GE and is the fastest expanding player in the North American telecommunications market.

In a world market dominated by global players, Ericsson has been able to compete successfully with rivals such as AT&T, Northern Telecom, Alcatel and Siemens. The company's current focus is on providing technical services that can genuinely be company specific. Ericsson has recognised that in the high tech world of telecommunications, each company's needs as a customer of Ericsson will be unique. A second important requirement is to facilitate integration with other businesses. While such an awareness of market trends and customer needs has figured prominently in Ericsson's success, so has the company's ability to maximise opportunities offered by the broader marketing environment. The NMT standard in Scandinavia gave Ericsson, perhaps by default, a viable standard on which to build. In North America, Ericsson used its joint venture with GE to penetrate the market, but its global knowledge and size allowed it to overcome many of the regulatory and political barriers impeding the growth of domestic US manufacturers. In the telecommunications market, however, the ground rules are continually changing, and regulatory bodies are particularly prone to protect domestic markets and specific consumers.

SOURCES: R. Olins, "Mobile phone war hots up", *Sunday Times*, 19 November 1995; T. Jackson, "New kids on the telephony block", *Financial Times*, 15 May 1995; T. Grey and C. Price, "Orange aims to float in March", *Financial Times*, 12 January 1996; Andrew Pickford, Combitech Traffic Systems; "A visit to telecom's magic kingdom", *America's Network*, 15 March 1995, pp. 52–54; Matthew Lynn, "Calling for partners", *Management Today*, July 1992, pp. 80–81.

Questions

1. Why is it important for Ericsson to monitor the marketing environment?
2. To compete in Europe with companies like Ericsson, what must Motorola or Sony find out about the marketing environment in these target markets?
3. What are likely to be the most significant aspects of the marketing environment for Ericsson as it continues its attack on world markets?

3 MARKETING IN INTERNATIONAL MARKETS

"An international perspective on marketing management is critical in the contemporary era of global competition."

Colin Egan
Leicester De Montfort University

OBJECTIVES

- To define international marketing and understand the nature of international involvement
- To understand the importance of international marketing intelligence
- To recognise the impact of environmental forces on international marketing efforts
- To become aware of regional trade alliances and markets
- To look at alternative market entry strategies for becoming involved in international marketing activities

Global hotel operator Holiday Inn boasts nearly 2,000 hotels, with over 350,000 rooms in more than 60 countries worldwide. This makes the chain, which is owned by the UK's Bass Plc and operates primarily on the basis of franchises, the largest in the world. In order to achieve its current size, the company has targeted travellers of all types through a series of subbrands: Holiday Inn Crowne Plaza Resorts, Holiday Inn Crowne Plaza Hotels, Holiday Inn Select, Holiday Inn Sunspree Resort, Holiday Inn, Holiday Inn Garden Court and Holiday Inn Express.

Most recently, special attention has been given to the "value for money" segment served, in particular, by the Holiday Inn Express brand.

With declared objectives to expand the chain by a further 1,000 hotels by 1998, it seems likely that Holiday Inn will soon exceed its eighth position in the hotel rooms rankings. This fits with the company's overall strategy, which is to provide for the needs of all travellers and to capitalise on the economies of scale generated by being a large global operator. According to Holiday Inn's UK marketing manager, "size and distribution are our

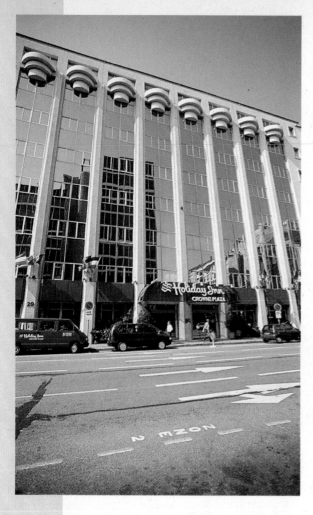

known as HIRO (Holiday Inn Reservation Optimiser), is vital to Holiday Inn's quest for scale economies. In the US alone, the global reservation network has already proved able to handle 120,000 calls a day. Such a system comes with a high price tag: in 1994 Holiday Inn spent £24 million on technology initiatives.

Encouraging hotel visitors to pay repeat visits plays an important part in Holiday Inn's growth strategy. Research has shown that more than 35 percent of hotel guests are repeat visitors. The company has therefore devised a frequent guest loyalty programme known as the Holiday Inn Priority Club. According to company literature, "The Priority Club programme is designed to recognise and reward frequent travellers worldwide with exclusive privileges and benefits at every Holiday Inn hotel". The loyalty scheme, which is available to visitors worldwide, allows members to redeem club points against a range of gifts, travel packages or frequent flier miles with airlines such as American Airlines, Delta, KLM, Lufthansa, Qantas and United Airlines. In addition, the scheme offers benefits such as guaranteed corporate and family rates, express reservations, personal cheque cashing services and discounts on car hire and hotel business services. The guest loyalty programme is just one technique Holiday Inn uses to appeal to its customers and just one aspect of its marketing programme—a programme that must be continually reviewed if the company's global standing is to be maintained. ∎

strategic marketing thrusts while we aim to build operational competitive advantage through consistency of guaranteed service and comfort. For this reason, Holiday Inn is largely a franchised business. Franchising allows us to grow quickly without taxing resources and yet take advantage of our infrastructure such as our worldwide computerised reservation systems and hotel management expertise". The computerised reservation system,

SOURCES: Jimmy K. H. Ang, *The Competitive Environment*, 1995, Warwick MBA Dissertation: Warwick Business School; "Operating and financial review", *Bass Plc Annual Report*, 1994; "Holiday Inn worldwide review", *Bass Plc Annual Report*, 1994 "Bass Plc", *Hoover's Handbook of World Business*, 1995–1996; "The supply structure", *Hotels*, Mintel Marketing Intelligence, February 1994; *Holiday Inn Worldwide Directory*, June 1995; C. Price, "Survey of international hotels—come back and see us", *The Financial Times*, 7 April 1994, p. 3.

International marketing generally refers to marketing activities performed across national boundaries.[1] Companies such as Holiday Inn, which operate globally, must manage all aspects of their operations with considerable care. In many cases, serving foreign target markets requires more than minor adjustments of marketing strategies.

This chapter looks closely at the unique features of international marketing. It begins by examining companies' level of commitment to and degree of involvement in international marketing and then considers the importance of international marketing intelligence when a firm is moving beyond its domestic market. Next the chapter focuses on the need to understand various environmental forces in international markets and discusses several regional alliances and markets. The concluding section describes alternative market entry strategies for becoming involved in international marketing.

• •

Involvement in International Marketing

Before international marketing could achieve its current level of importance, enterprises with the necessary resources had to develop an interest in expanding their businesses beyond national boundaries. Once interested, marketers engage in international marketing activities at several levels of involvement. Regardless of the level of involvement, however, they must decide on the degree to which it is possible to standardise their marketing strategies for different markets.

Levels of International Involvement

Domestic marketing
Marketing activities directed exclusively in a business's home market

Export marketing Marketing activities through which a business takes advantage of opportunities outside its home market but continues production in the home country

International marketing
Marketing activities in which a business reduces reliance on intermediaries and establishes direct involvement in the countries in which trade takes place

Multinational marketing
Adaptation of some of a company's marketing activities to appeal to local culture and differences in taste

Multinational companies
Companies that behave in their foreign markets as if they were local companies

The level of involvement in international marketing covers a wide spectrum, as shown in Figure 3.1. A business that undertakes marketing activities exclusively in its home market is involved in **domestic marketing**. Such organisations may have deliberately chosen to restrict their business to domestic customers or may simply not have considered the possibility of international marketing. **Export marketing** takes place when a business takes advantage of opportunities outside its home market. In some cases exporting activity begins almost by accident. For example, the products of a small medical supplies manufacturer might occasionally be purchased by hospitals or clinics in nearby countries; its products might also be purchased by other countries through an export agent. Whatever the reasons behind the initial export activity, production in the home country will be used to supply these new markets; for most businesses the domestic market will remain the key area of business. Companies that go beyond simple exporting become involved in **international marketing,** reducing their reliance on intermediaries and establishing direct links in the countries in which trade takes place. At this stage a foreign subsidiary may be set up, and products may be sourced away from the domestic market.

Multinational marketing takes marketing for non-domestic markets one step further by adapting some of the company's marketing activities, such as marketing communications, to appeal to local culture and differences in tastes. **Multinational companies** are those that behave in their foreign markets as if they were local companies. Full scale **global marketing** requires total commitment to international marketing and involves applying the organisation's assets, experience and products to develop and maintain marketing strategies on a global scale. Marketing Insight 3.1 explains the global marketing approach of ABB Asea Brown Boveri.

Understanding Global Marketing

Global marketing is the most extreme case of international involvement, representing the full integration of international marketing into strategic planning. The underlying principle is to identify products or services for which similarities across

The Logic of Global Business: An Interview with ABB's Percy Barnevik

Percy Barnevik, president and CEO of ABB Asea Brown Boveri, is a corporate pioneer. He is moving more aggressively than any CEO in Europe, perhaps in the world, to build the new model of competitive enterprise—an organisation that combines global scale and world-class technology with deep roots in local markets. He is working to give substance to the endlessly invoked corporate mantra, "Think global, act local".

Headquartered in Zurich, ABB is a young company forged through the merger of two venerable European companies. Asea, created in 1890, has been a flagship of Swedish industry for a century. Brown Boveri, which took shape in 1891, holds a comparable industrial status in Switzerland. In August 1987, Barnevik altered the course of both companies when he announced that Asea, where he was managing director, would merge with Brown Boveri to create a potent new force in the European market for electrical systems and equipment.

The creation of ABB became a metaphor for the changing economic map of Europe. Barnevik initiated a wrenching process of consolidation and rationalisation—lay offs, plant closings, product

exchanges between countries—that observers agreed will one day come to European industries from steel to telecommunications to cars. And soon more than a metaphor, Barnevik's bold moves triggered a wholesale restructuring of the Continent's electrical power industry.

In this interview, Percy Barnevik, 49, offers a detailed guide to the theory and practice of building a "multidomestic" enterprise.

The interview was conducted at ABB's Zurich headquarters by Harvard Business Review associate editor William Taylor.

HBR: Companies everywhere are trying to become global, and everyone agrees that ABB is more global than most companies. What does that mean?

Percy Barnevik: ABB is a company with no geographic centre, no national axe to grind. We are a federation of national companies with a global coordination centre. Are we a Swiss company? Our headquarters is in Zurich, but only 100 professionals work at headquarters and we will not increase that number. Are we a Swedish company? I'm the CEO, and I was born and educated in Sweden. But our headquarters is not in Sweden, and only two of

Global marketing A total commitment to international marketing, in which a company applies its assets, experience and products to develop and maintain marketing strategies on a global scale

many markets allow a single global strategy to be pursued. Various pressures make this approach attractive for managers. Perhaps the most significant is that if one marketing strategy can be used across a number of markets, a business can spread the costs of its research and development, technology and distribution, taking advantage of economies of scale in the process.

Despite the fact that global marketing strives for a single over-arching global strategy,[2] it is a mistake to assume that local differences can be ignored. During the 1980s marketers sought to globalise the marketing mix as much as possible by employing standardised products, promotion campaigns, prices and distribution channels for all markets. The potential economic and competitive pay offs for such an approach were certainly great. More recently marketers have realised that, while it may be feasible to standardise a company's offerings in different markets, a degree of adaptation to local differences is also required. While brand name, product characteristics, packaging and labelling may be relatively straightforward to standardise, media allocation, retail outlets and price may be more dif-the eight members of our board of directors are Swedes. Perhaps we are an American company. We report our financial results in US dollars, and English is ABB's official language. We conduct all high level meetings in English.

My point is that ABB is none of those things — and all of those things. We are not homeless. We are a company with many homes.

HBR: *Are all businesses becoming global?*

No, and this is a big source of misunderstanding. We are in the process of building this federation of national companies, a multidomestic organisation, as I prefer to call it. That does not mean all of our businesses are global. We do a very good business in electrical installation and service in many countries. That business is superlocal. The geographic scope of our installation business in, say, Stuttgart does not extend beyond a ten mile radius of downtown Stuttgart.

We also have businesses that are superglobal. There are not more than 15 combined-cycle power plants or more than three or four high voltage DC stations sold in any one year around the world. Our competitors fight for nearly every contract — they battle us on technology, price, financing — and

national borders are virtually meaningless. Every project requires our best people and best technology from around the world.

The vast majority of our businesses — and of most businesses — fall somewhere between the superlocal and the superglobal. These are the businesses in which building a multidomestic organisation offers powerful advantages. You want to be able to optimise a business globally — to specialise in the production of components, to drive economies of scale as far as you can, to rotate managers and technologists around the world to share expertise and solve problems. But you also want to have deep local roots everywhere you operate — building products in the countries where you sell them, recruiting the best local talent from the universities, working with the local government to increase exports. If you build such an organisation, you create a business advantage that's damn difficult to copy.

SOURCE: Reprinted by permission of *Harvard Business Review*. Adapted from, "The Logic of Global Business: An Interview with ABB's Percy Barnevik," by William Taylor, March/April 1991. Copyright © 1991 by the President and Fellows of Harvard College; all rights reserved.

ficult. For example, a construction equipment manufacturer may decide to send promotional literature about a new product to businesses across a range of different markets. Although the company's research may have identified a suitable global platform for the promotion, the types of businesses that purchase this equipment may vary on a country by country basis. The construction equipment manufacturer would therefore need to seek help from each country's marketing team to devise an appropriate mailing list.

Some companies have moved from customising or standardising products for a particular region of the world to offering globally standardised products that are advanced, functional, reliable and low in price.[3] Nike, for example, provides a standardised product worldwide. Examples of globalised products are electrical equipment, videos, films, soft drinks, rock music, cosmetics and toothpaste. Sony televisions, Levi jeans and UK confectionery brands seem to make annual gains in the world market. Even McDonald's restaurants seem to be widely accepted in markets throughout the world. Yet even here there is some adaptation to local

Domestic marketing	Export marketing	International marketing	Multinational marketing	Global marketing
Home market involvement only.	This is an attempt to create sales without significant changes in the firms's products and overall operations. An active effort to find foreign markets for existing products is most typical.	Greater commitment to international markets. International marketing activities are seen as part of overall planning. Direct investment in non-domestic markets is likely and products may also be sourced away from the home market.	Further steps are taken to adapt to local tastes. Modifications may be made to aspects of the marketing mix to make them more appealing to local markets.	Total commitment to international marketing which involves applying the organisation's assets, experience and products to develop and maintain marketing strategies on a global scale. Although a single global marketing strategy is required, some adaptation to local needs is still needed.

Domestic orientation ←————————————————————→ Global orientation

Figure 3.1 Levels of involvement in international marketing

tastes, with restaurants in certain countries serving alcoholic drinks. Some products that are regarded by many as globally standard, such as Coca-Cola (see Figure 3.2), are in fact adapted for certain markets.

Debate about the feasibility of globalised marketing strategies has continued since the birth of the idea in the 1960s. Surprisingly, questions about standardised advertising policies are the leading concern. However, it should be remembered that there are degrees of both customisation and globalisation. Neither strategy is implemented in its pure form.[4] The debate will doubtless continue, yet it seems that the feasibility of globalisation is ultimately determined by the degree of similarity among the various environmental and market conditions. For some products—such as soft drinks—a global marketing strategy, including advertising, seems to work well, while for other products—such as beer—strategies must make considerable concessions to accommodate local, regional and national differences.[5] Some marketers now believe that some of the best global opportunities are presented by "global market segments".

International Marketing Intelligence

Despite the debate over globalisation of markets, most firms perceive international markets as differing in some ways from domestic markets. Analyses of international markets and possible marketing efforts can be based on many dimensions. Table 3.1 lists the types of information that international marketers need. (Chapter 6 contains a detailed discussion of marketing research and data collection.)

Figure 3.2

Example of globalisation

Although Coca-Cola is available globally, in some markets the taste and packaging are adapted to local tastes.

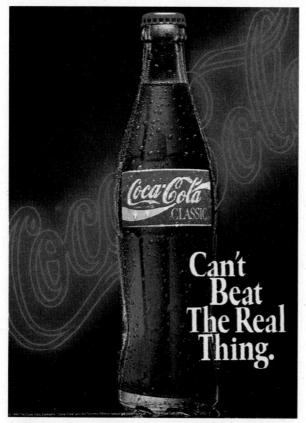

Source: "Coca-Cola" and the Dynamic Ribbon device are registered trademarks of the Coca-Cola company.

Gathering secondary data (see Table 3.2) should be the first step in analysing a foreign market. Sources of information include government publications, financial services firms, international organisations such as the United Nations, foreign governments and international trade organisations. UK firms seeking to market their products in Russia, for example, can obtain information about Russian markets and regulations from the Department of Trade and Industry (DTI), the Russian Chamber of Commerce and Industry, the Russian trade organisation Amtorg and numerous other organisations. Depending on the source, however, secondary data can be misleading. The reliability, validity and comparability of data from some countries are often problematic.

To overcome these shortcomings, marketers may need primary data to understand consumers' buying behaviour in the country under investigation. (Buyer behaviour is discussed in detail in Chapters 4 and 5.) Marketers may have to adjust their techniques of collecting primary data for foreign markets. Attitudes towards privacy, unwillingness to be interviewed, language differences and low literacy rates can be serious research obstacles. In a bi-cultural country such as Canada, a national questionnaire that uses identical questions cannot be used because of the cultural and language differences. In many areas of Africa, where the literacy rate is low, self-administered questionnaires would never work.

Primary research should uncover significant cultural characteristics before a product is launched so that the marketing strategy is appropriate for the target market. It may be necessary to investigate basic patterns of social behaviour,

Preliminary Screening

Demographic/Physical Environment

Population size, growth, density
Urban and rural distribution
Climate and weather variations
Shipping distance
Product significant demographics
Physical distribution and
    communications network
Natural resources

Political Environment

System of government
Political stability and continuity
Ideological orientation
Government in business
Government in communications
Attitudes towards foreign business
    (trade restrictions, tariffs, non-
    tariff barriers, bi-lateral trade
    agreements)
National economic and
    developmental priorities

Economic Environment

Overall level of development
Economic growth: GNP, industrial
    sector
Role of foreign trade in economy
Currency, inflation rate,
    availability, controls, stability
    of exchange rate
Balance of payments
Per capita income and distribution
Disposable income and
    expenditure patterns

Social/Cultural Environment

Literacy rate, educational level
Existence of middle class
Similarities and differences in
    relation to home market
Language and other cultural
    considerations

Analysis of Industry Market Potential

Market Access

Limitations on trade: tariff levels,
    quotas
Documentation and import
    regulations
Local standards, practices, and
    other non-tariff barriers
Patents and trade marks
Preferential treaties
Legal considerations: investment,
    taxation, repatriation,
    employment, code of laws

Product Potential

Customer needs and desires
Local production, imports,
    consumption
Exposure to and acceptance of
    product
Availability of linking products
Industry specific key indicators of
    demand
Attitudes towards products of
    foreign origin
Competitive offerings
Availability of intermediaries
Regional and local transport
    facilities
Availability of manpower
Conditions for local manufacture

Analysis of Company Sales Potential

Sales Volume Forecasting

Size and concentration of
    customer segments
Projected consumption statistics
Competitive pressures
Expectations of local
    distributors/agents

Landed Cost

Costing method for exports
Domestic distribution costs
International freight insurance
Cost of product modification

Cost of Internal Distribution

Tariffs and duties
Value added tax
Local packaging and assembly
Margins/commission allowed
    for the trade
Local distribution and
    inventory costs
Promotional expenditures

Other Determinants of Profitability

Going price levels
Competitive strengths and
    weaknesses
Credit practices
Current and projected exchange
    rates

SOURCE: Adapted from S. Tamer Cavusgil, "Guidelines for export market research", *Business Horizons*, November–December 1985, pp. 30–31. Used by permission.

Table 3.1 Information needed for international marketing analyses

Country/Region	Body Motions	Greetings	Colours	Numbers	Shapes, Sizes, Symbols
Japan	Pointing to one's own chest with a forefinger indicates one wants a bath. A forefinger to the nose indicates "me".	Bowing is the traditional form of greeting.	Positive colours are in muted shades. Combinations of black, dark grey, and white have negative overtones.	Positive numbers are 1, 3, 5, 8. Negative numbers are 4, 9.	Pine, bamboo or plum patterns are positive. Cultural shapes such as Buddha shaped jars should be avoided.
India	Kissing is considered offensive and is not usually seen on television, in films or in public places.	The palms of the hands touch and the head is nodded for greeting. It is considered rude to touch or shake hands with a woman.	Positive colours are bold such as green, red, yellow or orange. Negative colours are black and white if they appear in relation to weddings.	To create brand awareness, numbers are often used as a brand name.	Animals such as parrots, elephants, tigers or cheetahs are often used as brand names or on packaging. Sexually explicit symbols are avoided.
Europe	When counting on one's fingers, the number 1 is often indicated by thumb, 2 by thumb and forefinger.	It is acceptable to send flowers in thanks for a dinner invitation, but not roses (for sweethearts) or chrysanthemums (for funerals).	Generally, white and blue are considered positive. Black often has negative overtones.	The numbers 3 or 7 are usually positive; 13 is a negative number.	Circles are symbols of perfection. Hearts are considered favourably at Christmas time.
Latin America	General arm gestures are used for emphasis.	The traditional greeting is a hearty embrace and slap on the back.	Popular colours are generally bright or bold yellow, red, blue or green.	Generally, 7 is a positive number. Negative numbers are 13, 14.	Respect religious symbols. Avoid national symbols such as flag colours.
Middle East	The raised eyebrow facial expression indicates "yes".	The word "no" must be mentioned three times before it is accepted.	Positive colours are brown, black, dark blues and reds. Pink, violets and yellows are not favoured.	Positive numbers are 3, 5, 7, 9; 13, 15 are negative.	Round or square shapes are acceptable. Symbols of six-pointed star, raised thumb or Koranic sayings are avoided.

SOURCES: James C. Simmons, "A matter of interpretation", *American Way,* April 1983, pp. 106–111; "Adapting export packaging to cultural differences", *Business America,* 3 December 1979, pp. 3–7.

Table 3.3 Sampling of cultural variations

In Japan, an End to All Work and No Play

Every year about a hundred million Japanese spend about £50 each to see Mickey Mouse and wait two hours in line to ride Space Mountain at Tokyo Disneyland. They flock to hear Aron Narikiyo, "Elvis-san", a wildly popular Elvis impersonator. They ski, attend cultural events and play *pachinko,* a vertical version of pinball. They also shop. One hundred and twenty million Japanese consumers with rising disposable incomes translates into lots of buying power. Long considered a society of all work and no play, Japan finds both its culture and its consumers changing.

In the conventional picture of modern Japan, men work most of the time, and women are relegated to background positions of stay-at-home wives and mothers. Now this image is changing as Japanese men are discovering that fun is sometimes more important than earnest dedication to the workplace. Japanese women are assuming professional roles outside the home. Declaring that its citizens should start enjoying life, the government officially shortened the work week from forty-eight hours to forty and funded the Leisure Research and Development Centre to teach its citizens the value of leisure time. With more money to spend and more time in which to spend it, the Japanese are becoming active and experienced consumers, dedicated to making their country a *seikatsu taikoku* — a "lifestyle superpower".

Two of the most powerful groups of Japanese consumers are the eight million "second boomers", young people born in Japan's second population explosion following the Second World War, and women, whose status and affluence continue to grow. Raised during a prosperous time, young Japanese spend a lot of money on sports, audiovisual equipment, entertainment and fashion. One of their favourite places to go for fun is Namco's Wonder Eggs, an arcade specialising in virtual reality games. As for tastes in fashion, this group prefers American and European styles and colours. To attract these customers, some small shops in areas frequented by young people carry only imported clothing.

In today's Japan, women make up about 40 per cent of the workforce, and more than 50 per cent of mothers work outside the home. Following the Equal Employment Law of 1986, they became more educated, entered many professions, earned their own salaries and became champion consumers.

In addition to attending concerts and plays, travelling, playing sports and visiting "relaxation parlours", where the sounds of birds singing or waves crashing relieve stress, Japanese women go shopping. Choosy about labels, many Japanese women favour quality brands, such as Armani suits, Yves St. Laurent towels, and £1,000 Gucci handbags.

When Japanese leaders told the country to relax, the leisure industry rushed to provide places to do it. Just as retailing is profiting from larger numbers of Japanese shoppers, the leisure industry is profiting from the greater amount of time that Japanese consumers are spending engaged in leisure activities. In one year alone, two hundred companies applied for permits to develop new theme parks. To enable ski enthusiasts to make one day trips from Tokyo, a bullet train station opened at a popular ski resort, Gala Yuzawa. For those who prefer to have their skiing climate controlled, indoor ski slopes are available within city limits.

With all these choices and more, people don't have trouble deciding what to do with a day off, but the Japanese are still novices at relaxing. A Leisure Development Centre survey revealed that 40 per cent of the respondents said they wouldn't know what to do with a month off. To help them, the National Recreation Association offers a one year course on how to enjoy life.

SOURCES: Yumiko Ono, "Land of rising fun", *Wall Street Journal,* 2 October, 1992, pp. A1, A10; Merry White, "Home truths: woman and social change in Japan", *Daedalus,* Fall 1992, pp. 61–82; Gayle Hanson, "Japan at play", *Insight,* 27 April, 1992, pp. 6–13, 34–37; Gale Eisenstodt, "Value for yen," *Forbes,* 27 April, 1992, pp. 78–79; JETRO Video, *The Newest Waves of Japanese Consumers.*

those needs—it leads to increased customer satisfaction in marketing negotiations in France, Germany, the United Kingdom and the United States. However, the attractiveness of the salesperson and his or her similarity to the customer increase the levels of satisfaction only for Americans. Furthermore, marketing negotiations proceed differently in the various cultures, and the role and status of the seller are more important in both the UK and France.[8]

Social Forces

Marketing activities are primarily social in purpose; therefore they are structured by the institutions of family, religion, education, health and recreation (see Figure 3.3). For example, in the UK, where listening to music on hi-fi systems is a common form of relaxation, Japanese products have a large target market. In every nation, these social institutions can be identified. By finding major deviations in institutions among countries, marketers can gain insights into the adaptation of a marketing strategy. Although American football is a popular sport in the United States and a major opportunity for many television advertisers, soccer is the most popular television sport in Europe. Yet football hooliganism caused major advertisers in the United Kingdom to have second thoughts about supporting such events with vast sums spent on advertising.[9] The role of children in the family and a society's overall view of children also influence marketing activities. For example, the use of cute, cereal loving children in advertising for Kellogg's is illegal in France. In the Netherlands, children are banned from appearing in advertisements for sweets, and confectionery manufacturers are required to place a little toothbrush symbol at the end of each confectionery spot.[10]

Economic Forces

Economic differences dictate many of the adjustments that must be made in marketing abroad. The most prominent adjustments are caused by differences in standards of living, availability of credit, discretionary buying power, income distribution, national resources and conditions that affect transport.

Gross domestic product (GDP) The total value of all goods and services produced by a country's income

Gross domestic product (GDP) is the total value of all goods and services produced by a country's income. A comparison of GDP for Europe, America and Japan (see Table 3.4) shows that the United States has the largest gross domestic product in the world. However, in order to attain a measure of standard of living, it is necessary to divide this figure by the size of the population. In this way it is possible to gain insight into the level of discretionary income or "buying power" of individual consumers. This kind of knowledge about aggregate GDP, credit and the distribution of income provides general insights into market potential.

Opportunities for international marketers are certainly not limited to countries with the highest incomes. Some nations are progressing at a markedly faster rate than they were even a few years ago; and these countries—especially in Latin America, Africa, eastern Europe and the Middle East—have great market potential for specific products. However, marketers must first understand the political and legal environment before they can convert buying power into actual demand for specific products.

Political and Legal Forces

A country's political system, national laws, regulatory bodies, national pressure groups and courts all have great impact on global marketing. A government's policies towards public and private enterprise, consumers and foreign firms influence marketing across national boundaries. The types of measures a government can take to govern cross-border trade include the use of tariffs, quotas and non-tariff barriers. For example, the Japanese have established many barriers to imports into their country. Even though they are reducing the tariffs on certain items, many non-tariff barriers still make it difficult for other companies to export their

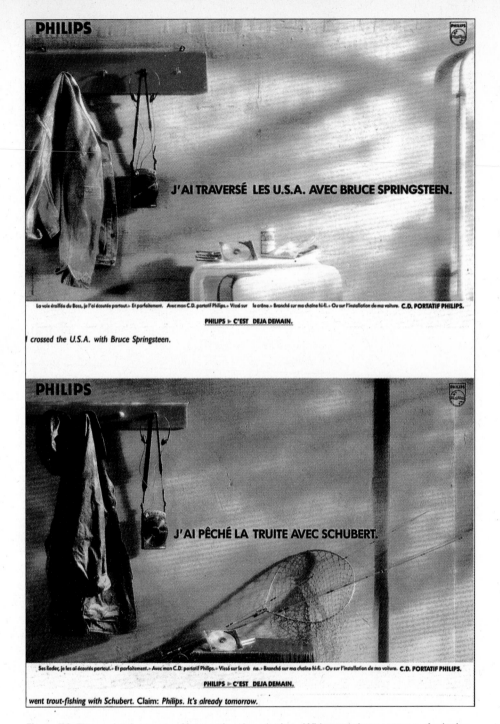

Figure 3.3 The societal aspects of international marketing. Widespread acceptance of relaxing to music enables Philips to produce a range of advertisements with relevance in many markets.

Source: © Philips Electronics N.V.

	GDP at Constant Prices				
	1990	**1991**	**1992**	**1993**	**1994**
World	2.7	1.7	3.2	3.0	—
Industrial countries	2.0	0.4	1.9	1.4	3.1
United States	0.8	−1.2	3.3	3.1	4.1
Canada	−0.2	−1.8	0.8	2.2	4.6
Australia	1.3	−1.6	2.5	4.0	4.9
Japan	4.8	4.3	1.4	0.1	0.6
New Zealand	−0.9	−2.5	1.9	5.2	—
Austria	4.2	2.9	1.8	−0.1	2.7
Belgium	3.2	2.3	1.9	−1.7	2.3
Denmark	1.4	1.3	0.8	1.5	4.4
Finland	—	−7.1	−3.6	−1.6	3.9
France	2.5	0.8	1.3	−1.5	2.7
Germany	4.9	3.6	1.2	−2.3	1.6
Greece	−0.9	3.2	0.8	−0.5	—
Iceland	0.6	1.2	−3.4	1.1	3.2
Ireland	8.6	2.9	5.0	4.0	—
Italy	2.1	1.3	0.9	—	—
Luxembourg	3.2	3.1	1.8	—	—
Netherlands	3.9	2.3	1.8	0.4	2.5
Norway	1.7	1.6	3.4	2.4	5.1
Portugal	4.1	2.1	1.1	—	—
Spain	3.7	2.2	0.7	−1.1	2.0
Sweden	1.4	−1.7	−1.4	−2.6	2.2
Switzerland	2.3	—	−0.3	−0.9	2.1
United Kingdom	0.4	−2.0	−0.5	2.3	3.8

NOTE: Percentage changes from previous year.
SOURCE: *International Financial Statistics Yearbook* (International Monetary Fund, 1995). Reprinted by permission of the International Monetary Fund.

Table 3.4 Growth of real GDP in some OECD countries

Tariffs Taxes that affect the movement of goods across economic or political boundaries and can also affect imports, exports or goods in transit

Quotas Physical restrictions on the amount of goods that can be imported into a particular country or region

Non-tariff barriers A wide range of rules, regulations and taxes that have an impact upon trade

products to Japan.[11] **Tariffs** are taxes that affect the movement of goods across economic or political boundaries and can affect imports, exports or goods in transit.[12] These taxes provide a useful source of government revenue and can provide domestic companies with an important advantage. For example, import tariffs in the form of import duties effectively increase the price of imported products, giving local companies an automatic advantage. **Quotas** involve physical restrictions on the amount of goods that can be imported into a particular country or region. The imposition of quotas is not always in the best interest of consumers, as choice is limited and allocations tend to be used up on imports of goods carrying the greatest profit margin. **Non-tariff barriers** are much more difficult to define; they include a wide range of rules, regulations and taxes that have an impact upon trade. As shown in Table 3.5, these barriers can include anything from port and border taxes to trademark and health and safety regulations. For example, just a few years ago, companies exporting electronic equipment to Japan had to wait for the Japanese government to inspect each item. A government's attitude towards co-operation with importers has a direct impact on the economic feasibility of

Formal Trade Restrictions	Administrative Trade Restrictions
A. Non-Tariff Import Restrictions (Price Related Measures)	**D. State Participation in Trade**

Formal Trade Restrictions

A. Non-Tariff Import Restrictions (Price Related Measures)

Surcharges at border
Port and statistical taxes
Non-discriminatory excise taxes and registration charges
Discriminatory excise taxes, government insurance requirements
Non-discriminatory turnover taxes
Discriminatory turnover taxes
Import deposit
Variable levies
Consular fees
Stamp taxes
Various special taxes and surcharges

B. Quantitative Restrictions and Similar Specific Trade Limitations (Quantity Related Measures)

Licensing regulations
Ceiling and quotas
Embargoes
Export restrictions and prohibitions
Foreign exchange and other monetary or financial controls
Government price setting and surveillance
Purchase and performance requirements
Restrictive business conditions
Discriminatory bi-lateral arrangements
Discriminatory regulations regarding countries of origin
International cartels
Orderly marketing agreements
Various related regulations

C. Discriminatory Freight Rates (Flag Protectionism)

Administrative Trade Restrictions

D. State Participation in Trade

Subsidies and other government support
Government trade, government monopolies, and granting of concessions or licences
Laws and ordinances discouraging imports
Problems relating to general government policy
Government procurement
Tax relief, granting of credit and guarantees
Boycott

E. Technical Norms, Standards, and Consumer Protection Regulations

Health and safety regulations
Pharmaceutical control regulations
Product design regulations
Industrial standards
Size and weight regulations
Packing and labelling regulations
Package marking regulations
Regulations pertaining to use
Regulations for the protection of intellectual property
Trade mark regulations

F. Customs Processing and Other Administrative Regulations

Anti-dumping policy
Customs calculation bases
Formalities required by consular officials
Certification regulations
Administrative obstacles
Merchandise classification
Regulations regarding sample shipment, return shipments and re-exports
Countervailing duties and taxes
Appeal law
Emergency law

SOURCE: Beatrice Bondy, *Protectionism: Challenge of the Eighties* (Zurich: Union Bank of Switzerland Economic Research Department, 1983), p. 19. Reprinted by permission.

Table 3.5 Non-tariff trade barriers

exporting to that country. As barriers to trade come down, opportunities are presented. Attempts to reduce trade barriers and improve the flow of goods between countries have come to the forefront in the post–Second World War period. The rules and frameworks for world trade are partly determined by the General Agreement on Tariffs and Trade (GATT). From a marketing standpoint, principles such as those defended by GATT increase competition.

Differences in political and government ethical standards are enormous. The use of pay offs and bribes is deeply entrenched in many governments, while in others direct involvement in pay offs and bribes is prohibited. European companies that do not engage in such practices may have a hard time competing with foreign firms that do. Some businesses that refuse to make pay offs are forced to hire local consultants, public relations firms or advertising agencies—resulting in indirect pay offs. The ultimate decision about whether to give small tips or gifts where they are customary must be based on a company's code of ethics.

Technological Forces

Much of the marketing technology used in Europe and other industrialised regions of the world may be ill suited for developing countries. For example, advertising on television or through direct mail campaigns may be difficult in countries that lack up to date broadcasting and postal services. Nonetheless, many countries—particularly China, South Korea, Mexico and the countries of the former Soviet Union—want to engage in international trade, often through partnerships with American, European and Japanese firms, so that they can gain valuable industrial and agricultural technology. However, in certain cases companies need permission to export goods. For example, in the UK and other EU countries, some level of government approval is needed before defence equipment can be exported, although in the post-Cold War period restrictions here are also decreasing. This is just one area where the reduction in conflicts between major powers is further freeing trade among nations.

• • • • • • • • • • • • • • • • • • •

Regional Trade Alliances and Markets

Although some firms are beginning to view the world as one huge marketplace, various regional trade alliances and specific markets may create difficulties or opportunities for companies engaging in international marketing. This section examines several regional trade alliances and changing markets, including the European Union, the Pacific Rim markets, changing conditions in central and eastern Europe, and the North American Free Trade Agreement.

European Union

European Union (EU) One of three major market groups in western Europe, the EU has 15 members: Austria, Belgium, Denmark, Finland, France, Germany, Greece, Ireland, Italy, Luxembourg, the Netherlands, Portugal, Spain, Sweden and the UK

Maastricht Treaty The treaty, signed in 1992, that established the European Union

The **European Union** (EU) is one of three major market groups in western Europe. Formed by the Treaty of European Union, the EU has its origins in the European Common Market, set up in 1958, which later became known as the European Community (EC). Following the signing of the **Maastricht Treaty** in 1992 and the creation of the single European market in 1993, the group became known as the European Union. Today the EU has 15 members: Austria, Belgium, Denmark, Finland, France, Germany, Greece, Ireland, Italy, Luxembourg, the Netherlands, Portugal, Spain, Sweden, United Kingdom. The objectives of the Union are set out in the following extract from Article B of the Treaty on European Union.[13]

—to promote economic and social progress which is balanced and sustainable, in particular through the creation of an area without internal frontiers, through the strengthening of economic and social cohesion and through the establishment of economic and monetary union, ultimately including a single currency in accordance with the provisions of this Treaty;

—to assert its identity on the international scene, in particular through the implementation of a common foreign and security policy including the eventual framing of a common defence policy, which might in time lead to a common defence;

Figure 3.4

EU and EFTA membership

Dates of accession
- 1958
- 1973
- 1981
- 1986
- 1995

Finland

Sweden

Ireland

Denmark

United Kingdom

Netherlands

Belgium   Germany

Luxembourg

France

Austria

Portugal   Spain   Italy

Greece

The members of EFTA

1959	1991	1995
Austria	Austria	Iceland
Denmark	Finland	Leichtenstein
Norway	Iceland	Norway
Portugal	Leichtenstein	Switzerland
Sweden	Norway	
Switzerland	Sweden	
United Kingdom	Switzerland	

Source: Eurostat: Europe in Figures, *4th edn, Office for Official Publications of the European Community: Brussels, 1994, pp. 9, 24.*

—to strengthen the protection of the rights and interests of the nationals of its Member States through the introduction of a citizenship of the Union;

—to develop close co-operation on justice and home affairs.

European Free Trade Association (EFTA)   Set up in 1960 to encourage free trade between member countries

The **European Free Trade Association (EFTA)** was set up in 1960 with the intention of encouraging free trade between member countries. In 1994, Austria, Finland and Sweden, formerly members of EFTA, joined the EU, bringing the number of member states to 15 (see Figure 3.4 for EU and EFTA membership as at the end of 1996). EFTA has been successful in meeting its objectives to eliminate customs duties and other restrictions on the trade of industrial products between members. However, in the period preceding the completion of the single European market, the need to reorganise the EFTA arrangement became apparent. Negotiations for a **European Economic Area (EEA)** were completed in 1993

European Economic Area (EEA)   An agreement, beginning in 1993, that encourages free trade between EFTA and the EU

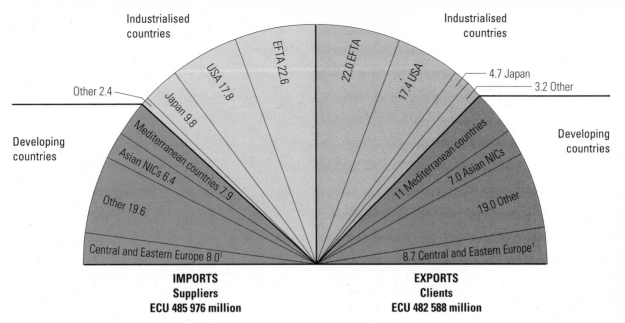

Industrialised countries

Industrialised countries

EFTA 22.6

USA 17.8

Japan 9.8

22.0 EFTA

17.4 USA

4.7 Japan

3.2 Other

Other 2.4

Developing countries

Mediterranean countries 7.9

Asian NICs 6.4

Other 19.6

Central and Eastern Europe 8.0¹

Developing countries

11 Mediterranean countries

7.0 Asian NICs

19.0 Other

8.7 Central and Eastern Europe¹

IMPORTS
Suppliers
ECU 485 976 million

EXPORTS
Clients
ECU 482 588 million

¹Including the former Soviet Union.

Figure 3.5 The EU's import and export trade

Source: Eurostat: Europe in Figures, 4th edn, Office for Official Publications of the European Community: 1994, pp. 367. Reprinted by permission.

and the EEA came into force on 1 January 1993. In addition to the 12 EU countries, the agreement also covered EFTA members (except Switzerland, which decided not to join, and Liechtenstein, which joined two years later). Since the initial agreement was signed, EFTA members Austria, Finland and Sweden have anyway joined the EU. The EEA agreement, which covers 377 million consumers, extends the earlier arrangement on free trade in industrial products to allow EFTA countries free movement of goods, services, people and capital within the EU. Figure 3.5 illustrates how the EU's import and export trade is made up. It is interesting to compare the ratio of imports to exports for different countries and regions. For example, imports from Japan still outnumber the exports it receives from the EU by a factor of 2:1; yet imports and exports to other regions are reasonably well balanced.

Although the 15 nations of the EU essentially function as one large market and consumers in the EU are likely to become more homogeneous in their needs and wants, marketers must be aware that cultural and social differences among the 15 member nations may require modifications in the marketing mix for consumers in each nation. Some researchers believe that eventually it will be possible to segment the European Union into six markets on the basis of cultural, geographic, demographic and economic variables. For example, the United Kingdom and Ireland would form one market, while Greece and southern Italy would form another.[14] Differences in taste and preferences among these markets are significant for international marketers. For example, the British prefer front loading washing machines; the French prefer top loading ones. Consumers in Spain eat far more poultry products than Germans do.[15] Preference differences may exist even within the same country, depending on the geographic region. Thus international marketing intelligence efforts are likely to remain very important in determining European consumers' needs and in developing marketing mixes that will satisfy those needs. It is also clear that EU organisations will have to face up to considerable changes in the way they operate, and for some, such as pharmaceutical companies, the prospects include harmonisation of prices and formulations and likely job losses.

Pacific Rim Nations

Countries in the Pacific Rim represent an enormous part of the world market with 60 per cent of the world's population living there. Although the region is characterised by considerable diversity, in general companies of the Pacific Rim nations—Japan, China, South Korea, Taiwan, Singapore, Hong Kong, the Philippines, Malaysia, Indonesia, Australia and Indochina—have become increasingly competitive and sophisticated in their marketing efforts in the last three decades. The performances of Japan and the four so called economic tigers of the region—South Korea, Singapore, Taiwan and Hong Kong—have been particularly impressive.[16] The Japanese in particular have made considerable inroads into the world consumer markets for cars, motorcycles, watches, cameras and audio-visual equipment. Products made by Sony, Sanyo, Toyota, Honda, Canon, Suzuki and others are sold all over the world and have set quality standards by which other products are often judged. Through direct investment in Europe, the Japanese have built strong distribution and have developed a keen understanding of the market. However, Japan's marketing muscle has attracted criticism in certain quarters, fuelled partly by fears that Japanese products may swamp the market. These concerns are compounded by Japan's reluctance to accept imports from other countries.[17] In practice, the sale of Japan's products in Europe is limited by the existence of quotas. However, with many of these quotas due to end in 1997, there will be repercussions for European manufacturers such as Citroën, Fiat and Peugeot.

South Korea has become very successful in world markets with familiar brands such as Samsung, Daewoo and Hyundai. But even before those companies became household names, their products achieved strong success under company labels such as RCA and JC Penney, for example, in America. Korean companies are now taking market share away from Japanese companies in the world markets for video cassette recorders, colour televisions and computers, despite the fact that the Korean market for these products is limited. In Canada, the Hyundai Excel overtook Japan's Honda in just 18 months.[18] Now Hyundai is taking on Japanese and American manufacturers for a piece of the US market.

Less visible Pacific Rim regions, such as Singapore, Taiwan and Hong Kong, are major manufacturing and financial centres. Singapore also has large world markets for pharmaceutical and rubber goods. Hong Kong, however, faces an uncertain future as it moves from British control to control by the People's Republic of China in 1997. Taiwan may have the most promising future of all the Pacific Rim nations. It has a strong local economy and has lowered many import barriers, sending imports up by 42 per cent, to nearly £35 billion in 1988. Taiwan has privatised state run banks and is also opening its markets to foreign firms. Some analysts believe that it may replace Hong Kong as a regional financial power centre when Hong Kong reverts to Chinese control.[19]

Much attention is now being given to the four Pacific Rim nations that have reached the point of massive industrial growth. Thailand, Malaysia, Indonesia and China all offer considerable marketing potential.[20] For example, the People's Republic of China has great market potential and opportunities for joint venture projects. Even the political instability of the 1980s and the 1989 student pro-democracy uprising in Beijing, which reversed several years of business progress in China, has done little to damage the long term potential of the market in China.

Central and Eastern Europe (CEE)

In general, attempts to form groups promoting trade and other links between Pacific Rim countries have not been particularly successful. Perhaps the best known is the **Association of South East Asian Nations (ASEAN),** formed in 1967, which aims to build trade and other links between its six members: Brunei, Indonesia, Malaysia, the Philippines, Singapore and Thailand. With 340 million consumers in the group and a combined GNP of some £300 billion, in practice the progress towards the trading links that the organisation sought has been hampered by the inability of member states to agree on key issues.[21] At the moment it seems that the future of ASEAN is in the balance, with an economic treaty being discussed that aims to set up a free trade area by the year 2008.[22] More recently, the **Asia Pacific Economic Co-operative (APEC)** has been set up to include the six ASEAN members, the United States, Australia, Canada, New Zealand, Japan, China, South Korea, Hong Kong and Taiwan.[23] Currently APEC is little more than a weakly joined group of countries aiming to promote trade, and what the future holds is unclear.

Central and Eastern Europe (CEE) encompasses the Commonwealth of Independent States (formerly the Soviet Union), the Balkan states, the Czech and Slovak Republics, Hungary and Poland. The decline of communism in central and eastern Europe, the fall of the Berlin Wall in 1989 and the break up of the former Soviet Union in 1990 have resulted in a host of new marketing opportunities in the region.

Following a policy of *perestroika*, encompassing considerable political and economic change, the CEE countries are replacing the Communist Party's centrally planned economies with marketing orientated democratic institutions. This process of market reforms, designed to lead to greater imports and exports, has not been without difficulty. Yet the challenge now for many of the eastern European countries is to move forward from the inefficiencies of state owned industry and to develop the marketing expertise, business culture, infrastructures and legal frameworks required to trade with capitalist countries.[24] If the CEE countries wish to compete effectively with nations from other parts of the world, these changes are essential. For example, the poorly developed distribution infrastructure in many parts of central and eastern Europe currently restricts the outlets where western products can be sold and limits the opportunities domestic companies can pursue.[25]

The **Commonwealth of Independent States (CIS)** emerged as a loosely connected group of former Soviet Union states. The member states of the CIS include Azerbaijan, Armenia, Belarus, Estonia, Georgia, Kazakhstan, Kyrgyzstan, Latvia, Lithuania, Moldova, Russia, Tajikistan, Turkmenistan, Ukraine and Uzbekistan. Reviewing key economic data for the CIS and comparing it with EU countries provides a stark reminder of the difficult position in which many eastern European nations find themselves. The highest GNP per capita figure for the CIS, £1,940, is found in Belarus, while the lowest for the region, £320, is in Tajikistan. These figures compare with an EU high of £23,507 in Luxembourg and a low of £4,787 in Greece.[26]

Although after it was set up there were potential opportunities for the CIS to trade as a market group, in practice this idea has been severely restricted by the lack of co-operation between member states and, in particular, by the continuing economic and political problems in Russia.[27] The importance of Russia—the largest market, with 150 million consumers—cannot be overlooked in the region's development.[28] For western companies, the potential is considerable. Hewlett-Packard enjoyed a four fold increase in sales in 1993 alone, and others—

such as Coca-Cola, RJR Nabisco and McDonald's—are just a few of those that have also taken advantage of the new opportunities.

The reformers of the CEE economies want to reduce trade restrictions on imports and offer incentives to encourage exports to and investment in their countries.[29] One such move involved seven UK companies, which formed a consortium to look at opportunities in the personal care and food and drink areas of the Russian market. So far, the initiative has led to a number of developments, including joint venture agreements between Tambrands and the Ukrainian ministry of public health to sell tampons to a market of 70 million women and between Allied Lyons and the Russian ministry of trade to market 8 million gallons of ice cream a year under the Baskin-Robbins label.[30] Because of these economic and political reforms, productivity in central and eastern Europe is expected to increase as workers are given more incentives and control, raising the possibility that the region will eventually become an economic powerhouse rivalling the United States and Japan. There is also speculation that some of the eastern European nations will ultimately join the European Union, allowing freer trade across all European borders.[31] In free elections, East Germany voted to re-unify with West Germany. Although there have been initial teething problems and some social unrest, the unification of Germany is also having a great impact on the European Union and world economy. Exactly how the changing face of the CEE in general will affect world trade remains to be seen. However, because of the swift and uncontrolled nature of the changes taking place in eastern Europe and the former Soviet Union, firms considering marketing their products in these countries must carefully monitor events and proceed cautiously.

The North American Free Trade Agreement: NAFTA

North American Free Trade Agreement (NAFTA)
Implemented in 1994 and designed to eliminate all tariffs on goods produced and traded between Canada, Mexico and the United States, providing for a totally free trade area by 2009

Implementation of the **North American Free Trade Agreement (NAFTA)** on 1 January 1994 created a market of about 374.2 million people. This market consists of Canada (population 27.3 million), the United States (population 254.5 million) and Mexico (population 92.4 million). The estimated annual output for this trade area is $7 trillion and has major implications for developing marketing strategies in the United States.

NAFTA is built on the Canadian Free Trade Agreement (FTA), signed by the United States and Canada in 1989, and on the substantial trade and investment reforms undertaken by Mexico since the mid-1980s. Initiated by the Mexican government, formal negotiations on NAFTA began in June 1991 between the governments of Canada, Mexico and the United States. In August 1992 trade representatives from the three countries announced the successful conclusion of the NAFTA negotiations. The support of NAFTA by President Bill Clinton, past US presidents Ronald Reagan and Jimmy Carter, and Nobel Prize winning economists provided support in the United States for ratifying NAFTA in November 1993.

NAFTA eventually eliminates all tariffs on goods produced and traded between Canada, Mexico and the United States to provide for a totally free trade area by 2009. In addition, the agreement liberalises US investment in Mexico and Canada, provides for intellectual property rights (of interest to producers of high tech goods and entertainment), expands trade in services by requiring equal treatment of US firms in both countries and simplifies country-of-origin rules, hindering Japan's use of Mexico as a staging ground for further penetration into US markets. Most competitive products immediately qualified for tariff-free treatment: aerospace equipment, semi-conductors, telecommunications and electronics, medical equipment, car parts, machine tools and paper.

Though tariffs on imports to the United States will be eliminated, duties on the more sensitive products, such as household glassware, footwear, and some fruits and vegetables, will be phased out over a 15 year period. For other US products, US export tariffs will be phased out over a 10 year period. NAFTA also contains special rules that allow re-instatement of certain tariffs or other measures to protect US farmers and workers in the case of injury from a sudden surge of imports from Mexico or Canada.

Additional supplemental agreements have also been negotiated concerning labour and the environment. The supplemental agreement on the environment provides measures for enforcing federal and international environmental laws. NAFTA is the first trade agreement in history to contain specific provisions for protecting the environment.

Alternative Market Entry Strategies

The level of commitment to international marketing is a major variable in deciding what kind of involvement is appropriate. A firm's options range from occasional exporting to expanding overall operations (production and marketing) into other countries. This section examines exporting, licensing, joint ventures, trading companies, direct ownership and other approaches to international involvement.

Exporting

Exporting Use of an intermediary that performs most marketing functions associated with selling to other countries; entails the minimum effort, cost and risk involved in international marketing

Exporting is the lowest level of commitment to international marketing and the most flexible approach. A firm may find an exporting intermediary that can perform most marketing functions associated with selling to other countries. This approach entails minimum effort and cost. Modifications in packaging, labelling, style or colour may be the major expenses in adapting a product. There is limited risk in using export agents and merchants because there is no direct investment in the foreign country.

Export agents bring together buyers and sellers from different countries; they collect a commission for arranging sales. Export houses and export merchants purchase products from different companies and then sell them to foreign countries. They specialise in understanding customers' needs in foreign countries.

Foreign buyers from companies and governments provide a direct method of exporting and eliminate the need for an intermediary. Foreign buyers encourage international exchange by contacting domestic firms about their needs and the opportunities available in exporting. Domestic firms that want to export with a minimum of effort and investment seek out foreign importers and buyers.

Licensing

Licensing System in which a licensee pays a commission or royalties on sales or supplies used in manufacturing

When potential markets are found across national boundaries—and when production, technical assistance or marketing know-how is required—**licensing** is an alternative to direct investment. The licensee (the owner of the foreign operation) pays commissions or royalties on sales or supplies used in manufacturing. An initial down payment or fee may be charged when the licensing agreement is signed. Exchanges of management techniques or technical assistance are primary reasons for licensing agreements. Yoplait yogurt is a French yogurt that is licensed for production in the United States; the Yoplait brand tries to maintain a French image.

Licensing is an attractive alternative to direct investment when the political stability of a foreign country is in doubt or when resources are unavailable for direct investment. Licensing is especially advantageous for small manufacturers wanting to launch a well known brand internationally. For example, all Spalding sporting products are licensed worldwide. The Questor Corporation owns the Spalding name but produces no goods itself. Pierre Cardin has issued 500 licences and Yves St Laurent 200 to make their products.[32] Löwenbrau has used licensing agreements to increase sales worldwide without committing capital to build breweries.

Franchising

Franchising A form of licensing granting the right to use certain intellectual property rights, such as trade names, brand names, designs, patents and copyright

Another alternative to direct investment in non-domestic markets is **franchising**. This form of licensing, which grants the right to use certain intellectual property rights such as trade names, brand names, designs, patents and copyright, is becoming increasingly popular in Europe.[33] Under this arrangement the franchiser grants a licence to the franchisee, who pays to be allowed to carry out business under the name owned by the franchiser. The franchiser retains control over the manner in which the business is conducted and assists the franchisee in running the business. The franchisee retains ownership of his or her own business, which remains separate from that of the franchiser.[34]

Franchising has recently experienced a period of rapid growth. Companies such as Benetton, Body Shop, Holiday Inn and IKEA are particularly well known for their commitment to growing global business in this way. The scale of the growth that can result is shown in Figure 3.6, which illustrates the increased retail surface area and store visitors that IKEA has recently enjoyed through franchising. There are various reasons why the popularity of franchising has increased so rapidly.[35] First, the general world decline in manufacturing and shift to service industries has increased the relevance of franchising. This is significant, because franchising is a very common internationalisation process for service organisations. Second, franchising has been relatively free of restrictions from legislation, especially in the EU. Third, an increase in self-employment has provided a pool of individuals willing to become involved in franchising, and this activity has generally been supported by the major clearing banks.

Figure 3.6

Growth of an international franchisor: IKEA

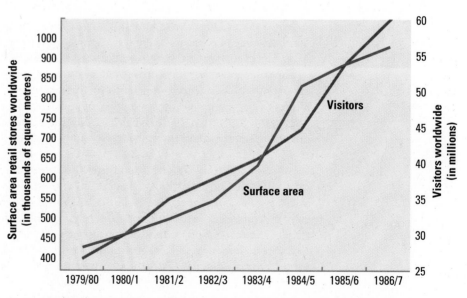

SOURCE: *Göran Götberg, 1989 "Franchising in International Marketing", in Karl Erik Gustafsson and Gunella Green, eds,* Marketing at the Gothenburg School of Economics: Proceedings from a Symposium for Bo Wickström, *BAS, Gothenburg, Sweden, pp. 83–93.*

Joint Ventures

Joint venture A partnership between a domestic firm and a foreign firm or government

In international marketing, a **joint venture** is a partnership between a domestic firm and a foreign firm or government. Joint ventures are especially popular in industries that call for large investments, such as natural resources extraction or car manufacturing. Control of the joint venture can be split equally, or one party may control decision-making. Joint ventures are often a political necessity because of nationalism and governmental restrictions on foreign ownership. They also provide legitimacy in the eyes of the host country's people. Local partners have first hand knowledge of the economic and socio-political environment, access to distribution networks, or privileged access to local resources (raw material, labour management, contacts and so on). Moreover, entrepreneurs in many less developed countries actively seek associations with an overseas partner as a ready means of implementing their own corporate strategy.[36]

Joint ventures are assuming greater global importance because of cost advantages and the number of inexperienced firms entering foreign markets. They may be the result of a trade-off between a firm's desire for completely unambiguous control of an enterprise and its quest for additional resources. They may occur when internal development or acquisition is not feasible or unavailable or when the risks and constraints leave no other alternative. As project sizes increase in the face of global competition and firms attempt to spread the huge costs of technological innovation, there is increased impetus to form joint ventures.[37] Several European truck makers are considering mergers and joint ventures with other European firms to consolidate their power after the unification of the EC in 1992 and the deregulation of the European haulage industry in 1993. Volvo and Renault have developed a partnership, and Britain's Leyland and the Netherlands' DAF joined forces.[38]

Joint ventures are sometimes criticised as being inherently unstable,[39] or because they result in linkages with a competitor, which may subsequently make a take-over attempt. For businesses trying to build longer term joint ventures, there is also the danger that the relationship stifles flexibility. Of course, it is important to stress that for many companies that become involved in joint ventures this may be their only feasible mode of entry at the time and may anyway be regarded purely as a transitional arrangement.[40] For example, European construction firms bidding for business in Saudi Arabia have found that joint ventures with Arab construction companies gain local support among the handful of people who make the contracting decisions.

Strategic alliances Partnerships formed to create a competitive advantage on a worldwide basis

Strategic alliances, the newest form of international business structure, are partnerships formed to create a competitive advantage on a worldwide basis. They are very similar to joint ventures. Strategic alliances have been defined as "co-operation between two or more industrial corporations, belonging to different countries, whereby each partner seeks to add to its competencies by combining its resources with those of its partner".[41] The number of strategic alliances is growing at an estimated rate of about 20 per cent per year.[42] In fact, in some industries, such as cars and high technology, strategic alliances are becoming the predominant means of competing. International competition is so fierce and the costs of competing on a global basis so high that few firms have the individual resources to go it alone. Thus individual firms that lack all the internal resources essential for international success may seek to collaborate with other companies.[43]

The partners forming international strategic alliances often retain their distinct identities, and each brings a distinctive competence to the union. However, the firms share common long term goals. What distinguishes international strategic alliances from other business structures is that member firms in the alliance may

Partners	Products
General Motors; Toyota	Cars
CompuServe; Microsoft	Internet
Recticel SA; Foamex	Autoparts
British Airways; American Airlines	Airlines
Lufthansa; Scandinavian Airlines Systems (SAS)	Airlines
Alfa Romeo; Nissan; Fiat	Cars
ATT; Olivetti	Office equipment; computers
Amdahl; Fujitsu	Computers
ICL; Fujitsu	Computers
ATT; Philips	Telecommunications equipment
Honeywell; L.M. Ericsson	PBX system
General Motors; Fanuc	Robotics
AEG Telefunken; JVC; Thorn-EMI; Thomson	Video recorders
General Electric; Matsushita	Electrical appliances
Corning Glass; Siemens	Optical cables
Hercules; Montedison	Polypropylene resin
United Technologies; Rolls Royce	Aircraft engines

SOURCE: Adapted from S. Young, J. Hamill, C. Wheeler and R. Davies, *International Market Entry and Development,* 1st edn (London: Harvester Wheatsheaf, 1989), p. 273, reprinted by permission of the publisher; *Information World Review,* 116, July/August 1996, p. 9; *Chemical Marketing Reporter,* 26, 24 June 1996, p. 31; *Economist,* 1 June 1996, p. 68; *Aviation Week,* 144, 22 January 1996, p. 21.

Table 3.6 Examples of international strategic alliances

have been traditional rivals competing for market share in the same product class.[44] Table 3.6 shows some examples of strategic alliances.[45]

Trading Companies

Trading company A company that provides a link between buyers and sellers in different countries

A **trading company** provides a link between buyers and sellers in different countries. A trading company, as its name implies, is not involved in manufacturing or owning assets related to manufacturing. It buys in one country at the lowest price consistent with quality and sells to buyers in another country. An important function of trading companies is taking title to products and undertaking all the activities necessary to move the products from the domestic country to a foreign country. For example, large grain trading companies control a major portion of the world's trade in basic food commodities. These trading companies sell agricultural commodities that are homogeneous and can be stored and moved rapidly in response to market conditions.

Trading companies reduce risk for companies interested in getting involved in international marketing. A trading company will assist producers with information about products that meet quality and price expectations in domestic or international markets. Additional services a trading company may provide include consulting, marketing research, advertising, insurance, research and development, legal assistance, warehousing and foreign exchange.

Foreign Direct Investment

Once a company makes a long term commitment to marketing in a foreign nation that has a promising political and economic environment, direct ownership of a

Foreign direct investment (FDI) A long term commitment to marketing in a foreign nation through direct ownership of a foreign subsidiary or division

foreign subsidiary or division is a possibility. **Foreign direct investment (FDI)** involves making a long term commitment to marketing in a foreign nation through direct ownership of a foreign subsidiary or division. Although most discussions of foreign investment concern only manufacturing equipment or personnel, the expenses of developing a separate foreign distribution system can be tremendous. The opening of retail stores in neighbouring countries can require a large financial investment in facilities, research and management. Disney's development of EuroDisney near Paris has been a huge drain on resources.

Multinational enterprise A firm with operations or subsidiaries in many countries

The term **multinational enterprise** refers to firms that have operations or subsidiaries located in many countries. Often the parent firm is based in one country and cultivates production, management and marketing activities in other countries. The firm's subsidiaries may be quite autonomous in order to respond to the needs of individual international markets. Firms such as ICI, Unilever and General Motors are multinational companies with worldwide operations. Table 3.7 lists the top 30 European companies, ranked by sales (turnover). Most of these companies are active in many countries and several continents.

A wholly owned foreign subsidiary may be allowed to operate independently of the parent company so that its management can have more freedom to adjust to the local environment. Co-operative arrangements are developed to assist in marketing efforts, production and management. A wholly owned foreign subsidiary may export products to the home country. Some car manufacturers, such as Ford and General Motors, for example, import cars built by their foreign subsidiaries. A foreign subsidiary offers important tax, tariff and other operating advantages. The greatest advantages of direct foreign investment are greater strategy control and enhanced market capacity. To maximise these, a subsidiary may operate under foreign management, so that a genuinely local identity can be developed. A company's success in achieving these advantages will tend to depend on whether the business has a competitive advantage allowing it to recover the costs of its investment.

Rank	Company Name	Sector	Period End Date	Net Profit Turnover Before Interest and Tax		No. of Emp's
				Latest £000	£000	
1	Royal Dutch/Shell Group, GBR/NLD[1]	Oil, gas and nuclear fuels	31/12/93	63,350,000	6,414,000	117,000
2	British Petroleum Company PLC (The), GBR	Oil, gas and nuclear fuels	31/12/93	47,655,000	1,977,000	84,500
3	Daimler-Benz AG, DEU	Transport—manufacture and distribution	31/12/93	38,042,000	1,230,000	371,107
4	IRI—Istituto per la Ricostruzione Industriale, ITA	Contracting, construction	31/12/92	34,034,000	3,016,000	41,318

(Continues)

Table 3.7 Top European companies, ranked by sales in £000s

| Rank | Company Name | Sector | Period End Date | Net Profit Turnover Before Interest and Tax | | No. of Emp's |
				Latest £000	£000	
5	Siemens AG, DEU	Electricals	30/09/93	33,378,845	1,896,897	391,000
6	ENI—Ente Nazionale Idrocarburi, ITA	Oil, gas and nuclear fuels	31/12/93	30,556,000	3,039,000	117,725
7	Volkswagen AG, DEU	Transport—manufacture and distribution	31/12/93	29,809,278	336,681	251,643
8	Unilever Group, GBR/NLD[1]	Food manufacturing	31/12/93	27,013,000	2,223,000	294,000
9	Nestlé SA, CHE	Food manufacturing	31/12/93	26,164,000	2,630,000	209,755
10	Elf Aquitaine SA [Ste], FRA	Oil, gas and nuclear fuels	31/12/93	24,002,000	366,000	10,795
11	Veba AG, DEU	Oil, gas and nuclear fuels	31/12/93	23,857,075	966,176	129,089
12	Fiat SpA, ITA	Transport—manufacture and distribution	31/12/93	21,539,000	951,000	256,600
13	Electricité de France, FRA	Electricity	31/12/93	21,016,000	2,606,000	13,510
14	Philips Electronics NV, NLD	Electronics	31/12/93	20,471,000	1,060,000	252,214
15	Alcatel-Alsthom Cie Generale d'Electricité, FRA	Communications	31/12/92	19,333,000	1,795,000	203,000
16	Peugeot SA, FRA	Transport—manufacture and distribution	31/12/92	18,586,000	821,000	150,800
17	Renault [Regie Nationale des Usines] SA, FRA	Transport—manufacture and distribution	31/12/93	18,288,000	548,000	15,996
18	ABB Asea Brown Boveri Ltd, CHE	Electricity	31/12/93	18,089,000	1,388,000	206,490
19	Hoechst AG, DEU	Chemicals	31/12/93	17,923,000	785,000	170,161
20	B.A.T Industries PLC, GBR	Tobacco	31/12/93	17,879,000	2,101,000	88,358
21	RWE AG, DEU	Electricity	30/06/93	17,721,900	897,230	113,642
22	Eaux [Cie Generale des], FRA	Contracting, construction	31/12/92	16,775,000	1,142,000	198,813
23	TOTAL, FRA	Oil, gas and nuclear fuels	31/12/92	16,335,000	992,000	51,139
24	Bayer AG, DEU	Chemicals	31/12/93	15,960,999	1,133,427	151,900
25	BASF AG, DEU	Chemicals	31/12/93	15,790,284	597,229	115,010
26	France Telecom, FRA	Communications	31/12/92	14,663,000	3,563,000	85,200
27	Carrefour, FRA	Stores	31/12/93	14,103,000	451,000	169,804
28	Bosch [Robert] GmbH, DEU	Electricals	31/12/92	14,047,567	571,580	136,975
29	Thyssen AG, DEU	Engineering—general	30/09/93	13,696,250	187,400	165,700
30	British Telecommunications PLC, GBR	Communications	31/03/94	13,675,000	3,145,000	

NOTE: [1]Multinational group incorporated part in Great Britain and part in The Netherlands.
SOURCE: *Times 1000 1995* (London Times Publishing, 1995), pp. 58–59. Reproduced by permission of Times Newspapers, Ltd.

Table 3.7 Top European companies, ranked by sales in £000s (cont.)

Summary

● Marketing activities performed across national boundaries are usually significantly different from domestic marketing activities. International marketers must have a profound awareness of the foreign environment. The marketing strategy is ordinarily adjusted to meet the needs and desires of markets across national boundaries.

● The level of involvement in *international marketing* covers a wide spectrum from *domestic marketing* to *export marketing, international marketing, multinational marketing* and *global marketing*. Although all companies involved in international marketing must make some modifications to their marketing effort, full scale global marketing requires total commitment to international marketing and involves applying the company's assets, experience and products to develop and maintain marketing strategies on a global scale. *Multinational companies* are those that operate in overseas markets as if they were local companies.

● Marketers must rely on international marketing intelligence to understand the complexities of the international marketing environment before they can formulate a marketing mix. Therefore, they collect and analyse secondary data and primary data about international markets.

● Environmental aspects of special importance include cultural, social, economic, political and legal forces. Cultural aspects of the environment that are most important to international marketers include customs, concepts, values, attitudes, morals and knowledge. Marketing activities are primarily social in purpose; therefore they are structured by the institutions of family, religion, education, health and recreation. The most prominent economic forces that affect international marketing are those that can be measured by income and resources. *Gross domestic product (GDP)* is the total value of all goods and services produced by a country's income. Credit, buying power and income distribution are aggregate measures of market potential. Political and legal forces include the political system, national laws, regulatory bodies, national pressure groups and courts.

● Measures that governments can take to govern cross-border trade include the use of tariffs, quotas and non-tariff barriers. *Tariffs* are taxes that affect the movement of goods across economic or political boundaries. *Quotas* involve physical restrictions on the amount of goods that can be imported. *Non-tariff barriers* include a wide range of rules, regulations and taxes that have an impact upon trade. The foreign policies of all nations involved in trade determine how marketing can be conducted. The level of technology helps define economic development within a nation and indicates the existence of methods to facilitate marketing.

● Various regional trade alliances and specific markets are creating both difficulties and opportunities for firms. In Europe there are three major market groups. The *European Free Trade Association (EFTA)* was set up in 1960 to promote trade between members. The creation of the single European market in 1993 by the Maastricht Treaty led to the formation of the *European Union (EU)*. The *European Economic Area (EAA)*, which was completed in 1993, attempts to encourage free trade between EU and EFTA members. The best known trading group in the Pacific Rim is the *Association of South East Asian Nations (ASEAN)*, which was formed in 1967. More recently, the *Asia Pacific Economic Co-operative (APEC)* has been set up to promote trade in the region. The group includes the US, Australia, Canada, New Zealand, Japan, China, South Korea, Hong Kong, Taiwan and ASEAN members. *Central and Eastern Europe (CEE)* encompasses the *Commonwealth of Independent States (CIS)*, the Balkan states, the Czech and Slovak Republics, Hungary and Poland. The *North American Free Trade Agreement (NAFTA)*, set up in 1994, aims to eliminate all tariffs on goods produced and traded between Canada, Mexico and the US and to provide for a totally free trade area by 2009.

● There are several ways of becoming involved in international marketing. *Exporting* is the easiest and most flexible method. *Licensing* is an alternative to direct investment; it may be necessitated by political and economic conditions. *Franchising* is a form of licensing granting the right to use certain intellectual property rights such as trade names, brand names, designs, patents and copyright. *Joint ventures* and *strategic alliances* are often appropriate when outside resources are needed, when there are governmental restrictions on foreign ownership or when changes in global markets encourage competitive consolidation. *Trading companies* are experts at buying products in the domestic market and selling to foreign markets, thereby taking most of the risk in international involvement. *Foreign Direct Investment (FDI)* in divisions or subsidiaries is the strongest commitment to international marketing and involves the greatest risk. When a company has operations or subsidiaries located in many countries, it is termed a *multinational enterprise.*

● ● ● ● ● ● ● ● ● ● ● ● ● ● ● ● ● ● ●

Discussion and Review Questions

1. How does international marketing differ from domestic marketing?
2. What must marketers consider before deciding whether to become involved in international marketing?
3. Are the largest industrial companies in Europe committed to international marketing? Why or why not?
4. Why do you think so much of this chapter is devoted to an analysis of the international marketing environment?
5. A manufacturer recently exported peanut butter with a green label to a nation in the Far East. The product failed because it was associated with jungle sickness. How could this mistake have been avoided?
6. How do religious systems influence marketing activities in foreign countries?
7. Which is more important to international marketers, a country's aggregate GDP or its GDP per capita? Why?
8. If you were asked to provide a small tip (or bribe) to have a document approved in a foreign nation where this practice was customary, what would you do?
9. What should marketers consider as they decide whether to license or to enter into a joint venture in a foreign nation?
10. Discuss the impact of strategic alliances on marketing strategies.

● ● ● ● ● ● ● ● ● ● ● ● ● ● ● ● ● ● ●

Important Terms

Domestic marketing
Export marketing
International marketing
Multinational marketing
Multinational companies
Global marketing
Gross domestic product (GDP)
Tariffs
Quotas
Non-tariff barriers
European Union (EU)
Maastricht Treaty

European Free Trade
   Association (EFTA)
European Economic Area (EEA)
Association of South East Asian
   Nations (ASEAN)
Asia Pacific Economic Co-
   operative (APEC)
Central and Eastern Europe
   (CEE)
Commonwealth of Independent
   States (CIS)

North American Free Trade
   Agreement (NAFTA)
Exporting
Licensing
Franchising
Joint venture
Strategic alliances
Trading company
Foreign direct investment (FDI)
Multinational enterprise

Recommended Readings

F. Bradley, *International Marketing Strategy*, 2nd ed. (Hemel Hempstead: Prentice-Hall, 1991).

J-P. Jeannet and D. H. Hennessey, *Global Marketing Strategies*, 3rd edn (Boston: Houghton Mifflin, 1995).

S. Paliwoda and J. K. Ryans, Jr., eds, *International Marketing Reader* (London: Routledge, 1995).

C. Bartlett, G. Hedlund and Y. Doz, *Managing the Global Firm* (London: International Thomson Business Publishing, 1996).

C. Egan and P. McKiernan, *Inside Fortress Europe: Strategies for the Single Market* (Wokingham: Addison Wesley, 1994).

Cases

3.1 Porsche AG: The International Tradition Continues

German high performance car maker Porsche AG was founded in 1930 by Dr Ferdinand Porsche as a research and development company. It accepted contracts from individuals and firms for new cars, aeroplanes and ships based on customer design. In 1948 Dr Ferry Porsche—Ferdinand Porsche's son—established a company that would itself design, as well as produce, sports cars under the Porsche name. Despite intermittent tough economic periods, the company persevered and prospered. By 1973, Porsche AG had built and sold some 200,000 cars, gaining worldwide recognition as the maker of the finest sports cars in the world. As the company promised the customer, to drive a Porsche was to experience "driving in its purest form".

The popularity of Porsche cars stems from their reputation for outstanding performance. Not only are the vehicles produced in painstakingly detailed fashion, but Porsche also takes maintenance and repair very seriously. Company mechanics receive five days of instruction annually at the Porsche Marketing Centre in Ludwigsburg, a higher level of training than that provided by any other car manufacturer in the world. Until 1984, Porsche mechanics in the United States also flew to Germany for this training. Now, however, they receive instruction at company training centres established in the United States.

Despite Porsche's impeccable reputation for excellence, the company has not been immune from trying times. For example, its sales suffered when it had to raise prices on cars sold in the United States because of fluctuating exchange rates and a new tax on luxury cars priced at over $30,000. These developments, a weak US dollar, and increased US- and Japanese-based competition in the American high performance sports car market brought down sales in its largest market from 30,000 in 1986 to about 3,700 in 1993. Since US sales traditionally account for about 60 per cent of the company's total global sales, such a drastic drop was particularly troublesome to its overall global operations. For example, Porsche sold only 23,000 cars worldwide in 1992, as compared with 50,000 in 1986. Consequently, the company made a loss of nearly £30 million in 1992, its first annual deficit in over 20 years, and even larger losses in 1993 as a result of what many industry observers considered the company's overdependence on the American market.

In an effort to combat its mounting problems, Porsche laid off more than 20 per cent of its US-based work force, lowered production output, cut manufacturing costs, reduced its prices, pulled out of the lower end of the American luxury car market and made public plans to enter promising new international markets such as Spain and Japan. In 1993 the company announced two additional moves designed to revive worldwide sales. Early in the year, Ferry Porsche, then 83 years old, asked to be relieved of his position as the company's chairman of the board. The appointment of Helmut Sihler as his replacement marked the first time in the organisation's 63 year history that someone from outside the controlling family was named to head the company. The move was applauded by many shareholders, who had attributed the company's financial troubles to the Porsche family's unwillingness to relinquish operational control. Besides this transition in leadership, the German company announced both the continuation of substantial cost cutting programmes and new developments on the product front. Specifically, Porsche AG disclosed plans to unveil five new versions of the company's three lines of sports cars. Porsche spent £13 million to launch a new redesigned 1995 911 Carrera. Launched at the Frankfurt motor show in September 1995, the 911 Targa and Carrera 4S arrived in the UK two months later with price tags starting from £64,250 and £74,795 respectively. The company also announced plans for production of a two-seat sports car similar to its highly acclaimed Boxster show car, which was launched in 1995.

SOURCES: Martha T. Moore, "Porsche smooths 'jerky' image", *USA Today,* 11 February 1994, p. 2B; "Business briefs", *Wall Street Journal,* 6 May 1993, p. B4; "Business briefs", *Wall Street Journal,* 9 March 1993, p. B4; Jerry Flint, "Porsche turns", *Forbes,* 1 February 1993, p. 104; "Porsche AG names Helmut Sihler to head Board of Supervisors", *Wall Street Journal,* 26 January 1993, p. B6; James R. Henley, "Porsche puts on brakes", *USA Today,* 29 January 1992, p. 2B; Karen Miller and Terrence Roth, "Porsche, a favorite in times of plenty, struggles to survive in a more frugal era", *Wall Street Journal,* 27 January 1992, pp. B1–B2; Thomas L. Bryant, "Miscellaneous ramblings", *Road and Track,* December 1991, p. 53; Jim Henry, "Luxury car tax may speed sales", *Advertising Age,* 10 December 1990, p. 17; David Vivian, "Heavenly bodies", *Marque,* Issue 2, 1995, pp. 6–7.

Questions for Discussion

1. Evaluate international marketing opportunities for Porsche AG. What are the company's strengths and weaknesses?
2. What obstacles must Porsche overcome to succeed in selling its cars in the United States?
3. What is the role of diversification in the Porsche AG corporate strategy?

3.2 MTV's Strategies in Global Markets

In 53 million American homes, pop music fans, mostly aged 16 to 34, tune in to enjoy superstars like Paula Abdul, Michael Jackson and Madonna. Working like a Top 40 radio station, MTV rotates through about 60 different music videos, selling and airing advertising to make its money. Viacom International, owner of MTV, reports that about 20 per cent of its £1 billion in revenue comes from its video network. In the last few years, the number of American MTV viewers has levelled off, and MTV's US market seems to be reaching saturation. Hoping to attract new audiences and still retain its established market, MTV is concentrating on international expansion. MTV's goal, says the network's CEO, is to be in every home in the world.

When MTV made its first foreign licensing deal in Japan, company executives were just beginning to think about overseas expansion. They gave their Japanese affiliate little supervision regarding style and content. However, after one MTV executive reviewed some of the Japanese videos, she decided that they didn't convey the trendy and sophisticated image MTV tries to impart. Renegotiating the deal, the network took tighter control over quality. Subsequent expansion into Europe, South America and Australia means that today, about 200 million fans in about 38 countries can enjoy the latest pop videos from around the world.

Other cable enterprises, including Cable News Network (CNN), broadcast internationally. Unlike executives at MTV, CNN's owner, cable giant Ted Turner, elects to broadcast solely in English, primarily targeting Americans travelling in all parts of the world. MTV, on the other hand, attempts to be sensitive to other countries' cultures by responding to their musical styles and tastes. Although every broadcast must fit into MTV guidelines, television networks outside the US employ native video jockeys who highlight locally popular stars. In Japan, MTV VJs speak almost entirely in Japanese and focus on Japanese and other international artists. English is the language of choice on 24 hour European MTV, but European and other international musicians are the stars of the videos. MTV depends on music instead of language to link its 25 country European market.

Recognised as the leading pop music expert in the United States, MTV is rapidly presenting itself as an authority on youth culture worldwide. The network is increasingly successful in convincing record companies that it can launch artists on a worldwide scale. Adding to its list of international advertisers like Nike, Levi's and Fruit of the Loom is going a long way towards keeping MTV one step ahead of its fast growing competitor, Video Jukebox Network. Recently, however, MTV in Europe has faced dropping audiences. The company has decided to abandon its long held belief that a single pan-European channel can serve audience needs across Europe. This is despite an MTV survey of three thousand 16 to 18 year olds in 20 European countries, showing them to have very similar tastes, lifestyles and attitudes irrespective of their country of residence. Language, though, is a problem: there genuinely is no single commonly spoken language throughout Europe. The decision by MTV to drop its single pan-European service is due in part to this language difficulty and in part to the arrival of the digital age, which is forcing a re-think generally in broadcasting, as well as competition—particularly in the form of rival youth network Viva in Germany. MTV is to offer several services for different parts of Europe.

SOURCES: "Pan-European idea is dead, says three-way MTV", *New Media Markets,* 14, 13, 1996, pp. 6–7; Nicole Dickenson, "Electronic generation", *Campaign,* 29 September 1995, pp. SS13–SS14; Andy Fry, "The year of European media revolution", *Marketing,* 28 March 1991, pp. 25–26; Peter Newcomb, "Music video wars", *Forbes,* 4 March 1991, pp. 68, 70; Sara Nelson, "What's the big idea", *Working Woman,* July 1990, pp. 96, 98, 108.

Questions for Discussion

1. Does MTV have a uniform product globally?
2. Have local or national needs altered MTV's marketing and its product format?
3. MTV's European network hinges on the English language. What problems may this cause? Are MTV's US bosses likely to be aware of these?

PART I POSTSCRIPT

Effective marketing hinges on satisfying customers and establishing relationships. There are many forces at work, however, which affect how organisations endeavour to achieve these goals. Part I of *Marketing: Concepts and Strategies* has explored the nature and scope of the concept of marketing, continuing to describe the forces of the marketing environment and the essential requirements for marketing in global markets.

The focus of *Marketing: Concepts and Strategies* now turns to the customer. As outlined in Figure 1.4, the customer must be at the centre of the marketing process. Businesses must target specific groups of customers, understand their needs and endeavour through their marketing activities to satisfy these needs. It is essential, though, to recognise that a business does not deal with its customers in a vacuum: there are many marketing environment forces at work, affecting the behaviour of customers and those organisations attempting to market to them. For businesses operating across national borders, involved with marketing in global markets, the impact of these forces and the trading decisions required are even more complex. These are the issues that have been examined in Part I.

Before progressing, readers should be confident that they are now able to do the following:

Define and explain the marketing concept

• What is marketing? • Why is marketing important? • What are the core stages of marketing strategy? • What is the marketing mix?

Outline the forces at work in the marketing environment

• What is environmental scanning? • Why are the forces of the marketing environment important considerations for marketers: economic and competitive, political, legal, regulatory, societal and technological?

Describe the additional complexities facing marketers engaged in international markets

• What is the nature of international marketing? • Why is marketing intelligence so important? • Why are the forces of the marketing environment integral to international marketing? • Why are regional trade alliances important considerations? • What market entry strategies can businesses use to become involved in international marketing activities?

Marketing Opportunity Analysis	Chapters
• The marketing environment	2
• Marketing in international markets	3
• Consumer markets and buyer behaviour	4
• Business-to-business markets and buyer behaviour	5
• Marketing research and information systems	6

Target Market Selection	Chapters
• Market segmentation and prioritisation	7, 22
• Product and brand positioning	7, 22
• Competitive advantage	7, 22

Marketing Mix Development	Chapters
• Product, branding, packaging and service decisions	8–11
• Distribution (place and channel) decisions	12–15
• Promotion decisions	16–18
• Pricing decisions	19, 20
• Supplementary decisions	3, 21, 24, 25

Marketing Management	Chapters
• Strategic marketing and competitive strategy	22, 23
• Marketing planning and sales forecasting	23
• Implementing strategies and measuring performance	24
• Marketing ethics and social responsibility	25

II UNDERSTANDING AND TARGETING MARKETS

As outlined in the figure, the customers must be at the centre of the marketing process. Businesses must target specific groups of customers, understand their needs and endeavour through their marketing activities to satisfy these customer needs. Part II of *Marketing: Concepts and Strategies* commences with a thorough examination of the nature of consumer buyer behaviour and buying processes and continues to examine the nature of buying in business-to-business organisational markets. There are times when managers' existing knowledge of their customers is sufficient for marketing decision-making, or when they are content to trust their intuition. On many occasions, however, marketers may not feel confident with the level of marketing intelligence available and will instigate marketing research in order to fill any gaps in their understanding of customers, competitors or market trends. The nature, uses and types of marketing research are introduced in Part II of *Marketing: Concepts and Strategies*. Having developed an understanding of a marketplace and particularly the customers within, marketers must then develop a marketing strategy. This should identify which customers they wish to target, what positioning they intend to use and which approach will provide an advantage over competitors. Part II concludes, therefore, with an examination of marketing strategy and, specifically, with target market selection.

Part II of *Marketing: Concepts and Strategies* examines buying behaviour for consumers and organisations, the nature of marketing research and the issues concerned with target market selection.

Chapter 4, "Consumer Buying Behaviour", describes the different types of consumer buying behaviour, the stages of consumer buying decision-making and the different categories of buying decisions. The chapter examines how personal, psychological and social factors influence the consumer buying decision process. Finally, it explains why marketers must understand consumer buying behaviour and use their understanding to determine marketing strategy.

Chapter 5, "Organisational Markets and Buying Behaviour", familiarises readers with the various types of business-to-business markets, identifies the major characteristics of organisational buyers and transactions, outlines the attributes of organisational demand and presents the concept of the buying centre. The chapter emphasises the notion of relationship marketing and exchanges between industrial buyers and sellers. The focus then shifts to the stages of the business-to-business organisational buying process and the factors that influence it. The chapter concludes by examining how to select and analyse business-to-business target markets.

Chapter 6, "Marketing Research and Information Systems", explains the importance of research and information systems in marketing decision-making, distinguishes between research and intuition in solving marketing problems, and outlines the five basic steps for conducting formal marketing research. The chapter then introduces the wide variety of marketing research tools and explains their relative pros and cons.

Chapter 7, "Segmenting Markets, Targeting and Positioning", explains the core aspect of developing a marketing strategy: the process of target market selection. The chapter commences by defining the concept of a market and outlining the various types of markets. The focus then shifts to how businesses segment markets, how they select which segments (groups of consumers) to target and how they determine a brand or product positioning strategy for each segment selected as a target market. The chapter also highlights how important it is for an organisation to attempt to develop an edge over its competitors in the market(s) it has chosen to target.

By the conclusion of Part II of *Marketing: Concepts and Strategies*, readers should understand buying behaviour in consumer and business-to-business markets, the nature and use of marketing research and the fundamentals of target market selection.

4 CONSUMER BUYING BEHAVIOUR

"Anticipating consumer behaviour is
not an option for marketing managers:
it is their job description."

Gordon Foxall
University of Birmingham

OBJECTIVES

* To understand the different types of consumer buying behaviour
* To recognise the stages of the consumer buying decision process and understand how this process relates to different types of buying decisions
* To explore how personal factors may affect the consumer buying decision process
* To learn about the psychological factors that may affect the consumer buying decision process
* To examine the social factors that influence the consumer buying decision process
* To understand why it is important for marketers to attempt to understand consumer buying behaviour and the role of this behaviour in marketing strategy

Most married couples regard their wedding day as one of the most important in their lives. Not surprisingly, then, getting married is big business. Each year in Europe vast amounts of currency are spent on the trappings traditionally associated with weddings: engagement rings and wedding bands for the bride and groom, photographers and wedding cars, catering and hotel accommodation for guests, wedding magazines and books. Family weddings not only provide an event to remember for the couple, they also offer relatives and friends the chance to meet up and socialise in happy circumstances.

For most brides-to-be, buying a wedding dress is a particularly important part of the event. Though traditions vary widely depending on religion and culture, many European brides traditionally marry dressed in white or ivory gowns. Whatever the culture, religion and nationality of the bride, it is common for the process of buying the dress to begin many months before the wedding day. The uniqueness of the purchase, its emotional significance, the length of time taken and the associated risk all make this a high involvement decision.

The complex buying process often begins with the bride paying a visit to a number of bridal wear retailers. Indeed, the significance of the purchase is reflected in the wide range of bridal wear retailers offering the latest range of fashionable gowns. Usually, the bride will be accompanied by her mother or a close female friend or relative as she visits her chosen store. Often the search for the dress will extend to several outlets, perhaps in more than one town. In some cases, the bride may have identified a particular designer whose gowns she likes. Wedding magazines and recommendations from friends and relatives may also be used to generate ideas. Many designs and fabrics will be considered and several tried. It is unlikely that a decision will be made on the first outing, as time is needed to think carefully about the options, costs, accessories and schedules. Sometimes the preferred store will be revisited several times before a final decision is reached. Even after the bride has made her choice, the buying process is not over. Further visits will be required, so that any required adjustments can be made to the dress, and matching accessories selected. It is difficult to believe that all of this buying activity leads to the purchase of an item that will probably be worn only once. Yet for most brides the significance of the occasion is sufficient justification for the effort involved. ■

SOURCES: Giles Laurent and Jean-Noel Kapferer, "Measuring consumer involvement profiles", *Journal of Marketing Research*, 22 February 1985, pp. 41–53; Henry Assael, *Consumer Behavior and Marketing Action* (Boston: PWS-Kent Publishing Co., 1992), p. 30; "Brides' wedding guide", *Brides and Setting Up Home,* March/April 1996.

Throughout their lives consumers purchase numerous products of all kinds. However, most consumers buy a wedding dress only once, and the uniqueness of the occasion is reflected in the care and time that is dedicated to the purchase. A wedding dress is, of course, distinctly different from many of the everyday items that individuals buy each week. Companies that supply products and services for weddings appreciate the significance their customers attach to this special event in their lives. Not surprisingly, such companies often make considerable efforts to determine their customers' needs and gain a better understanding of their buying behaviour.

Buying behaviour The decision process and actions of people involved in buying and using products

Consumer buying behaviour The buying behaviour of ultimate consumers—those who purchase products for personal or household use

The decision process and actions of people involved in buying and using products are termed their **buying behaviour.**[1] **Consumer buying behaviour** is the buying behaviour of ultimate consumers, those who purchase products for personal or household use. Consumer buying behaviour is not concerned with the purchase of items for business use.

There are important reasons for marketers to analyse consumer buying behaviour. The success of a company's marketing strategy will depend on how buyers react to it. As indicated in Chapter 1, the marketing concept stresses that the marketing mix companies develop must be designed with customer needs in mind. To find out what satisfies customers, marketers must examine the main influences on what, where, when and how consumers buy. By understanding these factors better, marketers are better able to predict how consumers will respond to marketing strategies. Ultimately, this information helps companies compete more effectively in the marketplace and leads to more satisfied customers.

Although marketers may try to understand and influence consumer buying behaviour, they cannot control it. Some critics credit them with the ability to manipulate buyers, but marketers have neither the power nor the knowledge to do so. Their knowledge of behaviour comes from what psychologists, social psychologists and sociologists know about human behaviour in general. Even if marketers wanted to manipulate buyers, the lack of laws and principles in the behavioural sciences would prevent them from doing so.

This chapter begins by examining the types of decision-making in which consumers engage. It then analyses the major stages of the consumer buying decision process and the personal, psychological and social factors that influence it. The chapter concludes by assessing the importance of understanding consumer buying behaviour.

Types of Consumer Buying Behaviour

Consumers usually want to create and maintain a collection of products that satisfy their needs and wants in both the present and future. To achieve this objective, consumers make many purchasing decisions. For example, people make many decisions daily regarding food, clothing, shelter, medical care, education, recreation or transport. As they make these decisions, they engage in different decision-making behaviour. The amount of time and effort, both mental and physical, that buyers expend in decision-making varies considerably from situation to situation—and from consumer to consumer. Consumer decisions can thus be classified into one of three broad categories: routine response behaviour, limited decision-making and extensive decision-making.[2]

Routine response behaviour
Behaviour that occurs when buying frequently purchased, low cost items that need little search and decision effort

A consumer practises **routine response behaviour** when buying frequently purchased, low cost items that need very little search and decision effort. When buying such items, a consumer may prefer a particular brand, but he or she is familiar with several brands in the product class and views more than one as being acceptable. The products a consumer buys through routine response behaviour are purchased almost automatically. Most buyers, for example, do not spend much time or mental effort choosing a loaf of bread or a confectionery bar. If the supermarket has run out of Mars bars, the buyers will probably select an alternative brand instead.

Limited decision-making
Behaviour that occurs when buying products purchased only occasionally, for which a moderate amount of information gathering and deliberation is needed

Buyers engage in **limited decision-making** when they buy products occasionally and when they need to obtain information about an unfamiliar brand in a familiar product category. This type of decision-making requires a moderate amount of time for information gathering and deliberation. For example, if Sega launches a new computer game aimed at teenagers, buyers may seek additional information about the new product, perhaps by asking a friend who has tested the game or seen it reviewed. Similarly, if a well known brand appears in a new form—for example, a new computer game format—the consumer will take extra time.

Extensive decision-making
Behaviour that occurs when a purchase involves unfamiliar, expensive or infrequently bought products for which the buyer spends much time seeking information and comparing brands before deciding on the purchase

The most complex decision-making behaviour, **extensive decision-making**, comes into play when a purchase involves unfamiliar, expensive or infrequently bought products—for instance, cars, homes, holidays or personal pensions. The buyer uses many criteria to evaluate alternative brands or choices and spends much time seeking information and comparing alternative brands before deciding on the purchase.

By contrast, **impulse buying** involves no conscious planning but a powerful, persistent urge to buy something immediately. For some individuals, impulse buying may be the dominant buying behaviour. Impulse buying, however, often provokes emotional conflicts. For example, a man may purchase a case of wine after seeing a special offer at his local supermarket, but later regret spending the money because the wine does not meet his expectations. Marketers often capitalise on the tendency towards impulse buying—for example, by placing magazines and confectionery next to supermarket checkout counters.

The purchase of a particular product does not always elicit the same type of decision-making behaviour.[3] In some instances, buyers engage in extensive decision-making the first time they purchase a certain kind of product but find that limited decision-making suffices when they buy the product again. If a routinely purchased, formerly satisfying brand no longer pleases, a consumer may use either limited or extensive decision processes to switch to a new brand. For example, if the video tapes a family usually buys are becoming damaged too easily, a better quality brand may be sought through limited or extensive decision-making.

• • • • • • • • • • • • • • • • • • •

The Consumer Buying Decision Process

As defined earlier, a major part of buying behaviour is the decision process used in making purchases. The **consumer buying decision process**, shown in Figure 4.1, includes five stages: (1) problem recognition, (2) information search, (3) evaluation of alternatives, (4) purchase and (5) post-purchase evaluation. Before examining each stage, consider these important points. First, the actual act of purchasing is only one stage in the process; the process is begun several stages before the actual purchase. Second, even though it is suggested that a purchase always occurs, not all decision processes lead to a purchase; the individual may end the process at any stage. It is also possible that a different sequence of stages will be followed, with buyers revisiting certain stages. Finally, consumer decisions do not always include all five stages. People engaged in extensive decision-making usually go through all stages of this decision process, whereas those engaged in limited decision-making and routine response behaviour may omit certain parts.

Problem Recognition

Problem recognition occurs when a buyer becomes aware that there is a difference between a desired state and an actual condition. For example, consider a sales manager who needs to keep a record of appointments. When, at the end of the year, her old diary is finished, she recognises that a difference exists between the desired state—a current diary—and the actual condition—an out-of-date one. She therefore makes the decision to buy a new diary.

Sometimes a person has a problem or need but is unaware of it. As shown in Figure 4.2, some consumers might be concerned about their weight but might not be aware that Hellmann's has introduced a low calorie mayonnaise. Marketers use sales personnel, advertising, sales promotion and packaging to help trigger recognition of such needs or problems. For example, travel agents may advertise package holidays immediately after the Christmas and New Year holidays. People who see the advertisements may realise that now is a good time to plan their summer holidays. The speed of consumer problem recognition can be either slow or rapid, depending on the individual concerned and the way in which need recognition was triggered.

Possible influences on the decision process

Personal influences

- Demographic
- Situational
- Involvement

Psychological influences

- Perception
- Motives
- Learning
- Attitudes
- Personality

Social influences

- Roles and family
- Reference groups
- Social classes
- Culture and subcultures

Consumer buying decision process

Problem recognition → Information search → Evaluation of alternatives → Purchase → Post-purchase evaluation

Feedback

Figure 4.1 Consumer buying decision process and possible influences on the process

Information Search

After recognising the problem or need, the buyer (if continuing the decision process) searches for information about products that will help resolve the problem or satisfy the need. For example, the people mentioned above, after recognising the need to plan their holiday, may search for information about different tour operators, travel options and possible locations. Information is acquired over time from the consumer's surroundings. However, it is important to remember that the impact of the information depends on how the consumer interprets it.

There are two aspects to an information search. In the **internal search,** buyers search their memory for information about products that might solve the problem. If they cannot retrieve enough information from their memory for a decision, they seek additional information in an **external search.** The external search may focus on communication with friends and colleagues, comparison of available brands and prices, marketer dominated sources, such as television or press advertisements, and/or public sources. An individual's personal contacts—friends, relatives, associates—are often viewed as credible sources of information because the consumer trusts and respects them. A consumer study has shown that word-of-mouth communication has a stronger impact on consumer judgements of products than do printed communications, unless the buyer has a well defined prior impression or unless printed information about a product is extremely negative.[4] Utilising marketer dominated sources of information, which include salespersons, advertising, package labelling, in-store demonstrations and displays, typically

Internal search One in which the buyer searches his or her memory for information about products

External search One that focuses on information not available from the consumer's memory

NOW YOU CAN GO HEAVIER ON THE MAYONNAISE.

NEW HELLMANN'S LIGHT MAYONNAISE. HALF THE FAT. HALF THE CALORIES. ALL THE TASTE OF HELLMANN'S. The only MAYONNAISE.

Figure 4.2 Problem Recognition. Recognising that many consumers are concerned about their weight, Hellmann's has introduced a low calorie mayonnaise.

SOURCE: Hellmann's is a registered trademark of CPC International.

does not require much effort on the consumers' part. Buyers can also obtain information from public sources—for instance, government reports, news stories, consumer publications and reports from product testing organisations. Consumers frequently value information from public sources highly because they perceive it as factual and unbiased. Many companies try to capitalise on these sources— when favourable to them—in their public relations. The external search is also characterised by the extensiveness, manner and order in which brands, stores, attributes and sources are considered. For example, a schoolboy choosing a new pair of training shoes may look at or try on several brands at a number of sports shops before reaching a final decision.

Consumer groups are increasingly demanding access to all relevant product information. However, the greater the quantity of information available, the more the buyer may be over-loaded with information. Research indicates that consumers make poorer choices when faced with large amounts of information.[5] Improving the quality of information and stressing features important to buyers in the decision process may help buyers make better purchase decisions.

How consumers use and process the information obtained in their search depends on features of the information itself, namely, availability, quantity, quality, repetition and format. If all the necessary information for a decision is available in the store, consumers may have no need to conduct an internal information search. Having all information externally available makes the consumers' decision process easier,[6] increases utilisation of the information and may thus facilitate a purchase. It is important to recognise that adequate information may not always be available. Sometimes consumers must make do with whatever data are on hand at the time of purchase. For example, a motorist replacing a broken windscreen following a road accident may not have enough time to review all relevant sources of information because the car is needed again urgently.

Repetition, a technique well known to advertisers, increases consumer learning of information. When seeing or hearing an advertising message for the first time, the recipient may not grasp all its important details but learns more details as the message is repeated. Nevertheless, even when commercials are initially effective, repetition eventually causes the phenomenon of "wear-out": consumers pay less attention to the commercial and respond to it less favourably than they did at first.[7] Consumers are more likely to be receptive to repetition when making a low involvement purchase. Involvement refers to the level of interest, emotion and activity which the consumer is prepared to expend on a particular purchase. For example, a consumer who purchases a kilogram of sugar may have very low interest in the product itself but may elect to buy the brand of a particular manufacturer because it is running a highly visible advertising campaign.

The format in which information is transmitted to the buyer may also determine its use. Information can be presented verbally, numerically or visually. For many consumer tasks, pictures are remembered better than words, and the combination of pictures and words further enhances learning.[8] Consequently, marketers pay great attention to the visual components of their advertising materials.

A successful information search yields a group of brands that a buyer views as possible alternatives. This group of products is sometimes called the buyer's **evoked set.** For example, an evoked set of compact disc players might be those manufactured by Sony, Aiwa, JVC and Philips.

Evoked set The group of products that a buyer views as possible alternatives after conducting an information search

Evaluation of Alternatives

When evaluating the products in the evoked set, a buyer establishes criteria for comparing the products. These criteria are the characteristics or features that the buyer wants (or does not want). For example, one compact disc player buyer may favour a compact machine with remote control, whereas another may have no preference as to the size of the machine but be unwilling to pay a premium for the remote control. The buyer also assigns a certain **salience,** or level of importance, to each criterion; some features and characteristics carry more weight than others. The salience of criteria varies from buyer to buyer. For example, when choosing a newspaper one buyer may consider the political stance of the editorial to be crucial, while another might place more importance on the quality and coverage of sports. Using the criteria, a buyer rates and eventually ranks the brands in the evoked set. Obviously this involves comparing the brands with each other as well as with the salient criteria. The evaluation stage may not yield a brand that the buyer is willing to purchase; in that case, a further information search may be necessary. Marketing Insight 4.1 considers how the criteria used by car buyers are changing.

Marketers can influence consumers' evaluation by *framing* the alternatives—that is, by the manner in which the alternative and its attributes are described. Framing can make a characteristic seem more important to a consumer and can facilitate its recall from memory. For example, by emphasising the whitening

Salience The level of importance assigned to each criterion for comparing products

Car Buyers Shun Speed and Sex

The annual national motor shows such as those staged in Paris, Frankfurt or at Birmingham's NEC feature bright lights, shiny paintwork, glamorous models, loud music and the latest in visual floorshows. For decades, car launches have focused on performance, sex appeal and sporty imagery. Results from the latest survey by the AA (Automobile Association) of 9,400 of its members reveal that car advertisements featuring speed and sex appeal now fail to seduce motorists in most markets. The average driver is more concerned with safety and reliability. Complex dashboards with trendy gadgets fall well behind features such as fuel economy and good brakes. Speed performance came only 27th in a list of 40 factors influencing car buyers. No longer included in this year's top 10 most desired attributes were high tech features, high speed and sex appeal.

According to the AA, "Mr and Mrs Ordinary Motorist are more turned on by mechanical reliability, good all-round vision, reassuring brakes and ease of getting in and out of the car … Theft and safety are fundamental concerns". Most drivers want comfortable cars suitable for school runs and long journeys, with hard wearing interiors, reasonable fuel economy and—befitting the latest promotional campaigns by Ford, Vauxhall or VW—safety and security. While some manufacturers have helped create this switch, government anti-theft campaigns have also instilled the changing attitudes of today's motorist. Ford recently ran a series of high profile television and press advertisements emphasising safety features such as anti-lock brakes, side impact protection mouldings, crumple zones and air bags—plus security features such as deadlocks, alarms, immobilisers and tracking systems. This focus on safety and security is taken right through Ford's communications package: advertising, press releases, dealer videos for showrooms, brochure features and sales force training. With the usual concern for reliability, the top 10 features from the AA's survey confirm the switch away from performance and sex appeal to safety and security as key requirements for car buyers.

Top 10 Features
1. Reliability
2. Vision
3. Accident avoidance
4. Fuel economy
5. Security against thieves
6. Air pollution control
7. Ease of getting in and out
8. Supportive, adjustable driving seat
9. Injury prevention
10. Roadholding ability

While companies such as Ford help determine the views of the car buying public, such consumer opinions are also influenced by media coverage, personal experience, the comments of family and friends, and the actions of regulatory bodies and consumer watchdogs, as well as by the marketing campaigns for other products and services. Safety and security are emotive issues that through a variety of sources have come to dominate customer needs in many segments of the car market. As the AA survey implies, far fewer motorists today are concerned with *911* acceleration or *XR3i* image appeal. There are still groups of car buyers who desire such performance and sex appeal, and manufacturers do cater for them with separate models or revved up model derivatives. The mainstream car buying segments, though, have changed significantly in their wants and worries as the 1990s have unfolded.

SOURCES: "Speed and sex appeal low down on list for drivers", *Evening Telegraph,* 18 June 1995; The AA PR Office, Hampshire, 1995/1996; *What Car?* magazine.

ingredient in a toothpaste, manufacturers can encourage the consumer to consider this particular aspect significant. Framing affects the decision processes of inexperienced buyers more than those of experienced ones.[9] If the evaluation of alternatives yields one or more brands that the consumer is willing to buy, the consumer is ready to move on to the next stage of the decision process—the purchase.

Purchase

The purchase stage, when the consumer chooses the product or brand to be bought, is mainly the outcome of the consumer's evaluation of alternatives, but other factors have an impact, too. The closeness of alternative stores and product availability can both influence which brand is purchased. For example, if the brand the buyer ranked highest is not available, the brand that is ranked second may be purchased instead.

During this stage, the buyer also picks the seller from whom the product will be purchased. The choice of the seller may affect the final product selection. The terms of sale, which, if negotiable, are determined during the purchase decision stage, will also be an important factor. Other issues such as price, delivery, guarantees, service agreements, installation and credit arrangements are discussed and settled. Finally, the purchase takes place, although in some cases the consumer terminates the buying decision process before reaching that point.

Post-purchase Evaluation

After the purchase has taken place, the buyer begins evaluating the product to check whether its actual performance meets expected levels. Many of the criteria used in evaluating alternatives are applied again during the post-purchase evaluation. This stage will determine whether the consumer is satisfied or dissatisfied. Either outcome strongly influences consumers' motivation and information processing. Consumers' satisfaction or dissatisfaction determines whether they make a complaint, communicate with other possible buyers or purchase the product again.[10] The impact of the post-purchase evaluation is illustrated by the feedback loop in Figure 4.1.

Cognitive dissonance
Doubts that occur as the buyer questions whether he or she made the right decision

Shortly after the purchase of an expensive product, the post-purchase evaluation may result in **cognitive dissonance**—doubts that occur because the buyer questions whether the right decision was made in purchasing the product. For example, after buying an expensive leather briefcase, a schoolteacher may feel guilty about the purchase or worry about whether it was the right brand and quality. A buyer who experiences cognitive dissonance may attempt to return the product or may seek positive information about it to justify the choice. For example, motoring journalists often note with amusement that car shows and exhibitions are frequented by consumers who have just recently purchased a new car.

As shown in Figure 4.1, three major categories of influences are believed to affect the consumer buying decision process: personal, psychological and social factors. These are the factors that determine which particular newspaper, chocolate bar, washing powder, camera, holiday, car or house a certain consumer will buy. Not surprisingly, understanding these aspects helps marketers build valuable insights into their customer base. The remainder of this chapter focuses on these factors. Although each major factor is discussed separately, it is important to realise that it is a combination of their effects which influences the consumer decision process.

Personal Factors Influencing
the Buying Decision Process

Personal factors Factors
unique to a particular individual

Personal factors are unique to a particular person. Many different personal factors can influence purchasing decisions. In this section three types are considered: demographic factors, situational factors and level of involvement.

Demographic Factors

Demographic factors
Individual characteristics such as age, sex, race, ethnic origin, income, family life cycle and occupation

Demographic factors are individual characteristics such as age, sex, race, ethnic origin, income, family life cycle and occupation. (These and other characteristics are discussed in Chapter 7 as possible variables for segmentation purposes.) Demographic factors have a bearing on who is involved in family decision-making. For example, it is estimated that by the mid- to late 1990s the UK will have the largest market for children's toys and clothes in the EU and the highest proportion of children in the population. Table 4.1 shows the EU official population projections by age and sex for the year 2000.

Children aged 6 to 17 are known to have more influence in the buying decision process for breakfast cereals, ice cream, soft drinks, holidays and even the family car than ever before.[11] This influence is increasingly reflected in the way such products are designed and marketed. For example, holiday brochures now contain pictures and information designed to appeal to children and teenagers. Demographic factors may also partially govern behaviour during a specific stage of the decision process. During the information stage, for example, a person's age and income may affect the number and types of information sources used and the amount of time devoted to seeking information. Marketing Insight 4.2 shows how demographics affect the choice of alcoholic drinks.

Country	Total	Male	Female	0–14	15–44	45–64	65+
Austria	8,109	3,948	4,161	1,399	3,516	1,926	1,268
Belgium	10,256	5,035	5,245	1,870	4,148	2,499	1,761
Denmark	5,312	2,626	2,686	994	2,178	1,355	786
Finland	5,172	2,528	2,644	946	2,068	1,391	768
France	59,412	28,845	30,567	11,420	24,939	13,606	9,444
Germany	83,741	41,615	42,125	13,049	35,541	21,557	13,593
Greece	10,351	5,145	5,207	1,608	4,409	2,547	1,788
Ireland	3,472	1,733	1,739	742	1,568	754	408
Italy	58,194	28,224	29,970	8,782	24,946	14,361	10,106
Luxembourg	394	196	198	67	168	100	60
The Netherlands	15,983	7,925	8,058	2,999	5,721	5,096	2,164
Portugal	10,595	5,128	5,467	1,756	4,906	2,315	1,620
Spain	39,615	19,451	20,164	6,199	18,263	8,744	6,409
Sweden	9,015	4,470	4,545	1,752	3,476	2,258	1,529
United Kingdom	59,613	29,360	30,253	11,640	24,716	13,904	9,353

SOURCE: *European Marketing Pocket Book 1996*, p. 14. Reprinted by permission of NTC Publications Ltd.

Table 4.1 Projected demographic population by age and sex for the year 2000 (in thousands)

Demographic factors also affect the extent and way in which a person uses products in a specific product category. While consumers aged 18 to 30 may purchase furniture, appliances and other household basics as they establish their own households, those aged 45 to 54 spend more money on luxury and leisure products after their children have left home.[12] Brand preferences, store choice and timing of purchases are other areas on which demographic factors have some impact. Consider, for example, how differences in occupation result in variations in product needs. A horse riding instructor and a secretary may earn roughly the same annual salary. Yet the riding instructor and the secretary spend their incomes differently, because different product needs arise from their respective jobs. Although both occupations require the purchase of work clothes, the riding instructor buys specialist outdoor clothing and the secretary buys suits and blouses/shirts. The cars they drive also vary to some extent. While the riding instructor opts for an old but robust Land Rover, the secretary drives a small town car. Where and what they eat for lunch are also quite different. Finally, the "tools" they purchase and use in their work are not the same. Thus occupation clearly affects consumer buying behaviour.

Situational Factors

Situational factors External circumstances or conditions that exist when a consumer is making a purchase decision

Situational factors are the external circumstances or conditions that exist when a consumer is making a purchase decision. These factors can influence the buyer at any stage of the consumer buying decision process and may cause the individual to shorten, lengthen or terminate the process. For example, a college lecturer who usually communicates with overseas colleagues by e-mail may be forced to use the fax machine when her computer breaks down, even if she would not usually do so. In other cases, a change in situation may arise which causes a person to lengthen or terminate the buying decision process. For instance, a consumer who is considering taking an exotic safari holiday and is laid off from work during the stage of evaluating alternatives may decide to reject the purchase entirely.

The effects of situational factors can be felt throughout the buying decision process in a variety of ways. Uncertainty about a family member's health may sway a consumer against making a purchase. On the other hand, a conviction that the supply of a particular product is sharply limited may impel a person to buy it. For example, consumers have purchased and hoarded petrol, food products and even toilet tissue when these products were believed to be in short supply. These and other situational factors can change rapidly; their influence on purchase decisions is generally as sudden as it is short lived.

The amount of time a consumer has available to make a decision is a situational factor that strongly influences buying decisions. If there is little time for selecting and purchasing a product, a person may quickly decide to buy a readily available brand. The amount of available time also affects the way consumers process the information contained in advertisements[13] and the length of the stages within the decision process. For example, if a family is planning to buy a new television set, its members may gather and consider a wide range of information from a variety of sources. They may read consumer magazines, consider mail order catalogues, talk to friends and salespersons, look at a number of advertisements and spend a good deal of time doing comparative shopping in a number of stores. However, if the family's 10 year old television set suddenly breaks down and cannot be repaired, the extent of the information search, the number of alternatives considered and the amount of comparative shopping may be much more restricted. Indeed, given the time factor, if these family members were reasonably satisfied

Changing Consumer Tastes: The Way Forward for White Spirits

A recent survey of 1,000 adults has highlighted changing tastes in the market for white spirits. As interest from younger consumers increases, the challenge is to appeal to the 18 to 25 year old market. For these drinkers, marketing pundits believe that vodka and white rum offer the way forward. Gin, it seems, is widely regarded by this younger group as an older person's drink—something their parents might enjoy. Market figures would appear to support this assumption, with 42 per cent of solus gin buyers being over 55 years old. Meanwhile, almost half of all vodka buyers are under 33 years old. With two thirds of those under 25 having purchased white spirits of one kind or another, it seems likely that the preference for vodka will increase.

For leading manufacturers in the white spirit market, the good news is that Smirnoff vodka, Gordons gin and Bacardi rum continue to dominate. Advertising recall also maps the purchase patterns, with each of the three leaders enjoying more than 10 per cent awareness among adults surveyed. Not surprisingly, brand loyalty also remains high, with 71 per cent of those surveyed claiming always to purchase the same brand. Only one third indicated that the cheapness of the brand influenced their choice, and this reason was skewed towards older buyers. For younger drinkers, advertising was still seen as an important contributor to brand choice, with 22 per cent of 18 to 34 year olds suggesting that they were influenced in this way.

In the UK market, vodka manufacturer Smirnoff is continuing its strategy of innovative product development backed up with heavy advertising spending. Soon the company's portfolio will include three sub-brands: Red, Blue (initially available through duty free) and now "super premium" Black, described by Jonathan Stordy, marketing controller, Smirnoff as "... the malt whisky of the vodka sector".

Meanwhile, Virgin's foray into the vodka market has stepped into controversial territory, with the launch of the first British television advertisement featuring a kiss and embrace between apparently gay men. As Virgin receives permission from satellite channel MTV to screen the advertisement, media interest is focused on whether Richard Branson's latest move will meet with disapproval or be quickly followed by other businesses directly targeting the gay community.

Age and Attitudes

"An ad featuring two men kissing would put me off buying that product ..."

	Agree	Unsure/ Don't know	Disagree
Total	59%	16%	25%
15-24	44%	15%	41%
25-34	41%	24%	35%
35-44	55%	16%	29%
45-54	66%	19%	15%
55-64	75%	3%	22%
65 +	77%	10%	13%
ABC1	59%	12%	29%
C2DE	59%	19%	22%
Men	61%	17%	22%
Women	57%	14%	29

SOURCE: CIA MediaLab, as reported in Ros Snowdon, "Virgin's spirit of acceptance", *Marketing*, 1 February 1996, p. 13.

Research to assess likely reaction to the advertisement shows attitudes among the young core of vodka drinkers to be much more open-minded than those among older consumers. In this respect, the Virgin brand is clearly aimed at the 18 to 34 year old market, and according to Virgin Trading Company's marketing director James Kydd, "People's reaction depends on what the product is. Our target 18 to 34 year olds won't be shocked; they will think it's good for Virgin Vodka".

SOURCES: "Spotlight: youth sector in high spirits", *Marketing Week*, 9 February 1996; Ros Snowdon, "Virgin's spirit of acceptance", *Marketing*, 1 February 1996; Ros Snowdon, "Virgin TV ad to show gay kiss", *Marketing*, 1 February 1996.

with the performance of the old set and service arrangements, they may buy an up to date model of the same brand.

Level of Involvement

Level of involvement The level of interest, emotional commitment and time spent searching for a product in a particular situation

Many aspects of consumer buying decisions are affected by the individual's **level of involvement.** This term refers to the level of interest, emotional commitment and time spent searching for a product in a particular situation. A buyer's level of involvement determines why he or she is motivated to seek information about certain products and brands but virtually ignores others. The extensiveness of the buying decision process varies greatly with the consumers' level of involvement. The sequence of the steps in this process may also be altered. Low involvement buyers may form an attitude towards a product—perhaps as a result of an advertising campaign—and evaluate its features after purchasing it rather than before.[14] Conversely, high involvement buyers spend much time and effort researching their purchase beforehand. For example, the purchase of a luxury car, such as the BMW shown in Figure 4.3, is a high involvement decision.

The level of consumer involvement experienced when making a purchase depends on a number of factors. Consumers tend to be more involved in the purchase of high priced goods and products that are visible to others, such as clothing, jewellery or houses. As levels of perceived risk increase, involvement levels are likely to rise. Furthermore, individuals may experience enduring involvement with a product class. *Enduring involvement* is an ongoing interest in a product class

Figure 4.3 Reaching consumers who have a high level of involvement. Choosing a luxury car is a high involvement purchase decision, as leading car manufacturer BMW knows.

Source: Courtesy of WCRS.

because of personal relevance. For example, people often have enduring involvement with products associated with their leisure activities. These individuals engage in ongoing search and information gathering processes for these products over extensive periods of time, irrespective of whether or not a purchase is imminent. Rock music enthusiasts often enjoy reading the music press, listening to new CDs and attending concerts; horse enthusiasts visit shows even if they are not taking part.

Buyers may also experience *situational involvement* resulting from the particular circumstance or environment in which they find themselves. This type of involvement, sometimes also called pre-purchase involvement, is temporary because the conditions that triggered the high degree of involvement may change.[15] If a man is searching for an engagement ring for his prospective fiancée, for example, he will probably experience a high level of involvement in the purchase decision. His information search and evaluation of alternatives may be extensive. However, once the selection has been made, he may no longer see an engagement ring as being personally relevant.

Many purchase decisions do not generate great involvement on the consumers' part. When the involvement level is low, as with routine response purchases, then buying is almost automatic, and the information search and evaluation of alternatives are extremely limited. For example, buying pet food represents a low involvement purchase decision for many consumers; the product is chosen out of habit and with minimal effort.

• • • • • • • • • • • • • • • • • •

Psychological Factors Influencing the Buying Decision Process

Psychological factors
Factors that influence consumer behaviour, including perceptions, motives, learning, attitudes and personality

Psychological factors operating within individuals partly determine people's general behaviour and thus influence their behaviour as consumers. The primary psychological influences on consumer behaviour are (1) perceptions, (2) motives, (3) learning, (4) attitudes and (5) personality. Even though these psychological factors operate internally, it will become apparent later in this chapter that they are very much affected by social forces external to the individual.

Perception

Perception The process of selecting, organising and interpreting information inputs to produce meaning

Information inputs The sensations received through sight, taste, hearing, smell and touch

Selective exposure The selection of inputs that people expose to their awareness

Are the horsemen in Figure 4.4 riding to the left or to the right? It could be either way depending on how you perceive the riders. Different people perceive the same thing at the same time in different ways. Similarly, the same individual at different times may perceive the same item in a number of ways. **Perception** is the process of selecting, organising and interpreting information inputs to produce meaning. **Information inputs** are the sensations received through sight, taste, hearing, smell and touch. Each time we see an advertisement, watch television, visit the shops or use a product, we receive information inputs.

As the definition indicates, perception consists of three steps. Although individuals receive numerous pieces of information at once, only a few of them reach awareness. Certain inputs are selected while others are ignored, because consumers do not have the ability to be conscious of every input at the same time. This phenomenon is sometimes called **selective exposure** because people select inputs that are to be exposed to their awareness. A student word-processing a report may be unaware that the light is on, that the computer is making a hum-

Figure 4.4

Perception

Are the horsemen riding to the left or to the right?

Source: © 1988 M. C. Escher c/o Cordon Art–Baarn–Holland.

ming sound, that there is background noise in the room or that other students are working at the same table. Even though these inputs are being received, the student will ignore them until they are mentioned.

Why do some types of information reach awareness while others do not? An input is more likely to reach awareness if it relates to an anticipated event. For example, a couple wishing to have their carpets cleaned are more likely to notice an advertisement in the local newspaper promoting a carpet cleaning service than are others with no interest in this service. An input is more likely to reach awareness if the information helps satisfy current needs. Thus, hungry people are more likely to notice a TGI Friday's sign than are those who are not. Finally, an input is more likely to reach awareness if its intensity changes significantly. When a store manager reduces a price slightly, consumers may not notice because the change is not significant, but if the manager cuts the price in half, they are much more likely to recognise the reduction.

The selective nature of perception leads to two other conditions: selective distortion and selective retention. **Selective distortion** is the changing or twisting of currently received information. This condition can occur when a person receives information that is inconsistent with personal feelings or beliefs. For example, an individual who reads some favourable publicity about a company he or she dislikes is likely to distort the information to make it more consistent with previous views. The publicity may therefore have much more impact on another consumer who views the same brand more positively. In the **selective retention** phenomenon, a person remembers information inputs that support personal feelings and beliefs and forgets inputs that do not. After hearing a sales presentation and leaving the shop, a customer may forget many of the selling points if they contradict pre-existing beliefs.

The information inputs that do reach awareness are not received in an organised form. For them to produce meaning, an individual must enter the second step of the perceptual process—organising and integrating the new information with that already stored in the memory. Although this step is usually carried out

Selective distortion The changing or twisting of currently received information

Selective retention The process of remembering information inputs that support personal feelings and beliefs and of forgetting those that do not quickly, it may take longer when the individual is considering an unfamiliar product area.

Interpretation—the third step in the perceptual process—is the assignment of meaning to what has been organised. A person bases interpretation on what is familiar, on knowledge already stored in memory. For this reason, a company that changes a package design or logo faces a major problem. Since people look for the product in the old, familiar package, they may not recognise it in the new one. Unless a package or logo change is accompanied by a promotional programme that makes people aware of the change, a firm may lose sales. Even in cases where such a programme is conducted, positive reaction from the consumer cannot be guaranteed. Companies often try to get around this difficulty by making only small changes to their logo or brand identity.

Although marketers cannot control people's perceptions, they often try to influence them. Several problems may arise from such attempts, however. First, a consumer's perceptual process may operate in such a way that a seller's information never reaches that person. For example, a buyer may block out a shop assistant's sales presentation. Second, a buyer may receive a seller's information but perceive it differently from the way the seller intended. For example, when a toothpaste producer advertises that "35 per cent of the people who use this toothpaste have less decay", a customer could infer that 65 per cent of the people who use the product have more tooth decay. Third, buyers who perceive information inputs to be inconsistent with their prior beliefs are likely to forget the information quickly. Thus if a prospective holidaymaker hears from a travel agent that accommodation in a particular location is keenly priced but has already been informed by friends that this area is expensive, he or she probably will not retain the information very long. The problem of interpreting information is made more complex by the large number of information inputs that consumers encounter each day.[16]

In addition to perceptions of packages, products, brands and organisations, individuals also have self-perceptions. That perception is called the person's **self-concept** or self-image. It is reasonable to believe that a person's self-concept affects purchase decisions and consumption behaviour. The results of some studies suggest that buyers purchase products that reflect and enhance their self-concepts. For instance, one individual might buy a Rolex watch to project an up-market image, while another might buy a Swatch to enhance acceptability among that person's peer group.

Self-concept A person's perception of himself or herself; self-image

Motives

A **motive** is an internal energy giving force that directs a person's activities towards satisfying a need or achieving a goal. Motivation is the set of mechanisms for controlling movement towards goals.[17] A buyer's actions at any time are affected by a set of motives rather than by just one. Each buyer's motives are unique and, at a single point in time, some motives in the set have priority, but the priorities of motives vary from one occasion to another. For example, a person's motives for taking a shower are particularly strong after a trip to the gym. Motivation also affects the direction and intensity of behaviour. Individuals must choose which goals to pursue at a particular time.

Motives influencing where a person purchases products on a regular basis are called **patronage motives**. A buyer may use a particular shop because of such patronage motives as price, service, location, honesty, product variety or friendliness of salespeople. To capitalise on patronage motives, a marketer should try to

Motive An internal energy giving force that directs a person's activities towards satisfying a need or achieving a goal

Patronage motives Those motives that influence where a person purchases a product determine why regular customers patronise a store and then emphasise these characteristics in the store's marketing mix. Useful lessons can also be learned by understanding people's reasons for patronising competing brands or outlets. In Figure 4.5, the manufacturer of Friskies cat food shows that it understands that many cat owners enjoy pampering their pets.

Motivation research can be used to analyse the major motives that influence consumers to buy or not buy their products. Measuring motive is not always straightforward. Motives that are subconscious are especially hard to judge, because people are by definition unaware of them and marketers thus cannot elicit them through direct questioning. Most motivation research relies on interviews or projective techniques.

In-depth interview The collection of data from an individual by an interview

When researchers study motives through interviews, they may use individual in-depth interviews, focus groups or a combination of the two. In an **in-depth interview,** the researcher tries to get the subject to talk freely about anything at all in order to create an informal atmosphere. Although there is some variation in approach, usually the researcher asks general, non-directed questions and then probes the subject's answers by asking for clarification. An in-depth interview may last for several hours. In a **focus group,** the moderator—through leadership

Focus group A semi-structured discussion involving 6 to 12 people, led by a moderator

that is not highly structured—tries to generate discussion about one or several topics in a group of 6 to 12 people. Through what is said in the discussion, the

Figure 4.5 Identifying consumer motives. As this advertisement for Friskies cat food shows, the manufacturer understands that many cat owners wish to pamper their pets.

Source: Courtesy of John Parker.

moderator attempts to discover people's motives relating to some issue such as the use of a product. The researcher usually cannot probe as far in a focus group as in an in-depth interview, and some products may not be suitable for such group discussion. To determine the subconscious motives reflected in the interviews, motivation researchers must exhibit a range of qualities: they must be perceived as non-threatening by members of the group, must be able to adopt a demeanour appropriate for the characteristics of the individuals in the group and must be extremely well trained in clinical psychology. The use of sound and video recordings can simplify the process of analysis. Moderators' skill in uncovering subconscious motives from what is said in an interview determines the effectiveness of their research. Both in-depth and focus group techniques can yield a variety of information. For example, they might help marketers discover why customers continue to buy high cholesterol red meats despite the fact that most say they are working towards reducing their intake of high fat foods.

Projective techniques Tests in which subjects are asked to perform specific tasks for particular reasons, while actually being evaluated for other purposes

Projective techniques are tests in which subjects are asked to perform specific tasks for particular reasons, while actually being evaluated for other purposes. Such tests are based on the assumption that subjects will unconsciously "project" their motives as they perform the required tasks. However, subjects should always be informed that the test is an unstructured evaluation. Researchers trained in projective techniques can analyse the materials a subject produces and make predictions about the subject's subconscious motives. Some common types of projective techniques are word association tests, sentence completion tests and bubble drawings. These are illustrated in Figure 4.6. Such tests can be useful to marketers in a number of ways. For example, attempts are currently being made to use projective techniques to make advertising more effective.[18]

Motivation research techniques can be reasonably effective but are far from perfect. Marketers who want to research people's motives should obtain the services of professional psychologists skilled in the methods of motivation research.

Learning

Learning Changes in a person's behaviour prompted by information and experience

Learning refers to changes in a person's behaviour caused by information and experience. The consequences of behaviour strongly influence the learning process. Behaviour that results in satisfying consequences tends to be repeated. For example, when a consumer buys a box of Bird's Eye Fish Fingers and enjoys them, he or she is more likely to buy the same brand next time. In fact, the individual will probably continue to purchase that brand until it no longer provides satisfaction. But when the effects of the behaviour are no longer satisfying, the person will perhaps switch to a different brand or start eating an alternative frozen food instead.

When making purchasing decisions, buyers have to process information. Individuals have differing abilities in this regard. For example, when purchasing a computer, a well educated potential buyer who has experience with computers may be able to read, comprehend and synthesise the considerable quantities of information found in the technical brochures for various competing brands. On the other hand, another buyer with more limited abilities may be incapable of performing this task and will have to rely on information obtained from advertisements or from a sales representative of a particular brand.

Knowledge Familiarity with a product and expertise—the ability to apply the product

A critical aspect of an individual's ability is knowledge. **Knowledge** has two components: familiarity with the product and expertise—the ability to apply the product.[19] The duration and intensity of the buying decision process depends on the buyer's familiarity with or prior experience in purchasing and using the product. For example, in Figure 4.7 AA builds consumer awareness by informing

Figure 4.6

Common types of projective techniques

Word Association Tests

Subjects are asked to say what words come into their minds when a particular topic/product is mentioned.

Fresh foods are . . .	Frozen foods are . . .
Natural	Processed
Fresh	Quick
Healthy	Simple
Expensive	Convenient
Good for you	Preservatives
Real	Manufactured

Sentence Completion Tests

Subjects are asked to complete the sentences.

"People who use re-cycled toilet tissue . . ."
"People who look for the ingredients on packets before they buy them are . . ."
"People who buy Caterpillar boots . . ."

Bubble Drawings

Subjects are asked to say what the man is thinking.

CAR SHOWROOM

I just love the one with flowers on it!

potential purchasers of the benefits of its Five Star Europe Service. The individual's knowledge influences his or her search for, re-call and use of information.[20]

When making purchase decisions, inexperienced buyers may use different types of information from more experienced shoppers who are familiar with the product and purchase situation. Inexperienced buyers use price as an indicator of quality more frequently than buyers who have some knowledge of a particular product category.[21] Thus two potential buyers of a pedigreed dog may use quite different

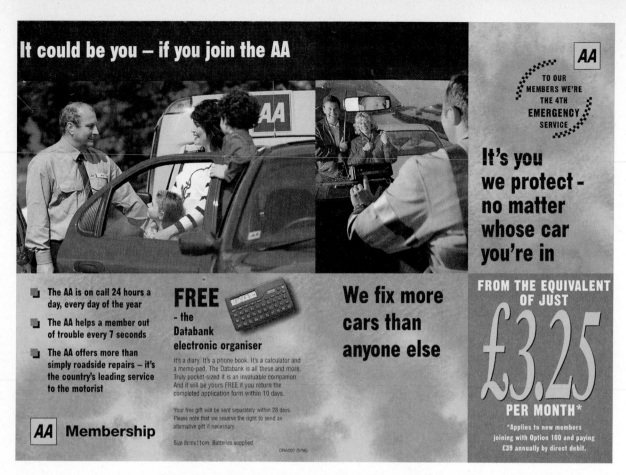

Figure 4.7 Building consumer awareness. The AA, the UK's leading motoring organisation, promotes awareness of its emergency road service.

Source: Courtesy of AA.

types of information in making their purchase decision. The more experienced buyer, wishing to take the animal to dog shows, may seek detailed information about the dog's pedigree; the less experienced buyer, looking for a loyal family pet, may judge the animal by how approachable and friendly it is.

Consumers who lack expertise are more likely to seek the advice of others when making a purchase. More experienced buyers have greater confidence; they also have more knowledge about the product or service and can tell which features are reliable indicators of product quality. For example, consider two families choosing a long haul holiday. Members of one family are unused to overseas travel, are unsure of the suitability of locations offered in travel brochures and do not understand how to investigate flight options or medical and insurance requirements. Members of the other family have taken holidays abroad regularly in many countries. Although on this occasion they intend to visit a country that is new to them, they are sufficiently conversant with this type of travel to make their purchase without assistance and with confidence.

Marketers sometimes help customers to learn about their products and to gain experience with them. Free samples encourage trial and reduce purchase risk. In-store demonstrations help consumers acquire knowledge of product uses. Visiting a homes and gardens exhibition gives potential customers an appreciation of the uses of new gardening equipment. Consumers also learn when they experience products indirectly, by way of information from salespeople, advertisements, friends and relatives. Through sales personnel and advertisements, marketers offer information before (and sometimes after) purchases to influence what consumers learn and to create a more favourable attitude towards the products.

Although marketers seek to influence what a consumer learns, their attempts are seldom fully successful. Marketers encounter problems in attracting and holding consumers' attention, providing consumers with the kinds of information that are important for making purchase decisions, and convincing them to try the product. These attempts are most likely to be successful when carefully designed to appeal to the target market.

Attitudes

Attitude An individual's enduring evaluation, feelings and behavioural tendencies towards an object or activity

An **attitude** refers to an individual's enduring evaluation, feelings and behavioural tendencies towards an object or activity. The objects or acts towards which we have attitudes may be tangible or intangible, living or non-living. Some attitudes relate to things that have a major impact on our lives, while others are less important. For example, we have attitudes towards relationships, culture and politics, just as we do towards rock music, skiing and pizza.

An individual learns attitudes through experience and interaction with other people. Just as attitudes are learned, they can also be changed. Nevertheless, an individual's attitudes remain generally stable and do not change from moment to moment. Likewise, at any one time, a person's attitudes do not all have equal impact; some are stronger than others. For example, members of a family which has recently suffered a house burglary may develop attitudes towards rising crime which are particularly clearly defined. An attitude consists of three major components: cognitive, affective and behavioural. The cognitive component is a person's knowledge and information about the object or idea, whereas the affective component comprises feelings and emotions towards the object or idea. The behavioural component is composed of the action tendencies one exhibits towards the object or idea. Changes in one of these components may or may not alter the other components. Thus consumers may become more knowledgeable about a specific brand without changing the affective or behavioural components of their attitude towards that brand.

Consumer attitudes towards a firm and its products greatly influence the success or failure of the firm's marketing strategy. When consumers have strong negative attitudes towards one or more aspects of a firm's marketing practices, they may not only stop using the firm's product but also urge their relatives and friends to do likewise. For example, following the execution of human rights activists in Nigeria, some motorists chose to boycott Shell petrol because of allegations about Shell's activities in Nigeria. Likewise, when an oil spill from Esso's supertanker *Valdez* fouled beaches and killed wildlife in Alaska's Prince William Sound, the public judged Esso's response to cleaning up the spill as inadequate and cosmetic. As a result, many consumers boycotted Esso products. Nearly 20,000 Esso credit card holders cut up their cards and sent them back to Esso, exhorting their friends to do the same.

Since attitudes can play such an important part in determining consumer behaviour, marketers should measure consumer attitudes towards prices, package designs, brand names, advertisements, salespeople, repair services, store locations, features of existing or proposed products, and social responsibility activities. Several methods can help marketers gauge these attitudes. One of the simplest ways is to question people directly. A marketing research agency carrying out attitude research for Diesel clothing, for example, might ask respondents for their opinions about the style and retailing of fashionable clothes. Projective techniques used in motivation research can also be employed to measure attitudes. Sometimes marketers evaluate attitudes through attitude scales. An **attitude scale** usually consists of a series of adjectives, phrases or sentences about an object. Subjects are asked to indicate the intensity of their feelings towards the object by reacting to the adjectives, phrases or sentences in a certain way. For example, a researcher measuring attitudes towards "green" products might ask respondents to state the degree to which they agree or disagree with a number of statements, such as "Recycling paper packaging is good for the environment".

Attitude scale A series of adjectives, phrases or sentences about an object used by a subject to indicate his or her feelings towards the object

When marketers determine that a significant number of consumers have strong negative attitudes towards an aspect of a marketing mix, they may try to change consumer attitudes to make them more favourable. This task is generally long, expensive and difficult and may require extensive promotional efforts. For example, in the UK, Post Office Counters has been advertising to draw customers' attention to the fact that local post offices offer a wide range of services. This publicity is attempting to alter customers' perceptions away from the traditional view that the Post Office exists purely for mailing letters and parcels. Similarly, manufacturers of detergents and household cleaners have been trying to respond to consumer desires for more environmentally sympathetic products.

Personality

Personality All the internal traits and behaviours that make a person unique

Personality includes all the internal traits and behaviours that make a person unique. Each person's unique personality arises from both heredity and personal experiences. Personalities are typically described as having one or more characteristics, such as compulsiveness, ambitiousness, gregariousness, dogmatism, authoritarianism, introversion, extroversion, aggressiveness and competitiveness. Marketing researchers attempt to find relationships among such characteristics and buying behaviour. Even though a few links between several personality characteristics and buyer behaviour have been determined, the results of many studies have been inconclusive. Some researchers see the apparently weak association between personality and buying behaviour as due to unreliable measures rather than because no such relationship exists.[22] A number of marketers are convinced that a consumer's personality does influence the types and brands of products purchased. For example, the type of clothing or cars that people buy, as well as the way their hair is styled and the leisure activities they engage in, may reflect one or more personality characteristics.

At times, marketers aim advertising campaigns at general types of personalities. In doing so, they use positively valued personality characteristics, such as gregariousness, independence or competitiveness. Products promoted in this way include drinks, cars, cigarettes, clothing and computer games. For example, Pepsi advertising aims to appeal to young, dynamic consumers.

• • • • • • • • • • • • • • • • • • •

Social Factors Influencing the Buying Decision Process

Social factors The forces other people exert on an individual's buying behaviour

The forces that other people exert on buying behaviour are called **social factors**. As shown in Figure 4.1, they can be grouped into four major areas: (1) roles and family, (2) reference groups, (3) social classes and (4) culture and sub-cultures.

Roles and Family

Role A set of actions and activities that a person in a particular position is supposed to perform, based on the expectations of both the individual and surrounding persons

All of us occupy positions within groups, organisations and institutions. Associated with each position is a **role**—a set of actions and activities that a person in a particular position is supposed to perform, based on the expectations of both the individual and surrounding persons. Because people occupy numerous positions, they also have many roles. For example, one man may perform the roles of father, husband, grandfather, son, machine tool operator, part time youth club organiser and member of the local rambling association. Thus there are several sets of expectations placed on each person's behaviour.

An individual's roles influence both general behaviour and buying behaviour. The demands of a person's many roles may be inconsistent and confusing. To illustrate, assume that a man is thinking about buying a boat. While he wants a boat for fishing, his children want one suitable for water skiing. His wife wants him to delay the boat purchase until next year. A colleague at work insists that he should buy a particular brand, known for high performance. Thus an individual's buying behaviour may be partially affected by the input and opinions of family and friends.

Family roles relate directly to purchase decisions. The male head of household is likely to be involved heavily in the purchase of products such as household insurance and alcohol. Although female roles have changed, women still make buying decisions related to many household items, including health care products, washing products, household cleaners and food. Husbands and wives participate jointly in the purchase of a variety of products, especially durable goods. Some students aged 16 to 24 may be rebellious; their brand loyalty can be quite changeable. Marketers frequently promote their products during school and college holidays to catch this hard-to-reach group at a time when they are more receptive to a promotional message.[23] Others in this age group may seek their parents' advice about products with which they are not personally familiar. For example, many college students bank with the same bank as their parents. Children are making many purchase decisions and influencing numerous household purchase decisions that traditionally were made only by husbands and wives. Some buying decisions are made by the whole family. For example, parents and children will usually all be involved in choosing a new house, although different family members may play different roles in the process. When two or more individuals participate in a purchase, their roles may dictate that each is responsible for performing certain tasks: initiating the idea, gathering information, deciding whether to buy the product, or selecting the specific brand. The particular tasks performed depend on the types of products being considered.

Marketers need to be aware of how roles affect buying behaviour. To develop a marketing mix that meets precisely the needs of the target market, marketers must know not only who does the actual buying but also what other roles influence the purchase. Because sex roles are changing so rapidly, marketers must ensure that their information is current and accurate.

Reference Groups

Reference group A group with which an individual identifies so strongly that he or she takes on many of the values, attitudes or behaviour of group members

A group becomes a **reference group** when an individual identifies with it so much that he or she takes on many of the values, attitudes or behaviour of group members. The person who views a group as a reference group may or may not know the actual size of the group. Most people have several reference groups, such as families, friends, work colleagues, religious and professional organisations.

A group can be a negative reference group for an individual. Someone may have been a part of a specific group at one time but later have rejected its values and members. One can also specifically take action to avoid a particular group.[24]

However, in this discussion reference groups mean those that the individual involved views positively.

A reference group may serve as a point of comparison and a source of information for an individual. A customer's behaviour may change to be more in line with the actions and beliefs of group members. For example, a student might stop buying one magazine and switch to another on the advice of members of the reference group. Generally, the more conspicuous a product, the more likely it is that the brand decision will be influenced by reference groups. An individual may also seek information from the reference group about other factors regarding a prospective purchase, such as where to buy a certain product. The degree to which a reference group will affect a purchase decision depends on an individual's susceptibility to its influence and the strength of his or her involvement with the group. Young people are often especially susceptible to this kind of influence.

A marketer sometimes tries to use reference group influence in advertisements by suggesting that people in a specific group buy a product and are highly satisfied with it. In this type of appeal, the advertiser hopes that many people will accept the suggested group as a reference group and buy (or react more favourably to) the product as a result. Whether this kind of advertising succeeds depends on three factors: how effectively the advertisement communicates the message, the type of product, and the individual's susceptibility to reference group influence.

In most reference groups, one or more members stand out as opinion leaders. An **opinion leader** provides information about a specific sphere that interests reference group participants who seek information. Opinion leaders are viewed by other group members as being well informed about a particular area and easily accessible. An opinion leader is not the foremost authority on all issues. However, because such individuals know that they are opinion leaders, they feel a responsibility to remain informed about the sphere of interest and thus seek out advertisements, manufacturers' brochures, salespeople and other sources of information.

Opinion leader The member of a reference group who provides information about a specific sphere of interest to reference group participants seeking information

Social Classes

Social class An open group of individuals with a similar social rank

Within all societies, people rank others into higher or lower positions of respect. This ranking results in social classes. A **social class** is an open group of individuals who have similar social rank. A class is referred to as "open" because people can move into and out of it. The criteria for grouping people into classes vary from one society to another. In the UK, as in other western countries, many factors are taken into account, including occupation, education, income, wealth, race, ethnic group and possessions. In the former Soviet Union, wealth and income are less important in determining social class than education and occupation: although Russian doctors and scientists do not make a great deal of money, they are highly valued in Russian society. A person who is ranking someone does not necessarily apply all of a society's criteria. The number and importance of the factors chosen depend on the characteristics of the individual being ranked and the values of the person who is doing the ranking. For example, one individual may particularly respect status within a church or religious sect, while another may regard it as having little relevance.

To some degree, persons within social classes develop and assume common patterns of behaviour. They may have similar attitudes, values, language patterns and possessions. Social class influences many aspects of people's lives. For example, it affects whom they marry, their likelihood of having children and the children's chances of surviving infancy. It influences childhood training, choice of religion, selection of occupation and the way in which people spend their time. Because social class has a bearing on so many aspects of a person's life, it also affects buying decisions. For example, upper class Europeans may choose luxury hotel accommodation when holidaying abroad, because they believe it symbolises their status, income and aspirations.

Social class determines to some extent the type, quality and quantity of products that a person buys and uses. Social class also affects an individual's shopping patterns and the types of stores patronised. Advertisements are sometimes based on an appeal to a specific social class. See Table 4.2 for an analysis of the categories of social class in the UK.

Culture and Sub-cultures

Culture All the things around us that are made by human beings: tangible items, such as food, furniture, buildings, clothing and tools; and intangible concepts, such as education, the legal system, health care and religion

Culture is everything in our surroundings that is made by human beings. It consists of tangible items, such as food, furniture, buildings, clothing and tools, and intangible concepts, such as education, the legal system, health care and religion. Culture also includes the values and wide range of behaviours that are acceptable within a specific society. The concepts, values and behaviours that make up a culture are learned and passed on from one generation to the next.

Culture influences buying behaviour because it permeates daily life. Culture determines what people wear and eat, where they live and travel. Certainly, society's interest in the healthiness of food has affected companies' approaches to developing and promoting their products. It also influences how consumers buy and use products and the satisfaction gained from them. In many western cultures, shortage of time is a growing problem because of the rise in the number of women who work and the current emphasis placed on physical and mental self-development. Many people do time saving shopping and buy convenience and labour saving products to cope with this problem.[25]

Because culture, to some degree, determines how products are purchased and used, it in turn affects the development, promotion, distribution and pricing of products. Food marketers, for example, have had to make a multitude of changes in their marketing efforts. Thirty years ago most families ate at least two meals a day together, and the mother devoted four to six hours a day to preparing those meals. Now more than 60 per cent of women aged 25 to 54 are employed outside the home, and average family incomes have risen considerably. These shifts, along with lack of time, have resulted in dramatic increases in per capita consumption of shelf-stable foods like Pot Rice and Pot Noodles, frozen meals and take-away foods.[26] As a result of increasing demands from those wishing to "eat on the move", petrol stations now stock a variety of prepared sandwiches and snacks.

When marketers sell products overseas, they often see the tremendous impact that culture has on the purchase and use of products. International marketers find that people in other regions of the world have different attitudes, values and needs, which in turn call for different methods of doing business, as well as different types of marketing mixes. Some international marketers fail because they do not or cannot adjust to cultural differences. The effect of culture on international marketing programmes was discussed in greater detail in Chapter 3.

Sub-cultures Sub-divisions of culture according to geographic regions or human characteristics, such as age or ethnic background

A culture can be divided into **sub-cultures** according to geographic regions or human characteristics, such as age or ethnic background. In any country, there are a number of different sub-cultures. Within these, there are even greater similarities in people's attitudes, values and actions than within the broader culture. Relative to other sub-cultures, individuals in a certain sub-culture may have stronger preferences for specific types of clothing, furniture or leisure activity. For example, the wearing of kilts tends to be confined to Scotland rather than England or Wales. Meanwhile, European teenagers seek out the latest trends in fashion from retailers like Benetton. Marketers must recognise that even though their

Approximate Social Grade	Social Status	Head of Household's Occupation	Percentage of Families
A	Upper middle class	Higher managerial, administrative or professional	3
B	Middle class	Intermediate managerial, administrative or professional	10
C1	Lower middle class	Supervisory or clerical and junior managerial, administrative or professional	24
C2	Skilled working class	Skilled manual workers	30
D	Working class	Semi- and unskilled manual workers	25
E	Those at lowest levels of subsistence	State pensioners or widows (no other earner), casual or lowest grade workers	8

A—Upper middle class: The head of the household is a successful business or professional person, senior civil servant, or has considerable private means. A young person in some of these occupations who has not fully established himself/herself may still be found in Grade B, though he/she should eventually reach grade A. In country or suburban areas, A-grade householders usually live in large detached houses or in expensive flats. In towns, they may live in expensive flats or town houses in the better parts of town.

B—Middle class: In general, the heads of B-grade households will be quite senior people but not at the very top of their profession or business. They are quite well off, but their style of life is generally respectable rather than rich or luxurious. Non-earners will be living on private pensions or on fairly modest private means.

C1—Lower middle class: In general it is made up of the families of small tradespeople and non-manual workers who carry out less important administrative, supervisory and clerical jobs, i.e. what are sometimes called "white-collar" workers.

C2—Skilled working class: Consists in the main of skilled manual workers and their families: the serving of an apprenticeship may be a guide to membership of this class.

D—Semi-skilled and unskilled working class: Consists entirely of manual workers, generally semi-skilled or unskilled.

E—Those at lowest levels of subsistence: Consists of old age pensioners, widows and their families, casual workers and those who, through sickness or unemployment, are dependent on social security schemes, or have very small private means.

SOURCE: From Peter M. Chisnall, *Marketing: A Behavioural Analysis* (Berkshire, England: McGraw-Hill Publishing Co. Ltd, 1976), pp. 114–115. Reprinted by permission.

Table 4.2 Socio-economic classification (JICNARS)

operations are confined to one country, state or city, sub-cultural differences may dictate considerable variations in what products people buy. There will also be differences in how people make purchases—and variations in when they make them as well. To deal effectively with these differences, marketers may have to alter their product, promotion, distribution systems, price or people to satisfy members of particular sub-cultures.

Understanding Consumer Behaviour

Marketers try to understand consumer buying behaviour so that they can offer consumers greater satisfaction. An appreciation of how and why individuals buy products and services helps marketers design more appealing marketing programmes. Yet a certain amount of customer dissatisfaction remains. Some marketers have not adopted the marketing concept, are not consumer oriented, do not regard customer satisfaction as a primary objective and fail to understand fully the process and motivations of consumer buying. Moreover, because the tools for analysing consumer behaviour are imprecise, marketers may not be able to determine accurately what is highly satisfying to buyers. Finally, even if marketers know what increases consumer satisfaction, they may not be able to provide it.

Understanding consumer behaviour is an important task for marketers. Even though research on consumer buying behaviour has not supplied all the knowledge that marketers need, progress has been made during the last 20 years and is likely to continue in the future. Not only will refinements in research methods yield more information about consumer behaviour, but the pressures of an increasingly competitive business environment will also make obtaining such information much more urgent for marketers.

Summary

● *Buying behaviour* refers to the decision processes and acts of people involved in buying and using products. *Consumer buying behaviour* refers to the buying behaviour of ultimate consumers, those who purchase products for personal or household use, not for business purposes. Analysing consumer buying behaviour is important to marketers; if they are able to determine what satisfies customers, they can implement the marketing concept and better predict how consumers will respond to different marketing programmes.

● Consumer decisions can be classified into three categories: routine response behaviour, limited decision-making and extensive decision-making. A consumer uses *routine response behaviour* when buying frequently purchased, low cost, low risk items that require very little search and decision effort. *Limited decision-making* is used for products purchased occasionally or when a buyer needs to acquire information about an unfamiliar brand in a familiar product category. *Extensive decision-making* is used when purchasing an unfamiliar, expensive, high risk or infrequently bought product. *Impulse buying* is an unplanned buying behaviour involving a powerful, persistent urge to buy something immediately.

The purchase of a certain product does not always elicit the same type of decision-making behaviour. Individuals differ in their response to purchase situations. Even the same individual may make a different decision in other circumstances.

● The *consumer buying decision process* includes five stages: problem recognition, information search, evaluation of alternatives, purchase and post-purchase evaluation. Decision processes do not always culminate in a purchase, and not all consumer decisions include all five stages. Problem recognition occurs when a buyer becomes aware that there is a difference between a desired state and an actual condition. After recognising the problem or need, the buyer searches for information about products that will help resolve the problem or satisfy the need. In the *internal search*, buyers search their memories for information about products that might solve the problem. If they are unable to retrieve from memory sufficient information to make a decision, they seek additional information through an *external search*. A successful search will yield a group of brands, called an *evoked set*, that a buyer views as possible alternatives. To evaluate the products in the evoked set, a buyer establishes certain criteria and assigns a certain *salience*—or importance—by which to compare, rate and rank the different products. Marketers can influence consumers' evaluation by framing the alternatives.

● In the purchase stage, the consumer selects the product or brand on the basis of results from the evaluation stage and on other dimensions. The buyer also chooses the seller from whom he or she will buy the product. After the purchase, the buyer evaluates the product to determine if its actual performance meets expected levels. Shortly after the purchase of an expensive product, for example, the post-purchase evaluation may provoke *cognitive dissonance,* dissatisfaction brought on by the consumer's doubts as to whether he or she should have bought the product in the first place or would have been better off buying another brand that had also ranked high in the evaluation. The results of the post-purchase evaluation will affect future buying behaviour.

● Three major categories of influences are believed to affect the consumer buying decision process: personal, psychological and social factors. A *personal factor* is one that is unique to a particular person. Personal factors include demographic factors, situational factors and level of involvement. *Demographic factors* are individual characteristics such as age, sex, race, ethnic origin, income, family life cycle and occupation. *Situational factors* are the external circumstances or conditions that exist when a consumer is making a purchase decision. The time available to make a decision is a situational factor that strongly influences consumer buying decisions. An individual's *level of involvement*—the importance and intensity of interest in a product in a particular situation—also affects the buying decision process. Enduring involvement is an ongoing interest in a product class because of personal relevance. Situational involvement is a temporary interest resulting from the particular circumstance or environment in which buyers find themselves.

● *Psychological factors* partly determine people's general behaviour and thus influence their behaviour as consumers. The primary psychological influences on consumer behaviour are perception, motives, learning, attitudes and personality. *Perception* is the process of selecting, organising and interpreting *information inputs* (the sensations received through sight, taste, hearing, smell and touch) to produce meaning. *Selective exposure* is the phenomenon of people selecting the inputs that are to be exposed to their awareness; *selective distortion* is the changing or twisting of currently received information. When a person remembers information inputs that support personal feelings and beliefs and forgets inputs that do not, the phenomenon is called *selective retention.* The second step of the perceptual process requires organising and integrating the new information with that already stored in memory. Interpretation—the third step in the perceptual process—is the assignment of meaning to what has been organised. In addition to perceptions of packages, products, brands and organisations, individuals also have a *self-concept,* or self-image.

● A *motive* is an internal, energy giving force directing a person's activities towards satisfying a need or achieving a goal. *Patronage motives* influence where a person purchases products on a regular basis. To analyse the major motives that influence consumers to buy or not buy their products, marketers conduct motivation research, using *in-depth interviews, focus groups* or *projective techniques.* Common types of projective techniques include word association tests, bubble drawings and sentence completion tests.

● *Learning* refers to changes in a person's behaviour caused by information and experience. *Knowledge* has two components: familiarity with the product and expertise—the individual's ability to apply the product.

● *Attitude* refers to knowledge and positive or negative feelings about an object or activity. Consumer attitudes towards a firm and its products greatly influence the success or failure of the firm's marketing strategy. Marketers measure consumers' attitudes with projective techniques and *attitude scales.*

● *Personality* comprises all the internal traits and behaviours that make a person unique. Some marketers believe that personality does influence the types and brands of products purchased.

● The forces that other people exert on buying behaviour are called *social factors.* Social factors include the influence of roles and family, reference groups, social classes, and culture and sub-cultures. All of us occupy positions within groups, organisations and institutions, and each position has a *role*—a set of actions and activities that a person in a particular position is supposed to perform, based on the expectations of both the individual and surrounding persons. A group is a *reference group* when an individual identifies with the group so much that he or she takes on many of the values, attitudes or behaviours of group members. In most reference groups, one or more members stand out as *opinion leaders*. A *social class* is an open group of individuals who have similar social rank. *Culture* is everything in our surroundings that is made by human beings. A culture can be divided into *sub-cultures* on the basis of geographic regions or human characteristics, such as age or ethnic background.

● Marketers try to understand consumer buying behaviour so that they can offer consumers greater satisfaction. Refinements in research methods will yield more information about consumer behaviour, and the pressure of an increasingly competitive business environment will spur marketers to seek a fuller understanding of consumer decision processes.

● ● ● ● ● ● ● ● ● ● ● ● ● ● ● ● ● ● ●

Important Terms

Buying behaviour
Consumer buying behaviour
Routine response behaviour
Limited decision-making
Extensive decision-making
Impulse buying
Consumer buying
   decision process
Internal search
External search
Evoked set
Salience
Cognitive dissonance
Personal factors

Demographic factors
Situational factors
Level of involvement
Psychological factors
Perception
Information inputs
Selective exposure
Selective distortion
Selective retention
Self-concept
Motive
Patronage motives
In-depth interview
Focus group

Projective techniques
Learning
Knowledge
Attitude
Attitude scale
Personality
Social factors
Role
Reference group
Opinion leader
Social class
Culture
Sub-cultures

● ● ● ● ● ● ● ● ● ● ● ● ● ● ● ● ● ●

Discussion and Review Questions

1. Name the types of buying behaviour consumers use. List some products that you have bought using each type of behaviour. Have you ever bought a product on impulse? In what circumstances?
2. What are the major stages in the consumer buying decision process? Are all these stages used in all consumer purchase decisions?
3. What are the personal factors that affect the consumer buying decision process? How do they affect the process?
4. How does a consumer's level of involvement affect his or her purchase behaviour?
5. What is the function of time in a consumer's purchasing decision process?
6. What is selective exposure and what effect does it have on consumer buying?
7. How do marketers attempt to shape consumers' learning?

8. Why are marketers concerned about consumer attitudes?
9. How do roles affect an individual's buying behaviour?
10. Describe reference groups. How do they influence buying behaviour? Name some of your own reference groups.
11. In what ways does social class affect a person's purchase decisions?
12. What is culture? How does it affect a person's buying behaviour?
13. Describe the sub-cultures to which you belong. Identify buying behaviour that is unique to your sub-culture.
14. What is the impact of post-purchase evaluation on future buying decisions?

Recommended Readings

G. R. Foxall and R. E. Goldsmith, *Consumer Psychology for Marketing* (London and New York: Routledge, 1994).

J. O'Shaughnessy, *Explaining Buyer Behaviour* (New York: Oxford University Press, 1992).

G. R. Foxall, *Consumers in Context* (London and New York: Routledge, 1996).

H. Assael, *Consumer Behaviour and Marketing Action* (Boston: PWS-Kent, 1992).

J. F. Engel, R. D. Blackwell and P. W. Miniard, *Consumer Behaviour* (Fort Worth: West, 1995).

Cases

4.1   IKEA: Stylish Home Furnishings at Affordable Prices

Swedish company IKEA is a mass market producer of cheap and stylish home furnishings that appear to transcend national boundaries. The company was founded in 1943 by Ingvar Kamprad, a small town handyman from southern Sweden, who devised the company name by combining his initials with the first initials of his farm (Elmtaryd) and the parish (Agunnaryd) where he was raised. Today, IKEA's business mission is clear. In the words of the company's founder, "We shall offer a wide range of furnishing items of good design and function, at prices so low that the majority of people can afford to buy them".

Since expanding internationally in 1973, IKEA's incremental growth approach to spreading into overseas markets has continued. Today the company is the world's largest retailer. Now located in more than twenty-five countries, with over 120 outlets, the company almost tripled its turnover worldwide between 1984 and 1990. Offering affordable and varied furniture is central to IKEA's strategy. The company maintains its cost advantages by doing what it does best and concentrates on its core business and on the adoption of a long term strategy.

IKEA's ability to maintain its success across so many markets is impressive. Some studies suggest that one possible reason for this success is that when prices are very competitive, cultural barriers become smaller and it becomes easier to reach a larger percentage of the total furniture buying population. To maintain its low cost base, the company needs to shift volume, which it does by selling broadly the same range of stylish, flat packed Swedish products in all of its stores worldwide.

Price is not the only reason for IKEA's success. In the design of its stores and products, IKEA has done much to appeal to consumers' underlying reasons for buying. The company understands that shopping is a purposeful activity: people buy in order to make their lives richer. In IKEA's case, the challenge has been to make the apparent essence of a Swedish lifestyle—beautiful homes and high quality living—available at affordable prices. IKEA has also used the opportunity to innovate where it can. For example, the retailer recently opened its first New York outlet, a 7,400 square foot scaled down version of its usual 200,000 square foot stores. The "boutique-style" outlet is essentially a marketing vehicle for the company. Known as the Marketing Outpost, the shop aims to concentrate on only one product at a time. Every eight to twelve weeks IKEA will close the store for a complete refit and transformation.

Consumer interest in IKEA has revived the flagging fortunes of furniture/retailers. In areas where new IKEA stores have opened, the company's lively approach has led to an increase in the time spent shopping for home related products. Research also suggests that the proportion of their income that consumers are prepared to spend on these products is increasing. IKEA therefore believes it is competing with purchases of new cars and holidays—anything that claims the disposable income in the consumers' pocket—not just from other furniture retailers.

Although the company does not deliberately use demographic and psychographic variables to segment its customer base, IKEA products seem to appeal particularly to people in their twenties and thirties. In order to expand the product line further into other life cycle stages, the company is trying to grow with its customers by adopting a policy of offering products that cater to families with teenage children and those whose children have left home.

While IKEA recognises that consumers shop to improve their lives, the company also acknowledges their practical needs. People are much more likely to visit retail outlets that are conveniently located and where the shopping experience is fun. IKEA meets these important needs by locating its stores close to motorways and major trunk roads and by offering extensive parking, child care, toilet and restaurant facilities. A full range of furnishings is presented in real room settings that combine expensive, high risk purchases such as living room suites and carpets with cheaper, lower involvement items such as pictures, ornaments and lampshades.

SOURCES: Jennifer Pellet, "IKEA takes Manhattan!", *Discount Merchandiser*, October 1995; "IKEA", *Retail Business—Retail Trade Reviews*, 33, March 1995; Peter Wingard, "A study of six Swedish firms' approach to marketing", Warwick Business School MBA Programme, 1991; S. Redmond, "Home truths", *Marketing*, 7 April 1988; J. Bamford and A. Dunlap Smith, "Why competitors shop for ideas at IKEA", *Business Week*, 9 October 1989; P. Corwin, "The Vikings are back—with furniture", *Discount Merchandiser*, 27 (4), April 1987; B. Saporito, "IKEA's got 'em lining up", *Fortune*, 123 (5), 11 March 1991; J. Reynolds, "IKEA: a competitive company with style", *Retail and Distribution Management*, 16 (3), 1988; "Report on the UK Furniture Market", *Key Note*, 1989.

Questions for Discussion

1. How do families go about purchasing a new item of furniture? Who influences and who is involved in the buying decision?
2. What factors influence the way in which a newly married couple buy furniture?
3. How important is price to IKEA because of its position as a retailer of home furnishings?

4.2 European White Goods Manufacturers Tune In to Customer Expectations

European manufacturers of white goods—washing machines, dishwashers, fridges and freezers—need to cater to many cultural and regional variations across the markets they serve. In the UK, consumer preference for front loading washing machines results in a product quite different from the top loading French equivalent. But not all variations are caused by differing consumer preferences. The warm, sunny climate in Italy also has an effect on product features. Here, much slower spin speeds are required by the clothes washing public than in Germany, where the climate is much colder and wetter. With the increasing use of electric tumble dryers, it is not clear for how long this difference will be significant.

Meanwhile, also in Germany, the powerful environmental movement is having an impact on the products offered to the consumer. For example, Freon gas in fridges and freezers has already been outlawed, and a move towards washing machines that use less water seems inevitable.

In 1995 Electrolux, Whirlpool Europe BV (WEBV) and Bosch-Siemens, three of Europe's top appliance manufacturers, signalled their intention to increase their pursuit of global expansion. The biggest player, Electrolux, with around 22 per cent market share (by retail value), aims to use one global brand and three pan-European brands to seg-ment its geographic market. Second placed Bosch-Siemens, with 14 per cent market share, sees future globalisation opportunities in markets in eastern Europe, China, South America and the US. Meanwhile WEBV, which serves its share of the European appliance market through 19 sales companies in 19 countries, aims to use the findings of extensive market research to identify and gear its marketing to the distinct needs of different segments. With a clearly stated intention to become the world's largest appliance manufacturer, Whirlpool will need to keep catering to regional differences in customer requirements.

Local and cultural differences have an important impact on the marketing programmes companies develop. WEBV has adopted an unusual approach in its attempts to implement its marketing and advertising effort in Europe. In 1989 WEBV launched the first pan-European advertising campaign. This approach has been developed in the company's current "Fantastic World" campaign, which is unusual in its product specific focus. Most manufacturers communicate at a local level, because they believe this helps to overcome differences in the way advertising messages are interpreted. Some also argue that traditional, American style advertising is unpopular in certain European markets.

Although there has been much discussion about possible convergence of product offerings in European markets, it is not yet clear how much regional differences can or will be ignored. For key industry players the challenge is to establish the values, opinions, attitudes, behaviour and expectations of consumers in order to identify similarities and differences between them.

Armed with a better understanding of the needs of key customer groups across Europe, manufacturers should be better able to match consumer requirements and make comparisons across national boundaries. Although the potential of merged marketing programmes is still unknown, opportunities exist to rationalise the way customers are grouped, thus reducing marketing costs.

SOURCES: Peter Wingard, "A study of six Swedish firms' approach to marketing", Warwick Business School MBA Programme, 1991; S. Whelan, "Scharp vision", *Marketing*, 26 January 1989, p. 29; T. A. Stewart, "A heartland industry takes on the world", *Fortune*, 121 (6), 12 March 1990, pp. 110–112; J. Kapstein, "The fast spinning machine that blew a gasket", *Business Week*, 10 September 1990, pp. 50–52; C. Harris, "Women of Europe put Whirlpool in a spin", *Financial Times*, 30 October 1990; Joe Jancsurak, "Group sales: Channel focused", *Appliance Manufacturer*, 43 (2), February 1995; "Holistic strategy pays off", *Appliance Manufacturer*, 43 (2), February 1995; "Marketing: phase 2", *Appliance Manufacturer*, 43 (2), February 1995; "Big plans for Europe's big three", *Appliance Manufacturer*, 43 (4), April 1995; James Stevens, "Electrolux market-share leader by units in Europe", *Appliance Manufacturer*, 42 (7), July 1994.

Questions for Discussion

1. What role do cultural and regional variations play in the purchase of white goods?
2. How might manufacturers of white goods cater for the regional variations that they encounter? Should the manufacturers try to ignore these variations?
3. What are the likely advantages and disadvantages of adopting a pan-European advertising campaign in this situation? Would you expect Whirlpool's strategy to be successful in the long term?

ORGANISATIONAL MARKETS AND BUYING BEHAVIOUR

"Business marketing is not simply about making sales. It's the task of establishing, developing and managing a portfolio of customer relationships."

David Ford
University of Bath

OBJECTIVES

- To become familiar with the various types of organisational markets

- To identify the major characteristics of organisational buyers and transactions

- To understand several attributes of organisational demand

- To become familiar with the major components of a buying centre

- To understand relationship marketing and exchanges between industrial buyers and sellers

- To understand the stages of the organisational buying decision process and the factors that affect this process

- To learn how to select and analyse business-to-business target markets

Despite difficult times in the roller bearings market, Swedish company Svenska Kullagerfabriken (SKF) is the world leader in this business and continues to enjoy success. Since 1990, bearings sales worldwide have diminished by more than 20 per cent. Demand for certain types of bearings is down by 50 per cent. Yet SKF has recently been awarded the project for the Tokyo Bay Tunnel, despite heavy competition from Japanese manufacturers.

SKF was founded in 1907 following the invention by its founder, Sven Wingquist, of a single groove ball-bearing. This product went on to form the basis of the organisation's success. Today, SKF's massive 20 per cent share of the world market comes from the efforts of 45,000 employees in

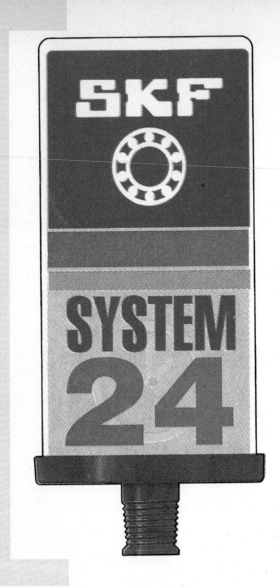

meeting the needs of a diverse customer base, the company is keen to maintain superior standards of quality and customer service across all areas of its business. These aspects form the central thrust of SKF's differential advantage and, therefore, the focus of the company's marketing activity.

Product quality standards are maintained through a programme of continual product checks, in both the research and development laboratories and manufacturing facilities. Although bearings may appear to be quite simple products, they are a critical component in many types of machine. Often the bearings must operate under extreme temperature conditions or cope with severe vibration. The dangers of bearing fatigue have led SKF to investigate alternative materials and develop new types of bearings. The company is proud of its investment in research and development, which is close to 2 per cent of sales. According to company literature, "If one were to magnify a ball from a standard bearing up to the size of Mount Everest, the largest irregularity would measure no more than 50 millimetres [2 inches]."

SKF has no intention of competing on the basis of price. The emphasis on product quality and suitability, coupled with efficient delivery and after sales service, means that price is not usually the customers' primary concern. SKF has invested considerable resources in its distribution network. Having its own subsidiaries in each country allows the organisation to keep control of the sales operation and maintain its high standards. It caters for the needs of the different national markets with promotional material in 17 languages and a carefully planned global promotion that takes into account the full range of customer cultures. In designing its marketing programmes, SKF has put the needs and wants of its diverse customer base at the forefront. ∎

130 different countries. Altogether, SKF has more than 100 factories and 8,000 distributors. The company has extended its product base, through acquisitions, to include, among others, machine tools, cutting tools, seals, aircraft components and textile machinery parts. The company's customer driven objectives aim to identify customer problems, devise solutions, provide the right product and offer appropriate service support.

SKF adopts a multi-level segmentation of the market, dividing customers first according to industry type and then by product application. In

SOURCES: Peter Wingard, Warwick Business School MBA Programme, 1990–91; *SKF Company Reports*, 1990, 1991; *The World of SKF*, SKF company literature, publication 3909 E, 1988; N. Webb, "The bearing industry: adding it all up", *Purchasing World*, vol. 34, issue 6, 1990, pp. 48–50; J. Arbrose, "SKF's strategy to counter the Japanese", *International Management* (UK), vol. 41, issue 6, pp. 40–47; Alan Shipman, "Sweden's high roller", *International Management*, v51.49, issue 2, pp. 22–24.

The Swedish company Svenska Kullagerfabriken supplies organisational or industrial markets with high quality roller bearings. An **organisational or industrial market** is defined as consisting of individuals or groups that purchase a specific type of product for re-sale, for use in making other products or for use in daily operations. To achieve its position in the world market, SKF has had to adapt its product and marketing offering to suit a wide ranging customer base. This has involved building an understanding of the characteristics of the companies that buy its products and an appreciation of their buyer behaviour.

This chapter looks more closely at organisational markets and organisational buying decision processes. In addition, it considers how such markets can be analysed and industrial targets identified. The first section discusses the various kinds of organisational markets and the types of buyers that make up these markets. The next section explores several dimensions of organisational buying, such as the characteristics of the transactions, the attributes and concerns of the buyers, the methods of buying and the distinctive features of the demand for products sold to organisational purchasers. The chapter then examines organisational buying decisions by considering how they are arrived at and who makes the purchases. The final section examines the selection and analysis of industrial markets.

●●●●●●●●●●●●●●●●●●●●

Types of Organisational Markets

There are four kinds of organisational, or industrial, markets: producers, resellers, governments and institutions (see also Chapter 7). The following section describes the characteristics of the customers that make up these markets. Table 5.1 shows the employment patterns in these markets across Europe.

Producer Markets

Individuals and business organisations that purchase products for the purpose of making a profit by using them to produce other products or by using them in their own operations are classified as **producer markets**. Producer markets include buyers of raw materials and semi-finished and finished items used to produce other products. For example, a manufacturer buys raw materials and component parts to use directly in the production of its products. Grocers and supermarkets are producer markets for numerous support products, such as paper and plastic bags, displays, scanners and floor care products. Farmers are producer markets for farm machinery, fertiliser, seed and livestock. Figure 5.1 illustrates a product aimed at farmers. Producer markets cover a broad array of industries, ranging from agriculture, forestry, fisheries and mining to construction, transport, communications and public utilities. The number of business units in European producer markets is enormous.

Manufacturers tend to be geographically concentrated. This concentration occurs in Europe too, with heavy industry centred on the Ruhr Valley in Germany and on the Midlands and North West in the UK. Sometimes an industrial marketer may be able to serve customers more efficiently as a result. Within certain areas, production in just a few industries may account for a sizeable proportion of total industrial output.

Sector

Sector	Austria	Belgium	Denmark	Finland	France	Germany	Greece	Ireland	Italy	Netherlands	Norway	Portugal	Spain	Sweden	Switzerland
Agriculture, forestry	7.1	2.9	5.2	8.6	5.1	3.0	21.3	10.5	7.5	4.0	5.3	11.3	10.1	3.4	5.6
Mining, quarrying	0.4	0.3	0.1	0.2	0.3	0.3	0.5	0.4	0.5	0.1	1.2	0.5	0.5	0.2	0.1
Manufacturing	26.0	20.7	19.8	19.5	19.6	29.1	15.6	16.3	22.9	17.8	14.9	23.8	20.3	18.3	23.6
Electricity, gas, water	1.1	0.8	0.6	1.1	0.9	1.2	1.1	0.9	1.1	0.7	1.1	0.7	0.7	0.8	0.6
Construction	8.1	7.1	5.8	6.2	6.8	6.5	7.0	5.2	8.5	6.0	5.8	8.1	9.2	5.6	8.9
Wholesale, retail, restaurants, hotels	18.8	17.9	15.8	14.8	16.9	17.1	21.3	18.0	21.7	17.3	17.1	19.4	21.0	14.5	20.3
Transport, storage and communications	6.6	6.9	7.2	7.8	6.4	5.8	6.7	5.1	5.7	6.3	8.1	4.7	5.9	6.9	6.3
Finance, insurance and business services	7.4	9.9	10.1	8.9	10.4	9.0	5.9	17.8	7.6	10.8	7.9	6.9	6.5	9.6	11.0
Community, social and personal services	23.9	33.0	34.6	32.8	33.5	28.0	20.6	4.8	24.5	34.7	38.5	24.6	25.7	40.5	23.6
Not defined	0.6	0.5	0.7	0.2	—	—	—	—	—	2.3	0.1	—	—	0.1	—

SOURCE: From *European Marketing Pocket Book*, 1996, p.14. Reprinted by permission of NTC Publications, Ltd.

Table 5.1 Percentage of the workforce employed in different sectors across Europe, 1993

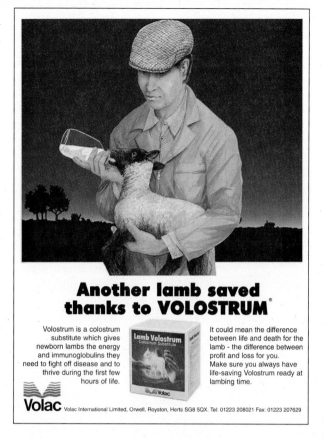
Reseller Markets

Reseller markets Intermediaries, such as wholesalers and retailers, who buy finished goods and re-sell them to make a profit

Wholesalers Intermediaries who purchase products for resale to retailers, other wholesalers and producers, governments and institutions

Retailers Intermediaries that purchase products and re-sell them to final consumers

Reseller markets consist of intermediaries, such as wholesalers and retailers, who buy finished goods and re-sell them to make a profit. (These intermediaries are discussed in Chapters 13 and 14.) Other than making minor alterations, resellers do not change the physical characteristics of the products they handle. With the exception of items that producers sell directly to consumers, all products sold to consumer markets are first sold to reseller markets.

Wholesalers purchase products for resale to retailers, to other wholesalers and to producers, governments and institutions. Although some highly technical products are sold directly to end users, many products are sold through wholesalers, who in turn sell products to other firms in the distribution system. Thus wholesalers are very important in helping to get a producer's product to customers. Wholesalers often carry many products, perhaps as many as 250,000 items. From the reseller's point of view, having access to such an array of products from a single source makes it much simpler to buy a variety of items. When inventories are vast, the re-ordering of products is normally automated and the wholesaler's initial purchase decisions are made by professional buyers and buying committees.

Retailers purchase products and re-sell them to final consumers. Some retailers carry a large number of items. Chemists, for example, may stock up to 12,000 items, and some supermarkets may handle as many as 20,000 different products. In small, family owned retail stores, the owner frequently makes purchasing decisions. Large department stores have one or more employees in each department who are responsible for buying products for that department. As for chain stores, a buyer or buying committee in the central office frequently decides whether a product will be made available for selection by store managers. For most products, however, local store managers make the actual buying decisions for a particular store.

When making purchase decisions, resellers consider several factors. They evaluate the level of demand for a product to determine in what quantity and at what prices it can be re-sold. They assess the amount of space required to handle a product relative to its potential profit. Sometimes resellers will put a product on trial for a fixed period, allowing them to judge customers' reactions and to make better informed decisions about shelf space and positions as a result. Retailers, for example, sometimes evaluate products on the basis of sales per square metre of selling area. Since customers often depend on a reseller to have a product when they need it, a reseller typically evaluates a supplier's ability to provide adequate quantities when and where wanted. Resellers also take into account the ease of placing orders and the availability of technical assistance and training programmes from the producer. More broadly, when resellers consider buying a product not previously carried, they try to determine whether the product competes with or complements products the firm is currently handling. These types of concerns distinguish reseller markets from other markets. Sometimes resellers will start stocking a new line of products in response to specific requests from customers. Marketers dealing with reseller markets must recognise these needs and be able to serve them.

Government Markets

Government markets
Departments that buy goods and services to support their internal operations and to provide the public with education, water, energy, national defence, road systems and health care

National and local governments make up **government markets**. They spend billions of pounds annually for a variety of goods and services to support their internal operations and to provide the public with education, water, energy, national defence, road systems and health care. Table 5.2 shows UK central government expenditure on goods and services from 1981 to 1994. In Europe, the amount spent by local governments varies from country to country depending on the level and cost of services provided. As a result of the European single market, the services provided by different governments may eventually become standardised.

The types and quantities of products bought by government markets reflect social demands on various government agencies. As the public's needs for government services change, so do the government markets' demands for products. Because government agencies spend public funds to buy the products they need to provide services, they are accountable to the public. This accountability is responsible for their relatively complex set of buying procedures. Some firms, unwilling to deal with so much red tape, do not even try to sell to government buyers. However, many marketers have learned to deal efficiently with government procedures and do not find them a stumbling block. For certain companies, such as British Aerospace, and for certain products, such as defence related items, the government may be one of only a few customers.

Governments usually make their purchases through bids or negotiated contracts. To make a sale under the bid system, a firm must apply and receive approval to be placed on a list of qualified bidders. When a government unit wants to buy, it sends out a detailed description of the products to these qualified bidders. Businesses that wish to sell such products then submit bids. The government unit is usually required to accept the lowest bid. When buying non-standard or highly complex products, a government unit often uses a negotiated contract. Under this procedure, the government unit selects only a few firms, negotiates specifications and terms, and eventually awards the contract to one of the negotiating firms. Most large defence contracts held by such companies as British Aerospace, GEC and Ferranti are reached through negotiated contracts.

	Percentages					
	1981	**1986**	**1991**	**1992**	**1993**	**1994**
Social security	27	31	32	33	34	34
Health	11	12	14	14	13	14
Education	12	12	13	13	12	13
Defence	11	12	10	10	9	8
Public order and safety	4	4	6	5	5	5
General public services	4	4	5	5	4	4
Housing and community amenities	6	5	4	4	4	4
Transport and communication	4	2	3	3	2	2
Recreational and cultural affairs	1	2	2	2	2	2
Agriculture, forestry and fishing	1	1	1	1	2	1
Other expenditure	19	16	11	11	12	13
All expenditure (=100%) (£ billion in real terms[1])	224.6	241.0	250.9	268.1	278.3	285.7

[1]Adjusted to 1994 prices using the GDP market prices deflator.
SOURCE: Central Statistical Office, *Social Trends: 1996 Edition*. British Crown Copyright 1995. Reproduced by permission of the Controller of HMSO and of the Office for National Statistics.

Table 5.2   UK central government expenditure: by function

Although government markets have complicated requirements, they can also be very lucrative. When government departments or health care providers modernise obsolete computer systems, for example, successful bidders can make many millions of pounds during the life of a contract, which may last for five years or more. Some firms have established separate departments to facilitate marketing to government units, while others specialise entirely in this area.

Institutional Markets

Institutional markets
Organisations with charitable, educational, community or other non-business goals

Organisations with charitable, educational, community or other non-business goals constitute **institutional markets**. Members of institutional markets include libraries, museums, universities, charitable organisations and some churches and hospitals. Institutions purchase millions of pounds' worth of products annually to provide goods, services and ideas to club members, congregations, students and others. For example, a community theatre group must buy materials for costumes and scenery; pay rent, fuel and water bills; provide refreshments for its members; and pay to produce programmes and to advertise its productions. Because such institutions often have different goals and fewer resources than other types of organisations, marketers may use special marketing activities to serve these markets.

• • • • • • • • • • • • • • • • • • •

Dimensions of Organisational Buying

Having clarified the different types of organisational customers, the next step is to consider the dimensions of organisational buying. After first examining several characteristics of organisational transactions, this section then discusses various attributes of organisational buyers and some of their primary concerns when making purchase decisions. Next it looks at methods of organisational buying and the major types of purchases organisations make. The section concludes with a discussion of how the demand for industrial products differs from the demand for consumer products.

Characteristics of Organisational Transactions

Although the marketing concept is equally applicable to organisational and consumer markets, there are several fundamental differences between the transactions that occur in each. Organisational buyers tend to order in much larger quantities than do individual consumers. Suppliers must often sell their products in large quantities to make profits; consequently, they prefer not to sell to customers who place small orders.

Generally, organisational purchases are negotiated less frequently than consumer sales. Some purchases involve expensive items, such as machinery or office equipment, that are used for a number of years. Other products, such as raw materials and component items, are used continuously in production and may have to be supplied frequently. However, the contract regarding the terms of sale of these items is likely to be a long term agreement, requiring periodic negotiations.

Although negotiations in organisational sales are less frequent than in consumer sales, they may take much longer. Purchasing decisions are often made by a committee; orders are frequently large, expensive and complex; and products may be custom built. There is a good chance that several people or departments in the purchasing organisation will be involved. One department might express a need for a product; a second department might develop its specifications; a third might stipulate the maximum amount to be spent; and a fourth might actually place the order. This approach allows individuals with relevant expertise to be incorporated into the process when required.

Reciprocity An arrangement in which two organisations agree to buy from each other

One practice unique to organisational sales is **reciprocity,** an arrangement in which two organisations agree to buy from each other. In some countries, reciprocal agreements that threaten competition are illegal and action may be taken to stop anti-competitive reciprocal practices. Nonetheless, it is reasonable to believe that a certain amount of reciprocal dealing occurs among small businesses and, to a lesser extent, among larger companies as well. Reciprocity can create a problem because coercive measures may be used to enforce it. Also, because reciprocity influences purchasing agents to deal only with certain suppliers, it can lower morale among agents and lead to less than optimal purchases.[1]

Attributes of Organisational Buyers

Organisational buyers are usually thought of as being different from consumer buyers in their purchasing behaviour because they are better informed about the products they purchase. To make purchasing decisions that fulfil an organisation's needs, organisational buyers demand detailed information about a product's functional features and technical specifications.

Organisational buyers, however, also have personal goals that may influence their buying behaviour. Most organisational buyers seek the psychological satisfaction that comes with promotion and financial rewards. In general, agents are most likely to achieve these personal goals when they consistently exhibit rational organisational buying behaviour and are thus performing their jobs in ways that help their firms achieve their organisational objectives. Suppose, though, that an organisational buyer develops a close friendship with a certain supplier. If the buyer values the friendship more than organisational promotion or financial rewards, he or she may behave irrationally from the firm's point of view. Dealing exclusively with that supplier regardless of better prices, quality or service from competitors may indicate an unhealthy or unethical alliance between the buyer and seller. Companies have different ways of dealing with such problems. Some require more than one person to be involved in buying products, while others periodically review their use of suppliers.

Primary Concerns of Organisational Buyers

When they make purchasing decisions, organisational customers take into account a variety of factors. Among their chief considerations are quality, delivery, service and price.[2] For example, in Figure 5.2 quality is stressed by the construction engineers. Product range and innovation may also be significant considerations.

Most organisational customers try to achieve and maintain a specific level of quality in the products they offer to their target markets. To accomplish this goal, they often buy their products on the basis of a set of expressed characteristics, commonly called *specifications*. These allow an organisational buyer to evaluate the quality of the products being considered according to a given list of features and thus to determine whether or not they meet the organisation's needs.

Meeting specifications is extremely important to organisational customers. If a product fails to meet specifications and malfunctions for the ultimate consumer, that product's supplier may be dropped and an alternative sought. On the other

Figure 5.2 Primary concerns of organisational buyers. In this instance, the construction engineers who built the bridge depended on the quality of the concrete supplied.

Source: Courtesy of Beton.

hand, an organisational buyer is usually cautious about buying products that exceed specifications, because such products often cost more and thus increase the organisation's production costs. Suppliers therefore need to design their products carefully to come as close as possible to their customers' specifications without incurring any unnecessary extras.

Organisational buyers also value service. The services offered by suppliers directly and indirectly influence organisational customers' costs, sales and profits. When tangible goods are the same or quite similar—as is true in the case of most raw materials—they may have the same specifications and be sold at the same price in the same kind of containers. Under such conditions, the mix of services an organisational marketer provides to its customers represents its greatest opportunity to gain a competitive advantage.

Among the most commonly expected services are market information, inventory maintenance, on-time delivery, warranty back-up repair services and credit facilities. Specific services vary in importance, however, and the mix of services companies need is also affected by environmental conditions.

Organisational buyers in general are likely to need technical product information, data regarding demand, information about general economic conditions or supply and delivery information. For example, when technology is changing rapidly, forcing companies to change their production machinery, the demand for consultancy support services and warranty assurances will be especially high. It is critical for suppliers to maintain an adequate inventory in order to keep products accessible when an organisational buyer needs them and to reduce the buyer's inventory requirements and costs. Furthermore, reliable, on-time delivery by suppliers is vital because it saves the organisational customers money, enabling them to carry less inventory. Organisational purchasers of machinery are especially concerned about adequate warranties. They are also keen to obtain repair services and replacement parts quickly, because equipment that cannot be used is costly.

Suppliers can also give extra value to organisational buyers by offering credit. Credit helps to improve an organisational customer's cash flow, reduces the peaks and troughs of capital requirements and thus lowers the firm's cost of capital. Although no single supplier can provide every possible service to its organisational customers, a marketing orientated supplier will try to create a service mix that satisfies the target market.

Providing service has become even more critical for organisational marketers because customer expectations of service have broadened. For instance, communication channels that allow customers to ask questions, complain, submit orders and trace shipments are indispensable. Organisational marketers also need to strive for uniformity of service, simplicity, truthfulness and accuracy; to develop customer service objectives; and to monitor or audit their customer service programmes. Firms can monitor the quality of their service by formally surveying customers or calling on them informally to ask questions about the service they have received. Marketers with a strong customer service programme reap a reward: their customers keep coming back long after the first sale.[3] For their programme to succeed, however, they must conduct research to determine customers' expectations in regard to product quality and service.[4] With customer expectations increasing, it is becoming more difficult for companies to achieve a differential advantage in these areas.[5] Marketing Insight 5.1 explains one company's efforts to stay in touch with customer expectations.

Price matters greatly to an organisational customer because it influences operating costs and costs of goods sold, and these costs affect the customer's selling price and profit margin. When purchasing major equipment, an industrial buyer views the price as the amount of investment necessary to obtain a certain level of return or savings. Thus an organisational purchaser is likely to compare the price of a machine with the value of the benefits that the machine will yield. Caterpillar lost market share to foreign competitors because its prices were too high. An organisational buyer does not compare alternative products by price alone, though; other factors, such as product quality and supplier services, are also major elements in the purchase decision. For example, one study found that in the buying decision process for mainframe computer software operating systems, intangible attributes, such as the seller's credibility and understanding of the buyer's needs, were very important in the buyers' decision process.[6]

Methods of Organisational Buying

Although no two organisational buyers go about their jobs in the same way, most use one or more of the following purchase methods: *description, inspection, sampling* or *negotiation*. When the products being purchased are commonly standardised according to certain characteristics (such as size, shape, weight and colour) and graded using such standards, an organisational buyer may be able to purchase simply by describing or specifying quantity, grade and other attributes. Agricultural produce often falls into this category. In some cases a buyer may specify a particular brand or its equivalent when describing the desired product. Purchases on the basis of description are especially common between a buyer and seller who have established an ongoing relationship built on trust.

Certain products, such as large industrial machinery, used vehicles and buildings, have unique characteristics and are likely to vary in condition. For example, a factory unit that is for sale may need to be redecorated and have a damp proof course inserted. Consequently, organisational buyers of such products must base their purchase decisions on inspection.

In buying based on sampling, a sample of the product is taken from the lot and evaluated. It is assumed that the characteristics of this sample represent the entire lot. This method is appropriate when the product is homogeneous—for instance, disposable pens—and examination of the entire lot is not physically or economically feasible.

Some industrial purchasing relies on negotiated contracts. In certain instances, an organisational buyer describes exactly what is needed and then asks sellers to submit bids. The buyer may take the most attractive bids and negotiate with those suppliers. In other cases, the buyer may not be able to identify specifically what is to be purchased but can provide only a general description—as might be the case for a special piece of custom made equipment. A buyer and seller might negotiate a contract that specifies a base price and contains provisions for the payment of additional costs and fees. These contracts are most likely to be used for one off projects, such as buildings and capital equipment.

Types of Organisational Purchases

New task purchase An organisation's initial purchase of an item to be used to perform a new job or to solve a new problem

Most organisational purchases are one of three types: new task purchase, modified re-buy purchase or straight re-buy purchase. The type of purchase affects the number of individuals involved and the length of the buying process. In a **new task purchase,** an organisation makes an initial purchase of an item to be used to perform a new job or to solve a new problem. A new task purchase may take a long time because it may require the development of product specifications, supplier specifications and procedures for future purchases. To make the initial purchase, the organisational buyer usually needs a good deal of information. A new task purchase is important to a supplier, for if the organisational buyer is satisfied with the product, the supplier may be able to sell the buyer large quantities of the product over a period of years.

Asea Brown Boveri Group: Combining Global Orientation and Local Flexibility

Swiss-Swedish international electrical engineering group Asea Brown Boveri Group (ABB) provides electrical systems and equipment worldwide to customers in the electrical power generation, transmission, industrial, environmental control and mass transit markets. Formed in 1987 from a merger between Asea from Sweden and Brown Boveri from Switzerland, the company's position as world leader in many of its key markets led to a restructuring of the global power industry.

At the centre of ABB's success is its ability to globalise engineering and production, while maintaining a local presence in the countries in which it operates. ABB does this by operating a matrix structure to its business. One dimension of the matrix consists of ABB's global network, where product strategy and sales development are the responsibility of business area managers around the world. Around 500 of ABB's managers are global managers, experts on maintaining the company's advantages globally. The second dimension consists of traditionally run national companies that are well established in their home markets. The role of the country managers is to ensure that responsiveness is maintained at the local level.

The company already has around 25,000 employees in a wide range of locations, and it is not afraid to enter markets other companies may not regard as particularly politically or economically stable. For example, ABB now has a presence in the Czech Republic, Estonia, Hungary, Kazakhstan, Latvia, Poland, Romania, Russia and Ukraine. All in all, the company now controls 58 companies in 16 eastern European countries. Such investment has been at a price, with profits falling during 1993. However, the company believes that investment in eastern Europe is an appropriate long term strategy.

To keep its diverse customer base satisfied, ABB has implemented its own mix of total quality management, just-in-time management and time-based management philosophies. The initiative aims to put the customer first and to offer higher standards of quality, delivery and customer support. Staff rotation and teamwork are encouraged; and sales and marketing, product development and production departments work together in functional units.

With interests in so many national markets, ABB is susceptible to a variety of important changes in environmental conditions. Most significant, the European power equipment industry is becoming increasingly oligopolistic as a result of mergers and acquisitions. Concern for the environment is also affecting ABB's market. As it moves forward into the late 1990s, the company seeks to capitalise on its experience in environmentally friendly technology by making products for use in "green" applications. For example, the company has been involved in a joint project with Volvo and the Royal Institute of Technology in Stockholm to create an environmental concept car. The Volvo ECC, as it is called, uses a gas turbine for highway driving and a rechargeable battery for electrically powered city driving. This project fits in with the company's relationship building philosophy, which helps it stay in touch with market needs by understanding and responding to changes in the environment in which it operates.

SOURCES: Paul Hofheinz, "Yes, you can win in eastern Europe", *Fortune*, 16 May 1994, pp. 110–112; John McClenahen, "Percy Barnevik ... and the ABBs of competition", *Industry Week*, 6 June 1994, pp. 20–24; "A local touch in global sales", *Business Europe*, 1 May 1995; Michael Maccoby, "Human engineering leads to operating principles for global management", *Research-Technology Management*, 38 (5), September/October 1995; Michael Valenti, "Hybrid car promises high performance and low emissions", *Mechanical Engineering*, 116 (7), July 1994, pp. 46–49; Peter Wingard, "A study of six Swedish firms' approach to marketing", *Warwick Business School MBA Programme*, 1991; "Asea Brown Boveri: power play", *The Economist*, 28 May 1988; W. Taylor, "The logic of global business: an interview with ABB's Percy Barnevik", *Harvard Business Review*, March–April 1991.

Modified re-buy purchase
A new task purchase that is
changed when it is re-ordered

In a **modified re-buy purchase,** a new task purchase is changed the second or third time it is ordered, or the requirements associated with a straight re-buy purchase are modified. For example, an organisational buyer might seek faster delivery, lower prices or a different quality of product specifications. When modified re-buying occurs, regular suppliers may become more competitive to keep the account. Competing suppliers may have the opportunity to obtain the business.

Straight re-buy purchase
One that occurs when a buyer
purchases the same products
again routinely under approximately the same terms of sale

A **straight re-buy purchase** occurs when a buyer purchases the same products again routinely under approximately the same terms of sale. For example, when re-ordering photocopying paper, a buyer requires little additional information and can usually place the order relatively quickly. The buyer tends to use familiar suppliers that have provided satisfactory service and products in the past. These suppliers try to set up automatic re-ordering systems to make re-ordering easy and convenient for organisational buyers and may even monitor the organisational buyer's inventory to indicate to the buyer what needs to be ordered.

Demand for Industrial Products

Products sold to organisational customers are called industrial products and, consequently, the demand for these products is called industrial demand. Unlike consumer demand, industrial demand is (1) derived, (2) inelastic, (3) joint and (4) more fluctuating. In discussing each of these characteristics, it is important to remember that the demand for different types of industrial products varies.

Derived Demand   As organisational customers, especially producers, buy products to be used directly or indirectly in the production of goods and services to satisfy consumers' needs, the demand for industrial products derives from the demand for consumer products; it is therefore called **derived demand.** For example, the demand for microwave oven turntables derives from the demand for microwave ovens. In the long run, no industrial demand is totally unrelated to consumer demand.

Derived demand   A name
given to the demand for industrial
products because it derives from
the demand for consumer
products

The derived nature of industrial demand usually occurs at a number of levels. For instance, consumers today are more concerned with good health and nutrition than ever before and as a result are purchasing food products containing less cholesterol, saturated fat, sugar and salt. When some consumers stopped buying high cholesterol cooking fats and margarine, the demand for equipment used in manufacturing these products also dropped. Thus factors influencing consumer buying of various food products ultimately affected food processors, equipment manufacturers, suppliers of raw materials and even fast food restaurants, which have had to switch to using lower cholesterol oils for frying. Changes in derived demand result from a chain reaction. When consumer demand for a product changes, a wave is set in motion that affects demand for all of the items involved in the production of that consumer product.

Inelastic Demand   The demand for many industrial products at the industry level is **inelastic demand,** that is, a price increase or decrease will not significantly alter demand for the item. (The concept of price elasticity of demand is discussed further in Chapter 20.) Because many industrial products contain a number of parts, price increases that affect only one or two parts of the product may yield only a slightly higher per unit production cost. Of course, when a sizeable price increase for a component represents a large proportion of the total product's cost, demand may become more elastic, because the component price increase will cause the price at the consumer level to rise sharply. For example, if manufacturers of

Inelastic demand   A condition in which a price increase or
decrease will not significantly
alter demand for an item

aircraft engines substantially increase the price of these engines, forcing Boeing in turn to raise the prices of its aircraft, the demand for aircraft may become more elastic as airlines reconsider whether they can afford them. An increase in the price of windscreens, however, is unlikely greatly to affect the price of the aircraft or the demand for them.

The characteristic of inelasticity applies only to industry demand for the industrial product, not to the demand curve faced by an individual firm. For example, suppose that a micro-chip manufacturer increases the price of micro-chips sold to manufacturers of personal computers, while its competitors continue to maintain their lower prices. The microchip manufacturer would probably experience reduced unit sales because most of its customers would switch to the lower priced brands. A specific organisation is vulnerable to elastic demand, even though industry demand for a particular product is inelastic.

Joint Demand   The demand for certain industrial products, especially raw materials and components, is subject to joint demand. **Joint demand** occurs when two or more items are used in combination to produce a product. For example, a firm that manufactures cork noticeboards for schools and colleges needs supplies of cork and wood to produce the item; these two products are demanded jointly. A shortage of cork will cause a drop in the production of wooden surrounds for noticeboards.

Joint demand   Demand that occurs when two or more products are used in combination to produce a product

Understanding the effects of joint demand is particularly important for a marketer selling multiple jointly demanded items. Such a marketer must realise that when a customer begins purchasing one of the jointly demanded items, a good opportunity exists for selling related products. Similarly, when customers purchase a number of jointly demanded products, the producer must exercise extreme caution to avoid shortages of any one of them, because such shortages jeopardise the marketer's sales of all the jointly demanded products. The susceptibility of producers to the shortage of a particular item is clearly illustrated when industrial action at companies producing car components results in a halt in production at major car manufacturers.

Fluctuating Demand   Because the demand for industrial products fluctuates according to consumer demand, when particular consumer products are in high demand, their producers buy large quantities of raw materials and components to ensure that they can meet long run production requirements. In addition, these producers may expand their production capacity, which entails the acquisition of new equipment and machinery, more workers, a greater need for industrial services, and more raw materials and component parts.

Conversely, a decline in the demand for certain consumer goods significantly reduces the demand for industrial products used to produce those goods. In fact, under such conditions, a marketer's sales of certain products may temporarily cease. When consumer demand is low, industrial customers cut their purchases of raw materials and components and stop buying equipment and machinery, even for replacement purposes. This trend is especially pronounced during periods of recession.

A marketer of industrial products may notice changes in demand when its customers change their inventory policies, perhaps because of expectations about future demand. For example, if several dishwasher manufacturers who buy timers from one producer increase their inventory of timers from a two week to a one month supply, the timer producer will experience a significant immediate increase in demand.

Sometimes price changes can lead to surprising temporary changes in demand. A price increase for an industrial item may initially cause organisational customers to buy more of the item because they expect the price to rise further. Similarly, demand for an industrial product may be significantly lower following a price cut as buyers wait for further price reductions. Such behaviour is often observed in companies purchasing information technology. Fluctuations in demand can be significant in industries in which price changes occur frequently.

● ● ● ● ● ● ● ● ● ● ● ● ● ● ● ● ● ● ●

Organisational Buying Decisions

Organisational (or industrial) buying behaviour The purchase behaviour of producers, resellers, government units and institutions

Organisational (or **industrial**) **buying behaviour** refers to the purchase behaviour of producers, resellers, government units and institutions. Although several of the same factors that affect consumer buying behaviour (discussed in Chapter 4) also influence organisational buying behaviour, a number of factors are unique to the latter. This section first analyses the buying centre to learn who participates in making organisational purchase decisions and then focuses on the stages of the buying decision process and the factors that affect it.

The Buying Centre

Buying centre The group of people within an organisation who are involved in making organisational purchase decisions

Most organisational purchase decisions are made by more than one person. The group of people within an organisation who are involved in making organisational purchase decisions are usually referred to as the **buying centre**. These individuals include users, influencers, buyers, deciders and gatekeepers, although one person may perform several of these roles.[7] Participants in the buying process share the goals and risks associated with their decisions.

Users are the organisation members who actually use the product being acquired. They frequently initiate the purchase process and/or generate the specifications for the purchase. After the purchase, they also evaluate the product's performance relative to the specifications. Although users do not ordinarily have sufficient power to make the final decision to buy, it is important that their views be considered. A user who is not happy with a piece of equipment may not work as efficiently as one who is. Influencers are often technical personnel, such as engineers, who help develop the specifications and evaluate alternative products. Technical personnel are especially important influencers when the products being considered involve new, advanced technology. For example, an insurance company about to change its telephone system may seek advice from a wide range of technical experts.

Buyers are responsible for selecting suppliers and actually negotiating the terms of purchase. They may also become involved in developing specifications. Buyers are sometimes called purchasing agents or purchasing managers. Their choices of suppliers and products, especially for new task purchases, are heavily influenced by individuals occupying other roles in the buying centre. For straight re-buy purchases, the buyer plays a major role in the selection of suppliers and in negotiations with them. Deciders actually choose the products and suppliers. Although buyers may be the deciders, it is not unusual for different people to occupy these roles. For routinely purchased items, buyers are commonly the deciders. However, a buyer may not be authorised to make purchases that exceed a certain monetary value, in which case higher level management personnel are the deciders. Gatekeepers, such as secretaries and technical personnel, control the flow of information to and among the persons who occupy the other roles in the buying centre. Buyers who deal directly with suppliers may also be gatekeepers because they can control the flow of information. The flow of information from supplier sales representatives to users and influencers is often controlled by personnel in the purchasing department. Unfortunately, relations between members of the buying centre at times can become strained.

The size and characteristics of an organisation's buying centres are affected by the number of its employees and its market position, the volume and types of products being purchased and the firm's overall managerial philosophy regarding exactly who should be involved in purchase decisions. A marketer attempting to sell to an organisational customer should determine who is in the buying centre, the types of decisions each individual makes and which individuals are the most influential in the decision process. Then, if it is not possible to contact all members of the buying centre, the marketer will be in a position to contact those who have the most influence.

Relationship Marketing and Managing Exchange Relationships

Relationship marketing All of the activities an organisation uses to build, maintain and develop customer relations

The relationship that exists between a supplying organisation and its customers is an important aspect of the buying process and one that deserves special consideration. In fact, marketing experts have recently become much more interested in marketing relationships in general.[8] The term **relationship marketing** has been used to express this particular development. Instead of being concerned about individual transactions between suppliers and buyers, the relationship marketing approach emphasises the importance of the whole relationship between the parties. Relationship marketing can therefore be regarded as all of the activities an organisation uses to build, maintain and develop customer relations.[9]

Put simply, relationship marketing is concerned with getting and keeping customers by ensuring that an appropriate combination of marketing, customer service and quality is provided.[10] Underlying the relationship marketing concept is the idea that the relationship between a supplying organisation and its buyers is essentially similar to the relationship between two individuals. For example, car parts manufacturer Lucas, featured in Case 5.1, has built up a relationship and shares a bond with car company Rover. This relationship is conducted over a period of time through a series of meetings, which allows each party to get to know the other, to share information, to adapt to each other and generally to build trust and co-operation.[11]

Although the concept of relationship marketing is changing the way in which marketers are looking at marketing, it is also particularly pertinent to this chapter's discussion of the exchange relationships that develop between buyers and sellers.[12] When a company buys a product or service from another company, both organisations become involved in an exchange process. During the transaction, both buyer and seller will exchange items of value in return for something else. For example, when a software company provides a printer with a desktop publishing package, it will provide the buyer with a package of benefits that include the software disks, detailed users' guide, warranty details, a variety of payment options and the opportunity to attend a training course. In exchange the buyer will agree to pay the price negotiated with the manufacturer. Figure 5.3 shows the range of factors that can be exchanged during the purchase process.

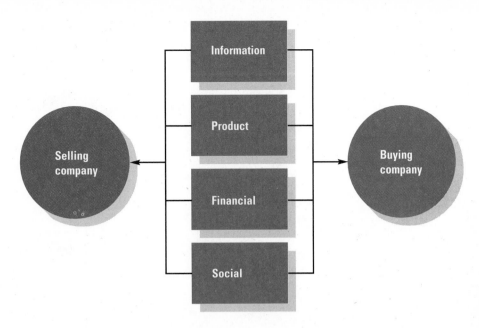

Figure 5.3

The exchange process in organisational buying

Information

Product

Financial

Social

Selling company

Buying company

It is often in the interests of both parties to develop long term relationships. If buying and selling companies are used to dealing with each other, they are more likely to be able to adapt to each other's needs and to reach an agreement quickly and easily. Long term relationships are often attractive to both companies because they reduce the level of risk (financial and practical) associated with the purchase. The trend towards long term relationships has resulted in the development of what is called **relationship management**.[13] This process encourages a match between the seller's competitive advantage and the buyer's requirements over the life cycle of the item being purchased.

Relationship management
The process of encouraging a match between the seller's competitive advantage and the buyer's requirements over an item's life cycle

Stages of the Organisational Buying Decision Process

Like consumers, organisations follow a buying decision process. This process is summarised on the right hand side of Figure 5.4. In the first stage, one or more individuals recognise that a problem or need exists. Problem recognition may arise under a variety of circumstances, either from inside or outside the company. For example, a machine might reach the end of its working life and need to be replaced, or changes in legislation concerning factory emissions might dictate the need for a new approach to manufacturing. Individuals in the buying centre, such as users, influencers or buyers, may be involved in problem recognition, but it may be stimulated by external sources, such as sales representatives or customers.

The second stage of the process—development of product specifications—requires organisational participants to assess the problem or need and to determine what is necessary to resolve or satisfy it. During this stage, users and influencers, such as technical personnel and engineers, often provide information and advice for developing product specifications. By assessing and describing needs, the organisation should be able to establish product specifications.

Searching for possible products to solve the problem and then locating suitable suppliers is the third stage in the decision process. Search activities may involve looking in company files and trade directories, contacting suppliers for information, visiting trade shows, soliciting proposals from known suppliers, and

Figure 5.4

Organisational buying decision process and factors that may influence it

Possible influencing factors

Environmental
- Competitive factors
- Legal and regulatory forces
- Economic conditions
- Sociocultural issues
- Technological changes

Organisational
- Objectives
- Purchasing policies
- Resources
- Buying centre structure

Interpersonal
- Co-operation
- Conflict
- Power relationships

Individual
- Age
- Education level
- Job status
- Personality
- Income

Decision process

Recognise problem

Develop product specifications to solve problem

Search for products and suppliers

Evaluate products and supplies relative to specifications

Select and order most appropriate products and supplies

Evaluate product and supplier performance

Feedback

SOURCE: Adapted from Frederick E. Webster, Jr, and Yoram Wind, Organisational Buying Behaviour (Englewood Cliffs, N.J.: Prentice-Hall, 1972), pp. 33–37. Adapted by permission.

examining catalogues and trade publications. Marketing Insight 5.2 illustrates the efforts of Intel to encourage prospective buyers to express a preference for computers with Intel inside. Some suppliers may be viewed as unacceptable because they are not large enough to supply the quantities needed, and others may have poor records of delivery and service. In some instances the product may not be available from any existing supplier and the buyer must then find an innovative company, such as 3M, that can design and build the product.

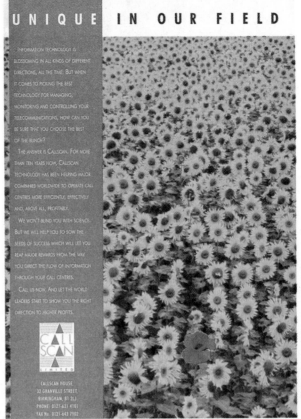

Figure 5.5 Does the product meet specifications? These advertisements from Kodak and Callscan illustrate the features of the product proposition.

SOURCE: left: *Courtesy of Kodak Ltd;* right: *Courtesy of Callscan House.*

If all goes well, the search stage will result in a list of several alternative products and suppliers. The fourth stage is evaluating the products on the list to determine which options (if any) meet the product specifications developed in the second stage. The advertisements in Figure 5.5 stress the particular product, service and supplier attributes that may help customers evaluate whether a particular offering meets their requirements. At this point, too, various suppliers are evaluated according to multiple criteria, such as price, service and ability to deliver.

The results of the deliberations and assessments in the fourth stage are used during the fifth stage to select the most appropriate product and supplier. In some cases the buyer may decide on several suppliers. In others only one supplier is selected—a situation known as **sole sourcing**. Sole sourcing has traditionally been discouraged except when a product is available from only one company; companies that have contracts with national governments are often required to have several sources for an item. Sole sourcing is becoming more popular today, partly because such an arrangement means better communications between buyer and supplier, stability and higher profits for the supplier, and often lower prices for the

Sole sourcing A buying process that involves the selection of only one supplier

Intel Builds Brand Awareness from the Inside Out

In 1986, thirty years after leaving his native Hungary, Andy Grove founded Intel Corp., pioneer manufacturer of microprocessing chips that provide the brainpower for most personal computers. The company's 8086 and 8088 chips powered early IBM personal computers, and today its 386 and 486 microprocessors dominate the market. Every year some 40 million personal computers are sold, and inside almost every one, including well known models such as the OS\2, NextStep, and Sun's Solaris, is at least one Intel chip.

When personal computing was in its infancy, companies designed, built and sold completely integrated systems, including chips, software and disk drives. Buyers had to choose a whole package or nothing. Because today's most successful products are all compatible, original equipment manufacturers can build computers with parts from various firms. Computers can easily contain Intel processors, Sharp displays, Toshiba memories, US Robotics modems and Microsoft operating systems. Although Intel continues to maintain its near monopoly of the microprocessor market, competition from firms such as Digital Equipment and Advanced Micro Devices is now making it necessary to differentiate Intel chips from its clones.

Recognising that most PC users never look inside their computers to see which microprocessors are providing the brains, Intel decided to make sure users think about who makes the silicon chips in there. To boost brand awareness and preference for its products, Intel launched its multi-million pound "Intel Inside" campaign. First, Intel created a logo, the words *Intel Inside* surrounded by an oval that doesn't quite close. In partnership with original equipment manufacturers (OEMs), the company is working to make that logo a symbol of quality and proven performance. Every time a participating manufacturer advertises 386sx and 486sx products and incorporates the "Intel Inside" logo, Intel reimburses that manufacturer for a percentage of its media placement costs. About a hundred OEMs, including industry front runners such as IBM, Zenith Data Systems, NCR and Dell Computer, feature Intel's logo in their advertisements; and another two hundred firms have signed up for the programme.

buyer. However, most organisations still prefer to purchase goods and services from several suppliers to reduce the possibility of disruption caused by strikes, shortages or bankruptcy. The actual product is ordered in this fifth stage and specific details regarding terms, credit arrangements, delivery dates and methods, and technical assistance are worked out.

During the sixth stage, the product's performance is evaluated by comparing it with specifications. Sometimes, even though the product meets the specifications, its performance does not adequately solve the problem or satisfy the need recognised in the first stage. In that case, the product specifications must be adjusted. The supplier's performance is also evaluated during this stage, and if it is found wanting, the organisational purchaser seeks corrective action from the supplier or searches for a new supplier. Buyers are increasingly concerned with obtaining high quality service from suppliers and may formally set performance targets for them. The results of such performance evaluations become feedback for the other stages and influence future organisational purchase decisions.

Intel provides its OEM partners with detailed and uncompromising guidelines for using the logo, including reproduction, placement and even colour. OEMs must always identify the Intel logo as a registered trademark of the Intel Corp. Official logo colours are blue, red and green only. Using supplied logo sheets, advertisers may not add graphics to the logo, place it on a patterned background, reduce its size, connect it to any other logo or type, or alter it in any other way. If firms put removable logo stickers on their products, they must place them on the top right or left hand corner, but not on the monitor, keyboard or other peripheral components.

By developing close partnerships with OEMs and directing them in effective logo use, Intel hopes both to heighten brand awareness and to increase its customers' preference for Intel components. When they see the "Intel Inside" logo, says the firm's marketing director, customers will instantly recognise a quality product with an Intel chip inside. Although participating computer firms claim that the logo has boosted their advertising effectiveness, industry sceptics predict that the campaign will not establish long term brand loyalty. Smart customers, they insist, will realise that there are no important differences between Intel and no-name brands and that choosing the latter can save them money.

These days Intel is too busy staying ahead of the market to listen to the doubters. In less than a decade, it has grown from a struggling operation into the world's largest microprocessor company. Despite competition from Cyrix Corporation, Intel maintains a near monopoly on sales of 486 computer chips. Its new Pentium microprocessor runs Compaq computers with twice their previous speed. Intel's president asserts that two essential steps will help the company maintain its preeminent status: continuing to pioneer better microprocessing technology and making sure that customers know that Intel products are better. Intel believes that its marketing investment in the "Intel Inside" campaign will help it achieve the second goal.

SOURCE: From Pride/Ferrell, Ninth Edition. Copyright © 1995 by Houghton Mifflin Company. Used by permission.

This organisational buying decision process is used in its entirety primarily for new task purchases. Several of the stages, but not necessarily all, are used for modified re-buying and straight re-buying, and fewer individuals are likely to be involved in these decisions.

Influences on Organisational Buying

Figure 5.4 also lists the four major categories of factors that influence organisational buying decisions: environmental, organisational, interpersonal and individual.

Environmental factors
Uncontrollable forces such as competitive and economic factors, legal and regulatory issues, technological changes and socio-cultural issues

Chapter 2 explained that **environmental factors** are uncontrollable forces such as politics, laws, regulations and regulatory agencies, activities of interest groups, changes in the economy, competitors' actions and technological changes. These forces generate a considerable amount of uncertainty for an organisation, which can make individuals in the buying centre apprehensive about certain types of purchases. Changes in one or more environmental forces can create new purchasing opportunities. For example, changes in competition and technology can make buying decisions difficult in the case of products like computers, a field in which competition is increasingly affected by new co-operative strategies between companies. Compaq Computer, for instance, grew into a billion dollar company by competing only against IBM and developing co-operative relationships with all other potential competitors.[14]

Organisational factors
Include the buyer's objectives, purchasing policies and resources, as well as the size and composition of its buying centre

Organisational factors influencing the organisational buying decision process include the buyer's objectives, purchasing policies and resources, as well as the size and composition of its buying centre. An organisation may have certain buying policies to which buying centre participants must conform. For instance, a firm's policies may require long term contracts, perhaps longer than most sellers desire. The nature of an organisation's financial resources may require special credit arrangements. Any of these conditions could affect purchase decision processes.

Interpersonal factors The relationships among the people in the buying centre

Interpersonal factors are the relationships among the people in the buying centre, where the use of power and the level of conflict significantly influence organisational buying decisions. Certain persons in the buying centre may be better communicators than others and thus more persuasive. Often these interpersonal dynamics are hidden, making them difficult for marketers to appraise.

Individual factors The personal characteristics of individuals in the buying centre, such as age, education, personality, and position in the organisation.

Individual factors are the personal characteristics of individuals in the buying centre, such as age, education, personality and position in the organisation. For example, a 60 year old manager who left school at 16 and has been with the organisation ever since may affect the decisions of the buying centre differently than a 30 year old person who left university with a business studies degree and an MBA and has been employed for only two years. How influential these factors will be depends on the buying situation, the type of product being purchased and whether the purchase is new task, modified re-buy or straight re-buy. The negotiating styles of people will undoubtedly vary within an organisation and from one organisation to another. To be effective, a marketer needs to know customers well enough to be aware of these individual factors and the effects they may have on purchase decisions.

●　●　●　●　●　●　●　●　●　●　●　●　●　●　●　●　●　●

Selection and Analysis of Business-to-Business Markets

Marketing research is becoming more important in industrial marketing, especially in selecting and analysing target markets. Most of the marketing research techniques discussed in Chapter 6 can be applied to **industrial marketing**. This section focuses on important and unique approaches to selecting and analysing industrial markets.

Industrial marketing
Activities directed towards facilitating and expediting exchanges between industrial markets and industrial producers

Industrial marketers have easy access to a considerable amount of information about potential customers, for much of this information appears in government and industry publications. However, comparable data about ultimate consumers are not available. Even though marketers may use different procedures to isolate and analyse target markets, most follow a similar pattern: (1) determining who potential customers are and how many there are, (2) locating where they are and (3) estimating their purchase potential.[15]

0	Agriculture, forestry and fishing
1	Energy and water supply industries
2	Extraction of minerals and ores other than fuels; manufacture of metals, mineral products and chemicals
3	Metal goods, engineering and vehicles
4	Other manufacturing industries
5	Construction
6	Distribution, hotels and catering; repairs
7	Transport and communication
8	Banking, finance, insurance, business services and leasing
9	Other services

Table 5.3 The Standard Industrial Classification (SIC) system for categorising industrial customers

Determining Who Potential Customers Are and How Many There Are

Standard Industrial Classification (SIC) system
A system that provides information on different industries and products, and classifies economic characteristics of industrial, commercial, financial and service organisations

Much information about industrial customers is based on the **Standard Industrial Classification (SIC) system,** which provides information on different industries and products and was developed to classify selected economic characteristics of industrial, commercial, financial and service organisations. In the UK this system is administered by the Central Statistical Office. Table 5.3 shows how the SIC system can be used to categorise products. The most recent SIC manual contains 10 broad divisions, each denoted by a single digit from 0 to 9. These are sub-divided into classes (each denoted by the addition of a second digit), the classes are divided into groups (three digits) and the groups into activity headings (four more digits). There are 10 divisions, 60 classes, 222 groups and 334 activity headings. For example, Division 4 (see Table 5.3), "Other manufacturing industries", has 8 classes, 50 groups and 91 activity headings. The numbering system follows that of NACE (Nomenclature Générale des Activités Économiques dans les Communautés Européennes) as far as possible.[16] To categorise manufacturers in more detail, the *Census of Distribution* further sub-divides manufacturers.

Data are available for each SIC category through various government publications and departments. Table 5.4 shows the types of information that can be obtained from government sources. Some data are available by town, county and

Value of industry shipments
Number of establishments
Number of employees
Exports as a percentage of shipments
Imports as a percentage of apparent consumption
Compound annual average rate of growth
Major producing areas

Table 5.4 Types of government information available about industrial markets (based on SIC categories)

metropolitan area. Business-to-business market data also appear in such non-government sources as Dun & Bradstreet's *Market Identifiers*.

The SIC system is a ready made tool that allows business-to-business marketers to divide industrial organisations into market segments based mainly on the type of product manufactured or handled. Although the SIC system is a vehicle for segmentation, it must be used in conjunction with other types of data to enable a specific business-to-business marketer to determine exactly which customers it can reach and how many of them can be targeted.

Input-output analysis works well in conjunction with the SIC system. This type of analysis is based on the assumption that the output or sales of one industry are the input or purchases of other industries. For example, component manufacturers provide products that form an input for manufacturers of white goods such as washing machines, dishwashers and fridges. **Input-output data** tell what types of industries purchase the products of a particular industry.

Input-output data
Information on the products that form an input for manufacturers

After discovering which industries purchase the major portion of an industry's output, the next step is to find the SIC numbers for those industries. Because firms are grouped differently in the input-output tables and the SIC system, ascertaining SIC numbers can be difficult. However, the Central Statistical Office does provide some limited conversion tables with the input-output data. These tables can assist business marketers in assigning SIC numbers to the industry categories used in the input-output analysis. Having determined the SIC numbers of the industries that buy the firm's output, a business-to-business marketer is in a position to ascertain the number of establishments that are potential buyers nationally, by town and by county. Government publications report the number of establishments within SIC classifications, along with other types of data, such as those shown in Table 5.4.

Locating Industrial Customers

At this point, industrial marketers know what industries purchase the kind of products their firm produces, as well as the number of establishments in those industries and certain other information. However, the marketers still have to find out the names and addresses of potential customers.

One approach to identifying and locating potential customers is to use business-to-business directories, such as *Kompass* and *Kelly's*. These sources contain such information about a firm as its name, SIC number, address, phone number and annual sales. By referring to one or more of these sources, an organisational marketer can isolate customers with certain SIC numbers, determine their locations and thus develop lists of potential customers by area.

A second approach, which is more expedient but also more expensive, is to use one of the many marketing research agencies. For example, Market Locations is able to provide lists of organisations which fall into particular SIC groups. Information can include name, location, sales volume, number of employees, type of products handled and names of chief executives.

Either approach can effectively identify and locate a group of potential organisational customers. However, an industrial marketer probably cannot pursue all firms on the list. Because some companies have a greater purchase potential than others, the marketer must weigh up the attractiveness of each and determine which segment or segments to pursue. Figure 5.6 illustrates the Dutch Automobile Association's attempts to target travel agencies.

In industrial marketing, situation specific variables may be more relevant in segmenting markets than general customer characteristics. Industrial customers concentrate on benefits sought; therefore, understanding the end use of the prod-

HOE BEREIK JE EEN VOLK VAN VASTBERADEN VAKANTIEGANGERS?

Hoe vaak heeft je grootvader het verhaal niet verteld? Dat hij op 'n He begon met werken. Dat vakantie toen nog niet bestond. Dat hij van 's maandags vroeg tot 's zaterdags laat zwoegde en zweette. En dat hij in stille voor 'n ideaten vocht z'n kinderen en kleinkinderen moesten 't beter krijgen dan hij.

Veel van zijn nakomelingen hebben 40 vrije dagen per jaar. Ze zwoegen en zweten als opa, maar alleen wanneer ze op vakantie zijn. Het zijn vastberaden en verwoede kanovaarders, bergbeklimmers, fietsers en wandelaars. Ze lezen Op Pad, een blad dat 100.000 mensen bereikt. Doorgaans hoog opgeleid en goed bij kas. Op Pad mag zich, evenals vele andere ANWB-titels, verheugen in de groeiende belangstelling van vastberaden adverteerders. Wilt u meer informatie, bel dan ANWB Media, telefoon 070-3146137.

Figure 5.6 Locating industrial customers. This advertisement for the Dutch Automobile Association targeted travel agencies.

Source: Courtesy ANWB Royal Dutch Touring Club.

uct is more important than the psychology of decisions or socio-economic characteristics. Segmenting by benefits rather than by customer characteristics can provide insight into the structure of the market and opportunities for new customers.[17]

Estimating Purchase Potential

To estimate the purchase potential of industrial customers or groups of customers, an industrial marketer must find a relationship between the size of potential customers' purchases and a variable available in SIC data, such as the number of employees. For example, a paint manufacturer might attempt to determine the average number of gallons purchased by a specific type of potential industrial customer relative to the number of persons employed. If the industrial marketer has no previous experience in this market segment, it will probably be necessary to survey a random sample of potential customers to establish a relationship between purchase sizes and numbers of persons employed. Once this relationship has been established, it can be applied to potential customer segments to estimate their purchases. After deriving these estimates, the industrial marketer selects the customers to be included in the target market.

● *Organisational* (or *industrial*) *markets* consist of individuals and groups that purchase a specific kind of product for re-sale, for direct use in producing other products, or for use in day-to-day operations. *Producer markets* include those individuals and business organisations that purchase products for the purpose of making a profit by using them either to produce other products or in their own operations. Intermediaries who buy finished products and re-sell them for the purpose of making a profit are classified as *reseller markets. Government markets* consist of national and local governments, which spend billions of pounds annually for goods and services to support their internal operations and provide citizens with needed services. Organisations that seek to achieve charitable, educational, community or other non-profit goals constitute *institutional markets.*

● Organisational transactions differ from consumer transactions in several ways. The transactions tend to be larger, and negotiations occur less frequently, though they are often lengthy. Organisational transactions sometimes involve more than one person or one department in the purchasing organisation. They may also involve *reciprocity,* an arrangement in which two organisations agree to buy from each other, although some countries have strict rules governing such agreements. Organisational customers are usually viewed as more rational and more likely to seek information about a product's features and technical specifications than are ultimate consumers.

● When purchasing products, organisational customers must be particularly concerned about quality, delivery, service and price. Quality is important because it directly affects the quality of the organisational buyer's ultimate product. To achieve an exact standard, organisations often buy their products on the basis of a set of expressed characteristics, called specifications. Reliable and quick delivery is crucial to many organisations whose production lines must be fed with a continuous supply of component parts and raw materials. Because services can have a direct influence on a firm's costs, sales and profits, such matters as market information, on-time delivery and availability of parts can be crucial to an organisational buyer. Although an organisational customer does not decide which products

to purchase solely by their price, cost is of prime concern because it directly influences a firm's profitability.

● Organisational buyers use several purchasing methods, including description, inspection, sampling and negotiation. Most organisational purchases are new task, modified re-buy or straight re-buy. In a *new task purchase,* an organisation makes an initial purchase of an item to be used to perform a new job or to solve a problem. In *modified re-buying,* a new task purchase is changed the second or third time it is ordered, or the requirements associated with a straight re-buy purchase are modified. A *straight re-buy purchase* occurs when a buyer purchases the same products routinely under approximately the same terms of sale.

● Industrial demand differs from consumer demand along several dimensions. *Industrial demand derives* from the demand for consumer products. At the industry level, industrial demand is *inelastic.* If the price of an industrial item changes, demand for the product will not change proportionally. Some industrial products are subject to *joint demand,* which occurs when two or more items are used in combination to make a product. Finally, because industrial demand ultimately derives from consumer demand, the demand for industrial products can fluctuate widely.

● *Organisational* (or *industrial*) *buying behaviour* refers to the purchase behaviour of producers, resellers, government units and institutions. Organisational purchase decisions are made through a *buying centre*—the group of people who are involved in making organisational purchase decisions. Users are those in the organisation who actually use the product. Influencers help develop the specifications and evaluate alternative products for possible use. Buyers are responsible for selecting the suppliers and negotiating the terms of the purchases. Deciders choose the products and suppliers. Gatekeepers control the flow of information to and among persons who occupy the other roles in the buying centre.

● When a company buys a product or service from another company, both organisations enter into a process during which items of value are exchanged in return for something else. This exchange process may lead to a long term relationship between buyer and seller. *Relationship marketing* is the term used to explain the special attention being given to this area and is defined as the activities an organisation uses to build, maintain and develop customer relations in *relationship management*.

● The stages of the organisational buying decision process are problem recognition, development of product specifications to solve the problem, search for products and suppliers, evaluation of products relative to specifications, selection and ordering of the most appropriate product and evaluation of the product's and the supplier's performance. The evaluation of product and supplies will directly affect future purchasing decisions. *Sole sourcing* is becoming more popular.

● Four categories of factors influence organisational buying decisions: environmental, organisational, interpersonal and individual. Environmental factors include laws and regulations, economic conditions, competitive forces and technological changes. Organisational factors include the buyer's objectives, purchasing policies and resources, as well as the size and composition of its buying centre. Interpersonal factors refer to the relationships among the people in the buying centre. Individual factors refer to the personal characteristics of individuals in the buying centre, such as age, education, personality, position in the organisation and income.

● *Industrial marketing* is a set of activities directed at facilitating and expediting exchanges involving industrial products and customers in industrial markets.

● Industrial marketers have a considerable amount of information available to them for use in planning their marketing strategies. Much of this information is based on the *Standard Industrial Classification (SIC) system,* which classifies businesses into major industry divisions, classes, groups and activities. The SIC system provides business marketers with information needed to identify market segments. It can best be used for this purpose in conjunction with other information, such as *input-output data*. After identifying target industries, the marketer can locate potential customers by using industrial directories or by employing a marketing research agency. The marketer must then estimate the potential purchases of organisational customers by finding a relationship between a potential customer's purchases and a variable available in published sources.

Important Terms

Organisational (or industrial) market
Producer markets
Reseller markets
Wholesalers
Retailers
Government markets
Institutional markets
Reciprocity
New task purchase

Modified re-buy purchase
Straight re-buy purchase
Derived demand
Inelastic demand
Joint demand
Organisational (or industrial) buying behaviour
Buying centre
Relationship marketing
Relationship management

Sole sourcing
Environmental factors
Organisational factors
Interpersonal factors
Individual factors
Industrial marketing
Standard Industrial Classification (SIC) system
Input-output data

Discussion and Review Questions

1. Identify, describe and give examples of four major types of organisational markets.
2. Why are organisational buyers generally considered more rational in regard to their purchasing behaviour than ultimate consumers?
3. What are the primary concerns of organisational buyers?
4. List several characteristics that differentiate organisational transactions from consumer ones.

5. What are the commonly used methods of organisational buying?

6. Why do buyers involved in a straight re-buy purchase require less information than those making a new task purchase?

7. How does industrial demand differ from consumer demand?

8. What are the major components of a buying centre?

9. What elements may be exchanged by a buyer and seller when a purchase transaction takes place?

10. Identify the stages of the organisational buying decision process. How is this decision process used when making straight re-buys?

11. What impact does the evaluation of a particular purchase have on future buying decisions?

12. How do environmental, organisational, interpersonal and individual factors affect organisational purchases?

13. What function does the SIC system help industrial marketers perform?

14. List some sources that an industrial marketer can use to determine the names and addresses of potential customers.

● ● ● ● ● ● ● ● ● ● ● ● ● ● ● ● ● ●

Recommended Readings

D. Ford, *Understanding Business Markets* (London: Academic Press, 1990).

M. D. Hutt and T. W. Speh, *Business Marketing Management: A Strategic View of Industrial and Organisational Markets* (Fort Worth: Dryden Press, 1992).

T. L. Powers, *Modern Business Marketing* (St. Paul, Minn.: West, 1990).

F. E. Webster, *Industrial Marketing Strategy* (New York: John Wiley, 1991).

● ● ● ● ● ● ● ● ● ● ● ● ● ● ● ● ● ●

Cases

5.1 Changing the Supply of Car Parts

Companies supplying automotive parts to garages that service and repair cars and other vehicles are having to respond to sweeping market changes. In the UK and Benelux countries, the balance of outlet types is shifting away from the traditional independent garages and franchises of car manufacturers towards specialist and "fast-fit" operations. Increasingly complex vehicle specifications seem to be responsible for the growing specialisation, with all its associated computer diagnostics—too expensive and complex for most garages. Meanwhile, the rise in fortunes of fast-fit operators, such as Kwik Fit, has stemmed from the increasing demands of car owners for competitive pricing and fast service. Their popularity looks set to spread throughout many other European countries in the near future.

While the needs of the car owning public are seen to be changing, most consumers have little idea of, or interest in, the actual parts that are fitted to their cars. It is true that car owners do have an interest in the availability, quality and price of parts used in their vehicles, but the choice of brand is invariably left to the garage installing the item. For Lucas Aftermarket Operations, the division of Lucas Automotive that provides vehicle parts, the buyer to be influenced is therefore the installer (garage) rather than the vehicle owner.

In order to hit its target customers, Lucas must gear its selling efforts to the needs of the changing installer base. In the present situation, the company must respond to the differing requirements of both new and old types of installers. Although each customer will require a slightly different mix of product, price, delivery, quality and service, Lucas seeks economies of scale by looking for similarities in the needs of the different types of installer.

To serve its customers, Lucas Aftermarket Operations has at its disposal a host of Lucas branded depots and fitting centres, as well as independent distributors and dealers. Altogether, 16 major Lucas distribution centres worldwide are supported by numerous independent distributors, and the company has access to a total of around 4,000 authorised outlets in more than 100 countries. The distribution channels are as complex as they are extensive, reaching a large number of alternative customer types via numerous different routes—and sometimes through many different intermediaries.

Although Lucas's wide ranging distribution coverage gives the company access to many markets worldwide, the complexity of the channels can impose undue distance between the points of supply and consumption. When the distance (both real and psychological) is great, it can be more difficult to understand and satisfy the installer's needs. One possible solution is to forge closer links between suppliers, distributors, retailers and garages, resulting in greater co-operation between players with jointly agreed product ranges and methods of installation. Shorter distribution channels, although implemented in response to changing customer needs, will cut out stages and people in the organisational buying process.

SOURCES: Sally Dibb, "Satisfying installer needs in the UK car parts market", *International Journal of Retail and Distribution Management*, 20(3), May–June 1992, pp. 20–26; T. Drakeford, "Distribution can change your business", *Logistics and Distribution Management*, December 1987, pp. 18–20; John Wormald and Erik Arnold, "Change and opportunities in the automotive aftermarket", Booz Allen and Hamilton International (UK) Ltd; *EIU, European Motor Business*, November 1989, pp. 125–151; "Garages/car servicing", *Mintel,* Marketing Intelligence Report, May 1988, pp. 101–117; Lucas annual report, 1992.

Questions for Discussion

1. Who are Lucas's customers?
2. What types of organisational markets (as classified in this chapter) purchase the products Lucas makes?
3. Would most purchases of Lucas's products be new task, modified re-buy or straight re-buy? Why?
4. What advantages might shorter distribution channels have for Lucas's customers?

5.2 Selling a White Powder: No Easy Matter

A white powder little known by most consumers appears as a core ingredient in all paints, inks and most plastics: TiO_2 or titanium dioxide, produced from ilmenite and synthetic rutile. With plants focused primarily in North America, Europe, Australia and southern Africa, the market is dominated by the UK's ICI—through its operating subsidiary Tioxide—and America's DuPont. In the Americas, DuPont has the edge, whereas in Europe Tioxide is the dominant player. Smaller companies such as Kemira, Kerr McGee, Kronos and SCM also have slices of the market. For this commodity product used in the production process for so many materials, continuity of supply and purity of the pigment are important considerations. Customers for Tioxide or Kerr McGee are quite diverse, ranging from international masterbatch companies requiring long production runs (perhaps producing packaging or film products) to PVC and linoleum flooring manufacturers, marine engineers producing boat mouldings, the paint giants ICI Dulux and Crown, and the manufacturers of road marking paints!

The task facing Tioxide or DuPont varies according to which type of customer the company is dealing with. An international packaging company may well have a buying centre comprising a senior purchasing officer, a technical manager, a laboratory technician for technical approval, a production manager whose job depends on having the right supplies and a senior financial controller to sign off on any orders. Not all will be involved throughout the buying process, but DuPont or Tioxide must be aware of their views and attempt to influence and comfort them as required. Such packaging companies will be very large and understand their own markets well, with the result that they will have very specific and well defined product requirements from suppliers such as DuPont or Kronos.

The key customer needs in such a market may include product consistency over time and throughout production runs, guarantee of supply and long term supplier relationships with reputable companies. The buying process will be much more complicated than for any consumer purchase. It will usually commence when the need for TiO_2 is noted and suppliers are contacted. Samples will be tested by the packaging company's own laboratory technical experts. If the samples are deemed fit, the production department will be asked for its approval. In some circumstances the packaging company's key customers will be asked to approve the quality, purity and appearance of the final products. At this point in the buying process, there will be a group meeting in the packaging company involving commercial and technical personnel to agree on order quantities, delivery requirements and payment terms. After a period of negotiation, DuPont, Kerr McGee or Tioxide may be lucky enough to be awarded a contract, after which the whole process will re-commence. During the course of such deliberations in the buying process, numerous market factors will influence those involved—opinions voiced at trade association meetings, customer specifications, sales agents, equipment manufacturers, technical seminars, EU legislation and even the sales efforts of the TiO_2 suppliers.

By contrast, if Kerr McGee or SCM wishes to sell to a flooring manufacturer, the process is relatively simple. The buying centre may consist only of a purchasing manager. The main influencing factors will usually relate to trends in the construction industry—which can be monitored easily—and to anti-PVC moves because of "green" concerns. Such manufacturers will require reliability of supply, but

any of the major players can meet that need. A competitive price and solid relationship with locally based sales personnel will continue to be dominant customer needs. Given that the product is a raw ingredient chemical, the buying process will still involve technical laboratory approval, production trial and senior level negotiation. With a much smaller buying centre, though, the process may be managed with more ease.

SOURCES: DuPont and Tioxide sales literature, 1996; Peter Fairly, "Tioxide grows materials group", *Chemical Week,* 5 July 1995, p. 18; Brent Shearer, "TiO2 producers mull new plants", *Chemical Marketing Reporter,* 9 January 1995, p. 3; Marjorie Coeyman, "DuPont, Tioxide plan capacity hike", *Chemical Week,* 19 October 1994, p. 14; Ian Young, "Kronos deal prompts Tioxide exit from minerals company", *Chemical Week,* 2 March 1994, p. 18.

Questions for Discussion

1. In industrial markets, why does the buying process often seem more complicated than in consumer goods markets? Explain your views.
2. Why is it so important to understand the factors that influence decision-makers in industrial buying?
3. How should DuPont or Tioxide attempt to monitor the buyer behaviour of its core customers? Describe with examples.

6 MARKETING RESEARCH AND INFORMATION SYSTEMS

"The researcher's challenge is not just generating data, but in creating a vision from that data."

Dave Birks
University of Bath

OBJECTIVES

- To understand the importance of and relationship between research and information systems in marketing decision-making
- To distinguish between research and intuition in solving marketing problems
- To learn the five basic steps for conducting a marketing research project
- To understand the fundamental methods of gathering data for marketing research
- To gain a sense of the relative advantages and disadvantages of marketing research tools

Retailers and providers of services depend increasingly not only on the products they sell or deliver but also on the ability, attitude and quality of their personnel and the internal environment of their branch outlets. The regional directors and head office managers who check such standards all too often enter through the staff door at the rear of the branch, focusing primarily on operations and not on customer concerns. The branch's customers enter from the front, having first seen the exterior of the branch. They deal with all levels of personnel, not just the manager or manageress to whom the visiting director talks. These customers are not wrapped up in the company's products and operations; they seek help and advice. They expect courtesy and professionalism.

Customers buy a company's products; quite often the company's management never does, instead requesting items direct from storage at staff discount rates without ever visiting shops or showrooms. Car manufacturers give their senior management vehicles and offer all employees

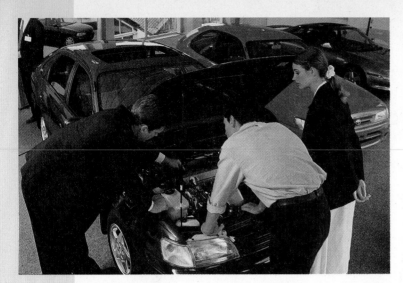

service by telephone and then phone again to cancel, judging the receptionist's response to the lost business. As a result of these frequent, always anonymous, visits, Rover was able to improve the standards of its dealers, the attitude of its personnel and ultimately the quality of its service and customer satisfaction.

This form of marketing research, "mystery shopper", is one of the fastest growing areas in the industry. The largest company in the UK, BEM, has 3,000 mystery shopper on its books, many working part time; and its annual sales exceed £5 million; £3.5 million from mystery shoppers surveys. BEM's employees are trained to evaluate how customers are greeted, how the store looks and whether shop assistants understand the products on sale. They are expected to blend in inconspicuously while assessing branches; they are not loud customers visibly asking awkward questions. For many businesses, mystery shopper researchers are evaluating standards and service quality and supplying management with measures of performance and benchmarks against which improvements can be made. ■

highly attractive deals. The result is that few senior managers ever visit a showroom or dealer—even their servicing is taken care of—so they never see the "sharp end", their dealers, as customers.

Rover Cars instigated a programme of "mystery shopper" surveys. This programme involved visits by bogus potential car buyers to dealers to rate the upkeep and appearance of showrooms, technical knowledge and attitude of personnel, quality of displays, negotiating criteria and adherence to company policies. Dealers did not know who the bogus buyers were, nor when they were to visit. Service reception staff were similarly targeted. A favourite ploy by the researchers was to book a car

SOURCES: *Marketing Guides: Market Research*, 13 June 1996; Customer Concern and BEM promotional literature; Rover Cars.

T o implement the marketing concept, marketers require information about the characteristics, needs and wants of their target markets. Given the intense competition in today's marketplace, it is unwise to develop a product and then look for a market where it can be profitably sold. The Sinclair C5 electric car is a prime example of product first, market second; it failed to satisfy customers' needs. Marketing research and information systems that provide practical, unbiased information help firms avoid assumptions and misunderstandings that could result in poor marketing performance, as detailed in the chapter opener's overview of mystery shopping research.

This chapter focuses on the ways of gathering information needed to make marketing decisions, first distinguishing between managing information within an organisation (a marketing information system) and conducting marketing research. The discussion next addresses the role of marketing research in decision-making and problem solving, compares it with intuition and examines the individual steps of the marketing research process. The chapter also takes a close look at experimentation and various methods of collecting data. The final section considers the importance of marketing research and marketing information systems.

Defining Marketing Research and Marketing Information Systems

Marketing research The process of gathering, interpreting and reporting information to help marketers solve specific problems or to take advantage of marketing opportunities

As the preceding chapters have made clear, marketers must understand customers, competitors, market trends and aspects of the marketing environment. To do this, they require information and marketing intelligence.[1] **Marketing research** is the systematic design, collection, interpretation and reporting of information to help marketers solve specific marketing problems or take advantage of marketing opportunities. It is a process for gathering information not currently available to decision-makers. Marketing research is conducted on a special project basis, and research methods are adapted both to the problems being studied and to changes in the environment. The marketing research industry is huge, highly competitive and increasingly dominated by international research agencies. Figure 6.1 reveals the scope of the marketing industry.

The Market Research Society defines research as follows:

> the collection and analysis of data from a sample of individuals or organisations relating to their characteristics, behaviour, attitudes, opinions or possessions. It includes all forms of marketing and social research such as consumer and industrial surveys, psychological investigations, observational and panel studies.[2]

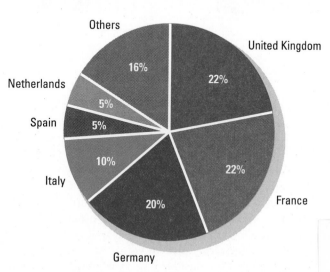

Figure 6.1 European marketing research markets, 1990. The total is 2,474 million ECUs.

Source: *ESOMAR, the European Society for Opinion and Marketing Resear[ch], Amsterdam, the Netherlands. Tel 31-20-664-2141; FAX: 31-20-664-2922.*

There are broadly two types of marketing research: quantitative and qualitative. In **quantitative research,** techniques and sample sizes lead to the collection of data that can be statistically analysed and whose results can be expressed numerically. These data tend to come from large surveys, sales data or market forecasts. **Qualitative research** deals with information that is too difficult or expensive to quantify: subjective opinions and value judgements that are not amenable to statistical analysis and quantification,[3] typically unearthed during depth interviews or discussion groups.

A **marketing information system (MIS)** is the framework for the day-to-day management and structuring of information gathered regularly from sources both inside and outside an organisation. As such, an MIS provides a continuous flow of information about prices, advertising expenditure, sales, competition and distribution expenses. When information systems are strategically created and then institutionalised throughout an organisation, their value is enhanced.[4] Figure 6.2 illustrates the chief components of an MIS.

The inputs into a marketing information system include the information sources inside and outside the firm assumed to be useful for future decision-making. Processing information involves classifying it and developing categories for meaningful storage and retrieval. Marketing decision-makers then determine which information—the output—is useful for making decisions. Finally, feedback enables those who are responsible for gathering internal and external data to adjust the information inputs systematically.[5]

Figure 6.2
An organisation's marketing information system

Regular reports of sales by product or market categories, data on inventory levels and records of salespeople's activities are all examples of information that is useful in making decisions. In the MIS, the means of gathering data receive less attention than do the procedures for expediting the flow of information. The main focus of the marketing information system is on data storage and retrieval, as well as on computer capabilities and management's information requirements. RJR Nabisco, for example, handles hundreds of thousands of consumer contacts each year, usually enquiries about product usage, nutrition and ingredients. This consumer feedback is computerised and made available on demand throughout the company's operating divisions.

The main difference between marketing research and a marketing information system is that the former is an information gathering process for specific situations, whereas the latter provides continuous data input for an organisation. Non-recurring decisions that deal with the dynamics of the marketing environment often call for a data search structured according to the problem and decision.

Marketing research is usually characterised by in-depth analyses of major problems or issues. Often the information needed is available only from sources outside an organisation's formal channels of information. For instance, an organisation may want to know something about its competitors or to gain an unbiased understanding of its own customers. Such information needs may require an independent investigation by a marketing research firm.

Data brought into the organisation through marketing research become part of its **marketing databank,** a file of data collected through both the MIS and marketing research projects. The marketing databank allows researchers to retrieve information that is useful for addressing problems quite different from those that prompted the original data collection. Often a research study developed for one purpose proves valuable for developing a research method of indicating problems in researching a particular topic. For instance, data obtained from a study by Ford Motors on the buying behaviour of purchasers of its models may be used in planning future models. Consequently, marketers should classify and store in the databank all data from marketing research and the MIS to facilitate their use in future marketing decisions.

Databanks vary widely from one organisation to another. In a small organisation, the databank may simply be a large notebook, but many organisations employ a computer storage and retrieval system to handle the large volume of data. Figure 6.3 illustrates how marketing decision-makers combine research findings with data from an MIS to develop a databank. Although many organisations do not use the term *databank,* they still have some system for storing information. Smaller organisations may not use the terms *MIS* and *marketing research,* but they normally do perform these marketing activities. All organisations have

Marketing databank   A file of data collected through the MIS and marketing research projects

Figure 6.3 Combining marketing research and the marketing information system

Marketing intelligence The composite of all data and ideas available within an organisation, a company or a marketing department

some **marketing intelligence,** although often it is found to be inadequate for specific problem solving, leading to ad hoc commissioning of marketing research. Marketing intelligence is the composite of all data and ideas available within an organisation, for example, a company or a marketing department.

After a marketing information system—of whatever size and complexity—has been established, information should be related to marketing planning.[6] The following section discusses how marketers use marketing information, intuition and judgement in making decisions. Marketing Insight 6.1 illustrates the importance of marketing research to marketing decision-makers.

. . . .

Information Needs and Decision-Making

The real value of marketing research and marketing information systems is measured by improvements in a marketer's ability to make decisions. Marketers should treat information in the same manner as other resources utilised by the firm, and they must weigh the costs of obtaining information against the benefits derived. Information is worthwhile if it results in marketing mixes that better satisfy the needs of the firm's target markets, leads to increased sales and profits, or helps the firm achieve some other goal.

Marketing research and marketing information systems provide the organisation with customer feedback, without which a marketer cannot understand the dynamics of the marketplace. As managers recognise its benefits, they assign marketing research a much larger role in decision-making. For example, Japanese managers, who put much more faith in information they get directly from wholesalers and retailers, are beginning to grasp the importance of consumer surveys and scientific methods of marketing research as they seek ways to diversify their companies.[7]

Intuition The personal knowledge and past experience upon which marketing managers may base decisions

The increase in marketing research activities represents a transition from intuitive to scientific problem solving. In relying on **intuition,** marketing managers base decisions on personal knowledge and past experience. However, in **scientific decision-making,** managers take an orderly and logical approach to gathering information. They seek facts on a systematic basis, and they apply methods other than trial and error or generalisation from experience.

Scientific decision-making An orderly and logical approach to gathering information

Despite the obvious value of formal research, marketing decisions are often made without it. Certainly, minor, low risk problems that must be dealt with at once can and should be handled on the basis of personal judgement and common sense. If good decisions can be made with the help of currently available information, costly formal research may be superfluous. However, as the financial, social or ethical risks increase or the possible courses of action multiply, full scale research as a prerequisite for marketing decision-making becomes both desirable and rewarding.

The suggestion here is not that intuition has no value in marketing decision-making. Successful decisions blend both research and intuition. Statistics, mathematics and logic are powerful tools in problem solving, and the information they provide can reduce the uncertainty of predictions based on limited experience. But these tools do not necessarily bring out the right answers. Consider an extreme example. A marketing research study conducted for Xerox Corporation in the late 1950s indicated a very limited market for an automatic photocopier. Xerox man-

	Research	**Intuition**
Nature	Formal planning, predicting based on scientific approach	Preference based on personal feelings
Methods	Logic, systematic methods, statistical inference	Experience and demonstration
Contributions	General hypotheses for making predictions, classifying relevant variables, carrying out systematic description and classification	Minor problems solved quickly through consideration of experience, practical consequences
Situation	High risk decision-making involving high costs, investment, strategic change or long term effects	Low risk problem solving and decision-making

Table 6.1 Distinctions between research and intuition in marketing decision-making

agement judged that the researchers had drawn the wrong conclusions from the study, and they decided to launch the product anyway. That product, the Xerox 914 copier, was an instant success. An immediate backlog of orders developed, and the rest is history. Although the Xerox example is certainly an extreme one, by and large a proper blend of research and intuition offers the best formula for a correct decision. Table 6.1 distinguishes between the roles of research and intuition in decision-making.

• • • • • • • • • • • • • • • • • • •

The Marketing Research Process

To maintain the control needed for obtaining accurate information, marketers approach marketing research in logical steps. The difference between good and bad research depends on the quality of the input, which includes effective control over the entire marketing research process. Figure 6.4 illustrates the five basic steps of the marketing research process: (1) defining and locating problems, (2) developing hypotheses, (3) collecting data with which to test and modify the hypotheses, (4) analysing and interpreting research findings, and (5) reporting research findings. These five steps should be viewed as an overall approach to conducting research rather than a rigid set of rules to be followed in each project. In planning research projects, marketers must think about each of the steps and how they can best be adjusted for each particular problem.

Why Products Fail: A Marketing Research Gap

The importance of marketing research and information systems is perhaps best understood by looking at product failures. Eight out of ten new products eventually fail. Strong marketing research can help companies reduce the likelihood of product failures.

In 1996, Britain's newest Sunday newspaper, *The Planet on Sunday,* closed after one issue. Sales were only 110,000, far fewer than the hoped for 250,000 copies. The ethos of "green" environmental issues, so important to the publisher, was not apparently a core concern to the majority of Sunday newspaper readers. This relatively unresearched product failed.

When the film *Crocodile Dundee* was popular in the 1980s, so too was anything Australian. In jumped Australia's Foster's Lager beer. Foster's promotion revolved around its Australian heritage. But when the Australian fever ended, Foster's lost more than 40 per cent of its sales. In a highly competitive market, Foster's failed to convey a clear image to consumers beyond its Australian origins, and the product never found a market niche of its own. Targeting a saturated market requires marketing research to determine niches that may have an interest in the product.

In the late 1980s, four new colognes for men and women were introduced. There was nothing too unusual about the colognes except their brand name: Bic. Upon introducing the product, Bic sank £13/£14 million into its marketing campaign, but disappointing sales contributed to a 22 per cent drop in company profits. Advertising for the colognes focused more on the novel shape of the package—similar to a cigarette lighter—and less on the fragrance. Consumers were confused by the packaging and reluctant to purchase a cologne that they could not test before purchasing. More extensive marketing research could have revealed that the Bic brand name had been over extended. What makes for a great pen, lighter or razor doesn't necessarily create a great cologne.

These examples highlight the importance of marketing research, test marketing and establishing marketing information systems both within and outside of the company. Without critical research, products may fail, resulting in substantial losses. Marketing research can identify successful product formulae—and pre-empt disastrous launches or marketing programmes.

SOURCES: *Private Eye,* June 1996; "Lighters and smokers' requisites", *Retail Business,* May 1995, pp. 118–137; Robert Lever, "Bic writes on the alchemy of success in a pen", *Europe,* February 1995, pp. 19–20; Ros Snowdon, "Courage's £5m backs Foster's", *Marketing,* 26 January 1995, p. 2; Jennifer Comiteau, "A Foster's four pack", *Adweek,* 16 January 1995, p. 6.

Stage 1: Defining and Locating Problems

Problem definition The process of uncovering the nature and boundaries of a negative, or positive, situation or question

Problem definition, the first step towards finding a solution or launching a research study, focuses on uncovering the nature and boundaries of a negative, or positive, situation or question. The first sign of a problem is usually a departure from some normal function, such as conflicts between or failures in attaining objectives. If a company's objective is a 12 per cent return on investment and the current return is 6 per cent, this discrepancy should be a warning flag. It is a symptom that something inside or outside the organisation has blocked the attainment of the desired goal or that the goal is unrealistic. Decreasing sales, increasing

Figure 6.4 The five steps of the marketing research process

expenses or decreasing profits also signal problems. Conversely, when an organisation experiences a dramatic rise in sales, or some other positive event, it may conduct marketing research to discover the reasons and maximise the opportunities stemming from them. In Figure 6.5 Taylor Nelson AGB promotes its ability to isolate and identify problems.

To pin down the specific causes of the problem through research, marketers must define the problem and its scope in a way that requires probing beneath the superficial symptoms. The interaction between the marketing manager and the

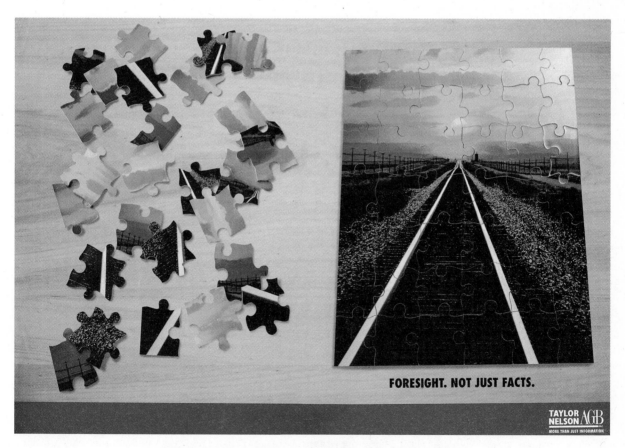

Figure 6.5 Defining and locating problems. Taylor Nelson AGB promotes its ability to target the most appropriate consumer types and their locations for profitable marketing investment.

Source: Courtesy of Taylor Nelson AGB.

marketing researcher should yield a clear definition of the problem. Depending on their abilities, the manager and the researcher can apply various methods to shape this definition. Traditionally, problem formulation has been viewed as a subjective, creative process. Today, however, more objective and systematic approaches are utilised. For example, the **Delphi method** for problem definition consists of a series of interviews with a panel of experts. With repeated interviews, the range of responses converges towards a "correct" definition of the problem.[8] This method introduces structure as well as objectivity into the process of problem definition. Researchers and decision-makers should remain in the problem definition stage until they have determined precisely what they want from the research and how they will use it.

Delphi method A method for problem definition that consists of a series of interviews with a panel of experts

The research objective specifies what information is needed to solve the problem. Deciding how to refine a broad, indefinite problem into a clearly defined and researchable statement is a prerequisite for the next step in planning the research: developing the type of hypothesis that best fits the problem.

• • • • • • • • • • • • • • • • • •

Stage 2: Developing Hypotheses

The objective statement of a marketing research project should include hypotheses drawn from both previous research and expected research findings. A **hypothesis** is an informed guess or assumption about a certain problem or set of circumstances. It is based on all the insight and knowledge available about the problem from previous research studies and other sources. As information is gathered, a researcher can test the hypothesis. For example, a food manufacturer such as H. J. Heinz might propose the hypothesis that children today have more influence than those of previous generations on their families' buying decisions in regard to ketchup and other grocery products. A marketing researcher would then gather data, perhaps through surveys of children and their parents, and draw conclusions as to whether or not the hypothesis was correct. Sometimes several hypotheses are developed during the actual study; the hypotheses that are accepted or rejected become the study's chief conclusions.

Hypothesis An informed guess or assumption about a certain problem or set of circumstances

• • • • • • • • • • • • • • • • • •

Stage 3: Collecting Data

The kind of hypothesis being tested determines which approach will be used for gathering general data: exploratory, descriptive or causal. When marketers need more information about a problem or want to make a tentative hypothesis more specific, they may conduct **exploratory studies**. Exploratory studies discover the general nature of a problem and the factors that relate to it. The design is deliberately flexible.[9] For instance, they may review the information in the firm's databank or examine publicly available data. Questioning knowledgeable people inside and outside the organisation may also yield new insights into the problem. An advantage of the exploratory approach is that it permits marketers to conduct mini-studies with a very restricted database. It also allows hypotheses to be developed further.

Exploratory studies Deliberately flexible data gathering used to discover the general nature of a problem and the factors that relate to it

Descriptive studies Data collection that focuses on providing an accurate description of the variables in a situation

If marketers need to understand the characteristics of certain phenomena to solve a particular problem, **descriptive studies** can aid them. Descriptive studies focus on providing an accurate description of the variables in a situation. Such studies may range from general surveys of consumers' education, occupation or age to specifics on how many consumers purchased Ice Cream Mars last month or how many adults between the ages of 18 and 30 eat some form of high fibre cereal at least three times a week. Some descriptive studies require statistical analysis and predictive tools. For example, a researcher trying to find out how many people will vote for a certain political candidate may have to survey registered voters to predict the results. Descriptive studies generally demand much prior knowledge and assume that the problem is clearly defined. The marketers' major task is to choose adequate methods of collecting and measuring data.

Hypotheses about causal relationships call for a more complex approach than a descriptive study. In **causal studies,** it is assumed that a particular variable X causes a variable Y. Marketers must plan the research so that the data collected prove or disprove that X causes Y. To do so, marketers must try to hold constant all variables except X and Y. For example, to find out whether new carpeting, curtains and ceiling fans increase the leasing rate in a block of flats, marketers need to keep all variables constant except the new furnishings and the leasing rate. Table 6.2 compares the features of these types of research studies.

Causal studies Data collection that assumes that a particular variable X causes a variable Y

Primary data Information gathered by observing phenomena or surveying respondents

Secondary data Information compiled inside or outside the organisation for some purpose other than the current investigation

Marketing researchers have two types of data at their disposal. **Primary data** are observed and recorded or collected directly from respondents. This type of data must be gathered by observing phenomena or surveying respondents. **Secondary data** are compiled inside or outside the organisation for some purpose other than the current investigation. Secondary data include general reports supplied to an enterprise by various data services. Such reports might concern market share, retail inventory levels and consumer buying behaviour. Figure 6.6 illustrates how primary and secondary sources differ. Commonly, secondary data are already available in private or public reports or have been collected and stored by the organisation itself. Because secondary data are already available—"second hand"—to save time and money they should be examined prior to the collection

Project Component	Exploratory Studies	Descriptive or Causal Studies
Purpose	Provide general insights	Confirm insights Verify hypotheses
Data sources	Ill defined	Well defined
Collection form	Open-ended	Structured
Sample	Small	Large
Collection procedure	Flexible	Rigid
Data analysis	Informal	Formal
Recommendations	Tentative	Conclusive

SOURCE: Adapted from A. Parasuraman, *Marketing Research,* First Edition, p. 122, © 1986 Addison-Wesley Publishing Company Inc. Reprinted by permission of Addison-Wesley Longman Inc.

Table 6.2 Comparison of data gathering approaches

Figure 6.6 Approaches to collecting data

of any primary data. Clearly, primary data collection is bespoke and therefore both time consuming and costly. For relatively straightforward problems, secondary data may prove adequate. More complex or risky situations may require specific primary data collection. Figure 6.7 illustrates Millward Brown International's data collection services. The next sections discuss the methods of gathering both secondary and primary data.

Secondary Data Collection

Marketers often begin the marketing research process by gathering secondary data. They may use available reports and other information from both internal and external sources to study a marketing problem.

Internal sources of secondary data can contribute tremendously to research. An organisation's marketing databank may contain information about past marketing activities, such as sales records and research reports, that can be used to test hypotheses and pinpoint problems. An organisation's accounting records are also an excellent source of data but, strangely enough, are often overlooked. The large volume of data that an accounting department collects does not automatically flow to the marketing area. As a result, detailed information about costs, sales, customer accounts or profits by product category may not be part of the MIS. This situation occurs particularly in organisations that do not store marketing information on a systematic basis.

Figure 6.7 Collecting data

Millward Brown International collects data to help organisations with their brand strategies and advertising campaigns.

Source: Courtesy of Millward Brown International.

Secondary data can also be gleaned from periodicals, government publications and unpublished sources. Periodicals such as *Investors' Chronicle, Marketing, Campaign, Marketing Week, Wall Street Journal* and *Fortune* print general information that is helpful for defining problems and developing hypotheses. *Business Monitor* contains sales data for major industries. Mintel publishes sector reports. Table 6.3 summarises the major external sources of secondary data, excluding syndicated services.

Syndicated data services
Organisations that collect general information and sell it to clients

Syndicated data services periodically collect general information, which they sell to clients. BARB, for example, supplies television stations and media buyers with estimates of the number of viewers at specific times. SAMI furnishes monthly information that describes market shares for specific types of manufacturers. Nielsen AGB provides data about products primarily sold through retailers. This information includes total sales in a product category, sales of clients' own brands and sales of important competing brands. In the US, the Market Research Corporation of America (MRCA) collects data through a national panel of consumers to provide information about purchases. The data on brands maintained by the MRCA are classified by age, race, sex, education, occupation and family size. Similar samples exist in most countries.

Another type of secondary data, which is available for a fee, is demographic analysis. Companies, such as CACI or CCN, that specialise in demographic data-banks have special knowledge and sophisticated computer systems to work with

Trade Journals	Virtually every industry or type of business has a trade journal. These journals give a feel for the industry—its size, degree of competition, range of companies involved and problems. To find trade journals in the field of interest, check *The Source Book,* a reference book that lists periodicals by subject.
Trade Associations	Almost every industry, product category and profession has its own association. Depending on the strength of each group, they often conduct research, publish journals, conduct training sessions and hold conferences. A telephone call or a letter to the association may yield information not available in published sources.
International Sources	Periodical indices, such as *Anbar,* are particularly useful for overseas product or company information. More general sources include the *United Nations Statistical Yearbook* and the *International Labour Organisation's Yearbook of Labour Statistics.*
Commercial Sources	Market survey/report organisations produce many sector reports and analyses of companies or brands, for example, *Mintel, Kompass, The Times 1000, Key British Enterprises.*
Governments	Governments, through their various departments and agencies, collect, analyse and publish statistics on practically everything. Government documents also have their own set of indices. A useful index for government generated information in the UK is the government's weekly *British Business.*
Books in Print (BIP)	*BIP* is a two volume reference book found in most libraries. All books issued by publishers and currently in print are listed by subject, title and author.
Periodical Indices	Library reference sections contain indices on virtually every discipline. *ABI Inform,* for example, indexes each article in all major periodicals.
Computerised Literature Retrieval Databases	Literature retrieval databases are periodical indices stored in a computer. Books and dissertations are also included. Key words (such as the name of a subject) are used to search a database and generate references. Examples include *Textline, Harvest* and *ABI Inform.*

Table 6.3 Guide to external sources of secondary data

the very complex census databanks. As a result, they are able to respond to specialised requests. Such information may be valuable in tracking demographic changes that have implications for consumer behaviour and the targeting of products.[10]

Primary Data Collection

The collection of primary data is a more lengthy and complex process than the collection of secondary data and is typically more costly. The acquisition of primary data often requires an experimental approach to determine which variable or variables caused an event to occur.

Experimentation Data collection that involves maintaining certain variables constant so that the effects of the experimental variables can be measured

Experimentation **Experimentation** involves keeping certain variables constant so that the effects of the experimental variables can be measured. For instance, when the Corel WordPerfect tests a change in its WordPerfect word processing computer program, all sales and marketing variables should be held constant except the change in the program. **Marketing experimentation** is a set of rules and procedures by which data gathering is organised to expedite analysis and interpretation.

Marketing experimentation A set of rules and procedures by which data gathering is organised to expedite analysis and interpretation

In experimentation, an **independent variable** (a variable not influenced by or dependent on other variables) is manipulated and the resulting changes measured in a **dependent variable** (a variable contingent on, or restricted to, one value or a set of values assumed by the independent variable). Figure 6.8 illustrates the relationship between these variables. For example, when Houghton Mifflin Company introduces a new edition of its *American Heritage Dictionary*, it may want to estimate the number of dictionaries that could be sold at various levels of advertising expenditure and prices. The dependent variable would be sales, the independent variables would be advertising expenditures and price. Researchers would design the experiment to control other independent variables that might influence sales, such as distribution and variations of the product.

Independent variable A variable not influenced by or dependent on other variables in experiments

Dependent variable A variable that is contingent on, or restricted to, one value or a set of values assumed by the independent variable

In designing experiments, marketing researchers must ensure that their research techniques are both reliable and valid. A research technique has **reliability** if it produces almost identical results in successive repeated trials. But a reliable technique is not necessarily valid. To have **validity**, the method must measure what it is supposed to measure, not something else. A valid research method provides data that can be used to test the hypothesis being investigated. For example, recent experiments on cold fusion by scientists at various institutions have been held to lack both reliability and validity because the results were not repeated in successive trials and the scientists are not sure whether their experiments were measuring energy produced as a result of fusion or some other process.

Reliability The quality of producing almost identical results in successive repeated trials

Validity A condition that exists when an instrument measures what it is supposed to measure

Figure 6.8 Relationship between independent and dependent variables

Technology Comes to Marketing Research

AGB's Superpanel, launched in 1990, took the supermarket barcode wands one step further. No longer was scanning only for the benefit of retailers' stock control. Some 8,500 households—28,000 individual consumers—were provided with barcode swipe wands in their kitchens. Weekly shopping purchases were swiped, first by the checkout assistants and a second time in the consumer's home. The collected data were automatically downloaded by telephone hook to AGB's central computer. The resulting analyses enabled AGB to relate consumer purchases by retailer and manufacturer brands to demographics and lifestyles. The sales of one brand could be examined by type of household, stockist retailers, competitive purchases and brand switching, pricing policies and promotional activity. Technology allowed this data collection to take place on a weekly—even daily—basis.

According to AGB, 12 million marketing research interviews now take place each year in the UK. Around 70 per cent are pen and paper or clipboard exercises—small scale, ad hoc surveys. Five hundred interviews in a survey do not warrant the use of software and lap-top computers by interviewers. Close to 70 per cent of all sales in America are barcoded, and Europe is following suit. Even most cars sold now have a barcode! Anticipating significant growth in electronic point-of-sale and in-home data capture, AGB has invested over £12 million in three years to create Superpanel.

In America, the barcode technology is being developed by leading food manufacturers to target specific consumers. Companies such as Quaker Oats, Kraft General Foods and Proctor & Gamble are developing in-house databases that should soon include the names and addresses of 25 per cent of their end user customers—the shoppers in the supermarkets. The names and data in this "relationship marketing" are collected from scanners at supermarket checkouts and from individually coded money back coupons mailed directly to millions of households. Once the personalised coupon has been redeemed, the consumer's code is instantly recorded in the scanner's database and purchases can be monitored.

Quaker Oats was a pioneer of this approach. It sent 10 coupons apiece to 18 million shoppers, each coupon inscribed with a separate family code and packaged with "involvement devices" such as competition entries and tie-ins with television programmes. Despite the high costs—double those for standard mailings—and the lengthy lead time before a database could be compiled from the feedback, other manufacturers quickly emulated Quaker Oats's initiative. Many US shoppers now carry "customer convenience cards", which reward—usually with price discounts—their compliance and brand loyalty.

Barcode scanning—in stores, at home and for manufacturers—is creating the biggest advance in data capture since the marketing research industry discovered telephone interviewing. The use of scanners, telecommunications and software has increased sample sizes and the amount and accuracy of the information collected, and it has reduced the time lags between data collection, analysis and interpretation of results.

Sources: Larry Black, "Homing in on the American household", *The Independent on Sunday,* 10 March 1991, p. IB21; Bill Blyth at AGB; Phil Dourado, "Clipboard makes way for barcode", *The Independent on Sunday,* 13 January 1991, p. IB21; AGB promotional video; Suzanne Bidlake, "Tesco plans smart loyalty breakthrough", *Marketing,* 14 January 1993, p. 3.

In the United States, one marketing research company, Information Resources Inc., has brought a new dimension to experimental research by combining cable television, supermarket scanners and computers. The company has placed its BehaviorScan microcomputers on televisions in thousands of households in major cities. The company can thus track every advertisement its panelists watch and every purchase they make in a supermarket or chemist's. The information provided by Information Resources helps marketers assess the effectiveness of their advertising by determining whether a viewer saw a particular advertisement and whether the advertisement led the viewer to buy the product.[11] Marketing Insight 6.2 discusses how the use of technology in marketing research assists with experimentation and marketing decision-making.

Experiments may be conducted in the laboratory or in the field; each research setting has advantages and disadvantages. In **laboratory settings,** participants or respondents are invited to a central location to react or respond to experimental stimuli. In such an isolated setting it is possible to control independent variables that might influence the outcome of an experiment. The features of laboratory settings might include a taste kitchen, video equipment, slide projectors, tape recorders, one-way mirrors, central telephone banks and interview rooms. In an experiment to determine the influence of price (independent variable) on sales of a new canned soup (dependent variable), respondents would be invited to a laboratory—a room with table, chairs and sample soups—before the soup was available in stores. The soup would be placed on a table with competitors' soups. Analysts would then question respondents about their reactions to the soup at various prices.

One problem with a laboratory setting is its isolation from the real world. It is simply not possible to duplicate all the conditions that affect choices in the marketplace. On the other hand, by controlling variables that cannot be controlled in the real world, laboratory experiments can focus on variables that marketers think may be significant for the success of a marketing strategy. Test market laboratories are being used more frequently today.[12]

The experimental approach can also be used in **field settings.** A field setting is a "real world" environment. A taste test of Stork SB margarine conducted in a supermarket is one example of an experiment in a field setting. Field settings give the marketer an opportunity to obtain a more direct test of marketing decisions than do laboratory settings.

There are, however, several limitations to field experiments. Field experiments can be influenced or biased by unexpected events, such as the weather or major economic news. Carry-over effects of field experiments are impossible to avoid. What respondents have been asked to do in one time period will influence what they do in the next. For example, evaluations of competing advertisements may influence attempts to obtain objective evaluations of a firm's proposed advertising. The fact that they have viewed previous advertising influences respondents' evaluation of future advertising. There is often an unfortunate experimental "effect". In **home placements** (where a product is used in the home in a real setting) or **diary tests** (when households log their weekly purchases and consumption patterns), people become too involved with the product—artificially so. They might sniff items they would not normally sniff, or ask for their children's opinions about a food item when normally they would just give their children the meal and expect them to eat it.[13] Respondents may not co-operate properly because they do not understand their role in the experiment. Finally, only a small number of variables can be controlled in field experiments. It is impossible, for

Laboratory settings Central locations at which participants or respondents are invited to react or respond to experimental stimuli

Field settings "Real world" environments in which experiments take place

Home placements Experiments in which a product is used in a home setting

Diary tests Experiments in which households log their weekly purchases and consumption patterns example, to control competitors' advertising or their attempts to influence the outcome of the experiment. Tactics that competitors can use to thwart field efforts include couponing, reducing prices temporarily and increasing advertising frequency.

Experimentation is used in marketing research to improve hypothesis testing. However, whether experiments are conducted in the laboratory or in the field, many assumptions must be made to limit the number of factors and isolate causes. Marketing decision-makers must recognise that assumptions may diminish the reliability of the research findings. For example, viewing proposed advertisements on a video cassette recorder in a laboratory is different from watching the advertisements on television at home.

The gathering of primary data through experimentation may involve the use of sampling, survey methods, observation or some combination of these techniques.

Sampling   By systematically choosing a limited number of units, or **sample,** to represent the characteristics of a total population, marketers can project the reactions of a total market or market segment. The objective of **sampling** in marketing research, therefore, is to select representative units from a total population. Sampling procedures are used in studying the likelihood of events based on assumptions about the future.

Since the time and the resources available for research are limited, it would be almost impossible to investigate all the members of a population. A **population,** or "universe", comprises all elements, units or individuals that are of interest to researchers for a specific study. For example, if a Gallup poll is designed to predict the results of an election, all the registered voters in the country would constitute the population. A representative national sample of several thousand registered voters would be selected in the Gallup poll to project the probable voting outcome. The projection would be based on the assumption that no major political events would occur before the election. Sampling techniques allow marketers to predict buying behaviour fairly accurately on the basis of the responses from a representative portion of the population of interest. Sampling methods include random sampling, stratified sampling, area sampling and quota sampling.

When marketers employ **random sampling,** all the units in a population have an equal chance of appearing in the sample. Random sampling is basic probability sampling. The various events that can occur have an equal or known chance of taking place. For example, a specific playing card in a pack has a 1/52 probability of being drawn at any one time. Similarly, if every student at a university or college has a unique identification number and these numbers are mixed up in a large basket, each student's number would have a known probability of being selected. Sample units are ordinarily chosen by selecting from a table of random numbers statistically generated so that each digit from zero to nine will have an equal probability of occurring in each position in the sequence. The sequentially numbered elements of a population are sampled randomly by selecting the units whose numbers appear in the table of random numbers.

In **stratified sampling,** the population of interest is divided into groups according to a common characteristic or attribute, and a probability sample is then conducted within each group. Employing a stratified sample may reduce some of the error that could occur as a result of using a simple random sample. By ensuring that each major group or segment of the population receives its proportionate share of sample units, investigators avoid including too many or too few sample units from each stratum. Usually, samples are stratified when researchers believe that there may be variations among different types of respondents. For example, many political opinion surveys are stratified by sex, race and age.

Area sampling involves two stages: (1) selecting a probability sample of geographic areas, such as streets, census tracts or census enumeration districts, and (2) selecting units or individuals within the selected geographic areas for the sample. This approach is a variation of stratified sampling, with the geographic areas serving as the segments, or primary units, used in sampling. To select the units or individuals within the geographic areas, researchers may choose every *n*th house or unit, or they may adopt random selection procedures to pick out a given number of units or individuals from a total listing within the selected geographic areas. Area sampling may be used when a complete list of the population is not available.

Quota sampling differs from other forms of sampling in that it is judgemental; that is, the final choice of respondents is left to the interviewers. A study of consumers who wear glasses, for example, may be conducted by interviewing any person who wears glasses. In quota sampling, there are some controls—usually limited to two or three variables such as age, sex and education—over the selection of respondents. The controls attempt to ensure that representative categories of respondents are interviewed. In the marketing research industry, quota sampling is by far the most commonly employed form of sampling.

Quota samples are unique because they are not probability samples; not everyone has an equal chance of being selected. Therefore, sampling error cannot be measured statistically. Quota samples are used most often in exploratory studies, in which hypotheses are being developed. Often a small quota sample will not be projected to the total population, although the findings may provide valuable insights into a problem. Quota samples are useful when people with some unusual characteristics are found and questioned about the topic of interest. They are also useful in focusing on a specific core target market segment. A probability sample used to study people allergic to cats would be highly inefficient. Readers who have been stopped in the street by a researcher with a clipboard and a few questions may well have been subject to quota sampling because they fitted, for example, an age or apparent social class "stereotype" deemed appropriate for the specific study.

Survey Methods **Survey methods** include interviews by mail or telephone and personal interviews. Selection of a survey method depends on the nature of the problem, the data needed to test the hypothesis and the resources, such as funding and personnel, that are available to the researcher. Table 6.4 summarises and compares the advantages of the various methods. Researchers must know exactly what type of information is needed to test the hypothesis and what type of information can be obtained through interviewing. Table 6.5 summarises marketing research issues and techniques in the UK.

Gathering information through surveys is becoming more difficult because respondent rates are declining. There is also an indication that people with higher incomes and education are the most likely to respond. Problems include difficulty in hiring qualified interviewers and respondents' reluctance to take part in surveys because of over-long questionnaires, dull topics and time pressures.[14] Moreover, fear of crime makes respondents unwilling to trust interviewers. The use of "sugging"—sales techniques disguised as market surveys—has also contributed to decreased respondent co-operation.

In **mail surveys**, questionnaires are sent to respondents by mail, who are encouraged to complete and return them. Mail surveys are used most often when

Area sampling A method that involves selecting a probability sample of geographic areas and selecting units or individuals within that area for the sample

Quota sampling A sampling method in which the final choice of respondents is left to the interviewers, who base their choices on one or two variables (such as age, sex and education)

Survey methods Interviews by mail or telephone and personal interviews

Mail surveys Questionnaires sent by mail to respondents, who are encouraged to complete and return them

	Mail Surveys	**Telephone Surveys**	**Personal Interview Surveys**
Economy	Potentially the lowest cost per interview if there is an adequate return rate; increased postage rates are raising costs	Avoids interviewers' travel expenses; less expensive than in-home interviews; most common survey method	In-home interviewing is the most expensive interviewing method; shopping mall and focus group interviewing may lower costs
Flexibility	Inflexible; questionnaire must be short, easy for respondents to complete; no probing questions; may take more time to implement than other survey methods	Flexible because interviewers can ask some probing questions, encourage respondents to answer questions; rapport may be gained, but observations are impossible	Most flexible method; respondents can react to visual materials, help fill out questionnaire; because observation is possible, demographic data are more accurate; in-depth probes are possible
Interviewer Bias	Interviewer bias eliminated; questionnaires can be returned anonymously (although often they are coded)	Some anonymity; may be hard to develop trust among respondents	Refusal may be decreased by interviewers' rapport building efforts; interviewers' personal attributes may bias respondents
Sampling and Respondents' Co-operation	Obtaining a complete mailing list is difficult; non-response is a major disadvantage—33 per cent response rates are common in consumer surveys; 1–2 per cent rates in business-to-business surveys	Sample must be limited to respondents with telephones and listed numbers; engaged signals, no answers and non-response—including refusals—are problems; samples must cope with out at work non-responses.	Not at homes are more difficult to deal with; focus groups, shopping mall interviewing may overcome these problems.

SOURCE: Adapted from Milton M. Pressley, "Try these tips to get 50% to 70% response rates from mail surveys of commercial populations", *Marketing News*, 21 January 1983, p. 16. Reprinted by permission of the American Marketing Association.

Table 6.4 Comparison of the three basic survey methods

the individuals chosen for questioning are spread over a wide area and funds for the survey are limited. A mail survey is the least expensive survey method as long as the response rate is high enough to produce reliable results. The main disadvantages of mail surveys are the possibility of a low response rate or of misleading results, if respondents are significantly different from the population being sampled.

Researchers can boost response rates in mail surveys by offering respondents some incentive to return the questionnaire. Incentives and follow-ups have consistently been found to increase response rates. On the other hand, promises of anonymity, special appeals for co-operation and questionnaire length have no apparent impact on the response rate. Other techniques for increasing the response rate, such as advance notification, personalisation of survey materials, type of postage, corporate or university sponsorship, or foot-in-the-door techniques, have had mixed results, varying according to the population surveyed.[15] Although such techniques may help increase the response rates, they can introduce sample composition bias, or non-response bias, which results when those responding to a survey differ in some important respect from those not responding to the survey. In other words, response enhancing techniques may alienate some people in the sample and appeal to others, making the results non-representative of the population of interest. Businesses devote relatively little funding to mail surveys.

Premiums or incentives encouraging respondents to return questionnaires have been effective in developing panels of respondents who are regularly interviewed

a. Expenditure on Market Research

Value of GB Commissioned Market Research						
	1989	1990	1991	1992	1993	1994
AMSO members' turnover £m	230	265	266	293	285	325

AMSO Members' Source of Income by Clients' Business, 1994					
	£m	%		£m	%
Food/soft drinks	42.4	+ 11	Alcoholic drinks	13.7	− 11
Public services and utilities	30.1	+ 13	Household products	13.4	—
Media	30.0	+ 13	Travel and tourism	10.7	+ 7
Financial services	26.0	+ 45	Advertising agencies	9.6	+ 12
Pharmaceuticals	21.4	+ 17	H'hold durables/hardware	3.8	+ 92
Business and industrial	18.6	+ 26	Oil	3.8	+ 13
Vehicles	18.2	+ 26	Tobacco	3.6	+ 73
Health and beauty	18.1	+ 11	Other direct clients	26.9	+ 13
Govt., public bodies	16.7	− 5	Other AMSO cos. (mainly	3.3	
Retailers	14.8	+ 13	subcontracted fieldwork)		

Nature of AMSO Members' Fieldwork (Percentage of total)					
	1993	1994		1993	1994
Personal interview	52	48	Focus group discussion	11	9
Telephone interview	16	19	Self-completion/postal	9	9
Hall test	12	12			

NOTE: The AMSO accounts for more than two-thirds of all marketing research conducted in the UK.
SOURCE: From *European Marketing Pocket Book*, 1996, p. 14. Reprinted by permission of NTC Publications, Ltd.

(Continues)

Table 6.5 The nature of the UK marketing research industry

	1994 Turnover £000s	Change % 1993–1994	Domestic Ranking	International Ranking
Overall Ranking by Turnover				
1. Taylor Nelson AGB Plc	58,052	+ 9.5	1	4
2. NOP Research Group Ltd	43,703	+ 26.3	2	3
3. Research International UK	40,006	+ 25.3	3	1
4. Millward Brown International	34,300	+ 14.0	4	2
5. BMRB International Ltd	20,227	+ 4.2	5	7
6. RSL—Research Services Ltd	17,804	+ 6.6	6	6
7. The Research Business Group	13,343	+ 10.3	8	5
8. MORI	12,799	+ 15.9	7	17
9. The MBL Group Plc	8,297	− 0.3	9	13
10. The Harris Research Centre	7,555	+ 17.0	13	8
11. Gordon Simmons Research Group Ltd	7,490	+ 54.1	10	12
12. Martin Hamblin Group	7,024	+ 10.7	12	11
13. Infratest Burke Group Ltd	6,368	+ 1.2	15	10
14. PAS (public attitude surveys)	5,107	+ 3.6	11	25
15. Simon Godfrey Associates	4,811	− 6.3	24	9
16. Pegram Walters Group	4,549	+ 46.6	16	18
17. FDS Market Research Group Ltd	4,485	+ 17.3	14	21
18. The Gallup Organisation	4,200	− 23.6	18	16
19. BEM	3,365	+ 45.0	17	—
20. Research and Auditing Services Ltd	3,269	− 5.6	19	—
21. Business and Market Research Plc	3,187	+ 38.4	20	22
22. Market Research Solutions Ltd	2,911	(—)	21	23
23. Marketing Sciences Ltd	2,571	+ 48.4	22	20
24. GfK Great Britain Ltd	2,112	+ 2.7	26	15
25. Surveyplan (market research)	1,961	(—)	23	—
26. Audits and Surveys Europe	1,944	(—)	29	14
27. IRB International Ltd	1,556	− 12.8	25	24
28. Scantel Ltd	1,300	+ 0.8	27	19
29. Marketing Direction Ltd	646	+ 1.1	28	—
Total Turnover of AMSO Members	**325,136**	**+ 13.9**		

SOURCE: Association of Market Survey Organisations, 1995.

Table 6.5 The nature of the UK marketing research industry (cont.)

Mail panels Groups of consumers selected to represent a market or market segment who agree to be regularly interviewed by mail

Consumer purchase diaries A marketing research tool in which consumers record their purchases

by mail. **Mail panels** of consumers selected to represent a market or market segment are especially useful for evaluating new products, providing general information about consumers and providing records of consumers' purchases. Many companies use consumer mail panels; others use **consumer purchase diaries.** These surveys are similar to mail panels, but consumers keep track of purchases only. Consumer mail panels and consumer purchase diaries are much more widely used than mail surveys, but they do have shortcomings. Research indicates that the people who take the time to fill out a consumer diary have a higher income and are better educated than the general population. If researchers include less well educated consumers in the panel, they must risk poorer response rates.[16]

In **telephone surveys,** respondents' answers to a questionnaire are recorded by interviewers on the phone. A telephone survey has some advantages over a mail survey. The rate of response is higher because it takes less effort to answer the telephone and talk than to fill out a questionnaire and return it. If there are enough interviewers, telephone surveys can be conducted very quickly. Thus they can be used by political candidates or organisations seeking an immediate reaction to an event. In addition, this survey technique permits interviewers to gain a rapport with respondents and ask some probing questions. According to a survey by the Council of American Survey Research Organizations (CASRO), telephone interviewing is the preferred survey method in more than 40 per cent of the projects conducted by commercial survey research firms.[17] Nearly all businesses engaged in marketing research at some time employ telephone interviewing.

Telephone interviews do have drawbacks. They are limited to oral communication; visual aids or observation cannot be included. Interpreters of results must make adjustments for subjects who are not at home or who do not have telephones. Surveys that specify quotas of respondents hit problems of non-response: secretaries "gatekeep" calls at businesses, thereby preventing researchers from talking to their targets; adult members of households who work outside the home are difficult to contact—and calls in the evening will not be welcome as people want to relax after work.

Telephone surveys, like mail and personal interview surveys, are sometimes used to develop panels of respondents who can be interviewed repeatedly to measure changes in attitudes or behaviour. Reliance on such panels is increasing.

Computer assisted telephone interviewing integrates questionnaire, data collection and tabulations, and provides data to aid decision-makers in the shortest time possible. In computer assisted telephone interviewing, the paper questionnaire is replaced by a computer monitor or video screen. Responses are entered on a terminal keyboard, or the interviewer can use a light pen (a pen shaped torch) to record a response on a light sensitive screen. On the most advanced devices, the interviewer merely points to the appropriate response on a touch sensitive screen with his or her finger. Open-ended responses can be typed on the keyboard or recorded with paper and pencil.

Computer assisted telephone interviewing saves time and facilitates monitoring the progress of interviews. Entry functions are largely eliminated; the computer determines which question to display on the screen, skipping irrelevant questions. Because data are available as soon as they are entered into the system, cumbersome hand computations are avoided and interim results can be quickly retrieved. With some systems, a lap-top computer may be taken to off-site locations for use in data analysis. Some researchers say that computer assisted telephone interviewing—including hardware, software and operation costs—is less expensive than conventional paper and pencil methods.[18]

Marketing researchers have traditionally favoured the **personal interview survey,** chiefly because of its flexibility. A personal interview is a face-to-face situation when the researcher meets the consumer and questions him or her about a specific topic.[19] Various audio-visual aids—pictures, products, diagrams or prerecorded advertising copy—can be incorporated into a personal interview. Rapport gained through direct interaction usually permits more in-depth interviewing, including probes, follow-up questions or psychological tests. In addition, because personal interviews can be longer, they can yield more information.

Depth interviews Lengthy, one-to-one structured interviews, examining in detail a consumer's views about a product

Shopping mall intercept interviews Personal interviewing of a percentage of individuals who pass by certain "intercept" points in a shopping centre

On-site computer interviewing A survey method that requires respondents to complete a self-administered questionnaire displayed on a computer monitor

Focus group interview A survey method that aims to observe group interaction when members are exposed to an idea or concept

Finally, respondents can be selected more carefully, and reasons for non-response can be explored. A **depth interview** is a lengthy, one-to-one structured interview examining a consumer's views about a product in detail.

The nature of personal interviews has changed. In the past, most personal interviews, which were based on random sampling or pre-arranged appointments, were conducted in the respondent's home. Today, most personal interviews are conducted in shopping centres or malls. **Shopping mall intercept interviews** involve interviewing a percentage of persons who pass by certain "intercept" points in a centre. Shopping mall intercept interviewing is a popular survey technique, after telephone and focus group interviewing.

Like any face-to-face interviewing method, shopping centre intercept interviewing has many advantages. The interviewer is in a position to recognise and react to respondents' non-verbal indications of confusion. Respondents can be shown product prototypes, video tapes of commercials and the like, and reactions can be sought. The environment lets the researcher deal with complex situations. For example, in taste tests, researchers know that all the respondents are reacting to the same product, which can be prepared and monitored from the mall test kitchen or some other facility. In addition, lower cost, greater control and the ability to conduct tests requiring bulky equipment make shopping mall intercept interviews popular.

Research indicates that given a comparable sample of respondents, shopping mall intercept interviewing is a suitable substitute for telephone interviewing.[20] In addition, there seem to be no significant differences in the completeness of consumer responses between telephone interviewing and shopping mall intercept interviewing. In fact, for questions dealing with socially desirable behaviour, shopping mall intercept respondents appear to be more honest about their past behaviour.[21]

In **on-site computer interviewing,** a variation of the mall intercept interview, respondents complete a self-administered questionnaire displayed on a computer monitor. For example, MAX (Machine Answered eXamination), a microcomputer based software package developed by POPULUS, conducts such interviews in shopping malls. After a brief lesson on how to operate MAX, respondents can proceed through the survey at their own pace. According to its developers, MAX provides not only faster and more accurate information but also consistency, for each respondent is asked questions in the same way. MAX is flexible because it can ask different sets of relevant questions depending on the respondents' previous answers. In addition, respondents' answers are entered directly into a computer and do not need to be coded and keyed in before being analysed; nor is there any chance of information being incorrectly encoded. Its developers assert that "MAX is the interviewer we would all like to be. MAX is patient, nonjudgmental, remembering all that he is taught, and he keeps track of every answer."[22]

The object of a **focus group interview** is to observe group interaction when members are exposed to an idea or concept. Focus groups frequently are held in viewing facilities as illustrated in Figure 6.9. Often these interviews are conducted informally, without a structured questionnaire. Consumer attitudes, behaviour, lifestyles, needs and desires can be explored in a flexible and creative manner through focus group interviews. Most firms use focus group interviewing. Questions are open-ended and stimulate consumers to answer in their own words. Researchers can ask probing questions to clarify something they do not fully understand or something unexpected and interesting that may help to explain consumer behaviour. When Cadbury used information obtained from focus

Figure 6.9

Primary data collection

Viewing facilities are often used for experiments or for running focus discussion groups.

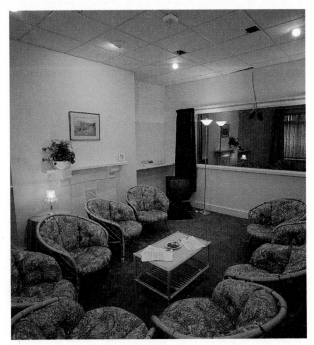

SOURCE: Courtesy of the West Midlands Viewing Facility.

groups to change its advertising and test product concepts, the new advertisements and product launches pushed up sales.[23] Case 6.2 describes the future of this marketing research technique. Focus group discussions commence with a general discussion, typically among eight consumers of the same sex, led by a moderator. This market researcher narrows the conversation during the session, homing in on a specific brand, product or advertisement—hence the term "focus" group.

Quali-depth interviews are 25 to 30 minute intercept interviews that incorporate some of the in-depth advantages of focus groups with the speed and researcher's flexibility for intercept studies. Typically, intercepted consumers are taken to a nearby hall or café and asked more probing and searching questions than is possible in a 3 to 4 minute intercept interview. They can also be shown a greater variety of stimulus material. This is a useful approach for sensitive issues that people might not wish to discuss in a group—gambling and drugs, for example.

Another research technique is the **in-home** (door-to-door) **interview**. Because it may be desirable to eliminate group influence, the in-home interview offers a clear advantage when thoroughness of self-disclosure is important. In an in-depth interview of 45 to 90 minutes, respondents can be probed to reveal their real motivations, feelings, behaviours and aspirations. In-depth interviews permit the discovery of emotional "hot buttons" that provide psychological insights.[24]

Questionnaire Construction A carefully constructed questionnaire is essential to the success of any survey. A **questionnaire** is a base document for research purposes that provides the questions and the structure for an interview or self-completion and has provision for respondents' answers.[25] Questions must be designed to elicit information that meets the study's data requirements. These questions must be clear, easy to understand and directed towards a specific objective.

Quali-depth interviews 25 to 30 minute intercept interviews that incorporate some of the in-depth advantages of focus groups with the speed and flexibility of intercept studies

In-home interview 45 to 90 minute interview in which the researcher visits the respondent in his or her home

Questionnaire Base document for research purposes, providing the questions and structure for an interview or self-completion and providing space for respondents' answers

Researchers need to define the objective before trying to develop a questionnaire because the objective determines the substance of the questions and the amount of detail. A common mistake in constructing questionnaires is to ask questions that interest the researchers but do not yield information useful in deciding whether to accept or reject a hypothesis. Finally, the most important rule in composing questions is to maintain impartiality.

The questions are usually of three kinds: open-ended, dichotomous and multiple choice:

1. OPEN-ENDED QUESTION
   What is your general opinion of the American Express Optima Card?

   _____
   _____
   _____

2. DICHOTOMOUS QUESTION
   Do you presently have an American Express Optima Card?
   Yes _____
   No _____

3. MULTIPLE CHOICE QUESTION
   What age group are you in?
   Under 20   _____
   20–29   _____
   30–39   _____
   40–49   _____
   50–59   _____
   60 and over   _____

The design of questionnaires is extremely important because it will affect the validity and usefulness of the results. It is therefore useful to test questionnaires on a few respondents before conducting the full survey. The questions must relate to the research objectives. The layout of the questionnaire must not be off-putting to respondents or to the researchers conducting the work. These days, carefully laid out questionnaires can be read and analysed by computers. Open-ended questions can be the most revealing, but are time consuming—and therefore off-putting—for respondents, as well as difficult to analyse across respondents. Dichotomous questions are straightforward but not very revealing; and often the answer is not a full yes or no. Multiple choice questions are popular, but care must be exercised in the choice of categories. Most questionnaires include a mix of question styles.

Researchers must be very careful in wording questions that a respondent might consider too personal or that might require him or her to admit to activities that other people are likely to condemn. Questions of this type should be worded in such a way as to make them less offensive, and are often placed towards the end of the questionnaire.

For testing special markets, where individuals (for instance, executives, scientists and engineers) are likely to own or have access to a personal computer, questionnaires may be programmed on a computer disk and the disk delivered through the mail. This technique may cost less than a telephone interview and eliminate bias by simplifying flow patterns in answering questions. Respondents see less clutter on the screen than on a printed questionnaire; the novelty of the approach may also spark their interest and compel their attention. The Internet is now being used for this purpose.[26]

Observation Methods When using **observation methods**, researchers record respondents' overt behaviour, taking note of physical conditions and events. Direct contact with respondents is avoided; instead, their actions are examined and noted systematically. For example, researchers might use observation methods to answer the question, "How long does the average McDonald's restaurant customer have to wait in line before being served?"

Observation may also be combined with interviews. For example, during personal interviews, the condition of a respondent's home or other possessions may be observed and recorded and demographic information such as ethnic origin, approximate age and sex can be confirmed by direct observation. Observation is not confined to consumers; shops and service establishments can be observed, too, through "mystery shopper" research—as detailed in the chapter opener.

Data gathered through observation can sometimes be biased if the respondent is aware of the observation process. An observer can be placed in a natural market environment, such as a grocery store, without biasing or influencing shoppers' actions. However, if the presence of a human observer is likely to bias the outcome or if human sensory abilities are inadequate, mechanical means may be used to record behaviour. **Mechanical observation devices** include cameras, recorders, counting machines and equipment to record physiological changes in individuals. For instance, a special camera can be used to record the eye movements of respondents looking at an advertisement and to detect the sequence of reading and the parts of the advertisement that receive greatest attention. Electronic scanners in supermarkets are mechanical observation devices that offer an exciting opportunity for marketing research. Scanner technology can provide accurate data on sales and consumers' purchase patterns, and marketing researchers may buy such data from the supermarket (see Case 6.1).

Observation is straightforward and avoids a central problem of survey methods: motivating respondents to state their true feelings or opinions. However, observation tends to be descriptive. When it is the only method of data collection, it may not provide insights into causal relationships. Another drawback is that analyses based on observation are subject to the biases of the observer or the limitations of the mechanical device.

Observation methods
Methods by which researchers record respondents' overt behaviour and take note of physical conditions and events

Mechanical observation devices Cameras, recorders, counting machines and other equipment that records physiological changes in individuals

● ● ● ● ● ● ● ● ● ● ● ● ● ● ● ● ● ● ● ●

Stage 4: Analysing and Interpreting Research Findings

After collecting data to test their hypotheses, marketers analyse and interpret the research findings. Interpretation is easier if marketers carefully plan their data analysis methods early in the research process. They should also allow for continual evaluation of the data during the entire collection period. They can then gain valuable insight into areas that ought to be probed during the formal interpretation. It is important to give consideration to data analysis techniques prior to the collection of data. Many students discover after a survey has been completed, for example, how different wording or ordering of questions, as well as of categories, could have reduced the complexity of the analysis. It also helps when interpreting findings to keep in mind the target audience for the results—the report or presentation—so that the level of analysis and interpretation of the findings can be geared to their understanding.

The first step in drawing conclusions from most research is displaying the data in table format. If marketers intend to apply the results to individual categories of the things or people being studied, cross-tabulation may be quite useful, especially in tabulating joint occurrences. For example, a cross-tabulation of data using the two variables gender and purchase rates of car tyres would show differences in how men and women purchase car tyres. Various statistical procedures exist that facilitate the simultaneous analysis and examine the interactions of many variables.[27]

Statistical interpretation An analysis of data that focuses on what is typical or what deviates from the average

After the data are tabulated, they must be analysed. **Statistical interpretation** focuses on what is typical or what deviates from the average. It indicates how widely responses vary and how they are distributed in relation to the variable being measured. This interpretation is another facet of marketing research that relies on marketers' judgement or intuition. Moreover, when they interpret statistics, marketers must take into account estimates of expected error or deviation from the true values of the population. The analysis of data may lead researchers to accept or reject the hypothesis being studied.

Data require careful interpretation by the marketer. If the results of a study are valid, the decision-maker should take action; however, if it is discovered that a question has been incorrectly worded, the results should be ignored. For example, if a study by an electricity company reveals that 50 per cent of its customers believe that meter-readers are "friendly", is that finding good, bad or indifferent? Two important benchmarks help interpret the result: how the 50 per cent figure compares with that for competitors and how it compares with a previous time period. The point is that managers must understand the research results and relate the results to a context that permits effective decision-making.[28]

● ● ● ● ● ● ● ● ● ● ● ● ● ● ● ● ● ● ●

Stage 5: Reporting Research Findings

The final step in the marketing research process is reporting the research findings. Before preparing the report, the marketer must take a clear, objective look at the findings to see how well the gathered facts answer the research question or support or negate the hypotheses posed in the beginning. In most cases, it is extremely doubtful that the study can provide everything needed to answer the research question. Thus in the report the researcher must point out the deficiencies and the reasons for them, perhaps suggesting areas that require further investigation.

The report presenting the results is usually a formal, written one. Researchers must allow time for the writing task when they plan and schedule the project. Since the report is a means of communicating with the decision-makers who will use the research findings, researchers need to determine beforehand how much detail and supporting data to include. They should keep in mind that corporate executives prefer reports that are short, clear and simply expressed. Often researchers will give their summary and recommendations first, especially if decision-makers do not have time to study how the results were obtained. A technical report allows its users to analyse data and interpret recommendations because it describes the research methods and procedures and the most important data gathered. Thus researchers must recognise the needs and expectations of the report user and adapt to them.

When marketing decision-makers have a firm grasp of research methods and procedures, they are better able to integrate reported findings and personal experience. If marketers can spot limitations in research from reading the report, their personal experience assumes additional importance in the decision-making process. Marketers who cannot understand basic statistical assumptions and data gathering procedures may misuse research findings. Consequently, report writers should be aware of the backgrounds and research abilities of those who will rely on the report in making decisions. Clear explanations presented in plain language make it easier for decision-makers to apply the findings and less likely that a report will be misused or ignored. Talking to potential research users before writing a report can help researchers supply information that will indeed improve decision-making.

The Importance of Ethical Marketing Research

Marketing research and systematic information gathering increase the chances of successful marketing. Many companies, and even entire industries, have failed because of a lack of marketing research. The conventional wisdom about the evaluation and use of marketing research by marketing managers suggests that in future managers will rely on marketing research to reduce uncertainty and to make better informed decisions than they could without such information.[29]

Clearly, marketing research and information systems are vital to marketing decision-making. Because of this, it is essential that ethical standards be established and followed. Attempts to stamp out shoddy practices and establish generally acceptable procedures for conducting research are important developments in marketing research. Other issues of great concern relate to researchers' honesty, manipulation of research techniques, data manipulation, invasion of privacy and failure to disclose the purpose or sponsorship of a study in some situations. Too often respondents are unfairly manipulated and research clients are not told about flaws in data.

One common practice that hurts the image of marketing research is "sugging" ("selling under the guise of marketing research"). A leading marketing research association, ESOMAR, is encouraging research companies and marketing research firms worldwide to adopt codes and policies prohibiting this practice.[30] In the UK, the Market Research Society lays down strict guidelines.

Because so many parties are involved in the marketing research process, developing shared ethical concern is difficult. The relationships among respondents who cooperate and share information, interviewing companies, marketing research agencies that manage projects, and organisations that use the data are interdependent and complex. Ethical conflict typically occurs because the parties involved in the marketing research process have different objectives. For example, the organisation that uses data tends to be results orientated, and success is often based on performance rather than a set of standards. On the other hand, a data gathering sub-contractor is evaluated on the ability to follow a specific set of standards or rules. The relationships among all participants in marketing research must be understood so that decision-making becomes ethical. Without clear understanding and agreement, including mutual adoption of standards, ethical conflict will lead to mistrust and questionable research results.[31]

Marketing research is essential in planning and developing marketing strategies. Information about target markets provides vital input in planning the marketing mix and controlling marketing activities. It is no secret that companies can use information technology as a key to gaining an advantage over the competition.[32] In short, the marketing concept—the marketing philosophy of customer orientation—can be implemented better when adequate information about customers, competition and trends is available.

● ● ● ● ● ● ● ● ● ● ● ● ● ● ● ● ● ●

Summary

● To implement the marketing concept, marketers need information about the characteristics, needs and wants of their target markets. Marketing research and information systems that furnish practical, unbiased information help firms avoid the assumptions and misunderstandings that could lead to poor marketing performance.

● *Marketing research* is the systematic design, collection, interpretation and reporting of information to help marketers solve specific marketing problems or take advantage of marketing opportunities. Marketing research is conducted on a special project basis, with the research methods adapted to the problems being studied and to changes in the environment. *Quantitative research* leads to findings that can be quantified and statistically analysed. *Qualitative research* examines subjective opinions and value judgements.

● The *marketing information system (MIS)* is a framework for the day-to-day managing and structuring of information regularly gathered from sources both inside and outside an organisation. The inputs into a marketing information system include the information sources inside and outside the firm considered useful for future decision-making. Processing information involves classifying it and developing categories for meaningful storage and retrieval. Marketing decision-makers then determine which information—the output—is useful for making decisions. Feedback enables those who are responsible for gathering internal and external data to adjust the information inputs systematically. Data brought into the organisation through marketing research become part of its *marketing databank,* a file of data collected through both the MIS and marketing research projects. Any information—an idea or piece of research—that assists in decision-making is *marketing intelligence.*

● The increase in marketing research activities represents a transition from intuitive to scientific problem solving. Intuitive decisions are made on the basis of personal knowledge and past experience. *Scientific decision-making* is an orderly, logical and systematic approach. Minor, non-recurring problems can be handled successfully by *intuition.* As the number of risks and alternative solutions increases, the use of research becomes more desirable and rewarding.

● The five basic steps of planning marketing research are (1) defining and locating problems, (2) developing hypotheses, (3) collecting data in order to test and further develop hypotheses, (4) analysing and interpreting research findings, and (5) reporting the findings.

● *Problem definition*—the first step towards finding a solution or launching a research study—means uncovering the nature and boundaries of a negative, or positive, situation or question. A problem must be clearly defined for marketers to develop a *hypothesis*—an informed guess or assumption about that problem or set of circumstances—which is the second step in the research process. The *Delphi method* can help develop hypotheses.

● To test the accuracy of hypotheses, researchers collect data—the third step in the research process. Researchers may use *exploratory, descriptive* or *causal studies. Secondary data* are compiled inside or outside the organisation for some purpose other than the current investigation. Secondary data may be collected from an organisation's databank and other internal sources; from periodicals, government publications and unpublished sources; and from *syndicated data services,* which collect general information and sell it to clients. Secondary data should be examined prior to the collection of any primary data.

● *Primary data* are observed and recorded or collected directly from respondents. *Experimentation* involves maintaining as constants those factors that are related to or may affect the variables under investigation, so that the effects of the experimental variables can be measured. *Marketing experimentation* is a set of rules and procedures according to which the task of data gathering is organised to expedite analysis and interpretation. In experimentation, an *independent variable* is manipulated and the resulting changes are measured in a *dependent variable*. Research techniques are *reliable* if they produce almost identical results in successive repeated trials; they are *valid* if they measure what they are supposed to measure and not something else. Experiments may take place in *laboratory settings*, which provide maximum control over influential factors, or in *field settings*, which are preferred when marketers want experimentation to take place in natural surroundings, such as with *home placements* and *diary tests*.

● Other methods of collecting primary data include sampling, surveys and observation. *Sampling* involves selecting representative units, or *samples*, from a total *population*. In *random sampling*, all the units in a population have an equal chance of appearing in the sample. In *stratified sampling*, the population of interest is divided into groups according to a common characteristics or attribute, and then a probability sample is conducted within each group. *Area sampling* involves selecting a probability sample of geographic areas such as streets, census tracts or census enumeration districts, and selecting units or individuals within the selected geographic areas for the sample. *Quota sampling* differs from other forms of sampling in that it is judgemental.

● *Survey methods* include *mail surveys* and *mail panels*, *consumer purchase diaries*, *telephone surveys*, *computer assisted telephone interviews* and *personal interview surveys*, such as *depth interviews*, *shopping mall intercept interviews*, *on-site computer interviews*, *focus group interviews*, *quali-depth interviews*, and *in-home interviews*. *Questionnaires* are instruments used to obtain information from respondents and to record observations; they should be unbiased and objective. *Observation methods* involve researchers recording respondents' overt behaviour and taking note of physical conditions and events. Observation may be facilitated by *mechanical observation devices*.

● To apply research findings to decision-making, marketers must interpret and report their findings properly. *Statistical interpretation* is analysis that focuses on what is typical or what deviates from the average. After interpreting their research findings, researchers must prepare a report of the findings that the decision-makers can use and understand.

● Marketing research and systematic information gathering increase the probability of successful marketing. Because marketing research is essential to the planning and development of marketing strategies, attempts to eliminate unethical marketing research practices and establish generally acceptable procedures for conducting research are important goals. However, because so many parties are involved in the marketing research process, shared ethical concern is difficult to achieve.

● ● ● ● ● ● ● ● ● ● ● ● ● ● ● ● ● ●

Important Terms

Marketing research	Exploratory studies	Laboratory settings
Quantitative research	Descriptive studies	Field settings
Qualitative research	Causal studies	Home placements
Marketing information system (MIS)	Primary data	Diary tests
	Secondary data	Sample
Marketing databank	Syndicated data services	Sampling
Marketing intelligence	Experimentation	Population
Intuition	Marketing experimentation	Random sampling
Scientific decision-making	Independent variable	Stratified sampling
Problem definition	Dependent variable	Area sampling
Delphi method	Reliability	Quota sampling
Hypothesis	Validity	Survey methods

Mail surveys	Personal interview survey	Quali-depth interviews
Mail panels	Depth interview	In-home interview
Consumer purchase diaries	Shopping mall intercept	Questionnaire
Telephone surveys	interviews	Observation methods
Computer assisted telephone	On-site computer interviewing	Mechanical observation devices
interviewing	Focus group interview	Statistical interpretation

• • • • • • • • • • • • • • • • •
Discussion and Review Questions

1. What is the MIS likely to include in a small organisation? Do all organisations have a marketing databank?
2. What is the difference between marketing research and marketing information systems? In what ways do marketing research and the MIS overlap?
3. What are the differences between quantitative and qualitative marketing research?
4. How do the benefits of decisions guided by marketing research compare with those of intuitive decision-making? How do marketing decision-makers know when it will be worthwhile to conduct research?
5. Give specific examples of situations in which intuitive decision-making would probably be more appropriate than marketing research.
6. What is the difference between defining a research problem and developing a hypothesis?
7. What are the major limitations of using secondary data to solve marketing problems?
8. List some of the problems of conducting a laboratory experiment on respondents' reactions to the taste of different brands of beer. How would these problems differ from those of a field study of beer taste preferences?
9. In what situation would it be best to use random sampling? Quota sampling? Stratified or area sampling?
10. *Non-response* is the inability or refusal of some respondents to co-operate in a survey. What are some ways to decrease non-response in personal door-to-door surveys?
11. Suggest some ways to encourage respondents to co-operate in mail surveys.
12. If a survey of all homes with listed telephone numbers is conducted, what sampling design should be used?
13. What are the benefits of the focus group technique?
14. Give some examples of marketing problems that could be solved through information gained from observation.
15. Why is questionnaire design important? Why should questionnaires be tested?
16. What is "sugging"? Why is it damaging to the marketing research industry?

• • • • • • • • • • • • • • • • •
Recommended Readings

R. P. Bagozzi, ed., *Principles of Marketing Research* (Oxford: Blackwell, 1994).

D. F. Birks "Market research" in M. J. Baker, ed., *The Marketing Book*, 3rd edn (Oxford: Butterworth-Heinemann, 1994), pp. 238–267.

E. F. McQuarrie, *The Market Research Toolbox: A Concise Guide for Beginners* (London: Sage, 1996).

D. S. Tull and D. I. Hawkins, *Marketing Research* (New York: Macmillan, 1990).

P. M. Chisnall *Marketing Research* (Maidenhead: McGraw-Hill, 1992).

Cases

6.1 Research Agencies Battle to Scan

A. C. Nielson is one of the world's largest marketing research companies. In the retail tracking business, Nielsen has close to 90 per cent of the market. Manufacturers and retailers use these data to monitor the performance of individual manufacturer brands such as Persil or Kellogg's Cornflakes; retailer own label brands such as Sainsbury's Novon; the relative success of separate food, grocery and electrical categories; the market shares of major retail groups or the impact of promotional campaigns and price variations by store, town, region or nation.

Nielsen's hold over the market for such supermarket scanning data is about to be broken with the appearance in Europe of fellow US research house, IRI. In the US, IRI's Infoscan has edged ahead of Nielsen's Scantrack. IRI plans to take the lead in Europe, too. Infoscan is jointly owned by IRI, Taylor Nelson and the German retail auditor GFK. IRI launched Infoscan in the UK, France and Germany in 1993, and during 1994 entered three additional countries' scanning data collection and analysis markets. IRI's Infoscan includes details on why goods are sold, not just when and where. Data come from over 1,000 stores, including convenience outlets; the major supermarket retailers Asda, Gateway, Tesco, Safeway and Sainsbury; and Superdrug (for data on beauty aids).

IRI claims to offer more user-friendly tracking data from more stores using leading edge software. Nielsen is retaliating by reminding the market that it offers a highly reliable and proven service as the "leading edge supplier of information systems around the world". Nielsen is stressing its overall knowledge of this market and its additional products, Scan*Pro and Homescan. Nielsen has signed up with superstore retailer Safeway to supply named account data, while IRI has opted for a similar deal with supermarket rival Asda. Nielsen's pioneering deal with Safeway, revealing specific sales data from Safeway suppliers and manufacturers, rather than general sales data not specific to a particular retailer or site, has broken new ground. It is likely that Nielsen's near monopoly of this £25 million UK market will become a buyer's market, with accounts playing off Nielsen and IRI in order to obtain the latest data at the most competitive rates.

The need for information has mushroomed, and the major research houses have invested heavily in developing these scanning research systems. Manufacturers need the information in order to plan brand strategies and identify market opportunities for new launches. These data prove invaluable in monitoring both the effects of their own marketing mixes and the impact of their rivals'. For retailers, the data assist in merchandise planning: ordering the desirable brands and products, taking account of rival retailers' performances and analysing regional variations.

Away from the market for scanning data, Nielsen has responded to IRI's threat by developing its strength as the leading coupon response and sales promotions monitoring agency. PPA is the result of Nielsen's co-operation with geodemographic house CCN. Instead of reporting just the number of responses received to consumer sales promotions, CCN's geodemographic profiling system Mosaic enables full geodemographic customer profiling of respondents, leading to more accurate targeting of future campaigns. Nielsen handles around 2 million sales promotion responses each day in the UK for around 500 manufacturers. The research giant believes that the combination of its coupon response analysis and CNN's Mosaic profiling provides the opportunity for retailers and manufacturers to

- produce geodemographic profiles of customers who respond to coupon based sales promotions.
- target more accurately next time those customers likely to be positive respondents.
- identify the "best" retail outlets for local and national promotions.
- select the most relevant media and promotions for specific brands.

The marketing research industry, like any other market, is constantly evolving: new technology in particular is altering the methods of data collection and analysis in retail tracking and large scale survey research. Major research houses are launching new products and entering more countries to compete head-on around the world. For the users of research data of this nature—manufacturers, distributors and retailers—the increased competition and investment in systems are leading to the rapid availability of more accurate data for more and more products.

SOURCES: Robert Dwek, "NDL and Pinpoint offer firms targeting plan", *Marketing*, 5 November 1992, p. 3; Robert Swek, "Nielsen sets up analysis service", *Marketing*, 3 December 1992, p. 12; "IRI to rival Nielsen with retail track", *Marketing Week*, 20 November 1992, p. 6; Alan Mitchell, "Information war sparked as US firm tackles Nielsen", *Marketing*, 19 November 1992, p. 3; "Safeway offers weekly monitor", *Marketing*, 9 July 1992, p. 4.

Questions for Discussion

1. What advantages do manufacturers gain from the rapid turnaround of Scantrack and Infoscan data?
2. How can manufacturers such as Kellogg's or Unilever use such data?
3. How can analysis of these scanning data help retailers such as Aldi, Carrefour, Safeway or Sainsbury?
4. Is the increasing competition between rival market research agencies detrimental to the services they offer or beneficial to their clients? Why?

6.2 Focus Group Interviewing: In-Depth Views from Group Discussions

Focus group interviews, which are generally informal group discussions about marketing ideas or concepts conducted by a marketer or marketing research firm, are used by most major organisations in developing marketing or business plans. In the 1980s, focus group interviewing became one of the most widely practised types of marketing research, expanding from the packaged goods industry into financial services, hard goods and industrial applications.

However, the function of focus group interviewing is expected to change. Traditionally, companies have relied on focus group interviews to define the input going into quantitative studies, but the new trend is to conduct focus group interviews after tabulating research results, to provide insight into why the results were achieved. The trend is also towards higher costs (the average today is £1,200 for 90 minutes and £1,750 for an extended, video recorded group lasting two and a half hours).

Other changes pertain to moderator guides and their reports. The moderator guides will be expected to involve clients in the development process. Their reports will concentrate on providing conclusions that interpret the findings and on making recommendations for action by the client. The reports will also contain fewer actual quotations from individual focus group participants. The post–focus group debriefing techniques are also being altered. The shift is towards disciplined debriefing that asks participants their reactions to the group session. Such debriefing can provide the link between concept development and application and can serve as a rough check on validity and reliability.

Another new development in focus group interviewing is the use of electronics to offer three-way capabilities. Computerised decision-making software can supplement research findings and consolidate opinions from three different audiences. For example, in health care research in a hospital setting, the three audiences would be former patients, physicians and employees. The advantages of using electronics include easier scheduling of participating groups and more interaction among the three audiences.

A major UK service retailer was faced with declining sales and two new competitors. In order to re-establish itself as the dominant force in its market, it decided to undertake some in-depth qualitative marketing research using focus groups. The retailer's new competitors were opening stores at the rate of six per month, and the company realised it had to act quickly to defend its position. However, it had conducted no consumer research for many years and was uncertain why its customer preferred its stores, how competitors were perceived and what types of people constituted its customer profile. Before modifying its marketing mix and launching an advertising campaign to combat its new competitors, the company had to gain a better understanding of its target market. For approximately £14,000, using a specialist consumer qualitative agency, in just three weeks the company had a good "feel" for its standing in its core trading area, as perceived by customers. The table shows that the information resulted from a fairly "standard" programme of focus groups.

Each group had eight consumers, four of whom were shoppers in the retailer's stores, four of whom shopped in competitors' stores. Each group lasted three hours, and a free merchandise voucher and buffet meal were provided for delegates. The same

Group Composition	Social Class*	Location
1. Male 25–39, white collar commuters[†]	A, B	Eastcheap
2. Male 40–55, white collar commuters	A, B	Hitchin
3. Female 25–44, executives/PAs	A, B, C1	Bristol
4. Female 25–44, semi-skilled	C2	Working
5. Female 35–40 "housewives"[†]	A, B	Leamington
6. Female 25–34, "housewives"	C1, C2	Sheffield
7. Males 18–29, young earners[†]	C1, C2	Ealing
8. Female 18-29, young earners	C1, C2	Telford

*For social class definitions, see Table 4.2, p. 126.
[†]Held in branches after hours

moderator ran all eight groups to maintain consistency. Each session was tape recorded, the tapes being transcribed later into a report and presentation to the retailer's board of directors. Two sessions were video recorded, and several were secretly viewed by the company's marketing executives.

SOURCES: Lynne Cunningham, "Electronic focus groups offer 3-way capability", *Marketing News,* 8 January 1990, pp. 22, 39; Thomas L. Greenbaum, "Focus group spurt predicted for the '90s", *Marketing News,* 8 January 1990, pp. 21, 22; Nino DeNicola, "Debriefing sessions: the missing link in focus groups", *Marketing News,* 8 January 1990, pp. 20, 22; Peter Jackson, Adsearch, Richmond.

Questions for Discussion

1. What are the strengths and benefits of focus group marketing research?
2. This retailer chose to commission a programme of focus groups. Given the aims of the company's research, what other research tools might the company have used? Explain your selection.

7

SEGMENTING MARKETS, TARGETING AND POSITIONING

"The essence of successful segmentation lies not in fragmentation but in building an excellent understanding of the marketplace."

Sally Dibb
Warwick Business School

OBJECTIVES

- To understand the definition of a market
- To recognise different types of markets
- To learn how firms segment markets
- To understand targeting decisions
- To learn about strategies for positioning
- To understand the importance of developing an edge over competitors

In mid-1995, the makers of Red Bull launched a £5 million campaign aimed at the fast growing market in energy enhancing non-alcoholic drinks. Targeted at the youth market, Red Bull, a proven success in Austria prior to its UK appearance, was expected to set the sector alive. By the end of the year, however, the headlines in the marketing press were very different: "Red Bull dumps 'confusing' ads", explained trade weekly *Marketing* magazine. Red Bull decided to abandon its launch advertising theme, replacing it with a £5 million branding drive, after marketing research revealed that consumers think the energy drink is in fact a beer. The brand positioning behind Red Bull had a big impact and was successful in that consumers remembered the brand and its advertising. The basic positioning platform, however, was apparently confusing target customers, who misunderstood the promotion to mean that the brand was yet another lager launch.

By the middle of 1996, the company had devised a new marketing strategy and planned a total re-launch to overcome this consumer confusion. Red Bull is now positioning itself as a hangover cure. New cans have been produced replacing the words "energy drink" with "Red Bull Stimulation". The managing director stated that he was positioning the drink "for people who want to burn the candle at both ends": office staff working long hours, long-distance lorry drivers, students, clubbers and people with hangovers. Although very different types of people, these targets for Red Bull all share the lifestyle trait of being active in the evenings and often during the night, thereby providing the producers of energy drinks with a clear target market.

The re-launch was pushed in an advertising campaign using graffiti artists spraying images of the drink. The advertisements mimicked cigarette advertising with the line "Caution: do not drink when you want to sleep". This novel positioning strategy was selected partly as a direct response to consumers who thought the product was a lager brand, but also because of the nature of the increasingly crowded energy drinks sector. With numerous new brands competing for the same group of consumers' attention, the management team behind Red Bull recognised that it had to set its brand apart not only from lagers but also from direct competitors. It remains to be seen whether the new positioning strategy appeals to the late night brigade. Modifying any marketing strategy, particularly the positioning as communicated to the target consumers, is a troublesome task. For Red Bull, the erroneous links with lager and increasing competition from other energy drinks have made the need for it to revise its marketing strategy essential. ▪

SOURCES: Sharon Marshall, "Red Bull dumps 'confusing' ads", *Marketing,* 7 December 1995, p. 2; Sharon Marshall, "Red Bull targets red-eye market", *Marketing,* 4 July 1996, p. 4; Gail Kemp, "Recent recruit hypes Red Bull", *Campaign,* 3 March 1995, p. 16; Jan Carruthers, "Energy drinks", *Beverage World,* March 1996, p. 120.

I n this example Red Bull advertisements confused customers into believing that the non-alcoholic drink was, in fact, a beer. The company was therefore forced to re-launch the drink by positioning it carefully as an "energy drink". This case shows the importance of focusing on the process of market segmentation, from the identification of different consumer needs right through to the identification and implementation of suitable marketing programmes for these individuals. Companies like Red Bull realise that not all consumers want the same things. To satisfy these different needs it is necessary for companies to single out groups of customers and aim some or all of their marketing activities at these groups. The key is then to develop and maintain a marketing mix that both satisfies the particular requirements of customers in these groups and is positioned in such a way as to be meaningful to them.

This chapter considers the nature of markets, first defining the term and describing the different types. It then reviews the concepts of segmentation, targeting and positioning by considering the variables used to segment markets. Next, it considers the strategies often used to select target markets and approaches to product positioning. It then reviews the importance of developing an edge over competitors. Finally, it discusses market measurement and primary sales forecasting techniques.

• • • • • • • • • • • • • • • • • •

What Are Markets?

The word *market* has a number of meanings. It used to refer primarily to the place where goods were bought and sold. It can also refer to a large geographic area. In some cases the word refers to the relationship between the demand and supply of a specific product. For instance, "What is the state of the market for oil?" Sometimes, "market" is used to mean the act of selling something.

Market An aggregate of people who as individuals or as organisations have a need for certain products and the ability, willingness and authority to purchase such products

For the purposes of this text, a **market** is an aggregate of people who, as individuals or in organisations, have needs for products in a product class and who have the ability, willingness and authority to purchase such products. In general use, the term *market* sometimes refers to the total population—or mass market—that buys products. However, the definition used here is more specific; it refers to individuals seeking products in a specific product category. For example, students are part of the market for textbooks, as well as being markets for calculators, pens and pencils, paper, food, music and other products. Obviously, there are many different markets in any economy. In this section, the requirements for markets are considered in conjunction with these different types.

Requirements for a Market

For a group of people to be a market, the members of the group must meet the following four requirements:

1. They must need or want a particular product or service.
2. They must have the ability to purchase the product. Ability to purchase is related to buying power, which consists of resources such as money, goods and services that can be traded in an exchange situation.
3. They must be willing to use their buying power.
4. They must have the authority to buy the specific products.

Individuals can have the desire, the buying power and the willingness to purchase certain products but may not be authorised to do so. For example, secondary school students may want, have the money for and be willing to buy alcoholic beverages; but a brewer does not consider them a market because until they are 18 years old, they are prohibited by law from buying alcohol. An aggregate of people that lacks any one of the four requirements thus does not constitute a market.

Types of Markets

Consumer market Purchasers or individuals in their households who personally consume or benefit from the purchased products and do not buy products primarily to make a profit

Organisational (or **industrial**) **market** Individuals or groups that purchase a specific kind of product to re-sell, use directly in producing other products or use in general daily operations

Markets can be divided into two categories: consumer markets and organisational or business-to-business markets. These categories are based on the characteristics of the individuals and groups that make up a specific market and the purposes for which they buy products. A **consumer market** consists of purchasers and/or individuals in their households who personally consume or benefit from the purchased products and who do not buy products primarily to make a profit. Each of us belongs to numerous consumer markets for such products as housing, food, clothing, vehicles, personal services, appliances, furniture and recreational equipment. Consumer markets are discussed in more detail in Chapter 4.

An **organisational** (or **industrial**) **market** consists of individuals or groups that purchase a specific kind of product for one of three purposes: resale, direct use in producing other products or use in general daily operations. The four categories of organisational (or industrial) markets—producer, reseller, government and institutional—are discussed in Chapter 5.

● ● ● ● ● ● ● ● ● ● ● ● ● ● ● ● ● ● ●

Selecting Target Markets

Chapter 1 defined a marketing strategy as having three components: (1) the analysis of marketing opportunities, (2) the selection of the organisation's target market and (3) the creation and maintenance of a marketing mix that satisfies that market's needs for a specific product. Irrespective of the general types of markets on which a firm focuses, marketing management must select the firm's target markets. The next section examines two general approaches to identifying target markets: the total market approach and market segmentation.

Total Market Approach or Market Segmentation?

Undifferentiated or **total market approach** An approach that assumes that all customers have similar needs and wants and can be served with a single marketing mix

Sometimes marketers define the total market for a particular product or service as their target market. Companies that develop a single marketing mix aimed at all potential customers in a market are said to be adopting an **undifferentiated** or **total market approach.** The assumption is that all customers in the market have similar needs and wants and can, therefore, be satisfied with a single marketing mix—a standard product or service, similar price levels, one method of distribution and a promotional mix aimed at everyone.

Increasingly, marketers in both consumer and industrial markets are accepting that because of the varying characteristics, needs, wants and interests of customers, there are few markets where a single product or service is satisfactory for all. The extensive array of goods on supermarket shelves reflects basic differences in customers' requirements. The trend, it seems, is away from a mass marketing approach, and even markets that were traditionally undifferentiated are changing, with an ever increasing number of products on offer. For instance, the market for food seasoning used to be dominated by salt. Now, low sodium substitutes are being offered as alternatives for the increasingly health conscious consumer.

The mass marketing approach is appropriate only under two conditions. The first, which is increasingly rare, is when there is little variation in the needs of customers for a specific product. The second condition is that the organisation must develop and sustain one marketing mix that satisfies everyone. If the number of customers is large, the commitment in terms of company resources and managerial expertise can be considerable.

When an undifferentiated approach is inappropriate or impractical, marketers use market segmentation to try to increase customer satisfaction. This technique involves identifying groups of customers in markets who share similar buying needs and characteristics. By identifying and understanding such groups, marketers are better able to develop product or service benefits that are appropriate for them (see Figure 7.1). They do this by designing products and brands to appeal to particular target segments and to be supported by an appropriate promotional campaign and suitable pricing and distribution strategies. For example, clothing sold through Victoria's Secret is manufactured for youthful female consumers. This is reflected in both the product styling and the promotional campaign.

Figure 7.1
Market segmentation
approach

Organisation   **Single marketing mix**   **Market**

Applying Market Segmentation

Heterogeneous markets
Markets in which all customers have different requirements

Markets in which all customers have different requirements are termed **heterogeneous markets.** For example, the market for wrist watches is quite diverse. Swatch designs relatively low priced watches for the fashion-conscious customer. Rotary markets much more conservative and expensive designs for an older customer group.

In completely heterogeneous markets the only way to satisfy everyone is by offering tailor made or bespoke products. This situation is more prevalent in organisational markets, where, for example, plant machinery is designed for a specific task and situation. However, while it may not be feasible to offer every customer a tailor made product, it is often possible to aggregate customers into groups with similar product needs and wants. **Market segmentation** is the process by which customers in markets with some heterogeneity can be grouped into smaller, more similar or homogeneous segments. In so doing, a balance is sought between obtaining reasonably substantial groups and ensuring sufficient similarity to allow individuals to be offered a standard marketing mix. As shown in Figure 7.2, Rover knows that customer needs in the car market vary.

Market segmentation The process of grouping customers in markets with some heterogeneity into smaller, more similar or homogeneous segments

Having identified market segments, marketers must decide which, if any, they intend to enter. A marketing programme covering all elements of the marketing mix can then be designed to suit the particular requirements of those segments tar-

Figure 7.2

Supplying a heterogeneous market

Rover knows that customer needs in the car market vary and accordingly offers a broad range of models.

SOURCE: *Courtesy of Rover Cars.*

geted. Sears-owned British Shoe Corporation dominated the UK footwear retailing sector, mainly through medium and budget priced chains such as Dolcis and Saxone. The company realised it was not catering for the upper end of the market, which had lower volumes but higher unit margins. Cable & Co. was duly launched to cater for this segment of the market.

Companies have turned to market segmentation with good reason. Burtons, Diner's Club and Bird's Eye Walls have all demonstrated that success can follow the effective implementation of market segmentation strategies. For example, the variety of offerings in the market for frozen, ready-to-eat meals illustrates the spread of customer needs.

Careful segmentation and the customer understanding underlying it can make it easier for firms to identify and exploit different market opportunities. For example, segmentation can help minor players in the market achieve a foothold in a particular niche, perhaps by identifying an opportunity not directly exploited by market leaders. In general, segmentation helps companies pursue four types of product and market opportunities:

1. *Market Penetration* involves increasing the percentage of sales in present markets by taking sales from the competition. For example, Coca-Cola and PepsiCo engage in advertising programmes that compete for each other's market share.
2. *Product Development* offers new or improved products to existing markets by expanding the range of products on offer. For example, the washing powder market has undergone much change over recent years with the introduction of new micro-powders and products aimed specifically at washing coloured clothing.
3. *Market Development* develops existing products in new markets by finding new applications and/or customer groups. Evian, one of the major players in the market for mineral water, now offers its product in a mist spray. The Evian Brumisateur atomiser (see Figure 7.3) is being marketed as a new concept in skin moisturisers.
4. *Diversification* involves moving into different markets by offering new products. For example, Bic followed its success in the ballpoint pen market by moving into disposable razors and perfumes.

· · · · · · · · · · · · · · · · · · ·

The Advantages of Market Segmentation

Segmentation is seen to offer businesses a number of advantages that make it easier to develop and capitalise on opportunities such as those described above. These advantages can be considered at the customer level, in relation to the competition or in terms of the effectiveness of resource allocation and strategic planning.

Customer Analysis Segmenting markets allows a better understanding of customers' needs, wants and other characteristics to be achieved. The sharper focus that segmentation offers allows the personal, situational and behavioural factors that characterise customers in a particular segment to be considered. In short, questions about how, why and what customers buy can be addressed. By being closely in touch with

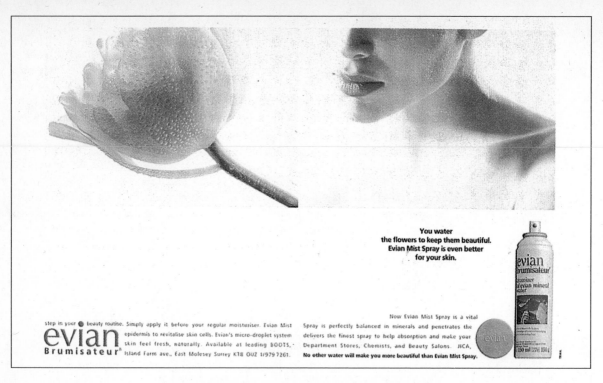

You water
the flowers to keep them beautiful.
Evian Mist Spray is even better
for your skin.

step in your beauty routine. Simply apply it before your regular moisturiser. Evian Mist epidermis to revitalise skin cells. Evian's micro-droplet system skin feel fresh, naturally. Available at leading BOOTS, Island Farm ave., East Molesey Surrey KT8 0UZ 1/979 7261.

Now Evian Mist Spray is a vital Spray is perfectly balanced in minerals and penetrates the delivers the finest spray to help absorption and make your Department Stores, Chemists, and Beauty Salons. JICA. **No other water will make you more beautiful than Evian Mist Spray.**

Figure 7.3 Developing existing products in new markets. Evian, one of the major players in the market for mineral water, now offers its product as a mist spray for skin care.

Source: Courtesy of PBWA Advertising, Inc. for Laboratoire d'Hygiene Dermatologique d'Evian.

segments, marketers can respond quickly to even slight changes in what target customers want.

Competitor Analysis Most markets are characterised by intense competition. Within this environment, companies need to understand the nature of the competition they face. Who are the main competitors? At which segments are they targeting their products? Answering these and other similar questions allows marketers to make decisions about which are the most appropriate segments to target and what kind of competitive advantage should be sought. Companies that do not understand how the market is divided up risk competing head-on against larger organisations with superior resources.

Effective Resource Allocation All companies have limited resources. To target the whole of the market is usually unrealistic. The effectiveness of personnel and material resources can be greatly improved when they are more narrowly focused on a particular segment of customers.

Strategic Marketing Planning Companies operating in a number of segments are unlikely to follow the same strategic plans in them all. Dividing markets up allows marketers to develop plans that give special consideration to the particular needs and requirements of customers in different segments. The time scale covered by the strategic plan can also be structured accordingly, because some segments change more rapidly than others. The market for recorded music is a typical example. While tastes in classical music remain fairly steady, tastes in pop change very rapidly. Companies like EMI clearly need to consider this factor when developing corporate plans.

The benefits of segmentation are illustrated in the following example. Despite recent problems, IBM is still regarded as something of a legend in the computer industry. During the 1960s, the company recognised that there was a need for certain industry standards. IBM argued that, when customers' needs changed, it would not be feasible for them to dispose of existing equipment and expertise and begin all over again. They had to be able to upgrade to equipment that spoke similar languages and had similar physiology. Through this insight, IBM became that standard. The company was able to offer a complete package of service, training, consultancy, maintenance and software support. It built its corporate image to the point where, according to an often quoted industry joke, "no-one ever got fired for buying IBM". For IBM's competitors this powerful competitive advantage presented a dilemma. How could they compete successfully against such odds? Curiously, for some companies the best solution was not to compete directly at all, but instead to specialise and focus on certain segments or niches in the market. For example, NCR concentrated on the retailing and banking markets, Apple on the education market.

• • • • • • • • • • • • • • • • • • • •

Segmenting, Targeting and Positioning

There are three stages to carrying out market segmentation: segmentation, targeting and positioning. Figure 7.4 gives an overview of these stages.

Figure 7.4

Basic elements of segmentation

Segmentation
- Consider variables for segmenting market.
- Look at profile of emerging segments.
- Validate segments emerging.

Targeting
- Decide on targeting strategy.
- Decide which and how many segments should be targeted.

Positioning
- Understand consumer perceptions.
- Position products in the mind of the consumer.
- Design appropriate marketing mix.

Segmenting the Market

There are many ways in which customers can be grouped and markets segmented. In different markets, the variables that are appropriate change. The key is to understand which are the most suitable for distinguishing between different product requirements. Understanding as much as possible about the customers in the segments is also important, as marketers who "know" their targets are more likely to design an appropriate marketing mix for them. For example, car company Daewoo used extensive customer research as the basis for its entry into the UK car market. The research revealed an inherent dislike of car showrooms and the high pressure selling techniques associated with them. Daewoo used its understanding to develop a new kind of distribution outlet, staffed by non-commissioned advisors. The impact of Daewoo's marketing approach is now being seen in the way other car manufacturers are gearing up their selling effort.

Targeting Strategy

Once segments have been identified, decisions about which and how many customer groups to target can be made. There are several options:

- Concentrate on a single segment with one product and marketing programme.
- Offer one product and marketing programme to a number of segments.
- Target a different product and marketing programme at each of a number of segments.

These options are explored in more detail later in this chapter. The choices companies make must take resource implications into consideration. The actions of NCR and Apple described above illustrate that careful focusing of resources is essential.

Positioning the Product

Companies must decide precisely how and where within the targeted segments to aim a product or products, brand or brands. The needs and wants of targeted customers must be translated into a tangible mix of product/service, price, promotion and distribution. The consumers' view of the product and where it is positioned relative to the competition is particularly critical. After all, the paying public does not always perceive a product or brand in the way the manufacturer would like. For example, to the dismay of those who developed it, the Sinclair C5 electric trike was perceived as an object of ridicule.

• • • • • • • • • • • • • • • • • •

Choosing Segmentation Variables

Segmentation variables or bases The dimensions or characteristics of individuals, groups or organisations that are used for dividing a total market into segments

Segmentation variables or bases are the dimensions or characteristics of individuals, groups or organisations that are used for dividing a total market into segments. There is rarely a single or best way to segment a market. Companies must choose from an array of different options.[1, 2] In consumer markets, background characteristics like age, sex and occupation—which are relatively easy to obtain and measure through observation and questioning—are very widely used. In organisational markets, customer size, location and product use are often the focus.

Several factors are considered in selecting segmentation variables. The variables chosen should relate to customers' needs for, uses of or behaviour towards the product. Indeed, there is no "magic" associated with segmentation. Clifford and Cavanagh succinctly put the technique into perspective:

High growth companies succeed by identifying and meeting the needs of certain kinds of customer, not all customers, for special kinds of products and service, not all products or all services. Business academics call this market segmentation. Entrepreneurs call it common sense.[3]

Stereo hi-fi equipment marketers might segment the stereo market on the basis of income and age—but not on the basis of religion, because one person's music equipment needs do not differ much from those of persons of other religions. Furthermore, if individuals or organisations in a total market are to be classified accurately, the segmentation variable must be measurable. For example, segmenting a market on the basis of intelligence or moral standards would be quite difficult because these attributes are hard to measure accurately.

Variables for Segmenting Consumer Markets

Companies developing their strategy for segmentation can choose one or several variables or bases from a wide range of choices. Table 7.1 comprehensively illustrates the options available for the marketer of consumer goods. These divide into variables like demographics and socio-economics that relate to basic customer

---

Basic Customer Characteristics

Because of the ease with which information concerning basic customer characteristics can be obtained and measured, the use of these variables is widespread.

Demographics

Age
Sex
Family
Race
Religion
The family life cycle concept is an imaginative way of combining demographic variables.

Socio-Economics

Income
Occupation
Education
Social class
Different income groups have different aspirations in terms of cars, housing, education, etc.

Geographic Location

Country
Region
Type of urban area (conurbation/village)
Type of housing (affluent suburbs/inner city)

Personality, Motives and Lifestyle

Holiday companies often use lifestyle to segment the market. Club Med, for example, concentrates on young singles while other tour operators cater especially for senior citizens or young families.

Product Related Behavioural Characteristics

Purchase Behaviour

Customers for frozen ready meals may be highly brand loyal to Heinz or Birds Eye or may shop purely on the basis of price.

Purchase Occasion

A motorist making an emergency purchase of a replacement tyre while on a trip far from home is less likely to haggle about price than the customer who has a chance to shop around.

Benefits Sought

When customers buy washing powder or fabric conditioner they seek different benefits. For some, cleaning power and softness are essential, whereas for others a product's environmental friendliness is the key. Ecover products try to cater for this latter group.

Consumption Behaviour and User Status

Examining consumption patterns can indicate where companies should be concentrating their efforts. Light or non-users are often neglected. The important question to ask is why consumption in these groups is low.

Attitude towards Product

Different customers have different perceptions of and preferences for products offered. Concern about environmental issues has altered many consumers' perceptions of household cleaning products and has resulted in a host of so called environmentally friendly products.

Table 7.1 Variables for segmenting consumer markets

characteristics and product related behavioural factors, such as purchase and usage behaviour.

Basic Customer Characteristics

Demographic Variables   The ease with which demographic variables can be measured has largely contributed to their widespread usage in segmenting markets. The characteristics most often used include age, sex, family, race and religion. Because these factors can be closely related to customers' product needs and purchasing behaviour, understanding them often helps target their efforts more effectively. For example, as shown in Figure 7.5, Heinz targets new parents with its baby foods. Manufacturers of ready-to-eat breakfast cereals, such as Kellogg's and Nabisco, offer their products in packages of different sizes to satisfy the needs of consumers ranging from singles to large families.

Financial institutions such as banks and building societies attempt to interest children in their products by offering free gifts such as book vouchers. Meanwhile, retired customers are targeted with products designed for a leisure orientated lifestyle. The emphasis is on tailoring the service package to suit the particular needs.

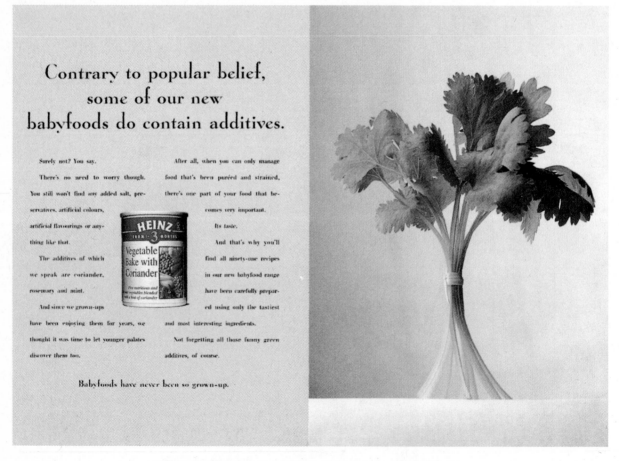

Figure 7.5 Demographic variables. Heinz baby food is promoted to new parents.
Source: Courtesy of Heinz.

a. Population of the EU by age group (%)

	0–19	20–59	≥ 60
1960	31.8	52.8	15.4
1965	32.2	51.4	16.4
1970	32.1	50.4	17.5
1975	31.5	50.3	18.2
1980	30.1	52.0	17.9
1985	27.8	53.4	18.8
1990	25.5	54.9	19.6
1995	24.2	55.4	20.4
2000	23.8	55.0	21.3
2005	23.4	54.6	22.0
2010	22.9	53.9	23.2
2015	22.2	53.5	24.3
2020	21.6	52.8	25.7

b. Population by age group at 1 January 1993 (%)

	0–19	20–39	40–59	≥ 60	Of Which ≥ 80
Austria	23.7	31.9	24.1	20.3	3.9
Belgium	24.3	30.5	24.2	21.1	3.7
Denmark	23.8	29.9	26.2	20.1	3.9
Finland	25.4	29.1	26.7	18.8	3.1
France	26.8	30.0	23.6	19.7	4.0
Germany	21.5	31.6	26.5	20.4	3.9
Greece	24.6	29.6	25.0	20.8	3.4
Ireland	34.9	28.9	21.0	15.3	2.4
Italy	22.6	30.9	25.3	21.3	3.6
Luxembourg	23.3	32.4	25.2	19.2	3.3
Netherlands	24.6	32.9	24.9	17.6	3.0
Portugal	27.4	29.4	23.7	19.5	2.7
Spain	26.5	31.3	22.7	19.6	3.0
Sweden	24.6	27.5	25.4	22.4	4.5
UK	24.3	29.9	23.6	22.2	3.8
EU	24.4	30.7	24.7	20.2	3.7

SOURCE: From *Eurostat: Europe in Figures,* 4th Edition, Office for Official Publications of the European Community, p. 142. Reprinted by permission.

Table 7.2 The changing age profile of the European Union

Population statistics help marketers to understand and keep track of changing age profiles. With the population of Europe increasing at a rate of 0.6 per cent a year, a 7 per cent fall in the 0 to 19 year old age band is expected between 1990 and 2000 (see Table 7.2). Over the same period, however, the number of 20 to 59 year olds is expected to stay steady, with the number of people over 60 likely to increase by 9 per cent. This will inevitably affect new opportunities for marketers, who must increasingly cater for an ageing population. Given the relative affluence of this particular group, a wide range of companies (for example, the leisure and service industries) might expect to reap the benefits of this increase by the turn of the century.

In some markets, including clothes, cosmetics, alcoholic drinks, books, magazines and even cigarettes, gender has long been a key demographic variable. In other markets, its use is more recent. European Union statistics show that while women and girls represent 51.4 per cent of the population, men and boys account for 48.6 per cent. The confectionery market is one that traditionally did not segment on the basis of sex. Chocolate manufacturers, including Cadburys, tried to change this by developing assortments aimed primarily at men. In general, despite the care taken in each product's design, packaging and promotion, they were not successful.

The way in which marketers treat ethnicity varies in different parts of the world. For instance, in the US, where one quarter of the population is made up of ethnic minorities, ethnicity is widely used as a means of segmenting markets for goods and services of all kinds. The US Hispanic population illustrates the importance of ethnicity as a segmentation variable. Comprising people of Mexican, Cuban, Puerto Rican, and Central and South American heritage, this ethnic group is growing five times faster than the general population. Consequently, it is being targeted by more and more companies—including AT&T, Campbell Soup Co., Nabisco and Procter & Gamble. However, targeting Hispanic customers is not an easy task. For example, although marketers have long believed that Hispanic consumers are exceptionally brand loyal and prefer Spanish language broadcast media, recent research has failed to support this notion. Not only do advertisers disagree about the merits of Spanish language media; they also question whether it is appropriate to advertise to Mexicans, Puerto Ricans and Cubans using a common Spanish language.[4] In other areas the proportion of ethnic minorities is much lower than in the US, affecting the level of marketing attention they receive. In the UK, where only 5 per cent of the population come from an ethnic minority, marketers are much more reluctant to develop bespoke marketing programmes for particular groups. As explained in Marketing Insight 7.1, they fear that such action may lead to accusations of ethnic stereotyping and racism.

Product needs also vary according to marital status and by number and age of children. Figure 7.6 illustrates patterns of expenditure on a full range of products for different household types. These factors are collectively taken into consideration by the *family life cycle* concept. Some of the more obvious markets in which the impact of different life cycles is seen are tourism, housing and financial services. The family life cycle has been broken down in several different ways. Table 7.3 illustrates a fairly comprehensive scheme that is sometimes used.

The scheme is based on the assumption that individuals at different life cycle stages have varying product needs. Marketers can respond to this by targeting such groups with marketing mixes designed to capitalise on the differences. For example, parents whose children have grown up and left home tend to have more disposable income than those with young children and tend to spend more on the home, holidays and new cars. Banks and financial institutions in particular are getting better at gearing their marketing efforts to life cycle changes. Critics of the life cycle concept point out that it can be difficult to decide to which categories families belong. In some cases, such as single-parent families and couples without children, households do not appear to fit in at all.

Figure 7.6

Pattern of expenditure by decile groups of gross income (1991)

Source: Family Expenditure Survey, 1991. *Crown Copyright 1991. Reproduced by permission of the Controller of HMSO and of the Office for National Statistics.*

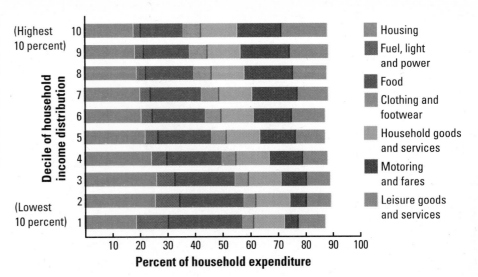

Note: Percentages are expenditure on commodity or service group as a percentage of total household expenditure.

Obviously, this discussion of demographic variables is not exhaustive. However, the variables described above probably represent the most widely used demographics. Other examples of the use of demographics include segmenting the cosmetic and hair care markets on the basis of race and directing certain types of foods and clothing towards people of specific religious sects.

Socio-Economic Variables   This group of variables includes income, occupation, education and social class. Some marketing academics and practitioners include certain of these variables under the demographics label.

Income can be a very useful way of dividing markets because it strongly influences people's product needs. It affects their ability to buy (discussed in Chapter 2) and their aspirations for a certain style of living. Obvious products in this

---

Bachelor stage (young single people not living with parents)
Newly married couples without children
Full nest I (youngest child under 6)
Full nest II (youngest child 6 or over)
Full nest III (older married couple with dependent children)
Empty nest I (no children living at home, family head in work)
Empty nest II (family head retired)
Solitary survivor (in work)
Solitary survivor (retired)

SOURCE: From *Consumer Market Research Handbook*, 3rd ed., R. Worcester and J. Downham, eds. (ESOMAR) (England: McGraw-Hill Book Company (UK) Ltd, 1986), p. 394. Courtesy of the European Society for Opinion and Marketing Research, Amsterdam.

Table 7.3 Wells and Gubar life cycle stages

Ethnic Marketing or Racial Stereotyping?

While their US counterparts are using a host of marketing tools and techniques specifically to target ethnic groups, many UK companies are still uncomfortable with the whole idea of ethnic marketing. At a time when the UK ethnic community is expected to double in the next three decades, the unwillingness of many businesses to capitalise on the new opportunities that are arising seems surprising. In practice, this reluctance stems from concerns that doing so may provoke accusations of racism, or of emphasising racial division. The outcome is that ethnic marketing in the UK tends to focus on ensuring that ethnic groups are not excluded, rather than being specifically targeted.

With new Office of National Statistics figures suggesting that the purchasing power of ethnic groups is on the increase, it seems inevitable that the situation will soon change. For example, there are now almost half a million Pakistani consumers in the UK, over half of whom hold managerial or professional positions. Since more than 60 per cent of these UK Pakistanis are under the age 25, the potential for future growth in this group is also large. These characteristics are vital, as it seems likely that the success of ethnic marketing will be driven by the economic affluence of the groups being targeted. For a host of religious, cultural or language reasons, some groups may be too fragmented or small to attract specifically designed products and marketing programmes. For example, the 800,000 strong Indian community, the UK's largest ethnic group, is broken down into sub-groups speaking five or more different languages, making targeting a complex affair.

The US, where more than 25 per cent of the population come from ethnic minorities, is not neces-sarily an appropriate point of comparison. The sheer size of the ethnic groups in the US simply cannot be ignored, and large companies such as Coca-Cola, Nabisco, P&G and Sears are all devel-oping specifically targeted marketing programmes for different ethnic minorities. In the UK, only around 5 per cent of the population come from eth-nic minorities, a much lower proportion. These eth-nic groups also tend to be more integrated into the population as a whole than in the US, so racial divi-sions are less clearly defined.

As companies in the UK continue to grapple with the strategic issue of ethnic marketing, attempts to include minorities at the tactical marketing level are increasing. For example, advertisers are making greater use of black, Chinese and Asian actors in their promotions than previously. Yet members of these ethnic minorities are still rarely used in cer-tain types of advertisements, such as those for cars, perfume, jewellery and financial services. The result is that accusations of tokenism and of rein-forcement of racial stereotypes still abound. For example, in 1996 a Vauxhall Astra television adver-tisement featuring hundreds of babies attracted criticism because almost all of them were white. In spite of this, a spokesperson for the Commission for Racial Equality believes that the advertising business has at least progressed in recent years. The challenge now, it seems, is for companies to move away from the passive, sometimes minimal-ist inclusion of ethnic minorities and actively seek the opportunities that this important part of the population represent.

SOURCES: Veronica Lyons, "Just a stereotype?", *Marketing Week*, 21 June 1996, pp. 40–41; Alicia Clegg, "Colour blind", *Marketing Week*, 21 June 1996, pp. 38–40; Peter Jackson, Adsearch, Richmond-upon-Thames, 1996.

category include housing, furniture, clothing, cars, food and certain kinds of sporting goods.

The occupations of the members of the household are known to have an impact on the types of products and services that are purchased. The type of housing individuals and families own or rent is strongly linked to this variable. It is obvious, for example, that sales of products for refurbishment and decoration, such as paints, fabrics and wallpapers, will occur predominantly among those professions that have owner-occupier status. Occupation is also known to affect the types of sporting and leisure activities people prefer (see Table 7.4).

Other socio-economic variables that may be used to segment markets include education level and social class.

Geographic Variables The needs of consumers in different geographic locations may be affected by their local climate, terrain, natural resources and population density. Markets may be divided into regions because one or more geographic variables may cause customers' needs to differ from one region to another. A company that sells products throughout the European Union will, for example, need to take the different languages spoken into account when labelling its goods.

City size can be an important segmentation variable. For example, one franchised restaurant organisation will not locate in cities of less than 100,000 people because experience shows that a smaller population base could make the operation unprofitable. The same company may add a second, or even a third, restaurant once the city reaches a certain size. Other firms, however, seek out opportunities in smaller towns. The major petroleum retailers, such as Esso and Shell, have traffic density thresholds, below which they perceive a local market as unviable. It is, therefore, quite common—particularly in villages and small towns in rural areas—for petroleum retailing to be dominated by independent garage owners and the smaller petroleum companies.

Market density The number of potential customers within a unit of land area

Market density refers to the number of potential customers within a unit of land area, such as a square kilometre. Although market density is generally related to population density, the correlation is not exact. For example, in two different geographic markets of approximately equal size and population, the market density for office supplies might be much higher in the first than in the second if the first contains a significantly greater proportion of business customers. Market density may be a useful segmentation variable because low density markets often require different sales, advertising and distribution activities from high density markets.

In Europe, climate can be used as a geographic segmentation variable. Companies entering new markets in Europe increasingly need to consider the impact of climate on their customer base. For example, washing machines sold in Italy do not require such fast spin speeds as those sold in Germany because the Italian climate is much sunnier. Other markets affected by climate include air conditioning and heating equipment, clothing, gardening equipment, recreational products and building materials.

Locality: ACORN ACORN (A Classification of Residential Neighbourhoods) develops geographic location as a segmentation base one stage further. Information taken from census data allows people to be grouped according to a number of factors, including geography, socio-economics and culture. In total, 40 different variables are considered, among them household size, number of cars, type of occupation, and family size and characteristics.

	Professional	Employers and Managers	Intermediate and Junior Non-manual	Skilled manual and Own Account Non-professional	Semi-skilled Manual and Personal Service	Unskilled Manual	All Socio-Economic Groups[3]
Walking	57	46	42	39	36	31	41
Swimming	27	19	18	10	11	8	15
Snooker/pool/billiards	11	12	8	17	10	9	12
Keep fit/yoga	13	12	18	6	9	8	12
Cycling	14	9	9	10	8	9	10
Darts	6	5	4	8	6	6	6
Weightlifting/training	7	5	5	6	4	3	5
Golf	9	10	5	6	2	2	5
Running/jogging	11	6	4	3	2	2	5
Soccer	6	3	3	6	3	3	4

[1] Percentage participating in the four weeks before interview.

[2] Socio-economic group is based on the person's current or most recent job.

[3] Includes full time students, members of the armed forces, those who have never worked and those whose job was inadequately described.

SOURCE: *Social Trends*, 1996. Crown Copyright 1996. Reproduced by permission of the Controller of HMSO and of the Office for National Statistics.

Table 7.4 Participation[1] in sports, games and physical activities: by socio-economic group,[2] Great Britain, 1993–94 (percentages)

The underlying concept is that customers living in different residential neighbourhoods have different profiles in respect of these variables. Their product needs in terms of styling and features therefore also vary. Consumers can be classified under ACORN on the basis of the postcode of their home address and then allocated to one of the groups in Table 7.5.

Categories	% Pop.	Groups	% Pop.
A Thriving	19.8	1 Wealthy achievers, suburban areas	15.1
		2 Affluent greys, rural communities	2.3
		3 Prosperous pensioners, retirement areas	2.3
B Expanding	11.6	4 Affluent executives, family areas	3.7
		5 Well-off workers, family areas	7.8
C Rising	7.5	6 Affluent urbanites, town and city areas	2.2
		7 Prosperous professionals, metropolitan areas	2.1
		8 Better-off executives, inner city areas	3.2
D Settling	24.1	9 Comfortable middle agers, mature home owning areas	13.4
		10 Skilled workers, home owning areas	10.7
E Aspiring	13.7	11 New home owners, mature communities	9.8
		12 White collar workers, better-off multi-ethnic areas	4.0
F Striving	22.8	13 Older people, less prosperous areas	3.6
		14 Council estate residents, better-off homes	11.6
		15 Council estate residents, high unemployment	2.7
		16 Council estate residents, greatest hardship	2.8
		17 People in multi-ethnic, low-income areas	2.1
Unclassified	0.5		0.5

Table 7.5 The ACORN consumer targeting classification

These categories further sub-divide to give a total of 17 groups and 54 neighbourhood types (see Figure 7.7). For example, the Aspiring (E) category splits into

- new home owners, mature communities.
- white collar workers, better-off multi-ethnic areas.

Personality, Motives and Lifestyle Variables such as personality characteristics, motives and lifestyle are sometimes used to segment markets. The variables can be used by themselves to segment a market or in combination with others, such as demographics or socio-economic statistics.

Personality characteristics are useful when a product is similar to many competing products and when consumers' needs are not significantly affected by other segmentation variables. However, attempting to segment a market according to personality characteristics has caused problems. Although marketing practitioners have long believed that consumer choice and product use should vary with personality and lifestyle, marketing research has shown only weak relationships. However, the weakness of such relationships may be due to the difficulty of accurately measuring personality traits, because most existing personality tests were developed for clinical use, not for segmentation purposes. As the reliability of more recent measurement instruments increases, a greater association between personality and consumer behaviour has been demonstrated.[5] For example, it has been shown that personality sometimes influences the clothes, make-up and hair styles individuals adopt.

When a market is segmented according to a motive, it is divided on the basis of consumers' reasons for making a purchase. Product durability, value for money, concern for the environment, convenience and status are all motives affecting the

Figure 7.7

ACORN Category C, Group 6, Type 17

CACI's ACORN classification, based on demographic data from the Census, is used extensively by marketers and planners in the UK for profiling purchasing and lifestyle behaviour. ACORN classifies people into 6 categories, which are sub-divided into 17 groups and 54 neighborhood types. This illustration is for ACORN category C, Group 6, Type 17: Flats and Mortgages, Singles and Young Working Couples. This type is found in affluent areas in London, the Home Counties and central Scotland.

Source: CACI and ACORN are the trademarks and/or servicemarks of CACI Limited.

types of product purchased and the choice of stores in which they are bought. For example, one consumer might be motivated to purchase recycled kitchen paper out of concern for the environment. Another might travel to a large supermarket in order to buy the most absorbent, high quality brand of kitchen towels.

Lifestyle segmentation groups individuals according to how they live and spend their time, the importance of items in their surroundings (their homes or their jobs, for example), their beliefs about themselves and broad issues, and some socio-economic characteristics, such as income and education.[6] Lifestyle analysis provides a broad view of buyers because it encompasses numerous characteristics related to people's activities, interests and opinions (see Table 7.6). It can be thought of as going beyond a simple understanding of personality.

Psychographics is the main technique used to measure lifestyle. However, its use continues to be limited because psychographic variables are more difficult to measure accurately than are other types of segmentation variables. In addition, the relationships between psychographic variables and consumers' needs are sometimes obscure and unproven, and the segments that result from psychographic segmentation may not be reachable.[7] For example, a marketer may determine that highly compulsive individuals want a certain type of clothing. However, no specific stores or particular media—such as television or radio programmes, newspapers or magazines—appeal precisely to this group and this group alone. Psychographic variables can sometimes offer a useful way of better understanding segments that have been defined using other base variables.

Product Related Behavioural Characteristics

Marketers can also segment markets on the basis of an aspect of consumers' behaviour towards the product. This might relate to the way the particular product is used or purchased, or perhaps to the benefits consumers require from it.

Purchase behaviour can be a useful way of distinguishing between groups of customers, giving marketers insight into the most appropriate marketing mix. For example, brand loyal customers may require a different kind of treatment from those who switch between brands. On pack sales promotions are often geared towards building loyalty in brand switchers.

Activities	Interests	Opinions
Work	Family	Themselves
Hobbies	Home	Social issues
Social events	Job	Politics
Vacation	Community	Business
Entertainment	Recreation	Economics
Club membership	Fashion	Education
Community	Food	Products
Shopping	Media	Future
Sports	Achievements	Culture

SOURCE: Reprinted, adapted, from Joseph Plummer, "The concept and application of life style segmentation", *Journal of Marketing*, January 1974, p. 34. Reprinted by permission of the American Marketing Association.

Table 7.6 Characteristics related to activities, interests and opinions

The occasion on which customers buy a particular product may impact upon product choice because in different sets of circumstances different product selection criteria may be applied. For instance, a customer who replaces a car tyre in an emergency will probably be less concerned about price than one who is routinely maintaining his or her car.

Benefit segmentation The division of a market according to the benefits consumers want from the product

Benefit segmentation is the division of a market according to the benefits consumers want from the product.[8] Although most types of market segmentation are based on the assumption that there is a relationship between the variable and customers' needs, benefit segmentation is different in that the benefits the customers seek *are* their product needs. By determining the benefits desired, marketers may be able to divide people into groups seeking certain sets of benefits.

The effectiveness of benefit segmentation depends on several conditions. First, the benefits people seek must be identifiable. Second, using these benefits, marketers must be able to divide people into recognisable segments. Finally, one or more of the resulting segments must be accessible to the firms' marketing efforts.

Product usage is another method marketers sometimes use to segment their customers. Individuals can be divided into users and non-users of a particular product. Users can then be classified further as heavy, moderate or light. To satisfy a specific user group, marketers sometimes create a distinctive product, set special prices or initiate special promotion and distribution activities. Thus airlines such as British Airways or KLM offer frequent flier programmes to reward their regular customers with free trips and discounts for car hire and hotel accommodation. Light users or non-users of products often receive little attention from manufacturers. There is a tendency sometimes to dismiss these groups when developing a marketing programme. For example, research in the holiday industry tends to focus on feedback from current customers, often forgetting to question why non-users failed to buy.

How customers apply the product may also determine segmentation. To satisfy customers who use a product in a certain way, some feature—say, packaging, size, texture or colour—may have to be designed with special care to make the product easier to use, more convenient or more environmentally friendly. For instance, Lever Brothers and Procter & Gamble are focusing more and more on the development of re-fill packs of detergents and other household products, to cater for increasing consumer concerns about the environment.

The varying attitude of customers towards products constitutes another set of variables that can be used to segment markets. Clothing retailers like River Island and Zy are particularly conscious of this. While one customer seeks outfits that are practical and comfortable, another is concerned with achieving a highly fashionable image.

As this brief discussion shows, consumer markets can be divided according to numerous characteristics. Ultimately, the choices marketers make will depend on a host of market and company factors.

Variables for Segmenting Organisational Markets

Like consumer markets, industrial or organisational markets are sometimes segmented, but the marketer's aim is to satisfy the needs of organisations for products. Marketers may segment organisational markets according to geographic location, type of organisation, customer size and product use. Marketing Insight 7.2 shows how construction equipment company JCB segments its market.

There are various reasons businesses may find it difficult to segment their markets.[9] The particular characteristics of the market or the distribution structure in place may restrict the types of segment bases that can be used. For example, many

Personal Characteristics of Buyers

Just as in consumer markets, the demographics, personality and lifestyle of those individuals in the buying centre impact upon purchase.

Situational Factors

The urgency of purchase or size of order can play an important role in the choices that are made.

Purchasing Approach

Buying centre structure, buying policies and balance of power among decision-makers may shape an organisation's purchase decisions.

Operating Variables

The technologies applied by an organisation or the manner in which products are used can fundamentally affect purchase choice.

Demographics

Company age, location, industry (SIC code) and size are likely to alter product requirements.

Table 7.7 Variables for segmenting organisational markets

European car manufacturers are dependent upon the fleet car market. This market tends to be structured on the basis of car engine and vehicle size, with companies providing their more senior managers with more powerful and expensive vehicles. It is likely that customers would resist a move away from this accepted structure by the car manufacturers, who are therefore not in a position to use possibly contradictory segmentation approaches. Various segmentation approaches have been developed to try to make it easier for companies to deal with these kinds of constraints.[10]

Whatever the approach adopted, just as in consumer markets, some segment bases are easier to measure and apply than others.[11] For example, it is much more straightforward to segment on the basis of company size, which is a measurable and visible characteristic, than on the basis of buying centre structure (see Chapter 5), which may be much more difficult to appraise. Table 7.7 provides an overview of the variables for segmenting organisational markets and illustrates the relative ease with which they can be measured. Variables at the base of the column, which are dealt with first, are easier to measure and more objective than those at the top.

Company Demographics Variables relating to the type of organisation or industry, geographic location, company age and size are probably the most widely used segmentation variables in organisational markets.

A company sometimes segments a market by the types of organisations within that market, perhaps on the basis of industry area or SIC code (see Chapter 5 and Table 5.3). Different types of organisations often require different product features, distribution systems, price structures and selling strategies. Given these variations, a firm may either concentrate on a single segment with one marketing mix (concentration strategy) or focus on several groups with multiple mixes (multi-segment strategy). A paint manufacturer could segment customers into several

Digging for Industrial Segments: The JCB Experience

Construction and agricultural equipment manufacturers produce a diversity of machines designed to cut and dig, carry and load, tunnel and excavate, climb on tracks up severe slopes or travel on public highways at speeds of up to 45 miles per hour. Some are designed to carry many tonnes of earth or rubble, others only small loads in often confined spaces.

The product ranges of most manufacturers have expanded gradually. Some companies have diversified and added new product groups, while others concentrate on developing improved models in existing product groups. Sales and marketing activities are often geared towards the different product groups, with teams of managers handling one set of products across national borders and customer groups. Distribution can be set up in a similar way: JCB customers may have to deal with several sales-people—even dealers—when sourcing machines from different product groups.

The customers are almost as varied as the product technology. Their needs are also diverse: the contractor, who wants a few telescopic handlers and backhoe loaders; the farmer, who uses harvesters, tractors, combines and telehandlers, but who perhaps purchases only tractors and telescopic handlers; the plant hirer, whose staple products are backhoe loaders, skid-steer loaders, mini-excavators and telescopic handlers, which are rented out to contractors and individual users; the large house building and quarrying companies, which have purchasing officers and large fleets. In general, the industry groups customers by product technology, industrial sector and country. These divisions have arisen historically for practical reasons and do not necessarily relate to different customer needs.

Although much of the company's success is built on the backhoe, JCB has a wide range of other construction products. In early 1993, the company launched its new skid-steer range, positioning it as the safest and most environmentally friendly in the industry. At the same time JCB realised that the needs of buyers of skid steers and other small

The Customers	The Products
Agriculture	All-terrain trucks
Civil engineering	Articulated dump trucks
Contractors	Asphalt finishers
Defence departments	Attachments
Earthmoving	Backhoe loaders
House building	Combines
Industrial services	Crawler dozers
Landscaping	Crawler excavators
Local authorities	Crawler loaders
Manufacturing services	Fork lifts
Mining and quarrying	Harvesters
Plant hire	Mini-excavators
Public utilities	Motor graders
Tool hire	Motor scrapers
Waste disposal	Rigid dump trucks
	Rough terrain lift trucks
	Skid-steer loaders
	Spreaders
	Telescopic handlers
	Tractors
	Wheeled excavators
	Wheeled loaders

equipment, such as the mini-excavator and smaller backhoe loaders, could be better served by a single division. With this in mind, the company has recently launched its Compact Division to handle the sales and service of these smaller machines.

The Compact Division cuts across traditional industry sectorisation of customers and selling, recognising that users of smaller equipment, irrespective of their business sector or country of origin, share common needs and expectations. These customers require a sales, service and distribution operation geared specifically to their needs. JCB's use of targeting and market segmentation through its Compact Division has given the company a significant advantage in its market.

Sources: Tony McBurnie and David Clutterbuck, *Give Your Company the Marketing Edge* (London: Penguin Books, 1988); "The JCB experience", JCB, 1992; JCB company reports; Matthew Lynn, "Digging for victory", *Business,* October 1990, pp. 112–115.

groups, such as paint wholesalers, do-it-yourself retail outlets, vehicle manufacturers, decorators and housing developers.

The demand for some consumer products can vary considerably by geographic area because of differences in climate, terrain, customer preferences or similar factors. Demand for organisational products also varies according to geographic location. For example, the producers of certain types of timber divide their markets geographically because their customers' needs vary regionally. Geographic segmentation may be especially appropriate for reaching industries that are concentrated in certain locations, for example, textiles in West Yorkshire, cutlery in Sheffield, brewing in Burton and lace in Nottingham. Examples of such concentration in Europe include heavy industry around Lille or in the Ruhr Valley and banking in Zurich.

An organisation's size may affect its purchasing procedures and the types and quantities of products it wants. To reach a segment of a particular size, marketers may have to adjust one or more marketing mix components. For example, customers who buy in extremely large quantities are sometimes offered discounts.

Operating Variables   Customer requirements can be affected in a range of ways by different operating variables such as the technology applied by the buying organisation or the product types used. Certain products, especially raw materials such as steel, petrol, plastics and timber, are used in numerous ways. Sometimes the technology used by a company will play an important role. How a company uses products affects the types and amounts it purchases, as well as the method of making the purchase.[12] For example, computers are used for engineering purposes, basic scientific research and business operations such as word processing and bookkeeping. A computer manufacturer may segment the computer market by types of use because organisations' needs for computer hardware and software depend on the purpose for which the products are purchased.

Purchasing Approach   Although it may be difficult for a company to appraise the buying approach of its customers, this is nonetheless sometimes an appropriate way for organisational markets to be segmented. The characteristics of the buying centre, including its structure (where the balance of buying power lies) and the nature of any buying policies can all affect the product requirements of customers. For example, suppliers of building materials must organise their sales efforts to satisfy a wide array of customer types who organise their buying activities in vastly different ways. While dealing with large buyers such as Wimpey will require an understanding of a relatively complex buying structure, small local builders may be perfectly satisfied with a much simpler supply arrangement.

Situational Factors   Sometimes it is appropriate to segment an organisational market on the basis of situational factors such as the urgency or size of the order. How urgently the order is required may have an impact on the importance a customer attaches to particular product features. For example, if a robot on a car production line has broken down, bringing the entire production process to a standstill, the price of replacement parts to fix it may be less important than their availability. However, if the same part is being replaced as part of a routine service, price may be the most important factor. The size of different orders can be an effective segmentation variable because it has ramifications concerning the way the customer relationship is handled. For example, a university that regularly orders vast amounts of stationery would expect a different level of service than a small business that only infrequently buys small quantities of paper and envelopes.

Personal Characteristics   Although individuals involved in organisational buying may not have as much control over the products and services selected as when they are making purchases for personal or family use, their individual characteristics still play a role in the preferences they demonstrate. For this reason it is sometimes appropriate to segment organisational markets on the basis of the characteristics of individuals within the buying centre. For example, the demographics, personality and lifestyle of managers tasked with buying a selection of new office furniture will influence the preferred designs. If power in the buying centre rests with one senior manager who strongly dislikes modern designs, this will influence the final selection of products.

Single Variable or Multivariable Segmentation

Selecting the appropriate variable for market segmentation is an important marketing management decision, because the variable is the primary factor in defining the target market. So far, segmentation by one variable has been discussed. In fact, more than one variable can be used, and marketers must decide on the number of variables to include.

Single variable segmentation
Segmentation achieved by using only one variable, the simplest type of segmentation to perform

Single variable segmentation, which is the simpler to perform, is achieved by using only one variable. The segmentation shown in Figure 7.8 is based on country of origin alone. (Although the areas on the graph are the same size, the segments are not necessarily equal in size or sales potential.) However, a single characteristic gives marketers only moderate precision in designing a marketing mix to satisfy individuals in a specific segment.

Multivariable segmentation
Segmentation using more than one characteristic to divide a total market

To achieve **multivariable segmentation,** more than one characteristic is used to divide a total market (see Figure 7.9). Notice in the figure that the market is segmented by three variables: annual income, population density and volume usage. The people in the highlighted segment earn more than £40,000, are urban dwellers and are heavy users. Multivariable segmentation provides more information about the individuals in each segment than does single variable segmentation. More is known about the people in each segment of Figure 7.9 than about those in the segments of Figure 7.8. This additional information may allow a company to develop a marketing mix that will satisfy customers in a given segment more precisely.

The major disadvantage of multivariable segmentation is that the larger the number of variables used, the greater the number of resulting segments. This proliferation reduces the sales potential of many of the segments. Compare, for example, the number and size of the segments in Figure 7.8 with the number and size of those in Figure 7.9. Another disadvantage is that it may be more complicated to resource and manage the proliferation of segments that result.

The use of additional variables can help create and maintain a more exact and satisfying marketing mix. However, when deciding on single variable or multi-

Figure 7.8
Single variable segmentation

| UK | France | Germany | Italy | Netherlands | Spain | Norway |

Annual income

Figure 7.9

Multivariable segmentation

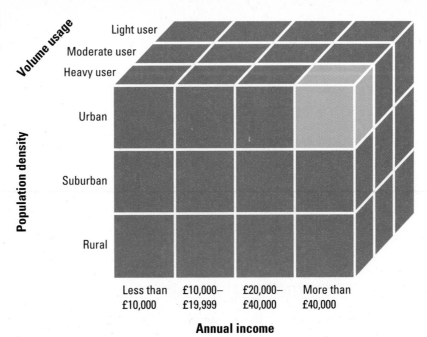

variable segmentation, a marketing manager must consider whether additional variables will actually help improve the firm's marketing mix. If using a second or third variable does not provide information that ensures greater precision, there is little reason to spend more money to gain information about the extra variables.

Segmentation Effectiveness

Whatever base variables are used, haphazard implementation can lead to ineffective market segmentation, missed opportunities and inappropriate investment. To avoid such difficulties marketers should take note of the following criteria. The first is that there must be real differences in the needs of consumers for the product or service. There is no value in segmenting a homogeneous market. In addition, segments revealed must be

- *measurable*—easy to identify and measure. Some basis must be found for effectively separating individuals into groups or segments with relatively homogeneous product or service needs.
- *substantial*—large enough to be sufficiently profitable to justify developing and maintaining a specific marketing mix.
- *accessible*—easy to reach with the marketing mix developed. For example, the promotional effort should target the relevant consumers.
- *stable*—the question of segment stability over time is not often addressed. If companies are to make strategic decisions on the basis of revealed segments, they need to be reasonably certain that those segments will be around long enough for action to be taken.

Using market segmentation also requires a good deal of common sense. It is often difficult for companies to implement totally new segmentation schemes because they would be at odds with the existing marketing structure and way of doing things. In such cases companies sometimes choose to make more minor changes to what is already in place.

Profiling Market Segments

Whatever the variable, or combination of variables, used to group customers, a more comprehensive understanding of the characteristics of individuals is likely to be required. For example, a company that segments the market for shoes on the basis of age, focusing on customers in their late teens, would do well to understand as much as possible about its particular target group in other respects. What reference groups influence them? Where do they live? Where and when do they shop? What social background are they from? What motivates them? The more comprehensive the image developed, the better the opportunity to develop an effective marketing mix with maximum appeal.

Profiling The task of building up a fuller picture of the target segments

Descriptors Variables used to profile or build a fuller picture of target segments

Profiling is the task of building up a fuller picture of target segments, and the variables being used in the description are termed **descriptors.** The types of descriptors available to marketers are broadly the same as the variables used to segment markets in the first place, that is, demographics, socio-economics and so on. This is sometimes a cause of confusion for students who struggle to remember whether they are dealing with base or descriptor variables. It helps to note that while base variables should discriminate between customer needs, descriptors are simply used to enrich the picture, to help summarise what else can be gleaned about the customers in a particular segment. This gives added inspiration to the creative team developing the product and promotional material and helps to fine-tune decisions on price and distribution. Overall, profiling segments in this way ensures that the impact of the marketing mix on the customer is maximised.

Targeting Strategies

Targeting The decision about which segment(s) a business decides to prioritise for its sales and marketing efforts

Targeting is the decision about which segment(s) a business decides to prioritise for its sales and marketing efforts. Decisions about targeting centre on two major segmentation strategies: the concentration strategy and the multisegment strategy. Whether a company chooses to adopt one or the other, the decision should be based on a clear understanding of company capabilities and resources, the nature of the competition and the characteristics of the product markets in question.

Concentration Strategy

Concentration strategy A process by which an organisation directs its marketing effort towards a single market segment

When an organisation directs its marketing efforts towards a single market segment by creating and maintaining one marketing mix, it is employing a **concentration strategy.** The fashion house Chanel, for example, targets the exclusive fashion segment, directing its marketing effort towards high income customers who want to own the most chic apparel. The chief advantage of the concentration strategy is that it allows a firm to specialise. The firm can analyse the characteristics and needs of a distinct customer group and then focus all its energies on satisfying that group's needs. A firm may be able to generate a large sales volume by reaching a single segment. In some cases, concentrating on a single segment permits a firm with limited resources to compete with much larger organisations, which may have overlooked some smaller segments.

Concentrating on one segment also means that a company puts "all its eggs in one basket"—clearly a disadvantage. If a company's sales depend on a single segment and the segment's demand for the product declines, the company's financial strength declines as well. Moreover, when a firm penetrates one segment and becomes well entrenched, its popularity may keep it from moving into other segments. For example, it is hard to imagine that Rolex would start producing low cost watches, or that Swatch might compete at the high end of the luxury watch segment.

Multisegment Strategy

Multisegment strategy A strategy by which an organisation directs its marketing efforts towards two or more market segments

With a **multisegment strategy** (see Figure 7.10), an organisation directs its marketing efforts at two or more segments by developing a marketing mix for each selected segment. Sometimes this is a natural progression from the successful application of a concentration strategy in one market segment. For example, Jockey underwear has traditionally been aimed at one segment: men. However,

Figure 7.10

Multisegment strategy

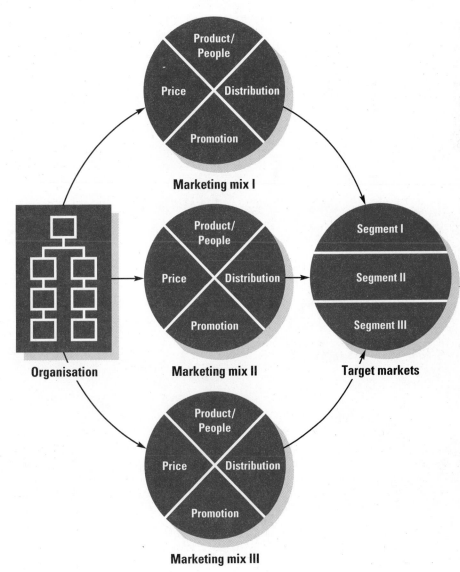

the company has expanded its efforts and now markets underwear for women and children as well. The marketing mixes used for a multisegment strategy may vary as to product/service differences, distribution methods, promotion methods and prices. The majority of users of Gatwick Airport near London are packaged holiday travellers. A significant minority, however, are business users as targeted in Figure 7.11.

A business can usually increase its sales in the aggregate market through a multisegment strategy because the organization's mixes are being aimed at more people. For example, a company with excess production capacity may find a multisegment strategy advantageous because the sale of products to additional segments may absorb this excess capacity. On the other hand, a multisegment strategy often demands a greater number of production processes, materials and people; thus production costs may be higher than with a concentration strategy. Keep in mind also that a firm using a multisegment strategy ordinarily experiences higher marketing costs. Because a multisegment strategy usually requires more research and several different promotion plans and distribution methods, the costs of planning, organising, implementing and controlling marketing activities increase.

Irrespective of whether or not a company chooses to adopt a concentration strategy or a multisegment strategy, when faced with the decision about whether or not to enter a new segment, it must consider a number of issues (see Figure 7.12). These issues include (1) the nature of the needs and wants of end users; (2) the size, structure and future potential of the segment; (3) the availability of company resources; (4) the intensity of the competition; (5) the size of the company's existing market share; and (6) the possibility of any production/marketing scale economies.

Figure 7.11 Targeting strategy. Gatwick Airport targets its business users.

Source: Courtesy of Gatwick Airport.

Figure 7.12

Factors affecting choice of
target market strategy

Positioning

Figure 7.4 illustrated the link between market segmentation, targeting and positioning. Having identified the segments in a market and decided on which segment (or segments) to target, a company must position its product, service or idea. According to Wind,

> a product's positioning is the place a product occupies in a given market, as perceived by the relevant group of customers; that group of customers is known as the target segment of the market.[13]

Harrison states that the position of a product is

> the sum of those attributes normally ascribed to it by the consumers—its standing, its quality, the type of people who use it, its strengths, its weaknesses, any other unusual or memorable characteristics it may possess, its price and the value it represents.[14]

Positioning The process of
creating an image for a product in
the minds of target customers

Positioning starts with a product—a piece of merchandise, a service, a company, an institution or even a person. **Positioning** is not what is done to the product—it is what is created in the minds of the target customers; the product is positioned in the minds of these customers and is given an image.[15] There may be a few cosmetic changes to the product—to its name, price, packaging, styling or channel of distribution—but these are to facilitate the successful promotion of the image desired by the target customers. The product must be perceived by the selected target customers to have a distinct image and position vis-à-vis its competitors. Product differentiation is widely viewed as the key to successful marketing; the product must stand out and have a clearly defined position.

Positioning is based on customers' perceptions and is therefore only partly within the control of marketers. Positions are described by variables and within parameters that are important to the customers and are essentially selected by them. Price may be the key in grocery shopping, service level in selecting a bank, quality and reliability in buying computer hardware, value for money in choosing which theme park to visit. In-depth market research (often focus group discussions) is required if customer motivations and expectations in a particular market are to be fully understood. Management's intuition is not always sufficient. For example, research revealed that consumers often have to decide between replacement living room or dining room furniture and a family package holiday abroad. Managers at most leading furniture retailers perceived other furniture retailers to be their competitors, when in reality they were additionally competing for consumers' disposable income against other diverse product areas. In this budget-conscious sector of the furniture buying market, retailers believed only price to be important. In-depth research proved that value for money, a concept that includes product quality and durability in addition to price, was perceived to be the main purchase consideration.

Consumers generally assign positions to a company or a product that is the market leader—and probably has the highest profile—and the limited number of competitors they can recollect are orientated to this market leader. For example, in the market for tomato ketchup, perceptions of brands are orientated towards market leader Heinz. Occasionally the brand consumers regard as the market leader may not be the genuine market leader in terms of market share, but simply the one most visible at that time, possibly because of heavy promotional exposure. Customers respond to the attributes of a product and to its promotional imagery, but the product's position as perceived by its target customers is affected by the reputation and image of the company, coupled with its other products, and by the activities of its competitors. For example, bad publicity, such as that recently experienced by British Airways following allegations of dirty tricks against Virgin Atlantic, can negatively affect a brand's positioning.

In-depth market research leads to an understanding of how consumers perceive different brands and companies, which marketing variables they believe to be most important and by what magnitude. **Perceptual mapping** is a tool commonly adopted by marketers and marketing researchers to visually depict such consumer perceptions and prioritising of brands and their perceived attributes. Figure 7.13 illustrates a hypothetical example in which consumers thought product range width and price were the key characteristics of the market. A cross marks the ideal position, with high product range width and above average price (typical of high quality shopping goods such as cameras or hi-fi systems). Brands (or companies) *A* and *C* are perceived as being relatively close to the ideal—their pricing policy does not fully match the image required—but brand (or company) *B* is viewed as being too cheap, with inadequate product range width. Figure 7.14 illustrates how consumers of children's wear in the UK realised that the positioning of Adams (see Case 7.1) had shifted to reflect improvements in the quality of its merchandise, stores and personnel. Adams had successfully repositioned its brand to move away from being perceived as a budget orientated retailer.

Perceptual mapping A tool used by marketers and marketing researchers to visually depict consumer perceptions and prioritising of brands and their perceived attributes

Steps in Determining a Positioning Plan

Although customers' perceptions play an important role in product positioning, the role of marketers is also crucial. There should be no mystique associated with positioning a product. Common sense and a step-by-step approach are essential in establishing a clear positioning for a product:

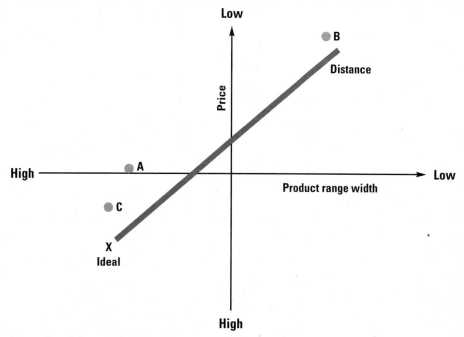

Figure 7.13

Positioning map of hypothetical consumer preferences

SOURCE: *From D. Knee and D. Walters,* Strategy in Retailing *(Herts, England: Philip Allan, 1985). p. 27. Reproduced by permission of Philip Allan, a division of Prentice-Hall International.*

1. Define the segments in a particular market.
2. Decide which segment (or segments) to target.
3. Understand what the target consumers expect and believe to be the most important considerations when deciding on the purchase.
4. Develop a product (or products) that caters specifically for these needs and expectations.
5. Evaluate the positioning and images, as perceived by the target customers, of competing products in the selected market segment (or segments).
6. Select an image that sets the product (or products) apart from the competing products, thus ensuring that the chosen image matches the aspirations of the target customers. (The selected positioning and imagery must be credible: consumers would not believe Lada or Skoda if they promoted their cars in the same manner as Porsche or Lotus.)
7. Inform target consumers about the product. Although this is primarily a promotional task, it is also vital that the product is made readily available at the right price, through the development of the full marketing mix.

Competitive Edge

Decisions about which marketing strategy to follow and which segments a business should target cannot possibly be made without considering the competitive arena.[16] Competitors' strengths and their ability to satisfy customers' needs may well influence the selection of target market priorities, particularly if a company feels certain that its competitors are much better equipped to match customer requirements in a particular market segment.[17] A business must identify what is

Figure 7.14

UK children's wear: positioning of major retailers, featuring the re-positioning of Adams

High quality

2 A

M & S

B

Low price ——— Bhs ——— **High price**

W   M

1

A

1 = Traditional perception of
    Adams' market position
2 = New market positioning
    of Adams

Low quality

A = Adams
M = Mothercare
W = Woolworth
B = Boots
Bhs = British Home Stores
M & S = Marks & Spencer

Basis for competing A differential advantage and any strengths held over competitors

Differential advantage An attribute of a product or a business that is not currently matched by rival companies or products and is highly desired by the target market's customers

referred to as a **basis for competing,** which hinges on identifying a differential advantage and making the most of any strengths held over rivals. A **differential advantage** is something that is highly desired by the target market's customers, which the business or its product has, that is not currently matched by rival companies or products. Without a differential advantage, success in the marketplace in the longer term is unlikely[18], and a business will be highly vulnerable to competitors' moves. Companies with a differential advantage should gear their marketing programmes around it so as to emphasise its existence to targeted customers through sales and marketing activities. It must be remembered that while companies strive for such a competitive edge, they are not always successful in achieving their goal. Specific product attributes are easy to substantiate if they genuinely provide an advantage over rivals, but aspects of the service product often assist in developing an edge over competitors (see Chapter 8). For example, Toyota stresses in its press advertising the capabilities and friendliness of its dealers; Chanel, the eminence of its brands and fragrances; the AA, its coverage and ability to help; 3M, its innovative creativity; DHL, its speed and reliability; Duracell, the longevity of its cells; BA Club Europe, the added service, comfort and convenience; and JCB, the value and reliability inherent in its brand. Where a differential advantage exists, a business's brand positioning and promotion must utilise and emphasise the attribute in question.

**Steps in Determining a
Differential Advantage**

There is a straightforward sequence of steps a particular business's marketers follow when attempting to identify a differential advantage.[19]

1. Identify the market's segments.
2. Establish what product and service attributes are desired and demanded by each segment.
3. Decide which of these attributes the business in question offers.
4. Determine which attributes the business's competitors offer.

5. Consider what the marketplace perceives the competitors' genuine strengths to be.
6. Identify whether any gaps exist between customer expectations of the product/service on offer and perceptions of the competitors' offers.
7. Consider whether any gaps identified in item 6 above are matched by the business and its own offerings. If the business is able to match one or more of these gaps, the potential exists for a differential advantage to be developed.
8. Question whether any of these potential advantages for the business can be emphasised through sales and marketing programmes.
9. Consider the sustainability of these advantages for the business. How easily and quickly can competitors catch up? Is it possible for the business to defend these advantages?
10. If there are no current advantages for the business, given the gaps identified between competitors' offerings and customer expectations, consider which areas offer potential for developing a future differential advantage.
11. In order to maximise any existing or potential differential advantages, detail the changes the business must make to its research and development, engineering, sales and marketing activities.

It is important to remember that companies frequently examine their relative strengths and weaknesses in relation to their rivals. A strength is not the same as a differential advantage. For example, many rivals may also have strong brand awareness or high profitability. A differential advantage is something that targeted customers want and value and that only one supplier is able to provide. It is also important to avoid stressing aspects of the product or marketing mix as though they are differential advantages when they are, in effect, "givens" in a marketing programme. Indeed, customers take these aspects for granted. Most competitors in a market will in any case include these features, for example, guaranteed delivery or product quality, in their marketing programmes. Without such attributes—the "givens"—a customer may not even consider a particular company's products or services to be of interest. The basic requirements of customers and a business's numerous strengths may be important aspects of a company's basis for competing, but they do not constitute a differential advantage, which is the ultimate and most desirable basis for competing. Strategic issues of competition are addressed more extensively in Chapter 22.

● ●

Evaluating Markets and Forecasting Sales

Whatever segmentation choices businesses make, measuring the sales potential of the chosen target market or markets is crucial. Moreover, a marketing manager must determine the portion or share of the selected market that the firm can capture relative to its objectives, resources and managerial skills, as well as to those of its competitors. Developing and maintaining a marketing mix consume a considerable amount of a company's resources. Thus the target market or markets selected must have enough sales potential to justify the costs of developing and maintaining one or more marketing mixes.

The potential for sales can be measured along several dimensions, including product, geographic area, time and level of competition.[20] With respect to product, potential sales can be estimated for a specific product item (for example, Diet Coke) or an entire product line (for example, Coca-Cola, Coca-Cola Classic, Diet Coke, Diet caffeine-free Coke, and Cherry Coca-Cola are one product line). A manager must also determine the geographic area to be included in the estimate. In relation to time, sales potential estimates can be short range (one year or less), medium range (one to five years), or long range (longer than five years). The competitive level specifies whether sales are being estimated for a single firm or for an entire industry. Thus marketers measure sales potential both for the entire market and for their own firms and then develop a sales forecast. A detailed discussion of market potential, sales potential and sales forecasting is given in Chapter 20.

• • • • • • • • • • • • • • • • • • • •

Summary

● A *market* is an aggregate of people who, as individuals or as organisations, have needs for products in a product class and who have the ability, willingness and authority to purchase such products. A *consumer market* consists of purchasers and/or individuals in their households who intend to consume or benefit from the purchased products and who do not buy products for the main purpose of making a profit. An *organisational* (or *industrial*) *market* consists of persons and groups who purchase a specific kind of product for re-sale, direct use in producing other products or use in day-to-day operations. Profit is not always necessarily a motive. Because products are classified according to use, the same product may be classified as both a consumer product and an organisational product.

● Marketers use two general approaches to identify their target markets: the total market and the market segmentation approaches. A firm using an *undifferentiated* or *total market approach* designs a single marketing mix and directs it at an entire market for a particular product. The total market approach can be effective when a large proportion of individuals in the total market have similar needs for the product and the organisation can develop and maintain a single marketing mix to satisfy those needs.

● Markets made up of individuals with diverse product needs are called *heterogeneous markets*. The *market segmentation* approach divides the total market into groups of customers who have similar product needs. *Profiling* segments using *descriptor* variables can help the marketer build up a fuller picture and design a marketing mix (or mixes) that more precisely matches the needs of people in a selected segment (or segments). A market segment is a group of individuals, groups or organisations sharing one or more similar characteristics that cause them to have relatively similar product needs.

● *Targeting* is the task of prioritising which market segment(s) to address. There are two major types of targeting strategy. In the *concentration strategy*, the organisation directs its marketing efforts towards a single market segment through one marketing mix. In the *multisegment strategy*, the organisation develops different marketing mixes for two or more segments. The decisions about which segment or segments to enter are linked to considerations about company resources, expertise and the nature of customers and competitors.

● Certain conditions must exist for market segmentation to be effective. First, consumers' needs for the product should be heterogeneous. Second, the segments of the market should be measurable so that the segments can be compared with respect to estimated sales potential, costs and profits. Third, at least one segment must be substantial enough to have the profit potential to justify developing and maintaining a special marketing mix for that segment. Fourth, the firm must be able to access the chosen segment with a particular marketing mix. Fifth, the segment should be reasonably stable over time.

● *Segmentation variables* or *bases* are the dimensions or characteristics of individuals, groups or organisations used for dividing a total market into segments. The segmentation variable should be related to customers' needs for, uses of or behaviour towards the product. Segmentation variables for consumer markets can be grouped into two broad categories that relate either to customer characteristics—demographics (age, sex, family, race, religion), socio-economics (income, occupation, education, social class), geography (country, region, urban area, housing), personality, motives and lifestyle—or to product related behaviour—purchase behaviour and occasion, benefits sought (*benefit segmentation*), consumption behaviour and user status, and attitude towards product. Segmentation variables for organisational markets include demographic factors, operating variables, purchasing approach, situational factors and the personal characteristics of buyers. Besides selecting the appropriate segmentation variable, a marketer must also decide how many variables to use. *Single variable segmentation* involves only one variable, but in *multivariable segmentation,* more than one characteristic is used to divide a total market. *Market density* refers to the number of potential customers within a unit of land area.

● Having decided which segment or segments to target, the marketer must position the product in order to create a clearly defined image in the minds of its target consumers. The product's *positioning* must be perceived by its consumers to be different from the positions of competing products. *Perceptual maps* assist marketers in graphically depicting the relative positions of the products in a particular market. Although a product's attributes and styling, along with its pricing, service levels and channel of distribution, contribute to how consumers perceive the product, a marketer uses mainly promotion to establish a product's positioning. Whichever segments marketers target, irrespective of the positioning adopted, they must be able to measure the sales potential of the target market or markets.

● To trade successfully, a business must endeavour to satisfy its target customers in a manner that gives it a competitive edge over its rival businesses. Companies therefore create a basis for competing as part of their marketing strategy. A *basis for competing* hinges on identifying a differential advantage and making the most of any edge over competitors. A *differential advantage* is something that is highly desired by target customers, which a business or its product has, that is not currently matched by rival companies or products. It is important to remember that a differential advantage is not merely an edge over competitors, as several other rivals could actually share a certain business strength. Aspects taken for granted by customers as basic entry points in a market's product and marketing offerings, the "givens", must also not be designated as a business's differential advantage.

● ● ● ● ● ● ● ● ● ● ● ● ● ● ● ● ● ●

Important Terms

Market	Segmentation variables or bases	Concentration strategy
Consumer market	Market density	Multisegment strategy
Organisational (or industrial) market	Benefit segmentation	Positioning
	Single variable segmentation	Perceptual mapping
Undifferentiated or total market approach	Multivariable segmentation	Basis for competing
	Profiling	Differential advantage
Heterogeneous markets	Descriptors	
Market segmentation	Targeting	

● ● ● ● ● ● ● ● ● ● ● ● ● ● ● ● ●

Discussion and Review Questions

1. What is a market? What are the requirements for a market?
2. In the area where you live, is there a group of people with unsatisfied product needs who represent a market? Could this market be reached by a business organisation? Why or why not?
3. Identify and describe the two major types of market. Give examples of each.
4. What is the total market approach? Under what conditions is it most useful? Describe a current situation in which a company is using a total market approach. Is the business successful? Why or why not?
5. What is the market segmentation approach? Describe the basic conditions required for effective segmentation. Identify several firms that use the segmentation approach.
6. List the differences between the concentration and the multisegment strategies. Describe the advantages and disadvantages of each strategy.
7. Identify and describe four major categories of variables that can be used to segment consumer

markets. Give examples of product markets that are segmented by variables in each category.

8. What dimensions are used to segment industrial or organisational markets?

9. How do marketers decide whether to use single variable or multivariable segmentation? Give examples of product markets that are divided through multivariable segmentation.

10. Choose a product and discuss how it could best be positioned in the market.

11. Explain what is meant by the term *differential advantage*.

12. Describe the steps a business should take to create a differential advantage.

• • • • • • • • • • • • • • • • • •

Recommended Readings

S. Dibb and L. Simkin, *The Market Segmentation Workbook: Target Marketing for Marketing Managers* (London: International Thomson Business Publishing, 1996).

S. Dibb, "Developing a decision tool for identifying operational and attractive segments", *Journal of Strategic Marketing,* vol. 3, 1995, pp. 189–203.

G. Hooley and J. Saunders, *Competitive Positioning: The Key to Market Success* (London: Prentice-Hall, 1993).

M. McDonald and I. Dunbar, *Market Segmentation* (London: Macmillan Press, 1995).

S. Dibb and L. Simkin, "Implementation problems in industrial market segmentation", *Industrial Marketing Management,* vol. 23, 1994, pp. 55–63.

• • • • • • • • • • • • • • • • • •

Cases

7.1 Targeting in Children's Wear

Until the launch of Terence Conran's Mothercare chain, children's clothes had been marketed through large department stores and independently owned single shops, with each town generally having two or three such specialists. Mothercare, offering clothes and hardware such as cots and prams to parents of infants and toddlers, was a tremendous success. Mothercare's financial worries in the 1980s coincided with the rise of Adams Childrenswear, part of the Sears retailing group. From its humble origins as a budget driven family business in the Midlands, Adams has become one of the UK's most successful retailers, with expansion plans in South East Asia, the Middle East and mainland Europe. Its success is the result of sound marketing principles: a well defined retailing formula clearly targeted at a specific market segment, with customer satisfaction a priority.

"Our mission is simple … To become the No. 1 specialist children's wear retailers in the United Kingdom through the achievement of excellence throughout our business." From being a loss-making "me too" in a market dominated by Mothercare, Woolworth and Boots, Adams has emerged as market leader. In 1987–88 net sales were £18 million from 126 stores; now they are close to £200 million from 300 stores nationwide. The possibility of franchising the name, merchandise and concept outside the UK offers an opportunity for continued growth. Sears was sufficiently committed to the Adams operation and its proven ability to push sales beyond £300 per square foot to allocate £50 million for new store openings and refurbishment.

What has led to the success and turnaround of Adams? Clear thinking and the development of a marketing strategy have enabled the management to take advantage both of range omissions in Marks & Spencer and BhS and financial problems in Mothercare. Adams researched its market, evaluating each competitor and determining the positioning of the major players (see Figure 7.14). This analysis was supported by extensive marketing research designed to determine the needs and expectations of targeted consumers: children up to the age of eight and their parents and grandparents.

Traditionally, Adams's trading proposition had been price driven, but as the company knew, "Price alone will not be a sufficient differential advantage to take Adams forward to market leadership". Adams opted to focus on design—of stores and merchandise—and on quality, service, value and convenience. The consumer research revealed that product quality and durability dominated buyers' decision-making. Adams has a well resourced in-house quality control and product testing department that increasingly sets industry standards. Young mothers often lack time and mobility, so convenience of branch locations, entrances and store layout are key determinants of store choice. First-time parents are often inexperienced shoppers for children's wear, so Adams's training emphasises customer service and advice. With clothing retailer Next, furniture manufacturers IKEA, grocers Sainsbury and skin care products chain Body Shop all helping to create fashion- and design-conscious consumers, Adams's colourfully co-ordinated merchandise and stores have proved popular with its target market.

Behind the scenes, the company has invested heavily in systems and computer programmes to facilitate its expansion. All branches are networked to the Nuneaton headquarters with EPOS (electronic point-of-sale data capture), resulting in automatic stock replenishment and sales records. Major suppliers are directly linked to Adams's headquarters, with orders arriving as required to a fully automated and robotised warehouse and distribution centre. Computer packages assist with store location, layout and shelf space allocation, merchandise planning, stock control and distribution, credit control and financial planning.

Adams's understanding of its marketplace has led to further innovations. In 1992, the first branches of its new Pride & Joy chain opened. While rivals Boots and Mothercare cater for parents of infants, toddlers and young children, Adams has split these consumers into two segments. Prams, pushchairs and cots are bulky, slow moving items that shoppers with babies and very young children need, but they eat up space in a children's clothing store. These consumers have more functional requirements for clothes and baby equipment than do families with children aged three to eight. Adams has focused its Pride & Joy operation directly on mothers-to-be and parents of very young children, leaving its Adams chain to target the children's market for clothes.

Sources: "Adams 1987–1992", Adams Childrenswear Ltd; John Thornhill, "Why eight is a lucky number", *Financial Times,* 13 December 1990; "Sears—Adams Childrenswear", *Harvest,* 1990 and 1993.

Questions for Discussion

1. What is Adams's target market?
2. How has Adams used the steps of the positioning process?
3. How is Adams positioned relative to its competitors?

7.2 No Longer *Just* the Mini-Van or an Espace: The MPV Market Comes of Age

The famous VW Camper mini-van with its removable bench seats, sink unit and versatility was throughout the 1960s and 1970s the only real alternative to the large estate car for many large families. Then came Renault's Espace: more carlike than vanlike, with space for seven passengers and some luggage at levels of speed and comfort almost equivalent to those of a car. Certainly not cheap—the latest models are priced between £18,000 and £28,000—the Espace quickly established a reputation for reliability, comfort, utility and a dash of French flair in what is now classed as the multipurpose vehicle (MPV) or "people carrier" market.

As the 1980s drew to a close, yet another category of vehicles in the car market took off and expanded: the 4x4 off-roader. Led initially by the genuine working vehicles built by Land Rover, more often than not mud-coated and prone to a harsh existence, Land Rover identified a market segment requiring 4x4 versatility combined with the comfort of the executive car. The resulting Range Rover and then the Discovery were trend setters in the growing 4x4 market, just as the Renault Espace had led the way in the MPV market.

In the 4x4 market, Land Rover's success was noted by the major Japanese players with the arrival of the Shogun, Land Cruiser and Trooper. Now the 4x4 market has been further segmented: the Toyota Rav4 and Suzuki Vitara cater for the cheaper, "fun" leisure users; the Ford Maverick and GM Monterey aim at the middle family market; and the Mitsubishi Shogun and Range Rover target company executives and country gentry. Few of these versatile off-roaders, increasingly bought as "fashion statements" by their image-conscious owners, ever see a muddy embankment or field. Despite a record year in terms of sales, Land Rover no longer has the 4x4 market to itself. The latest development has been the entry of the South Korean manufacturers into this seemingly crowded market. The SSang Yong Musso is big, brash and glitzy; it has the off-road performance of the Range Rover and the design flair of Ken Greenley, the man behind Aston Martin's supercar, the Virage. German giant Mercedes has confidence in the new South Korean player: it owns 5 per cent of the company, provides the engines and permits the use of its logo and brand in the Musso's advertising. New entrant Ford Explorer aims to compete with the Range Rover and Jeep Cherokee at the top of the market. Even the creator of the breed, Land Rover, is bringing out a new model, the CB40, to compete in the "fun" sector against the Toyota Rav4 and Suzuki Vitara.

A similar competitive pattern is evident in the MPV market. For well over a decade, the Espace was not really challenged by any major manufacturer outside North America. Honda launched the Shuttle and Daihatsu the Hijet in 1993; the VW Sharan, Fiat Ulysee, Peugeot 806, Citroën Synergie and Chrysler Voyager appeared in 1994 and 1995. Ford formed the AutoEuropa joint venture with VW to produce the Ford Galaxy and VW Sharan. Even mighty Mercedes entered the European MPV market, aiming for a slice of the 300,000 vehicles sold annually with its Viano (V-class). In the middle of 1995, the Espace still had 50 per cent of the market, followed by Toyota, Nissan and Mitsubishi. However, despite a decade's lead over its rivals, significant brand awareness and re-styling, the Ford Galaxy is now outselling Renault's ageing Espace. The Ford-VW plant in Portugal, which has the capacity to produce 180,000 Sharan/Galaxy models a year, is clearly intended to dominate the market-place for MPVs. Ford's high spending promotional campaigns, pan-European branding, extensive dealer network and long standing customer base perhaps give cause for surprise only that the company waited until late 1995 to enter this rapidly growing market sector.

Perhaps the most significant development, though, is the re-emergence of America's Chrysler in European markets, not seen since the late 1970s. In the mid-1990s, the US giant re-launched the famous Jeep 4x4 range in Europe. In 1996 the top selling MPV Chrysler Voyager arrived, "the Espace of the US market". To universal press and critical acclaim, the "people eating" Voyager looks set to revolutionise the people carrier market so long dominated by Renault's Espace. With the Ford-VW joint venture and recent new MPV launches by Mercedes (the V-class) and Vauxhall/GM (US-made Sintra), the market is becoming crowded. The entry of these manufacturers is, however, an indication of the importance they place on this market.

The 4x4 off-road market was created during the aftermath of World War II as Land Rovers and Jeeps were converted for commercial use and farming applications. Land Rover built on its expertise in the consumer-orientated 1970s to create the larger Range Rover. Originally also a work horse, the Range Rover was re-positioned at the executive and country estate markets. Now there are 4x4 off-road product offerings from most major manufacturers, catering for executives, farmers, outdoor enthusiasts and families at all price points and specifications. There are initial signs that a similar evolution of models and targeting is about to be evident in the MPV market. Few manufacturers do not have an MPV on offer, and success will depend increasingly on more carefully honed target market strategies and marketing programmes. Rival manufacturers are having to further segment the people carrier market and are working even harder to create brand and product identities that differentiate their MPVs.

SOURCES: *The New Portugal Magazine*, February 1995, p. 6; *The Renault Magazine*, 131, Winter/Spring 1995, pp. 11–14; K. Done, "Espace—the final frontier", *Financial Times*, 12 April 1995; I. Morton, "Car makers scramble into people carriers", *Evening Standard*, 9 June 1995; Stewart Smith, "Far East flash of the Musso", *Evening Telegraph*, December 1995; *What Car?*, January 1996.

Questions for Discussion

1. What market and consumer trends have led to the growth of the MPV market?

2. In the 4x4 market, separate segments have emerged. Is this likely to happen in the MPV market? If so, why?

3. How might a new MPV be positioned in the existing marketplace?

PART II POSTSCRIPT

Academics and practitioners define marketing as involving the understanding and satisfying of customers. It is not possible to accomplish these requirements without a sound understanding of buying behaviour, the processes involved and the associated influencing factors. Accordingly, Part II of *Marketing: Concepts and Strategies* has presented a comprehensive examination of the nature of consumer buying behaviour and then business-to-business buying behaviour.

Over time, marketers develop knowledge of their markets. Many marketing decisions are based on this experience and on the intuition of the managers concerned. Frequently, though, marketers recognise that they do not fully understand their customers, competitors or aspects of the marketing environment forces. In such instances they conduct marketing research. The nature and use of marketing research have also been discussed in Part II, along with an examination of the principal element of marketing strategy: target market selection.

Before progressing, readers should be confident that they are now able to:

Describe consumer buying behaviour

• What are the types and stages of consumer buying decision-making and the associated influencing personal, psychological and social factors? • Why should marketers understand consumer buying behaviour?

Describe business-to-business buying behaviour

• What are the types of business-to-business markets and the characteristics of organisational buyers and transactions, organisational demand and the buying centre? • Why are relationships so important? • What are the stages of the buying process? • How can business-to-business markets be selected and analysed?

Outline the core aspects of marketing research and information systems

• What is the importance of research and information systems in marketing? • What distinguishes intuition from marketing research? • What are the steps of the marketing research process and the basic tools for conducting marketing research?

Explain the process of target market selection

• Why is target market selection so important? • What types of markets are there? • How do marketers determine market segments? • What is the role of positioning in the target market process? • Why should companies strive for a differential advantage over competitors?

Marketing Opportunity Analysis	Chapters
• The marketing environment	2
• Marketing in international markets	3
• Consumer markets and buyer behaviour	4
• Business-to-business markets and buyer behaviour	5
• Marketing research and information systems	6

Target Market Selection	Chapters
• Market segmentation and prioritisation	7, 22
• Product and brand positioning	7, 22
• Competitive advantage	7, 22

Marketing Mix Development	Chapters
• Product, branding, packaging and service decisions	8–11
• Distribution (place and channel) decisions	12–15
• Promotion decisions	16–18
• Pricing decisions	19, 20
• Supplementary decisions	3, 21, 24, 25

Marketing Management	Chapters
• Strategic marketing and competitive strategy	22, 23
• Marketing planning and sales forecasting	23
• Implementing strategies and measuring performance	24
• Marketing ethics and social responsibility	25

III PRODUCT, BRANDING, PACKAGING AND SERVICE DECISIONS

In Chapter 1, marketing was said to involve marketing opportunity analysis, target market selection and the development of a marketing mix for each target market. The marketing mix is the tactical tool kit deployed by marketing managers in order to implement a company's agreed marketing strategy. The marketing mix centres on the "5Ps" of product, people, place, promotion and pricing decisions. The marketing mix must endeav-our to match the identified needs of target customers in order to satisfy these customers' requirements. It must also communicate the desired brand or product positioning and emphasise any differential advantage held by an organisation over its rivals.

Part III of *Marketing: Concepts and Strategies* examines the product and people ingredients of the marketing mix, along with the integral issues of branding, packaging and customer service.

Chapter 8, "Product Decisions", introduces the concepts of how marketers define and classify products; examines the differences between product item, product line and product mix; and explores the product life cycle. The chapter then discusses organisational structures available to manage products, and concludes by examining the importance of the levels of a product in determining a competitive edge over rivals' products.

Chapter 9, "Branding and Packaging", recognises the fundamental importance of brands in marketing and looks at different types of brands, their benefits, selection, protection and licensing. The chapter goes on to discuss the functions of packaging, design considerations and the role of packaging in marketing strategy. Finally, it explores the functions of labelling and the associated legal issues.

Chapter 10, "Developing and Managing Products", outlines the organisational alternatives for managing products, explains how a business develops a product idea into a commercial product and analyses the role of product development in the marketing mix. The chapter includes a discussion of how existing products can be modified and how product deletion can sometimes benefit a marketing mix. In conclusion, it discusses how products should be managed during the various stages of a product's life cycle.

Chapter 11, "The Marketing of Services", explores how services differ from tangible goods and explores the implications for marketers. The chapter begins by explaining the nature and characteristics of services, classifying services and the development of strategies for services. It goes on to discuss the significant problems encountered in developing a differential advantage for a service. Services are growing in importance for marketing as they contribute increasingly to the economy and employment. A sub-sector is a non-business or not-for-profit activity such as the public sector and charities. The chapter then explores the concept of marketing in non-business situations and the development of service strategies and methods for controlling non-business service activities.

By the conclusion of Part III of *Marketing: Concepts and Strategies*, readers should understand the core product decisions that must be made in determining a marketing mix, including branding, packaging, people and service issues.

PRODUCT DECISIONS

"Developing great new products is not just about great ideas. It's about transforming them into products and services that customers want, that competitors have difficulty in copying and that exploit the strengths of the company."

Susan Hart
University of Stirling

OBJECTIVES

- To learn how marketers define products
- To understand how to classify products
- To become familiar with the concepts of product item, product line and product mix and understand how they are connected
- To understand the concept of product life cycle
- To understand the types of organisational structures used to manage products
- To grasp the importance of the levels of a product in determining a competitive edge

Whitbread once just brewed beers and ran pubs. But now it does much more than simply produce leading beer brands such as Boddington's (the "cream of Manchester") or Director's bitter. With restaurant chains including TGI Friday's, Beefeater and Pizza Hut; fun pubs; beer brands such as Stella Artois, Heineken and Murphy's; David Lloyd Tennis Centres; championship golf courses such as the Forest of Arden (home of the English Open); and hotel chains Marriott (in the UK), Country Club and Travel Inn, there is much more to Whitbread than brewing beer. The company's evolution has been customer driven, led by a highly professional marketing culture. Whitbread's senior managers have purposefully innovated and expanded in the chosen domain of the leisure sector. The company constantly monitors market trends, customers' lifestyles and leisure requirements, perceptions of its brands and services, and competitor activity. While non-beer businesses are important to the company, the traditional focus for the business continues to be supported and new beer products developed.

Pioneer Brewing Company, Whitbread's specialist new product development division. Researchers had noted a growing tendency by drinkers to add a measure of spirits to a pint of beer and were aware of the tradition of the "chaser", the glass of whisky drunk immediately after a pint of beer, that exists in many parts of the country.

The Pioneer Brewing Company's marketers have as their targets young, socially comfortable drinkers who enjoy dabbling with new products and experiences. Unlike the often criticised alcopops—the lemonades and sodas with a "hint" of alcohol—Kentucky Black and Arkansas are overtly alcoholic, distributed through pubs and clubs and aimed at consumers well used to drinking and enjoying alcohol. Although they are not as quirky as the company's chocolate flavoured beer, being based on traditional and quite widely consumed alcohol mixes, it remains to be seen whether Whitbread's marketers have identified a target market large enough to sustain the new brands. The boffins have not finished with new concoctions. Wild Brew is an intriguing mix of fruit juice, alcohol and bitter tasting Guarana stimulant. A few years ago, the company launched Murphy's Irish stout to rival the long standing market leader Guinness. In only a few years, Murphy's has taken a significant slice of the market and established a strong brand presence. Wild Brew and Kentucky Black may just be the first in a long line of successful product launches designed to keep Whitbread firmly at the forefront of the brewing industry. ■

Whitbread's research and development department has created a whole new sector in the alcoholic beverages market. Spirits have been mixed with beer in the same bottle in a move that the company hopes will emulate the successful introduction of the alcopop drinks sector a few years ago. A Kentucky bourbon mixed with beer—Kentucky Black—and a vodka beer mix—Arkansas—went on trial initially in 250 pubs and clubs in the UK in mid-1996. Both products were created by the

SOURCES: Sharon Marshall, "Whitbread puts beer and spirits drinks on trial", *Marketing*, 23 May 1996, p. 1; Caroline Marshall, "BBH unveils latest Boddington's ad", *Campaign*, 29 March 1996, p. 6; David Benady, "Inn jeopardy", *Marketing Week*, 15 March 1996, pp. 38–41; David Benady, "Whitbread rejigs alcopop launch for 'adult' appeal", *Marketing Week*, 9 February 1996, p. 8.

The product is an important variable in the marketing mix. Products such as the Murphy's beer brand are among a firm's most crucial and visible contacts with buyers. If a company's products do not meet its customers' desires and needs, the company will have to adjust its offering in order to survive. Developing a successful product, as Whitbread has done, requires knowledge of fundamental marketing and product concepts.

This chapter's first section introduces and defines the concepts that help clarify what a product is and looks at how buyers view products. The next section examines the concepts of product mix and product line as an introduction to product planning. The chapter then explores the stages of the product life cycle. Each life cycle stage generally requires a specific marketing strategy, operates within a certain competitive environment and has its own sales and profit pattern. The final section discusses the elements that make up a product.

What Is a Product?

Product Everything, both favourable and unfavourable, tangible and intangible, received in an exchange of an idea, service or good

Good A tangible physical entity

Service The application of human and mechanical efforts to people or objects in order to provide intangible benefits to customers

Ideas Concepts, philosophies, images or issues that provide the psychological stimulus to solve problems or adjust to the environment

A **product** is everything, both favourable and unfavourable, that is received in an exchange. It is a complexity of tangible and intangible attributes, including functional, social and psychological utilities or benefits.[1] A product can be an idea, a service, a good or any combination of these three. This definition also covers supporting services that go with goods, such as installation, guarantees, product information and promises of repair or maintenance. A **good** is a tangible physical entity, such as a box of Lindt chocolate or a Disney video tape. A **service**, by contrast, is intangible; it is the result of the application of human and mechanical efforts to people or objects. Examples of services include TNT overnight delivery, medical examinations and child care. (Chapter 11 provides a detailed discussion of services marketing.) **Ideas** are concepts, philosophies, images or issues. They provide the psychological stimulus to solve problems or adjust to the environment. For example, Oxfam provides famine relief and attempts to improve the long term prospects of people in hunger stricken countries.

When buyers purchase a product, they are really buying the benefits and satisfaction they think the product will provide. An MG sports car, for example, is purchased for excitement and fun, not just for transport. Services, in particular, are bought on the basis of promises of satisfaction. Promises, with the images and appearances of symbols, help consumers make judgements about tangible and intangible products.[2] Often, symbols and cues are used to make intangible products more tangible or real to the consumer. MasterCard, for example, uses globes to symbolise the firm's financial power and worldwide coverage.

Classifying Products

Consumer products Items purchased to satisfy personal or family needs

Industrial or **business-to-business products** Items bought for use in a company's operations or to make other products

Products fall into one of two general categories. Products purchased to satisfy personal and family needs are **consumer products**. Those bought for use in a firm's operations or to make other products are **industrial** or **business-to-business products**. Consumers buy products to satisfy their personal wants, whereas industrial buyers seek to satisfy the goals of their organisations.

The same item can be both a consumer product and an industrial product. For example, when consumers purchase light bulbs for their homes, light bulbs are classified as consumer products. However, when a large corporation purchases light bulbs to provide lighting in a factory or office, the light bulbs are considered industrial products because they are used in the daily operations of the firm. Thus the buyer's intent—or the ultimate use of the product—determines whether an item is classified as a consumer or an industrial product. It is common for more people to be involved in buying an industrial product than in a consumer purchase. Chapters 4 and 5 explain the differences in buying and decision-making for consumer and business-to-business products.

Why is it important to know about product classifications? The main reason is that classes of products are aimed at particular target markets and classification affects distribution, promotion and pricing decisions. Furthermore, the types of marketing activities and efforts needed—in short, the entire marketing mix—differ according to how a product is classified. This section examines the characteristics of consumer and industrial products and explores the marketing activities associated with some of them.

Consumer Products

The most widely accepted approach to classifying consumer products relies on the common characteristics of consumer buying behaviour. It divides products into four categories: convenience, shopping, speciality and unsought products. However, not all buyers behave in the same way when purchasing a specific type of product. Thus a single product can fit into all four categories. To minimise this problem, marketers think in terms of how buyers *generally* behave when purchasing a specific item. In addition, they recognise that the "correct" classification can be determined only by considering a particular firm's intended target market. The four traditional categories of consumer products should be examined with these thoughts in mind.

Convenience Products   Relatively inexpensive, frequently purchased and rapidly consumed items on which buyers exert only minimal purchasing effort are called **convenience products.** They range from bread, soft drinks and chewing gum to petrol and newspapers. The buyer spends little time planning the purchase or comparing available brands or sellers. Even a buyer who prefers a specific brand will readily choose a substitute if the preferred brand is not conveniently available.

Convenience products
Inexpensive, frequently purchased and rapidly consumed items that demand only minimal purchasing effort

Classifying a product as a convenience product has several implications for a firm's marketing strategy. A convenience product is normally marketed through many retail outlets. Because sellers experience high inventory turnover, per unit gross margins can be relatively low. Producers of convenience products such as Smiths crisps and Crest toothpaste expect little promotional effort at the retail level and thus must provide it themselves in the form of advertising and sales promotion. Packaging is also an important element of the marketing mix for convenience products. The package may have to sell the product, because many convenience items are available only on a self-service basis at the retail level. The use of on-pack sales promotion is one way to maximise the impact of the package.

Shopping Products   Items that are more carefully chosen than convenience products are called **shopping products.** Buyers are willing to expend considerable effort in planning and purchasing these items. They allocate time for comparing stores and brands with respect to prices, credit, product features, qualities, services and perhaps guarantees. Appliances, furniture, bicycles, stereos, jewellery and cameras (as shown in Figure 8.1) are examples of shopping products. These products are expected to last a fairly long time and are bought less often than convenience items. Even though shopping products are more expensive than convenience products, few buyers of shopping products are particularly brand loyal. If they were, they would be unwilling to shop and compare among brands.

Shopping products   Items chosen more carefully than convenience products; consumers will expend considerable effort in planning and purchasing these items

To market a shopping product effectively, a marketer considers several key issues. Shopping products require fewer retail outlets than convenience products. Because they are purchased less frequently, inventory turnover is lower and middlemen expect to receive higher gross margins. Although large sums of money may be required to advertise shopping products, an even larger percentage of resources is likely to be used for personal selling. Indeed, the quality of the service

ZONDER EEN SONY TRAVELLER BLIJFT 'T EEN STERK VERHAAL.

Als je serieus genomen wilt worden, heb je soms meer nodig dan een leuke babbel. Een Sony Handycam Traveller dus.

Superkleine en vederlichte Video 8 camera's, die ideaal zijn voor op reis. En daarmee leg je alles haarscherp vast.

Om te beginnen is er de TR45 (f 1.999,-). De kleinste en lichtste (700 gram) ter wereld. Uitgerust met een krachtige

zoomlens (6x), digitale Superimpose en een sluitertijd tot 1/4000 seconde, zodat niets hem meer te snel af is.

Ben je nog veeleisender, dan kies je voor de TR50. (f 2.299,-) Die heeft ook nog eens een handige Auto Lock Cover, een Fader, LCD-display en liefst 8x zoom.

Wie helemaal het onderste uit de kan wil, neemt de TR75

(f 2.599,-). Dan geniet je tevens van Hifi-stereo en een superieure beeldkwaliteit (470.000 beeldpunten).

Wat je allemaal hebben, is 't gemak van Video 8: perfect geluid, drie uur op één bandje en direct afspelen op je tv.

En zelfs 't afrekenen word je makkelijk gemaakt met The Sony Card. Dus loop snel eens binnen bij de Sony-

dealer. Dan kun je de sterke verhalen voortaan aan anderen overlaten. UITEINDELIJK WIL JE TÓCH EEN SONY

Figure 8.1 Shopping product. Sony cameras, as well as most other brands of camera, are shopping products.

Source: Courtesy of Sony Europa.

may be a factor in the consumer's choice of outlet. Usually, the producer and the middlemen expect some co-operation from one another with respect to providing parts and repair services and performing promotional activities.

Speciality Products   Products that possess one or more unique characteristics and for which a significant group of buyers is willing to expend considerable effort to obtain are called **speciality products**. Buyers actually plan the purchase of a speciality product; they know exactly what they want and will not accept a substitute. An example of a speciality product is a painting by L. S. Lowry or a Cartier watch. When searching for speciality products, buyers do not compare alternatives; they are concerned primarily with finding an outlet that has a pre-selected product available.

The fact that an item is a speciality product can affect a firm's marketing efforts in several ways. Speciality products are often distributed through a limited number of retail outlets. For some consumers this limited availability accentuates the exclusivity of the product. Some companies, for example Chanel, go to considerable lengths to control this aspect of their distribution. Like shopping goods, spe-

Speciality products Items that possess one or more unique characteristics; consumers of speciality products plan their purchases and will expend considerable effort to obtain them ciality products are purchased infrequently, causing lower inventory turnover and thus requiring relatively high gross margins.

Unsought Products   Products that are purchased when a sudden problem must be solved or when aggressive selling is used to obtain a sale that otherwise would not take place are called **unsought products.** In general, the consumer does not think of buying these products regularly. Emergency car repairs and headstones are examples of unsought products. Life insurance and encyclopaedias, in contrast, are examples of products that need aggressive personal selling. The salesperson tries to make consumers aware of the benefits that can be derived from buying such products.

Industrial Products

Industrial products are usually purchased on the basis of an organisation's goals and objectives. Generally, the functional aspects of the product are more important than the psychological rewards sometimes associated with consumer products. Industrial products can be classified into seven categories according to their characteristics and intended uses: raw materials, major equipment, accessory equipment, component parts, process materials, consumable supplies and industrial services.[3]

Raw Materials   The basic materials that become part of physical products are **raw materials.** They include minerals, chemicals, agricultural products and materials from forests and oceans. They are usually bought and sold in relatively large quantities according to grades and specifications.

Major Equipment   Large tools and machines used for production purposes, such as cranes and spray painting machinery, are considered **major equipment.** Normally, major equipment is expensive and intended to be used in a production process for a considerable length of time. Some major equipment is custom made to perform specific functions for a particular organisation. For example GEC Large Machines manufactures purpose built large gears and turbines. Other items are standardised and perform similar tasks for many types of firms. Because major equipment is so expensive, purchase decisions are often made by high level management. In some cases the purchase process will be long and complicated. Marketers of major equipment frequently must provide a variety of services, including installation, training, repair and maintenance assistance, and even help in financing the purchase. Often manufacturers of major equipment build up long term relationships with their customers so that they can better adapt to their needs.

Accessory Equipment   Equipment that does not become a part of the final physical product but is used in production or office activities is referred to as **accessory equipment.** Marketing Insight 8.1 discusses computer software packages used by companies to expedite other activities. Other examples include typewriters, fractional horsepower motors, calculators and tools. Compared with major equipment, accessory items are usually much cheaper, are purchased routinely with less negotiation and are treated as expenditure items rather than capital items because they are not expected to last as long. Accessory products are standardised items that can be used in several aspects of a firm's operations. More outlets are required for distributing accessory equipment than for major equipment, but sellers do not have to provide the multitude of services expected of major equipment marketers.

Unsought products   Items that are purchased when a sudden problem must be solved or when aggressive selling is used to obtain a sale that otherwise would not take place

Raw materials   The basic materials that become part of physical products

Major equipment   Large tools and machines used for production purposes

Accessory equipment   Tools and equipment used in production or office activities that do not become part of the final physical product

Microsoft Windows

Once again the brilliant minds at computer software company Microsoft have developed a winner: Microsoft Windows. Described as a "pick and click" system, version 3.1 precipitated a meteoric rise in Windows' fortunes following its launch in May 1990. In the first six weeks alone over 3 million copies were sold. Now it is estimated that more than 45 million copies are in use around the world, with an estimated one million more being shipped to customers each month. The latest version, Windows 95, a totally new package, is already dominating markets throughout Europe. For software companies the popularity of the Windows system means that software programs can run on a number of different operating systems—including PC operating system, MS-DOS and, most recently, Windows. However, the intrinsic appeal and simplicity of the mouse driven Windows look set to ensure its long term popularity for the innovative Microsoft company.

For many industrial customers the Windows operating system offers a host of benefits: it is easy to use, attractive to look at and—perhaps most significant—has a common user interface (CUI). The CUI means that users apply the same commands, through the same system of menus, to a wide range of different programs. The result is that once users have become familiar with commands from one software package, they can move on to another with minimum fuss.

It is perhaps not surprising that Microsoft Windows has attracted positive interest and feedback across all industry sectors. According to brewery giant Bass, the installation of Windows in its marketing department is helping to improve coordination of projects by making analysis, planning, data access and communications more efficient. Advertising agency Saatchi & Saatchi is also a strong convert, claiming that the installation of Windows allows personnel to switch easily from machine to machine and move quickly through a variety of packages. This maximum flexibility with minimum learning is particularly welcome in Saatchi's high pressured and fast moving environment. Although the agency does not force employees to use computer based technology, those who do are unstinting in their praise. Of course, switching to a new operating system is not without its costs. Some organisations, such as Mars, are getting around this difficulty in the short term by offering managers a choice of systems when replacing hardware. But whatever routes companies are taking to convert to Windows, the widespread acceptance of another Microsoft masterpiece seems clear.

SOURCES: Chris Long, "Bill Gates: one man as his brand", *Marketing,* 18 February 1993, pp. 24–26; "See the stars of page and screen", Windows for Marketers, *Marketing,* 11 February 1993, p. 4; Ron Condon, "It's the sound and vision thing", Windows for Marketers, *Marketing,* 11 February 1993, pp. 12–13; "Laptop lunacy licked", Windows for Marketers, *Marketing,* 11 February 1993, pp. 10–11; Microsoft publicity 1996; Dell sales office, Dublin, 1996.

Component parts   Parts that become incorporated into the physical product and are either finished items ready for assembly or products that need little processing before assembly

Component Parts   Parts that become a part of the physical product and are either finished items ready for assembly or products that need little processing before assembly are called **component parts.** Although they become part of a larger product, component parts can often be easily identified and distinguished. Microchips, switches, screws and wires are all component parts of a personal computer. Buyers purchase such items according to their own specifications or industry standards. They expect the parts to be of specified quality and delivered on time so that production is not slowed or stopped. Producers that are primarily assemblers, such as most lawn mower or car manufacturers, depend heavily on the suppliers of component parts.

Process Materials   Materials that are used directly in the production of other products are called **process materials.** Unlike component parts, however, process materials are not readily identifiable. For example, Reichhold Chemicals markets a treated fibre product: a phenolicresin, sheet moulding compound used in the production of flight deck instrument panels and aircraft cabin interiors. Although the material is not identifiable in the finished aircraft, it retards burning, smoke and formation of toxic gas when subjected to fire or high temperatures. In Figure 8.2, Henkel promotes the fact that its chemicals are used by industries around the world. As with component parts, process materials are purchased according to industry standards or the purchaser's specifications.

Process materials   Materials used directly in the production of other products, but not readily identifiable

Consumable Supplies   Supplies that facilitate production and operations but do not become part of the finished product are referred to as **consumable supplies.** Paper, pencils, oils, cleaning agents and paints are in this category. Because such supplies are standardised items used in a variety of situations, they are purchased by many different types of organisations. Consumable supplies are commonly sold through numerous outlets and are purchased routinely. To ensure that supplies are available when needed, buyers often deal with more than one seller.

Consumable supplies   Supplies that facilitate production and operations but do not become part of the finished product

Figure 8.2

An example of a process material

Henkel produces chemicals used in a wide range of manufacturing processes.

Source: Courtesy of Henkel Corporation.

Because these supplies can be divided into three sub-categories—maintenance, repair and operating (or overhaul) supplies—they are sometimes called **MRO items.**

Industrial Services **Industrial services** are the intangible products that many organisations use in their operations. They include financial, legal, marketing research, computer programming and operation, caretaking and printing services for business. Purchasers must decide whether to provide their own services internally or obtain them outside the organisation. This decision depends largely on the costs associated with each alternative and the frequency with which the services are needed.

The Three Levels of Product

The product may appear obvious—a tin of baked beans or a JCB digger—but generally the purchaser is buying much more than some beans or an earthmover. To be motivated to make the purchase, there must be a perceived or real core benefit or service to be gained from the product. This level of product, termed the **core product**, is illustrated in Figure 8.3. The **actual product** is a composite of several factors: the features and capabilities offered, quality and durability, design and product styling, packaging and, often of great importance, the brand name.

In order to make the purchase, the consumer will often require the assistance of sales personnel; there may be delivery and payment credit requirements and, for bulky or very technical products, advice regarding installation. The level of warranty back-up and after sales support, particularly for innovative, highly technical or high value goods, will be of concern to most consumers. Increasingly, the overall level of customer service constitutes part of the purchase criteria, and in many markets it is deemed integral to the product on offer. These "support" issues form what is termed the **augmented product** (see Figure 8.3).

When a £20,000 Rover 800 executive car is purchased, the vehicle's performance specification and design may have encouraged the sale. Speed of delivery and credit payment terms may have been essential to the conclusion of the deal. The brand's image, particularly in the case of a car costing £20,000, will also have influenced the sale. Once behind the wheel of the Rover car, its new owner will expect reliability and efficient, friendly, convenient service in the course of maintenance being required. The purchase might have been lost at the outset had the salesperson mishandled the initial enquiry. Repeat servicing business and the subsequent sale of another new car would equally be ruled out if the owner encountered incompetent, unhelpful service engineers. The core benefit may have been a car to facilitate journeys to work, transport for the family or the acquisition of a recognised status symbol. Customer satisfaction will depend on the product's actual performance and also on service aspects of the augmented product.

This example is not unusual. For most consumer or industrial products and services, the consumer is aware of—and influenced by—the three levels of the product: core, actual and augmented. Of growing importance to many marketers is the role of personnel, who facilitate most product exchanges. Without people, there would be no marketing. In companies they design, produce, market and sell products and services. In the distribution channel they help to make products available to the marketplace. As consumers, people make decisions and ultimately adopt

Figure 8.3

The three levels of product:
core, actual and augmented

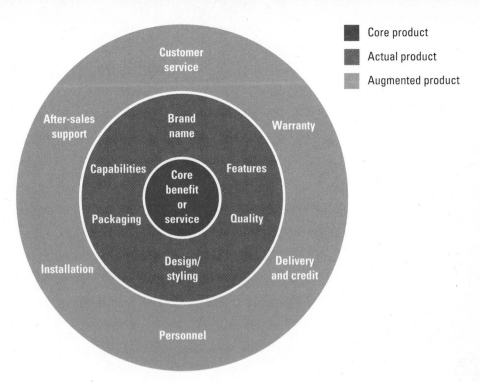

products for use and consumption. Companies endeavour to educate their target customers: promotional activity explains product usage, presents an image for the product and convinces customers that they have a reason to purchase. More attention is now being paid to the skills, attitudes and motivations of personnel involved in the marketing channel. Most companies are recognising the key role played by their personnel, particularly in their interaction with consumers. As explained in Chapter 11, this role is especially significant for services, but as discussed in Chapter 1, personnel also constitutes an essential ingredient of the marketing mix for consumer and industrial goods.

• • • • • • • • • • • • • • • • • • •

Product Line and Product Mix

Marketers must understand the relationships among all the products of their organisation if they are to co-ordinate the marketing of the total group of products. The following concepts help describe the relationships among an organisation's products. A **product item** is a specific version of a product that can be designated as a distinct offering among an organisation's products, for example, Cadbury's Dairy Milk chocolate. A **product line** includes a group of closely related product items that are considered a unit because of marketing, technical or end use considerations. All the chocolate bars manufactured by Cadbury's constitute one of its product lines. Figure 8.4 illustrates the product line for Neutradol. To come up with the optimum product line, marketers must understand buyers' goals. Specific items in a product line reflect the desires of different target markets or the different needs of consumers.

Product item   A specific version of a product that can be designated as a distinct offering among an organisation's products

Product line   A group of closely related product items that are considered a unit because of marketing, technical or end use considerations

Product mix   The composite group of products that an organisation makes available to customers

Depth (of product mix)   The number of different products offered in each product line

Width (of product mix)   The number of product lines a company offers

A **product mix** is the composite, or total, group of products that an organisation makes available to customers. For example, all the personal care products, laundry detergent products and other products that Procter & Gamble manufactures constitute its product mix. The **depth** of a product mix is measured by the number of different products offered in each product line. The **width** of a product mix is measured by the number of product lines a company offers. Figure 8.5 shows the width of the product mix and the depth of each product line for selected Procter & Gamble products in the US. Procter & Gamble is known for using distinctive technology, branding, packaging and consumer advertising to promote individual items in its detergent product line. Tide, Bold, and Ariel—all Procter & Gamble detergents—share similar distribution channels and manufacturing facilities. Yet due to variations in product formula and attributes, each is promoted as distinct, adding depth to the product line.

Product Life Cycles

Product life cycle   The four major stages for products: introduction, growth, maturity and decline

Just as biological cycles progress through growth and decline, so do **product life cycles.** A new product is introduced into the marketplace; it grows; it matures; and when it loses appeal and sales decline, it is terminated.[4] Recall that the earlier definition of a product focused on tangible and intangible attributes. The total prod-

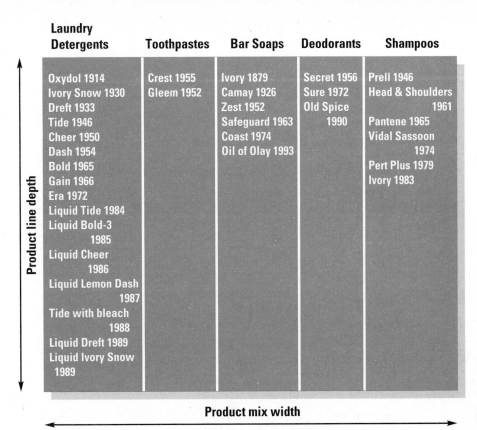

Laundry Detergents	Toothpastes	Bar Soaps	Deodorants	Shampoos
Oxydol 1914	Crest 1955	Ivory 1879	Secret 1956	Prell 1946
Ivory Snow 1930	Gleem 1952	Camay 1926	Sure 1972	Head & Shoulders 1961
Dreft 1933		Zest 1952	Old Spice 1990	Pantene 1965
Tide 1946		Safeguard 1963		Vidal Sassoon 1974
Cheer 1950		Coast 1974		Pert Plus 1979
Dash 1954		Oil of Olay 1993		Ivory 1983
Bold 1965				
Gain 1966				
Era 1972				
Liquid Tide 1984				
Liquid Bold-3 1985				
Liquid Cheer 1986				
Liquid Lemon Dash 1987				
Tide with bleach 1988				
Liquid Dreft 1989				
Liquid Ivory Snow 1989				

Product line depth (vertical axis) · **Product mix width** (horizontal axis)

SOURCE: *Information provided and reprinted by permission of The Procter & Gamble Company, Public Affairs Division, 1 Procter & Gamble Plaza, Cincinnati, OH 45202-3315.*

uct might be not just a good, but also the ideas and services attached to it. Packaging, branding and labelling techniques alter or help create products, so marketers can modify product life cycles. (Marketing strategies for different life cycle stages are discussed in Chapter 10.)

As Figure 8.6 shows, a product life cycle has four major stages: (1) introduction, (2) growth, (3) maturity and (4) decline. As a product moves through its cycle, the strategies relating to competition, promotion, distribution, pricing and market information must be periodically evaluated and possibly changed. Astute marketing managers use the life cycle concept to make sure that the introduction, alteration and termination of a product are timed and executed properly. By understanding the typical life cycle pattern, marketers are better able to maintain profitable products and drop unprofitable ones.

Introduction

Introduction stage A product's first appearance in the marketplace, before any sales or profits have been made

The **introduction stage** of the life cycle begins at a product's first appearance in the marketplace, when sales are zero and profits are negative. Profits are below zero because a new product incurs development cases, initial revenues are low and at the same time a company must generally incur large expenses for promotion a distribution. As time passes, sales should move upwards from zero and p should build up from the negative position due to high expenses (see Figu

Because of cost, very few product introductions represent major i Developing and introducing a new product can mean an outlay of m

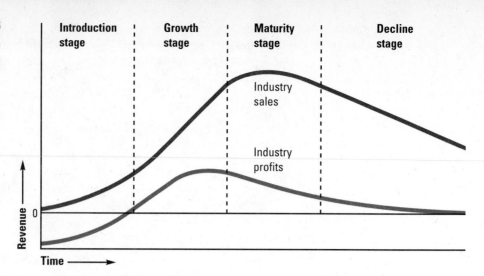

Figure 8.6

The four stages of the product life cycle

During the **growth stage,** sales rise rapidly and profits reach a peak and then start to decline (see Figure 8.6). The growth stage is critical to a product's survival because competitive reactions to its success during this period will affect the product's life expectancy.

Introduction stage | **Growth stage** | **Maturity stage** | **Decline stage**

Industry sales

Industry profits

Revenue

0

Time

of pounds. The failure rate for new products is quite high, ranging from 60 to 90 per cent depending on the industry and how product failure is defined. For example, in the food and drinks industry, 80 per cent of all new products fail.[5] More typically, product introductions involve a new magazine, a new type of portable phone or a new fashion in clothing rather than a major product innovation.

Potential buyers must be made aware of the new product's features, uses and advantages. Two difficulties may arise at this point. Only a few sellers may have the resources, technological knowledge and marketing know-how to launch the product successfully; and the initial product price may have to be high in order to recoup expensive marketing research or development costs. Given these difficulties, it is not surprising that many products never get beyond the introduction stage; indeed many are never launched commercially at all.

Growth

Growth stage The stage at which a product's sales rise rapidly and profits reach a peak, before levelling off into maturity

During the **growth stage,** sales rise rapidly and profits reach a peak and then start to decline (see Figure 8.6). The growth stage is critical to a product's survival because competitive reactions to its success during this period will affect the product's life expectancy. For example, Mars successfully launched Ice Cream Mars, the first ice cream version of an established confectionery product. Today the product competes with around a dozen other brands. Already some of the competing brands have failed—time will show how many others follow. Profits decline late in the growth stage as more competitors enter the market, driving prices down and creating the need for heavy promotional expenses. At this point a typical marketing strategy encourages strong brand loyalty, perhaps using sales promotion, and competes with aggressive emulators of the product. During the growth stage, an organisation tries to strengthen its market share and develop a competitive position by emphasising the product's benefits. Marketing Insight 8.2 reveals how easyJet and Virgin Express are enjoying the growth in the market for no frills air travel at a budget price.

Aggressive promotional pricing, including price cuts, is typical during the growth stage. The mobile telephone industry is currently in the growth stage, and competitors are entering the market. Cellnet and Vodaphone are having to battle hard to maintain their existing positions in this competitive arena.

PRODUCT, BRANDING, PACKAGING AND SERVICE DECISIONS

Maturity stage The stage during which a product's sales curve peaks and starts to decline, and profits continue to decline

During the **maturity stage,** the sales curve peaks and starts to decline, and profits continue to decline (see Figure 8.6). This stage is characterised by severe competition, with many brands in the market. Competitors emphasise improvements and differences in their versions of the product. Inevitably, during the maturity stage some weaker competitors are squeezed out or switch their attentions to other products. For example, some brands of compact disc players will perish as the product moves through the maturity stage.

During the maturity phase, the producers who remain in the market must make fresh promotional and distribution efforts. These efforts must focus on dealers as much as on consumers to ensure that brand visibility is maintained at the point of sale. Advertising and dealer orientated promotions are typical during this stage of the product life cycle. The promoters must also take into account the fact that, as the product reaches maturity, buyers' knowledge of it attains a high level. Consumers of the product are no longer inexperienced generalists but rather experienced specialists.

Decline

Decline stage The last stage of a product's life cycle, during which sales fall rapidly

During the **decline stage,** sales fall rapidly (see Figure 8.6). New technology or a new social trend may cause product sales to take a sharp turn downwards. When this happens, the marketer considers pruning items from the product line to eliminate those not earning a profit. At this time, too, the marketer may cut promotion efforts, eliminate marginal distributors and, finally, plan to phase out the product.

Because most businesses have a product mix consisting of multiple products, a firm's destiny is rarely tied to one product. A composite of life cycle patterns is formed when various products in the mix are at different stages in the cycle. As one product is declining, other products are in the introduction, growth or maturity stage. Marketers must deal with the dual problems of prolonging the life of existing products and introducing new products to meet organisational sales goals. For example, Kodak has prolonged the product life cycle of its 110mm cameras by adding built-in flashes, waterproof bodies and other features. But Kodak has also continued to introduce new products, including the disposable 35mm Kodak Fling; Breeze, a new line of 35mm cameras; and Ektar, a new line of colour films designed specifically for 35mm single-lens reflex cameras. Chapter 10 further explores the development of new products and considers how they can be managed in their various life cycle stages.

● ● ● ● ● ● ● ● ● ● ● ● ● ● ● ● ● ●

Other Product Related Characteristics

When developing products, marketers make many decisions. Some of these decisions involve the physical characteristics of the product; others focus on less tangible support services that are very much a part of the total product.

Physical Characteristics of the Product and Quality

Quality The core product's ability to achieve the basic functional requirements expected of it

A crucial question that arises during product development is how much **quality** to build into the product. In the core product, quality constitutes the product's ability to achieve the basic functional requirements expected of it. A major dimension of quality is durability. Higher quality often demands better materials and more expensive processing, increasing production costs and, ultimately, the product's price. In determining the specific level of quality required, a marketer must decide approximately what price the target market views as acceptable. In addition, a

A New Market in Air Travel: Virgin Express Enters the Fray

In 1984, music entrepreneur and multi-millionaire Richard Branson formed Virgin Atlantic Airways, a low cost alternative airline for people travelling from London to New York. Before launching this transatlantic route with a fanfare of publicity, Virgin analysed the service offerings of its rival operators to try to improve on the competition and avoid the "cattle train" atmosphere inherent in most US-bound services. Entertainment was a focus. Travellers' desire to alleviate their boredom dovetailed nicely with Branson's music business interests. Show business celebrities were encouraged to fly with Virgin Atlantic, free or at reduced rates, if they were prepared to perform on board. In-seat video players and TV screens were installed, followed more recently by computer games and—for business use—full computer/telecommunications facilities. Within a matter of months, the airline had built a reputation for fun, less hassle and better customer service than its rivals.

When in 1989 Virgin began flying to Tokyo, the new route forced Virgin to re-assess its customer service. Japan's recession had reduced business travel, forcing major carriers to compete for reduced levels of business by improving even economy class service. Virgin opted for at least 50 per cent Japanese cabin staff, Japanese food and a Japanese pop music channel. The company strove to understand the culture of its new market and to give travellers a service that genuinely satisfied their distinctive needs. The result was success in an increasingly hostile marketplace. The airline has continued to expand, flying to six US cities, Japan and Athens. It has recently embarked on a series of partnership deals and acquisitions with smaller airlines to boost route and destination coverage.

The latest development for the ever expanding Virgin airline is the creation of Virgin Express, formed after Virgin bought Belgian airline EBA for £36.5 million. Deregulation in the European airline market has prompted a rise in the number of small companies offering low cost, no frills flights. With US operators pointing the way, these airlines are turning air travel into a commodity item. Newcomer airline easyJet offers Scotland to London (Luton) for around £30 by cutting out the travel agent and offering a direct booking telesales operation. EasyJet now also flies to Nice and Barcelona. Other low price rivals include World Airlines, Denim, Debonair and now Virgin Express. The market leader in this budget sector, easyJet's philosophy is straightforward: on flights less than two hours, passengers will happily do without any cabin service in return for low cost travel, with significant staff savings for the airline. The company also offers one-way tickets and, unlike its rivals, requires no Saturday night stayover.

Virgin chairman Richard Branson bought Belgian airline EBA with the stated intention of creating a new marketing offer with a no frills service offering the lowest prices on chosen routes. Prices may be up to 50 per cent cheaper than those offered currently by rival operators on the same routes. By purchasing an existing airline, Virgin has also taken over a ready made selection of slots at the big airports and guaranteed routes. The major airlines are fighting back. In Italy and Spain, where the state airlines also run many of the airport services, the discount operators have found it difficult to obtain check-in desks and computer hook-ups. Air UK has cut its scheduled prices to combat its new rivals, and in Germany domestic fares dropped by over 20 per cent as Lufthansa fought back. Virgin Express is opening up a new market for the Virgin business, but it will not be without fierce competition. The indication, however, is that a significant market segment exists in which low prices do compensate for reduced customer services; Branson clearly aims to cater for this market with Virgin Express.

SOURCES: Jon Rees, "Wings of desire", *Marketing Week,* 17 May 1996, pp. 36–37; "Virgin Airlines soars to success in Japan", *Focus Japan,* April 1995, p. 7; "Virgin flies in", *Marketing,* 23 June 1994, p. 2.

marketer usually tries to set a level for a specific product consistent with the firm's other products that carry a similar brand. Obviously, the quality of competing brands is another consideration. It is important to understand how the targeted customers perceive quality and what levels they believe to be acceptable.

A product's physical features require careful consideration by marketers and by those in research and development. For example, product development personnel at Gillette spent considerable resources dealing with the Sensor razor's physical features. The prime basis for decisions about the physical features of a product should be the needs and wants of the target market. If marketers do not know what physical features people in the target market want in a product, it is highly unlikely that the product will be satisfactory. For example, Rover and JCB hold customer clinics offering people the opportunity to examine their product range and comment on desired features. Even a firm whose existing products have been designed to satisfy target market desires should continue to assess these desires periodically to determine whether they have changed enough to require alterations in the product.

Supportive Product Related Services

All products, whether they are goods or not, possess intangible qualities. "When prospective customers can't experience the product in advance, they are asked to buy what are essentially promises—promises of satisfaction. Even tangible, testable, feelable, smellable products are, before they're bought, largely just promises."[6] There are many product related services and product intangibles, but three of the most common are guarantees, repairs/replacements and credit.

Guarantee An agreement specifying what the producer or supplier will do if the product malfunctions

The type of guarantee a company provides can be a critical issue for buyers, especially when expensive, technically complex goods such as appliances are involved. A **guarantee** specifies what the producer or supplier will do if the product malfunctions. In recent years, government actions have required a guarantor to state more simply and specifically the terms and conditions under which the firm will take action. Because guarantees must be more precise today, marketers are using them more vigorously as tools to give their brands a competitive advantage. Retailers, such as Dixons, which sells electrical brown goods, including compact disc players and camcorders, are increasingly using guarantees as a competitive tool by providing longer periods of guarantee protection.

Although it is more difficult to provide guarantees for services than for goods, some service marketers do guarantee customer satisfaction. An effective service guarantee should be unconditional, easy to understand and communicate, meaningful, easy to invoke, and quick and easy to collect on. The customer can return a product and get a replacement, a refund or a credit for the returned good. Photographic processors such as SupaSnaps offer free processing on prints not ready within 24 hours. Such guarantees of satisfying the customer are beneficial because they force the service provider to focus on customers' definitions of good service. They also provide clear performance standards, generate feedback from customers on the quality of the service and help build customer loyalty and sales.[7]

A marketer must also be concerned with establishing a system to provide replacement parts and repair services. This support service is especially important for expensive, complex industrial products that buyers expect to last a long time. For example, farmers expect agricultural machinery manufacturers like Massey Ferguson to be able to provide replacement parts quickly and without fuss. Although the producer may furnish these services directly to buyers, it is more common for the producer to provide such services through regional service centres or middlemen. Regardless of how services are provided, it is important to customers that they be performed quickly and correctly.

Finally, a company must sometimes provide credit services to customers. Even though credit services place a financial burden on an organisation, they can yield several benefits. One of them is that a firm may acquire and maintain a stable market share. Many major oil companies, for example, have competed effectively against petrol discounters by providing credit services. For marketers of relatively expensive items, offering credit services enables a larger number of people to buy the product, thus enlarging the market for the item. Another reason for offering credit services is to earn interest income from customers. The types of credit services offered depend on the characteristics of target market members, the company's financial resources, the type of products sold and the types of credit services that competitors offer.

· · · · · · · · · · · · · · · · · · · ·

Competitive Edge

Marketing must aim to satisfy customers. In the context of products, this goal demands an understanding of the *core* product requirement. However, it depends on marketers identifying and providing the *actual* product features expected and—with ever increasing importance—aspects of the *augmented* product such as customer service, warranty, delivery and credit, personnel, installation and after sales support. Product quality is a subject fundamentally linked to both customer satisfaction and a business's ability to compete. The question that taxes the brand manager of a range of video recorders is not just what features the machines should incorporate but how long the machines should last and with what level of reliability.

Differential advantage An attribute of a product or brand highly desired by targeted customers and not currently offered by rival companies or products

A **differential advantage** is the requirement desired by targeted customers that only one company has the capability to offer: it is a unique differentiator, if utilised in that business's sales and marketing activity. Invariably, differential advantages are difficult to identify, particularly in crowded and mature markets with a plethora of similar product offers from rival companies. Even when a differential advantage exists, it is rarely sustainable in the medium term as envious competitors copy and follow suit. Nevertheless, a differential advantage does provide a competitive edge. For many years stunning off-road performance combined with the luxury of a limousine gave the Range Rover an edge over its rivals. The Shogun and Jeep now match Range Rover on both counts. With its new single arm skid steer, JCB is virtually alone amongst mainstream construction manufacturers in providing drivers with such safe access to and from the cab. As businesses strive to derive a differential advantage over rivals, they look not just to the actual product but also, increasingly, to aspects of product quality and the augmented product features.[8]

· · · · · · · · · · · · · · · · · · · ·

Summary

● A *product* is everything, both favourable and unfavourable, that is received in an exchange. It is a complex set of tangible and intangible attributes, including functional, social and psychological utilities or benefits. A product can be an *idea,* a *service,* a *good* or any combination of these three. When consumers purchase a product, they are buying the benefits and satisfaction that they think the product will provide.

● Products can be classified on the basis of the buyer's intentions. Thus *consumer products* are those purchased to satisfy personal and family needs. *Industrial* or *business-to-business products,* on the other hand, are purchased for use in a company's operations or to make other products. Consumer products can be sub-divided into *convenience, shopping, speciality* and *unsought products.* Industrial products can be divided into *raw materials, major equipment, accessory equipment, component parts, process materials, consumable supplies, MRO items* and *industrial services.*

● The purchaser buys a core benefit or service (the *core product*) in addition to the product's brand name, features, capabilities, quality, packaging and design (the *actual product*). Increasingly, aspects of the *augmented product* are important considerations for purchasers of consumer goods, services and industrial goods. Guarantees, delivery and credit, personnel, installation, after sales support and customer service are integral to the actual product's appeal and perceived benefits. The role of personnel in particular is of fundamental concern to marketers; people now form a central part of the marketing mix. It is important to remember that a product has three levels: core, actual and augmented.

● A *product item* is a specific version of a product that can be designated as a distinct offering among an organisation's products. A *product line* is a group of closely related product items that are considered a unit because of marketing, technical or end use considerations. The composite, or total, group of products that an organisation makes available to customers is called the *product mix.* The *depth* of a product mix is measured by the number of different products offered in each product line. The *width* of the product mix is measured by the number of product lines a company offers.

● The *product life cycle* describes how product items in an industry move through (1) *introduction,* (2) *growth,* (3) *maturity* and (4) *decline.* The life cycle concept is used to make sure that the introduction, alteration and termination of a product are timed and executed properly. The sales curve is at zero on introduction, rises at an increasing rate during growth, peaks at maturity and then declines. Profits peak towards the end of the growth stage of the product life cycle. The life expectancy of a product is based on buyers' wants, the availability of competing products and other environmental conditions. Most businesses have a composite of life cycle patterns for various products. It is important to manage existing products and develop new ones to keep the overall sales performance at a desired level.

● When creating products, marketers must take into account other product related considerations, such as physical characteristics and less tangible support services. Specific physical product characteristics that require attention are the level of *quality,* product features, textures, colours and sizes. Support services that may be viewed as part of the total product include *guarantees,* repairs/replacements and credit services. The desire to establish a *differential advantage* over rivals is an important consideration for marketers. Product attributes are important for this aim, but so too are product quality and aspects of the augmented product.

● ● ● ● ● ● ● ● ● ● ● ● ● ● ● ● ● ● ●

Important Terms

Product	Major equipment	Product mix
Good	Accessory equipment	Depth (of product mix)
Service	Component parts	Width (of product mix)
Ideas	Process materials	Product life cycle
Consumer products	Consumable supplies	Introduction stage
Industrial or business-to-business products	MRO items	Growth stage
	Industrial services	Maturity stage
Convenience products	Core product	Decline stage
Shopping products	Actual product	Quality
Speciality products	Augmented product	Guarantee
Unsought products	Product item	Differential advantage
Raw materials	Product line	

Discussion and Review Questions

1. List the tangible and intangible attributes of a spiral notebook. Compare the benefits of the spiral notebook with those of an intangible product such as life insurance.
2. A product has been referred to as a "psychological bundle of satisfaction". Is this a good definition of a product? Why or why not?
3. Is a roll of carpet in a shop a consumer product or an industrial product? Defend your answer.
4. How do convenience products and shopping products differ? What are the distinguishing characteristics of each type of product?
5. Would a stereo system that sells for £400 be a convenience, shopping or speciality product?
6. In the category of industrial products, how do component parts differ from process materials?
7. How does an organisation's product mix relate to its development of a product line? When should an enterprise add depth to its product lines rather than width to its product mix?
8. How do industry profits change as a product moves through the four stages of its life cycle?
9. What is the relationship between the concepts of product mix and product life cycle?
10. What factors must marketers consider when deciding what quality level to build into a product? What support services can be offered to back up product quality?
11. What are aspects of the augmented product for a new car?
12. Why is the augmented product increasingly important when determining a differential advantage?

Recommended Readings

P. Doyle, *Marketing Management and Strategy* (London: Prentice-Hall, 1994).

Y. J. Wind, *Product Policy: Concepts, Methods and Strategy* (Reading, Mass.: Addison-Wesley, 1982).

A. Craig and S. Hart, "Where to now in new product development research?", *European Journal of Marketing*, vol. 26, no. 11, 1992, pp. 1–49.

R. J. Calantone, C. A. Di Benedetto and T. Haggblom, "Principles of new product management: exploring the beliefs of product practitioners", *Journal of Product Innovation Management*, vol. 12, no. 3, 1995, pp. 235–247.

G. Rifkin, "Product development: the myth of short life cycles", *Harvard Business Review*, vol. 72, no. 4, 1994, p. 11.

Cases

8.1 Heineken's Portfolio of Brands

Heineken is Europe's largest brewer. While more than half of its sales are European, worldwide, Heineken is second only to US based Anheuser-Busch. Heineken beer is recognised around the globe. With a presence in 170 countries and more than three quarters of sales originating outside the domestic Dutch market, Heineken has been described as the most international beer brand.

Despite its activities in the US, South East Asia and Asia, Heineken recognises the significance of its strength in Europe—a particularly important market, which accounts for over 40 per cent of world beer sales. Here, despite the mass appeal of the Heineken brand, to stay a step ahead of the competition the company has to adjust its product mix to suit the needs of different countries, fitting in with local cultures and tastes. In general, Heineken achieves this goal by offering a choice of three core brands in each European country:

- A local brand, aimed at the standard and largest market segment. In Italy this is Dreher, in France "33" and in Spain Aguila Pilsener.
- A brand targeted at the "upper" end of the market. Sometimes this is a locally produced brand, such as the Spanish Aguila Master; in other cases a newer Heineken brand, Amstel, is preferred.

- The Heineken brand itself, aimed at the premium market segment. The beer offered may be manufactured locally or it may be exported from the Netherlands. Either way, the Dutch head office works hard to maintain product quality and brand image.

Chairman Karel Vuursteen believes that it is the proven combination of the Heineken brand with local mainstream brands that creates the successful level of distribution in the market and adequate economies of scale in production. Heineken has a share in over 60 brewing companies around the globe to help facilitate this strategy. The company also keeps up with trends, including iced beers and non-alcoholic brews such as Buckler.

Branding policy in the UK differs slightly from that implemented in other parts of Europe. The standard Heineken brand there is a lower strength version of the beer offered in Europe. The lower strength lager first became popular in pubs across the UK in the 1960s. Now, with the increasing sophistication of the UK beer drinker, the company has introduced the Heineken Export Strength brand—more closely akin to the "standard" Heineken offered throughout Europe.

The competition was caught unawares, however, in 1996 when Heineken re-launched its standard,

original Heineken brand, with new packaging and heavy promotional support. Heineken deliberately ambushed arch rival Carlsberg, high profile sponsors of the Euro '96 football championships. The Heineken brand re-launch was successful in its own right but additionally proved an interesting spoiling tactic against Carlsberg's football sponsorship.

SOURCES: Caroline Farquhar, Warwick MBA, 1991–92; "The Netherlands trade review—the beverage market", Economic Intelligence Unit, *Marketing in Europe*, No. 347, October 1991, p. 36; Heineken annual report and accounts, 1991, 1994 and 1996; David Benardy, "Heineken Euro '96 plot", *Marketing Week*, 23 February 1996, p. 7; Nina Munk, "Make mine Hoegaarden", *Forbes*, 18 December 1995, pp. 124–126; Havis Dawson, "Brand brewing", *Beverage World*, October 1995, pp. 50–60; "Heineken stresses sponsorship in marketing non-alcoholic beer", *Crossborder Monitor*, 11 January 1995, p. 9.

Questions for Discussion

1. Why was the UK's version of Heineken lager weaker than its counterpart in the rest of Europe? What problems has this product variation caused Heineken?
2. Why does Heineken opt for a mix of internationally known brands marketed alongside local beers?
3. In what ways is Heineken continuously up-dating its product portfolio and its marketing mix?

8.2 Disney Expands Its Product Mix

After the death of its founder, Walt Disney, in 1966, the Walt Disney Company seemed to lose its creative edge. As other studios diversified into television and video, Disney seemed content with its library of feature films and animated classics. The company was producing only three or four new films a year, most of which failed at the box office. Disney also pulled out of television after 29 years of network programming. By the mid-1980s, Disney was dependent on theme parks and property development for about 75 per cent of its revenues.

Today, however, Disney executives are intent on recapturing—and building on—the old Disney magic. Company executives say that the Disney name, culture, films and library are the company's biggest resources, and Disney's plan is to rejuvenate old assets and simultaneously develop new ones. While continuing its traditional appeal to the family segment of the film market, Disney, through its Touchstone Pictures division, is turning out films for

adult audiences as well. The company is releasing both old and new programmes for television syndication and testing new promotional and licensing projects. In addition, the Disney theme park has been exported. The Tokyo Disneyland is attracting millions of people a year, and a $2 billion Euro Disneyland opened near Paris in 1992. Disney's overall strategy is to channel the company's revived creativity into improved theme parks, to use the parks to generate interest in Disney films and to promote both parks and merchandise through Disney television shows.

The year 1995 proved a watershed and emphasised the company's turnaround: a blockbuster merger with Capital Cities/ABC, a management coup in hiring Hollywood superagent Michael Ovitz, a turnaround at EuroDisney near Paris, two smash movies—*Pocahontas* and *Toy Story*—and the headhunting of Nickelodeon executive Geraldine Laybourne. The ABC link is perhaps the most significant aspect; never before has a company with the marketing, merchandising and management expertise of Disney owned a television network. ABC is expected to become a powerful promotional vehicle for Disney.

Disney received its new lease on life a few years ago when threats of a corporate takeover prompted the company to replace its top executives. The new management moved quickly to tap the resources of the Disney television and film library. About two hundred Disney films and cartoon packages are now available on video cassette; other classic films, such as *Snow White,* will now be released every five years instead of every seven. The studio plans to release one new animated film for children every 18 months and about a dozen adult films a year.

Disney is back on network television as well, with the return of the *Disney Sunday Movie.* The company also produces the comedy show *The Golden Girls,* along with two top rated Saturday morning cartoon shows. Following the lead of other studios, Disney has moved into television syndication by marketing packages of feature films, old cartoons and *Wonderful World of Disney* programmes. The company is syndicating *The Disney Afternoon,* a block of children's cartoons that will run from 3 p.m. to 5 p.m. New shows are also being produced for syndication. They include the popular game show *Win, Lose or Draw,* a business news programme and film reviews by Gene Siskel and Roger Ebert. In an otherwise flat cable television market, the number of subscribers to the family orientated Disney Channel has jumped dramatically—to 4 million. The channel now offers 24 hour features and more original programming than any other pay service. Disney has even signed an agreement with the Chinese government to broadcast a weekly television series starring Mickey Mouse and Donald Duck. The company may license the Chinese to produce Disney merchandise as well.

In the United States, too, marketing of Disney characters is receiving considerable emphasis. Recently, Mickey, Donald and others visited hospital wards and marched in parades in a 120 city tour. Snow White and all seven dwarfs made a special appearance on the floor of the New York Stock Exchange to promote the celebration of Snow White's 50th birthday. Minnie Mouse now has a trendy new look and appears on clothing and watches and in a fashion doll line. Disney is also working with toy companies to develop new characters, such as Fluppy Dogs and Wuzzles, both of which will be sold in stores and featured in television shows. In addition, the company has opened non-tourist retail outlets. Located primarily in shopping malls, Disney stores carry both licensed products and exclusive theme park merchandise. Disney Stores are now found in most large cities across Europe. The latest generation opened in Las Vegas and San Francisco, providing an inventive and colourful display of wizardry and entertainment far beyond the traditional retail store.

Disney's revitalised market presence has been credited with increasing attendance at the Disney theme parks to more than 50 million people. In Florida, Disney has recently completed new hotels and a movie studio/tour attraction. Moreover, Disney is constructing a 50 acre water park and adding $1.4 billion worth of new attractions to Walt Disney World. The company is also considering regional centres that would combine restaurants and shopping with evening entertainment. In a recent move, Disney announced plans to extend its expertise into the European time-share business by launching the Disney Vacation Club. The new concept offers holidaymakers accommodations in purpose built facilities at Florida's Disney World. The price is a once only payment of £7,000, which will give club members access to accommodation at Disney World, or over 100 other destinations around the world. It is not yet clear whether the company plans to build vacation clubs at other Disney sites.

Disney intends eventually to reduce the company's financial dependence on parks and hotels. The strategy is to triple the proportion of company profits from films and television and to acquire such distribution outlets as cinemas, television stations and record companies. Recent business deals with Procter & Gamble, McDonald's, Coca-Cola, Time, M&M/Mars, and Sears will help increase Disney's profits and market presence still further.

SOURCES: Stanley Bing, "More magic from Mickey's and Michael's kingdom", *Fortune,* 15 January 1996, p. 51; "Disney's ABC buy creates media co of the future", *Brandweek,* 7 August 1995, p. 4; Marianne Wilson, "Disney's one-two punch", *Chain Store Executive,* July 1995, pp. 92–93; Dudley Clendinen, "Disney's mouse of marketing", *New York Times,* 22 November 1986, p. 41–L; Pamela Ellis-Simon, "Hi ho, hi ho", *Marketing & Media Decisions,* September 1986, pp. 52–54; Andrea Gabor and Steve L. Hawkins, "Of mice and money in the magic kingdom", *U.S. News & World Report,* 22 December 1986, pp. 44–46; Ronald Grover, "Disney's magic", *Business Week,* 9 March 1987, pp. 62–65; Scott Hume, "Sears gains exclusivity with Disney contract", *Advertising Age,* 23 November 1987, p. 63; Stephen Koepp, "Do you believe in magic?", *Time,* 25 April 1988, pp. 66–76; Marcy Magiera, "Disney tries retailing", *Advertising Age,* 1 June 1987, p. 80; Myron Magnet, "Putting magic back in the kingdom", *Fortune,* 5 January 1987, p. 65; Raymond Roel, "Disney's marketing touch", *Direct Marketing,* January 1987, pp. 50–53; Stephen J. Sansweet, "Disney Co. cartoons are going to China in commercial foray", *Wall Street Journal,* 23 October 1986, p. 19; Susan Spillman, "Animation draws on its storied past", *USA Today,* 15 November 1989, pp. 1B–2B; Wayne Walley, "Disney enlists Time Inc., Mars to honor Mickey", *Advertising Age,* 6 June 1988, pp. 3, 110; Wayne Walley, "P & G, Disney link videos, products", *Advertising Age,* 18 January 1988, p. 1; and Wayne Walley, "Roger Rabbit makes splash", *Advertising Age,* 27 June 1988, pp. 3, 110; "Disney hunts marketer for Euro timeshare club", *Marketing Week,* 19 February 1993, p. 5.

Questions for Discussion

1. Disney's product mix consists of many products. Does Disney have product lines? If so, what are they?
2. Disney labels many of its new films for adults as Touchstone Pictures. With a famous name like Disney, why does the company not use the Disney name?
3. Do the products in the Disney product mix have product life cycles? Explain.

9 BRANDING AND PACKAGING

"Brands are at the very heart of
marketing. When a company creates
a strong brand it attracts customer
preference and builds a defensive
wall against competition."

Peter Doyle
Warwick Business School

OBJECTIVES

- To recognise the importance of brands
- To understand the types and benefits of brands and how to select, protect and license them
- To become aware of the major packaging functions and design considerations and of the way in which packaging is used in marketing strategies
- To examine the functions of labelling and the legal issues associated with labelling

Packaging giant Tetra Pak came in for much criticism from consumers and retailers alike during the mid-1990s. For more than two decades, consumers have struggled to open cardboard cartons of milk, juice and soups with flaps that had to be pulled down, then apart, then … well, they were not the easiest of items with which to do battle! The alarm bells rang when supermarket giants Sainsbury's and Tesco responded to consumer views and opted for plastic containers with screw caps for milk and juice, threatening to de-stock Tetra Pak cartons totally.

Tetra Pak responded by mounting a successful publicity campaign to persuade the media that its cartons were simple to use and indeed were well loved by consumers. The company also modified its packaging design, adding a pop-open spout and top to the traditional carton for easy opening. For a one-product company with 16,000 employees operating in 117 countries and shipping 70 billion cartons annually, the negative consumer reaction had to be addressed speedily and with care.

The consumer backlash against the difficult-to-open cartons occurred across all types of shoppers.

Tetra Pak came in for significant criticism during the "Through Other Eyes" campaign, particularly for its milk cartons. However, Ulf Brasen, Tetra Pak's managing director, was a keen participant in the workshops. "Wearing view-restricting goggles, armbands and ankle weights made simple tasks such as reading the cooking instructions on a food package significantly harder than I would ever have considered possible," he commented. Those involved in this particular awareness campaign universally acknowledge the significant strides made by Tetra Pak to eliminate some of the most common problems. The Tetra Pak ring-pull tops on cartons are significantly better. As Ulf Brasen explained, "we have been looking at this issue for a number of years and are introducing easy-open packaging designs. If disabled people can safely and readily open, pour and reclose our cartons, then so can the rest of the community". Of course, the packaging companies are looking into this issue for economic reasons, too. In light of the ageing population, more and more consumers will find easier to open packaging appealing, and manufacturers and retailers will have to supply merchandise in more user friendly containers and packaging. Companies like Tetra Pak are responding to both the needs of the community and the requirements stipulated by their immediate customers, the manufacturers and supermarket chains. ■

But what about those with disabilities? If consumers with no physical limitations have problems with packaging, then what of those with disabilities? As the 1990s unfold, more and more companies are redesigning their packaging to reflect ease of opening and use. Charity Age Concern ran a programme called "Through Other Eyes" for marketing and sales directors. Dressed in rubber gloves, goggles, armbands and ankle weights, those attending the workshop were helped to understand the problems faced by the elderly and disabled.

As Roger Saunders, responsible for the campaign, explained, "how often have you struggled to open a carton of orange juice or a jar of jam, or unwrap the cellophane from around a compact disc? It is often frustrating and ends in broken nails and lost tempers. If you have arthritis or Parkinson's disease, for example, then it is doubly difficult". The Royal College of Art has advised the programme and has indeed developed many innovative packaging applications. One good design is the new flip-top toothpaste tube, which prevents the top from being dropped or lost.

SOURCES: Helen Jones, "It's open war with the Pack", *Independent on Sunday*, 17 December 1995; "Veryfine tuning", *Adweek*, 13 November 1995, p. 6; Liz Dunning, "Design choice: Tetra Pak", *Marketing*, 3 August 1995, p. 11; Emma Hall, "KLD to counter image problem for Tetra Pak", *Campaign*, 28 April 1995, p. 4; Helen Slingsby, "Leader of the Pak", *Marketing Week*, 8 July 1994, pp. 36–37.

Brands and packages are part of a product's tangible features, the verbal and physical cues that help customers identify the products they want and influence their choices when they are unsure. A good brand is distinct and memorable; without one, firms could not differentiate their products, and shoppers' choices would essentially be arbitrary. A good package design like the one produced by Tetra Pak, is cost effective, safe, environmentally responsible and valuable as a promotional tool.

The first part of this chapter defines branding, its benefits to customers and sellers, and the various types of brands. The next section explores how companies choose brands, how they protect them, the various branding policies that companies employ and brand licensing. The chapter goes on to discuss how businesses manage brands and ensure that they contribute effectively to the company's fortunes. It then examines the critical role of packaging as part of the product and how it is marketed. The following section explores the functions of packaging, issues to consider in packaging design, how the package can be a major element in marketing strategy and packaging criticisms. The chapter concludes with a discussion of labelling and other product related features, including the product's physical characteristics and supportive product related services.

● ● ● ● ● ● ● ● ● ● ● ● ● ● ● ● ● ● ● ●

Branding

Brand A name, term, design, symbol or any other feature that identifies one seller's good or service as distinct from those of other sellers

Brand name That part of a brand that can be spoken, including letters, words and numbers

Brand recognition The extent to which consumers are aware of a brand

Brand mark The element of a brand that cannot be spoken—often a symbol or design

In addition to making decisions about actual products, marketers must make many decisions associated with branding, such as brands, brand names, brand marks, trademarks and trade names. A **brand** is a name, term, design, symbol or any other feature that identifies one seller's good or service as distinct from those of other sellers. A brand may identify one item, a family of items or all items of that seller.[1] A **brand name** is that part of a brand that can be spoken—including letters, words and numbers—such as Coca-Cola. A brand name is often a product's only distinguishing characteristic. Without the brand name, a firm could not identify its products. To consumers, brand names are as fundamental as the product itself. Brand names simplify shopping, guarantee a specific level of quality and allow self-expression.[2] Table 9.1 lists the 20 most powerful brands in the world based on surveys of over 10,000 respondents in the US, Japan and Europe. These ratings reflect both **brand recognition** (awareness) and esteem scores. Subsequent chapters on promotion decisions highlight the importance of brand recognition.

The element of a brand that is not made up of words but is often a symbol or design is called a **brand mark.** One example is the symbol of a baby on Procter & Gamble's Fairy Liquid detergent. Occasionally brand marks are modified for local

World Brands

1. Coca-Cola	8. McDonald's	15. Kleenex
2. Sony	9. IBM	16. Ford
3. Mercedes-Benz	10. Pepsi Cola	17 Volkswagen
4. Kodak	11. Rolls Royce	18. Kellogg's
5. Disney	12. Honda	19. Porsche
6. Nestlé	13. Panasonic	20. Polaroid
7. Toyota	14. Levi's	

SOURCE: Landor Associates' ImagePower Survey, 1990 (New York). Used by permission.

Table 9.1 Top world brands

markets. For example, Microsoft tops its brand name with a butterfly in France, a fish in Portugal and a sun in Spain. A **trademark** is a legal designation indicating that the owner has exclusive use of a brand or a part of a brand and that others are prohibited by law from using it. To protect a brand name or brand mark a company must register it as a trademark with the appropriate patenting office. Finally, a **trade name** is the full and legal name of an organisation, such as Ford Motor Company or Safeway Stores, rather than the name of a specific product.

Trademark Legal designation indicating that the owner has exclusive use of a brand

Trade name The full and legal name of an organisation

Benefits of Branding

Branding provides benefits for both buyers and sellers.[3] Brands help buyers identify specific products that they do and do not like, a process that in turn facilitates the purchase of items that satisfy their needs and reduces the time required to purchase the product. Without brands, product selection would be quite random, because buyers could have no assurance that they were purchasing what they preferred. Imagine the chaos in a supermarket if every shopper entered not knowing which products and brands to purchase! Research indicates, however, that the bulk of supermarket shoppers are highly brand loyal. So much so, that in-store redesigns and new shelf-space allocations cause significant distress and generate high levels of customer complaints. A brand also helps buyers evaluate the quality of a product, especially when they are unable to judge its characteristics. In other words, a purchaser for whom a brand symbolises a certain quality level will transfer that perception of quality to the unknown item. A brand thus helps to reduce a buyer's perceived risk of purchase. In addition, it may offer the psychological reward that comes from owning a brand that symbolises status. Certain brands of watches (Rolex) and cars (Rolls Royce) fall into this category.

Sellers benefit from branding because each company's brands identify its products, which makes repeat purchasing easier for consumers. Branding helps a firm introduce a new product that carries the name of one or more of its existing products, because buyers are already familiar with the firm's existing brands. For example, Heinz regularly introduces new tinned products. Because consumers are used to buying the brand and have a high regard for its quality, they are likely to try the new offerings. Branding also facilitates promotional efforts because the promotion of each branded product indirectly promotes all other products that are similarly branded.

Branding also helps sellers by fostering brand loyalty. **Brand loyalty** is a strongly motivated and long standing decision to purchase a product or service. To the extent that buyers become loyal to a specific brand, the company's market share for that product achieves a certain level of stability, allowing the firm to use its resources more efficiently.[4] When a firm succeeds in fostering some degree of customer loyalty to a brand, it can charge a premium price for the product. For example, brand loyal buyers of Anadin aspirin are willing to pay two or three times more for Anadin than for a generic brand of aspirin with the same amount of pain relieving agent. However, brand loyalty is declining, partly because of marketers' increased reliance on sales, coupons and other short term promotions and partly because of the sometimes overwhelming array of similar new products from which consumers can choose. In the brand dominated US, a *Wall Street Journal* survey found that 12 per cent of consumers are not loyal to any brand, whereas 47 per cent are brand loyal for one to five product types. Only 2 per cent of the respondents were brand loyal for more than 16 product types (see Figure 9.1). To stimulate loyalty to their brands, some marketers are stressing image advertising, mailing personalised catalogues and magazines to regular users and creating membership clubs for brand users.[5] Sometimes consumers make repeat

Brand loyalty A strongly motivated and long standing decision to purchase a particular product or service

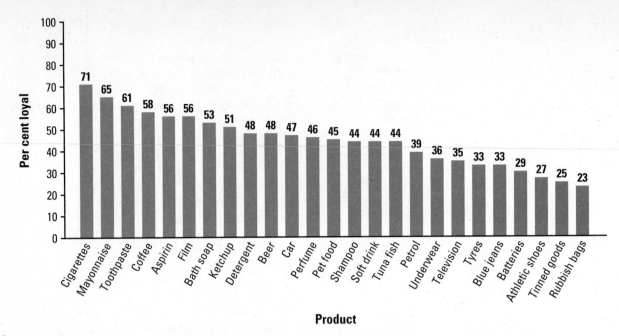

Figure 9.1 Percentage of users of selected products who are loyal to one brand

Source: Wall Street Journal, *19 October 1989, p. B1. ©1989 Dow Jones & Company, Inc. All rights reserved worldwide.*

purchases of products for reasons other than brand loyalty. Spurious loyalty is not stable and may result from non-availability of alternative brands or the way in which products are displayed in retail outlets.

Types of Brands

Manufacturer brands
Brands initiated by producers to ensure that they are identified with their products at the point of purchase

Own label brands Brands initiated and owned by resellers— wholesalers or retailers

There are three categories of brands: manufacturer brands, own label brands (also called private brands, store brands or dealer brands) and generic brands. **Manufacturer brands** are initiated by producers and ensure that producers are identified with their products at the point of purchase—for example, Green Giant, Apple Computer and Wall's ice cream. A manufacturer brand usually requires a producer to become involved in distribution, promotion and, to some extent, pricing decisions. Brand loyalty is encouraged by promotion, quality control and guarantees; it is a valuable asset to a manufacturer. The producer tries to stimulate demand for the product, which tends to encourage middlemen to make the product available. Figure 9.2 presents a well known manufacturer brand, Levi's.

Own label brands are initiated and owned by resellers—wholesalers or retailers. The major characteristic of own label brands is that the manufacturers are not identified on the products. Retailers and wholesalers use these brands to develop more efficient promotion, to generate higher gross margins and to improve store images. Own label brands give retailers or wholesalers freedom to purchase products of a specified quality at the lowest cost without disclosing the identity of the manufacturer. Wholesale brands include Roca, Family Choice, Happy Shopper and Lifestyle. Familiar retailer brand names include St. Michael (Marks & Spencer), Yessica (C & A) and George (Asda). Many successful own label brands are distributed nationally. Matsui domestic appliances (Currys) are as well known as most name brands. Sometimes retailers with successful distributor brands start manufacturing their own products to gain more control over product costs, qual-

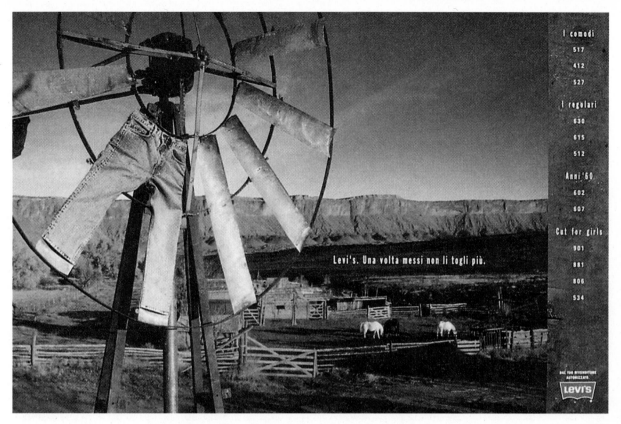

Figure 9.2 Types of brands. Levi's is a manufacturer brand.

SOURCE: Levi Strauss and Company.

ity and design in the hope of increasing profits. While one might think that store brands appeal most strongly to lower income shoppers or to up-market shoppers who compare labels, studies indicate that buyers of own label brands have characteristics that match those of the overall population.[6]

Generic brand A brand that indicates only the product category and does not include the company name or other identifying terms

Some marketers of products that have traditionally been branded have embarked on a policy of not branding, often called generic branding. A **generic brand** indicates only the product category (such as aluminum foil) and does not include the company name or other identifying terms. Usually generic brands are sold at prices lower than those of comparable branded items. Although at one time generic brands may have represented as much as 10 per cent of all retail grocery sales, today they account for less than 1 per cent.[7] They are popular for pharmaceuticals and in some discount grocery stores.

Competition between manufacturer brands and own label brands (sometimes called "the battle of the brands") is intensifying in several major product categories, particularly tinned foods, breakfast cereal, sugar and soft drinks. Own label brands now account for around 13 per cent of all supermarket sales.[8] As shown in Figure 9.3, both men and women are quite favourable towards own label brands of food products, with women (still the major grocery purchasers) even more favourable than men. For manufacturers, developing multiple manufacturer brands and distribution systems has been an effective means of combating the increased competition from own label brands. By developing a new brand

Figure 9.3

Preference for own label brands of food products by age and sex

SOURCE: Yankelovich Monitor®, ©1991. Used with permission.

name, a producer can adjust various elements of a marketing mix to appeal to a different target market. For example, Scott Paper has developed lower priced brands of paper towels; it has tailored its new products to a target market that tends to purchase own label brands.

Manufacturers find it hard to ignore the marketing opportunities that come from producing own label brands for resellers. If a manufacturer refuses to produce an own label brand for a reseller, a competing manufacturer will. Moreover, the production of own label brands allows the manufacturer to use excess capacity during periods when its own brands are at non-peak production. The ultimate decision whether to produce an own label or a manufacturer brand depends on a company's resources, production capabilities and goals.

Choosing a Brand Name

Marketers should consider a number of factors when they choose a brand name. The name should be easy for customers—including foreign buyers, if the firm intends to market its products in other countries—to say, spell and recall. Short, one syllable names such as Mars or Tide satisfy this requirement. The brand name should indicate the product's major benefits and, if possible, should suggest in a positive way the product's uses and special characteristics: negative or offensive references should be avoided. For example, a deodorant should be branded with a name that signals freshness, dryness or long lasting protection, as do Sure, Right Guard and Arrid Extra Dry. The brand should be distinctive, to set it apart from competing brands. If a marketer intends to use a brand for a product line, it must be compatible with all products in the line. Finally, a brand should be designed so that it can be used and recognised in all of the various types of media. Finding the right brand name has become a challenging task, because many obvious product names have already been used.

How are brand names derived? Brand names can be created from single or multiple words—for example, Bic or Findus Lean Cuisine. Initials, numbers or sometimes combinations are used to create brands such as IBM PC. At times, words, numbers and initials are combined to yield brand names such as Mazda MX5 or Mitsubishi 3000GT. To avoid terms that have negative connotations, marketers sometimes use fabricated words that have absolutely no meaning at the point when they are created—for example, Kodak and Esso. Occasionally, a brand is simply brought out of storage and used as is or modified. Firms often maintain banks of registered brands, some of which may have been used in the past. Cadillac, for example, has a bank of approximately 360 registered trademarks. The LaSalle brand, used in the 1920s and 1930s, may be called up for a new Cadillac model soon to be introduced.[9] Possible brand names are sometimes tested in focus groups or in other settings to assess customers' reactions.

Who actually creates brand names? Brand names can be created internally by the organisation. Sometimes a name is suggested by individuals who are close to the development of the product. Some organisations have committees that participate in brand name creation and approval. Large companies that introduce numerous new products annually are likely to have a department that develops brand names. Increasingly, outside consultants are used in the process of developing brand names. An organisation may also hire a company that specialises in brand name development.

Even though most of the important branding considerations apply to both goods and services, services branding has some additional dimensions. The brand of the service is usually the same as the company name. For example, American Express, Vidal Sassoon, ProntoPrint and Sheraton are names of companies and the services that they provide. Whereas companies that produce tangible goods (such as Procter & Gamble) can use separate brand names for separate products (such as Ariel, Head & Shoulders, Flash and Camay), service providers (such as British Airways) are perceived by customers as having one brand name, even though they offer multiple products (first class, business class and economy). Because the service brand name and company name are so closely interrelated, a service brand name must be flexible enough to encompass a variety of current services, as well as new ones that the company might offer in the future. Geographical references like "western" and descriptive terms like "trucking" limit the scope of associations that can be made with the brand name. "Northwest Airlines" is not a good name if the company begins flying south and east.[10] Frequently, a service marketer will employ a symbol along with its brand name to make the brand distinctive and to communicate a certain image.

Protecting a Brand Marketers need to design brands that can be protected easily through registration. Amongst the most difficult to protect are generic words, such as aluminum foil, surnames and descriptive geographic or functional names.[11] Because of their designs, some brands can be legally infringed upon more easily than others. Although registration provides trademark protection, a firm should develop a system for ensuring that its trademarks will be renewed as needed. To protect its exclusive rights to a brand, the company must make certain that the selected brand is not likely to be considered an infringement on any existing brand already registered with the relevant patent office. This task may be complex because infringement is determined by the courts, which base their decisions on whether a brand causes consumers to be confused, mistaken or deceived about the source of the product. McDonald's is one company that aggressively protects its trademarks against infringement; it has brought charges against a number of companies with "Mc" names because it fears that the use of the "Mc" will give consumers the impression that these companies are associated with or owned by McDonald's. In Figure 9.4, Prudential includes a symbol within its logo to enhance the recognition of its brand.

If possible, marketers must guard against allowing a brand name to become a generic term used to refer to a general product category. Generic terms cannot be protected as exclusive brand names. For example, names such as aspirin,

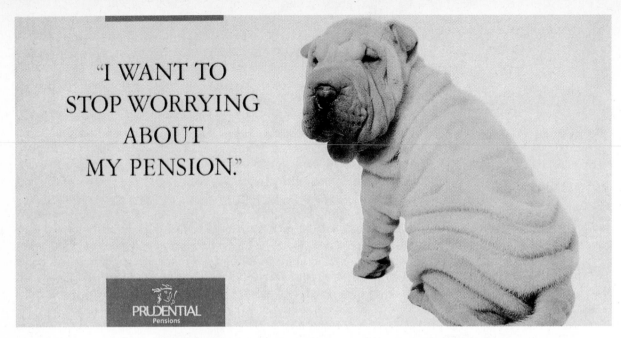

Figure 9.4 Using a symbol with a brand name. Prudential uses a symbol to make its brand distinctive. Marketers hope this symbol will conjure up images of safety and protection for customers.

SOURCE: Courtesy of The Prudential.

escalator and shredded wheat—all brand names at one time—were eventually declared generic terms that refer to product classes; thus they no longer could be protected. To keep a brand name from becoming a generic term, the firm should spell the name with a capital letter and use it as an adjective to modify the name of the general product class, as in Kellogg's Coco Pops.[12] Including the word *brand* just after the brand name is also helpful. An organisation can deal with this problem directly by advertising that its brand is a trademark and should not be used generically. The firm can also indicate that the brand is a registered trademark by using the symbol ®.

Firms that try to protect a brand in a foreign country frequently encounter problems. In many countries, brand registration is not possible; the first firm to use a brand in such a country has the rights to it. In some instances, a company has actually had to buy its own brand rights from a firm in a foreign country because the foreign firm was the first user in that country.

Marketers trying to protect their brands must also contend with brand counterfeiting. In many countries, for instance, it is possible to buy fake General Motors parts, fake Rolex watches, fake Chanel perfume, fake Microsoft software, fake Walt Disney character dolls and a host of other products illegally marketed by manufacturers that do not own the brands. Many counterfeit products are manufactured overseas—in South Korea, Italy, Taiwan or China, for example—but some are counterfeited in the countries in which they are sold. The International Anti-Counterfeiting Coalition estimates that roughly $60 billion in annual world trade involves counterfeit merchandise. The sale of this merchandise obviously reduces the brand owners' revenues from marketing their own legitimate products.

Brand counterfeiting is particularly harmful because the usually inferior counterfeit product undermines consumers' confidence in the brand and their loyalty to it. After unknowingly purchasing a counterfeit product, the buyer may blame the legitimate manufacturer if the product is of low quality or—even worse—if its use results in damage or injury. Since counterfeiting has become such a serious problem, many firms are taking legal action against counterfeiters. Others have adopted such measures as modifying the product or the packaging to make counterfeit items easier to detect, conducting public awareness campaigns and monitoring distributors to ensure that they stock only legitimate brands.[13]

Branding Policies

Before it establishes branding policies, a firm must first decide whether to brand its products at all. If a company's product is homogeneous and similar to competitors' products, it may be difficult to brand. Raw materials—such as coal, salt, sand and milk—are hard to brand because of the homogeneity of such products and their physical characteristics. Marketers must also consider the degree to which consumers differentiate among brands of a product. For example, while brand may be an important factor in the purchase of coffee, snacks and frozen foods, it is not usually so important a consideration in buying light bulbs, cheese and cling film.

If a firm chooses to brand its products, it may opt for one or more of the following branding policies: individual, overall family, line family and brand extension branding. **Individual branding** is a policy of naming each product differently. Procter & Gamble relies on an individual branding policy for its line of fabric washing products, which includes Tide, Bold, Daz and Dreft.

Individual branding A policy of naming each product differently

A major advantage of individual branding is that if an organisation introduces a poor product, the negative images associated with it will not contaminate the company's other products. An individual branding policy may also facilitate market segmentation when a company wishes to enter many segments of the same market. Separate, unrelated names can be used, and each brand can be aimed at a specific segment.

Overall family branding A policy of branding all of a firm's products with the same name or at least part of a name

In **overall family branding**, all of a firm's products are branded with the same name or at least part of the name, such as Kraft, Heinz, Microsoft or Ford. In some cases, a company's name is combined with other words to brand items. Heinz uses its name on its products along with a generic description of the item, such as Heinz Salad Cream, Heinz Baked Beans, Heinz Spaghetti and Heinz Tomato Soup. The quality image of its products increases consumer confidence in what they are buying. This brand consistency is stressed in Heinz advertisements (see Figure 9.5). Unlike individual branding, overall family branding means that the promotion of one item with the family brand promotes the firm's other products.

Line family branding A policy of using family branding only for products within a single line

Sometimes an organisation uses family branding only for products within a single line. This policy is called **line family branding**. Colgate-Palmolive, for example, produces a line of cleaning products that includes a cleanser, a powdered detergent and a liquid cleaner—all with the name Ajax. Colgate also produces several brands of toothpaste, none of which carries the Ajax brand.

Brand extension branding A firm's use of one of its existing brand names as part of an improved or new product, usually in the same product category as the existing brand

Brand extension branding occurs when a firm uses one of its existing brand names as part of a brand for an improved or new product that is usually in the same product category as the existing brand. The makers of Timotei Shampoo extended the name to hair conditioner and skin care products. There is one major difference between line family branding and brand extension branding. With line family branding, all products in the line carry the same name, but with brand

Name Change for Kentucky Fried Chicken

Customers of Kentucky Fried Chicken will have seen a change at their favourite fast food outlet. In response to changing market conditions, the company is looking at ways to overhaul its brand identity. As part of this move, it is testing a take-away only concept, using red and blue livery in place of the famous red. While Colonel Sanders retains his role as brand mascot and prominence on the shop fascia, the name Kentucky Fried Chicken has been shortened to "KFC" or "KFC Express". In the UK, initially around 50 of the 290 outlets were switched to the KFC branding. Over two years, the whole chain was rebranded, and worldwide KFC has rebranded 9,000 outlets.

The reasons for the change are almost certainly linked to the increasing challenges presented by the fast food market. Up-dating the Kentucky Fried Chicken brand identity should help provide a welcome boost to an image that has become slightly tired and should make it easier to position the brand away from the host of copycats such as Favourite Chicken and Southern Fried Chicken. Management at Kentucky Fried Chicken is also testing dishes with grilled, baked and rotisserie cooked chicken in order to respond to the increasingly health-conscious consumer. Removing the word *fried* from the company's branding further emphasises this shift. The latest development is to move away from the burger orientated fast food market by positioning KFC as "the best family meal provider in the UK fast food industry". To appeal to children, KFC has allied with the universally recognised Jim Davis cartoon character Garfield.

It is not just Kentucky Fried Chicken's brand identity that has changed. Location policy is also being up-dated: management is improving the brand's visibility by reducing the number of secondary sites that outlets occupy and moving into prime high street and "drive thru" positions. Such changes are vital to enable the company to respond to an increasingly competitive marketplace that includes McDonald's, Burger King, Pizza Hut and Pizzaland, as well as a host of independents—all offering the fast food consumer more choice than ever before. For Kentucky Fried Chicken (KFC) the threat from giants McDonald's and Burger King is particularly acute as both these companies increase their range of chicken dishes.

The rewards for success are considerable in a market where the key players are set for growth. During the 1990s alone, it is anticipated that McDonald's will open a further 400 to 500 outlets outside the US, while PepsiCo (whose portfolio includes Pizza Hut and Taco Bell as well as Kentucky Fried Chicken) plans to increase its international outlets by 80 per cent.

SOURCES: Paul Meller, "KFC cooks up new look for food fight", *Marketing,* 11 March 1993; "Kentucky Fried Chicken pushes take away option", *Marketing Week,* 12 March 1993; Karen Benezra, "Garfield next name of KFC kid biz", *Brandweek,* 13 November 1995, p. 4; David Benady, "KFC hires Ross Man for top job", *Marketing Week,* 14 July 1995, p. 10; Tabitha Cole, "KFC plays on Kentucky roots", *Campaign,* 12 May 1995, p. 20.

extension branding this is not the case. The producer of Arrid deodorant, for example, also makes other brands of deodorants.

An organisation is not limited to a single branding policy. Instead, branding policy is influenced by (1) the number of products and product lines the company produces, (2) the characteristics of its target markets, (3) the number and types of competing products available and (4) the size of its resources. Anheuser-Busch, for example, uses both individual and brand extension branding. Most of the brands

Figure 9.5 Overall family branding. Heinz uses its name on its products, along with a generic description of the item.

Source: Courtesy of Heinz.

are individual brands; however, the Michelob Light brand is an extension of the Michelob brand. Sometimes companies must up-date brands so that they remain fresh and interesting (see Marketing Insight 9.1).

Brand Licensing

A recent trend in branding strategies involves the licensing of trademarks. By means of a licensing agreement, a company may permit approved manufacturers to use its trademark on other products for a licensing fee. Royalties may be as low as 2 per cent of wholesale revenues or higher than 10 per cent. The licensee is responsible for all manufacturing, selling and advertising functions and bears the costs if the licensed product fails. Not long ago, only a few firms licensed their corporate trademarks but today the licensing business is worth billions of pounds and is growing. Harley-Davidson, for example, has authorised the use of its name on non-motorcycle products such as cologne, wine coolers, gold rings and shirts. Disney also licenses its brand for use on a range of products.

The advantages of licensing range from extra revenues and low cost to free publicity, new images and trademark protection. For example, Coca-Cola has licensed its trademark for use on glassware, radios, trucks and clothing in the hope of protecting its trademark. Similarly, Jaguar has licensed a range of leisure wear. However, brand licensing is not without drawbacks. The major disadvantages are a lack of manufacturing control, which could hurt the company's name, and the undesirability of bombarding consumers with too many unrelated products bearing the same name. Licensing arrangements can also fail because of poor timing, inappropriate distribution channels or mismatching of product and name.

Managing Brands

With the need for brands to create product differentiation, assist in establishing a competitive advantage and encourage product awareness, marketers must manage their brands with care. As explained in detail in the next chapter, this involves understanding when a brand requires re-positioning, modifying, deleting or simply being left alone. Most companies operate with a portfolio of separate brands and products and must make difficult decisions in terms of which are to receive support and the bulk of a business's marketing resource and which are to be killed off or given only minimal support. Chapter 22 explores these strategic choices. As explained in Chapter 4's discussion of consumer buyer behaviour, without an understanding of brand loyalty and brand switching, it is difficult to manage a business's brands effectively. It is essential, therefore, for companies to make an effort to research brand loyalty and brand perceptions to help them make sensible decisions that accurately reflect consumers' views.

Research shows that to create **successful brands,** a company must

Successful brands Brands for which a company must prioritise quality, offer superior service, get there first, differentiate brands, develop a unique positioning concept, have a strong communications programme and be consistent and reliable

- Prioritise quality—the top brands are all "high" quality in their product fields
- Offer "superior" service—less easily copied by competitors than pure product attributes
- Get there first—not necessarily technologically, but in the minds of targeted customers, by

  1. Exploiting new technology (Rank Xerox, Sony)
  2. New positioning concepts (Body Shop, First Direct)
  3. New distribution channels (Argos, Direct Line)
  4. New market segments (Amstrad, Orange)
  5. Using gaps resulting from environmental change (Ecover, Daz Ultra)

- Differentiate its brands—so that consumers perceive the brands on offer as being different
- Develop a unique positioning concept—making the brand and its differentiating characteristics stand out with a clear image and positioning message against rival brands
- Support the brand and its positioning with a strong communications programme—so that target consumers are aware of the brand and its positioning proposition
- Deliver consistency and reliability over time—keeping the brand's values trustworthy as perceived by target consumers.

Levels of brands The tangible product, the "basic" brand, the "augmented" brand and the "potential" brand

Branding expert Peter Doyle[14] states that to build effective brands it is essential for a business to understand that there is more to a brand than simply a catchy name and visible logo. There are, in fact, four **levels of brands:** the tangible product, the "basic" brand, the "augmented" brand and the "potential" brand. Level 1, the tangible product, is the degree of quality, performance, features and actual attributes. Level 2, the "basic" brand, is the identity, differentiation and positioning. Level 3, the "augmented" brand, is the aggregated impact from including supplementary products and service support. Level 4, the "potential" of the brand, is reached when customers will not willingly accept substitutes and are unhappy to switch to rival brands; psychological benefits and barriers in the minds of target customers are important determinants of brand potential. There are three essential acid tests for whether a brand is successful. Although most companies consider only the overall profit contribution to the end-of-year financial annual report and accounts, when determining a brand's success they should ask the following three fundamental questions:

1. Has the brand captured the leading share in its market segment or distribution channel?
2. Does the brand command prices sufficiently high enough to produce a high profit margin?

3. Will the brand sustain its strong share of profits when rival and generic versions of the product enter the market?

Using these criteria, many brands are relatively unsuccessful. For marketers, managing brands must include knowing when a brand is succeeding, when it is faltering but may be saved, and when a brand is a lost cause and should be deleted from the company's range of brands. Chapter 22, "Marketing Strategy and Competitive Forces", examines this difficult issue in more detail.

• • • • • • • • • • • • • • • • •

Packaging

Packaging The development of a product's container and label, complete with graphic design

Packaging involves the development of a container and label, complete with graphic design for a product. A package can be a vital part of a product, making it more versatile, safer or easier to use. Like a brand name, a package can influence customers' attitudes towards a product and thus affect their purchase decisions. For example, several producers of sauces, salad dressings and ketchups have packaged their products in squeezable containers to make use and storage more convenient. Package characteristics help shape buyers' impressions of a product at the time of purchase or during use. This section examines the main functions of packaging and considers several major packaging decisions. The role of the package in marketing strategy is also analysed.

Packaging Functions

Effective packaging means more than simply putting products into containers and covering them with wrappers. First of all, packaging materials serve the basic purpose of protecting the product and maintaining its functional form. Fluids such as milk, orange juice and hair spray need packages that preserve and protect them; the packaging should prevent damage that could affect the product's usefulness and increase costs. Since product tampering has become a problem for marketers of many types of goods, several packaging techniques have been developed to counter this danger. Some packages are also designed to foil shoplifters.

Another function of packaging is to offer convenience for consumers. For example, small, sealed packages—individual sized boxes or plastic bags that contain liquids and do not require refrigeration—strongly appeal to children and young adults with active lifestyles. The size or shape of a package may relate to the product's storage, convenience of use or replacement rate. Small, single serving tins of fruit, such as Del Monte's Fruitinni, may prevent waste and make storage easier. Low, regular shaped packets may be easier to stack and use cupboard space more efficiently. A third function of packaging is to promote a product by communicating its features, uses, benefits and image. At times, a re-usable package is developed to make the product more desirable. For example, some ice cream containers can be used again as food storage containers.

Major Packaging Considerations

When developing packages, marketers must take many factors into account. Some of these factors relate to consumers' needs; others relate to the requirements of resellers. Obviously, one major consideration is cost. Although a variety of packaging materials, processes and designs are available, some are rather expensive. In recent years buyers have shown a willingness to pay more for improved packaging, but there are limits. Marketers should try to determine, through research, just how much customers are willing to pay for packages.

As already mentioned, developing tamper resistant packaging is very important. Although no package is totally tamper proof, marketers can develop packages that are difficult to tamper with and also make any tampering evident to resellers and consumers. Because new, safer packaging technologies are being explored, marketers should be aware of changes in packaging technology and legislation and be prepared to make modifications that will ensure consumer safety. One packaging innovation includes an inner pouch that displays the word *open* when air has entered the pouch after opening. Marketers also now have an obligation to inform consumers of the possibilities and risks of product tampering by educating them to recognise possible tampering and by placing warnings on packaging.[15] For example, the tops of many sauce and condiment bottles now have plastic seals around them, so that consumers can be confident that they have not been opened. Baby food manufacturers such as Cow & Gate and Heinz have taken this protection method one step further by using special metal jar tops with pop-up discs showing when a jar has been opened. This move followed cases of tampering in which foreign bodies were introduced into baby foods. Now the special tops expressly warn consumers to watch out for tampering. Although effective tamper resistant packaging may be expensive to develop, when balanced against the costs of lost sales, loss of consumer confidence and a company's reputation, and potentially expensive product liability lawsuits, the costs of ensuring consumer safety are minimal.[16]

Marketers should consider how much consistency is desirable in an organisation's package designs. The best policy may be not to attempt consistency, especially if a firm's products are unrelated or aimed at vastly different target markets. To promote an overall company image, a firm may decide that all packages are to be similar or include one major element of the design. This approach is called **family packaging.** Sometimes it is used only for lines of products, as with Campbell's soups, Weight Watchers foods and Planters nuts.

A package's promotional role is an important consideration. Through verbal and non-verbal symbols, the package can inform potential buyers about the product's content, features, uses, advantages and hazards. A firm can create desirable images and associations by its choice of colour, design, shape and texture. Many cosmetics manufacturers, for example, design their packages to create impressions of richness, luxury and exclusiveness. A package performs a promotional function when it is designed to be safer or more convenient to use, if such characteristics help stimulate demand.

To develop a package that has a definite promotional value, a designer must consider size, shape, texture, colour and graphics. Beyond the obvious limitation that the package must be large enough to hold the product, a package can be designed to appear taller or shorter. For instance, thin vertical lines make a package look taller; wide horizontal stripes make it look shorter. A marketer may want a package to appear taller because many people perceive something that is taller as being larger.

Colours on packages are often chosen to attract attention. People associate specific colours with certain feelings and experiences. Red, for example, is linked with fire, blood, danger and anger; yellow suggests sunlight, caution, warmth and vitality; blue can imply coldness, sky, water and sadness.[17] When selecting packaging colours, marketers must decide whether a particular colour will evoke positive or negative feelings when it is linked to a specific product. Rarely, for example, do processors package meat or bread in green materials, because customers may associate green with mould. However, recent concern about the state of the environment has, in general, led to an increase in the use of green coloured

Family packaging An approach in which all of a firm's packages are similar or include one major element of the design packaging. Marketers must also decide whether a specific target market will respond favourably or unfavourably to a particular colour. Cosmetics for women are more likely to be sold in pastel packaging than are personal care products for men. Packages designed to appeal to children often use primary colours and bold designs.

Packaging must also meet the needs of resellers. Wholesalers and retailers consider whether a package facilitates transportation, storage and handling. Packages must allow these resellers to make maximum use of storage space, both in transit and in the shops. Products should be packed so that sales staff can transfer them to the shelves with ease. Shape and weight of packaging are also important. Resellers may refuse to carry certain products if their packages are cumbersome. Figure 9.6 shows how these factors have been taken into consideration by Cuprinol's Castlepak™ woodcare varnish container.

A final consideration is whether to develop packages that are environmentally responsible. A Cable News Network report on the growing refuse disposal problem in the US stated that nearly 50 per cent of all rubbish consists of discarded plastic packaging, such as polystyrene containers, plastic soft drink bottles, carrier bags and other packaging.[18] Plastic packaging material does not biodegrade, and paper requires the destruction of valuable forest lands. Consequently, a number of companies are recycling more materials and exploring packaging alternatives, helped by packaging experts such as Tetra Pak. H.J. Heinz, for example, is looking for alternatives to its plastic ketchup squeeze bottles. Marketing Insight 9.2 examines some of the latest packaging innovations.

Figure 9.6 Cuprinol's Castlepak™ woodcare varnish container highlights how environmental consumer usage and operation needs can be incorporated into a single packaging solution.

Source: Courtesy of Marketing Magazine, London.

New Developments in 3D Packaging Design—Good Packaging and Design Help Increase Consumer Loyalty

Three dimensional packaging does much more than protect products and make them easy to distribute, handle and use.

For marketers, 3D packaging can help differentiate a brand, add value or simply aid consumer recognition. The distinctive shape of the Coca-Cola bottle, recognised worldwide, is synonymous with the brand. The importance of creative packaging design is well established. Maximising packaging design benefits requires an integrated approach that considers financial, manufacturing, distribution and marketing requirements. In some companies this total business approach is achieved by forming staff teams with representatives from all business areas. The teams will consider all aspects of packaging design—materials, size and shape, opening and closure features, material conversion efficiency, retail storage and display, transportability, disposability, filling speed and costs.

Research shows that for some products, innovative packaging is seen to add value in the eyes of target consumers. There is the sensual pleasure of handling the product, a perception of creativity and added prestige from the purchase, as well as the implication that the manufacturer "cares" about the consumer.

Growing consumer concern about the environment and government targets for recycling are putting new pressures on packaging design and development, in addition to all the other marketing and operational requirements of the process. As they look for ways to increase the environmental friendliness of their packaging, companies need to ask a series of questions:

- Can the amount of material in the package be reduced?
- Can the size of the package be reduced?
- Is recyclable material a possibility?
- Are the necessary recycling processes available?
- Are the raw materials used easy to replenish?

Environmental concerns are causing companies to reconsider the appropriateness of traditional packaging materials. For example, glass is coming back to supermarket shelves, while new developments in the use of plastics and paper/board are leading to improvements in recyclability. Even when companies are able to move towards more ecologically sympathetic packaging, there may be hidden problems. For example, the process of recycling itself may waste energy and create pollution. To ensure that the disadvantages of changing packaging design do not outweigh the benefits, a company should undertake a "cradle to grave" analysis of the proposed packaging, looking at all aspects of its manufacture, distribution, use and disposal.

In the rush to meet consumer demands and regulatory requirements, companies are in danger of introducing ineffective packaging solutions. For example, manufacturers have recently introduced flexible re-fill pouches as a replacement for plastic bottles. To the consumer, who sees plastic bottles as bulky and difficult to dispose of, this seems to be a positive step. In practice, the lightweight alternative may look better; but it is awkward to distribute, problematic to stock, hard to open and difficult to recycle. Packaging must be sensible and capable of adding to the brand's image.

Sources: CGM, *Marketing Guide 14: 3D Packaging Design*, Haymarket Publishing Services Ltd, 1992; John S. Blyth, "Packaging for competitive advantage", *Management Review*, May 1990, p. 64; Dagmar Mussey and Juliana Kanteng, "Packaging strict green rules", *Advertising Age*, 2 December 1991, p. S-10; Katrina Carl, "Good package design helps increase consumer loyalty", *Marketing News*, 19 June 1995, p. 4; Andy Gilgrist, "The shape of things to come", *Marketing Week*, 16 September 1994, pp. 43–47.

Companies that decide to develop environmentally responsible packaging have not always received a positive response. For example, customers' responses to Wendy's new paper plates and coffee cups have been mixed; some customers prefer the old non-biodegradable foam packages. Other companies searching for alternatives to environmentally harmful packaging have experienced similar problems.[19] Thus marketers must carefully balance society's desires to preserve the environment against consumers' desires for convenience.

Packaging and Marketing Strategy

Packaging can be a major component of a marketing strategy. A new cap or closure, a better box or wrapping, or a more convenient container may give a product a competitive advantage. The right type of package for a new product can help it gain market recognition very quickly. In the case of existing brands, marketers should periodically re-evaluate packages. Especially for consumer convenience products, marketers should view packaging as a major strategic tool. This section examines ways in which packaging can be used strategically.

Altering the Package   At times, a marketer changes a package because the existing design is no longer in style, especially when compared with competitive products. Smith and Nephew has recently redesigned its simple range of toiletries to show that the products have evolved with the times. A package also may be redesigned because new product features need to be highlighted on the package, or because new packaging materials have become available. An organisation may decide to change a product's packaging to make the product more convenient or safer to use, or to re-position the product. A major redesign of a simple package costs about £15,000, and the redesign for a line of products may cost up to £200,000.[20] Choosing the right packaging material is an important consideration when redesigning. Different materials vary in popularity at different times. For example, glass is becoming more popular as views on the environment and the need for recyclability come to the fore.[21]

Secondary use package   A package that can be re-used for purposes other than its initial use

Secondary Use Packaging   A **secondary use package** is one that can be re-used for purposes other than its initial use. For example, a margarine container can be re-used to store leftovers, a jam jar can be used as a drinking glass, and shortbread tins can be re-used for storing cakes and biscuits. Secondary use packages can be viewed by customers as adding value to products. If customers value this type of packaging, then its use should stimulate unit sales.

Category consistent packaging   The packaging of a product according to the packaging practices associated with that particular product category

Category Consistent Packaging   **Category consistent packaging** means that the product is packaged in line with the packaging practices associated with a particular product category. Some product categories—for example, mayonnaise, mustard, ketchup and jam—have traditional package shapes. Other product categories are characterised by recognisable colour combinations—red and white for soup; red and yellow for tea; red, white and blue for Ritz-like crackers. When an organisation introduces a brand in one of these product categories, marketers will often use traditional package shapes and colour combinations to ensure that customers will recognise the new product as being in that specific product category.

Innovative Packaging   Sometimes, a marketer will employ a unique cap, design, applicator or other feature to make the product competitively distinctive, as illustrated in Figure 9.7. Such packaging can be effective when the innovation makes

Figure 9.7 Innovative packaging. The importance of packaging design cannot be underestimated.

Source: top: *Courtesy of* Van den Bergh Foods; bottom: *Courtesy of Kalon Group PLC.*

the product safer or easier to use, or when the unique package provides better protection for the product. In some instances, marketers use innovative or unique packages that are inconsistent with traditional packaging practices to make the brand stand out relative to its competitors. Procter & Gamble, for example, used an innovative, crush proof cylinder to package its Pringles potato crisps. Innovative packaging generally requires considerable resources, not only for the package design itself but also to make customers aware of the unique package and its benefit. Sometimes, innovative packaging can change the way in which consumers use a product. The introduction of cardboard boxed, single serving soft drinks made it easier for consumers to have a drink while travelling by car, train and plane. Even cyclists can drink with ease while on the move!

Multiple Packaging   Rather than packaging a single unit of the product, marketers sometimes use twin packs, tri-packs, six-packs or other forms of **multiple packaging**. For certain types of products, multiple packaging is used to increase demand because it increases the amount of the product available at the point of consumption (in consumers' houses, for example). However, multiple packaging does not work for all types of products. Consumers would not use additional table salt simply because an extra box is in the pantry. Multiple packaging can make products easier to handle and store, as in the case of six-packs for soft drinks; it can also facilitate special price offers, such as two-for-one sales. In addition, multiple packaging may increase consumer acceptance of the product by encouraging the buyer to try the product several times.

Multiple packaging
Packaging that includes more than one unit of a product, such as twin packs, tri-packs and six-packs

Handling Improved Packaging   Packaging of a product may be changed to make it easier to handle in the distribution channel—for example, changing the outer carton, special bundling, shrink wrapping or palletising. In some cases the shape of the package may need to be changed. For example, an ice cream producer may change from a cylindrical package to a rectangular one to facilitate handling. In addition, at the retail level the ice cream producer may be able to get more shelf facings with a rectangular package as opposed to a round one. Outer containers for products are sometimes changed so that they will proceed more easily through automated warehousing systems.

As package designs improve, it becomes harder for any one product to dominate because of packaging. However, marketers still attempt to gain a competitive edge through packaging. Case 9.2 looks at the benefits offered by a new type of packaging. Skilled artists and package designers who have experience in marketing research test packaging to see what sells well, not just what is aesthetically appealing. Since the typical large store stocks 15,000 items or more, products that stand out are more likely to be bought.

Criticisms of Packaging

The last several decades have seen a number of improvements in packaging. However, some packaging problems still need to be resolved. This chapter's opener incident highlights how leading packaging company Tetra Pak is responding to complaints about the ease of use of its containers.

Some packages simply do not work well. The packaging for flour and sugar is, at best, not much better than poor. Both grocers and consumers are very much aware that these packages leak and are easily torn. Can anyone open and close a bag of flour without spilling at least a little bit? Certain packages such as biscuit tins, milk cartons with fold-out spouts and potato crisp bags are frequently difficult to open. The traditional shapes of packages for products such as ketchup and salad dressing make the products inconvenient to use. Have you ever questioned when tapping on a ketchup bottle why the producer didn't put ketchup in a mayonnaise jar?

As discussed earlier, certain types of packaging are being questioned in regard to recyclability and biodegradability. For example, throw-away bottles take considerably more resources to produce than do re-usable glass bottles.

Although many steps have been taken to make packaging safer, critics still focus on the safety issues. Containers with sharp edges and easily broken glass bottles are sometimes viewed as a threat to safety. Certain types of plastic packaging and aerosol containers represent possible health hazards.

At times, packaging is viewed as being deceptive. Package shape, graphic design and certain colours may be used to make a product appear larger than it actually is. The inconsistent use of certain size designations—such as "giant", "economy", "family", "king" and "super"—can certainly lead to customer confusion. Although customers have traditionally liked attractive, effective, convenient packaging, the cost of such packaging is high. For some products, such as cosmetics, the cost of the package is higher than the cost of the product itself.

Labelling

Labelling Packaging information that can be used for a variety of promotional, informational and legal purposes

Labelling is very closely related to packaging and can be used in a variety of promotional, informational and legal ways. The label can be used to facilitate the identification of a product by presenting the brand and a unique graphic design. For example, Heinz's ketchup is easy to identify on a supermarket shelf because the brand name is easy to read and is coupled with a distinctive, crown-like graphic design. Labels have a descriptive function. For certain types of products, the label indicates the grade of the product, especially for tinned fruit. Labels can describe the source of the product, its contents and major features, how to use the product, how to care for the product, nutritional information, type and style of the product, and size and number of servings. The label can play a promotional function through the use of graphics that attract attention. The food and drug administrations and consumer protection agencies in different countries have varying requirements concerning warnings, instructions, certifications and manufacturers' identifications. Increasingly, however, the EU is demanding similar standards in all member countries. Despite the fact that consumers have responded favourably to the inclusion of this type of information on labels, evidence as to whether they actually use it has been mixed. Several studies indicate that consumers do not use nutritional information, whereas other studies indicate that the information is useful. Labels can also promote a manufacturer's other products or encourage proper use of products and therefore greater satisfaction with them.

Universal product code (UPC) or barcode A series of thick and thin lines that identifies the product and provides inventory and pricing information readable by an electronic scanner

The label for many products includes a **universal product code (UPC)**, sometimes known as a **barcode,** which is a series of thick and thin lines that identifies the product and provides inventory and pricing information that can be read by an electronic scanner. The UPC is read electronically at the retail checkout counter. This information is used by retailers and producers for price and inventory control purposes.

Colour and eye catching graphics on labels overcome the jumble of words—known to designers as "mouse print"—that have been added to satisfy government regulations. Because so many similar products are available, an attention getting device or silent salesperson is needed to attract interest. As one of the most visible parts of a product, the label is an important element in a marketing mix.

● ● ● ● ● ● ● ● ● ● ● ● ● ● ● ● ●

Summary

● A *brand* is a name, term, design, symbol or any other feature that identifies one seller's good or service, creates *brand recognition* and distinguishes the product from those of other sellers. A *brand name* is that part of a brand that can be spoken; the element that cannot be spoken is called a *brand mark*. A *trademark* is a legal designation indicating that the owner has exclusive use of a brand or part of a brand and that others are prohibited by law from using it. A *trade name* is the legal name of an organisation.

● Branding helps buyers identify and evaluate products, helps sellers facilitate repeat purchasing and product introduction, and fosters *brand loyalty.* A *manufacturer brand,* initiated by the producer, makes it possible to associate the firm more easily with its products at the point of purchase. An *own label brand* is initiated and owned by a reseller, such as a retailer. A *generic brand* indicates only the product category and does not include the company name or other identifying terms. Manufacturers combat the growing competition from own label brands by developing multiple brands. When selecting a brand, a marketer should choose one that is easy to say, spell and recall, and that alludes to the product's uses, benefits or special characteristics.

● Brand names are created inside an organisation by individuals, committees or branding departments, or by outside consultants. Brand names can be devised from words, initials, numbers, nonsense words or a combination of these. Services as well as products are branded, often with the company name and an accompanying symbol that makes the brand distinctive or conveys a desired image.

● Producers protect ownership of their brands through patent and trademark offices. Marketers at a company must make certain that their selected brand name does not infringe on an already registered brand by confusing or deceiving consumers about the source of the product. In many countries, brand registration is on a first-come, first-served basis, making protection more difficult. Brand counterfeiting, increasingly common, has potential for undermining consumer confidence in and loyalty to a brand.

● Companies brand their products in several ways. *Individual branding* designates a unique name for each of a company's products; *overall family branding* identifies all of a firm's products with the single name; *line family branding* assigns all products within a single line the same name; and *brand extension branding* applies an existing name to a new or improved product. Trademark licensing enables producers to earn extra revenue, receive low cost or free publicity and protect their trademarks. Through a licensing agreement, and for a licensing fee, a firm may permit approved manufacturers to use its trademark on other products.

● Strong brands usually command premium prices, obtain greater market share, have high levels of customer loyalty in their target markets and demand a significant amount of management and control. There is far more to a good brand than a catchy name and appealing logo. Four *levels of brands* need to be addressed: the tangible product behind the brand, the "basic" brand, the "augmented" brand and the "potential" of the brand. *Successful brands* tend to prioritise quality, offer relatively superior service, get to market or the targeted segment first, be clearly differentiated from rival brands, have a unique positioning concept supported by a strong communications programme and be consistent over time. To be successful, a brand should capture the leading share in its market segment or distribution channel, command prices sufficiently high to offer high profit margins and be likely to maintain its profit position after more brands and generic versions enter the market. Many companies should be more ruthless in managing their brands, many of which do not live up to these success criteria.

● *Packaging* involves development of a container and graphic design for a product. Effective packaging offers protection, economy, safety and convenience. It can influence the customer's purchase decision by promoting features, uses, benefits and image. When developing a package, marketers must consider costs relative to how much the target market is willing to pay. Other considerations include how to make the package tamper resistant, whether to use *multiple packaging* and *family packaging, secondary use packaging* and *category consistent packaging,* how to design the package as an effective promotional tool, how best to accommodate resellers and whether to develop environmentally responsible packaging.

● Packaging can be an important part of an overall marketing strategy. Firms choose particular colours, designs, shapes and textures to create desirable images and associations. Producers alter packages to convey new features or to make them safer or more convenient. If a package has a secondary use, the product's value to the consumer may be increased. Category consistent packaging makes products more easily recognised by consumers, and innovative packaging enhances a product's distinctiveness. Consumers may criticise packaging that doesn't work well, poses health or safety problems, is deceptive in some way, or is not biodegradable or recyclable.

● *Labelling* is an important aspect of packaging for promotional, informational and legal reasons.

Because labels are attention getting devices, they are significant features in the marketing mix. Various regulatory agencies can require that products be labelled or marked with warnings, instructions, certifications, nutritional information and the manufacturer's identification. Increasingly, most products —even cars—have a *universal product code (UPC)* or *barcode*.

● ● ● ● ● ● ● ● ● ● ● ● ● ● ● ● ● ●
Important Terms

Brand	Own label brand	Packaging
Brand name	Generic brand	Family packaging
Brand recognition	Individual branding	Secondary use package
Brand mark	Overall family branding	Category consistent packaging
Trademark	Line family branding	Multiple packing
Trade name	Brand extension branding	Labelling
Brand loyalty	Successful brands	Universal product code (UPC)
Manufacturer brand	Levels of brands	Barcode

● ● ● ● ● ● ● ● ● ● ● ● ● ● ● ● ● ●
Discussion and Review Questions

1. What is the difference between a brand and a brand name? Compare and contrast the terms *brand mark* and *trademark*.
2. How does branding benefit customers and organisations?
3. What are the advantages associated with brand loyalty?
4. What are the distinguishing characteristics of own label brands?
5. Given the competition between own label brands and manufacturer brands, should manufacturers be concerned about the popularity of own label brands? How should manufacturers fight back in the brand battle?
6. Identify and explain the major considerations consumers take into account when selecting a brand.
7. The brand name Xerox is sometimes used generically to refer to photocopying machines. How can Xerox Corporation protect this brand name?
8. Identify and explain the four major branding policies and give examples of each. Can a firm use more than one policy at a time? Explain your answer.
9. What are the major advantages and disadvantages of licensing?
10. Why is there more to a brand than its name? Explain your response.
11. What are the most commonly found foundations for successful brands? Illustrate your response with brand examples.
12. What are the three core criteria for assessing the success of a brand?
13. Describe the functions that a package can perform. Which function is most important? Why?
14. When developing a package, what are the major issues that a marketer should consider?
15. In what ways can packaging be used as a strategic tool?
16. What are the major criticisms of packaging?
17. What are the major functions of labelling?

● ● ● ● ● ● ● ● ● ● ● ● ● ● ● ● ● ●
Recommended Readings

P. Doyle, "Building successful brands: the strategic options", *The Journal of Consumer Marketing,* vol. 7, no. 2, 1993, pp. 5–20.

P. Doyle, *Marketing Management and Strategy* (London: Prentice-Hall, 1994).

C. Macrae, *The Brand Chartering Handbook* (London: EIU and Addison-Wesley, 1996).

C. Macrae, S. Parkinson and J. Sheerman, "Managing marketing's DNA: the role of branding", *Irish Marketing Review,* vol. 8, 1995, pp. 13–20.

G. S. Low and R. A. Fullerton, "Brands, brand management and the brand manager system: a critical-historical evaluation", *Journal of Marketing Research,* vol. 31, no. 2, 1994, pp. 173–190.

Cases

9.1 KP Heads for Market Leadership

Snack giant KP has its sights set on half of the snacks, crisps and nuts markets. The company has given itself until the year 2000 to achieve a 50 per cent share of this £1.5 billion market in the UK. Such a goal does not seem unreasonable considering that since 1982, KP has managed to increase its market share by 10 per cent to 40 per cent.

The threat to KP comes from giant PepsiCo, which the company managed to topple from market leadership for the first time in 1990. In a closely fought contest for market share, PepsiCo disputes the figures that put KP on top. While KP bases its market share on volume tonnes sold (19.2 per cent of KP's business comes from its production of own label products for supermarkets), PepsiCo says that branded sales are what matters and calculates its success using figures for branded products only—putting it at 42.6 per cent—ahead by around 14 per cent. Now PepsiCo plans to merge its Smiths and Walkers subsidiaries to strengthen its branding further, a move that KP hopes will distract PepsiCo's attention from the battle for market supremacy.

New products provide the key to KP's strategy. According to the company's marketing director, around two-thirds of growth will be centred on new products. As new products are added to the range, the company will consider rationalising its existing portfolio. Those snacks and crisps that fail to reach the £20 million level are likely to be dropped. Currently, the values of KP's top four nibbles are £95 million for Hula Hoops, followed by £90 million for KP Nuts, followed by The Real McCoys and Skips, worth £48 million and £45 million respectively.

The merger between Walkers and Smiths means that the PepsiCo range will soon undergo a transition. Monster Munch and Smiths Quavers are to be re-launched as Walkers Quavers and Walkers Monster Munch. This is part of a PepsiCo move, backed by £6.5 million marketing spend, to use the Walkers brand to support its key products. Other changes include the introduction of salt and vinegar flavoured Quavers (to attract children) and mixed cheese to appeal to "housewives".

KP's recent launch of Roysters Steam Nuts is indicative of the company's drive for innovative products. Representing the company's first move to extend a brand into a new sector, the product follows naturally on from the 1992 introduction of Roysters. The extra large peanuts will be available in three tempting flavours: Kentucky Smoke, Louisiana Hot Spice and New York Smoke. KP hopes that the move will provide it with a 5 per cent stake of the £136 million nuts market. According to KP's Marketing Director, the Steam Nuts brand has connotations of tradition and intrigue, which should boost a flagging market.

Core Snack Brands	
KP	
Hula Hoops	KP Nuts
The Real McCoys	Skips
Solo Lower Fat Crisps	Frisps
Roysters	Discos
Brannigans	
PepsiCo	
Walkers Crisps	Smiths Quavers
Monster Munch	Smiths Crisps
Tudor Crisps	French Fries
Ruffles	Looney Tunes
Planters Nuts	Smiths Squares
Smiths Tuba Loops	Smiths Crinkles
Frazzles	Smiths Chip
Sticks	
Big D Nuts	

SOURCES: Suzanne Bidlake, "Snack attack by KP demands a crisp reply", *Marketing*, 21 January 1993; "KP extends Roysters to grab 5% of market", *Marketing*, 21 January 1993; Juliana Koranteng, "Quavers revamp for battle with Hula Hoops", *Marketing*, 21 January 1993.

Questions for Discussion

1. To what category of consumer products do snacks, crisps and nuts belong?
2. Is branding important in this market? Why?
3. What is meant by "brand extension"? Why is KP engaging in brand extension?

9.2 Stepcan: Innovative Packaging Design

In 1988, Metal Box (MB) developed a container to rival the tin can: the Stepcan. The unique packaging, manufactured by the Stretch Tube Extrusion Process (STEP), was made of flexible, transparent plastic with a metal, ring-pull lid. Stepcan was resealable and gave consumers the opportunity of viewing the container's contents. Initial marketing research justified the company's belief that consumers would prefer the non-breakable Stepcan with its clearly viewed contents. Indeed, according to the research, consumers claimed they would happily pay a price premium. From the resellers' viewpoint, the Stepcan offered a range of advantages over some other types of packaging: it was simple to fill, convenient and light to transport, and easy to display at the point of sale. Some of the more apparent benefits of the Stepcan package were as follows:

- *Clarity.* Consumers could view the product they were buying and seemingly judge its quality for themselves.
- *High quality image.* Consumers used to eating tinned fruit but who fancied a change from their usual products felt that Stepcan offered a more socially acceptable alternative, especially for guests.
- *Long shelf life.* Stepcan offered similar benefits to tinned foods for retailers and consumers not wishing to continually re-stock.
- *Lightweight and shatter proof.* In parts of Europe, bottled fruit and vegetables sold in glass packaging have been popular for many years. Stepcan offered the same visibility benefits of its glass cousin while being light to carry and non-breakable.
- *Easy to open ends.* The use of plastic overlids to re-seal the packing allowed easy storage in the refrigerator after opening.
- *Stackable.* Many packaging innovations have come to grief because they fail to take distributors' needs into consideration. But Stepcan was as easy to store as conventional tinned foods.
- *Re-usable.* Stepcan could be used as a handy storage container once its contents had been used.
- *Interchangeable on canning lines.* From an operational viewpoint, Stepcan offered many of the same benefits as the traditional tin can, being easy to switch into the canning process. Even the need to label was minimal.

Marks & Spencer wanted exclusivity for the packaging innovation. Sainsbury's, Waitrose and Tesco all expressed an interest. Marks & Spencer won the first round, and Stepcans containing fruit cocktail were test marketed in a number of locations at a variety of price levels. Eventually, the product was given a price tag of £1.29, some three times the price of a similar weight of conventional tinned fruit cocktail. When put on supermarket shelves adjacent to competing tinned brands, Stepcan consistently outsold them, sometimes by more than three times as much. As more retailers started to stock Stepcans for their own label products, more product lines were found to be suitable for this type of packaging, from fruit cocktail to soups. The simple design allowed new labels to be added with the minimum of fuss. All in all, Stepcan represented a packaging design that appeared to fulfil a mix of operational and marketing requirements.

For Metal Box, the problem was in meeting orders and persuading its sales force to price Stepcan well ahead of its ordinary tin cans. After all, the retailers were charging consumers a premium, so why not Metal Box for its packaging? The sales force, in a commodity business, found this a difficult concept to grasp. Most of the price benefit and profit potential went to the food packers and the retailers, not to Metal Box. For the renamed Carnaud Metalbox company, perhaps the story is not all bad news. Even in 1988, the environmentally concerned Germans and Scandinavians worried about the difficulty of recycling Stepcans. They preferred glass containers. Today, as most European consumers worry about such issues, is there a place for Stepcan?

SOURCES: "M and S adopts clear plastics Stepcan for premium fruit pack presentation", *Packaging News,* May 1988; "Stepcan: the choice is clear", Metal Box food promotional literature, 1988; "What's in a can?", *Inside News,* Marks & Spencer plc. April/May 1989; "Full speed ahead", *Metal Box News,* April 1988, p. 1; "Technology is the key in Crown-CHB deal", *Modern Plastics,* July 1995, p. 15.

Questions for Discussion

1. What benefits did Stepcan offer customers? Which do you think were the most important?
2. Why might Metal Box have had difficulty maintaining its premium price in the long term?
3. How practical was Stepcan for retailers and distributors?
4. What long term threats might Stepcan have faced?

10 DEVELOPING AND MANAGING PRODUCTS

"In the globally competitive world, product and brand management represents the most important resource responsibility in the portfolio of the marketing manager's job."

Michael J. Thomas
University of Strathclyde

OBJECTIVES

- To become aware of organisational alternatives for managing products
- To understand how businesses develop a product idea into a commercial product
- To understand the importance and role of product development in the marketing mix
- To acquire knowledge of the management of products during the various stages of a product's life cycle
- To become aware of how existing products can be modified
- To learn how product deletion can be used to improve product mixes

In early April 1996, PepsiCo International dramatically re-launched Pepsi-Cola and Diet Pepsi in the UK. The move, which replaces the red, white and blue caps with a new blue design, is backed by a £2 million television advertisement featuring Cindy Crawford, Claudia Schiffer and Andre Agassi. These modern-day icons are shown being processed together in a large machine to produce the new Pepsi can. The campaign is accompanied by the statement, "Change the script".

Although the new advertisement has been billed as the most expensive ever, it will play a relatively small part in the £200 million makeover. Other launch initiatives include possible sponsorship deals with football clubs wearing blue kits, the publication of a blue coloured *Daily Mirror* newspaper and painting Concorde blue. The icons theme is also developed in an extensive poster campaign, where familiar red icons, such as strawberries and tomato ketchup bottles, are turned

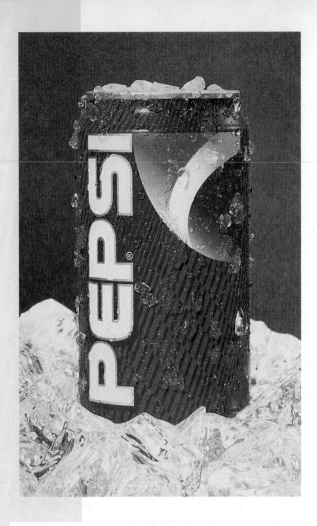

launched worldwide a year after first appearing in the UK. PepsiCo's decision to re-launch has followed two years of declining UK market share: between 1993 and 1995 Pepsi-Cola's share by volume fell by nearly 2 per cent. The decline has been caused by aggressive competition from Virgin Cola and own label brands—Coca-Cola has seen its market share drop by 9 per cent during the same period.

PepsiCo hopes that the new deep blue packaging, which was one of more than 3,000 designs considered, should be easy to differentiate on supermarket shelves. The company also hopes that the new look will build on the success of sugar free Pepsi Max, which is already sold in deep blue cans. In the first two years of sales the youth orientated drink has built up a 4.7 per cent share of the UK cola market and now accounts for one fifth of Pepsi-Cola sales. Early signals for the new blue image look promising, with immediate short term gains for the brand. In the month preceding the launch of the blue can, UK sales were 12 per cent up on the previous year. In the month immediately after the launch a sales increase of 27 per cent over 12 months has been recorded. Now, as it looks to roll out the new branding across Europe, PepsiCo is anxiously awaiting the impact on long term market share. ■

SOURCES: Sharon Marshall, "UK leads global Pepsi relaunch", *Marketing,* 22 February 1996, p. 1; Sharon Marshall, "Pepsi struggles to be heard by a New Generation", *Marketing,* 22 February 1996, p. 16; "Turning Pepsi blue", *The Economist,* 13–19 April 1996, p. 17; "Pepsi to turn the *Daily Mirror* blue", *Marketing Week,* 29 March 1996, p. 7; "Pepsi signs up Schiffer for 'blue' ads", *Marketing Week,* 22 March 1996, p. 7; Michele Simpson, "Pepsi courts UK football teams sporting blue kit….", *Marketing Week,* 12 April 1996, p. 9; Emma Hall, "Pepsi launches $500m blue can", *Campaign,* 5 April 1996, p. 2; Patrick Barrett, "Pepsi elevates UK 'blue' chief",*Marketing,* 16 May 1996, p. 3.

blue. All in all, PepsiCo has covered one quarter of the available six sheet UK poster sites with the advertisements.

If successful, the company plans to roll out the new livery to the rest of the world. This strategy would mirror the launch of Pepsi Max, which was

To compete effectively and achieve their goals, organisations such as PepsiCo must be able to adjust their product mix in response to changes in buyers' preferences. A firm often has to modify existing products, introduce new products or eliminate products that were successful perhaps only a few years ago. For companies such as PepsiCo, this may include quite a radical change to an existing, well known brand. Sometimes, as in the chapter opener, product alterations are required for competitive reasons. Whatever the reasons for altering products, the product mix must be managed. For example, a marketer may need to delete a product from the mix because a competitor dominates the market. In other circumstances it may be appropriate to expand a firm's product mix to take advantage of excess marketing and production capacity. The product portfolio approach, which is reviewed in Chapter 22, tries to create specific marketing strategies to achieve a balanced mix of products that will maximise a firm's long term profits. This chapter is more concerned with the management of the resulting product mix. It begins by considering how businesses are organised to develop and manage products. Next, several ways to improve an organisation's product mix, including new product development from idea generation to commercialisation, are reviewed. Different types of product modifications are also examined. The chapter then considers issues and decisions associated with managing a product through the growth, maturity and declining stages of its life cycle. Finally, the deletion of weak products from the product mix is examined.

Organising to Manage Products

A company must often manage a complex set of products, markets or both. Often, too, it finds that the traditional functional form of organisation—in which managers specialise in business functions such as advertising, sales and distribution—does not fit its needs. Consequently, management must find an organisational approach that accomplishes the tasks necessary to develop and manage products. Alternatives to functional organisation include the product or brand manager approach, the marketing manager approach and the venture or joint team approach.

Product manager The person responsible for a product, a product line or several distinct products that make up an interrelated group within a multi-product organisation

A **product manager** is responsible for a product, a product line or several distinct products that make up an interrelated group within a multi-product organisation. A **brand manager,** on the other hand, is responsible for a single brand, for example, Lipton's Yellow Label tea or Virgin Cola. A product or brand manager operates cross-functionally to co-ordinate the activities, information and strategies involved in marketing an assigned product. Product managers and brand managers plan marketing activities to achieve objectives by co-ordinating a mix of distribution, promotion (especially sales promotion and advertising) and price. They must consider packaging and branding decisions and work closely with research and development, engineering and production departments. The product manager or brand manager approach is used by many large, multiple product companies in the consumer goods business.

Brand manager The person responsible for a single brand

Marketing manager The person responsible for managing the marketing activities that serve a particular group or class of customers

A **marketing manager** is responsible for managing the marketing activities that serve a particular group or class of customers. This organisational approach is particularly effective when a firm engages in different types of marketing activities to provide products to diverse customer groups. A company might have one marketing manager for industrial markets and another for consumer markets. These broad market categories might be broken down into more limited market responsibilities.

Venture or **project team** The group that creates entirely new products, perhaps aimed at new markets, and is responsible for all aspects of the products' development

A **venture** or **project team** is designed to create entirely new products that may be aimed at new markets. Unlike a product or marketing manager, a venture team is responsible for all aspects of a product's development: research and development, production and engineering, finance and accounting, and marketing. Venture teams work outside established divisions to create inventive approaches to new products and markets. As a result of this flexibility, new products can be developed to take advantage of opportunities in highly segmented markets.

The members of a venture team come from different functional areas of an organisation. When the commercial potential of a new product has been demonstrated, the members may return to their functional areas, or they may join a new or existing division to manage the product. The new product may be turned over to an existing division, a marketing manager or a product manager. Innovative organisational forms such as venture teams are especially important for well established firms operating in mature markets. These companies must take a dual approach to marketing organisation. They must accommodate the management of mature products and also encourage the development of new ones.[1]

New Product Development

Developing and introducing new products is frequently expensive and risky. The development of Gillette's Sensor razor took over eight years and resulted in a £150 million investment.[2] Thousands of new consumer products are introduced annually, and, as indicated in Chapter 8, anywhere from 60 to 90 per cent of them fail. Lack of research, technical problems in design or production and errors in timing the product's introduction are all causes of failure. Although developing new products is risky, so is failing to introduce new products. For example, the makers of Timex watches gained a large share of the watch market through effective marketing strategies during the 1960s and early 1970s. By 1983, Timex's market share had slipped considerably, in part because the company had failed to introduce new products. More recently, Timex has regained market share by introducing a number of new products.

The term *new product* can have more than one meaning. It may refer to a genuinely new product—such as the digital watch once was—offering innovative benefits. But products that are merely different and distinctly better are also often viewed as new. The following items (listed in no particular order) are product innovations of the last 30 years: Post-It notes, birth control pills, personal computers, felt tip pens, anti-ulcer drugs, video cassette recorders, deep fat fryers, compact disc players, soft contact lenses and telephone banking. Thus, a new product can be an innovative variation of an existing product, such as Mars Miniatures shown in Figure 10.1. It can also be a product that a given firm has not marketed previously, although similar products may be available from other companies. The first company to introduce a video cassette recorder clearly was launching a new product, yet if Boeing introduced its own brand of video cassette recorder, this would also be viewed as a new product for Boeing, because it has not previously marketed such products.

New product development
The process a product goes through before introduction, involving six phases: idea generation, screening, business analysis, product development, test marketing and commercialisation

Before a product is introduced, it goes through the six phases of **new product development** shown in Figure 10.2: (1) idea generation, (2) screening, (3) business analysis, (4) product development, (5) test marketing and (6) commercialisation. A product may be dropped, and many are, at any of these stages of development. This section examines the process through which products are developed from the inception of an idea to a product offered for sale. Table 10.1 shows how companies can improve their new product success rate.

Idea generation The process by which businesses and other organisations seek product ideas that will help them achieve their objectives

Idea Generation **Idea generation** involves businesses and other organisations seeking product ideas that will help them achieve their objectives. This task is difficult because only a few ideas are good enough to be commercially successful. Although some organisations get their ideas almost by chance, firms trying to manage their product mixes effectively usually develop systematic approaches for generating new product ideas. At the heart of innovation is a purposeful, focused

Figure 10.1
A new product

Mars Miniatures is an
example of a new product

*Source: Courtesy of Mars
Confectionery.*

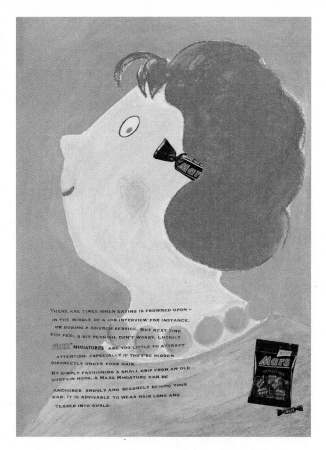

effort to identify new ways to serve a market. Unexpected occurrences, incongruities, new needs, industry and market changes, and demographic changes may all indicate new opportunities.[3]

New product ideas can come from several sources. They may come from internal sources—marketing managers, researchers, sales personnel, engineers or other organisational personnel. Brainstorming and incentives or rewards for good ideas are typical intra-firm devices for stimulating the development of ideas. The company 3M is well known for encouraging the generation of new ideas. The idea for 3M's Post-It adhesive backed yellow notes came from an employee. As a church choir member, he used slips of paper for marking songs in his hymn book. Because the pieces of paper fell out, he suggested developing an adhesive backed note.[4] Hewlett-Packard keeps its labs open to engineers 24 hours a day to help generate ideas; it also encourages its researchers to devote 10 per cent of company time to exploring their own ideas for new products.[5]

Figure 10.2 Phases of new product development

1. Talk with consumers; don't introduce a product just because you can technologically make it.

2. Set realistic sales goals. Unrealistic goals can result in potentially successful products being terminated.

3. Make all parts of the firm (research, manufacturing, marketing and distribution) work together for customer orientation.

4. At each stage of development, the product should have consumer acceptance, the ability to be manufactured at an acceptable cost and sales support.

5. Test market a product long enough to get an accurate assessment. Some products fail because consumers buy them early as a novelty only.

6. Carefully evaluate all product failures to provide information for future product introductions.

SOURCE: Christopher P. Power, Kathleen Kerwin, Ronald Grover, Keith Alexander and Robert D. Hof, "Flops: too many new products fail. Here's why—and how to do better", *Business Week*, 16 August 1993, pp. 78–79.

Table 10.1 How to improve new product success

New product ideas may also arise from sources outside the firm—customers, competitors, advertising agencies, management consultants and private research organisations. Johnson & Johnson, for example, acquired the technology for its new, clear orthodontic braces through a joint venture with Saphikon, the developer of the technology behind the braces.[6] Sometimes ideas come from potential buyers of a product. Asking weekend fishermen what they wanted in a sonar fish finder led Techsonic to develop its LCR (liquid crystal recorder) fish finder. The practice of asking customers what they want from its products has helped Techsonic maintain its leadership in the industry.[7]

Screening ideas The process by which a company assesses whether product ideas match its organisational objectives and resources

Screening Ideas **Screening ideas** involves first assessing whether they match organisational objectives and resources and then choosing the best ideas for further review. Next the company's overall ability to produce and market the product is analysed. Other aspects of an idea that should be weighed are the nature and wants of buyers and possible environmental changes. More new product ideas are rejected during the idea screening phase than during any other phase.

Sometimes a checklist of new product requirements is used to ensure that the screening process is as systematic as possible. If a critical factor on the checklist remains unclear, the type of formal marketing research described in Chapter 6 may be needed. To screen ideas properly, it may be necessary to test product concepts; a product concept and its benefits can be described or shown to consumers. Several product concepts may be tested to discover which might appeal most to a particular target market.

Business analysis A company's evaluation of a product idea to determine its potential contribution to the firm's sales, costs and profits

Business Analysis During the **business analysis** stage, the product idea is evaluated to determine its potential contribution to the firm's sales, costs and profits. In the course of a business analysis, evaluators ask a variety of questions: Does the product fit in with the organisation's existing product mix? Does the company have the right expertise to develop the new product? Is demand strong enough to justify entering the market and will the demand endure? What types of environmental and competitive changes can be expected and how will these changes affect the product's future sales, costs and profits? Are the organisation's research, development, engineering and production capabilities adequate? If new facilities must be constructed, how quickly can they be built and how much will they cost? Is the necessary financing for development and commercialisation on hand or obtainable at terms consistent with a favourable return on investment? Will the new product or idea benefit the company's existing portfolio of products? Is there any danger that existing products or services will be cannibalised?

In the business analysis stage, firms seek market information. The results of consumer polls, along with secondary data, supply the specifics needed for estimating potential sales, costs and profits. At this point, a research budget should explore the financial objectives and related considerations for the new product. Table 10.2 addresses key questions to consider in new product development.

Product development The phase in which the organisation determines if it is technically and financially feasible to produce a new product

Product Development   **Product development** is the phase in which the organisation finds out if it is technically feasible to produce the product and if it can be produced at costs low enough to make the final price reasonable. To test its acceptability, the idea or concept is converted into a prototype, or working model. Case 10.1 considers the role of concept cars in the development of new vehicles and shows how manufacturers such as Peugeot and Citroën invest considerable energy and resources in developing new products. The prototype should reveal tangible and intangible attributes associated with the product in consumers' minds. The product's design, mechanical features and intangible aspects must be linked to wants in the marketplace. This includes the service aspects of the product, which, as Marketing Insight 10.1 shows, are a vital component of many products. Failure to determine how consumers feel about the product and how they would use it may lead to the product's failure. For example, the Sinclair C5 electric buggy was developed as a serious on-road, single seater car for city or country use. However, drivers felt unsafe in the buggy, and campus students ended up using the remaining stocks as on-pavement runabouts.

The development phase of a new product is frequently lengthy and expensive; thus a relatively small number of product ideas are put into development. If the product appears sufficiently successful during this stage to merit testing, then during the latter part of the development stage marketers begin to make decisions regarding branding, packaging, labelling, pricing and promotion for use in the test marketing stage.

Test marketing The limited introduction of a product into certain geographic areas chosen to represent the intended market

Test Marketing   A limited introduction of a product in geographic areas chosen to represent the intended market is called **test marketing**. Its aim is to determine the reactions of probable buyers. For example, after McDonald's developed fried chicken products for its fast food menu, it test marketed the idea in certain McDonald's restaurants to find out how those customers felt about eating chicken at McDonald's.[8] The company followed a similar strategy for test marketing its range of salads and pizza. Test marketing is *not* an extension of the development stage; it is a sample launching of the entire marketing mix and should be conducted only after the product has gone through development and initial plans regarding the other marketing mix variables have been made.

Companies of all sizes use test marketing to lessen the risk of product failure. The dangers of introducing an untested product include undercutting already profitable products and, should the new product fail, loss of credibility with

Customer Service—Becoming Part of the Product?

Toy Story (PG): new from Walt Disney Pictures, this computer-generated animated fantasy features an all-star line up of vocal talent including Tom Hanks, Tim Allen, Annie Potts, Don Rickles and Jim Varney. With music from Randy Newman, this family story tells the tale of a group of toys who come to life whenever their owner, a boy named Andy, is not around. Toy Story the movie "product", as described by leading multiplex cinema operator National Amusements, known to millions of cinema-goers as Showcase.

People visit cinemas to watch a movie for many reasons: to catch the latest release, because friends are going, to be entertained, to go courting, to occupy the kids, to escape from the kids, to be with people, to have an emotional experience, to "kill" time, to have a rest, or "just because it's somewhere to go". The choice of which movie may often be the first decision, but these days, with the growth of multiplex complexes and increased cinema attendances, the choice may be which multiplex: MGM, UCI or Showcase? For rival operators, the "augmented" product is becoming increasingly important as they seek to develop an edge and to encourage customer loyalty. For example, Showcase strongly emphasises many once secondary or minor features in an attempt to add to the appeal of its cinemas:

State of the art film projection
Acres of free, illuminated car parking
Best seats in town—exclusive rocking loungers
Bargain matinees daily
Freshly popped popcorn
Cinema hire and special group rates
Main coach routes
Dolby stereo equipped auditoria
Air conditioning
Excellent facilities for the disabled
Late night shows every Friday and Saturday

distributors and customers. When Lever Brothers launched Wisk—previously only a washing powder—in liquid form in 1986, the firm had misjudged consumer usage. Many blocked washing machines later, P&G offered liquid Ariel with Arielettes, containers to be placed inside the machines together with the clothes. Reformulations have now overcome these problems.

Test marketing provides several benefits. It lets marketers expose a product in a natural marketing environment to gauge its sales performance. While the product is being marketed in a limited area, the company can seek to identify weaknesses in the product or in other parts of the marketing mix. Corrections can be made more cheaply than if the product had already been introduced nationwide. Test marketing also allows marketers to experiment with variations in advertising, price and packaging in different test areas and to measure the extent of brand awareness, brand switching and repeat purchases that result from alterations in the marketing mix.

The accuracy of test marketing results often hinges on where the tests are conducted. Selection of appropriate test areas is very important. The validity of test market results depends heavily on selecting test sites that provide an accurate representation of the intended target market. The criteria used for choosing test cities

Efficient, courteous service
Gift certificates always available
Art gallery with prints for sale

Car giant Daewoo entered the European market spectacularly in 1995 with an innovative, mould breaking proposition and marketing strategy: selling direct rather than through franchised garages and without commission paid sales staff. Daewoo's entire proposition was intended to identify customers' "pet hates" in car buying and to eliminate them from Daewoo's sales and marketing. Daewoo's used car operation received a similar treatment. The company's intention was to re-assure its customers and to reduce the stress and uncertainty inherent in purchasing a second hand car. While it is still ultimately the car that the Daewoo customer buys, the company has put together an impressive package of additional benefits:

12 month comprehensive Daewoo guarantee
116 point AA approved inspection
Independent mileage check

12 months' AA roadside assistance
Free MOT tests for as long as you own the car
An HPI check to make sure the car hasn't
   been stolen or written off and that it has
   no outstanding hire purchase
   agreements
30 day exchange or money back guarantee
Full service to manufacturer's specification
Where possible, direct contact with all
   previous owners
6 months' road tax
Free mobile phone
Menu priced servicing with free courtesy car in
   mainland UK.

For many companies, not only Showcase or Daewoo, the augmented product is an increasingly important element in marketing strategy and the search for customer satisfaction.

SOURCES: Showcase Cinema, Coventry; Daewoo UK; *Coventry Evening Telegraph*, 5 April 1996, p. 64.

or television regions depend on the product's characteristics, the target market's characteristics and the firm's objectives and resources.

Test marketing can be risky because it is expensive and a firm's competitors may try to interfere. A competitor may invalidate test results in an attempt to "jam" the test programme by increasing advertising or promotions, lowering prices or offering special incentives—all to combat the recognition and purchase of a new brand. Sometimes, too, competitors copy the product in the testing stage and rush to introduce a similar product. It is therefore desirable to move quickly and commercialise as soon as possible after testing.

To avoid these risks, companies may use alternative methods to gauge consumer preferences. One such method is simulated test marketing. Typically, consumers at shopping centres are asked to view an advertisement for a new product and are given a free sample to take home. These consumers are subsequently interviewed over the phone and asked to rate the product. The major advantages of simulated test marketing are lower costs, tighter security and, consequently, a reduction in the flow of information to competitors and the elimination of jamming. Scanner based test marketing is another, more sophisticated version of the traditional test marketing method.[9] Some marketing research firms, such as A. C.

Concept/Product

1. Do consumers understand your product and is it unique?
2. Is the product perceived as a good value?
3. Does your product perform at an acceptable level?
4. What promotion methods are appropriate?
5. What are the sales projections?
6. What is the perceived profitability of the product?

Company

7. Does this product fit the company's product portfolio?
8. Does this product give the company the advantage to move in a new direction or strengthen current positioning?
9. Is current technology being maximised?
10. What are the capital investment requirements?

Target Market

11. Who is the target market for the product?
12. Is there a perception of long term demand for the product?
13. What are the perceived benefits to the customer?
14. What are the requirements to gain distribution?
15. When is the product launch scheduled and what market tests are required?

Competition

16. Who is your primary competition?
17. How do you expect the competition to react to the product?

Final Considerations

18. Where do you derive your information and do you trust the sources?
19. What are the unanswered questions related to new product success?
20. What is the probability of success after considering the above questions?

SOURCE: Adapted from Larry A. Constantineau, "The twenty toughest questions for new product proposals", *Journal of Consumer Marketing*, Spring 1992, pp. 51–53. © 1992 MCB University Press, Ltd. Used by permission.

Table 10.2 Key questions to address in new product development

Nielsen, offer test marketing services to help provide independent assessment of products.

Commercialisation The process of refining and settling plans for full scale manufacturing and marketing

Commercialisation During the **commercialisation** phase, plans for full scale manufacturing and marketing must be refined and settled, and budgets for the project must be prepared. Early in the commercialisation phase, marketing management analyses the results of test marketing to find out what changes in the marketing mix are needed before the product is introduced. For example, the results of test marketing may tell the marketers to change one or more of the product's physical attributes, modify the distribution plans to include more retail outlets, alter promotional efforts or change the product's price. During this phase, the organisation also has to gear up for production and may therefore face sizeable capital expenditure and personnel costs.

The product enters the market during the commercialisation phase. One study indicates that only 8 per cent of new product projects started by major companies reach this stage.[10] When introducing a product, marketers often spend enormous sums of money for advertising, personal selling and other types of promotion. These expenses, together with capital outlays, can make commercialisation extremely costly; such expenditures may not be recovered for several years. For example, when Citroën introduced its new Saxo model, the company spent millions of pounds on advertising to communicate the new car's attributes.

Commercialisation is easier when customers accept the product rapidly, which they are more likely to do if marketers can make them aware of its benefits.

Product Adoption Process

Product adoption process
The stages buyers go through in accepting a product: awareness, interest, evaluation, trial and adoption

The following stages of the **product adoption process** are generally recognised as those that buyers go through in accepting a product:

1. *Awareness.* The buyer becomes aware of the product.
2. *Interest.* The buyer seeks information and is generally receptive to learning about the product.
3. *Evaluation.* The buyer considers the product's benefits and determines whether to try it.
4. *Trial.* The buyer examines, tests or tries the product to determine its usefulness relative to his or her needs.
5. *Adoption.* The buyer purchases the product and can be expected to use it when the need for this general type of product arises again.[11]

In the first stage, when individuals become aware that the product exists, they have little information about it and are not concerned about obtaining more. Consumers enter the interest stage when they are motivated to get information about the product's features, uses, advantages, disadvantages, price or location. During the evaluation stage, individuals consider whether the product will satisfy certain criteria that are crucial for meeting their specific needs. In the trial stage, they use or experience the product for the first time, possibly by purchasing a small quantity, by taking advantage of a free sample or demonstration or by borrowing the product from someone. Supermarkets, for instance, frequently offer special promotions to encourage consumers to taste products. During this stage, potential adopters determine the usefulness of the product under the specific conditions for which they need it.

Individuals move into the adoption stage by choosing the specific product when they need a product of that general type. However, the fact that a person enters the adoption process does not mean that she or he will eventually adopt the new product. Rejection may occur at any stage, including adoption. Both product adoption and product rejection can be temporary or permanent.

This adoption model has several implications for the commercialisation phase. First, the company must promote the product to create widespread awareness of its existence and its benefits. Samples or simulated trials should be arranged to help buyers make initial purchase decisions. Marketers should also emphasise quality control and provide solid guarantees to reinforce buyer opinion during the evaluation stage. Finally, production and physical distribution must be linked to patterns of adoption and repeat purchases. (The product adoption process is also discussed in Chapter 16.) When launching a new product, companies should be aware that buyers differ in the speed with which they adopt a product. Identifying buyers who are most open to new products can help expedite this process.

Products are not usually launched nationwide overnight but are introduced through a process called a roll out. In a roll out, a product is introduced in stages, starting in a set of geographic areas and gradually expanding into adjacent areas. Thus, Cadbury's Wispa bar appeared initially in the North East of England. It may take several years to market the product nationally. Sometimes the test cities are used as initial marketing areas, and the introduction becomes a natural extension of test marketing.

Gradual product introduction reduces the risks of introducing a new product. If the product fails, the firm will experience smaller losses. Furthermore, it may take some time for a company to develop a suitable distribution network. Also, the number of units needed to satisfy the national demand for a successful product can be enormous, and a firm usually cannot produce the required quantities in a short time.

Despite the good reasons for introducing a product gradually, marketers realise that this approach creates some competitive problems. A gradual introduction allows competitors to observe what a firm is doing and to monitor results, just as the firm's own marketers are doing. If competitors see that the newly introduced product is successful, they may enter the same target market quickly with similar products.

Avoiding competition is critical when a firm introduces a brand into a market in which it already has one or more brands. Marketers usually want to avoid cannibalising sales of their existing brands, unless the new brand generates substantially larger profits. When Coca-Cola re-introduced Tab, it attempted to position the cola so as to minimise the adverse effects on Diet Coke sales. Similarly, when KP introduces a new snack brand, it must take care to ensure that sales of other KP brands do not suffer.

If a product has been planned properly, its attributes and brand image will give it the distinctive appeal needed. Style, shape, construction, quality of work and colour help create the image and the appeal. Of course buyers are more likely to purchase the product if they can easily identify the benefits. When the new product does not offer some preferred attributes, there is room for another new product or for re-positioning an existing product.[12]

• • • • • • • • • • • • • • • • • • • •

Product Life Cycle Management

Most new products start off slowly and seldom generate enough sales to produce profits immediately. As buyers learn about the new product, marketers should be alert for weaknesses and ready to make corrections quickly, in order to prevent the product's early demise. Computer software companies expect to modify "bugs" when launching new software packages. Consumers must be informed quickly and efficiently of any difficulties if damage to the brand image is to be avoided. Marketing strategy should be designed to attract the segment that is most interested in and has the fewest objections to the product. If any of these factors need adjustment, this action, too, must be taken quickly to sustain demand. As the sales curve moves upwards and the break even point is reached, the growth stage begins.

Marketing Strategy in the Growth Stage

As sales increase, management must support the momentum by adjusting the marketing strategy. The goal is to establish the product's position and to fortify it by encouraging brand loyalty. As profits increase, the organisation must brace itself for the entrance of aggressive competitors, who may make specialised appeals to selected market segments.

During the growth stage, product offerings may have to be expanded. To achieve greater penetration of an overall market, segmentation may have to be used more intensely. That would require developing product variations to satisfy the needs of customers in several different market segments. Marketers should analyse the product position regarding competing products and correct weak or omitted attributes. Further quality, functional or style modifications may be required.

Gaps in the marketing channels should be filled during the growth period. Once a product has won acceptance, new distribution outlets may be easier to obtain. Sometimes marketers tend to move from an **exclusive** or **selective distribution** to a more **intensive distribution** of dealers to achieve greater market penetration. Marketers must also make sure that the physical distribution system is running efficiently and delivering supplies to distributors before their inventories are exhausted. Because competition increases during the growth period, good service and an effective mechanism for handling complaints are important.

Advertising expenditure may be lowered slightly from the high level of the introductory stage but still needs to be quite substantial. As sales increase, promotion costs should drop as a percentage of total sales. A falling ratio between promotion expenditure and sales should contribute significantly to increased profits. The advertising messages should aim to stress brand benefits and emphasise the product's position. Coupons and samples may be used to increase market share.

After recovering development costs, a business may be able to lower prices. As sales volume increases, efficiencies in production can result in lower costs. These savings may be passed on to buyers. If demand remains strong and there are few competitive threats, prices tend to remain stable. If price cuts are feasible, they can improve price competition and discourage new competitors from entering the market. For example, when compact disc players were introduced in the early 1980s, they carried an £800 price tag. Primarily because of the price, the product was positioned as a "toy for audiophiles"—a very small market segment. To generate mass market demand, compact disc player manufacturers dropped their prices to around £150, and the cost of discs also dropped. The price is now at a point where the margin is low but the turnover is high, and more homes are now investing in compact disc players. A similar pattern has emerged in the sale of mobile phones.

Marketing Strategy for Mature Products

As many products are in the maturity stage of their life cycles, marketers must always be ready to improve the product and marketing mix. During maturity, the competitive situation stabilises and some of the weaker competitors drop out. It has been suggested that as a product matures, its customers become more experienced and their requirements more diverse, so that market segmentation opportunities increase. As customers' needs change, new marketing strategies may be called for.[13] For example, in the wake of new competition from Eurotunnel, ferry operator P&O now stresses its excellent on-board shopping facilities in its advertising (see Figure 10.3). Marketers may also need to modify the product. Symptoms of a mature product include price cutting, increased competitive

Exclusive distribution
Market coverage in which only one outlet is used in a geographic area

Selective distribution
Market coverage in which only some available outlets in an area are chosen to distribute a product

Intensive distribution
Market coverage in which all available outlets are used for distributing a product

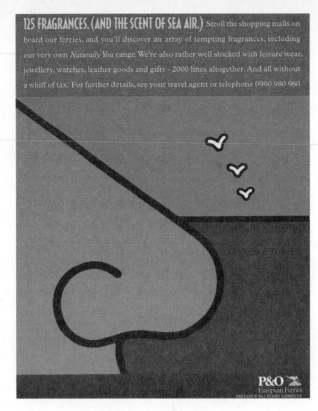

125 FRAGRANCES. (AND THE SCENT OF SEA AIR.) Stroll the shopping malls on board our ferries, and you'll discover an array of tempting fragrances, including our very own *Naturally You* range. We're also rather well stocked with leisure wear, jewellery, watches, leather goods and gifts - 2000 lines altogether. And all without a whiff of tax. For further details, see your travel agent or telephone 0990 980 980.

P&O
European Ferries
BRITAIN'S No.1 FERRY COMPANY

action and shifting from a product orientation to a non-product orientation (price, promotion and distribution adaptation); in addition, market growth slows.[14]

Product modification means changing one or more characteristics of a firm's product. This strategy is most likely to be used in the maturity stage of the product life cycle to give a firm's existing brand a competitive advantage. Marketing Insight 10.2 shows how even well established brands such as Sellotape must be modified from time to time. Altering a product mix in this way entails less risk than developing a new product because the product is already established in the market. For example, publishers may launch new editions of popular reference books up-dated with the latest information.

If certain conditions are met, product modification can improve a firm's product mix. First, the product must be modifiable. Second, existing customers must be able to perceive that a modification has been made (assuming that the modified item is still aimed at them). Third, the modification should make the product more consistent with customers' desires so that it provides greater satisfaction. If these conditions are not met, it is unlikely that the product modification, however innovative, will be successful. Product modifications fall into three major categories: quality, function and style modifications.

Quality Modifications Changes concerning a product's dependability and durability are called **quality modifications**. Usually, they are executed by altering the materials or the production process. Reducing a product's quality may allow an organisation to lower its price and direct the item at a larger target market.

Product modification The alteration of one or more characteristics of a firm's product

Quality modifications Changes that affect a product's dependability and durability

By contrast, increasing the quality of a product may give a firm an advantage over competing brands. During the last 20 years, marketers have been forced by increased global competition, technological change and more demanding customers to improve product integrity.[15] Higher quality may enable a company to charge a higher price by creating customer loyalty and by lowering customer sensitivity to price. However, higher quality may require the use of more expensive components, less standardised production processes and other manufacturing and management techniques that force a firm to charge higher prices.[16] At the beginning of the 1990s, concern for quality increased significantly, with many firms, such as Rover, Volvo and Caterpillar, finding ways to both increase quality and reduce costs.

Functional Modifications Changes that affect a product's versatility, effectiveness, convenience or safety are called **functional modifications;** they usually require the product to be redesigned. Typical product categories that have undergone considerable functional modifications include home computers, audio equipment and cleaning products. Functional modifications can make a product useful to more people, thus enlarging its market, or improve the product's competitive position by providing benefits competing items do not offer. Functional modifications can also help an organisation achieve and maintain a progressive image. For example, washing machine manufacturers such as Whirlpool have developed appliances that use less heat and water. At times, too, functional modifications are made to reduce the possibility of product liability claims.

Functional modifications Changes that affect a product's versatility, effectiveness, convenience or safety

Style Modifications **Style modifications** change the sensory appeal of a product by altering its taste, texture, sound, smell or visual characteristics. Such modifications can be important, because when making a purchase decision a buyer is swayed by how a product looks, smells, tastes, feels or sounds. As illustrated in Figure 10.4 and Case 10.2, even successful products such as Tango may benefit from this kind of modification.

Although style modifications can be used by a firm to differentiate its product from competing brands, their major drawback is that their value is highly subjective. A company may strive to improve the product's style, but customers may actually find the modified product less appealing. Some organisations try to minimise these problems by altering product style in subtle ways. For example, Mattel's Barbie doll has gradually changed over the years to reflect changing fashions.

Style modifications Changes that alter a product's sensory appeal—taste, texture, sound, smell or visual characteristics

Figure 10.4

Style modification

The new look Tango has undergone style modification.

SOURCE: *Courtesy of Tango.*

Sellotape or Mustard? Increasing Market Penetration

Just as *JCB* is a generic term for backhoe diggers in the construction industry, *Hoover* for vacuum cleaners, *Post-It* for those useful sticky stationery tags, and *Bic* for disposable pens, for many decades *Sellotape* has been the term applied to sticky transparent tape. Over the years, however, many other brands and suppliers have entered the market and eaten away Sellotape's once dominant market share. So where next for Sellotape?

At the end of 1995, following nearly two years of research and planning, Sellotape enjoyed a £2 million re-launch. This represented the "most significant change in the brand's 60 year history", according to Neil Ashley, executive director of the company, renamed the Sellotape Company. The name Sellotape has been the company's core marketing asset for many decades, with nine out of ten consumers familiar with the brand. However, the company has for some time sold a wider range of products than its sticky tape association implies. Michael Peters of the branding specialist Identica, responsible for the Sellotape re-think, was more fervent in his view: "While it is a very famous trademark, it's a grey one." Qualitative market research revealed that although well known, hardly any consumer asked for Sellotape by name. Worse, they readily accepted other brands because they could see no obvious product or brand features that gave Sellotape a competitive edge.

The re-launch aimed to address the inherent weakness in becoming a generic name for a product by re-establishing a new brand identity alongside existing core brand values. Rival products not using cellulose are cheaper, so alongside its traditional tape, the Sellotape Company now offers a range of tape made from other source materials. Elephant Tape, for example, is a heavy duty fabric tape that is targeted at the do-it-yourself (DIY) market.

Under the sub-brand Sellotape Office, a range of products aimed at office use has been launched. Ranges have also been targeted at the children's market and the home security market. The view that there are in effect three distinct markets—retail, DIY and office—has led to the development of novel product applications and totally separate ranges.

The key problem to overcome has been "the Colman's mustard dilemma". Colman's, the market

During the maturity stage of the cycle, marketers actively encourage dealers to support the product, perhaps by offering promotional assistance or help in lowering their inventory costs. In general, marketers go to great lengths to serve dealers and to provide incentives for selling the manufacturer's brand, partly because own label or retailer brands are a threat at this time. As discussed in Chapter 9, own label brands are both an opportunity and a threat to manufacturers, who may be able to sell their products through recognised own label or retailer brand names as well as their own. However, own label or retailer brands frequently undermine manufacturers' brands.

Maintaining market share during the maturity stage requires moderate and sometimes heavy advertising expenditure. Advertising messages focus on differentiating a brand from numerous competitors, and sales promotion efforts are aimed at both consumers and resellers.

leader, had tremendously high brand awareness, and consumers perceived their mustards to be of high quality. Unfortunately, these consumers usually bought only one type of mustard, English; and that one jar lasted for years! Colman's had to increase usage. It achieved this by (1) demonstrating in advertisements and cookery supplements that mustard could be used in a variety of ways, particularly as an additional ingredient in many sauces, just like a herb or spice, and (2) bringing out a range of different mustards, each with unique strengths, flavours and applications: French, Italian and American mustards, along with the traditional English. Consumers were encouraged to have several jars in their cupboards.

For Sellotape, research showed that most customers bought only one roll of sticky tape each year, often around Christmas. The launch of ranges designed for different target audiences—retail, DIY and office—and for various applications—children's activities and home security uses—emulated the brand extension principles so well deployed by Colman's.

Sellotape's strong brand awareness and identity mean that the company does not need to advertise heavily. Instead, the Sellotape Company is relying on direct marketing and point-of-sale promotion to create awareness of its new sub-brands and their applications. A core task for the company has been to break down traditional views of the product and its customers held by employees and to establish additional channels of distribution through toy shops and garden centres to reflect the extended and additional product ranges. It is away from the once core stationery retailers that the Sellotape Company expects to see the strongest growth, particularly in the DIY sector. There, pan-European sales are rising by around 8 per cent each year and now amount to £60 million.

If the Sellotape Company can, like Colman's, encourage its customers to buy two products annually instead of just one and to look for its branded products by name, the heritage of the brand and the re-organisation of the company will reap significant rewards.

Sources: "Sellotape acts to avoid getting stuck in a rut", *Independent on Sunday,* 26 November, 1995, IB8; the Sellotape Company, 1996; B&Q, 1996; Sainsbury's Homebase, 1996. With grateful thanks to Meg Carter.

A greater mixture of pricing strategies is used during the maturity stage. In some cases, strong price competition occurs and price wars may break out. Sometimes marketers develop price flexibility to differentiate offerings in product lines. Mark-downs and price incentives are more common, but prices may rise if distribution and production costs increase. Marketers of mature products also often alter packaging and even positioning strategies. For example, in the US, Heinz re-packaged and re-positioned its vinegar as an all natural cleaning product.

Marketing Strategy for Declining Products

As a product's sales curve turns downwards, industry profits continue to fall. A business can justify maintaining a product as long as it contributes to profits or enhances the overall effectiveness of a product mix. In this stage, marketers must determine whether to eliminate the product or seek to re-position it in an attempt to extend its life. Usually, a declining product has lost its distinctiveness because similar competing products have been introduced. Competition engenders increased substitution and brand switching as buyers become insensitive to minor product differences. For these reasons, marketers do little to change a product's style, design or other attributes during its decline. New technology, product substitutes or environmental considerations may also indicate that the time has come to delete a product. For example, the ill fated Betamax video cassette technology was quickly pushed out by the VHS format.

During a product's decline, outlets with strong sales volumes are maintained and unprofitable outlets are weeded out. An entire marketing channel may be eliminated if it does not contribute adequately to profits. Sometimes a new marketing channel, such as a factory outlet, will be used to liquidate remaining inventory of an obsolete product.

Advertising expenditure is at a minimum. Advertising or special offers may slow the rate of decline. Sales promotions, such as coupons and premiums, may temporarily regain buyers' attention. As the product continues to decline, the sales staff shifts its emphasis to more profitable products.

To have a product return a profit may be more important to a firm than to maintain a certain market share. To squeeze out all possible remaining profits, marketers may maintain the price despite declining sales and competitive pressures. Prices may even be increased as costs rise if a loyal core market still wants the product. In other situations, the price may be cut to reduce existing inventory so that the product can be deleted. Severe price reductions may be required if a new product is making an existing product obsolete.

Deleting Products

Product deletion The process of eliminating a product that no longer satisfies a sufficient number of customers

Product deletion is the process of eliminating a product that no longer satisfies a sufficient number of customers. Products usually cannot contribute to an organisation's goals indefinitely, and a declining product reduces an organisation's profitability, draining resources that could be used to modify other products or develop new ones. A marginal product may require shorter production runs, which can increase per unit production costs. Finally, when a dying product completely loses favour with customers, the negative feelings may transfer to some of the company's other products.

Most organisations find it difficult to delete a product. It was probably a hard decision for Austin Rover to drop the TR7 sports car and admit that it was a failure. A decision to drop a product may be opposed by management and other employees who feel that the product is necessary in the product mix, or by salespeople who still have some loyal customers. Considerable resources and effort are sometimes spent in trying to improve the product's marketing mix enough to increase sales and thus avoid having to delete it.

Some organisations delete products only after they have become heavy financial burdens. Robert Maxwell's London newspaper the *Daily News* closed after only a few weeks, having lost £25 million. A better approach is to institute some form of systematic review to evaluate each product and monitor its impact on the overall effectiveness of the firm's product mix. Such a review should analyse a product's contribution to the company's sales for a given period and should include estimates of future sales, costs and profits associated with the product. It should also gauge the value of making changes in the marketing strategy to improve the product's performance. A systematic review allows an organisation to improve product performance and to ascertain when to delete products.

Figure 10.5 Product deletion process

Source: Martin L. Bell, Marketing: Concepts and Strategy, *3rd ed., p. 267; copyright © 1979, Houghton Mifflin Company. Reproduced by permission of Mrs. Martin L. Bell.*

Although many companies do systematically review their product mixes, one research study found that few firms have formal, written policies concerning the process of deleting products. The study also found that most companies base their decisions to delete weak products on poor sales and profit potential, low compatibility with the firm's business strategies, unfavourable market outlook and historical declines in profitability.[17]

Basically, there are three ways to delete a product: phase it out, run it out or drop it immediately (see Figure 10.5). A **phase out** approach lets the product decline without a change in the marketing strategy. No attempt is made to give the product new life. A **run out** policy exploits any strengths left in the product. Intensifying marketing efforts in core markets or eliminating some marketing expenditures, such as advertising, may cause a sudden profit increase. This approach is commonly taken for technologically obsolete products, such as older models of camcorders or computers, and is often accompanied by a price reduction. Some car manufacturers use a run out approach to dispose of certain models just before a new launch. The third option, an **immediate drop** of an unprofitable product, is the best strategy when losses are too great to prolong the product's life.

Phase out   An approach that lets the product decline without a change in marketing strategy

Run out   A policy that exploits any strengths left in the product

Immediate drop   An option that drops an unprofitable product immediately

• • • • • • • • • • • • • • • • • •

Summary

● Developing and managing products is critical to an organisation's survival and growth. The various approaches available for organising product management share common activities, functions and decisions necessary to guide a product through its life cycle. A *product manager* is responsible for a product, a product line or several distinct products that make up an interrelated group within a multi-product organisation. A *brand manager* is a product manager who is responsible for a single brand. *Marketing managers* are responsible for managing the marketing activities that serve a particular group or class of customers. A *venture* or *project team* is sometimes used to create entirely new products that may be aimed at new markets.

● To maximise the effectiveness of a product mix, an organisation usually has to alter its mix through modification of existing products, deletion of a product or new product development.

● A new product may be an innovation that has never been sold by any organisation, or it can be a product that a given firm has not marketed previously, although similar products have been available from other organisations. Before a product is introduced, it goes through the six phases of *new product development*. (1) In the *idea generation* phase, new product ideas may come from internal or external sources. (2) In the process of *screening ideas*, those with the greatest potential are selected for further review. (3) During the *business analysis* stage, the product idea is evaluated to determine its potential contribution to the firm's sales, costs and profits. (4) *Product development* is the stage in which the organisation finds out if it is technically feasible to produce the product and if it can be produced at costs low enough for the final price to be reasonable. (5) *Test marketing* is a limited introduction of a product in areas chosen to represent the intended market. (6) The decision to enter the *commercialisation* phase means that full scale production of the product begins and a complete marketing strategy is developed. The *product adoption process* that buyers go through in accepting a product includes awareness, interest, evaluation, trial and adoption.

● As a product moves through its life cycle, marketing strategies may require continual adaptation. In the growth stage, it is important to develop brand loyalty and a market position. Marketers may move from *exclusive* or *selective distribution* using an *intensive distribution* of dealers. In the maturity stage, a product may be modified or new market segments may be developed to rejuvenate its sales.

Product modification involves changing one or more characteristics of a firm's product. This approach to altering a product mix can be effective when the product is modifiable, when customers can perceive the change and when customers want the modification. *Quality modifications* are changes that relate to a product's dependability and durability. Changes that affect a product's versatility, effectiveness, convenience or safety are called *functional modifications*. *Style modifications* change the sensory appeal of a product.

● *Product modification* involves changing one or more characteristics of a firm's product. This approach to altering a product mix can be effective when the product is modifiable, when customers can perceive the change and when customers want the modification. *Quality modifications* are changes that relate to a product's dependability and durability. Changes that affect a product's versatility, effectiveness, convenience or safety are called *functional modifications*. *Style modifications* change the sensory appeal or a product.

● A product that is declining may be maintained as long as it makes a contribution to profits or enhances the product mix. Marketers must determine whether to eliminate the declining product or to re-position it to extend its life.

● *Product deletion* is the process of eliminating a product that is unprofitable, consumes too many resources and no longer satisfies a sufficient number of customers. A product may be *phased out, run out* or *dropped immediately*. A product mix should be systematically reviewed to determine when to delete products.

●●●●●●●●●●●●●●●●●●●

Important Terms

Product manager
Brand manager
Marketing manager
Venture or project team
New product development
Idea generation
Screening ideas
Business analysis

Product development
Test marketing
Commercialisation
Product adoption process
Exclusive distribution
Selective distribution
Intensive distribution
Product modification

Quality modifications
Functional modifications
Style modifications
Product deletion
Phase out
Run out
Immediate drop

Discussion and Review Questions

1. What organisational alternatives are available to a firm with two product lines, each consisting of four product items?
2. When is it more appropriate to use a product manager than a marketing manager? When might an alternative or combined approach be used?
3. What type of organisation might use a venture team to develop new products? What are the advantages and disadvantages of such a team?
4. Do small companies that manufacture one or two products need to be concerned about developing and managing products? Why or why not?
5. Why is product development a cross-functional activity within an organisation? That is, why must finance, engineering, manufacturing and other functional areas be involved?
6. Develop information sources for new product ideas for the car industry.
7. What are the advantages and disadvantages of test marketing?
8. Compare and contrast three ways of modifying a product.
9. What are the stages of the product adoption process, and how do they affect the commercialisation phase?
10. How can a company prolong the life of a mature product? What actions should be taken to try to stem the product's decline?
11. Give several reasons why an organisation might be unable to eliminate an unprofitable product.

Recommended Readings

P. Doyle, "Product life cycle management", in *Companion Encyclopaedia of Marketing*, M. J. Baker, ed. (London: Routledge, 1995).

S. Majaro, "Product planning", in *Gower Handbook of Marketing*, 4th edn, M. J. Thomas, ed. (Aldershot: Gower Press, 1995).

M. J. Thomas, "Product development and management", in *The Marketing Book*, 3rd edn, M. J. Baker, ed. (Oxford: Butterworth-Heinemann, 1994).

C. Macrae, *The Brand Chartering Handbook*, (London: EIU and Addison-Wesley, 1996).

L. de Chernatony and M. H. B. McDonald, *Creating Powerful Brands* (Oxford: Butterworth-Heinemann, 1992).

Cases

10.1 New Product Development and the Concept Car

Car manufacturers are well used to the stresses associated with new product development. The costs and difficulties of the process must be vigorously tackled by companies wishing to generate high sales and remain in the forefront of technological development. In spite of recessionary pressures and falling car sales, the industry is investing in the future with a host of new and revised model designs. The year 1997 witnesses the introduction of the new Renault Clio, VW baby Polo, Fiat Marea, new VW Passat, BMW Z3, Ford Puma (Fiesta coupé), Mercedes-Benz CLK coupé, Toyota MR2, Volvo 850 coupé, Ford Explorer off-roader, Vauxhall Sintra MPV and Daewoo's Mondeo challenger the J100, to mention a few. Even those manufacturers not launching new models in the near future are seeking to improve and upgrade their existing portfolios.

For many manufacturers, developing so called concept cars is an important part of the new product development process, which helps new techniques, technologies, materials and production processes to be tested and evaluated. Renault's striking model, the Racoon, described by the company as a "freedom car of tomorrow", is just one example of the concept cars that appear at motor shows around the world. The four wheel drive vehicle is amphibious, has a telephone, fax machine and computer based navigation aids, and was designed using revolutionary product development techniques. Although the vehicle may look unusual to today's consumers, precedents show that today's concept cars do sometimes appear in showrooms in the future. The "ladybird" shaped Ford Ghia Saetta is either Ford's most extravagant test car camouflage ever, or a wacky roadster concept car—or both. According to *Autocar's* Peter Robinson, the Saetta is basically a two-seater version of Ford's new £7,000 city car, the Ka. The Saetta roadster concept car enables Ford to show buyers and management what is possible.

When it was introduced at the Geneva motor show, the Aston Martin Lagonda Vignale created quite a sensation. However, despite the high performance, excellent standards of accommodation and obvious good looks of the model, this too is a concept car. The company's reason for developing the Vignale was to test the future potential for producing hand-built cars by investigating a range of design and production techniques and materials. According to Aston Martin's Lagonda chief executive, Walter Haynes, "There is a place for the hand-made luxury car in the future but it has to be fuel efficient and innovative and capable of being a car for life". While the company does not intend to begin commercial production of the Vignale, the development of the car is considered to have been very beneficial to the company's plans for new product development.

Aston Martin is not alone in trying to predict the changes that the twenty-first century will bring. According to the UK Motor Industry Research Association (MIRA), a move towards electrically powered vehicles is likely. It is estimated that by 2010 there may be over 10 million electric cars worldwide, with annual sales running as high as 2 million. The growth seems likely, given increasing concerns about the harmful impact of petrol driven vehicles on the environment. If European companies are to maintain their stake in car production, inevitably they must direct more attention towards developing low emission, electrical vehicle technology. Such programmes will no doubt be accompanied by the development of further concept cars, vehicle trials and long run testing.

Already, the Japanese government is doing much to encourage the development of such technology. So far there has been less activity in Europe, where only the French government displays a similar degree of commitment. According to MIRA's head of automotive services, Dr. Martin White, "People believe the well publicised problems of pollution in Los Angeles are unique to that city and its suburbs sitting as they do in a geographic bowl. But even our own inner-city areas, with their tower blocks and poor air circulation, can suffer the consequences of a similar and relatively effective pollution trap".

Whatever developments the future may bring for car manufacturing, the use of product and concept testing will continue to play an important role in the changing face of car design.

SOURCES: Stewart Smith, "Peugeot keeps it in the family", Telegraph Motoring, *Coventry Evening Telegraph,* 16 March 1993, p. 23; "Face of the future", Telegraph Motoring, *Coventry Evening Telegraph,* 16 March 1993, p. 24; "Luxurious Lagonda", Fast Lane 93, *Coventry Evening Telegraph,* February 1993, p. 11; "The shape of things to come", Fast Lane 93, *Coventry Evening Telegraph,* February 1993, p. 11; *What Car?* magazine, 1996, 1997; Peter Robinson, "Saetta shows how far Ka can go", *Autocar,* 22 May 1996, pp. 26–29.

Questions for Discussion

1. Why is it important for car manufacturers to develop concept cars?
2. What other forms of research and testing are relevant to the launch of a new model?
3. How can consumers' views of concept cars displayed at motor shows feed into the new product development process for production cars?

10.2 Soft Drinks Wars Continue As Tango Marches On

For decades the "cola wars" have been making headlines in the marketing press. The battle between Coca-Cola and Pepsi is long established, with escalating marketing budgets fuelling the campaign for market share. The recent multi-million spend by Pepsi on re-launching its products in blue livery is the latest stage in the battle. In the last few years the entry of a host of so called copy-cat rivals has intensified the war. Canadian cola manufacturer Cott, responsible for some of the key copy-cat brands, has become a significant player in the rivalry. Through its links with Virgin, Sainsbury's and Woolworths, the manufacturer has played a key role in offering the consumer a new choice of good quality and keenly priced colas. Virgin's deal with retailer Tesco gives new Virgin Cola access to around 10 per cent of UK grocery buyers, while Cott's links with Sainsbury's and Woolworths extend the availability of Cott products much further.

Now there is a new battle in the soft drinks market, this time in the fruit drinks sector. The impetus for this fight comes from Britvic's plans to spend £124 million over the next five years re-launching Tango. In a move code named "Operation Breakthrough" Britvic has ambitious plans for the brand, which was originally launched in 1981 and achieved sales of 199 million litres in 1995. Currently available only in the UK, Ireland, Germany, the Netherlands and Hungary, the massive investment may signal the first step in the global launch of the brand. Certainly the company hopes to increase sales to around 688 million litres by the year 2001.

Britvic has already proved its marketing expertise where Tango is concerned. In 1992 the company successfully re-launched orange Tango in a black can, with the award winning "You've been Tangoed" campaign. However, the success of the orange flavoured drink (drunk by 23 per cent of the population) has tended to overshadow subsequent launches of apple, lemon and blackcurrant variants,

enjoyed by only between 5 and 9 per cent of consumers. Now Britvic sees revitalising the whole range as an opportunity to increase penetration figures. The company will try to achieve this by "re-engineering" the brand and giving each flavour its own packaging theme and distinctive identity. While the background black coloration currently seen on Tango cans and bottles will be continued, this will be combined with a green lips motif for its apple flavour, a wild spattering of lemon drops for the lemon version, blackcurrants crackling in electricity for the blackcurrant flavour and an orange explosion for the original Tango. The themes for the packaging design come from recent and planned advertising campaigns. Diet versions of the drinks will appear in silver cans with the same motifs. When the new cans appear on supermarket shelves, they will be accompanied by point-of-sale displays using the slogan "Ignore them. They're just trying to get attention".

As a first step in its massive marketing campaign, Britvic has run a series of "Euphoria" television advertisements that have already created a stir in advertising circles. The underlying concept of the campaign is the worshipping of lemons in the cult of "Jim". This idea, which is carried through a number of advertisements, builds on the product values of refreshment and the taste explosion. As a result of the advertisements 80,000 consumers have telephoned the hotline featured to ask to join the make-believe cult. Campaigns for Still Tango and the Apple and Blackcurrant Tangos are also scheduled.

Tango's Build-Up Schedule	Fizzy Orange Volume Share	
Lemon Tango ("Euphoria" TV ads) February–March 1996	Tango (Britvic)	39.0%
	Sunkist (CCSB)	16.7%
Still Tango ("Pants" refreshment ads) April 1996	Other	14.6%
Apple Tango ('Seduction' ads, calendar and sampling) May–June 1996	Own label	15.5%
	Orangina (Orangina)	8.2%
Re-engineering (new packaging enters shops) July 1996	Fanta (CCSB)	6.0%
Blackcurrant Tango (TV work) Autumn 1996		
Lemon Tango (new TV work) late 1996		

NOTE: In the total fruit market, the overall share for Tango is around 20 per cent, according to Nielsen.

SOURCE: Sharon Marshall, "Be fruitful, and multiply", *Marketing*, 16 May 1996, p. 12. Reproduced by permission.

Competition for the fruit sector of the soft drinks market is intense. Existing incumbents such as Sunkist, 7-Up, Sprite, Dr Pepper, Fanta and Orangina are already battling with a host of own label brands. In this sector, as for cola, the range and quality of these own label offerings are increasing. In addition, consumers are faced with an array of new products including Fruitopia, Virgin Lips, Oasis and Mountain Dew. In such a confusing arena, Britvic's brand building efforts will need to be powerful. The evidence so far is encouraging: consumer response to earlier Tango campaigns, which make heavy use of comedy, has been excellent. In addition to the Lemon Tango advertisement success, 300,000 consumers requested plastic orange dolls, while two and a half million telephoned the Apple Tango "help" line. Yet despite its successes with Orange Tango, it remains to be seen whether Britvic can genuinely develop the identity of the apple, lemon and blackcurrant variants to the same level.

Furthermore, success away from its existing markets will depend on the degree to which the Tango sense of humour can transcend the cultural divide.

SOURCES: "The marketing story: CopyCotting catches on", *Marketing,* 20 October 1996, p. 17; Paul Cowan, "Campaign of the week: Lemon Tango", *Marketing,* 7 March 1996, p. 8; Sharon Marshall, "Tango's £124m for global goal", *Marketing,* 16 May 1996, p. 1; Sharon Marshall, "Be fruitful, and multiply", *Marketing,* 16 May 1996, p. 12.

Questions for Discussion

1. At what stages in their product life cycle are the different Tango products, and what are the management implications?
2. Why has it been necessary for Britvic to re-launch its Tango range?
3. How might product modification help Britvic to develop its competitive position in this market?

THE MARKETING OF SERVICES

OBJECTIVES

- To understand the nature and characteristics of services
- To classify services
- To understand the development of strategies for services
- To understand the problems involved in developing a competitive advantage in services
- To explore the concept of marketing services in non-business situations
- To understand the development of service strategies in non-business organisations
- To describe methods for controlling non-business service activities

In the early 1990s, Gatwick Airport, situated 27 miles south of London, found itself in an unhappy situation. Passenger traffic was declining, most Gatwick based airlines were not profitable and the airport was operating at well below optimum levels of business. Meanwhile, neighbouring Heathrow was facing congestion due to lack of space. The main reason for Gatwick's problems was that business travellers perceived it as a "charter only" leisure airport, subject to associated delays and congestion. As a result, airlines' passenger yields were low owing to a lack of first and business class passengers. While Heathrow was seen by travellers to be the "main" airport and Stanstead the newest and most modern, Gatwick had become the "anonymous" London airport, without a clear market position.

Owner BAA established the Airport Marketing Department specifically to determine a marketing strategy for Gatwick Airport. The department's aims were to (1) know and understand customers' needs, (2) identify and build on the organisation's strengths, (3) address weaknesses and (4) develop an innovative "product" offering for the 1990s.

Marketing research established that while not many major airlines used Gatwick for scheduled services—because of its distance from London's centre—once fliers had in fact used and experienced the airport, they preferred it to nearby rivals. UK travel agents were not used to pushing Gatwick to their clients. UK business travellers associated Gatwick with crowds, delays and clowns vainly trying to entertain bored children due to long delayed charter flights. Non-UK passengers did not even know about Gatwick, associating London only with Heathrow.

The new strategy to re-position Gatwick as a business airport commenced in 1993. The *Fast Track* brand was developed in response to business fliers' wishes: a quick, clear route through the airport, with no queues, bespoke security desks and no early arrival for check-in, thus putting busy travellers in control of their own time. This "we save you time" positioning was promoted through advertising posters, direct mail and public rela-tions to business fliers and the corporate travel agencies that arrange so much of business travel. This use of marketing to develop a service provider's business has certainly been fruitful for Gatwick. More business users are flying from Gatwick; a greater proportion now claim to prefer Gatwick than before the re-positioning exercise, so customer satisfaction is rapidly increasing; the airport's image as a location for charters is declining; and more airlines are seeking to offer scheduled mainstream routes using Gatwick. In 1996, readers of the *Travel Trade Gazette* voted Gatwick the best UK airport. The role of the airport's personnel has not been over looked; the marketing team encourages all employees—be they porters, clerks, security officers, cleaners, shop workers, courtesy bus drivers or managers—to remember that their performance is integral to the service and satisfaction experienced by users of this busy airport. ■

SOURCES: Adam Watson, Marketing Development Manager, Gatwick Airport Ltd; *Travel Trade Gazette*; BAA plc.

This chapter presents concepts that apply specifically to the marketing of services. Services marketing involves marketing in non-profit organisations such as education, health care, charities and government, as well as for profit areas such as entertainment, tourism, finance, personal services and professional services. As detailed in the chapter opener, BAA, owner of Gatwick Airport, has deployed marketing to considerable effect to enhance the image of its facility and to boost customer satisfaction.

The chapter first focuses on the growing importance of service industries in the economy. Second, it addresses the unique characteristics of services and the problems they present to marketers. Third, it presents various classification schemes that can help service marketers develop marketing strategies. In addition, it discusses a variety of marketing mix considerations, along with the associated problems of creating and sustaining a differential advantage (competitive edge). Finally, the chapter defines non-business marketing and examines the development of non-business marketing strategies and the control of non-business marketing activities.

The Nature and Characteristics of Services

Service An intangible product involving a deed, performance or effort that cannot be physically possessed

As mentioned in Chapter 8, all products—goods, services and ideas—possess a certain amount of intangibility. A **service** is an intangible product involving a deed, a performance or an effort that cannot be physically possessed.[1] It should be noted that few products can be classified as a pure good or a pure service. Consider, for example, a car. When consumers purchase a car, they take owner-

Figure 11.1 A continuum of product tangibility and intangibility

ship of a physical item that provides transport, but the warranty associated with the purchase is a service. When the car is returned to the dealer for routine maintenance, the dealer is providing a service. When consumers hire a car, they purchase a transport service that is provided through temporary use of a car. Most products, such as cars and car hire, contain both tangible and intangible components. One component, however, will dominate, and it is this dominant component that leads to the classification of goods, services and ideas.

Figure 11.1 illustrates the tangibility concept by placing a variety of "products" on a continuum of tangibility and intangibility. Tangible dominant products are typically classified as goods, and intangible dominant products are typically considered services. An airline seat or hotel bed may be tangible and physical, but the airline or hotel operator is in fact providing a service: transportation or temporary accommodation. Thus, as defined in Chapter 8, services are intangible dominant products that involve the application of human and mechanical efforts to people or objects.

Growth and Importance of Services

In the United States, the increasing importance of services in the economy has led many people to call the country the world's first service economy. Service industries—encompassing trade, communications, transport, food and lodging, financial and medical services, education, government and technical services—account for about 60 per cent of the US national income and three quarters of the non-farm jobs in the United States. In the UK and in Europe, the service sector is now just as important (see Tables 11.1 and 11.2), employing 67 per cent of the workforce in the UK and 61 per cent in the rest of the European Union. There are services intended for consumers—**consumer services**—and those designed to satisfy businesses—**business services**.

One major catalyst of the growth in consumer services has been general economic prosperity, which has led to an increase in financial services, travel, entertainment and personal care, with more mundane activities contracted out. Lifestyle changes have similarly encouraged expansion of the service sector. Smaller families result in more free time and relatively higher disposable income. A widespread desire for self-fulfillment—experience rather than ownership—leads consumers to "buy in" outside services. In the past 40 years, the number of women in the workforce has more than doubled. Consumers want to avoid tasks such as meal preparation, house cleaning, home maintenance and preparation of tax returns. Furthermore, Europeans have become more fitness and recreation orientated, and with greater leisure time, the demand for fitness and recreational facilities has escalated. In terms of demographics, the population is growing older, and this change has promoted tremendous expansion of health care services. Finally, the number and complexity of goods needing servicing have spurred demand for repair services.

Not only have consumer services grown in the economy, business services have prospered as well. Business or industrial services include repairs and maintenance,

Consumer services Services such as house cleaning, home maintenance, preparation of tax returns and other services to help consumers

Business services Services such as repairs and maintenance, consulting and professional advice, installation, equipment leasing, marketing research, advertising, temporary office personnel and caretaking services

Standard Industrial Classification, 1980	June 1971		March 1995	
	'000s	%	'000s	%
Agriculture, forestry and fishing	421	1.9	244	1.2
Coal, oil and natural gas extraction and processing	400	1.8	73	0.3
Electricity, gas, other energy and water supply	390	1.8	212	1.0
Manufacturing industries	7,890	36.4	4,282	20.3
Construction	1,159	5.4	850	4.0
Wholesale, distribution and repairs	972	4.5	1,087	5.1
Retail distribution	1,954	9.0	2,299	10.9
Hotels and catering	687	3.2	1,236	5.9
Transport	1,096	5.1	849	4.0
Postal services and telecommunications	436	2.0	337	1.6
Banking, insurance, finance	1,318	6.1	2,756	13.0
Public administration, etc.	1,730	8.0	1,738	8.2
Education	1,272	5.9	1,830	8.7
Medical and other services, veterinary services	943	4.4	1,555	7.4
Other services	978	4.5	1,778	8.4
All employees in employment	21,648	100.0	21,122	100.0

NOTE: *Adjusted for seasonal variation.

SOURCE: *Employment Gazette* Historical Supplement No. 3, June 1992, and *Employment Gazette*, August 1995, Table 1.2 in both issues (published by HMSO). Please see this source for definitions and footnotes.

Table 11.1 Analysis by industry of employees in employment*—Great Britain

consulting and professional advice, installation, equipment leasing, marketing research, advertising, temporary office personnel and caretaking services. Expenditures for business and industrial services have risen even faster than expenditures for consumer services. This growth has been attributed to the increasingly complex, specialised and competitive business environment. Large retailers such as IKEA or Marks & Spencer are successfully incorporating additional services into their retail stores. Providing additional services at one location is an excellent way to satisfy and keep customers who need and want more and more services. Burton Group operates its traditional department stores (Debenhams) but in addition offers optical services, financial services and so on. If customers enter a store for one service, they are more likely to shop at the store again or try another service that the retailer provides.[2]

For non-consumer services there are three key reasons behind the growth of business-to-business services:

- *Specialisation*—the delegation of non-care tasks such as advertising, executive recruitment and car fleet management.
- *Technology*—the increase in sophistication leading to the "buying in" of expert knowledge and skills such as IT computing consultants.
- *Flexibility*—the need in many organisations to avoid fixed overhead costs. Marketing research, maintenance and cleaning are frequently brought in only on an ad hoc basis.

	Agriculture		Industry		Services		Total	
	1,000	%	1,000	%	1,000	%	1,000	%
EU	8,705	5.8	48,718	32.6	92,205	61.6	149,628	100
Austria	250	7.1	1,261	35.5	2,036	57.4	3,547	100
Belgium	109	2.9	1,164	30.9	2,498	66.2	3,770	100
Denmark	136	5.2	715	27.2	1,780	67.7	2,637	100
Finland	187	8.6	602	27.7	1,382	63.7	2,171	100
France	1,301	5.9	6,497	29.6	14,187	64.5	22,021	100
Germany	1,368	3.7	14,273	39.1	20,887	57.2	36,528	100
Greece	804	21.9	933	25.4	1,942	52.8	3,680	100
Ireland	157	13.7	322	28.1	667	58.2	1,149	100
Italy	1,657	7.9	6,962	33.1	12,396	59.0	21,015	100
Luxembourg	5	3.3	47	29.5	107	67.1	165	100
Netherlands	247	3.9	1,571	24.9	4,503	71.2	6,614	100
Portugal	517	11.5	1,468	32.6	2,523	56.0	4,509	100
Spain	1,257	10.1	4,075	32.7	7,126	57.2	12,458	100
Sweden	140	3.3	1,112	26.5	2,935	69.9	4,195	100
UK	569	2.2	7,715	30.2	17,237	67.5	25,630	100

SOURCE: Eurostat, 1996.

Table 11.2 Share of economic sectors in employment in 1992

Characteristics of Services

Intangibility An inherent quality of services that are performed and therefore cannot be tasted, touched, seen, smelled or possessed

Search qualities The tangible attributes of a service that can be viewed prior to purchase

Experience qualities Attributes that can be assessed only after purchase and consumption, including satisfaction, courtesy and the like

Credence qualities Attributes that cannot be assessed even after purchase and consumption

The problems of the marketing of services are distinct from those of goods marketing.[3] To understand them, it is first necessary to understand the distinguishing characteristics of services. Services have four basic characteristics: (1) intangibility, (2) inseparability of production and consumption, (3) perishability and (4) heterogeneity.[4] Table 11.3 summarises these characteristics and the marketing problems they entail.

Intangibility stems from the fact that services are performances. They cannot be seen, touched, tasted or smelled; nor can they be possessed. Intangibility also relates to the difficulty that consumers may have in understanding service offerings.[5] Services have a few tangible attributes, called **search qualities,** that can be viewed prior to purchase. When consumers cannot view a product in advance and examine its properties, they may not understand exactly what is being offered. Even when consumers do gain sufficient knowledge about service offerings, they may not be able to evaluate the possible choices. On the other hand, services are rich in experience and credence qualities. **Experience qualities** are those qualities that can be assessed only after purchase and consumption (satisfaction, courtesy and the like). **Credence qualities** are those qualities that cannot be assessed even after purchase and consumption.[6] An appendix operation is an example of a service that is high in credence qualities. How many consumers are knowledgeable enough to assess the quality of an appendectomy, even after the surgery has been performed?

A Volvo car can be test driven before being purchased. It can be viewed in the dealer's showroom and on the streets. It can—to an extent—be consumed prior

Unique Service Features	Resulting Marketing Problems
Intangibility	Cannot be stored
	Cannot be protected through patents
	Cannot be readily displayed or communicated
	Prices difficult to set
Inseparability	Consumer involved in production
	Other consumers involved in production
	Centralised mass production difficult
Perishability	Services unable to be stock-piled
Heterogeneity	Standardisation and quality difficult to control

SOURCE: Valarie A. Zeithaml, A. Parasuraman and Leonard L. Berry, "Problems and strategies in services marketing", *Journal of Marketing*, Spring 1985, pp. 33–46. Used by permission of the American Marketing Association.

Table 11.3 Service characteristics and marketing problems

to the risk taking purchase. The same is not true of a meal in a top restaurant or a theatre seat. The meal may be disappointing, as may the play, but by the time the disappointment is recognised it is too late; the service has been—at least partially—consumed and paid for.

Related to intangibility, therefore, is **inseparability** of production and consumption. Services are normally produced at the same time they are consumed. A medical examination is an example of simultaneous production and consumption. In fact, the doctor cannot possibly perform the service without the patient's presence, and the consumer is actually involved in the production process. Dining out in a restaurant is a similar example. With other services, such as air travel, many consumers are simultaneously involved in production. Because of *high consumer involvement* in most services, standardisation and control are difficult to maintain. Marketing Insight 11.1 (on page 318) illustrates how Dutch banking giant ABN AMRO addresses this difficulty.

Because production and consumption are simultaneous, services are also characterised by **perishability**. The consumer of a service generally has to be present and directly involved in the consumption of the service at the time of its production. In other words, unused capacity in one time period cannot be stockpiled or inventoried for future time periods. Consider the airlines' seating capacity dilemma. Each carrier maintains a sophisticated reservations system to juggle ticket prices and ensure maximum revenues for every flight. This attempt to maximise profit on each flight has led to over booking, which means that airlines may sell tickets for more seats than are available so as to compensate for "no shows"— people who have made reservations but do not actually take that particular flight. The airlines' dilemma illustrates how service perishability presents problems very different from the supply and demand problems encountered in the marketing of goods.[7] Unoccupied seats on an airline flight cannot be stored for use on another flight that is booked to capacity. Hotel operators offer bargain breaks—discount deals—to fill under utilised capacity in slack periods; an empty room one night is a sale lost for ever. In contrast, cans of soup remaining on the supermarket shelf

Inseparability In relation to production and consumption, a characteristic of services that means they are produced at the same time as they are consumed

Perishability A characteristic of services whereby unused capacity on one occasion cannot be stock-piled or inventoried for future occasions or a Volvo car left unsold in a dealer's showroom at the close of business will be available for sale the following day.

Finally, because most services are labour intensive, they are susceptible to **heterogeneity.** For the service to be provided and consumed, the client generally meets and deals directly with the service provider's personnel: *direct contact* and *interaction*. People typically perform services, and people do not always perform consistently. There may be variation from one service to another within the same organisation or variation in the service that a single individual provides from day to day and from customer to customer. A good branch manager is crucial for a company such as Pizza Hut. Poor customer reaction and branch performance can often be traced back to a poor branch manager.[8] Queuing times in McDonald's can vary greatly, often due to teamwork, speed and efficiency variations between branches. A hotel general manager has a significant impact on the attitude of the hotel's staff and thus on the running of the hotel. There may be a considerable variation in guest satisfaction, therefore, between one Hilton and another. Thus standardisation and quality are extremely difficult to control. But this fact may also lead to customising services to meet consumers' specific needs. Because of these factors, service marketers often face a dilemma: how to provide efficient, standardised service at some acceptable level of quality while simultaneously treating each customer as a unique person. Giving "good service" is a major concern of all service organisations, and it is often translated into more personalised service.

Heterogeneity Variability in the quality of service because services are provided by people, and people perform inconsistently

● ● ● ● ● ● ● ● ● ● ● ● ● ● ● ● ● ●

Classification of Services

Services are a very diverse group of products, and an organisation may provide more than one kind. Examples of services include car hire, repairs, health care, hair dressers, health centres, child care, domestic services, legal advice, banking, insurance, air travel, education, entertainment, catering, business consulting, dry cleaning and accounting. Nevertheless, services can be meaningfully analysed by using a **five category classification** scheme: (1) type of market, (2) degree of labour intensiveness, (3) degree of customer contact, (4) skill of service provider and (5) goal of the service provider. Table 11.4 summarises this scheme.

Services can be viewed in terms of the market or type of customer they serve—consumer or industrial. The implications of this distinction are very similar to those for all products and therefore are not discussed here. In Figure 11.2, the National Exhibition Centre in Birmingham aims to attract conferences to Britain's "second city".

A second way to classify services is by degree of labour intensiveness. Many services, such as repairs, education and hair care, rely heavily on human labour. Other services, such as telecommunications, health farms/fitness centres and public transport, are more equipment intensive (although people are still integral).

Labour (people) based services are more susceptible to heterogeneity than are most equipment based services. Marketers of people based services must recognise that the service providers are often viewed as the service itself. Therefore, strategies relating to selecting, training, motivating and controlling employees are very important to the success of most service businesses. A bad attitude from counter staff in Barclays would colour the customer's view not just of the employee concerned but also of the company and all of its service products. A customer who

Five category classification A method of analysing services according to five criteria: type of market, degree of labour intensiveness, degree of customer contact, skill of service provider and goal of the service provider

Dutch Bankers Build Relationships—ABN AMRO Leads Through Services

The 1991 merger between Algemene Bank Nederland and Amsterdam-Rotterdam Bank to create Dutch based ABN AMRO Bank produced the dominant financial institution in the Netherlands, the seventh largest bank in Europe and one of the world's top 20. With branches throughout Benelux, and over 500 in 55 other countries, ABN AMRO deals daily with thousands of customers face to face or through telecommunications.

The company's policy is to buy relatively small banking operations around the globe and integrate them fully within its existing business. It does not seek mega-mergers with other large international banks. ABN AMRO North America has agreed to buy Chicago Corp: the business will be merged with ABN AMRO Securities Inc., resulting in the addition of 1,400 employees and a significant New York based operation destined for rapid growth. Hoare Govett has already been so integrated, creating the seventeenth largest insurance broker in the world. Nordic Alfred Berg is now also part of the network.

Significant alliances have been established in South East Asia, with China now seen to be an important market. The strategy is recognised as successful well beyond the banking fraternity; ABN has received many prestigious awards for the competitive success of its global operation.

To facilitate this growth, the bank is one of the world's leading spenders on information systems, maintaining that today's technology helps it to offer an efficient and reliable service to its most valuable asset—its customer base. Customers are kept to the fore through the company's policy of relationship management, a core strategy since 1980. The

bank targets only a small number of clients, who are subsequently handled by a large team of relationship managers.

Many consumers find banks' history and formal procedures intimidating and view them as powerful institutions with which they can enjoy little personal interaction. ABN AMRO has tackled this perception head-on, recognising that as fundamentally a service provider dealing with people, its success depends on the attitude and ability of the bank's own personnel. In this respect, ABN AMRO realises it must behave as a service provider and adopt the practices of services marketing.

ABN AMRO places significant emphasis on its employees, who are integral to its products, marketing and the services it provides. The bank's internal marketing focuses on training and motivating its staff worldwide to deliver a consistent, friendly, proficient and superior service to ABN AMRO's many customers. ABN AMRO acknowledges that it is only as good as its personnel—those people who to many customers epitomise the bank's products and services. Its human resource and marketing executives highlight these employees' skills in handling customer contact and delivering the bank's services.

Sources: "European 100", *Information Week,* 11 December 1995, pp. 32–41; Yvette Kantrow, "ABN AMRO/Chicago Corp will expand 'significantly' in N.Y.", *Investment Dealers' Digest,* 2 October 1995, pp. 8–9; "Jan Kalff, chairman, ABN AMRO", *Euromoney,* September 1995, p. 64; John Anderson et al., "The 1995 industry all stars", *Independent Energy,* September 1995, pp. 24–30; Matthew Ball, "ABN AMRO aims for 380 of the best", *Corporate Finance,* July 1995, p. 40; "Berg sale raises broking stakes", *Euroweek,* June 1995, p. 45; Caroline Farquhar; ABN AMRO annual report and accounts; Barclays de Zoete Wedd Securities; Credit Suisse First Boston; Financial Times Analysis; "Banking industry report", Salomon Brothers, April 1992; ABN AMRO Utrecht.

Category	Examples
Type of Market	
Consumer	Repairs, child care, legal advice
Industrial	Consulting, caretaking services, installation
Degree of Labour Intensiveness	
Labour based	Repairs, education, haircuts
Equipment based	Telecommunications, health farms, public transport
Degree of Customer Contact	
High	Health care, hotels, air travel
Low	Repairs, home deliveries, postal service
Skill of the Service Provider	
Professional	Legal advice, health care, accountancy
Non-professional	Domestic services, dry cleaning, public transport
Goal of the Service Provider	
Profit	Financial services, insurance, tourism
Non-profit	Health care, education, government

Table 11.4 Classification of services

has banked quite happily with Barclays for many years may be prompted to consider taking his or her business to a rival company because of one negative encounter with a clerk in a branch.

The third way in which services can be classified is by customer contact. High contact services include health care, hotels, estate agencies and restaurants; low contact services include repairs, theatres, dry cleaning and spectator sports.[9] Note that high contact services generally involve actions that are directed towards individuals. Because these services are directed at people, the consumer must be present during production. Although it is sometimes possible for the service provider to go to the consumer, high contact services typically require that the consumer goes to the production facility. Thus the physical appearance and ambience of the facility may be a major component of the consumer's overall evaluation of the service. The enjoyment of an evening out in a restaurant stems not just from the taste of the food but also from the decor and furnishings, general ambience, and the ability and attitude of the staff. Because the consumer must be present during production of a high contact service, the process of production may be just as important as its final outcome. For example, open plan banks and quick queue systems aim to improve the transaction process and make the service more enjoyable for the consumer.

Low contact service, in contrast, commonly involves actions directed at things. Consequently, the consumer is usually not required to be present during service delivery. The consumer's presence, however, may be required to initiate or terminate the service. The Post Office maintains a network of branches, sorting offices and vehicles. The process of sending a parcel from Cardiff to London or Lille is lengthy. Although they must be present to initiate the provision of the service,

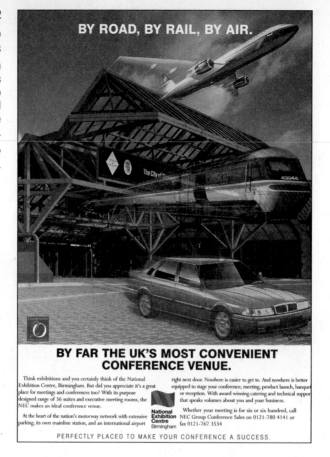

consumers need not be present during the process. The appearance of the production facilities and the interpersonal skills of actual service providers are thus not as critical in low contact services as they are in high contact services.[10]

Skill of the service provider is a fourth way to classify services. Professional services tend to be more complex and more highly regulated than non-professional services. In the case of legal advice, for example, consumers often do not know what the actual service will involve or how much it will cost until the service is completed, because the final product is very situation specific. Additionally, solicitors are regulated both by law and by professional associations.

Finally, services can be classified according to the goal of the service provider—profit or non-profit. The second half of this chapter examines non-business marketing, that is, marketing by not-for-profit organisations, such as the public sector and charities. Most non-business organisations provide services rather than goods.

● ● ● ● ● ● ● ● ● ● ● ● ● ● ● ● ● ● ●

Developing Marketing Strategies for Services

Strategic Considerations

In developing marketing strategies, the marketer must first understand what benefits the customer wants, how the company's service offer and brand are perceived relative to the competition and what services consumers buy.[11] In other words, the marketer must develop the right service for the right people at the right price, in the right place with the right positioning and image. The marketer must remember to communicate with consumers so that they are aware of the need satisfying services available to them. The key aspects of effective target marketing—as explained in Chapter 7—and of managing the implementation of the determined marketing strategy—as detailed in Chapters 21 and 24—apply very strongly to the marketing of services.

One of the unique challenges service marketers face is matching supply and demand. Price can be used to help smooth out demand for a service. There are other ways, too, in which marketers can alter the marketing mix to deal with the problem of fluctuating demand. Through price incentives, advertising and other promotional efforts, marketers can remind consumers of busy times and encourage them to come for service during slack periods. Additionally, the product itself can be altered to cope with fluctuating demand. Restaurants, for example, may change their menus, vary their lighting and decor, open or close the bar and add or delete entertainment. A ski resort may install an alpine slide to attract customers during the summer. Finally, distribution can be modified to reflect changes in demand. Theatres have traditionally offered matinées during the weekend, when demand is greater, and some libraries have mobile units that travel to different locations during slack periods.[12]

Before understanding such strategies, service marketers must first grasp the pattern and determinants of demand. Does the level of demand follow a cycle? What are the causes of this cycle? Are the changes random?[13] An attempt to use price decreases to shift demand for public transport to off-peak periods would most likely fail because of the cause of the cyclical demand for public transport: employment hours. Employees have little control over working hours and are therefore unable to take advantage of pricing incentives. Therefore, marketers of services must understand their customers' needs.

Table 11.5 summarises ways in which service firms may deal with the problem of fluctuating demand. Note that the strategies fall into two categories: marketing and non-marketing strategies. Non-marketing strategies essentially involve internal, employee related actions.[14] They may be the only available choices when fluctuations in demand are random. For example, a strike or natural disaster may cause fluctuations in consumer demand for public transport.

Creating a Differential Advantage in Services

Differential advantage
Something desired by the customer that only one company—not its rivals—can offer

The aim of marketing is to satisfy customers, achieving product or brand differentiation with an advantage over competitors' products. This **differential advantage**, sometimes termed a *competitive edge*, is determined by customers' perceptions. A differential advantage is something desired by the customer that only one company—not its rivals—can offer. If the targeted customers do not perceive an advantage, in marketing terms the product offers no benefit over rival products.

For any product, achieving—and sustaining—a differential advantage is difficult, but for services the challenge is even greater. The intangibility of the service product and the central role of people are the prime causes of this difficulty, but there are also others:

- Intangibility minimises product differentiation.
- No—or little—patent protection exists.
- Few barriers to entry enable competitors to set up and copy successful initiatives.

Marketing Strategies	Non-marketing Strategies
Use different pricing	Hire extra staff/lay off employees
Alter product	Work employees over time/part time
Change distribution	Cross-train employees
Use promotional efforts	Use employees to perform non-vital tasks during slack times
Modify customer service levels	Sub-contract work/seek sub-contract work
Alter branding and positioning	Slow the pace of work
	Turn away business

Table 11.5 Strategies for coping with fluctuations in demand for services

- The interface with customers is difficult to control.
- Growth is hard to achieve, particularly since key personnel can only be spread so far.
- Service quality is irregular.
- It is difficult to improve productivity and lower the cost to the consumer.
- Innovation leads to imitation.
- Restrictive regulations abound, particularly in the professions.

The difficulty encountered in creating a differential advantage in services underscores the importance of many of the fundamental steps in marketing. In services it is increasingly important for businesses to identify well defined target market segments in order to bring service products and the marketing mix into line with consumers' exact requirements, to evaluate competitors' service offerings and marketing programmes, and to research customers' satisfaction levels. Branding, supported with well constructed promotional campaigns, is even more central to the reinforcement and communication of any differential advantage for services.

The Extended Marketing Mix for Services

The standard marketing mix comprises the "4 Ps":

- Product
- Promotion
- Price
- Place (distribution)

The discussion about the classification of services has emphasised the importance of these additional elements:

- Process
- Physical evidence (ambience)
- People

Extended marketing mix for services In addition to the standard "4 Ps" marketing mix—product, promotion, price and place (distribution)—there are 3 Ps: process, physical evidence (ambience) and people

Collectively, these seven elements—the "7 Ps"—form what is termed the **extended marketing mix for services** (see Figure 11.3), which is discussed in detail in Chapter 21.

Figure 11.3

The extended marketing mix for services

Customer Satisfaction

It is essential to reiterate a major point: the marketing concept is equally applicable to goods, services and ideas. The marketing of services, like the marketing of goods, requires the identification of a viable target market segment; the development of a service concept that addresses consumers' needs within that segment; the creation and implementation of an operating strategy that will adequately support the service concept; and the design of a service delivery system that will support the chosen operating strategy.[15]

Table 11.6 illustrates the approaches that marketers of services can take to achieve consumer satisfaction. A basic requirement of any marketing strategy, however, is a development phase, which includes defining target markets and finalising a marketing mix. The following seven preconditions need to be considered when developing a service marketing strategy:

1. Make sure that marketing occurs at all levels, from the marketing department to the point where the service is provided.
2. Allow flexibility in providing the service—when there is direct interaction with the customers, customise the service to their wants and needs.
3. Hire and maintain high quality personnel and market the organisation or service to them; often it is the people in a service organisation who differentiate the organisation from competitors.
4. Consider marketing to existing customers to increase their use of the service or to create loyalty to the service provider.
5. Quickly resolve any problems in providing the service, to avoid damaging the firm's reputation for quality.
6. Use high technology to provide improved services at a lower cost. Continually evaluate how to customise the service to each consumer's unique needs.
7. Brand the service to distinguish it from that of the competition. For example, instead of simply seeking a pest controller, a customer would seek assistance from Rentokil because of Rentokil's name recognition.[16]

Service Industry	Outcome Sought By Buyer	Technical Possibilities	Strategic Possibilities
Higher education	Educational attainment	Help lecturers to be effective teachers; offer tutoring	Admit better prepared students (or, for a fee, give them better preparation before entry)
Hospitals	Health	Instruct patients in how to manage their current problems and prevent others	Market preventive medicine services (weight loss, stress reduction and so on)
Banks	Prosperity	Offer money management courses; provide management assistance to small businesses	Market financial expertise, probably by industry specialisation
Plumbing repairs	Free flowing pipes	Provide consumers with instructions and supplies to prevent further blockages	Diversity (for example, point-of-use water purification system)

SOURCE: Adapted from Betsy D. Gelb, "How marketers of intangibles can raise the odds for consumer satisfaction", *Journal of Services Marketing*, Summer 1987, p. 15. Reprinted by permission of the publisher.

Table 11.6 Examples of approaches to consumer satisfaction for marketers of services

• • • • • • • • • • • • • • • • • • •

Non-business Marketing

Marketing was broadly defined earlier as a set of individual and organisational activities aimed at facilitating and expediting satisfying exchanges in a dynamic environment through the creation, distribution, promotion and pricing of goods, services and ideas. Most of the previously discussed concepts and approaches to managing marketing activities also apply to non-business situations such as the public sector and charities. Of special relevance is the material offered in the first half of this chapter, because many non-business organisations provide services. As a discipline, marketing is becoming increasingly important in the non-business sector, as illustrated in Marketing Insight 11.2, which looks at marketing in charities.

Non-business marketing includes marketing activities conducted by individuals and organisations to achieve some goal other than ordinary business goals of profit, market share or return on investment. Non-business marketing can be divided into two categories: non-profit organisation marketing and social marketing. Non-profit organisation marketing is the application of marketing concepts and techniques to organisations such as hospitals and colleges. Social marketing is the development of programmes designed to influence the acceptability of social ideas, such as contributing to a foundation for AIDS research or getting people to recycle more newspapers, plastics and aluminum.[17]

As discussed in Chapter 1, an exchange situation exists when individuals, groups or organisations possess something that they are willing to give up in an

Non-business marketing
Activities conducted by individuals and organisations to achieve some goal other than ordinary business goals of profit, market share or return on investment

exchange. In non-business marketing, the objects of the exchange may not be specified in financial terms. Usually, such exchanges are facilitated through **negotiation** (mutual discussion or communication of terms and methods) and **persuasion** (convincing and prevailing upon by argument). Often negotiation and persuasion are conducted without reference to or awareness of the role that marketing plays in transactions. The discussion here concerns non-business performance of marketing activities, whether the exchange is consummated or not.

The rest of this chapter first examines the concept of non-business marketing to determine how it differs from marketing activities in business organisations. Next it explores the overall objectives of non-business organisations, their marketing objectives and the development of their marketing strategies. The discussion closes by illustrating how an audit of marketing activities can promote marketing awareness in a non-business organisation.

Why Is Non-business Marketing Different?

Traditionally and mistakenly, people have not thought of non-business exchange activities as marketing. But consider the following example. Warwick Business School used to promote its degree courses solely through the University of Warwick's prospectuses. In the early 1980s, its main programmes received small advertising budgets. As courses were improved, the wider use of advertising increased awareness of the school and its programmes. A new corporate identity was developed by Coley Porter Bell of London, and each programme, led by the MBA, developed its own full marketing mix and more extensive promotional strategy—all in line with the school's new mission statement. Many university departments and state maintained schools are now engaging in marketing strategy.

Many non-business organisations strive for effective marketing activities. Charitable organisations and supporters of social causes are major non-business marketers. Political parties, unions, religious groups and student organisations also perform marketing activities, yet they are not considered businesses. Whereas the chief beneficiary of a business enterprise is whoever owns or holds shares in it, in theory the only beneficiaries of a non-business organisation are its clients, its members or the public at large.

Non-businesses have a greater opportunity for creativity than most business organisations, but trustees or board members of non-businesses are likely to have trouble judging performance when services can be provided only by trained professionals. It is harder for administrators to evaluate the performance of doctors, lecturers or social workers than it is for sales managers to evaluate the performance of salespeople in a for-profit organisation.

Another way in which non-business marketing differs from for-profit marketing is that non-business organisations are sometimes quite controversial. Greenpeace, CND and Shelter spend lavishly on lobbying efforts to persuade government and even the courts to support their interests, in part because acceptance of their aims is not always guaranteed. However, marketing as a field of study does not attempt to define an organisation's goals or debate the issue of non-business versus business goals. Marketing attempts only to provide a body of knowledge to further an organisation's goals. Individuals must decide whether they approve of an organisation's goal orientation. Most marketers would agree that profit and consumer satisfaction are appropriate goals for business enterprises, but there probably would be considerable disagreement about the goals of a controversial non-business organisation.

Marketing Charities

Many people see marketing as a selling or advertising activity undertaken by companies such as Ford, McDonald's or Kodak. While such commercial organisations seek high returns and profits, charities seek to increase their revenues to fund their laudable causes. During the past five or ten years, many leading charities and fund raising bodies have appointed marketing managers, strategists and professional public relations executives. While there is a cost to bear for recruiting such marketers, the extra revenue attracted through their efforts is expected to more than justify the additional expense.

At the NEC Marketing Show, one of the most prominent stands promotes the animal welfare charity, the RSPCA. The aim is not to persuade visitors to this exhibition to make donations. Instead the display and supporting brochure illustrate the charity's numerous joint promotional campaigns with leading household brands. The manufacturers have promoted the RSPCA on their brands' packaging and in their advertising, gaining a more "caring" image in return. In addition to exposure, the RSPCA receives a donation from these manufacturers for each item purchased during the promotion.

The RSPCA is not alone in discovering marketing. A hard hitting Christmas appeal for the leading children's charity, the NSPCC—which included one of the most successful TV charity adverts, "Ellie"—was awarded the gold award in the Direct Marketing Association's Streamline awards. Television was also selected by the Royal National Lifeboat Institution (RNLI), the UK's third largest charity, for a direct response campaign. The advertising was scheduled to coincide with a six week documentary series about the RNLI and was supported with a direct mail drop to half a million

homes. The promotional activity was part of a carefully orchestrated strategy to broaden the charity's donor base. As the recession bites, charities have had to compete more aggressively for consumers' disposable income. St. John's Ambulance increased its use of direct mail campaigns in an attempt to enlarge its 15,000 strong database of regular donors. The accuracy of the mail shots was improved through the profiling of existing donors' lifestyles and geodemographic characteristics by research specialists CACI and NDL.

The World Wide Fund for Nature (WWF) is going further. In the aftermath of the Earth Summit in Rio de Janeiro, the WWF recruited a UK marketing campaigns director. The intention was to develop a more coherent marketing planning and strategy function using innovative and high profile fund raising activities instead of relying on the direct mail method traditionally used by charities. With operations in 28 countries, the WWF has achieved a significant increase in income through enhanced marketing and better image building—from £5 million per annum in the mid-1980s to £22 million.

The launch of the National Lottery has repeatedly hit donations to charities as consumers save their money for a stake to win a fortune. The growing band of professional marketers in the leading charities now have an even more pressing need to increase their organisations' revenues.

SOURCES: Oxfam; RSPCA; Daz Valladares, "Charities find relief in targeted advertising", *Marketing Week,* 27 November 1992, p. 16; Ken Gofton, "NSPCC wins DMA prize", *Marketing,* 17 December 1992, p. 4; Paul Meller, "Amherst picks up St. John's account", *Marketing,* 26 November 1992, p. 8; "RNLI takes plunge with TV ad move", *Marketing,* 19 November 1992, p. 14; "Charities face shortage of marketers", *Marketing Week,* 29 January 1993, p. 8; "RSPCA Christmas ads help recession hit pets", *Marketing Week,* 27 November 1992, p. 8.

Non-business Marketing Objectives

The basic aim of non-business organisations is to obtain a desired response from a target market. The response could be a change in values, a financial contribution, the donation of services or some other type of exchange. Non-business marketing objectives are shaped by the nature of the exchange and the goals of the organisation. BBC sponsored Children in Need and Comic Relief telethons have raised millions of pounds. Telethons have three specific marketing objectives: (1) to raise funds to support programmes, (2) to plead a case on behalf of disadvantaged groups and (3) to inform the public about the organisation's programmes and services. Tactically, telethons have received support by choosing good causes; generating extensive grass-roots support; portraying disadvantaged people in a positive and dignified way; developing national, regional and local support; and providing quality entertainment.[18] Figure 11.4 illustrates how the exchanges and the purpose of the organisation can influence marketing objectives. (These objectives are used as examples and may or may not apply to specific organisations.)

Non-business marketing objectives should state the rationale for an organisation's existence. An organisation that defines its marketing objective as providing a product can be left without a purpose if the product becomes obsolete. However, serving and adapting to the perceived needs and wants of a target public, or market, enhances an organisation's chance to survive and achieve its goals.

Developing Non-business Marketing Strategies

Non-business organisations must also develop marketing strategies by defining and analysing a target market and creating and maintaining a marketing mix that appeals to that market.

Figure 11.4

Examples of marketing objectives for different types of exchanges

Police's marketing objective: To serve the public by enforcing laws and to gain public support and co-operation.

Protection and security

Taxes, co-operation and support

Church's marketing objective: To inform the public about the church's doctrine and convince people to become members.

Religious values and services

Contributions, service and acceptance of values

Charity's marketing objective: To serve the needs and wants of clients and the donor public.

Satisfaction from solving social problems or promoting a cause

Financial contributions, time and support

Source: Philip Kotler, Marketing for Non-profit Organisations, *2nd edn, © 1982, p. 38. Adapted by permission of Prentice-Hall, Inc., Englewood Cliffs, N.J.*

Target public A collective of individuals who have an interest in or concern about an organisation, product or social cause

Target Markets   The concept of target markets needs to be revised slightly to apply to non-business organisations. Whereas a business is supposed to have target groups that are potential purchasers of its product, a non-business organisation may attempt to serve many diverse groups. A **target public** is broadly defined as a collective of individuals who have an interest in or concern about an organisation, a product or a social cause. The terms *target market* and *target public* are difficult to distinguish for many non-business organisations. The target public for campaigns warning about the dangers of solvent abuse is parents, adults and concerned teenagers. However, the target market for many of the advertisements is potential and current solvent users. When an organisation is concerned about changing values or obtaining a response from the public, it views the public as a market.[19]

Client publics In non-business organisations, direct consumers of a product

General publics In non-business organisations, indirect consumers of a product

In non-business organisations, direct consumers of the product are called **client publics** and indirect consumers are called **general publics**.[20] For example, the client public for a university is its student body, and its general public includes parents, graduates, employers and the University Senate. The client public usually receives most of the attention when an organisation develops a marketing strategy. The techniques and approaches to segmenting and defining target markets discussed in Chapter 7 also apply to non-business target markets.

Developing a Marketing Mix   A marketing mix strategy limits choices and directs marketing activities towards achieving organisation goals. The strategy should outline or develop a blueprint for making decisions about product, distribution, promotion, price and personnel. These decision variables should be blended to serve the target market.

In tackling the product variable, non-business organisations deal more often with ideas and services than with goods. Problems may evolve when an organisation fails to define what is being provided. What products do the Women's Institute, the Scout Movement or the Chamber of Commerce provide? They offer a forum for social gatherings, courses, outings and a sense of co-operation. Their products are more difficult to define than the average business product. As indicated in the first part of this chapter, services are intangible and therefore need special marketing efforts. The marketing of ideas and concepts is likewise more abstract than the marketing of tangibles, and it requires considerable effort to present benefits.

Because most non-business products are ideas and services, distribution decisions relate to how these ideas and services will be made available to clients. If the product is an idea, selecting the right media (the promotional strategy) to communicate the idea will facilitate distribution. The availability of services is closely related to product decisions. By nature, services consist of assistance, convenience and availability. Availability is part of the total service. For example, making a product such as health services available calls for knowledge of such retailing concepts as site location analysis and logistics management.

Developing a channel of distribution to co-ordinate and facilitate the flow of non-business products to clients is a necessary task, but in a non-business setting the traditional concept of the marketing channel may need to be reviewed. The independent wholesalers available to a business enterprise do not exist in most non-business situations. Instead, a very short channel—non-business organisation to client—is prevalent, because production and consumption of ideas and services are often simultaneous. For example, local government departments often deal directly with householders. Charities generally pitch their fund raising activities directly to their target customers/householders/donors.

Making promotional decisions may be the first sign that non-business organisations are performing marketing activities. Non-business organisations use advertising and publicity to communicate with clients and the public. Direct mail remains the primary means of fund raising for services such as those provided by the Red Cross or Oxfam. In addition to direct mail, Oxfam uses press advertising, public relations and sponsorship. Personal selling is also used by many non-business organisations, although it may be called something else. Churches and charities rely on personal selling when they send volunteers to recruit new members or request donations. The armed forces use personal selling when recruiting officers attempt to persuade men and women to enlist. Special events to obtain funds, communicate ideas or provide services are sales promotion activities. Contests, entertainment and prizes offered to attract donations resemble the sales promotion activities of business enterprises. Amnesty International, for example, has held worldwide concert tours, featuring artists such as Sting and Phil Collins, to raise funds and increase public awareness of political prisoners around the world.

The number of advertising agencies that are donating their time for public service announcements (PSAs) or public information films is increasing, and the quality of print PSAs is improving noticeably. Not-for-profit groups are becoming more interested in the impact of advertising on their organisations, and they realise that second rate PSAs can cause a credibility loss.[21]

Although product and promotion techniques might require only slight modification when applied to non-business organisations, pricing is generally quite different and the decision-making more complex. The different pricing concepts that the non-business organisation faces include pricing in user and donor markets. There are two types of monetary pricing: *fixed* and *variable*. Membership fees, such as the amount paid to become a friend of a zoo, represent a fixed approach to pricing, whereas zoo fund raising activities that lead to donations represent a variable pricing structure.[22]

The broadest definition of price (valuation) must be used to develop non-business marketing strategies. Financial price, an exact monetary value, may or may not be charged for a non-business product. Economists recognise the giving up of alternatives as a cost. **Opportunity cost** is the value of the benefit that is given up by selecting one alternative rather than another. This traditional economic view of price means that if a non-business organisation can persuade someone to donate time to a cause or to change his or her behaviour, the alternatives given up are a cost to (or a price paid by) the individual. Volunteers who answer phones for a university counselling service or suicide hotline, for example, give up the time they could have spent studying or doing other things, as well as the income they might have earned from working in a business organisation.

For other non-business organisations, financial price is an important part of the marketing mix. Non-business organisations today are raising money by increasing the prices of their services or starting to charge for services if they have not done so before. They are using marketing research to determine for what kinds of products people will pay.[23] Pricing strategies of non-business organisations often stress public and client welfare over equalisation of costs and revenues. If additional funds are needed to cover costs, then donations, contributions or grants may be solicited.

The additional elements of the marketing mix for services are also important in non-business marketing. The physical environment quite often poses problems: subscribers and donors want an organisation that looks "professional" but not head administrative offices that look as if precious funds have been wasted on office equipment, fittings and furniture. There needs to be a compromise: an

Opportunity cost The value of the benefit that is given up by selecting one alternative instead of another appearance of business-like efficiency without any extravagance. The process for transactions is increasingly important: regular donors are offered direct debits, automatic payment methods and regular information packs or leaflets detailing the recipient organisation's activities, expenditures and plans. People, too, are of importance: capable administrators, sympathetic helpers, trustworthy fund raisers—they too, must project a caring yet efficient image to the client and general publics.

Controlling Non-business Marketing Activities

To control marketing activities in non-business organisations, managers use information obtained in the marketing audit to make sure that goals are achieved. Table 11.7 lists several helpful summary statistics. It should be obvious that the data in Table 11.7 are useful for both planning and control. Control is designed to identify what activities have occurred in conformity with the marketing strategy and to take corrective action where any deviations are found. The purpose of control is not only to point out errors but to revise organisational goals and marketing objectives as necessary. One way to measure the impact of an advertisement is to audit the number of requests for information or applications, such as those received by Oxfam, the Royal Navy (see Figure 11.5) or the WWF.

Many potential contributors decide which charities to support based on the amount of money actually used for charitable purposes. Charities are more aggressively examining their own performance and effectiveness. For example, compared with other charities, the Salvation Army contributes the most of every pound it receives to the needy; its employees are basically volunteers who work for almost nothing. Charities are making internal changes to increase their effec-

1. **Product mix offerings**
   A. Types of product or services
   B. Number of organisations offering the product or service

2. **Financial resources**
   A. Types of funding used
      1. Local government grants
      2. Government grants
      3. Foundations
      4. Public appeals
      5. Fees/charges
   B. Number using each type of funding
   C. Number using combinations of funding sources

3. **Size**
   A. Budget (cash flows)

   B. Number of employees
      1. By organisation
      2. Total industry wide
   C. Number of volunteers
      1. By organisation
      2. Total industry wide
   D. Number of customers serviced
      1. By type of service
      2. By organisation
      3. Total industry wide

4. **Facilities**
   A. Number and type
      1. By organisation
      2. Total industry wide
   B. Location
      1. By address
      2. By postal code

SOURCE: Adapted from Philip D. Cooper and George E. McIlvain, "Factors influencing marketing's ability to assist non-profit organizations", John H. Summey and Ronald D. Taylor, eds., *Evolving Marketing Thought for 1980, Proceedings of the Southern Marketing Association* (19–22 November 1980), p. 315. Used by permission.

Table 11.7 Examples of data useful in controlling non-business marketing activities

LIFE. ADD SALT TO TASTE.

EVER SAT QUIETLY IN A CHAIR AND WONDERED WHAT LIFE WAS ALL ABOUT? HERE'S A CLUE: IT'S GOT VERY

LITTLE TO DO WITH SITTING QUIETLY IN CHAIRS WONDERING WHAT LIFE IS ALL ABOUT. SO SEND US THE COUPON

OR CALL 0345 300 123 AND WE'LL SEND YOU AN INFORMATION PACK THAT'LL REALLY GET YOU THINKING.

The Royal Navy is looking for men and women to fill vacancies now. Send to: The Royal Navy and Royal Marines Careers Service, Department (3BJ05443), FREEPOST 4335, Bristol, BS1 3YX. No stamp needed. Internet: http://www.open.gov.UK/navy/RNHM.HTM.

NAME (MR, MS) _____ DATE OF BIRTH _____

ADDRESS _____

_____ POSTCODE _____ TELEPHONE _____

We are equal opportunity employers under the Race Relations Act and welcome enquiries and applications from all ethnic groups. **JOIN THE NAVY AND SEE THE WORLD. DIFFERENTLY.** ROYAL NAVY

Figure 11.5 Measuring the impact of advertising. The Royal Navy can measure the impact of its advertising by keeping count of the number of requests for information.

SOURCE: Courtesy of Andy Griffiths and the Royal Navy.

tiveness, and many are hiring professional managers and fund raisers to help with strategic planning in developing short term and long range goals, marketing strategies and promotional plans.

To control non-business marketing activities, managers must make a proper inventory of activities performed and prepare to adjust or correct deviations from standards. Knowing where and how to look for deviations and knowing what types of deviations to expect are especially important in non-business situations. Because non-business marketing activities may not be perceived as marketing, managers must clearly define what activity is being examined and how it should function.

It may be difficult to control non-business marketing activities, because it is often hard to determine whether goals are being achieved. A homeless support group that wants to inform community members of its services may not be able to find out whether it is communicating with people who need assistance. Surveying to discover the percentage of the population that is aware of a pro- gramme to help the homeless can show whether the awareness objective has been achieved, but it fails to indicate what percentage of people without housing has been assisted. The detection and correction of deviations from standards are certainly major purposes of control, but standards must support the organisation's overall goals. Managers can refine goals by examining the results that are being achieved and analysing the ramifications of those results.

Techniques for controlling overall marketing performance must be compatible with the nature of an organisation's operations. Obviously, it is necessary to control the marketing budget in most non-business organisations, but budgetary control is not tied to standards of profit and loss; responsible management of funds is the objective. Central control responsibility can facilitate orderly, efficient administration and planning. For example, most universities evaluate graduating students' progress to control and improve the quality of the educational product. The audit phase typically relies on questionnaires sent to students and eventual employers. The employer completes a questionnaire to indicate the former student's progress; the graduate completes a questionnaire to indicate what additional concepts or skills were needed to perform duties. In addition, a number of faculty members may interview certain employers and former students to obtain information for control purposes. Results of the audit are used to develop corrective action if university standards have not been met. Corrective action might include an evaluation of the deficiency and a revision of the curriculum.

● ● ● ● ● ● ● ● ● ● ● ● ● ● ● ● ● ●

Summary

● *Services* are intangible dominant products that cannot be physically possessed—the result of applying human or mechanical efforts to people or objects. They are a growing part of the economy. There are *consumer services* and *business services*. Services have four distinguishing characteristics: (1) *intangibility,* (2) *inseparability* of production and consumption, (3) *perishability* and (4) *heterogeneity.* Intangibility places greater importance on *search, experience* and *credence qualities.* Because services include a diverse group of industries, classification schemes are used to help marketers analyse their products and develop the most appropriate marketing mix. Services can be viewed in terms of a *five category classification:* type of market, degree of labour intensiveness, degree of customer contact, skill of the service provider and goal of the service provider.

● The intangibility of the service product, together with the importance of the people component of the extended marketing mix for services, leads to significant difficulties in creating—and sustaining—a *differential advantage* or competitive edge. Increasingly, strong branding and associated promotional strategy are playing more of a role in the marketing strategy for services. The basic marketing mix is augmented for services through the addition of people, physical evidence (ambience) and the process of transaction in order to produce the "7 Ps" or the *extended marketing mix.*

● Fluctuating demand is a major problem for most service firms. Marketing strategies (the marketing mix) as well as non-marketing strategies (primarily internal, employee-based actions) can be used to deal with the problem. Before attempting to undertake any such strategies, however, service marketers must understand the patterns and determinants of demand.

● *Non-business marketing* includes marketing activities conducted by individuals and organisations to achieve goals other than normal business goals. Non-business marketing uses most of the concepts and approaches applied to business situations. The chief beneficiary of a business enterprise is whoever owns or holds shares in the business, but the beneficiary of a non-business enterprise should be its clients, its members or its public at large. The goals of a non-business organisation reflect its unique philosophy or mission. Some non-business organisations have very controversial goals, but many organisations exist to further generally accepted social causes.

● The marketing objective of non-business organisations is to obtain a desired response from a target market, often from *negotiation* or *persuasion*. Developing a non-business marketing strategy consists of defining and analysing a target market and creating and maintaining a marketing mix. *Target, client* and *general publics* must all be identified. In non-business marketing, the product is usually an idea or service. Distribution is involved not so much with the movement of goods as with the communication of ideas and the delivery of services, which results in a very short marketing channel. Promotion is very important in non-business marketing; personal selling, sales promotion, advertising and publicity are all used to communicate ideas and inform people about services. Price is more difficult to define in non-business marketing because of *opportunity costs* and the difficulty of quantifying the values exchanged.

● It is important to control marketing strategies in non-business situations. Control is designed to identify what activities have occurred in conformity with marketing strategy and to take corrective action where deviations are found. The standards against which performance is measured must support the non-business organisation's overall goals.

Important Terms

Service
Consumer services
Business services
Intangibility
Search qualities
Experience qualities
Credence qualities

Inseparability
Perishability
Heterogeneity
Five category classification
Differential advantage
Extended marketing mix for
    services

Non-business marketing
Negotiation
Persuasion
Target public
Client publics
General publics
Opportunity cost

Discussion and Review Questions

1. Identify and discuss the distinguishing characteristics of services. What problems do these characteristics present to marketers?
2. What is the significance of "tangibles" in service industries?
3. Analyse a house cleaning service in terms of the five classification schemes and discuss the implications for marketing mix development.
4. How do search, experience and credence qualities affect the way consumers view and evaluate services?
5. What additional elements must be included in the marketing mix for services? Why?
6. Why is it difficult to create and maintain a differential advantage in many service businesses?
7. Analyse the demand for dry cleaning and discuss ways to cope with fluctuating demand.
8. Compare and contrast the controversial aspects of non-business versus business marketing.
9. Relate the concepts of product, distribution, promotion and price to a marketing strategy aimed at preventing drug abuse.
10. What are the differences between clients, publics and consumers? What is the difference between a target public and a target market?
11. What is the function of control in a non-business marketing strategy?
12. Discuss the development of a marketing strategy for a university. What marketing decisions should be made in developing this strategy?

Recommended Readings

W. J. Glynn and J. G. Barnes, *Understanding Services Management, Integrating Marketing, Organisational* *Behaviour, Operations and Human Resource Management* (Chichester: John Wiley and Sons, 1995).

B. Edvardsson, B. Thomasson and J. Ovretveit, *Quality of Service, Making It Really Work* (London: McGraw Hill, 1994).

C. Grönroos, *Service Management and Marketing* (Lexington, Mass.: Lexington Books, 1990).

L. Berry, *On Great Service* (New York: The Free Press, 1995).

C. H. Lovelock, *Managing Services* (Englewood Cliffs, N.J.: Prentice-Hall, 1992).

● ● ● ● ● ● ● ● ● ● ● ● ● ● ● ● ● ●

Cases

11.1   Multiplex Cinemas: The Promise of UCI

In 1991 over 107 million cinema seats were sold in Germany. In the UK the number was 91 million, a significant rise from 72 million in 1985. Now around 11 per cent of the population claim to be "regular" film goers. Despite additional television channels and transmitting hours, relaxed regulations in terms of television censorship, the introduction of more cable and satellite television services and the increasing range of competing activities for leisure time, the cinema industry is booming. This boom can be attributed mainly to two factors: better, more attractive cinemas in more accessible locations and a regular stream of US made "blockbuster" movies.

United Cinemas International (UCI), a joint venture between MCA and Paramount, leads the development of the new generation of cinemas: the multiplex. Each multiplex has 8 to 10 screens offering a wide choice of movies for all social groups and ages. In addition to the mainstream releases there are children's clubs, late night adult clubs and showings of critically acclaimed "art" films. The luxuriously appointed auditoria have air conditioning, extra leg room, comfortable seating, wide screens and Dolby stereo Surroundsound. All multiplexes offer extensive refreshment facilities and some, such as the Milton Keynes complex "The Point", house restaurants, a nightclub and an amusement area.

These large, often out-of-town developments are quite different from the traditional Victorian Regal or Roxy with one screen and limited amenities. The consumer of the 1980s came to expect more comfortable, glitzy surroundings, with easy car parking and access. The boom in cinema attendance, though, has also benefited the older, traditional town centre cinemas. High Street chains are reporting increased ticket sales, as are the remaining independent cinemas.

MGM, Showcase and UCI have brought a new generation of cinemas to Europe with plans for expansion throughout the EU and Scandinavia. The UCI ethos is well defined:

> It is the philosophy of United Cinemas International to offer a complete cinematic entertainment package to every member of the family, and, in so doing, become an important part of the community. Through the concept of the multiplex cinema this philosophy will be "screened" worldwide, with UCI acting as the catalyst which will bring people back to the cinema—truly recreating the magic of the movies.

From the first UK UCI in 1985, the company now operates over 30 sites. Each, whether it has 6 or 18 screens, aims to present a wide choice of films, with top picture and sound quality based on the latest technology in luxurious, clean and well maintained surroundings. High management and staff service levels, the convenience of easily accessible sites in or near shopping and leisure complexes that have easy public transport links and ample parking, and value for money complete the UCI offer.

The goal of becoming part of the community is central to UCI's marketing. Months before a new cinema opening, UCI liaises with community leaders to discuss ways in which the cinema and the company can help with special events or activities. Links with local arts festivals, charity fund raising, sponsorship of events, special interest films for the community, exhibitions and publicity are just a few of the activities in which UCI becomes involved. Opening galas are always staged in aid of a prominent local charity and involve people from all sectors of the local community. Celebrities turn out and often a spectacular event is staged free for everyone—perhaps a fireworks display or one off Drive-In movie, an event pioneered in Europe by UCI.

UCI believes that staff training "provides the essential foundation upon which all successful organisations base their business". A smart appearance and friendly personality are essential qualities, but "attitude" is of central importance. New recruits are taught basic skills in each main area—box office, refreshment, usher, health and hygiene, fire safety and first aid. They take written and oral exams, gaining in status and pay as they pass each stage. The very best employees reach the coveted "Top Gun" status and receive the opportunity to enter management posts. For managers, training is equally rigorous and includes orientation programmes for the UCI and multiplex philosophies and courses at UCI's Manchester training department in employment law, cinema administration, discipline and grievance procedures, communication and training skills, leadership and teamwork. Ultimately, the individual cinema can be run efficiently and for the consumers' benefit only if the manager is caring and well versed in UCI's philosophy, which is reiterated in UCI's "promise":

Thank You for Choosing a UCI Cinema

We promise that when you visit one of our cinemas,

Our staff will be friendly, courteous and helpful.

The foyers, corridors and auditoriums will be clean and tidy.

The toilets will be clean and fully stocked.

Refreshment areas will be clean, and refreshments will be served hot or cold as intended.

The film presentation will be of the highest quality, with crystal clear pictures and top quality sound.

If for any reason your visit is not up to our promise or your expectations, please see one of our duty managers, and let us know your views.

We value your impressions as much as we do your custom.

The attention to detail highlighted by UCI's charter is important given the increasing competition from home entertainment systems and services, as well as from the growing chains of rival multiplex operators. For example, the 120 strong MGM chain was recently bought by the ever expanding leisure force Virgin in a £200 million deal. Virgin is already developing a more aggressive and varied marketing strategy. Promotional spend has been increased to over £5 million and activity will move away from the traditional newspaper "what's on" advertisements. With the launch of *Take 2,* a new cinema concept showing second run blockbuster films at bargain prices, MGM is fighting the triple onslaught of multiplex cinemas, in-home entertainment and consumer spending on the National Lottery. Ten years ago, cinema attendances stood at half today's level and the video age seemed set to wipe out the industry. The multiplex turned the situation round, but in a maturing market major players such as UCI must endeavour to maintain service standards and to seek an edge over their rivals.

SOURCES: David Teather, "Virgin to cinema's rescue", *Marketing,* 13 July 1995, p. 10; "MGM ditches 'listings' approach", *Marketing,* 10 November 1994, p. 5; "MGM fends off rivals with Take 2 cinema launch", *Marketing,* 18 August 1994, p. 1; "Movies eclipse films", *The Economist,* 5 February 1994, pp. 95–96; *Screen Digest,* August 1990; "The cinema industry", *Key Note,* 1990; Kok Bon; "General household survey", HMSO; UCI, "Projecting a philosophy"; "Bright lights, big picture show", *Marketing Week,* 6 February 1993, p. S6; UCI information pack.

Questions for Discussion

1. What has led to the "re-birth" of the cinema industry?
2. Compared with its numerous competitors, what advantages are offered by the multiplex concept?
3. How do the core lessons of services marketing reveal themselves in UCI's trading formula?

11.2   Expansion of Health Care Marketing: BUPA Fights for Continued Leadership

Private health care is far removed from the marketing of Sony Walkmans or Caterpillar earthmovers. What is the product? The consultation with a specialist? The treatment? Perhaps the speed from diagnosis to operation? The en suite, comfortable facilities? Or the improved condition and lifestyle of the patient? In the UK, BUPA is a leader in the provision of private (non-government provided) health care and has just recruited car hire company

Avis's marketing director in order to rekindle its marketing.

Although there are dozens of health care companies—and more from Europe entering the UK market each year—only a handful offer the complexity of products available from BUPA. The insurance operation sells health cover policies, which to many consumers represent the most visible side of BUPA. There is much more, however. BUPA owns its own hospitals, operating theatre units and health clinics. The organisation both buys and sells health care provision and increasingly works in localised partnerships with the state run national health service (NHS). The company is thus far more than an insurance broker; and as a result, it has many publics. These include companies that subscribe for insurance cover on behalf of their employees as a "perk"; suppliers of medical equipment and drugs; the medical profession, which recommends its hospitals and facilities; NHS trust managers; insurance brokers, who recommend policies to their clients; the general and specialist media; and consumers as private purchasers of policies and as patients.

The principal market for BUPA insurance is the corporate sector; it therefore targets sales activity at companies taking out policies for their employees. In addition, BUPA is now devoting more attention to promoting its services directly to consumers in order to increase its membership and enlarge its customer base. Television advertisements emphasise the relatively low cost of private health cover "from as little as £17 per month". With *fund holding* GPs taking a fresh look at private medicine, BUPA is also publicising its facilities and locations to the general medical profession.

In the recent rapid expansion of the private health care sector, Nuffield Hospitals and AMI have taken market share from BUPA. BUPA's marketing used to be handled regionally, but with over 30 hospitals, 30 health screening clinics, homes for the elderly and an occupational health service, BUPA feels the need for a formal marketing strategy and centralised control. Already the enhanced marketing activity has turned a £63 million loss at the end of the 1980s into a pre-tax profit to be reinvested in BUPA's facilities.

BUPA's actions coincided with the launch of a new rival, Firstchoice, led by ex-BUPA executives. Claiming to be the UK's first health insurance broker, Firstchoice develops tailor made insurance packages and sells services from over 20 health care companies. It has established agreements with all of the market's major players, except with BUPA. Whereas most competitors target the corporate sector primarily, Firstchoice believes there is growing consumer interest in private health care cover and services. Firstchoice is segmenting the marketplace and developing marketing programmes aimed at specific target audiences, employing many tools created by the marketers of the consumer goods giants.

Towards the end of 1995, however, private medical insurer PPP launched a £30 million drive to close the gap on rival BUPA, commencing with a branding campaign featuring its first ever mainstream advertising campaign, designed to distance the company from the insurance industry's "uncaring image". The £15 million year long campaign began with a 60 second brand building and awareness generating advertisement, followed by a series of product feature and cost benefit commercials. PPP became the biggest spending health care advertiser in the UK, although this expenditure was indicative primarily of the overall growth of the sector. Private medical insurance is now worth £1.5 billion per annum in the UK, and volume is rising sharply as more consumers strive to safeguard their families' medical provision in the light of strained resources in the state funded NHS. BUPA now pays out over £2 million each day in benefits to its policy holders requiring medical treatment or consultation. Despite the efforts of Firstchoice as a broker, PPP as a rival insurer, or Nuffield with competing private hospitals, BUPA is still the market leader. In the insurance operation alone, it has 45 per cent of the market. Its unique mix of activities, from insurance to hospital and screening clinic owner to purchaser and provider of health care, provides a good base in this highly competitive marketplace, but also a highly complex organisation to market.

SOURCES: Liz Fisher, "Careful nursing in the private bag", *Accountancy,* July 1995, pp. 34–36; John Owen, "PPP challenges BUPA with £15 million blitz", *Campaign,* 13 October 1995, p. 8; David Teather, "PPP plans push on health rival", *Marketing,* 12 October 1995, p. 5; "Firstchoice claims new line in health insurance", *Marketing Week,* 26 February 1993, p. 9.

Questions for Discussion

1. Why are leading private medical insurance companies such as BUPA and PPP turning more to the marketing tactics deployed by consumer goods companies?
2. To which groups of people must BUPA appeal? Will this mix impact on the marketing strategy BUPA follows? Use specific examples to explain your answers.
3. What exactly is the product BUPA offers its customers? How can BUPA define this product for its target customers?

PART III POSTSCRIPT

Having identified marketing opportunities, a business should recommend a marketing strategy that involves selecting the target market, determining the required positioning and developing a differential advantage. For the recommended target market strategy to be implemented, a marketing mix must be developed. The marketing mix centres on the "5Ps" of product, people, place, promotion and pricing decisions.

Part III of *Marketing: Concepts and Strategies* has addressed the product ingredient of the marketing mix and its integral component, the people ingredient. It has also examined the associated aspects of branding, packaging, labelling and services. Special consideration has been given to the role of marketing in non-business or not-for-profit organisations.

Before progressing, readers should be confident that they are now able to:

Describe the basic product decisions

• What are the definitions and classifications of products adopted by marketers? • What distinguishes product items, product lines and product mixes? • Why is the product life cycle so important? • What organisational structures are available to manage products? • Why are the different levels of a product so important in determining an edge over competitors' products?

Explain the importance of branding and packaging

• Why are brands important? • What are the types of brands, their benefits and the ways in which they can be selected, protected and licensed? • What are the functions and design considerations of packaging? • What is the role of packaging in marketing strategy? • What are the functions of labelling and the associated legal issues?

Outline the requirements for developing and managing products

• What alternatives are there for managing products? • How does a business develop a product idea into a commercial product? • What is the role of product development in the marketing mix? • How can product modification or product deletion benefit the marketing mix? • Why must products be managed differently in the various stages of the product life cycle?

Understand the special requirements for the marketing of services

• What are the nature and characteristics of services? • How can services be classified? • How can strategies be developed for services? • Why are there difficulties in creating a differential advantage for services? • Why is marketing in non-business situations unique? • How can service strategies be developed and controlled for non-business activities?

Marketing Opportunity Analysis	Chapters
• The marketing environment	2
• Marketing in international markets	3
• Consumer markets and buyer behaviour	4
• Business-to-business markets and buyer behaviour	5
• Marketing research and information systems	6

Target Market Selection	Chapters
• Market segmentation and prioritisation	7, 22
• Product and brand positioning	7, 22
• Competitive advantage	7, 22

Marketing Mix Development	Chapters
• Product, branding, packaging and service decisions	8–11
• Distribution (place and channel) decisions	12–15
• Promotion decisions	16–18
• Pricing decisions	19, 20
• Supplementary decisions	3, 21, 24, 25

Marketing Management	Chapters
• Strategic marketing and competitive strategy	22, 23
• Marketing planning and sales forecasting	23
• Implementing strategies and measuring performance	24
• Marketing ethics and social responsibility	25

IV PLACE (DISTRIBUTION AND CHANNEL) DECISIONS

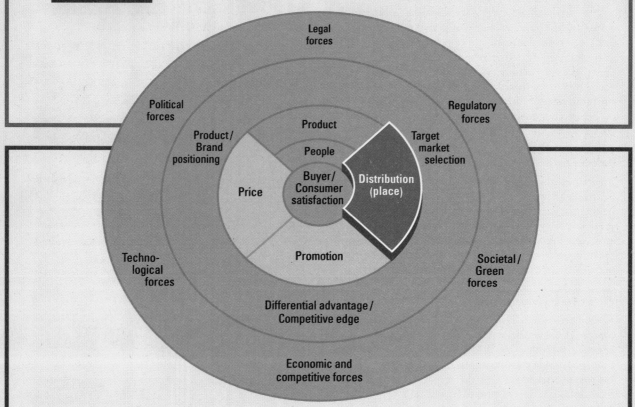

Legal forces

Political forces

Regulatory forces

Product/Brand positioning

Product

People

Target market selection

Price

Buyer/Consumer satisfaction

Distribution (place)

Techno-logical forces

Promotion

Societal/Green forces

Differential advantage/Competitive edge

Economic and competitive forces

Having identified a marketing opportunity and selected a target market, the marketer must design a product and service package that will satisfy the consumers targeted while maximising the marketing opportunity for the business in question. The product may be exactly what the targeted consumers desire, but if it is not made available to them, they will not be able to adopt the product. The place ingredient of the marketing mix addresses the distribution and marketing channel decisions that are necessary to provide the target market with convenient and ready access to the product or service, but in a manner that is beneficial to the supplier of the product or service. **Part IV of Marketing: Concepts and Strategies** examines the nature of marketing channels, wholesalers and distributors, retailing and the physical distribution of products and services.

Chapter 12, "Marketing Channels", explains the marketing channel concept and the functions, different types and structures of marketing channels. The chapter considers the selection of marketing channels; explores the behavioural aspects of channels, particularly the concepts of co-operation, relationship building, conflict and leadership; and examines legal issues in channel management.

Chapter 13, "Wholesalers and Distributors", presents a description of the nature of wholesaling in its broadest forms (i.e. including dealers and distributors) in the marketing channel, explains wholesalers' activities and their classification, examines the organisations that facilitate wholesaling and concludes by examining some changing patterns in wholesaling and distribution.

Chapter 14, "Retailing", explains the purpose and function of retailers in the marketing channel, provides an overview of the principal types and locations of retailing and describes non-store retailing and franchising. The chapter highlights the many strategic issues concerning modern retailing and shows that retail marketing is a specialist area requiring a modified approach by marketers.

Chapter 15, "Physical Distribution", illustrates how physical distribution activities are fundamental to channel management. It explains customer service, total distribution costs and cost trade-offs and then introduces order processing, materials handling, warehousing, storage, inventory management and the selection of transport modes—all essential for effective physical distribution.

By the conclusion of Part IV of *Marketing: Concepts and Strategies*, readers should understand the essential place decisions concerning marketing channels and distribution required in the marketing mix.

MARKETING CHANNELS

"Effective management of
manufacturer-dealer relationships is
formidably problematic but
strategically imperative."

David Shipley
Trinity College
University of Dublin

OBJECTIVES

- To understand the marketing channel concept and the nature of marketing channels
- To discuss the functions of channels
- To examine different types of channels
- To examine the structure and function of the channel system
- To consider the selection of channels
- To explore the behavioural aspects of channels, especially the concepts of co-operation, relationship building, conflict and leadership
- To examine legal issues in channel management

The distribution of petrol has entered a period of change as fuel companies Esso, Shell and BP are challenged by food retailers offering cut-price petrol from forecourts adjacent to their supermarket outlets. For food retailers such as Tesco and Sainsbury's, which purchase petrol at the lowest prices on the world oil markets, the fuel sales are treated as a loss leader aimed at drawing customers in to buy groceries. Meanwhile, the vertically integrated fuel companies are realising that petrol sales may no longer be profitable on their own. In such an environment the ability to generate business away from the core area of fuel sales is essential; new ways must therefore be found to encourage customers to visit petrol forecourts. For this reason, most of the fuel companies have given considerable attention to the stocking and pricing of other goods offered by their petrol forecourts.

It is perhaps ironic that in the longer term these pressures look likely to reduce consumer choice. Some industry experts believe that as petrol prices involved first reducing prices to win customers back and then offering to match supermarket prices within a three mile radius. In the first two months of 1996 the company spent £4.1 million promoting the campaign. Shell has adopted a different approach, that of aggressively promoting its Smart Card, which allows customers to collect points that can be exchanged for a wide range of gifts. Yet despite these efforts, at the end of 1995 the supermarkets' share of the market had risen to 27 per cent.

Now BP and Mobil have announced a joint venture in Europe aimed at achieving greater economies of scale and providing access to over three thousand more forecourts around Europe. In the UK, the combined forces of BP and Mobil will move the venture into second place behind Esso. In other markets in Europe it will become market leader. The main benefits to the companies will revolve around supply efficiencies, as the companies share costs and cut down on duplication. The move will entail switching over Mobil's outlets to BP's green livery and shedding between two and three thousand jobs from the European network. Yet despite the fact that the joint venture will enjoy a 15 per cent market share in the UK, it remains to be seen whether the sites will be profitable. ■

spiral downwards, smaller and more remote petrol outlets will be forced out of business, with sales becoming focused on fewer, higher volume sites. This view seems to be at odds with research results, which suggest that 55 per cent of consumers are unaware of petrol prices, choosing their petrol forecourt on the basis of location.

The challenge to the fuel giants does not end with low prices. Tesco has rolled out its Clubcard scheme for its national network of petrol stations. Now the 6.5 million customers who hold a card can enjoy cost saving benefits to their fuel as well as their grocery bills. The Clubcard allows customers to collect points as they spend; these are later exchanged for money-off coupons. Asda's recently launched Fill and Save card offers similar benefits.

Not surprisingly, the fuel companies have responded quickly to the competitive attack from the supermarkets. Esso's Pricewatch scheme has

SOURCES: Julian Lee, "Clubcard move fuels price war", *Marketing*, 29 February 1996, p. 1; Martin Payne and Phillip Wisson, "Retailscan: ads fuel petrol's risky price war", *Marketing Week*, 19 April 1996, pp. 30–31; Claire Murphy, "Why sites are key to fuel fight", *Marketing*, 7 March 1996, p. 16; Ken Gofton, "Coupons flourish as distribution shifts", *Marketing*, 7 March 1996, p. 12.

Distribution involves activities that make products available to customers when and where they want to purchase them. It is sometimes referred to as the *place* element in the marketing mix of the *Ps:* product, place (distribution), promotion, price and people. Choosing which channels of distribution to use is a major decision in the development of marketing strategies. Changes in the manner in which products are distributed have a major impact on customers. For example, the moves by food retailers to sell petrol from sites adjacent to their supermarkets has affected the UK petrol market in a number of important ways. Reducing petrol prices and increasing promotional activity are damaging margins to a point where profitability is severely threatened. In the long term this may force small suppliers out of business, thus reducing consumer choice.

This chapter focuses on the description and analysis of marketing channels, first discussing the nature of channels and their functions and then explaining the main types of channels and their structures. These sections are followed by a review of several forms of channel integration. Consideration is given to how marketers determine the appropriate intensity of market coverage for a product and to the factors that are considered when selecting suitable channels of distribution. After examining behavioural patterns within marketing channels and the relationships that develop between channel members, the chapter concludes by looking at several legal issues affecting channel management.

● ● ● ● ● ● ● ● ● ● ● ● ● ● ● ● ● ● ● ●

The Nature of Marketing Channels

Channel of distribution (or **marketing channel**)   A group of individuals and organisations that direct the flow of products from producers to customers

A **channel of distribution** (sometimes called a **marketing channel**) is a group of individuals and organisations that direct the flow of products from producers to customers. Providing customer benefits should be the driving force behind all marketing channel activities. Buyers' needs and behaviour are therefore important concerns of channel members. Channels of distribution make products available at the right time, in the right place and in the right quantity by providing such product enhancing functions as transport and storage.

Marketing intermediary   A middleman who links producers to other middlemen or to those who ultimately use the products

Most, but not all, channels of distribution have marketing intermediaries. A **marketing intermediary**, or middleman, links producers to other middlemen or to those who ultimately use the products. Marketing intermediaries perform the activities described in Table 12.1. There are two major types of intermediaries: merchants and functional middlemen (agents and brokers). **Merchants** take title to products and re-sell them, whereas **functional middlemen** do not take title to products.

Merchants   Intermediaries who take title to products and re-sell them

Functional middlemen   Intermediaries who do not take title to products

Both retailers and wholesalers are intermediaries. Retailers purchase products for the purpose of reselling them to users. Merchant wholesalers resell products to other wholesalers and to retailers. Functional wholesalers, such as agents and brokers, expedite exchanges among producers and resellers and are compensated by fees or commissions. For purposes of discussion in this chapter, all wholesalers are considered merchant middlemen unless otherwise specified.

Channel members share certain significant characteristics. Each member has different responsibilities within the overall structure of the distribution system, but mutual profit and success can be attained only if channel members co-operate in delivering products to the market. The area of relationship management has recently received a great deal of attention in marketing circles.

Although distribution decisions need not precede other marketing decisions, they do exercise a powerful influence on the rest of the marketing mix. Channel decisions are critical because they determine a product's market presence and buyers' accessibility to the product. The strategic significance of these decisions is further heightened by the fact that they entail long term commitments. For example, it is much easier for an organisation to change prices or packaging than to change existing distribution systems.

It may be necessary for companies to use different distribution paths in different countries. The links in any channel, however, are the merchants (including producers) and agents who oversee the movement of products through that channel. Marketing channels are commonly classified into channels for consumer products or channels for industrial products.

Category of Marketing Activities	Possible Activities Required
Marketing information	Analyse information such as sales data; perform or commission marketing research studies
Marketing management	Establish objectives; plan activities; manage and co-ordinate financing, personnel and risk taking; evaluate and control channel activities
Facilitating exchange	Choose and stock product assortments that match the needs of buyers
Promotion	Set promotional objectives, co-ordinate advertising, personal selling, sales promotion, publicity, direct mail and packaging
Price	Establish pricing policies and terms of sales
Physical distribution	Manage transport, warehousing, materials handling, inventory control and communication

Table 12.1 Marketing channel activities performed by intermediaries

Functions of Marketing Channels

Marketing channels serve many functions. Although some of these functions may be performed by a single channel member, most functions are accomplished through both independent and joint efforts of channel members. These functions include creating utility, facilitating exchange efficiencies, alleviating discrepancies, standardising transactions and providing customer service.

Creating Utility Marketing channels create three types of utility: time, place and possession. Time utility is having products available when the customer wants them. Place utility is created by making products available in locations where customers wish to purchase them. Possession utility is created by giving the customer access to the product to use or to store for future use. Possession utility can occur through ownership or through arrangements such as lease or rental agreements that give the customer the right to use the product. Channel members sometimes create form utility by assembling, preparing or otherwise refining the product to suit individual customer needs.

Facilitating Exchange Efficiencies Marketing intermediaries can reduce the costs of exchanges by efficiently performing certain services or functions. Even if producers and buyers are located in the same city, there are costs associated with exchanges. As Figure 12.1 shows, when four buyers seek products from four producers, sixteen transactions are possible. If one intermediary serves both producers and buyers, the number of transactions can be reduced to eight. Intermediaries are specialists in facilitating

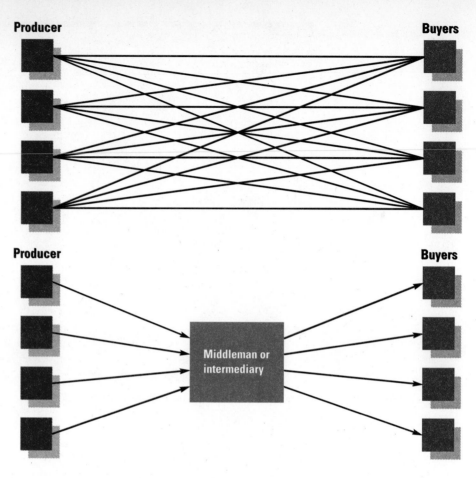

Figure 12.1

Efficiency in exchanges
provided by an intermediary

Producer

Buyers

Producer

Buyers

Middleman or
intermediary

exchanges. They provide valuable assistance because of their access to, and control over, important resources used in the proper functioning of marketing channels.

Nevertheless, the press, consumers, public officials and other marketers freely criticise intermediaries, especially wholesalers. Table 12.2 indicates that in a US survey of the general public 74 per cent believed that "wholesalers frequently make high profits, which significantly increase prices that consumers pay". Critics accuse wholesalers of being inefficient and parasitic. Consumers often wish to make the distribution channel as short as possible, assuming that the fewer the intermediaries, the lower the price. For example, Virgin's new financial services operation aims to offer competitive prices by cutting out brokers. Because suggestions to eliminate them come from both ends of the marketing channel, wholesalers must be careful to perform only those marketing activities that are truly desired. To survive, they must be more efficient and more customer focused than alternative marketing institutions.

Critics who suggest that eliminating wholesalers would lower consumer prices do not recognise that doing so would not remove the need for services that wholesalers provide. Although wholesalers can be eliminated, the functions they perform cannot. Other channel members would have to perform those functions, and customers would still have to fund them. In addition, all producers would have to deal directly with retailers or consumers, so that every producer would have to

Statement: Wholesalers frequently make high profits, which significantly increase prices that consumers pay.

	Total %	Male %	Female %
Strongly agree	35.5	33	38
Somewhat agree	38	40	36
Neither agree nor disagree	16	14	18
Somewhat disagree	8	9	7
Strongly disagree	2.5	4	1
	100	100	100

SOURCE: O. C. Ferrell and William M. Pride, national sample of 2,045 households.

Table 12.2 Consumer misunderstanding about wholesalers

keep voluminous records and hire enough personnel to deal with a multitude of customers. Customers might end up paying a great deal more for products because prices would reflect the costs of less efficient channel members.

To illustrate wholesalers' efficient services, assume that all wholesalers have been eliminated. Because there are more than 1.5 million retailers, a widely purchased consumer product—say, toilet paper—would require an extraordinary number of sales contacts, possibly more than a million, to maintain the current level of product exposure. For example, Scott would have to deliver its paper products, establish warehouses all over Europe and maintain fleets of trucks. Selling and distribution costs for Scott's products would rocket. Instead of a few contacts with food brokers, large retail organisations and merchant wholesalers, such manufacturers would face thousands of expensive contacts with and shipments to smaller retailers. Such an operation would be highly inefficient, and costs would be passed on to consumers. Wholesalers are often more efficient and less expensive.

Alleviating Discrepancies

The functions performed within marketing channels help to overcome two major distribution problems: discrepancies in quantity and discrepancies in assortment. With respect to discrepancies in quantity, consider a firm that manufactures jeans. The company specialises in goods it can produce most efficiently, denim clothing. To make jeans most economically, the producer turns out a hundred thousand pairs of jeans each day. Few persons, however, want to buy a hundred thousand pairs of jeans; they just want a few pairs. Thus the quantity of jeans the company can produce efficiently is more than the average customer wants. This is called *discrepancy in quantity*.

Assortment A combination of products put together to provide customer benefits

An **assortment** is a combination of products put together to provide benefits. Consumers create and hold an assortment. The set of products made available to customers is an organisation's assortment. Most consumers want a broad assortment of products. Besides jeans, they want to buy shoes, food, cars, stereos, soft drinks and many other products. Yet our jeans manufacturer has a narrow assortment because it makes only jeans and a few other denim clothes. A *discrepancy in assortment* exists because a consumer wants a broad assortment, but an individual manufacturer produces a narrow assortment.

Sorting activities Functions that let channel members divide roles and separate tasks

Sorting out Separating products into uniform, homogeneous groups

Accumulation The development of a bank of homogeneous products with similar production or demand requirements

Allocation The breaking down of large homogeneous inventories into smaller lots

Assorting The grouping of products that buyers want to have available in one place

Quantity and assortment discrepancies are resolved through sorting activities of channel members. **Sorting activities** are functions allowing channel members to divide roles and separate tasks; they include sorting out, accumulation, allocation and assorting of products (see Figure 12.2).[1] **Sorting out,** the first step in developing an assortment, is separating conglomerates of heterogeneous products into relatively uniform, homogeneous groups based on product characteristics such as size, shape, weight or colour. Sorting out is especially common in the marketing of agricultural products and other raw materials, which vary widely in size, grade and quality and would be largely unusable in an undifferentiated mass. A grape crop, for example, must be sorted into grapes suitable for making wine, those best for turning into grape juice and those to be sold by food retailers. **Accumulation** is the development of a bank, or inventory, of homogeneous products with similar production or demand requirements. Farmers who grow relatively small quantities of grapes, for example, transport their sorted grapes to central collection points, where they are accumulated in large lots for movement into the next level of the channel. Accumulation lets producers continually use up stocks and replenish them, thus minimising losses from interruptions in the supply of materials. **Allocation** is the breaking down of large homogeneous inventories into smaller lots. This process, which addresses discrepancies in quantity, enables wholesalers to buy efficiently in lorry loads or railway car loads and apportion products by cases to other members. A food wholesaler, for instance, serves as a depot, allocating products according to market demand. The wholesaler may divide a single lorry load of Del Monte canned tomatoes among several retail food stores. **Assorting** is the process of combining products into collections or assortments that buyers want to have available in one place. Assorting eliminates discrepancies in assortment by grouping products in ways that satisfy buyers. Assorting is especially important to retailers, for they strive to create assortments matching the demands of consumers who patronise their stores. Although no single customer is likely to buy one of everything in the store, retailers must anticipate the probability of purchase and provide a satisfactory range of product choices. For example, the same food wholesaler that supplies supermarkets with Del Monte tomato products may also buy canned goods from competing food processors so that the grocery store can choose from a wide assortment of canned fruit and vegetables.

Standardising Transactions

Marketing channels help to standardise the transactions associated with numerous products. In many purchase situations, the price is not negotiable; it is predetermined. Although there may be some variation in units of measure, package sizes, delivery schedules and location of the exchange, marketing channel members tend to limit customers' options with respect to these types of issues. When a

Figure 12.2

Sorting activities conducted by channel members

Sorting out	Accumulation	Allocation	Assorting
Classifying heterogeneous supplies into homogeneous groups	Developing a bank or stock of homogeneous products to provide aggregate inventory	Breaking down homogeneous stocks (inventories) into smaller units	Combining products into collections or assortments that buyers want

customer goes to a supermarket to purchase a loaf of bread, it is unlikely that the individual will be able to buy a half loaf of bread, buy a loaf sliced lengthwise, negotiate the price, obtain a written warranty or return an unused portion of the loaf. Many of the details associated with the purchase of a loaf of bread are standardised.

Providing Customer Service

Channel members participate in providing customer service. Retailers of durable goods are expected to provide delivery, installation, repair services, parts and perhaps instruction or training. Channel members above the retailers are responsible for supporting retailers' efforts to provide end user service and satisfaction even though they may not come into direct contact with ultimate customers. To gain and maintain a competitive advantage, channel members make decisions and take actions to provide excellent customer service and support.

Types of Channels

Because marketing channels appropriate for one product may be less suitable for others, many different distribution paths have been developed. The various marketing channels can be classified generally as channels for consumer products or channels for industrial products.

Channels for Consumer Products

Figure 12.3 illustrates several channels used in the distribution of consumer products. Besides the channels listed, a manufacturer may use sales branches or sales offices.

Channel A describes the direct movement of goods from producer to consumers. Customers who pick their own fruit from commercial orchards or buy

Figure 12.3

Typical marketing channels for consumer products

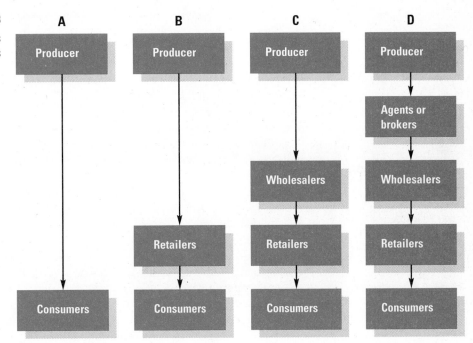

cosmetics from door-to-door salespeople are acquiring products through a direct channel. A producer who sells goods directly from the factory to end users and ultimate consumers is using a direct marketing channel. Although this channel is the simplest, it is not necessarily the cheapest or the most efficient method of distribution.

Channel B, which moves goods from producer to retailers and then to consumers, is often used by large retailers that can buy in quantity from a manufacturer. Such retailers as Marks & Spencer, Sainsbury's, Aldi and Carrefour, for example, sell clothing, food and many other items they have purchased directly from the producers. Cars are also commonly sold through this type of marketing channel.

A long standing distribution channel, especially for consumer products, channel C takes goods from producer to wholesalers, then to retailers and finally to consumers. This option is very practical for a producer who sells to hundreds of thousands of consumers through thousands of retailers. A single producer finds it hard to do business directly with thousands of retailers. For example, consider the number of retailers that stock Coca-Cola. It would be extremely difficult, if not impossible, for Coca-Cola to deal directly with all the retailers that sell its brand of soft drink. Manufacturers of tobacco products, confectionery, some home appliances, hardware and many convenience goods sell their products to wholesalers, who then sell to retailers, who in turn do business with individual consumers.

Channel D—through which goods pass from producer to agents to wholesalers to retailers, and only then to consumers—is frequently used for products intended for mass distribution, such as processed food. For example, to place its biscuit line in specific retail outlets, a food processor may hire an agent (or a food broker) to sell the biscuits to wholesalers. The wholesalers then sell the biscuits to supermarkets, vending machine operators and other retail outlets.

Contrary to popular opinion, a long channel may be the most efficient distribution channel for certain consumer goods. When several channel intermediaries are available to perform specialised functions, costs may be lower than if one channel member is responsible for all the functions in all territories.

Channels for Industrial Products

Figure 12.4 shows four of the most common channels for industrial products. Like their consumer products counterparts, manufacturers of industrial products sometimes work with more than one level of wholesalers.

Channel E illustrates the direct channel for industrial products. In contrast with consumer goods, many industrial products—especially expensive equipment, such as steam generators, aircraft and mainframe computers—are sold directly to the buyers. For example, Airbus Industries sells aircraft directly to airlines such as British Airways and Air France. The direct channel is most feasible for many manufacturers of industrial goods because they have fewer customers, and those customers may be clustered geographically. Buyers of complex industrial products can also receive technical assistance from the manufacturer more easily in a direct channel. In some cases the provision of such information may continue for the life time of the product.

Industrial distributor An independent business organisation that takes title to industrial products and carries inventories

If a particular line of industrial products is aimed at a larger number of customers, the manufacturer may use a marketing channel that includes **industrial distributors,** merchants who take title to products (channel F). Construction products made by Case or JCB, for example, are sold through industrial distributors as are building materials, operating supplies and air conditioning equipment.

Figure 12.4

Typical marketing channels for industrial products

Industrial distributors can be most effectively used when a product has broad market appeal, is easily stocked and serviced, is sold in small quantities and is needed rapidly to avoid high losses.[2]

Channel G—producer to agents to industrial buyers—may be chosen when a manufacturer without a marketing department needs market information, when a company is too small to field its own sales force or when a firm wants to introduce a new product or to enter a new market without using its own salespeople. Thus a large soya bean producer might sell its product to animal food processors through an agent.

Channel H is a variation of channel G: goods move from producer to agents to industrial distributors and then to industrial buyers. A manufacturer without a sales force may rely on this channel if its industrial customers purchase products in small quantities or if they must be resupplied frequently and therefore need access to decentralised inventories. Japanese manufacturers of electronic components, for example, work through export agents who sell to industrial distributors serving small producers or dealers overseas. Chapter 21 presents more information about marketing channels for industrial products.

Multiple Marketing Channels

When aiming at diverse target markets, it may be appropriate for a manufacturer to use several marketing channels simultaneously, with each channel involving a different group of intermediaries. For example, a manufacturer turns to multiple channels when the same product is directed to both consumers and industrial customers. When Procter & Gamble sells cleaning products for household use, the products are sold to supermarkets through grocery wholesalers or, in some cases, directly to the retailers, whereas the cleaning products going to restaurants or institutions follow a different distribution channel. In some instances, a producer may prefer **dual distribution:** the use of two or more marketing channels for distributing the same products. Villeroy & Boch is a respected supplier of fine china and glassware to households across the world. The company also has ranges for the catering industry, sold and promoted through a separate marketing channel.

Dual distribution A channel practice whereby a producer distributes the same product through two or more different channels

Strategic channel alliance
Arrangement for distributing the products of one organisation through the marketing channels of another

A **strategic channel alliance** exists when the products of one organisation are distributed through the marketing channels of another organisation. The products are often similar with respect to target markets or product uses, but they are not direct competitors. For example, a brand of bottled water might be distributed through a marketing channel for soft drinks, or a US cereal producer might form a strategic channel alliance with a European food processor. Alliances can provide benefits both for the organisation that owns the marketing channel and for the company whose brand is being distributed through the channel.

• • • • • • • • • • • • • • • • • • • •

Channel Integration

Channel functions may be transferred among intermediaries, to producers and even to customers. This section examines how channel members can either combine and control most activities or pass them on to another channel member. Remember, though, that the channel member cannot eliminate functions; unless buyers themselves perform the functions, they must pay for the labour and resources needed for the functions to be performed. The statement that "you can eliminate middlemen but you can't eliminate their functions" is an accepted principle of marketing.

Many marketing channels are determined by consensus. Producers and intermediaries co-ordinate their efforts for mutual benefit. Some marketing channels, however, are organised and controlled by a single leader, which can be a producer, a wholesaler or a retailer, depending on the industry. The channel leader may establish channel policies and co-ordinate the development of the marketing mix. Marks & Spencer and IKEA, for example, are channel leaders for several of the many products they sell.

The various links or stages of the channel may be combined under the management of a channel leader either horizontally or vertically. Integration may stabilise supply, reduce costs and increase co-ordination of channel members. Marketing Insight 12.1 shows how deregulation in the electricity market is changing the integration of channels in one industry.

Vertical Channel Integration

Vertical channel integration
The combination of two or more stages of the channel under one management

Combining two or more stages of the channel under one management is **vertical channel integration**. One member of a marketing channel may purchase the operations of another member or simply perform the functions of the other member, eliminating the need for that intermediary as a separate entity. For example, changes in the regulations controlling the UK electricity industry have led to an increase in vertical channel integration, as some companies controlling the supply and distribution of electricity have merged. Total vertical integration encompasses all functions from production to ultimate buyer; it is exemplified by oil companies that own oil wells, pipelines, refineries, terminals and service stations.

Whereas members of conventional channel systems work independently and seldom co-operate, participants in vertical channel integration co-ordinate their efforts to reach a desired target market. This more progressive approach to distribution enables channel members to regard other members as extensions of their own operations. Vertically integrated channels are often more effective against competition because they result in increased bargaining power, the ability to inhibit competitors and the sharing of information and responsibilities.[3] At one end of an integrated channel, for example, a manufacturer might provide advertising and training assistance, and the retailer at the other end would buy the manufacturer's products in quantity and actively promote them.

In the past, integration has been successfully institutionalised in marketing channels called vertical marketing systems. A **vertical marketing system (VMS)** is a marketing channel in which a single channel member co-ordinates or manages channel activities to achieve efficient, low cost distribution aimed at satisfying target market customers. Because the efforts of individual channel members are combined in a VMS, marketing activities can be co-ordinated for maximum effectiveness and economy, without duplication of services. Vertical marketing systems are also competitive, accounting for a growing share of retail sales in consumer goods.

Most vertical marketing systems today take one of three forms: corporate, administered or contractual. The *corporate* VMS combines all stages of the marketing channel, from producers to consumers, under a single ownership. Supermarket chains that own food processing plants and large retailers that purchase wholesaling and production facilities are examples of corporate VMSs. Figure 12.5 contrasts a conventional marketing channel with a VMS, which consolidates marketing functions and institutions.

In an *administered* VMS, channel members are independent, but a high level of inter-organisational management is achieved by informal co-ordination. Members of an administered VMS may agree, for example, to adopt uniform accounting and ordering procedures and to co-operate in promotional activities. Although individual channel members maintain their autonomy, as in conventional marketing channels, one channel member (such as the producer or a large retailer) dominates the administered VMS, so that distribution decisions take into account the system as a whole. Because of its size and power as a retailer, Marks & Spencer exercises a strong influence over the independent manufacturers in its marketing channels, as do Kellogg's (cereals) and Volvo (cars and trucks).

Under a *contractual* VMS, the most popular type of vertical marketing system, inter-organisational relationships are formalised through contracts. Channel members are linked by legal agreements that spell out each member's rights and obligations. For instance, franchise organisations such as McDonald's and KFC are contractual VMSs. Other contractual VMSs include wholesaler sponsored groups such as Mace or IGA (Independent Grocers' Alliance) stores, in which independent retailers band together under the contractual leadership of a wholesaler.

Horizontal Channel Integration

Horizontal channel integration The combination of institutions at the same level of operation under one management

Combining institutions at the same level of operation under one management constitutes **horizontal channel integration**. An organisation may integrate horizontally by merging with other organisations at the same level in a marketing channel level. For example, the owner of a bistro may buy another bistro and then rebrand it in the same way as the existing business. Horizontal integration may enable a firm to generate sufficient sales revenue to integrate vertically as well.

Although horizontal integration permits efficiencies and economies of scale in purchasing, marketing research, advertising and specialised personnel, it is not always the most effective method of improving distribution. The increase in size may result in decreased flexibility, difficulties in co-ordination, and the need for additional marketing research and large scale planning. Unless distribution functions for the various units can be performed more efficiently under unified management than under the previously separate managements, horizontal integration will not reduce costs or improve the competitive position of the integrating firm.

Deregulation and Distribution Changes for the Utilities

In 1990 the British government began the process of privatising the state owned electricity industry. The aims of the scheme, which followed the privatisation of the telephone, water and gas industries, were clear: greater efficiency, more choice and lower prices for consumers. The UK's twelve regional electricity companies (RECs) experienced the first stage of privatisation in 1994, when the business market (those spending more than £12,000 annually on electricity) was opened up to competition. For the first time the RECs were able to compete for customers away from their own geographical area. For some, the impact was devastating. According to a senior marketing manager at one of the RECs, "In London, it was a huge shock. Almost overnight we lost 30 per cent of our business". With deregulation in the domestic market set for 1998, the RECs are now faced with balancing their desire to retain existing customers with their ambitions for capturing new business.

An important characteristic of the privatisation approach was to separate electricity generation, distribution and supply. The intent of this move away from vertical integration was to ensure that the large generators (such as the newly created companies National Power and PowerGen) were kept apart from those supplying business and consumers (the RECs). This, it was stated, would reduce the power of the generators to control prices by making them compete to find buyers of their electricity. The government was also responding to criticism of its privatisation of the gas industry, which resulted in a vertically integrated distribution system from the gas field through to the end consumer.

In practice, anticipation of the market changes resulted in a host of merger and acquisition activity involving gas, electricity and water companies. With Scottish Power being allowed to buy REC Manweb and Hanson's acquisition of Eastern Electricity, it seemed inevitable that the industry would soon consist of a small number of vertically integrated businesses. Yet the government then surprised industry experts by refusing to allow generators PowerGen and National Power to bid for the RECs Midland Electric and Southern Electric. Meanwhile, US firms Houston Industries, Texas-Utilities and Pacific Gas and Electric have all signalled interest in the supply businesses and sought to acquire RECs.

An interesting aspect of the privatisation of the utilities has been the degree to which supply companies may re-position themselves as total providers of utility services. According to Rick Peel, a consultancy expert in the field, "The benefits of such an arrangement include access to a partner's markets, a stronger brand, new technology or simply bundling one product with another". Not surprisingly, considerable interest in this approach has already been shown. For example, some of the RECs have participated in the South West gas trial. This was a test market experiment run in 1996 to allow half a million residential customers to "shop around" for their gas supply from a range of competing companies. It was hoped that the pilot scheme would allow testing of the complex distribution and billing mechanisms in a relatively controlled manner.

While many questions about how suppliers will differentiate their products and how the practicalities of billing and meter reading systems will be handled remain unanswered, the biggest unknown is how the change in distribution will really affect consumers and what their reaction will be to the changes.

SOURCES: "Britain's electricity shocker", *Economist,* 13 April 1996, p. 15; "Britain: short circuit", *Economist,* 13 April 1996 pp. 27–29; Meg Carter, "The mains attraction", *Marketing Week,* 8 December 1995, pp. 36–39; George Pitcher, "MMC's change of heart turns privatisation policy on its head", *Marketing Week,* 19 April 1996, p. 27.

Figure 12.5

Comparison of a conventional marketing channel and a vertical marketing system

Source: Adapted from Strategic Marketing, *by David J. Kollat et al., copyright © 1972. Reprinted by permission.*

A conventional marketing channel

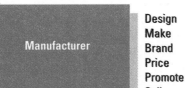

Members	Functions
Manufacturer	Design Make Brand Price Promote Sell

Members	Functions
Wholesaler	Buy Stock Promote Display Sell Deliver Finance

Members	Functions
Retailer	Buy Stock Promote Display Sell Deliver Finance

Members
Consumer

A vertical marketing channel

Members	Functions
Manufacturer Wholesaler Retailer	Design Make Brand Price Promote Buy Stock Display Sell Deliver Finance

Members
Consumer

Different Levels of Market Coverage

The kind of coverage that is appropriate for different products is determined by the characteristics and behaviour patterns of buyers. Chapter 8 divides consumer products into three categories—convenience products, shopping products and speciality products—according to how the purchase is made. In considering products to buy, consumers take into account replacement rate, product adjustment (services), duration of consumption, time required to find the product and similar factors.[4] Three major levels of market coverage are intensive, selective and exclusive distribution.

Intensive Distribution

Intensive distribution The use of all available outlets for distributing a product

In **intensive distribution,** all available outlets are used for distributing a product. Intensive distribution is appropriate for convenience products such as bread, chewing gum, beer and newspapers. To consumers, availability means a store located nearby and minimal time necessary to search for the product at the store.

Sales may have a direct relationship to availability. The successful sale of bread and milk at service stations or of petrol at convenience grocery stores has shown that the availability of these products is more important than the nature of the outlet. Convenience products have a high replacement rate and require almost no service. To meet these demands, intensive distribution is necessary, and multiple channels may be used to sell through all possible outlets.

Producers of packaged consumer items rely on intensive distribution. In fact, intensive distribution is one of Procter & Gamble's key strengths. It is fairly easy for this company to formulate marketing strategies for many of its products (soaps, detergents, food and juice products, and personal care products) because consumers want availability provided quickly and intensively.

Selective Distribution

Selective distribution The use of only some available outlets in an area to distribute a product

In **selective distribution,** only some available outlets in an area are chosen to distribute a product. Selective distribution is appropriate for shopping products. Durable goods such as electrical appliances and exclusive fragrances usually fall into this category. Such products are more expensive than convenience goods. Consumers are willing to spend more searching time visiting several retail outlets to compare prices, designs, styles and other features.

Selective distribution is desirable when a special effort—such as customer service from a channel member—is important. Shopping products require differentiation at the point of purchase. To motivate retailers to provide adequate pre-sale service, selective distribution and company owned stores are often used. Many industrial products are sold on a selective basis to maintain a certain degree of control over the distribution process. For example, agricultural herbicides are distributed on a selective basis because dealers must offer services to buyers, such as instructions about how to apply the herbicides safely or the option of having the dealer apply the herbicide.

Exclusive Distribution

Exclusive distribution The use of only one outlet in a relatively large geographic area to distribute a product

In **exclusive distribution,** only one outlet is used in a relatively large geographic area. Exclusive distribution is suitable for products that are purchased rather infrequently, are consumed over a long period of time, or require service or information to fit them to buyers' needs. Exclusive distribution is not appropriate for convenience products and many shopping products. It is often used as an incentive to sellers when only a limited market is available for products. For example, cars such as the Rolls Royce are sold on an exclusive basis. Royal Copenhagen's premium china is retailed through carefully selected, exclusive retail outlets (see Figure 12.6). A producer who uses exclusive distribution generally expects a dealer to be very co-operative with respect to carrying a complete inventory, sending personnel for sales and service training, participating in promotional programmes and providing excellent customer service. Exclusive distribution gives a company tighter image control because the types of distributors and retailers that distribute the product are closely monitored.[5]

• • • • • • • • • • • • • • • • • • • •

Choosing Distribution Channels

Choosing the most appropriate distribution channels for a product can be complex. Producers must choose specific intermediaries carefully, evaluating their sales and profit levels, performance records, other products carried, clientele, availability and so forth. In addition, producers must also examine other factors that influence distribution channel selection, including organisational objectives

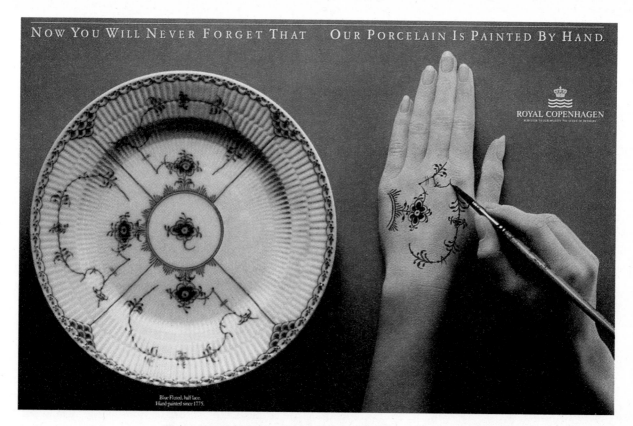

NOW YOU WILL NEVER FORGET THAT   OUR PORCELAIN IS PAINTED BY HAND.

Figure 12.6 Using exclusive distribution. Royal Copenhagen china controls its choice of retail outlets.

SOURCE: Courtesy of Royal Copenhagen A/S Denmark.

and resources, market characteristics, buyer behaviour, product attributes and environmental forces. In some markets, such as the distribution of insurance products, these factors may indicate that multiple channels should be used.[6]

Organisational Objectives and Resources

Producers must carefully consider their objectives and the cost of achieving them in the marketplace. A company's objectives may be broad—such as higher profits, increased market share and greater responsiveness to customers—or narrow, such as replacing an intermediary that has left the channel. The organisation may possess sufficient financial and marketing clout to control its distribution channels, for example, by engaging in direct marketing or by operating its own fleet of lorries. On the other hand, an organisation may have no interest in performing distribution services or may be forced by lack of resources and experience to depend on middlemen.

Companies must also consider how effective their past distribution relationships and methods have been and question their appropriateness in regard to current objectives. One firm might decide to maintain its basic channel structure but add members for increased coverage in new territories. Another company mig[ht] alter its distribution channel so as to provide same day delivery on all order[s]

Market Characteristics

Beyond the basic division between consumer markets and industrial ma[rkets, sev]eral market variables influence the design of distribution channels. [Geography is] one factor; in most cases, the greater the distance between the pr[oducer] markets, the less expensive is distribution through intermediaries rather than through direct sales. Market density must also be considered; when customers tend to be clustered in several locations, the producer may be able to eliminate middlemen. Transport, storage, communication and negotiation are specific functions performed more efficiently in high density markets. Market size—measured by the number of potential customers in a consumer or industrial market—is yet another variable. Direct sales may be effective if a producer has relatively few buyers for a product, but for larger markets the services of middlemen may be required.[7] Figure 12.7 shows how warehouses are often promoted on the basis of location.

Buyer Behaviour

Buyer behaviour is a crucial consideration in selecting distribution channels. To be able to match intermediaries with customers, the producer must have specific, current information about customers who are buying the product and how, when and where they are buying it.[8] A manufacturer might find direct selling economically feasible for large volume sales but inappropriate for small orders.

The producer must also understand how buyer specifications vary according to whether buyers perceive products as convenience, shopping or speciality items (see Chapter 8). Customers for magazines, for example, are likely to buy the product frequently (even impulsively) from a variety of outlets. Buyers of home computers, however, carefully evaluate product features, dealers, prices and after sales services.

Buyers may be reached most effectively when producers are creative in opening up new distribution channels. In the UK, effective distribution, the essential tool in the highly competitive soft drinks sector, is forcing brand leader Coca-Cola and Schweppes Beverages (CCSB) to find creative ways of extending distribution. CCSB has launched a company, Vendleader, to increase penetration of sales through vending machines.

Product Attributes

Another variable in the selection of distribution channels is the product itself. Because producers of complex industrial products must often provide technical services to buyers both before and after the sale, these products are usually shipped directly to buyers. Perishable or highly fashionable consumer products with short shelf lives are also marketed through short channels. In other cases, distribution patterns are influenced by the product's value; the lower the price per unit, the longer the distribution chain. Additional factors to consider are the weight, bulkiness and relative ease of handling the products. Producers may find wholesalers and retailers reluctant to carry items that create storage or display problems.[9] For example, manufacturers of breakfast cereals such as Kellogg's and Nabisco must use packaging that retailers find easy to handle and display.

Environmental Forces

Finally, producers making decisions about distribution channels must consider forces in the total marketing environment—that is, such issues as competition, ecology, economic conditions, technology, society and law. Technology, for example, has made possible electronic scanners, computerised inventory systems such as EPOS (electronic point-of-sale) and electronic shopping devices, all of which are altering present distribution systems and making it harder for technologically unsophisticated firms to remain competitive. Changing family patterns and the emergence of important minority consumer groups are driving producers to seek new distribution methods for reaching market segments. Interest rates, inflation

Figure 12.7 Market characteristics. Warehouses are often promoted on the basis of location.

SOURCE: left: *Courtesy of Central Leeds;* right: *Courtesy of Quayside.*

and other economic variables affect members of distribution channels at every level. Environmental forces are numerous and complex and must be taken into consideration if distribution efforts are to be appropriate, efficient and effective. For example, EU regulation changes in 1993 had an impact on the retailing of cars, resulting in a power shift away from the car manufacturers (see Marketing Insight 12.2).

Behaviour of Channel Members

The marketing channel is a social system with its own conventions and behaviour patterns. Each channel member performs a different role in the system and agrees (implicitly or explicitly) to accept certain rights, responsibilities, rewards and sanctions for non-conformity. Channel members have certain expectations of other channel members. Retailers, for instance, expect wholesalers to maintain

EU Car Distribution: A Period of Change

Car distribution in the European Union is changing. For decades, most car manufacturers have maintained networks in Europe for retailing and servicing their models alone. In Germany, Portugal or the UK car showrooms are decorated in the corporate colours of BMW, Rover or Saab. A few showrooms are owned by the manufacturers themselves: French manufacturers Citroën and Renault operate a small proportion of the Citroën and Renault retail outlets in several countries. In general, however, car showrooms are owned by companies independent of the manufacturers on whose behalf they display, stock, sell and service vehicles.

Manufacturers design and produce vehicles with the intention of gaining market share and making profits. The showroom franchise holders are also profit motivated. Despite this interdependent relationship, the power and control have tended to be in the hands of the manufacturers. Most manufacturers in the past used their position to establish control over their dealers' stock levels, site standards, training of personnel, computing systems and financial arrangements. Consequently, most showrooms sold only one manufacturer's vehicles.

With the relaxation of trading regulations in the EU in 1993, dealers have found the power shifting towards them. Some dealers have introduced a second manufacturer's models alongside their existing franchise. Others have built separate showrooms adjacent to their existing operation, offering the consumer several manufacturers' cars at one location. Dealers have started to specialise: the four wheel drive, off-road showroom containing vehicles from five or six manufacturers; or high performance sports coupés from several manufacturers under one roof.

Meanwhile, in the UK the entry of Daewoo, which plans to capture a 1 per cent market share in two years, is bringing about new changes in the way that cars are sold. Although relatively unknown in Europe, Daewoo is South Korea's third biggest car manufacturer. Achieving a foothold in the UK market is seen by the company as a possible point of access into the rest of Europe. The company has shocked existing incumbents with its innovative three tier system for selling its range. The system, which has been developed as a result of considerable customer research, moves away from the franchised dealer/manufacturer relationship upon which the sale of cars in the UK has been based for so long.

The first tier of the Daewoo system consists of out-of-town Motor Shows, which mimic international motor shows in style, offer customers crèche and café facilities, are run by non-commissioned staff and offer high tech IT systems to help in the choice of car model and colour. The second tier consists of Car Centre outlets which are geared to sell new and used cars. Servicing facilities are available at Car Centres or at branches of Halfords, a well established national retailer of car and bicycle spares and accessories. Halfords, which already offers servicing and repairs, is the third tier of the Daewoo selling system.

Not surprisingly, this move has aroused considerable interest from other car manufacturers, many of which are attracted by the prospect of reducing their dependence on dealer networks. As manufacturers continue to adjust to the post-1993 trading changes, the industry expects that the success or failure of the Daewoo venture will be a key factor in shaping the future of car distribution in Europe.

Sources: Tom O'Sullivan, "Daewoo bids to make its marque", *Marketing Week,* 31 March 1995, pp. 20–21; Andy Fry, "Channels of communication", *Marketing,* October 1995, pp. 3–5; Robert Dwek, "Car firms push ahead", *Marketing,* 14 January 1993, p. 2; Willem Molle, *The Economics of European Integration* (Aldershot: Dartmouth, 1990); Guy de Jonquières and David Buchan, "Japanese car import agreement threatened by EC disarray", *Financial Times,* 25 September 1990, p. 1c; Paolo Cecchini, *The European Challenge 1992* (Wildwood House, 1988); Tony Cutler, Colin Haslam, John Williams and Karel Williams, *1992—The Struggle for Europe* (New York: BERG, 1989).

adequate inventories and to deliver goods on time. For their part, wholesalers expect retailers to honour payment agreements and to keep them informed of inventory needs. This section discusses several issues related to channel member behaviour, including co-operation, conflict and leadership. Marketers need to understand these behavioural issues to make effective channel decisions.

Channel Co-operation and Relationship Building

Channel co-operation is vital if each member is to gain something from other members.[10] Without co-operation, neither overall channel goals nor member goals can be realised. Policies must be developed that support all essential channel members; otherwise, failure of one link in the chain could destroy the channel.

There are several ways to improve channel co-operation. A marketing channel should consider itself a unified system, competing with other systems. This way, individual members will be less likely to take actions that would create disadvantages for other members. Similarly, channel members should agree to direct their efforts towards a common target market so that channel roles can be structured for maximum marketing effectiveness, which in turn can help members achieve their individual objectives. It is crucial to define precisely the tasks that each member of the channel is to perform. This definition provides a basis for reviewing the intermediaries' performance and helps reduce conflicts because each channel member knows exactly what is expected of it. As explained in Chapter 5, it is often in the interests of channel members to build long term relationships. These relationships can improve channel co-operation and help individual channel members better adapt to the needs of the others.[11]

Channel Conflict

Although all channel members work towards the same general goal—distributing products profitably and efficiently—members may sometimes disagree about the best methods for attaining this goal. Each channel member wants to maximise its own profits while maintaining as much autonomy as possible. However, if this self-interest creates misunderstanding about role expectations, the end result is frustration and conflict for the whole channel. For individual organisations to function together in a single social system, each channel member must clearly communicate and understand role expectations. Communication difficulties are a potential form of channel conflict and can lead to frustration, misunderstandings and ill co-ordinated strategies.[12]

Channel conflict often arises when a given channel member does not conduct itself in the manner expected by other channel members. Wholesalers expect producers to monitor quality control and production scheduling, and they expect retailers to market products effectively. Producers and retailers expect wholesalers to provide co-ordination, functional services and communication. But if members do not fulfil their roles—for example, if wholesalers or producers fail to deliver products on time or the producers' pricing policies cut into the margins of downstream channel members—conflict may ensue.

Channel conflicts also arise when dealers over emphasise competing products or diversify into product lines traditionally handled by other, more specialised intermediaries. In some cases, conflict develops because producers strive to increase efficiency by circumventing intermediaries, as is happening in marketing channels for microcomputer software and video games. Many software-only stores are establishing direct relationships with software producers, bypassing wholesale distributors altogether. Some dishonest retailers are also pirating software or making unauthorised copies, thus cheating other channel members out of their due compensation. Consequently, suspicion and mistrust are heightening tensions in software marketing channels.[13]

Although there is no single method for resolving conflict, an atmosphere of co-operation can be re-established if two conditions are met. First, the role of each channel member must be specified. To minimise misunderstanding, all members must be able to expect unambiguous, agreed-on levels of performance from one another. Second, channel members must institute certain measures of channel co-ordination, a task that requires leadership and the benevolent exercise of control.[14] To prevent channel conflict, producers or other channel members may provide competing resellers with different brands, allocate markets among resellers, define direct sales policies to clarify potential conflict over large accounts, negotiate territorial issues between regional distributors and provide recognition to certain resellers for the importance of their role in distributing to others. Hallmark, for example, distributes its Ambassador greetings card line in discount stores and its name brand Hallmark line in up-market department and specialist card stores, thus limiting the amount of competition among retailers carrying its products.[15]

Channel Leadership

Channel power The ability to influence another channel member's goal achievement

The effectiveness of marketing channels hinges on channel leadership, which may be assumed by producers, retailers or wholesalers. To become a leader, a channel member must want to influence and direct overall channel performance. Furthermore, to attain desired objectives, the leader must possess **channel power**, which is the ability to influence another channel member's goal achievement. As Figure 12.8 shows, the channel leader derives power from seven sources, two of them economic and five non-economic.

Figure 12.8
Determinants of channel leadership

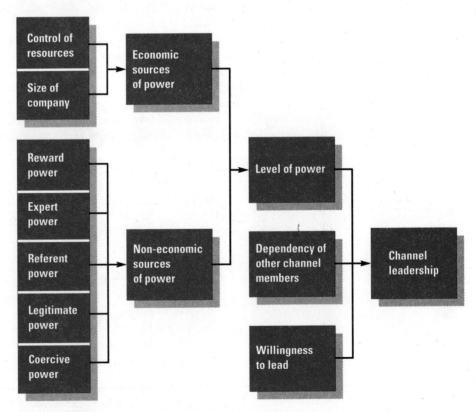

Source: R. D. Michman and S. D. Sibley, Marketing Channels and Strategies, 2nd edn (Worthington, Ohio: Publishing Horizons, Inc., 1980), p. 413. Reproduced by permission.

The five non-economic sources of power—reward, expert, referent, legitimate and coercive—are crucial for establishing leadership. A channel leader gains reward power by providing financial benefits. Expert power exists when other channel members believe that the leader provides special expertise required for the channel to function properly. Referent power emerges when other members strongly identify with and emulate the leader. Legitimate power is based on a superior-subordinate relationship. Coercive power is a function of the leader's ability to punish other channel members.[16]

In many countries, producers assume the leadership role in marketing channels. A manufacturer—whose large scale production efficiency demands increasing sales volume—may exercise power by giving channel members financing, business advice, ordering assistance, advertising and support materials.[17] For example, BMW and Mercedes-Benz control their dealers totally, specifying showroom design and layout, discount levels and quotas of models. Coercion causes dealer dissatisfaction that is stronger than any impact from rewards, so the use of coercive power can be a major cause of channel conflict.[18]

Retailers can also function as channel leaders, and with the domination of national chains and own label merchandise they are increasingly doing so. For example, Sainsbury's challenged Coca-Cola with its own label of cola, which was similarly packaged to that of the market leader. Small retailers, too, may share in the leadership role when they command particular consumer respect and patronage in local or regional markets. Among large retailers, Carrefour, IKEA, Marks & Spencer and Sainsbury's base their channel leadership on wide public exposure to their products. These retailers control many brands and sometimes replace uncooperative producers. Marks & Spencer exercises power by dictating manufacturing techniques, lead times, quality levels and product specifications.

Wholesalers assume channel leadership roles as well, although they were more powerful decades ago, when most manufacturers and retailers were small, underfinanced and widely scattered. Today, wholesaler leaders may form voluntary chains with several retailers, which they supply with bulk buying or management services or which market their own brands. In return, the retailers shift most of their purchasing to the wholesaler leader. In Scandinavia, buying groups act as wholesalers, with bulk ordering price advantages, expert advertising and purchasing. Other wholesaler leaders such as Intersport or Mace might also help retailers with store layouts, accounting and inventory control.

• • • • • • • • • • • • • • •

Legal Issues in Channel Management

The multitude of laws governing channel management are based on the general principle that the public is best served when competition and free trade are protected. Under the authority of such national legislation as the UK's Monopolies and Mergers Commission, Fair Trading Act, Prices Act, Trade Description Act and Consumer Protection Act, or EU Competition Laws and dictates, the courts and regulatory agencies determine under what circumstances channel management practices violate this underlying principle and must be restricted and when these practices may be permitted. Although channel managers are not expected to be legal experts, they should be aware that attempts to control distribution functions may have legal repercussions. The following practices are among those frequently subject to legal restraint.

Restricted Sales Territories

Restricted sales territories
System by which a producer tries to prohibit intermediaries from selling its products outside designated sales territories

To tighten its control over the distribution of its products, a manufacturer may try to prohibit intermediaries from selling its products outside designated sales territories, creating **restricted sales territories.** The intermediaries themselves often favour this practice, because it lets them avoid competition for the producer's brands within their own territories. Many companies have long followed the policy of restricting sales in this fashion. In recent years, the courts have adopted conflicting positions in regard to restricted sales territories. Although they have deemed restricted sales territories a restraint of trade among intermediaries handling the same brands (except for small or newly established companies), the courts have also held that exclusive territories can actually promote competition among dealers handling different brands. At present, the producer's intent in establishing restricted territories and the overall effect of doing so on the market must be evaluated for each case individually.

Tying Contracts

Tying contracts Arrangement whereby a supplier (usually a manufacturer or franchiser) furnishes a product to a channel member with the stipulation that the channel member must purchase other products as well

When a supplier (usually a manufacturer or franchiser) furnishes a product to a channel member with the stipulation that the channel member must purchase other products as well, a **tying contract** exists.[19] Suppliers, for instance, may institute tying arrangements to move weaker products along with more popular items. To use another example, a franchiser may tie the purchase of equipment and supplies to the sale of franchises, justifying the policy as necessary for quality control and protection of the franchiser's reputation.

A related practice is full-line forcing. In this situation, a supplier requires that channel members purchase the supplier's entire line to obtain any of the products. Manufacturers sometimes use full-line forcing to ensure that intermediaries accept new products and that a suitable range of products is available to customers.

The courts accept tying contracts when the supplier alone can provide products of a certain quality, when the intermediary is free to carry competing products as well and when a company has just entered the market. Most other tying contracts are considered illegal.

Exclusive Dealing

Exclusive dealing System by which a manufacturer forbids an intermediary to carry products of competing manufacturers

When a manufacturer forbids an intermediary to carry products of competing manufacturers, the arrangement is called **exclusive dealing.** A manufacturer receives considerable market protection in an exclusive dealing arrangement and may cut off shipments to an intermediary that violates such an agreement.

An exclusive dealing contract is generally legally permitted if dealers and customers in a given market have access to similar products or if the exclusive dealing contract strengthens an otherwise weak competitor.

Refusal to Deal

Refusal to deal Situation in which suppliers will not do business with wholesalers or dealers simply because these wholesalers or dealers have resisted policies that are anti-competitive or in restraint of trade

Producers have the right to choose the channel members with whom they will do business (and the right not to choose others). Within existing distribution channels, however, suppliers may not refuse to deal with wholesalers or dealers just because these wholesalers or dealers have resisted policies that are anticompetitive or in restraint of trade. Suppliers are further prohibited from organising some channel members in **refusal to deal** actions against other members who choose not to comply with illegal policies.[20]

Summary

● Distribution refers to activities that make products available to customers when and where they want to purchase them. A *channel of distribution* (or *marketing channel*) is a group of individuals and organisations that direct the flow of products from producers to customers. In most channels of distribution, producers and customers are linked by *marketing intermediaries* or middlemen, called *merchants* if they take title to products and *functional middlemen* if they do not take title. Channel structure reflects the division of responsibilities among members.

● Although intermediaries can be eliminated, their functions are vital and cannot be dropped; these activities must be performed by someone in the marketing channel or passed on to customers. Because intermediaries serve both producers and buyers, they reduce the total number of transactions that would otherwise be needed to move products from producer to ultimate users. Intermediaries' specialised functions also help keep down costs.

● An *assortment* is a combination of products assembled to provide benefits. Intermediaries perform *sorting activities* essential to the development of product assortments. Sorting activities allow channel members to divide roles and separate tasks. Through the basic tasks of *sorting out, accumulating, allocating* and *assorting* products for buyers, intermediaries resolve discrepancies in quantity and assortment. The number and characteristics of intermediaries are determined by the assortments and the expertise needed to perform distribution activities.

● Channels of distribution are broadly classified as channels for consumer products or channels for industrial products. Within these two broad categories, different marketing channels are used for different products. Although some consumer goods move directly from producer to consumers, consumer product channels that include wholesalers and retailers are usually more economical and efficient. Industrial goods move directly from producer to end users more frequently than do consumer goods. Channels for industrial products may also include agents, *industrial distributors* or both. Most producers use *dual distribution* or multiple channels so that the distribution system can be adjusted for various target markets. Sometimes *strategic channel alliances* are used so that the products of one organisation can be distributed through the marketing channels of another.

● Integration of marketing channels brings various activities under the management of one channel member. *Vertical integration* combines two or more stages of the channel under one management. The *vertical marketing system (VMS)* is managed centrally for the mutual benefit of all channel members. Vertical marketing systems may be corporate, administered or contractual. *Horizontal integration* combines institutions at the same level of channel operation under a single management.

● A marketing channel is managed so that products receive appropriate market coverage. In choosing *intensive distribution*, producers strive to make a product available to all possible dealers. In *selective distribution*, dealers are screened to choose those most qualified for exposing a product properly. *Exclusive distribution* usually gives one dealer exclusive rights to sell a product in a large geographic area.

● When selecting distribution channels for products, manufacturers evaluate potential channel members carefully. Producers also consider the organisation's objectives and available resources; the location, density and size of a market; buyers' behaviour in the target market; characteristics of the product; and outside forces in the marketing environment.

● A marketing channel is a social system in which individuals and organisations are linked by a common goal: the profitable and efficient distribution of goods and services. The positions or roles of channel members are associated with rights, responsibilities and rewards, as well as sanctions for non-conformity. Channels function most efficiently when members co-operate, but when they deviate from their roles, channel conflict can arise. Effective marketing channels are usually a result of channel leadership and of relationship building between channel members.

● Channel leaders can facilitate or hinder the attainment of other members' goals, and they derive this *channel power* from authority, coercion, rewards, referents or expertise. Producers are in an excellent position to structure channel policy and to use technical expertise and consumer acceptance to influence other channel members. Retailers gain channel control through consumer confidence, wide product mixes and intimate knowledge of consumers. Wholesalers and buying groups become channel leaders when they have expertise that other channel members value and when they can co-ordinate functions to match supply with demand.

● Channel management is governed by a variety of legal issues. These are based on the principle that the public is best served when free competition and free trade are protected. Various practices may be sub-ject to legal restraint. To tighten its distribution control, manufacturers may try to operate *restricted sales territories,* where intermediaries are barred from selling products outside designated areas. A *tying contract* occurs when a supplier stipulates that another channel member must purchase other products in addition to the one originally supplied. *Exclusive dealing* occurs when a manufacturer forbids an intermediary to carry products from competing manufacturers. *Refusal to deal* means that a producer will not do business with a wholesaler or dealer that has resisted the manufacturer's anti-competitive practice.

• • • • • • • • • • • • • • • • • • •

Important Terms

Channel of distribution
  (or marketing channel)
Marketing intermediary
Merchants
Functional middlemen
Assortment
Sorting activities
Sorting out
Accumulation

Allocation
Assorting
Industrial distributor
Dual distribution
Strategic channel alliance
Vertical channel integration
Vertical marketing system
  (VMS)
Horizontal channel integration

Intensive distribution
Selective distribution
Exclusive distribution
Channel power
Restricted sales territories
Tying contracts
Exclusive dealing
Refusal to deal

• • • • • • • • • • • • • • • • • • •

Discussion and Review Questions

1. Compare and contrast the four major types of marketing channels for consumer products. Through which type of channel is each of the following products most likely to be distributed: (a) new cars, (b) cheese biscuits, (c) cut-your-own Christmas trees, (d) new textbooks, (e) sofas, (f) soft drinks?

2. "Shorter channels are usually a more direct means of distribution and therefore are more efficient." Comment on this statement.

3. Describe an industrial distributor. What types of products are marketed through industrial distributors?

4. Under what conditions is a producer most likely to use more than one marketing channel?

5. Why do consumers often blame intermediaries for distribution inefficiencies? List several reasons.

6. How do the major functions that intermediaries perform help resolve the discrepancies in assortment and quantity?

7. How does the number of intermediaries in the channel relate to the assortments retailers need?

8. Can one channel member perform all channel functions?

9. Identify and explain the major factors that influence decision-makers' selection of marketing channels.

10. Name and describe firms that use (a) vertical integration and (b) horizontal integration in their marketing channels.

11. Explain the major characteristics of each of the three types of vertical marketing systems (VMSs).

12. Explain the differences among intensive, selective and exclusive methods of distribution.

13. "Channel co-operation requires that members support the overall channel goals to achieve individual goals." Comment on this statement.

14. How do power bases within the channel influence the selection of the channel leader?

Recommended Readings

J. C. Anderson and J. A. Narus, "A model for distributor firm and manufacturing firm working relationships", *Journal of Marketing,* vol. 54, no. 1, 1990, pp. 42–58.

J. A. Quelch and D. Harding, "Brands versus private labels: fighting to win", *Harvard Business Review,* vol. 74, no. 1, 1996, January–February pp. 99–109.

S. D. Hunt, M. M. Ray and V. R. Wood, "Behavioural dimensions of channels of distribution: review and synthesis", *Journal of the Academy of Marketing Science,* vol. 13, no. 3, 1985, pp. 1–24.

D. Shipley and C. Egan, "Power, conflict and co-operation in brewer-tenant distribution channels", *International Journal of Service Industry Management,* vol. 3, no. 4, 1992, pp. 44–62.

Cases

12.1 *Firstdirect:* Innovative Banking Channels

With *Firstdirect* you can do your banking when it suits you, not when it suits us. We're open every hour, of every day, 365 days a year. So, if you want to transfer cash on a Sunday or set up a standing order late at night, you just ring up. And yes, you always talk to a real person. Because everything's done by phone, you can also bank from wherever you are … at home or in the office. And all calls are charged at local rate.

Most consumers have a bank cheque account from which cash is drawn, bills are paid and cheques written, and into which salaries, pensions or grant cheques are paid. For many consumers, the bank is a high street or shopping mall office—imposing, formal and often intimidating. Whether it's National Westminster, Barclays or TSB in the UK; ABN AMRO or Rabobank in the Netherlands, each high street bank is fairly alike, with similar products and services, personnel, branch layouts, locations and opening hours. Differentiation has been difficult to achieve and generally impossible to maintain over any length of time as competitors have copied rivals' moves. Promotional strategy and brand image have been the focus for most banking organisations, supported with more minor tactical changes in, for example, opening hours or service charges. For the majority of bank account holders, however, the branch—with its restricted openings, formal ambience and town centre location—is the only point of contact for the bulk of transactions.

Firstdirect, owned by Midland Bank, but managed separately, broke the mould in 1989. Launched with a massive £6 million promotional campaign, *Firstdirect* bypassed the traditional marketing channel. *Firstdirect* has no branches, no branch overhead and operating costs. It provides free banking, unlike its high street competitors with their system of bank charges combined with interest paid on positive balances. *Firstdirect* is a telephone banking service that offers full current and deposit account facilities, cheque books, automatic bill payment and ATM "hole in the wall" cash cards through Midland's international service-till network.

Midland has established a purpose built administrative centre for *Firstdirect* in Leeds, guaranteeing immediate, personal response to calls 24 hours a day. All normal banking transactions can be completed over the telephone. Initial reactions were positive, with many non-Midland account holders switching to the innovative new style of banking. The more traditional consumer—who equates the marbled halls of the Victorian branches with heritage, security and traditional values—has been less easily converted. For the targeted, more financially aware and independent income earner, *Firstdirect* is proving very popular.

Firstdirect's services and products are not new, but the chosen marketing channel—no branches, only the telephone—is innovative. Customers no longer have to reach inaccessible, parked-up, town centre branches with queues and restricted opening hours. *Firstdirect* has introduced a service, alien to some more traditional tastes perhaps, which is more readily available and with fewer costs. Many thousands of consumers have welcomed the launch of this new option, but millions have preferred to bank the traditional way. The start for *Firstdirect* has been highly encouraging, and now other high street banks are beginning to offer similar banking services.

SOURCES: "Midland fails to bank on a third successive win", *Marketing*, 19 July 1990, p. 7; Mat Toor, "Taxis fare well with Firstdirect", *Marketing*, 19 April 1990, p. 1; "Banking industry report", Salomon Brothers, 1992; *Firstdirect* advertising, 1993; *Firstdirect* fact file, 1993; Beverly Crany, "Reading your MIND", *Marketing*, 22 February 1996, pp. 33–34.

12.2   Bols: Revitalised for the 1990s

Bols liqueurs are well known throughout the world, but there is much more to the Dutch distiller than creamy yellow advocate. Just in the world's top 10 spirits manufacturers and distributors, Bols employs 2,000 people and produces spirits, aperitifs, non-alcoholic wines, mineral water, fruit juices and soft drinks. Bols produces its own branded drinks as well as own label brands for various buying groups and retailers. Founded by Lucas Bols in 1575, the company's heritage is based upon distilling high quality liqueurs. During the 1980s, Bols had to make some difficult decisions, the most significant of which was to diversify from its main spirits business and enter the low and non-alcoholic beverage market in line with growing consumer demand for these products. Bols also divested third party agency business—brand franchises held to produce and distribute other manufacturers' brands.

The shift away from the traditional liqueur business was quite fundamental. The Netherlands' trading position and ties with the Spice Islands in the Far East had allowed Bols' products to take on a very distinctive character: highly coloured, with a consistent, premium quality taste. The non-alcoholic drinks share few of these traits. Bols' distribution had traded the company's liqueur spirits throughout Europe for centuries. The 1980s distribution focused on establishing Bols' spirit liqueur brands in bars and restaurants, as well as off-licences and retail outlets. In most countries the distribution for soft drinks and low alcohol wines was quite different.

In Benelux, Bols and leading rival Heineken were both suffering from severe price competition and eroding margins. As a result, the two companies formed the joint venture Bols Benelux, with Heineken under Bols management. The combined muscle saw margins improve by 8 per cent and sales of spirits rise by 30 per cent. Today, Bols Benelux has 40 per cent of the Dutch market. In Italy, Bols took advantage of the rise in sparkling wine and non-alcoholic drink consumption, purchasing Ottavio Riccadonna (now Bols Italy) to become the fourth largest producer of sparkling wines in Italy. Bols' lemonade, Lemonsoda, is the brand leader, and in mineral water the company has a toe-hold of 2 per cent and is seeking further acquisitions.

In France a number of strategically prudent acquisitions has led to Bols becoming a major force in the high quality wine market, exporting to the USA, the UK and the Netherlands. Bols Strothmann, created in the 1980s with the acquisition of the Strothmann distillery, has given Bols a presence in Germany at a time when German unification has opened up significant new markets to the east. There are successes in Spain, where sherries are exported to the UK, and in Switzerland; and agreements have been entered into in Hungary, Czechoslovakia and other eastern European countries. Only 14 per cent of business comes from outside Europe, but recently this proportion has expanded rapidly, particularly through new offices in Singapore, New York, Brazil and Argentina.

Bols had to make hard decisions as its historical core product, spirits, declined worldwide and beers, wines and non-alcoholic beverages gained market share. The company diversified, but only within the drinks industry with which it was familiar. New lines, particularly soft drinks and low alcohol sparkling wines, have heralded an up turn in the company's fortunes, coupled with wider geographic activity away from the European heartland. Sales in 1989 had dropped 10 per cent, but they rose 8 per cent in 1990 and 11.3 per cent in 1991, by which time profits were Dfl 144,300,000 at a margin of 10.8 per cent.

Distribution in the drinks industry is complicated and highly competitive. Several countries, including the UK, are dominated by third party specialist distributors who have access to retail chains and independent shops through wholesalers, bars, res-

Questions for Discussion

1. Why is innovation in marketing channels generally difficult to achieve?
2. Why is *Firstdirect* different from its rivals? What gives it differentiation?
3. Why might some potential customers of *Firstdirect* have reservations about the innovative nature of the service?

taurants and entertainment facilities. Bols has adopted a variety of methods to expand its activities, including organic growth—mainly in its Benelux base—acquisition and contractual arrangements with leading distributors such as JR Phillips. Bols' experience in spirits gave it access to several markets, but the most direct approach to expanding and achieving distribution penetration came through the acquisition of leading players that already had distribution networks and outlets.

SOURCES: "Bols–company report", Barclays De Zoete Wedd Securities, January 1992; Bols: Review of operations, 1990; "Bols", UBS Phillips & Drew, April 1992; "Bols", FT Analysis, May 1992; "Spirits and liqueurs in the Netherlands", Economist Intelligence Unit, Issue 338, 1991; "The beverages industry", Economist Intelligence Unit, Issue 347, 1991; Caroline Farquhar (with thanks).

Questions for Discussion

1. What forced Bols to consider diversification?
2. What possible options were available to Bols to help the company reverse its declining fortunes?
3. What implications did Bols' new strategy in the 1980s have for the company's distribution and channel management?

13 WHOLESALERS AND DISTRIBUTORS

"In order to achieve greater profitability throughout the supply chain, greater collaboration is required between members of the marketing channel to achieve cost reductions and improve sales."

John Fernie
University of Abertay Dundee

OBJECTIVES

- To understand the nature of wholesaling in its broadest forms in the marketing channel
- To learn about wholesalers' activities
- To understand how wholesalers are classified
- To examine organisations that facilitate wholesaling
- To explore changing patterns in wholesaling

When Korean Daewoo entered the European car market it was an unknown brand. The company makes everything from fork lift trucks to electrical appliances, aeroplanes to earthmovers, but it is for its competitively priced family cars that Daewoo is now best known. In its first six months of operation in the UK it sold an incredible 14,000 cars. With South Korea now ranked the sixth largest producer of cars in the world, but with slow domestic sales, such a successful launch into Europe should come as no surprise. The company has established sales operations in most of northern Europe and bought into Austrian and Polish manufacturers in order to capitalise on market opportunities in eastern Europe.

The launch marketing blitz itself was innovative and inspired. The company's marketing research revealed all the aspects of car buying that consumers mistrusted or despised: dealers on commission, hard-sell aggressive sales personnel, over exaggerated promotional campaigns and poor after service. The promotional executions used the following themes to explain how Daewoo is different: good value, reliable cars with ABS brakes, door impact protection and power steering, non-commission sales advisers, three year warranties, courtesy cars or pick up and collection for services, AA road cover, no-fuss guarantees. More important, in a market known for its hype, all these features have been shown to be true.

Daewoo has also managed to differentiate itself and to be innovative in its choice of distribution. Most car manufacturers opt for a network of franchised dealerships: independent companies that operate a particular manufacturer's franchise. Such franchises are often notoriously over hungry for business: sales staff, paid on commission, traditionally pounce on customers as they enter showrooms, and they have poor reputations for looking after customers who have their cars serviced there after making a purchase.

Daewoo avoided this traditional distribution channel. Instead it owns its own dealerships and sells direct. These are genuinely places for showing rather than selling cars. Personnel are sales advisers earning full salaries rather than commissions on hard-fought sales, and they are trained to respond to queries with helpful information rather than "foot in the door" sales tactics. The showrooms have crèches and children's play areas, plus café facilities. Cars are serviced not at the same location, but by carefully trained technicians at Halfords, the do-it-yourself out-of-town service centres. The innovative choice of channel to market is intended to take the pressure off consumers as they make what is generally their hardest and most expensive purchasing decision after buying a house. ■

SOURCES: *What Car?*, February 1996, p. 27; Andy Fry, "Channels of communication", *Marketing*, 5 October 1995, p. III–V; Tony Taylor, "Campaign of the week: Daewoo", *Marketing*, 3 August 1995, p. 8; Michael Newman, "Driving for exports", *Far Eastern Economic Review*, 158 (25), 1995, pp. 54–55; Neil Merrick, "Putting pushy salespeople out of commission", *People Management*, 1 (9) 1995, pp. 10–11.

This chapter addresses wholesalers' and distributors' activities within a marketing channel. Wholesaling is viewed here as *all* exchanges among organisations and individuals in marketing channels, except transactions with ultimate consumers. The focus is on (1) merchant wholesalers and distributors; (2) agents and brokers; and (3) manufacturers' own branches (such as in Daewoo's case) and offices—the "middlemen" in many marketing channels. This chapter examines the importance of wholesalers and their functions, noting the services they render to producers and retailers alike; it then classifies various types of wholesalers and facilitating organisations. Finally, changing patterns in wholesaling are explored.

● ● ● ● ● ● ● ● ● ● ● ● ● ● ● ● ● ● ●

The Nature and Importance of Wholesaling

Wholesaling Service comprising all transactions in which the purchaser intends to use the product for re-sale, for making other products or for general business operations

Wholesaler An individual or organisation engaged in facilitating and expediting exchanges that are primarily wholesale transactions

Wholesaling comprises all transactions in which the purchaser intends to use the product for re-sale, for making other products or for general business operations. It does not include exchanges with ultimate consumers. Wholesaling establishments are engaged primarily in selling products directly to industrial, reseller (e.g. retailers), government and institutional users.

A **wholesaler** is an individual or organisation engaged in facilitating and expediting exchanges that are primarily wholesale transactions. Only occasionally does a wholesaler engage in retail transactions, which are sales to ultimate consumers.

The Activities of Wholesalers

In the United States and in Europe more than 50 per cent of all products are exchanged, or their exchange is negotiated, through wholesaling institutions. Owing to the strength of large, national retailers, in the UK wholesaling is not as important in consumer markets. There are also far fewer wholesalers. For example, just 27 wholesale companies and buying groups account for 85 per cent of the grocery wholesale market. In Scandinavia, Iberia and much of eastern Europe, wholesaling companies (or buying groups) account for the bulk of exchanges. Of course, it is important to remember that the distribution of all goods requires wholesaling activities, whether or not a wholesaling institution is involved. Table 13.1 lists the major activities wholesalers perform. The activities are not mutually exclusive; individual wholesalers may perform more or fewer activities than Table 13.1 shows. Wholesalers provide marketing activities for organisations above and below them in the marketing channel.

Services for Producers   Producers, above wholesalers in the marketing channel, have a distinct advantage when they use wholesalers. Wholesalers perform specialised accumulation and allocation functions for a number of products, thus allowing producers to concentrate on developing and manufacturing products that match consumers' wants.

Activity	Description
Wholesale management	Planning, organising, staffing and controlling wholesaling operations
Negotiating with suppliers	Serving as the purchasing agent for customers by negotiating supplies
Promotion	Providing a sales force, advertising, sales promotion and publicity
Warehousing and product handling	Receiving, storing and stock keeping, order processing, packaging, shipping outgoing orders and materials handling
Transport	Arranging and making local and long distance shipments
Inventory control and data-processing	Controlling physical inventory, book keeping, recording transactions, keeping records for financial analysis
Security	Safeguarding merchandise
Pricing	Developing prices and providing price quotations
Financing and budgeting	Extending credit, borrowing, making capital investments and forecasting cash flow
Management and marketing assistance to clients	Supplying information about markets and products and providing advisory services to assist customers in their sales efforts

Table 13.1 Major wholesaling activities

Wholesalers provide other services to producers as well. By selling a manufacturer's products to retailers and other customers and by initiating sales contacts with the manufacturer, wholesalers serve as an extension of the producer's sales force. Wholesalers also provide four forms of financial assistance: (1) they often pay the costs of transporting goods; (2) they reduce a producer's warehousing expenses and inventory investment by holding goods in inventory; (3) they extend credit and assume the losses from buyers who turn out to be poor credit risks; and (4) when they buy a producer's entire output and pay promptly or in cash, they are a source of working capital. In addition, wholesalers are conduits for information within the marketing channel, keeping manufacturers up to date on market developments and passing along the manufacturers' promotional plans to other middlemen in the channel.

Ideally, many producers would like more direct interaction with retailers, as close contact with major retail chains may lead to greater shelf space allocation and higher margins for the producer's goods, there being no middlemen to take a cut. Wholesalers, however, usually have closer contact with retailers because of their strategic position in the marketing channel. Besides, even though a producer's own sales force is probably more effective in its selling efforts, the costs of maintaining a sales force and performing the activities normally done by wholesalers are usually higher than the benefits received from better selling. Wholesalers can also spread their costs over many more products than most producers, resulting in lower costs per product unit. For these reasons, many producers have chosen to control promotion and influence the pricing of products and have shifted transport, warehousing and financing functions to wholesalers.

Services for Retailers Wholesalers help their retailer customers select inventory. In industries where obtaining supplies is important, skilled buying is essential. A wholesaler that buys is a specialist in understanding market conditions and an expert at negotiating final purchases. For example, based on its understanding of local customer needs and market conditions, a building supply wholesaler purchases inventory ahead of season so that it can provide its retail customers with the building supplies they want when they want them.[1] A retailer's buyer can thus avoid the responsibility of looking for and coordinating supply sources. Moreover, if the wholesaler makes purchases for several different buyers, expenses can be shared by all customers. Another key advantage is that a manufacturer's salespeople can offer retailers only a few products at a time, but independent wholesalers have a wide range of products always available.

By buying in large quantities and delivering to customers in smaller lots, a wholesaler can perform physical distribution activities—such as transport, materials handling, inventory planning, communication and warehousing—more efficiently and can provide more service than a producer or retailer would be able to do with its own physical distribution system. Furthermore, wholesalers can provide quick and frequent delivery even when demand fluctuates. They are experienced in providing fast delivery at low cost, thus allowing the producer and the wholesalers' customers to avoid risks associated with holding large product inventories.[2]

Because they carry products for many customers, wholesalers can maintain a wide product line at a relatively low cost. Often wholesalers can perform storage and warehousing activities more efficiently, permitting retailers to concentrate on other marketing activities. When wholesalers provide storage and warehousing, they generally take on the ownership function as well, an arrangement that frees retailers' and producers' capital for other purposes.

Wholesalers are very important in reaching global markets. Approximately 85 per cent of all prescription drugs sold in Europe go through wholesalers that are within national borders. In the future, it is anticipated that more wholesalers will operate across borders, particularly as changing EU regulations reduce EU restrictions.[3]

● ●

Classifying Wholesalers

Many types of wholesalers meet the different needs of producers and retailers. In addition, new institutions and establishments develop in response to producers and retail organisations that want to take over wholesaling functions. Wholesalers adjust their activities as the contours of the marketing environment change.

Wholesalers are classified along several dimensions. Whether a wholesaler is owned by the producer influences how it is classified. Wholesalers are also grouped according to whether they take title to (actually own) the products they handle. The range of services provided is another criterion used for classification. Finally, wholesalers are classified according to the breadth and depth of their product lines. Using these dimensions, this section discusses three general categories, or types, of wholesaling establishments: (1) merchant wholesalers, (2) agents and brokers, and (3) manufacturers' sales branches and offices.

Merchant Wholesalers

Merchant wholesalers
Wholesalers that take title to goods and assume the risks associated with ownership

Distributors Firms that buy and sell on their own account but tend to deal in the goods of only certain specified manufacturers

Merchant wholesalers are wholesalers that take title to goods and assume the risks associated with ownership. These independently owned businesses, which make up about two-thirds of all wholesale establishments, generally buy and re-sell products to industrial or retail customers. A producer is likely to use merchant wholesalers when selling directly to customers would not be economically feasible. From the producer's point of view, merchant wholesalers are also valuable for providing market coverage, making sales contacts, storing inventory, handling orders, collecting market information and furnishing customer support.[4] Some merchant wholesalers are even involved in packaging and developing own label brands to help their retailer customers be competitive. **Distributors** are firms that buy and sell on their own account but tend to deal in the goods of only certain specified manufacturers.

During the past 30 years, merchant wholesalers have expanded their share of the wholesale market despite competition from other types of intermediaries. Now, they often account for more than half of all wholesale revenues.[5] As a rule, merchant wholesalers for industrial products are better established and earn higher profits than consumer goods merchant wholesalers; the latter normally deal in products of lower unit value and face more competition from other middlemen. Industrial product wholesalers are also more likely to have selective distribution arrangements with manufacturers because of the technical nature of many industrial products.

Merchant wholesalers go by various names, including wholesaler, jobber, distributor, assembler, exporter and importer.[6] They fall into one of two broad categories: full service and limited service. Figure 13.1 illustrates the different types of merchant wholesalers.

Figure 13.1

Types of merchant
wholesalers

Merchant wholesalers
Merchants take title,
assume risk and are
usually involved in
buying and reselling
products to other
wholesalers, industrial
customers or retailers

Full service
wholesalers
■ General merchandise
■ Limited line
■ Speciality line

Limited service
wholesalers
■ Cash and carry
■ Truck
■ Rack jobber *
■ Drop shipper
■ Mail order

* Rack jobbers, in many cases, provide such a large number of services that they can be
classified as full service, speciality line wholesalers.

Full service wholesalers
Middlemen who offer the widest
possible range of wholesaling
functions

Full Service Merchant Wholesalers **Full service wholesalers** are middlemen who
offer the widest possible range of wholesaling functions. Their customers rely on
them for product availability, suitable assortments, bulk breaking (breaking large
quantities into smaller ones), financial assistance, and technical advice and service.[7] Full service wholesalers provide numerous marketing services to interested
customers. Many large grocery wholesalers, for example, help retailers with store
design, site selection, personnel training, financing, merchandising, advertising,
coupon redemption and scanning. Although full service wholesalers often earn
higher gross margins than other wholesalers, their operating expenses are also
higher because they perform a wider range of functions. Full service merchant
wholesalers may handle either consumer products or industrial products and are
categorised as general merchandise, limited line or speciality line wholesalers.

**General merchandise whole-
salers** Middlemen who carry a
wide product mix but offer limited
depth within the product lines

    General merchandise wholesalers are middlemen who carry a wide product
mix but offer limited depth within the product lines. They deal in such products
as medicines, hardware, non-perishable foods, cosmetics, detergents and tobacco.
General merchandise wholesalers develop strong, mutually beneficial relationships with local grocery stores, hardware and appliance shops, and local department stores, which are their typical customers. The small retailers often obtain
everything they need from these wholesalers. General merchandise wholesalers
for industrial customers provide supplies and accessories and are sometimes called
industrial distributors or *mill supply houses*.

Limited line wholesalers
Wholesalers that carry only a few
product lines but offer an extensive assortment of products
within those lines

    Limited line wholesalers are wholesalers that carry only a few product lines,
such as groceries, lighting fixtures, oil well drilling equipment or construction
equipment, but offer an extensive assortment of products within those lines.
Marketing Insight 13.1 discusses the evolving role of pharmaceuticals wholesaler
Unichem. They provide a range of services similar to those of full service merchant wholesalers. Limited line wholesalers for industrial goods serve relatively large geographic areas and provide technical expertise; in consumer goods,
they supply single or limited line retailers. Computerworld, for example, is a

Unichem Seeks Unique Distributor/Retailer Combination

Unichem is the leading wholesale distributor of health care products in the UK. Though it also distributes beauty aids, general merchandise, speciality foods and children's goods, its primary line of business is drug/pharmaceutical wholesaling. Throughout its existence, Unichem has revolutionised the health care industry by providing retailers with distribution innovations, new avenues of customer support and electronic information systems.

Decades ago, Unichem executives realised that because their firm offered the same physical products as its competitors, the company needed to differentiate itself from other drug wholesalers by offering retailers more services and benefits. An electronic order entry system assists retailers in cutting costs. Giving retailers the capability to order products automatically using hand-held order entry devices, Unichem reduces retailers' labour and product costs and inventory holdings. Unichem provides regular deliveries on guaranteed days, but it also supports its pharmacists with a "panic wagon" top-up delivery service.

Unichem set out to assist in particular smaller retail chemists that were competing with the larger health care chains, such as Boots, Lloyds or Superdrug. It organised these stores into purchasing co-operatives, which could then receive volume discounts comparable to the ones given to giant chain operations. Using research gathered by its sales force, Unichem learned that the smaller stores wanted help with marketing research, shelf management planning, centralised warehousing and storage, and co-operative advertising and joint marketing. With the aid of this large wholesaler, the smaller chemists are now able to offer consumers reduced prices and better services—making them more profitable and stable enterprises.

In 1996 Unichem, until then only a wholesaler, launched an agreed £650 million takeover for Lloyds Chemists. Lloyds had risen in less than a decade from a small family business to one with over 1,000 retail pharmacies and the number two position in the marketplace (behind Boots). Unichem argued it would still give full support to its wholesale clients, while its increased market share would provide greater purchasing power and thereby better deals for the smaller chemists. For Unichem, the move marked a departure from its role as a middleman in the marketing channel, to additionally seeking to be a retailer selling directly to the general public. Ultimately, Unichem was outbid for Lloyds by Germany's Gehe, but the intention to branch out into retailing is clear.

SOURCES: Meghan O'Leary, "Getting the most out of buying at cost", *CIO*, August 1989, pp. 86–88; William L. Trombetta, "Channel systems: an idea whose time has come in health care marketing", *Journal of Health Care Marketing,* September 1989, pp. 26–35; *Marketing,* 18 May 1995, p. 3; Unichem promotional literature; Lloyds Chemists financial reports, 1996.

limited line wholesaler of single and multi-user computer systems, dealing in six manufacturers' hardware but a limited number of product lines.

Speciality line wholesalers
Middlemen who carry the narrowest range of products, usually a single product line or a few items within a product line

Speciality line wholesalers are the middlemen who carry the narrowest range of products, usually a single product line or a few items within a product line. For example, wholesalers who carry shellfish, fruit or other food delicacies such as cheeses are speciality line wholesalers. Speciality line wholesalers understand the particular requirements of the ultimate buyers and offer customers detailed product knowledge and depth of choice. To provide sales assistance to retailers, speciality wholesalers may set up displays and arrange merchandise. In industrial markets, speciality wholesalers are often better able than manufacturers to give customers technical advice and service.

Rack jobbers Speciality line wholesalers that own and maintain their own display racks in supermarkets and drugstores

Rack jobbers are speciality line wholesalers who own and maintain their own display racks in supermarkets and drugstores. They specialise in non-food items—particularly branded, widely advertised products sold on a self-service basis—which the retailers themselves prefer not to order and stock because of risk or inconvenience. Health and beauty aids, toys, books, magazines, hardware, housewares and stationery are typical products rack jobbers handle. The rack jobbers send out delivery people to set up displays, mark merchandise, stock shelves and keep billing and inventory records; retailers need only furnish the space. Most rack jobbers operate on consignment and take back unsold products.

Limited service wholesalers Middlemen who provide only some marketing services and specialise in a few functions

Limited Service Merchant Wholesalers **Limited service wholesalers** provide only some marketing services and specialise in a few functions. Producers perform the remaining functions, or the functions are passed on to customers or other middlemen. Limited service wholesalers take title to merchandise, but in many cases they do not deliver merchandise, grant credit, provide marketing information, store inventory or plan ahead for customers' future needs. Because they offer only restricted services, limited service wholesalers are compensated with lower rates and thus earn smaller profit margins than full service wholesalers.

Although certain types of limited service wholesalers are few in number, they are important in the distribution of such products as speciality foods, perishable items, construction materials and coal. This section discusses the specific functions of four typical limited service wholesalers: cash and carry wholesalers, truck wholesalers, drop shippers and mail order wholesalers. (Table 13.2 summarises the services these wholesalers provide.)

Cash and carry wholesalers Middlemen whose customers will pay cash and furnish transport

Cash and carry wholesalers are middlemen whose customers—usually small retailers and small industrial firms—will pay cash and furnish transport. In some cases, full service wholesalers set up cash and carry departments because they cannot otherwise supply small retailers profitably. Cash and carry middlemen usually handle a limited line of products with a high turnover rate—for instance, groceries, building materials, electrical supplies or office supplies. Marketing Insight 13.2 highlights the growth of Dutch cash and carry giant Makro.

Booker Cash and Carry has a national network in the UK of retail warehouses stocking fresh and frozen foods, cigarettes, wines and spirits, and meat and provisions. Selling to the trade only, Booker offers bulk discounts to hotels, restaurants, the catering industry and small, local shops.

	Cash and Carry	Drop Shipper[a]	Mail Order
Physical possession of merchandise	Yes	No	Yes
Personal sales calls on customers	No	No	No
Information about market conditions	No	Yes	Yes
Advice to customers	No	Yes	No
Stocking and maintenance of merchandise in customers' stores	No	No	No
Credit to customers	No	Yes	Some
Delivery of merchandise to customers	No	No	No

[a]Also called desk jobber.

Table 13.2 Various services provided by limited service merchant wholesalers

The March of Makro—The Dutch Are Coming Your Way

The cash and carry sector was shaken up with the entry of Holland's Makro, a self-service wholesaler. Makro is part of SHV Holdings, a large international distribution and energy company and the sixth largest company in the Netherlands (after Shell, Unilever, Philips, AKZO and Ahold). With sales of £7 billion, the company is now active throughout Europe. Its recent growth has been in Brazil, Colombia, Taiwan, Thailand and North America. In the UK, Makro has 7,000 employees and 21 UK sites, and has quickly moved into fifth place with around 8 per cent of the cash and carry market and sales around £800 million.

Makro's latest two openings in Aberdeen and Croydon are, at over 3,000 square metres (about 100,000 square feet), more than twice the average size of a cash and carry warehouse. These depots have the latest computer systems, customer service points and in-store displays. Makro serves the trade as a cash and carry wholesaler of groceries, fresh foods, wines, spirits, beer and cigarettes, household goods, clothing, toys and sports equipment. The company retails a clutch of own label brands in these categories, including Aro, Louis Chevalier and Roca.

In a relatively traditional sector dominated by four long standing companies, Dutch Makro has had a major impact in a short time. Its mix of merchandise is more comprehensive than its competitors, forcing several, such as Booker and Landmark, to re-think their merchandising strategies. Because depth and breadth of stock within individual product categories are not as extensive as those of UK rivals, the industry has been prompted to re-think, and most companies have reduced the number of lines stocked. Although not the first wholesaler with own label products, Makro's promotion of its own ranges has encouraged its competitors to divert more attention to this area, which now accounts for 20 per cent of all sales in the cash and carry sector.

Perhaps Makro's biggest impact has been in the sales and marketing techniques it has brought to the UK. Cash and carry warehouses used to be dowdy depots that paid little attention to layout, upkeep, design or ambience, and demonstrated even less regard for customer service and satisfaction. Price was the name of the game: customers could buy in bulk at a discount but were offered few additional benefits. Makro's philosophy brings to the cash and carry sector the retailing techniques of the hypermarket: carefully controlled branch designs and layouts, high levels of staff training and a significant emphasis on building ongoing relationships with customers. Customers are wooed with more enticing warehouse stores and better customer service. In addition, sales teams monitor customers' orders and offer incentives to regular purchasers. As customer needs and buying habits change, so do Makro's depots, merchandising and marketing. The secretive Dutch company has earned a glowing reputation in its UK market.

SOURCES: Makro Leicester; *Marketing Pocket Book* (NTC Publications, 1996); "Cash and carry outlets", Keynote Publications, 1992; Harvest; Charles Thurston, "Testing Latin waters", *Global Finance*, June 1995, p. 25; Ian Fraser, "Retailer to the World", *Director*, June 1994, pp. 48–52.

Cash and carry wholesaling developed after 1920, when independent retailers began experiencing competitive pressure from large chain stores. Today cash and carry wholesaling offers advantages to wholesalers and customers alike.[8] The wholesaler has no expenditures for outside salespeople, marketing, research, promotion, credit or delivery, and the customer benefits from lower prices and immediate access to products. Many small retailers whose accounts were refused by other wholesalers have survived because of cash and carry wholesalers.

Truck wholesalers Limited service wholesalers that transport products directly to customers for inspection and selection

Truck wholesalers, sometimes called truck jobbers or wagon jobbers, transport a limited line of products directly to customers for on-the-spot inspection and selection. These wholesalers are often small operators who own and drive their own trucks. Usually, truck wholesalers have regular routes, calling on retailers and institutions to determine their needs.

Truck wholesalers sometimes supply small grocery stores with perishables, such as fruits and vegetables, which other wholesalers often do not carry. They may also sell meat, service station supplies and tobacco products. Although truck wholesalers sell, promote and transport goods, they are generally classified as limited service wholesalers because they do not extend credit. Their low volume sales and wide range of customer services result in high operating costs. Although not particularly common in northern Europe, truck wholesalers do exist in southern and eastern Europe.

Drop shippers Intermediaries who take title to goods and negotiate sales but never take actual possession of products

Also known as desk jobbers, **drop shippers** are intermediaries who take title to goods and negotiate sales but never take actual possession of products. They forward orders from retailers, industrial buyers or other wholesalers to manufacturers and then arrange for large shipments of items to be delivered directly from producers to customers. The drop shipper assumes responsibility for the products during the entire transaction, including the costs of any unsold goods.

Drop shippers are most commonly used in large volume purchases of bulky goods, such as coal, coke, oil, chemicals, lumber and building materials. Normally sold in wagon loads, these products are expensive to handle and ship relative to their unit value; extra loading and unloading is an added (and unnecessary) expense. One trend in this form of wholesaling is the use of more drop shipping from manufacturers to supermarkets.[9] A drop shipment eliminates warehousing and deferred deliveries to the stores, and large supermarkets can sell entire lorry loads of products rapidly enough to make drop shipping profitable.[10]

Because drop shippers incur no inventory costs and provide only minimal promotional assistance, they have low operating costs and can pass along some of the savings to their customers. In some cases drop shippers do offer planning services, credit and personal selling.

Mail order wholesalers Wholesalers that use catalogues instead of sales forces to sell products to retail, industrial and institutional buyers

Mail order wholesalers use catalogues instead of sales forces to sell products to retail, industrial and institutional buyers. This is a convenient and effective method of selling small items to customers in remote areas. Mail order enables buyers to choose particular catalogue items and then send in their orders and receive shipments through the postal service or other carriers. Wholesalers can thus generate sales in locations that would otherwise be unprofitable to service.

Wholesale mail order houses generally feature cosmetics, speciality foods, hardware, sporting goods, business and office supplies, and car parts. They usually require payment in cash or by credit card, and they give discounts for large orders. Mail order wholesalers hold goods in inventory and offer some planning services but seldom provide assistance with promotional efforts.

Agents and Brokers

Functional middlemen Intermediaries who perform a limited number of marketing activities in exchange for a commission

Agents and brokers (see Figure 13.2) negotiate purchases and expedite sales but do not take title to products. They are **functional middlemen,** intermediaries who perform a limited number of marketing activities in exchange for a commission, which is generally based on the product's selling price. **Agents** are middlemen who represent buyers or sellers on a permanent basis. **Brokers** are usually middlemen whom either buyers or sellers employ temporarily.

Agents Middlemen who represent buyers or sellers on a permanent basis

Although agents and brokers perform even fewer functions than limited service wholesalers, they are usually specialists in particular products or types of customer and can provide valuable sales expertise. They know their markets well and

Figure 13.2

Types of agents and brokers

Agents and brokers
These functional middlemen do not take title to products and are compensated with commissions for negotiating exchanges between sellers and buyers

Agents
Represent either buyer or seller usually on a permanent basis
- Manufacturers' agents
- Selling agents
- Commission merchants

Brokers
Bring buyers and sellers together on a temporary basis
- Food brokers
- Land/property brokers
- Other brokers, e.g., securities, insurance

Brokers Middlemen employed temporarily by either buyers or sellers

often form long lasting associations with customers. Agents and brokers enable manufacturers to expand sales when resources are limited, to benefit from the services of a trained sales force and to hold personal selling costs down. However, despite the advantages they offer, agents and brokers face increased competition from merchant wholesalers, manufacturers' sales branches and offices, and direct sales efforts.

This section concentrates on three types of agents: manufacturers' agents, selling agents and commission merchants, as well as examining the brokers' role in bringing about exchanges between buyers and sellers. Table 13.3 summarises these services.

Manufacturers' agents Independent middlemen or distributors who represent two or more sellers and usually offer customers complete product lines

Agents **Manufacturers' agents**—who account for over half of all agent wholesalers—are independent middlemen or distributors who represent two or more sellers and usually offer customers complete product lines. They sell and take orders year round, much as a manufacturer's sales office does. Restricted to a particular territory, a manufacturers' agent handles non-competing and complementary products. The relationship between the agent and each manufacturer is governed by written agreements explicitly outlining territories, selling price, order handling and terms of sale relating to delivery, service and warranties. Manufacturers' agents are commonly used in the sale of clothing and accessories, machinery and equipment, iron, steel, furniture, automotive products, electrical goods and certain food items.

Although most manufacturers' agents run small enterprises, their employees are professional, highly skilled salespeople. The agents' major advantages, in fact, are their wide range of contacts and strong customer relationships. These intermediaries help large producers minimise the costs of developing new sales territories and adjust sales strategies for different products in different locations. Agents are also useful to small producers who cannot afford outside sales forces of their

	Brokers	Manufacturers' Agents	Selling Agents	Commission Merchants
Physical possession of merchandise	No	Some	No	Yes
Long term relationship with buyers or sellers	No	Yes	Yes	Yes
Representation of competing product lines	Yes	No	No	Yes
Limited geographic territory	No	Yes	No	No
Credit to customers	No	No	Yes	Some
Delivery of merchandise to customers	No	Some	Yes	Yes

Table 13.3 Various services agents and brokers provide

own, because they incur no costs until the agents have actually sold something. By concentrating on a limited number of products, agents can mount an aggressive sales effort that would be impossible with any other distribution method except producer owned sales branches and offices. In addition, agents are able to spread operating expenses among non-competing products and thus offer each manufacturer lower prices for services rendered.

The chief disadvantage of using agents is the higher commission rate (usually 10 to 15 per cent) they charge for new product sales. When sales of a new product begin to build, total selling costs go up, and producers sometimes transfer the selling function to in-house sales representatives. For this reason, agents try to avoid depending on a single product line; most work for more than one manufacturer.

Manufacturers' agents have little or no control over producers' pricing and marketing policies. They do occasionally store and transport products, assist with planning and provide promotional support. Some agents help retailers advertise and maintain a service organisation. The more services offered, the higher the agents' commission.

Selling agents market either all of a specified product line or a manufacturer's entire output. They perform every wholesaling activity except taking title to products. Selling agents usually assume the sales function for several producers at a time and are often used in place of a marketing department. In contrast to other agent wholesalers, selling agents generally have no territorial limits and have complete authority over prices, promotion and distribution. They play a key role in the advertising, marketing research and credit policies of the sellers they represent, at times even advising on product development and packaging.

Selling agents, who account for about 1 per cent of the wholesale trade, are used most often by small producers or by manufacturers who find it difficult to maintain a marketing department because of seasonal production or other factors. A producer having financial problems may also engage a selling agent. By so doing, the producer relinquishes some control of the business but may gain working capital by avoiding immediate marketing costs.

To avoid conflicts of interest, selling agents represent non-competing product lines. The agents play an important part in the distribution of coal and textiles, and they also sometimes handle canned foods, household furnishings, clothing, lumber and metal products. In these industries, competitive pressures increase the importance of marketing relative to production, and the selling agent is a source of essential marketing and financial expertise.

Selling agents Agents who market either all of a specified product line or a manufacturer's entire output

Commission merchants
Agents who receive goods on consignment from local sellers and negotiate sales in large central markets

Commission merchants are agents who receive goods on consignment from local sellers and negotiate sales in large central markets. Most often found in agricultural marketing, commission merchants take possession of commodities in lorry loads, arrange for any necessary grading or storage and transport the commodities to auction or markets where they are sold. When sales have been completed, an agent deducts a commission plus the expense of making the sale and then turns over the profits to the producer.

Sometimes called factor merchants, these agents may have broad powers regarding prices and terms of sale, and they specialise in obtaining the best price possible under market conditions. Commission merchants offer planning assistance and sometimes extend credit, but they do not usually provide promotional support. Because commission merchants deal in large volumes, their per unit costs are usually low. Their services are most useful to small producers who must get products to buyers but choose not to field a sales force or accompany the goods to market themselves. In addition to farm products, commission merchants may handle textiles, art, furniture or seafood products. Businesses—including farms—that use commission merchants have little control over pricing, although the seller can specify a minimum price. Generally, the seller is able to supervise the agent's actions through a check of the commodity prices published regularly in newspapers. Large producers, however, need to maintain closer contact with the market and so have limited need for commission merchants.

Brokers   Brokers seek out buyers or sellers and help negotiate exchanges. In other words, brokers' primary purpose is to bring buyers and sellers together. Thus brokers perform fewer functions than other intermediaries. They are not involved in financing or physical possession, have no authority to set prices and assume almost no risks. Instead, they offer their customers specialised knowledge of a particular commodity and a network of established contacts.

Brokers are especially useful to sellers of certain types of products who market those products only occasionally. Sellers of used machinery, seasonal food products, financial securities and land/property may not know of potential buyers. A broker can furnish this information. The party who engages the broker's services—usually the seller—pays the broker's commission when the transaction is completed. Many consumers these days deal with insurance brokers when insuring a car or house contents, or with a mortgage broker when buying a house or moving. It is likely that energy brokers will set up to market gas and electricity supplies in the newly deregulated marketplace for utilities.

Food brokers   Intermediaries who sell food and general merchandise items to retailer owned and merchant wholesalers, grocery chains, industrial buyers and food processors.

Food brokers—the most common type of broker—are intermediaries who sell food and general merchandise items to retailer owned and merchant wholesalers, grocery chains, industrial buyers and food processors. Food brokers enable buyers and sellers to adjust to fluctuating market conditions. They also aid in grading, negotiating and inspecting foods, and in some cases they store and deliver products. Because of the seasonal nature of food production, the association between broker and producer is temporary—though many mutually beneficial broker-producer relationships are resumed year after year. Because food brokers provide a range of services on a somewhat permanent basis and in specific geographic territories, they can more accurately be described as manufacturers' agents.

Manufacturers' Sales Branches and Offices

Sometimes called manufacturers' wholesalers, manufacturers' sales branches and offices resemble merchant wholesalers' operations. These producer owned middlemen account for about 9 per cent of wholesale establishments and generate approximately one-third (31 per cent) of all wholesale sales.[11]

Sales branches are manufacturer owned middlemen selling products and providing support services to the manufacturer's sales force, especially in locations where large customers are concentrated and demand is high. They offer credit, deliver goods, give promotional assistance and furnish other services. In many cases, they carry inventory (although this practice often duplicates the functions of other channel members and is now declining). Customers include retailers, industrial buyers and other wholesalers. Branch operations are common in the electrical supplies, plumbing, lumber and car parts industries.

Sales offices are manufacturer owned operations that provide services which are normally associated with agents. Like sales branches, they are located away from manufacturing plants, but unlike branches, they carry no inventory. A manufacturer's sales offices or branches may sell products that enhance the manufacturer's own product line. For example, Hiram Walker, a distiller, imports wine from Spain to increase the number of products that its sales offices can offer wholesalers.

Manufacturers may set up sales branches or sales offices so that they can reach customers more effectively by performing wholesaling functions themselves. A manufacturer may also set up these branches or offices when required specialised wholesaling services are not available through existing middlemen. In some situations, however, a manufacturer may bypass its wholesaling organisation entirely—for example, in the case of Daewoo's showrooms or if the producer decides to serve large retailer customers directly. One major distiller bottles own label spirits for a UK grocery chain and separates this operation completely from the company's sales office, which serves other retailers.

• • • • • • • • • • • • • • • •

Facilitating Agencies

The total marketing channel is more than a chain linking the producer, intermediary and buyer. **Facilitating agencies**—transport companies, insurance companies, advertising agencies, marketing research agencies and financial institutions—may perform activities that enhance channel functions. Note, however, that any of the functions these facilitating agencies perform may be taken over by the regular marketing intermediaries in the marketing channel.

The basic difference between channel members and facilitating agencies is that channel members perform the negotiating functions (buying, selling and transferring title), whereas facilitating agencies do not: they perform only the various tasks that are detailed below.[12] In other words, facilitating agencies assist in the operation of the channel, but they do not sell products. The channel manager may view the facilitating agency as a sub-contractor to which various distribution tasks can be farmed out according to the principle of specialisation and division of labour.[13]

Channel members (producers, wholesalers, distributors or retailers) may rely on facilitating agencies because they believe that these independent businesses will perform various activities more efficiently and more effectively than they themselves could. Facilitating agencies are functional specialists that perform special tasks for channel members without getting involved in directing or controlling channel decisions. The following sections describe the ways in which facilitating agencies provide assistance in expediting the flow of products through marketing channels.

Public Warehouses

Public warehouses are storage facilities available for a fee. Producers, wholesalers and retailers may rent space in a warehouse instead of constructing their own facilities or using a merchant wholesaler's storage services. Many warehouses also order, deliver, collect accounts and maintain display rooms where potential buyers can inspect products.

To use goods as collateral for a loan, a channel member may place products in a bonded warehouse. If it is too impractical or expensive to transfer goods physically, the channel member may arrange for a public warehouser to verify that goods are in the member's own facilities and then issue receipts for lenders.[14] Under this arrangement, the channel member retains possession of the products but the warehouser has control. Many field public warehousers know where their clients can borrow working capital and are sometimes able to arrange low cost loans.

Finance Companies

Wholesalers and retailers may be able to obtain financing by transferring ownership of products to a sales finance company or bank while retaining physical possession of the goods. Often called "floor planning", this form of financing enables wholesalers and retailers—especially car and appliance dealers—to offer a greater selection of products for customers and thus increase sales. Loans may be due immediately upon sale, so products financed this way are usually well known, sell relatively easily and present little risk.

Other financing functions are performed by factors—organisations that provide clients with working capital by buying their accounts receivable or by lending money, using the accounts receivable as collateral. Most factors minimise their own risks by specialising in particular industries, in order to better evaluate individual channel members within those industries. Factors usually lend money for a longer time than banks. They may help clients improve their credit and collection policies and may also provide management expertise.

Transport Companies

Rail, road, air and other carriers are facilitating organisations that help manufacturers and retailers transport products. Each form of transport has its own advantages. Railways ship large volumes of bulky goods at low cost; in fact, outside the UK, a "unit train" is the cheapest form of over-land transport for ore, grain or other commodities. Air transport is relatively expensive but is often preferred for shipping high value or perishable goods. Trucks, which usually carry short haul, high value goods, now carry more and more products because factories are moving closer to their markets. As a result of technological advances, pipelines now transport powdered solids and fluidised solid materials, as well as petroleum and natural gas.

Transport companies sometimes take over the functions of other middlemen. Because of the ease and speed of using air transport for certain types of products, parcel express companies (see Figure 13.3) can eliminate the need for their clients to maintain large inventories and branch warehouses. In other cases, freight forwarders perform accumulation functions by combining less than full shipments into full loads and passing on the savings to customers—perhaps charging a wagon rate rather than a less than wagon rate.

Trade Shows and Trade Markets

Trade shows and trade markets enable manufacturers or wholesalers to exhibit products to potential buyers and thus help the selling and buying functions. **Trade shows** are industry exhibitions that offer both selling and non-selling benefits.[15]

Figure 13.3

Facilitating agencies

Parcel express companies such as DHL, FedEx, UPS and Securicor Omega Express facilitate and sometimes perform functions of marketing channel members.

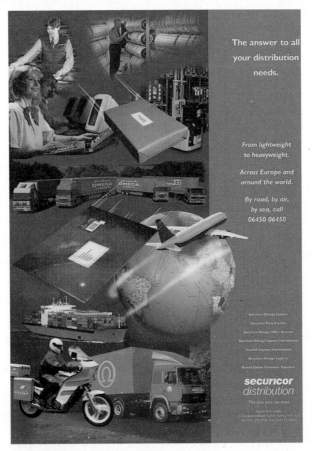

SOURCE: Courtesy of Securicor Distributors.

Trade shows Industry exhibitions that offer both selling and non-selling benefits

On the selling side, trade shows let vendors identify prospects; gain access to key decision-makers; disseminate facts about their products, services and personnel; and actually sell products and service current accounts through contacts at the show.[16] Trade shows also allow a firm to reach potential buyers who have not been approached through regular selling efforts. In fact, research indicates that most trade show visitors have not been contacted by a sales representative of any company within the past year, and many are therefore willing to travel several hundred miles to attend trade shows to learn about new goods and services.[17] The non-selling benefits include opportunities to maintain the company image with competitors, customers and the industry; gather information about competitors' products and prices; and identify potential channel members.[18] Trade shows have a positive influence on other important marketing variables, such as maintaining or enhancing company morale, product testing and product evaluation.

Trade shows can permit direct buyer-seller interaction and may eliminate the need for agents. Companies exhibit at trade shows because of the high concentration of prospective buyers for their products. Studies show that it takes, on average, 5.1 sales calls to close an industrial sale but less than 1 sales call (0.8) to close a trade show lead. The explanation for the latter figure is that more than half of the customers who purchase a product based on information gained at a trade show order the product by mail or by phone after the show. When customers use these more impersonal methods to gather information, the need for major sales calls to provide such information is eliminated.[19]

Trade markets   Relatively permanent facilities that firms can rent to exhibit products all year round

Trade markets are relatively permanent facilities that firms can rent to exhibit products year round. At these markets, such products as furniture, home decorating supplies, toys, clothing and gift items are sold to wholesalers and retailers. In the United States, trade markets are located in several major cities, including New York, Chicago, Dallas, High Point (North Carolina), Atlanta and Los Angeles. The Dallas Market Center, which includes the Dallas Trade Mart, the Home Furnishing Mart, the World Trade Center, the Decorative Center, Market Hall, InfoMart and the Apparel Mart, is housed in six buildings designed specifically for the convenience of professional buyers. Paris, Rotterdam and London all have centres similar in scale to Birmingham's National Exhibition Centre, which offers a 240 hectare (600 acre) site, with open display areas, plus 125,000 square metres (156,000 square yards) of covered exhibition space, hotels, parking for thousands of cars, plus rail and air links.

● ● ● ● ● ● ● ● ● ● ● ● ● ● ● ● ● ● ● ●

Changing Patterns in Wholesaling

The nature of the wholesaling industry is changing. The distinction between wholesaling activities that any business can perform and the traditional wholesaling establishment is becoming blurred. Changes in the nature of the marketing environment itself have transformed various aspects of the industry. For instance, they have brought about an increasing reliance on computer technology to expedite the ordering, delivery and handling of goods. The trend towards globalisation of world markets has resulted in other changes to which astute wholesalers are responding. The predominant shifts in wholesaling today are (1) the consolidation of the wholesaling industry and (2) the development of new types of retailers.

Wholesalers Consolidate Power

Like most major industries, the wholesale industry is experiencing a great number of mergers. Wholesaling firms are acquiring or merging with other firms primarily to achieve more efficiency in the face of declining profit margins.[20] Consolidation also gives larger wholesalers more pricing power over producers. Some analysts have expressed concern that wholesalers' increased price clout will increase the number of single source supply deals, which may reduce competition among wholesalers as well as retailers and producers. Nevertheless, the trend towards consolidation of wholesaling firms appears to be continuing.[21] It is also crossing national borders, as many European companies take advantage of the EU's cross-border trade and regulatory improvements.

One of the results of the current wave of consolidation in the wholesale industry is that more wholesalers are specialising. For example, McKesson once distributed chemicals, wines and spirits but now focuses only on medicines. The new larger wholesalers can also afford to purchase and use more modern technology to manage inventories physically, provide computerised ordering services and even help manage their retail customers' operations.[22]

New Types of Wholesalers

The trend towards larger retailers—superstores and the like (discussed in Chapter 14—will offer opportunities as well as dangers for wholesaling establishments. Opportunities will develop from the expanded product lines of these mass merchandisers. A merchant wholesaler of groceries, for instance, may want to add other low cost, high volume products sold in superstores. On the other hand, some limited function merchant wholesalers may no longer have a role to play. For example, the volume of sales may eliminate the need for rack jobbers, who usually handle slow moving products that are purchased in limited quantities. The future of independent wholesalers, agents and brokers depends on their ability to delineate markets and furnish desired services. The trend is also towards large global groups such as Makro, now present throughout Latin America, Asia and the Pacific as well as the European heartland.

● ● ● ● ● ● ● ● ● ● ● ● ● ● ● ● ● ● ●

Summary

● *Wholesaling* includes all transactions in which the purchaser intends to use the product for re-sale, for making other products or for general business operations. It does *not* include exchanges with the ultimate consumers. Although people may think of wholesale markets and suppliers to small grocery stores when the term wholesaling is used, wholesaling is in fact much broader in scope in the marketing channel, encompassing merchant wholesalers and distributors, agents and brokers, and manufacturers' sales branches. *Wholesalers* are individuals or organisations that facilitate and expedite primarily wholesale transactions.

● Except in the UK consumer markets, where the large multiple retailers dominate, more than half of all goods are exchanged through wholesalers, although the distribution of any product requires that someone must perform wholesaling activities, whether or not a wholesaling institution is involved. For producers, wholesalers perform specialised accumulation and allocation functions for a number of products, letting the producers concentrate on manufacturing the products. For retailers, wholesalers provide buying expertise, wide product lines, efficient distribution, and warehousing and storage services.

● Various types of wholesalers serve different market segments. How a wholesaler is classified depends on whether the wholesaler is owned by a producer, whether it takes title to products, the range of services it provides, and the breadth and depth of its product lines. The three general categories of wholesalers are merchant wholesalers, agents and brokers, and manufacturers' sales branches and offices.

● *Merchant wholesalers* are independently owned businesses that take title to goods and assume risk; they make up about two thirds of all wholesale firms. They are either full service wholesalers, offering the widest possible range of wholesaling functions, or limited service wholesalers, providing only some marketing services and specialising in a few functions. *Distributors* buy and sell on their own account but tend to deal in the goods of only certain manufacturers. *Full service wholesalers* include (1) *general merchandise wholesalers,* which offer a wide but relatively shallow product mix; (2) *limited line wholesalers,* which offer extensive assortments in a few product lines; and (3) *speciality line wholesalers,* which offer great depth in a single product line or in a few items within a line. *Rack jobbers* are speciality line wholesalers that own and service display racks in supermarkets and chemists. There are four types of *limited service wholesalers.* (1) *Cash and carry wholesalers* sell to small businesses, require payment in cash and do not deliver. (2) *Truck wholesalers* transport products directly to customers for inspection and selection. (3) *Drop shippers* own goods and negotiate sales but never take possession of products. (4) *Mail order wholesalers* sell to retail, industrial and institutional buyers through direct mail catalogues.

● Agents and brokers, sometimes called *functional middlemen,* negotiate purchases and expedite sales but do not take title to products. They are usually specialists and provide valuable sales expertise. *Agents* represent buyers or sellers on a permanent basis. *Manufacturers' agents* offer customers the complete product lines of two or more sellers; *selling agents* market a complete product line or a producer's entire output and perform every wholesaling function except taking title to products; *commission merchants* receive goods on consignment from local sellers and negotiate sales in large central markets. *Brokers*, such as *food brokers*, negotiate exchanges between buyers and sellers on a temporary basis.

● Manufacturers' sales branches and offices are vertically integrated units owned by manufacturers. *Sales branches* sell products and provide support services for the manufacturer's sales force in a given location. *Sales offices* carry no inventory and function much as agents do.

● *Facilitating agencies* do not buy, sell or take title but perform certain wholesaling functions. They include *public warehouses*, finance companies, transport companies, and *trade shows* and *trade markets*. In some instances, these organisations eliminate the need for a wholesaling establishment.

● The nature of the wholesaling and distribution industry is changing in response to changes in the marketing environment. The predominant changes are the increasing consolidation of the wholesaling industry and the growth of new types of wholesalers.

● ● ● ● ● ● ● ● ● ● ● ● ● ● ● ● ● ●

Important Terms

Wholesaling	Limited service wholesalers	Commission merchants
Wholesaler	Cash and carry wholesalers	Food brokers
Merchant wholesalers	Truck wholesalers	Sales branches
Distributors	Drop shippers	Sales offices
Full service wholesalers	Mail order wholesalers	Facilitating agencies
General merchandise wholesalers	Functional middlemen	Public warehouses
Limited line wholesalers	Agents	Trade shows
Speciality line wholesalers	Brokers	Trade markets
Rack jobbers	Manufacturers' agents	
	Selling agents	

● ● ● ● ● ● ● ● ● ● ● ● ● ● ● ● ● ●

Discussion and Review Questions

1. Is there a distinction between wholesalers and wholesaling? If so, what is it?
2. Would it be appropriate for a wholesaler to stock both interior wall paint and office supplies? In what circumstances would this product mix be logical?
3. What services do wholesalers provide to producers and retailers?
4. Drop shippers take title to products but do not accept physical possession. Commission merchants take physical possession of products but do not accept title. Defend the logic of classifying drop shippers as wholesale merchants and commission merchants as agents.
5. What are the advantages of using agents to replace merchant wholesalers? What are the disadvantages?

6. What, if any, are the differences in the marketing functions that manufacturers' agents and selling agents perform?
7. Why are manufacturers' sales offices and branches classified as wholesalers? Which independent wholesalers are replaced by manufacturers' sales branches? Which independent wholesalers are replaced by manufacturers' sales offices?
8. "Public warehouses are really wholesale establishments." Please comment.
9. Discuss the role of facilitating organisations. Identify three facilitating organisations and explain how each type performs this role.
10. Why has car manufacturer Daewoo opted for a new approach to car distribution?

Recommended Readings

J. Fernie, "Quick response: an international perspective", *International Journal of Physical Distribution and Materials Management,* vol. 24, no. 6, 1994, pp. 38–46.

J. Fernie, "International comparisons of supply chain management in grocery retailing", *Service Industries Journal,* vol. 15, no. 4, 1995, pp. 134–147.

GEA, *Supplier-Retailer Collaboration in Supply Chain Management* (London: Coca-Cola Retailing Research Group, 1994).

R. C. Laming, *Beyond Partnership—Strategies for Innovation and Lean Supply* (New York: Prentice-Hall, 1993).

D. Shipley, ed., "Industrial distribution channel management", special edition, *European Journal of Marketing,* vol. 23, no. 2, 1989.

Cases

13.1 JCB Benelux—Part of the Family

JCB is the family owned Staffordshire construction equipment manufacturer renowned for its backhoe digger, telehandlers, distinctive yellow livery and prominent branding. Throughout Europe its name is used as the generic description for perhaps the most versatile piece of construction equipment, the backhoe loader. Established soon after the end of the Second World War, creating farm machinery from old air raid shelters, the company is now a billion pound success story selling its wares across the world, principally in the Pacific Rim, Europe and North America. The choice for distribution, however, is not straightforward: a variety of routes to market is deployed.

In the UK, six dealer groups operate around fifty depots. Each dealer is an independently owned company concentrating on a geographic region of the UK. While some of these companies may retail cars and trucks, thereby holding other vehicle manufacturers' franchises, in earthmoving and construction equipment they are totally focused on JCB's extensive range of products. With over half of the UK market, it is not surprising that JCB inspires tremendous loyalty and enthusiasm from its dealer groups. JCB does much more than supply high quality machines to its dealers. Extensive training programmes are run for all levels of dealer personnel, and help is offered for business planning, marketing and promotional activity. Now, under its "Keep It Genuine" initiative, even the after-market for spares and service is strongly supported by the company.

Away from the UK domestic market, JCB maintains a mix of different marketing approaches. In core European territories such as Benelux, France or Germany there are wholly owned JCB subsidiaries that take their lead from the UK head office but have local responsibility for sales forecasts, sales and marketing, and business planning. These subsidiaries choose individual dealers or small dealer groups in their particular country of responsibility. This additional tier of management—the subsidiaries—enables JCB to carefully reflect local market conditions and to monitor performance more closely. The subsidiaries import JCB's machines from its UK factories before "selling them on" to the local dealers. In contrast with the UK, however, the European dealer depots are not solus JCB outlets—they may retail and service a variety of other construction equipment manufacturers' models. In Portugal JCB uses a different approach again. Two dealer groups dominate JCB's sales throughout the country. While they do deal in other companies' machines, they are principally JCB orientated and very focused on assisting JCB to dominate the market. JCB's head office team works very closely and directly with the principals of the two large independently owned Portuguese dealer groups. In most other countries in which JCB has a significant presence, the company deals with numerous one-off or small local dealer groups to ensure that most major conurbations have a JCB presence—JCB machines readily available, with knowledgeable personnel and full local servicing and parts back-up. In territories where only small numbers of machines are sold, JCB uses local agents to represent the company.

The company maintains this diverse mix of channel members to support its range not by accident but to reflect local market conditions, sales forecasts and levels of business, future strategy requirements—and to guarantee an adequate level of market coverage in a controllable manner. To JCB, the quality reputation of its brand and products is crucial and must be reflected in its choice of dealers and the effectiveness of its channels to market. The picture recently has been further complicated. Marketing research has revealed several distinct market segments. Customers of smaller equipment such as mini-excavators and skid steers were different and had their own set of purchasing requirements compared with the customers of JCB's core backhoe digger and telehandler ranges. Different again were the users of the very large excavators deployed in major road building or quarrying schemes. A joint venture with Japan's Sumitomo prompted the company to treat its newly expanded "heavy line" excavators as a separate market, requiring specialist dealer expertise from fewer locations (sales are more infrequent, unit prices into six figures and stockholding for dealers very difficult, given the cost and size of the big excavators). For the smaller equipment, JCB set up its "Compact Division" of dealers within dealers. Specialist departments in carefully selected dealers concentrate on the mini-excavators, skid steers and hydropower packs. Only JCB's detailed knowledge of its markets and dealers, coupled with its shrewdly honed mix of channel members, permitted it to implement successfully its revised approach to its product portfolio.

The variety in dealer styles, loyalty and geographic coverage forces JCB to devote a great deal of attention to motivating and communicating with its dealers. For example, in March 1994 JCB flew in over 1,500 delegates, mostly dealer principals, to de luxe accommodation in Malaga, Spain. Close to 30 new models were on display, complete with the fanfare usually associated with a motor show launch for a new Jaguar or Porsche. Apart from reassuring dealers that the company was still innovating and developing exciting products despite the recession, the two week event, costing around half a million pounds, orientated dealers to the company's evolving machine range and strategic plans. It also introduced them to *Trident*. Through the three prongs of *Trident*, JCB instigated the launch of its Compact Division, heavy line and staple medium range marketing initiatives designed to keep the company as the leader in Europe.

SOURCES: JCB sales literature, 1994÷1997; *Trident* promotional material, 1994; Ken Gofton, "JCB digs for marketing gold", *Marketing*, 14 April 1994, pp. 28–29; Amanda Burnside, "Keeping the faith", *Marketing*, 27 July 1995, pp. IV–VI.

Questions for Discussion

1. JCB operates through a variety of dealer types. Why? Does this mix of styles present difficulties for the company's head office staff?
2. Most machinery and vehicle manufacturers use a network of dealers and franchised depots. Why?

13.2 Cash and Carry No Longer Just Discounts

Heinz boss Tony O'Reilly heads Fitzwilton group, a major Irish motor, cash and carry, and industrial group, trading as M6 Cash and Carry in Britain. Despite the sector's worth of close to £8.5 billion in 1992, O'Reilly described UK cash and carry trading conditions as the "toughest in recent years, with volumes and sales just keeping pace with inflation". The boom years of the mid-1980s encouraged numerous new entrants, but now there is over capacity, with declining numbers of depots and increasing liquidations. This squeeze has hit the smaller operators most; the largest companies are consolidating their grip on the sector: Booker, Landmark, Nurdin & Peacock, and NISA-Today's have over 70 per cent of the market. This concentration replicates the grocery retailing scene of the late 1960s, when supermarket groups merged to produce a handful of dominant players.

Although price remains a core trading proposition, service and brand image are increasingly important. Customers are being offered better service, together with assistance in building their own company image through local press and television advertising. The leading cash and carry companies are offering marketing support to their key accounts not just to stimulate sales but also to build up those customers' loyalty to their nearby warehouse. These changes have been accompanied by a rise in average

Company	Market Share (%)	Number of Depots	
		1989	1992
Booker	22.0	171	166
Today's	15.5	86	90
Landmark	17.0	75	90
Nurdin & Peacock	15.0	38	50
Sterling	4.7	31	39
Mojo	1.4	25	24
Makro	7.6	15	21
Watson & Philip	2.0	14	12
Batleys	5.0	11	11

SOURCE: Key Note, 1992.

sales per depot from £9.2 million in 1986 to £14.9 million in 1991.

Depots have been up-rated by the leading groups, with new equipment, better stocking systems and improved physical distribution. They have also initiated sales promotions campaigns and incentive programmes. Computerisation has helped lower costs and improve efficiency. With Germany's Siemens Nixdorf, Booker has created MIDAS (management information depot application system), giving each of its depots a comprehensive invoicing, mailing, sales data, customer information and stock control system. This system has improved Booker's ability to target customers and monitor stock needs. Systems such as MIDAS have enabled the leading companies to reduce their product lines. For example, Nurdin & Peacock used to carry 60,000 lines but has now reduced its coverage to 40,000 and is aiming to reach 30,000 without alienating customers.

Branches are being rationalised, both to respond to the recession and to benefit from cost economies and enhanced computer systems. For example, companies are either consolidating three out-dated neighbouring depots into one central, spacious, service orientated depot, or they are closing a branch while extending and refurbishing a neighbouring one. Own label lines are taking up to 20 per cent of cash and carry sales; among the most popular are Booker's grocery Family Choice label and its catering Chef's Larder range, Landmark's Lifestyle, and Nurdin & Peacock's Happy Shopper. There are own label brands in most of the key product areas: grocery, catering (for the catering trade), confectionery, wines, spirits, lager and beer, and cigarettes. Own label brands are even available for some fresh foods, shirts and sports equipment (Makro), and garden products (Nurdin & Peacock). Companies have also established specialist sales teams to provide expert advice and service. For example, Nurdin & Peacock has separate teams handling independent grocers, garage forecourts and newsagents, and the catering trade.

Significant investment has gone into staff training, new stores, computer systems, sales teams and the development of own label products. The overriding aim has been to provide customers with a better service that is closely in tune with their needs, even down to offering marketing advice and support for customers' promotional campaigns. As the sector has evolved, customer service and modernised operations have taken a prime position. The cash and carry sector now involves much more than pure discounting.

SOURCES: "Cash & carry outlets", Key Note, 1992; IGD Research Services; Harvest; Booker promotional material; Nick Higham, "Independent—at any price?", *Marketing Week,* 11 February 1994, p. 19.

Questions for Discussion

1. How are the major cash and carry companies responding to changing customer needs?
2. How are computerised retailing systems contributing to improved customer service?
3. Why are cash and carry companies offering marketing and promotional advice to their customers?

14 RETAILING

"The power, prestige and proactivity of major retailers now exceeds that of their manufacturer suppliers."

Peter J. McGoldrick
Manchester Business School

OBJECTIVES

- To understand the purpose and function of retailers in the marketing channel
- To describe and distinguish major types of retailers and locations
- To understand non-store retailing and franchising
- To learn about strategic issues in retailing
- To realise that retailing *per se* is a specialist area requiring a modified approach to marketing

BAA owns and operates seven airports in the UK, including Heathrow, Gatwick and rapidly expanding Stanstead. BAA's 80 million passengers account for 70 per cent of the UK's air passenger traffic. The company, privatised in 1987, builds and manages terminals and runways and handles security. Chief executive Sir John Egan, former champion of Jaguar Cars, intends to keep London as the "hub of Europe", ahead of challengers Paris, Frankfurt, Amsterdam and Vienna.

A couple of years ago Egan instigated a policy review emphasising a commitment to quality service, on-site competition, and the introduction of branded operations and concessions. All proposals followed extensive marketing research. Three tax-free operators currently compete for the available business: Allders, Forte and Harrods. SAS, Häagen-Dazs and Garfunkels compete for catering business, along with big names such as Upper Crust, Granary, Casey Jones and Burger King. The BAA Skyshop brand disappeared and was replaced

Machine have well equipped him for the task. Some 90,000 square metres (1 million square feet) of new shopping space will open before the end of 1998, and pre-tax profits are expected to reach £450 million by 1997.

BAA has taken restless passengers waiting for flights and put them into shops selling well known brands and a variety of merchandise. Research from 120,000 interviews each year has shown that retail outlets are a high priority for passengers. The following are now offered: Bally, Benetton, Body Shop, Sock Shop, Aquascutum, Burberry, Harrods, Thomas Cook. The captive audience is appreciative of the changes, as are the retailers. Tie Rack's sales at Heathrow are £27,000 per square metre (£3,000 per square foot) annually, 10 times the ratio the company's high street stores achieve. Heathrow's Terminal 4 houses BAA's first "serious" shopping mall, with 20 retailers, natural daylight, shopping trolleys and big brands. ■

with Forte bookshops and market leaders W. H. Smith and John Menzies. Only well known retail brands are now welcome.

With the EU planning to phase out intra-community duty free trade from 1996, Egan sees retail operations as the way to continue BAA's impressive profits record. Already 10 per cent of terminal space—46,000 square metres (500,000 square feet)—is devoted to retailing. Egan intends to expand space significantly, with the help of retailing director Barry Gibson, whose record of senior positions at Littlewoods, Burton Group and Jean

SOURCES: BAA press office; Bunhill, *The Independent on Sunday,* 21 February 1993, p. IB40; Clare Sambrook, "BAA talks shop on airport retailing", *Marketing,* 29 October 1992, pp. 25–30; *The Independent on Sunday,* 11 February 1996, p. IB5; "It's not easy being green", *The Economist,* 6 January 1995, p. 29.

Marketing research has enabled BAA to develop facilities in line with passengers' wishes and a marketing strategy that has enhanced its profits. Marketing methods that satisfy consumers serve well as the guiding philosophy of retailing. Retailers are an important link in the marketing channel because they are both marketers and customers for producers and wholesalers. They perform many marketing activities, such as buying, selling, grading, risk taking and developing information about consumers' wants. Of all marketers, retailers are the most visible to ultimate consumers. They are in a strategic position to gain feedback from consumers and to relay ideas to producers and intermediaries in the marketing channel. Retailing is an extraordinarily dynamic area of marketing.

This chapter examines the nature of retailing and its importance in supplying consumers with goods and services. It discusses the major retail locations and types of retail stores and describes several forms of non-store retailing, such as in-home retailing, telemarketing, automatic vending and mail order retailing. This chapter also looks at franchising, a retailing form that continues to grow in popularity. Finally, it presents several strategic issues in retailing: location, product assortment, retail positioning, atmospherics, store image, scrambled merchandising, the wheel of retailing, the balance of retailing, retail technology and the impact of the deregulation of the European Union.

• • • • • • • • • • • • • • • • • • •

The Nature of Retailing

Retailing All transactions in which the buyer intends to consume the product through personal, family or household use

Retailer An organisation that purchases products for the purpose of re-selling them to ultimate consumers, the general public, often from a shop or store

Retailing includes all transactions in which the buyer intends to consume the product through personal, family or household use. The buyers in retail transactions are ultimate consumers. A **retailer,** then, is an organisation that purchases products for the purpose of re-selling them to ultimate consumers, the general public, often from a shop or store. Although most retailers' sales are to consumers, non-retail transactions occasionally occur when retailers sell products to other businesses. Retailing activities usually take place in a store or in a service establishment, but exchanges through telephone selling, vending machines, mail order retailing and the Internet occur outside stores.

It is common knowledge that retailing is important to the economy, being a large employer and major service sector component. Table 14.1, for example, shows the level of retail sales in the UK between 1988 and 1994. As the table shows, sales have increased signicantly over this period. Also, most personal income is spent in retail stores.

By providing assortments of products to match consumers' wants, retailers create place, time and possession utilities. *Place utility* means moving products from wholesalers or producers to a location where consumers want to buy them. *Time utility* involves maintaining specific business hours to make products available when consumers want them. *Possession utility* means facilitating the transfer of ownership or use of a product to consumers.

In the case of services such as hairdressing, dry cleaning, restaurants and car repairs, retailers themselves develop most of the product utilities. The services of such retailers provide aspects of *form utility* associated with the production process. Retailers of services usually have more direct contact with consumers and more opportunity to alter the product in the marketing mix.

• • • • • • • • • • • • • • • • • • •

Retail Locations

Central Business District

Central business district (CBD) The traditional hub of most cities and towns; the focus for shopping, banking and commerce and, hence, the busiest part of the whole area

The traditional hub of most cities and towns is the **central business district** (CBD), the focus for shopping, banking and commerce and hence the busiest part of the whole area for traffic, public transport and pedestrians. Examples are London's Oxford and Regent streets, the Champs Elysées in Paris and Berlin's Kurfürstendamm.[1] The CBD is sub-divided into zones: generally, retailers are clustered together in a zone; banking and insurance companies locate together; legal offices occupy neighbouring premises; municipal offices and amenities are built on adjoining plots (town hall, library, law courts, art galleries).

Within the shopping zone certain streets at the centre of the zone will have the main shops and the highest levels of pedestrian footfall. In this area, known as the

Prime pitch   The area at the
centre of the shopping zone with
the main shops and the highest
levels of pedestrian footfall

prime pitch, the key traders or magnets (Marks & Spencer, Boots or major department stores) will occupy prominent sites, so generating much of the footfall. Other retailers vie to be located close to these key traders so as to benefit from the customer traffic they generate. The highest rents are therefore paid for such sites. The CBD shopping centre—the city or town centre—generally offers shopping goods and some convenience items. Clothing, footwear, jewellery, cosmetics and financial services dominate the CBD. For the most part, grocers have moved out of town.

	Current Prices, £ Billion						
	1988	**1989**	**1990**	**1991**	**1992**	**1993**	**1994**
All Retailers	113.29	120.92	129.32	135.40	140.32	148.33	155.06
Food retailers	40.53	43.72	47.52	51.03	53.69	56.83	60.06
Grocers	32.48	35.61	39.13	42.65	45.39	48.91	52.04
Dairymen	2.43	2.40	2.31	2.36	2.29	2.20	2.13
Butchers	2.68	2.82	2.82	2.79	2.65	2.54	2.43
Fishmongers	0.24	0.26	0.28	0.28	0.25	0.25	0.24
Greengrocers, fruiterers	1.36	1.49	1.59	1.59	1.52	1.46	1.44
Bread and flour confectioners	1.18	1.28	1.39	1.43	1.47	1.53	1.57
Clothing and footwear retailers	11.22	11.99	12.75	12.88	12.88	13.52	14.15
Men's and boys' wear	1.95	2.06	2.19	2.06	1.93	1.95	1.95
Women's, girls', children's and infants' wear; general clothing; leather and travel goods	6.95	7.34	7.72	7.88	8.11	8.42	8.88
Footwear	2.38	2.58	2.84	2.84	2.90	3.09	3.38
Household goods	21.12	21.80	22.47	23.37	24.05	26.07	27.42
Furniture, carpet and textiles	7.05	7.27	7.34	7.56	8.00	9.18	9.69
Electrical, music goods, gas and electricity showrooms	7.12	7.26	7.41	7.56	7.63	8.08	8.45
Hardware, china and fancy goods	1.79	1.92	2.06	2.14	2.25	2.37	2.43
DIY	3.78	4.12	4.25	4.59	4.76	5.01	5.39
TV and other hire and repair	1.34	1.34	1.41	1.50	1.41	1.37	1.41
All other non-food retailers	20.57	22.53	24.49	25.23	25.96	26.94	27.19
CTNs	8.84	9.35	10.05	10.65	11.16	11.36	11.26
Off-licences	2.77	2.93	3.15	3.31	3.66	3.66	3.75
Chemists[1]	2.06	2.31	2.49	2.59	2.68	2.88	2.93
Booksellers, stationers, specialist newsagents	1.66	2.02	2.44	2.46	2.58	2.68	2.73
Jewellers	1.72	1.98	2.02	1.92	1.80	1.84	1.78
Toys, hobby, sports goods and cycles	1.52	1.72	1.97	1.97	1.77	1.87	1.93
Other non-food	1.90	2.16	2.38	2.38	2.38	2.57	2.71
Mixed retail businesses	19.84	20.92	22.09	22.86	23.61	25.09	26.31
Very large mixed businesses[2]	15.51	16.38	17.24	17.93	18.44	19.65	20.51
Other mixed businesses	0.90	1.02	1.15	1.22	1.21	1.28	1.29
General mail order houses	3.48	3.55	3.70	3.77	3.92	4.22	4.47

(Continues)

Table 14.1 Retail sales by type of business: Great Britain, 1988–94

	Constant 1990 Prices, £ Billion						
	1988	**1989**	**1990**	**1991**	**1992**	**1993**	**1994**
All Retailers	133.69	132.37	129.32	127.91	127.79	133.01	135.68
Food retailers	47.83	47.86	47.52	48.21	48.90	50.96	52.55
Grocers	38.33	38.98	39.13	40.29	41.34	43.86	45.54
Dairymen	2.86	2.63	2.31	2.23	2.08	1.97	1.86
Butchers	3.16	3.09	2.82	2.64	2.41	2.28	2.12
Fishmongers	0.28	0.28	0.28	0.26	0.23	0.22	0.21
Greengrocers, fruiterers	1.61	1.63	1.59	1.50	1.39	1.31	1.26
Bread and flour confectioners	1.39	1.40	1.39	1.35	1.34	1.37	1.37
Clothing and footwear retailers	13.24	13.12	12.75	12.17	11.73	12.12	12.39
Men's and boys' wear	2.30	2.25	2.19	1.94	1.75	1.75	1.70
Women's, girls', children's and infants' wear; general clothing; leather and travel goods	8.20	8.03	7.72	7.44	7.39	7.55	7.77
Footwear	2.81	2.83	2.84	2.68	2.64	2.77	2.96
Household goods	24.93	23.86	22.47	22.08	21.90	23.38	23.99
Furniture, carpet and textiles	8.32	7.96	7.34	7.15	7.29	8.23	8.48
Electrical, music goods, gas and electricity showrooms	8.40	7.95	7.41	7.14	6.95	7.24	7.39
Hardware, china and fancy goods	2.12	2.10	2.06	2.02	2.04	2.12	2.13
DIY	4.46	4.51	4.25	4.33	4.33	4.49	4.72
TV and other hire and repair	1.58	1.47	1.41	1.41	1.29	1.23	1.23
All other non-food retailers	24.28	24.67	24.49	23.83	23.64	24.16	23.79
CTNs	10.44	10.23	10.05	10.06	10.16	10.18	9.85
Off-licences	3.27	3.21	3.15	3.13	3.33	3.28	3.28
Chemists[1]	2.44	2.53	2.49	2.44	2.45	2.59	2.57
Booksellers, stationers, specialist newsagents	1.95	2.21	2.44	2.32	2.35	2.40	2.39
Jewellers	2.02	2.16	2.02	1.81	1.64	1.65	1.55
Toys, hobby, sports goods and cycles	1.79	1.88	1.97	1.86	1.62	1.68	1.69
Other non-food	2.25	2.37	2.38	2.25	2.17	2.30	2.37
Mixed retail businesses	23.41	22.90	22.09	21.60	21.51	22.50	23.02
Very large mixed businesses[2]	18.31	17.93	17.24	16.94	16.80	17.62	17.95
Other mixed businesses	1.06	1.11	1.15	1.16	1.10	1.15	1.13
General mail order houses	4.10	3.89	3.70	3.56	3.57	3.78	3.92

NOTES: Deflated by the Retail Prices Index (1990 = 100).
[1]Excluding receipts under the National Health Service.
[2]With turnovers of £12 million or more in 1991.
SOURCE: *The Retail Pocket Book* 1996 (Henley, Oxon: NTC Publications, 1996), pp. 38–39. Reprinted by permission.

Table 14.1 Retail sales by type of business: Great Britain, 1988–94 (cont.)

Property developers build shopping malls or centres in and around the CBD. Each development has one or more magnets (big name variety or department stores) both to attract shoppers and to encourage other retailers to locate within the development. Most city centres now have one covered shopping centre development (Eldon Square in Newcastle, Arndale Centre in Manchester).[2] On streets adjacent to this area of prime pitch, rents are lower but so is footfall. These secondary sites are suitable for speciality retailers or discounters, which have either lower margins or lower **customer thresholds** (the number of customers required to make a profit). Figure 14.1 shows the composition of a typical central business district (CBD).

Customer threshold The number of customers required to make a profit

Suburban Centres

Suburban centres Shopping centres created at major road junctions that cater for local shopping needs

Historically, as urban areas expanded during the early part of the twentieth century, they joined and subsequently swallowed up neighbouring towns and villages. The shopping centres of these settlements survived to become **suburban centres** of the now larger city or town. Where the expansion of the town was planned, suburban centres were created at major road junctions to cater for local shopping

Figure 14.1

The composition of a typical central business district (CBD)

SOURCE: Lyndon Simkin and Sally Dibb

⌐¬ CBD	▨ Banks, building societies, insurance companies	B Town hall, art gallery, library
1 Bus station	▩ Solicitors/legal	▨ Covered shopping centres/malls
2 Railway station	Central shopping area	
3 Coach station	Head Post Office	O Peak land value intersection (retail)
▬ Main road	Department stores	Zone in transition*
— Minor road	▨ Market hall	
╫╫ Railway	A Law courts	● Peak overall land value (CBD)
▬ Canal		Sports stadium
		+ Cinema/theatre

*The zone in transition is the land use between the CBD and suburban housing areas: light manufacturing, transport termini, wholesaling, garages, medical, multi-family residences.

needs and reduce demands and congestion in the CBD.[3] Suburban centres tend to offer convenience goods (frequently demanded, cheaper items such as groceries and drugs) and some shopping goods (clothing and footwear). Apart from a supermarket or limited range variety store (such as Woolworth), the shops tend to be small store outlets from 150 to 250 square metres (1,650 to 2,750 square feet); many are privately owned—unlike those in the CBD—and are not part of national chains.

Edge of Town

During the 1970s, as rents in the CBD rose and sites sufficient for large, open-plan stores became harder to obtain, retailers looked to the green fields adjacent to outer ring roads for expansion. The superstore era had dawned as the major grocery, carpets and furniture, electrical and DIY* retailers opened free-standing "sheds". Needing more space to display stock and sell their goods than they could afford or obtain in the CBD or even suburban centre, but still requiring high traffic levels, they sought sites adjacent to major road arteries into the CBD. Initially, planning authorities protected green belt and undeveloped land, so the retailers occupied disused warehouses and factory units in once thriving industrial and commercial areas.

The planners then began to realise that stylish retail outlets could brighten up areas, create employment, attract traffic and rejuvenate decaying zones. Major retail chains such as the grocery retailers with their frequently purchased convenience goods attracted large volumes of traffic. Relocating these stores to non-retail areas of the city, and particularly to **edge of town sites,** helped redistribute traffic volumes and make use of the latest infrastructure. Retailers no longer had to occupy run down warehouses; they could acquire undeveloped land on the edge of built up areas and provide purpose built stores, parking facilities and amenities for their customers.[4]

Edge of town sites Retail locations on undeveloped land, providing purpose built stores, parking facilities and amenities for their customers on the edge of a built up area

Retail Parks

The progression of the out of town concept and relaxation of planning regulations by local authorities led to the mid-1980s initiation of the **retail park,** in which free-standing superstores, each over 2,500 square metres (27,500 square feet) are grouped together to form retail villages or parks. Located close to major roads, they offer extensive free parking. Most of the stores offer one floor shopping with wide ranges. Grocery superstores locate so as to be easily accessible to their consumers, as do the retailers of large, expensive shopping goods: carpets, furniture, electrical goods, toys. The extensive ranges and displays of DIY retailers make such locations viable.

Retail park Groupings of free-standing superstores, forming a retail village

Increasingly, planners are for the first time allowing clothing and footwear retailers to locate out of town. They initially feared the demise of the CBD, but forecasts now show that both CBD and out of town centres can survive serving the same town or city.

Most retail parks provide only superstores, but some have shopping malls of speciality and chain stores, such as Birmingham's Merry Hill or Gateshead's Metro Centre. Leisure facilities are frequently incorporated to cater for a family day out: ice skating rinks, cinemas, children's play areas, restaurants, fast food outlets and food courts (see Figure 14.2).

*DIY (do-it-yourself) merchandise includes building materials, hardware, plumbing and electrical goods, kitchen units and gardening requirements.

Figure 14.2

The out of town shopping mall has reached Europe

Gateshead's Metro Centre offers the major retail chains plus extensive leisure amenities and catering facilities.

SOURCE: *Courtesy of The Metro Centre.*

• • • • • • • • • • • • • • • •

Major Store Types

Department and Variety Stores

Department stores
Physically large stores that occupy prominent positions in the traditional heart of the town or city

Department stores are physically large—around 25,000 square metres (275,000 square feet)—and occupy prominent positions in the traditional heart of the town or city, the central shopping centre. Most towns have at least one such store; larger towns and cities have the population size to support several. The smaller town's department store is generally independently owned, whereas the larger store groups—Debenhams, House of Fraser, John Lewis or Allders in the UK; AuHPrintemps in France; El Corte Ingles in Spain; or Karlstadt in Germany—have stores in many cities. Within a department store, related product lines are organised into separate departments such as cosmetics, men's and women's fashions and accessories, housewares, home furnishings, haberdashery and toys. Each department functions as a self-contained business unit and the buyers for individual departments are fairly autonomous. Financial services, hairdressing and restaurants or coffee shops act as additional "pulls" to attract customers into the store.

Quite often concessionaires operate shops within shops. Brides is the largest retailer of wedding apparel in the UK. The company has its own bridal shops and agencies in secondary locations but also operates the bridal departments in most Debenhams and House of Fraser department stores (see Figure 14.3). Brides either pays a fixed rental per square metre of space occupied in the host department store or pays a percentage commission on its volume of business. In department stores, concessions or shops within shops are typical for fashion clothing, cosmetics and housewares.

Throughout the 1970s and 1980s, with the growth of shopping malls and covered centres, the explosion in the number of speciality shops and the move to out of town shopping, the demise of department stores was predicted. Yet they are still at the heart of many CBD shopping centres. With new management teams and investment, most departmental store groups are once again thriving and expanding, building new stores in towns where they were not previously represented and in out of town retail parks, as well as refurbishing existing outlets.

Variety stores   Slightly smaller stores than department stores, offering a reduced range of merchandise

Variety stores tend to be slightly smaller and often are more specialised, offering a reduced range of merchandise. Their appeal tends to be middle market, price points are more critical and the selection of additional services is limited, usually

Figure 14.3

A shop within a shop

Brides occupies a prominent position in this Debenhams store.

Source: Courtesy of Bridal Fashions Ltd.

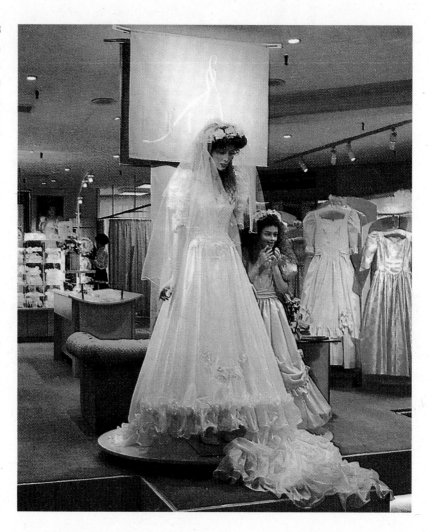

just coffee shops. C&A focuses on men's, women's and children's clothing; Marks & Spencer on clothing and food; BhS and Littlewoods on clothing and housewares; Woolworth on housewares, records and tapes, children's clothes and confectionery. Variety stores are characterised by low cost facilities, self-service shopping, central payment points and multiple purchases; they appeal to large, heterogeneous target markets, especially price-conscious customers.

Grocery Supermarkets, Superstores and Hypermarkets

In the 1960s, grocery retailers, led by Sainsbury's, Tesco and Fine Fare, expanded into 1,000 square metre (11,000 square foot) supermarkets, either in the city centre or within suburban centres. As product ranges grew, self-service requirements called for more space; and as city centre rents rose, the age of the superstore arrived. Size requirements grew further still, and there was an exodus from the city centre. In the 1980s the average grocery superstore grew from 2,500 square metres to 5,500 square metres (27,500 to 61,000 square feet) and moved away from the suburban centre to either free-standing superstore sites or edge of town retail parks.

Supermarkets and **super-stores** Large, self-service stores that carry a complete line of food products as well as other convenience items

Supermarkets and grocery **superstores** are large, self-service stores that carry a complete line of food products as well as other convenience items—cosmetics, non-prescription drugs and kitchenwares. Some, such as Asda or Tesco, sell clothing and small electrical appliances. Grocery superstores are laid out in departments for maximum efficiency in stocking and handling products but have central checkout facilities by the exits to the ample, free parking. Prices are considerably lower than in the independently owned supermarkets based in suburban shopping centres or in neighbourhood grocery shops. An increase in the number of price-conscious consumers demanding greater choice, improved packaging and refrigeration, as well as the advent of widespread car ownership, spurred the huge growth of major grocery superstore retailers Sainsbury's, Tesco, Asda, Somerfield and Safeway.

EPOS Electronic point-of-sale scanning of barcodes for inventory management

Of the top retailers in Europe (see Table 14.2, Table 14.3, Table 14.4 and Table 14.5), many are superstore trading grocery companies. They are at the forefront of retail technology—barcode scanning **EPOS** (electronic point-of-sale) tills, shelf allocation modelling, robotised warehouse stacking—and of monitoring changes in customer attitudes and expectations. Increasingly, to gain an edge over the competition, they are launching more own label products with attributes equal to, if not better than, the manufacturers' brands also on sale. Marketing Insight 14.1 describes how the grocery retailers have led the transition in Europe, crossing national borders to trade in many countries. This move has been led by the discounters, such as Aldi, Netto and Carrefour.

Hypermarkets Stores that take the benefits of the superstore even further, using their greater size to give the customer a wider range and depth of products

Hypermarkets take the benefits of the superstore even further, using their greater size—over 9,000 square metres (100,000 square feet)—to give the customer a wider range and depth of products. They are common in the US, France and Germany, but there are few genuine hypermarkets in the UK, except perhaps for Sainsbury's Savacentre.

Asda, based in Leeds, began as a discount retailer of grocery products in the northern industrial regions of the UK. Needing large premises but unable to gain planning permission to build on green field sites, the company operated initially from redundant cinemas and converted industrial warehouses. As the superstore era blossomed, Asda was a guiding force. Today the company is a leader in superstore grocery retailing, with over two hundred purpose built free-standing superstores offering manufacturer and Asda branded goods. The stores have over 4,500 square metres (50,000 square feet) of one floor retail space, pleasing ambience

Rank	Retailer	Sales[1] £ million	Rank	Retailer	Sales[1] £ million
	Supermarket Chains			**Furniture and Carpets**	
1	Tesco	8,347	1	MFI	659
2	J. Sainsbury	8,339[2]	2	Berisford–Magnet	175
3	Argyll Group	5,608	3	IKEA (excluding Habitat)	166
4	Asda Group	4,794	4	Allied Carpets	164
5	Somerfield Group	3,110	5	DFS	135
	Chemists and Drugstores			**Clothing**	
1	Boots	2,806[3]	1	Burton	999
2	Kingfisher–Superdrug	617	2	C & A/Brenninkmeyer	780[4]
3	Lloyds	537	3	Sears–various fascias	443
4	AAH	145	4	Next	392
5	Unichem	114	5	Storehouse–Mothercare, Blazer, etc.	295
	CTNs			**Footwear**	
1	Gallaher–Forbuoys, NSS, etc. (now sold)	660	1	Sears–British Shoe Corporation	547
2	Martin Retail Group	355	2	C & J Clark Group	275[4]
3	T & S Stores	352	3	Stylo–Barratts	102
4	United News Shops	76	4	Oliver Group	74
5	Claverley–Star News, Bunces, etc.	72	5	Harrods Holdings–Kurt Geiger, etc.	53
	DIY			**Department Stores**	
1	Kingfisher–B & Q	1,151	1	John Lewis Partnership	1,091
2	Ladbroke–Texas (now J. Sainsbury)	692	2	House of Fraser	1,070
3	Do It All (Boots/W. H. Smith, now Boots)	389	3	The Burton Group–Debenhams	910
4	J. Sainsbury–Homebase	280	4	Allders	297
5	Wickes	230	5	Sears–Selfridges	217
	Electrical and Gas Appliances			**Mixed Goods**	
1	Dixons Group	1,402	1	Marks & Spencer	5,420[4]
2	Kingfisher–Comet	526	2	Boots	2,806
3	British Gas	276	3	Kingfisher–Woolworths	1,314
4	Powerhouse Retail	259	4	Argos	1,110
5	THORN EMI–Rumbelows (now sold)	195	5	W. H. Smith Group–W. H. Smith	896[4]

NOTES: [1]Sales, excluding VAT, for the financial year ending in 1994.
[2]Excluding grocery sales through Savacentre.
[3]Also classified as a mixed goods retailer.
[4]Corporate Intelligence Group estimates.

SOURCES: *The Retail Pocket Book 1996* (Henley, Oxon: NTC Publications, 1996), pp. 102–103. Reprinted by permission.

Table 14.2 The top five retailers in the UK: by sector, 1994

Rank	Retailer Group	Sales £ billion
1	J. Sainsbury	9.22
2	Tesco	8.80
3	Argyll Group	5.61
4	Marks & Spencer	5.42
5	Asda Group	4.79
6	Kingfisher	3.72
7	The Boots Company	3.46
8	Isosceles	3.11
9	Kwik Save Group	2.80
10	John Lewis Partnership	2.18

NOTE: UK retail sales, excluding VAT, for the financial year ending in 1994, including any acquisitions and excluding any disposals during the year.

SOURCES: *The Retail Pocket Book 1996* (Henley, Oxon: NTC Publications, 1996), p. 101; The Corporate Intelligence Group.

Table 14.3 The top ten retailer groups in the UK

	Number One	Number Two	Number Three	Combined Share
Austria	BML	Spar	Konsum	56
Belgium	GIB	Delhaize	Aldi	58
Denmark	FDB	Dansk Supermarkt	Supervib	77
Finland	Kesko	Suomen Spar	SOK	80
France	Intermarché	Leclerc	Carrefour	38
Germany	Edeka	Rewe	Aldi	46
Greece	Marinopoulos	Sklaventis	Veropoulos	17
Ireland	Dunnes	Power Supermarket	SuperQuinn	43
Italy	Coop	Despar	GS	11
Netherlands	A. Heyn	Super Unie	Vendex	47
Norway	Norgesdetalj	Hakon	Coop	86
Portugal	Sonae	Pão de Acucar	Pingo Doce	41
Spain	Pryca	Continente	Alcampo	20
Sweden	ICA	D-Gruppe	Coop	95
Switzerland	Migros	Coop	Denner	75
UK	Sainsbury	Tesco	Argyll	43

SOURCES: *The Retail Pocket Book 1996* (Henley, Oxon: NTC Publications, 1996), p. 169; Reprinted by permission.

Table 14.4 The top three retailers in European countries

Supermarketers Lead the Way Across Europe

The German company Aldi, one of Europe's largest retailers, led the assault into the UK grocery sector. In late 1992, the French giant Carrefour announced its intention to launch its Ed discount operation in southern England, becoming the first non-UK discounter to challenge Kwik Save in the south of the country. Unlike Aldi, or Danish Netto, which operates in the North East, Ed will sell more manufacturers' brands than the retailer's own label. German discounter Norma, which has 700 stores outside the UK, is also entering South East England with an operation similar to Aldi's.

Although some retailers have dabbled outside their country of origin, hardly any retailers outside the grocery sector have spread their marque away from their original heartland. The few exceptions are IKEA and, previously, Habitat in home furnishings, C & A and Marks & Spencer in clothing and, most notably, Body Shop in skin and body care.

There are signs in many sectors, from electricals to footwear, that this situation is changing. The grocery sector, however, has long led the way, and not just through the quickly growing Aldi or Carrefour.

Voluntary group SPAR has a significant presence throughout Europe. Most SPAR stores are owned by individual entrepreneurs or companies trading from small regional chains of 20 to 30 shops. In 1992 SPAR ran its first pan-European promotion—pushing well known manufacturers' brands at low prices across 14 countries. Simultaneously, SPAR developed a new image for its own label products,

an image that could be used throughout its network of convenience stores in Europe. The company has encountered various problems. For its pan-European promotions, supplying manufacturers were concerned about maintaining uniform brand positioning and pricing from country to country. Most brands, including SPAR's own label, occupy different positionings from one country to the next. This problem was to prove more fundamental to the roll out and strategic use of the SPAR own label brand, particularly between Spain, Germany, Holland and the UK. The brand occupies a discount position, except in the UK, where it enjoys a slightly more up-market image.

Perhaps such problems should not be too unexpected, given that SPAR is active in most countries across Europe except Hungary and Poland. This inevitably means a huge mix of brands, brand positionings, styles of retailing, customer buying processes and cultural/economic conditions. However, with the current trend towards pan-European retail networks of branches, many retail marketers will soon experience SPAR's teething problems for themselves.

SOURCES: "Cut price Carrefour targets UK", Suzanne Bidlake, *Marketing*, 19 November 1992, p. 3; "Norma and Carrefour invade UK", *Marketing Week*, 22 January 1993, p. 6; "Aldi appointments", *The Independent on Sunday*, 7 March 1993, p. IB39; Kate Trollope, "Spar slashes brand prices over Europe", *Marketing*, 11 June 1992, p. 8; James Martin, "Price wars dampen hopes", *European Retail*, 30 August 1994, pp. 6–9; *Retail Business*, December 1994, pp. 92–99; *The Retail Pocket Book 1996* (Oxford: NTC Publications, 1996).

Rank	Company Name	Country	Retail Activity	Retail Sales £m*	Year End
1	Metro International[1]	Switz./Ger.	Multi-sector	32,219[2,5]	31-12-93
2	Tengelmann	Germany	Multi-sector	20,206[2]	30-06-94
3	Rewe Group	Germany	Grocery	17,175[3]	31-12-94
4	Carrefour	France	Grocery	16,329[4]	31-12-94
5	Centres Leclerc	France	Grocery	14,955[4]	31-12-94
6	Aldi	Germany	Grocery	14,948[2,5]	31-12-94
7	Intermarché	France	Grocery	14,512[4]	31-12-94
8	Edeka Group	Germany	Grocery	12,621[4]	31-12-94
9	J. Sainsbury	UK	Grocery	11,357[4,6]	13-03-95
10	Promodès	France	Grocery	11,339[4]	31-12-94
11	Tesco	UK	Grocery	10,101[4]	25-02-95
12	Otto Versand	Germany	Mail order	10,064[2]	28-02-95
13	Karstadt	Germany	Dept. stores	9,974[4,7]	31-12-94
14	Ahold	Netherlands	Grocery	9,286[4]	31-12-94
15	Pinault-Printemps	France	Dept. stores	8,489[4]	30-12-94
16	Auchan	France	Grocery	7,903[2,5]	31-12-94
17	Groupe Delhaize le Lion	Belgium	Grocery	7,647[4]	31-12-94
18	Co-operative Societies	UK	Grocery	7,500[2]	31-12-94
19	Casino/Rallye	France	Grocery	7,483[4]	31-12-94
20	Crai	Italy	Grocery	7,094[2,8]	31-12-94
21	Lidl & Schwarz	Germany	Grocery	7,012[2,5]	31-12-94
22	SHV Holdings	Netherlands	Cash and carry	6,875[4]	31-12-94
23	Marks & Spencer	UK	Variety	6,671[4]	31-03-95
24	Migros	Switzerland	Grocery	6,307[3]	31-12-94
25	GIB Group	Belgium	Multi-sector	6,109[3,9]	31-01-95
26	Quelle Schickedanz	Germany	Mail order	6,063[3]	31-01-94
27	Argyll Group	UK	Grocery	5,815[4]	01-04-95
28	Spar Handels	Germany	Grocery	5,264[4,8]	31-12-94
29	Asda Group	UK	Grocery	5,257[4]	29-04-95
30	Docks de France	France	Grocery	5,220[4]	31-12-94
31	El Corte Inglés	Spain	Dept. stores	5,146[2]	28-02-94
32	Système U	France	Grocery	5,136[4]	31-12-94
33	Co-op Switzerland	Switzerland	Grocery	4,891[2]	31-12-94
34	Kingfisher	UK	Multi-sector	4,851[4]	28-01-95
35	ICA	Sweden	Grocery	4,841[3]	31-12-94
36	Co-op Italia	Italy	Grocery	4,439[3]	31-12-94
37	Conad	Italy	Grocery	4,135[2]	31-12-94
38	The Boots Company	UK	Multi-sector	3,846[4]	31-03-95
39	Kesko	Finland	Grocery	3,651[4]	31-12-94
40	Co-op Denmark	Denmark	Grocery	3,631[3]	31-12-94
41	Galeries Lafayette	France	Dept. stores	3,532[4]	31-12-94
42	AVA	Germany	Grocery	3,423[3,10]	31-12-94
43	C & A Brenninkmeyer	Germany	Fashion	3,370[3]	31-12-93
44	SOK (S Group)	Finland	Multi-sector	3,330[4]	31-12-94
45	Cora	France	Grocery	3,233[4]	31-12-94
46	IKEA	Sweden	Furniture	3,139[2]	31-08-94
47	Somerfield Holdings	UK	Grocery	3,110[4]	24-04-94
48	Comptoirs Modernes	France	Grocery	3,077[4]	31-12-94
49	Kwik Save Group	UK	Grocery	2,800[4]	27-08-94
50	Vendex International	Netherlands	Multi-sector	2,794[4]	31-01-95

NOTES: *Exchange rates are averages for the calendar year. [1]Includes Asko, Kaufhof and Masso. [2]The source for this figure does not specify whether VAT is included or not. [3]Figure includes VAT. [4]Figure excludes VAT. [5]Estimated figure. [6]Group sales only. [7]Includes Hertie (acquired in 1994). [8]Includes sales of all associated retailers. [9]Includes franchise sales. [10]Excludes Nanz.

SOURCES: *The Retail Pocket Book 1996* (Henley, Oxon: NTC Publications, 1996), p. 130. Reprinted by permission.

Table 14.5 The top fifty West European retailers

and additional amenities such as cafés, crèche facilities and ample free parking. The company has a new distribution network, fully computerised and centralised, with on-line EPOS systems monitoring the exact stock requirements of each store.

Discount Sheds and Superstores

The move away from the city or town centre was not confined to multiple grocery retailers. Furniture, carpets and electrical appliances require large display areas, ranges with strength in depth and, if possible, one floor shopping. The concentration of retailers in the city centre led to limited store opening opportunities (large enough sites were hard to find) and to high rents. When the electrical retailer Comet and furniture retailers Queensway and MFI sought out of town sites, they too were initially forced by the planning authorities to occupy disused warehouses and industrial units along arteries into the city centre. As the planners reviewed their regulations, these firms, along with the major DIY and toy retailers, developed purpose built discount "sheds" or retail warehouses. Originally free-standing, these 2,000 to 3,500 square metre (22,000 to 39,000 square foot) stores are increasingly found in edge of town retail parks.

Discount sheds Cheaply constructed, one storey retail stores with no window displays and few add-on amenities; orientated towards car-borne shoppers

The **discount sheds** are cheaply constructed, one storey retail stores with no window displays and few add-on amenities. Orientated towards car-borne shoppers, they have large, free car parks and spacious stock facilities to enable shoppers to take delivery of their purchases immediately. Checkout points and customer services are kept to a minimum. As major retail groups have seen the cost benefits of location out of town, more companies have opened out of town, free-standing or retail park superstores. Many customers would not tolerate the minimalist approach to ambience and service levels. Construction is still basic, but more resources are devoted to shop fitting expertise and customer service. US Toys "R" Us and Sweden's IKEA typify the new generation of superstores. Most retail groups selling electrical goods, carpets, furniture, toys, groceries or DIY goods, not just the discounters, now operate superstores. Increasingly, major variety store companies, departmental store groups, and clothing and footwear retailers are developing superstores: Marks & Spencer, Debenhams and Sears are among them.

Warehouse Clubs

Warehouse clubs Large scale, members only selling operations combining cash and carry wholesaling with discount retailing

A rapidly growing form of mass merchandising, **warehouse clubs** are large scale, members only selling operations combining cash and carry wholesaling with discount retailing. For a nominal annual fee, small retailers purchase products at wholesale prices for business use or for re-sale. Warehouse clubs also sell to ultimate consumers affiliated with government credit unions, schools, hospitals and banks, but instead of paying a membership fee, individual consumers pay about 5 per cent more on each item than do business customers.

Sometimes called buying clubs, warehouse clubs offer the same types of products as discount stores but in a limited range of sizes and styles. Warehouse clubs offer a broad product mix, including non-perishable foods, beverages, books, appliances, housewares, automotive parts, hardware and furniture. Their facilities, often located in industrial areas, have concrete floors and aisles wide enough for fork lifts. Merchandise is stacked on pallets or displayed on pipe racks. All payments must be in cash, and customers must transport purchases themselves. Warehouse clubs appeal to many price-conscious consumers and small retailers unable to obtain wholesaling services from larger distributors. CostCo was the first US-style warehouse club to enter the UK.

Speciality Shops

Most shopping centres and towns have a major department store. At the other end of the spectrum is the traditional corner shop. Few small shops these days retail a variety of product groups. In suburban areas such shops tend to specialise in retailing one convenience product category—newsagents with cigarettes and newspapers, greengrocers, chemists, hair salons, etc. In the town centre (CBD) few retailers of convenience goods, with their low margins, can afford the rents and business tax. Instead, the small store retailers—250 square metres (2,750 square feet) and under—in the town centre specialise in shopping or comparison items: clothing, footwear, records and tapes, cosmetics, jewellery. Ownership of such retail outlets is increasingly concentrated in the hands of a few major retail groups (see Table 14.6), some of which also have retail brands that operate as department stores or out of town superstores. **Speciality shops** offer self-service but a greater level of assistance from store personnel. A typical 300 square metre (3,300 square feet) footwear or clothing retail store will have window displays to entice passing pedestrians, one or two checkout points and three or four assistants. Such stores depend on the town centre's general parking facilities and on proximity to a key trader, such as Boots or Marks & Spencer, which will generate pedestrian traffic.

Speciality shops Stores that offer self-service but a greater level of assistance from store personnel than department stores and carry a narrow product mix with deep product lines

Boots (chemists, opticians, car accessories, DIY)	Boots, Halfords, Do It All, A.G. Stanley, FADS Homestyle
Burton Group (fashion clothing shops and department stores)	Burton, Top Man, Principles/Principles for Men, Top Shop, Evans, Dorothy Perkins and Debenhams
Dixons (electricals, computers)	Dixons, Currys, PC World
John Menzies (books, newsagency, toys)	Hammicks; John Menzies; Early Learning Centres
Kingfisher (variety stores, chemists, electricals, DIY, office supplies)	Woolworth, Superdrug, Comet, B&Q, Staples
J. Sainsbury (grocery, DIY)	Sainsbury, Savacentre; Homebase, Texas
Sears (footwear, fashion clothing, jewellery, children's wear, mail order, discounters)	British Shoe Corporation (Dolcis, Bertie, Cable & Co., Saxone, Roland Cartier, Shoe City); Fosters, Hornes, Your Price; Miss Selfridge, Wallis, Richards Warehouse; Milletts Leisure; Adams Childrenswear, Pride & Joy; Selfridges; Freemans; Stage 1, Stage 2
Thorn EMI (TV rental, books, records, household goods)	Radio Rentals; Dillons; HMV; Crazy George's
W. H. Smith (newsagency, books, records/tapes)	W. H. Smith, Waterstone, Paperchase, Our Price, Virgin, Wee Three Records (USA), Playhouse
Storehouse (fashion clothing, children's wear, variety stores)	Blazer, Mothercare, BhS, One Up, Childrensworld

Table 14.6 Large retail groups

Convenience Stores

As the number of neighbourhood grocery stores declined in the 1960s and 1970s with the expansion of the superstore based national grocery chains, a niche emerged in the market to be filled by **convenience stores**. These shops sell essential groceries, alcoholic drinks, drugs and newspapers outside the traditional 9.00 a.m. to 6.00 p.m. shopping hours. The major superstores extended their opening hours to 8.00 p.m. to facilitate after work shopping, but no major retailers catered for "emergency" or top-up shopping. There was a resurgence of the traditional corner shop located in suburban housing estates, offering limited ranges but extended opening hours. Consumers pay a slight price premium but receive convenience in terms of location and opening hours. In the 1970s and 1980s, the voluntary groups (Spar, Mace, VG) and national retail groups such as Circle K and 7/Eleven re-positioned their brands into the "open all hours" top-up or emergency shopping niche.

Discounters

An emerging trend is for un-let units in malls and the CBD to be taken on very short term leases, sometimes even weekly, by "pile it high, sell it cheap" **discounters** selling items such as stationery, toys, confectionery, gifts—often at "everything under a £1!!" Understandably, these operations invest little in shop fitting, promotion or staff training. For their landlords, such tenants may not be ideal, but they do generate rental income in what would otherwise be empty shop units.

Markets and Cash and Carry Warehouses

In most towns there are wholesale **markets** selling meat, greengrocery, fruit, flowers and fish from which speciality retailers make their inventory purchases. Traditional, too, is the general retail market selling to the general public, either in recently refurbished Victorian market halls or in council provided modern halls adjacent to the town centre shopping malls. Such market halls sell fresh foods, clothing and housewares, and they cater for budget-conscious shoppers who typically have a middle and down-market social profile.

Cash and carry warehouses, such as Booker or Makro, retail extensive ranges of groceries, tobacco, alcohol, beverages and confectionery to newsagents, small supermarkets and convenience stores, and the catering trade (hotels, guest houses, restaurants and cafés). By purchasing from manufacturers in bulk, cash and carry companies can offer substantial price savings to their customers, who in turn can add a retail margin without alienating their customers. Many countries, particularly Scandinavia, have hybrid outlets that combine the speciality shop, convenience store and cash and carry warehouse. Buying groups link small, often privately owned local retailers with similar shops; collectively their purchasing power is enhanced, and they increasingly operate their own wholesale warehouses and offer own label brands.

Catalogue Showrooms

In a **catalogue showroom** one item of each product class is on display and the remaining inventory is stored out of the buyer's reach. Using catalogues that have been mailed to their homes or are on counters in the store, customers order the goods at their leisure. Shop assistants usually complete the order form and then collect the merchandise from the adjoining warehouse. Catalogue showrooms, such as Argos or Index, regularly sell goods below the manufacturers' list price and often provide goods immediately. Higher product turnover, fewer losses through damage or shoplifting and lower labour costs lead to their reduced retail prices. Jewellery, luggage, photographic equipment, toys, small appliances, housewares, sporting goods, garden furniture and power tools are the most commonly available items, listed by category and brand in the company's catalogue.

Categories Table 14.1 summarised the sales of the major categories of retailing. It is worth noting that the categories with the most stores do not necessarily top the league for highest turnover or profitability. The superstore and department store retailers have relatively few outlets, but they account for large floor areas and include many of the UK's main retail groups. European, and UK in particular, retail statistics are notoriously poor, being based on infrequent estimates rather than regular censuses. Agencies such as AGB, Euromonitor, Jordans, Mintel and Verdict produce regular reports on retail sectors and consumer expectations based on commissioned marketing research surveys. These are available by subscription or occasionally, for the newest versions, through business libraries. These agencies tend to use categories similar to those discussed by the retail trade itself rather than the stilted, amalgamated official classification:

Food/grocery • CTN (confectionery, tobacco, news) • Off-licence beverages
Men's/women's wear • Children's wear • Footwear/leather goods
Furniture/carpets/soft furnishings
Electrical (small appliances, brown and white goods)
Hardware • DIY
Chemist/druggist
Books/greeting cards
Jewellers
Toys
Mixed retail businesses
Mail order
Restaurants/cafés/catering • Hotels
Banking/financial services

• • • • • • • • • • • • • • • • • • •

Non-store Retailing and Home Retailing

Non-store retailing The selling of goods or services outside the confines of a retail facility

Non-store retailing is the selling of goods or services outside the confines of a retail facility. This form of retailing accounts for an increasing percentage of sales (see Table 14.7) and includes personal sales methods, such as in-home retailing and telemarketing, and non-personal sales methods, such as automatic vending and mail order retailing (which includes catalogue retailing). A growing form of non-store retailing is the use of the Internet to promote goods and services; orders can be placed using a credit card via a home based PC.

Direct marketing The use of non-personal media or telesales to introduce products to consumers, who then purchase the products by mail or telephone

Certain non-store retailing methods are in the category of **direct marketing**: the use of non-personal media or telesales to introduce products to consumers, who then purchase the products by mail or telephone. In the case of telephone orders, salespeople may be required to complete the sales. Telemarketing, mail order and catalogue retailing are all examples of direct marketing, as are sales generated by coupons, direct mail and Freephone, bell gratis, 0800 numbers.

a. Mail Order

	Mail Order Sales Value £ billion	Annual Growth %	Mail Order vs. All Retailers		Mail Order % of Total Retail Sales
			Index 1990 = 100		
			Mail Order	All Retailers	
1987	3.40	7.0	92	80	3.3
1988	3.48	2.2	94	88	3.1
1989	3.55	2.1	96	94	2.9
1990	3.70	4.2	100	100	2.9
1991	3.77	2.0	102	105	2.8
1992	3.92	3.9	106	109	2.8
1993	4.22	7.5	114	115	2.8
1994	4.48	6.1	121	120	2.9

b. Home Shopping: Share of Markets, 1994

Market	Total Market (£ m)	Home Shopping (£ m)	%
Clothing and footwear	24,392	2,770	11.3
Electrical goods	10,260	539	5.3
Furniture and carpets	7,938	319	4.0

SOURCES: *The Retail Pocket Book 1996* (Henley, Oxon: NTC Publications) Reprinted by permission. 1996, pp. 134–135.

Table 14.7 Trends in non-store retailing

In-Home Retailing

In-home retailing Selling via personal contacts with consumers in their own homes

In-home retailing is selling via personal contacts with consumers in their own homes. Organisations such as Avon, Amway and Betterware send representatives to the homes of pre-selected prospects. Traditionally, in-home retailing relied on a random, door-to-door approach. Some companies now use a more efficient approach. They first identify prospects by reaching them by phone or mail or intercepting them in shopping malls or at consumer trade fairs. These initial contacts are limited to a brief introduction and the setting of appointments.

Some in-home selling, however, is still undertaken without information about sales prospects. Door-to-door selling without a pre-arranged appointment represents a tiny proportion of total retail sales, less than 1 per cent. Because it has so often been associated with unscrupulous and fraudulent techniques, it is illegal in some communities. Generally, this method is regarded unfavourably because so many door-to-door salespeople are under trained and poorly supervised. A big disadvantage of door-to-door selling is the large expenditure, effort and time it demands. Sales commissions are usually 25 to 50 per cent (or more) of the retail price; as a result, consumers often pay more than a product is worth. Door-to-door selling is used most often when a product is unsought—for instance, encyclopaedias or double glazed windows, which most consumers would not be likely to purchase in a store.

A variation of in-home retailing is the home demonstration or party plan, which such companies as Tupperware, Ann Summers and Mary Kay Cosmetics use successfully. One consumer acts as host and invites a number of friends to view merchandise at his or her home, where a salesperson is on hand to demonstrate the products. The home demonstration is more efficient for the sales representative than contacting each prospect door-to-door, and the congenial atmosphere partly overcomes consumers' suspicions and encourages them to buy. Home demonstrations also meet the buyers' needs for convenience and personal service. Commissions and selling costs make this form of retailing expensive, however. Additionally, successful party plan selling requires both a network of friends and neighbours who have the time to attend such social gatherings and a large number of effective salespeople. With so many household members now holding full time jobs, both prospects and sales representatives are harder to recruit. The growth of interactive telephone-computer home shopping and the growing use of the Internet may also cut into party plan sales.

Telemarketing

Telemarketing The direct selling of goods and services by telephone based on either a cold canvass of the telephone directory or a pre-screened list of prospective clients

More and more organisations—IBM, Merrill Lynch, Avis, Ford, Quaker Oats, Time and American Express, to name a few—are using the telephone to strengthen the effectiveness of traditional marketing methods. **Telemarketing** is direct selling of goods and services by telephone based on either a cold canvass of the telephone directory or a pre-screened list of prospective clients. (In some areas, certain telephone numbers are listed with an asterisk to indicate the people who consider sales solicitations a nuisance and do not want to be bothered.) Telemarketing can generate sales leads, improve customer service, speed up collection of over due accounts, raise funds for not-for-profit groups and gather market data.[5]

In some cases, telemarketing uses advertising encouraging consumers to initiate a call or to request information about placing an order. Such advertisements will include "a call to action" to prompt target consumers to dial an 0800 Freephone number. This type of retailing is only a small part of total retail sales, but its use is growing. Telephone Marketing Resources, a US telemarketing firm, estimates telephone sales of goods and services at $75 billion annually (the figure includes business-to-consumer sales and business-to-business sales).[6] Experts believe that similar growth will be seen in Europe in the next few years. Research indicates that telemarketing is most successful when combined with other marketing strategies, such as direct mail or advertising in newspapers, radio and television.

Automatic Vending

Automatic vending The use of coin operated self-service machines to sell small, standardised, routinely purchased products such as chewing gum, sweets, newspapers, cigarettes, soft drinks and coffee

Automatic vending makes use of machines and accounts for less than 1 per cent of all retail sales. In the UK there are approximately 800,000 vending machines. Locations and the percentage of sales each generates are as follows:[7]

Plants and factories	38%
Public locations (e.g. stores)	26
Offices	16
Colleges and universities	6
Government facilities	3
Hospitals and nursing homes	3
Primary and secondary schools	2
Others	6

Video game machines provide an entertainment service, and many banks now offer machines that dispense cash or offer other services, but these uses of vending machines are not reported in total vending sales volume.

Automatic vending is one of the most impersonal forms of retailing. Small, standardised, routinely purchased products (chewing gum, sweets, newspapers, cigarettes, soft drinks, coffee) can be sold in machines because consumers usually buy them at the nearest available location. Machines in areas of heavy traffic provide efficient and continuous services to consumers. The elimination of sales personnel and the small amount of space necessary for vending machines give this retailing method some advantages over stores. The advantages are partly offset by the expense of the frequent servicing and repair needed.

Mail Order Retailing

Mail order retailing   Selling by description because the buyers usually do not see the actual product until it arrives in the mail

Mail order retailing involves selling by description because buyers usually do not see the actual product until it arrives in the mail. Sellers contact buyers through direct mail, catalogues, television, radio, magazines and newspapers. A wide assortment of products such as compact discs, books and clothing is sold to consumers through the mail. Placing mail orders by telephone is increasingly common. The advantages of mail order selling include efficiency and convenience. Mail order houses, such as Freemans or Grattan, can be located in remote, low cost areas and avoid the expenses of store fixtures. Eliminating personal selling efforts and store operations may result in tremendous savings that can be passed along to consumers in the form of lower prices. On the other hand, mail order retailing is inflexible, provides limited service and is more appropriate for speciality products than for convenience products. As shown in Table 14.7, mail order is on the increase.

Catalogue retailing   A type of mail order retailing in which customers receive their catalogues by mail, or pick them up if the catalogue retailer has stores

When **catalogue retailing** (a specific type of mail order retailing) is used, customers receive their catalogues by mail, or they may pick them up if the catalogue retailer has stores, as does Littlewoods. Although in-store visits result in some catalogue orders, most are placed by mail or telephone. In the US, General Foods created Thomas Garroway Ltd., a mail order service supplying gourmet pasta, cheese, coffee and similar items. Other packaged goods manufacturers involved in catalogue retailing include Hanes, Nestlé, Thomas J. Lipton, Sunkist and Whitman Chocolates.[8] These catalogue retailers are able to reach many two income families who have more money and less time for special shopping. In the UK, manufacturers and store focused retail groups tend not to be involved with catalogue or home shopping. The specialist mail order companies such as GUS and Freemans dominate this sector. The UK mail order market is worth over £5.4 billion, having grown by 113 per cent since 1982.[9] As described in Case 14.2, it is a sector likely to be assisted by new technology and the changing leisure habits of consumers.

• • • • • • • • • • • • • • • • • • •

Franchising

Franchising   An arrangement whereby a supplier (franchisor) grants a dealer (franchisee) the right to sell products in exchange for some type of consideration

Franchising is an arrangement whereby a supplier, or franchisor, grants a dealer, or franchisee, the right to sell products in exchange for some type of consideration. For example, the franchisor may receive some percentage of total sales in exchange for furnishing equipment, buildings, management know-how, marketing assistance and branding to the franchisee. The franchisee supplies labour and capital, operates the franchised business and agrees to abide by the provisions of the franchise agreement. This next section looks at the major types of retail franchises, the advantages and disadvantages of franchising and trends in franchising.

Major Types of Retail Franchises

Retail franchise arrangements can generally be classified as one of three general types. In the first arrangement, a manufacturer authorises a number of retail stores to sell a certain brand name item. This franchise arrangement, one of the oldest, is common in the sales of cars and trucks, farm equipment, earthmoving equipment and petroleum. The majority of all petrol is sold through franchised independent retail service stations, and franchised dealers handle virtually all sales of new cars and trucks. In the second type of retail franchise, a producer licenses distributors to sell a given product to retailers. This franchising arrangement is common in the soft drinks industry. Most international manufacturers of soft drink syrups—Coca-Cola, Pepsi-Cola—franchise independent bottlers, which then serve retailers. In the third type of retail franchise, a franchisor supplies brand names, techniques or other services, instead of a complete product. The franchisor may provide certain production and distribution services, but its primary role in the arrangement is the careful development and control of marketing strategies. This approach to franchising, which is the most typical today, is used by many organisations, including Holiday Inn, McDonald's, Avis, Hertz, KFC, Body Shop, Holland & Barrett, Pronuptia and Benetton, as described in Marketing Insight 14.2.

Advantages and Disadvantages of Franchising

Franchising offers several advantages to both the franchisee and the franchisor. It enables a franchisee to start a business with limited capital and to make use of the business experience of others. Moreover, an outlet with a nationally advertised name, such as Body Shop or Burger King, is often assured of customers as soon as it opens. If business problems arise, the franchisee can obtain guidance and advice from the franchisor at little or no cost. Franchised outlets are generally more successful than independently owned businesses: only 5 to 8 per cent of franchised retail businesses fail during the first two years of operation, whereas approximately 54 per cent of independent retail businesses fail during that period.[10] The franchisee also receives materials to use in local advertising and can take part in national promotional campaigns sponsored by the franchisor.

The franchisor gains fast and selective distribution of its products through franchise arrangements without incurring the high cost of constructing and operating its own outlets. The franchisor therefore has more capital available to expand production and to use for advertising. At the same time, it can ensure, through the franchise agreement, that outlets are maintained and operated to its own standards. The franchisor also benefits from the fact that the franchisee, being a sole proprietor in most cases, is likely to be very highly motivated to succeed. The success of the franchise means more sales, which translate into higher royalties for the franchisor.

Despite their numerous advantages, franchise arrangements also have several drawbacks. The franchisor can dictate many aspects of the business: decor, the design of employees' uniforms, types of signs and numerous details of business operations. In addition, franchisees must pay to use the franchisor's name, products and assistance. Usually, there is a one-time franchise fee and continuing royalty and advertising fees, collected as a percentage of sales. In addition, franchisees often must work very hard, putting in 10 and 12 hour days, six days a week. In some cases, franchise agreements are not uniform: one franchisee may pay more than another for the same services. The franchisor also gives up a certain amount of control when entering into a franchise agreement. Consequently, individual establishments may not be operated exactly as the franchisor would operate them.

Franchising All Over the McDonald's Globe

hanks to franchising, the familiar golden arches of McDonald's now serve more than 14,000 communities around the world. Most of these restaurants, however, are locally owned and managed: they are franchised from the US parent company.

A press campaign in 1993 by McDonald's was not targeted at its customers. Instead, it sought franchisees, as the advertisement's header explained:

Here's something for hungry entrepreneurs to get their teeth into.

In the UK McDonald's owns the bulk of its 550 restaurants, but in many other territories most are owned and operated by franchise holders. The fast food giant, eager to speed up its expansion and reduce its capital outlay, is offering budding entrepreneurs the chance to own and run their own McDonald's restaurant. The requirements include entrepreneurial spirit, the ability to lead and motivate staff, sound financial skills, the successful completion of a vigorous training programme and £50,000 to lease an existing restaurant or £150,000 to £240,000 to purchase a new or existing restaurant.

McDonald's offers one of the best known brands in the world, a proven trading concept, training, advice and promotional support. For the franchisee, however, individual success depends on his or her own abilities, commitment and business skills.

McDonald's has a successful track record of viable franchises all around the world. Not all franchises have been so fortunate. From dry cleaning operations to mobile car maintenance, baked potato outlets to security systems, the bankruptcy courts are littered with the records of failed franchises. Nevertheless, the annual Franchise Exhibi-

Trends in Franchising   Franchising has been used since the early 1950s, primarily for service stations and car dealerships. However, it has grown enormously since the mid-1960s.[11] This growth has generally paralleled the expansion of the fast food industry—the industry in which franchising is widely used. Of course, franchising is not limited to fast foods. Franchise arrangements for health clubs, pest control, hair salons and travel agencies are widespread. The estate agency industry has also experienced a rapid increase in franchising. The largest franchising sectors, ranked by sales, are: car and truck dealers (52 per cent), service stations (14 per cent), restaurants (10 per cent) and non-food retailing (5 per cent).[12] Many internationally known brands, such as Burger King, McDonald's, Benetton and Body Shop, use franchising as their core means of rapid global expansion.

Strategic Issues in Retailing

Consumers often have vague reasons for making a retail purchase. Whereas most industrial purchases are based on economic planning and necessity, consumer purchases often result from social influences and psychological factors. Because consumers shop for a variety of reasons—to search for specific items, to escape boredom or to learn about something new—retailers must do more than simply fill space with merchandise; they must make desired products available, create stimulating environments for shopping and develop marketing strategies that tion sees thousands of visitors seeking information and business opportunities offered by franchising. For well known brands such as Pizza Hut, McDonald's, Body Shop and the print shop Kall-Kwik, franchising has brought considerable rewards for both brand owner and franchise holder.

For the franchisee, it is essential that there be a clearly defined brand proposition, and one that is in demand. The franchise holder must be paying for a marketing asset that is well perceived by the target market. It must be a well thought out business proposition. Identified customer needs, competitive forces and environmental trends all need to support a viable financial analysis and cash flow forecast. The British Franchise Association stresses that a franchise is not something for nothing; taking on a franchise is not a cut-price way to establish a high profile, well branded operation and make the

franchisee's fortune overnight. A franchise agreement is a business deal. The brand and concept must be in sufficient demand by the target public to warrant the purchase of the franchise and the setting up of the business. Like any other type of business, stresses the Association, a franchise opportunity requires thorough marketing and financial analyses. With annual sales approaching £5 billion, franchising in the UK is quickly emulating patterns in Europe and North America.

SOURCES: Roger Trapp, "A low risk guide to franchising", *The Independent on Sunday*, 11 October 1992, p. IB23; McDonald's advertisements, February 1993; Roger Trapp, "Buy yourself a brand name", *The Independent on Sunday,* 21 February 1993, p. IB26; British Franchise Association literature; Ed Rensi, "Franchising: American business in high gear", *Franchising World*, January 1995, pp. 7–10; Mariana Crespo, "Burgers'n Champagne", *Financial World,* 21 June 1994, p. 54.

increase store patronage. Research indicates that for many consumers, shopping is far more than the task of purchasing and collecting goods: it is a social, leisure orientated activity. This section discusses how store location, property ownership, product assortment, retail positioning, atmospherics/design, store image, scrambled merchandising, central/regional management, technology, distribution, the wheel of retailing and EU deregulation affect these retailing objectives.

Location

Location The strategic retailing issue that dictates the limited geographic trading area from which a store must draw its customers

Location, the least flexible of the strategic retailing issues, is one of the most important, because location dictates the limited geographic trading area from which a store must draw its customers.[13] Thus retailers consider a variety of factors when evaluating potential locations, including the location of the firm's target customers within the trading area, the economic climate in the region, the kinds of products being sold, the availability of public transport, customer characteristics and competitors' locations.[14] The relative ease of movement to and from the site is important, so that pedestrian and vehicular traffic, parking and transport must all be taken into account. Most retailers prefer sites with high pedestrian traffic; preliminary site investigations often include a pedestrian count to determine how many of the passers-by are truly prospective customers. Similarly, the nature of the area's vehicular traffic is analysed. Certain retailers, such as service stations and convenience stores, depend on large numbers of carborne customers but try to avoid overly congested locations. In addition, parking space must be adequate, and transport networks (major thoroughfares and public transport) must be able to accommodate customers and delivery vehicles.

Retailers also evaluate the characteristics of the site itself: the other stores in the area, particularly the proximity of key traders or magnets; the size, shape and visibility of the plot or building under consideration; and the rental, leasing or ownership terms under which the building may be occupied. Retailers also look for compatibility with nearby retailers because stores that complement one another draw more customers for everyone. This is particularly true for clothing, footwear and jewellery retailers.[15] When making site location decisions, retailers must select from among several general types of location: free-standing structures, traditional business districts, neighbourhood/suburban shopping centres, out of town superstores and retail parks. In recent years retailers have been moving away from the traditional store assessment procedure of pedestrian counts and "eyeballing" the site's immediate location. Various agencies—notably CACI and SAMI—have detailed databases examining each shopping centre. Computer modelling, such as SLAM (Store Location Assessment Model), has become more widespread, bringing a basis of objectivity to what was previously an intuitive decision-making process based on few hard facts.[16]

Property Ownership

Property ownership is perpetually an issue in retailing. Some companies, such as Marks & Spencer, own the majority of their property portfolio. This gives security of tenure, saves on rents and lease negotiations, and adds to the book value of the company. To release operating funds, companies often engage in "sale and leaseback" deals. Property companies buy the freehold to add to their assets but immediately give a favourable lease to the retailer. In recent years companies that once held the freehold for most of their stores have sold off property to make available operating funds for new computer systems, store refurbishment or new store openings. Companies such as the Burton Group or Next argue that they are primarily retailers and should not tie up funds in property ownership. Retailers that locate mainly in covered shopping centres and in retail parks generally have to accept lease agreements as the centre's developer maintains ownership of the property.

Product Assortment

The product assortments that retailers develop vary considerably in breadth and depth. As discussed earlier, retail stores are often classified according to their product assortments. Conversely, a store's type affects the breadth and depth of its product offerings, as shown in Figure 14.4. Thus a speciality store has a single product line but considerable depth in that line. Tie Rack stores and Fannie May Candy Shops, for example, carry only one line of products but many items within that line. In contrast, discount stores may have a wide product mix (such as housewares, automotive services, clothing and food). Department stores may have a wide product mix with different product line depths. Nevertheless, it is usually difficult to maintain both a wide and a deep product mix because of the inventories required. In addition, some producers prefer to distribute through retailers that offer less variety so that their products gain more exposure and are less affected by the presence of competing brands. As already discussed, discounters like Everything Under £1 have a wide product mix with little depth. The limited line grocery chains, led by Kwik Save, Netto and Aldi, have a moderate product mix with restricted depth—an approach that has brought them significant success as they target the budget-conscious.[17]

Issues of product assortment are often a matter of what and how much to carry. When retailers decide what should be included in their product assortments, they consider an assortment's purpose, status and completeness.[18] *Purpose* relates to how well an assortment satisfies consumers and at the same time furthers the

Discount store

Department store

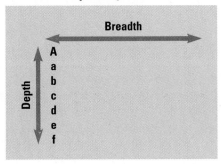

Specialty store

The capital letters represent the number of product lines, and the small letters depict the choices in any one product line. Thus it can be seen that discount stores are wide and shallow in merchandise assortment. Specialty stores, at the other extreme, have few product lines, but much more depth in the few they carry. The typical department store falls in between, having a broad assortment with many merchandise lines and medium depth in each line.

retailer's goals. *Status* identifies by rank the relative importance of each product in an assortment: for example, motor oil might have low status in a store that sells convenience foods. *Completeness* means that an assortment includes the products necessary to satisfy a store's customers; the assortment is incomplete when some products are missing. An assortment of convenience foods must include milk to be complete because most consumers expect to be able to buy milk when purchasing other food products. New products are added to (and declining products are deleted from) an assortment when they meet (or fail to meet) the retailer's standards of purpose, status and completeness.

The retailer also considers the quality of the products to be offered. The store may limit its assortments to expensive, high quality goods for upper income market segments; it may stock cheap, low quality products for low income buyers; or it may try to attract several market segments by offering a range of quality within its total product assortment.

How much to include in an assortment depends on the needs of the retailer's target market. A discount store's customers expect a wide and shallow product mix, whereas speciality store shoppers prefer narrow and deep assortments. If a retailer can increase sales by increasing product variety, the assortment may be enlarged. If a broader product mix ties up too much floor space or creates storage problems, however, the retailer may stock only the products that generate the greatest sales. Other factors that affect product assortment decisions are personnel, store image, inventory control methods and the financial risks involved.[19]

Retail Positioning   Because of the emergence of new types of store (discount warehouses, superstores, hypermarkets) and the expansion of product offerings by traditional stores, competition among retailers is intense. Thus it is important for management to

Retail positioning The strategy of identifying a highly attractive market segment and serving it in a way that distinguishes the retailer from others in the minds of consumers in that segment

consider the retail organisation's market positioning.[20] **Retail positioning** involves identifying an unserved or under served market niche, or a highly attractive market segment, and serving it through a strategy that distinguishes the retailer from others in the minds of people in that segment.[21] The retailer must have a proposition, trading concept, brand image or merchandise policy that is visibly different from its competitors.

There are several ways in which retailers position themselves.[22] A retailer may position itself as a seller of high quality, premium priced products providing many services. A store such as Selfridges, which specialises in expensive high fashion clothing and jewellery, sophisticated electronics and exclusive home furnishings, might be expected to provide wrapping and delivery services, personal shopping consultants and restaurant facilities. Fortnum & Mason, for example, emphasises superlative service and even hires pianists to play in the entrance of its store.[23] Dixons, the electrical retailer, is often referred to as "the grown man's toy shop". Another type of retail organisation, such as IKEA, may be positioned as a marketer of reasonable quality products at low prices.

Atmospherics

Atmospherics The physical elements in a store's design that appeal to consumers' emotions and encourage them to buy

Atmospherics are often used to help position a retailer. **Atmospherics** are the physical elements in a store's design that appeal to consumers' emotions and encourage them to buy. Exterior and interior characteristics, layout and displays all contribute to a store's atmosphere. Department stores, restaurants, hotels, service stations and shops combine these elements in different ways to create specific atmospheres that may be perceived as warm, fresh, functional or exciting.

Exterior atmospheric elements include the appearance of the store front, the window displays, store entrances and degree of traffic congestion. Exterior atmospherics are particularly important to new customers, who tend to judge an unfamiliar store by its outside appearance and may not enter the store if they feel intimidated by the building or inconvenienced by the car park. Because consumers form general impressions of shopping centres and business districts, the businesses and neighbourhoods surrounding a store will affect how buyers perceive the atmosphere of a store.

Interior atmospheric elements include aesthetic considerations such as lighting, wall and floor coverings, changing rooms and store fixtures. Interior sensory elements also contribute to atmosphere. Colour, for example, can attract shoppers to a retail display. Many fast food restaurants use bright colours such as red and yellow because these have been shown to make customers feel hungrier and eat faster, thus increasing turnover. Sound is another important sensory component of atmosphere and may consist of silence, soft music or even noisiness. Scent may be relevant as well; within a store, the odour of perfume suggests an image different from that suggested by the smell of prepared food. A store's layout—arrangement of departments, width of aisles, grouping of products and location of cashiers— is yet another determinant of atmosphere. Closely related to store layout is the element of crowding. A crowded store may restrict exploratory shopping, impede mobility and decrease shopping efficiency. An apparently empty store, however, may imply unpopularity and deter shoppers from entering.

Once the exterior and interior characteristics and store layout have been determined, displays are added. Displays enhance the store's atmosphere and give customers information about products. When displays carry out a store-wide theme, during the Christmas season, for instance, they attract customers' attention and generate sales. So do displays that present several related products in a group, or ensemble. Interior displays of products stacked or hanging neatly on racks create one kind of atmosphere; marked down items grouped together on a bargain table produce a different kind.

Retailers must determine the atmosphere the target market seeks and then adjust atmospheric variables to encourage the desired awareness and action in consumers. High fashion boutiques generally strive for an atmosphere of luxury and novelty; discount department stores must not seem too exclusive and expensive. To appeal to multiple market segments, a retailer may create different atmospheres for different operations within the store; for example, the discount basement, the sports department and the women's shoe department may each have a distinctive atmosphere.

Store Image

Image A functional and psychological picture in the consumer's mind

To attract customers, a retail store must project an **image**—a functional and psychological picture in the consumer's mind—that is acceptable to its target market. Although heavily dependent on atmospherics and design, a store's image is also shaped by its reputation for integrity, the number of services offered, location, merchandise assortments, pricing policies, promotional activities, community involvement and the retail brand's positioning.[24]

Characteristics of the target market—social class, lifestyle, income level and past buying behaviour—help form store image as well. How consumers perceive the store can be a major determinant of store patronage. Consumers from lower socio-economic groups tend to patronise small, high margin, high service food stores and prefer small, friendly building societies/loan companies over large, impersonal banks, even though these companies charge high interest. Affluent consumers look for exclusive, high quality establishments that offer prestige products and labels.

Retailers should be aware of the multiple factors that contribute to store image and recognise that perceptions of image vary. For example, one study found that in the United States consumers perceived Wal-Mart and Kmart differently, although the two sold almost the same products in stores that looked quite similar, offered the same prices and even had similar names. Researchers discovered that Wal-Mart shoppers spent more money at Wal-Mart and were more satisfied with the store than Kmart shoppers were with Kmart, in part because of differences in the retailers' image. For example, Wal-Mart employees wore waistcoats; Kmart employees did not. Wal-Mart purchases were packed in paper bags while Kmart used plastic bags. Wal-Mart had wider aisles, recessed lighting and carpeting in some departments. Even the retailers' logos affected consumers' perceptions: Wal-Mart's simple white and brown logo appeared friendly and "less blatantly commercial", while K mart's red and turquoise blue logo conveyed the impression that the stores had not changed much since the 1960s. These atmospheric elements gave consumers the impression that Wal-Mart was more "upmarket", warmer and friendlier than Kmart.[25]

Scrambled Merchandising

Scrambled merchandising The addition of unrelated products and product lines, particularly fast moving items that can be sold in volume, to an existing product mix

When retailers add unrelated products and product lines, particularly fast moving items that can be sold in volume, to an existing product mix, they are practising **scrambled merchandising**. For example, a convenience store might start selling lawn fertiliser. Retailers adopting this strategy hope to accomplish one or more of the following: (1) to convert their stores into one-stop shopping centres, (2) to generate more traffic, (3) to realise higher profit margins, (4) to increase impulse purchases.

In scrambling merchandise, retailers must deal with diverse marketing channels and thus may reduce their own buying, selling and servicing expertise. The practice can also blur a store's image in consumer's minds, making it more difficult for a retailer to succeed in today's highly competitive, saturated markets. Finally, scrambled merchandising intensifies competition among traditionally distinct types of stores and forces suppliers to adjust distribution systems so that new channel members can be accommodated. Asda is predominantly a grocery retailer; however, most Asda stores carry the "George" clothing ranges. The company retails small electrical appliances, DIY goods and car accessories in some stores but not in others. During the summer months, gardening supplies and equipment are sold. In the months leading up to Christmas, that floor space is given over to children's toys and gifts.

The Wheel of Retailing

Wheel of retailing The hypothesis that new retailers often enter the marketplace with low prices, margins and status and eventually emerge at the high end of the price/cost/services scales to compete with newer discount retailers

As new types of retail businesses come into being, they strive to fill niches in the dynamic environment of retailing. One hypothesis regarding the evolution and development of new types of retail stores is the **wheel of retailing**.[26] According to this theory, new retailers often enter the marketplace with low prices, margins and status. The new competitors' low prices are usually the result of innovative cost cutting procedures, and they soon attract imitators. Gradually, as these businesses attempt to broaden their customer base and increase sales, their operations and facilities become more elaborate and more expensive. They may move to more desirable locations, begin to carry higher quality merchandise or add customer services. Eventually, they emerge at the high end of the price/cost/service scales, competing with newer discount retailers who are following the same evolutionary process.[27]

For example, supermarkets have undergone many changes since their introduction in the 1920s. Initially, they provided limited services in exchange for lower food prices. However, over time they developed a variety of new services, including free coffee, gourmet food sections and children's play areas. Now supermarkets are being challenged by superstores and hypermarkets, which offer more product choices than the original supermarkets and have under cut supermarket prices.

Figure 14.5 illustrates the wheel of retailing for department stores and discounters. Department stores such as Debenhams started out as high volume, low cost merchants competing with general stores and other small retailers; discount houses developed later, in response to the rising expenses of services in department stores. Many discounters now appear to be following the wheel of retailing by offering more services, better locations, high quality inventories and, therefore, higher prices. Some discount houses are almost indistinguishable from department stores.

Like most hypotheses, the wheel of retailing may not fit every case. For example, it does not adequately explain the development of convenience stores, speciality stores, department store branches and vending machine operations. Another major weakness of the theory is that it does not predict what retailing innovations will develop, or when. Still, the hypothesis works reasonably well in industrialised, expanding economies.

Current Trends

Balance of retailing power The balance of negotiating and buying power between retailers and their suppliers

In addition to the strategic issues highlighted above, mention must also be made of some current trends with strategic implications. The **balance of retailing power** is a well documented subject: the balance of negotiating and buying power between retailers and their suppliers.[28] As more retailers devote shelf space to their own label branded goods, the major manufacturers find themselves squeezed out.[29] In the clothing market nearly all retailers now give precedence to their own

Figure 14.5

The wheel of retailing, which explains the origin and evolution of new types of retail stores

SOURCE: *Adapted from Robert F. Hartley,* Retailing: Challenge and Opportunity, *3rd edn, p. 42. Copyright © 1984 by Houghton Mifflin Company. Used by permission.*

High prices and mark-ups, many services, expensive surroundings

Low prices and mark-ups, few services, austere surroundings

General stores and miscellaneous small retailers

Department stores

Department stores

Department stores

Discount stores

Discounters (such as factory outlet malls)

Department stores

Entry of discount stores

Large "members only" discount outlets

1890–1910   1955–1970   1990s

If the "wheel" is considered to be turning slowly in the direction of the arrows, then the department stores around 1900 and the discounters later can be viewed as coming on the scene at the low end of the wheel. As it turns slowly, they move with it, becoming higher price operations, and at the same time leaving room for lower price firms to gain entry at the low end of the wheel.

label goods. Marks & Spencer takes the situation to the extreme: only St. Michael (Marks & Spencer's own label) goods are on sale. The company dictates quality levels, lead times, packaging and delivery conditions, and often the price it will pay to its suppliers![30] A few years ago retailer Sainsbury's threatened to de-stock Kellogg's cereals totally and Kellogg's refused to supply Sainsbury's. Two giant brands were locked in a power struggle. Increasingly compromise and negotiation are leading to deals beneficial to both sides of the equation: retailers receive preferential treatment and buying terms while manufacturers receive contracts to supply major retail chains exclusively with their own label needs, often alongside their own manufacturer brands.[31] Certainly for most of the large retail chains, the power is in the hands of the retailers, not the manufacturers.

Retail technology Systems that increase retailers' efficiency and productivity and often create a competitive edge

Technology   Retailers are turning to **retail technology** for improved productivity and often to create a competitive edge.[32] Table 14.8 shows the current levels of electronic systems penetration in retailing. Barcode scanning and electronic point-of-sale (EPOS) systems enable companies to monitor exact consumer spending patterns on a store-by-store basis, to prevent stock-outs and to have detailed sales data to add weight to negotiations with suppliers. EFTPOS (electronic funds transfer at point of sale) equipment facilitates speedy payment for goods, thereby reducing checkout queues; the rapid debiting of customer accounts is to the benefit of the retailer's bank account and cash flow. Video screens and video walls bring a new medium for the promotion of goods and services, as well as for the transfer of information. Retailers such as Sainsbury's are already using sites on the World Wide Web (the Internet) to promote ranges and even to take home delivery orders. The spread of computer systems has enabled consultants to develop computer graphic tools for the modelling of store location choice, customer demographics and shelf space allocation.[33]

a. Number of Grocery Scanning Stores by Group, Great Britain

Group	Number of Stores Scanning	% of Stores	% of All Commodity Volume Scanned
Kwik Save	951	100.0	100.0
Tesco	484	96.2	99.0
Somerfield	436	69.1	88.4
Safeway	367	100.0	100.0
Sainsbury	352	100.0	100.0
Alldays	253	100.0	100.0
Asda	201	99.0	99.8
M & W	118	100.0	100.0
Waitrose	111	100.0	100.0
Presto	90	51.7	76.4
Netto	82	100.0	100.0
Wm Morrison	72	100.0	100.0
Budgens	39	38.2	43.0
Jacksons	39	83.0	82.4
Savacentre	10	100.0	100.0
Lidl	10	100.0	—
Hunt Spar	9	47.4	52.6
Healds Day & Nite	7	20.0	21.8
Walter Wilson	6	10.7	26.8
Normans	3	13.6	24.0
One Stop	2	2.4	2.4
All multiples	3,642	75.5	94.9
Co-operatives	575	23.7	53.3
Independents	647	2.0	3.2
Total	4,864	12.2	81.9

b. Trend in the Number of Grocery Scanning Stores, Great Britain

Year	Number of Stores Scanning	Year	Number of Stores Scanning
April 1986	382	January 1991	1,894
April 1987	473	June 1992	2,695
April 1988	535	June 1993	3,710
January 1989	972	December 1993	3,932
January 1990	1,497	December 1994	4,864
			(Continues)

Table 14.8 Current levels of electronic systems penetration in retailing

c. International Comparisons: Grocery Stores Equipped With Scanners, 1993*

Country	Turnover Scanned (%)	Country	Turnover Scanned (%)
Finland	85	Spain	49
Sweden	75	Portugal	47
Belgium	69	Austria	41
UK	69	Italy	41
Denmark	65	Germany	32
France	60	Ireland	29
Netherlands	55	Switzerland	6
Norway	51	Greece	1

*Ranked by percentage of turnover scanned.

SOURCES: *The Retail Pocket Book 1996* (Henley, Oxon: NTC Publications, 1996), pp. 132–133. Reprinted by permission.

Table 14.8 Current levels of electronic systems penetration in retailing (cont.)

Retail technology is not cheap—£80,000 to bring a typical shoe shop on-line with an EPOS system—but it often allows decision-makers to be fully aware of sales trends and customer needs. When linked to the warehouse network, the EPOS process brings increased speed and efficiency to the physical distribution process. Most national retail groups are centralising their distribution.[34] The grocery companies, for instance, have one or two huge, centrally located warehouses close to the heart of the motorway network. Through EPOS data, each store's exact requirements are dispatched from the central warehouse to match actual daily or weekly sales patterns. Often the warehouse is automated, with robotised handling. This reduces stockholdings in the store itself and centrally, and minimises safety stocks (the "extra" stock held to cater for surges in demand or supplier delays).[35]

Dixons and Currys have two major warehouses that receive most of their deliveries from manufacturers. Small appliances are dispatched to individual stores—to match each store's sales patterns—but white goods (too large to occupy branch space productively) are held at regional warehouses, each of which serves 30 or 40 branches and delivers direct to customers rather than to the shops. Prior to the introduction of EPOS and the move to warehouse centralisation, such fine-tuning would not have been possible.

Europe 1992/93 Deregulation of the European Community in 1992/93 had various implications for European retailers.[36] Market leaders in the UK, for example, once perceived as unassailable, are relatively small on a European scale. A grocery retailer with 8 per cent of the UK market may have 0.5 per cent of the European market. Large UK groups that previously bought out smaller regional UK retailers now find themselves being targeted for takeover by French and German retail groups. More non-UK based companies are establishing footholds in the UK market, which was previously relatively free from Continental European competition (see Case 14.1). Increasingly, the major French, German, Italian and Scandinavian retailers operate throughout Europe.[37] For many years, particularly in more affluent South East England, retailers have found it difficult to attract high calibre sales assistants and managers in competition for employment with other industrial sectors. Current research is anticipating an exaggeration of the problem as many UK residents move across the English Channel to find employment in France and beyond.

● ● ● ● ● ● ● ● ● ● ● ● ● ● ● ● ● ● ●

Summary

● *Retailing* includes all transactions in which the buyer intends to consume the product through personal, family or household use. *Retailers,* organisations that sell products primarily to ultimate consumers, are important links in the marketing channel because they are customers for wholesalers and producers. Most retailing takes place inside stores or service establishments, but retail exchanges may also occur outside stores through telemarketing, vending machines, mail order catalogues and the Internet. Retail institutions provide place, time and possession utilities. In the case of services, retailers develop most of the product's form utility as well.

● Retail stores locate in the *central business district (CBD)*—the traditional centre of the town on the *prime pitch,* or in locations that provide an adequate *customer threshold*—in *suburban centres,* in *edge of town,* free-standing superstores, or in *retail parks.* The national chains occupy the prime pitch sites in the CBD and the edge of town sheds. Locally based independent retailers tend to dominate in the suburbs and focus on convenience and some comparison goods.

● Retail stores are often classified according to width of product mix and depth of product lines. The major types of retail stores are *department stores, variety stores, hypermarkets, superstores* and *supermarkets, discount sheds, warehouse clubs, speciality shops, convenience stores, discounters, markets, cash and carry warehouses* and *catalogue showrooms.* Department stores are large retail employers characterised by wide product mixes in considerable depth for most product lines. Their product lines are organised into separate departments that function much as self-contained businesses do.

● Speciality retailers offer substantial assortments in a few product lines. They include traditional speciality retailers, which carry narrow product mixes with deep product lines.

● *Non-store retailing* is the selling of goods or services outside the confines of a retail facility. *Direct marketing* is the use of non-personal media or telesales to introduce products to consumers, who then purchase the products by mail or telephone. Forms of non-store retailing include: *in-home retailing* (selling via personal contacts with consumers in their own homes), *telemarketing* (direct selling of goods and services by telephone based either on a cold canvass of the telephone directory or on a pre-screened list of prospective clients), the Internet, *automatic vending* (selling through machines) and *mail order* and *catalogue retailing* (selling by description because buyers usually do not see the actual product until it arrives in the mail).

● *Franchising* is an arrangement whereby a supplier grants a dealer the right to sell products in exchange for some type of consideration. Retail franchises are of three general types: (1) a manufacturer may authorise a number of retail stores to sell a certain brand name item; (2) a producer may license distributors to sell a given product to retailers; or (3) a franchisor may supply brand names, techniques or other services instead of a complete product. Franchise arrangements have a number of advantages and disadvantages over traditional business forms, and their use is increasing.

● To increase sales and store patronage, retailers must consider several strategic issues. *Location* determines the trading area from which a store must draw its customers and should be evaluated carefully. When evaluating potential sites, retailers take into account a variety of factors, including the location of the firm's target market within the trading area, the kinds of products being sold, the availability of public transport, customer characteristics and competitors' locations. The retailer must decide whether to invest heavily in owning freeholds or to negotiate leases. Retailers can choose among several types of locations: free-standing structures, traditional business districts, neighbourhood/suburban shopping centres, regional shopping centres or retail parks. The width, depth and quality of the product assortment should be of the kind that can satisfy the retailer's target market customers.

● *Retail positioning* involves identifying an unserved or under served market niche, or clear market segment, and serving the segment through a strategy that distinguishes the retailer from others in people's minds. *Atmospherics* and design comprise the physical elements of a store's design that can be adjusted to appeal to consumers' emotions and thus induce them to buy. Store *image* derives not only from atmosphere but also from location, products offered, customer services, prices, promotion and the store's overall reputation. *Scrambled merchandising* adds unrelated product lines to an existing product mix and is being used by a growing number of stores to generate sales.

● The *wheel of retailing* hypothesis holds that new retail institutions start as low status, low margin and low price operators. As they develop, they increase service and prices and eventually become vulnerable to newer institutions, which enter the market and repeat the cycle. However, the hypothesis may not apply in every case. There is an ever changing *balance of retailing power* between retailers and their suppliers, emphasised by the growth of retailers' own label brands, which compete with manufacturers' brands. *EPOS* (electronic point of sale) and other *retail technology* systems have revolutionised retailing and—when coupled with new, often centralised warehouse networks—have reduced stockholdings, improved productivity and minimised the risk of stock-outs. The reduction of European Union border controls and regulations is making the retailing environment much more fluid and dynamic: it holds new opportunities for expansion or strategic alliances in other countries, but it also carries the risk of takeover and increased competition in domestic markets.

● ● ● ● ● ● ● ● ● ● ● ● ● ● ● ● ●

Important Terms

Retailing	Discount sheds	Mail order retailing
Retailer	Warehouse clubs	Catalogue retailing
Central business district (CBD)	Speciality shops	Franchising
Prime pitch	Convenience stores	Location
Customer threshold	Discounters	Retail positioning
Suburban centres	Markets	Atmospherics
Edge of town sites	Cash and carry warehouses	Image
Retail park	Catalogue showroom	Scrambled
Department stores	Non-store retailing	merchandising
Variety stores	Direct marketing	Wheel of retailing
Supermarkets and superstores	In-home retailing	Balance of retailing power
EPOS	Telemarketing	Retail technology
Hypermarkets	Automatic vending	

● ● ● ● ● ● ● ● ● ● ● ● ● ● ● ● ●

Discussion and Review Questions

1. What are the major differences between speciality shops and department stores?
2. How does a superstore differ from a supermarket?
3. Evaluate the following statement: "Direct marketing and non-store retailing are roughly the same thing."
4. Why is door-to-door selling a form of retailing? Some consumers feel that direct mail orders skip the retailer. Is this true?
5. If you were to open a retail business, would you prefer to open an independent store or to own a store under a franchise arrangement? Explain your preference.
6. What major issues should be considered when determining a retail site location?
7. Describe the major types of shopping centre. Give examples of each type in your area.

8. How does atmosphere add value to products sold in a store? How important are atmospherics for convenience stores?

9. How should one determine the best retail store atmosphere?

10. Discuss the major factors that help determine a retail store's image.

11. Is it possible for a single retail store to have an overall image that appeals to sophisticated shoppers, extravagant shoppers and bargain hunters? Why or why not?

12. In what ways does the use of scrambled merchandising affect a store's image?

13. In what ways has technology improved retail productivity?

14. What are the likely effects of EU deregulation on retailing in the EU?

Recommended Readings

P. J. McGoldrick, *Retail Marketing,* 2nd edn (London: McGraw-Hill, 1997).

P. J. McGoldrick and G. Davies, *International Retailing: Trends and Strategies* (London: Pitman, 1995).

S. Brown, *Retail Location: A Micro-Scale Perspective* (Aldershot: Avebury, 1992).

A. Ghosh, *Retail Management* (Orlando: Dryden Press, 1993).

D. Cook and R. D. Walters, *Retail Marketing* (London: Prentice-Hall, 1991).

Cases

14.1 Aldi Expands Across Europe

While the major UK grocery retailers recently positioned themselves as middle to up-market, providing extensive ranges, own label goods, improved customer service and large stores with carefully conceived facilities and atmospherics, the budget-conscious sector of the market was left in the hands of Kwik Save.

With only 2,500 lines and concentrating on manufacturer brands, no frills service and small supermarkets in town centres or in the suburbs, Kwik Save has become one of the UK's most successful companies.

Now, however, the market is changing. Aldi, the German discounter, has opened its first branches in the UK. Already one of Europe's largest grocery retailers, with total sales of £13 billion worldwide, Aldi offers no luxuries, no customer services and secondary sites with no expense devoted to store design and fitting out. Aldi concentrates on many of its own label products but they—along with manufacturer brands—are displayed in their shipping containers (in boxes). A limited range of essentials for C2/DE shoppers, for whom price is the key, is the Aldi approach.

Discount grocery retailing has not been successful in the UK. Tesco is still shaking off its former discount image; Supasave went into liquidation in 1982; Pricerite was carved up by Shoppers Paradise and Argyll; Shoppers Paradise itself was devoured and rebranded by Gateway in 1986. The only success story has been Kwik Save. For Aldi, however, UK grocery margins of 5 to 7 per cent are perceived as high, enticing the company into the UK. It remains to be seen whether Aldi can create a network of branches large enough to give it the necessary scale economies to trade on price. UK consumers have yet to accept its discount, limited range positioning in a market led by such high profile retailers as Sainsbury's, Tesco, Somerfield, Argyll (Safeway), Asda and Marks & Spencer.

Aldi describes its UK operation as "new", "dynamic", and "fast moving". In its first three years it opened 65 stores, predominantly in the Midlands and northern England, centred on two state-of-the-art regional distribution centres in Leicestershire and Manchester. With 3,500 stores in Europe and the US, the German discount supermarket chain has succeeded in each country it has

Different Views of Successful UK Food Retailers, Selected Ratios and Ranking

Company	Turnover (£m)	Operating Profit (£m)	Market Value (£m)	% Return on Net Assets	% Return on Equity	Sales Growth	PE Ratio	Added Value[1]
Sainsbury	5,659(1)[2]	369(1)	3,365(1)	21(4)	21(3)	11(2)	13.5(2)	12.3(3)
Tesco	4,717(2)	274(2)	2,350(2)	23(3)	18(4)	7(3)	12.6(4)	12.5(2)
Somerfield	4,516(3)	205(3)	1,703(4)	21(5)	17(6)	−19(6)	10.8(6)	6.6(5)
Argyll	3,500(4)	156(4)	1,661(5)	25(2)	24(2)	1(4)	13.3(3)	10.1(4)
Asda	2,708(5)	156(5)	1,913(3)	18(6)	18(5)	1(5)	11.5(5)	1.2(6)
Kwik Save	1,181(6)	58(6)	848(6)	41(1)	27(1)	18(1)	17.6(1)	26.8(1)

[1] As percentage of input costs.
[2] All rankings in brackets.

SOURCE: John Kay, "Different Views of Successful UK Food Retailers, Selected Ratios and Ranking", *Accountancy*. Reprinted by permission.

entered. Compared with UK discount rival Kwik Save and more up-market leaders Sainsbury's, Tesco or Safeway, Aldi is still a niche player in a highly competitive market. The success of Kwik Save, one of the UK's most profitable retailers, shows that price driven supermarkets can compete with their superstore rivals. Danish, French and German discount rivals have also targeted the UK, and Kwik Save has speeded up its store opening programme.

However, Aldi is still behind in its target of 200 UK stores in its first five years. Away from the Midlands and North East, where Aldi is now seeking sites, discounting is not as popular with the more affluent consumers. In addition, Aldi is now in head to head competition for scarce sites with arch rivals Kwik Save, Lo-Cost and Netto, as well as late-comers Lidl, Ed and Rewe. Denmark's Netto entered the UK in the Tyne Tees area, trading with a similar concept to Aldi. Despite quickly establishing a regional network of 77 stores, it traded at a loss for its first few years and shared Aldi's problems in striving for scale economies with restricted new

store opening opportunities. Nevertheless, as Kwik Save will testify, Aldi and Netto have had a significant impact in the UK.

SOURCES: "King of the discounts invades the south", *Marketing*, 13 September 1990, pp. 38–39; "Aldi arrives", *Marketing*, 9 May 1990, p. 3; Nigel Cope, "Aldi cuts the cackle", *Business*, June 1990, pp. 78–80; Suzanne Bidlake, "Cut price Carrefour targets UK", *Marketing*, 19 November 1992, p. 3; "Norma and Carrefour invade UK", *Marketing Week*, 22 January 1993, p. 6; "Aldi appointments," *The Independent on Sunday*, 7 March 1993, p. IB39; "Netto", *Retail Business*, December 1994, pp. 96–99; "Aldi", *Retail Business*, December 1994, pp. 92–95; David Benady, "UK discounters face up to high street war", *Marketing Week*, 7 April 1995, p. 21.

Questions for Discussion

1. Why are retailers targeting other countries for store expansion?
2. What market opportunities has Aldi exploited in the UK?
3. What problems now oppose the continued rapid expansion of Aldi's no frills discount chain?

14.2 Technology to Increase Home Shopping: Catalogue Retailer Littlewoods Stays Ahead

Throughout the 1970s and 1980s, pundits were predicting the demise of the traditional home catalogue shopping companies such as Littlewoods, Freemans, Great Universal Stores and Otto Versand's Grattan. Instead, Next's Directory and a whole host of specialist operators such as Innovations entered a market that turned out to be far from obsolete. One in three consumers now buys goods at home through catalogue retailing, a market set for important technological changes.

John Moores started his mail order business from one office, a little warehouse, with one secretary.

a. Home Shopping: Market Shares

Company	Market Share (%)
GUS	30.4
Littlewoods	18.0
Freemans	9.7
Grattan	7.8
Empire	4.4
N. Brown	3.8
Fine Art	3.7
Next	2.4
Direct selling	15.7
Other	4.0
Total	100.0

SOURCE: Verdict Research.

b. Some Mail Order Houses

Great Universal Stores: incl. Great Universal; Choice; Family Album; Fashion Extra; Marshall Ward; Kays; Accolade; Kit; Style Plus; One And All. Over 50 Catalogue Bargain Shop outlets.

Littlewoods Organisation: incl. John Moores; Brian Mills; Burlington; Littlewoods; Janet Frazer; Peter Craig; 127 Index Catalogue shops (many within chain stores); 16 Hitchens catalogue surplus shops.

Freemans (Sears): incl. Freemans; Editions.

Grattan (Otto Versand): incl. Grattan; Kaleidoscope; Scotcade; Look Again; Curiosity Shop; Class; Mode.

Empire Stores (Bradford) (La Redoute): incl. Empire; La Redoute.

SOURCES: Companies concerned, 1994; *The Retail Pocket Book 1996* (Henley, Oxon: NTC Publications, 1996), p. 134. Reprinted by permission. Verdict.

Already a millionaire from his football pools operation, Moores wanted to see if he could "make another million from nothing". Pools customers were recruited as customers for mail order, and they in turn persuaded relatives, friends and neighbours to buy from Moores' catalogues. In its first year, the Littlewoods catalogue division had sales of £100,000. In 1936, sales hit £4 million. Today Littlewoods accounts for 18 per cent of the home shopping market and 25 per cent of the mail order sector, a market worth £5.4 billion; the company deals with £2 million worth of orders each working day and despatches 40 million parcels annually to UK homes.

Sixty years of Littlewoods' catalogue sales have echoed consumer changes. When it all began in the 1930s, most people had never travelled more than 50 miles from their birthplace, there was an economic slump, women "slaved" as housewives, few houses had electricity, even large towns had only a few shops, and there was no such entity as a supermarket. In the 1940s Littlewoods joined the war effort, supplying 13,000 food packs daily for troops in Burma, 12 million shells, 750 Wellington bomber bodies, 50,000 rubber dinghies and 5 million parachutes. A fireside chair cost £2, a three-piece suite £8, a double bed or vacuum cleaner £3, a diamond ring £1.50 and gas irons 50p. By the present Queen's coronation in 1953, half the population crammed into bars and lucky neighbours' houses to watch the ceremony on television. Tea, sugar, butter and cheese were still rationed, an electric iron cost £2.40 and a ballpoint pen £1.74 in the still austere 1950s.

The swinging 1960s ushered in a credit driven society seeking consumer durables and more stylish merchandise: transistor radios for £12.60, cine cameras at £55, a sewing machine for £38. In the 1970s inflation soared to 15.9 per cent and Britain joined the European Common Market. A radio cost £6.65 or 20 weeks at 33p; a superior three-piece suite £75.75 or £1.51 a week for 50 weeks. A Hotpoint washing machine cost £131.29 and a Hoovermatic £103.85. The 1980s, the decade of Margaret Thatcher, heralded increased consumer spending and prosperity, rising unemployment and crime, and inner city riots. The microchip arrived in nearly every household, and the yuppies wheeled and dealed their way to inherit the land! Health foods and non-smoking grew in popularity, home ownership rocketed and nearly all households had a television set, a fridge and central heating. AIDS imposed its tragic effects on society, and people worried more about the world's starving millions and under privileged.

Throughout all of these evolving, and at times dramatic, consumer changes, Littlewoods led the catalogue sector. In retailing, the burgeoning of retail chains nationwide and even internationally created a shopping-conscious consumer happy to see increased choice and rapid development of new shopping centres, malls and retail parks. With the adoption of the US superstore concept and out of town retailing, many analysts predicted the demise of high street retailers and home catalogue shopping. Sears, Freemans, Grattan, GUS and Littlewoods all suffered during the early 1980s, but the adoption of sound marketing principles led to rekindled fortunes.

These companies monitored changing consumer tastes and trends more closely, altering their merchandise ranges and prices accordingly. They created new identities for separate catalogues, each targeted at slightly different groups of customers. For example, German-acquired Grattan trades through several catalogues: Grattan—a household name—Kaleidoscope, Scotcade, You & Yours, Look Again, Curiosity Shop, Class and Mode. Freemans operates as Freemans, Editions, Complete Essentials, Clothkits, We Are, Direct Collection and the Jan Harvey Collection. Each catalogue has a different mix of styles and merchandise, price points and sourcing, giving each its own positioning in a highly competitive marketplace. In addition to the clothing and household goods dominated catalogues of the major companies, there are niche specialists offering narrowly focused ranges, including perfumes and cosmetics, toys and novelty goods, home/office stationery and equipment, photographic products, car accessories and speciality foods.

The sector is far from in decline (see Table 14.7). Littlewoods believes that leisure trends and the increasing use of in-home technology favour the continued success of catalogue retailing. The company expects technology to make it possible to buy almost anything while sitting in an armchair at home. Already, personal financial business from insurance to current account banking can be conducted over the telephone or through home computers. Catalogues can be made available on home computers or displayed through video discs on television screens. Investments in such technologies are high, but the competitive advantage is potentially great so long as consumers accept the innovations. In the interim, Littlewoods has kept its options open; in addition to its catalogue business, the company operates a chain of high street variety stores, Littlewoods and over one hundred Index catalogue stores in town centres and retail parks. In mail order, though, Littlewoods and its rivals anticipate the dawning of a whole new era of catalogue retailing and home shopping.

SOURCES: Littlewoods; Freemans; Grattan; *The Marketing Pocket Book 1993* (Henley-on-Thames: NTC), p. 60; Barbara Argument, "Rise and rise of mail order shopping", *Coventry Evening Telegraph*, 1 September 1992, pp. L2–3; with grateful thanks to the *Coventry Evening Telegraph* and Littlewoods; "Great Universal Stores", *Retail Business*, September 1994, pp. 70–76, 82–87; David Martin, "Catalogues face some home truths", *Marketing Week*, 9 September 1994, pp. 21–22; David Benady, "Retail dinosaurs go on a revival course", *Marketing Week*, 9 June 1995, p. 20.

Questions for Discussion

1. What threats have faced the catalogue retailers? How have these been addressed?
2. What are the current trends in the home shopping sector?
3. Why does Littlewoods anticipate the dawning of a whole new era?

15

PHYSICAL DISTRIBUTION

"One of the most neglected, yet potentially most powerful, elements of the marketing mix is the way we reach and service the customer."

Martin Christopher
Cranfield University School of Management

OBJECTIVES

* To understand how physical distribution activities are integrated into marketing channels and overall marketing strategies
* To examine three important physical distribution objectives: customer service, total distribution costs and cost trade-offs
* To learn how efficient order processing facilitates product flow
* To illustrate how materials handling is a part of physical distribution activities
* To learn how warehousing facilitates the storage and movement functions in physical distribution
* To understand how inventory management is conducted to develop and maintain adequate assortments of products for target markets
* To gain insight into how transport modes, which bridge the producer-customer gap, are selected and co-ordinated

For over forty years, East Germans had seen Coca-Cola ads on West German television, but couldn't buy Coke. When the borders opened in 1989, East Germans flocked into West Germany, snapping up products that politics and borders had denied them. Of the many sought after items, the two most popular were bananas and Coke.

Coca-Cola's German subsidiary, Coca-Cola Erfrischungsgetränke GmbH (known popularly as CCEG), moved quickly to satisfy what it recognised as the soft drink's fastest growing market in the world. In its first year on former East German grocery shelves, Coke sales catapulted from zero to 21 million cases. The next year, that number more than tripled to 74 million, leaving Pepsi far behind. According to industry experts, what is contributing to Coca-Cola's victory in the ongoing cola wars is its decision to buy and build bottling plants and distribution centres in eastern Germany.

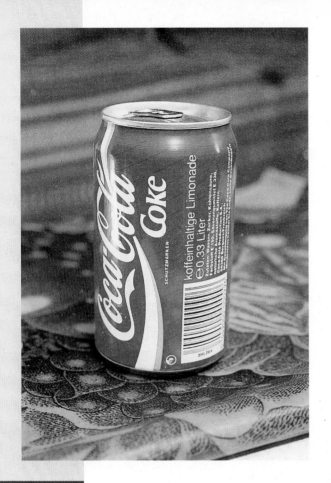

To satisfy eastern German demands for its product, Coca-Cola immediately stocked 8,000 vending machines, initiated fountain service, consolidated more than 100 antiquated German bottlers into 30 efficient state-of-the-art factories, and set up a temporary distribution network using any vehicle with wheels. Coca-Cola then built new distribution centres and bottling plants and upgraded its motorised fleet. At its bottling plants, fully automated bottle cleaners and fillers prepare the soft drink for transfer to warehouses, where fork lifts speed pallets of Coke into delivery trucks. By bottling its product throughout eastern Germany, Coke can take orders in the afternoon and make deliveries by 9 A.M. the next day.

Coca-Cola now patronises local suppliers, spending about 150 million marks a year in eastern Germany alone for sugar, glass, labels, plastic caps and cups. Prompt and easy access to supplies enhances Coca-Cola's already impressive ability to provide its customers with their favourite soft drink. ■

SOURCES: Walecia Konrad, "The real thing is thundering eastward", *Business Week,* 13 April 1992, pp. 55, 98; Robert J. Guttman, "Coca-Cola president, Donald Keough", *Europe,* May 1992, pp. 30–32; Greg Farrell, "We got the Achtung, baby!" *Brandweek,* 18 January 1993, pp. 23–26.

C oca-Cola provides quality customer service to marketing channel members. The company's service orientation helps manufacturers, wholesalers and retailers in the physical distribution of their products. Physical distribution deals with the movement and handling of goods and the processing of orders, activities necessary to provide a level of service that will satisfy customers. Even though physical distribution is costly, it creates time and place utility, which maximises the value of products by delivering them when and where they are wanted. The product may be the best in the world, but if the eager customer or distributor does not receive it when and where promised, customer satisfaction will be zero!

This chapter describes how marketing decisions are related to physical distribution. After considering basic physical distribution concepts, it outlines the major objectives of physical distribution. Next it examines each major distribution function: order processing, materials handling, warehousing, inventory management and transport. The chapter closes with a discussion of marketing strategy considerations in physical distribution. In reading this chapter, it is important to keep in mind how significant customer service is to physical distribution and how physical distribution is related to marketing channels. Without the smooth and efficient movement and handling of goods from one channel member to the next, the chosen marketing channel simply will not function.

The Importance of Physical Distribution

Physical distribution is a set of activities—consisting of order processing, materials handling, warehousing, inventory management and transport—used in the movement of products from producers to consumers and end users. Planning an effective physical distribution system can be a significant decision in developing a marketing strategy. A company that has the right goods in the right place at the right time in the right quantity and with the right support services is able to sell more than competing firms that fail to accomplish these goals. Physical distribution is an important variable in a marketing strategy because it can decrease costs and increase customer satisfaction. In fact, speed of delivery, along with service and dependability, is often as important to buyers as cost. In some situations, for example the emergency provision of a spare part for vital production line machinery, it may even be the single most important factor.

Physical distribution deals with physical movement and inventory holding (storing and tracking inventory or stock until it is needed) both within and among marketing channel members. Often one channel member will arrange the movement of goods for all channel members involved in exchanges. For example, a packing company ships fresh salmon and champagne (often by air) to remote markets on a routine basis. Frequently, buyers are found while the goods are in transit.

The physical distribution system is often adjusted to meet the needs of a channel member. For example, an agricultural equipment dealer who keeps a low inventory of replacement parts requires the fastest and most dependable service when parts not in stock are needed. In this case, the distribution cost may be a minor consideration when compared with service, dependability and promptness. Grocery retailers such as Aldi or Asda receive some deliveries to central and regional warehouses, whereas other deliveries from manufacturers such as Heinz or Kellogg's go directly to individual stores as required, and insisted upon, by the retail companies.

Physical Distribution Objectives

For most companies, the main **objective of physical distribution** is to decrease costs while increasing service. In the real world, however, few distribution systems manage to achieve these goals in equal measure. The large inventories and rapid transport essential to high levels of customer service drive up costs. On the other hand, reduced inventories and slower, cheaper shipping methods cause customer dissatisfaction because of stock-outs or late deliveries. Physical distribution managers strive for a reasonable balance of service, costs and resources. They determine what level of customer service is acceptable yet realistic, develop a "system" outlook of calculating total distribution costs and trade higher costs at one stage of distribution for savings in another. In this section these three performance objectives are examined more closely.

Customer Service

In varying degrees, all organisations attempt to satisfy customer needs and wants through a set of activities known collectively as **customer service**. Many companies claim that service to the customer is their top priority. These companies see service as being as important in attracting customers and building sales as the cost or quality of the organisation's products.

Customers require a variety of services. At the most basic level, they need fair prices, acceptable product quality and dependable deliveries.[1] There are many facets of service as described throughout this text, but in the physical distribution area, availability, promptness and quality are the most important dimensions of customer service. These are the main factors that determine how satisfied customers are likely to be with a supplier's physical distribution activities.[2] Customers seeking a higher level of customer service may also want sizeable inventories, efficient order processing, availability of emergency shipments, progress reports, post-sale services, prompt replacement of defective items and warranties. Customers' inventory requirements influence the level of physical distribution service they expect. For example, customers who want to minimise inventory storage and shipping costs may require that suppliers assume the cost of maintaining inventory in the marketing channel, or the cost of premium transport.[3] Because service needs vary from customer to customer, companies must analyse—and adapt to—customer preferences. Attention to customer needs and preferences is crucial to increasing sales and obtaining repeat sales. A company's failure to provide the desired level of service may mean the loss of customers. Without customers there can be no profit.

Companies must also examine the service levels competitors offer and match those standards, at least when the costs of providing the services can be balanced by the sales generated. For example, companies may step up their efforts to identify the causes of customer complaints or institute corrective measures for billing and shipping errors. In extremely competitive businesses, such as the market for vehicle parts, firms may concentrate on product availability. To compete effectively, manufacturers may strive for inventory levels and order processing speeds that are deemed unnecessary and too costly in other industries.[4]

Services are provided most effectively when service standards are developed and stated in terms that are specific, measurable and appropriate for the product: for example, "Guaranteed delivery within 48 hours". Standards should be communicated clearly to both customers and employees and rigorously enforced. In many cases, it is necessary to maintain a policy of minimum order size to ensure that transactions are profitable; that is, special service charges are added to orders smaller than a specified quantity. Many carrier companies operate on this basis. Many service policies also spell out delivery times and provisions for back ordering, returning goods and obtaining emergency shipments. The overall objective of any service policy should be to improve customer service just to the point beyond which increased sales would be negated by increased distribution costs.

Total Distribution Costs

Although physical distribution managers try to minimise the costs of each element in the system—order processing, materials handling, inventory, warehousing and transport—decreasing costs in one area often raises them in another. By using a total cost approach to physical distribution, managers can view the distribution system as a whole, not as a collection of unrelated activities. The emphasis shifts from lowering the separate costs of individual functions to minimising the total cost of the entire distribution system.

The total cost approach calls for analysing the costs of all possible distribution alternatives, even those considered too impractical or expensive. Total cost analyses weigh inventory levels against warehousing expenses, materials handling costs against various modes of transport and all distribution costs against customer service standards. The costs of potential sales losses from lower performance levels are also considered. In many cases, accounting procedures and statistical methods can be used to figure total costs. Where hundreds of combinations of distribution variables are possible, computer simulations may be helpful. In no case is a distribution system's lowest total cost the result of using a combination of the cheapest functions; instead, it is the lowest overall cost compatible with the company's stated service objectives.

Cost Trade-offs

Cost trade-offs The offsetting of higher costs in one area of the distribution system by lower costs in another area, to keep the total system cost effective

A distribution system that attempts to provide a specific level of customer service for the lowest possible total cost must use **cost trade-offs** to resolve conflicts about resource allocations. That is, higher costs in one area of the distribution system must be offset by lower costs in another area if the total system is to remain cost effective.

Trade-offs are strategic decisions to combine (and re-combine) resources for greatest cost effectiveness. When distribution managers regard the system as a network of interlocking functions, trade-offs become useful tools in a unified distribution strategy. The furniture retailer IKEA uses a system of trade-offs. To ensure that each store carries enough inventory to satisfy customers in the area, IKEA groups its retail outlets into regions, each served by a separate distribution centre. In addition, each IKEA store carries a five week back stock of inventory. Thus IKEA has chosen to trade higher inventory warehousing costs for improved customer service.[5]

Now that several of the physical distribution objectives that marketers may pursue have been considered, it is time to take a closer look at specific physical distribution activities. The remainder of the chapter focuses on order processing, materials handling, warehousing, inventory management and transport.

• • • • • • • • • • • • • • • • • • • •

Order Processing

Order processing The receipt and transmission of sales order information

Order processing—the first stage in a physical distribution system—is the receipt and transmission of sales order information. Although management sometimes overlooks the importance of these activities, efficient order processing facilitates product flow. Computerised order processing, used by many firms, speeds the flow of information from customer to seller.[6] Indeed, in many industries key suppliers are linked "live" to retailers' or distributors' tills and order books. They are thus able to replenish or supply exactly in line with demand and actual sales. When carried out quickly and accurately, order processing contributes to customer satisfaction, repeat orders and increased profits.

Generally, there are three main tasks in order processing: order entry, order handling and order delivery.[7] Order entry begins when customers or salespeople place purchase orders by mail, telephone, fax or computer. In some companies, sales service representatives receive and enter orders personally and also handle complaints, prepare progress reports and forward sales order information.[8]

The next task, order handling, involves several activities. Once an order has been entered, it is transmitted to the warehouse, where the availability of the product is verified, and to the credit department, where prices, terms and the customer's credit rating are checked. If the credit department approves the purchase, the warehouse begins to fill the order. If the requested product is not in stock, a production order is sent to the factory or the customer is offered a substitute item.

When the order has been filled and packed for shipment, the warehouse schedules pick up with an appropriate carrier. If the customer is willing to pay for rush service, priority transport, such as overnight courier, is used. The customer is sent an invoice, inventory records are adjusted and the order is delivered.

Order processing can be manual or electronic, depending on which method provides the greatest speed and accuracy within cost limits. Manual processing suffices for a small volume of orders and is more flexible in special situations; electronic processing is more practical for a large volume of orders and lets a company integrate order processing, production planning, inventory, accounting and transport planning into a total information system.[9] Many leading retail groups, with products from groceries to electrical goods, have their stores networked to the head office. Suppliers are also electronically linked to the retailers' head offices, so that stock can be ordered electronically.

Materials Handling

Materials handling The physical handling of products

Materials handling, or physical handling of products, is important for efficient warehouse operations, as well as in transport from points of production to points of consumption. The characteristics of the product itself often determine how it will be handled. For example, fresh dairy produce has unique characteristics that determine how it can be moved and stored.

Materials handling procedures and techniques should increase the usable capacity of a warehouse, reduce the number of times a good is handled, improve service to customers and increase their satisfaction with the product. Packaging, loading, movement and labelling systems must be co-ordinated to maximise cost reduction and customer satisfaction.

In Chapter 9 it was noted that the protective functions of packaging are important considerations in product development. Appropriate decisions about packaging materials and methods allow for the most efficient physical handling; most companies employ packaging consultants or specialists to accomplish this important task. Materials handling equipment is used in the design of handling systems.

Unit loading Grouping one or more boxes on a pallet or skid, permitting movement of efficient loads by mechanical means

Unit loading is grouping one or more boxes on a pallet or skid; it permits movement of efficient loads by mechanical means, such as fork lifts, trucks or conveyor systems. **Containerisation** is the practice of consolidating many items into a single large container that is sealed at its point of origin and opened at its destination. The containers are usually 2.5 metres (8 feet) wide, 2.5 metres (8 feet) high, and 3, 6, 7.5 or 12 metres (10, 20, 25, or 40 feet) long. They can be conveniently stacked and sorted as units at the point of loading. Because individual items are not handled in transit, containerisation greatly increases efficiency and security in shipping.

Containerisation The practice of consolidating many items into a single large container that is sealed at its point of origin and opened at its destination, greatly increasing efficiency and security in shipping

Warehousing

Warehousing The design and operation of facilities for storing and moving goods

Warehousing, the design and operation of facilities for storing and moving goods, is an important physical distribution function. Warehousing provides time utility by enabling firms to compensate for dissimilar production and consumption rates. That is, when mass production creates a greater stock of goods than can be sold immediately, companies may warehouse the surplus goods until customers are ready to buy. Warehousing also helps stabilise the prices and availability of seasonal items. Following is a description of the basic functions of warehouses and the different types of warehouses available. Distribution centres, special warehouse operations designed so that goods can be moved rapidly, are also examined.

Steel Stockholding—Ad Hoc Distribution Moves Into the 21st Century

Steel stockholding in Europe is dominated by the nationalised industries' stockholding subsidiaries; in the UK the privatised British Steel subsidiaries have nearly half of the market. British Tubes Stockholding (BTS), for example, accounted for a quarter of the market with seven warehouses throughout the UK as well as two central distribution centres. BTS customers ranged from small general engineers to major oil companies. Market sectors included general engineering, shipbuilding, pipework fabricators, power generation contractors, management contractors, offshore fabricators, oil companies, petrochemical and gas industries. BTS provided an international service for direct shipment to worldwide destinations. With the acquisition of its direct rival, Walkers, BTS—now called BSD—became the market leader.

BSD Tubes, like the other major stockholders, Brown and Tawse, has grown by acquiring smaller, often locally orientated independents. Its distribution network is, therefore, rather ad hoc: two new, purpose built warehouses that can handle the whole product range; some warehouses capable of stocking only a limited range; some out-dated premises built many years ago with limited vehicle access and poor handling facilities; non-uniform coverage areas—some deal nationally, others locally, many intrude on neighbouring sales or delivery territories. In one case, the area sales force is capable of generating 40 per cent more business volume than its warehouse can supply.

A new network of warehouses is now being developed. Large, infrequently demanded, bulky items are to be stocked centrally, still providing delivery in under 24 hours—better, according to market research, than the market requires—and all regional warehouses will have a product range in line with their customer requirements. New locations close to motorways will enable easy delivery from factories and importers while allowing easy collection from or delivery to customers in each region. Warehousing in the South East will be able to cater for exports into Europe and act as a deterrent to Dutch, Belgian and French competitors targeting the UK markets around the ports and the Channel Tunnel. A computer monitors all stockholding, orders and deliveries, minimising stockouts and excess holdings. The new distribution system will be in line with customer needs and will totally modernise the company's operation.

SOURCES: BTS management, 1988–1990; BTS promotional material, "Buying from your local winning team", 1988; "British Steel's solid strength", *Investors Chronicle,* 16–22 February 1990, p. 50; "British Steel: manufacturer and distributor", *Investors Chronicle,* 15–21 June 1990, p. 52; Robert Heller, "British Steel rolls ahead", *Management Today,* June 1995, pp. 42–46; BSD sales literature, 1996.

Warehousing Functions   Warehousing is not limited simply to the storage of goods. When warehouses receive goods by wagon loads or lorry loads, they break the shipments down into smaller quantities for individual customers; when goods arrive in small lots, the warehouses assemble the lots into bulk loads that can be shipped out more economically.[10] Warehouses perform these basic distribution functions:

1. *Receiving goods*—The merchandise is accepted, and the warehouse assumes responsibility for it.
2. *Identifying goods*—The appropriate stock keeping units are recorded, along with the quantity of each item received. The item may be marked with a physical code, tag or other label; or it may be identified by an item code (a code on the carrier or container) or by physical properties.

3. *Sorting goods*—The merchandise is sorted for storage in appropriate areas.
4. *Despatching goods to storage*—The merchandise is put away so that it can be retrieved when necessary.
5. *Holding goods*—The merchandise is kept in storage and properly protected until needed.
6. *Recalling and picking goods*—Items customers have ordered are efficiently retrieved from storage and prepared for the next step.
7. *Marshalling the shipment*—The items making up a single shipment are brought together and checked for completeness or explainable omissions. Order records are prepared or modified as necessary.
8. *Despatching the shipment*—The consolidated order is packaged suitably and directed to the right transport vehicle. Necessary shipping and accounting documents are prepared.[11]

Types of Warehouses

A company's choice of warehouse facilities is an important strategic consideration. By using the right warehouse, a company may be able to reduce transport and inventory costs or improve its service to customers; the wrong warehouse may drain company resources. For example, a company that produces processed foods must locate its warehousing close to main transport routes to facilitate delivery to supermarkets in different parts of the country. Besides deciding how many facilities to operate and where to locate them, a company must determine which type of warehouse will be most appropriate. Warehouses fall into two general categories: private and public. In many cases, a combination of private and public facilities provides the most flexible approach to warehousing.

Private warehouse A warehouse operated by a company for shipping and storing its own products

Private Warehouses A **private warehouse** is operated by a company for shipping and storing its own products. Private warehouses are usually leased or purchased when a firm believes that its warehouse needs in given geographic markets are so substantial and so stable that it can make a long term commitment to fixed facilities. They are also appropriate for firms that require special handling and storage features and want to control the design and operation of the warehouse. Marketing Insight 15.1 describes BSD's warehousing and distribution functions.

Some of the largest users of private warehouses are retail chain stores.[12] Retailers such as Aldi, Marks & Spencer, Texas or Carrefour find it economical to integrate the warehousing function with purchasing for and distribution to their retail outlets. When sales volumes are fairly stable, ownership and control of a private warehouse may provide benefits, such as property appreciation. Private warehouses, however, face fixed costs, such as land rents, insurance, taxes, maintenance and debt expense. They also allow little flexibility when firms wish to move inventories to more strategic locations. Before tying up capital in a private warehouse or entering into a long term lease, a company should consider its resources, the level of its expertise in warehouse management and the role of the warehouse in its overall marketing strategy.

Public warehouses Warehouses that rent storage space and related physical distribution facilities to other companies and sometimes provide distribution services such as receiving and unloading products, inspecting, re-shipping, filling orders, financing, displaying products and co-ordinating shipments

Public Warehouses **Public warehouses** rent storage space and related physical distribution facilities to other companies and sometimes provide distribution services such as receiving and unloading products, inspecting, re-shipping, filling orders, financing, displaying products and co-ordinating shipments. They are especially useful to firms with seasonal production or low volume storage needs, companies with inventories that must be maintained in many locations, firms that are testing or entering new markets and business operations that own private warehouses but occasionally require additional storage space. Public warehouses

Benetton's New "Sell Direct" Policy Benefits from Its International Electronic Data Interchange System

How important can eight people be to a multinational clothing manufacturer and retailer? To Benetton, the Italian casual wear company, the eight people who run the warehouse that handles the distribution of 50 million pieces of clothing a year are extremely important. These eight people are responsible for processing 230,000 articles of clothing a day to serve 6,500 stores in 110 countries, of which 1,500 are located in Italy, 800 in the United States and 400 in the UK. Though sales in the garment industry have sagged recently, Benetton is still moving tremendous amounts of knit and cotton clothing. After their small clothing business expanded into an international fashion sensation, executives at Benetton realised that highly efficient physical distribution methods were a must.

Benetton has linked its sales agents, factory and warehouse together using an international electronic data interchange (EDI) system managed by General Electric Information Services. Suppose a student in Maastricht wants to buy a Benetton sweater identical to his older brother's. He goes to a Benetton store and searches for it, only to be disappointed when he finds that the sweater is not there. The salesperson assures him that the sweater will arrive in a month. The salesperson then calls a Benetton sales agent, who places the sweater order on a personal computer. Three times a day, this information is collected and sent to the company's mainframe system in Italy, where the computer searches inventory data to find out if the requested item is in stock. If not, an order automat-

ically travels to a machine that cuts the materials and immediately starts to knit the sweater. Workers put the finished sweater in a box with a barcoded label and send it to the warehouse. In the warehouse, a computer commands a robot to retrieve the sweater and any other merchandise that needs to be transported to the same store.

In the mid-1990s, Benetton surprised the rag trade (the clothing industry) by announcing that it was to launch a "direct sell" operation—home shopping via catalogues and courier delivery firms. Benetton in the UK is the first high street store based retailer to opt for direct home shopping since Next launched its *Next Directory* in 1986. Effective stock control and distribution will now be even more important for Italy's Benetton.

Through efficient management of physical distribution activities and the use of technologically advanced equipment, Benetton ensures that its products are available to consumers when and where they want them. Close attention to physical distribution activities has helped the company achieve its objectives and become a major competitor in the fashion industry. With the addition of a home shopping operation, it is essential for Benetton's logistical support to be "state-of-the-art".

SOURCES: Barbara DePompa, "More power at your fingertips", *Information Week,* 23 December 1991, p. 22; Lory Zottola, "The united systems of Benetton", *Computerworld,* 2 April 1990, p. 70; Harriet Fox, "Benetton opts for direct sell", *Marketing,* 16 March 1995, p. 5; Tom O'Sullivan and David Benady, "Unravelling of Benetton?", *Marketing Week,* 3 February 1995, pp. 21–22; Fiorenza Belussi, "The Italian job", *RDM,* Summer 1994, pp. ix–x.

can also serve as collection points during product recall programmes. Whereas private warehouses have fixed costs, public warehouses' costs are variable (and often lower) because users rent space and purchase warehousing services only as needed.

In addition, many public warehouses furnish security for products that are being used as collateral for loans, a service that can be provided at either the warehouse or the site of the owner's inventory. A **field public warehouse** is a warehouse

Field public warehouse A warehouse established by a public warehouse at the owner's inventory location established by a public warehouse at the owner's inventory location. The warehouser becomes the custodian of the products and issues a receipt that can be used as collateral for a loan. Public warehouses can also provide **bonded storage,** a warehousing arrangement under which imported or taxable products are not released until the owners of the products have paid customs duties, taxes or other fees. Bonded warehouses enable firms to defer tax payments on such items until the products are delivered to customers.

Bonded storage A warehousing arrangement by which imported or taxable products are not released until the owners of the products have paid customs duties, taxes or other fees

The Distribution Centre   A **distribution centre** is a large, centralised warehouse that receives goods from factories and suppliers, re-groups them into orders and ships them to customers quickly; its focus is on active movement of goods rather than passive storage.[13] Distribution centres are specially designed for the rapid flow of products. They are usually one storey buildings (to eliminate lifts) and have access to transport networks, such as motorways or railway lines. Many distribution centres are highly automated operations in which computer directed robots, fork lifts and hoists collect and move products to loading docks. Although some public warehouses offer such specialised services, most distribution centres are privately owned. They serve customers in regional markets and in some cases function as consolidation points for a company's branch warehouses.

Distribution centre   A large, centralised warehouse that receives goods from factories and suppliers, regroups them into orders and quickly ships them to customers

Distribution centres offer several benefits, the most important of which is improved customer service. Distribution centres ensure product availability by maintaining full product lines. The speed of their operations cuts delivery time to a minimum. In addition, they reduce costs. Instead of having to make many smaller shipments to scattered warehouses and customers, factories can ship large quantities of goods directly to distribution centres at bulk load rates, thus lowering transport costs; furthermore, rapid turnover of inventory lessens the need for warehouses and cuts storage costs. Some distribution centres also facilitate production by receiving and consolidating raw materials and providing final assembly for some products.

· · · · · · · · · · · · · · · · · · · ·

Inventory Management

Inventory management   The development and maintenance of sufficient assortments of products to meet customers' needs

Inventory management involves developing and maintaining adequate assortments of products to meet customers' needs. Because a firm's investment in inventory usually represents 30 to 50 per cent of its total assets, inventory decisions have a significant impact on physical distribution costs and the level of customer service provided. When too few products are carried in inventory, the result is **stock-outs,** or shortages of products, which result in brand switching, fewer sales and loss of customers. But when too many products (or too many slow moving products) are carried, costs increase, as do the risks of product obsolescence, pilferage and damage. The objective of inventory management, therefore, is to minimise inventory costs while maintaining an adequate supply of goods. Marketing Insight 15.2 shows how staff at Benetton use high technology equipment to ensure that the company's inventory is managed efficiently.

Stock-outs   Shortages of products resulting from a lack of products carried in inventory

There are three types of inventory costs. *Carrying costs* are holding costs; they include expenditures for storage space and materials handling, financing, insurance, taxes and losses from spoilage of goods. *Replenishment costs* are related to the purchase of merchandise. The price of goods, handling charges and expenses for order processing contribute to replenishment costs. *Stock-out costs* include sales lost when demand for goods exceed supply on hand and the clerical and processing expenses of back ordering. A company must control all the costs of obtaining and maintaining inventory in order to achieve its profit goals. Management must therefore have a clear idea of the level of each type of cost incurred.

Inventory managers deal with two issues of particular importance. They must know when to re-order and how much merchandise to order. For example, many high street banks no longer require current account customers to order new cheque books. Once a certain cheque number is reached, a new book is automatically sent to the customer. The **re-order point** is the inventory level that signals that more inventory should be ordered. Three factors determine the re-order point: (1) the expected time between the date an order is placed and the date the goods are received and made ready for re-sale to customers; (2) the rate at which a product is sold or used up; and (3) the quantity of **safety stock** on hand, or inventory needed to prevent stock-outs. The optimum level of safety stock depends on the general demand and the standard of customer service to be provided. If a firm is to avoid shortages without tying up too much capital in inventory, some systematic method for determining re-order points is essential.

The inventory manager faces several trade-offs when re-ordering merchandise. Large safety stocks ensure product availability and thus improve the level of customer service; they also lower order processing costs because orders are placed less frequently. Small safety stocks, on the other hand, cause frequent re-orders and high order processing costs but reduce the overall cost of carrying inventory. Figure 15.1 illustrates two order systems involving different order quantities but the same level of safety stocks. Figure 15.1(a) shows inventory levels for a given demand of infrequent orders; Figure 15.1(b) illustrates the levels needed to fill frequent orders at the same demand.

To quantify this trade-off between carrying costs and order processing costs, a model for an **economic order quantity** (EOQ) has been developed (see Figure 15.2); it specifies the order size that minimises the total cost of ordering and carrying inventory.[14] The fundamental relationships underlying the widely accepted EOQ model are the basis of many inventory control systems. Keep in mind, however, that the objective of minimum total inventory cost must be balanced against the customer service level necessary for maximum profits. Therefore, because increased costs of carrying inventory are usually associated with a higher level of customer service, the order quantity will often lie to the right of the optimal point in the figure, leading to a higher total cost for ordering and larger carrying inventory.

Re-order point   The inventory level that signals the need to order more inventory

Safety stock   Inventory needed to prevent stock-outs

Economic order quantity (EOQ)   The order size that minimises the total cost of ordering and carrying inventory

Q = quantity.

Figure 15.1 Effects of order size on an inventory system

Figure 15.2

Economic order quantity (EOQ) model

Fluctuations in demand, for example in times of economic recession, mean that it is not always easy to predict changing inventory levels. When management miscalculates re-order points or order quantities, inventory problems develop. Warning signs include an inventory that grows at a faster rate than sales, surplus or obsolete inventory, customer deliveries that are consistently late or lead times that are too long, inventory that represents a growing percentage of assets, and large inventory adjustments or write-offs.[15] However, there are several tools for improving inventory control. From a technical standpoint, an inventory system can be planned so that the number of products sold and the number of products in stock are determined at certain checkpoints. The control may be as simple as tearing off a code number from each product sold so that the correct sizes, colours and models can be tabulated and re-ordered. Many bookshops insert re-order slips of paper into each item of stock, which can be removed at the checkout. A sizeable amount of technologically advanced electronic equipment is available to assist with inventory management. In many larger stores, such as Tesco and Toys "R" Us, checkout terminals connected to central computer systems instantaneously up-date inventory and sales records. For continuous, automatic up-dating of inventory records, some firms use pressure sensitive circuits installed under ordinary industrial shelving to weigh inventory, convert the weight to units and display any inventory changes on a video screen or computer printout.

Various techniques have also been used successfully to improve inventory management. The just-in-time concept, widely used in Japan, calls for companies to maintain low inventory levels and purchase products and materials in small quantities, just at the moment they are needed for production. Ford Motor Company, for example, sometimes receives supply deliveries as often as every two hours.[16] Just-in-time inventory management depends on a high level of co-ordination between producers and suppliers, but the technique enables companies to eliminate waste and reduce inventory costs significantly. When Polaroid implemented just-in-time techniques as part of its zero base pricing programme to reduce the overall cost of purchased materials, equipment and services, it saved an average of £15 million per year.[17]

Another inventory management technique, the 80/20 rule, holds that fast moving products should generate a higher level of customer service than slow moving products, on the theory that 20 per cent of the items account for 80 per cent of the sales. Thus an inventory manager attempts to keep an adequate supply of fast selling items and a minimal supply of the slower moving products.

• • • • • • • • • • • • • • • • • • •

Transportation

Transportation The process of moving a product from where it is made to where it is purchased and used

Transportation adds time and place utility to a product by moving it from where it is made to where it is purchased and used.[18] Because product availability and timely deliveries are so dependent on transport functions, a firm's choice of transport directly affects customer service and satisfaction. A firm may even build its distribution and marketing strategy around a unique transport system if the system ensures on-time deliveries that will give the firm a competitive edge. This section considers the principal modes of transport, the criteria companies use to select one mode over another and several methods of co-ordinating transport service. Table 15.1 illustrates typical transport modes for various products.

Transport Modes

Transport modes Methods of moving goods; these include railways, motor vehicles, inland waterways, airways and pipelines

There are five major **transport modes,** or methods of moving goods: railways, motor vehicles, inland waterways, airways and pipelines. Each mode offers unique advantages; many companies have adopted physical handling procedures that facilitate the use of two or more modes in combination (see Table 15.2).

Motor Vehicles Motor vehicles provide the most flexible schedules and routes of all major transport modes because they can go almost anywhere. Lorries have a unique ability to move goods directly from factory or warehouse to customer, so they are often used in conjunction with other forms of transport that cannot provide door-to-door deliveries.

Although motor vehicles usually travel much faster than trains, they are more vulnerable to bad weather, and their services are more expensive. Lorries are also subject to the size and weight restrictions of the products they carry. In addition, carriers are sometimes criticised for high levels of loss and damage to freight and for delays due to re-handling of small shipments. In response, the road haulage industry is turning to computerised tracking of shipments and is developing new equipment to speed loading and unloading.[19] Companies are paying more attention to route planning to ensure that goods are delivered as efficiently as possible.

Railways*	Motor Vehicles	Waterways*	Pipelines	Airways
Coal	Clothing	Petroleum	Oil	Flowers
Grain	Paper goods	Chemicals	Processed coal	Perishable food
Chemicals	Computers	Iron ore	Natural gas	Instruments
Timber	Books	Bauxite	Water	Emergency parts
Cars	Fresh fruit	Grain		Overnight mail
Iron	Livestock			

*Not so much in the UK, but common in the rest of Europe.

Table 15.1 Typical transport modes for various products

Mode	Imports (000 Tonnes)	Exports (000 Tonnes)
Railways	540	481
Road	6,281	4,513
Ship	53,344	82,920

Table 15.2 UK trade by transport modes

Figure 15.3 illustrates three types of routes that can be used. The choice of route will depend on vehicle capacity, order size, geographical characteristics of the territory and existence of suitable major routes.[20] In Europe, particularly the UK, road haulage dominates in the distribution of most consumer and industrial products. Quick, flexible and relatively cost efficient, it has overtaken rail, and motorway improvements will further strengthen its position.

Railways Railways carry heavy, bulky freight that must be shipped over land for long distances. Railways commonly carry minerals, sand, timber, pulp, chemicals and farm products, as well as low value manufactured goods and an increasing number of cars. They are especially efficient for transporting full car loads, which require less handling—and can therefore be shipped at lower rates—than smaller quantities. Some companies locate their factories or warehouses near major rail lines or on spur lines for convenient loading and unloading.

Although railways haul intercity freight, their share of the transport market has declined in recent years. High fixed costs, shortages of rail wagons during peak periods, poor maintenance of tracks and equipment, and increased competition from other carriers, mainly road hauliers, have plagued European rail operators. The Channel Tunnel will be rail orientated. Rail freight depots have been constructed at numerous strategic locations in anticipation of increased rail freight. The partial privatisation of British Rail is further complicating the situation in the UK.

Inland Waterways Water transport is the cheapest method of shipping heavy, low value, non-perishable goods such as coal, grain, sand and petroleum products. Water carriers offer considerable capacity. Barges that travel along inland rivers,

Area routes connect customers in concentratred areas.

Arc (circumferential) routes link customers in arcs at different distances from the distribution centre.

Radial routes link customers in radial groups to and from the distribution centre.

Figure 15.3 Planning distribution routes

canals and navigation systems can haul many times the weight of one railway wagon. In Benelux and parts of Europe, it is a popular freight method, but not so much in the UK.

However, many markets are accessible to water only with supplementary rail or road transport. Furthermore, water transport is extremely slow and sometimes comes to a standstill during freezing weather. Companies that depend on water may ship their entire inventory during the summer and then store it for winter use. Droughts and floods also create difficulties for users of inland waterway transport. Because water transport is extremely fuel efficient, its volume is expected to double by the year 2000, but it will still represent only a very small percentage of total shipping.[21]

Airways   Air transport is the fastest and most expensive form of shipping. It is used most often for perishable goods; for high value, low bulk items; and for products that must be delivered quickly over long distances, such as emergency shipments (see Figure 15.4). The capacity of air transport is limited only by the capacity of individual aircraft. Medium-range jets can carry about 18,000 kilos (40,000 pounds) of freight, and some new jet cargo planes equipped to carry containers can accommodate more than 90,000 kilos (200,000 pounds). Most air car-

FASTER FOR SURE.

If time is money, SIA Cargo's Swiftrider service could save you a fortune. Swiftrider shipments take off with priority handling and clearance, later close-out times, money-back guaranteed uplift, tracking and proof of delivery from FORSC–SIA Cargo's reservation and tracking computer system. Not to mention our new airport-to-door delivery when flying goods to Singapore. It all adds up to a service that puts you miles ahead. Working across a network of more than 70 cities in over 40 countries, Swiftrider is faster, that's for sure.

Figure 15.4 Air transport. Singapore Airlines promotes its cargo services.

Source: Courtesy of Swiftrider/Singapore Airlines Cargo.

riers transport a combination of passengers, freight and mail.[22] Although air transport accounts for less than 1 per cent of total tonne-miles carried, its importance as a mode of transport is growing. Despite its expense, air transit can reduce warehousing and packaging costs and also losses from theft and damage, thus helping to offset total costs. However, the ground transport needed for pick up and final delivery adds to cost and transit time.

Pipelines   Pipelines, the most automated transport mode, usually belong to the shipper and carry the shipper's products. Most pipelines carry petroleum products or chemicals. For example, the Trans-Alaska Pipeline, owned and operated by a consortium of oil companies that includes Exxon, Mobil and BP, transports crude oil for its owners from remote oil drilling sites in central Alaska to shipping terminals on the coast. Slurry pipelines have been developed to carry pulverised coal, grain or wood chips suspended in water.

Pipelines move products slowly but continuously and at relatively low cost. They are a reliable mode of transport and ensure low product damage and theft. However, their contents are subject to as much as 1 per cent shrinkage, usually from evaporation, and products must be shipped in minimum quantities of 25,000 barrels for efficient pipeline operation.[23] British and Scandinavian North Sea oil and natural gas depend on pipelines for transport and distribution. They have also been a source of concern to environmentalists, who fear that installation and leaks could harm plants and animals. Time will tell whether the safety record of pipelines is better or worse than traditional methods, for example oil tankers, for moving oil.

Criteria for Selecting Transport

Marketers select a transport mode on the basis of costs, transit time (speed), reliability, capability, accessibility, security and traceability.[24] Table 15.3 summarises various cost and performance considerations that help determine the selection of transport modes. It is important to remember that these relationships are approximations and that the choice of a transport mode involves many trade-offs.

Costs   One consideration that helps determine transportation mode, involving comparison of alternative modes to determine whether the benefits of a more expensive mode are worth the higher costs

Costs   Marketers compare alternative means of transport to determine whether the benefits from a more expensive mode are worth the higher **costs.** Air freight carriers provide many benefits, such as high speed, reliability, security and traceability, but at higher costs relative to other transport modes. When speed is less important, marketers prefer lower costs.

	Cost	Transit Time	Reliability	Capability	Accessibility	Security	Traceability
Most	Air	Water	Pipeline	Water	Road	Pipeline	Air
	Pipeline	Rail	Rail	Road	Rail	Water	Road
	Rail	Pipeline	Road	Rail	Air	Rail	Rail
	Road	Road	Air	Air	Water	Air	Water
Least	Water	Air	Water	Pipeline	Pipeline	Road	Pipeline

Source: Selected information adapted from J. L. Heskett, Robert Ivie and J. Nicholas Glaskowsky, *Business Logistics* (New York: Ronald Press, 1973). Reprinted by permission of John Wiley & Sons, Inc.

Table 15.3 Ranking of transport modes by selecting criteria, highest to lowest

Recently, marketers have been able to cut expenses and increase efficiency. Railways, airlines, road hauliers, barges and pipeline companies have all become more competitive and more responsive to customers' needs. Surveys reveal that in recent years transport costs per tonne and as a percentage of sales have declined, now averaging 7.5 per cent of sales. This figure varies by industry, of course: electrical machinery, textiles and instruments have transport costs of only 3 or 4 per cent of sales, whereas timber products, chemicals and food have transport costs close to 15 per cent of sales.

Transit time The total time a carrier has possession of goods

Transit Time **Transit time** is the total time a carrier has possession of goods, including the time required for pick up and delivery, handling and movement between the points of origin and destination. Closely related to transit time is frequency, or number of shipments per day. Transit time obviously affects a marketer's ability to provide service, but there are some less obvious implications as well. A shipper can take advantage of transit time to process orders for goods en route, a capability especially important for agricultural and raw materials shippers. Some railways also let shipments already in transit be redirected, for maximum flexibility in selecting markets. For example, a consignment of seafood may be shipped to a closer destination if the seafood is in danger of going bad.

Reliability The consistency of service provided

Reliability The total **reliability** of a transport mode is determined by the consistency of service provided. Marketers must be able to count on their carriers to deliver goods on time and in an acceptable condition. Along with transit time, reliability affects a marketer's inventory costs, which include sales lost when merchandise is not available. Unreliable transport necessitates maintaining higher inventory levels to avoid stock-outs. Reliable delivery service, on the other hand, enables customers to save money by reducing inventories; for example, if a pharmacist knows that suppliers can deliver drugs within hours of ordering, he or she can carry a smaller inventory.

Capability The ability of a transport mode to provide the appropriate equipment and conditions for moving specific kinds of goods

Capability **Capability** is the ability of a transport mode to provide the appropriate equipment and conditions for moving specific kinds of goods. For example, many products must be shipped under controlled temperature and humidity. Other products, such as liquids or gases, require special equipment or facilities for their shipment.

Accessibility The ability to move goods over a specific route or network

Accessibility A carrier's **accessibility** refers to its ability to move goods over a specific route or network (rail lines, waterways or roads).

Security The measure of the physical condition of goods upon delivery

Security A transport mode's **security** is measured by the physical condition of goods upon delivery. A business organisation does not incur costs directly when goods are lost or damaged, because the carrier is usually held liable in these cases. Nevertheless, poor service and lack of security will indirectly lead to increased costs and lower profits for the firm, since damaged or lost goods are not available for immediate sale or use. In some cases companies find it necessary to transport products using courier companies such as Securicor.

Traceability The relative ease with which a shipment can be located and transferred

Traceability **Traceability** is the relative ease with which a shipment can be located and transferred (or found if it is lost). Quick traceability is a convenience that some firms value highly. Shippers have learned that the ability to trace shipments, along with prompt invoicing and processing of claims, increases customer loyalty and improves a firm's image in the marketplace.[25]

Co-ordinating Transport Services

Intermodal transport The combination and co-ordination of two or more modes of transport

To take advantage of the benefits various types of carriers offer, and to compensate for their deficiencies, marketers often must combine and co-ordinate two or more modes of transport. In recent years, **intermodal transport,** as this integrated approach is sometimes called, has become easier because of new developments within the transport industry.

Several kinds of intermodal shipping are available, all combining the flexibility of road haulage with the low cost or speed of other forms of transport. Containerisation, discussed earlier, facilitates intermodal transport by consolidating shipments into sealed containers for transport by piggyback (shipping that combines truck trailers and railway flatcars), fishyback (truck trailers and water carriers), and birdyback (truck trailers and air carriers). As transport costs increase, intermodal services gain popularity. Intermodal services have been estimated to cost 25 to 40 per cent less than all-road transport in the US, where they account for about 12 to 16 per cent of total transport business.[26]

Freight forwarders Specialised agencies that co-ordinate and combine shipments from several organisations into efficient lot sizes

Specialised agencies, **freight forwarders,** provide other forms of transport co-ordination. These firms combine shipments from several organisations into efficient lot sizes. Small loads—less than 225 kilos (500 pounds)—are much more expensive to ship than full lorry loads and frequently must be consolidated. The freight forwarder takes small loads from various shippers, buys transport space from carriers and arranges for the goods to be delivered to their respective buyers. The freight forwarder's profits come from the margin between the higher, less than car load rates charged to each shipper and the lower car load rates the agency pays. Because large shipments require less handling, the use of a freight forwarder can speed transit time. Freight forwarders can also determine the most efficient carriers and routes and are useful for shipping goods to foreign markets.

Megacarriers Freight companies that provide several methods of shipment, such as rail, road and air service

One other transport innovation is the development of **megacarriers,** freight companies that provide several methods of shipment, such as rail, road and air service. Air carriers have increased their ground transport services. As they have expanded the range of transport alternatives, carriers have also put greater stress on customer service.

• •

Strategic Issues in Physical Distribution

The physical distribution functions discussed in this chapter—order processing, materials handling, warehousing, inventory management and transport—account for about one third of all marketing costs. Moreover, these functions have a significant impact on customer service and satisfaction, which are of prime importance to marketers. Effective marketers accept considerable responsibility for the design and control of the physical distribution system. They work to ensure that the organisation's overall marketing strategy is enhanced by physical distribution, with its dual objectives of decreasing costs while increasing customer service. Remember, to ensure that customers are satisfied, they must be able to obtain within reason the product or service when and where they want it.

The strategic importance of physical distribution is evident in all elements of the marketing mix. Product design and packaging must allow for efficient stacking, storage and transport; decisions to differentiate products by size, colour and style must take into account the additional demands that will be placed on warehousing and shipping facilities. Competitive pricing may depend on a firm's ability to provide reliable delivery or emergency shipments of replacement parts; a firm trying to lower its inventory costs may offer quantity discounts to encourage large purchases. Promotional campaigns must be co-ordinated with distribution functions so that advertised products are available to buyers; order processing departments must be able to handle additional sales order information efficiently. Distribution planners must consider warehousing and transport costs, which may influence—for example—the firm's policy on stock-outs or its choice to centralise (or decentralise) its inventory.

No single distribution system is ideal for all situations, and any system must be evaluated continually and adapted as necessary. For instance, pressures to adjust service levels or reduce costs may lead to a total re-structuring of the marketing channel relationships; changes in transport, warehousing, materials handling and inventory may affect speed of delivery, reliability and economy of service. Marketing strategists must consider customers' changing needs and preferences and recognise that changes in any one of the major distribution functions will necessarily affect all other functions. Consumer orientated marketers will analyse the various characteristics of their target markets and *then* design distribution systems to provide products at acceptable costs.

● ● ● ● ● ● ● ● ● ● ● ● ● ● ● ● ● ● ●

Summary

● *Physical distribution* is a set of activities that moves products from producers to consumers, or end users. These activities include order processing, materials handling, warehousing, inventory management and transport. An effective physical distribution system can be an important component of an overall marketing strategy, because it can decrease costs and lead to higher levels of customer satisfaction. Physical distribution activities should be integrated with marketing channel decisions and should be adjusted to meet the unique needs of a channel member. For most firms, physical distribution accounts for about one-fifth of a product's retail price.

● The main *objective of physical distribution* is to decrease costs while increasing customer service. Physical distribution managers therefore try to balance service, distribution costs and resources. Companies must adapt to customers' needs and preferences, offer service comparable to—or better than—that of their competitors, and develop and communicate desirable *customer service* policies. The costs of providing service are minimised most effectively through the total cost approach, which evaluates the costs of the system as a whole rather than as a collection of separate activities. *Cost trade-offs* must often be used to offset higher costs in one area of distribution against lower costs in another area.

● *Order processing*, the first stage in a physical distribution system, is the receipt and transmission of sales order information. Order processing consists of three main tasks. (1) Order entry is the placement of purchase orders from customers or salespeople by mail, telephone or computer. (2) Order handling involves checking customer credit, verifying product availability and preparing products for shipping. (3) Order delivery is provided by the carrier most suitable for a desired level of customer service. Order processing may be done manually or electronically, depending on which method gives greater speed and accuracy within cost limits.

● *Materials handling*, or the physical handling of products, is an important element of physical distribution. Packaging, loading and movement systems must be co-ordinated to take into account both cost reduction and customer requirements. Basic handling systems include *unit loading* on pallets or skids, movement by mechanical devices and *containerisation*.

- *Warehousing* involves the design and operation of facilities for storing and moving goods. It is important for companies to select suitable warehousing conveniently located close to main transport routes. *Private warehouses* are owned and operated by a company for the purpose of distributing its own products. *Public warehouses* are business organisations that rent storage space and related physical distribution facilities to other firms. Public warehouses may furnish security for products that are being used as collateral for loans by establishing *field public warehouses*. They may also provide *bonded storage* for companies wishing to defer tax payments on imported or taxable products. *Distribution centres* are large, centralised warehouses specially designed to facilitate the rapid movement of goods to customers. In many cases, a combination of private and public facilities provides the most flexible approach to warehousing.

- The objective of *inventory management* is to minimise inventory costs while maintaining a supply of goods adequate for customers' needs. All inventory costs—carrying, replenishment and stock-out costs—must be controlled if profit goals are to be met. To avoid *stock-outs* without tying up too much capital in inventory, a firm must have a systematic method of determining a *re-order point*, the inventory level at which more inventory is ordered. The trade-offs between the costs of carrying larger average *safety stocks* and the costs of frequent orders can be quantified using the *economic order quantity (EOQ)* model. Inventory problems may take the form of surplus inventory, late deliveries, write-offs and inventory that is too large in proportion to sales or assets. Methods for improving inventory management include systems that continuously monitor stock levels and techniques such as just-in-time management and the 80/20 rule.

- *Transportation* adds time and place utility to a product by moving it from where it is made to where it is purchased and used. The five *transport modes* are motor vehicles, railways, inland waterways, airways and pipelines. Marketers evaluate transport modes with respect to *costs, transit time* (speed), *reliability, capability, accessibility, security* and *traceability;* final selection of a transport mode involves many trade-offs. *Intermodal transport* allows marketers to combine the advantages of two or more modes of transport; this method is facilitated by containerisation, *freight forwarders*—who co-ordinate transport by combining small shipments from several organisations into efficient lot sizes—and *megacarriers*—freight companies that offer several methods of shipment.

- Physical distribution affects every element of the marketing mix: product, price, promotion, distribution and personnel/customer service. To give customers products at acceptable prices, marketers consider consumers' changing needs and any shifts within the major distribution functions. They then adapt existing physical distribution systems for greater effectiveness. Physical distribution functions account for about one-third of all marketing costs and have a significant impact on customer satisfaction. Therefore, effective marketers are actively involved in the design and control of physical distribution systems.

● ● ● ● ● ● ● ● ● ● ● ● ● ● ● ● ●

Important Terms

Physical distribution	Public warehouses	Costs
Objective of physical distribution	Field public warehouse	Transit time
	Bonded storage	Reliability
Customer service	Distribution centre	Capability
Cost trade-offs	Inventory management	Accessibility
Order processing	Stock-outs	Security
Materials handling	Re-order point	Traceability
Unit loading	Safety stock	Intermodal transport
Containerisation	Economic order quantity (EOQ)	Freight forwarders
Warehousing	Transportation	Megacarriers
Private warehouse	Transport modes	

Discussion and Review Questions

1. Discuss the cost and service trade-offs involved in developing a physical distribution system.
2. What factors must physical distribution managers consider when developing a customer service mix?
3. Why should physical distribution managers develop service standards?
4. What is the advantage of using a total cost approach to distribution?
5. What are the main tasks involved in order processing?
6. Discuss the advantages of using an electronic order processing system. Which types of organisation are most likely to use such a system?
7. How does a product's package affect materials handling procedures and techniques?
8. What is containerisation? Discuss the major benefits of containerisation.
9. Explain the major differences between private and public warehouses. What is a field public warehouse?
10. What characteristics should a suitable warehouse possess?
11. In what circumstances should a firm use a private warehouse instead of a public one?
12. The focus of distribution centres is on active movement of goods. Discuss how distribution centres are designed for the rapid flow of products.
13. Describe the costs associated with inventory management.
14. Explain the trade-offs inventory managers face when re-ordering merchandise.
15. How can managers improve inventory control? Give specific examples of techniques.
16. Compare the five major transport modes in terms of costs, transit time, reliability, capability, accessibility, security and traceability.
17. What is transit time, and how does it affect physical distribution decisions?
18. Discuss how marketers can combine or co-ordinate two or more modes of transport. What advantage do they gain by doing this?
19. Identify the type of containerised shipping available to physical distribution managers.
20. Discuss how the elements of the marketing mix affect physical distribution strategy.

Recommended Readings

M. Christopher, *Logistics and Supply Chain Management* (London: Pitman, 1992).

M. Christopher, *Marketing Logistics* (Oxford: Butterworth-Heinemann, 1996).

D. M. Lambert and J. R. Stock, *Strategic Logistics Management* (Homewood, Ill.: Richard D. Irwin, 1993).

J. Gattorna, ed., *The Physical Distribution Handbook* (Aldershot: Gower, 1983).

Cases

15.1 Transportation Industry Faces a Packaging Dilemma

Many companies are facing a dilemma in their choice of cushioning materials to protect their products during distribution. The use of polystyrene peanuts, the most common cushioning material, is provoking increasing criticism from both consumers and environmentalists for several reasons. First, polystyrene peanuts are made from petroleum, a non-renewable resource. Second, the peanuts are not biodegradable; they remain in the environment anywhere from 400 to 1,000 years. Third, some peanuts contain chlorofluorocarbons (CFCs) that are released during incineration. CFCs are widely known for their damaging effects on the earth's ozone layer. Finally, the peanuts produce static electricity, making them useless for cushioning sensitive electronic equipment.

The purpose of any cushioning material is to protect a package's contents from harm during the distribution process. Internal packaging is important because if it fails to do its job, the quality of the package's contents becomes a secondary concern. However, in the face of increased environmental awareness, many companies are discovering that their choice of packaging materials is fast becoming an important issue with their customers.

There are several alternatives to polystyrene peanuts, each having advantages and disadvantages. One of the cleverest alternatives is popcorn, which many industry experts say could be the answer to the dilemma. Popcorn is attractive because it is biodegradable and costs one quarter as much as polystyrene peanuts. Likewise, unpopped popcorn is less expensive to ship and store before it is needed. However, in some countries popcorn is not an option at present because it is considered a food, not a packaging material. Many countries forbid the use of popcorn as a cushioning material until a method can be found to prevent people from eating it after it has been used for shipping purposes.

Billed as a direct alternative to polystyrene peanuts, Eco-Foam is made from a special hybrid corn and is composed of 95 per cent cornflour, making it fully biodegradable and less prone to static electricity. Eco-Foam, which looks a lot like polystyrene peanuts, is attractive because it can be used with the same dispensing equipment as peanuts.

Thus a company that currently uses peanuts can switch to Eco-Foam with very little inconvenience. However, Eco-Foam is more expensive and has one major drawback: it fully disintegrates when it gets wet. This makes Eco-foam impractical for use in shipping liquid-filled containers or in situations in which the threat of water damage is high. In addition, Eco-foam has a tendency to shrink when exposed to high heat and humidity, which is always a possibility in a vehicle trailer or on a train.

Quadra-Pak, a third choice, is fully biodegradable and recyclable, contains no CFCs and is produced totally from refuse materials. Quadra-Pak is made by stacking heavyweight paper in layers that are then cut into strips 10 centimetres (4 inches) long and 0.3 centimetres (0.125 inches) wide. The cut lengths are then compacted into an accordion shape that makes them act as if spring loaded. The finished product measures about 2.5 centimetres (1 inch) long but expands when it is jostled. The result is a packing material that protects from all sides while preventing a carton's contents from moving about. Although Quadra-Pak possesses superior cushioning properties to peanuts, it is more expensive to manufacture and cannot be used with current dispensing equipment.

Other options include Bio-Puffs—a loose-fill foam packaging peanut that biodegrades within weeks or months—and vermiculite, a naturally occurring mineral used by the military to ship munitions in Operation Desert Storm. With so many alternatives and the relentless pressure of environmentalists to use more environmentally friendly packing materials, the Polystyrene Packaging Council (PPC) is crying foul. PPC admits that CFCs were once a problem, but even then, it argues, only 2 per cent of all polystyrene contained CFCs, and their use was phased out of polystyrene production in 1989. To curb negative publicity, the PPC—along with four producers of polystyrene peanuts—is creating a peanut recycling programme.

While many packaging options exist, there is no perfect answer to the current dilemma. All of the options have good and bad characteristics. For the most part, companies currently choose a packing material on the basis of cost and performance.

Ultimately, however, the choice of material will depend more and more upon the needs of the customer and the material's impact on the environment.

SOURCES: Jerry Drisaldi, "Protective packaging: it's your responsibility", *Inbound Logistics*, November 1991, p. 39; Walter L. Weart, "Packaging dilemmas: the sequel", *Inbound Logistics*, June 1991, pp. 27–29; Bob Friday, "Popcorn, peanuts, and Quadra-Paks", *Inbound Logistics*, February 1991, pp. 25–28; "Environmental concerns influence packaging", *Inbound Logistics*, June 1990, p. 4.

Questions for Discussion

1. What are the advantages and disadvantages of each of the packaging options discussed above?
2. How does a company's choice of packaging materials affect its ability to serve customer needs?
3. Overall, which packaging material would you choose? Why? How would your decision change if you were shipping electronic equipment? Glass? Liquid-filled containers?

15.2 Rapidly Changing Sales Opportunities for Excel

Under the EU's direction, much regulation within Europe has been *harmonised*. In the area of physical distribution management, this has had significant impact on day-to-day operations and longer term planning. In the airline industry, most major carriers are either state owned or state subsidised. British Airways (BA) is unusual in having been privatised and returned to the free market economy without state hand-outs and financial support to the balance sheet. For decades, "state" airlines have enjoyed a degree of protection over routes into and out of their country of origin. Often, for example, on a particular route, only two airlines were permitted to fly—those from each of the host countries: BA from Heathrow, London, and Lufthansa from Munich, Germany. Smaller airlines were excluded, as were major airlines from "third party" points of origin; BA would have found it virtually impossible to be allowed to fly between Portugal and France. In line with the EU's policies, member governments have, sometimes slowly and reluctantly, made moves to open up the skies. Such liberalisation of routes is happening slowly, but some airlines are being allowed to fly on increasing numbers of routes. Favouritism and reciprocal agreements between governments or airlines will eventually, travellers are assured, become a quirk of the past.

For freight transport, the impact of regulation is more apparent. Until January 1993, each EU member state operated its own border patrols and customs checks. Now there is standardisation of paper work; vehicles; product and vehicle labelling; and legal, taxation and driving regulations across the EU. Before, a relatively straightforward journey across Europe's motorways from, for example, the UK to Italy might have taken the best part of a week, with delays for bureaucracy at customs posts accounting for over a day! Now, it tends to be only on journeys into eastern Europe and the former communist bloc countries that such delays are commonplace.

For hauliers, perhaps the most significant change has been the ending of "cabotage". Operators' trucks travelling from Belgium to, for example, Spain would have made their return journeys empty: they would have been barred from picking up return loads from Spanish companies or depots. Such loads would have been transported by Spanish hauliers, who in turn would have been forced to return from Belgium to Spain with empty vehicles. With fewer borders to negotiate and significantly less bureaucracy, interstate trade is expected to increase quite dramatically as Europe genuinely becomes a pan-European marketplace. For hauliers now permitted to seek contracts and loads in other countries and for the financial incentive of having trucks travelling in both directions with full loads, this situation presents significant opportunities.

Companies such as Excel Logistics, the re-branded National Freight Company, have been forced to re-think their sales and marketing programmes. Excel is the combination of once separate operators BRS, Lynx Express, SPD and Hoults. With close to 20,000 employees, it is one of Europe's largest freight businesses. The UK's island status has long forced Excel to develop links throughout Europe. Strategic alliances with national companies and shipping agencies across Europe have given Excel a network of contacts through which to generate sales leads for seeking return loads for vehicles heading back from mainland Europe and into Britain. Excel, though, is having to do much more, establishing its own branch network and regional sales operations throughout the EU.

The company believes that within a decade or so there will be only four or five logistics companies that truly trade and operate across Europe. More significantly, such players will provide much more than physical distribution services for clients' merchandise: they will be offering to manage the entire supply chains of client businesses, incoming and outgoing distribution needs and inventory management. The changing regulations within the EU help to make this a possibility, but such major logistics operators will need also to be very shrewd marketers—assessing markets, determining customer requirements and developing very specific target market strategies. The days of winning local distri-bution contracts with neighbourhood firms have long gone for pan-European businesses such as Excel.

SOURCES: Stephen Dearden, "Air transport regulation in the EU", *European Business Review,* 94 (5), 1994, pp. 15–19; Gonzalo Cedrum and Gines de Rus, "Developments in transport policy", *Journal of Transport Economics & Policy,* 28 (2), 1994, pp. 211–214; "Towards the 21st century", *Logistics in Focus,* 2 (8), 1995, p. 26; Clyde E. Witt, "Third-party logistics: first choice for managers", *Material Handling Engineering,* 49 (2), 1994, pp. 47–52.

Questions for Discussion

1. How real are the benefits of EU transport deregulation?
2. What impact will regulatory changes have on major airlines? Explain your views.
3. For Excel Logistics, changing regulation and customer requirements pose opportunities and threats. Describe the situation facing the Excel marketing team.

The place ingredient of the marketing mix addresses the distribution and marketing channel decisions necessary to provide the target market with convenient and ready access to a product or service. The place specification developed in the marketing mix must be beneficial to the supplier of the product or service if it is to remain in business and be commercially viable. Part IV of *Marketing: Concepts and Strategies* has examined the nature of marketing channels, wholesalers and distributors, retailing and the physical distribution of products and services.

Before progressing, readers should be confident that they are now able to:

Explain the concept of the marketing channel

• What is the marketing channel? What are the functions, types and structures of marketing channels? • What issues determine the selection of a marketing channel? • What are the concepts of co-operation, relationship building, conflict and leadership important in marketing channel management? • What legal issues concern marketers as they manage marketing channels?

Describe the functions of wholesalers and distributors

• What is meant, in its broadest sense, by wholesaling? • What activities do wholesalers undertake and how can they be classified? • What organisations facilitate wholesaling? • What are the current patterns and trends in wholesaling and distribution?

Outline the nature of retailing and the specialist requirements for retail marketers

• What is the function of retailing in the marketing channel? • What are the principal types and locations of retailing? • What are non-store retailing and franchising? • What are the strategic issues in retailing? • Why is retailing a specialist area for marketers?

Discuss the tasks of physical distribution management

• Why are physical distribution activities fundamental to marketing channel management? • What do customer service, total distribution costs and cost trade-offs mean? • What are the roles of order processing, materials handling, warehousing, storage, inventory management and transport modes in effective physical distribution?

Marketing Opportunity Analysis	Chapters
• The marketing environment	2
• Marketing in international markets	3
• Consumer markets and buyer behaviour	4
• Business-to-business markets and buyer behaviour	5
• Marketing research and information systems	6

Target Market Selection	Chapters
• Market segmentation and prioritisation	7, 22
• Product and brand positioning	7, 22
• Competitive advantage	7, 22

Marketing Mix Development	Chapters
• Product, branding, packaging and service decisions	8–11
• Distribution (place and channel) decisions	12–15
• Promotion decisions	16–18
• Pricing decisions	19, 20
• Supplementary decisions	3, 21, 24, 25

Marketing Management	Chapters
• Strategic marketing and competitive strategy	22, 23
• Marketing planning and sales forecasting	23
• Implementing strategies and measuring performance	24
• Marketing ethics and social responsibility	25

V PROMOTION DECISIONS

Legal forces

Political forces

Regulatory forces

Product/Brand positioning

Product

People

Target market selection

Price

Buyer/Consumer satisfaction

Distribution (place)

Promotion

Techno-logical forces

Societal/Green forces

Differential advantage/Competitive edge

Economic and competitive forces

The term *promotion* encompasses all of the various tools of marketing communications. These include advertising, public relations and publicity, the growing area of sponsorship, personal selling, sales promotion and direct mail. Together, these elements are generally referred to as the *promotional mix*. Many consumers believe that the promotional aspect of marketing is all that marketing encompasses. For many marketing personnel, the layperson's familiar view that "marketing is advertising" is a tiresome but frequently encountered attitude. It must be emphasised that promotion is just another ingredient of the marketing mix, the tactical toolkit marketers use to implement marketing strategies. Nevertheless, it is a very important ingredient, one that accounts for the vast proportion of most businesses' marketing budgets, employs millions of people in Europe alone and constitutes an essential aspect of communicating an organisation's product or service proposition and its associated brand positioning strategy.

Part V of *Marketing: Concepts and Strategies* presents a thorough overview of the elements of promotion and how the promotional mix fits into marketing strategy.

Chapter 16, "Promotion: An Overview", discusses the role of promotion in the marketing mix, the process of communication *per se* and the way in which the concept of the product adoption process relates to promotional activity. The chapter goes on to explain the aims of promotion and then explores the elements of the promotional mix, the major promotional methods and the way in which organisations select which ones to use.

Chapter 17, "Advertising, Publicity and Sponsorship", takes these three aspects of the promotional mix and explores their use in more detail. The chapter commences by describing the uses of advertising, the steps involved in developing an advertising campaign and the personnel involved. The emphasis then switches to the nature of publicity and public relations; following this discussion, the chapter highlights some of the current trends in the spheres of advertising and public relations (PR). Finally, it explores the rapidly evolving world of corporate sponsorship.

Chapter 18, "Personal Selling, Sales Promotion and Direct Mail", begins by examining the purposes, steps and types of personal selling. It goes on to explain the nature of sales management and then outlines in detail the use of sales promotion and the wide range of related activities. The chapter concludes with an overview of the role of direct mail in the promotional mix.

By the conclusion of Part V of *Marketing: Concepts and Strategies,* readers should understand the essential promotion decisions and composition of the promotional mix within the marketing mix.

PROMOTION: AN OVERVIEW

"Marketing communication is the art of seducing a consumer on his way to your competitor."

Patrick De Pelsmacker
University of Antwerp

OBJECTIVES

- To understand the role of promotion in the marketing mix
- To examine the process of communication
- To understand the product adoption process and its implications for promotional efforts
- To understand the aims of promotion
- To explore the elements of the promotional mix
- To acquire an overview of the major methods of promotion
- To explore factors that affect the choice of promotional methods

When mighty Kodak launched its Advantix range it faced quite a dilemma. To recoup its significant development costs, the promotional message at the heart of its launch and brand building campaigns had to appeal to both the dedicated photographer and the "happy snapper". Large sales volumes were essential. By using some technical information in its advertising within a simple, memorable execution, Kodak's advertising proved a successful ingredient in the marketing mix for the Advantix.

Five of the biggest players in the photographic market have spent five years and £750 million developing a new mass consumer system: the Advanced Photo System (APS). As the products came to the market in the summer of 1996, two intriguing issues attracted the attention of observers: which company would gain market leadership and whether consumers would really want this innovation. As with the development of the CD player and video recorder, rival manufacturers were forced to pool technical resources in expensive models enable the user to switch a film mid-roll and re-use it later. Because the films are 24mm—as opposed to the currently dominant 35mm format—they allow for smaller and lighter cameras. The films are priced similarly to their 35mm counterparts, although the cameras cost around 20 per cent more than 35mm models. Developed jointly by Kodak, Fujifilm, Minolta, Nikon and Canon, the new technology is already being used by over 50 licensees. In year one, the combined marketing spend of the five creators was thought to be around £100 million.

Kodak believes that for Advantix to succeed, consumers must trust in the technology and the quality of the product. To help communicate the credentials of its Advantix brand, Kodak UK has doubled its advertising spend to nearly £10 million, much of which is promoting the new product. To reassure customers, Kodak's advertising plays on the company's reputation, record of constant product innovation and position as the most established name in the market. A good reputation is not enough, however, as Kodak knows. Its campaign includes advertising with 30 and 60 second executions, supported by sales promotion and point-of-sale activity. Fuji entered the market first with a range of six cameras, film and a photo player enabling customers to view their holiday snaps on their television screens. This launch gave Fuji an initial 60 per cent of the fledging APS market. Kodak's promotional activity quickly helped to knock Fuji back, although the APS market has yet to take off in a manner that will give the major players adequate returns. ■

order to develop the new technology. Once it was created, the erstwhile partners divided, each to launch competing products. The market for cameras and films had declined in the core European, American and Japanese markets: APS was intended to revitalise a slumbering market, just as CD players and video cameras had done previously in the brown goods market.

APS has a film that drops into the camera like a battery into a Walkman. The cameras permit three different picture sizes to be selected, and more

SOURCES: Roger Baird, "Stakes high in bid to boost photo sector", *Marketing Week,* 28 June 1996, p. 23; Loredana Roberts, "Kodak Advantix", *Marketing,* 22 February 1996, p. 9; Mark Maremont, "Will a new film click?", *Business Week,* 5 February 1996, p. 46; Amy Dunkin, "The next great leap for Shutterbugs", *Business Week,* 22 April 1996, pp. 150–152.

Organisations use various promotional approaches to communicate with target markets, as Kodak did when it launched its Advantix APS photographic range. This chapter looks at the general dimensions of promotion, defining promotion in the context of marketing and examining its roles. Next, to understand how promotion works, the chapter analyses the meaning and process of communication, as well as the product adoption process. The remainder of the chapter discusses the major types of promotional methods and the factors that influence an organisation's decision to use specific methods of promotion: advertising, personal selling, public relations, sales promotion, sponsorship and direct mail.

● ● ● ● ● ● ● ● ● ● ● ● ● ● ● ● ● ●

The Role of Promotion

People's attitudes towards promotion vary. Some hold that promotional activities, particularly advertising and personal selling, paint a distorted picture of reality because they provide the customer with only selected information. According to this view, the repetition of similar themes in promotion has brought about changes in social values, such as increased materialism.[1] Proponents of this view hold that promotional activities are unnecessary and wasteful and that promotion costs (especially advertising) are high—sometimes excessively so—resulting in higher prices. Others take a positive view. They believe that advertising messages often project wholesome values—such as affection, generosity or patriotism[2]—or that advertising, as a powerful economic force, can free countries from poverty by communicating information.[3] It has also been argued that advertising of consumer products was a factor in the decline of Communism and the move towards a free enterprise system in eastern Europe. However, none of these impressions is completely accurate.

Promotion Communication with individuals, groups or organisations in order to facilitate exchanges by informing and persuading the audience to accept the firm's products

The role of **promotion** in a company is to communicate with individuals, groups or organisations with the aim of directly or indirectly facilitating exchanges by informing and persuading one or more of the audiences to accept the firm's products.[4] PepsiCo, for example, recruited pop star Michael Jackson to communicate the benefits of its cola drink. Rock Against Drugs (RAD), a not-for-profit organisation, employs popular rock musicians, such as Lou Reed, to communicate its anti-drug messages to teenagers and young adults. Like PepsiCo and RAD, marketers try to communicate with selected audiences about their company and its goods, services and ideas in order to facilitate exchanges. Marketing Insight 16.1 describes how the music business utilises promotion.

Marketers indirectly facilitate exchanges by focusing information about company activities and products on interest groups (such as environmental and consumer groups), current and potential investors, regulatory agencies and society in general. Some marketers use *cause related marketing,* which links the purchase of their products to philanthropic efforts for a particular cause. Cause related marketing often helps a marketer boost sales and generate goodwill through contributions to causes that members of its target markets want to support. For example, American Express used cause related marketing to encourage its credit card holders to use their cards more often and thus help to re-build the Statue of Liberty. American Express pledged to donate a percentage of the value of all purchases charged on its cards to rebuilding the statue.[5] Similarly, Procter & Gamble has tied promotional efforts for some of its products with contributions to the Special Olympics. Oxfam promotes use of the Visa card.

Viewed from this wider perspective, promotion can play a comprehensive communication role.[6] Some promotional activities, such as publicity and public relations, can be directed towards helping a company justify its existence and maintain positive, healthy relationships between itself and various groups in the marketing environment. Record companies, television stations, media and personalities gave their services free to facilitate the global Live Aid fund raising activities.

Plugging Music—Promoting Pop

The music industry depends not only on the ability of artists to record and perform but also on the skills of marketing managers and publicity officers in the large recording companies such as EMI, Sony or Virgin. In 1980 the Postcard label released "Falling and Laughing" by Orange Juice in a plain brown paper sleeve, arguing that the record would sell on merit alone. The recording is reported to have notched up 41 sales. In 1983 the ZTT label released the debut single by Frankie Goes to Hollywood, "Relax", supported by personal selling, advertising, sales promotion and significant publicity. The result was 2.4 million sales.

Although the ability and quality of artists are critical factors, promotional support is clearly essential for commercial success. The death of Queen lead singer Freddie Mercury did not end sales of either Queen recordings or Mercury's solo singles. Instead, through shrewd marketing that capitalised on the loyalty of Queen fans, both Queen and Mercury topped the charts worldwide.

In the case of a newly signed band, the record company uses PR to "hype" the signing, the band and any newsworthy characteristics of its music, gigs or individual members. Contacts are used to gain gig bookings, and "promo" recordings are made for distribution to clubs and radio stations.

With luck, the recording is picked up and given air time, which—supported with more publicity—leads to media coverage and the possible play-listing of the recording for regular broadcasting. Flyers, posters and other printed items will add to the increasing promotional coverage. Indeed, "guerrilla" tactics are very important, including fly-posting and leaflet drops or street corner handouts. "Pluggers" work on behalf of the record companies to gain air time on radio and in clubs, visiting DJs and station managers to peddle their wares. Sales activity may warrant promotional videos aimed at television coverage and further, more polished recordings. These then form the foundation for additional publicity, interviews and media coverage. If the record (CD) sells, a television appearance may encourage the record company to bring out new format special editions and re-mixes. Low sales will lead to discounting and a new strategy: different promotional activity or the end of the recording contract.

SOURCES: Neal Martin; Fives Records; HMV; Mute Records; Damien Lanigan, "Guerrilla media", *Campaign,* 5 April 1996, pp. 26–27; "Europop raves on", *Economist,* 12 August 1995, p. 69; Allyson Stewart, "Europe's music business: a sound success", *Marketing News,* 4 July 1994, p. 9.

Although a company can direct a single type of communication—such as an advertisement—towards numerous audiences, marketers often design a communication precisely for a specific target market. A company frequently communicates several different messages concurrently, each to a different group. For example, McDonald's may direct one communication towards customers for its Big Mac, a second message towards investors about the firm's stable growth and a third communication towards society in general regarding the company's Ronald McDonald Houses, which provide support to families of children suffering from cancer.

To gain maximum benefit from promotional efforts, marketers must make every effort to properly plan, implement, co-ordinate and control communications. Effective promotional activities are based on information from the marketing environment, often obtained from an organisation's marketing information

Figure 16.1
Information flows into and out of an organisation

system (see Figure 16.1). How effectively marketers can use promotion to maintain positive relationships depends largely on the quantity and quality of information an organisation takes in. For example, scares in the UK about the contamination of baby food led manufacturers to inform customers about specially developed safety tops. The problem was that the customers could see if a tinned food had been tampered with, but found it more difficult to detect tampering when it came to food sold in glass jars. The manufacturers therefore stressed the safety "button" on jar lids, which popped up when the seal was broken. Because the basic role of promotion is to communicate, it is important to analyse what communication is and how the communication process works.

• • • • • • • • • • • • • • • • • •

Promotion and the Communication Process

Communication can be viewed as the transmission of information.[7] For communication to take place, however, both the sender and the receiver of the information must share some common ground. They must share an understanding of the symbols used to transmit information, usually pictures or words. For instance, an individual transmitting the following message may believe he or she is communicating with readers of *Marketing: Concepts and Strategies*:

在工廠吾人製造化粧品，在商店吾人銷售希望。

However, communication has not taken place, because few readers understand the intended message.[8] Thus **communication** is defined here as a sharing of meaning.[9] Implicit in this definition is the notion of transmission of information, because sharing necessitates transmission.

As Figure 16.2 shows, communication begins with a source. A **source** is a person, group or organisation that has a meaning it intends and attempts to share with an audience. For example, a source could be a salesperson who wishes to communicate a sales message or an organisation that wants ~~~nd a message to thousands of consumers through an advertisement. A rece~~ group or organisation that decodes a coded message. A rec~~ or more receivers who decode a message. The intended rec~~ an advertisement for Cellnet cellular telephones, for exam~~ people who must frequently travel by car. The source ma~~ nies such as Securicor Communications, which install~~ phones.

Communication A sharing of meaning through the transmission of information

Source A person, group or organisation that has an intended meaning it attempts to share with an audience

Receiver An individual, group or organisation that decodes a coded message

460

PART V

Figure 16.2

The communication process

Coding process The process
of converting meaning into a
series of signs that represent
ideas or concepts; also called
encoding

To transmit meaning, a source must convert the meaning into a series of signs that represent ideas or concepts. This is called the **coding process,** or *encoding.* When coding meaning into a message, a source must take into account certain characteristics of the receiver or audience. First, to share meaning, the source should use signs that are familiar to the receiver or audience. Marketers who understand this fact realise how important it is to know their target market and to make sure that an advertisement, for example, is written in language that the target market can understand. Thus when Du Pont advertised its Stainmaster carpeting, it did not mention the name of the chemical used to make the carpet resistant to stains, because it would have had little meaning to consumers seeing the advertisement. There have been some notable problems in the translation of advertisements. For example, a beer advertisement translated from English to Spanish using the tag line *"Sueltate"* was supposed to mean "Let go!" but actually invited readers to "Get diarrhoea!". An airline advertisement translated to entice Spanish speakers to fly first class on leather seats invited them instead to fly naked.[10] Thus it is important that people fully understand the language used in promotion.

Second, when coding a meaning, a source should try to use signs that the receiver or audience uses for referring to the concepts the source intends. Marketers should generally avoid signs that can have several meanings for an audience. For example, an international advertiser of soft drinks should avoid using the word *soda* as a general term for soft drinks. Although in some places soda is taken to mean "soft drink", in others it may connote bicarbonate of soda, an ice cream drink, or something that one mixes with Scotch whisky.

Medium of transmission
The tool used to carry the coded
message from the source to the
receiver or audience

To share a coded meaning with the receiver or audience, a source must select and use a medium of transmission. A **medium of transmission** carries the coded message from the source to the receiver or audience. Transmission media include ink on paper, vibrations of air waves produced by vocal cords, chalk marks on a chalkboard and electronically produced vibrations of air waves, as in radio and television signals.

When a source chooses an inappropriate medium of transmission, several problems may arise. A coded message may reach some receivers, but not the right ones. For example, suppose a local theatre group spends most of its advertising budget on radio advertisements. If theatre goers depend mainly on newspapers for information about local drama, then the theatre will not reach its intended target audience. Coded messages may also reach intended receivers in an incomplete form because the intensity of the transmission is weak. For example, radio signals can be received effectively only over a limited range that may vary depending on climatic conditions. Members of the target audience who live on the fringe of the broadcasting area may receive a weak signal; others well within the broadcasting area may also receive an incomplete message if they listen to their radios while driving or studying.

In the **decoding process,** signs are converted into concepts and ideas. Seldom does a receiver decode exactly the same meaning that a source coded. When the result of decoding is different from what was coded, **noise** exists. Noise has many sources and may affect any or all parts of the communication process. When a source selects a medium of transmission through which an audience does not expect to receive a message, noise is likely to occur. Noise sometimes arises within the medium of transmission itself. Radio static, faulty printing processes and laryngitis are sources of noise. Interference on viewers' television sets during an advertisement is noise and lessens the impact of the message. Noise also occurs when a source uses a sign that is unfamiliar to the receiver or that has a different meaning from the one the source intended. Noise may also originate in the receiver. As Chapter 4 discusses, a receiver may be unaware of a coded message because his or her perceptual processes block it out or because the coded message is too obscure.

The receiver's response to a message is **feedback** to the source. The source usually expects and normally receives feedback, although it may not be immediate. During feedback, the receiver or audience is the source of a message that is directed towards the original source, which then becomes a receiver. Feedback is coded, sent through a medium of transmission and then decoded by the receiver, the source of the original communication. It is logical, then, to think of communication as a circular process.

During face-to-face communication, such as in personal selling or product sampling, both verbal and non-verbal feedback can be immediate. Instant feedback lets communicators adjust their messages quickly to improve the effectiveness of their communication. For example, when a salesperson realises through feedback that a customer does not understand a sales presentation, he or she adapts the presentation to make it more meaningful to the customer. In interpersonal communication, feedback occurs through talking, touching, smiling, nodding, eye movements and other body movements and postures.

When mass communication such as advertising is used, feedback is often slow and difficult to recognise. If EuroDisney increased its advertising in order to increase the number of visitors, it might be 6 to 18 months before the theme park could recognise the effects of the expanded advertising. Although it is harder to recognise, feedback does exist for mass communication. Figure 16.3 illustrates a unique programme developed by NEXT Interiors to obtain feedback on whether its message was received by its target market. Advertisers, for example, obtain feedback in the form of changes in sales volume or in consumers' attitudes and awareness levels, monitored through tracking research.

Each communication channel has a limit on the volume of information it can handle effectively. This limit, called **channel capacity,** is determined by the least efficient component of the communication process. Communications that depend on vocal speech provide a good illustration of this. An individual source can talk only so fast, and there is a limit to how much an individual receiver can take in aurally. Beyond that point, additional messages cannot be decoded; thus meaning cannot be shared. Although a radio announcer can read several hundred words a minute, a one minute advertising message should not exceed 150 words because

Decoding process The process in which signs are converted into concepts and ideas

Noise A condition that exists when the decoded message is different from what was coded

Feedback The receiver's response to a message

Channel capacity The limit of information that a particular communication channel can handle effectively

Figure 16.3

Getting feedback

With this direct response press advertisement, NEXT Interiors can judge the impact of its campaign.

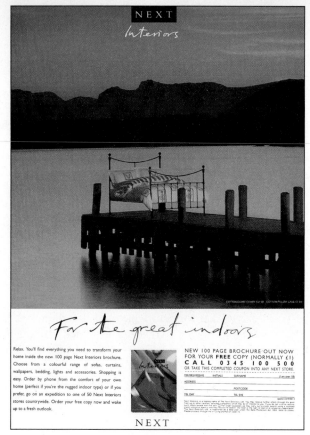

SOURCE: Courtesy of NEXT Interiors.

most announcers cannot articulate the words into understandable messages at a rate beyond 150 words per minute. This figure is the limit for both source and receiver, and marketers should keep this in mind when developing radio commercials. At times, a firm creates a television advertisement that contains several types of visual material and several forms of audio messages, all transmitted to viewers at the same time. Such communication may not be totally effective, because receivers cannot decode all the messages simultaneously.[11]

Now that the basic communication process has been explored, it is worth considering more specifically how promotion is used to influence individuals, groups or organisations to accept or adopt a firm's products. Although the product adoption process was briefly touched upon in Chapter 10, it is discussed more fully in the following section in order to provide a better understanding of the conditions under which promotion occurs.

• • • • • • • • • • • • • • • • • • •

Promotion and the Product Adoption Process

Marketers do not promote simply to inform, educate and entertain; they communicate to facilitate satisfying exchanges. One long run purpose of promotion is to influence and encourage buyers to accept or adopt goods, services and ideas. At times, an advertisement may be informative or entertaining, yet it may fail to get the audience to purchase the product. For example, some ads for business computers seem to be weak in communicating benefits—they focus instead on getting customers to feel good about the product. The ultimate effectiveness of promotion is determined by the degree to which it affects product adoption among potential buyers or increases the frequency of current buyers' purchases.

To establish realistic expectations about what promotion can do, product adoption should not be viewed as a one-step process. Rarely can a single promotional activity cause an individual to buy a previously unfamiliar product. The acceptance of a product involves many steps. Although there are several ways to look at the **product adoption process,** it is commonly divided into five stages: (1) awareness, (2) interest, (3) evaluation, (4) trial and (5) adoption.[12]

In the **awareness stage,** individuals become aware that the product exists, but they have little information about it and are not concerned about obtaining more. When Peugeot launched its 405 model, for example, it used provocative teaser advertisements, which showed burning fields but no car. Later adverts did show the 405. In Figure 16.4 JCB's teaser advertisement (left) did not reveal its innovative single arm skid steer; later adverts did (right). Consumers enter the **interest stage** when they are motivated to obtain information about the product's features, uses, advantages, disadvantages, price or location. During the **evaluation stage,** individuals consider whether the product will satisfy certain criteria that are crucial for meeting their specific needs. In the **trial stage,** they use or experience the product for the first time, possibly by purchasing a small quantity, by taking advantage of a free sample or demonstration or by borrowing the product from someone. Supermarkets, for example, frequently offer special promotions to encourage consumers to taste products such as cheese, cooked meats, snacks or pizza. During this stage, potential adopters determine the usefulness of the product under the specific conditions for which they need it.

Individuals move into the **adoption stage** by choosing the specific product when they need a product of that general type. It cannot be assumed, however, that because a person enters the adoption process she or he will eventually adopt the new product. Rejection may occur at any stage, including adoption. Both product adoption and product rejection can be temporary or permanent.

For the most part, people respond to different information sources at different stages of the adoption process. Figure 16.5 illustrates the most effective sources for each stage. Mass communication sources, such as television advertising, are often effective for moving large numbers of people into the awareness stage. Producers of consumer goods commonly use massive advertising campaigns when introducing new products. They do so to create product awareness as quickly as possible within a large portion of the target market.

Mass communications may also be effective for people in the interest stage who want to learn more about a product. During the evaluation stage, individuals often seek information, opinions and reinforcement from personal sources—relatives, friends and associates. In the trial stage, individuals depend on salespeople for information about how to use the product properly to get the most out of it. Marketers must use advertising carefully when consumers are in the trial stage. If advertisements greatly exaggerate the benefits of a product, the consumer may be disappointed when the product does not meet expectations.[13] It is best to avoid creating expectations that cannot be satisfied, because rejection at this stage will prevent adoption. Friends and peers may also be important sources during the trial stage. By the time the adoption stage has been reached, both personal

Product adoption process A series of five stages in the acceptance of a product: awareness, interest, evaluation, trial and adoption

Awareness stage The beginning of the product adoption process, when individuals become aware that the product exists but have little information about it

Interest stage The stage of the product adoption process when customers are motivated to obtain more information about the product's features, uses, advantages, disadvantages, price or location

Evaluation stage The stage of the product adoption process when customers decide whether the product will meet their individual needs

Trial stage The stage of the product adoption process when individuals use or experience the product for the first time

Adoption stage The final stage of product acceptance, when customers choose the specific product when they need a product of that type

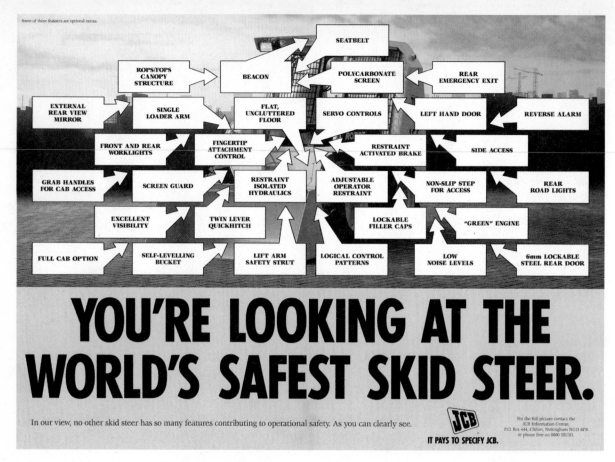

Figure 16.4 Building awareness. JCB launched its skid steer initially with this teaser advertisement (left) before running the second advertisement, which revealed the actual product (right).

Source: Client: John Bradley, JCB Sales Ltd Agency: CB Brookes Advertising Ltd.

communication from sales personnel and mass communication through advertisements may be required. Even though the particular stage of the adoption process may influence the types of information sources consumers use, marketers must remember that other factors, such as the product's characteristics, price and uses, as well as the characteristics of customers, also affect the types of information sources that buyers desire and believe.

Because people in different stages of the adoption process often require different types of information, marketers designing a promotional campaign must determine what stage of the adoption process a particular target audience is in before they can develop the message. Potential adopters in the interest stage will need different information from people who have already reached the trial stage.

When an organisation introduces a new product, people do not all begin the adoption process at the same time and they do not move through the process at the same speed. Of those people who eventually adopt the product, some enter the adoption process rather quickly, whereas others start considerably later. For most products, too, there is a group of non-adopters who never begin the process.

Some of these features are optional extras.

SAFETY FIRST, SECOND, THIRD, FOURTH, FIFTH...

[1] Side access. [2] Left hand door. [3] Servo controls. [4] Adjustable operator restraint. [5] Restraint isolated hydraulics. [6] Restraint activated brake. [7] Seatbelt. [8] ROPS/FOPS canopy structure. [9] "Green" engine. [10] Low noise levels. [11] Twin lever quickhitch. [12] Self-levelling bucket. [13] Polycarbonate screen. [14] Screen guard. [15] 6mm lockable steel rear door. [16] Lockable filler caps. [17] Grab handles for cab access. [18] Excellent visibility. [19] Flat, uncluttered floor. [20] Rear emergency exit. [21] Logical control patterns. [22] Front and rear worklights. [23] Reverse alarm. [24] Lift arm safety strut. [25] Beacon. [26] Rear road lights. [27] Non-slip step for access. [28] Single loader arm. [29] Fingertip attachment control. [30] External rear view mirror. [31] Full cab option. For more detailed information on the world's safest skid steer, contact JCB at the address below. First.

Write to: JCB Information Centre, P.O. Box 444, Clifton, Nottingham NG11 6PR. Or phone free on 0800 501761.

JCB

IT PAYS TO SPECIFY JCB.

Product Adopter Categories

Adopter categories Five groups into which customers can be divided according to the length of time it takes them to adopt a product: innovators, early adopters, early majority, late majority and laggards

Innovators The first people to adopt a new product

Early adopters People who choose new products carefully and are often consulted by people from the remaining adopter categories

Early majority People who adopt products just prior to the average person

Late majority People who are quite sceptical about new products but eventually adopt them because of economic necessity or social pressure

Depending on the length of time it takes them to adopt a new product, people can be divided into five major **adopter categories:** innovators, early adopters, early majority, late majority and laggards.[14] Figure 16.6 shows each adopter category and indicates the percentage of total adopters that it typically represents. **Innovators** are the first to adopt a new product. They enjoy trying new products and tend to be venturesome. **Early adopters** choose new products carefully and are viewed as "the people to check with" by those in the remaining adopter categories. People in the **early majority** adopt just prior to the average person; they are deliberate and cautious in trying new products. **Late majority** people, who are quite sceptical about new products, eventually adopt them because of economic necessity or social pressure. **Laggards,** the last to adopt a new product, are orientated towards the past. They are suspicious of new products, and when they finally adopt the innovation, it may already have been replaced by a newer product. When microwave ovens first appeared, only technocrats or food boffins—the innovators—bought them. Then "trend setters", the early adopters, came into the market. After several years and prompted by many frozen food manufacturers' new product launches, many more consumers—the early majority—decided to adopt the microwave oven. Eventually, the rest of the masses—the late majority—decided that they, too, should have a microwave oven "given that most people have one now". There are, though, some households only now deciding to buy one—the laggards; and some—the non-adopters—never will. When developing

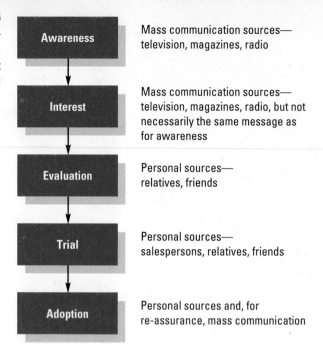

Awareness	Mass communication sources— television, magazines, radio
Interest	Mass communication sources— television, magazines, radio, but not necessarily the same message as for awareness
Evaluation	Personal sources— relatives, friends
Trial	Personal sources— salespersons, relatives, friends
Adoption	Personal sources and, for re-assurance, mass communication

Laggards The last people to adopt a new product, suspicious of new products and orientated towards the past

promotional efforts, a marketer should bear in mind that people in different adopter categories often need different forms of communication and different types of information.

Aims of Promotion Communication

Five communication effects Communication aims that include category need, brand awareness, brand attitude, brand purchase intention and purchase facilitation

Product adoption is a major focus for any promotional activity. There are, though, five basic communications aims, known as the **five communication effects,** which are defined as follows.[15]

Category Need The consumer must realise he or she wants a particular product— particularly for innovative new category product launches—and must perceive a **category need** in order to be motivated even to consider a product. When compact disc players were launched, many consumers had perfectly adequate album and/or

Figure 16.6

Distribution of product adopter categories

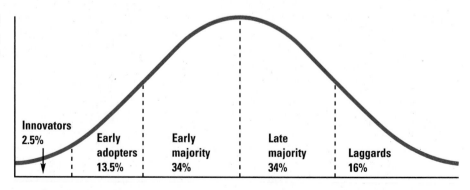

| Innovators 2.5% | Early adopters 13.5% | Early majority 34% | Late majority 34% | Laggards 16% |

Source: Reprinted with the permission of the Free Press, a division of Simon & Schuster, from Diffusion of Innovations, *Third Edition by Everett M. Rogers. Copyright © 1962, 1971, 1983 by The Free Press.*

Category need The consumer's perception of his or her need for a product in a certain category

Brand awareness The consumer's ability to identify a manufacturer's brand in sufficient detail to distinguish it from other brands

Brand attitude A consumer's particular impression of a brand, formed by emotions, logic and cognitive beliefs

Brand purchase intention The consumer's decision and efforts to purchase the particular product

Purchase facilitation Circumstances that make it possible for the consumer to purchase the product: availability, location, price and familiarity of vendor

cassette based hi-fi systems and did not see any need to purchase a compact disc player.

Brand Awareness The consumer must be able to identify (recognise or recall) a manufacturer's brand within the category in sufficient detail to make a purchase. **Brand awareness** means that the manufacturer must make its brand stand out, initially through product attributes supported by distinctive promotional activity. Sony wants consumers to be aware of *its* compact disc players rather than Aiwa or Amstrad players.

Brand Attitude Emotions and logic or cognitive beliefs combine to give the consumer a particular impression of a product. This **brand attitude** directs consumer choice towards a particular brand. Companies need customers to have a positive view of their brands.

Brand Purchase Intention Once a category need and brand awareness are established, if the consumer's brand attitude is favourable, he or she will decide to purchase the particular product and take steps to do so, showing **brand purchase intention.**

Purchase Facilitation Having decided to buy, the consumer requires the product to be readily available at a convenient location, at a suitable price and from a familiar dealer: **purchase facilitation.** The manufacturer must ensure that other marketing mix factors (product, people, distribution and price) do not hinder the purchase. Sony customers expect wide distribution from reputable retailers, with no budget pricing. Sony produces high quality goods, but it has several well respected competitors and must ensure product availability and continued product improvement to prevent brand switching.

To provide a better understanding of how promotion can move people closer to the acceptance of goods, services and ideas, the next section focuses on the major promotional methods available to an organisation—the promotional mix.

● ● ● ● ● ● ● ● ● ● ● ● ● ● ● ● ● ●

The Promotional Mix

Promotional mix The specific combination of ingredients an organisation uses to promote a product, traditionally including four ingredients: advertising, personal selling, public relations and sales promotion

Several types of promotional methods can be used to communicate with individuals, groups and organisations. When an organisation combines specific ingredients to promote a particular product, that combination constitutes the promotional mix for that product. The four traditional ingredients of a **promotional mix** are advertising, personal selling, public relations and sales promotion. Increasingly, sponsorship and direct mail are elements of the promotional mix in their own right (see Figure 16.7). For some products, firms use all these ingredients; for other products, two or three will suffice. This section analyses the major ingredients of a promotional mix and the chief factors that influence an organisation to include specific ingredients in the promotional mix for a specific product. Chapters 17 and 18 examine the promotional mix in greater detail.

Figure 16.7

Possible ingredients of an organisation's promotional mix

Promotional Mix Ingredients

At this point consideration is given to some general characteristics of advertising, personal selling, public relations, sales promotion, sponsorship and direct mail.

Advertising A paid form of non-personal communication about an organisation and its products that is transmitted to a target audience through a mass medium

Advertising **Advertising** is a paid form of non-personal communication about an organisation and its products that is transmitted to a target audience through a mass medium such as television, radio, newspapers, magazines, direct mail, public transport, outdoor displays or catalogues. Individuals and organisations use advertising to promote goods, services, ideas, issues and people. Because it is highly flexible, advertising offers the options of reaching an extremely large target audience or focusing on a small, precisely defined segment of the population. For instance, McDonald's advertising focuses on a large audience of potential fast food consumers, ranging from children to adults, whereas advertising for DeBeers' diamonds focuses on a much smaller and specialised target market.

Advertising offers several benefits. It can be an extremely cost efficient promotional method because it reaches a vast number of people at a low cost per person. For example, if the cost of a four colour, one page advertisement in the *Sunday Telegraph* magazine is £7,000, and the magazine reaches 700,000 readers, the cost of reaching 1,000 subscribers is only £10 per person. Advertising also lets the user repeat the message a number of times. Unilever advertises many of its products (cleaning products, foods, cosmetics) on television, in magazines and through outdoor advertising. In addition, advertising a product in a certain way can add to its value. For example, BMW cars are advertised as having more sophistication, style and technical innovation than Honda, Toyota and other Japanese companies' vehicles. The visibility that an organisation gains from advertising enhances the firm's public image.

Advertising also has several disadvantages. Even though the cost per person reached may be low, the absolute monetary outlay can be extremely high, especially for advertisements shown during popular television programmes. These high costs can limit, and sometimes prevent, the use of advertising in a promotional mix. Moreover, advertising rarely provides rapid feedback. Measuring its effect on sales is difficult, and it ordinarily has a less persuasive impact on customers than, for example, personal selling.[16]

Personal Selling   Selling that involves informing customers and persuading them to purchase products through personal communication in an exchange situation is called **personal selling**. The phrase *to purchase products* should be interpreted broadly to encompass the acceptance of ideas and issues. **Telemarketing**, described in Chapter 14 as direct selling over the telephone, relies heavily on personal selling.

Personal selling has both advantages and limitations when compared with advertising. Advertising is general communication aimed at a relatively large target audience, whereas personal selling involves more specific communication aimed at one person or several people. Reaching one person through personal selling costs considerably more than doing so through advertising, but personal selling efforts often have a greater impact on customers. Personal selling also provides immediate feedback, which allows marketers to adjust their message to improve communication. It helps them determine and respond to customers' needs for information.

When a salesperson and customer meet face-to-face, they use several types of interpersonal communication. Obviously, the predominating communication form is language—both speech and writing. In addition, a salesperson and customer frequently use **kinesic communication**, or body language, by moving their heads, eyes, arms, hands, legs or torsos. Winking, head nodding, hand gestures and arm motions are forms of kinesic communication. A good salesperson can often evaluate a prospect's interest in a product or presentation by watching for eye contact and head nodding. **Proxemic communication**, a less obvious form of communication used in personal selling, occurs when either person varies the physical distance that separates the two people. When a customer backs away from a salesperson, for example, that individual may be indicating that he or she is not interested in the product or may be expressing dislike for the salesperson. Touching, or **tactile communication**, can also be used; shaking hands is a common form of tactile communication in many countries.

Publicity and Public Relations   **Publicity** refers to non-personal communication in news story form about an organisation or its products, or both, that is transmitted through a mass medium at no charge. Examples of publicity include magazine, newspaper, radio and television news stories about new retail stores, new products or personnel changes in an organisation. Although both advertising and publicity are transmitted through mass communication, the sponsor does not pay the media costs for publicity and is not identified. Nevertheless, publicity should never be viewed as free communication. There are clear costs associated with preparing news releases and encouraging media personnel to broadcast or print them. A firm that uses publicity regularly must have employees to perform these activities or obtain the services of a public relations firm or an advertising agency. Either way, the firm bears the costs of the activities.

Publicity must be planned and implemented so that it is compatible with, and supportive of, other elements in the promotional mix.[17] However, publicity cannot always be controlled to the extent that other elements of the promotional mix can be. For example, just as Perrier's contamination problems appeared to be easing, a BBC television programme showed that the "bottled at source" packaging was misleading because the bubbles were added during the bottling process. Sainsbury's, the UK's major grocery retailer, refused for many months to re-stock Perrier until the wording on the packaging was altered, creating further adverse

Personal selling   The use of personal communication in an exchange situation to inform customers and persuade them to purchase products

Telemarketing   Direct selling over the telephone, relying heavily on personal selling

Kinesic communication   Body language, including winking, head nodding, hand gestures and arm motions

Proxemic communication   A subtle form of communication used in face-to-face interactions when either party varies the physical distance that separates the two

Tactile communication   Interpersonal communication through touching, including shaking hands

Publicity   Non-personal communication in news story form about an organisation and/or its products that is transmitted through a mass medium at no charge

Benetton Bares All

Italian clothing giant Benetton, known for its vibrant colours and fashionable knitwear, has never been shy of seeking media attention in order to gain consumer awareness. In the early 1990s two campaigns not only created headlines but also provoked shock around the world. First, huge billboards brought a blood covered newborn baby still attached to the umbilical cord to the streets of many towns and cities. With not an item of Benetton clothing in sight, complaints broke all records; watchdog bodies forced Benetton to remove the offending advertisements. In the UK the Advertising Standards Authority received over 800 complaints, while members of the public also contacted Trading Standards officials and even the police. On previous occasions Benetton's awareness generating, colourful campaigns had tackled such weighty issues as racial equality, civil rights, birth control and world peace.

A year later, the world's media covered Benetton's new campaign, which broke in the US and featured an AIDS victim lying dead in hospital in the arms of his grieving father, surrounded by distraught family members. Public opinion was again outraged, and the campaign never reached most European markets. The adverts were branded sensational, insensitive and irrelevant to the promotion of Benetton's merchandise and shops.

In 1993, the company's $25 million global campaign replaced the images of a dying AIDS victim and oil drenched gulls with that of a naked Luciano Benetton, the company's chairman. The strap line read, "I want my clothes back". Still as bizarre as previous Benetton campaigns, this one avoided adverse media coverage and aimed to present a more sympathetic, caring image for the company. The new adverts "combined the advertising of a brand with concrete social concerns", being run in association with the International Red Cross and clothing charity Coritas. The adverts appealed to consumers to take their old, unwanted clothes to any Benetton shop where collection bins were located. The clothes were sent to the world's numerous trouble spots.

According to Benetton, the campaign was not just an attempt to patch up its battle-scarred brand image. "There will always be the cynical point of view, but we never expected everyone to be with us." The company remains unrepentant about past campaigns. "All we ever wanted was for people to understand our point of view." Either way, the new charity orientated campaign caught the positive attention of the world's media while continuing to attract the attention of consumers worldwide and reinforce the Benetton brand. By the late 1990s, images of human hearts were splashed over Benetton's advertising—the sensationalist, attention grabbing advertising had returned. Punching the audience in the face certainly gains Benetton attention!

SOURCES: ASA; Mat Toor, "Benetton bares all for charity", *Marketing*, 28 January 1993, p. 4; Stefano Hatfield, "Toscani hits out at Benetton critics in D&AD talk", *Campaign*, 29 September 1995, p. 1; "Benetton ad warning", *Marketing*, 7 March 1996, p. 2; Karen Yates, "Benetton rules out any change from maverick ad image", *Campaign*, 21 April 1995, p. 2; "It's not so much what as where", *Marketing*, 20 April 1995, p. 3.

Public relations Managing and controlling the process of using publicity effectively

publicity for the French company. Marketing Insight 16.2 explains how Benetton's advertising caused the Italian company to re-think its promotion and provided extra work for its publicity department. The **public relations** mechanism manages and controls the process of effectively using publicity (see Chapter 17).[18]

Sales promotion An activity or material that acts as a direct inducement by offering added value to or incentive for the product to resellers, salespeople or consumers

Sales Promotion A **sales promotion** is an activity or material that acts as a direct inducement by offering added value to or incentive for the product to resellers, salespeople or consumers.[19] Examples of sales promotion include gift certificates and tokens, bonuses and contests used to enhance the sales of a product. The term *sales promotion* should not be confused with *promotion;* sales promotion is but a part of the more comprehensive area of promotion that encompasses personal selling, advertising, publicity, sponsorship and direct mail. Some sales promotions, however, are closely associated with additional elements of the promotional mix (see Chapter 17). Currently, marketers spend about half as much on sales promotion as they do on advertising. Sales promotion appears to be growing in use more than advertising.

Marketers frequently rely on sales promotion to improve the effectiveness of other promotional mix ingredients, especially advertising and personal selling. For example, some firms allocate 25 per cent of their annual promotional budget to trade shows in order to introduce new products, meet key industry personnel and identify likely prospects.[20]

Marketers design sales promotion to produce immediate, short run sales increases. For example, the major brewers such as Heineken and Whitbread use a continuous programme of sales promotion techniques to boost sales in the highly competitive beer and lager market: free drinks and prize competitions, scratch cards and trade incentives.

Generally, if a company employs advertising or personal selling, it either depends on them continuously or turns to them cyclically. However, a marketer's use of sales promotion tends to be irregular. Many products are seasonal. For example, Thomas Cook and Lunn Poly promote summer package holidays predominantly in the winter and spring months. Qualcast pushes its lawn mowers and other gardening equipment from Easter onwards. On the whole, sales promotions are infrequent, ad hoc campaigns.

Sponsorship The financial or material support of an event, activity, person, organisation or product by an unrelated organisation or donor

Sponsorship The financial or material support of an event, activity, person, organisation or product by an unrelated organisation or donor is called **sponsorship.** Funds are made available to the recipient of the sponsorship in return for the prominent exposure of the benefactor's generosity, products and brands. Sponsorship is no longer confined to the arts or the sporting world, although many galleries, theatrical companies, sports events and teams could not survive without sponsorship. Research and development, buildings, degree courses, charitable events—all often benefit from sponsorship. The donor or sponsor gains the benefits of enhanced company, brand or individual reputation and awareness, as well as possibly improved morale and employee relations. Note the number of prestigious or well known brands sponsoring the Olympics.

Direct mail A method of communication used to entice prospective customers or charitable donors to invest in products, services or worthy causes

Direct Mail The direct mail industry takes a significant slice of the promotional budgets for many companies and organisations. Few households and companies fail to receive direct mail solicitations. **Direct mail** is used to entice prospective customers or charitable donors directly to invest in products, services or worthy causes. Throughout Europe, direct mail is used as a pre-sell technique prior to a sales call, to generate orders, qualify prospects for a sales call, follow up a sale, announce special or localised sales and raise funds for charities and not-for-profit organisations. Good database management is essential, and the material must be carefully targeted to overcome the growing public aversion to "junk mail".

Now that the basic components of an organisation's promotional mix have been discussed, it is important to consider how that mix is created. The factors and conditions that affect the selection of the promotional methods a specific organisation uses in its promotional mix for a particular product need to be examined.

Selecting Promotional Mix Ingredients

Marketers vary the composition of promotional mixes for many reasons. Although all six ingredients can be included in a promotional mix, frequently a marketer selects fewer than six. In addition, many firms that market multiple product lines use several promotional mixes simultaneously.

An organisation's promotional mix (or mixes) is not an unchanging part of the marketing mix. Marketers can and do change the composition of their promotional mixes. The specific promotional mix ingredients employed and the intensity with which they are used depend on a variety of factors, including the organisation's promotional resources, objectives and policies; characteristics of the target market; characteristics of the product; and cost and availability of promotional methods.

Promotional Resources, Objectives and Policies   The quality of an organisation's promotional resources affects the number and relative intensity of promotional methods that can be included in a promotional mix. If a company's promotional budget is extremely limited, the firm is likely to rely on personal selling because it is easier to measure a salesperson's contribution to sales than to measure the effect of advertising. A business must have a sizeable promotional budget if it is to use regional or national advertising and sales promotion activities. Organisations with extensive promotional resources can usually include more ingredients in their promotional mixes. However, larger promotional budgets do not necessarily imply that the companies will use a greater number of promotional methods.

An organisation's promotional objectives and policies also influence the types of promotion used. If a company's objective is to create mass awareness of a new convenience good, its promotional mix is likely to lean heavily towards advertising, sales promotion and possibly publicity. If a company hopes to educate consumers about the features of durable goods, such as home appliances, its promotional mix may combine a moderate amount of advertising, possibly some sales promotion efforts designed to attract customers to retail stores and a great deal of in-store personal selling, this being an excellent way to inform customers about these types of products. If a firm's objective is to produce immediate sales of consumer non-durables, such as paper products and many grocery goods, the promotional mix will probably stress advertising and sales promotion efforts. Business-to-business marketers often use detailed trade advertising, personal selling through sales representatives, sales promotions—often in the guise of bulk discounts and trade show exhibits—and direct mail of brochures and price lists.

Characteristics of the Target Market   The size, geographic distribution and socio-economic characteristics of an organisation's target market also help dictate the ingredients to be included in a product's promotional mix. To some degree, market size determines the composition of the mix. If the size is quite limited, the promotional mix will probably emphasise personal selling, which can be quite effective for reaching small numbers of people. Organisations that sell to industrial markets and firms that market their products through only a few wholesalers frequently make personal selling the major component of their promotional mixes. When markets for a product consist of millions of customers, organisations use advertising and sales promotion because these methods can reach masses of people at a low cost per person. The Coca-Cola Company attempted to reach consumers through a non-traditional vehicle when it placed a commercial for Diet Coke in the introduction to the home video version of the 1989 blockbuster *Batman*. Warner Home Video, the distributor of *Batman*, believed that it would sell more than 10 million copies of the video cassette, exposing millions of consumers to the Diet Coke message at a low cost per person.[21]

The geographic distribution of a firm's customers can affect the combination of promotional methods used. Personal selling is more feasible if a company's customers are concentrated in a small area than if they are dispersed across a vast region. When the company's customers are numerous and dispersed, advertising may be more practical.

The distribution of a target market's socio-economic characteristics, such as age, income or education, may dictate the types of promotional techniques that a marketer selects. For example, personal selling may be much more successful than print advertisements for communicating with poorly educated people, because it allows meaning or product attributes to be explained face-to-face.

Characteristics of the Product   Generally, promotional mixes for industrial products concentrate on personal selling. In promoting consumer goods, on the other hand, advertising plays a major role. This generalisation should be treated cautiously, however. Industrial goods producers do use some advertising to promote their goods, particularly in the trade press. Advertisements for computers, road building equipment and aircraft are not altogether uncommon, and sales promotion is used to promote industrial goods. Personal selling is used extensively for services and consumer durables, such as insurance, leisure and education, home appliances, cars and houses, and consumer convenience items are promoted mainly through advertising and sales promotion. Publicity appears in promotional mixes for industrial goods, consumer goods and services. Many organisations use direct mail, and more are now examining the growing use of corporate sponsorship.

Marketers of highly seasonal products are often forced to emphasise advertising, and possibly sales promotion, because off-season sales will not support an extensive year round sales force. Although many toy producers have sales forces to sell to resellers, a number of these companies depend to a large extent on advertising to promote their products.

The price of a product also influences the composition of the promotional mix. High priced products call for more personal selling because consumers associate greater risk with the purchase of such products and usually want the advice of a salesperson. Few consumers, for example, would be willing to purchase a refrigerator or personal computer from a self-service establishment. For low priced convenience items, marketers use advertising rather than personal selling at the retail level. The profit margins on many of these items are too low to justify the use of salespeople, and most customers do not need advice from sales personnel when buying such products.

A further consideration in creating an effective promotional mix is the stage of the product life cycle. During the introduction stage, a good deal of advertising may be necessary for both industrial and consumer products to make potential users aware of a new product. For many products, personal selling and sales promotion are helpful as well at this stage. In the case of consumer non-durables, the growth and maturity stages call for a heavy emphasis on advertising. Industrial products, on the other hand, often require a concentration of personal selling and some sales promotion efforts during these stages. In the decline stage, marketers usually decrease their promotional activities, especially advertising. Promotional efforts in the decline stage often centre on personal selling and sales promotion efforts.

The intensity of market coverage is still another factor affecting the composition of the promotional mix. When a product is marketed through intensive distribution, the firm depends strongly on advertising and sales promotion. A number of convenience products, such as lotions, cereals and coffee, are promoted through samples, coupons and cash refunds. Where marketers have opted for selective distribution, marketing mixes vary considerably as to type and amount of promotional methods. Items handled through exclusive distribution frequently demand more personal selling and less advertising. Expensive watches, furs and high quality furniture are typical products that are promoted heavily through personal selling. Intensive, selective and exclusive distribution are discussed in Chapter 12.

A product's use also affects the combination of promotional methods. Manufacturers of highly personal products, such as non-prescription contraceptives, feminine hygiene products and haemorrhoid treatments, count on advertising for promotion because many users do not like to talk to sales personnel about such products.

Cost and Availability of Promotional Methods   The cost of promotional methods is a major factor to analyse when developing a promotional mix. National advertising and sales promotion efforts require large expenditures. For example, some detergent brands have annual advertising budgets of £10 to £15 million. However, if the efforts are effective in reaching extremely large numbers of people, the cost per individual reached may be quite small, possibly a few pennies per person. Moreover, not all forms of advertising are expensive. Many small, local businesses advertise their products through local newspapers, magazines, radio stations, outdoor signs and public transport.

Another consideration that marketers must explore when formulating a promotional mix is the availability of promotional techniques. Despite the tremendous number of media vehicles, a firm may find that no available advertising medium effectively reaches a certain market. For example, a product may be banned from being advertised on television, as cigarettes are in many countries. A stockbroker may find no suitable advertising medium for investors in Manchester United Football Club: should the stockbroker use financial publications, sports magazines or general media? The problem of media availability becomes even more pronounced when marketers try to advertise in other countries. Some media, such as television, simply may not be available to advertisers. Television advertising in Scandinavia is minimal. In the UK only seven and a half minutes of advertising are permitted per average hour of terrestrial television, with a maximum of twelve minutes in any one "real" hour.[22] The media that are available may not be open to certain types of advertisements. For example, in Germany, advertisers were forbidden to make brand comparisons in television advertisements. Other promotional methods have limitations as well. An organisation may wish to increase the size of its sales force but be unable to find qualified personnel. In the United States, some state laws prohibit the use of certain types of sales promotion activities, such as contests. Such prohibited techniques are thus "unavailable" in those locales.

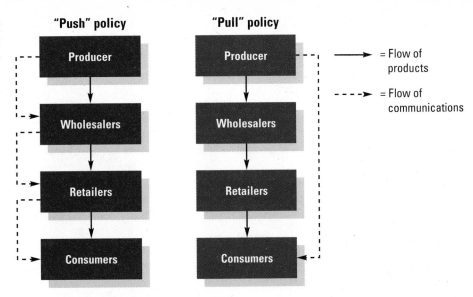

Figure 16.8

Comparison of push and pull promotional strategies

"Push" policy

Producer → Wholesalers → Retailers → Consumers

"Pull" policy

Producer → Wholesalers → Retailers → Consumers

——→ = Flow of products

- - -→ = Flow of communications

Push Policy Versus Pull Policy

Push policy A promotional policy in which the producer promotes the product only to the next institution down the marketing channel

Pull policy A promotional policy in which a firm promotes directly to consumers in order to develop a strong demand for its products

Another element that marketers should consider when they plan a promotional mix is whether to use a push policy or a pull policy. With a **push policy**, the producer promotes the product only to the next institution down the marketing channel. For instance, in a marketing channel with wholesalers and retailers, the producer promotes to the wholesaler, in this case the channel member just below the producer (see Figure 16.8). Each channel member in turn promotes to the next channel member. A push policy normally stresses personal selling. Sometimes sales promotion, direct mail and advertising are used in conjunction with personal selling to push the products down through the channel.

As Figure 16.8 shows, a firm using a **pull policy** promotes directly to consumers with the intention of developing a strong consumer demand for the products. It does so through advertising, sales promotion, direct mail, sponsorship and packaging that helps manufacturers build and maintain market share.[23] Because consumers are persuaded to seek the products in retail stores, retailers will in turn go to wholesalers or the producer to buy the products. The policy is thus intended to "pull" the goods down through the channel by creating demand at the consumer level.

A push policy can be combined with a pull policy. Mars, for example, has a pull policy aimed at the consumer: sponsorship of events and advertising create awareness; packaging, sales promotions—such as competitions or discounts—and direct mail prompt product trial and adoption. Simultaneously, the company's push policy of trade advertising, sales promotions and personal selling persuades channel members to stock and retail its products.

● ● ● ● ● ● ● ● ● ● ● ● ● ● ● ● ● ●

Summary

● The primary role of *promotion* is to communicate with individuals, groups or organisations in the environment with the aim of directly or indirectly facilitating exchanges.

● *Communication* is a sharing of meaning. The communication process involves several steps. Using the *coding process*, the *source* first translates the meaning into a series of signs that represent concepts. The source should employ signs familiar to the *receiver* or audience and choose signs that the receiver or audience uses for referring to the concepts or ideas being promoted. The coded message is sent through a *medium of transmission* to the receiver or audience. The receiver or audience then uses the *decoding process* to convert the signs into concepts and usually supplies *feedback* to the source. When the decoded message differs from the encoded one, a condition called *noise* exists. Occasionally, *channel capacity* is reached when the volume of information can no longer be handled effectively.

● The long run purpose of promotion is to influence and encourage customers to accept or adopt goods, services and ideas. The *product adoption process* consists of five stages. (1) In the *awareness stage,* individuals become aware of the product. (2) People move into the *interest stage* when they seek more information about the product. (3) In the *evaluation stage,* individuals decide whether the product will meet certain criteria that are crucial for satisfying their needs. (4) During the *trial stage,* the consumer actually tries the product. (5) In the *adoption stage,* the consumer decides to use the product on a regular basis. Product rejection may occur at any stage. The *adopters* can be divided into five major categories—*innovators, early adopters, early majority, late majority* and *laggards*—according to how long it takes them to start using a new product.

● There are *five communication effects*. A manufacturer or retailer must establish a *category need* for a product. Consumers must be *aware* of a company's *brands* and have a favourable *brand attitude* towards the products. If the consumer decides to make a purchase—*brand purchase intention*—the company's overall marketing policy must guarantee distribution, suitable product quality and attributes and set the relevant price points—*purchase facilitation*. These are all areas of successful promotional activity.

● The *promotional mix* for a product may include the four major promotional methods—advertising,

personal selling, publicity and sales promotion—as well as the growing areas of direct mail and sponsorship. *Advertising* is a paid form of non-personal communication about an organisation and its products that is transmitted to a target audience through a mass medium. *Personal selling* is a process of informing customers and persuading them to purchase products through personal communication in an exchange situation. *Kinesic, proxemic* and *tactile communication* are important in personal selling. *Telemarketing* often supports personal selling. *Publicity* is non-personal communication in news story form, about an organisation, its products, or both, that is transmitted through a mass medium at no charge, controlled by the *public relations* mechanism. *Sales promotion* is an activity or material that acts as a direct inducement by offering added value to or incentive for the product to resellers, salespeople or consumers. *Sponsorship* involves financial or material support for an organisation, product or event in return for prominent public recognition and display of the sponsor's name, products or services. *Direct mail* involves mailing information, selling or donation packages to consumers and businesses to solicit interest in products or services, purchases or charitable donations.

● There are several major determinants of what promotional methods to include in a promotional mix: the organisation's promotional resources, objectives and policies; the characteristics of the target market; the characteristics of the product; and the cost and availability of promotional methods. Marketers must also consider whether to use a push policy or a pull policy, or a combination of the two. With a *push policy,* the producer promotes the product only to the next institution down the marketing channel. Normally, a push policy stresses personal selling. A firm that uses a *pull policy* promotes directly to consumers with the intention of developing a strong consumer demand for the products. Once consumers are persuaded to seek the products in retail stores, retailers in turn go to wholesalers or the producer to buy the products.

● ● ● ● ● ● ● ● ● ● ● ● ● ● ● ● ● ● ●

Important Terms

Promotion	Receiver	Decoding process
Communication	Coding process	Noise
Source	Medium of transmission	Feedback

Channel capacity
Product adoption process
Awareness stage
Interest stage
Evaluation stage
Trial stage
Adoption stage
Adopter categories
Innovators
Early adopters
Early majority

Late majority
Laggards
Five communication effects
Category need
Brand awareness
Brand attitude
Brand purchase intention
Purchase facilitation
Promotional mix
Advertising
Personal selling

Telemarketing
Kinesic communication
Proxemic communication
Tactile communication
Publicity
Public relations
Sales promotion
Sponsorship
Direct mail
Push Policy
Pull policy

● ● ● ● ● ● ● ● ● ● ● ● ● ● ● ● ● ● ●

Discussion and Review Questions

1. What is the major task of promotion? Do firms ever use promotion to accomplish this task and fail? If so, give several examples.
2. What is communication? Describe the communication process. Is it possible to communicate without using all the elements in the communication process? If so, which ones can be omitted?
3. Identify several causes of noise. How can a source reduce noise?
4. Describe the product adoption process. In certain circumstances, is it possible for a person to omit one or more of the stages in adopting a new product? Explain your answer.
5. Describe a product that many people are in the process of adopting. Have you begun the adoption process for this product? If so, what stage have you reached?
6. What is category need? Illustrate your answer with examples.
7. Identify and briefly describe the major promotional methods that can be included in an

organisation's promotional mix. How does publicity differ from advertising?
8. What forms of interpersonal communication in addition to language can be used in personal selling?
9. How do market characteristics determine which promotional methods to include in a promotional mix? Assume that a company is planning to promote a cereal to both adults and children. Along what major dimensions would these two promotional efforts have to be different?
10. How can a product's characteristics affect the composition of its promotional mix?
11. Evaluate the following statement: "Appropriate advertising media are always available if a company can afford them."
12. Explain the difference between a pull policy and a push policy. Under what conditions should each policy be used?

● ● ● ● ● ● ● ● ● ● ● ● ● ● ● ● ● ● ●

Recommended Readings

J. Engel, M. Warshaw and T. Kinnear, *Promotional Strategy: Managing the Marketing Communications Process,* 8th edn (Boston, Mass.: Irwin, 1994).

J. J. Burnett, *Promotion Management* (Boston, Mass.: Houghton Mifflin, 1993).

C. R. Evans, *Marketing Channels—Informercials and the Future of Televised Marketing* (London: Prentice-Hall, 1994).

M. M. A. Mirabito, *The New Communication Technologies* (Boston, Mass.: Butterworth-Heinemann, 1994).

C. Petersen and A. Toer, *Sales Promotion in Post-Modern Marketing* (Aldershot: Gower, 1995).

Cases

16.1 The Energizer Bunny Marches On and On … Straight into Duracell's Pink Bunny

"Nothing outlasts the Energizer. They keep going and going…." To effectively communicate the message that its Energizer batteries last a long, long time, the Ever Ready Battery Co. introduced in America what has been called one of the cleverest advertising campaigns in television history. With the Energizer brand's introduction into Europe, the Energizer Bunny has encountered an aggressive pink rival.

In a series of television advertisements, the Energizer Bunny's batteries last so long that he escapes from a real advertisement for the batteries and marches through parodied advertisements for fictional products such as instant coffee, air freshener, late-night albums by obscure artists, soft drinks and Château Marmoset wine. After several seconds of a seemingly real advertisement for "Chug-a-Cherry Cola", for example, E.B. encounters a young man dancing upside down on the ceiling. In an advertisement for a fictitious phone company, the bunny knocks down the partition dividing two callers, poking fun at telephone trunk call advertising. After following the real 60 second battery advertisement for several weeks, the 15 second parody spots now air alone, enhancing the surprise effect.

Chiat/Day, the campaign's creators, pay attention to the tiniest details in the parodied advertisements, even down to a "use only as directed" disclaimer for the fake nasal spray. The ads emphasise that "nothing outlasts the Energizer. They keep going and going and going…," just as E.B. keeps going and going, even into other commercials. The campaign works because of the elements of surprise and humour. The long lasting message is clearly evident, and the phoney spots amuse consumers while standing out from the barrage of television advertising. Company executives say they have received hundreds of positive letters about the campaign and one Energizer Bunny ad won a Clio award for the year's best video spot.

One nagging concern for both Ever Ready and its advertising agency is continuing customer confusion over which brand of battery the bunny advertisements promote. In a recent American survey by Video Storyboard Tests, 40 per cent of the respondents who remember the bunny think he advertises Duracell batteries, Ever Ready's number one competitor. Research in the UK similarly showed that consumers link pink toy rabbits with Duracell. This is a throwback to an earlier Duracell advertisement that featured toy bunnies. Although some experts are advising Ever Ready to spend more time advertising the Energizer name and less on the bunny, the company is confident that this is a normal "lag time" before people consistently link the bunny to the battery.

Despite its overwhelming popularity, the campaign's effect on sales is ambiguous. Nielsen figures place Duracell in the number one spot in America with 44 per cent of all alkaline battery sales, and Ever Ready in second place with 37 per cent, down slightly from the previous year. Ever Ready consumer research shows unaided brand awareness up 33 per cent, television commercial awareness up 43 per cent and recall of the product's "long lasting" message up 49 per cent. In the UK, the launch of Energizer has finally enabled Ever Ready to peg back the march of Duracell.

Increasing consumer demand from the campaign has forced retailers to respond by moving Energizer battery displays to more prominent spaces in their stores. In fact, E.B. is so popular that an offer for a stuffed E.B. doll in the US drew 20,000 requests in two weeks—a response 20 times larger than a typical mail offer generates. The bunny gained some extra publicity when an impostor E.B. appeared on the *Late Night with David Letterman* television programme. In a Coors Brewing Company advertisement, actor Leslie Nielsen—dressed in bunny ears, cottontail and pink bunny feet—marched through an advertisement for light beer while a voice-over announced that Coors Light sales keep on "growing and growing". Although Ever Ready initiated talks with Coors to try to stop the advertisement from airing, some analysts assert that battery sales will actually benefit from the humour and extra exposure. Many other companies sought to utilise E.B.'s popularity, too.

In time for 1993 Christmas sales, however, Duracell rekindled its "enormously popular" pink bunny property with a £4 million national television campaign in the UK through agency BSB Dorland. Observers thought this was a clever way of spiking Ever Ready's guns just as the company imported the US brand Energizer and its drum beating bunny to replace the flagging Ever Ready Gold Seal alkaline battery line. Research in the UK shows the pink bunny to be clearly associated with Duracell, which has 30 per cent of the market compared with Ever Ready's 25.5 per cent. The Energizer Bunny has hit Europe, though, with Duracell spreading its pink bunny rival to stem Ever Ready's Energizer introduction. E.B. in Europe has been truly nobbled by Duracell's own pink bunny.

SOURCES: Julie Liesse, "Bunny back to battle Duracell", *Advertising Age*, 17 September 1990, pp. 4, 78; Joanne Lipman, "Too many think the Bunny is Duracell's, not Ever Ready's", *Wall Street Journal*, 31 July 1990, pp. B1, B7; Stuart Elliott, "He's back: Energizer Bunny's beat goes on", *USA Today*, 6 December 1989, p. 2B; Bob Garfield, "Energizer's parody campaign is one bunny of a concept", *Advertising Age*, 23 October 1989, p. 120; Mat Toor, "Bunny leaps back into Duracell's defence", *Marketing*, 8 October 1992, p. 7; Mat Toor, "Energizer: the birth of a brand", *Marketing*, 4 March 1993, pp. 20–21; David Benardy, "Three battle for £26 million Energizer", *Marketing Week*, 2 February 1996, p. 13; Alex Benady, "Energizer fires up battery row", *Marketing*, 18 August 1994, p. 4; Paul LaMonica, "Battling batteries", *Financial World*, 30 January 1996, pp. 58–62.

Questions for Discussion

1. In America, why are the Energizer battery advertisements so successful?
2. What is the advertising platform for the Energizer Bunny campaign?
3. What is the nature of the publicity that Ever Ready gained with the Energizer Bunny campaign? Distinguish between the publicity and the advertising in this campaign.
4. How can Ever Ready's Energizer Bunny work to Duracell's advantage?

16.2 Häagen-Dazs: Promoting an Adult Ice Cream

Häagen-Dazs makes the best selling superpremium ice cream in North America. Its luscious ingredients include chocolate from Benelux, vanilla from Madagascar, Brazilian coffee, Oregon strawberries, nuts from Hawaii and Switzerland—and the text on the packaging serenely asserts that it is the world's best ice cream. Since Grand Metropolitan's takeover of Pillsbury, Häagen-Dazs has come to Europe in a big way. In just six years, sales in Britain, France and Germany have climbed from £3 million to £70 million, with consumers happily paying two or three times the cost of rival, traditional brands for this premium product.

London's Leicester Square shop served close to one million ice cream lovers in its first year. The success of the Victor Hugo Plaza shop in Paris, now the company's second busiest, led to the establishment of its first European factory in France. Häagen-Dazs shops have opened in Italy, Spain, Benelux and Scandinavia. The appealing flavours can now be found not only in the company's shops but also at airports, in cafés and in carefully selected delicatessens, with rapidly growing popularity.

The product's high quality has been essential in maintaining a loyal customer following, but it was promotional work that led to the successful take-off of what was, until recently, an unheard-of brand in Europe. Free tasting was a major prong of attack; over 5 million free cupfuls of ice cream were given away during the company's European launch. Thousands of retailers, cafés and delis were supplied with branded freezers both to display and carefully look after the new premium ice cream. Häagen-Dazs spent £30 million on advertising, stressing the de luxe ingredients, unusual flavours and novelty of the product. Europeans currently eat 25 per cent of the 3 billion gallons of ice cream consumed worldwide. Häagen-Dazs plans to increase consumption by appealing to more than traditional ice cream lovers.

The summer afternoon stroll with an ice cream cornet, the family trip to a fun park or beach, a snack during a film or concert, the sticky climax of a birthday party feast had long been the core market for Wall's and Lyons Maid. Ice Cream Mars changed all that by creating an ice cream bar suitable for any occasion and particularly attractive to adults. Häagen-Dazs goes further! Award winning press adverts, artistically shot, often in black and white, feature lithe, semi-nude couples entwined in exotic poses while feeding each other Häagen-Dazs ice cream. The appeal of vanilla ice cream bars hand-dipped in Belgian chocolate and rolled in roasted almonds now seems hard to resist for adults everywhere. The advertising imagery promotes an adult, up-market, glamorous positioning for this superpremium ice cream. The Häagen-Dazs range has been expanded to include frozen yogurts, sorbets and now ice cream novelties, such as the ice cream sandwich made with cookies.

SOURCES: "Dairy produce", *Campaign,* 15 March 1996, p. 34; "Häagen-Dazs cinema first", *Campaign,* 26 March 1995, p. 5; "Pillsbury's global training plan", *Crossborder Monitor,* 19 April 1995, p. 9; G. Mead, "Sex, ice and video beer", *Financial Times,* 26 September 1992, p. 5; "Saucy way to sell a Knickerbocker Glory—Häagen-Dazs' new ice cream campaign", *Financial Times,* 8 August 1991, p. 8; "Häagen-Dazs is using sex to secure an up market niche in Britain's £400m ice cream market", *Observer,* 4 August 1991, p. 25; M. Carter, "The luxury ice cream market", *Marketing Week,* 22 May 1992, p. 30.

Questions for Discussion

1. Why did the London launch of Häagen-Dazs utilise so many stunts and such a mix of promotional activity?
2. Why did Häagen-Dazs target the adult market rather than families or children?
3. Was the "adult" positioning and promotional execution risky? Why did Häagen-Dazs deploy this positioning strategy?

17 ADVERTISING, PUBLICITY AND SPONSORSHIP

"The strengths and weaknesses of
publicity provide a mirror image to
those of advertising which, when
combined, complement one another
synergistically."
Norman Hart

OBJECTIVES

- To explore the uses of advertising
- To become aware of the major steps involved in developing an advertising campaign
- To find out who is responsible for developing advertising campaigns
- To gain an understanding of publicity and public relations
- To analyse how public relations can be used
- To be aware of current trends in advertising and public relations
- To understand the nature of corporate sponsorship

The Internet connects a rapidly growing number of homes, businesses and schools across the globe to a huge array of information and, increasingly, to the sales particulars of many companies' products and services. In its early years, the Internet was purely a vehicle for communicating information. Now, with scrambling techniques to safeguard credit card details, the Internet can be used as an interactive advertising, product information, ordering and payment tool within the marketing mix. Experts believe that within a few years, the Internet could be taking a staggering £200 billion in orders for all types of products and services, notably banking and financial services, which are predicted to be the fastest growing sector of the Internet for promoting and selling products, as well as for small firms with limited advertising budgets.

German car giant BMW has used the Internet to create a service only available on-line, the BMW Approved Used Car Directory. This service is interactive, providing a search and find facility, as well

The screen shows a Netscape browser window with menu bar: File Edit View Go Bookmarks Options Directory Window. Title: Netscape: Westin Hotels & Resorts. Toolbar buttons: Back, Forward, Home, Reload, Images, Open, Print, Find, Stop. Location: http://www.westin.com/#acrobat. Buttons: What's New? What's Cool? Handbook Net Search Net Directory Newsgroups. The page displays: WESTIN HOTELS & RESORTS — Travel Guide — Discover the world of Westin and you may never want to leave. Icons: What's New, World of Westin, Listings & Reservations, Special Offers, Westin Premier.

as general BMW information support. Users may either specify a desired model/colour/specification/age/price combination for the BMW system to locate or scroll through comprehensive lists of used BMWs for sale through the dealer network. All local BMW dealers are on the Internet, promoting their site through local media and press advertising.

To work, a "good" Internet site must attract target customers' attention and fulfil their expectations, just as any other product or service must. The information being offered by BMW and its dealers must be of interest to target BMW customers and relevant users of the Internet. The site must be interactive, offering users the chance to become involved. The Internet site must be interesting and of high quality. It must be promoted; otherwise either users will not track it down, or it will be swamped by the plethora of sites being set up. It must pay for itself: a good Internet site costs around £30,000 to set up. The Internet site must be staffed, particularly if users are likely to seek responses to very specific queries or to place an order. Above all, advertisers need to remember that the imagery and message used on the Internet must be consistent and fully integrated with the rest of their promotional mix. Whether it is for Newcastle United Football Club, Condé Nast's *Vogue* and *Tatler* or Richard Branson's Virgin, the Internet is playing an increasingly significant role in many businesses' promotional activity. The Internet is now very much part of the promotional mix and indeed also of the overall marketing mix. ■

SOURCES: *Marketing Guides*: "The Internet", 27 June 1996; C. Lloyd, "On a quest to bring the Internet to the masses", *Sunday Times,* 26 November 1995; "Innovation", *Sunday Times,* 19 and 26 November, 31 December 1995; "Scramble to build a super showroom in cyberspace", *Independent on Sunday,* 4 February 1996, p. IB 8; "Pay by plastic plan on internet", *Evening Telegraph,* 3 February 1996, p. 15.

This chapter explores the many dimensions of advertising, public relations and sponsorship. Initially focusing on how advertising is used, it goes on to examine the major steps by which an advertising campaign is developed, describing who is responsible for developing such campaigns. After analysing publicity and public relations and comparing their characteristics with those of advertising, the chapter explores the different forms publicity may take. The following section considers how publicity is used and what is required for an effective public relations programme. After discussing negative publicity and some problems associated with the use of publicity, the chapter examines some of the current trends in advertising and public relations, as typified by the growing use of the Internet in marketing. It concludes with a look at the increasing use of corporate sponsorship in the promotional mix.

The Nature of Advertising

Advertising permeates everyone's daily lives.[1] At times people view it positively; at other times they avoid it by taping television programmes and then zapping over the advertisements as they watch later by pressing the video cassette recorder's fast forward button.[2] Some advertising informs, persuades or entertains; some of it bores, even offends. For example, consumer groups have been whitewashing billboards advertising tobacco products because they believe such advertisements encourage children to smoke.[3]

Advertising A paid form of non-personal communication that is transmitted through mass media such as television, radio, newspapers, magazines, direct mail, public transport vehicles, outdoor displays and the Internet

As mentioned in Chapter 16, **advertising** is a paid form of non-personal communication that is transmitted through mass media such as television, radio, newspapers, magazines, direct mail, public transport vehicles, outdoor displays and now also the Internet. An organisation can use advertising to reach a variety of audiences, ranging from small, precise groups, such as the stamp collectors of the Highlands, to extremely large audiences, such as all the buyers of fax machines in Sweden.

When people are asked to name major advertisers, most immediately mention business organisations. (See Table 17.1 for a listing of the top 10 advertisers by country in Europe for 1994.) However, many types of organisations—including governments, churches, universities, civic groups and charitable organisations—take advantage of advertising. For example, the UK government is one of the largest advertisers: "Heroin Screws You Up", Employment Training, the DTI Enterprise Initiative are just a few examples. So even though advertising is analysed here in the context of business organisations, it should be borne in mind that much of the discussion applies to all types of organisations.

Marketers sometimes give advertising more credit than it deserves. This attitude causes them to use advertising when they should not. For example, manufacturers of basic products such as sugar, flour and salt often try to differentiate their products, with minimal success. Over the years, Saxa has nevertheless tried to position its salt as different from the competition with the advertising slogan "Saxa Table Salt—lets the flavour flow".

Under certain conditions, advertising can work effectively for an organisation. The questions in Table 17.2 raise some general points that a marketer should consider when assessing the potential value of advertising as an ingredient in a product's promotional mix. The list is not all-inclusive. Numerous factors have a bearing on whether advertising should be used at all, and if so, to what extent.

The Uses of Advertising

Advertising can serve a variety of purposes. Individuals and organisations use it to promote products and organisations, to stimulate demand, to offset competitors' advertising, to make sales personnel more effective, to increase the uses of a product, to remind and reinforce customers, and to reduce sales fluctuations (see Figure 17.1).

Promoting Products and Organisations

Advertising is used to promote goods, services, ideas, images, issues, people and indeed anything that the advertiser wants to publicise or foster. Depending on what is being promoted, advertising can be classified as institutional or product

Austria
Unilever
Procter & Gamble
Leiner/Kika
BML Konzern
Jacobs/Suchard
Konsum Österreich
Media Markt
Henkel Austria
Spar Waren
Raiffeisen

Belgium
Procter & Gamble
GIB Group
Unilever
Etat Belge
Philip Morris Group
BSN-Gervais Danone
L'Oréal Belgilux
D'Ieteren
Master Foods
Interbrew Belgium

Denmark
FDB
Dansk Supermarkt
Teledanmark
Carlsberg
Procter & Gamble
Unilever
Egmont Gruppen
Det Berlingske Hus
Nestlé
Politiken

Finland
Valio (food)
Tele (telecommunications)
Lever
Procter & Gamble
Orion (pharmaceuticals)
Volvo-Auto (car sales)
Silja Line (shipping)
Veikkaus (lottery)
Korprivaara (cars)
Van den Bergh Foods

France
PSA
L'Oréal
Nestlé Enterprises
Danone
Renault
Unilever
Procter & Gamble
Mulliez
Philips
Lagardere

Germany
Procter & Gamble
Kraft Jacobs Suchard
Henkel Waschmittel GMbH
Ferrero
Opel Adam AG
Volkswagen AG
C&A
Union Dt. Lebensm. Werke
Effem
Zusatzgeschäft

Greece
Lever
Procter & Gamble
Public services
Elais (Unilever)
Delta
Sopral (Nestlé)
Fage
Colgate-Palmolive
Coca-Cola (3E)
Lambrakis Publishing Gp

Italy
Ferrero
Fiat Auto
Procter & Gamble
Barilla
Sagit
Spec. Localita
Telecom Italia
Saipo
Renault
Nestlé

Netherlands
Procter & Gamble Benelux
Lever
Albert Heijn
PTT Telecom
Heineken Nederland
Nestlé Nederland
Van den Bergh Foods
ABN Amro Bank
Postbank
Molnlycke Netherlands

Portugal
Procter & Gamble
Nestlé Portugal
Renault Portuguesa
Unicer-União Cervejeira
Indústrias Lever Portuguesa
Sincoral
Santa Casa Misericórdia
 Lisboa
Fiat Auto Portuguesa
Fima Indústria Alimentar
Central Cervejas

Spain
El Corte Ingles
Procter & Gamble España
Fasa Renault
Citroën Hispania
S.E.A.T.
Ford España
Henkel Iberica
Org. Nat. Loterias Estado
Nestlé España
Peugeot-Talbot España

Sweden
ICA
Procter & Gamble
Telia
Kooperativa Förbundet
Volvo
Elida Robert Group
Hennes & Mauritz
Sparbanken Sverige
Colgate-Palmolive
Lever

NOTE: For the UK, see Table 17.3, page 494.
SOURCE: From *The Marketing Pocket Book 1996* (Henley, Oxon: NTC Publications, 1995). Reprinted by permission.

Table 17.1 Top 10 advertisers by country in Europe, 1994

1. **Does the product possess unique, important features?**

Although homogeneous products such as cigarettes, petrol and beer have been advertised successfully, they usually require considerably more effort and expense than other products. On the other hand, products that are differentiated on physical rather than psychological dimensions are much easier to advertise. Even so, "being different" is rarely enough. The advertisability of product features is enhanced when buyers believe that those unique features are important and useful.

2. **Are "hidden qualities" important to buyers?**

If by viewing, feeling, tasting or smelling the product buyers can learn all there is to know about the product and its benefits, advertising will have less chance of increasing demand. Conversely, if not all product benefits are apparent to consumers on inspection and use of the product, advertising has more of a story to tell, and the probability that it can be profitably used increases. The "hidden quality" of vitamin C in oranges once helped explain why Sunkist oranges could be advertised effectively, whereas the advertising of lettuce has been a failure.

3. **Is the general demand trend for the product favourable?**

If the generic product category is experiencing a long term decline, it is less likely that advertising can be used successfully for a particular brand within the category.

4. **Is the market potential for the product adequate?**

Advertising can be effective only when there are sufficient actual or prospective users of the brand in the target market.

5. **Is the competitive environment favourable?**

The size and marketing strength of competitors and their brand shares and loyalty will greatly affect the possible success of an advertising campaign. For example, a marketing effort to compete successfully against Kodak film, Heinz baked beans, or Campbell soups would demand much more than simply advertising.

6. **Are general economic conditions favourable for marketing the product?**

The effects of an advertising programme and the sale of all products are influenced by the overall state of the economy and by specific business conditions. For example, it is much easier to advertise and sell luxury leisure products (stereos, sailing boats, video cameras) when disposable income is high.

7. **Is the organisation able and willing to spend the money required to launch an advertising campaign?**

As a general rule, if the organisation is unable or unwilling to undertake an advertising expenditure that as a percentage of the total amount spent in the product category is at least equal to the market share it desires, advertising is not likely to be effective.

8. **Does the firm possess sufficient marketing expertise to market the product?**

The successful marketing of any product involves a complex mixture of product and consumer research, product development, packaging, pricing, financial management, promotion and distribution. Weakness in any area of marketing is an obstacle to the successful use of advertising.

SOURCE: Adapted from Charles H. Patti, "Evaluating the role of advertising", *Journal of Advertising*, Fall 1977, pp. 32–33. Reprinted by permission of the *Journal of Advertising*.

Table 17.2 Some issues to consider when deciding whether to use advertising

Institutional advertising The type of advertising that promotes organisational images, ideas or political issues

advertising. **Institutional advertising** promotes organisational images, ideas or political issues. For example, some of Seagram's advertising promotes the idea that drinking and driving do not mix, in order to create and develop a socially responsible image. Hanson Trust and BOC have successfully used advertising to

Figure 17.1

Major uses of advertising

- Promote products, organisations and causes
- Stimulate primary and selective demand
- Offset competitors' advertising
- **Advertising uses**
- Aid sales personnel
- Increase uses of a product
- Remind and reinforce
- Reduce sales fluctuations

explain and promote their different subsidiaries and products: their corporate composition.

Product advertising promotes goods and services. Business, government and private non-business organisations turn to it to promote the uses, features, images and benefits of their products. When Monsanto introduced a new pesticide to help farmers clean up weeds in the post-harvest stubble, it used press advertising to tout the benefits of Sting CT, including a competition (a trip to Italy) and a coupon to send off for further technical details of the product. It is this type of advertising that readers, as consumers, will be familiar with, be it the advertisements for Ford cars, Kellogg's cereals or Barclays Bank's services. Marketing Insight 17.1 examines Reebok's high profile advertising.

Product advertising The type of advertising that promotes goods and services

Stimulating Primary and Selective Demand

When a specific firm is the first to introduce an innovation, it tries to stimulate *primary demand*—demand for a product category rather than a specific brand of the product—through pioneer advertising. **Pioneer advertising** informs people about a product: what it is, what it does, how it can be used and where it can be purchased. Because pioneer advertising is used in the introductory stage of the product life cycle when there are no competitive brands, it neither emphasises the brand name nor compares brands. The first company to introduce the compact

Pioneer advertising The type of advertising that informs people about a product: what it is, what it does, how it can be used and where it can be purchased disc player, for instance, initially tried to stimulate primary demand (create category need) by emphasising the benefits of compact disc players in general rather than the benefits of its brand. Product advertising is also used sometimes to stimulate primary demand for an established product. Occasionally, an industry trade group, rather than a single firm, sponsors advertisements to stimulate primary demand. For example, to stimulate demand for milk, the old Milk Marketing Board sponsored advertisements that demonstrated how healthy and pleasant milk is to drink. In Figure 17.2, advertising promotes the use of potatoes.

To build *selective demand*, or demand for a specific brand, an advertiser turns to competitive advertising. **Competitive advertising** points out a brand's uses, features and advantages that benefit consumers but may not be available in competing brands. For example, Volvo heavily promotes the safety and crash-worthiness of Volvo cars in its advertising.

Another form of competitive advertising is **comparative advertising,** in which two or more brands are compared on the basis of one or more product attributes. Companies must not, however, misrepresent the qualities or characteristics of the comparison product.

Competitive advertising The type of advertising that points out a brand's uses, features, and advantages that may not be available in competing brands

Comparative advertising The type of advertising that compares two or more brands on the basis of one or more product attributes

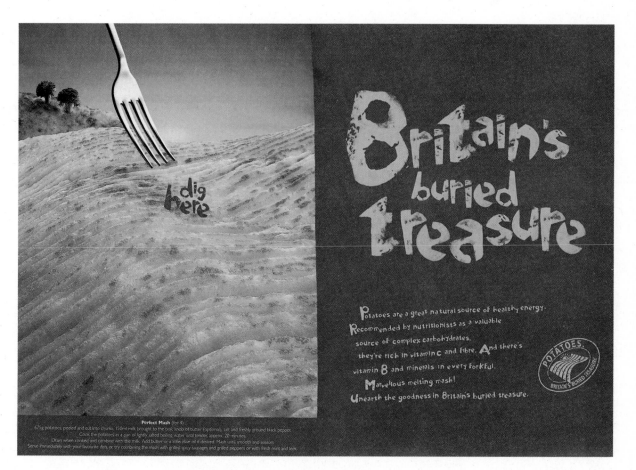

Figure 17.2 Stimulating primary demand. This advertisement aims to stimulate demand for potatoes in general, rather than for a specific brand.

Source: Courtesy of the Potato Marketing Board.

High Profile Brand Building: Risks for Reebok

In the furious competition for market share in the huge but maturing £17 billion global athletic shoe industry, some companies are willing to take high risks. One such company is Reebok International. For several years, Reebok and its rival Nike have engaged in an intense strategic marketing war. In early 1990 Reebok's ad agency struggled to come up with a brilliant ad campaign for the Reebok Pump shoe that would challenge the successful Nike Air campaign. The result was a television advertisement featuring bungee jumpers — people who leap from high places tethered at the ankles by giant elastic ropes. Two men are standing on a bridge, 50 metres (180 feet) above whitewater rapids and rocks, both wearing basketball shoes — one man in Nike Air hightops and the other in

Reebok's Pump. Then the two men jump. At the end, the Reebok wearer is shown safely hanging upside down above the water; the other cord holds only a pair of empty Nike Airs. The announcer says, "The Pump from Reebok — it fits a little better than your ordinary athletic shoe".

The advertisement certainly caught people's attention and generated publicity, but it was the wrong kind. Many people viewed the sly joke about violent death as extraordinarily cruel, and consumers complained that children might try the dangerous stunt. Although the advertisement was originally planned as a £20 million, three week campaign, in several territories, including North America, Europe and South East Asia, Reebok took it off the air after six days. The company later

Offsetting Competitors' Advertising

Defensive advertising The type of advertising that aims to offset or lessen the effects of a competitor's promotional programme

When marketers advertise to offset or lessen the effects of a competitor's promotional programme, they are using **defensive advertising.** Although defensive advertising does not necessarily increase a company's sales or market share, it may prevent a loss in these areas. For example, when McDonald's first test marketed pizza, Pizza Hut countered with defensive advertising to protect its market share and sales. Pizza Hut advertised both on television and in newspapers in the two test cities, emphasising that its product is made from scratch, whereas McDonald's uses frozen dough.[4] Defensive advertising is used most often by firms in extremely competitive consumer product markets, such as the fast food industry.

Making Sales Personnel More Effective

Business organisations that stress personal selling often use advertising to improve the effectiveness of sales personnel. Advertising created specifically to support personal selling activities tries to pre-sell a product to buyers by informing them about its uses, features and benefits and by encouraging them to contact local dealers or sales representatives. This form of advertising helps salespeople find good sales prospects. Advertising is often designed to support personal selling efforts for industrial products, insurance and consumer durables, such as cars and major household appliances. For example, advertising may bring a prospective buyer to a showroom, but usually a salesperson plays a key role in actually closing the sale.

attempted to re-run the commercial with dis-claimers, but many major television companies refused to air it.

Amongst the clutter of television advertising, how does a company get attention, make a statement? What is certain is that associating a competitor's product with death raises an ethical issue. The Reebok campaign generated a great deal of adverse publicity: Reebok's public relations team had to work overtime to calm critics in the media and to re-assure consumers. Stockists of Reebok footwear also were unhappy and did not want their reputations damaged by Reebok's apparent insensitivity. Existing advertisements filled gaps in the schedule, but Reebok's agency had to think up a whole new campaign in a hurry. Meanwhile, Nike benefited from Reebok's promotional error.

The major global brands such as Nike and Reebok depend on high brand awareness for suc-cess. Sponsorship of leading sports stars, teams and events; advertisements featuring well known personalities; sensationalist stunts such as explosions and bungee jumping or photographic trickery—all assist the brand building cause. Recently Reebok put a new slant on the marketing of sports shoes with a £4 million advertising campaign aimed at women. It hopes not to attract adverse publicity or criticism from women's groups.

Sources: Harriet Green, "Reebok reaches for the stars", *Campaign,* 29 March 1996, p. 16; Margaret Hood, "Lowes targets women in £4m Reebok sports shoe TV push", *Campaign,* 14 April 1995, p. 4; "Sports clothing", *Retail Business,* May 1994, pp. 53–74; Bob Garfield, "Good taste takes deep dive in bungee ad for Reebok Pump", *Advertising Age,* 26 March 1990, p. 52; Marcy Mageira, "Nike edges Reebok, L.A. Gear sprinting", *Advertising Age,* 25 September 1989, p. 93; Lindsay McMurdo, "Above the plimsoll line", *Marketing Week,* 8 November 1992, pp. 32–35.

Increasing the Uses of a Product

Reminder advertising The type of advertising that reminds customers of the uses, characteristics and benefits of an established brand

The absolute demand for any product is limited because people in a market will consume only so much of it. Given both this limit on demand and competitive conditions, marketers can increase sales of a specific product in a defined geographic market only to a certain point. To improve sales beyond this point, they must either enlarge the geographic market and sell to more people or develop and promote a larger number of uses for the product. If a firm's advertising convinces buyers to use its products in more ways, the sales of the products go up. For example, Nabisco used advertising to inform consumers that its Shredded Wheat cereal contains no added sugar and is high in natural fibre, which is essential to a healthy, balanced diet. The company is thus attempting to position Shredded Wheat as part of a wholesome diet, as well as a popular children's cereal. When promoting new uses, an advertiser attempts to increase the demand for its own brand without driving up the demand for competing brands.

Reminding and Reinforcing Customers

Reinforcement advertising The type of advertising that tries to assure current users that they have made the right choice and tells them how to get the most satisfaction from the product

Marketers sometimes employ **reminder advertising** to let consumers know that an established brand is still around and that it has certain uses, characteristics and benefits. Procter & Gamble, for example, reminds consumers that its Crest toothpaste is still the best one for preventing cavities. **Reinforcement advertising,** on the other hand, tries to assure current users that they have made the right choice and tells them how to get the most satisfaction from the product. Both reminder and reinforcement advertising aim to prevent a loss in sales or market share.

Reducing Sales Fluctuations

The demand for many products varies from month to month because of such factors as climate, holidays, seasons and customs. A business, however, cannot operate at peak efficiency when sales fluctuate rapidly. Changes in sales volume translate into changes in the production or inventory, personnel and financial resources it requires. To the extent that marketers can generate sales during slow periods, they can smooth out the fluctuations. When advertising reduces fluctuations, a manager can use the firm's resources more efficiently.

Advertising is often designed to stimulate business during sales slumps. For example, advertisements promoting price reductions of lawncare equipment or package holidays can increase sales during the winter months. On occasion, a business advertises that customers will get better service by coming in on certain days rather than others. During peak sales periods, a marketer may refrain from advertising to prevent over stimulating sales to the point where the firm cannot handle all the demand. For example, coupons for the delivery of pizza are often valid only from Monday to Thursday, not Friday to Sunday, which are the peak delivery days.

A firm's use of advertising depends on the firm's objectives, resources and environmental forces. The degree to which advertising accomplishes the marketer's goals depends in large part on the advertising campaign.

● ● ● ● ● ● ● ● ● ● ● ● ● ● ● ● ● ● ●

Developing an Advertising Campaign

Advertising campaign An attempt to reach a particular target market by designing a series of advertisements and placing them in various advertising media

An **advertising campaign** involves designing a series of advertisements and placing them in various advertising media to reach a particular target market. As Figure 17.3 indicates, the major steps in creating an advertising campaign are (1) identifying and analysing the advertising target, (2) defining the advertising objectives, (3) creating the advertising platform or property, (4) determining the advertising budget, (5) developing the media plan, (6) creating the advertising message, (7) executing the campaign and (8) evaluating the effectiveness of the advertising. The number of steps and the exact order in which they are carried out may vary according to an organisation's resources, the nature of its product, the types of target markets or audiences to be reached and the advertising agency selected.[5] These general guidelines for developing an advertising campaign are appropriate for all types of organisations.

Figure 17.3

General steps for developing and implementing an advertising campaign

Identifying and Analysing the Advertising Target

Advertising target The group of people at which advertisements are aimed

The **advertising target** is the group of people at which advertisements are aimed. For example, the target audience for Special K and All-Bran cereals is health-conscious adults. Identifying and analysing the advertising target are critical processes; the information they yield helps determine the other steps in developing the campaign. The advertising target often includes everyone in a firm's target market. Marketers may, however, seize some opportunities to slant a campaign at only a portion of the target market.

Advertisers analyse advertising targets to establish an information base for a campaign. Information commonly needed includes the location and geographic distribution of the target group; the distribution of age, income, ethnic origin, sex and education; and consumer attitudes regarding the purchase and use of both the advertiser's products and competing products. Qualitative marketing research is very important in this process, particularly the use of focus group discussions.[6] The exact kinds of information that an organisation will find useful depend on the type of product being advertised, the characteristics of the advertising target, and the type and amount of competition. Generally, the more advertisers know about the advertising target, the more likely they are to develop an effective advertising campaign. When the advertising target is not precisely identified and properly analysed, the campaign may not succeed.

Defining the Advertising Objectives

The advertiser's next step is to consider what the firm hopes to accomplish with the campaign. Because advertising objectives guide campaign development, advertisers should define their objectives carefully to ensure that the campaign will achieve what they want. Advertising campaigns based on poorly defined objectives seldom succeed.

Advertising objectives should be stated clearly, precisely and in measurable terms. Precision and measurability allow advertisers to evaluate advertising success: to judge, at the campaign's end, whether the objectives have been met, and if so, how well. To provide precision and measurability, advertising objectives should contain benchmarks—the current condition or position of the firm—and indicate how far and in what direction the advertiser wishes to move from these benchmarks. For example, the advertiser should state the current sales level (the benchmark) and the amount of sales increase that is sought through advertising. An advertising objective also should specify a time frame, so that advertisers know exactly how long they have to accomplish the objective. Thus an advertiser with average monthly sales of £450,000 (the benchmark) might set the following objective: "Our primary advertising objective is to increase average monthly sales from £450,000 to £540,000 within 12 months." This also tells the advertiser when evaluation of the campaign should begin.

If an advertiser defines objectives by sales, the objectives focus on raising absolute monetary sales, increasing sales by a certain percentage or increasing the firm's market share. However, even though an advertiser's long run goal is to increase sales, not all campaigns are designed to produce immediate sales. Some campaigns are designed to increase product or brand awareness, make consumers' attitudes more favourable or increase consumers' knowledge of a product's features. These objectives are stated in terms of communication. For example, when Apple Computers introduced home computers, its initial campaign did not focus on sales but on creating brand awareness and educating consumers about the features and uses of home computers. A specific communication objective might be to increase product feature awareness from 0 to 40 per cent in the target market at the end of six months. The RAC's £5 million annual spend aims to increase membership, while Rolling Rock, the premium bottled lager distributed by Whitbread, spends £3 million annually to boost sales and increase brand awareness.[7]

Creating the Advertising Platform

Advertising platform The basic issues or selling points that an advertiser wishes to include in the advertising campaign

Before launching a political campaign, party leaders develop a political platform, which states the major issues that will be the basis of the campaign. Like a political platform, an **advertising platform** consists of the basic issues or selling points that an advertiser wishes to include in the advertising campaign. A single advertisement in an advertising campaign may contain one or several issues in the platform. Although the platform sets forth the basic issues, it does not indicate how they should be presented.

A marketer's advertising platform should consist of issues that are important to consumers. One of the best ways to determine what those issues are is to survey consumers about what they consider most important in the selection and use of the product involved. For example, Procter & Gamble has developed re-fill packages for some of its cleaning products. The re-fill packages provide a unique benefit by not adding to solid waste disposal problems.[8] Environmentally conscious consumers consider this a positive selling feature. The selling features of a product must not only be important to consumers; if possible, they should also be features that competitive products do not have.

Although research is the most effective method for determining the issues of an advertising platform, it is expensive. As a result, the advertising platform is most commonly based on the opinions of personnel within the firm and of individuals in the advertising agency, if an agency is used. This trial and error approach generally leads to some successes and some failures.

Because the advertising platform is a base on which to build the message, marketers should analyse this stage carefully. A campaign can be perfect in the selection and analysis of its advertising target, the statement of its objectives, its media strategy and the form of its message. But the campaign will still fail if the advertisements communicate information that consumers do not consider important when they select and use the product.

Determining the Advertising Budget

Advertising budget The total amount of money that a marketer allocates for advertising over a period of time

The **advertising budget** is the total amount of money that a marketer allocates for advertising over a period of time. It is difficult to determine this amount, because there is no way to measure the precise effects of spending a certain amount of money on advertising.

Many factors affect a firm's decision about how much to spend for advertising. The geographic size of the market and the distribution of buyers within the market have a great bearing on this decision. Both the type of product being advertised and a firm's sales volume relative to competitors' sales volumes play a part in determining what proportion of a firm's revenue is spent on advertising. Advertising budgets for industrial products are usually quite small relative to the sales of the products, whereas consumer convenience items, such as soft drinks, soaps and cosmetics, generally have large budgets. The UK launch of Ragu pasta sauce, for example, had a budget of £2 million for two weeks' advertising and below-the-line support.

Objective and task approach A technique for determining an advertising budget that involves determining campaign objectives and then attempting to list the tasks required to accomplish them

Of the many techniques used to determine the advertising budget, one of the most logical is the **objective and task approach.** Using this approach, marketers initially determine the objectives that a campaign is to achieve and then attempt to list the tasks required to accomplish them. The costs of the tasks are then calculated and added to arrive at the amount of the total budget. This approach has one main problem: marketers usually find it hard to estimate the level of effort needed to achieve certain objectives. A coffee marketer, for example, might find it extremely difficult to determine by what amount it should increase national television advertising in order to raise a brand's market share from 8 to 12 per cent. As a result of this problem, advertisers do not often use the objective and task approach.

In the more widely used **percentage of sales approach,** marketers simply multiply a firm's past sales, plus a factor for planned sales growth or declines, by a standard percentage, based on both what the firm traditionally spends on advertising and what the industry averages. This approach has one major flaw: it is based on the incorrect assumption that sales create advertising, rather than the reverse. Consequently, a marketer using the approach at a time of declining sales will reduce the amount spent on advertising. But such a reduction may further diminish sales. Though illogical, this technique has gained wide acceptance because it is easy to use and less disruptive competitively; it stabilises a firm's market share within an industry. However, in times of declining sales, many firms do increase their contribution to advertising in the hope of reversing the decline.

Another way to determine the advertising budget is the **competition matching approach.** Marketers who follow this approach try either to match their major competitors' budgets or to allocate the same percentage of sales for advertising as their competitors do. Although a wise marketer should be aware of what competitors spend on advertising, this technique should not be used by itself, because a firm's competitors probably have different advertising objectives and different resources available for advertising. Many companies and advertising agencies engage in quarterly competitive spending reviews, comparing competitors' expenditures in print, radio and television with their own spending levels. Competitive tracking of this nature occurs at both the national and regional levels.

At times, marketers use the **arbitrary approach:** a high level executive in the firm states how much can be spent on advertising for a certain time period. The arbitrary approach often leads to under spending or over spending. Although hardly a scientific budgeting technique, it is expedient.

Establishing the advertising budget is critically important. If it is set too low, the campaign cannot achieve its full potential for stimulating demand. When too much money is allocated for advertising, the over spending that results wastes financial resources.

Developing the Media Plan

As Table 17.3 shows, advertisers spend tremendous amounts of money on advertising media. These amounts have grown rapidly during the past two decades. To derive the maximum results from media expenditures, a marketer must develop an effective media plan. A **media plan** sets forth the exact media vehicles to be used (specific magazines, television channels, newspapers and so forth) and the dates and times when the advertisements will appear. The effectiveness of the plan determines how many people in the advertising target will be exposed to the message. It also determines, to some degree, the effects of the message on those individuals. Media planning is a complex task that requires thorough analysis of the advertising target, as well as of any legal restrictions that might apply. For example, the EU has strict regulations pertaining to the advertising of tobacco, foods, pharmaceuticals and comparative advertising. More regulations are coming in connection with alcohol, financial services, cars, environmental labelling and the portrayal of women.

To formulate a media plan, the planner selects the media for a campaign and draws up a time schedule for each medium. The media planner's primary goal is to reach the largest possible number of people in the advertising target for the

Percentage of sales approach   A budgeting technique that involves multiplying a firm's past sales, plus a factor for planned sales growth or decline, by a standard percentage based on both what the firm traditionally spends on advertising and what the industry averages

Competition matching approach   A budgeting technique in which marketers match their major competitors' budgets or allocate the same percentage of sales for advertising as their competitors

Arbitrary approach   A budgeting technique in which a high level executive in the firm states how much can be spent on advertising over a certain time

Media plan   The process of establishing the exact media vehicles to be used for advertising, and the dates and times when the advertisements will appear

		Advertising Expenditure			
Rank	Advertiser	Total £'000s	TV %	Radio %	Press %
1	Procter & Gamble	117,444	94.3	0.2	5.5
2	British Telecommunications	94,682	55.9	2.1	42.1
3	Lever Brothers (Unilever)	69,338	70.5	0.5	29.0
4	Ford Motor Company	66,827	86.3	2.0	11.6
5	Kellogg Company	66,224	94.2	—	5.8
6	Vauxhall Motors	55,312	94.5	1.0	4.6
7	Procter & Gamble (Health & Beauty)	52,022	44.3	1.1	54.6
8	Dixons Stores	48,829	6.3	2.9	90.8
9	Birds Eye Wall's (Unilever)	43,666	80.3	0.1	19.5
10	Peugeot Talbot Motors	39,010	38.8	0.6	60.6
11	Renault (UK)	38,780	57.4	3.6	39.1
12	Elida Gibbs (Unilever)	35,883	84.0	0.4	15.6
13	Rover Group	34,932	45.9	1.2	52.9
14	Mars Confectionery	33,900	42.9	1.2	55.9
15	Citroën (UK)	32,514	94.6	0.5	4.9
16	Nestlé Rowntree	32,380	42.4	1.8	55.8
17	VAG (UK)	32,136	46.3	0.6	53.1
18	Nissan (GB)	32,035	37.3	0.5	62.2
19	Tesco	31,845	—	1.1	98.9
20	Gallaher Tobacco	29,554	33.1	0.1	66.9

NOTE: Outdoor, cinema, industrial and overseas publications are excluded. TV expenditure reflects an average discount of 1.3 per cent. Comparisons with previous years should be made with caution.

SOURCE: *The Marketing Pocket Book 1996* (Henley, Oxon: NTC Publications Ltd, 1995). Reprinted by permission.

Table 17.3 The top 20 UK advertisers, 1994 (compiled by Register-MEAL)

amount of money spent on media. In addition, a secondary goal is to achieve the appropriate message reach and frequency for the target audience while staying within the budget. *Reach* refers to the percentage of consumers in the advertising target actually exposed to a particular advertisement in a stated time period. *Frequency* is the number of times these targeted consumers were exposed to the advertisement.

Media planners begin with rather broad decisions; eventually, however, they must make very specific choices. A planner must first decide which kinds of media to use: radio, television, newspapers, magazines, direct mail, outdoor displays, public transport, the Internet,[9] or a combination of two or more of these. After making the general media decision, the planner selects specific sub-classes within each medium. Estée Lauder, for example, might advertise its Clinique cosmetic line in women's magazines, as well as during daytime, prime time and late night television.

Media planners take many factors into account as they devise a media plan. They analyse the location and demographic characteristics of people in the advertising target because the various media appeal to particular demographic groups in particular locations. For example, there are radio stations directed mainly at teenagers, magazines for men in the 18 to 34 age group and television programmes aimed at adults of both sexes. Media planners should also consider the size and type of audiences that specific media reach. Several data services collect and periodically publish information about the circulations and audiences of various media.

The cost of media is an important but troublesome consideration. Planners try to obtain the best coverage possible for the amount of money spent, yet there is no accurate way of comparing the cost and impact of a television advertisement with the cost and impact of a newspaper advertisement.

The content of the message sometimes affects the choice of media. Print media can be used more effectively than broadcast media to present many issues or numerous details. The makers of Tartare Light Fromage Frais produce wordy magazine advertisements, including recipes as well as product details, to boost demand and educate consumers about the product's uses. The advertisements appear in most women's and food magazines. If an advertiser wants to promote beautiful colours, patterns or textures, media that offer high quality colour reproduction—magazines or television—should be used instead of newspapers. For example, cosmetics can be far more effectively promoted in a full colour magazine advertisement than in a black and white newspaper advertisement.

Table 17.4 provides data on the amounts of advertising expenditure in Europe by media. The data indicate that different countries give greater priority to certain types of advertising media. The medium selected is determined by the

Country	Total	News-papers	Magazines	TV	Radio	Cinema	Outdoor/Transport
Germany	18,352.3	9,229.2	3,698.0	3,855.1	777.1	189.3	603.6
UK	11,518.5	4,911.8	2,032.4	3,740.2	338.7	66.6	428.8
France	8,753.6	2,183.0	2,026.3	2,792.7	666.4	50.4	1,034.8
Italy	4,997.5	1,076.1	848.6	2,866.0	68.7	n/a	138.1
Spain	4,223.8	1,350.8	686.5	1,573.7	395.8	34.7	192.2
Netherlands	2,982.4	1,403.3	757.7	587.4	123.6	11.5	98.9
Switzerland	2,415.0	1,389.2	438.7	210.6	69.5	21.9	285.2
Sweden	1,581.9	1,010.9	170.8	294.5	21.3	10.4	74.1
Austria	1,480.4	653.7	268.5	328.5	146.2	5.5	77.9
Belgium	1,354.3	356.4	349.4	416.6	104.6	12.0	115.3
Denmark	1,179.5	734.6	188.6	202.3	25.9	6.9	21.1
Greece	967.3	135.0	135.7	634.9	42.6	n/a	19.0
Norway	847.1	512.7	106.5	151.6	50.8	5.1	20.5
Finland	832.7	509.1	111.1	159.9	29.6	0.8	22.2
Portugal	704.2	120.2	118.0	385.8	34.9	n/a	45.3
Ireland	463.3	265.9	22.5	115.5	35.6	3.4	20.2

NOTES: Data are net of discounts; they include agency commission and press classified advertising but exclude production costs. Data are ranked on total ad spend.

SOURCE: *The European Marketing Pocket Book 1996* (Henley, Oxon: NTC Publications Ltd, 1995). Reprinted by permission.

Table 17.4 Advertising expenditure by country and medium (US$m)—1994

Medium	Types	Unit of Sale	Factors Affecting Rates	Cost Comparison Indicator	Advantages	Disadvantages
Newspaper	National Local Morning Evening Sunday Sunday supplement Weekly Special	Column cms/inches Counted words Printed lines Agate lines	Volume and frequency discounts Number of colours Position charges for preferred and guaranteed positions Circulation level	Milline rate = cost per agate line × 1,000,000 divided by circulation Cost per column cm/inch	Almost everyone reads a newspaper; purchased to be read; selective for socio-economic groups; national geographic flexibility; short lead time; frequent publication; favourable for co-operative advertising; merchandising services	Short life; limited reproduction capabilities; large advertising volume limits exposure to any one advertisement
Magazine	Consumer Farm Business Sports Travel	Pages Partial pages Column cms/inches	Circulation level Cost of publishing Type of audience Volume discounts Frequency discounts Size of advertisement Position of advertisement (covers) Number of colours Regional issues	Cost per thousand (CPM) = cost per page × 1,000 divided by circulation	Socio-economic selectivity; good reproduction; long life; prestige; geographic selectivity when regional issues are available; read in leisurely manner	High absolute monetary cost; long lead time
Direct mail	Letters Catalogues Price lists Calendars Brochures Coupons Circulars Newsletters Postcards Booklets Samples	Not applicable	Cost of mailing lists Postage Production costs	Cost per contact	Little wasted circulation; highly selective; circulation controlled by advertiser; few distractions; personal; stimulates action; use of novelty; easy to measure performance; hidden from competitors	Expensive; no editorial matter to attract readers; considered junk mail by many; criticised as invasion of privacy

(Continues)

Table 17.5 Characteristics, advantages and disadvantages of major advertising media

Radio	AM FM	Programme types Spots: 5, 10, 20, 30, 60 seconds	Time of day Audience size Length of spot or programme Volume and frequency discounts	Cost per thousand (CPM) = cost per minute $\times$ 1,000 divided by audience size	Highly mobile; low cost broadcast medium; message can be quickly changed; geographic selectivity; socio-economic selectivity	Little national radio advertising; provides only audio message; has lost prestige; short life of message; listeners' attention limited because of other activities while listening
Television	ITV Satellite Cable	Programme types Spots: 15, 20, 30, 60 seconds	Time of day Length of spot Volume and frequency discounts Audience size	Cost per thousand (CPM) = cost per minute $\times$ 1,000 divided by audience size	Reaches large audience; low cost per exposure; uses both audio and video; highly visible; high prestige; geographic and socio-economic selectivity	High monetary costs; highly perishable message; size of audience not guaranteed; prime time limited
Inside public transport	Buses Underground	Full, half and quarter showings are sold on a monthly basis	Number of passengers Multiple-month discounts Production costs Position	Cost per thousand passengers	Low cost; "captive" audience; geographic selectivity	Does not secure quick results
Outside public transport	Buses Taxis	Full, half and quarter showings; space also rented on per unit basis	Number of advertisements Position Size	Cost per 100 exposures	Low cost; geographic selectivity; reaches broad, diverse audience	Lacks socio-economic selectivity; does not have high impact on readers
Outdoor	Papered posters/billboards Painted displays Spectaculars Poster vans	Papered posters: sold on monthly basis in multiples Painted displays and spectaculars; sold on per unit basis	Length of time purchased Land rental Cost of production Intensity of traffic Frequency and continuity discounts Location	No standard indicator	Allows for repetition; low cost; message can be placed close to the point of sale; geographic selectivity; works 24 hours a day	Message must be short and simple; no socio-economic selectivity; seldom attracts readers' full attention; criticised for being traffic hazard and blight on countryside

SOURCES: Some of the information in this table is from S. Watson Dunn and Arnold M. Barban, *Advertising: Its Role in Modern Marketing*, 6th edn (Hinsdale, Ill.: Dryden Press, 1986); and Anthony F. McGann and J. Thomas Russell, *Advertising Media* (Homewood, Ill.: Irwin, 1981).

characteristics, advantages and disadvantages of the major media available (see Table 17.5).

Given the variety of vehicles within each medium, media planners must deal with a vast number of choices. The multitude of factors that affect media rates obviously adds to the complexity of media planning. A **cost comparison indicator** lets an advertiser compare the costs of several vehicles within a specific medium (such as two newspapers) in relation to the number of people reached by each vehicle. For example, the "milline rate" is the cost comparison indicator for newspapers; it shows the cost of exposing a million people to a space equal to one agate line.*

Cost comparison indicator A measure that allows an advertiser to compare the costs of several vehicles within a specific medium in relation to the number of people reached by each vehicle

Creating the Advertising Message

The basic content and form of an advertising message are a function of several factors. The product's features, uses and benefits affect the content of the message. Characteristics of the people in the advertising target—their sex, age, education, ethnic origin, income, occupation and other attributes—influence both the content and form. When Procter & Gamble promotes its Crest toothpaste to children, the company emphasises the importance of daily brushing and decay control. When it markets Crest to adults, it discusses tartar and plaque. To communicate effectively, an advertiser must use words, symbols and illustrations that are meaningful, familiar and attractive to the people who constitute the advertising target.

The objectives and platform of an advertising campaign also affect the content and form of its messages. For example, if a firm's advertising objectives involve large sales increases, the message demands hard hitting, high impact language and symbols. When campaign objectives aim at increasing brand awareness, the message may use much repetition of the brand name and words and illustrations associated with it. Thus the advertising platform is the foundation on which campaign messages are built.

The choice of media obviously influences the content and form of the message. Effective outdoor displays and short broadcast spot announcements require concise, simple messages. Magazine and newspaper advertisements can include more detail and long explanations. Because several different kinds of media offer geographic selectivity, a precise message can be tailored to a particular geographic section of the advertising target. Some magazine and national newspaper publishers produce **regional issues**: for a particular issue, the advertisements and editorial content of copies appearing in one geographic area differ from those appearing in other areas. A clothing manufacturer might decide to use one message in London and another in the rest of the UK. A company may also choose to advertise in only a few regions. Such geographic selectivity lets a firm use the same message in different regions at different times.

Regional issues Versions of a magazine or newspaper that differ across geographic regions in their advertising and editorial content

The basic components of a print advertising message are shown in Figure 17.4. The messages for most advertisements depend on the use of copy and artwork. These two elements are now examined in more detail.

Copy The verbal portion of an advertisement

Copy The verbal portion of an advertisement is **copy**. It includes headlines, subheadlines, body copy and the signature (see Figure 17.4). When preparing advertising copy, marketers attempt to move readers through a persuasive sequence called **AIDA**: attention, interest, desire and action. Not all copy need be this extensive, however.

AIDA A persuasive sequence used in advertisements: attention, interest, desire and action

*An agate line is one column wide and the height of the smallest type normally used in classified newspaper advertisements. There are fourteen agate lines in one column inch.

Figure 17.4

Copy and artwork elements of printed advertisements

This advertisement clearly differentiates the basic elements of print advertising.

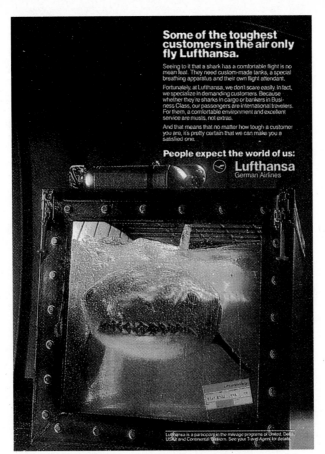

Headline

Body Copy

Sub-headline
Signature

Illustration

SOURCE: *Courtesy of Lufthansa German Airlines.*

The headline is critical because often it is the only part of the copy that people read. It should attract readers' attention and create enough interest to make them want to read the body copy. The sub-headline, if there is one, links the headline to the body copy. Sometimes it helps explain the headline.

Body copy for most advertisements consists of an introductory statement or paragraph, several explanatory paragraphs and a closing paragraph. Some copywriters have adopted a pattern or set of guidelines to develop body copy systematically: (1) identify a specific desire or problem of consumers, (2) suggest the good or service as the best way to satisfy that desire or solve that problem, (3) state the advantages and benefits of the product, (4) indicate why the advertised product is the best for the buyer's particular situation, (5) substantiate the claims and advantages, and (6) ask the buyer for action.[10]

The signature identifies the sponsor of the advertisement. It may contain several elements, including the firm's trademark, logo, name and address. The signature should be designed to be attractive, legible, distinctive and easy to identify in a variety of sizes.

Because radio listeners often are not fully "tuned in" mentally, radio copy should be informal and conversational to attract their attention and achieve greater impact. The radio message is highly perishable. Thus radio copy should consist of short, familiar terms. Its length should not require a delivery rate exceeding approximately two and a half words per second.

COGENT
Advertising Copy

Client: Premier–
    Cadbury's Fingers

Job No: 3149   Date: 26.1.94

Job Name: 30" TV
    Fingular Fiddle

Ref No: SS/jw   Issue: Final post
                   production

VISUAL	SOUND
Open on a light purple stage set with purple curtains and a flight of Hollywood-Musical style chocolate Finger steps reaching up into the distance.	MUSIC THROUGHOUT
Michael Barrymore is standing in front of a music stand. He taps a chocolate Finger on the stand in the manner of a conductor. He holds the Finger up to camera.	Michael Barrymore: Ohhhh!
He holds it up length-ways and sideways, then runs it across his arm like a violin bow.	They're singular, they're fingular.... They're only as tall as they're wide ....
He's tickled by a large Finger coming from off screen.	....Their middles are thick, As the stick on a fiddle.... ....And they tickle your middle inside....
He dissolves with laughter.	

VISUAL	SOUND
A large finger swings across, chasing him off stage, and re-appears with Barrymore sitting astride swinging off the opposite side of the stage.	....The creamy coat delights your throat.... ....Goes down like chocolate silk....
Barrymore's head pops up in front of screen with normal sized chocolate Finger.	
The voice-over comes in. Barrymore tries to hold the note over the message. His face shows the strain.	But the most singular thing in a Finger....
He finishes the high note with some relief, and holds up the box, which, until now, made up the purple band.	MVO: Chocolate Fingers. The fingular biscuit from Cadbury.
(CADBURY TEAR APPEARS) (PACKSHOT)	Barrymore: ....the Cadbury's Dairy Milk.
He pops a chocolate finger in his mouth.	Lovely bisc-ew-its!
Super: The fingular biscuit from Cadbury.	

Figure 17.5   Example of a parallel script. Agency Cogent advertises Cadbury's Fingers.

SOURCE: *Courtesy of Cogent Elliott Ltd.*

In television copy, the audio material must not over power the visual material and vice versa. However, a television message should make optimal use of its visual portion. As Figure 17.5 illustrates, copy for a television advertisement is initially written in parallel script form. The video is described in the left column and the audio in the right column. When the parallel script is approved, the copywriter and the artist combine the copy with the visual material through use of a **storyboard** (see Figure 17.6), which depicts a series of miniature television screens showing the sequence of major scenes in the advertisement. Technical personnel use the storyboard as a blueprint when they produce the advertisement.

Storyboard A series of miniature television screens used to show the sequence of major scenes in the advertisement

Artwork   **Artwork** consists of the illustration and layout of the advertisement (see Figure 17.4). Although **illustrations** are often photographs, they can also be drawings, graphs, charts or tables. Illustrations are used to attract attention, to encourage the audience to read or listen to the copy, to communicate an idea quickly or to communicate an idea that is difficult to put into words.[11] They are especially important because consumers tend to recall the visual portion of advertisements better than the verbal portions. Advertisers use a variety of illustration techniques, which are identified and described in Table 17.6.

Artwork The illustration and layout of the advertisement

Illustrations Photographs, drawings, graphs, charts or tables used in advertisement artwork

The **layout** of an advertisement is the physical arrangement of the illustration, headline, sub-headline, body copy and signature. The arrangement of these parts in Figure 17.4 is only one possible layout. These same elements could be arranged in many ways. The final layout is the result of several stages of preparation. As it moves through these stages, the layout helps people involved in developing the

Layout The physical arrangement of the illustration, headline, sub-headline, body copy and signature of an advertisement

Figure 17.6 Final storyboard for Cadbury's Fingers advertisement

Source: Courtesy of Cogent Elliott Ltd.

advertising campaign exchange ideas. It also provides instructions for production personnel.

Executing the Campaign

The execution of an advertising campaign requires an extensive amount of planning and co-ordination. Regardless of whether or not an organisation uses an advertising agency, many people and organisations are involved in the execution of a campaign.[12] Production companies, research organisations, media firms, printers, photo engravers and commercial artists are just a few of the people and organisations that contribute to a campaign.

Implementation requires detailed schedules to ensure that various phases of the work are done on time. Advertising management personnel must evaluate the quality of the work and take corrective action when necessary. In some instances, changes have to be made during the campaign so that it meets campaign objectives more effectively.

Evaluating the Effectiveness of the Advertising

Pre-tests Evaluations performed before an advertising campaign begins to assess the effectiveness of one or more elements of the message

Consumer focus group A semi-structured discussion, led by a moderator, involving actual or potential buyers of advertised products who are asked to judge one or several dimensions of the advertisements

There are various ways to test the effectiveness of advertising. They include measuring achievement of advertising objectives; assessing the effectiveness of copy, illustrations or layouts; and evaluating certain media.

Advertising can be evaluated before, during and after the campaign. Evaluations performed before the campaign begins are called **pre-tests** and usually attempt to evaluate the effectiveness of one or more elements of the message. To pre-test advertisements, marketers sometimes use a **consumer focus group,** a number of people who are actual or potential buyers of the advertised product. Members are asked to judge one or several dimensions of two or more advertisements. Such tests are based on the belief that consumers are more likely than advertising experts to know what will influence them.

To measure advertising effectiveness during a campaign, marketers usually take advantage of "enquiries". In the initial stages of a campaign, an advertiser may use several direct response advertisements simultaneously, each containing a coupon or a form requesting information. The advertiser records the number of coupons that are returned from each type of advertisement. If an advertiser receives 78,528 coupons from advertisement A, 37,072 coupons from advertisement B and 47,932

Illustration Technique	Description
Product alone	Simplest method; advantageous when appearance is important, when identification is important, when trying to keep a brand name or package in the public eye, or when selling through mail order
Emphasis on special features	Shows and emphasises special details or features as well as advantages; used when product is unique because of special features
Product in setting	Shows what can be done with product; people, surroundings or environment hint at what product can do; often used in food advertisements
Product in use	Puts action into the advertisement; can remind readers of benefits gained from using product; must be careful not to make visual cliché; should not include anything that will divert attention from product; used to direct readers' eyes towards product
Product being tested	Uses test to dramatise product's uses and benefits versus competing products
Results of product's use	Emphasises satisfaction from using product; can liven up dull product; useful when nothing new can be said
Dramatising headline	Appeal of illustration dramatises headline; can emphasise appeal but dangerous to use illustrations that do not correlate with headlines
Dramatising situation	Presents problem situation or shows situation in which problem has been resolved
Comparison	Compares product with "something" established; the something must be positive and familiar to audience
Contrast	Shows difference between two products or two ideas or differences in effects between use and non-use; before and after format is a commonly used contrast technique
Diagrams, charts and graphs	Used to communicate complex information quickly; may make presentations more interesting
Phantom effects	X-ray or internal view; can see inside product; helpful to explain concealed or internal mechanism
Symbolic	Symbols used to represent abstract ideas that are difficult to illustrate; effective if readers understand symbol; must be positive correlation between symbol and idea
Testimonials	Actually shows the testifier; should use famous person or someone to whom audience can relate

SOURCES: Dorothy Cohen, *Advertising* (New York: Wiley, 1972), pp. 458–464; and S. Watson Dunn and Arnold M. Barban, *Advertising: Its Role in Modern Marketing*, 6th edn (Hinsdale, Ill.: Dryden Press, 1986), pp. 497–498.

Table 17.6 Illustration techniques for advertisements

coupons from advertisement C, advertisement A is judged superior to advertisements B and C. For advertisements that do not demand action—coupon filling or dialling an 0800 Freephone number—enquiries are difficult to monitor.

Evaluation of advertising effectiveness after the campaign is over is called a **post-campaign test** or **post-test**. Advertising objectives often indicate what kind of post-test will be appropriate. If an advertiser sets objectives in terms of communication—product awareness, brand awareness or attitude change—then the post-test should measure changes in one or more of these dimensions. Typically, qualitative marketing research (focus groups or depth interviews) is used before, during and after a campaign to monitor shifts in consumers' perceptions. It is

Post-campaign test or **post-test** The evaluation of advertising effectiveness after a campaign hoped that brand awareness will have improved following the running of a particular advertising campaign. Advertisers sometimes use consumer surveys or experiments to evaluate a campaign based on communication objectives. These methods are costly, however.

For campaign objectives that are stated in terms of sales, advertisers should determine the change in sales or market share that can be attributed to the campaign. Unfortunately, such changes brought about by advertising cannot be measured precisely;[13] many factors independent of advertisements affect a firm's sales and market share. Competitive actions, government actions and changes in economic conditions, consumer preferences and weather are only a few factors that might enhance or diminish a company's sales or market share. However, by using data about past and current sales and advertising expenditures, an advertiser can make gross estimates of the effects of a campaign on sales or market share.

Because consumer surveys and experiments are so expensive, and because it is so difficult to determine the direct effects of advertising on sales, many advertisers evaluate print advertisements according to the degree to which consumers can remember them. The post-test methods based on memory include recognition and recall tests. Such tests are usually performed by research organisations through consumer surveys. If a **recognition test** is used, individual respondents are shown the actual advertisement and asked whether they recognise it. If they do, the interviewer asks additional questions to determine how much of the advertisement each respondent read. When recall is evaluated, the respondents are not shown the actual advertisement but instead are asked about what they have seen or heard recently.

Recall can be measured through either unaided or aided recall methods. In an **unaided** or **spontaneous recall test,** subjects are asked to identify advertisements that they have seen recently but are given no clues to help them remember. A similar procedure is used with **aided** or **prompted recall test,** except that subjects are shown a list of products, brands, company names or trademarks to jog their memories. Several research organisations, such as Nielsen, Audience Selection and Gallup, provide research services that test recognition and recall of advertisements (see Table 17.7).

The major justification for using recognition and recall methods is that people are more likely to buy a product if they can remember an advertisement about it than if they cannot. However, recalling an advertisement does not necessarily lead to buying the product or brand advertised. Research shows that the more "likeable" an advertisement is, the more it will influence consumers. People who enjoy an advertisement are twice as likely to be persuaded that the advertised brand is best. Of about 16 per cent of those who liked an advertisement, a significant number increased their preference for the brand. Only a small percentage of those who were neutral about the advertisement felt more favourable towards the brand as a result of the advertisement.[14] The type of programme in which the product is advertised can also affect consumers' feelings about the advertisement and the product it promotes. Viewers judge advertisements placed in happy programmes as more effective and recall them somewhat better.[15]

Researchers are also using a sophisticated technique called single source data to help evaluate advertisements. With this technique, individuals' behaviour is tracked from television sets to the checkout counter. Monitors are placed in preselected homes, and microcomputers record when the television set is on and which channel is being viewed. At the supermarket checkout, the individual in the sample household presents an identification card. The cashier records the

Recognition test A test in which an actual advertisement is shown to individual respondents, who are then asked whether they recognise it

Unaided or **spontaneous recall test** A test in which subjects are asked to identify advertisements that they have seen recently but are given no clues to help them remember

Aided or **prompted recall test** A test in which subjects are asked to identify advertisements while being shown a list of products, brands, company names or trademarks to jog their memory

	Last Week	Account	Agency/TV Buyer	%
1	(1)	BT	Abbott Mead Vickers BBDO/IDK	88
2	(3)	Coca-Cola	Wieden & Kennedy/Universal McCann	71
3	(2)	Safeway	Bates Dorland/Zenith	69
4	(–)	Vodafone	BMP DDB/Needham	66
5	(–)	Tango	HHCL/BBJ Media	63
6	(–)	VW Polo	BMP DDB/BBJ Media	61
7	(–)	Gillette Right Guard	Saatchi & Saatchi/BMP Media	52
8	(–)	Somerfield	Butler Lutos Sutton Wilkinson/CIA Medianetwork	49
9	(16=)	Royal Mail Stamps	Bates Dorland/The Media Centre	47
10=	(–)	Impulse	Ogilvy & Mather/Initiative Media	46
10=	(–)	Railtrack Privatisation	WCRS	46
12	(–)	Lenor	Grey Advertising/P&G Media	45
13	(–)	Royal Bank of Scotland	Faulds Advertising	42
14	(–)	Wall's Too Good to Be True	McCann-Erickson/Initiative Media	36
15	(–)	Intel	Dahlin Smith White (US)/Optimedia	35
16	(–)	Saab 900	Barker & Ralston/Universal McCann	34
17	(–)	Monster Munch	Abbott Mead Vickers BBDO/The Media Centre	29
18	(–)	Elida Organics	J. Walter Thomspon/Initiative Media	28
19	(–)	Nivea Active Hydro Lotion	TBWA/Eurospace	25
20	(–)	Clairol Natural Instincts	JWT New York/Zenith	21

NOTE: Adwatch research was conducted 14 June to 16 June 1996 by Audience Selection (0171-608 3618) using Phonebus, a weekly telephone omnibus survey among more than 1,000 adults. Advertisements were selected by CTC (0171-439 7096) and CIA Medianetwork (0171-633 9999). Analysis and further information from The Planning Partnership (0171-430 1641). Full sets of Adwatch data including demographic analysis are available from Jonti Campbell at Audience Selection tel 0171-608 3618. Fee £150.

SOURCE: Adwatch research reprinted from *Marketing*, 27 June 1996, p. 14. Used by permission of *Marketing* magazine and Audience Selection.

Table 17.7 Results of tested recall of advertisements

purchases by scanner, and the data are sent to the research facility. This technique is bringing more insight into people's buying patterns than ever before. The use of technology and scanning techniques is discussed in more detail in Chapter 6.

• • • • • • • • • • • • • • • • • •

Who Develops the Advertising Campaign?

An advertising campaign may be handled by (1) an individual or a few people within the firm, (2) an advertising department within the organisation or (3) an advertising agency.

In very small firms, one or two individuals are responsible for advertising and many other activities as well. Usually these individuals depend heavily on personnel at local newspapers and broadcasting stations for copywriting, artwork and advice about scheduling media.

In certain types of large businesses—especially in larger retail organisations—advertising departments create and implement advertising campaigns. Depending on the size of the advertising programme, an advertising department may consist of a few multi-skilled people or a sizeable number of specialists, such as copywriters, artists, media buyers and technical production co-ordinators. An advertising department sometimes obtains the services of independent research organisations and also hires freelance specialists when they are needed for a particular project.

When an organisaton uses an advertising agency, such as Ogilvy & Mather or JWT, the firm and the agency usually develop the advertising campaign jointly. How much each party participates in the campaign's total development depends on the working relationship between the firm and the agency. Ordinarily, a firm relies on the agency for copywriting, artwork, technical production and formulation of the media plan.

An advertising agency can assist a business in several ways. An agency, especially a larger one, supplies the firm with the services of highly skilled specialists—not only copywriters, artists and production co-ordinators but also media experts, researchers and legal advisers. Agency personnel have often had broad experience in advertising and are usually more objective than a firm's employees about the organisation's products. Figure 17.7 outlines the composition of a typical advertising agency.

Because an agency traditionally receives most of its income from a 15 per cent commission on media purchases, a firm can obtain some agency services at a low or moderate cost. For example, if an agency contracts for £400,000 of television time for a firm, it receives a commission of £60,000 from the television company. Although the traditional compensation method for agencies is changing and now includes other factors, the media commission still offsets some costs of using an agency. BMP DDB Needham is considering breaking the mould; the agency would be paid by results. Clients would pay a bonus to the agency for meeting targets or receive a payback (refund) if the advertising failed to deliver.[16]

Now that advertising has been explored as a potential promotional mix ingredient, it is time to consider a related ingredient, publicity, and its controlling mechanism, public relations.

Figure 17.7
A typical advertising agency structure

Strategy co-ordination
Production liaison

Concept
Art direction and copywriting

Client services

Creative

Account planning

Media

Marketing research
Strategy development

Planning and buying

Publicity and Public Relations

As indicated in Chapter 16, **publicity** is communication in news story form about an organisation, its products or both that is transmitted through a mass medium at no charge (although the publicity activity will incur production and personnel costs). Publicity can be presented through a variety of vehicles, several of which are examined here.

Within an organisation, publicity is sometimes viewed as part of public relations—a larger, more comprehensive communications function. **Public relations** is the planned and sustained effort to establish and maintain goodwill and mutual understanding between an organisation and its **target publics:** customers, employees, shareholders, trade bodies, suppliers, government officials and society in general.[17] Publicity is the result of various public relations efforts. For example, when Tesco decided to make a special effort to stock environmentally safe products and packaging, its public relations department sent out press releases to various newspapers, magazines and television contacts, as well as to its suppliers. The result was publicity in the form of magazine articles, newspaper acknowledgements and television coverage. Towards the end of the 1980s, public relations was the fastest growing element in the promotional mix.[18]

Publicity and Advertising Compared

Although publicity and advertising both depend on mass media, they differ in several respects. Advertising messages tend to be informative or persuasive, whereas publicity is primarily informative. Advertisements are sometimes designed to have an immediate impact on sales; publicity messages are more subdued. Publicity releases do not identify sponsors; advertisements do. The sponsor pays for media time or space for advertising, but not for publicity, and there is therefore no guarantee of inclusion. Communications through publicity are usually included as part of a programme or a print story, but advertisements are normally separated from the broadcast programmes or editorial portions of print media so that the audience or readers can easily recognise (or ignore) them. Publicity may have greater credibility than advertising among consumers because as a news story it may appear more objective. Finally, a firm can use advertising to repeat the same messages as many times as desired; publicity is generally not subject to repetition.

Kinds of Publicity

There are several types of publicity mechanism.[19] The most common is the **press (news) release** which is usually a single page of typewritten copy containing fewer than 300 words. A press release, sometimes called a news release, also gives the firm's or agency's name, its address and phone number, and the contact person.[20] Car makers often use press releases to introduce new products. Figure 17.8 is an example of a press release. A **feature article** is a longer manuscript (up to 3,000 words) that is usually prepared for a specific publication. A **captioned photograph** is a photograph with a brief description explaining the picture's content. Captioned photographs are especially effective for illustrating a new or improved product with highly visible features.

There are several other kinds of publicity. A **press conference** is a meeting called to announce major news events. Media personnel are invited and are usually supplied with written materials and photographs. In addition, letters to the editor and editorials are sometimes prepared and sent to newspapers and magazines. However, newspaper editors frequently allocate space on their editorial pages to

Figure 17.8

Example of a press release
Countrywide's press release
for client Blue Circle
Cement capitalises on the
growing awareness of environmental issues.

COUNTRYWIDE PORTER NOVELLI

**press
information**

BC661/011/96
8 May 1996

ENVIRONMENTAL FIRST FOR BLUE CIRCLE

Blue Circle, the country's largest cement manufacturer, has been awarded a
'first' for its commitment to environmental management at its Aberthaw Works
in South Wales.

The site, which employs 125 people, has become UK's first (and, it is believed,
the world's first) cement works to receive certification against the requirements
of British Standard BS7760 (Environmental Management Systems).

The award recognises the company's commitment to environmental management
through the establishment of effective procedures and systems across the whole
of its operation at Aberthaw, which started producing cement back in 1914.

This first award of its kind for Blue Circle Cement marks the start of its
programme to aim to attain this standard for all its 11 Business Units across
the country.

"Blue Circle Cement is sending a clear message that it takes its environmental
responsibilities seriously", said Alan Whitehead, Managing Director of Lloyds
Register Quality Assurance, the certicating authority.

-ends-

<u>For further information please contact:</u>

Michele Sutton
Countrywide Porter Novelli
Tel: 01295 272288   Fax: 01295 270659

FS 24906
SC 9001

Countrywide Porter Novelli
Communications House
51 The Green
South Bar, Banbury
Oxfordshire OX16 9AB
Tel: +44 (0) 1295 272288
Fax: +44 (0) 1295 270859

A MEMBER OF PORTER NOVELLI INTERNATIONAL
THE MANAGEMENT OF REPUTATION WORLDWIDE

SOURCE: *Reproduced by kind permission of the Countrywide
Communications Group, England.*

local writers and national columnists. Finally, films and tapes may be distributed
to broadcasting companies in the hope that they will be aired. The broader remit
of public relations also includes training personnel to meet and handle the media
(journalists); arranging interviews; establishing links with VIPs and influential
bodies; managing visits, seminars and meetings; and maintaining information
flows within the organisation.

A marketer's choice of specific types of publicity depends on considerations
that include the type of information being transmitted, the characteristics of the
target audience, the receptivity of media personnel, the importance of the item to
the public, and the amount of information that needs to be presented. Sometimes
a marketer uses a single type of publicity in a promotional mix. In other cases, a
marketer may use a variety of publicity mechanisms, with publicity being the primary ingredient in the promotional mix. **Third party endorsement** increases the
credibility of publicity and public relations; this is a recommendation (written,
verbal or visual) from an opinion leader or respected personality.

Third party endorsement A
recommendation from an opinion
leader or respected personality
used to increase the credibility of
publicity and public relations

Uses of Publicity

Publicity has a number of uses. It can make people aware of a firm's products,
brands or activities; help a company maintain a certain level of positive public visibility; and enhance a particular image, such as innovativeness or progressiveness.
Companies also try to overcome negative images through publicity. Some firms

Marketing Developments

New products
New uses for old products
Research developments
Changes of marketing personnel
Large orders received
Successful bids
Awards of contracts
Special events

Company Policies

New guarantees
Changes in credit terms
Changes in distribution policies
Changes in service policies
Changes in prices

News of General Interest

Annual election of directors
Meetings of the board of directors
Anniversaries of the organisation
Anniversaries of an invention
Anniversaries of the senior directors
Holidays that can be tied to the organisation's
    activities
Annual banquets
Conferences and special meetings
Open house to the community
Athletic events
Awards of merit to employees
Laying of cornerstone
Opening of an exhibition

Reports on Current Developments

Reports of experiments
Reports on industry conditions
Company progress reports
Employment, production and sales statistics
Reports on new discoveries
Tax reports
Speeches by principals
Analyses of economic conditions
Employment gains
Financial statements
Organisation appointments
Opening of new markets
Government trade awards

Personalities—Names Are News

Visits by famous persons
Accomplishments of individuals
Winners of company contests
Employees' and directors' advancements
Interviews with company officials
Company employees serving as judges for
    contests
Interviews with employees

Slogans, Symbols, Endorsements

Company's slogan—its history and
    development
A tie-in of company activities with slogan
Creation of a slogan
The company's trademark
The company's name plate
Product endorsements

SOURCE: Albert Wesley Frey, ed., *Marketing Handbook*, Second Edition. (New York: Ronald Press, 1965), pp. 19–35. Copyright © 1965. Reprinted by permission of John Wiley & Sons, Inc.

Table 17.8 Possible topics for publicity releases

seek publicity for a single purpose and others for several purposes. As Table 17.8 shows, publicity releases can tackle a multitude of specific issues. It must be remembered that an organisation has a number of audiences—customers, suppliers, distributors, shareholders, journalists—as well as its internal market: its employees and management. Publicity needs to target all of these publics.

Requirements of a Publicity Programme

For maximum benefit, a firm should create and maintain a systematic, continuous publicity programme.[21] A single individual or department—within the organisation or from its advertising agency or public relations firm—should be responsible for managing the programme. Relationships must be maintained with the media, particularly to facilitate crisis management public relations.

It is important to establish and maintain good working relationships with media personnel. Often personal contact with editors, reporters and other news personnel is essential; without their input a company may find it hard to design its publicity programme so as to facilitate the work of newspeople.

Media personnel reject a great deal of publicity material because it is poorly written or not newsworthy. To maintain an effective publicity programme, a firm must strive to avoid these flaws. Guidelines and checklists can aid it in this task. Material submitted must match the particular newspaper's style, for example in length, punctuation and layout.

Finally, an organisation has to evaluate its publicity efforts.[22] Usually, the effectiveness of publicity is measured by the number of releases actually published or broadcast. To monitor print media and determine which releases are published and how often, an organisation can hire a cuttings service—a firm that cuts out and sends published news releases to client companies. To measure the effectiveness of television publicity, a company can enclose a card with its publicity releases and request that the television company record its name and the dates when the news item is broadcast, but companies do not always comply. Though some television and radio tracking services do exist, they are extremely costly.

| **Dealing with Unfavourable Publicity** | Up to this point publicity has been discussed as a planned promotional mix ingredient. However, companies may have to deal with unfavourable publicity regarding an unsafe product, an accident, the actions of a dishonest employee or some other negative event. For example, when British Airways' Lord King had to apologise publicly to a rival airline, Virgin Atlantic Airways, and its boss, Richard Branson, for a "dirty tricks campaign", BA's credibility was severely damaged and seat reservations reportedly declined significantly.[23] The BSE beef crisis has forced government departments, farming bodies, meat producers, supermarket companies and consumer associations to deal with unfavourable publicity. |

Such unfavourable publicity can arise quickly and dramatically. A single negative event that produces unfavourable publicity can wipe out a company's favourable image and destroy consumer attitudes that took years to build through promotional efforts. Moreover, the mass media today can disseminate information faster and to larger audiences than ever before, and bad news generally receives much attention in the media. Thus the negative publicity surrounding an unfavourable event now reaches more people.[24] By dealing effectively with a negative situation, an organisation can minimise the damage from unfavourable publicity.

To protect an organisation's image, it is important to avoid unfavourable publicity or at least to lessen its effects. First and foremost, the organisation can directly reduce negative incidents and events through safety programmes, inspections and effective quality control procedures. However, because organisations obviously cannot eliminate all negative occurrences, they need to establish policies and procedures for the news coverage of such events. These policies and procedures should aim at reducing negative impact.

In most cases, organisations should expedite news coverage of negative events rather than try to discourage or block it. The expediting approach not only tends to diminish the fall out from negative events but also fosters a positive relationship with media personnel. Such a relationship is essential if news personnel are to co-operate with a company and broadcast favourable news stories about it. Facts are likely to be reported accurately, but if news coverage is discouraged, rumours and misinformation may be passed along. An unfavourable event can easily be blown up into a scandal or a tragedy. It can even cause public panic.

Crisis management A process in which a company responds to negative events by identifying key targets (publics) for which to provide publicity, developing a well rehearsed contingency plan and providing access for journalists

Crisis management involves the identification of key targets (publics) for which to provide material or publicity; the need for a well rehearsed contingency plan and public relations exercise; the ability and skills of the organisation to report quickly and accurately details of the crisis itself; and the provision of immediate access by journalists to information and personnel. Above all, the organisation must remain in control of the situation and the material being published or broadcast.

Limitations in Using Publicity

Free media publicity is a double-edged sword: the financial advantage comes with several drawbacks. If company messages are to be published or broadcast, media personnel must judge them newsworthy. Consequently, messages must be timely, interesting and accurate. Many communications simply do not qualify. It may take time and effort to convince media personnel of the news value of publicity releases. Even a top public relations consultancy achieves a hit rate of only one out of every four press releases being published in the press.

Although marketers usually encourage media personnel to air a publicity release at a certain time, they control neither the content nor the timing of the communication. Media personnel alter the length and content of publicity releases to fit publishers' or broadcasters' requirements and may even delete the parts of the message that the firm deems most important. Furthermore, media personnel use publicity releases in time slots or positions that are most convenient for them; thus the messages often appear at times or in locations that may not reach the firm's target audiences. These limitations can be frustrating. Nevertheless, properly managed publicity offers an organisation substantial benefits at relatively low cost.

Trends Impacting on Advertising and Public Relations

The world of advertising is facing significant changes. Briefly, these include a mixture of business trends and client-induced pressures. For example, a growing number of agencies are having to offer pan-European capabilities as major advertisers believe they must consider pan-European campaigns. The major international agencies already have widespread office networks, but for the smaller agencies there is a need to establish links with small agencies in other countries. With the concentration of media ownership across borders, agencies and clients have to be able to negotiate package deals across countries.[25] Rupert Murdoch's media empire, which covers newspapers, magazines, radio, satellite and terrestrial television all the way from the Pacific Rim through North America and across Europe, is a prime illustration. There is increasing pressure on advertising agencies and public relations consultancies to justify the value of their activities and campaigns. Simple qualitative research into the visual appeal of a particular campaign is not seen as sufficient by major advertisers. These clients have short term sales gains as a motivation for advertising; many advertising personnel, however, believe that the role of advertising is also critical for longer term **brand building**, as a brand's image and standing are developed with intended long term benefits for brand awareness and brand value.[26]

Brand building Developing a brand's image and standing with a view to creating long term benefits for brand awareness and brand value

Senior advertising agency figures are also aware that the recession of the early 1990s caused many clients to downgrade their advertising budgets and to re-evaluate their promotional spend. The result has been the rationalisation of agencies, leading to mergers, even closures, and an urgency among agencies to seek competitive edges over their rivals. There are now also far fewer medium sized advertising agencies, the field having polarised into major international advertising agencies and numerous local or regional small firms.[27] This trend has also affected public relations. There is now an increasing tendency for clients and agencies to develop closer and longer term relationships, as tight budgets require a close, mutual understanding of what the advertising must achieve for a particular brand or product.

The sphere of public relations is also undergoing significant change. Clients are demanding pan-European and international services. Through the development of technology—such as the Internet and interactive television—plus new advertising formats—such as the growing use of mini-documentary style lengthy "advertorials" and infomercials—there is a move to more overt competition between public relations consultancies and advertising agencies. Advertising agencies perceive these developments to be part of their toolkit, whereas public relations consultancies have begun to include these innovations in their armoury. In addition, the public relations industry believes it is maturing and accordingly needs to become more professional, recruiting higher calibre personnel and providing better training, while ensuring their output is assessed in terms of client goals and expectations.[28] These enhancements require time and high budgets in an ever more competitive market. With all these changes, there is little doubt that both the marketing environment and client requirements are significantly affecting the nature of the services offered by advertising agencies and public relations consultancies.

This chapter concludes with an overview of corporate sponsorship—an element of the promotional mix that is increasingly apparent to many consumers and a promotional tool now used by many organisations.

● ● ● ● ● ● ● ● ● ● ● ● ● ● ● ● ● ●

Sponsorship

Sponsorship The financial or material support of an event, activity, person, organisation or product by an unrelated organisation or donor

Sponsorship is the financial or material support of an event, activity, person, organisation or product by an unrelated organisation or donor. Generally, funds will be made available to the recipient of the sponsorship deal in return for the prominent exposure of the sponsor's name or brands.[29]

Increasing Popularity of Sponsorship

A decade or so ago sponsorship in the arts became an established form of funding for individual performances, tours, whole seasons or exhibitions; indeed some theatrical companies and galleries came to depend on it.[30] Many orchestras, ballet, opera or theatre companies, museums and art galleries would not have survived in the face of declining government subsidies for the arts had it not been for corporate sponsorship. Sport was soon to follow, as numerous football teams found that gate receipts and pitch advertising revenues were no longer adequate to cover wage bills and operating costs. While the larger clubs earn seven figure revenues from shirt sponsorship by companies such as Sony, JVC or Heineken, deals for as little as £20,000 are not uncommon in the lower leagues; either way this form of financial support is becoming essential to guarantee the survival of many clubs.

The popularity of corporate sponsorship has grown dramatically: few leading sports or arts events are without corporate sponsorship, as detailed in Table 17.9 and Marketing Insight 17.2. Sponsors believe there are two key benefits to the

Sponsorship in Sport

Along with the arts, sport is the prime target for sponsorship. High profile, well attended and often televised sporting events prove popular targets for companies wishing to increase the visibility of their products. With "professional" players entering rugby union, many leading clubs such as Bath and Leicester have sought sponsorship to retain the services of their leading stars by providing adequate financial rewards.

It is not always so easy, though, to seek sponsorship. The Brighton indoor women's tennis tournament began in 1978 and was rated one of the most important events outside the Grand Slam tour. In 1980, Martina Navratilova beat Chris Evert there, replacing her as world number one. Past sponsors included Daihatsu, Pretty Polly, Midland Bank and Autoglass. In 1994 for the first time there was no sponsor. With no world ranked British women players, there was no public interest in the event and little for sponsors to "buy". Instead, with five British males in the top 150 players and the arrival of Greg Rusedski, the Lawn Tennis Association has dropped the Brighton tournament and bought a men's clay court event in Bournemouth. Sponsorship for this event is not so problematic.

As the following table reveals, sponsorship in sport is widespread and costly, but the rewards are considered highly attractive.

Sports Event	Sponsor	Reason for Sponsorship	Cost and Benefit	Spin-Offs
Cricket Sunday league cricket	AXA Equity & Law	Cricket attracts the male AB audience that the insurance company seeks. AXA Equity & Law provides Family Awards to those counties that promote attendance of families—they feel that it is imperative to get kids hooked early before Nintendo takes over.	Costs £1.2m a year. Sponsorship to be extended until 1998—a £3.5m investment which shows that AXA Equity & Law is getting what it wants. As well as goodwill and opportunities for corporate entertaining, it reports greater awareness of the company.	Corporate hospitality for key business clients and staff. Sponsorship campaign supported by vigorous merchandising (baseball caps, bags with AXA logo). Perimeter boards at matches.
Bowls National championships	Sanatogen Cod Liver Oil	Sanatogen Cod Liver Oil is designed to alleviate stiffness in the joints; the comparatively elderly bowls audience is the ideal target.	Net cost for three tournaments £50,000, including marketing support. Increased sales represent a six-fold return on Sanatogen's spending.	Logos on hoardings at events, and free samples handed out (but not forcibly administered to spectators). A questionnaire distributed to the EBA's membership enabled Sanatogen to target them with literature on cod liver oil.
Rugby league 1995 World Cup	Halifax	The Halifax and rugby league share common northern roots, but the game is developing internationally. So the sponsor gains local goodwill and international connections.	The Halifax, true to its status as a trustworthy custodian of others' funds, will not reveal how much it has paid to be main sponsor. It is the Halifax's first sports sponsorship of any kind, and it is "very happy" with the response so far.	The Halifax is not overplaying its presence at matches, but is instead promoting the competition through its branches and advertising. It is also keen to develop business links through corporate entertainment.

Sports Event	Sponsor	Reason for Sponsorship	Cost and Benefit	Spin-Offs
Motor racing Williams Formula One team	Rothmans	Cigarette manufacturers are concerned to associate their product with glamour, excitement and high achievement. Formula One, the pinnacle of motor sport, delivers these ingredients, as well as offering invaluable television air-time to companies that are banned from advertising on the medium.	A top F1 team spends around £40m a year. Rothmans gets a chunk of the most-watched sport on television apart from the World Cup and the Olympics. In the first five grands prix this year, Williams, Ferrari and Benetton occupied 83 per cent of grand prix coverage.	Hospitality for Rothmans' VIPs. Kiosks selling base-ball caps, T-shirts and team jackets. Full-size mock-up Williams computer simula-tions at the track-side for would-be Damon Hills.
Snooker World Championship	Embassy	Severe advertising restric-tions for tobacco companies mean the cham-pionships are vital for cre-ating brand awareness. The company is banned from using players, equipment or even brand colours in any ads or logos so it needs some way of accessing smokers, who make up the bulk of snooker watchers and players.	Total prize money for the next championships (spon-sored by Embassy for the twenty-first time) is £1,132,000. Add a hefty six-figure sum for accom-modation and staging. In return, a recent survey showed instant recognition of Embassy through its association with snooker.	Corporate hospitality for Embassy clients.
Boat Race Oxford vs. Cambridge rowing contest	Beefeater Gin	The Boat Race is a uniquely English sporting event. Beefeater wanted to link a classic brand with a classic British event. The race location also helps: Beefeater is the only gin distilled in the capital. Beefeater is gunning for the ABC1 market, and alumni of the two competing uni-versities fit the bill.	Cost: £1.35m over 3 years, plus the same again on pro-moting the race. Beefeater is paying for exposure of a product that until recently could not be advertised on British TV. Won the Institute of Sports Spon-sorship's Best Televised Event award.	Hospitality for trade and international distributors of the brand. Merchan-dising of T-shirts, anoraks, umbrellas, etc. Sampling opportunities at pub pro-motions and rowing nights in London, Oxford, Cambridge and overseas.
Football FA Premiership	Carling	Most ardent football fans are between 18 and 30— Carling's target group of consumers. Aim: to raise profile and image among younger drinkers and attract new consumers. Pre-miership occupies more TV time, column inches and pub conversations than any other sport.	The deal will cost Carling £12m over four years. Research shows that since the deal kicked off in 1993, there has been extremely high awareness of Carling's role, particularly among the targeted younger drinkers.	Plentiful: hospitality for Carling customers at matches; perimeter adver-tising; editorial space in match programmes; Man of the match competition on Sky Sports; pub promo-tions, newspaper and radio competitions.

SOURCE: Table adapted from "A word about our sponsors: how the money men benefit from sport", *Independent on Sunday*, 15 October 1995, p. 24. Copyright © 1995 by The Independent on Sunday. Reprinted by permission.

Table 17.9 — Sports Sponsorship and Arts Sponsorship

Sports Sponsorship: Total Expenditure

	1989	1990	1991	1992	1993	1994
Market size, £m	200	230	238	239	250	265

Corporate Sponsorship of Sport, 1993/94

	1993	1994		1993	1994
Drink (alcohol)	108	139	Grocery	23	35
Insurance	43	68	Media	32	34
Cars/allied trades	61	67	Power/gas/electricity/steel	22	30
Banks/finance	40	56	Tobacco	23	29
Sports goods/clothing	46	53	Communications	18	28

Corporate Sponsorship of the Arts[1], 1993/94 (Expenditure by art form)

Music	18.9%	Arts centres	2.7%
Opera	17.8	Heritage	1.1
Museums	12.0	Literature	0.7
Theatre	10.9	Photography	0.5
Arts festivals	9.6	Services	0.2
Film and video	5.0	Crafts	—
Dance	4.5	Other	5.9
Visual arts and sculpture	4.1	Awards and prizes	6.1

NOTE: [1]Based on Business Sponsorship Incentive Scheme (BSIS). Total corporate sponsorship in 1993/94 was £69.5m (54.9m from sponsorship and £14.6m from corporate membership and donations).

SOURCE: *The Marketing Pocket Book 1996* (Henley, Oxon: NTC Publications, 1995). Reprinted by permission.

Table 17.9 Expenditure on sponsorship

company and its products. First and foremost, media coverage is unbridled. Volvo estimates that its £2 million investment in tennis sponsorship has been worth the equivalent of £15 million spent on advertising. Its banners are displayed at its tournaments, as are examples of its model range. Volvo advertisements and publicity appear in the programmes. The Volvo brand appears in advertising for the event, and usually the company's cars transport the celebrity players during the tournaments. Not only does the public see the company's advertisements, they cannot fail to see its brand name displayed extensively. In addition, the product is on hand for demonstration, while television coverage of the events takes the Volvo name into every tennis fan's home; radio and press coverage prominently features Volvo's name.

Few spectators at the Atlanta Olympics or Euro 96 football championships, could have failed to notice the identities of the leading sponsors. To many sports enthusiasts, the leading competitions become generically known as the Gillette Cup, Nat West Trophy, Prudential Series or Coca-Cola Cup. In equestrian events, the horses' names often include the name of the sponsoring company. Visitors to the Royal Shakespeare Company's performances are clearly informed of the support given by leading sponsors. Montserrat Caballe's performance at Birmingham's prestigious new Symphony Hall was made possible largely by the sponsorship of Forward Trust Group, a fact made clear in all promotional material—leaflets, advertising and publicity—and in the concert's programme.

The second benefit of corporate sponsorship is internal. Many organisations believe that their sponsorship of events helps improve the morale of their workforce. On one level, high profile, brand building sponsorship, such as Prudential Insurance's involvement with cricket, re-assures the workforce and re-affirms the company's leading position in its marketplace. On a more human level, sponsorship for altruistic projects, such as worthy community causes, helps give employees a "warm", positive feeling towards their employer. McDonald's support of Ronald McDonald Homes close to children's hospitals and its sponsorship of local school events not only help the community but also make its employees feel more positive towards the company.

Applications for Sponsorship

Sponsorship used to be a tool of public relations and the domain of public relations consultancies. Increasingly, it is a specialist area and a separate component of the promotional mix. Public relations consultancies still handle many sponsorship deals, but a growing number of specialist sponsorship advisers now introduce sponsors to appropriate recipients. It should not be thought that sponsorship is prominent only in the sports and arts worlds. It is an activity of growing importance in many fields. Universities and colleges seek sponsorship for students, technical equipment, buildings and even degree programmes. Hospitals receive and welcome the sponsorship of buildings, operating theatres, and fund raising events. Engineering and scientific research, particularly in universities and "research clubs", benefit from the sponsorship of research and development, often from organisations in completely unrelated fields of business.

No matter what the area, if a company believes its brand reputation will be enhanced and its brand awareness improved by its involvement with an organisation or an event, sponsorship becomes an important element in its promotional mix. Sponsorship can be for events or competitions, equipment or buildings, ideas or research, learning or development, animals or people, commercial or charitable causes, television programmes, products or services, single activities or ongoing programmes.

Reputable Partnerships

Reputable partnerships
Reputable and ethical dealings between a recognised, welcome and acceptable sponsoring organisation and a recipient organisation

There are ground rules to be considered by the prospective sponsor. As with any promotional activity, the sponsor must ensure that the recipient organisation, event or product is recognised by the sponsor's target audience, that it is welcome and acceptable to its target audience and that it is reputable and ethical in its dealings. **Reputable partnerships** are essential. The sponsor does not want to invest its promotional budget in activities not recognised by its own target market. The sponsor cannot risk becoming involved with an event or organisation which has a risqué reputation and unprofessional management; such a situation threatens the sponsor's reputation and brands. Consider the effect on a prestigious brand if an athlete sponsored by that brand failed a dope test or was found guilty of cheating. The recipient, too, needs to be wary of the donor's image and reputation.

● ● ● ● ● ● ● ● ● ● ● ● ● ● ● ● ● ● ●

Summary

● *Advertising* is a paid form of non-personal communication that is transmitted to consumers through mass media, such as television, radio, newspapers, magazines, direct mail, public transport and outdoor displays. Both non-business and business organisations use advertising.

● Marketers use advertising in many ways. *Institutional advertising* promotes organisations' images and ideas, as well as political issues and candidates. *Product advertising* focuses on the uses, features, images and benefits of goods and services. To make people aware of a new or innovative product's existence, uses and benefits, marketers rely on *pioneer advertising* in the introductory stage to stimulate primary demand for a general product category. Then they switch to *competitive advertising* to boost selective demand by promoting a particular brand's uses, features and advantages. *Comparative advertising* is a form of competitive advertising in which two or more brands are compared for one or more attributes.

● Through *defensive advertising,* a company can sometimes lessen the impact of a competitor's promotional programme or make its own sales force more effective. To increase market penetration, an advertiser sometimes focuses a campaign on promoting a greater number of uses for the product. *Reminder advertising* for an established product lets consumers know that the product is still around and that it has certain characteristics and uses. Marketers may use *reinforcement advertising* to assure users of a particular brand that they are selecting the best brand. Marketers also use advertising to smooth out fluctuations in sales.

● Although marketers may vary in how they develop *advertising campaigns,* they should follow a general pattern. First, they must identify and analyse the *advertising target.* Second, they should establish what they want the campaign to accomplish by defining the advertising objectives. The third step is creating the *advertising platform,* which contains the basic issues to be presented in the campaign. Fourth, advertisers must decide on the *advertising budget,* that is, how much money will be spent on the campaign; they arrive at this decision through the *objective and task approach,* the *percentage of sales approach,* the *competition matching approach*, or the *arbitrary approach*. Fifth, they must develop the *media plan* by selecting and scheduling the media to be used in the campaign, taking into account *cost comparison indicators* and *regional issues.* In the sixth stage, advertisers use *copy, artwork* and *illustrations* to create the message, with the aid of *storyboards* and careful *layouts,* bearing in mind *AIDA,* the persuasive sequence of attention, interest, desire and action. In the seventh stage, they

execute their advertising campaign, after extensive planning and co-ordination. Finally, advertisers must devise one or more methods for evaluating the effectiveness of the advertisements, including *pretests,* the use of *consumer focus groups, post-tests, recognition tests,* and *unaided* or *aided recall tests.*

● Advertising campaigns can be developed by personnel within the firm or in conjunction with advertising agencies. When a campaign is created by the firm's personnel, it may be developed by only a few people, or it may be the product of an advertising department within the firm. The use of an advertising agency may be advantageous to a firm because an agency can provide highly skilled, objective specialists with broad experience in the advertising field at low to moderate costs to the firm.

● *Publicity* is communication in news story form about an organisation, its products or both, transmitted through a mass medium at no charge. Generally, publicity is part of the larger, more comprehensive communications function of *public relations.* Publicity is mainly informative and usually more subdued than advertising. There are many types of publicity, including *press (news) releases, feature articles, captioned photographs, press conferences,* editorials, films and tapes. In addition, public relations includes training managers to handle journalists and publicity, establishing links with influential bodies and VIPs, managing visits and seminars, and providing information to employees. *Third party endorsement,* in which a VIP or celebrity publicly endorses a product or a brand, is particularly effective. Marketers can use one or more of these forms to achieve a variety of objectives. *Target publics* include consumers, suppliers, distributors, journalists and shareholders, as well as employees and managers inside the firm. Effective public relations depends on thorough identification of target publics. To have an effective publicity programme, someone—either in the organisation or in the firm's agency—must be responsible for creating and maintaining systematic and continuous publicity efforts.

● An organisation should avoid negative publicity by reducing the number of negative events that result in unfavourable publicity. To diminish the impact of unfavourable publicity, an organisation should institute policies and procedures for dealing with news personnel when negative events do occur. Problems that organisations confront when seeking publicity include the reluctance of media personnel to print or broadcast releases and a lack of control over the timing and content of messages. *Crisis management* is an integral part of public relations.

● There are significant client pressures and market trends affecting advertising agencies and public relations consultancies. These include client demands for international and pan-European service, accountability over the effectiveness of the promotional activity, short term goals versus longer term *brand building,* concentration of media ownership, reduced client budgets, rationalisation in terms of the number and size of agencies, the growing use of technology such as the Internet, conflict between advertising agencies and public relations consultan-

cies over advertorials and infomercials, and the need to offer an increasingly professional service.

● *Sponsorship* is the financial or material support of an event, activity, person, organisation or product by an unrelated organisation or donor in return for the prominent exposure of the sponsor's name and brands. Once the domain of arts and sports, sponsorship applications are broadening. An organisation's target audiences can be communicated with through sponsorship. An additional benefit can be to raise the morale of employees within the donor organisation. Sponsor recipients and donors must be certain of each other's ethics and behaviour. *Reputable partnerships* are essential.

● ● ● ● ● ● ● ● ● ● ● ● ● ● ● ● ● ●

Important Terms

Advertising	Competition matching approach	Unaided or spontaneous recall test
Institutional advertising	Arbitrary approach	Aided or prompted recall test
Product advertising	Media plan	
Pioneer advertising	Cost comparison indicator	Publicity
Competitive advertising	Regional issues	Public relations
Comparative advertising	Copy	Target publics
Defensive advertising	AIDA	Press (news) release
Reminder advertising	Storyboard	Feature article
Reinforcement advertising	Artwork	Captioned photograph
Advertising campaign	Illustrations	Press conference
Advertising target	Layout	Third party endorsement
Advertising platform	Pre-tests	Crisis management
Advertising budget	Consumer focus group	Brand building
Objective and task approach	Post-campaign test or post-test	Sponsorship
Percentage of sales approach	Recognition test	Reputable partnership

● ● ● ● ● ● ● ● ● ● ● ● ● ● ● ● ● ●

Discussion and Review Questions

1. What is the difference between institutional and product advertising?
2. When should advertising be used to stimulate primary demand? When should advertising be used to stimulate selective demand?
3. What are the major steps in creating an advertising campaign?
4. What is an advertising target? How does a marketer analyse the target audience after it has been identified?
5. Why is it necessary to define advertising objectives?
6. What is an advertising platform, and how is it used?
7. What factors affect the size of an advertising budget? What techniques are used to determine this budget?
8. Describe the steps required in developing a media plan.
9. What is the role of copy in an advertising message?
10. What role does an advertising agency play in developing an advertising campaign?

11. Discuss several ways to post-test the effectiveness of an advertisement.
12. What is publicity? How does it differ from advertising?
13. How do organisations use publicity? Give several examples of publicity releases that you have observed recently in local media.
14. What are target publics? Why must they be carefully identified and handled by a public relations department?
15. How should an organisation handle negative publicity? Identify a recent example of a firm that received negative publicity. Did the firm deal with it effectively?
16. Explain the problems and limitations associated with using publicity. How can some of these limitations be minimised?
17. How can corporate sponsorship enhance brand awareness for a sponsoring organisation?
18. What factors must an organisation consider before selecting a sponsor or recipient organisation?

● ● ● ● ● ● ● ● ● ● ● ● ● ● ● ● ●

Recommended Readings

C. L. Bovee, J. V. Thill, G. P. Dovel and M. B. Wood, *Advertising Excellence* (New York: McGraw-Hill, 1995).

D. Parente, B. V. Bergh, A. Barban and J. Marra, *Advertising Campaign Strategy: A Guide to Marketing Communication Plans* (Fort Worth: Dryden Press, 1996).

T. Hunt and J. E. Grunig, *Public Relations Techniques* (Fort Worth: Harcourt Brace, 1994).

N. A. Hart, *Industrial Marketing Communications* (London: Kogan Page, 1993).

N. A. Hart, *Strategic Public Relations* (London: Macmillan Press, 1995).

● ● ● ● ● ● ● ● ● ● ● ● ● ● ● ● ●

Cases

17.1 British Airways' Evolving Promotion

In the late 1970s British Airways (BA) had lost its way as the UK's national airline. The merger of BOAC and BEA had not gone smoothly, financial performance was poor and travel surveys showed customer satisfaction to be low. The 1979 election of a Conservative government gave new impetus to improve, as the government wished to privatise the state owned airline. Lord King was appointed chairman in 1983, and under him the airline quickly became operationally sound, although customers had not perceived the change.

The subsequent promotional strategy can be divided into three distinct phases. From 1983 to 1985 the global campaigns of Saatchi & Saatchi aimed "to make the airline feel proud again". Employees were to feel valued and part of a successful organisation, customers were to believe BA was superior to competitors and financial institutions were to see the turnaround in BA as a prelude to privatisation. The now famous "Manhattan Landing" commercial made no attempt to demonstrate product benefits, create category need or purchase intention. The message was that BA was large and "the world's favourite airline". The campaign was hugely successful in the UK and US—BA's main markets. Sales increased by 28 per cent in the US and 13 per cent elsewhere; the US voted the commercial the best of all airlines' promotion in 1984. Perceptions of BA changed.

By 1985, awareness of BA had grown. The objective then was to alter customer attitudes, particularly in the lucrative business class sector. Stressing service and comfort, advertisements were targeted at business travellers, particularly in the United States; "Superclub Seats", "Supercare", and "Putting People First" are examples of such advertisements. The campaign was influenced by Colin Marshall, who had recently joined BA from Avis and believed in service as a means of differentiation. Training programmes improved service levels so that the reality of the product offer matched the message of BA's promotion.

Since 1987, BA's advertising has concentrated on its "pillar" brands. BA had previously promoted a recognisable corporate image but had only haphazardly promoted its various services, such as Club Class and the Shuttles. Mike Batt joined the airline from Mars and brought marketing techniques that focused on the product rather than on the company or corporate image. He introduced the concept of pillar brands, the key products that supported the global and corporate branding already in place. The corporate identity remained part of the promotion, but the focus turned to selling specific products to particular market segments using distinctive brands—for example, Club World, Saver Shuttle, Executive Shuttle. The "Boardroom" advertisement sold Club World—a long haul service providing comfort and convenience and enabling passengers to arrive fit for work—to businesspeople. Following these branding and promotion exercises, the number of business class passengers increased by 31 per cent worldwide and 12 per cent in Europe.

Through M&C Saatchi, BA still spends over £70 million annually on is global advertising account, one of the most prestigious accounts in the world of advertising. The result is very high brand awareness and an image for being an ultra-high service provider at competitive fare rates. The latest advertising has executions aimed separately at business and leisure users, concentrating on the hopes and dreams of BA's passengers. The message, though, is consistent with the platform adopted throughout the 1980s: BA is big, convenient, friendly and looks after its customers.

SOURCES: John Tylee, "BA confirms M&C Saatchi's position", *Campaign*, 12 April 1996, p. 1; Douglas Nelms, "Imaging's new demands", *Air Transport World*, April 1996, pp. 34–38; Noreen O'Leary, "Limits of illusion", *Adweek*, 15 January 1996, pp. 14–18; Laurel Wentz, "BA's $150m campaign makes worldwide debut", *Advertising Age*, 8 January 1996, p. 33; John Tylee, "M&C Saatchi unveils new look ads in BA branding drive", *Campaign*, 5 January 1996, p. 1; Saatchi & Saatchi directors; *Sunday Times*, 27 May 1990; John Francis, "BA promotions in the 1980s", University of Warwick, 1990.

Questions for Discussion

1. How important is a strong corporate identity in the successful advertising of services?
2. Creating a successful platform is difficult. Keeping it fresh is more so. Discuss the problems of building on BA's powerful and innovative "Manhattan Landing" advertisement.

17.2   Public Relations and Perrier's Crisis

On 10 February 1990, in North Carolina, bottles of Perrier were found to be contaminated with benzene. For the best selling brand of mineral water in the world this meant a huge crisis. "Once a critical situation arises the most vital task is to do everything you can to reduce damage to the absolute minimum. We were fortunate that we had agreed procedures in advance and these procedures were followed absolutely", stated Perrier spokesperson Wenche Marshall Foster. "From the very beginning we were determined to keep everyone fully informed."

Perrier's crisis team in the UK moved quickly; senior executives of Perrier, its PR agency Infoplan and advertising agency Leo Burnett had been briefed before the contamination scare on the needs of crisis management. Within hours of the contamination announcement Perrier had set up tests with independent consultant Hydrotechnica so as to have accurate information to give out. The crisis team knew it had to be truthful throughout. Infoplan immediately set up a telephone information service, which dealt with 1,700 calls each day from distributors, retailers and consumers. Within three days of the crisis breaking, shelves worldwide had been cleared and all stocks returned to Perrier. The company achieved goodwill by moving so decisively. No press conferences were given. Instead, the five members of the crisis team individually met journalists for in-depth, head to head interviews to give precise and clear information and to minimise poor publicity.

Perrier risked competitors moving to take advantage of the crisis, since retailers would not leave shelves empty. Perrier, though, was the clear brand leader with the only established image worldwide. Competitors would take time to develop such strength, and their stocks were not high. Evian and others had nothing to gain from drawing further attention to Perrier's crisis, which was damaging the industry as a whole.

Perrier handled the crisis in PR textbook fashion. With 85 per cent of the American and 60 per cent of the UK market it had a great deal to lose. The company informed its publics of its difficulties, tackled the contamination problems and re-launched the product with new packaging and bottle sizes—clearly to be seen as new stock—with a "Welcome Back" promotional campaign. Within months, Perrier's market share was climbing back and shelf space had been regained. The company did not hide anything, it identified the various audiences to brief and it tackled its production to ensure that there were no repeat problems. Consumers, distributors, public health bodies and the media were made to feel part of Perrier's solution through the effective use of PR.

Perrier handled its crisis very efficiently, but never fully regained its domination of the bottled mineral water market—the fastest expanding sector of the beverages market in the 1990s. Perrier's success had been noted by major beverage suppliers; the removal of its bottles from shelves and the contamination scare gave rivals the opportunity to move in. Despite re-packaging, fresh designs and a new advertising agency, Publicis, Perrier struggled to re-kindle its former glory days and was taken over by the mighty Swiss company, Nestlé. Today, supermarket shelves have a multitude of rival mineral water brands, many mixed with exotic fruit flavours or energy enhancing ingredients. Nevertheless, Perrier still has very high brand awareness, significant market share and a loyal customer base.

SOURCES: John Tylee, "Publicis extends 'eau' theme for Perrier blitz", *Campaign*, 19 May 1995, p. 7; Greg Prince, "In hot water", *Beverage World*, March 1995, pp. 90–95; "Perrier aims to recapture lost young drinkers", *Marketing*, 24 March 1994, p. 1; *Marketing Week*, 2 March 1990; *Personally Speaking*, 27 March 1990; *Fortune*, 23 April 1990.

Questions for Discussion

1. How important is it to have an ongoing commitment to public relations in the event of a crisis?
2. Could Perrier's competitors have taken more advantage of the crisis?
3. Did the same publicity message go out to all of Perrier's publics or target audiences?

18 PERSONAL SELLING, SALES PROMOTION AND DIRECT MAIL

"If we are what we do, then we all of us, are salespeople."

Antonis Simintiras
The Open University

OBJECTIVES

- To understand the major purposes of personal selling
- To learn the basic steps in the personal selling process
- To identify the types of sales force personnel
- To gain insight into sales management decisions and activities
- To become aware of what sales promotion activities are and how they can be used
- To become familiar with specific sales promotion methods used
- To understand the role of direct mail in the promotional mix

Not too long ago Green Shield trading stamps were the most widely encountered frequent user sales promotion. Today, it is the loyalty card. The current wave was instigated by the petrol forecourts, which offer points with petrol towards prizes or catalogue merchandise. In 1995 supermarket giant Tesco introduced its loyalty card, the Tesco Clubcard, to ridicule by competitors. Tremendously successful, the cards have accordingly increased the number of Tesco shoppers, and in 1996 the company over-took arch rival Sainsbury's as the number one grocery retailer in the UK. Not resting on its laurels, Tesco surprised many of its rivals—including Sainsbury's—which by then had introduced their own loyalty cards, by launching Clubcard Plus.

Within a year the original Clubcard had 6.5 million regular customers who used their cards to earn discounts against their spending. Clubcard Plus goes further: it offers holders interest paid on their balances and can be used like any other debit card. This move into financial services is not new.

other financial services on the back of its highly visible and reputable brand name. The difference with Tesco is that instead of using its brand name to sell financial services, it is using its loyalty card based financial product to sell its brand name and successful chain of supermarkets.

Tesco's Clubcard has enabled the company to overtake its rivals and has, analysts believe, increased the frequency of shopping visits to Tesco stores. Within twelve months of being launched, the Clubcard had become the most popular loyalty scheme in the UK, ahead of the more established schemes run by companies such as Esso and Air Miles. Thanks also to operators like Shell with its Smart Card and the widely accepted Air Miles, it is expected that by the end of the decade, most UK consumers will be enrolled in one or more of the leading loyalty card schemes, making available to the schemes' marketers a wealth of demographic, lifestyle and spending data. The opportunities for more carefully honed target marketing are thereby much increased. The loyalty card has proved to be a major success story and not only as a sales promotion tool, particularly for Tesco. ∎

Marks & Spencer has a very successful division handling its payment card, which now also sells PEPs and pensions. Once a music business, now a hotelier and airline, Virgin sells life insurance and

SOURCES: David Benardy, "Tesco plays its Clubcard right", *Marketing Week,* 3 November 1995, pp. 30–31; "Tesco's Clubcard tops loyalty", *Marketing,* 25 May 1995, p. 4; Martin Croft, "It's all in the cards", *Marketing Week,* 24 March 1995; Anthony Bailey, "There's lolly in your trolley", *Independent on Sunday,* 9 June 1996, p. IB18.

As indicated in Chapter 16, personal selling, sales promotion and direct mail are possible ingredients in a promotional mix. Personal selling is the most widely used. Sometimes it is a company's sole promotional tool, although it is generally used in conjunction with other promotional mix ingredients. Personal selling is becoming more professional and sophisticated, with sales personnel acting more as consultants and advisers. Sales promotion and direct mail are also playing an increasingly important role in marketing strategies.[1] The sales promotion vehicle Clubcard has been very important in establishing Tesco's market leadership.

This chapter focuses on personal selling, sales promotion and direct mail, examining the purposes of personal selling, its basic steps, the types of salespeople and how they are selected. It also discusses the major sales management decisions and activities, which include setting objectives for the sales force and determining its size; recruiting, selecting, training, compensating and motivating salespeople; managing sales territories; and controlling sales personnel. The discussion then goes on to explore several characteristics of sales promotion, the reasons for using sales promotion and the sales promotion methods available for use in a promotional mix. The chapter concludes with a look at the role of direct mail.

The Nature of Personal Selling

Personal selling The process of using personal communication in an exchange situation to inform customers and persuade them to purchase products

Personal selling is the process of informing customers and persuading them to purchase products through personal communication in an exchange situation. For example, a salesperson describing the benefits of a Braun shaver to a customer in a Boots store is using personal selling. Personal selling gives marketers the greatest freedom to adjust a message to satisfy customers' information needs. In comparison with all other promotional methods, personal selling is the most precise, enabling marketers to focus on the most promising sales prospects. Other promotional mix ingredients are aimed at groups of people, some of whom may not be prospective customers. A major disadvantage of personal selling is its cost. Generally, it is the most expensive ingredient in the promotional mix, owing to the associated costs of salaries, cars and expenses. Personal selling costs are increasing faster than advertising costs.

Businesses spend more money on personal selling than on any other promotional mix ingredient. Millions of people, including increasing numbers of women, earn their living through personal selling. In the UK it is estimated that 600,000 people are directly employed as salespeople.[2] A selling career can offer high income, a great deal of freedom, a high level of training and a high level of job satisfaction.[3] Unfortunately, consumers often view personal selling negatively. A study of marketing students' perceptions of personal selling showed that approximately 25 per cent of the survey group associated it directly with door-to-door selling. In addition, 59 per cent of all students surveyed had a negative impression of personal selling. Major businesses, professional sales associations and academic institutions are making an effort to change the negative stereotypes associated with salespeople.[4]

Personal selling goals vary from one firm to another. However, they usually involve finding prospects, persuading prospects to buy and keeping customers satisfied. Identifying potential buyers who are interested in an organisation's products is critical. Because most potential buyers seek information before they make a purchase, salespeople must ascertain prospects' information needs and then provide the relevant information. To do so, sales personnel must be well trained, both in regard to their products and in regard to the selling process in general.[5]

Salespeople need to be aware of their competitors. They need to monitor new products being developed, and they should be aware of all competitors' sales activities in their sales territories. Salespeople must emphasise the advantages their products provide when their competitors' products do not offer that specific advantage.[6] This issue is discussed in greater detail later in this chapter.

Few businesses survive solely on profits from one sale customers. For long run survival, most marketers depend on repeat sales. A company has to keep its customers satisfied to obtain repeat purchases. Besides, satisfied customers help attract new ones by telling potential customers about the organisation and its products. Even though the whole organisation is responsible for providing customer satisfaction, much of the burden falls on salespeople. The salesperson is almost always closer to customers than anyone else in the company and often provides buyers with information and service after the sale. Such contact not only gives salespeople an opportunity to generate additional sales but also offers them a good vantage point from which to evaluate the strengths and weaknesses of the company's products and other marketing mix ingredients. Their observations are helpful in developing and maintaining a marketing mix that better satisfies both customers and the firm.

A salesperson may be involved in achieving one or more of the three general goals. In some organisations, there are people whose sole job is to find prospects. This information is relayed to salespeople, who then contact the prospects. After the sale, these same salespeople may do the follow up work, or a third group of employees may have the job of maintaining customer satisfaction. In many smaller organisations, a single person handles all these functions. No matter how many groups are involved, several major sales tasks must be performed to achieve these general goals.

● ● ● ● ● ● ● ● ● ● ● ● ● ● ● ● ● ● ● ●

Elements of the Personal Selling Process

The exact activities involved in the selling process vary from one salesperson to another and differ for particular selling situations. No two salespeople use exactly the same selling methods. Nonetheless, many salespeople—either consciously or unconsciously—move through a general selling process as they sell products. This process consists of seven elements, or steps: (1) prospecting and evaluating, (2) preparing, (3) approaching the customer, (4) making the presentation, (5) overcoming objections, (6) closing and (7) following up.

Prospecting and Evaluating

Prospecting Developing a list of potential customers

Developing a list of potential customers is called **prospecting.** A salesperson seeks the names of prospects from the company's sales records, referrals, trade shows, newspaper announcements (of marriages, births, deaths and so on), public records, telephone directories, trade association directories, telemarketing lists[7] and many other sources. Sales personnel also use responses from advertisements that encourage interested people to send in an information request form. Seminars and meetings may produce good leads. Seminars may be targeted at particular types of clients, such as solicitors, accountants, the over-55s or specific business-people.

After developing the prospect list, a salesperson evaluates whether each prospect is able, willing and authorised to buy the product. On the basis of this evaluation, some prospects may be deleted, while others are deemed acceptable and ranked according to their desirability or potential.

Preparing

Before contacting acceptable prospects, a salesperson should find and analyse information about each prospect's specific product needs, current use of brands, feelings about available brands and personal characteristics. The most successful salespeople are thorough in their preparation. They prepare by identifying key decision-makers, reviewing account histories and reports, contacting other clients for information, assessing credit histories and problems, preparing sales presentations, identifying product needs and obtaining all relevant literature.[8] Being well informed about a prospect makes a salesperson better equipped to develop a presentation that precisely communicates with the prospect.

For example, Xerox developed an automated sales process to help sales personnel prepare for complex sales situations after discovering that its salespeople spent half their time on sales inhibiting activities, such as looking for forms and gathering information. Preparing an order required 5 to 13 forms, and one third of all orders were rejected because of mistakes on the forms. To overcome the problem, Xerox developed computer work stations to assist its sales force in shaping proposals, prospecting and preparing, and to link salespeople throughout the company without a piece of paper having to be touched.[9]

Approaching the Customer

Approach The way in which a salesperson contacts a potential customer

The **approach,** the manner in which a salesperson contacts a potential customer, is a critical step in the sales process. In more than 80 per cent of initial sales calls, the purpose is to gather information about the buyer's needs and objectives. Creating a favourable impression and building rapport with the prospective client are also important tasks in the approach, because the prospect's first impression of the salesperson is usually a lasting one, with long run consequences. During the initial visit, the salesperson strives to develop a relationship rather than just push a product. The salesperson may have to call on a prospect several times before the product is considered.[10]

One type of approach is based on referrals. The salesperson approaches the prospect and explains that an acquaintance, an associate or a relative suggested the call. The salesperson who uses the cold canvass method calls on potential customers without their prior consent. Repeat contact is another common approach; when making the contact, the salesperson mentions a prior meeting. The exact type of approach depends on the salesperson's preferences, the product being sold, the firm's resources and the characteristics of the prospect.

Making the Presentation

During the sales presentation, the salesperson must attract and hold the prospect's attention to stimulate interest and stir up a desire for the product. The salesperson should have the prospect touch, hold or actually use the product. If possible, the salesperson should demonstrate the product and get the prospect more involved with it to stimulate greater interest. Audio-visual materials may be used to enhance the presentation.

During the presentation, the salesperson must not only talk but also listen. The sales presentation gives the salesperson the greatest opportunity to determine the prospect's specific needs by listening to questions and comments and observing responses. Even though the salesperson has planned the presentation in advance, she or he must be able to adjust the message to meet the prospect's information needs.

Overcoming Objections

An effective salesperson usually seeks out a prospect's objections in order to address them. If they are not apparent, the salesperson cannot deal with them, and they may keep the prospect from buying. One of the best ways to overcome a prospect's objections is to anticipate and counter them before the prospect has an opportunity to raise them. However, this approach can be risky because the salesperson may mention some objections that the prospect would not have raised. If possible, the salesperson should handle objections when they arise. They can also be dealt with at the end of the presentation.

Closing

Closing The stage in the selling process when the salesperson asks the prospect to buy the product or products

Closing is the stage in the selling process in which the salesperson asks the prospect to buy the product or products. During the presentation, the salesperson may use a "trial close" by asking questions that assume the prospect will buy the product. For example, the salesperson might ask the potential customer about financial terms, desired colours or sizes, delivery arrangements or the quantity to be purchased. The reactions to such questions usually indicate how close the prospect is to buying. A trial close allows prospects to indicate indirectly that they will buy the product without having to say those sometimes difficult words, "I'll take it".

A salesperson should try to close at several points during the presentation, because the prospect may be ready to buy. One closing strategy involves asking the potential customer to take a trial order. The sales representative should either guarantee a refund if the customer is not satisfied or make the order a free offer.[11] Often an attempt to close the sale will result in objections. Thus closing can be an important stimulus that uncovers hidden objections, which can then be addressed.

Following Up
After a successful closing, the salesperson must follow up the sale. In the follow up stage, the salesperson should determine whether the order was delivered on time and installed properly, if installation was required. He or she should contact the customer to learn what problems or questions have arisen regarding the product. The follow up stage can also be used to determine customers' future product needs.

● ● ● ● ● ● ● ● ● ● ● ● ● ● ● ● ● ● ● ●

Types of Salespeople

To develop a sales force, a marketing manager must decide what kind of salesperson will sell the firm's products most effectively. Most business organisations use several different categories of sales personnel. Based on the functions they perform, salespeople can be classified into three groups: order getters, order takers and support personnel. One salesperson can, and often does, perform all three functions.

Order Getters

Order getters Employees who increase their firm's sales by selling to new customers and by increasing sales to present customers

To obtain orders, a salesperson must inform prospects and persuade them to buy the product. The **order getter's** job is to increase the firm's sales by selling to new customers and by increasing sales to present customers. This task is sometimes called creative selling. It requires salespeople to recognise potential buyers' needs and then give them the necessary information. Order getting activities are sometimes divided into two categories: current customer sales and new business sales.

Current Customer Sales   Sales personnel who concentrate on current customers call on people and organisations that have purchased products from the firm at least once. These salespeople seek more sales from existing customers by following up previous sales. Current customers can also act as leads for new prospects.

New Business Sales   Business organisations depend on sales to new customers, at least to some degree. New business sales personnel locate prospects and convert them to buyers. Salespeople in many industries help to generate new business, but industries that depend in large part on new customer sales are insurance, heavy industrial machinery, fleet cars and office stationery.

The time share industry uses various sales promotion techniques (direct mail, competitions, free offers) to attract potential buyers to attend seminars or open days at the time share site. Once they are there, however, the sales force has to explain the concept of time sharing, show the site's facilities and close the deal. It is unlikely that other promotional techniques alone would be sufficient to sign up new customers. The Internet, as described in Marketing Insight 18.1, is increasingly part of the promotional mix. For many businesses, like BMW with its Internet used car service, the leads generated from "the Net" are followed up by the sales force.

Order Takers

Order takers Employees who ensure that repeat customers have sufficient quantities of the desired product where and when they are needed in order to perpetuate long lasting relationships

Taking orders is a repetitive task that sales staff perform to perpetuate long lasting, satisfying relationships with customers. **Order takers** seek repeat sales. One of their major objectives is to be absolutely certain that customers have sufficient product quantities where and when they are needed. Most order takers handle orders for standardised products that are purchased routinely and therefore do not require extensive sales efforts.[12] There are two groups of order takers: inside order takers and field order takers.

Inside Order Takers In many businesses, inside order takers work in sales offices and receive orders by mail and telephone (telesales). Certain producers, wholesalers and even retailers have sales personnel who sell from within the firm rather than in the field. That does not mean that inside order takers never communicate with customers face-to-face. For example, salespersons in retail stores are classified as inside order takers.

Field Order Takers Salespeople who travel to customers are referred to as "outside", or "field", order takers: the field force. Often a customer and a field order taker develop an interdependent relationship. The buyer relies on the salesperson to take orders periodically, and sometimes to deliver them, and the salesperson counts on the buyer to purchase a certain quantity of product periodically. Use of lap-top computers can improve the field order taker's tracking of inventory and orders.

Field and inside order takers should not be thought of as passive functionaries who simply record orders in a machine-like manner. Order takers generate the bulk of many organisations' total sales.

Support Personnel

Support personnel Employees who facilitate the selling process but are not usually involved solely in selling

Support personnel facilitate the selling function but are not usually involved solely in making sales. They are engaged primarily in marketing industrial products. They locate prospects, educate customers, build goodwill and provide service after the sale. Although there are many kinds of sales support personnel, the three most common are missionary, trade and technical.

Missionary salespeople Support salespeople, usually employed by the manufacturer, who assist the producer's customers in selling to their own customers

Missionary salespeople Usually employed by manufacturers, **missionary salespeople** assist the producer's customers in selling to their own customers. A missionary salesperson may call on retailers to inform and persuade them to buy the manufacturer's products. If the call is successful, the retailers purchase the products from wholesalers, who are the producer's customers. Manufacturers of medical supplies and pharmaceutical products often use missionary sales staff to promote their products to doctors, hospitals and retail chemists.

Trade salespeople Employees who are not strictly classified as support personnel because they take orders as well as help customers, especially retail stores, promote the product

Trade salespeople Not strictly support personnel, **trade salespeople** usually perform the order taking function as well. However, they direct many of their efforts towards helping customers, especially retail stores, promote the product. They are likely to re-stock shelves, obtain more shelf space, set up displays, provide in-store demonstrations and distribute samples to store customers. Food producers and cosmetics companies commonly employ trade salespeople.

Technical salespeople Employees who give technical assistance to the organisation's current customers

Technical salespeople **Technical salespeople** give technical assistance to the organisation's current customers. They advise customers on product characteristics and applications, system designs and installation procedures. Because this job is often highly technical, the salesperson usually needs to have formal training in

Internet into the Dictionary—the New Revolution in Marketing Communications

Few consumers have not yet heard about the Internet: television documentaries, news items and schoolchildren's games have all established the concept of a global network of easily accessible information available in the home through a hooked up PC. From its beginnings in the US in the early 1980s at a research institute, the Internet now extends to over 40 million users worldwide, and the number is expanding at the rate of around 60 per cent per year. The Internet was created as a means of (1) transmitting information between sites, irrespective of location or country, and (2) for education. Presently, most companies see "the Net" as an additional tool in the promotional mix toolkit. Oxford Instruments, for example, created a page on the Net to keep its scientific customers, long standing users of the Internet, up to date with product modifications and service issues. Now the company promotes new services and product launches using its space on the Net. Oxford Instruments is not alone: more and more television advertisements conclude with an e-mail address or Internet code for use by interested consumers who wish to find out more about the company, product or service in question.

Netscape was founded only in 1994, yet the company is now worth over $700 million. Netscape provides Internet browsing software and has around two-thirds of the market. Its proposition is unusual: it gives its software free to users and makes its revenue by selling promotional space on the Net to advertisers. Many commercial companies would like the Net to be for more than games, information and advertising. Why not direct response advertising, so that orders for goods and services could be placed over the Net? For home shopping and catalogue ordering, too? Only Sainsbury's in the UK used the Internet for order placing in 1995, and then only for wines. Since the networks were not secure, a credit card number, password or PIN number given to a supplier via the Net could all too easily fall into the hands of an unscrupulous third party, who could then use it to run up a hefty bill for the unsuspecting consumer. Netscape, though, believes it may now have the solution to providing secure communications for traders and their customers.

The real breakthrough came in early 1996 when the two leading card suppliers Visa and MasterCard agreed on a new way of scrambling payment information to prevent hackers and fraudsters raiding accounts. Experts believe that within a few years, the Internet could be taking a staggering £200 billion in orders for all types of products and services. Visa executive Edmund Jensen believes that the technical breakthrough in scrambling and decoding is the key to making cyberspace attractive to banks and financial services, predicted to be the fastest growing users of the Net for promoting and selling products. It is expected that the new tool will also

one of the physical sciences or in engineering. Technical sales personnel often sell technical industrial products, such as computers, heavy equipment and steel.

When hiring sales personnel, marketers seldom restrict themselves to a single category, because most firms require different types. Several factors dictate how many of each type of salesperson a particular company should have. A product's uses, characteristics, complexity, price and margin influence the kind of sales personnel used, as do the number of customers and their characteristics. The kinds of marketing channels and the intensity and type of advertising also have an impact on the selection of sales personnel.

prove highly popular with small firms that have limited marketing and advertising budgets.

Already, the decision whether or not to set up a site on the World Wide Web is no longer the issue. For many, the emphasis is on how a business can differentiate its on-line presence and exploit the potential of the Net. Yellow Pages and BMW set up sites and used press advertising to announce and promote their arrival on the Net! "The challenge now is to create something people choose to come to. Companies can no longer rely on people visiting their [Web] sites out of curiosity", stated Mark Curtis of CHBi, the creator for Yellow Pages of Yell, the first comprehensive directory of UK Web sites. Yell has several sections: its core UK Yellow Web, listing what is on and where; Film Finder, with reviews and showing times of major films; and Electronic Yellow Pages, an on-line version of the original Yellow Pages directory. Yell is a new, stand-alone service, separate from the traditional Yellow Pages.

BMW, too, has used the Internet to create a service only available on-line, the BMW Approved Used Car Directory, which offers an interactive search and find catalogue, as well as general BMW information support. All local BMW dealers will eventually be on the Internet, promoting the company's site through local media and press advertising, and they will be able to run their own locally focused promotions.

Netscape's success is not unusual in a market that is itself still in its introductory stage, and in which consumer understanding, technology and competition are far from steady. Since it is difficult for even the huge multinationals such as Microsoft and Apple to gauge truly this market's development, opportunities abound for niche suppliers such as Netscape to enter the market and seize a dominant market share. For potential traders via the Internet such as Barclays, GA, Sainsbury's or IKEA, and the resulting beneficiaries such as Visa or Amex, it is also a challenging task to evaluate how the market will develop and what their own requirements will be. Nevertheless, the Net is here to stay and it is being evaluated by a huge variety of organisations. Businesses, however, recognise that simply having a site on the Web is not sufficient. Increasingly, even a site on the Web requires differentiation and creativity to stand out against a growing number of businesses selling their wares through this new inroad into the lifestyles of a growing part of the population.

SOURCES: IEE Conference, "The Internet", Cambridge, 7 December 1995; C. Lloyd, "On a quest to bring the Internet to the masses", *The Sunday Times,* 26 November 1995; "How Netscape found a web full of dollars", *Financial Times,* 20 September 1995; "Innovation", *The Sunday Times,* 19 and 26 November, 31 December 1995; "Scramble to build a super showroom in cyberspace", *Independent on Sunday,* 4 February 1996, p. IB8; "Pay by plastic plan on Internet", *Evening Telegraph,* 3 February 1996, p. 15.

• • • • • • • • • • • • • • • • • •

Management of the Sales Force

The sales force is directly responsible for generating an organisation's primary input: sales revenue. Without adequate sales revenue, a business cannot survive long. A firm's reputation is often determined by the ethical conduct of its sales force. On the other hand, the morale and, ultimately, the success of a firm's sales force are determined in large part by adequate compensation, room for advancement, sufficient training and management support—all key areas of sales management. When these elements are not satisfactory, sales staff may leave for more satisfying jobs elsewhere. It is important to evaluate the input of salespeople because effective sales force management determines a firm's success.

This section explores eight general areas of sales management: (1) establishing sales force objectives, (2) determining sales force size, (3) recruiting and selecting sales personnel, (4) training sales personnel, (5) compensating sales personnel, (6) motivating salespeople, (7) managing sales territories and (8) controlling and evaluating sales force performance.

Establishing Sales Force Objectives

To manage a sales force effectively, a sales manager must develop sales objectives. Sales objectives tell salespeople what they are expected to accomplish during a specified time period. These objectives give the sales force direction and purpose and serve as performance standards for the evaluation and control of sales personnel. For example, in Figure 18.1, Matbro uses direct response advertising to produce leads and thereby help salespeople meet their sales goals. As with all types of objectives, sales objectives should be stated in precise, measurable terms and should specify the time period and the geographic areas involved.

Sales objectives are usually developed for both the total sales force and each salesperson. Objectives for the entire force are normally stated in terms of sales volume, market share or profit. Volume objectives refer to a quantity of money or sales units. For example, the objective for an electric drill manufacturer's sales force might be to sell £6 million worth of drills annually or 600,000 drills annu-

Figure 18.1

Assisting the sales force

Matbro's direct response advertising produces sales leads for the company's sales force.

SOURCE: Courtesy of Matbro.

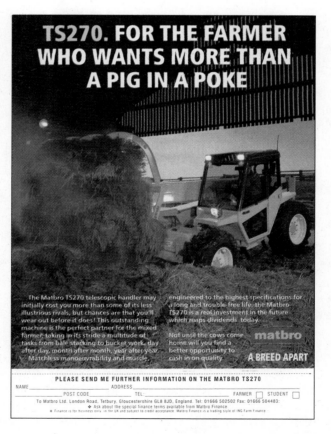

ally. When sales goals are stated in terms of market share, they usually call for an increase in the proportion of the company's sales relative to the total number of products sold by all businesses in that particular industry. When sales objectives are based on profit, they are generally stated in terms of monetary amounts or in terms of return on investment.

Sales objectives, or quotas, for an individual salesperson are commonly stated in terms of monetary or unit sales volume. Other bases used for individual sales objectives include average order size, average number of calls per time period and the ratio of orders to calls.

Determining Sales Force Size

Deciding how many salespeople to use is important because the size of the sales force influences the company's ability to generate sales and profits. Moreover, sales force size affects the compensation methods used, salespeople's morale and overall sales force management. Sales force size must be adjusted from time to time because a firm's marketing plans change, as do markets and forces in the marketing environment. It is dangerous, however, to cut back the size of the sales force to increase profits by cutting costs. The sales organisation could then lose its strength and resilience, preventing it from rebounding when growth returns or better market conditions prevail. The organisation that loses capacity through cutbacks may not have the energy to accelerate.[13]

There are several analytical methods for determining the optimal size of the sales force; however, a detailed discussion of these methods is beyond the scope of this text. Although marketing managers may use one or several analytical methods, they normally temper their decisions with a good deal of subjective judgement.[14]

Recruiting and Selecting Salespeople

Recruiting A process by which the sales manager develops a list of applicants for sales positions

To create and maintain an effective sales force, a sales manager must recruit the right type of salespeople. **Recruiting** is a process by which the sales manager develops a list of applicants for sales positions. The cost of hiring, training and retaining a salesperson is soaring; currently, costs in the UK can reach £60,000 or more.[15]

To ensure that the recruiting process results in a pool of qualified salespeople from which to choose, a sales manager should establish a set of required qualifications before beginning to recruit. Although for years marketers have attempted to identify a set of traits that characterise effective salespeople, there is currently no such set of generally accepted characteristics. Therefore, a sales manager must develop a set tailored to the sales tasks in a particular company. Two activities can help establish this set of requirements. The sales manager should prepare a job description that lists the specific tasks salespeople are to perform. The manager should also analyse the characteristics of the firm's successful salespeople, as well as those of its ineffective sales personnel. From the job description and the analysis of traits, the sales manager should be able to develop a set of specific requirements and be aware of potential weaknesses that could lead to failure.

A sales manager generally recruits applicants from several sources: departments within the firm, other firms, employment agencies, educational institutions, respondents to advertisements and individuals recommended by current employees. The specific sources a sales manager uses depend on the type of salesperson required and the manager's experiences with particular sources.

The process of hiring a sales force varies tremendously from one company to another. One technique used to determine whether potential candidates will be good salespeople is an assessment centre. Assessment centres are intense training environments that place candidates in realistic problem settings in which they must assign priorities to their activities, make decisions and act on their decisions. Candidates are judged by experienced managers or trained observers. Assessment centres have proved to be valuable in selecting good salespeople.[16]

Sales management should design a selection procedure that satisfies the company's specific needs. The process should include enough steps to yield the information needed to make accurate selection decisions. However, because each step incurs a certain expense, there should be no more steps than necessary. The stages of the selection process should be sequenced so that the more expensive steps, such as physical examination, are near the end. Fewer people will then move through the higher cost stages.

Recruitment should not be sporadic; it should be a continuous activity aimed at reaching the best applicants. The selection process should systematically and effectively match applicants' characteristics and needs with the requirements of specific selling tasks. Finally, the selection process should ensure that new sales personnel are available where and when they are needed.

Recruitment and selection of salespeople are not one-off decisions. The market and marketing environment change, as do an organisation's objectives, resources and marketing strategies. Maintaining the proper mix of salespeople thus requires the firm's sales management's continued attention.

Training Sales Personnel

Many organisations have formal training programmes; others depend on informal, on-the-job training. Some systematic training programmes are quite extensive; others are rather short and rudimentary. Regardless of whether the training programme is complex or simple, its developers must consider what to teach, whom to train and how to train them.

A sales training programme can concentrate on the company, on products or on selling methods. Training programmes often cover all three areas. For experienced company sales staff, training usually emphasises product information, although it also describes new selling techniques and any changes in company plans, policies and procedures.

Training programmes can be aimed at newly hired salespeople, experienced sales staff or both. Ordinarily, new sales personnel require comprehensive training, whereas experienced personnel need both refresher courses about established products and training in new product information. Training programmes can be directed at the entire sales force or at one segment of it.

Sales training may be done in the field, at educational institutions, in company facilities or in several of these locations. Some firms train new employees before assigning them to a specific sales position. Other businesses, however, put them into the field immediately and provide formal training only after they have gained a little experience. Training programmes for new personnel can be as short as several days or as long as three years, or even longer. Sales training for experienced personnel is often scheduled during a period when sales activities are not too demanding. Because training experienced salespeople is usually an ongoing effort, a firm's sales management must determine the frequency, sequencing and duration of these activities.

Sales managers, as well as other salespeople, often engage in sales training—whether daily on-the-job or periodically in sales meetings. Salespeople sometimes receive training from technical specialists within their own organisations. In addition, a number of individuals and organisations sell special sales training programmes. Appropriate materials for sales training programmes range from films, texts, manuals and cases to programmed learning devices and audio and video cassettes. As for teaching methods, lectures, demonstrations, simulation exercises and on-the-job training can all be effective. The choice of methods and materials for a particular sales training programme depends on the type and number of trainees, the programme's content and complexity, its length and location, the size of the training budget, the number of teachers and the teachers' preferences.

Compensating Salespeople

To develop and maintain a highly productive sales force, a business must formulate and administer a compensation plan that attracts, motivates and retains the most effective individuals. The plan should give sales management the desired level of control and provide sales personnel with an acceptable level of freedom, income and incentive. It should also be flexible, equitable, easy to administer and easy to understand. Good compensation programmes facilitate and encourage proper treatment of customers.

Even though these requirements appear to be logical and easily satisfied, it is actually quite difficult to incorporate them all into a simple programme. Some of them will be satisfied, and others will not. Studies evaluating the impact of financial incentives on sales performance indicate four general responses. (1) For price sensitive individuals, an increase in incentives will usually increase their sales efforts, and a decrease in financial rewards will diminish their efforts. (2) Unresponsive salespeople will sell at the same level regardless of the incentive. (3) Leisure sensitive salespeople tend to work less when the incentive system is implemented. (4) Income satisfiers normally adjust their performance to match their income goal. Understanding potential reactions and analysing the personalities of the sales force can help management evaluate whether an incentive programme might work.[17] Therefore, in formulating a compensation plan, sales management must strive for a proper balance of freedom, income and incentives.

The developer of a compensation programme must determine the general level of compensation required and the most desirable method of calculating it. In analysing the required compensation level, sales management must ascertain a salesperson's value of the company on the basis of the tasks and responsibilities associated with the sales position. The sales manager may consider a number of factors, including salaries of other types of personnel in the firm, competitors' compensation plans, costs of sales force turnover and the size of non-salary selling expenses and perks.

Sales compensation programmes usually reimburse salespeople for their selling expenses, provide a certain number of fringe benefits and deliver the required compensation level. To do that, a firm may use one or more of three basic compensation methods: straight salary, straight commission or a combination of salary and commission. In a **straight salary compensation plan,** salespeople are paid a specified amount per time period. This sum remains the same until they receive a pay increase or decrease. In a **straight commission compensation plan,** salespeople's compensation is determined solely by the amount of their sales for a given time period. A commission may be based on a single percentage of sales or on a sliding scale involving several sales levels and percentage rates. In a **combination compensation plan,** salespeople are paid a fixed salary plus a commission based on sales volume. Some combination programmes require a salesperson to exceed a certain sales level before earning a commission; others offer commissions for any level of sales.

Straight salary compensation plan A plan according to which salespeople are paid a specified amount per time period

Straight commission compensation plan A plan according to which salespeople are paid solely on the basis of their sales for a given time period

Combination compensation plan A plan according to which salespeople are paid a fixed salary plus a commission based on sales volume

Compensation Method	Frequency of Use (%)*	When Especially Useful	Advantages	Disadvantages
Straight salary	17.4	Compensating new salespeople; firm moves into new sales territories that require developmental work; salespeople need to perform many non-selling activities	Gives salesperson maximum amount of security; gives sales manager large amount of control over sales force; easy to administer; yields more predictable selling expenses	Provides no incentive; necessitates closer supervision of salespeople's activities; during sales declines, selling expenses remain at same level
Straight commission	6.5	Highly aggressive selling is required; non-selling tasks are minimised; company cannot closely control sales force activities	Provides maximum amount of incentive; by increasing commission rate, sales managers can encourage salespeople to sell certain items; selling expenses relate directly to sales resources	Salespeople have little financial security; sales manager has minimum control over sales force; may cause salespeople to give inadequate service to smaller accounts; selling costs less predictable
Combination	76.1	Sales territories have relatively similar sales potentials; firm wishes to provide incentive but still control sales force activities	Provides certain level of financial security; provides some incentive; selling expenses fluctuate with sales revenue	Selling expenses less predictable; may be difficult to administer

*The figures are computed from "Alternative sales compensation and incentive plans", *Sales & Marketing Management*, 17 February 1986, p. 57. *Note:* The percentage for Combination includes compensation methods that involved any combination of salary, commission or bonus.

SOURCE: Based on John P. Steinbrink, "How to pay your sales force", *Harvard Business Review,* July/August 1978.

Table 18.1 Characteristics of sales force compensation methods

Traditionally, department stores have paid salespeople straight salaries, but combination compensation plans are becoming popular. Concessionaries in Debenhams, for example, are offering commissions (averaging 6 to 8 per cent) to a large segment of their sales force. The practice has made the salespeople more attentive to a customer's presence and needs; it has also attracted older, more experienced salespeople, who tend to be in short supply.[18] Car salespeople traditionally receive low basic salaries (£5,000 to £9,500 p.a.), with the remainder coming from commission.

Table 18.1 lists the major characteristics of each sales force compensation method. Notice that the combination method is most popular. When selecting a compensation method, sales management weighs the advantages and disadvantages shown in Table 18.1.

Proper administration of the sales force compensation programme is crucial for developing high morale and productivity among sales personnel. A good salesperson is highly marketable in today's workplace, and successful sales managers switch industries on a regular basis. Basic knowledge and skills related to sales management are in demand, and sometimes new insights can be gained from different work experiences. For example, one of British Steel's best sales managers was recruited from the grocery sector. To maintain an effective compensation programme and retain productive employees, sales management should periodically review and evaluate the plan and make necessary adjustments.

Motivating Salespeople

A sales manager should develop a systematic approach for motivating the sales force to be productive. Motivating should not be viewed as a sporadic activity reserved for periods of sales decline. Effective sales force motivation is achieved through an organised set of activities performed continuously by the company's sales management. For example, scheduled sales meetings can motivate salespeople. Periodic sales meetings have four main functions: (1) recognising and reinforcing the performance of salespeople, (2) sharing sales techniques that are working, (3) focusing employees' efforts on matching the corporate goals and evaluating their progress towards achieving these goals, and (4) teaching the sales staff about new products and services.[19]

Although financial compensation is important, a motivational programme must also satisfy non-financial needs. Sales personnel, like other people, join organisations to satisfy personal needs and achieve personal goals. Sale managers must become aware of their sales personnel's motives and goals and then attempt to create an organisational climate that lets their salespeople satisfy their personal needs.

A sales manager can use a variety of positive motivational incentives as well as financial compensation (see Figure 18.2). For example, enjoyable working conditions, power and authority, job security and an opportunity to excel can be effective motivators. Salespeople can also be motivated by their company's efforts to make their job more productive and efficient. For example, Honeywell Information Systems developed a computerised sales support system that increased sales productivity by 31 per cent and reduced sales force turnover by 40 per cent within a year. This system can track leads and provide customer profiles and competitor data.[20]

Sales contests and other incentive programmes can also be effective motivators. Sales contests can motivate salespeople to focus on increasing sales or new accounts, promote special items, achieve greater volume per sales call, cover territories better and increase activity in new geographic areas.[21] Some companies have found such incentive programmes to be powerful motivating tools that marketing managers can use to achieve corporate goals. Properly designed, an incentive programme can pay for itself many times over. However, for an incentive system to succeed, the marketing objectives must be accepted by the participants and prove effective in the marketplace. Some organisations also use negative motivational measures: financial penalties, demotions, even terminations of employment.

Managing Sales Territories

The effectiveness of a sales force that must travel to its customers is influenced to some degree by sales management's decisions regarding sales territories. Sales managers deciding on territories must consider size, shape, routing and scheduling.

Figure 18.2

Motivating sales force performance through an organised set of activities

Creating Sales Territories Several factors enter into the design of the size and shape of sales territories. First, sales managers must construct the territories so that sales potentials can be measured. Thus sales territories often consist of several geographic units for which market data are obtainable, such as census tracts, cities, counties or regions. Sales managers usually try to create territories that have similar sales potentials or require about the same amount of work. If territories have equal sales potentials, they will almost always be unequal in geographic size. The salespeople who are assigned the larger territories will have to work longer and harder to generate a certain sales volume. Conversely, if sales territories that require equal amounts of work are created, sales potentials for those territories will often vary. If sales personnel are partially or fully compensated through commissions, they will have unequal income potentials. Many sales managers try to balance territorial workload and earnings potential by using differential commission rates. Although a sales manager seeks equity when developing and maintaining sales territories, some inequities will always prevail.

A territory's size and shape should also be designed to enable the sales force to provide the best possible customer coverage and to minimise selling costs. Sales territory size and shape should take into account the density and distribution of customers.

Routing and Scheduling Salespeople   The geographic size and shape of a sales territory are the most important factors affecting routing and scheduling of sales calls. Next are the number and distribution of customers within the territory, followed by the frequency and duration of sales calls. The person in charge of routing and scheduling must consider the sequence in which customers are called on, the specific roads or transport schedules to be used, the number of calls to be made in a given period and what time of day the calls will occur. In some firms, salespeople plan their own routes and schedules with little or no assistance from the sales manager; in other organisations, the sales manager draws up the routes and schedules. No matter who plans the routing and scheduling, the major goals should be to minimise salespeople's non-selling time (the time spent travelling and waiting) and maximise their selling time. The planners should try to achieve these goals in a way that holds a salesperson's travel and accommodation costs to a minimum. Many companies use agencies, such as SPA Ltd, to construct databases of actual and potential customers and associated sales territories. SPA has a database of car and lorry drive-times, even taking account of road works, which allows sales territories to be delineated. These territories can share out actual and potential customers and allocate the sales force in relation to the time taken to service them.

Controlling and Evaluating Sales Force Performance

To control and evaluate sales force activities properly, sales management needs information. A sales manager cannot observe the field sales force daily and so relies on call reports, customer feedback and invoices. Call reports identify the customers called on and present detailed information about interaction with those clients. Travelling sales personnel must often file work schedules indicating where they plan to be during specific future time periods.

The dimensions used to measure a salesperson's performance are determined largely by sales objectives. These objectives are normally set by the sales manager. If an individual's sales objective is stated in terms of sales volume, then that person should be evaluated on the basis of sales volume generated. Even though a salesperson may be assigned a major objective, he or she is ordinarily expected to achieve several related objectives as well. Thus salespeople are often judged along several dimensions. Sales managers evaluate many performance indicators, including average number of calls per day, average sales per customer, actual sales relative to sales potential, number of new customer orders, average cost per call and average gross profit per customer.

To evaluate a salesperson, a sales manager may compare one or more of these dimensions with a pre-determined performance standard. However, sales management commonly compares one salesperson's current performance either with the performance of other employees operating under similar selling conditions or with his or her past performance. Sometimes management judges factors that have less direct bearing on sales performance, such as personal appearance, knowledge of the product and competitors.

After evaluating their sales force, sales managers must take any corrective action needed, because it is their job to improve the performance of the sales force. They may have to adjust performance standards, provide additional sales training or try other motivational methods. Corrective action may demand comprehensive changes in the sales force.

Many industries, especially technical ones, are monitoring their sales forces and increasing productivity through the use of lap-top computers. In part, the increasing use of computers in technical sales is a response to customers' greater technical sophistication. Product information—especially information on price, specifications and availability—helps salespeople to be more valuable. Some companies that have provided their sales forces with lap-tops expect a 15 to 20 per cent increase in sales.[22]

● ● ● ● ● ● ● ● ● ● ● ● ● ● ● ● ● ●

Sales Promotion

The Nature of Sales Promotion

Sales promotion An activity or material that acts as an inducement and offers added value or incentive to buy the product

As defined earlier, **sales promotion** is an activity or material (or both) that acts as a direct inducement and offers added value to or incentive to buy the product to resellers, salespeople or consumers.[23] The sale probably would have taken place without the sales promotion activity, but not for a while; the promotion has brought the sale forward. For example, a consumer loyal to Persil washing powder may purchase a packet every four weeks. If, however, in the third week Sainsbury's or Tesco has Persil on offer or with an on-pack promotion, the consumer will probably buy a week early to take advantage of the deal. Sales promotion encompasses all promotional activities and materials other than personal selling, advertising and publicity. In competitive markets, where products are very similar, sales promotion provides additional inducements to encourage purchases. Sales promotions are designed to generate short term sales and goodwill towards the promoter.

Sales promotion has grown dramatically in the last 10 years, largely because of the focus of business on short term profits and value and the perceived need for promotional strategies to produce short term sales boosts.[24] Current estimates in the UK suggest that consumer sales promotion is worth £2 billion annually. Include price discounting and the figure could be £4 billion higher; include trade sales promotion and the total reaches £8 billion.[25] The most significant change in promotion expenditures in recent years has been the transfer of funds usually earmarked for advertising to sales promotion. Companies now spend 54 per cent of their combined marketing services budgets on advertising and 21 per cent on sales promotion.[26] Fundamental changes in marketing, which have led to a greater emphasis on sales promotion, mean that specialist sales promotion agencies have increased and many major advertising agencies have developed sales promotion departments.

Ratchet effect The impact of using sales promotion and advertising together

An organisation often uses sales promotion activities in concert with other promotional efforts to facilitate personal selling, advertising or both.[27] Figure 18.3 depicts what is known as the **ratchet effect**—the impact of using sales promotion (short term sales brought forward) and advertising (longer term build up to generate sales) together. Sales promotion efforts are not always secondary to other promotional mix ingredients. Companies sometimes use advertising and personal selling to support sales promotion activities. For example, marketers frequently use advertising to promote contests, free samples and premiums. Manufacturers' sales personnel occasionally administer sales contests for wholesale or retail salespeople. The most effective sales promotion efforts are closely interrelated with other promotional activities. Decisions regarding sales promotion therefore often affect advertising and personal selling decisions, and vice versa.

Figure 18.3 The "ratchet effect". Sales promotion (SP) brings forward sales but has an immediate effect. An advertising campaign (A) takes time to take off and to generate sales, but can switch other brand users and non-users. The ratchet effect has been identified in most consumer and service markets.

SOURCE: W. T. Moran, "Insights from pricing research", in E. B. Bailey, ed., Pricing Practices and Strategies (New York: The Conference Board, 1978), pp. 7 and 13. Used by permission.

Sales Promotion Opportunities and Limitations

Sales promotion can increase sales by providing an extra incentive to purchase. There are many opportunities to motivate consumers, resellers and salespeople to take a desired action. Some kinds of sales promotion are designed specifically to stimulate resellers' demand and effectiveness; some are directed at increasing consumer demand; still others focus on both resellers and consumers. Regardless of the purpose, marketers need to ensure that the sales promotion objectives are consistent with the organisation's overall objectives, as well as with its marketing and promotion objectives.[28]

Although sales promotion can support a brand image, excessive price reduction sales promotion, such as coupons, can affect it adversely. Firms therefore must decide between short term sales increases and the long run need for a desired reputation and brand image.[29] As already noted, sales promotion has been catching up with advertising in total expenditure; but in the future, brand advertising may become more important relative to sales promotion. Some firms that shifted from brand advertising to sales promotion have lost market share, particularly in consumer markets where advertising is essential to maintain awareness and brand recognition. Advertising does not necessarily work better than sales promotion. There are trade-offs between these two forms of promotion, and the marketing manager must determine the right balance to achieve maximum promotional effectiveness.

• • • • • • • • • • • • • • • • •

Sales Promotion Methods

Consumer sales promotion techniques Techniques that encourage or stimulate consumers to patronise a specific retail store or to try a particular product

Trade sales promotion methods Techniques that encourage wholesalers, retailers or dealers to carry and market a producer's products

Most sales promotion methods can be grouped into the categories of consumer sales promotion and trade sales promotion. **Consumer sales promotion techniques** encourage or stimulate consumers to patronise a specific retail store or to try a particular product. **Trade sales promotion methods** stimulate wholesalers, retailers or dealers to carry a producer's products and to market these products aggressively.

Marketers consider a number of factors before deciding which sales promotion methods to use.[30] They must take into account both product characteristics (size, weight, costs, durability, uses, features and hazards) and target market characteristics (age, sex, income, location, density, usage rate and shopping patterns). How the product is distributed and the number and types of resellers may determine the type of method used. The competitive and legal environment may also influence the choice.

This section looks closely at several consumer and trade sales promotion methods to show what they entail and what goals they can help marketers achieve. Figure 18.4 shows how all members of a marketing channel can be engaged in sales promotion activities with different target audiences and techniques.

Consumer Sales Promotion Methods

The principal consumer sales promotion methods include coupons, demonstrations, frequent user incentive programmes, point-of-sale displays, free samples, money refunds, premiums, price-off offers, and consumer contests and sweepstakes.

Coupons A promotion method that reduces the purchase price of an item in order to stimulate consumers to try a new or established product, to increase sales volume quickly, to attract repeat purchasers or to introduce new package sizes or features

Coupons are used to stimulate consumers to try a new or established product, to increase sales volume quickly, to attract repeat purchasers or to introduce new package sizes or features. Coupons usually reduce the purchase price of an item. The savings may be deducted from the purchase price or offered as cash. For best results, coupons should be easy to recognise and state the offer clearly. The nature of the product (seasonality, maturity, frequency of purchase and so on) is the prime consideration in setting up a coupon promotion.

Several thousand manufacturers distribute coupons, which are used by approximately 80 per cent of all households. One study found that pride and satisfaction from obtaining savings through the use of coupons and price-consciousness were the most important determinants of coupon use.[31] Coupons are distributed through free-standing inserts (FSIs), print advertising, direct mail/leaflet drops and in stores. Historically, FSIs have been the dominant vehicle for coupons.[32] When deciding on the proper vehicle for their coupons, marketers should consider strategies and objectives, redemption rates, availability, circulation and exclusivity. The whole coupon distribution and redemption business has become very competitive. To draw customers to their stores, grocers may double and some-

Figure 18.4

Uses of sales promotion in the marketing channel

Consumer: Coupons, free samples, demonstrations, competitions.
Trade (at wholesalers, retailers, salespeople): Sales competitions, free merchandise, P-O-S. displays, plus trade shows and conferences.

SOURCE: John Rossiter and Larry Percy, Advertising and Promotion Management. Copyright © 1987 by McGraw-Hill, Inc. Used with permission of The McGraw-Hill Companies.

times even triple the value of the coupons they bring in. But because the practice of doubling and tripling coupons is expensive, many of these retailers have asked manufacturers to reduce the face value of the coupons they offer.[33]

There are several advantages to using coupons. Print advertisements with coupons are often more effective than non-promotional advertising in generating brand awareness. Generally, the larger the coupon's cash offer, the better the recognition generated. Another advantage is that coupons are a good way to reward present users of the product, win back former users and encourage purchasers in larger quantities. Coupons also let manufacturers determine whether the coupons reached the intended target market because they get the coupons back.

Coupons also have drawbacks. Fraud and misredemption are possible, and the redemption period can be quite lengthy. Table 18.2 illustrates coupon distribution and redemption rates in the UK. In addition, some experts believe that coupons are losing their value because so many manufacturers are offering them, and consumers have therefore learned not to buy without some incentive, whether it be a

Coupons—Volume and Expenditure			
	1990	**1992**	**1994**
Number of coupons distributed (millions)	5,074	5,402	4,286
Number of coupons redeemed (millions)	376	365	194
Total value of coupons redeemed (£m)	92.0	105.1	65.6
Coupons' average face value (pence)	24.4	28.8	34.0
Manufacturers' average handling allowance* to retailers (pence per 100 coupons)	186	230	251
Distribution medium of coupons redeemed* (%)			
Newspaper	7	5.5	4.9
Magazine	3	3.5	6.0
Door-to-door	26	22.7	13.1
In/on pack	25	37.0	39.1
In store	28	27.8	18.3
Direct mail	—	—	13.4
Others	11	4.1	5.2
Average redemption rates by media (%)			
Newspaper	1.7	1.6	1.2
Magazine	1.2	1.6	1.2
Door-to-door	12.8	8.6	4.5
In/on pack	15.4	16.7	20.3
In store	—	—	3.7
Direct mail	—	—	16.0

*Excluding retailer tailor-made promotions. (1994 figure is the recommended retailer handling allowance.)

SOURCE: From *The Marketing Pocket Book 1996*. Copyright © 1995 by NTC Publications. Used by permission.

Table 18.2 Coupon redemption rates in the UK

coupon, a rebate or a refund. There has been a general decline in brand loyalty among heavy coupon users. On the other hand, many consumers redeem coupons only for products they normally buy. Studies have shown that about 75 per cent of coupons are redeemed by people who already use the brand on the coupon. So, as an incentive to try to use a new brand or product, coupons have questionable success. Another problem with coupons is that stores often do not have enough of the coupon item in stock. This situation can generate ill-will towards both the store and the product.[34]

Although the use of coupons as a sales promotion technique is expected to grow in the next few years, marketers' concerns about their effectiveness could well diminish their appeal. However, coupons will probably remain a major sales promotion component for stimulating trial of new products. Coupons will also be used to increase the frequency of purchase for established products that show sluggish sales. On the other hand, successful, established products may be reducing their profits if 75 per cent of the coupons are redeemed by brand loyal customers.[35]

Demonstrations of products at dealers, retailers, or trade shows are excellent attention-getters. Manufacturers often use them temporarily either to encourage trial use and purchase of the product or to show how the product actually works. Because labour costs can be extremely high, demonstrations are not widely used. They can, however, be highly effective for promoting certain types of products, such as appliances, cosmetics and cars. Cosmetics marketers, such as Clinique (owned by Estée Lauder), sometimes offer potential customers "makeovers" to demonstrate their products' benefits and proper application.

Many firms develop **frequent user incentive** programmes to reward individual consumers who engage in repeat purchases. For example, most major international airlines offer a frequent flier programme through which customers who have flown a specified number of miles are rewarded with free tickets for additional travel. Air Miles takes this concept further, extending it across many products. As the chapter's opening example shows, supermarket loyalty cards are another popular incentive. A **loyalty card** offers discounts or free merchandise to regular customers. Thus frequent user incentives help foster customer loyalty to a specific company or group of co-operating companies that provides extra incentives for patronage. Frequent user incentives have also been used by service businesses, such as car hire companies, hotels and credit card companies, as well as by marketers of consumer goods.

An older frequent user incentive is trading stamps. **Trading stamps** are dispensed in proportion to the amount of a consumer's purchase and can be accumulated and redeemed for goods. Retailers use trading stamps to attract consumers to specific stores. Stamps are attractive to consumers as long as they do not drive up the price of goods. They are effective for many types of retailers. Trading stamps were very popular in the 1960s, but their use as a sales promotion method declined dramatically in the 1970s. However, Green Shield stamps made a comeback, and petrol retailers are now offering in-house stamps redeemable for limited collections of goods.

Point-of-sale (P-O-S) materials include such items as outside signs, window displays, counter pieces, display racks and self-service cartons. Innovations in P-O-S displays include sniff teasers, which give off a product's aroma in the store as consumers walk within a radius of four feet, and computerised interactive displays, which ask a series of multiple choice questions and then display information on a

Demonstrations Occasions on which manufacturers show how a product actually works in order to encourage trial use and purchase of the product

Frequent user incentives Incentive programmes that reward customers who engage in repeat purchases

Loyalty card A mechanism whereby regular customers who remain loyal to a particular company are rewarded with discounts or free merchandise

Trading stamps Stamps, dispensed in proportion to the amount of a consumer's purchase, that can be accumulated and redeemed for goods

Point-of-sale (P-O-S) materials Enhancements designed to increase sales, such as outside signs, window displays, counter pieces, display racks and self-service cartons screen to help consumers make a product decision.[36] IKEA stores offer interactive monitors on which room layouts and colour combinations may be tested prior to purchases. These items, which are often supplied by producers, attract attention, inform customers and encourage retailers to carry particular products. A retailer is likely to use point-of-sale materials if they are attractive, informative, well constructed and in harmony with the store. With two-thirds of all purchases resulting from in-store decisions, P-O-S materials can help sustain incremental sales if a brand's essential components—brand name, positioning and visual image—are the basis of the P-O-S display.[37]

A survey of retail store managers indicated that almost 90 per cent believed that P-O-S materials sell products. The retailers surveyed also said that P-O-S is essential for product introductions. Different forms of display materials are carried by different types of retailers. Convenience stores, for example, favour window banners and "shelf talkers" (on-the-shelf displays or signs), whereas chain chemists prefer floor stands and devices that provide samples.[38]

Free samples   Give-aways used to stimulate customers to try a product, to increase sales volume in the early stages of a product's life cycle or to obtain desirable distribution

Free samples of merchandise are used for several reasons: to stimulate trial of a product, to increase sales volume in the early stages of a product's life cycle or to obtain desirable distribution. The sampling programme should be planned as a total event, not merely a give-away.[39] Sampling is the most expensive of all sales promotion methods; production and distribution through such channels as mail delivery, door-to-door delivery, in-store distribution and on-package distribution entail very high costs. In designing a free sample, marketers should consider factors such as the seasonality of the product, the characteristics of the market and prior advertising. Free samples are not appropriate for mature products and products with a slow turnover.

Money refunds   A specific amount of money mailed to customers who submit proof of purchase

With **money refunds**, consumers submit proof of purchase and are mailed a specific amount of money. Usually, manufacturers demand multiple purchases of the product before a consumer can qualify for a refund. For example, Panasonic marketed a line of VHS tapes that featured a £1 rebate per tape for up to 12 purchases. A customer had to send in the sales receipt and a proof of purchase from inside each tape package. This method, used primarily to promote trial use of a product, is relatively inexpensive. Nevertheless, because money refunds sometimes generate a low response rate, they have limited impact on sales.

One of the problems with money refunds or rebates is that many people perceive the redemption process as too complicated. Consumers also have negative perceptions of manufacturers' reasons for offering rebates. They may believe that these are new, untested products or products that have not sold well. If these perceptions are not changed, rebate offers may degrade the image and desirability of the product being promoted. If the promotion objective in the rebate offer is to increase sales, an effort should be made to simplify the redemption process and proof of purchase requirements.[40]

Premiums   Items offered free or at minimum cost as a bonus for purchasing a product

Premiums are items offered free or at minimum cost as a bonus for purchasing a product. Vidal Sassoon offered a free, on-pack 50 ml "travel size" container of shampoo with its 200 ml size of Salon Formula shampoo. Kellogg's offered easy art books with its Variety Packs. Premiums can attract competitors' customers, introduce different sizes of established products, add variety to other promotional efforts and stimulate loyalty. Inventiveness is necessary, however; if an offer is to stand out and achieve a significant number of redemptions, the premium must be matched to both the target audience and the brand's image.[41] To be effective, premiums must be easily recognisable and desirable. Premiums are usually

Promoting Free Flights: Hoover Comes Unstuck

Whether it's Sainsbury's and Boots with BA, Boots and British Rail, Sony and Thomas Cook, or Bird's Eye Menumaster and National Express Coaches, retailers and manufacturers have frequently negotiated with carriers to offer free travel or holidays to boost sales. The depressed holiday industry has welcomed the opportunity to use excess capacity and increase demand. It was not too surprising when consumer electronics giant Hoover joined the ranks of manufacturers offering free trips in order to stimulate demand for its white goods, first by offering free tickets to Europe with purchases of more than £100, then by extending the promotion to include free tickets to the US. What was not predictable was the adverse publicity the scheme brought for Hoover.

The second promotion was supported by a high profile £1 million television campaign. The offer included two free flights to either Orlando or New York for every purchase over £100, with an additional £60 towards car hire and accommodation for purchases over £300. Hoover claimed that the tickets into Europe had constituted its most successful promotion ever, putting its £130 vacuum cleaner ahead of its £100 model and making its £380 washing machine more popular than its £300 model.

In November 1992 a *Daily Record* story, "Hoover's flight shocker", started the trouble. This story alleged that none of the airlines Hoover claimed was involved in the US deal had any knowledge of the scheme and that Hoover had yet to reserve a single airline seat. The article also stated that the sales promotion company behind the offer was £500,000 in debt. In response, Hoover launched a major damage limitation exercise, including full page adverts assuring people that there was no mystery, that the offer was genuine and that free flights were available. Hoover's problems did not end there, however. Media attention increased, as did stories of disgruntled consumers.

From BBC consumer affairs programme *Watchdog* to the House of Commons, questions were asked about the ethics of the deal and the apparently unfair treatment of hundreds of annoyed consumers who, having purchased a Hoover product and received their vouchers, had actually attempted to claim their prizes. Many potential holidaymakers could not get first or even second choices of dates or destination. Many were refused their choices so often that Hoover's promotions company refused to permit any travel! Over 70 MPs demanded a parliamentary investigation. Eventually, the Office of Fair Trading was brought in to investigate.

Hoover had intended neither to mislead nor to disappoint its customers, but the promotion nevertheless severely affected the firm's reputation. Circumstances combined in several well publicised cases to make a deteriorating situation even worse for the company. What began as a sales boosting, attention grabbing sales promotion rapidly turned into a damaging public relations nightmare for Hoover. Key directors were dismissed and the US parent company had to shell out millions of pounds to meet travellers' demands for their prizes. Twelve months later, disputes had still to be settled.

US parent Maytag Corp. had bought Britain's Hoover for $320 million in 1989. In 1995, Maytag sold its European operation to an Italian company at a loss of $135 million. The free flights promotion was, as described in many newspapers, "a fiasco", damaging not just this type of promotional activity but, more severely, the Hoover brand name.

Sources: Clare Sambrook, "Do free flights really build brands?", *Marketing*, 15 October 1992, p. 11; Mat Toor, "Hoover retaliates over flights offer", *Marketing*, 3 December 1992, p. 3; Robert Dwek, "Hoover extends its free flights deal", *Marketing*, 29 October 1992, p. 16; BBC and ITN television news broadcasts, March and April 1993; Chris Knight, "Direct route", *Marketing Week*, 8 September 1995, pp. 58–59; Marcia Berss, "Whirlpool's bloody nose", *Forbes*, 11 March 1996, pp. 90–92.

Price-off offers A method of encouraging customers to buy a product by offering a certain amount off the regular price shown on the label or package

Consumer contests Contests designed to generate traffic at the retail level in which consumers compete for prizes based on their analytical or creative skill

Consumer sweepstakes A method of stimulating sales in which consumers submit their names for inclusion in a drawing for prizes

Trade Sales Promotion Methods

Buy back allowance A certain sum of money given to a purchaser for each unit bought after an initial deal is over

Buying allowance A temporary price reduction given to resellers who purchase specific quantities of a product

Counts and recounts A promotion method based on the payment of a specifc amount of money for each product unit moved from a reseller's warehouse in a given time period

distributed through retail outlets or the mail, but they may also be placed on or in packages. Marketing Insight 18.2 relates the sorry tale of Hoover's free flight promotion.

Price-off offers give buyers a certain amount off the regular price shown on the label or package. Similar to coupons, this method can be a strong incentive for trying the product; it can stimulate product sales, yield short lived sales increases and promote products in off-seasons. It is an easy method to control and is used frequently for specific purposes. However, if used on an ongoing basis, it reduces the price to customers who would buy at the regular price and frequent use of price-off offers may cheapen a product's image. In addition, the method often requires special handling by retailers.

Consumer contests encourage individuals to compete for prizes based on their analytical or creative skill. This method generates traffic at the retail level. Marriott and Hertz co-sponsored a scratch-card contest with a golf theme to boost sales during the slow winter travel season. Contestants received game cards when they checked in at a Marriott hotel or hired a Hertz car and scratched off spots to see if they had won prizes, such as cars, holidays or golf clubs.[42] However, marketers should exercise care in setting up a contest. Problems or errors may anger consumers or result in legal action. Contestants are usually more involved in consumer contests than they are in sweepstakes (see below), even though the total participation may be lower. Contests may be used in conjunction with other sales promotion methods, such as coupons.

The entrants in a **consumer sweepstake** submit their names for inclusion in a drawing for prizes. Sweepstakes are used to stimulate sales and, as with contests, are sometimes teamed with other sales promotion methods. Sweepstakes are used more often than consumer contests and tend to attract a greater number of participants. The cost of a sweepstake is considerably less than the cost of a contest.[43] Successful sweepstakes or competitions can generate widespread interest and short term increases in sales or market share.

Producers use sales promotion methods to encourage resellers, especially retailers and dealers, to carry their products and promote them effectively. The methods include buy back allowances, buying allowances, counts and recounts, free merchandise, merchandise allowances, co-operative advertising, dealer listings, premium or push money, sales contests and dealer loaders.

A **buy back allowance** is a certain sum of money given to a purchaser for each unit bought after an initial deal is over. This method is a secondary incentive in which the total amount of money that resellers can receive is proportional to their purchases during an initial trade deal, such as a coupon offer. Buy back allowances foster co-operation during an initial sales promotion ... ulate re-purchase afterwards. The main drawback ...

A **buying allowance** is a temporary pr... specified quantities of a product. A soap p... ers £1 for each case of soap purchased. Suc... a new product, achieve a temporary price ... an item in larger than normal quantities. T... form of money, yields profits to resellers and ... There are no restrictions on how resellers ... method's effectiveness.

The **count and recount** promotion method ... cific amount of money for each product unit ...

546

Sales ...vate distr... sales person... and rewarding achievements in a given time period. Units of a product are counted at the start of the promotion and again at the end to determine how many have moved from the warehouse. This method can reduce retail stock-outs by moving inventory out of warehouses and can also clear distribution channels of obsolete products or packages and reduce warehouse inventories. The count and recount method might benefit a producer by decreasing resellers' inventories, making resellers more likely to place new orders. However, this method is often difficult to administer and may not appeal to resellers who have small warehouses.

Free merchandise is sometimes offered to resellers who purchase a stated quantity of the same or different products. Occasionally, free merchandise is used as payment for allowances provided through other sales promotion methods. To avoid handling and bookkeeping problems, the usual method of giving away merchandise free is by reducing the invoice.

A **merchandise allowance** is a manufacturer's agreement to pay resellers certain amounts of money for providing special promotional efforts, such as advertising or displays. This method is best suited to high volume, high profit, easily handled products. One major problem with using merchandise allowances is that some retailers or dealers perform their activities at a minimally acceptable level simply to obtain the allowances. Before paying retailers or dealers, manufacturers usually verify their performance. Manufacturers hope that the retailers' or dealers' additional promotional efforts will yield substantial sales increases.

Co-operative advertising is an arrangement whereby a manufacturer agrees to pay a certain amount of a retailer's or dealer's media costs for advertising the manufacturer's products. The amount allowed is usually based on the quantities purchased. Before payment is made, a retailer or dealer must show proof that advertisements did appear. These payments give retailers or dealers additional funds for advertising. They can, however, put a severe burden on the producer's advertising budget. Some retailers or dealers exploit co-operative advertising programmes by crowding too many products into one advertisement. Some retailers or dealers cannot afford to advertise; others can afford it but do not want to advertise. Still others actually put out advertising that qualifies for an allowance but are not willing to undertake the paperwork required for reimbursement from producers.[44]

A **dealer listing** is an advertisement that promotes a product and identifies the names of participating retailers or dealers who sell the product. Dealer listings can influence retailers or dealers to carry the product, build traffic at the retail level and encourage consumers to buy the product at participating dealers.

Premium or **push money** is used to push a line of goods by providing additional compensation to salespeople. This promotion method is appropriate when personal selling is an important part of the marketing effort; it is not effective for promoting products that are sold through self-service. Although this method often helps a manufacturer obtain commitment from the sales force, it can also be very expensive.

Sales contests are designed to motivate distributors, retailers and sales personnel by recognising outstanding achievements. The Colt Car Company, importer of Japanese made Mitsubishi cars into the UK, designed a sales contest that offered dealers an incentive trip for two to Barbados if they improved their sales figures by 10 to 12 per cent. Approximately 50 per cent of the dealers met this sales goal and won the trip.[45] To be effective, this method must be equitable for all sales personnel involved. One advantage of the method is that it can achieve participation

Free merchandise Giveaways sometimes offered to resellers who purchase a specific quantity of the same or different products

Merchandise allowance A manufacturer's agreement to pay resellers certain amounts of money for providing special promotional efforts, such as advertising or displays

Co-operative advertising An arrangement whereby a manufacturer agrees to pay a certain amount of a retailer's or dealer's media costs for advertising the manufacturer's products

Dealer listing An advertisement that promotes a product and identifies the names of retailers or dealers who sell it

Premium or **push money** Additional compensation provided to salespeople in order to push a line of goods

contest A way to motivate ibutors, retailers and nel by recognising outstanding at all levels of distribution. However, the results are temporary, and prizes are usually expensive.

Dealer loaders are gifts to a retailer or dealer who purchases a specified quantity of merchandise. Often dealer loaders are used to obtain special display efforts from retailers by offering essential display parts as premiums. For example, a manufacturer might design a display that includes a sterling silver tray as a major component and give the tray to the retailer. Marketers use dealer loaders to obtain new distributors and push larger quantities of goods.

This chapter concludes with an examination of direct mail, an increasingly important ingredient in the promotional mix.

Dealer loader A gift to a retailer or dealer who purchases a specified quantity of merchandise

• • • • • • • • • • • • • • • • • • • •

Direct Mail

Direct mail Printed advertising material delivered to a prospective customer's or donor's home or work address

Direct mail and telephone selling are part of the *direct selling* category described in Chapter 14. Direct mail is the delivery to the target's home or work address of printed advertising material to contact prospective customers or donors. The use of direct mail to contact prospective customers and to solicit interest in products or services is not new.[46] Advertising agencies, public relations consultancies and in particular sales promotion houses have been using mail shots for several decades. With approximately 6 per cent of all promotional budgets in consumer goods and services, its own professional bodies and trade associations, and the growing sophistication of consumer databases, the direct mail industry believes it warrants recognition as a separate element of the promotional mix alongside advertising, sales promotion, personal selling, public relations and sponsorship.

Uses for Direct Mail

Direct mail is not confined to consumers; it is an important promotional activity in many business-to-business markets. Direct mail delivers the promotional message—and sometimes the product—through the postal service, private delivery organisations and the expanding network of in-home fax machines. Direct mail is used to create brand awareness and stimulate product adoption.[47] Throughout Europe, direct mail is widely used to generate orders, pre-sell prior to a sales call, qualify prospects for a sales call, screen out non-prospects, follow up a sale, announce special sales and localised selling initiatives and raise funds for charities and non-profit organisations. In the UK, the average household receives six items of direct mail each month (see Table 18.3).

Attention Seeking Flashes

Junk mail Unwanted mail binned unread by uninterested recipients

Flashes Headers printed on a direct mail package to gain the recipients' attention

Direct mail packages must prompt the recipient to open them, rather than treat them as **junk mail**—unwanted mail binned unread by uninterested recipients. "Prize inside", "Your opportunity to win", "Not a circular", "Important documentation enclosed" are just some of the popular headers or **flashes** printed prominently on the address labels. In some markets, these are sufficient at least to persuade the recipient to open the package. With the boom in direct mail and the growing adverse reaction to junk mail, however, persuasive phrases are often not enough. Packaging design is becoming more important in enticing recipients, through attractive or unusual shapes and designs, to examine the detail of the direct mail shot.

The Package

Direct mail package A mix of mailing envelope, covering or explanatory letter, circular, response device and return device

The **direct mail package** is more than just the envelope. Often it is a mix of mailing envelope, covering or explanatory letter, circular, response device and return device. The mailing envelope has to overcome the recipient's inertia, often through catchy flashes and design flair. The letter needs to be personalised and clear, appeal to the beliefs and lifestyle of the recipient and elicit interest in the product or service in question. The circular contains the service or product details and specifications: colour, sizes, capabilities, prices, photographs or illustrations, and guarantees and endorsements from satisfied customers or personalities. The circular is the primary selling tool in the pack and often takes the form of a booklet, broadsheet, jumbo folder, brochure or flyer. The response device is typically an order form, which must be legally correct, must repeat the selling message and product benefits, must be simple to read and fill out and comprehensive in the information requested. Alternatively, the response device can be an 0800 Freephone telephone number or credit card hotline. The return device is any mechanism that enables the recipient to respond with an order or donation. It can be an information request form, order form or payment slip and is usually accompanied by a pre-printed—and often pre-paid—return envelope.

a. Direct Mail Advertising—Volume and Expenditure, UK

	1989	1990	1991	1992	1993	1994
Volume (millions of items)	2,117	2,272	2,122	2,246	2,436	2,730
Expenditure (£millions)						
Production	485	682	605	603	555	646
Postage	273	297	290	342	352	404
Total	758	979	895	945	907	1,050

b. Direct Mail Costs, UK

The average British household receives six and a half items of direct mail per month. Direct mail is defined as personally addressed advertising that is delivered through the post. Direct mail suppliers will provide quotations on request. Prices can vary dramatically with volume and type of material. Specimen charges range as follows:

Service	Approx. Cost per '000
List rental cost by type:	
Consumer list (responders/purchasers)	£80
Consumer lifestyle database	£85
Electoral register—geodemographic selection	£50
Named subscribers to business magazines	£95
Companies classified by SIC code	£90
Laser printing	£12–£20
Inserting: 1–2 items by machine	£10–£16
3–4 items by machine	£14–£20

(Continues)

Table 18.3 The direct mail industry

c. Addressed Direct Mail Volume, Europe

Items per capita	1989	1990	1991	1992	1993	1994
Belgium	75	78	80	85	85	87
Denmark	45	47	49	50	44	50
Finland	48	50	49	44	44	46
France	53	55	55	61	62	65
Germany*	60	61	72	63	67	68
Ireland	11	11	14	16	16	20
Netherlands	57	60	43	66	66	72
Norway	45	48	50	50	49	53
Portugal	10	11	5	9	11	13
Spain	20	24	24	23	21	21
Sweden	71	74	77	46	62	64
Switzerland	101	103	106	107	104	104
United Kingdom	37	41	40	39	42	47

*Figures from 1989 to 1993 for West Germany only.

SOURCES: *The Marketing Pocket Book 1996* (Henley, Oxon: NTC Publications, 1995) and *The European Marketing Pocket Book 1996* (Henley, Oxon: NTC Publishing, 1995). Reprinted by permission.

Table 18.3 The direct mail industry (cont.)

Mailing Lists

Mailing lists Directories of suitable, relevant recipients or targets

Eighty per cent of direct mail is opened: only 63 per cent is partially read; less still leads to an order or donation. Depending on the scale of the targeted audience, however, the costs are relatively low: design, printing, postage and the purchase or compilation of **mailing lists**—directories of suitable, relevant recipients or targets. To be effective, appropriate targeting of direct mail is essential. Mailing lists must be as up to date as possible. There is a rule of thumb in the industry that one-third of addresses on a list change each year owing to deaths and re-locations. Within a year or two a list can be obsolete. Internal lists are those compiled in-house from customer addresses, account details and records of enquiries. External lists are produced by list brokers or mailing houses and bought—or rented—at commercial rates.

The suppliers of these external lists often undertake the complete direct mail operation for clients, from identification of recipients and compilation of lists to production of printed material, postage and even receipt of response devices. External lists can be either addresses of product category customers, including those of competing businesses if available, or general lists of targets with apparently suitable demographic profiles and lifestyles. Many of the leading geodemographic databases, such as ACORN or MOSAIC, were originally developed to assist in the targeting of direct mail. The Royal Mail can also be a good data source (see Figure 18.5).

Copy Writing

Copy writing The creation and wording of the promotional message

The targeting does not stop with the acquisition of a mailing list. The printed and product material included in the direct mail package must be written, designed and produced to appeal to the targets. The material must be prepared by people who understand the emotions and attitudes of the prospective customers. **Copy writing,** the creation and wording of the promotional message, is an important

Figure 18.5

Collecting data

The Royal Mail promotes a range of services to the marketing research and direct mail industries, emphasising its comprehensive and up to date databases.

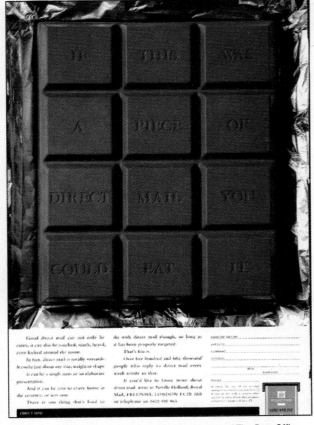

SOURCE: Advertisement reproduced by permission of The Post Office.

skill in the promotional mix, especially in the production of direct mail. The text must appeal to the target audience; sell the product; re-assure the reader; be informative, clear and concise; and lead to a positive response.

Strengths and Weaknesses of Direct Mail

There are many advantages associated with direct mail. The medium offers a wide variety of styles and formats—more than offered by a radio or press advertisement, for example. The package can be personalised and customised. Often it will be received and read alone, not in competition with other promotions from other products and services. Marketing research and database management can lead to accurate targeting of direct mail. Sending material directly to people's homes and workplaces can hit targets otherwise inaccessible to promotional activity.

The primary disadvantage is the growing consumer view that direct mail is junk mail that should be consigned to the dustbin without even being opened. If used on a large scale, direct mail can prove costly—perhaps less so than a sales force or television advertising, but more expensive than many public relations activities and some local or trade advertising. The direct mail packages and campaigns need to be up-dated to remain fresh in the fight against the junk mail image. In many countries, the paucity of up to date mailing lists increases the cost of direct mail, reduces the response rates and adds to consumer dislike of the concept of unsolicited direct selling through the post.

For organisations as diverse as retailer Marks & Spencer, financial services group American Express, catalogue retailer GUS, charity Oxfam, consumer goods manufacturer Unilever or British Airways, direct mail is an important, everyday component of the promotional mix. Whether it is on behalf of the starving in the Third World, double glazing for windows, fast food or book clubs, direct mail is familiar to consumers in most countries. For office supplies, maintenance services, security, computing products, and raw materials and components, in organisational markets direct mail is another important promotional tool, often supporting trade advertising and personal selling campaigns.

● ● ● ● ● ● ● ● ● ● ● ● ● ● ● ● ● ●

Summary

● *Personal selling* is the process of informing customers and persuading them to purchase products through personal communication in an exchange situation. The three general purposes of personal selling are finding prospects, convincing them to buy and keeping customers satisfied.

● Many salespeople—either consciously or unconsciously—move through a general selling process as they sell products. In *prospecting*, the salesperson develops a list of potential customers. Before contacting acceptable prospects, the salesperson prepares by finding and analysing information about the prospects and their needs. The *approach* is the manner in which a salesperson contacts a potential customer. During the sales presentation, the salesperson must attract and hold the prospect's attention to stimulate interest and desire for the product. If possible, the salesperson should handle objections when they arise. *Closing* is the stage in the selling process when the salesperson asks the prospect to buy the product or products. After a successful closing, the salesperson must follow up the sale.

● In developing a sales force, marketing managers must consider which types of salespeople will sell the firm's products most effectively. The three classifications of salespeople are *order getters, order takers* and *support personnel*. Order getters inform both current customers and new prospects and persuade them to buy. Order takers seek repeat sales and fall into two categories: inside order takers and field order takers. Sales support personnel facilitate the selling function, but their duties usually extend beyond making sales. The three types of support personnel are *missionary, trade* and *technical salespeople*.

● The effectiveness of sales force management is an important determinant of a firm's success because the sales force is directly responsible for generating an organisation's sales revenue. The major decision areas and activities on which sales managers must focus are establishing sales force objectives, determining sales force size, *recruiting* and selecting salespeople, training sales personnel, compensating salespeople, motivating salespeople, managing sales territories, and controlling and evaluating the sales force.

● Sales objectives should be stated in precise, measurable terms and specify the time period and the geographic areas involved. The size of the sales force must be adjusted from time to time because a firm's marketing plans change, as do markets and forces in the marketing environment.

● The task of recruiting and selecting salespeople involves attracting and choosing the right type of salesperson to maintain an effective sales force. When developing a training programme, managers must consider a variety of dimensions, such as who should be trained, what should be taught and how the training should occur. Compensation of salespeople involves formulating and administering a compensation plan that attracts, motivates and holds the right types of salespeople for the firm. Choices include a *straight salary compensation plan*, a *straight commission compensation plan* and a *combination compensation plan*. Motivation of salespeople should allow the firm to attain high productivity. Managing sales territories, another aspect of sales force management, focuses on such forces as size, shape, routing and scheduling. To control and evaluate sales force performance, the sales manager must use information obtained through sales personnel's call reports, customer feedback and invoices.

● *Sales promotion* is an activity or material (or both) that acts as a direct inducement, offering added value or incentive for the product, to resellers, salespeople or consumers. Marketers use sales promotion to identify and attract new customers, to introduce a new product and to increase reseller inventories. Sales promotion techniques fall into two general categories: consumer and trade. *Consumer sales promotion techniques* encourage consumers to trade at specific stores or dealerships or to try a specific product. These methods include *coupons, demonstrations, frequent user incentives,* such as *loyalty cards, trading stamps, point-of-sale (P-O-S) materials, free samples, money refunds, premiums, price-off offers,* and *consumer sweepstakes* and *contests. Trade sales promotion methods* stimulate resellers to handle a manufacturer's products and market these products aggressively. These techniques include *buy back allowances, buying allowances, counts and recounts, free merchandise, merchandise allowances, co-operative advertising, dealer listings, premium* or *push money, sales contests* and *dealer loaders.* The *ratchet effect* is the impact of using sales promotion and advertising together.

● *Direct mail* uses the postal service to contact prospective customers and to solicit interest in products or services. The main problem facing the direct mail industry is the growing adverse reaction to it as *junk mail.* Nevertheless, direct mail is widely used for consumer goods and services and also in business-to-business marketing. Increasingly, it is also important to non-profit organisations and charitable fund raising. Direct mail must be carefully designed with an attention seeking *flash,* good *copy writing* and a well constructed *direct mail package. Mailing lists* quickly become obsolete, and good database management is essential for the effective targeting of mail shots.

● ● ● ● ● ● ● ● ● ● ● ● ● ● ● ● ●

Important Terms

Personal selling	Ratchet effect	Buying allowance
Prospecting	Consumer sales promotion techniques	Count and recount
Approach	Trade sales promotion methods	Free merchandise
Closing	Coupons	Merchandise allowance
Order getters	Demonstrations	Co-operative advertising
Order takers	Frequent user incentives	Dealer listing
Support personnel	Loyalty card	Premium or push money
Missionary salespeople	Trading stamps	Sales contest
Trade salespeople	Point-of-sale (P-O-S) materials	Dealer loader
Technical salespeople	Free samples	Direct mail
Recruiting	Money refunds	Junk mail
Straight salary compensation plan	Premiums	Flashes
Straight commission compensation plan	Price-off offers	Direct mail package
Combination compensation plan	Consumer contests	Mailing lists
Sales promotion	Consumer sweepstakes	Copy writing
	Buy back allowance	

● ● ● ● ● ● ● ● ● ● ● ● ● ● ● ● ●

Discussion and Review Questions

1. What is personal selling? How does personal selling differ from other types of promotional activities?
2. What are the primary purposes of personal selling?
3. Identify the elements of the personal selling process. Must a salesperson include all these elements when selling a product to a customer? Why or why not?
4. How does a salesperson find and evaluate prospects? Do you find any of these methods ethically questionable?
5. Are order getters more aggressive or creative than order takers? Why or why not?
6. Identify several characteristics of effective sales objectives.

7. How should a sales manager establish criteria for selecting sales personnel? What are the general characteristics of a good salesperson?
8. What major issues or questions should be considered when developing a sales force training programme?
9. Explain the major advantages and disadvantages of the three basic methods of compensating salespeople. In general, which method do you prefer? Why?
10. What major factors should be taken into account when designing the size and shape of a sales territory?
11. How does a sales manager—who cannot be with each salesperson in the field on a daily basis—control the performance of sales personnel?

12. What is sales promotion? Why is it used?
13. Does sales promotion work well in isolation from the other promotional mix elements?
14. For each of the following, identify and describe three techniques and give several examples: (a) consumer sales promotion methods, (b) trade sales promotion methods, (c) retail sales promotion methods.
15. What types of sales promotion methods have you observed recently?
16. How does direct mail gain the interest of its recipients?
17. What are the problems facing users of direct mail?

● ● ● ● ● ● ● ● ● ● ● ● ● ● ● ● ● ● ●

Recommended Readings

A. C. Semintiras, J. W. Cadogan and G. A. Lancaster, "Salesforce behaviour: in search of motivational determinants", *Industrial Marketing Management,* vol. 25, no. 5, 1996, pp. 1–17.

G. Lancaster and D. Jobber, *Selling and Sales Management* (London: Pitman, 1994).

T. A. Shimp, *Promotion Management and Marketing Communication,* 3rd edn (Fort Worth: Dryden Press, 1993).

D. Bird, *Commonsense Direct Marketing* (London: Kogan Page, 1989).

J. Cummins, *Sales Promotion* (London: Kogan Page, 1989).

● ● ● ● ● ● ● ● ● ● ● ● ● ● ● ● ● ●

Cases

18.1   DEC's Sales Force Goes On-Line

Since 1957, when Digital Equipment Corporation was established, it has risen to be a leader in the computer market, alongside Compaq and IBM. Faced with more hardware and software challengers in the market, as well as an industry wide slowdown, DEC is now struggling to remain at the top. Only a few years ago company profits rose 38 per cent, but more recently DEC has experienced a drop in its market share and has cut its workforce by 10,000. Declining sales have served as a catalyst for change. By linking personal computers to information networking technology, DEC is automating its sales force—to establish a more efficient sales force capable of maintaining a competitive edge.

With buzzwords like "Microserver", "Microvax II", and "ethernet" in its vocabulary, networking conjures images of science fiction full of robots and other futuristic technology usurping humanity's place in the world. However, it is really only a tool designed to serve, and in large and small companies alike, it is doing just that. Hewlett-Packard, Fina Oil and Chemical equip all their salespeople with laptop computers, and several small businesses have saved themselves from going under by automating their sales forces. House-to-house interviewers in marketing research surveys use keyboards instead of clipboards. Meter readers for the utilities and delivery drivers for FedEx use barcode readers and data capture equipment during their calls. All that is needed is a computer, a modem and the communications software, which is becoming increasingly available. The most recent *Directory of Marketing Software*, a comprehensive list of sales marketing and sales software, catalogues almost 800 packages available for microcomputers, minicomputers and mainframes, compared with only 250 entries just a few years earlier. Turn on the switch and there is an electronic sales assistant, a desktop library with 24 hour access to current information and a worldwide communication system.

DEC's software, called Easynet Network, links sales, marketing and service personnel in 500 offices and 33 countries, allowing communication anytime and anyplace. Every DEC salesperson has an Easynet account accessible at the office, the customer site or at home via a personal computer. Sales personnel can use three different electronic ordering systems. Electronic Store provides customers with descriptions and pricing for every DEC product and service; over 100,000 customers have used this option to place orders. DECdirect, with a "mailing list" of 500,000 customers, is an electronic catalogue for lower priced items, with salespeople available for on-line customer assistance. One of DEC's goals over the next few years is to use DECdirect to place at least 80 per cent of its orders. EDI (electronic data interchange) provides computer-to-computer exchange of documents, such as purchase orders, enabling the sales force to respond to orders and ship products sooner. Sales representatives receive credit toward bonuses and membership in "top sales" clubs for all orders they place electronically.

Asked what they like most about being on-line, DEC salespeople place access to information, as well as to others in the company, at the top of the list. Seventeen informational databases satisfy the sales representatives' "need to know," offering information on topics such as account management, customer service and telemarketing. One DEC sales manager reports that Easynet saves sales representatives more than one hour of research time for every sale, as well as about 60 phone calls a month, translating into a savings of over £15 million. Easynet provides communication between sales, marketing, finance and engineering personnel through electronic mail (person-to-person messages), conferencing (group discussions) and electronic bulletin boards (company wide information). As communication becomes easier, geography becomes less relevant to the sales process. On a large project, the

sales manager in Frankfurt can communicate with the project manager in London, who can talk to the support personnel in Maryland—without playing telephone tag or waiting for conventional mail. Thanks to Easynet, DEC is now re-structuring its sales organisation from territory based to industry based. A person formerly responsible for a geographic area—Benelux, for example—may become the sales manager for a specific industry, such as insurance or banking.

Why automate a sales force? Critics warn that computer technology may be difficult for new people to learn and that the amount of available information may overwhelm the sales force. DEC believes that computerised selling frees people from paperwork and streamlines the ordering process, giving sales personnel more time to create demands for their products and to propose solutions to meet those demands. DEC saves money and gets a better prepared, more knowledgeable sales force. After more than 20 years in business, the president of DEC remains committed to his vision of a technology driven operation. His goal is to use electronics in a continuous effort to satisfy any customer's needs for any of DEC's 100,000 products or services in less and less time at lower and lower cost.

DEC is not alone in its new philosophy. Marketing research, door-to-door selling, retailing and business-to-business selling situations are increasingly supported by IT (information technology) hardware and software. Prospect screening, order taking, delivery and after sales service can all be assisted with IT solutions, to the benefit of customers, suppliers and employees alike.

SOURCES: Jaikumar Vijayan, "DEC points finger at flagging PC sales", *Computerworld*, 25 March 1996, p. 28; Philip Sellers, "DEC unleashes new Net initiatives", *Computing*, 1 February 1996, pp. 25–26; Thayer C. Taylor, "DEC gets its house in order", *Sales & Marketing Management*, July 1990, pp. 59–66; "Our 1990 marketing software directory", *Business Marketing*, June 1990, pp. 54, 56–58, 60–61, 70, 72; "DEC fires up an enterprise wide networking strategy", *Electronics*, September 1988; Leslie Helm, "What's next for Digital?" *Business Week*, 16 May 1988, pp. 88–92; Russ Lockwood, "What's new in on-line services", *Personal Computing*, June 1987, pp. 151–161; "Digital's high tech coup", *Dun's Business Month*, December 1986, pp. 28–29; Nick Sullivan, "Making on-line information work for you", *Working Woman*, April 1986, pp. 111–113.

Questions for Discussion

1. In what ways does the automation of DEC's sales force help the company's sales managers do their jobs more effectively?

2. What competitive advantages are gained by equipping DEC's sales force with advanced information technology?

3. What problems may be encountered during the implementation of such automation?

18.2 Trade Shows Launch New Zanussi Range

Italian white goods giant, Zanussi, part of the leading electrical appliances Electrolux group, chose a massive trade show as the central element in its new product launch. The 1993 new generation of cookers, fridges, dishwashers and washing machines premiered to the trade at a "no expense spared" extravaganza at Birmingham's National Exhibition Centre (NEC) organised by corporate events specialist Park Avenue. During the three day spring trade show, close to 3,000 retailers of white goods were "educated" into the new Zanussi range and brand positioning. Although in Italy Zanussi has a fairly utilitarian image, in many countries it is perceived to stand for design and innovation. Parent company Electrolux, locked in a global battle with Philips-Whirlpool, has injected substantial resources into Zanussi's new range in an attempt to maintain Zanussi's dominant position alongside the Electrolux brand, enabling a double-pronged attack on Whirlpool.

Hoover, too, launched New Wave and Classica washing machines and driers, stressing environmental benefits in terms of their production, reduced use of water and less reliance on harmful detergents. Zanussi's range had not been fully re-vamped for close to a decade and needed to match both competitors' developments and changing consumer concerns.

Zanussi's well remembered "appliance of science" television campaigns from the early 1980s firmly established the trademark as a brand in consumers' minds. Television advertising has now dropped to 10 per cent of such levels and focuses on maintaining awareness of the brand in short bursts. Seventy per cent of the company's promotional budget goes on below-the-line activities such as sales promotions. The NEC "mega" trade show was part of a regular series of road shows that began to develop links with retailers in 1986.

Zanussi recognises the importance of the white goods retailer in the buying process. Retailers' in-store displays are influential, as is the advice of sales personnel. Stock levels and product availability also influence the consumer's choice. As Zanussi's marketing director explains, "the need to support and work closely with retailers is more crucial than ever".

The move away from above-the-line advertising to various sales promotions activities—including road shows, trade shows, point-of-sale displays, retailer incentives and training—has coincided with Zanussi's gain of 1.5 per cent of the white goods market. With the recession-hit electrical appliance market still led by Hotpoint with 16 per cent and Philips-Whirlpool's attack on Europe making significant inroads, Zanussi is steadily building its share. With 12 per cent of the market, the Electrolux subsidiary hopes to become the market leader in the UK before the end of the 1990s.

In such a competitive market, Zanussi has not turned away from mainstream advertising totally. Its new Jetsystem washing machine range was given a high profile launch in 1995. In the same year, sales events like that held at Birmingham's NEC and Germany's regular Demotechnica exhibition continued to play an important role within the marketing channel, ensuring good product awareness and stockholding amongst retailers and wholesalers. In recent years, Zanussi has taken advantage of the high consumer recall of those famous "appliance of science" advertisements to produce a series of spoof advertisements along the same theme, but also tapping into the public's fascination with aliens and UFOs.

SOURCES: Robert Dwek, "Zanussi trade show to boost new image", *Marketing*, 28 January 1993, p. 13; "Zanussi adopts UFO theme", *Campaign*, 12 April 1996, p. 7; "Show stoppers", *Appliance Manufacturer*, April 1995, pp. 34–35; "Zanussi film leads £5m brand push", *Marketing*, 26 January 1995, p. 6; Lindsay McMurdo, "Advertisers favour revival of the fittest", *Marketing Week*, 10 June 1994, p. 21.

Questions for Discussion

1. Why does Zanussi employ a mix of advertising and sales promotion?
2. Zanussi's use of trade shows and exhibitions is part of a push promotional strategy. Why does the company not put its entire promotional budget behind advertising and adopt a pull policy?
3. What was so good about Zanussi's "appliance of science" advertising that justified the use of the same theme over 20 years later?

The promotion ingredient of the marketing mix addresses how a business promotes itself and its products to its target publics and target audiences. The decisions made by marketers concerning promotion affect how an organisation communicates with its target markets, how consumers are made aware of its products, services and activities, and how marketers expect to explain their determined brand positioning strategies. The chapters in Part V of *Marketing: Concepts and Strategies* have explained the core aspects of the promotional mix—advertising, public relations and publicity, sponsorship, personal selling, sales promotion and direct mail—and many of the key current trends and developments in the sphere of marketing communications.

Before progressing, readers should be confident that they are now able to:

Explain the role of promotion and communication in marketing

• What is the role of promotion in the marketing mix? • What is the process of communication? How does promotional activity relate to the product adoption process? • What are the aims of promotion? What is the promotional mix? • How do businesses choose which promotional tools to use?

Describe the use of advertising, publicity and sponsorship

• What are the uses of advertising? • What are the steps involved in developing an advertising campaign and whom does it involve? • What is publicity? • What is the nature of public relations? • What current trends are altering the work of advertising agencies and public relations consultancies? • What is meant by sponsorship in marketing terms? • How is sponsorship used by marketers?

Describe the use of personal selling, sales promotion and direct mail

• What are the purposes, steps and types of personal selling? • What are the principal tasks of sales management? • What are the uses of sales promotion? • What are the tools of sales promotion? What does direct mail involve? • What is the role of direct mail within the promotional mix?

Marketing Opportunity Analysis	Chapters
• The marketing environment	2
• Marketing in international markets	3
• Consumer markets and buyer behaviour	4
• Business-to-business markets and buyer behaviour	5
• Marketing research and information systems	6

Target Market Selection	Chapters
• Market segmentation and prioritisation	7, 22
• Product and brand positioning	7, 22
• Competitive advantage	7, 22

Marketing Mix Development	Chapters
• Product, branding, packaging and service decisions	8–11
• Distribution (place and channel) decisions	12–15
• Promotion decisions	16–18
• Pricing decisions	19, 20
• Supplementary decisions	3, 21, 24, 25

Marketing Management	Chapters
• Strategic marketing and competitive strategy	22, 23
• Marketing planning and sales forecasting	23
• Implementing strategies and measuring performance	24
• Marketing ethics and social responsibility	25

VI PRICING DECISIONS

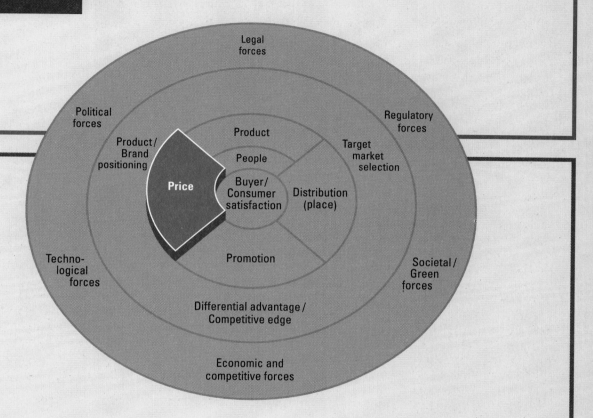

Legal forces

Political forces

Regulatory forces

Product/Brand positioning

Product

People

Target market selection

Price

Buyer/Consumer satisfaction

Distribution (place)

Techno-logical forces

Societal/Green forces

Promotion

Differential advantage/Competitive edge

Economic and competitive forces

T he price of a product or service will determine how consumers perceive it, reflect on its brand positioning, influence the choice of marketing channel, affect how it is promoted and have an impact on the level of customer service expected by target consumers. The price ingredient of the marketing mix will also strongly affect the viability of the supplying organisation. The pricing decisions for a business must take into account con-sumers' notion of value. The concept of pricing is complex, but as a marketing mix ingredient it is of fundamental importance to the successful imple-mentation of a marketing strategy. **Part VI of** *Marketing: Concepts and Strategies* explains the principal concepts of pricing and the setting of prices.

Chapter 19, "Pricing Concepts", explains the nature and importance of price in marketing, out-lines the characteristics of price and non-price competition, examines various pricing objectives and explores the key factors that influence marketers' pricing decisions. The chapter pays special attention to the complex aspect of pricing in industrial or business-to-business markets, and it concludes by discussing consumers' price versus value decisions.

Chapter 20, "Setting Prices", presents a detailed examination of the eight major stages in the process used to establish prices. The chapter also explores various issues that must be addressed when determining pricing objectives; the target market's evaluation of price; the relationship between demand curves and price elasticity; and links between demand, costs and profits. It next presents an analysis of competitive prices and then examines different pricing policies. The chapter concludes with an examination of the major pricing methods and the "pricing balance".

By the conclusion of Part VI of *Marketing: Concepts and Strategies,* readers should understand the essential pricing decisions required in the formulation of the marketing mix.

PRICING CONCEPTS

"The task of setting a price is one
of the most important decisions in
determining the marketing mix."

Peter Leeflang
Rijksuniversiteit Groningen

OBJECTIVES

- To understand the nature and importance of price
- To be aware of the characteristics of price and
  non-price competition
- To examine various pricing objectives
- To explore key factors that may influence marketers'
  pricing decisions
- To consider issues affecting the pricing of products for
  industrial markets
- To understand consumers' price versus value decisions

At the Dutch Annual Congress on Sales Promotion in 1994, the hot topic was EDLP (everyday low pricing). The notion is that by creating efficiencies in distribution and logistics, and by temporarily or permanently ceasing certain promotional activities, the budget savings incurred can be passed on by the manufacturer to the consumer through reduced prices on many leading brands. In most cases such price cuts can be achieved for prolonged periods and are therefore not simply short term sales boosting campaigns. The intent, too, is to reduce prices to the consumer through these savings in logistics and promotion without cutting retailers' margins, thereby avoiding alienating retail stockists.

Procter & Gamble deployed everyday low pricing in the UK in a bid to stem the tide of own label market share gains. The first two categories to benefit were the core markets of dishwashing liquids and nappies. P&G funded the reduced retail prices by cutting advertising and sales promotions budgets for brands such as Fairy Liquid and ference between Fairy Liquid and Tesco or Sainsbury's own brands to just 3p. Rival Lever Brothers cut the price of Persil, forcing the supermarkets to reduce their own label prices. In the highly competitive nappy market, P&G dropped the price of Pampers from £6.45 to £5.99. Rival Kimberly-Clark followed suit with its Huggies, and supermarket giant Tesco cut its own Advances brand price by 50p to £5.39. The consumer clearly is the beneficiary. It remains to be seen what the overall impact of EDLP will be on the advertising and sales promotions industries as manufacturers aim for savings in their promotional budgets to support lower prices for their consumer goods. ∎

Pampers. The company hopes that by lowering prices permanently, consumer loyalty to its brands will be strengthened and the role of retailers' own label products weakened.

In dishwashing products, own label products now account for one quarter of the market. Fairy Liquid's price was cut by 10 per cent as part of P&G's EDLP campaign, narrowing the price dif-

SOURCES: Amanda Richards, "P&G price cuts to hit own label", *Marketing,* 15 February 1996, p. 1; "P&G censures press over memo coverage", *Marketing Week,* 23 February 1996, pp. 8–9; Allan Mitchell, "Two sides of the same argument", *Marketing Week,* 16 February 1996, pp. 26–27; Stephen Hoch, Xavier Dreze and Mary Purk, "EDLP—hi-lo, and margin arithmetic", *Journal of Marketing,* 58 (4), 1994, pp. 16–27.

P&G is using price, along with other elements, to distinguish its products from competitive brands. For it and other firms, as for most organisations, pricing is a crucial element in the marketing mix. After focusing first on the nature of price and its importance to marketers, this chapter considers some of the characteristics of price and non-price competition. It next explores the various types of pricing objectives that marketers may establish and examines in some detail the numerous factors that can influence pricing decisions. The chapter then discusses selected issues related to the pricing of products for industrial markets and concludes with a look at the important debate over price versus value for money.

● ● ● ● ● ● ● ● ● ● ● ● ● ● ● ● ● ●

The Nature of Price

Price The value placed on what is exchanged

To a buyer, **price** is the *value* placed on what is exchanged. Something of value—usually buying power—is exchanged for satisfaction or utility. As described in Chapter 2, buying power depends on a buyer's income, credit and wealth. It is a mistake to believe that price is always money paid or some other financial consideration. In fact, trading of products—barter—is the oldest form of exchange.

Money may or may not be involved. In most organisations, however, the price element of the marketing mix means setting monetary price points and levels. Such businesses should broaden their understanding of price to consider ease of payment and payment terms as well as their target customers' perceptions of value for money.

Buyers' interest in price stems from their expectations about the usefulness of a product or the satisfaction they may derive from it. Because buyers have limited resources, they must allocate their buying power so that they can obtain the most desired products. Buyers must decide whether the utility gained in an exchange is worth the buying power sacrificed. Almost anything of value—ideas, services, rights and goods—can be assessed at a price, because in many societies the financial price is the measurement of value commonly used in exchanges. Thus a painting by Picasso may be valued, or priced, at £1 million. **Financial price**, then, quantifies value: it is the basis of most market exchanges.

Financial price The quantified value of what is exchanged; the basis of most market exchanges

Terms Used to Describe Price

Price is expressed in different terms for different exchanges. For instance, motor insurance companies charge a *premium* for protection from the cost of injuries or repairs stemming from a car accident. A police officer who stops a motorist for speeding writes a ticket that requires a *fine* to be paid. A lawyer charges a *fee,* and a *fare* is charged for a railway or taxi. A *toll* is sometimes charged for the use of bridges. *Rent* is paid for the use of equipment or for a flat. An estate agent receives a *commission* on the sale of a property. A *deposit* is made to reserve merchandise. A *tip* helps pay waitresses or waiters for their services. *Interest* is charged for loans, and *taxes* are paid for government services. The value of many products is called *price.*

Although price may be expressed in a variety of ways, it is important to remember that the purpose of this concept is to quantify and express the value of the items in a market exchange.

The Importance of Price to Marketers

As pointed out in Chapter 10, developing a product may be a lengthy process. It takes time to plan promotion and to communicate benefits. Distribution usually requires a long term commitment to dealers who will handle the product. Often price is the only aspect a marketer can change quickly to respond to changes in demand or to the actions of competitors. It must be borne in mind, however, that under certain circumstances the price variable may be relatively inflexible. Distributors and/or consumers may be alienated by significant price changes.

Price is also a key element in the marketing mix because it relates directly to the generation of total revenue. The following equation is an important one for the entire organisation:

$$\text{Profits} = \text{Total Revenues} - \text{Total Costs}$$
$$\text{or}$$
$$\text{Profits} = (\text{Price} \times \text{Quantities Sold}) - \text{Total Costs}$$

Prices affect an organisation's profits, which are its life-blood for long term survival. Price affects the profit equation in several ways. It directly influences the equation because it is a major component. It has an indirect impact because it can be a major determinant of the quantities sold. Even more indirectly, price influences total costs through its impact on quantities sold.

Because price has a psychological impact on customers, marketers can use it symbolically. By raising a price, they can emphasise the quality of a product and

Figure 19.1 Price competition. Budget Car Rental emphasises low price in its advertising.

Source: Courtesy of Budget Car Rental.

try to increase the status associated with its ownership. By lowering a price, they can emphasise a bargain and attract customers who go out of their way—spending extra time and effort—to save a small amount. In Figure 19.1, Budget advertises low price in addition to other service features.

· · · · · · · · · · · · · · · · · · · ·

Price and Non-price Competition

A product offering can compete on a price or non-price basis. The choice will affect not only pricing decisions and activities but also those associated with other marketing mix decision variables.

Price Competition

Price competition A policy whereby a marketer emphasises price as an issue and matches or beats the prices of competitors

When **price competition** is used, a marketer emphasises price as an issue and matches or beats the prices of competitors. Bic engages in price competition by pricing its perfume or pens low and emphasising price in its advertisements. To compete effectively on a price basis, a firm should be the low cost producer of the product. If all firms producing goods in an industry charge the same price, the firm with the lowest costs is the most profitable. Firms that stress low price as a key element in the marketing mix tend to produce standardised products. A seller using price competition may change prices frequently or at least must be willing and able to do so. Whenever competitors change their prices, the seller must respond quickly and aggressively. In many countries, the postal service and United Parcel Service or DHL engage in direct price competition in their pricing of overnight air express services. In the UK, fast printing services adopt a similar approach.

Price competition gives a marketer flexibility. Prices can be altered to account for changes in the firm's costs or in demand for the product. If competitors try to gain market share by cutting prices, an organisation competing on a price basis can react quickly to such efforts. However, a major drawback of price competition is that competitors, too, have the flexibility to adjust their prices. Thus they can quickly match or beat an organisation's price cuts. A price war may result. In the UK in the 1970s, both grocery and petrol retailers engaged in highly visible price wars. Many grocery retailers—led by Fine Fare and Tesco—traded purely on price; and their promotional material (newspaper advertisements and window posters) pushed the latest price reductions on major brands. The petrol companies and independent forecourt operators were locked in a price war in which neighbouring competing garages might reduce pump prices several times in one day in tit-for-tat reactions. Furthermore, if a user of price competition is forced to raise prices, competing firms that are not under the same pressures may decide not to raise their prices. As the 1990s draw to a close, the supermarket giants and petrol forecourts are again locked in severe price competition and price wars. EDLP,[1] described in this chapter's opener, is the latest variation on price competition. Companies like P&G hope to strengthen consumer loyalty by permanently cutting prices of key brands. By reducing promotions budgets, retail prices can be cut while retailers' margins remain static.

Non-price Competition

In **non-price competition,** a seller elects not to focus on price but instead emphasises distinctive product features, service, product quality, promotion, packaging or other factors to distinguish the product from competing brands. Since non-price competition is based on factors other than price, this approach gives an organisation the opportunity to increase its brand's unit sales through means other than changing the brand's price. For example, Galway Irish Crystal stresses heritage and product quality rather than competitive price. One major advantage of non-price competition is that a firm can build customer loyalty towards its brand. If customers prefer a brand because of non-price issues, they may not be easily lured away by competing firms and brands. Customers whose primary attraction to a store is based on non-price factors are less likely to leave their regular store for a lower competitive price. Price is not the most durable factor from the standpoint of maintaining customer loyalty.[2] But when price is the primary reason that customers buy a particular brand, the competition can attract such customers through price cuts.

Non-price competition is workable under the right conditions. A company must be able to distinguish its brand through unique product features, higher quality, customer service, promotion, packaging and the like (see Figure 19.2). Buyers must not only be able to perceive these distinguishing characteristics but must also view them as desirable. Marketing Insight 19.1 looks at how Parker uses its brand image in non-price competition. The distinguishing features that set a particular brand apart from its competitors should be difficult, if not

Parker Targets Its Pricing

Status symbols are expensive by nature—sleek European sports cars, 18-carat gold watches and ostrich skin briefcases are all very costly. Though smaller and less expensive, fancy fountain pens have become a common sight in the hands of influential business people. Such pens have high price tags and are much more difficult to maintain than ballpoints, felt tip pens or roller ball pens. However, recent sales figures indicate that the semi-obsolete fountain pen is making a comeback as the writing instrument of choice for status minded individuals.

Of the premium priced fountain pens, Montblanc pens are probably the most prestigious. Named after the highest mountain in Europe, these German made fountain pens cost from about £100 to £5,000 (for a solid gold one). The most popular model costs about £300. Prestige pricing has worked well for Montblanc, placing the pen in the same category as Rolex watches, Porsche sunglasses, BMW cars and Gucci luggage. Former US president Ronald Reagan, ex–Prime Minister Margaret Thatcher and fictional super-spy James Bond all use Montblanc pens.

Parker also makes high priced "power" pens, including its revived Duofold model, which was popular during the 1920s. The Duofold comes in a blue and maroon marbled finish and sells for about £175. Waterman and S.T. Dupont also sell fine fountain pens. The Waterman Le Man series, which comes in seven sizes, is priced at around £160. Dupont pens have a distinctive Chinese lacquer finish and are priced from £200 to £300 (for the gold flecked models).

Consumers can pay just 20 pence to write with a disposable biro pen, yet many thousands choose to spend £20, £50 or even £150 on a pen. Why? The product's image and the individual consumer's own aspirations dictate that such pens must do more than simply write. For Parker, this psychological pricing influence is not to be ignored. The company has developed a comprehensive approach to determining pricing for its various ranges. This involves a rigorous process of target market identification and analysis—per target market—of desired product and brand attributes for writing instruments. Various pricing algorithms are then applied, taking into account brand image and qualitative issues in addition to straightforward cost analyses. The approach concludes with an exhaustive investigation to determine customer willingness to pay a premium for the company's de luxe products.

Sources: Chuck Tomkovick and Kathryn Dobie, "Apply hedonic pricing models and factorial surveys at Parker Pen to enhance new product success", *Journal of Product Innovation Management*, 12 (4), 1995, pp. 334–335; Allen Norwood, "Pen offers status", *Charlotte Observer*, 20 November 1988, pp. 1c–3c; Parker Pen Co. sales literature, 1996.

impossible, for competitors to imitate. Finally, the organisation must extensively promote the distinguishing characteristics of the brand to establish its superiority and to set it apart from competitors in the minds of buyers.

Many European and non-US firms put less emphasis on price than do their American counterparts. They look for a competitive edge by concentrating on promotion, research and development, marketing research and marketing channel considerations. In a study of pricing strategy, many firms stated specifically that they emphasise research and development and technological superiority; competition based on price was seldom a major marketing consideration.[3]

A marketer attempting to compete on a non-price basis is still not able simply to ignore competitors' prices, however. The organisation must be aware of com-

Figure 19.2

Non-price competition
In this advertisement, the
Port of Calais stresses its
easy accessibility rather
than the price of channel
crossings.

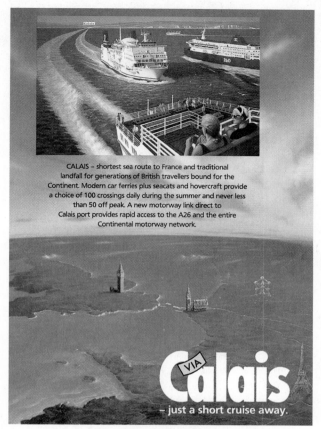

CALAIS – shortest sea route to France and traditional
landfall for generations of British travellers bound for the
Continent. Modern car ferries plus seacats and hovercraft provide
a choice of 100 crossings daily during the summer and never less
than 50 off peak. A new motorway link direct to
Calais port provides rapid access to the A26 and the entire
Continental motorway network.

Calais
– just a short cruise away.

SOURCE: *Chambre de Commerce et d'industrie de Calais France.*

petitors' prices and will probably price its brand near or slightly above competing brands. As an example, Sony sells television sets in a highly competitive market and charges higher prices for its sets; but it is successful nonetheless. Sony's emphasis on high product quality both distinguishes it from its competitors and allows it to set higher prices. Therefore, price remains a crucial marketing mix component in situations that call for non-price competition.

Pricing Objectives

Pricing objectives Overall
goals that describe what a firm
wants to achieve through its pricing efforts

Pricing objectives are overall goals that describe what the firm wants to achieve through its pricing efforts. Because pricing objectives influence decisions in most functional areas—including finance, accounting and production—the objectives must be consistent with the organisation's overall mission and purpose. Banking is an area where pricing is a major concern. As competition has intensified, bank executives have realised that their products must be priced to meet not only short term profit goals but also long term strategic objectives.[4] Because of the many areas involved, a marketer often uses multiple pricing objectives. This section looks at a few of the typical pricing objectives that companies might set for themselves.

Survival

A fundamental pricing objective is survival. Most organisations will tolerate difficulties such as short run losses and internal upheaval if they are necessary for survival. Because price is a flexible and convenient variable to adjust, it is sometimes used to increase sales volume to levels that match the organisation's expenses.

Profit

Although businesses may claim that their objective is to maximise profits for their owners, the objective of profit maximisation is rarely operational, because its achievement is difficult to measure. Because of this difficulty, profit objectives tend to be set at levels that the owners and top level decision-makers view as satisfactory. Specific profit objectives may be stated in terms of actual monetary amounts or in terms of percentage change relative to the profits of a previous period.

Return on Investment

Pricing to attain a specified rate of return on the company's investment is a profit related pricing objective. Most pricing objectives based on return on investment (ROI) are achieved by trial and error, because not all cost and revenue data needed to project the return on investment are available when prices are set. General Motors (Vauxhall), for example, uses ROI pricing objectives.

The objective of return on investment may be used less as managers and marketers in diversified companies stress the creation of shareholder value. When shareholder value is used as a performance objective, strategies—including those involving price—are evaluated on the basis of the impact they will have on the value investors perceive in the firm.[5]

Market Share

Many firms establish pricing objectives to maintain or increase market share, that is, a product's sales in relation to total industry sales. For example, Volkswagen AG cut prices on its 1990 model Jettas, Golfs, Cabriolets and Carats by 5 to 14 per cent and introduced two new models—the Corrado and Passat—at unexpectedly lower prices to boost its share of the car market.[6]

Maintaining or increasing market share need not depend on growth in industry sales. Remember that an organisation can increase its market share even though sales for the total industry are decreasing. On the other hand, assuming that the overall market is growing, an organisation's sales volume may actually increase as its market share within the industry decreases.

Cash Flow

Some organisations set prices to recover cash as fast as possible. Financial managers are understandably interested in quickly recovering capital spent to develop products. This objective may have the support of the marketing manager who anticipates a short product life cycle.

Although it may be acceptable in some situations, the use of cash flow and recovery as an objective over simplifies the value of price in contributing to profits. A disadvantage of this pricing objective could be high prices, which might allow competitors with lower prices to gain a large share of the market.

Status Quo

In some cases, an organisation may be in a favourable position and, desiring nothing more, may set an objective of status quo. Such objectives can focus on several dimensions—maintaining a certain market share, meeting (but not beating) competitors' prices, achieving price stability or maintaining a favourable public image. A status quo pricing objective can reduce a firm's risks by helping to stabilise demand for its products. The use of status quo pricing objectives sometimes minimises pricing as a competitive tool, leading to a climate of non-price competition in an industry.

Product Quality   A company might have the objective of product quality leadership in the industry. For example, the construction equipment manufacturer JCB aims to be ranked as one of the leading companies in its industry in terms of product quality and customer satisfaction.[7] Having such a goal normally dictates a relatively high price to cover the high product quality and, in some instances, the high cost of research and development.

• • • • • • • • • • • • • • • • • •

Factors Affecting Pricing Decisions

Pricing decisions can be complex because of the number of details that must be considered. Frequently there is considerable uncertainty about the reactions to price on the part of buyers, channel members, competitors and others. Price is also an important consideration in marketing planning, market analysis and sales forecasting. It is a major issue when assessing a brand's position relative to competing brands. Most factors that affect pricing decisions can be grouped into one of the eight categories shown in Figure 19.3. This section explores how each of these eight groups of factors enters into price decision-making.

Organisational and   Marketers should set prices that are consistent with the organisation's goals and
Marketing Objectives   mission. For example, a retailer trying to position itself as offering value for money may wish to set prices that are quite reasonable relative to product quality. In this case, a marketer would not want to set premium prices on products but would strive to price products in line with this overall organisational goal. Marketing Insight 19.2 discusses how BMW used the price of its new 3 Series Compact to broaden its target market.

Figure 19.3
Factors that affect pricing
decisions

BMW's Discounting Causes a Stir

At the 1988 Paris Motor Show, BMW launched its Z1 two-seater sports car. Intended initially as a limited edition pilot project, critical acclaim and consumer interest persuaded the German car giant to put the Z1 into production, but only in limited, deliberately withheld numbers. The quota for the UK in 1989 was just 25 cars, rising to 50 the next year. Many months before the launch, BMW was swamped with orders, which required a mandatory £5,000 deposit. The official price of the Z1 in August 1989 was £36,925. In the press that summer, however, 16 Z1s were advertised by owners or dealers with an average asking price of £46,822. Some cars were even re-sold for over £50,000. While BMW had purposely held down production levels, the company was still surprised by the prices being attained by the lucky recipients of the first 25 Z1s shipped to the UK.

For a company whose products represent up-market allure and superior brand image, the success of Z1 reflected the demand for the rest of the BMW range of luxury executive cars. A departure came with the launch of the new BMW 3 Series. Previously, the 3 Series range had been priced at the top end of the more middle market Ford Sierra or Vauxhall Cavalier prices, so keeping the BMW marque out of range of most car buyers. Arch rival Mercedes, however, had enjoyed significant success with the launch of its 190 range, priced significantly under anything previously sold by the company. Ironically, while Mercedes' 190 range was priced to compete with BMW's original 3 Series, Mercedes' success in winning a new market gave BMW a pointer. With its 190, Mercedes captured a significant market of people who had not previously been able to afford a Mercedes car, but who genuinely aspired to own one.

When BMW re-launched its re-modelled 3 Series, it slightly lowered the price of its entry point model, the 316i, to only £16,000. This pricing decision was popular with the motoring press and target customers alike. Two years later, though, to everyone's surprise, came the BMW 3 Series Compact. Slightly shorter and with a downgraded specification, the new Compact was sold at only £14,000. This price was intended to win over VW Golf drivers and owners of some of the more mass market models available from rival manufacturers. The risk for BMW was that its reduced entry point price might downgrade and thereby devalue the BMW marque in consumers' minds. BMW need not have worried; the marque retains its premium, luxury image but now appeals to a moderately broader target audience. So successful is the BMW 316 Compact that it won the "brand of the year" award at the annual ITV ceremony in 1995.

SOURCES: Douglas Hamilton, *Reuters*, 30 September and 17 October 1988; *Autocar*, 19 July 1989; "BMW", *Marketing Week*, 3 February 1995, p. 50; "Consistent innovation wins BMW top award", *Marketing*, 22 October 1994, p. 1.

The firm's marketing objectives must also be considered. Decision-makers should make pricing decisions that are compatible with the organisation's marketing objectives. Say, for instance, that one of a producer's marketing objectives is a 12 per cent increase in unit sales by the end of the next year. Assuming that buyers are price sensitive, increasing the price or setting a price above the average market price would not be in line with the firm's sales objective. A case in point: Ford has introduced high performance, well specified model variants to the top of each of its model ranges, for example, the £25,000 Escort RS Cosworth and the £28,000 Granada Scorpio 24v. Such prices ensure that these particular models have only limited appeal. Ford's stated objective, however, is to be market leader in terms of sales volume. The company, therefore, is careful to price the great majority of its cars in line with the price expectations of the bulk of the car buying public and fleet operators—far below these £25,000 and £28,000 levels.[8]

Types of Pricing Objectives

The type of pricing objectives a marketer uses will obviously have considerable bearing on the determination of prices.[9] An objective of a certain target return on investment requires prices to be set at a level that will generate a sales volume high enough to yield the specified target. A market share pricing objective usually causes a firm to price a product below competing brands of similar quality to attract competitors' customers to the company's brand. This type of pricing can lead to lower profits. A marketer sometimes uses temporary price reductions in the hope of gaining market share. A cash flow pricing objective may cause an organisation to set a relatively high price, which can place the product at a competitive disadvantage. On the other hand, a cash flow pricing objective sometimes results in a low price sustained in the long term. However, this type of objective is more likely to be addressed by using temporary price reductions, such as sales, refunds and special discounts.

Costs

Obviously, costs must be an issue when establishing price. A firm may temporarily sell products below cost to match the competition, to generate cash flow or even to increase market share; but in the long run it cannot survive by selling its products below cost. Even when a firm has a high volume business, it cannot survive if each item is sold slightly below what it costs to produce and market. A marketer should be careful to analyse all costs so that they can be included in the total costing associated with a product.

Besides considering the costs associated with a particular product, marketers must also take into account the costs that the product shares with others in the product line. Products often share some costs, particularly those of research and development, production and distribution. Services are especially subject to cost sharing. For example, the costs of a bank building are spread over the costs of all services the bank offers.[10] Most marketers view a product's cost as a minimum, or floor, below which the product cannot be priced. Cost analysis is discussed in more detail in the next two chapters

Other Marketing Mix Variables

All marketing mix variables are closely interrelated. Pricing decisions can influence decisions and activities associated with product, distribution, promotion and customer service variables. A product's price frequently affects the demand for the item. A high price, for instance, may result in low unit sales, which in turn may lead to higher production costs per unit. Conversely, lower per unit production costs may result from a low price. For many products, buyers associate better product quality with a high price and poorer product quality with a low price. This perceived price-quality relationship influences customers' overall image of products or brands. The price sometimes determines the degree of status associated with ownership of the product.

Pricing decisions influence the number of competing brands in a product category. When a firm introduces a product, sets a relatively high price and achieves high unit sales, competitors may be attracted to this product category. If a firm uses a low price, the low profit margin may be unattractive to potential competition.

The price of a product is linked to several dimensions of its distribution. Premium priced products are often marketed through selective or exclusive distribution; lower priced products in the same product category may be sold through intensive distribution. For example, Cross pens are distributed through selective distribution and Bic pens through intensive distribution. The manner in which a product is stored and transported may also be associated with its price. When a producer is developing the price of a product, the profit margins of marketing channel members such as wholesalers and retailers must be considered. Channel members must be adequately compensated for the functions they perform. Inadequately compensated channel members will withdraw from a marketing channel or be poorly motivated.

The way a product is promoted can be affected by its price. Bargain prices are often included in advertisements, whereas premium prices are less likely to appear in advertising messages. The issue of a premium price is sometimes included in advertisements for up-market items, such as luxury cars or fine jewellery. Higher priced products are more likely to require personal selling efforts than lower priced ones. A customer may purchase an inexpensive watch in a self-service environment but hesitate to buy an expensive watch in the same store, even if it is available there.

The price structure can affect a salesperson's relationship with customers. A complex pricing structure takes longer to explain to customers, is more likely to confuse the buyer and may cause misunderstandings that result in long term customer dissatisfaction. For example, the pricing structures of many airlines are complex and frequently confuse ticket sales agents and travellers alike. Customer service expectations are generally greater for expensive goods and services. The price charged for a product relates to income and profit levels: these must be able to sustain the required customer service levels and personnel.

Channel Member Expectations

When making price decisions, a producer must consider what distribution channel members (such a wholesalers, retailers and dealers) expect. A channel member certainly expects to receive a profit for the functions performed. The amount of profit expected depends on the amount that would be gained by handling a competing product instead. The amount of time and the resources required to carry the product also influence intermediaries' expectations.

Channel members often expect producers to provide discounts for large orders and quick payment. (Discounts are discussed later in this chapter.) At times, resellers expect producers to provide several support activities, such as sales training, service training, repair advisory service, co-operative advertising, sales promotions and perhaps a programme for returning unsold merchandise to the producer. These support activities clearly incur associated costs, and a producer must consider these costs when determining prices. Failure to price the product so that the producer can provide some of these support activities may cause resellers to view the product less favourably.

Buyers' Perceptions

One important question that marketers should assess when making price decisions is, "How important is the price to people in the target market?" The importance of price is not absolute; it can vary from market segment to market segment and from person to person. Members of one market segment may be more sensitive to price than members of a different target market. Moreover, the importance of price will vary across different product categories. Price may be a more important factor in the purchase of petrol than in the purchase of a pair of jeans, because buyers may be more sensitive to the price of a frequently purchased item such as petrol than to the price of jeans.

For numerous products, buyers have a range of acceptable prices. This range can be fairly narrow in some product categories but wider in others. A marketer should become aware of the acceptable range of prices in the relevant product category. (This issue and related ones are discussed in more detail in the next chapter.)

Consumers' perceptions of price may also be influenced by all the products in a firm's product line. The perception of price depends on a product's actual price plus the consumers' reference price, that is, the consumers' expectation of price. Exposure to a range of prices in a product line affects the consumers' expectations and perceptions of acceptable prices.[11]

Buyers' perceptions of a product relative to competing products may allow or encourage a firm to set a price that differs significantly from the prices of competing products. If the product is deemed superior to most of the competition, a premium price may be feasible. Strong brand loyalty sometimes makes it possible for the firm to charge a premium price for its product. On the other hand, if buyers view the product relatively unfavourably (without being extremely negative), a lower price may be required to generate sales. There is a considerable body of research on the relationship between price and consumers' perceptions of quality. Consumers use price as an indicator of quality when brands are unfamiliar and when the perceived risk of making unsatisfactory choices is high. They also rely on price as an indicator if there is little information available and judging a product's attributes is difficult.[12]

Competition

A marketer needs to know competitors' prices so that the firm can adjust its own prices accordingly. This does not mean that a company will necessarily match competitors' prices; it may set its price above or below theirs. However, matching competitors' fares is an important strategy for survival in the airline industry.[13]

When adjusting prices, a marketer must assess how competitors will respond. Will they change their prices (some, in fact, may not), and if so, will they raise or lower them? For example, it is likely that as Hertz stresses its keen pricing, competitors will adjust their pricing. Chapter 2 describes several types of competitive market structures. The structure that characterises the industry to which a firm belongs affects the flexibility of price setting.

When an organisation operates as a monopoly and is unregulated, it can set whatever prices the market will bear. However, the company may avoid pricing the product at the highest possible level for fear of inviting government regulation or because it wants to penetrate a market by using a lower price. If the monopoly is regulated, it normally has less pricing flexibility; the regulatory body lets it set prices that generate a reasonable, but not excessive, return. A government owned monopoly may price products below cost to make them accessible to people who otherwise could not afford them. However, government owned monopolies sometimes charge higher prices to control demand.

In an oligopoly, only a few sellers operate, and there are high barriers to competitive entry. The motor, mainframe computer, telecommunications and steel industries exemplify oligopolies. A firm in such an industry can raise its price, hoping that its competitors will do the same. When an organisation cuts its price to gain a competitive edge, other firms are likely to follow suit. Thus very little is gained through price cuts in an oligopolistic market structure.

A market structure characterised by monopolistic competition means numerous sellers with differentiated product offerings. The products are differentiated by physical characteristics, features, quality and brand images. The distinguishing characteristics of its product may allow a company to set a different price from its competitors. However, firms engaged in a monopolistic competitive market structure are likely to practice non-price competition, discussed earlier in this chapter.

Under conditions of perfect competition, there are many sellers. Buyers view all sellers' products as the same. All firms sell their products at the going market price, and buyers will not pay more than that. This type of market structure, then, gives a marketer no flexibility in setting prices.

Legal and Regulatory Issues

At times government action sways marketers' pricing decisions. To curb inflation, the government may invoke price controls, "freeze" prices at certain levels or determine the rates at which prices can be increased. With the privatisation of once public utilities, the UK government has set up regulatory bodies that stress minimum and maximum charges (for example, OFTEL for telecommunications).

Many regulations and laws affect pricing decisions and activities. Not only must marketers refrain from fixing prices, they must also develop independent pricing policies and set prices in ways that do not even suggest collusion. Over the years, legislation has been established to safeguard the consumer and organisations from the sharp practices of other companies. In the UK, the Monopolies and Mergers Commission prevents the creation of monopolistic situations. The consumer is protected by the Trade Descriptions Act, the Fair Trading Act, the Consumer Protection Act and many more. All countries have similar legislation, and the European Union legislates to protect consumers within the community.

• • • • • • • • • • • • • • • • • • •

Pricing for Industrial Markets or Organisational Markets

Industrial markets consist of individuals and organisations that purchase products for re-sale, for use in their own operations or for producing other products. Establishing prices for this category of business-to-business buyers is sometimes different from setting prices for consumers. Industrial marketers have experienced much change because of economic uncertainty, sporadic supply shortages and an increasing interest in service. Differences in the size of purchases, geographic factors and transport considerations require sellers to adjust prices. This section discusses several issues unique to the pricing of industrial products and business-to-business markets—including discounts, geographic pricing, transfer pricing and price discrimination.

Price Discounting

Producers commonly provide intermediaries with discounts off list prices. Although there are many types of discounts, they usually fall into one of five categories: trade, quantity, cash and seasonal discounts, and allowances.

Trade Discounts   A reduction off the list price given by a producer to an intermediary for performing certain functions is called a **trade** or **functional discount**. A trade discount is usually stated in terms of a percentage or series of percentages off the list price. Intermediaries are given trade discounts as compensation for performing various functions, such as selling, transporting, storing, final processing

Trade or **functional discount**
A reduction off the list price given by a producer to an intermediary for performing certain functions

and perhaps providing credit services. Although certain trade discounts are often a standard practice within an industry, discounts do vary considerably from one industry to another.

Quantity Discounts Deductions from list price that reflect the economies of purchasing in large quantities are called **quantity discounts.** Price quantity discounts are used to pass on cost savings, gained through economies of scale, to the buyer. Cost savings usually occur in four areas. First, fewer but larger orders reduce per unit selling costs. Second, fixed costs, such as invoicing and sales contracts, remain the same or may even go down. Third, costs for raw materials are lower, because quantity discounts are often available to the seller. Fourth, longer production runs mean no increases in holding costs.[14] In addition, a large purchase may shift some of the storage, finance and risk taking functions to the buyer. Thus quantity discounts usually reflect legitimate reductions in costs.

Quantity discounts can be either cumulative or non-cumulative. **Cumulative discounts** are aggregated over a stated period of time. Purchases of £10,000 in a three month period, for example, might entitle the buyer to a 5 per cent, or £500, rebate. Such discounts are supposed to reflect economies in selling and encourage the buyer to purchase from one seller. **Non-cumulative discounts** are one-off reductions in prices based on the number of units purchased, the monetary value of the order or the product mix purchased. Like cumulative discounts, these discounts should reflect some economies in selling or trade functions.

Cash Discounts A **cash discount,** or simple price reduction, is given to a buyer for prompt payment or payment in cash. Accounts receivable are an expense and a collection problem for many organisations. A policy to encourage prompt payment is a popular practice and sometimes a major concern in setting prices.

Discounts are based on cash payments or cash paid within a stated time. For example, "2/10 net 30" means that a 2 per cent discount will be allowed if the account is paid within 10 days. However, if the buyer does not pay within the 10 day period, the entire balance is due within 30 days without a discount. If the account is not paid within 30 days, interest may be charged.

Seasonal Discounts A price reduction to buyers who purchase goods or services out of season is a **seasonal discount.** These discounts let the seller maintain steadier production during the year. For example, car hire companies offer seasonal discounts in winter and early spring to encourage firms to use cars during the industry's slow months.

Allowances Another type of reduction from the list price is an **allowance**—a concession in price to achieve a desired goal. Trade-in allowances are price reductions granted for turning in a used item when purchasing a new one. For example, £50 for an old washing machine is credited against the purchase of a new machine. Allowances help give the buyer the ability to make the new purchase. This type of discount is popular in the aircraft industry. Another example is promotional allowances, which are price reductions granted to dealers for participating in advertising and sales support programmes intended to increase sales of a particular item.

Quantity discounts
Reductions off the list price that reflect the economies of purchasing in large quantities

Cumulative discounts
Quantity discounts aggregated over a stated period of time

Non-cumulative discounts
One-time only quantity discounts

Cash discount A simple price reduction given to a buyer for prompt payment or payment in cash

Seasonal discount A price reduction given to buyers who purchase goods or services out of season

Allowance A concession in price to achieve a desired goal

Geographic Pricing

Geographic pricing Pricing that involves reductions for transport costs or other costs associated with the physical distance between the buyer and the seller

F.O.B. factory price The price of the merchandise at the factory before it is loaded onto the carrier vehicle, i.e. excluding transport costs, which must be paid by the buyer

F.O.B. destination price A price quotation indicating that the producer absorbs the costs of shipping the merchandise to the customer

Uniform geographic pricing Pricing in which the same price is charged to all customers regardless of their geographic location

Zone prices Regional prices that take advantage of a uniform pricing system in which prices are adjusted for major geographic zones as the transport costs increase

Base point pricing A geographic pricing policy that includes the price at the factory, plus freight charges from the base point nearest the buyer

Freight absorption pricing A pricing policy in which the seller absorbs all or part of the actual freight costs

Geographic pricing involves reductions for transport costs or other costs associated with the physical distance between the buyer and the seller. Prices may be quoted as being F.O.B. (free-on-board) factory or destination. An **F.O.B. factory price** indicates the price of the merchandise at the factory, before it is loaded onto the carrier vehicle; it thus excludes transport costs. The buyer must pay for shipping. An **F.O.B. destination price** means that the producer absorbs the costs of shipping the merchandise to the customer. This policy may be used to attract distant customers.

Although F.O.B. pricing is an easy way to price products, it is sometimes difficult for marketers to administer, especially when a firm has a wide product mix or when customers are widely dispersed. Because customers will want to know about the most economical method of shipping, the seller must keep abreast of shipping rates.

To avoid the problems involved in charging different prices to each customer, **uniform geographic pricing**, sometimes called postage stamp pricing, may be used. The same price is charged to all customers regardless of geographic location, and the price is based on average shipping costs for all customers. Petrol, paper products and office equipment are often priced on a uniform basis.

Zone prices are regional prices that take advantage of a uniform pricing system; prices are adjusted for major geographic zones as the transport costs increase. For example, the prices of a manufacturer located in the northern French town of Lille may be higher for buyers in the south of France than for buyers in Paris.

Base point pricing is a geographic pricing policy that includes the price at the factory, plus freight charges from the base point nearest the buyer. This approach to pricing has virtually been abandoned because its legal status has been questioned. This policy can result in all buyers paying freight charges from one location, regardless of where the product was manufactured!

When the seller absorbs all or part of the actual freight costs, **freight absorption pricing** is being used. The seller might choose this method because it wishes to do business with a particular customer or to get more business; more business will cause the average cost to fall and counter-balance the extra freight cost. This strategy is used to improve market penetration and to retain a hold in an increasingly competitive market.

Transfer Pricing

Transfer pricing The type of pricing used when one unit in a company sells a product to another unit

When one unit in a company sells a product to another unit, **transfer pricing** occurs. The price is determined by one of the following methods:

Actual full cost—calculated by dividing all fixed and variable expenses for a period into the number of units produced.
Standard full cost—calculated on what it would cost to produce the goods at full plant capacity.
Cost plus investment—calculated as full cost, plus the cost of a portion of the selling unit's assets used for internal needs.
Market based cost—calculated at the market price less a small discount to reflect the lack of sales effort and other expenses.

The choice of a method of transfer pricing depends on the company's management strategy and the nature of the units' interaction. The company might initially choose to determine price by the actual full cost method. But later price changes could result in a market based method or another method that the management of the company decides is best for its changed business situation.[15] An organisation must also ensure that transfer pricing is fair to all units that must purchase its goods or services.

Price Discrimination

Price discrimination A policy in which different prices are charged in order to give a particular group of buyers a competitive advantage

A policy of **price discrimination** results in different prices being charged to give a group of buyers a competitive advantage. In some countries price discrimination is regarded as illegal in certain circumstances. For example, in the US price differentials are legal only when they can be justified on the basis of cost savings, when they are used to meet competition in good faith or when they do not damage competition. Thus, if customers are not in competition with one another, different prices may be charged legally. The EU is keen to stamp out price discrimination.

Price differentiation is a form of market segmentation that companies use to provide a marketing mix that satisfies different segments. Because different market segments perceive the value of a particular product differently, depending on the product's importance and value to the industrial buyer, marketers may charge different prices to different market segments. Price discrimination can also be used to modify demand patterns, support sales of other products, help move obsolete goods or excessive inventories, fill excess production capacity and respond to competitors' activities in particular markets.[16] Table 19.1 shows the principal forms of price discrimination. For price discrimination to work, several conditions are necessary:

1. The market must be segmentable.
2. The cost of segmenting should not exceed the extra revenue from price discrimination.
3. The practice should not breed customer discontent.
4. Competition should not be able to steal the segment that is charged the higher price.
5. The practice should not violate any applicable laws.

Bases of Discrimination	Examples
Buyers' income	Low priced admission to leisure and recreation facilities for the unemployed
Buyers' age	Children's haircuts, lower admission charges for students and senior citizens
Buyers' location	Zone prices and season ticket reductions for bus and train travel
Buyers' status	Lower prices to new customers, quantity discounts to big buyers
Use of product	Eat in and take away prices for fast foods
Qualities of products	Relatively higher prices for de luxe models
Labels on products	Lower prices for unbranded products
Sizes of products	Relatively lower prices for larger sizes (the "giant economy" size)
Peak and off-peak services	Lower prices for off-peak services (excursion rates on public transport, off-season rates at resorts, holiday and evening telephone rates)

Table 19.1 Principal forms of price discrimination

Value

Value for money The benefit consumers perceive to be inherent in a product or service, weighed against the price demanded

When determining a marketing mix, in many organisations the discussion of pricing often revolves around the actual monetary value—*the price*—to be charged for the good or service. It is important for marketers to consider also the payment terms and conditions they will permit or foster, such as interest free credit on household furniture or 60 days to pay for construction equipment. It is also necessary for marketers to recognise that raw price cannot be isolated from perceived **value for money** when consumers consider making a purchase. Consumers will not pay more than they value the benefit inherent in a product or service. Consumers balance the price demanded, typically in monetary terms, against the anticipated level of use and satisfaction to be gained from buying and using the specific product. Various factors will influence this equation: the consumers' previous experience of the brand and similar products, the perceived quality of the product in question, its brand image, purpose, anticipated usage, overall appeal and the nature of competing offers. These emotive issues are difficult to quantify, but through qualitative marketing research, most organisations are able to assess their target market's views of value. These findings have to be included in the decision-making surrounding the setting of prices (see Marketing Insight 19.1).

● ● ● ● ● ● ● ● ● ● ● ● ● ● ● ● ● ●

Summary

● *Price* is the value placed on what is exchanged. The buyer exchanges buying power—which depends on the buyer's income, credit and wealth—for satisfaction or utility. Price is not always money paid; barter, the trading of products, is the oldest form of exchange. Price is a key element in the marketing mix because it relates directly to the generation of total revenue. The profit factor can be determined mathematically by first multiplying price by quantity sold to calculate total revenues and then subtracting total costs. Price is the only variable in the marketing mix that can be adjusted quickly and easily to respond to changes in the external environment. *Financial price* is the quantified value of what is exchanged.

● A product offering can compete on either a price or a non-price basis. *Price competition* emphasises price as the product differential. Prices fluctuate frequently, and price competition among sellers is aggressive. *EDLP*, everyday low pricing, is a budget savings passed on from the manufacturer to the consumer. *Non-price competition* emphasises product differentiation through distinctive features, services, product quality or other factors. Establishing brand loyalty by using non-price competition works best when the product can be physically differentiated and the customer can recognise these distinguishing characteristics.

● *Pricing objectives* are overall goals that describe the role of price in a firm's long range plans. The most fundamental pricing objective is the organisation's survival. Price can be easily adjusted to increase sales volume or to combat competition so that the organisation can stay alive. Profit objectives, which are usually stated in terms of monetary sales volume or percentage change, are normally set at a satisfactory level rather than at a level designed for profit maximisation. A sales growth objective focuses on increasing the profit base by increasing sales volume. Pricing for return on investment (ROI) sets a specified profit as its objective. A pricing objective to maintain or increase market share implies that market position is linked to success. Other types of pricing objectives include cash flow and recovery, status quo and product quality.

● A group of eight factors enters into pricing decisions: (1) organisational and marketing objectives, (2) pricing objectives, (3) costs, (4) other marketing mix variables, (5) channel member expectations, (6) buyers' perceptions, (7) competition and (8) legal and regulatory issues. When setting prices, marketers should make decisions consistent with the organisation's goals and mission. Pricing objectives heavily influence price setting decisions. Most marketers view a product's cost as the floor below which a product cannot be priced. Due to the interrelation of the marketing mix variables, price can affect product, promotion, distribution and service level decisions. The revenue that channel members expect for the functions they perform must also be considered when making price decisions.

● Buyers' perceptions of price vary. Some consumer segments are sensitive to price, but others may not be; before determining the price, therefore, a marketer needs to be aware of its importance to the target market. Knowledge of the prices charged for competing brands is essential so that the firm can adjust its prices relative to those of competitors. Government regulations and legislation can also influence pricing decisions through laws to enhance competition and by invoking price controls—for example, to curb inflation.

● Unlike consumers, industrial or business-to-business buyers purchase products to use in their own operations or for producing other products. When adjusting prices, industrial sellers take into consideration the size of the purchase, geographical factors and transport requirements. Producers commonly provide *trade* or *functional discounts* off list prices to intermediaries. The categories of discounts include (1) trade, (2) quantity, (3) cash and (4) seasonal discounts, and allowances. A trade discount is a price reduction for performing such functions as storing, transporting, final processing or providing credit services. If an intermediary purchases in large enough quantities, the producer gives a *quantity discount,* which can be either *cumulative* or *non-cumulative.* A *cash discount* is a price reduction for prompt payment or payment in cash. Buyers who purchase goods or services out of season may be granted a *seasonal discount.* A final type of reduction from the list price is an *allowance,* such as a trade-in allowance.

● *Geographic pricing* involves reductions for transport costs or other costs associated with the physical distance between the buyer and the seller. An *F.O.B. factory price* means that the buyer pays for shipping from the factory; an *F.O.B. destination price* means that the producer pays for shipping. This is the easiest way to price products, but it can be difficult for marketers to administer. When the seller charges a fixed average cost for transport, the practice is known as *uniform geographic pricing. Zone prices* take advantage of a uniform pricing system adjusted for major geographical zones as the transport costs increase. *Base point pricing* resembles zone pricing; prices are adjusted for shipping expenses incurred by the seller from the base point nearest the buyer. A seller who absorbs all or part of the freight costs is using *freight absorption pricing. Transfer pricing* occurs when one unit in a company sells a product to another unit within the company.

● When a *price discrimination* policy is adopted, different prices are charged to give a group of buyers a competitive advantage. In some countries, price differentials are legal only when they can be justified on the basis of cost savings, when they meet competition in good faith or when they do not attempt to damage competition.

● *Value for money* is an important consideration when setting prices. Consumers do not regard price purely as the monetary value being demanded in exchange for a good or a service. The quality of the item, its brand image, purpose, usage and overall appeal—along with the consumers' previous experiences—dictate the consumers' view of value for money.

● ● ● ● ● ● ● ● ● ● ● ● ● ● ● ● ● ●

Important Terms

Price	Cumulative discounts	Uniform geographic pricing
Financial price	Non-cumulative discounts	Zone prices
Price competition	Cash discount	Base point pricing
EDLP	Seasonal discount	Freight absorption pricing
Non-price competition	Allowance	Transfer pricing
Pricing objectives	Geographic pricing	Price discrimination
Trade or functional discount	F.O.B. factory price	Value for money
Quantity discounts	F.O.B. destination price	

Discussion and Review Questions

1. Why are pricing decisions so important to an organisation?
2. Compare and contrast price and non-price competition. Describe the conditions under which each form works best.
3. How does a pricing objective of sales growth and expansion differ from a pricing objective to increase market share?
4. Why is it crucial to consider both marketing objectives and pricing objectives when making pricing decisions?
5. In what ways do other marketing mix variables affect pricing decisions?
6. What types of expectations may channel members have about producers' prices, and how do these expectations affect pricing decisions?
7. How do legal and regulatory forces influence pricing decisions?
8. Compare and contrast a trade discount and a quantity discount.
9. What is the reason for using the term F.O.B.?
10. What is the difference between a price discount and price discrimination?
11. What is EDLP (everyday low pricing)? How does it work?
12. Why must marketers consider consumers' perceptions of value for money when setting prices?

Recommended Readings

E. Gijsbrechts, "Pricing and pricing research in consumer marketing: some recent developments", *International Journal of Research in Marketing,* vol. 10, 1993, pp. 15–151.

B. K. Monroe, *Pricing: Making Profitable Decisions* (New York: McGraw-Hill, 1990).

M. H. Morris, "Separate prices as a marketing tool", *Industrial Marketing Management,* vol. 16, 1987, pp. 79–86.

J. Winckler, *Pricing for Results* (Oxford: Butterworth-Heinemann, 1983).

B. K. Munroe, "Buyers' subjective perceptions of price", *Journal of Marketing Research,* February 1973, pp. 70–80.

Cases

19.1   Pricing Risks to Brand Positioning: Mumm Champagne

As the Christmas 1992 festivities died down and revellers looked to New Year's Eve celebrations, few realised the significant changes occurring throughout the European Community. Britain's Prime Minister John Major lit one of hundreds of beacons to mark the dawning of a new era in intra-European trade and co-operation. The customs posts had a new, more limited focus: travellers entering the EU from other parts of the world. For EU business people and tourists alike, the formalities of passport checks and duty free allowances when passing from country to country in the EU had changed beyond recognition. Passport checks were few, and car-borne travellers could load more goods in their cars than—according to leading motoring organisations and the police—their vehicles could safely transport.

Many EU consumers noticed no changes until their annual holidays took them into Europe. For some more alert consumers, the changes in EU regulations had an immediate impact. Car ferry operators reported brisk business and above average passenger levels as UK consumers headed for the French coastal hypermarkets to load up with cut price wines and spirits. Coach operators from the South of England were joined by operators from the Midlands and the North running "away days" to the French hypermarkets. For the hypermarkets, extra stocks were brought in and English language signage became more prominent.

There had been much talk about 1992's EU deregulation. Governments had been preparing companies and trade organisations for several years, but the low cost wines of France were the first concrete manifestation of the changes for many UK consumers. Not only the French hypermarkets were facing new and changing opportunities. The new regulations were to cause upheaval for many companies, including Seagram's, makers of Mumm champagne.

Seagram's decided to sell its Mumm brand in the UK at prices similar to Mumm's French prices. Why? "We had to align our prices with those charged in France, to prevent the French coming over and buying it cheaper from here [the UK]," explained Seagram's. The price per case to the trade was to increase £23, pushing the wholesale price per bottle up from £14.33 to £16.25. The retail price to the consumer was £17.99 but rose to over £20, pushing Mumm ahead of arch rivals Moet Chandon, Mercier and Piper Heidsieck. "We are trying to re-position Mumm with a more premium image because the current positioning is not enough to support the new bottle price."

Seagram's had to re-think its pricing differential between France and the UK for its Mumm brand as trade barriers altered and consumers had an incentive to travel further to purchase, even potentially crossing the English Channel. The existing press advertising for Mumm, through Ogilvy & Mather, had to be shelved as Mumm was re-positioned. Seagram's second champagne marque, Perrier Jouet, also received additional marketing attention to reduce any loss to the re-positioned Mumm brand.

The French hypermarkets, UK coach operators, car ferry companies and alcoholic beverages giant Seagram's were not the only companies to notice changes caused by the macro marketing environment: EU deregulation. In Seagram's case, the pricing policies of major brands had to be altered and brand positioning reassessed.

SOURCES: Paul Meller, "Mumm price follows in French fashion", *Marketing,* 28 January 1993, p. 6; the Automobile Association; BBC and ITN television news broadcasts, 1 and 2 January 1993; Paul Meller, "Champagne: missing the marque?" *Marketing,* 17 December 1992, pp. 16–19; Seagram's 1995; Oddbins, 1996.

Questions for Discussion

1. In raising prices for Mumm, what considerations influenced Seagram's decision? Why did these complicate the issue for Seagram's?
2. What was the impact on Mumm's positioning? What are the risks of a radical price revision to positioning? Explain your answer.

19.2 Perfume Discounting—Pricing Policies to Rattle the Leading Brands

For decades the leading perfume houses of Paris, London and New York have sought exclusive, premium brand positioning: Joy, Chanel No. 5 and Givenchy have been marketed as high priced, de luxe lines available only from carefully selected retailers: leading department stores, fragrance houses and only those chemists with a genuine perfumery. Even a company as reputable as Boots has failed to gain Chanel's permission to retail Chanel fragrances throughout its chain of stores. Chanel permits only the larger, more exclusive branches of Boots to stock its brands, sometimes giving preference to an independent specialist fragrance house in a town to retail its products.

While these up-market brands have controlled distribution, they have also prevented price discounting. The more mass market brands, such as Revlon, Max Factor or Boots' own No. 7, have been

left to take the bulk of the market on volume, pricing way below Joy, Chanel No. 5 or Givenchy. In this way, these more expensive, selectively distributed brands have nurtured an exclusive, premium image to support their higher prices.

Kingfisher, owners of Woolworths and B&Q DIY, has created the UK's leading chain of discount drugstores. Towards the end of 1992, Kingfisher's Superdrug chain caught the marketplace by surprise. It brought in full in-store pharmacies to rival Boots but kept its discounting focus by reducing prices of proprietary medicines by around 10 per cent. Superdrug also looked to the perfume market, reducing the prices of the more mass market brands it stocked. Why, though, should Superdrug not create full perfumery sections in its larger branches and stock the more up-market, exclusive brands? More importantly, why should Superdrug not discount the prices of these leading exclusive brands of perfume, in line with the chain's general trading philosophy as a discounter?

Shock waves were felt throughout the industry. The perfume producers had spent decades creating premium priced, exclusive brands. Discounting by a retail chain was the antithesis of this strategy. Independent perfume retailers had been able to occupy prime pitch sites with high staffing levels and glamorous shop fittings on the basis of the higher margins offered by the slower selling exclusive brands. The pricing and images of these brands had for decades protected them from the national retail chains and buying groups. The large department stores were less dependent on maintaining the premium pricing, but they similarly saw their sales decline as Superdrug followed through with its plans. EU and UK trading laws and anti-price fixing legislation seemed to be on Superdrug's side, too.

It was not easy going for Superdrug. Along with the other discounters, Superdrug was refused supplies from the perfume manufacturers; the company had to source from "the grey market", mainly overseas wholesalers. The producers' PR mechanisms mobilised many industry players against the moves. Superdrug's first press advertising campaign for its discounting of fine fragrances was rejected by a string of up-market colour supplements and publishing houses. According to the marketing press, the colour supplements of *The Independent on Sunday, The Sunday Times* and *The Observer* refused to carry the Superdrug advertisements for fear of provoking repercussions from the up-market perfume houses, all leading advertisers in these newspapers' supplements.

Prior to Christmas, the peak selling season for all perfumes—including brands such as Joy, Chanel and Givenchy—leading department store operator House of Fraser, which owns Harrod's and stores in most large cities in the UK, reduced prices of many leading perfumes. Boots, too, retaliated against Superdrug's move. For example, in branches of Boots permitted to sell Chanel, a smaller Chanel No. 5 perfume dropped from around £28 to £21, a price still well ahead of the more mass market brands, but the largest discount for such a brand seen in one of its core retail outlets. Boots and House of Fraser admitted they were "reviewing daily" their pricing policies.

Years of brand building and image cultivation were in jeopardy. More to the point, the retailers were to risk reducing sales of these still lucrative brands. Superdrug wanted to enter the upper echelons of the fragrance market, but not to let discounting devalue the worth of stocking some of these brands. There were no intentions to replicate the price discounting and tit-for-tat retaliations in the DIY or grocery sectors of retailing, or in the holiday industry. The fragrance market, though, witnessed quite dramatic upheavals in a very conservative market. The entry of Superdrug, with its aggressive pricing policy and discounting, caused changes in strategies throughout the industry, by perfume producers, retailers and the media.

SOURCES: "Superdrug finds refuge in women's magazines", *Marketing Week,* 13 November 1992, p. 6; Helen Slingsby, "House of Fraser reviews scent pricing", *Marketing Week,* 18 December 1992, p. 5; "Stop press", *Marketing,* 19 November 1992, p. 7; "Eau Zone expands with new name", *Marketing Week,* 6 November 1992, p. 8; Suzanne Bidlake, "Givenchy TV ads 'plug' discounters", *Marketing,* 17 December 1992, p. 6, Suzanne Bidlake, "Perfume firms fear wrath of retailers", *Marketing,* 29 October 1992, p. 5; Suzanne Bidlake, "Asda apes Superdrug with discount scent", *Marketing,* 22 October 1992, p. 5.

Questions for Discussion

1. What were the pricing objectives of perfume manufacturers such as Chanel and Givenchy? Explain.
2. What impact could a price war have on brand loyalty in this market? Why?
3. On what criteria has competition in this market previously been based? Was the new focus on price a sensible development?

SETTING PRICES

"Price is the most dangerous
marketing weapon a firm can
use. It should be handled with
great care."

Eric Waarts
Erasmus University, Rotterdam

OBJECTIVES

- To understand the eight major stages of the process used to establish prices
- To explore issues connected with selecting pricing objectives
- To grasp the importance of identifying the target market's evaluation of price
- To gain insight into demand curves and the price elasticity of demand
- To examine the relationships between demand, costs and profits
- To learn how to analyse competitive prices
- To understand the different types of pricing policies
- To scrutinise the major kinds of pricing methods
- To grasp the "pricing balance"

For decades Heinz has built up an enviable range of products—far more than the old positioning statement of "57 varieties"— and significant brand reputation. Rarely in any marketing research do consumers voice complaints about Heinz products. Apart from soups, tomato ketchup and salad cream, the company is perhaps best known for its baked beans in tomato sauce. Few observers thought the baked bean market, already differentiated with the addition of sausages and burgers, would see any development.

Then came the budget lines. A~ ~~
average branded ~~~
retailed at aroun
were priced at 1
as 6p a can! L~
chains, but the ca
brands. Nestlé re
standing Crosse &
totally from the ma

The major branc
situations has been

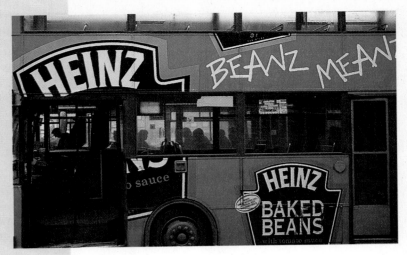

there is no reason to pay more to purchase Heinz branded cans. The share of own label baked beans moved up from 28.6 per cent in 1994 to 33.7 per cent in 1995, with predictions that it would achieve 40 per cent by the end of 1998. The growth has not all been at Heinz's expense by any means, as the departure of Crosse & Blackwell created a void into which many retailers pushed their own label lines. However, Heinz's share has dropped from 41.2 per cent to 40.3 per cent.

Heinz refuses to supply its "standard" recipes to the retailers as own label budget priced lines, thereby sustaining differentiation of its branded product. Heinz believes it will maintain its domination of the baked bean market while enhancing its scale economies by utilising excess capacity to supply a limited number of supermarket chains with own label brands. In a market where the retail price has dropped from around 30p a can to only 5p or 6p, the risks for Heinz are nevertheless great. Its balancing act in supplying some budget lines to Tesco, Sainsbury's and Kwik Save therefore poses an even greater dilemma. For the consumer, the sensational price reductions are very welcome, but the longer term effects on brand values are far from clear. ■

priced products could not possibly have been sourced from them: Coca-Cola and Kellogg's frequently use advertising to state that they do not manufacture own label or budget brands for supermarket chains. In the baked bean battle, however, the situation has been destabilised by Heinz's very determined entry into the supply of own label beans. Heinz claims that the downward price spiral was instigated by the retailers well before it decided to supply own label brands. Heinz uses own label supply contracts, which account for only 3 per cent of its output, to utilise spare capacity in its factories.

For the consumer, the situation is uncertain: did Heinz produce those discounted own label baked beans or not? As word spreads that some own label beans are originating from Heinz sites, the risk is that consumers will come to believe that all low cost baked beans are in fact Heinz products so

SOURCES: Stephanie Bentley, "Heinz own label hits supply snag", *Marketing Week*, 16 February 1996, p. 9; Stephanie Bentley, "Budget brands cook up trouble for Heinz", *Marketing Week*, 1 March 1996, p. 24; Julian Lee and Claire Murphy, "Cracking the lookalike code", *Marketing*, 29 February 1996, p. 12.

I n the baked bean market, the economic recession and the price wars between rival retailers have brought price points into prominence. Leader Heinz has responded with the launch of own label lines for some supermarket chains. Setting prices of products requires careful analysis of numerous issues. This chapter examines the eight stages of a process that marketers can use when setting prices.

Figure 20.1 illustrates these eight stages. Stage 1 is the development of a pricing objective that is congruent with the organisation's overall objectives and its marketing objectives. In stage 2, both the target market's evaluation of price and the ability of these consumers to buy must be assessed. Stage 3 requires marketers to determine the nature and price elasticity of demand. Stage 4, which consists of analysing demand, cost and profit relationships, is necessary for estimating the

Figure 20.1
Stages for establishing prices

economic feasibility of alternative prices. Evaluation of competitors' prices, which constitutes stage 5, helps determine the role of price in the marketing strategy. Stage 6 is the selection of a pricing policy, or the guidelines for using price in the marketing mix. Stage 7 involves choosing a method for calculating the price charged to customers. Stage 8, the determining of the final price, depends on environmental forces and marketers' understanding and use of a systematic approach to establishing prices. These stages are not rigid steps that all marketers must follow but rather guidelines that provide a logical sequence for establishing prices. In some situations, additional stages may need to be included in the price setting process: in others, certain stages may not be necessary.

Stages for Establishing Prices

In considering the stages for establishing prices, it is important for marketers to grasp target customers' evaluation of price and perceived value for money, as well as understand market trends and competitors' pricing moves. The "economics" of pricing—demand curves and price elasticity, plus the relationship in the market in question between demand, costs and profits—must also be addressed. The marketer must ultimately choose from a variety of pricing policies and specific pricing methods. In reviewing the eight stages for establishing prices, the remainder of this chapter examines these issues in greater depth. The final section explains that in the reality of day-to-day operational situations, many marketers are forced to take a broader look at pricing concerns and to exercise a degree of pragmatism in determining the price element of the marketing mix.

Selection of Pricing Objectives (Stage 1)

Chapter 19 considered the various types of pricing objectives. Selecting pricing objectives is an important task because they form the basis for decisions about other stages of pricing. Thus pricing objectives must be explicitly stated. The

Waterford: Crystal Maker Moves "Downscale"

Irish crystal manufacturer Waterford Glass Group acquired the famous chinaware manufacturer Josiah Wedgwood in 1986. The china division became profitable, but the crystal operation suffered a 73 per cent drop in profits. Gradually, there has been an overall recovery, and Waterford Wedgwood is now the world's leading manufacturer of high quality china and glassware. The company is particularly strong in North America, with expanding markets in Japan and Europe. Its products, premium priced giftware, are bought for special occasions or as notable gifts—emotional purchases supported by its strong, reputable brand names of Waterford and Wedgwood. The declining fortunes for the company in the late 1980s/early 1990s forced the company to re-examine its ranges and price levels.

With its new Marquis line targeted at the North American market, the venerable crystal maker has taken a new approach to manufacturing and marketing. Waterford has moved its production into Europe and scaled down its price points, which now start at $30 for smaller pieces, on average 30 per cent cheaper than traditional Waterford lines.

Seen by some observers as risky, this new line for "the less well heeled", manufactured in Germany, Portugal and parts of the former Yugoslavia, has led to labour unease at Waterford's Irish plants.

In the US, where Waterford has 28 per cent of the luxury crystal market, "Marquis by Waterford Crystal" is positioned in the $30 to $40 niche (although larger platters and bowls retail at $135) in order to compete more directly with crystal suppliers Mikasa, Lenox, Miller Rogasks and Gorham. The 1991 launch into 30 stores proved immediately profitable, but it is unclear how the range can be taken into other territories. Marquis is a huge gamble; it moves the company away from the "finest hand-crafted Irish" traditions and the Waterford brand heritage, which in the USA and Japan puts it alongside names such as Rolls Royce and Rolex.

The traditional Wedgwood and Waterford ranges are not generally intended to be day-to-day functional lines. They are premium priced and intended as "special", lasting purchases. This is an image well cultivated by the company's advertising and public relations and its refusal to become involved with discounting and retailer promotions.

statement of pricing objectives should include the time within which the objectives are to be accomplished.

Marketers must be certain that the pricing objectives they set are consistent with the organisation's overall objectives and marketing objectives. Marketing Insight 20.1 shows that Waterford priced its new range deliberately low to enable its corporate goals to be achieved. Inconsistent objectives cause internal conflicts and confusion and can prevent the organisation from achieving its overall goals. Furthermore, pricing objectives inconsistent with organisational and marketing objectives may cause marketers to make poor decisions during the other stages in the price setting process.

Organisations normally have multiple pricing objectives, some short term and others long term. For example, the pricing objective of gaining market share is normally short term in that it often requires the firm to price its product quite low relative to competitors' prices. An organisation should have one or more pricing objectives for each product. For the same product aimed at different market segments, marketers sometimes choose different pricing objectives. A marketer typically alters pricing objectives over time.

Carefully controlled distribution through only leading china/crystal showrooms and department stores further enhances the exclusive branding. The core market is the giftware sector, which its ceramics and glassware share with cutlery, jewellery (by far the dominant gift category) toys and games, and leather goods. Within crystal giftware there are five distinct segments: general giftware, weddings, investment giftware, business gifts/incentives and specials such as sporting trophies.

The giftware market depends on emotions. The selection of a gift, no matter what the occasion, is a personal, subjective and often risky action. Nowhere are individual consumer tastes and social influences more to the fore. Innovative, individually crafted, expensive crystal is a difficult purchase over which buyers agonise. High ticket prices and the very "personal" nature of the merchandise often extend the buying process as family and friends' opinions are sought. Will the choice be liked? Is it right for the intended home? Is it correct for the occasion? Is it value for money?

Waterford's enviable worldwide reputation is built upon a heritage of hand-crafted superior workmanship at its Irish birthplace. The company has been able to command premium prices in expanding international markets. The giftware market is idiosyncratic and very much consumer driven. In an economic recession, premium priced crystal is not at the top of every consumer's shopping list. Waterford is striving to build on its roots, while taking its wares into more countries and to a wider audience with its new ranges and lower pricing. In each segment, customers have specific needs and expectations, not always matched by the premium priced Waterford products. To expand the appeal and sales of a de luxe product without alienating the core target market is no easy task, particularly for such an emotive product as crystal.

SOURCES: Waterford Company Statements, 1992–1996; Harvest; Warwick University's Business Information Service; Caroline Farquhar; Sally Dibb and Lyndon Simkin, *The Marketing Casebook* (Routledge: London, 1994); Robert Gray, "A green and pleasant brand", *Marketing*, 20 July 1995, pp. 22–23; "Gifts galore", *Incentive*, 169 (4), 1995, pp. 77–86; "Give 'em a hand", *Incentive*, 168 (6), 1994, pp. 79–82.

• • • • • • • • • • • • • • • • • •

Assessing the Target Market's Evaluation of Price and Its Ability to Buy (Stage 2)

Although it is generally assumed that price is a significant issue for buyers, the importance of price depends on the type of product, the type of target market and the purchase situation. For example, in general, buyers are probably more sensitive to petrol prices than to luggage prices. With respect to the type of target market, the price of an airline ticket is much more important to a tourist than to a business traveller. The purchase situation also affects the buyer's view of price. Most movie goers would never pay, in other situations, the prices asked for soft drinks, popcorn and confectionery in cinema foyers. By assessing the target market's evaluation of price, a marketer is in a better position to know how much emphasis to place on price. Information about the target market's price evaluation may also help a marketer determine how far above the competition a firm can set its prices.

As discussed in Chapter 7, the people who make up a market must have the ability to buy a product. Buyers must need a product, be willing to use their buying power and have the authority (by law or social custom) to buy. Their ability to buy, like their evaluation of price, has direct consequences for marketers. The ability to purchase involves such resources as money, credit, wealth and other products that could be traded in an exchange. Understanding customers' buying power and knowing how important a product is to them in comparison with other products helps marketers correctly assess the target market's evaluation of price. As outlined in the previous chapter, it is also important to understand the consumers' view of actual price versus perceived value for money.

• • • • • • • • • • • • • • • • • •

Determining Demand (Stage 3)

Determining the demand for a product is the responsibility of marketing managers, who are aided in this task by marketing researchers and forecasters. Marketing research and forecasting techniques yield estimates of sales potential or the quantity of a product that could be sold during a specific period. (Chapter 23 describes such techniques as surveys, time series analyses, correlation methods and market tests.) These estimates are helpful in establishing the relationship between a product's price and the quantity demanded.

The Demand Curve

For most products, the quantity demanded goes up as the price goes down and goes down as the price goes up. Thus there is an inverse relationship between price and quantity demanded. As long as the marketing environment and buyers' needs, ability (purchasing power), willingness and authority to buy remain stable, this fundamental inverse relationship will continue.

Figure 20.2 illustrates the effect of one variable—price—on the quantity demanded. The classic **demand curve** (D1) is a graph of the quantity of products expected to be sold at various prices, if other factors remain constant.[1] It illustrates that as price falls, the quantity demanded usually rises. Demand depends on

Demand curve   The graph of the quantity of products expected to be sold at various prices

Figure 20.2

Demand curve illustrating the price-quantity relationship and an increase in demand

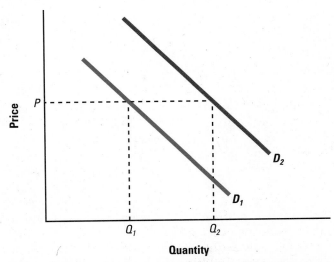

SOURCE: *Reprinted from* Dictionary of Marketing Terms, *Peter D. Bennett, ed., 1988, p. 54, published by the American Marketing Association. Used by permission.*

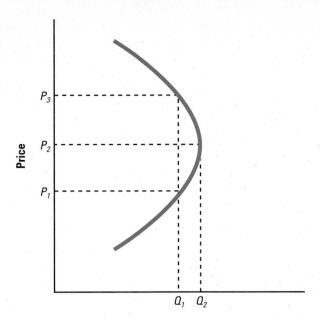

other factors in the marketing mix, including product quality, promotion and distribution. An improvement in any of these factors may cause a shift to, say, demand curve D2. In such a case, an increased quantity (Q2) will be sold at the same price (P).

There are many types of demand, and not all conform to the classic demand curve shown in Figure 20.2. Prestige products, such as selected perfumes and jewellery, seem to sell better at high prices than at low ones. These products are desirable partly because their cost makes buyers feel superior. If the price fell drastically and many people owned them, they would lose some of their appeal.

The demand curve in Figure 20.3 shows the relationship between price and quantity for prestige products. Demand is greater, not less, at higher prices. For a certain price range—from P1 to P2—the quantity demanded (Q1) goes up to Q2. After a point, however, raising the price backfires. If the price of a product goes too high, the quantity demanded goes down. The figure shows that if the price is raised from P2 to P3, quantity demanded goes back down from Q2 to Q1.

Demand Fluctuations

Changes in buyers' needs, variations in the effectiveness of other marketing mix variables, the presence of substitutes and dynamic environmental factors can influence demand. Restaurants and utility companies experience large fluctuations in demand daily. Toy manufacturers, fireworks suppliers, and air conditioning and heating contractors also face demand fluctuations because of the seasonal nature of these items. The demand for fax machines, single serving low calorie meals and fur coats has changed significantly over the last few years. In some cases, demand fluctuations are predictable. It is no surprise to restaurants and public utilities that demand fluctuates. However, changes in demand for other products may be less predictable, leading to problems for some companies. Although demand can fluctuate unpredictably, some firms have been able to anticipate changes in demand by correlating demand for a specific product with demand for the total industry or with some other economic variable. If a brand maintains a fairly constant market share, its sales can be estimated as a percentage of industry sales.

Figure 20.4

Elasticity of demand

SOURCE: *Reprinted from* Dictionary of Marketing Terms, *Peter D. Bennett, ed., 1988, p. 54, published by the American Marketing Association. Used by permission.*

Gauging Price Elasticity of Demand

Price elasticity of demand
A measure of the sensitivity of demand to changes in price

Up to this point, the discussion has considered how marketers identify the target market's evaluation of price and its ability to purchase and how they examine demand to learn whether price is related inversely or directly to quantity. The next stage in the process is to gauge price elasticity of demand. **Price elasticity of demand** provides a measure of the sensitivity of demand to changes in price. It is formally defined as the percentage change in quantity demanded relative to a given percentage change in price (see Figure 20.4).[2] The percentage change in quantity demanded caused by a percentage change in price is much greater for elastic demand than for inelastic demand. For a product such as electricity, demand is relatively inelastic. When its price is increased, say from P1 to P2, quantity demanded goes down only a little, from Q1 to Q2. For products such as recreational vehicles, demand is relatively elastic. When price rises sharply, from P1 to P2, quantity demanded goes down a great deal, from Q1 to Q2.

If marketers can determine price elasticity of demand, it is much easier for them to set a price. By analysing total revenues as prices change, marketers can determine whether a product is "price elastic". Total revenue is price times quantity: thus 10,000 rolls of wallpaper sold in one year at a price of £10 per roll equals £100,000 of total revenue. If demand is *elastic,* a change in price causes an opposite change in total revenue—an increase in price will decrease total revenue, and a decrease in price will increase total revenue. An *inelastic* demand results in a change in the same direction in total revenue—an increase in price will increase total revenue, and a decrease in price will decrease total revenue. The following formula determines the price elasticity of demand:

$$\text{Price Elasticity of Demand} = \frac{\text{\% Change in Quantity Demanded}}{\text{\% Change in Price}}$$

For example, if demand falls by 8 per cent when a seller raises the price by 2 per cent, the price elasticity of demand is −4 (the negative sign indicating the inverse relationship between price and demand). If demand falls by 2 per cent when price is increased by 4 per cent, then elasticity is −$\frac{1}{2}$. The less elastic the demand, the more beneficial it is for the seller to raise the price. Products for which substitutes are not readily available and for which consumers have strong needs (for example, electricity or petrol) usually have inelastic demand.

Marketers cannot base prices solely on elasticity considerations. They must also examine the costs associated with different volumes and see what happens to profits.

● ● ● ● ● ● ● ● ● ● ● ● ● ● ● ● ● ● ● ●

Analysis of Demand, Cost and Profit Relationships (Stage 4)

The previous section examined the role of demand in setting prices and the various costs and their relationships; this section explores the relationships between demand, cost and profit. There are two approaches to understanding demand, cost and profit relationships: (1) marginal analysis and (2) break even analysis.

Marginal Analysis

Fixed costs Those costs that do not vary with changes in the number of units produced or sold

Average fixed cost The fixed cost per unit produced, calculated by dividing fixed costs by the number of units produced

Variable costs Those costs that vary directly with changes in the number of units produced or sold

Average variable cost The variable cost per unit produced, calculated by dividing the variable costs by the number of units produced

Total cost The sum of average fixed costs and average variable costs multiplied by the quantity produced

Average total cost The sum of the average fixed cost and the average variable cost

Marginal cost (MC) The extra cost a firm incurs when it produces one more unit of a product

Marginal revenue (MR) The change in total revenue that occurs when a firm sells an additional unit of a product

Marginal analysis is the examination of what happens to a firm's costs and revenues when production (or sales volume) is changed by one unit. Both production costs and revenues must be evaluated. To determine the costs of production, it is necessary to distinguish between several types of costs. **Fixed costs** do not vary with changes in the number of units produced or sold. The cost of renting a factory does not change because production increases from one shift to two shifts a day, or because twice as much wallpaper is sold. Rent may go up, but not because the factory has doubled production or revenue. **Average fixed cost,** the fixed cost per unit produced, is calculated by dividing fixed costs by the number of units produced.

Variable costs vary directly with changes in the number of units produced or sold. The wages for a second shift and the cost of twice as much paper are extra costs that occur when production is doubled. Variable costs are usually constant per unit; that is, twice as many workers and twice as much material produce twice as many rolls of wallpaper. **Average variable cost,** the variable cost per unit produced, is calculated by dividing the variable costs by the number of units produced.

Total cost is the sum of average fixed costs and average variable costs multiplied by the quantity produced. The **average total cost** is the sum of the average fixed cost and the average variable cost. **Marginal cost (MC)** is the extra cost a firm incurs when it produces one more unit of a product. Table 20.1 illustrates various costs and their relationships. Notice that the average fixed cost declines as the output increases. The average variable cost follows a U shape, as does the average total cost. Because the average total cost continues to fall after the average variable cost begins to rise, its lowest point is at a higher level of output than that of the average variable cost. The average total cost is lowest at 5 units at a cost of £22, whereas the average variable cost is lowest at 3 units at a cost of £11.67. As shown in Figure 20.5, marginal cost equals average total cost at the latter's lowest level. In Table 20.1 this occurs between 5 and 6 units of production. Average total cost decreases as long as the marginal cost is less than the average total cost, and it increases when marginal cost rises above average total cost.

Marginal revenue (MR) is the change in total revenue that occurs when a firm sells an additional unit of a product. Figure 20.6 depicts marginal revenue and a demand curve. Most firms in Europe face downward sloping demand curves for their products. In other words, they must lower their prices to sell additional units. This situation means that each additional product sold provides the firm

Figure 20.5

Typical marginal cost and average cost relationships

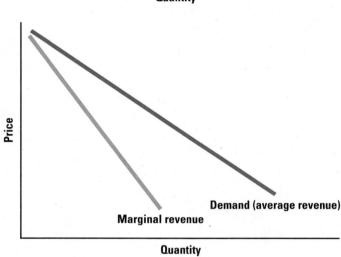

Figure 20.6

Typical marginal revenue and average revenue relationships

with less revenue than the previous unit sold. MR then becomes less than average revenue, as Figure 20.6 shows. Eventually, MR reaches zero, and the sale of additional units merely hurts the firm.

However, before the firm can determine whether a unit makes a profit, it must know its cost, as well as its revenue, because profit equals revenue minus cost. If MR is a unit's addition to revenue and MC is a unit's addition to cost, then MR

1	2	3	4	5	6	7
Quantity	Fixed Cost	Average Fixed Cost (2) ÷ (1)	Average Variable Cost	Average Total Cost (3) + (4)	Total Cost (5) × (1)	Marginal Cost
1	£40	£40.00	£20.00	£60.00	£60	£10
2	40	20.00	15.00	35.00	70	5
3	40	13.33	11.67	25.00	75	15
4	40	10.00	12.50	22.50	90	20
5	40	8.00	14.00	22.00	110	30
6	40	6.67	16.67	23.33	140	40
7	40	5.71	20.00	25.71	180	

Table 20.1 Costs and their relationships

1	2	3	4	5	6	7
Price	Quantity Sold	Total Revenue (1) × (2)	Marginal Revenue	Marginal Cost	Total Cost	Profit (3) − (6)
£57.00	1	£ 57	£57	£—	£ 60	£ −3
55.00	2	110	53	10	70	40
40.00	3	120	10	5	75	45
33.75*	4	135	15	15	90	45
30.00	5	150	15	20	110	40
27.00	6	162	12	30	140	22
25.00	7	175	13	40	180	−5

*Boldface indicates best price-profit combination.

Table 20.2 Marginal analysis: method of obtaining maximum profit producing price

minus MC tells whether the unit is profitable or not. Table 20.2 illustrates the relationships between price, quantity sold, total revenue, marginal revenue, marginal cost and total cost. It indicates where maximum profits are possible at various combinations of price and cost.

Profit is maximised where MC = MR (see Table 20.2). In this table MC = MR at 4 units. The best price, therefore, is £33.75 and the profit is £45. Up to this point, the additional revenue generated from an extra unit of sale exceeds the additional total cost. Beyond this point, the additional cost of another unit sold exceeds the additional revenue generated, and profits decrease. If the price was based on minimum average total cost—£22 (Table 20.1)—it would result in less profit: only £40 (Table 20.2) or 5 units at a price of £30 versus £45 for 4 units at a price of £33.75.

Graphically combining Figures 20.5 and 20.6 into Figure 20.7 shows that any unit for which MR exceeds MC adds to a firm's profits, and any unit for which MC exceeds MR subtracts from a firm's profits. The firm should produce

Figure 20.7

Combining the marginal cost and marginal revenue concepts for optimal profit at the point where MR equals MC, because this is the most profitable level of production.

This discussion of marginal analysis may give the false impression that pricing can be highly precise. If revenue (demand) and cost (supply) remained constant, then prices could be set for maximum profits. In practice, however, cost and revenue change frequently. The competitive tactics of other firms or government action can quickly undermine a company's expectations of revenue. Thus marginal analysis is only a model from which to work. It offers little help in pricing new products before costs and revenues are established. On the other hand, in setting prices of existing products, especially in competitive situations, most marketers can benefit by understanding the relationship between marginal cost and marginal revenue.

Break Even Analysis

Break even point The point at which the costs of producing a product equal the revenue made from selling the product

The point at which the costs of producing a product equal the revenue made from selling the product is the **break even point.** If a wallpaper manufacturer has total annual costs of £100,000 and in the same year sells £100,000 worth of wallpaper, then the company has broken even: no profits, no losses.

Figure 20.8 illustrates the relationships of costs, revenue, profits and losses involved in determining the break even point. Knowing the number of units necessary to break even is important in setting the price. If a product priced at £100 per unit has an average variable cost of £60 per unit, then the contribution to fixed costs is £40. If total fixed costs are £120,000, here is the way to determine the break even point in units:

$$\text{Break Even Point} = \frac{\text{Fixed Costs}}{\text{Per Unit Contribution to Fixed Costs}}$$

$$\frac{\text{Fixed Costs}}{\text{Price-Variable Costs}}$$

$$\frac{£120,000}{£40}$$

$$= 3,000 \text{ Units}$$

To calculate the break even point in terms of cash sales volume, multiply the break even point in units by the price per unit. In the preceding example, the break even point in terms of cash sales volume is 3,000 (units) times £100, or £300,000.

Figure 20.8
Determining the break even point

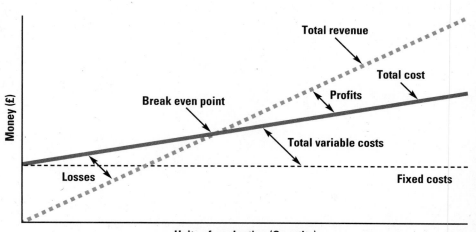

To use break even analysis effectively, a marketer should determine the break even point for each of several alternative prices. This determination allows the marketer to compare the effects on total revenue, total costs and the break even point for each price under consideration. Although this comparative analysis may not tell the marketer exactly what price to charge, it will identify highly undesirable price alternatives that should definitely be avoided.

Break even analysis is simple and straightforward. It does assume, however, that the quantity demanded is basically fixed (inelastic) and that the major task in setting prices is to recover costs. It focuses more on how to break even than on how to achieve a pricing objective, such as percentage of market share or return on investment. Nonetheless, marketing managers can use this concept to determine whether a product will achieve at least a break even volume. In other words, it is easier to answer the question "Will we sell at least the minimum volume necessary to break even?" than the question "What volume of sales will we expect to sell?"

• • • • • • • • • • • • • • • • • •

Evaluation of Competitors' Prices (Stage 5)

In most cases, marketers are in a better position to establish prices when they know the prices charged for competing brands. Learning competitors' prices may be a regular function of marketing research. Some grocery and department stores, for example, have full time comparative shoppers who systematically collect data on prices. Companies may also purchase price lists, sometimes weekly, from syndicated marketing research agencies.

Finding out what prices competitors are charging is not always easy, especially in producer and reseller markets. Competitors' price lists are often closely guarded. Even if a marketer has access to price lists, they may not reflect the actual prices at which competitive products are sold because those prices may be established through negotiation.

Knowing the prices of competing brands can be very important for a marketer. Marketing Insight 20.2 reveals how some companies allow their awareness of rivals' pricing to dictate their own marketing programmes. Competitors' prices and the marketing mix variables that they emphasise partly determine how important price will be to customers. Marketers in an industry in which non-price competition prevails need competitive price information to ensure that their organisation's prices are the same as its competitors' prices. In some instances, an organisation's prices are designed to be slightly above competitors' prices to give its products an exclusive image. Alternatively, another company may use price as a competitive tool and attempt to set its prices below those of competitors. Aldi, Toys "R" Us and Superdrug, for example, have all acquired a large market share through aggressive competitive prices.

• • • • • • • • • • • • • • • • • •

Selection of a Pricing Policy (Stage 6)

Pricing policy A guiding philosophy or course of action designed to influence and determine pricing decisions

A **pricing policy** is a guiding philosophy or course of action designed to influence and determine pricing decisions. Pricing policies set guidelines for achieving pricing objectives. They are an important component of an overall marketing strategy. Generally, pricing policies should answer this recurring question: "How will

Price Wars: Supermarkets Copy the Holiday Business

For television viewers throughout Europe, the winter months after Christmas throughout the 1970s and 1980s were brightened by holiday programmes and television advertisements promoting resorts, destinations, tour operators and travel agencies. As the 1980s came to a close, the market witnessed two changes. First, the promotional season began to start well before Christmas. Travel companies saw the need to compete more aggressively not only with one another but also for Christmas shoppers' disposable income. In addition, the retailers' post-Christmas January sales were a significant draw on consumers' available cash. Second, the core message was no longer brochure choice or exotic destinations but price: value for money, low cost holidays.

In the 1960s and 1970s supermarket chains and petrol forecourts had competed largely on the basis of price; they attempted little or no product or service differentiation, and their promotional campaigns emphasised only low prices. The resulting price wars sometimes led to several price reductions for the same merchandise within a working day. Motorists would travel the extra half mile to save 1 or 2 per cent on the price of a tank of petrol. Neighbouring garage forecourts would alter the advertised price of their petrol in tit-for-tat retaliations. Shoppers would visit neighbouring supermarkets to compare prices on major lines such as branded soups or breakfast cereals.

Although not as frenetic, the price wars in the holiday industry were equally fierce. Poor weather in 1992, coupled with the economic recession throughout much of Europe, made 1993 a crucial season for many travel firms. In the UK in 1992 several major operators had been forced out of business. Even Intersun, once the market leader, had ceased trading.

The first shots were fired by Thomas Cook, which not only guaranteed no surcharges for its new season's holidays but reduced list prices in its brochures by 10 per cent. Leading travel agent rivals Lunn Poly and Pickford's followed suit, reducing prices. Not only the travel agencies offered reductions. Leading rival tour operators such as Thomsons and Airtours slashed their 1993 brochure prices. Europe's latest resort, EuroDisney, found itself having to offer hefty price discounts.

price be used as a variable in the marketing mix?" This question may relate to (1) introduction of new products, (2) competitive situations, (3) government pricing regulations, (4) economic conditions or (5) implementation of pricing objectives. Pricing policies help marketers solve the practical problems of establishing prices. This section examines the most common pricing policies.

Pioneer Pricing Policies

Pioneer pricing   The setting of a base price for a new product

Pioneer pricing—setting the base price for a new product—is a necessary part of formulating a marketing strategy. The base price is easily adjusted (in the absence of government price controls), and its establishment is one of the most fundamental decisions in the marketing mix. The base price can be set high to recover development costs quickly or to provide a reference point for developing discount prices to different market segments.

When marketers set base prices, they also consider how quickly competitors will enter the market, whether they will mount a strong campaign on entry, and what effect their entry will have on the development of primary demand. If com-

Industry observers were concerned that the latest price wars would harm everyone and force more companies into liquidation, as well as causing service standards for the consumer to fall as companies pared their operating costs to the bone. The independent travel agents were squeezed even more by their chain rivals, many of which were part of larger holding companies with significant funds and resources. Noel Josehides of the Association of Independent Tour Operators warned that multiples such as Lunn Poly and Pickford's were conditioning the consumer to expect constant give-aways by offering a wider range of cut price deals than ever before. Industry observers believed that several operators were selling holidays at well below cost price and that travel agents were waiving their commissions. The emphasis was on reduced prices, cash flow generation and, for many companies, short term survival.

As the 1990s roll on, the cash orientated offers and heavy discounting continue in the "holiday wars". The consumer now expects such discounting, and few people who book a holiday pay the list or published price. This trend may no longer be sur-

prising. The price wars between the pre-eminent supermarket giants, however, are. For decades, Tesco and Sainsbury's rivalled each other in location, store openings, range selection and customer service. In a bid to prevent Tesco from becoming the market leader, Sainsbury's resorted to price cutting and launched its Economy range. The result for Sainsbury's has been reduced profits, a bad situation made worse by the negative reaction of financial journalists and shareholders. Sainsbury's crown has slipped in the eyes of some—and clearly, price wars are not necessarily the best weapon in the marketer's armoury. Differentiation is important in all areas of marketing, but that based on product or service—as Sainsbury's had developed—generally works better than trading on price.

SOURCES: Thomas Cook, Airtours, Thomson, Lunn Poly, Pickford's promotional literature, 1992–93; "Holiday discounts are 'unfair trading'", *Marketing Week,* 22 January 1992, p. 8; Juliana Koranteng, "Travel agents unite for ad campaign", *Marketing,* 29 October 1992, p. 10; Stephen Buck, "Sainsbury's strategy goes back to basics", *Marketing Week,* 6 October 1995, p. 24; Julian Lee, "Economy range takes the softly, softly approach", *Marketing Week,* 14 September 1995, p. 1; Sainsbury's AGM 1996.

petitors will enter quickly with considerable marketing force and with limited effect on the primary demand, a firm may adopt a base price that will discourage their entry.

Price skimming A pricing policy whereby an organisation charges the highest possible price that buyers who most desire the product will pay

Price Skimming **Price skimming** is charging the highest possible price that buyers who most desire the product will pay. This pioneer approach provides the most flexible introductory base price. Demand tends to be inelastic in the introductory stage of the product life cycle (for example, the compact disc player and the pocket calculator).

Price skimming can provide several benefits, especially when a product is in the introductory stage of its life cycle. A skimming policy can generate much needed initial cash flows to help offset sizeable developmental costs. When introducing a new model of camera, Polaroid initially uses a skimming price to defray large research and development costs. Price skimming protects the marketer from problems that arise when the price is set too low to cover costs. When a firm introduces a product, its production capacity may be limited. A skimming price can help keep demand consistent with a firm's production capabilities. The use of a skimming price may attract competition into an industry because the high price makes that type of business appear to be quite lucrative.

Penetration price A price set below the prices of competing brands in order to penetrate a market and produce a larger unit sales volume

Penetration Price   A **penetration price** is a price set below the prices of competing brands in order to penetrate a market and produce a larger unit sales volume. When introducing a product, a marketer sometimes uses a penetration price to gain a large market share quickly. As shown in Figure 20.9, SAS stresses its competitive cargo rates. This approach places the marketer in a less flexible position than price skimming because it is more difficult to raise a penetration price than to lower or discount a skimming price. It is not unusual for a firm to use a penetration price after having skimmed the market with a higher price.

Penetration pricing can be especially beneficial when marketers suspect that competitors could enter the market easily. First, if the penetration price lets one marketer gain a large market share quickly, competitors might be discouraged from entering the market. Second, entering the market may be less attractive to competitors when a penetration price is used, because the lower per unit price results in lower per unit profit; this may cause competitors to view the market as not being especially lucrative.

A penetration price is particularly appropriate when demand is highly elastic. Highly elastic demand means that target market members would purchase the

Figure 20.9

Penetration pricing

SAS hopes to persuade customers that the airline offers highly competitive cargo rates and value for money.

Source: Courtesy of SAS Cargo.

product if it was priced at the penetration level but that few would buy the item if it was priced higher. A marketer should consider using a penetration price when a lower price would result in longer production runs, increasing production significantly and reducing the firm's per unit production costs.

Psychological Pricing

Psychological pricing A pricing method designed to encourage purchases that are based on emotional rather than rational responses

Odd-even pricing A pricing method that tries to influence buyers' perceptions of the price or the product by ending the price with certain numbers

Psychological pricing encourages purchases based on emotional rather than rational responses. It is used most often at the retail level. Psychological pricing has limited use for industrial products.

Odd-Even Pricing   Through **odd-even pricing**—that is, ending the price with certain numbers—marketers try to influence buyers' perceptions of the price or the product. Odd pricing assumes that more of a product will be sold at £99.95 than at £100. Supposedly, customers will think, or at least tell friends, that the product is a bargain—not £100, mind you, but £99, plus a few insignificant pence. Also, customers are supposed to think that the store could have charged £100 but instead cut the price to the last penny or so, to £99.95. Some claim, too, that certain types of customers are more attracted by odd prices than by even ones. However, no substantial research findings support the notion that odd prices produce greater sales. Nonetheless, even prices are far more unusual today than odd prices.

Even prices are used to give a product an exclusive or up-market image. An even price supposedly will influence a customer to view the product as being a high quality, premium brand. A tie manufacturer, for example, may print on a premium silk tie packet a suggested retail price of £32 instead of £31.95; the even price of the tie is used to enhance its up-market image.

Customary pricing A pricing method whereby goods are priced primarily on the basis of tradition

Customary Pricing   In **customary pricing**, certain goods are priced primarily on the basis of tradition. Recent economic uncertainties have caused most prices to fluctuate fairly widely, but the classic example of the customary, or traditional, price is the telephone call. Until the mid-1980s, UK public telephones were geared to the use of particular coins. For years the 2p and, later, the 10p slots were widely recognised. BT's initial response to rising prices was to alter the cost of units so that less call time was allowed for the same money. Since then, demands for greater flexibility of use have seen public call boxes altered to accept most British coins.

Prestige pricing A pricing method whereby prices are set at an artificially high level to provide prestige or a quality image

Prestige Pricing   In **prestige pricing**, prices are set at an artificially high level to provide prestige or a quality image. In the United States, pharmacists report that some consumers complain if a prescription does not cost enough. Apparently, some consumers associate a drug's price with its potency. Consumers in Europe often associate the quality of service provided by a hairdresser with price. In some cases, this is demonstrated by a willingness to pay more than twice as much for a perm at an establishment like Vidal Sassoon than at the local hairdresser, even though the treatment given may be comparable.

Prestige pricing is used especially when buyers associate a higher price with higher quality. Typical product categories in which selected products are given prestige prices include perfumes, cars, alcoholic beverages, jewellery, cameras, and electrical appliances. Dramatically lowering the prices of products with prestige prices would be inconsistent with the perceived images of such products.

Price lining A pricing method whereby an organisation sets a limited number of prices for selected groups or lines of merchandise

Price Lining When an organisation sets a limited number of prices for selected groups or lines of merchandise, it is using **price lining.** A retailer may have various styles and brands of men's shirts of similar quality that sell for £10. Another line of higher quality shirts may sell for £20. Price lining simplifies consumers' decision-making by holding constant one key variable in the final selection of style and brand within a line. In product line pricing, the company should look at the prices of the overall product line to ensure that the price of the new model lies within the range of existing prices for that line. Failure to consider the impact of the new model's price relative to the existing product line may change buyers' perceptions of all the models in the line.[3]

The basic assumption in price lining is that the demand is inelastic for various groups or sets of products. If the prices are attractive, customers will concentrate their purchases without responding to slight changes in price. Thus a women's dress shop that carries dresses priced at £85, £55 and £35 might not attract many more sales with a drop to, say, £83, £53 and £33. The "space" between the prices of £55 and £35, however, can stir changes in consumer response. With price lining, the demand curve looks like a series of steps, as shown in Figure 20.10.

Professional Pricing

Professional pricing Pricing used by people who have great skill or experience in a particular field or activity

Professional pricing is used by people who have great skill or experience in a particular field or activity. Some professionals who provide such products as medical services feel that their fees (prices) should not relate directly to their time and involvement in specific cases; rather, they charge a standard fee regardless of the problems involved in performing the job. Some estate agents' and solicitors' fees are prime examples: 2 per cent of a house sale price, plus VAT, and £300 for house conveyancing. Other professionals set prices in other ways.

The concept of professional pricing carries with it the idea that professionals have an ethical responsibility not to over charge unknowing customers. In some situations, a seller can charge customers a high price and continue to sell many units of the product. Medicine offers several examples. If a patient with high blood pressure requires four tablets a day to survive, the individual will pay for the prescription whether it costs £3 or £30 per month. In fact, the patient would

Figure 20.10
Price lining

purchase the pills even if the price went higher. In these situations sellers could charge exorbitant fees. Drug companies claim that despite their positions of strength in this regard, they charge "ethical" prices rather than what the market will bear. In 1989 Burroughs-Wellcome reduced the price of its AIDS drug AZT by 20 per cent, partly in response to pressure from AIDS patients and activists. However, some feel that the annual price tag for AZT treatments is still far too high.[4]

Promotional Pricing

Promotional pricing Pricing related to the short term promotion of a particular product

Price is an ingredient in the marketing mix, and it is often co-ordinated with promotion. The two variables sometimes are so interrelated that the pricing policy is promotion orientated. Examples of **promotional pricing** include (1) price leaders, (2) special event pricing, (3) everyday low pricing and (4) experience curve pricing.

Price leaders Products sold below the usual mark-up, near cost or below cost

Price Leaders   Sometimes a firm prices a few products below the usual mark-up, near cost, or below cost, which results in prices known as **price leaders.** This type of pricing is used most often in supermarkets and department stores to attract consumers by giving them special low prices on a few items. Management hopes that sales of regularly priced merchandise will more than offset the reduced revenue from the price leaders.

Special event pricing Advertised sales or price cutting that is linked to a holiday, season or event to increase sales volume

Special Event Pricing   To increase sales volume, many organisations co-ordinate price with advertising or sales promotion for seasonal or special situations. **Special event pricing** involves advertised sales or price cutting that is linked to a holiday, season or event. Many companies, such as Christian Dior, organise sales linked to holidays, for example. If the pricing objective is survival, special sales events may be designed to generate the necessary operating capital. Special event pricing also entails co-ordination of production, scheduling, storage and physical distribution. Whenever there is a sales lag, special event pricing is an alternative that marketers should consider.

Everyday low pricing (EDLP) The reduction of retail prices of leading brands for a prolonged period

Everyday Low Pricing   With **everyday low pricing (EDLP)** retailers choose to reduce retail prices of leading brands for a prolonged period. Reduced promotional budgets and improvements in logistics create financial savings that are used to support such price cuts to the consumer.[5] The use of EDLP is not a short term price promotion or sales promotion. It is, however, usually given high visibility within the store.

Experience curve pricing A pricing policy in which a company expands its market share by fixing a low price that high cost competitors cannot match

Experience Curve Pricing   In **experience curve pricing,** a company fixes a low price that high cost competitors cannot match and thus expands its market share. This practice is possible when a firm gains cumulative production experience and is able to reduce its manufacturing costs at a predictable rate through improved methods, materials, skills and machinery. Texas Instruments used this strategy in marketing its calculators.

The experience curve depicts the inverse relationship between production costs per unit and cumulative production quantity. To take advantage of the experienc curve, a company must gain a dominant market share early in a product's l cycle. An early market share lead, with the greater cumulative production ex ence that it implies, will place a company further down the experience cur its competitors.

Misleading Prices

Misleading prices Pricing policies that confuse or dupe consumers

The UK Consumer Protection Act (1987) contains a code of practice intended to give advice on **misleading prices**. The act makes it illegal to mislead customers about the price at which products or services are offered for sale. However, the code—which is not legally binding—encourages companies to offer explanations whenever price comparisons or reductions are made. According to the *Which?* handbook of consumer law, "Unexplained reductions from a store's own prices should be used only if the goods have been on sale at the same store for 28 days in the preceding six months, and if the price quoted was the last price at which the goods were on sale.[6] South Korean car manufacturer Daewoo is mounting a campaign against the asterisk, common in most rivals' advertisements. These state a list price for a car model, yet the "small print", as referenced by the asterisk, reveals additional costs for delivery, number plates and road tax that may be as much as £450. Daewoo argues that hiding these extra charges is misleading.[7]

● ● ● ● ● ● ● ● ● ● ● ● ● ● ● ● ● ●

Development of a Pricing Method (Stage 7)

Pricing method A mechanical procedure for setting prices on a regular basis

After selecting a pricing policy, a marketer must choose a **pricing method**, a mechanical procedure for setting prices on a regular basis. The pricing method structures the calculation of the actual price. The nature of a product, its sales volume or the amount of product the organisation carries will determine how prices are calculated. For example, a procedure for pricing the thousands of products in a supermarket must be simpler and more direct than that for calculating the price of a new earthmoving machine manufactured by Caterpillar or JCB. This section examines three market orientated pricing methods: cost orientated, demand orientated and competition orientated pricing.

Cost Orientated Pricing

Cost orientated pricing A pricing method whereby a monetary amount or percentage is added to the cost of a product

In **cost orientated pricing**, a monetary amount or percentage is added to the cost of a product. The method thus involves calculations of desired margins or profit margins. Cost orientated pricing methods do not necessarily take into account the economic aspects of supply and demand, nor do they necessarily relate to a specific pricing policy or ensure the attainment of pricing objectives. They are, however, simple and easy to implement. Two common cost orientated pricing methods are cost plus and mark-up pricing.

Cost plus pricing A pricing method based on adding a specified amount or percentage to the seller's cost after that cost is determined

Cost Plus Pricing   In **cost plus pricing**, the seller's costs are determined (usually during a project or after a project is completed), and the price is then set by adding a specified amount or percentage of the cost to the seller's cost. Cost plus pricing is appropriate when production costs are difficult to predict or production takes a long time. Custom made equipment and commercial construction projects are often priced by this method. The government frequently uses cost orientated pricing in granting defence contracts. One pitfall for the buyer is that the seller may ⎿crease costs to establish a larger profit base. Furthermore, some costs, such as ⎿verheads, may be difficult to determine.

In periods of rapid inflation, cost plus pricing is popular, especially when the producer must use raw materials that are fluctuating in price. For industries in which cost plus pricing is common and sellers have similar costs, price competition may not be especially intense.

599

Mark-Up Pricing A common pricing method among retailers is **mark-up pricing.** In mark-up pricing, a product's price is derived by adding a predetermined percentage of the cost, called *mark-up*, to the cost of the product. Although the percentage mark-up in a retail store varies from one category of goods to another (35 per cent of cost for hardware items and 100 per cent of cost for greeting cards, for example), the same percentage is often used to determine the price of items within a single product category, and the same or similar percentage mark-up may be standardised across an industry at the retail level. Using a rigid percentage mark-up for a specific product category reduces pricing to a routine task that can be performed quickly.

Mark-up can be stated as a percentage of the cost or as a percentage of the selling price. The following example illustrates how percentage mark-ups are determined and points out the differences between the two methods. Assume that a retailer purchases a tin of tuna at 45p, adds 15p to the cost, and then prices the tuna at 60 pence. Here are the figures:

$$\text{Mark-Up as a Percentage of Cost} = \frac{\text{Mark-up}}{\text{Cost}}$$

$$\text{Mark-Up as a Percentage of Selling Price} = \frac{\text{Mark-up}}{\text{Selling Price}}$$

$$= \frac{15}{60}$$

$$= 25\%$$

Obviously, when discussing a percentage mark-up, it is important to know whether the mark-up is based on cost or selling price.

Mark-ups normally reflect expectations about operating costs, risks and stock turnovers. Wholesalers and manufacturers often suggest standard retail mark-ups that are considered profitable. An average percentage mark-up on cost may be as high as 100 per cent or more for jewellery or as low as 20 per cent for this textbook. To the extent that retailers use similar mark-ups for the same product category, price competition is reduced. In addition, using rigid mark-ups is a convenient method for retailers who face numerous pricing decisions.

Demand Orientated Pricing

Rather than basing the price of a product on its cost, marketers sometimes use a pricing method based on the level of demand for the product: **demand orientated pricing.** This method results in a high price when demand for the product is strong and a low price when demand is weak. Admission to night clubs often operates on this basis, with higher prices when demand is highest, on Friday nights and at weekends. To use this method, a marketer must be able to estimate the amounts of a product that consumers will demand at different prices. The marketer then chooses the price that generates the highest total revenue. Obviously, the effectiveness of this method depends on the marketer's ability to estimate demand accurately.

A marketer may favour a demand orientated pricing method called **price differentiation** when the firm wants to use more than one price in the marketing of a specific product. Price differentiation can be based on such considerations as type of customer, type of distribution channel used or the time of the purchase. Here are several examples. A 12 ounce can of soft drink costs less from a supermarket than from a vending machine. London hotel accommodation is more expensive in the summer than in the winter. Christmas tree ornaments and cards are usually cheaper on 27 December than on 16 December.

For price differentiation to work properly, the marketer must be able to segment a market on the basis of different strengths of demand and then keep the segments separate enough so that segment members who buy at lower prices cannot then sell to buyers in segments that are charged a higher price. This isolation could be accomplished, for example, by selling to geographically separated segments.

Price differentiation is often facilitated in international marketing by the geographic distance between markets. For example, the price Matsushita Electric Co. charges for cordless Panasonic telephones in Japan is eight times the price charged for cordless telephones of slightly lower quality in the United States. When a Japanese trading company re-imported the US cordless phones and sold them for $80 instead of the Japanese model, which cost $657, consumers lined up to buy the cheaper telephone. To combat the re-importation, Matsushita bought up all the unsold, made for export Panasonic telephones it could find to eliminate the wide price differential. The major difference between the telephones was that the US telephone had a range of 40 metres (130 feet) and the Japanese telephone had a range of 50 metres (165 feet), which is surprising, because the average Japanese home is much smaller than the average US home.[8]

Price differentiation can also be based on employment in a public service position. For example, many bookshops offer a 15 per cent discount to teachers.

Compared with cost orientated pricing, demand orientated pricing places a firm in a better position to reach higher profit levels, assuming that buyers value the product at levels sufficiently above its actual cost. To use demand orientated pricing, however, a marketer must be able to estimate demand at different price levels, which is often difficult to do accurately.

Competition Orientated Pricing

Competition orientated pricing
A pricing method whereby an organisation considers costs and revenue to be secondary to competitors' prices

In using **competition orientated pricing**, an organisation considers costs and revenue to be secondary to competitors' prices. The importance of this method increases if competing products are almost homogeneous and the organisation is serving markets in which price is the key variable of the marketing strategy. A firm that uses competition orientated pricing may choose to be below competitors' prices, above competitors' prices or at the same level. The price of this textbook paid by the bookshop to the publishing company was determined using competition orientated pricing. Competition orientated pricing should help attain a pricing objective to increase sales or market share. Competition orientated pricing methods may be combined with cost approaches to arrive at price levels necessary for a profit.

● ● ● ● ● ● ● ● ● ● ● ● ● ● ● ● ● ●

Determining a Specific Price (Stage 8)

Pricing policies and methods should direct and structure the selection of a final price. If they are to do so, it is important for marketers to establish pricing objectives, to know something about the target market and to determine demand, price elasticity, costs and competitive factors. In addition to those economic factors, the manner in which pricing is used in the marketing mix will affect the final price.

Although a systematic approach to pricing is suggested here, in practice prices are often finalised after only limited planning; or they may be set without planning, just by trial and error. Marketers then determine whether the revenue minus costs yields a profit. This approach to pricing is not recommended, because it makes it difficult to discover pricing errors. If prices are based on both unrealistic pricing methods and unrealistic sales forecasts, a firm may resort to price gimmickry to sell its products. This approach should be avoided because it can become permanent. The car industry is a current example of how pricing incentives, such as discounts, cheap credit facilities and trade-in deals, can become an essential and permanent part of pricing.

In the absence of government price controls, pricing remains a flexible and convenient way to adjust the marketing mix. In most situations, prices can be adjusted quickly—in a matter of minutes or over a few days. This flexibility and freedom do not characterise the other components of the marketing mix. Because so many complex issues are involved in establishing the right price, pricing is indeed as much an art as a science.

●●●●●●●●●●●●●●●●●●●

The Pricing Balance—The Need for Pragmatism

This chapter has presented a sequence of the stages a marketer must address in determining a price that will reflect customer expectations, match market developments and still produce a suitable financial return for the company in question. These eight stages identified for establishing prices must be tackled. However, in the reality of many markets, the external trading environment can change quickly and constantly: consumers are relatively fickle and revise their expectations, market developments alter the pattern of the market, and competitors are always modifying their marketing mix—a price cutting campaign, a new model launch, a high profile advertising campaign or, perhaps, a customer service initiative. To respond to such quick-fire events, marketers may be forced to react pragmatically by modifying their own pricing policy and method.

In the context of the marketing mix, price is, after all, an element that in most cases can be altered relatively quickly, that is, when compared with the time and resources required to launch a new product, modify a channel of distribution, improve customer service or create and run a new advertising campaign. Even in this context, however, the shrewd marketer should endeavour to minimise price cutting and discounting. Generally, the only beneficiary of a price war in the short term is the consumer, not the business, its distributors, the brand and the long term flexibility of the marketing mix. The marketer, though, will make such decisions on the basis of marketing intelligence, market trends, customer perceptions and competitor activity. Pragmatism must never lose sight of the "economics" of pricing and the fundamental relationship between demand, costs and profits: there must be a sensible trade-off between economic analysis and pragmatism.

●●●●●●●●●●●●●●●●●

Summary

● The eight stages in the process of establishing prices are as follows: (1) selecting pricing objectives; (2) assessing the target market's evaluation of price and its ability to purchase; (3) determining demand; (4) analysing demand, cost and profit relationships; (5) evaluating competitors' prices; (6) selecting a pricing policy; (7) developing a pricing method; and (8) determining a specific price.

● The first stage, setting pricing objectives, is critical because pricing objectives form a foundation on which the decisions of subsequent stages are based. Organisations may use numerous pricing objectives: short term and long term ones, and different ones for different products and market segments.

● The second stage in establishing prices is an assessment of the target market's evaluation of price and its ability to purchase. This stage tells a marketer how much emphasis to place on price and may help the marketer determine how far above the competition the firm can set its prices. Understanding customers' buying power and knowing how important a product is to the customers in comparison with other products helps marketers correctly assess the target market's evaluation of price.

● In the third stage, the organisation must determine the demand for its product. The classic *demand curve* is a graph of the quantity of products expected to be sold at various prices, if other factors are held constant. It illustrates that, as price falls, the quantity demanded usually increases. However, for prestige products, there is a direct positive relationship between price and quantity demanded: demand increases as price increases. Next, *price elasticity of demand*—the percentage change in quantity demanded relative to a given percentage change in price—must be determined. If demand is elastic, a change in price causes an opposite change in total revenue. Inelastic demand results in parallel change in total revenue when a product's price is changed.

● Analysis of demand, cost and profit relationships—the fourth stage of the process—can be accomplished through marginal analysis or break even analysis. Marginal analysis is the examination of what happens to a firm's costs and revenues when production (or sales volume) is changed by one unit. Marginal analysis combines the demand curve with a firm's costs to develop an optimum price for maximum profit. *Fixed costs* do not vary with changes in the number of units produced or sold; *average fixed cost* is the fixed cost per unit produced. *Variable costs* vary directly with changes in the number of units produced or sold. *Average variable cost* is the variable cost per unit produced. *Total cost* is the sum of average fixed costs and average variable costs multiplied by the quantity produced. *Average total cost* is the sum of the average fixed cost and average variable cost times the quantity produced. The optimum price is the point at which *marginal cost* (the cost associated with producing

one more unit of the product) equals *marginal revenue* (the change in total revenue that occurs when one additional unit of the product is sold). Marginal analysis is only a model; it offers little help in pricing new products before costs and revenues are established.

● Break even analysis—determining the number of units necessary to break even—is important in setting the price. The point at which the costs of production equal the revenue made from selling the product is the *break even point*. To use break even analysis effectively, a marketer should determine the break even point for each of several alternative prices. This determination makes it possible to compare the effects on total revenue, total costs and the break even point for each price under consideration. However, this approach assumes that the quantity demanded is basically fixed and that the major task is to set prices to recover costs.

● A marketer needs to be aware of the prices charged for competing brands. This awareness allows a firm to keep its prices the same as competitors' prices when non-price competition is used. If a company uses price as a competitive tool, it can price its brand below competing brands.

● A *pricing policy* is a guiding philosophy or course of action designed to influence and determine pricing decisions. Pricing policies help marketers solve the practical problems of establishing prices. Two types of *pioneer pricing* policies are *price skimming* and *penetration pricing*. With price skimming, an organisation charges the highest price that buyers who most desire the product will pay. A penetration price is a lower price designed to penetrate the market and produce a larger unit sales volume. Another pricing policy, *psychological pricing*, encourages purchases that are based on emotional rather than rational responses. It includes *odd-even pricing, customary pricing, prestige pricing* and *price lining*. A third pricing policy, *professional pricing*, is used by people who have great skill or experience in a particular field. *Promotional pricing*, in which price is co-ordinated with promotion, is another type of pricing policy. *Price leaders* and *special event pricing* are examples of promotional pricing, as is *everyday low pricing*. *Experience curve pricing* fixes a low price that high cost competitors cannot match. Experience curve pricing is possible when experience reduces manufacturing costs at a predictable rate. *Misleading prices*—where consumers are misled about the true cost or value of a product or service—are increasingly monitored and tackled through consumer protection legislation.

● A *pricing method* is a mechanical procedure for assigning prices to specific products on a regular basis. Three types of pricing methods are cost orientated, demand orientated and competition orientated pricing. In using *cost orientated pricing,* a firm determines price by adding a monetary amount or percentage to the cost of the product. Two common cost orientated pricing methods are *cost plus* and *mark-up* pricing. *Demand orientated pricing* is based on the level of demand for the product. To use this method, a marketer must be able to estimate the amounts of a product that buyers will demand at different prices, particularly if the company wishes to use *price differentiation* for the marketing of a specific product. Demand orientated pricing results in a high price when demand for a product is strong and a low price when demand is weak. In the case of competition orientated pricing, costs and revenues are secondary to competitors' prices. *Competition orientated pricing* and cost approaches may be combined to arrive at price levels necessary to generate a profit.

● Pragmatism may require the marketer to revise pricing on an ad hoc basis in response to market developments. While such reactions are to some extent inevitable, marketers must never lose sight of the longer term implications for the brand, or for the fundamental relationship between demand, costs and profits.

Important Terms

Demand curve
Price elasticity of demand
Fixed costs
Average fixed cost
Variable costs
Average variable cost
Total cost
Average total cost
Marginal cost (MC)
Marginal revenue (MR)
Break even point
Pricing policy

Pioneer pricing
Price skimming
Penetration price
Psychological pricing
Odd-even pricing
Customary pricing
Prestige pricing
Price lining
Professional pricing
Promotional pricing
Price leaders

Special event pricing
Everyday low pricing (EDLP)
Experience curve pricing
Misleading prices
Pricing method
Cost orientated pricing
Cost plus pricing
Mark-up pricing
Demand orientated pricing
Price differentiation
Competition orientated pricing

Discussion and Review Questions

1. Identify the eight stages that make up the process of establishing prices.
2. Why do most demand curves demonstrate an inverse relationship between price and quantity?
3. List the characteristics of products that have inelastic demand. Give several examples of such products.
4. Explain why optimum profits should occur when marginal cost equals marginal revenue.
5. The Chambers Company has just gathered estimates in preparation for a break even analysis for a new product. Variable costs are £7 a unit. The additional plant will cost £48,000. The new product will be charged £18,000 a year for its share of general overheads. Advertising expenditure will be £80,000, and £55,000 will be spent on distribution. If the product sells for £12, what is the break even point in units? What is the break even point in sales volume?
6. Why should a marketer be aware of competitors' prices?
7. For what type of products would a pioneer price skimming policy be most appropriate? For what type of products would penetration pricing be more effective?
8. Why do consumers associate price with quality? When should prestige pricing be used?
9. In setting prices, why must marketers take a "balanced" view of a broad set of issues?

Recommended Readings

H. Simon, "Pricing opportunities—and how to exploit them", *Sloan Management Review,* vol. 33, no. 2, 1992, pp. 55–65.

M. V. Marn and R. L. Rosiello, "Managing price, gaining profit", *Harvard Business Review,* vol. 70, no. 5, 1992, pp. 84–94.

K. Steward, "Fixing the price", in *Effective Industrial Marketing*, N. Hart, ed. (London: Kogan Page, 1994).

T. Nagle, *Strategy and Tactics of Pricing: A Guide to Profitable Decision-Making* (Hemel Hempstead: Prentice-Hall, 1994).

M. Campanelli, "The price to pay", *Sales & Marketing Management,* vol. 146, no. 10, 1994, pp. 96–102.

Cases

20.1 The Burgeoning Budget Hotels Sector: The UK, Benelux and Now Italy

The hotel industry had been dominated by two extremes: small, privately owned, no frills hotels aimed at sales representatives travelling on tight budgets and at families seeking low cost accommodation for their summer holidays; and larger hotel groups operating chains of mid- and up-market hotels. In the last few years, however, there have been several fundamental changes. Many operators are truly international and own properties in many countries. Hotel groups geared to the business market have invested heavily in conference and meeting facilities. Benelux, France, the UK and Germany have seen the growth of de luxe, small, rural country house hotels. Perhaps one of the most significant developments, however, has been the expansion of chains of low cost, well appointed motorway lodges. Typically of AA two star standard, with en suite bedrooms but limited catering facilities and no leisure amenities, these hotels have sprung up close to most major settlements and motorway intersections.

The small, privately owned hotels offer basic accommodation at around £25 per night with few extra facilities or amenities. The larger hotels in most town and city centres, such as the three and four star hotels owned by Forte, Queens Moat Houses, Hilton or Holiday Inn, offer more in-room amenities plus leisure and conference facilities, but at prices from £70 to £120 per night. In the 1980s several operators identified a niche in the market between the cheaper private hotels and the more expensive branded chains: a budget-conscious segment that, though price driven, requires convenient,

safe locations, clean, comfortable bedrooms with television and bathroom, and somewhere close at hand for a bite to eat.

Most of the major hotel groups have entered this market, led by Forte's Travelodge chain, which now has close to 150 locations in the UK and properties in key business locations in Europe. Travelodge, now run by Granada, provides comfortable bedrooms, easy access and the reassurance of a major brand, but without any extras such as a fitness centre or business services. Indeed, the chain has no restaurants; instead, each site is shared by one of three diner chains: Happy Eater, Little Chef or Relais. A room at the Travelodge—"little luxuries, little prices"—costs just over £30 per night, irrespective of whether it is occupied by one person or a family of four. Travelodge's latest target is Italy, where 24 motorway lodges are under construction following a deal with petrol giant Agip. Granada Lodges and Sleep Inns are similarly targeted.

Marriott (Courtyard by Marriott) and Holiday Inn (Garden Court) have also entered this budget-conscious arena, but with slightly higher pricing and more facilities. Still pitched beneath Holiday Inns or Hiltons, the Garden Courts are "competitively priced three star hotels featuring all the benefits of luxury accommodation but without the extras like swimming pools and a choice of restaurants". Each does provide a bistro-style dining area, open plan bar and fitness centre, as well as in-room movies in its four star standard bedrooms. Prices per night, though, are £64.50 Sunday to Thursday and £49.50 at weekends. Locations tend to be close to major motorways—ideal for business travellers, who represent the core weekday market. Courtyard by Marriott is £62 during the week and £38 at weekends £24 room only without breakfast). The variable pricing positions the hotels more towards bargain breaker tourists at weekends in order to use slack capacity.

The market has been further shaken up with the entry of France's Formule group. Visitors to a Formule 1 hotel are greeted by a cash point machine that checks how many nights they want to stay, debits their credit cards and gives out a six-figure code allowing them to pass through the locked lobby doors and into a room. Once by their beds, red and green lights tell them when it is safe to have a bath without risk of being sluiced with detergents in the self-cleaning bathrooms. The hotel consists of prefabricated, factory built, interlocking cabins and is maintained without staff, except for a husband and wife management team. There are no catering facilities, but fast food chains and pubs are nearby. The price is under £20 per night for up to three people sharing a room. Formule is talking about opening close to 200 such hotels in the UK. "A lot of people like the idea of staying in a quiet, cheap place without meeting anybody."

Price is a key differentiating aspect of the marketing mix for these hotel operators, but it is not always the only issue of importance to these target consumers. The hotel business, after all, is increasingly strongly branded and, as a service industry, depends on additional elements of the marketing mix. Nevertheless, as France's Formule and the UK's Travelodge have demonstrated, there is room in this industry to trade on the basis of price, augmented with balanced supporting marketing programmes and clear positioning strategies.

SOURCES: Nick Cohen, "Anonymity for any number at automatic hotel", *The Independent,* November 1992; Holiday Inn and Travelodge promotional literature; *Marketing,* 16 August 1992, p. 4; *Leamington Spa Business Times,* August 1990, p. 5; Clare Sambrook, "Marriott: a name to contend with", *Marketing,* 3 September 1992, pp. 16–18; Tim Troy, "Forte acquisitions fuel Travelodge growth", *Hotel and Motel Management,* 209 (6), 1994, pp. 3–7; "Brand builders: its Forte is mascots", *Brandweek,* 36 (38), 1995, pp. 24–26.

Questions for Discussion

1. What opportunities is Travelodge aiming to exploit? Do its aims differ from those of Courtyard by Marriott or Holiday Inn's Garden Court?

2. Why do many hotel companies alter their price points at weekends? Is such a pricing policy seen in other industries? Why or why not?

3. Is price alone a basis for competing in this budget sector of the hotel market? Why or why not?

20.2 Toys "R" Us—Sweden Faces Stiff Price Competition

Toys "R" Us, which leads the US toy market with its chain of over 400 warehouse-style toy supermarkets spread across the country, is expanding rapidly in Europe and the Pacific Rim. In Europe its growth is fast bringing a new style and scale of toy retailing to the UK (50 branches), Germany (40), France (25), Spain (12) and Austria (5). The company has long been an innovator in both its pricing policies and its toy supermarket design. Toys "R" Us brings customers into the store by discounting such baby care products as buggies and disposable nappies below cost. The strategy is that once parents are in the store, they will spend on toys the money they saved on the discounted baby goods.

Toys "R" Us stores are usually located along road arteries, well away from central business district (CBD) shopping malls, to keep down costs and prevent customers from being distracted by other toy merchants. Isolation from shopping malls also means that customers will load up their shopping trolleys because they do not have to lug their purchases through crowded malls.

The first Toys "R" Us store was opened in 1957 as the Children's Supermarket (the "Rs" were printed backwards to encourage name recognition), offering brand name toys and baby goods below normal retail prices. Today, it still offers brand name toys at 20 to 50 per cent below retail price. Each store has a full stock of thousands of different toys and baby goods tracked by a computer system that almost eliminates stock-outs. Managers don't place orders for toys, the toys just arrive on time, thus averting the Toys "R" Us definition of a major disaster—not having a certain toy on display and ready to sell.

Toys "R" Us sets its price for a particular item based on how much it projects customers will pay for it. The company then determines the price at which it is willing to purchase the toy from the manufacturer and negotiates fiercely with the manufacturer to get the toy at that price. The company has a definite advantage in negotiations because it buys in such large volume. Toy manufacturers also treat Toys "R" Us well because the company is often a testing ground for new toys. Price is so important to the Toys "R" Us strategy that even when demand for a toy is high and supplies are short, the company will not raise its price on the toy to make a quick profit.

Market share is the Toys "R" Us main pricing objective; and at present it is the number one toy store in the United States. In the UK, local independent toy shops still account for the bulk of the toy market share, but in only a few years Toys "R" Us has become the leading national chain. The company says it is willing to cut prices to retain its leading position. Other toy stores are scrambling to meet the competition from Toys "R" Us; those that do not change their strategies wind up out of the toy market altogether. Many stores, such as Kmart, or Asda in the UK, expand their toy lines only for the six week Christmas season and bring customers in with sales. Although Toys "R" Us never holds sales, it maintains its huge selection and discount prices year round. Customers who found good buys at Toys "R" Us at Christmas will also shop there for children's birthdays and other special days, when other retail stores have a limited selection. Even new parents who drop in to Toys "R" Us for discounted baby products tend to return to buy toys. The company also sells sporting goods "toys", such as footballs and bicycles, suitable for teens, young adults and family members of almost any age.

Some competitors (in the UK, Mothercare owned Children's World) have adopted the Toys "R" Us supermarket approach and have tried to meet Toys "R" Us prices throughout the year. Other stores are trying non-price competition by offering educational and babysitting services. However, Toys "R" Us intends to rely on its non-price attributes of convenience, selection and inventory, as well as price competition, to hold its position.

Toys "R" Us has expanded internationally, into Europe, Canada, Japan and other parts of Asia with close to 200 stores outside the US. The company has plans for many more stores overseas to take advantage of the world toy market, which is nearly double that of the United States. Additionally, it opened Kids "R" Us in the United States, a chain of children's clothing stores similar to the toy stores. The latest country to receive the famous reversed R logo is Sweden. Much to the chagrin of the Swedish Federation of Toy Retailers, Toys "R" Us has announced that by the end of the decade, a chain of 15 toy superstores will be operational in Sweden.

Toys "R" Us has customer loyalty behind it. Customers know that they can find *the* toy that a child wants, at the best price, at Toys "R" Us. And if the child does not like the toy, the purchaser may return it for a full refund with no questions asked.

SOURCES: Robert J. Cole, "Toys "R" Us to open stores in Japan within two years", *The New York Times,* 27 September 1989, pp. D1, D6; Dan Dorfman, "Toys "R" Us: Mattel play?" *USA Today,* 28 June 1987, p. 2B; Trish Hall, "Finding gold in overalls and bibs", *The New York Times,* 25 December 1988, pp. F1, F10; Mark Maremont, Dori Jones Yang and Amy Dunkin, "Toys "R" Us goes overseas—and finds that toys 'R' them, too", *Business Week,* 26 January 1987, pp. 71–72; David Owen, "Where toys come from", *Atlantic Monthly,* October 1986, pp. 64–78; Jesus Sanchez, "Toymakers make a play for market", *USA Today,* 10 February 1987, pp. 1B–2B; Toys "R" Us UK HQ, 1993; "Toys "R" Us launches UK loyalty, credit card", *Marketing Week,* 6 October 1995, p. 11; Claes Philipson, "Toys embarks on important initiative", *European Retail,* 30 August 1994, p. 12.

Questions for Discussion

1. What are the major pricing objectives of Toys "R" Us?

2. Assess the Toys "R" Us practice of not raising the prices of products that are scarce and in high demand.

3. A major disadvantage of using price competition is that competitors can match prices. Or can they? Evaluate this potential threat for Toys "R" Us.

PART VI POSTSCRIPT

The price of a product or service is the value placed on what is exchanged by the supplying business and the consumer. There is much more to pricing, however, than the setting of a specific monetary figure. The price of a product or a service will affect how it is perceived by consumers, how it is distributed and promoted, the level of customer service expected and the brand positioning strategy to be pursued. The pricing strategy developed by an organisation will also fundamentally relate to its performance and even to its viability. Pricing is not one of the more "glamorous" ingredients of the marketing mix, such as product development or promotional activity, but it is very important and relatively easy to manipulate.

Before progressing, readers should be confident that they are now able to:

Outline the central concepts of pricing

• What is the nature and importance of price in marketing? • What are the characteristics of price and non-price competition? • What are the principal pricing objectives? • What factors influence marketers' pricing decisions? • What is required in setting prices in business-to-business markets? • Why is it important to consider the consumers' view of value versus price?

Explain the requirements of setting prices

• What are the eight major steps in setting a price? • What issues are faced when determining pricing objectives? • Why must marketers understand the target market's evaluation of price? • What are the relationships between demand curves and price elasticity, and between demand, costs and profits? • Why must marketers analyse competitors' pricing? • What are the core pricing policies? • What is the pricing balance?

Marketing Opportunity Analysis	Chapters
• The marketing environment	2
• Marketing in international markets	3
• Consumer markets and buyer behaviour	4
• Business-to-business markets and buyer behaviour	5
• Marketing research and information systems	6

Target Market Selection	Chapters
• Market segmentation and prioritisation	7, 22
• Product and brand positioning	7, 22
• Competitive advantage	7, 22

Marketing Mix Development	Chapters
• Product, branding, packaging and service decisions	8–11
• Distribution (place and channel) decisions	12–15
• Promotion decisions	16–18
• Pricing decisions	19, 20
• Supplementary decisions	3, 21, 24, 25

Marketing Management	Chapters
• Strategic marketing and competitive strategy	22, 23
• Marketing planning and sales forecasting	23
• Implementing strategies and measuring performance	24
• Marketing ethics and social responsibility	25

VII MANIPULATING THE MARKETING MIX

C hapter 1 of *Marketing: Concepts and Strategies* explained how marketers, after analysing marketing opportunities, must develop marketing strategies that include target market selection. In order to implement the recommended marketing strategy, marketing programmes must be formulated based on a bespoke marketing mix for each market targeted. The basic ingredients of the marketing mix are product, people, place, promotion and pricing decisions. Parts III to VI have examined in detail these ingredients of the marketing mix. There are, however, situations in which market characteristics or the nature of the product require the standard marketing mix to be modified. These situations occur most notably for business-to-business markets, the marketing of services and when organisations are engaged in marketing in international markets.

Part VII of *Marketing: Concepts and Strategies* explores the manipulation of the marketing mix to cater for business-to-business markets, the marketing of services and marketing in international markets.

Chapter 21, "Modifying the Marketing Mix for Various Markets", new for this third edition of *Marketing: Concepts and Strategies,* recognises the reality of formulating the marketing mix in a variety of complex business situations. The chapter commences by explaining why in many situations the basic marketing mix requires modification. It examines the nature of the marketing mix for business-to-business markets and presents the complex and extended marketing mix for services. To conclude, the chapter highlights the many additional issues considered by marketers involved with global markets and relates them to the development of the marketing mix.

By the conclusion of Part VII of *Marketing: Concepts and Strategies,* readers should understand why in certain circumstances the standard marketing mix requires modification and manipulation.

21 MODIFYING THE MARKETING MIX FOR VARIOUS MARKETS

"Expanding the traditional boundaries of the marketing mix is imperative for international and services contexts."

Constantine Katsikeas
Cardiff Business School

OBJECTIVES

- To recognise that in many situations the basic marketing mix requires modification
- To examine the nature of the marketing mix for business-to-business markets
- To understand the more complex and extended marketing mix required for services
- To recognise that for marketers involved with global marketing, the marketing mix requires consideration of additional issues

Aer Lingus is Eire's de facto national carrier. It competes in four distinct markets: the transatlantic long haul sector, against such giants as American Airlines or British Airways; within the European Union, against a plethora of national carriers such as Lufthansa or TAP; in the London/UK provincial market, against British Airways, British Midland and a host of smaller airlines; and locally within Eire, where it competes with train and road. Aer Lingus's marketing programmes must reflect the nuances and requirements of its international and national markets, while the company must acknowledge that as the provider of a service (transportation) it must accept that its marketing mix is complex and difficult to control. Aer Lingus is "a people business," and as such believes that its future depends on its ability not only to satisfy its target customers but also, in doing so, to give the airline an edge over its competitors.

Chief executive Gary McGann is on record as stating that "Aer Lingus is in the service business, not a supplier of seats on aircraft—a traditional international organisational focus of many airlines—but as a supplier of a total travel experience". To compete successfully, the airline knows it must increase its already strong focus on service and quality. The Aer Lingus brand is strong in its core markets and can only be strengthened by the company's desire to offer ever improved levels of customer service and satisfaction. This emphasis inevitably leads to a focus on the airline's personnel; their training, attitudes, ability and motivation to give customers "good" service. It also extends to any environment—terminal, aircraft or booking point—in which passengers encounter Aer Lingus, as well as the ease with which customers can book, travel and experience the airline's service product.

This focus on customer service and the importance of personnel is highlighted strongly in Aer Lingus's stated mission:

The Aer Lingus mission is to be a strong niche airline, primarily carrying passengers and freight into and out of Ireland, capable of sustained profitability through commercially viable products and practices and a keen customer focus, delivered by committed and well motivated staff. It will strive to attain a position in which its subsidiaries are profitable and viable within themselves, are strategic to the core airline business and the ownership of which enhances the achievability of the airline's objectives. ■

SOURCES: Jimmy Ang; Aer Lingus; Aer Lingus report and accounts; T. McEnaney, "Aer Lingus set to profit on Dublin/London route", *The Times*, 19 January 1995; D. Churchill, "Cabin pressures", *Management Today*, 4 October 1994; "A fighting chance—Aer Lingus", *Airline Business*, 1 June 1995.

The core ingredients of the marketing mix—the marketing manager's tactical toolkit—have been examined in detail in Parts III to VI of *Marketing: Concepts and Strategies*. While these chapters have broadly covered consumer, business-to-business, service and not-for-profit markets, inevitably there has been some bias towards the marketing of consumer goods. In part this reflects the plethora of consumer brands and their coverage in the media, while in part it has been deliberate: as consumers themselves, all readers of this text will be familiar with many of the products and services featured so far. It is important to acknowledge, however, that marketing services and business-to-business products is moderately different from marketing consumer goods, as airline Aer Lingus has recognised. Those organisations involved in international marketing, trading across national borders and cultures, are faced with additional issues that have an impact on their marketing activity.

These differences are not major: "marketing is marketing", and the approach outlined in this text holds true across consumer, business-to-business, services and not-for-profit markets. The marketing environment must be analysed, as must consumer behaviour and customer needs, the competitive situation and general trends. A marketing strategy must be determined that identifies segments, prioritises target markets, judges the ability to compete and defines a desired brand or product positioning. Once the analysis and strategy stages are complete, programmes must be developed that—through the marketing mix—implement the recommended target market strategy. Control mechanisms must be in place to ensure effective implementation of both the marketing strategy and the associated marketing mix programmes. This is true no matter what the market in question.

Nevertheless, there are differences in the characteristics of the respective markets for consumer, business-to-business and service products. These are evident in the practices of business-to-business marketers, but particularly for those responsible for the marketing of services. This chapter presents a summary of some of the most important, if at times subtle, differences encountered when marketing business-to-business products and marketing services. The chapter concludes by suggesting how international marketing requires consideration of additional issues in formulating a marketing mix.

Characteristics of Business-to-Business Marketing Mixes

As with consumer marketers, business-to-business marketers must also create a marketing mix that will satisfy the customers in the target market. In many respects, the general concepts and methods involved in developing a business-to-business marketing mix are similar to those used in consumer product marketing and outlined in Parts III to VI of this text. In this section the focus is on the features of business-to-business marketing mixes that differ from the marketing mixes for consumer products. Each of the main components in a business-to-business marketing mix is examined: product, distribution, promotion, price and people. Personnel are not particularly part of the product, but they are integral to the selling and promotional activity in all markets, and are important in developing ongoing relationships in many industrial markets.

Product   After selecting a target market, the business-to-business marketer has to decide how to compete. Production orientated managers fail to understand the need to develop a distinct appeal for their product to give it a competitive, or differential advantage. Positioning the product (discussed in Chapters 7 and 10) is necessary to serve a market successfully, whether it is consumer or business-to-business.[1]

Compared with consumer marketing mixes, the product ingredients of business-to-business marketing mixes often include a greater emphasis on services, both before and after sales. Services, including on-time delivery, quality control, custom design (see Figure 21.1) and a comprehensive parts distribution system, may be important components of the product. Marketing Insight 21.1 reveals the importance of a service "package" in the truck market.

Before making a sale, business-to-business marketers provide potential customers with technical advice regarding product specifications, installation and applications. Many business-to-business marketers depend heavily on long term customer relationships that perpetuate sizeable repeat purchases. Therefore, business-to-business marketers also make a considerable effort to provide services after the sale. Because business-to-business customers must have products available when needed, on-time delivery is another service included in the product component of many business-to-business marketing mixes. A business-to-business marketer unable to provide on-time delivery cannot expect the marketing mix to satisfy business-to-business customers. Availability of parts must also be included in the product mixes of many business-to-business marketers in order to prevent costly production delays. The business-to-business marketer that includes availability of parts within the product component has a competitive advantage over one that fails to offer this service. Furthermore, customers whose average purchases are large often desire credit; thus some business-to-business marketers include credit services in their product mixes. When planning and developing a business-to-business product mix, a business-to-business marketer of component parts and semi-finished products must realise that a customer may decide to make the items instead of buying them. In some cases, then, business-to-business marketers compete not only with one another, but with their own potential customers as well.

Frequently, industrial products must conform to standard technical specifications that business-to-business customers want. Thus business-to-business mar-

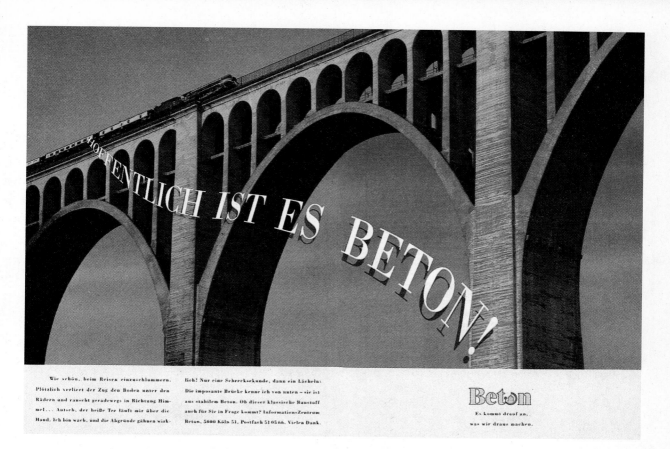

Figure 21.1 Business-to-business services. Beton offers its services to the building industries.
SOURCE: Courtesy of Beton.

keters often concentrate on functional product features rather than on marketing considerations. This fact has important implications for business-to-business salespeople. Rather than concentrating just on selling activities, they must assume the role of consultants, seeking to solve their customers' problems and influencing the writing of specifications.[2] For example, salespeople for computer hardware often act as consultants for software as well as the basic computer kit. Most customers now expect this level of service. In the UK many suppliers have gone out of business because of their inability to offer such a service.

Because industrial products are rarely sold through self-service, the major consideration in package design is protection. There is less emphasis on the package as a promotional device.

Research on business-to-business customer complaints indicates that such buyers usually complain when they encounter problems with product quality or delivery time. On the other hand, consumers' complaints refer to other problems, such as customer service and pricing. This type of buyer feedback allows business-to-business marketers to gauge marketing performance. It is important that business-to-business marketers respond to valid complaints, because the success of most industrial products depends on repeat purchases. Because buyer complaints serve a useful purpose, many industrial firms facilitate this feedback by providing customer service departments.[3]

Volvo Trucks Fights Back—Aftermarket Opportunities Help Recovery

Volvo Trucks is a wholly owned subsidiary of Volvo. It is the division that handles the importing, manufacturing, sales and marketing, and after sales support for all Volvo heavy goods vehicles. Throughout the 1990s, truck sales have declined in most key markets, but some manufacturers have performed better owing to their exposure to the stronger US market. In western Europe, sales are down from 100,000 in 1992 to 80,000 vehicles in the light/medium category, and in the heavy category to 120,000 from 150,000. Italy, Germany and France have seen sales decline by 20 per cent, Spain by 40 per cent, but there has recently been a recovery in the UK, where sales have increased by 8 per cent. Mercedes-Benz, Volvo Trucks and Renault have been the dominant players in an increasingly competitive marketplace.

For most of the major players in the European truck market, two major trends are dictating current marketing strategies. The decline in new vehicle sales is leading to an increased focus on the after market. The market for replacement parts is more stable and offers some degree of cushioning against the more extreme fluctuations in demand for new vehicles. Similarly, tyres, fuels and lubricants continue to sell steadily even when there is a downturn in truck sales. Most truck manufacturers are devoting more of their marketing effort to servicing, maintenance and provision of parts.

The second trend has been a move by hauliers and large companies with their own transport fleets away from purchasing new vehicles outright. There has been a switch to leasing and contract hire, whereby the truck manufacturer ultimately retains ownership of the vehicle and has to off-load the vehicles when they are returned by the haulier. This development has forced marketers to learn a variety of new financial skills. They have to set leasing and contract hire rates sufficiently high to make an operating profit, bearing in mind the increased competition in the market. They must also be prepared to take back and re-sell large numbers of used vehicles. For the business-to-business marketer working in the truck business, the task is no longer simply one of marketing and selling new vehicles—the provision of after sales services and parts and the negotiating of complex leasing and contract hire agreements are becoming increasingly important. The pattern, however, differs country by country, causing problems for Volvo's marketers and necessitating prudent marketing planning that takes into account each country's trading characteristics.

SOURCES: "Looking up, looking down—tracing an entire chain", *Works Management,* July 1995, pp. 37–41; "The West European truck sector: recovery in prospect?", *European Motor Business,* 4th quarter, 1994, pp. 90–130; Jim Mele, "Volvo builds a city truck for the future", *Fleet Owner,* October 1995, p. 16. "Heavy going", *Automotive Management,* 13 September 1990; John Griffiths, "Truck sales suffer fall in September of nearly 40%", *Financial Times,* 17 October 1990; Richard Longworth, "Glitter shadows and lights at the ends of tunnels", *Transport Week,* 22 September 1990, pp. 40–41.

If a business-to-business marketer is in a mature market, growth can come from attracting market share from another business; alternatively, a company can look at new applications or uses for its products. JCB dominates the backhoe digger market in Europe, but the economic recession, which resulted in reduced construction of buildings and infrastructures, hit its key customers hard. The company used its existing skills and facilities to design an innovative range of very safe, single arm skid steer machines. These nimble, compact "mini-diggers" are now appearing on most building sites and are entering the hire market, proving very successful for JCB. Putting user safety and environmental concerns to the fore, they lend themselves particularly well to buyer needs in Germany and

Scandinavia. JCB's success stems from winning sales from its competitors, seeking new applications for its products and designing innovative products.

Distribution

The distribution ingredient in organisational marketing mixes differs from that for consumer products with respect to the types of channels used, the kinds of intermediaries available, and the transport, storage and inventory policies. Nonetheless, the primary objective of the physical distribution of industrial products is to ensure that the right products are available when and where needed.

Distribution channels tend to be shorter for industrial products than for consumer products. (Figure 21.2 shows the four commonly used industrial distribution channels that were described in Chapter 12). Although **direct distribution channels,** in which products are sold directly from producers to users, are not used frequently in the distribution of consumer products, they are the most widely used for industrial products. More than half of all industrial products are sold through direct channels (channel E in Figure 21.2). Industrial buyers like to communicate directly with producers, especially when expensive or technically complex products are involved. For this reason organisational buyers prefer to purchase expensive and highly complex mainframe and mini-computers directly from the producers. In these circumstances, an industrial customer wants the technical assistance and personal assurances that only a producer can provide.

A second industrial distribution channel involves an industrial distributor to facilitate exchanges between the producer and customer (channel F in Figure 21.2). A **business-to-business distributor** is an independent business organisation that takes title to products and carries inventories. Such distributors are merchant wholesalers; they assume possession and ownership of goods, as well as the risks associated with ownership. Business-to-business distributors usually sell standardised items, such as maintenance supplies, production tools and small operating equipment. Some carry a wide variety of product lines; others specialise in one or a small number of lines. Industrial distributors can be used most effectively when a product has broad market appeal, is easily stocked and serviced, is sold in

Direct distribution channels Distribution channels in which products are sold directly from producers to users

Business-to-business distributor An independent business organisation that takes title to products and carries inventories

Figure 21.2

Typical marketing channels for industrial products/business-to-business markets

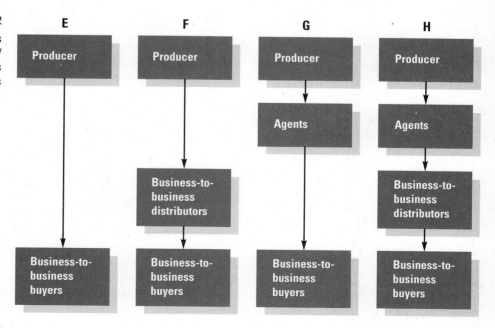

small quantities and is needed rapidly to avoid high losses (such as a part for an assembly line machine).[4]

Business-to-business distributors or dealers offer sellers several advantages. They can perform the needed selling activities in local markets at relatively low cost to a manufacturer. They can reduce a producer's financial burden by providing their customers with credit services. And because industrial distributors usually maintain close relationships with their customers, they are aware of local needs and can pass on market information to producers. By holding adequate inventories in their local markets, these distributors reduce the producers' capital requirements.

There are, though, several disadvantages to using business-to-business distributors. They may be difficult to control because they are independent firms. Because they often stock competing brands, an industrial seller cannot depend on them to sell a specific brand aggressively. Furthermore, industrial distributors maintain inventories, for which they incur numerous expenses; consequently, they are less likely to handle bulky items or items that are slow sellers relative to profit margin, need specialised facilities or require extraordinary selling efforts. In some cases, business-to-business distributors lack the technical knowledge necessary to sell and service certain industrial items.

In the third business-to-business distribution channel (Channel G in Figure 21.2), a manufacturer's agent is employed. As described in Chapter 12, a manufacturer's agent or representative is an independent business person who sells complimentary products of several producers in assigned territories and is compensated through commissions. Unlike an industrial distributor, a manufacturer's agent does not acquire title to the products and usually does not take possession. Acting as a salesperson on behalf of the producers, a manufacturer's agent has no latitude, or very little, in negotiating prices or sales terms.

Using manufacturer's agents can benefit a business marketer. These agents usually possess considerable technical and market information and have an established set of customers. For an industrial seller with highly seasonal demand, a manufacturer's agent can be an asset because the seller does not have to support a year round sales force. The fact that manufacturers' agents are paid on a commission basis may also make them an economical alternative for a firm that has extremely limited resources and cannot afford a full time sales force.

Certainly, the use of manufacturers' agents is not problem-free. Even though straight commissions may be cheaper for an organisational seller, the seller may have little control over manufacturers' agents. Because of the compensation method, manufacturers' agents generally want to concentrate on their larger accounts. They are often reluctant to spend adequate time following up sales, to put forward special selling efforts or to provide sellers with market information when such activities reduce the amount of productive selling time. Because they rarely maintain inventories, manufacturers' agents have a limited ability to provide customers quickly with parts or repair services.

The fourth business-to-business distribution channel (Channel H in Figure 21.2) has both a manufacturer's agent and an industrial distributor between the producer and the organisational customer. This channel may be appropriate when the business marketer wishes to cover a large geographical area but maintains no sales force because demand is highly seasonal or because the firm cannot afford one. This type of channel can also be useful for a business-to-business marketer that wants to enter a new geographic market without expanding the firm's existing sales force.

So far, this discussion has implied that all channels are equally available and that an industrial producer can select the most desirable option. However, in a number of cases, only one or perhaps two channels are available for the distribution of certain types of products. An important issue in channel selection is the manner in which particular products are normally purchased. If customers ordinarily buy certain types of products directly from producers, it is unlikely that channels with intermediaries will be effective. Other dimensions that should be considered are the product's cost and physical characteristics, the costs of using various channels, the amount of technical assistance customers need and the size of product and parts inventory needed in local markets.

Physical distribution decisions regarding transport, storage and inventory control are especially important for business-to-business marketers. Some raw materials and other industrial products may require special handling; for example, toxic chemicals used in the manufacture of some products must be shipped, stored and disposed of properly to ensure that they do not harm people or the environment. In addition, the continuity of most organisational buyer-seller relationships depends on the seller having the right products available when and where the customer needs them. This requirement is so important that business-to-business marketers must sometimes make a considerable investment in order processing systems, materials handling equipment, warehousing facilities and inventory control systems. Tioxide, a subsidiary of chemicals giant ICI, holds extensive stocks of TiO_2 for distribution to a variety of business markets—ranging from PVC, paint to inks—worldwide. Without high stocks and a quickly responsive distribution system, rival DuPont would gain an edge.

Many industrial purchasers are moving away from traditional marketing exchange relationships—where the buyer purchases primarily on price from multiple suppliers—to more tightly knit, relational exchanges, which are long lasting, less price driven agreements between manufacturers and suppliers.[5] Just-in-time inventory management systems are providing the rationale underlying these new types of relationships. In order to reduce inventory costs and to eliminate waste, buyers purchase new stock just before it is needed in the manufacturing process. To make this system effective, they must share a great deal of information with their suppliers, since these relationships are collaborative.

Promotion

The combination of promotional efforts used in business-to-business marketing mixes generally differs from those for consumer products, especially convenience goods. The differences are evident in the emphasis on various promotional mix ingredients and the activities performed in connection with each promotional mix ingredient.

Personal selling The task of informing and persuading customers to purchase through personal communication

For several reasons, most organisational marketers rely on **personal selling,** informing and persuading customers to purchase through personal communication, to a much greater extent than do consumer product marketers (except, perhaps, marketers of consumer durables). Because an industrial seller often has fewer customers, personal contact with each customer is more feasible. Some industrial products have technical features that are too numerous or too complex to explain through non-personal forms of promotion. Moreover, business-to-business purchases are frequently high in value and must be suited to the job and available where and when needed; thus business buyers want reinforcement and personal assurances from industrial sales personnel. Because business marketers depend on repeat purchases, sales personnel must follow up sales to make certain that customers know how to use the purchased items effectively, as well as to

Figure 21.3

A typical business-to-
business advertisement

In industrial selling, advertising often supplements
personal selling efforts.

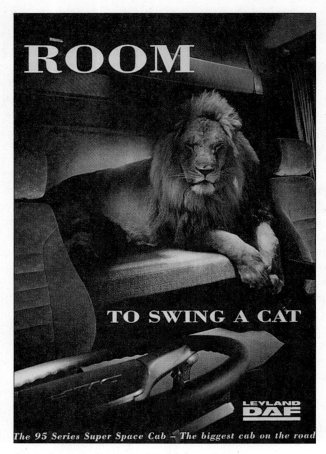

SOURCE: Courtesy of Leyland DAF.

ensure that the products work properly. Personal selling is often supported with advertising activity (see Figure 21.3).

Salespeople need to perform the role of educators, showing buyers clearly how the product fits their needs. When the purchase of a product is critical to the future profitability of the business-to-business buyer, buying decision-makers gather extensive amounts of information about all alternative products. To deal with such buyers successfully, the seller must have a highly trained sales force that is knowledgeable not only about its own company's products but also about competitors' offerings. Besides, if sales representatives offer thorough and reliable information, they can reduce the organisational buyer's uncertainty, as well as differentiate their firm's product from the competition. Finally, the gathering of information lengthens the decision-making process. Thus it is important for salespeople to be patient; not to pressure their clients as they make important, new and complex decisions; and to continue providing information to their prospects throughout the entire process.[6]

As Table 21.1 illustrates, the average cost of an industrial sales call varies from industry to industry. Selling costs comprise salaries, commissions, bonuses, and travel and entertainment expenses. In the United States, the average cost of an industrial call is $229.70.[7] It should also be noted, however, that some business-to-business sales are very large. A Boeing salesperson, for instance, closed a sale

Industry	Number of Business-to-Business Companies Reporting	Average Daily Number of Sales Calls Per Salesperson	Average Cost of Business-to-Business Sales Call	Average Daily Sales Call Costs[b] Per Sales-Person
Printing and publishing	18	3.2	$148.60	$ 475.52
Chemicals and allied products	41	4.0	$155.20	$ 620.80
Petroleum and coal products	12	5.3	$ 99.10	$ 525.23
Primary metal industries	15	3.9	$363.90	$1,419.21
Fabricated metal products	113	3.9	$186.10	$ 725.79
Machinery, except electrical	275	3.5	$257.30	$ 900.55
Electronic computing equipment (computer hardware)	17	4.2	$452.60	$1,900.92
Electrical and electronic equipment	137	3.5	$238.40	$ 834.40
Transport equipment	41	2.9	$255.90	$ 742.11
Instruments and related products	73	3.9	$209.50	$ 817.05
Wholesale trade-durable goods	29	5.1	$139.80	$ 712.98
Business services	30	2.8	$227.20	$ 636.16

[a]No comparable UK/EU statistics available.
[b]This cost is determined by multiplying the average daily number of calls per salesperson by the average cost per sales call for each industry.

SOURCE: Laboratory of Advertising Performance (LAP), report no. 8052.3 (date unavailable), McGraw-Hill Research. Reprinted by permission of McGraw-Hill, Inc.

Table 21.1 The average cost of a business-to-business sales call between selected industries in America[a]

with Delta Air Lines for commercial aircraft worth $3 billion.[8] But on average, only 350 aircraft are sold each year, resulting in sales of $105 billion. Generally, aircraft salespeople work hardest in the three to five years before a sale is made.[9]

Because of the escalating costs of advertising and personal selling, telemarketing—the creative use of the telephone to enhance the salesperson's function—is on the increase. Some of the activities in telemarketing include Freephone 0800 phone lines and personal sales workstations—assisted by data terminals—that take orders, check stock and order status, and provide shipping and invoicing information.

Although not all business-to-business sales personnel perform the same sales activities, they can generally be grouped into the following categories, as described in Chapter 18: technical, missionary, and trade or inside order takers. An inside order taker could effectively use telemarketing. Regardless of how sales personnel are classified, industrial selling activities differ from consumer sales efforts. Because organisational sellers are frequently asked for technical advice about product specifications and uses, they often need technical backgrounds and are more likely to have them than consumer sales personnel. Compared with typical buyer-seller relationships in consumer product sales, the interdependence that develops between industrial buyers and sellers is likely to be stronger. Sellers count on buyers to purchase their particular products; and buyers rely on sellers to provide information, products and related services when and where needed. Although business-to-business salespeople do market their products aggressively, they almost never use "hard sell" tactics because of their role as technical consultants and the interdependence between buyers and sellers.

Advertising is emphasised less in business sales than in consumer transactions. Some of the reasons given earlier for the importance of personal selling in business-to-business promotional mixes explain why. However, advertising often supplements personal selling efforts. Because the cost of a business-to-business sales call is high and continues to rise, advertisements that allow sales personnel to perform more efficiently and effectively are worthwhile for business-to-business marketers. Advertising can make organisational customers aware of new products and brands; inform buyers about general product features, representatives and organisations; and isolate promising prospects by providing enquiry forms or the addresses and phone numbers of company representatives. To ensure that appropriate information is sent to a respondent, it is crucial for the enquiry to specify the type of information desired, the name of the company and respondent, the company's SIC (Standard Industrial Classification) number and the size of the organisation.

Because the demand for most business-to-business products is derived demand—for example, demand for construction equipment stems from consumer demand for more new houses, which in turn prompts building firms to require more plants and equipment—marketers can sometimes stimulate demand for their products by stimulating consumer demand. Thus an organisational marketer occasionally sponsors an advertisement promoting the products sold by the marketer's customers.

When selecting advertising media, organisational marketers primarily choose print media such as trade publications and direct mail; they seldom use broadcast media. Trade publications and direct mail reach precise groups of industrial customers and avoid wasted circulation. In addition, they are best suited for advertising messages that present numerous details and complex product information (which are frequently the types of messages that business-to-business advertisers wish to convey).

Compared with consumer product advertisements, industrial advertisements are usually less persuasive and more likely to contain a large amount of copy and numerous details. In contrast, marketers that advertise to reach ultimate consumers sometimes avoid extensive advertising copy because consumers are reluctant to read it. Business-to-business advertisers, however, believe that industrial purchasers with any interest in their products will search for information and read long messages.

Sales promotion activities, too, can play a significant role in business-to-business promotional mixes. They encompass such efforts as catalogues, trade shows and trade sales promotion methods, including merchandise allowances, buy back allowances, displays, sales contests and other methods discussed in Chapter 18. Business-to-business marketers go to great lengths and considerable expense to provide catalogues that describe their products to customers. Customers refer to various sellers' catalogues to determine specifications, terms of sale, delivery times and other information about products. Catalogues thus help buyers decide which suppliers to contact.

Trade shows can be effective vehicles for making many customer contacts in a short time. One study found that firms allocate 25 per cent of their annual promotional budgets to trade shows in order to communicate with their current and potential customers, promote their corporate image, introduce new products, meet key account executives, develop mailing lists, identify sales prospects and find out what their competitors are doing. Although trade shows take second place to personal selling, they rank above print advertising in influencing business-to-business purchases, particularly as the organisational buyers reach the stages in the buying process of need recognition and supplier evaluation.

Many firms that participate in trade shows lack specific objectives regarding what they hope to accomplish by such participation. Firms with the most successful trade show programmes have written objectives for the tasks they wish to achieve, and they carefully select the type of show in which to take part so that those attending match the firm's target market.[10]

The way in which business marketers use publicity in their promotional mixes may not be much different from the way in which marketers of consumer products use it. As described in Chapter 17, more companies are incorporating public relations automatically into their promotional mixes.

Price
Compared with consumer product marketers, organisational or business-to-business marketers face many more price constraints from legal and economic forces. With respect to economic forces, an individual industrial firm's demand is often highly elastic, requiring the firm to approximate competitors' prices. This condition often results in non-price competition and a considerable amount of price stability.

Today's route to sustainable *differential advantage* (competitive edge) lies in offering customers something that the competition does not offer—something that helps them increase their productivity and profitability. Firms achieve high market share not by offering low prices but by offering their customers superior value and product quality.[11] Customers are willing to pay higher prices for quality products.[12] Companies such as Caterpillar Tractor, Hewlett-Packard and 3M have shown that a value based strategy can win a commanding lead over competition. Such firms emphasise the highest quality products at slightly higher prices.

Many industrial companies are devoting increased resources to training, so that their personnel are better qualified and more willing to provide full customer service. Corporate image, reliability and flexibility in production and delivery, technical innovation and well executed promotional activity also present opportunities to create a differential advantage. Price used to be the basis for differentiation in industrial markets, but price can be reduced only so far if companies are to remain viable. Although cost is still important, in most markets companies have attempted to move away from a selling proposition based purely on low price. They have realised that *value* is not necessarily equal to a low price. Service, reliability, image and design are just a few factors in addition to price that influence many sales. Today, value—keen price coupled with a product/service offer—and not raw, low price is often the deciding factor for many business-to-business customers.

Although there are various ways to determine prices of industrial products, the three most common are administered pricing, bid pricing and negotiated pricing. With **administered pricing,** the seller determines the price (or series of prices) for a product, and the customer pays that specified price. Marketers who use this approach may employ a one price policy in which all buyers pay the same price,

Administered pricing A pricing method in which the seller determines the price for a product and the customer pays the specified price or they may set a series of prices that are determined by one or more discounts. In some cases, list prices are posted on a price sheet or in a catalogue. The list price is a beginning point from which trade, quantity and cash discounts are deducted. Thus the actual (net) price a business-to-business customer pays is the list price less the discount(s). When a list price is used, an industrial marketer sometimes specifies the price in terms of list price times a multiplier. For example, the price of an item might be quoted as "list price x .78", which means the buyer can purchase the product at 78 per cent of the list price. Simply changing the multiplier lets the seller revise prices without having to issue new catalogues or price sheets.

With **bid pricing**, prices are determined through sealed or open bids. When a buyer uses sealed bids, selected sellers are notified that they are to submit their bids by a certain date. Normally, the lowest bidder is awarded the contract, as long as the buyer believes that the firm is able to supply the specified products when and where needed. In an open bidding approach, several, but not all, sellers are asked to submit bids. In contrast to sealed bidding, the amounts of the bids are made public. Finally, an organisational purchaser sometimes uses negotiated bids. Under this arrangement, the customer seeks bids from a number of sellers and screens the bids. Then the customer negotiates the price and terms of sale with the most favourable bidders, until either a final transaction is consummated or negotiations are terminated with all sellers.

Sometimes a buyer will be seeking either component parts to be used in production for several years or custom built equipment to be purchased currently and through future contracts. In such instances, an industrial seller may submit an initial, less profitable bid to win "follow on" (subsequent) contracts. The seller that wins the initial contract is often substantially favoured in the competition for follow on contracts. In such a bidding situation, a business-to-business marketer must determine how low the initial bid should be, the probability of winning a follow on contract and what combination of bid prices on both the initial and the follow on contract will yield an acceptable profit.[13]

For certain types of business markets, a seller's pricing component may have to allow for **negotiated pricing**. That is, even when there are stated list prices and discount structures, negotiations may determine the actual price an organisational customer pays. Negotiated pricing can benefit seller and buyer because price negotiations frequently lead to discussions of product specifications, applications and perhaps product substitutions. Such negotiations may give the seller an opportunity to provide the customer with technical assistance and perhaps sell a product that better fits the customer's requirements; the final product choice might also be more profitable for the seller. The buyer benefits by gaining more information about the array of products and terms of sale available and may acquire a more suitable product at a lower price.

Some business-to-business marketers sell in markets in which only one of these general pricing approaches prevails. Such marketers can simplify the price components of their marketing mixes. However, a number of business marketers sell to a wide variety of organisational customers and must maintain considerable flexibility in pricing.

People

This chapter has already emphasised the importance of people in the marketing of business-to-business products. The role of personal selling is especially important in many business markets, particularly those in which the purchase is deemed risky because of its size, value or complexity. For many technologically advanced products, the need to have face-to-face explanation and guidance is fundamental to the customers' perceived level of satisfaction. The development of long term **relationships**—regular, ongoing contacts—with business-to-business customers, is increasingly a driving factor in the development of marketing mixes for businesses supplying other businesses. Where products are high value or complex, customers often expect such relationships. Even in commodity markets, for example basic components, computer consumerables or the provision of electricity, relationships are seen as a means of maintaining contact with customers, ensuring re-orders and enabling a supplying business to differentiate itself through customer service rather than price alone. More attention is being given to the effective recruitment, training and motivation of personnel who are often in regular contact with a business's immediate customers, typically other organisations in the marketing channel.

Relationships Regular, ongoing contacts between businesses and their customers

• • • • • • • • • • • • • • • • • • • •

Amending the Marketing Mix for Services

The original marketing mix defined by McCarthy included the now well known "4Ps" of product, promotion, price and place (distribution/channels). Most authors now mention an additional ingredient of the marketing mix: people. Originally suggested by services marketers who acknowledged that consumers often view the personnel providing a service as part and parcel of the service "product" being offered, the people aspect of the marketing mix has become an accepted part of most businesses' marketing programmes, not only for organisations marketing services. The nature of services, however, as described in Chapter 11, has led marketers to further adapt the marketing mix.[14] The intangibility of service products, inseparability of production and consumption, perishability and heterogeneity—the key characteristics of services—force the marketing mix to be amended in two ways: (1) the traditional 4Ps of product, promotion, price and place have some important extra dimensions unique to the marketing of services, and (2) the marketing mix is itself modified to include the additional core ingredients of people, physical evidence or ambience and process, thereby creating the "7Ps" of what is termed the **extended marketing mix for services**.[15] Figure 21.4 presents this revised marketing mix for services. This section examines in more detail the amendments required when determining a marketing mix for services, commencing with the traditional 4Ps, before reviewing the additional ingredients of the extended marketing mix.

Extended marketing mix for services Besides the traditional 4 Ps of product, promotion, price and place, the additional 3 Ps of people, physical evidence and process

Product

Goods can be defined in terms of their physical attributes, but services, because of their **intangibility**, cannot. As pointed out earlier in the chapter, it is often difficult for consumers to understand service offerings and to evaluate possible service alternatives. British Gas, for example, offers schemes to spread bill payments and to assist the financially disadvantaged, plus several methods for making payments. These services are explained in the company's advertisements.

Intangibility Services that cannot be defined in terms of their physical attributes because they cannot be perceived by any of the five senses

There may also be tangibles (such as facilities, employees or communications) associated with a service. These tangible elements help form a part of the product and are often the only aspects of a service that can be viewed prior to purchase. Consequently, marketers must pay close attention to associated tangibles and make sure that they are consistent with the selected image of the service product.[16] For example, consumers perceive public transport at night as plagued by crime and therefore hesitate to use it. Improvements in the physical appearance of tube

Figure 21.4

The extended marketing mix for services

stations and reductions in the time between trains are tangible cues that consumers can use to judge public transport services.

    The service product is often equated with the **service provider**, for example, the bank clerk or the stylist becomes the service a bank or a beauty salon provides. Because consumers tend to view services in terms of the service personnel and because personnel are inconsistent in their behaviour, it is imperative that marketers effectively select, train, motivate and control contact people.

    After testing many variables, the Strategic Planning Institute (SPI) in the United States developed an extensive database on the impact of various business strategies on profits. The institute found that "relative perceived product *quality*" is the single most important factor in determining long term profitability. In fact, because there are generally no objective measures to evaluate the quality of professional services (medical care, legal services and so forth), the customer is actually purchasing confidence in the service provider.[17] The strength or weakness of the service provided often affects consumers' perceptions of **service product quality**. Of the companies in the SPI database, businesses that rate low on service lose market share at the rate of 2 per cent a year and average a 1 per cent return on sales. Companies that score high on service gain market share at the rate of 6 per cent a year, average a 12 per cent return on sales and charge a significantly higher price.[18] These data indicate that firms having service dominant products must score high on service quality.

    Because services are performances rather than tangible goods, the concept of service quality is difficult to grasp. However, price, quality and value are important considerations of consumer choice and buying behaviour for both goods and services.[19] It should be noted that it is not objective quality that matters, but the consumer's subjective perceptions. Instead of quality meaning conformity to a set of specifications—which frequently determine levels of product quality—service quality is defined by customers.[20] Moreover, quality is frequently determined through a comparison—in the case of services, by contrasting what the consumer expected of a service with her or his actual experience.[21]

Service provider   A person who offers a service, such as a bank clerk or hairstylist

Service product quality   The consumer's perception of the quality of service he or she receives

Service providers and service consumers may have quite different views of what constitutes service quality. Consumers frequently enter service exchanges with a set of pre-determined expectations. Whether a consumer's actual experiences exceed, match or fall below these expectations will have a great effect on future relationships between the consumer and the service provider. To improve service quality, a service provider must adjust its own behaviour to be consistent with consumers' expectations or re-educate consumers so that their expectations will parallel the service levels that can be achieved.[22]

A study of doctor-patient relationships proposed that when professional service exceeds client expectations, a true person-to-person bonding relationship develops. However, the research also revealed that what doctors viewed as being quality service was not necessarily what patients perceived as quality service. Although interaction with the doctor was the primary determinant of the overall service evaluation, patients made judgements about the entire service experience, including factors such as the appearance and behaviour of receptionists, nurses and technicians; the decor; and even the appearance of the building.[23]

Other product concepts discussed in Chapters 9 and 10 are also relevant here. Management must make decisions regarding the product mix, positioning, branding and new product development of services. It can make better decisions if it analyses the organisation's service products in terms of **complexity** and **variability**. Complexity is determined by the number of steps required to perform the service. Variability reflects the amount of diversity allowed in each step of service provision. In a highly variable service, every step in performing the service may be unique, whereas in cases of low variability, every performance of the service is standardised.[24] For example, services provided by doctors are both complex and variable. Patient treatment may involve many steps, and the doctor has considerable discretion in shaping the treatment for each individual patient.

An examination of the complete service delivery process, including the number of steps and decisions, enables marketers to plot their service products on a complexity/variability grid, such as the one in Figure 21.5. The position of a service on the grid has implications for its positioning in the market. Furthermore, any alterations in the service delivery process that shift the position of the service on the complexity/variability grid have an impact on the positioning of the service in the marketplace. Table 21.2 details the effects of such changes. When structuring the service delivery system, marketers should consider the firm's marketing goals and target market.

Complexity In services marketing, the number of steps required to perform a service

Variability The amount of diversity allowed in each step of service provision

Figure 21.5

Complexity/variability grid for medical services

SOURCE: Adapted from Lynn Shostack, 1985 American Marketing Association Faculty Consortium on Services Marketing, Texas A&M University, 7–11 July. Reprinted by permission of the American Marketing Association.

Downgrading Complexity/Variability	Upgrading Complexity/Variability
Standardises the service	Increases costs
Requires strict operating controls	Indicates higher margin/lower volume strategy
Generally widens potential market	Personalises the service
Lowers costs	Generally narrows potential market
Indicates lower margin/higher volume strategy	Makes quality more difficult to control
Can alienate existing markets	

SOURCE: Adapted from Lynn Shostack, 1985 American Marketing Association Faculty Consortium on Services Marketing, Texas A&M University, 7–11 July. Reprinted by permission of the American Marketing Association.

Table 21.2 Effects of shifting positions on the complexity/variability grid

Promotion

As intangible dominant products, services are not easily promoted. The intangible is difficult to depict in advertising, whether the medium is print or broadcast. Service advertising should thus emphasise tangible cues that will help consumers understand and evaluate the service. The cues may be the physical facilities in which the service is performed or some relevant tangible object that symbolises the service itself.[25] For example, restaurants may stress their physical facilities—clean, elegant, casual and so on—to provide clues as to the quality or nature of the service. Insurance firms, such as Legal and General, use objects as symbols to help consumers understand their services. Legal and General's umbrella symbol reflects an image of paternalistic protection. Midland Bank's slogan "The Listening Bank" gives the impression of understanding, helpfulness and service. Service providers may also focus their advertising on the characteristics they believe customers want from their services. National Westminster Bank's promotion stresses its ability to offer unbiased, independent advice about pensions. Commercial Union Assurance—"We won't make a drama out of a crisis"—emphasises speed of service in dealing with insurance claims and the provision of assistance in sorting out the problem.

The symbols, catch lines and imagery common to most financial organisations reflect the increasing importance of branding in services.[26] Differentiation between rival services is difficult, as is effective promotion. Branding is helping to distinguish competing services and to provide a platform for promotional activity.[27]

To be successful, firms must not only maximise the difference between the value of the service to the customer and the cost of providing it; they must also design the service with employees in mind. Contact personnel are critical to the perception of quality service. They must be provided with sufficient tools and knowledge to furnish the type of service that the customer desires. Because service industries are information driven, they can substitute knowledgeable, highly trained personnel for the capital assets used in more product orientated businesses.[28]

Thus employees in a service organisation are an important secondary audience for service advertising. Variability in service quality, which arises from the labour intensive nature of many services, is a problem for service marketers, because consumers often associate the service with the service provider. Advertising can have a positive effect on customer contact personnel. It can shape employees' perceptions of the company, their jobs and how management expects them to perform. It can be a tool for motivating, educating and communicating with employees.[29] For example, British Airways' famous strapline on its advertising throughout the 1980s, "the world's favorite airline", was designed not just to remind air travellers that more people flew with BA than with any other airline but also to develop a sense of pride among BA's flight and ground personnel.

Personal selling is potentially powerful in services because this form of promotion lets consumers and salespeople interact. When consumers enter into a service transaction, they must, as a general rule, interact with service firm employees. Customer contact personnel can be trained to use this opportunity to reduce customer uncertainty, give reassurance, reduce dissonance and promote the reputation of the organisation.[30] Once again, therefore, properly managing contact personnel is important.

Although consumer service firms have the opportunity to interact with actual customers and those potential customers who contact them, they have little opportunity to go out into the field and solicit business from all potential consumers. The very large number of potential customers and the high cost per sales call rule out such efforts. On the other hand, marketers of industrial services, like the marketers of industrial goods, are dealing with a much more limited target market and may find personal selling the most effective way of reaching their customers.

Sales promotions, such as contests, are feasible for service firms, but other types of promotions are more difficult to implement. How does a firm display a service? How does it provide a free sample without giving away the whole service? A complimentary visit to a health club or a free skiing lesson could possibly be considered a free sample to entice a consumer into purchasing a membership or taking lessons. Although the role of publicity and the implementation of a publicity campaign do not differ significantly in the goods and service sectors, service marketers appear to rely on publicity much more than goods marketers do.[31]

Consumers tend to value word-of-mouth communications more than company sponsored communications. This preference is probably true for all products, but especially for services, because they are experimental in nature. For this reason, service firms should attempt to stimulate word-of-mouth communications.[32] They can do so by encouraging consumers to tell their friends about satisfactory performance. Many firms, for instance, prominently display signs urging customers to tell their friends if they like the service and to tell the firm if they do not. Some service providers, such as hairdressers, give their regular customers discounts or free services for encouraging friends to come in for a haircut. Word-of-mouth can be simulated through communications messages that feature a testimonial—for example, television advertisements showing consumers who vouch for the benefits of a service a particular firm offers.

One final note should be made in regard to service promotion. The promotional activities of most professional service providers, such as doctors, lawyers and accountants, are severely limited. Until recently, all these professionals were prohibited by law from advertising. Although these restrictions have now been lifted in many countries, there are still many obstacles to be overcome. Not used to seeing professionals advertise, consumers may reject the advertisements of those who do. Furthermore, professionals are not familiar with advertising and consequently do not always develop advertisements appropriate for their services. In many countries, lawyers are being forced to consider advertising, both because many potential clients do not know that they need legal services and because there is an over supply of lawyers. Consumers want more information about legal services, and lawyers have a very poor public image.[33] On the other hand, doctors and dentists are more sceptical about the impact of advertising on their image and business. Despite the trend towards professional services advertising, the professions themselves exert pressure on their members to advertise or promote only in a limited way because such activities are still viewed as somewhat risqué.

Price

Price plays both an economic and a psychological role in the service sector, just as it does with physical goods. However, the psychological role of price in respect to services is magnified; after all, consumers must rely on price as the sole indicator of service quality when other quality indicators are absent. In its economic role, price determines revenue and influences profits. Knowing the real costs of each service provided is vital to sound pricing decisions.[34]

Services may also be bundled together and then sold for a single price. Service bundling is a practical strategy, because in many types of service there is a high ratio of fixed to variable costs and high cost sharing amongst service offerings. Moreover, the demand for certain services is often interdependent. For example, banks offer packages of banking services—current and savings accounts and credit lines that become active when customers overdraw their other accounts. Price bundling may help service marketers cross-sell to their current customers or acquire new customers. The policy of price leaders also may be used by discounting the price of one service product when the customer purchases another service at full price.[35] Visitors to a safari park may be offered discounted entry to the attached fairground and amusements.

Service intangibility may also complicate the setting of prices. When pricing physical goods, management can look to the cost of production (direct and indirect materials, direct and indirect labour, and overheads) as an indicator of price. It is often difficult, however, to determine the cost of service provision and thus identify a minimum price. Price competition is severe in many service areas characterised by standardisation. Usually, price is not a key variable when marketing is first implemented in an organisation. Once market segmentation and specialised services are directed to specific markets, specialised prices are set. Next comes comparative pricing as the service becomes fairly standardised. Price competition is quite common in the hotel and leisure sectors, banking and insurance.

Many services, especially professional services, are situation specific. Thus neither the service firm nor the consumer knows the extent of the service prior to production and consumption. Once again, because cost is not known beforehand, price is difficult to set. Despite the difficulties in determining cost, many service firms use cost plus pricing. Others set prices according to the competition or market demand.

Pricing of services can also help smooth out fluctuations in demand. Given the perishability of service products, this is an important function. A higher price may be used to deter or off-set demand during peak periods, and a lower price may be used to stimulate demand during slack periods. The railways offer cheap day returns and savers to minimise sales declines in slack periods. Airlines rely heavily on price to help smooth out their demand, as do many other operations, such as pubs and entertainment clubs, cinemas, resorts and hotels.

Place (Distribution)   In the service context, distribution is making services available to prospective users. Marketing intermediaries are the entities between the actual service provider and the consumer that make the service more available and more convenient to use.[36] The distribution of services is very closely related to product development. Indirect distribution of services may be made possible by a tangible representation or a facilitating good, for example, a bank credit card.[37]

Almost by definition, service industries are limited to direct channels of distribution. Many services are produced and consumed simultaneously; in high contact services in particular, service providers and consumers cannot be separated. In low contact services, however, service providers may be separated from customers by intermediaries. Dry cleaners, for example, generally maintain strategically located retail stores as drop-off centres, and these stores may be independent or company owned. Consumers go to the branch to initiate and terminate service, but the actual service may be performed at a different location. The separation is possible because the service is directed towards the consumer's physical possessions, and the consumer is not required to be present during delivery.

Other service industries are developing unique ways to distribute their services. To make it more convenient for consumers to obtain their services, airlines, car hire companies and hotels have long been using intermediaries: travel agencies. In financial services marketing, the two most important strategic concerns are the application of technology and the use of electronic product delivery channels— such as automatic cash dispensers and electronic funds transfer systems—to provide customers with financial services in a more widespread and convenient manner.[38] Consumers no longer have to go to their bank for routine transactions; they can now receive service from the nearest cash dispenser or conduct transactions via telephone or fax. Indeed, Midland Bank's First Direct banking operation is managed entirely through telecommunications: there is no bank branch network. Bank credit cards have enabled banks to extend their credit services to consumers over widely dispersed geographic areas through an international network of intermediaries, namely, the retailers who assist consumers in applying for and using the cards.

Process   The acts of purchasing and consumption are important in all markets—consumer, industrial or service. The direct involvement of consumers in the production of most services and the perishability of these services place greater emphasis on the process of the transaction for services. Friendliness of staff and flows of information affect the customer's perception of the service product offer. Appointment or queuing systems become part of the service. Ease of payment can enhance or spoil the consumption of a service. Diners in a TGI Friday's or Old Orleans expect prompt service, informative menus, no waiting and no delays in paying their bills at the conclusion of their meals. These are operational issues that *directly* affect customer perceptions and satisfaction: they are important aspects of the marketing of services.[39]

Physical Evidence/Ambience   The environment in which a service is offered, and consumed, is central to the consumer's understanding of the service and to her or his enjoyment or satisfaction. The "feel" is very much part of the service offer. Whether in a restaurant, hospital, sports club or bank, the appearance and ambience matter. Layout, decor, up-keep; noise and aroma; general ease of access and use—all become part of the service product.

People   The nature of most services requires direct interaction between the consumer and personnel representing the service provider's organisation. In many services, customers interact with one another; the organisation's staff also interact with one another. This level of human involvement must be given maximum attention if customers are to maximise their use of the service and, ultimately, their satisfaction.[40] Employee selection, training and motivation are central considerations. A restaurant may have a superb operation, but if the chef or waiters become demoralised and unmotivated, they will begin to deliver low quality meals and inefficient service, resulting in a poor product from the consumer's point of view. Operational staff often help "produce" the service product, sell it and assist in its consumption. Many service businesses are totally dependent on their personnel, as Leo Burnett, founder of the international advertising agency that bears his name, summed up: "All our assets go down the elevator every evening"—people!

• • • • • • • • • • • • • • • • • • •

Strategic Adaptation of Marketing Mixes for International Markets

As explained in Chapter 3, marketing in non-domestic markets requires an understanding of the marketing environment and a specifically devised strategy. Once a company determines overseas market potential and understands the foreign environment, it develops and adapts its marketing mix(es). Creating and maintaining the marketing mix are the final steps in developing the international marketing strategy. Only if foreign marketing opportunities justify the risk will a company go to the expense of adapting the marketing mix. Of course, in some situations new products are developed for a specific country. In these cases, there is no existing marketing mix and no extra expense to consider in serving the foreign target market.

Product and Promotion   As Figure 21.6 shows, there are five possible strategies for adapting product and promotion across national boundaries: (1) keep product and promotion the same worldwide, (2) adapt promotion only, (3) adapt product only, (4) adapt both product and promotion and (5) invent new products.[41]

Keep Product and Promotion the Same Worldwide   This strategy attempts to use in the foreign country the product and promotion developed for the home market, an approach that seems desirable wherever possible because it eliminates the expenses of marketing research and product re-development. American companies PepsiCo and Coca-Cola use this approach in marketing their soft drinks. Although both translate promotional messages into the language of a particular country, they market the same product and promotion messages around the world. Despite certain inherent risks that stem from cultural differences in interpretation, exporting advertising copy does provide the efficiency of international standardisation, or globalisation. As the following examples imply, not all brands/products are suitable for export in their existing forms: *Zit* fizzy drink (Greece), *Bum's* biscuits (Sweden), *Krapp* toilet paper (Sweden), *Grand Dick* red

Figure 21.6

International product and promotion strategies

SOURCE: *Adapted from Warren J. Keegan,* Global Marketing Management, *4th edn, Englewood Cliffs, N.J.: Prentice-Hall, 1989, pp. 378–382. Used by permission.*

wine (France), and *Sor Bits* mints (Denmark).[42] Global advertising embraces the same concept as global marketing, discussed in Chapter 3. An advertiser can save hundreds of thousands of pounds by running the same advertisement worldwide.

Adapt Promotion Only   This strategy leaves the product basically unchanged but modifies its promotion. For example, McDonald's provides similar products throughout the world but may modify the media for its advertising messages. This approach may be necessary because of language, legal or cultural differences associated with the advertising copy. When Polaroid introduced its SX-70 camera in Europe, for example, it used the same television and print advertisements featuring the same "celebrities" that it had used in the United States. However, because those featured were in fact not well known in Europe, the advertisements were not effective, and sales of the SX-70 were initially low. Only when Polaroid adapted its promotion to appeal to regional needs and tastes did the SX-70 begin to achieve success.[43] Promotional adaptation is a low cost modification compared with the costs of re-developing engineering and production and physically changing products.

Generally, the strategy of adapting only promotion infuses advertising with the culture of the people who will be exposed to it (see Figure 21.7). Often promotion combines thinking globally and acting locally. At company headquarters, a basic global marketing strategy is developed, but promotion is modified to fit each market's needs.

Adapt Product Only   The basic assumption in modifying a product without changing its promotion is that the product will serve the same function under different conditions of use. Soap and washing powder manufacturers have adapted their products to local water conditions and washing equipment without changing their promotions. Household appliances also have been altered to use different power voltages.

A product may have to be adjusted for legal reasons. Japan, for example, has some of the most stringent car emission requirements in the world. European cars that fail emission standards cannot be marketed in Japan. Sometimes, products

TREAUPHÄE

Treauphy.

EIGENLEAUB

Bleau your own trumpet.

PREAUPAGANDE

Preaupaganda.

FEAUREVER

Figure 21.7 Adapting promotion across national boundaries

SOURCE: Courtesy Perrier Exports.

must be adjusted to overcome social and cultural obstacles. American Jell-O introduced a powdered jelly mix that failed in Britain because Britons were used to buying jelly in cube form. Resistance to a product is frequently based on attitudes and ignorance about the nature of new technology. It is often easier to change the product than to overcome technological biases.

Adapt Both Product and Promotion   When a product serves a new function or is used differently in a foreign market, then both the product and its promotion need to be altered. For example, when Procter & Gamble marketed its Cheer washing powder in Japan, it promoted the product as being effective in all temperatures. Most Japanese, however, wash clothes in cold water and therefore do not care about all temperature washing. Moreover, the Japanese often add a lot of fabric softener to the wash, and Cheer did not produce many suds under those conditions. Procter & Gamble thus reformulated Cheer so that it would not be affected by the addition of fabric softeners and changed the promotion to emphasise "superior" cleaning in cold water. Cheer then became one of Procter & Gamble's most successful products in Japan.[44] Adaptation of both product and promotion is the most expensive strategy discussed so far, but it should be considered if the foreign market appears large enough and competitively attractive.

Invent New Products   This strategy is selected when existing products cannot meet the needs of a foreign market. General Motors developed an all purpose, jeep-like motor vehicle that can be assembled in developing nations by mechanics with no special training. The vehicle is designed to operate under varied conditions; it has standardised parts and is inexpensive. Colgate-Palmolive developed an inexpensive, all plastic, hand-powered washing machine that has the tumbling action of a modern automatic machine. The product, marketed in less developed countries, was invented for households that have no electricity. Strategies that involve the invention of products are often the most costly, but the pay-off can be great. The clockwork radio was designed as a low cost and effective educational medium for poor regions of southern Africa. It proved a success in this context, but surprisingly also in the United States and developed economies, where it took on cult status and sold for a high price as an up-market, trendy status symbol.

Distribution and Pricing   Decisions about the distribution system and pricing policies are important in developing an international marketing mix. Figure 21.8 illustrates different approaches to these decisions.

Distribution   A company can sell its product to an intermediary that is willing to buy from existing marketing channels, or it can develop new international marketing channels. Obviously, some service companies, such as Citicorp or ABN AMRO, need to develop their own distribution systems to market their products. However, many products, such as toothpaste, are distributed through intermediaries and brokers. The firm must consider distribution both between countries and within the foreign country. Marketing Insight 21.2 reveals how confectionery giant Suchard seeks to acquire local companies in order to gain both ready-made production facilities and the acquired companies' distribution networks.

In determining distribution alternatives, the existence of retailers and wholesalers that can perform marketing functions between and within countries is one major factor. If a country has a segmented retail structure consisting primarily of one person shops or street sellers, it may be difficult to develop new marketing channels for products such as packaged goods and prepared foods. Quite often in

Pan-European Suchard Thinks Globally, Operates Locally

The chocolate confectionery business of US-Swiss Kraft Jacob Suchard represents 65 per cent of its Sw. fr. 9 billion turnover. Suchard has been gearing up for global markets since the late 1960s, by developing global brands, such as Milka and Toblerone, and undertaking a number of strategically important acquisitions. In taking over other European confectionery companies, such as Du Lac (Italian), Pavlides (Greek) and Terry's (UK), Suchard has sought established distribution and retail channels in areas where it was not traditionally strong. This has helped the company to develop its own global brands alongside smaller, local products. The acquisition of the West German cocoa trader Van Houten in 1987 has given Suchard closer control over its raw materials.

At the pan-European level, global brands are now assisted by the single market allowing unrestricted flow of goods between EU countries. Companies with pan-European brands, including Suchard, benefit from the advertising opportunities offered by European satellites, which are less exploited by national brands. It is probable that over several years preferences and eating habits within Europe will gradually converge as communication of this type increases. Companies such as Suchard have evolved from operating within a domestic market to being international players. As such, they must now seek additional marketing intelligence and data, re-think strategies and modify their marketing mixes.

In the UK, Terry's of York was a major player, though relatively small next to the mighty Cadbury's and Rowntree's (now owned by Nestlé). It did, however, have many well known brands and products, good distribution coverage and modern production facilities. Acquisition by Suchard immediately increased the company's share of the UK confectionery market and improved distribution coverage for the existing range of Suchard products. Suchard is currently focusing on eastern Europe. A new automated logistics centre in Fallingbostel in Germany caters for retail and wholesale customers throughout unified Germany. The company has a 99.2 per cent stake in Rumania's state confectionery maker, Poiana SA, and has promised to invest £30 million over the next five years. In Lithuania, it has acquired production facilities from Kaunas, rather than supplying the market with imported chocolate. Kaunas's sales have doubled since the 1993 takeover. While mainstream brands are taken into these new markets, Suchard prefers to acquire locally based production and to supply existing national brands alongside those international "best sellers" it believes have local potential.

SOURCES: Terry's of York; "'Krafting' bar code and EDI technology", *Automatic ID News,* December 1995, p. 22; "KJS to put further $17m in confectioner", *Finance East Europe,* 6 October 1995, p. 12; "Chocolate maker stirs pot in Lithuania", *Crossborder Monitor,* 4 October 1995, p. 8; "Making a marque", *Corporate Location,* Sept/Oct 1995, pp. 42–43.

Third World countries, certain channels of distribution are characterised by ethnodomination. *Ethnodomination* occurs when an ethnic group occupies a majority position within a marketing channel. Indians, for example, own approximately 90 per cent of the cotton gins in Uganda; the Hausa tribe in Nigeria dominates the trade in kola nuts, cattle and housing; and Chinese merchants dominate the rice economy in Thailand. Marketers must be sensitive to ethnodomination and recognise that the ethnic groups operate in sub-cultures with a unique social and economic organisation.[45]

Figure 21.8

Strategies for international distribution and pricing

Distribution

	No effort to establish new marketing channels	Establish new marketing channels
Do not change price policies	1. Same price policies; no control over distribution	3. Establish new channels and use same price policies
Change price policies	2. Price policies changed for international markets; no control over distribution	4. Develop new channels and change price policies

Price policies

If the product being sold across national boundaries requires service and information, then control of the distribution process is desirable. Caterpillar, for example, sells more than half its construction and earthmoving equipment outside its native US. Because it must provide services and replacement parts, Caterpillar has established its own dealer in foreign markets. Regional sales offices and technical experts are also available to support local dealers. A manufacturer of paint-brushes, on the other hand, would be more concerned about agents, wholesalers or other manufacturers (for example, of paint) that would facilitate the product's exposure in a foreign market. Control over the distribution process would not be so important for that product because services and replacement parts are not needed.

Research suggests that international firms use independently owned marketing channels when they market in countries perceived to be highly dissimilar to their home markets. However, when they market complex products, they develop vertically integrated marketing channels to gain control of distribution. To manage the distribution process from manufacturer to customer contact requires an expert sales force that must be trained specifically to sell the firm's products. Moreover, when products are unique or highly differentiated from those of current competitors, international firms also tend to design and establish vertically integrated channels.[46]

It is crucial to realise that a country's political instability can jeopardise the distribution of goods. For example, when the United States invaded Panama in late 1989, the Panama Canal was closed for several days, delaying shipments of goods through the canal. Similarly, during the political unrest in China, military activity and fighting made it difficult to move goods into and out of certain areas. Instability centring on Iraq and the Persian Gulf had a similar effect. Thus it must be stressed again how important it is to monitor the environment when engaging in international marketing. Companies that market products in unstable nations may need to develop alternative plans to allow for sudden unrest or hostility and to ensure that the distribution of their products is not jeopardised.

It is important to have the "right" product or service to appeal to the target market in an international market. A significant impediment to effective international marketing, however, is distribution. It is not always easy to grasp how marketing channels operate in an alien territory. Companies setting up in Russia find the channels, bureaucracy and corruption difficult to manage. It is never easy to identify the most suitable channel members and players with which to do business, or to find those that should be permitted to sell a company's products.

Pricing   The domestic and non-domestic prices of products are usually different. For example, the prices charged for Walt Disney videos in the UK, Germany and Spain will all vary, as well as being different from US prices. The increased costs of transport, supplies, taxes, tariffs and other expenses necessary to adjust a firm's operations to international marketing can raise prices. A key decision is whether the basic pricing policy will change (as discussed in Chapter 20). If it is a firm's policy not to allocate fixed costs to non-domestic sales, then lower foreign prices could result.

It is common practice for EU countries to sell off foodstuffs and pharmaceuticals at knock down prices to eastern bloc and African states respectively. This kind of sale of products in non-domestic markets—or vice versa—at lower prices (when all the costs have not been allocated or when surplus products are sold) is called **dumping**. Dumping is illegal in some countries if it damages domestic firms and workers.

Dumping   The sale of products in non-domestic markets at lower prices than those charged in domestic markets, when all costs are not allocated or when surplus products are sold

A cost plus approach to international pricing is probably the most common method used because of the compounding number of costs necessary to move products from their country of origin. Of course, as the discussion of pricing policies in Chapter 20 points out, understanding consumer demand and the competitive environment is a necessary step in selecting a price.

The price charged in other countries is also a function of foreign currency exchange rates. Fluctuations in the international monetary market can change the prices charged across national boundaries on a daily basis. There has been a trend towards greater fluctuation (or float) in world money markets. For example, a sudden variation in the exchange rate, which occurs when a nation devalues its currency, can have wide ranging effects on consumer prices.

There are also pricing issues that stem from transfer pricing practices and the problems of parallel imports. **Transfer pricing** is the price charged between profit centres, for example a manufacturing company and its foreign subsidiary. Company policies can force subsidiaries to sell products at higher prices than the local competition, even though the true costs of their manufacture may be no different. The manufacturer tries to make a profit even from its "internal" customer, its own subsidiary.[47] **Parallel imports**, that is, goods exported from low price to high price countries, are an increasing problem. For example, French and Belgian beer producers export to the UK at set price levels, but consumers and small independent retailers cross by car ferry to Calais and stock up with similar brands at much lower prices than those the manufacturers "officially" offer to UK customers. Independent operators have set up import/export businesses to take well known beer brands into the UK to be sold at prices higher than in their native markets, but still lower than those offered by the manufacturers' official export agents.

Transfer pricing   The price charged between profit centres, for example between a manufacturing company and its foreign subsidiary

Parallel imports   Goods that are imported through "non-official" channels from low price to high price countries

There are also important price ramifications to consider stemming from product or brand positioning and any differences between countries. For example, in the UK Stella Artois beer is marketed as "reassuringly expensive", whereas in its native Belgium it is more of a commodity, mass market brand competing against brands such as Duval or the specialist "Trappist monk" beers. Pricing, in any market, must reflect the brand positioning adopted.[48]

People   As noted earlier, great importance is now attached to the people ingredient of the marketing mix. The nature of many business-to-business markets and the form of most service products often lead businesses to determine formally the role of people within their marketing mixes. In the context of international marketing, the people ingredient is also important. Chapter 3 highlighted how marketers performing across national boundaries must be aware of often striking differences, country by country or region by region, in the marketing environment. Often, cultural and social forces are the most varied—and also the most difficult for marketers based in another country and culture to understand. Companies must deploy people with the "right" skills to address such issues either from their own ranks or from third parties in the territories under scrutiny. Channel members such as agents can often assist in this respect. Having personnel who understand the nuances of an international market is a fundamental requirement for effective marketing, but so too is the need for those personnel with the cultural and local knowledge to be able to implement a marketing mix, which itself may well have been modified to reflect the nuances of the relevant marketing environment.

● ● ● ● ● ● ● ● ● ● ● ● ● ● ● ● ● ●

Summary

● This chapter has explained why and how the marketing mix must be manipulated differently for business-to-business markets, services and international markets.

● Business-to-business marketing is a set of activities directed at facilitating and expediting exchanges involving industrial products and customers in industrial markets. Like marketers of consumer products, business-to-business marketers must develop a marketing mix that satisfies the needs of customers in the industrial target market. Personnel are not generally seen as integral to the product itself, but perhaps more than in consumer marketing they are central to the selling process and are a key part of promotional activity. The product component frequently emphasises services, which are often of primary interest to business customers. The marketer must also consider that the customer may elect to make the product rather than buy it. Industrial products must meet certain standard specifications that organisational users want.

● The distribution of business-to-business products differs from that of consumer products in the types of channels used, the kinds of intermediaries available, and transport, storage and inventory policies. A *direct distribution channel* is common in business marketing. Also used are channels containing manufacturers' agents, *business-to-business distributors* or both agents and distributors. Channels are chosen on the basis of availability, the typical mode of purchase for a product and several other variables.

● *Personal selling* is a primary ingredient of the promotional component in business-to-business marketing mixes. Sales personnel often act as technical advisers both before and after a sale. Advertising is sometimes used to supplement personal selling efforts. Business-to-business marketers generally use print advertisements containing more information but less persuasive content than consumer advertisements. Other promotional activities include catalogues and trade shows.

● The price component for business marketing mixes is influenced by legal and economic forces to a greater extent than it is for consumer marketing mixes. *Administered*, *bid* and *negotiated pricing* are additional possibilities in many business-to-business markets. Pricing may be affected by competitors' prices, as well as by the type of customer who buys the product. Increasingly, though price is still important, many companies are seeking new ways of creating a differential advantage. Value for money is important in most markets, but low price is not an effective differential advantage except in the very short term. Flexibility and reliability in production and delivery can be differentiating factors, as can technical innovation, personnel and customer service, promotional activity and even payment terms. People, important in the context of personal selling, are also often required to establish ongoing long term *relationships* with key customers.

● When developing a marketing mix for services, several aspects deserve special consideration.

Regarding product, service offerings are often difficult for consumers to understand and evaluate. The tangibles associated with a service may be the only visible aspect of the service, and marketers must manage these scarce tangibles with care. Because services are often viewed in terms of the *service providers,* service firms must carefully select, train, motivate and control employees, particularly to guarantee *service product quality.* Service marketers are selling long term relationships as well as performance. It is important to understand the *complexity* of the service product and to seek to limit its *variability.*

● Promoting services is problematic because of their *intangibility.* Advertising should stress the tangibles associated with the service or use some relevant tangible object. Personnel in direct contact with customers should be considered an important secondary audience for advertising. Personal selling is very powerful in service firms because customers must interact with personnel; some forms of sales promotion, however, such as displays and free samples, are difficult to implement. The final principal component of the promotion mix, publicity, is vital to many service firms. Because customers value word-of-mouth communications, messages should attempt to stimulate or simulate word-of-mouth. Many professional service providers, however, are severely restricted in their use of promotional activities.

● Price plays three major roles in service firms. It plays a psychological role by indicating quality and an economic role by determining revenues. Price is also a way to help smooth out fluctuations in demand.

● Service distribution channels are typically direct because of simultaneous production and consumption. However, innovative approaches such as drop-off points, intermediaries and electronic distribution are being developed.

● The basic marketing mix is augmented for services through the addition of people, physical evidence (ambience) and the process of transaction in order to produce the "7 Ps" or the *extended marketing mix.*

● International marketing requires careful planning. Marketing activities performed across national boundaries are usually significantly different from domestic marketing activities. International marketers must have a profound awareness of the foreign environment. The marketing strategy is ordinarily adjusted to meet the needs and desires of markets across national boundaries.

● After a country's environment has been analysed, marketers must develop a marketing mix and decide whether to adapt product or promotion. There are five possible strategies for adapting product and promotion across national boundaries: (1) keep product and promotion the same worldwide, (2) adapt promotion only, (3) adapt product only, (4) adapt both product and promotion and (5) invent new products. Foreign distribution channels are nearly always different from domestic ones. Identifying and understanding channels in foreign markets are not easy tasks. Distribution channels can become a major impediment in international marketing. The allocation of costs, transport considerations or the costs of doing business in foreign nations will affect pricing. *Transfer pricing* and *parallel imports* are important considerations, as are the regulations pertaining to *dumping.* It is also necessary to set pricing levels that reflect the nuances of a product's brand positioning in a particular market: the same brand may occupy distinctly different positions in separate territories.

● ● ● ● ● ● ● ● ● ● ● ● ● ● ● ● ● ● ●

Important Terms

Direct distribution channels
Business-to-business distributor
Personal selling
Administered pricing
Bid pricing
Negotiated pricing

Relationships
Extended marketing mix for services
Intangibility
Service provider
Service product quality

Complexity
Variability
Dumping
Transfer pricing
Parallel imports

Discussion and Review Questions

1. How do business marketing mixes differ from those of consumer products?
2. What are the major advantages and disadvantages of using industrial distributors?
3. Why do organisational marketers rely on personal selling more than consumer products marketers?
4. Why would a business-to-business marketer spend resources on advertising aimed at stimulating consumer demand?
5. Compare three methods of determining the price of industrial products.
6. Why must a differential advantage be based on more than just low prices?
7. Discuss the role of promotion in services marketing.
8. What additional elements must be included in the marketing mix for services? Why?
9. Why is it difficult to create and maintain a differential advantage in many service businesses?
10. Why do the marketers of services place so much emphasis on the people ingredient of the marketing mix?
11. What are the principal choices a company can make when manipulating the marketing mix for international markets?
12. How and why can the *distribution* (place) ingredient of the marketing mix cause problems for international marketers?
13. What additional factors determine a company's pricing policy in foreign markets?

Recommended Readings

T. L. Powers, *Modern Business Marketing* (St. Paul, Minn.: West, 1990).

C. Lovelock, *Managing Services* (Englewood Cliffs, N.J.: Prentice-Hall, 1992).

A. Payne, *The Essence of Services Marketing* (Hemel Hempstead: Prentice-Hall, 1993).

F. Bradley, *International Marketing Strategy*, 2nd edn (Hemel Hempstead: Prentice-Hall, 1991).

C. S. Katsikeas, N. F. Piercy and C. Ioannides, "Determinants of export performance in a European context", *European Journal of Marketing*, vol. 30, no. 6, 1996, pp. 6–35.

Cases

21.1 Porsche AG: Striving for Recovery

Founded in 1930 by Dr. Ferdinand Porsche, the company known today as Porsche AG began as a research and development firm. The original company accepted contracts from individuals and firms to design new cars, aeroplanes and ships. The company built prototypes of each design and thoroughly tested them. If the firm that commissioned the work approved the design, the product was then produced by one of the large manufacturing companies in Germany. After World War II, the Porsche family experienced a period of hardship, disappointment and personal tragedy. Porsche's son, Dr Ferry Porsche, began a company to manufacture family designed sports cars in 1948. Despite depressed economic conditions, the company persevered and prospered. By 1973, Porsche AG had built and sold some 200,000 Porsches, gaining world recognition for its cars and their promise of "driving in its purest form".

Porsche today is organised into three divisions located in three suburbs of Stuttgart: the factory, in Zuffenhausen; testing, engineering and design, in Weissach; and marketing, in Ludwigsburg. The Porsche Research and Development Centre has produced the 959 race car, an aircraft engine, the TAG motor and designs for ambulances, mobile surgery units, gliders, fire engines and fork lift trucks. The company holds more than 2,000 patents, and innovations developed by Porsche are in several manufacturers' car models.

Despite Porsche's reputation for excellence, the company has fallen on hard times. It was forced to raise prices on cars sold in the US because of changes in the dollar exchange rate. Because of the price increases, a weakening US dollar, and lower priced Japanese imitations, sales in the United States dropped significantly in the late 1980s. Roughly 60 per cent of all Porsches were sold in the United States. Production dropped from 50,000 cars annually to 20,000.

Porsche is successful in markets where the social climate favours people who want to demonstrate their success and where the economic climate is conducive to the entrepreneur. Recessions have caused Porsche major problems. Porsche management believes that its customers have high personal goals, are ambitious, do not like to compromise and give their best efforts every time. Although not averse to risk, they prepare thoroughly for new ventures. Porsche customers are apparently goers and doers, but not show-offs. To succeed, Porsche AG must exhibit some of its customers' traits. Customers must be able to identify with the firm, to see in the company the same characteristics they see in themselves.

Wendelin Wiedeking became chairman in 1993. After six years of deteriorating sales, by 1995 the company was at last breaking even. Sales recovered to 30,000 units and Japanese consultants re-engineered the whole manufacturing operation, bringing significant cost savings. Close to £1 billion is currently being invested in re-vamping the model range to include a two-seater roadster and the 996, the next generation 911. To reduce the company's dependence on the ever more crowded market for high performance sports cars, Wiedeking has returned to the company's roots and is seeking more engineering and design contracts through Weissach, Porsche's legendary research and development arm.

Work for VW Seat and development of the first mainstream Chinese family car are supported by the production of designer sun glasses, audio equipment and tableware. The main business of manufacturing and selling cars is not taking a back seat, however. Aside from introducing new models, the company has revolutionised customer databases to take account of national buying characteristics and loyalty levels. In the UK and US, this effort has helped dealers boost the proportion of repeat buyers to close to three out of four Porsche drivers. The databases, supplemented by extensive marketing research, have helped the company to re-define its customer groups into "top guns", "elitists", "proud owners", "bon vivants" and "fantasists", each with a bespoke marketing mix.

SOURCES: Porsche UK, Reading; *Marque* magazine, 1996; Dyan Machan, "Salvation in Stuttgart", *Forbes,* 11 September 1995, pp. 154–155; Regina Eisman, "Porsche", *Incentive*, June 1995, pp. 54–55; Alex Taylor, "Porsche slices up its buyers", *Fortune,* 16 January 1995, p. 24; "Japan to the rescue", *German Brief*, 6 May 1994, pp. 4–5.

Questions for Discussion

1. Why has the Porsche company broadened its product portfolio by encouraging Weissach to undertake more design contracts? What benefits or disadvantages does this policy bring to Porsche?
2. Recessions in various parts of Porsche's global operation have brought the company problems. In developing an international marketing strategy, how can Porsche take account of various economic trends?
3. Porsche undertakes projects for rival car manufacturers, most notably VW SEAT. What are the benefits of such ventures for these clients? Are there any potential problems in following this strategy for Porsche's own car marketers?

21.2 Compaq Computer Targets All Users As It Takes Over in Europe

In businesses, banks, doctors' surgeries, department stores and homes, computers in general make work and life easier. But no single class of computer is a perfect fit for every job, and computer companies continually develop and market a variety of models to fill a variety of niches. Compaq initially produced high quality, high priced versions for businesses and professional organisations that required fast, rugged and reliable machines and were willing to pay premium prices to get them. Compaq targeted *Times 1000* type companies, including in its impressive clientele such organisations as the Louvre Museum in Paris, Dole Foods of Thailand and Lego Toys.

In 1982, Rod Canion, Bill Murto and Jim Harris left their executive positions with Texas Instruments, formed their own company and introduced the Compaq Portable Computer. Just four years later, Compaq made *Fortune* magazine's list of the top 500 companies in the world, achieving that position faster than any other business in the history of the list. By the end of 1987, sales topped the £666 million mark. Compaq succeeded in attracting the high end of the computer market by maintaining premium prices, low key advertising and a dealership distribution strategy. In the early 1990s, however, slowing US sales and intense competition from lower priced catalogue companies forced the company to re-evaluate its methods and initiate some changes. Compaq began to discount prices up to 40 per cent on several of its most advanced PCs. Calling it "creative pricing", one company executive said that his organisation was responding to the growing view that its products were becoming too costly, especially for smaller companies that were previously loyal Compaq customers. Responding to the reality that few computer retailers were equipped to sell machines as complicated as the £15,000–£25,000 SystemPro, Compaq signed agreements with several computer consulting firms to sell the SystemPro line and opened up demonstration centres in major conurbations in its core territories to help sell the network systems. Expanding its marketing techniques beyond simple and straightforward advertising, Compaq introduced a joint worldwide promotion with Microsoft to introduce the Microsoft BallPoint Mouse, the first such pointing device designed specifically for use with lap-top PCs. Compaq offered free BallPoints to buyers of any of its lap-top or notebook computers. Advertisements for the promotion appeared in leading business magazines and newspapers, reinforced with direct mail packs to business users and telemarketing support.

By 1995, Compaq's strategy had paid off. The company overtook arch rivals IBM and Apple to become leader in the world's personal computer market, with a 10 per cent market share. In Europe, Compaq's share reached an impressive 13 per cent.

Success has not come easily. A management shake-up brought a new CEO, Eckhard Pfeiffer, Compaq's former head of its European operations. The target market was re-defined, away from a focus on *Times 1000* type organisations. Pfeiffer declared that it was the company's intention to sell computers in all segments of the market. Costs were slashed and the company's infrastructure streamlined to free up resources that would enable the company to offer propositions to many more target market segments. Wholly owned subsidiaries were established in 19 countries to ensure that the characteristics of customers and local distribution requirements could properly be met. Customer support was identified as a potential source of competitive advantage, but it was also noted that the requirement differed segment by segment and between countries. In targeting more segments in greater detail across so many countries, Compaq has recognised the importance of developing bespoke marketing operations and of emphasising customer service.

SOURCES: Michael Fitzgerald, "Compaq Europe beefs up", *Computerworld,* 21 March 1994, p. 37; Peter Gwin, "King Compaq", *Europe,* April 1995, pp. 16–18; "Compaq, Microsoft team for joint promotion", *Adweek,* 11 March 1991, p. 61; Jim Bartimo and Deidre A. Depke, "Compaq's muscular mini isn't knocking them out", *Business Week,* 2 July 1990, pp. 34–35.

Questions for Discussion

1. Compare Compaq's new marketing strategy with its previous one.
2. Will the new strategy that Compaq is using to remain competitive diminish its premium image and thus adversely affect its efforts to market its products in the premium business segment of the personal computer market?
3. In trading globally, what issues will dictate how Compaq must modify its marketing mix between countries?

The marketing mix is the tactical toolkit deployed by marketers to implement their marketing strategy and to take their product or service offering to their target market. The basic ingredients of the marketing mix are the "5Ps" of product, people, place, promotion and pricing, described in Parts III to VI of *Marketing: Concepts and Strategies*. There are, however, situations in which either market characteristics or the nature of the product requires modification of the standard marketing mix—most notably, for business-to-business markets, services marketing and international markets. Part VII of *Marketing: Concepts and Strategies* has explored how the marketing mix must be manipulated in these situations.

Before progressing, readers should be confident that they are now able to:

Explain why, when and how the basic marketing mix requires additional manipulation

• In what situations does the standard marketing mix require modification? • What is the nature of the marketing mix in business-to-business markets? • What is the extended marketing mix for services?
• Why does the marketing of services require additional ingredients in the marketing mix? • What issues do marketers encounter in international markets? • Why must the marketing mix be manipulated for international markets?

Marketing Opportunity Analysis	Chapters
• The marketing environment	2
• Marketing in international markets	3
• Consumer markets and buyer behaviour	4
• Business-to-business markets and buyer behaviour	5
• Marketing research and information systems	6

Target Market Selection	Chapters
• Market segmentation and prioritisation	7, 22
• Product and brand positioning	7, 22
• Competitive advantage	7, 22

Marketing Mix Development	Chapters
• Product, branding, packaging and service decisions	8–11
• Distribution (place and channel) decisions	12–15
• Promotion decisions	16–18
• Pricing decisions	19, 20
• Supplementary decisions	3, 21, 24, 25

Marketing Management	Chapters
• Strategic marketing and competitive strategy	22, 23
• Marketing planning and sales forecasting	23
• Implementing strategies and measuring performance	24
• Marketing ethics and social responsibility	25

VIII MARKETING MANAGEMENT

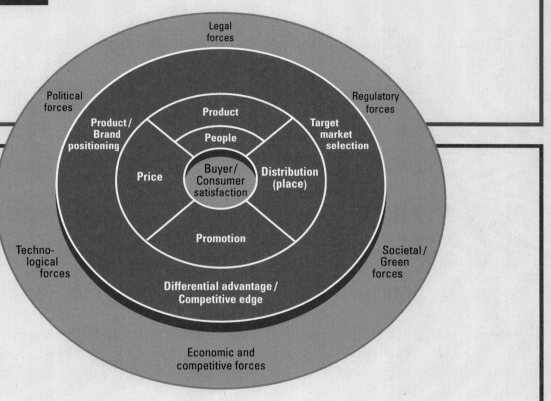

I n Chapter 1, Figure 1.5, the generic tasks of marketing strategy were identified as marketing opportunity analysis, target market selection, marketing mix development and marketing management. Parts I to VII of *Marketing: Concepts and Strategies* examined the first three of these generic tasks, while target market selection was discussed in detail in Chapter 7. There are, however, additional concepts to be addressed when develop-

ing a marketing strategy. These are explained at the beginning of **Part VIII of *Marketing: Concepts and Strategies.*** The focus then becomes the management, implementation and control of marketing strategy and marketing activity, in particular the popular and important technique of marketing planning. Finally, of growing concern to marketers and consumers are the topics of ethics and social responsibility in marketing. These issues must be of central concern to marketers when they determine marketing strategies and then strive to implement these strategies. Part VIII of *Marketing: Concepts and Strategies* explores further the central issues of marketing strategy, marketing planning and sales forecasting, implementing strategies and measuring performance, and the role of ethics and social responsibility in marketing.

Chapter 22, "Marketing Strategy and Competitive Forces", presents an overview of marketing strategy and the strategic planning process. Four tools to assist in strategic marketing decision-making are discussed: product portfolio analysis, the market attractiveness-business position model, Profit Impact on Marketing Strategy (PIMS) and the ABC sales: contribution analysis. The chapter concludes by returning to the all important topic of competition, notably competitors' strategies and competitive positions.

Chapter 23, "Marketing Planning and Assessing Sales Potential", details the popular and core process of formal marketing planning, highlighting the important relationship between marketing analyses, marketing strategy and marketing programmes. After examining the role of the SWOT analysis in marketing planning, the chapter presents an overview of a typical marketing plan. The discussion then turns to the related issue of assessment of sales potential and of the principal forecasting techniques. Finally, the components of the marketing audit are described.

Chapter 24, "Implementing Strategies and Measuring Performance", commences by explaining how the marketing unit fits into a company's organisational structure, describes ways of organising a marketing unit, examines issues related to implementing marketing strategies, presents some of the principal control processes used by marketers and explains how cost and sales analyses can be used to evaluate the performance of marketing strategies.

Chapter 25, "Marketing Ethics and Social Responsibility", defines marketing ethics and explains the importance of this concept in today's marketing world. The chapter explores the factors that influence ethical and unethical decisions, discussing some of the important ethical issues marketers face. Next it presents ways of improving ethical decisions in marketing. The focus of the chapter then switches to social responsibility: explaining the concept, exploring important issues and describing strategies for dealing with social dilemmas.

By the conclusion of Part VIII of *Marketing: Concepts and Strategies,* readers should understand more about the complexities of developing marketing strategies, the importance of competition, the role of marketing planning and forecasting sales, ways of implementing marketing strategy and measuring performance, and the significant influence of ethics and social responsibility in marketing.

MARKETING STRATEGY AND COMPETITIVE FORCES

"A proper analysis of the strategic aspects of any competitive marketplace may not result in certain success, but it almost always helps to avoid failures."

Robin Wensley
Warwick Business School

OBJECTIVES

- To understand the basis of marketing strategy and the strategic market planning process

- To explore and examine four major tools to assist in strategic marketing decision-making, the analysis of market opportunities, use of resources and effective market targeting: product portfolio analysis, the market attractiveness-business position model, Profit Impact on Marketing Strategy (PIMS) and the ABC sales: contribution analysis

- To evaluate the role of competition and competitors' strategies in relation to the development of functional marketing strategies and activities

As they still are in many European countries, Britain's utilities used to be state owned and operated. The Central Electricity Generating Board generated and the National Grid physically distributed the energy to both domestic and business users, with regional electricity boards acting as the customer interface, connecting supplies, determining consumption through meter reading and billing customers for the electricity consumed. In the mid-1980s the government decided to continue its privatisation programme and create a commercially run elec-tricity supply industry with shareholders and competition as in most other industries. The sale raised over £10 billion in equity and debt for the government and created over 12 million shareholders. The entire privatisation scheme lasted four years and cost an estimated £1 billion to facilitate. Upon its dissolution in 1990 the Central Electricity Generating Board employed 47,000 people. The new look industry employs only 25,000.

Before the break up of the state run electricity industry, a household or factory in one part of the country would have dealt primarily with just one the logo on the bill. From 1998, this freedom of competition will extend to consumers of less than 100kW— small businesses and residential households. Even if a customer lives in YEB's traditional geographic territory, he or she will be contacted by the other 11 RECs, perhaps by some generators, and even by organisations as diverse as BP, Currys, Direct Line, Tesco or Virgin, which may choose to enter the retail end of the electricity supply market by buying in bulk from the RECs, the generators or private generators entering the marketplace.

In a market where previously there was no competition, this situation is likely to be highly confusing to customers. It is also a major shift in orientation for the RECs. They must determine which customers they should target; where in the country they should target them; what proposition and levels of customer service, pricing, payment terms and promotional support they should offer; and what channels of distribution they should use. The need to identify a differential advantage over rivals in a commodity market and to develop a distinctive and plausible positioning strategy is taxing all of the RECs as they strive to come to terms with such a rapidly evolving market and stiff competition. It remains to be seen whether customers will genuinely benefit or whether bills will rise to cover the huge sales and marketing expenditure suddenly required. There is no doubt, though, that throughout every REC, a tremendous amount of research and strategic thinking is currently under way as the companies gear up to a deregulated market. ■

regional electricity board: YEB (Yorkshire Electricity Board) in Yorkshire, MEB (Midlands Electricity Board) in Birmingham, EMEB (East Midlands Electricity Board) in Leicester and so on. To all intents and purposes, customers would have had no dealings with a generator, which in any case was the same organisation throughout the country. Privatisation divided the generating side of the industry among five new and publicly quoted companies, such as PowerGen and National Power. The regional electricity boards became regional electricity companies, still with a focus on their own geographic region, but with shareholders and a renewed profit making motivation.

Then came deregulation in earnest. First, customers using more than 100kW of electricity per annum were told that they could "shop around" to seek better tariffs from suppliers other than their local regional electricity company (REC). In practice, this enabled large companies, institutions and retail groups, whose consumption beat the 100kW threshold, to seek alternative quotes from other RECs and even, at times, directly from some generators. The infrastructure did not alter. There remained only one network of cables and pylons. The customer interface with a particular REC might have changed, as might the tariff agreed and

SOURCES: "Energy market report: electricity", *Energy Economist,* October 1995, pp. 29–32; "Energy market report: electricity", *Energy Economist,* January 1995, pp. 30–31; Nick Hasell, "Power bargaining", *Management Today,* July 1994, pp. 68–70; Alex Henney, "Challenging the status quo", *Fortnightly,* 15 July 1994, pp. 26–31; Margaret McKinlay, "100kW users test the water in the electricity pool", *Purchasing & Supply Management,* February 1994, pp. 20–21.

Parts I and II of this text explored the analysis of marketing opportunities, in particular the need to understand the moves and trends in a marketplace, customer behaviour and needs, and the importance of targeting the right market segments. Parts III to VII focused on the marketing mix ingredients that ultimately take a product or service into a marketplace to reach the targeted consumers. This chapter aims to highlight which strategic marketing considerations help to ensure that the product or service is marketed for the benefit of the organisation as well as its targeted customers, and differently enough from its competitors' marketing programmes to give the organisation's product or service a perceived advantage over these competitors that will lead to success in the marketplace. These core components of marketing strategy are illustrated in Figure 22.1 and are clearly of great concern to the electricity companies, described in this

Figure 22.1 The components of marketing strategy

SOURCE: Adapted by permission from John Saunders and Veronica Wong, "In search of excellence in the UK", Journal of Marketing Management, 1 (2), 1985, Fig. 2, p. 130.

chapter's opener, now facing a fully competitive marketplace for the first time. Although for simplicity's sake this text has deliberately discussed the tactics of marketing first (Parts III to VII), it is important to realise that marketers must have developed a clearly thought out marketing strategy *before* specifying the marketing mix issues of product/service/people, place, promotion and pricing. This strategy must reflect the organisation's corporate goals, market trends, opportunities and the competitive situation, while aiming to give the targeted customers satisfaction.

The chapter first explores how to develop marketing strategies and then discusses strategic market planning, stressing the importance of organisational goals and corporate strategy. The next section presents some of the related analytical tools associated with the planning of a marketing strategy: the product portfolio analysis, the market attractiveness-business position model, Profit Impact on Marketing Strategy (PIMS) and the ABC sales: contribution analysis. The chapter then focuses on competitive strategies for marketing: the role of competition, its ramifications for strategy, competitive positions and warfare strategies. Other aspects of the strategic marketing management process—marketing forecasting and marketing planning; organising, implementing and controlling—are covered in Chapters 23 and 24 respectively.

● ● ● ● ● ● ● ● ● ● ● ● ● ● ● ● ● ● ●

Marketing Strategy Defined

Marketing strategy A strategy indicating the specific target markets and the types of competitive advantages that are to be developed and exploited

Strategic market plan
An outline of the methods and resources required to achieve an organisation's goals within a specific target market

Strategic business unit (SBU)
A division, product line or other profit centre within a parent company

Strategic market planning
A process that yields a marketing strategy constituting the framework for a marketing plan

Marketing plan A written document that includes the framework and set of activities for implementing and controlling an organisation's marketing activities

Marketing strategy indicates the specific markets towards which activities are to be targeted and the types of competitive advantages that are to be developed and exploited.[1] Implicitly, as described in Figure 22.1, the strategy requires clear objectives and a focus in line with an organisation's corporate goals; the "right" customers must be targeted more effectively than they are by its competitors, and associated marketing mixes must be developed into marketing programmes that successfully implement the marketing strategy.

A **strategic market plan** is an outline of the methods and resources required to achieve an organisation's goals within a specific target market. It takes into account not only marketing but also all functional aspects of a business unit that must be co-ordinated. These functional aspects include production, finance and personnel. Environmental issues are an important consideration as well. The concept of the strategic business unit is used to define areas for consideration in a specific strategic market plan. Each **strategic business unit** (SBU) is a division, product line or other profit centre within the parent company. Each sells a distinct set of products to an identifiable group of customers, and each competes with a well defined set of competitors. Each SBU's revenues, costs, investments and strategic plans can be separated and evaluated apart from those of the parent company. SBUs operate in a variety of markets, which have differing growth rates, opportunities, degrees of competition and profit making potential. Construction giant JCB, for example, includes the Compact Division for smaller machines, a strategic business unit (see Figure 22.2). Strategic planners therefore must recognise the different performance capabilities of each SBU and carefully allocate resources.

The process of **strategic market planning** yields a marketing strategy that is the framework for a marketing plan. A **marketing plan** (see Chapter 23) includes the framework and entire set of activities to be performed; it is the written document

Figure 22.2 An SBU in operation. JCB's Compact Division caters for users of construction equipment requiring small machines.

Source: Client: *John Badley, JCB Sales Ltd.* Agency: *CD Brookes Advertising Ltd.*

or blueprint for implementing and controlling an organisation's marketing activities. Thus a strategic market plan is *not* the same as a marketing plan—it is a plan of *all* aspects of an organisation's strategy in the marketplace.[2] A marketing plan, in contrast, deals primarily with implementing the market strategy as it relates to target markets and the marketing mix.[3]

Figure 22.3 shows the components of strategic market planning. The process is based on the establishment of an organisation's overall goals, and it must stay within the bounds of the organisation's opportunities and resources. When the firm has determined its overall goals and identified its resources, it can then assess its opportunities and develop a corporate strategy. Marketing objectives must be designed so that their achievement will contribute to the corporate strategy and so that they can be accomplished through efficient use of the firm's resources.

To achieve its marketing objectives, an organisation must develop a marketing strategy, or a set of marketing strategies, as shown in Figure 22.3. The set of marketing strategies that are implemented and used at the same time is referred to as the organisation's **marketing programme**. Through the process of strategic market planning, an organisation can develop marketing strategies that, when properly implemented and controlled, will contribute to the achievement of its

Marketing programme A set of marketing strategies that are implemented and used at the same time

The InterCity Brand Risks Confusion

British Rail used to run the railway network in Britain, through three operating divisions. Now broken up ready for privatisation and sale by the British government, the railways are operated by 25 separate companies. InterCity, still the flagship brand for long distance travel, predominantly focuses on the business traveller but is also aimed at leisure users.

Every business regularly needs to re-appraise its activities, and InterCity is no exception. Recognising the importance of the business market, InterCity consults customers to ascertain what they seek and whether their requirements are being met. Products may need re-launching, improving or promoting to make customers aware of them. InterCity conducted a major programme of consumer research, comparing the advantages and disadvantages for customers of rail, car and air travel. Consumers most often indicated these advantages:

Car	Privacy/flexibility/accessibility/control/speed
Plane	Standard of service/thrill of flying/arrive fresh
InterCity	Space to move around/work while travelling/centre to centre

The major finding from the research, however, was that business travellers cared greatly about the status accompanying their choice of transport. Because InterCity offered less privacy and appeared less exclusive, it did not adequately meet status needs.

Knowing the problems, InterCity decided to alter its perceived position and to take steps to be viewed as a more up-market product. To carry out this re-positioning, InterCity designed a marketing package aimed at increasing the status of business travel by rail, coupled with the existing advantages of lack of strain, space to move and ability to work while travelling. Executive tickets, for example,

marketing objectives and its overall goals. Marketing Insight 22.1 discusses InterCity's strategy appraisal and resulting marketing programme. To formulate a marketing strategy, the marketer identifies and analyses the target market and develops a marketing mix to satisfy individuals in that market. Marketing strategy is best formulated when it reflects the overall direction of the organisation and is co-ordinated with all the firm's functional areas.

As indicated in Figure 22.3, the strategic market planning process is based on an analysis of the environment, by which it is very much affected. Environmental forces can place constraints on an organisation and possibly influence its overall goals; they also affect the amount and type of resources that a firm can acquire. However, these forces can create favourable opportunities as well—opportunities that can be translated into overall organisational goals and marketing objectives. For example, when oil prices declined during the second half of the 1980s, consumers viewed cars with high petrol consumption more favourably. This situation created an opportunity for manufacturers of large vehicles, such as BMW and Volvo.

Marketers differ in their viewpoints concerning the effect of environmental variables on marketing planning and strategy. Some take a deterministic perspective, believing that firms must react to external conditions and tailor their strategies and organisational structures to deal with these conditions. According to others, however, companies can influence their environments by choosing in include seat reservations, 24 hours' car parking, refreshment voucher and London Underground travel. Pullman luxury carriages have been added on more services, and Pullman executive lounges have been built at various major stations. Advertising campaigns emphasised this re-positioning and the benefits of InterCity. The rail operator identified what its business travellers wanted, provided the required service and communicated the improvements and changes to existing and potential customers.

With rail privatisation and the selling off of separate regional networks, the sales and marketing department responsible for InterCity's success is now a free-standing advertising agency and marketing consultancy. Replacing Saatchi & Saatchi (Cordiant), the Travel and Rail Marketing Company has just seen its first InterCity advertisements screened. However, there is real competition for the now disparate parts of the InterCity account. Operated by five separate companies, InterCity's

branded advertising is being produced by a host of agencies, including the now commercially independent Travel and Rail Marketing Company, plus TBWA, GGK and Collet Dickenson Pearce. Without shrewd strategic thinking and careful planning, a once very identifiable and cohesive brand, InterCity, could become a very confused proposition in the eyes of the consumer.

SOURCES: "How InterCity caters for its business customers", Wetherby: Target, 1990; Michael Benn and Associates, 1990; Fiona Plant, "Agencies vie for BR's £4m", *Campaign*, 19 October 1990, p. 4; Nicholas Faith, "British Rail's market express", *Business*, July 1989, pp. 52–62; Roland Rudd, "Full steam ahead for the big state sell off", *Independent on Sunday*, 13 January 1991, pp. 4–5; Harriet Green, "TBWA debuts InterCity films", *Campaign*, 25 August 1995, p. 6; "Colletts nets InterCity new-products launch", *Campaign*, 31 May 1995, p. 3; Simon Watkins, "TRMC unveils first InterCity TV ad", *Campaign*, 10 March 1995, p. 8; Tabitha Cole, "The train-spotter on an inside track with InterCity", *Campaign*, 9 December 1994, p. 10; Tom O'Sullivan, "Crossed lines", *Marketing Week*, 18 November 1994, pp. 40–43.

which markets to compete. They can also change the structures of their industries, engaging in activities such as mergers and acquisitions, demand creation or technological innovation.[4]

Regardless of which viewpoint is adopted, environmental variables play a part in the creation of a marketing strategy. When environmental variables affect an organisation's overall goals, resources, opportunities or marketing objectives, they also affect its marketing strategies, which are based on these factors. Environmental forces more directly influence the development of a marketing strategy through their impact on consumers' needs and desires. In addition, these forces have a bearing on marketing mix decisions. For instance, competition strongly influences marketing mix decisions. The organisation must diagnose the marketing mix activities it performs, taking into account competitors' marketing mix decisions, and develop some competitive advantage to support a strategy. Thus as Honda and Toyota entered the luxury car market with the Acura and Lexus models, European car makers BMW, Mercedes and Jaguar had to change their marketing strategies to maintain their market shares. They did so by lowering prices to compete with the new Japanese models.

The next sections discuss the major components of the strategic market planning process: organisational goals, organisational opportunities and resources, and corporate strategy, as well as the tools that aid in strategic market planning and some competitive marketing strategies.

Figure 22.3

Components of strategic
market planning

Legal forces

**Political
forces**

**Regulatory
forces**

Overall
organisational
goals

Organisational
opportunities

Corporate
strategy

Organisational
resources

Marketing
objectives

Marketing strategies
or programme

- Selection and
  analysis of
  target markets

- Development
  of marketing
  mixes

**Technological
forces**

**Societal/Green
forces**

**Economic and
competitive forces**

• • • • • • • • • • • • • • • • •

Organisational Mission and Goals

Mission The broad, long term
tasks that the organisation wants
to accomplish

A firm's organisational goals should be derived from its **mission,** the broad, longer
term tasks that the organisation wants to accomplish. IBM, for example, has
stated that its mission is helping business people make decisions. When a company
decides on its mission, it really answers two questions: what is our business? and
what should our business be?[5] Although these questions seem very simple, they
are in fact two of the hardest yet most important questions that any business can
answer.

Creating or revising a mission statement is very difficult because of the many
complex variables that must be examined. However, having a mission statement
can greatly benefit the organisation in at least five ways.[6]

• A mission statement gives the organisation a clear purpose and direction,
  keeping it on track and preventing it from drifting.

- A mission statement describes the unique aim of the organisation that helps to differentiate it from similar competing organisations.
- A mission statement keeps the organisation focused on customer needs rather than its own abilities. This ensures that the organisation remains externally rather than internally focused.
- A mission statement provides specific direction and guidelines to top managers for selecting alternative courses of action. It helps them decide which business opportunities to pursue, as well as which opportunities not to pursue.
- A mission statement provides guidance to all employees and managers of an organisation, even if they work in different parts of the world. As a result, the mission statement acts like glue to hold the organisation together.

A company's mission and overall organisational goals should guide all its planning efforts. Its goals should specify the ends, or results, that are sought. Examples of organisational goals include profit, return on investment or an increase in market shares. Organisations can also have short term and long term goals. Companies experiencing financial difficulty may be forced to focus solely on the short term results necessary to stay in business, such as increasing cash flow by lowering prices or selling off parts of the business. Other organisations may have more optimistic, long term goals. In many cases, companies that pursue long term goals have to sacrifice short term results to achieve them.

A firm in serious financial trouble may be concerned solely with short run results needed for staying in business. There usually is an airline or major retailer being forced by cash shortages to take drastic action to stay in business. Lowndes Queensway, once the UK's largest retailer of carpets and furniture, had to renegotiate its financing several times with city institutions, alter payment and credit times and terms with its suppliers, and ultimately identify which of its 500 superstores should be closed to save costs. The company went into receivership despite all its efforts. On the other hand, some companies have more optimistic goals. Often manufacturers such as General Motors have goals that relate to return on investment. A successful company, however, may want to sacrifice the current year's profits for the long run and at the same time pursue other goals, such as increasing market share.

• • • • • • • • • • • • • • • • • • • •

Organisational Opportunities and Resources

There are three major considerations in assessing opportunities and resources: evaluating marketing opportunities, environmental scanning (discussed in Chapter 2) and understanding the firm's capabilities. An appreciation of these elements is essential if an organisation is to build up a sustainable differential or competitive advantage.

Differential Advantage

Differential advantage A competitive edge that results when a marketing mix matches target market needs and is superior to those offered by competitors

If a marketing mix is developed that matches target market needs and expectations and is superior to those offered by competitors, there is a real—or perceived—**differential advantage**. A differential advantage is inherent in an organisation's marketing mix if it is desired by consumers and not matched by competitors. Achieving a differential advantage, or competitive edge, requires an organisation to make the most of its opportunities and resources while offering customers a satisfactory mix of tangible and intangible benefits (see Figure 22.4).[7]

Figure 22.4

Differential advantage

With innovative features, Whirlpool strives to create a differential advantage by responding to consumer needs.

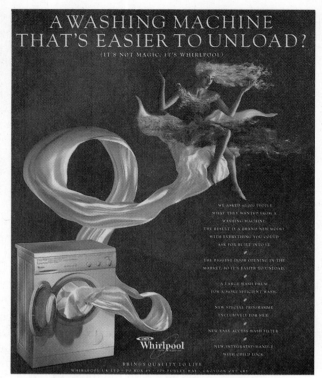

A WASHING MACHINE
THAT'S EASIER TO UNLOAD?
(IT'S NOT MAGIC, IT'S WHIRLPOOL)

Whirlpool

BRINGS QUALITY TO LIFE

Source: Courtesy of Whirlpool Home Appliances.

When striking a balance between customer requirements on the one hand and company resources on the other, competitor activity must also be monitored. For example, there is little sense in promoting speedy distribution to customers if several large competing organisations offer a faster service. There are many different sources of differential advantage that firms can pursue.

For some firms, such as 3M, innovativeness is the focus, while for others, like Vidal Sassoon hair salons, image plays an important part. The Body Shop concentrates on environmentally friendly cosmetics, whereas for multiplex cinemas the differential advantage is the choice of multiple screens at one location. Some of these ways of gaining an edge are easier to sustain than others. For example, many UK companies that have traditionally focused on low price have found this advantage difficult to maintain in the long term.[8] The airline industry is just one to be plagued by periodic price wars.

Marketing Opportunities

Marketing opportunity
Circumstances and timing that allow for an organisation to take action towards reaching a target market

A **marketing opportunity** arises when the right combination of circumstances occurs at the right time to allow an organisation to take action towards reaching a target market. An opportunity provides a favourable chance or opening for the firm to generate sales from identifiable markets. For example, in reaction to the overwhelming growth in cereals and other foods containing oat bran (which some researchers believe helps lower cholesterol levels), the Quaker Oats Company developed an advertising campaign to remind consumers that Quaker porridge oats have always contained oat bran. The advertisements told consumers that eating porridge is "the right thing to do" and helped boost sales of Quaker Oats dramatically.[9] Increasing concerns about cancer and heart disease gave Quaker a marketing opportunity to reach consumers who are especially health-conscious by touting the health benefits of its oats. Kellogg's also took advantage of the popularity of oat bran by creating its Common Sense™ Oat Bran cereal. Interestingly, in 1990 a study published in a leading medical journal questioned the effectivness of oat bran in lowering cholesterol, concluding that it was the elimination of high cholesterol animal products that really lowered cholesterol. Therefore, some of the oat bran mystique vanished overnight. The term **strategic window** has been used to describe what are often temporary periods of optimum fit between the key requirements of a market and the particular capabilities of a firm competing in that market.[10]

The attractiveness of marketing opportunities is determined by market factors, such as size and growth rate, as well as competitive, financial, economic, technological, social, ecological, legal and political factors.[11] Because each industry and product are somewhat different, the factors that determine attractiveness tend to vary.

Market requirements relate to customers' needs or desired benefits. Market requirements are satisfied by components of the marketing mix that provide buyers with these benefits. Of course, buyers' perceptions of what requirements fulfil their needs and provide the desired benefits determine the success of any marketing effort. Marketers must devise strategies to out-perform competitors by finding out what product attributes buyers use to select products. An attribute must be important and differentiating if it is to be useful in strategy development. When marketers fail to understand buyers' perceptions and market requirements, the result may be failure. For example, prior to its takeover by Sears, Freemans launched its by mail "Specialogue" for yuppie men. What the company failed to realise was that its target customers wanted branded goods from prestigious speciality retail outlets; they just did not perceive mail order shopping to be suitable for them.

Environmental Scanning

In Chapter 2 **environmental scanning** was defined as the process of collecting information about the marketing environment to help marketers identify opportunities and assist in planning. Some companies have derived substantial benefits from establishing an "environmental scanning (or monitoring) unit" within the strategic planning group or from including line management in teams or committees to conduct environmental analysis. This approach engages management in the process of environmental forecasting and enhances the likelihood of successfully integrating forecasting efforts into strategic market planning.[12] Results of forecasting research show that even simple quantitative forecasting techniques out-perform the unstructured intuitive assessments of experts.[13] Many builders and developers in the UK believe that the house buying public is unwilling to pay the increased cost of energy efficient new housing. However, research suggests that consumers *are* happy to pay extra, within reason, for the increased comfort levels and reduced fuel bills associated with such property.[14]

Environmental scanning to detect changes in the environment is extremely important if a firm is to avoid crisis management. An environmental change can suddenly alter a firm's opportunities or resources. Re-formulated, more effective strategies may then be needed to guide marketing efforts. For example, after the UK government legislated against heavy emissions from cars and gave unleaded fuel tax advantages, petrol suppliers and vehicle manufacturers had to re-formulate their strategies and marketing programmes.[15] Because car manufacturers had engaged in environmental scanning and were aware that such legislation might

Strategic window A temporary period of optimum fit between the key requirements of a market and the particular capabilities of a firm competing in that market

Market requirements Requirements that relate to customers' needs or desired benefits

Environmental scanning The process of collecting information about the marketing environment to help marketers identify opportunities and assist in planning indeed be enacted because of social and political concerns, most had already begun developing plans for cars powered by clean fuel. Ford Motor Company, for example, is already testing a car that can run on methanol, ethanol, petrol or any combination of those fuels.[16] Similarly, increased concern about the cleanliness of the environment has left manufacturers looking for ways to pass on the costs of catalytic converters, which are necessary if some cars are to run on lead-free fuels, to the consumer. Environmental scanning should identify new developments and determine the nature and rate of change.

Capabilities and Resources

Capabilities A firm's distinctive competencies to do something well and efficiently

Marketing assets Capabilities that managers and the marketplace view as beneficially strong

A firm's **capabilities** relate to *distinctive competencies* that it has developed to do something well and efficiently. A company is likely to enjoy a *differential advantage* in an area where its competencies out-do those of its potential competitors.[17] Often a company may possess manufacturing or technical skills that are valuable in areas outside its traditional industry. For example, BASF, known for its manufacture and development of audio and video tapes, produced a new type of lightweight plastic that has uses in other industries. **Marketing assets** highlight capabilities that managers and the marketplace view as beneficially strong. These capabilities can then be stressed to the company's advantage. *Customer based assets* include brand image and reputation; *distribution based assets* may involve density of dealers and geographic coverage; *internal marketing assets* include skills, experience, economies of scale, technology and resources.[18]

Today marketing planners are especially concerned with external resource constraints. Shortages in energy and other scarce economic resources often limit strategic planning options. On the other hand, planning to avoid shortages can back-fire. In many countries electricity suppliers decided to build nuclear power plants in the 1970s to compensate for an expected shortfall of fossil fuels—only to find the political, social and technological problems of nuclear power almost impossible to overcome. Moreover, an adequate supply of fossil fuels still exists to power traditional plants that generate electricity. But as the public grows more concerned about pollution and the so called "greenhouse effect"—the increased warming of the earth caused by pollution—nuclear power plants may once again become a plausible alternative.

• • • • • • • • • • • • • • • • • • • •

Corporate Strategy

Corporate strategy A strategy that determines how resources are to be used to meet the organisation's goals in the areas of production, finance, research and development, personnel and marketing

Corporate strategy determines the means for utilising resources in the areas of production, finance, research and development, personnel and marketing to reach the organisation's goals. A corporate strategy determines not only the scope of the business but also its resource deployment, competitive advantages and overall co-ordination of production, finance, marketing and other functional areas. The term *corporate* in this context does not apply only to corporations; corporate strategy is used by all organisations, from the smallest sole proprietorship to the largest multinational corporation.

Corporate strategy planners are concerned with issues such as diversification, competition, differentiation, interrelationships among business units and environmental issues. Strategic planners attempt to match the resources of the organisation with the various opportunities and risks in the environment. Corporate strategy planners are also concerned with defining the scope and role of the strategic business units of the organisation so that they are co-ordinated to reach the ultimate goals desired.

Tools for Strategic Market Planning

A number of tools have been proposed to aid marketing managers in their planning efforts. Based on ideas used in the management of financial portfolios, several models that classify an organisation's product portfolio have been proposed. These models allow strategic business units or products to be classified and visually displayed according to the attractiveness of various markets and the business's relative market share within those markets. Four of these tools—the Boston Consulting Group (BCG) product portfolio analysis, the market attractiveness-business position model, the Profit Impact on Marketing Strategy (PIMS) and the ABC sales: contribution analysis—are discussed next.

The Boston Consulting Group (BCG) Product Portfolio Analysis

Product portfolio analysis
A strategic planning tool that takes a product's market growth rate and its relative market share into consideration in determining a marketing strategy

Just as financial investors have different investments with varying risks and rates of return, firms have a portfolio of products characterised by different market growth rates and relative market shares. **Product portfolio analysis,** the Boston Consulting Group approach, is based on the philosophy that a product's market growth rate and its relative market share are important considerations in determining its marketing strategy. All the firm's products should be integrated into a single, overall matrix and evaluated to determine appropriate strategies for individual SBUs and the overall portfolio strategies. However, a balanced product portfolio matrix is the end result of a number of actions—not just the analysis alone. Portfolio models can be created on the basis of present and projected market growth rates and proposed market share strategies (build share, maintain share, harvest share or divest business). Managers can use these models to determine and classify each product's expected future cash contributions and future cash requirements.

Generally, managers who use a portfolio model must examine the competitive position of a product (or product line) and the opportunities for improving that product's contribution to profitability and cash flow.[19] The BCG analytical approach is more of a diagnostic tool than a guide for making strategy prescriptions.

Figure 22.5, which is based on work by the BCG, enables the marketing manager to classify a firm's products into four basic types: stars, cash cows, dogs and problem children.[20] **Stars** are products with a dominant share of the market and good prospects for growth. However, they use more cash than they generate to finance growth, add capacity and increase market share. **Cash cows** have a dominant share of the market but low prospects for growth; typically, they generate more cash than is required to maintain market share. Cash cows generate much needed funds to support the stars and problem children. **Dogs** have a subordinate share of the market and low prospects for growth; these products are frequently found in mature markets and often should be phased out. **Problem children,** sometimes called "question marks", have a small share of a growing market and generally require a large amount of cash to build share. The question is, are they capable of becoming star products or are they destined to be dogs?

The growth-share matrix in Figure 22.5 can be expanded to show a firm's whole portfolio by providing for each product (1) its cash sales volume, illustrated by the size of a circle on the matrix; (2) its market share relative to competition, represented by the horizontal position of the product on the matrix; and (3) the growth rate of the market, indicated by the position of the product in the vertical direction. It should be noted that relative market share is a company's own

Stars Products with a dominant share of the market and good prospects for growth

Cash cows Products with a dominant share of the market but low prospects for growth

Dogs Products that have a subordinate share of the market and low prospects for growth

Problem children Products that have a small share of a growing market, generally requiring a large amount of cash to build share

Figure 22.5

Illustrative growth-share
matrix developed by the
Boston Consulting Group

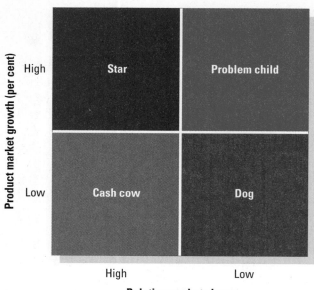

SOURCE: Perspectives, *No. 66, "The product portfolio". Reprinted by permission from The Boston Consulting Group, Inc., Boston, MA. Copyright © 1970.*

market share relative to the biggest competitor's. Figure 22.6 suggests marketing strategies appropriate for cash cows, stars, dogs and problem children.

The long term health of an organisation depends on having some products that generate cash (and provide acceptable profits) and others that use cash to support growth. Among the indicators of overall health are the size and vulnerability of the cash cows, the prospects for the stars, if any, and the number of problem children and dogs. Particular attention must be paid to those products with large cash appetites. Unless the company has an abundant cash flow, it cannot afford to sponsor many such products at one time. If resources, including debt capacity, are spread too thinly, the company will end up with too many marginal products and will be unable to finance promising new product entries or acquisitions in the future.

Market Attractiveness-Business Position Model

Market attractiveness-business position model A two dimensional matrix that helps determine which SBUs have an opportunity to grow and which should be divested

The **market attractiveness-business position model,** illustrated in Figure 22.7, is another two dimensional matrix. However, rather than using single measures to define the vertical and horizontal dimensions of the matrix, the model employs multiple measurements and observations. The vertical dimension, *market attractiveness,* includes all strengths and resources that relate to the market, such as seasonality, economies of scale, competitive intensity, industry sales and the overall cost and feasibility of entering the market. The horizontal axis, *business position,* is a composite of factors such as sales, relative market share, research and development, price competitiveness, product quality and market knowledge as they relate to the product in building market share. A slight variation of this matrix is called General Electric's Strategic Business Planning Grid because General Electric is credited with extending the product portfolio planning tool to examine market attractiveness and business strength. Marketing Insight 22.2 (on page 664) explains how the chemicals giants deploy this tool.

The best situation for a firm is to have a strong business position in an attractive market. The upper left area in Figure 22.7 represents the opportunity for an

Stars

Characteristics

- Market leaders
- Fast growing
- Substantial profits
- Require large investment to finance growth

Strategies

- Protect existing share
- Reinvest earnings in the form of price reductions, product improvements, providing better market coverage, production efficiency, and so on
- Obtain a large share of the new users

Problem children

Characteristics

- Rapid growth
- Poor profit margins
- Enormous demand for cash

Strategies

- Invest heavily to get a disproportionate share of new sales
- Buy existing market shares by acquiring competitors
- Divestment (see Dogs)
- Harvesting (see Dogs)
- Abandonment (see Dogs)
- Focus on a definable niche where dominance can be achieved

Cash cows

Characteristics

- Profitable products
- Generate more cash than needed to maintain market share

Strategies

- Maintain market dominance
- Invest in process improvements and technological leadership
- Maintain price leadership
- Use excess cash to support research and growth elsewhere in the company

Dogs

Characteristics

- Greatest number of products fall in this category
- Operate at a cost disadvantage
- Few opportunities for growth at a reasonable cost
- Markets are not growing; therefore, little new business

Strategies

- Focus on a specialised segment of the market that can be dominated and protected from competitive inroads
- Harvesting—cut back all support costs to a minimum level; supports cash flow over the product's remaining life
- Divestment—sale of a growing concern
- Abandonment—deletion from the product line

Product market growth — High / Low

Relative market share — High / Low

Figure 22.6 Characteristics and strategies for the four basic product types in the growth-share matrix

Source: Concepts in this figure adapted from George S. Day, "Diagnosing the product portfolio", Journal of Marketing, April 1977, pp. 30–31. Reprinted by permission of the American Marketing Association.

invest/grow strategy, but the matrix does not indicate how to implement this strategy. The purpose of the model is to serve as a diagnostic tool to highlight SBUs that have an opportunity to grow or that should be divested or approached selectively.[21] SBUs that occupy the invest/grow position can lose their position through faulty marketing strategies.

Decisions on allocating resources to SBUs of medium overall attractiveness should be arrived at on a basis relative to other SBUs that are either more or less

Figure 22.7 Market attractiveness-business position model

Source: Adapted from Derek F. Abell and John S. Hammond, Strategic Market Planning: Problems and Analytical Approaches *(Englewood Cliffs, N.J.: Prentice-Hall, 1979), p. 213. Used by permission.*

attractive. The lower right area of the matrix is a low growth harvest/divest area. Harvesting is a gradual withdrawal of marketing resources on the assumption that sales will decline at a slow rate but profits will still be significant at a lower sales volume. Harvesting and divesting may be appropriate strategies for SBUs characterised by low overall attractiveness.

Profit Impact on Marketing Strategy (PIMS)

Profit Impact on Marketing Strategy (PIMS) A research programme that compiled a databank of information on 3,000 strategic business units of 200 different firms in order to assist in analysing marketing performance and formulating marketing strategies

The US Strategic Planning Institute (SPI) developed a databank of information on 3,000 strategic business units of 200 different firms during the period 1970 to 1983 for the **Profit Impact on Marketing Strategy (PIMS)** research programme.[22] The sample is somewhat biased because it is composed primarily of large, profitable manufacturing firms marketing mature products; service firms and distribution companies are under represented. However, 19 per cent of the sample is composed of international businesses.[23] The member organisations of the Institute provide confidential information on successes, failures and marginal products. Figure 22.8 shows a PIMS data form. The data are analysed to provide members with information about how similar organisations have performed under a given set of circumstances and about the factors that contribute to success or failure in given market conditions.

The unit of observation in PIMS is the SBU. Table 22.1 shows the types of information provided on each business in the PIMS database. The PIMS database includes both diagnostic and prescriptive information to assist in analysing marketing performance and formulating marketing strategies. The analysis focuses on options, problems, resources and opportunities.

The PIMS project has identified more than 30 factors that affect the performance of firms. These factors can be grouped into three sets of variables: (1) those relating to the structure of the marketplace in which the firm competes; (2) those

Characteristics of the Business Environment	Structure of the Production Process
Long run growth rate of the market	Capital intensity (degree of automation, etc.)
Short run growth rate of the market	Degree of vertical integration
Rate of inflation of selling price levels	Capacity utilisation
Number and size of customers	Productivity of capital equipment
Purchase frequency and magnitude	Productivity of people
	Inventory levels
Competitive Position of the Business	**Discretionary Budget Allocations**
Share of the served market	Research and development budgets
Share relative to largest competitors	Advertising and promotion budgets
Product quality relative to competitors	Sales force expenditures
Prices relative to competitors	**Strategic Moves**
Pay scales relative to competitors	Patterns of change in the controllable elements above
Marketing efforts relative to competitors	
Pattern of market segmentation	**Operating Results**
Rate of new product introductions	Profitability results
	Cash flow results
	Growth results

SOURCE: Reproduced by permission of the Strategic Planning Institute [PIMS programme], Cambridge, Mass.

Table 22.1 Types of information provided on each business in the PIMS database

that describe the firm's competitive position within that market; and (3) those that relate to the strategy chosen by the firm.[24] These factors may interact, as well as directly affect performance and profitability. Some of the main findings of the PIMS project are discussed briefly below.

Strong Market Position   Market position refers to the relative market share that a firm holds in relation to its competition. Firms that have a large share of a market tend to be the most profitable. However, it should be noted that market share does not necessarily create profitability. Business strategies, such as the marketing of high quality products, and the provision of good service result in profitability.

High Quality Products   Organisations that offer products of higher quality tend to be more profitable than their competitors. They are able to demand higher prices for those products. Moreover, high quality offerings instil customer loyalty, foster repeat purchases, insulate firms from price wars and help build market share. In Figure 22.9, Coca-Cola promotes its ongoing commitment to quality. It appears impossible for firms to overcome inferior offerings with high levels of marketing expenditures. Advertising is no substitute for product quality.

Lower Costs   Firms achieve lower costs through economies of scale, ability to bargain with suppliers or backward integration. Low costs heighten profitability levels.

To Market Waste—ICI's Strategists Hit on the Right Formula

Originally a joint venture, but now a wholly owned subsidiary of ICI, Tioxide Group vies head to head with America's Du Pont organisation for leadership worldwide of the TiO_2, titanium dioxide, market. This innocuous powder appears in all paints, inks, PVCs and plastics. As a commodity it is predominantly sold on price, although for certain applications the purity of the pigment is important. With some customers, such as car manufacturers, a significant level of technical expertise and laboratory support is required too.

Although TiO_2 is a commodity, the major players such as Du Pont, Kemira, Kerr McGee, Kronos, SCM and Tioxide do attempt in certain markets to create a differential advantage over their rivals. This may be based on the purity of the pigment from a particular plant, the volume of production, guaranteeing supplies to customers dependent on TiO_2 to finish their products, innovative distribution through tankers or variable pack sizes, delivery times, expertise in the customers' technical needs or long term relationships permitting the sharing of both technical product and market knowledge.

Because there are relatively few competitors—perhaps only 20 major production sites around the world—there is significant rivalry to secure supplies of the raw materials used to produce TiO_2. In addition to the occasional but inevitable production failures and plant closings, this market endures significant cyclical hitches in the supply of TiO_2 to customers. The dilemma then for the major operators is which customers to continue to supply. Should those that take the largest tonnages be given priority? In terms of cash flow, perhaps; but as these customers exercise huge purchasing power, they often buy at the lowest profit margins for companies such as Du Pont or Tioxide. However, to alienate such large customers as ICI Paints or BMW would jeopardise a TiO_2 supplier's long term viability. There has to be a balance between guaranteeing to supply long standing, large customers—particularly those that also operate globally and may well buy from a network of a TiO_2 supplier's plants—and supporting smaller but highly profitable accounts. In times of restricted supply, the use of portfolio models, such as the market attractiveness-business position model or the ABC sales: contribution analysis, plays an active role in these chemicals giants' decision-making.

For the strategists in Du Pont or Tioxide, a persistent problem has been what to do with the waste slurry left from the production of TiO_2 in its purest forms for the major ink, packaging or paint companies. Tioxide tackled this dilemma head-on. Chairman Alan Pedder set up a management group to investigate the possibilities for marketing the waste slurry (or "co-product") in its own right. To the surprise of some industry observers, this effort has proved highly successful, both in finding existing applications and customers that could easily tolerate a lower grade pigment (i.e. with some co-product included) and in identifying totally new applications and customers for the slurry product. In 1994, Tioxide sold more tonnes of co-products from the production of titanium dioxide production than TiO_2 itself.

SOURCES: Peter Fairly, "Tioxide grows materials group", *Chemical Week,* 5 July 1995, p. 18; Sean Milmo, "Tioxide embraces TiO_2 by-products", *Chemical Marketing Reporter,* 12 June 1995, p. 9; Marjorie Coeyman, "Du Pont, Tioxide plan capacity hike", *Chemical Week,* 19 October 1994, p. 14; Brent Shearer, "Tio_2 producers mull new plants", *Chemical Marketing Reporter,* 9 January 1995, p. 3.

Figure 22.8

Sample page from PIMS data forms

103: "LIFE CYCLE" STAGE OF PRODUCT CATEGORY

How would you describe the stage of development of the types of products or services sold by this business during the last three years? *(Check one)*

. . . Introductory Stage: Primary demand for product just starting to grow; products or services still unfamiliar to many potential users □ 1

. . . Growth Stage: Demand growing at 10% or more annually in real terms: technology or competitive structure still changing □ 2

. . . Maturity Stage: Products or services familiar to vast majority of prospective users; technology and competitive structure reasonably stable □ 3

. . . Decline Stage: Products viewed as commodities: weaker competitors beginning to exit □ 4

104: What was this business's first year of commercial sales? *(Check one)*

Prior to 1930	1930–1949	1950–1954	1955–1959	1960–1964	1965–1969	1970–1974	1975–
□ 0	□ 1	□ 2	□ 3	□ 4	□ 5	□ 6	□ 7

105: At the time this business first entered the market, was it . . . *(Check one)*

. . . One of the pioneers in first developing such products or services? □ 1

. . . An early follower of the pioneer(s) in a still growing, dynamic market? □ 2

. . . A later entrant into a more established market situation? □ 3

106–07: PATENTS AND TRADE SECRETS

Does this business benefit *to a significant degree* from patents, trade secrets, or other proprietary methods of production or operation . . .

106: Pertaining to products or services?   NO □ 0   YES □ 1   **107:** Pertaining to processes?   NO □ 0   YES □ 1

108: STANDARDIZATION OF PRODUCTS OR SERVICES

Are the products or services of this business . . *(Check one)*.

. . . More or less standardized for all customers? □ 0

. . . Designed or produced to order for individual customers? □ 1

109: FREQUENCY OF PRODUCT CHANGES

Is it typical practice for the business and its major competitors to change all or part of the line of products or services offered . . . *(Check one)*

. . . Annually (for example, annual model changes)? □ 1

. . . Seasonally? □ 2

. . . Periodically, but at intervals longer than one year? □ 3

. . . No regular, periodic pattern of change? □ 4

110: TECHNOLOGICAL CHANGE

Have there been major technological changes in the products offered by the business or its major competitors, or in methods of production, during the last 8 years? *(If in doubt about whether a change was "major," answer NO.)*   NO □ 0   YES □ 1

Source: *PIMS Data Form reproduced by permission of the Strategic Planning Institute (PIMS programme), Cambridge, Mass., 1979.*

Investment and Capital Intensity   The higher the required investment to compete in an industry, the more pressure there is on a firm to use fully its production capacity. Moreover, these factors tend to have a negative impact on profitability.

The ABC Sales: Contribution Analysis

ABC sales: contribution analysis An approach that examines the financial worth to a company of its products, product groups or customers

The **ABC sales: contribution analysis** can be conducted at either product group or product line level; for the total market, territories or sub-markets; for customer groups/market segments; or for individual customer accounts. The aim is to show both the amount of sales and the financial contribution from these sales to the company's fortunes. Financial success, after all, is not confined to sales volume figures; a business must have an adequate level of contribution (sales revenue minus all variable costs) from its sales. This analysis helps companies to identify the relative value of different products, markets or even individual customer accounts, helping with the allocation of resources. An example of an ABC sales: contribution chart is shown in Figure 22.10. The 45 degree diagonal line from bottom left to top right is the optimum. It is a straightforward rule, not a regression line, however. In an ideal world, the dots on the chart would be located on the line (good sales and contribution) and be at the top right of the graph (high

Figure 22.9

A commitment to quality

Coca-Cola offers a high
quality product and
remains the number one
selling soft drink.

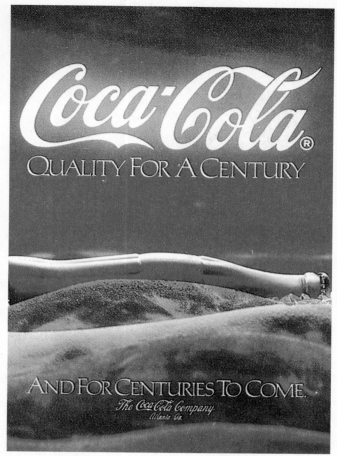

SOURCE: "Coca-Cola" and the Dynamic Ribbon device are registered
trademarks of The Coca-Cola Company

sales and high contribution). These "sell a lot, make a lot" are the "A" class. Typically, however, this is not the case. The majority of customers or markets fall at the bottom left of the graph (low sales and low contribution: the "C" class), or they have reasonably high sales, but low contributions (the "B" class).

Three important conclusions can be drawn from an ABC analysis. (1) It can identify highly attractive customers, markets or products in terms of the associated contributions, but where sales are relatively low. For such accounts, an increase in sales (no matter how slight), with associated high prices and good financial returns, will be highly rewarding. (2) It can determine accounts with high sales figures but low or pitiful contributions. Cash flow may be good, but profitability is not helped; even a slight increase in contribution is most desirable. (3) It can challenge the historical perspective that often clouds judgement as to what constitutes a "good" product, market or customer. Every business has its historically most rewarding customers and products that are no longer performing in sales terms, contribution or both. Often, managers still believe the historical rhetoric rather than recognise that the situation has moved on; new priorities must benefit from the available resources and marketing effort. The ABC analysis generally unearths a few such instances.

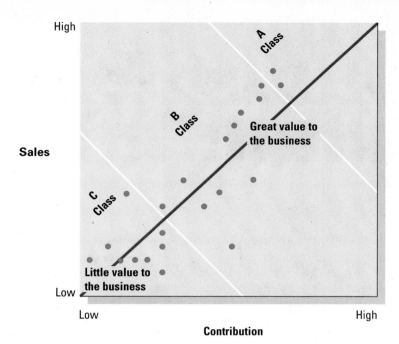

High

A
Class

B
Class

Great value to
the business

Sales

C
Class

The dots could be products,
product groups, market
territories, segments or even
individual customer accounts
depending on the chosen
level of analysis

Little value to
the business

Low

Low   High

Contribution

Figure 22.10 Example of ABC sales: contribution chart

Significance of Strategic Market Planning Approaches

The approaches presented here provide an overview of the most popular analytical methods used in strategic market planning. However, the Boston Consulting Group's portfolio analysis, the market attractiveness-business position model, the Profit Impact on Marketing Strategy research programme and the ABC sales: contribution analysis are used not only to diagnose problem areas or to recognise opportunities but also to facilitate the allocation of resources among business units. They are not intended to serve as formulae for success or prescriptive guides, which lay out cut-and-dried strategic action plans.[25] These approaches are supplements to, not substitutes for, the marketing manager's own judgement. The real test of each approach, or any integrated approach, is how well it helps management diagnose the firm's strengths and weaknesses and prescribe strategic actions for maintaining or improving performance. The emphasis should be on making sound decisions with the aid of these analytical tools.[26]

Another word of caution regarding the use of portfolio approaches is necessary. The classification of SBUs into a specific portfolio position hinges on four factors: (1) the operational definition of the matrix dimensions; (2) the rules used to divide a dimension into high and low categories; (3) the weighting of the variables used in composite dimensions, if composite dimensions are used; and (4) the specific model used.[27] In other words, changes in any of these four factors may well result in a different classification for a single SBU.

The key to understanding the tools for strategic market planning described in this chapter is recognition that strategic market planning takes into account all aspects of a firm's strategy in the marketplace. Most of this book is about functional decisions and strategies of marketing as a part of business. This chapter focuses on the recognition that all functional strategies, including marketing, production and finance, must be co-ordinated to reach organisational goals. Results of a survey of top industrial firms sponsored by the *Harvard Business Review*

Figure 22.11

Ansoff's competitive strategies

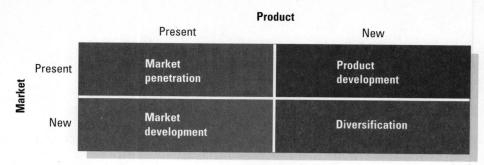

SOURCE: H. I. Ansoff, The New Corporate Strategy (New York, N.Y.: John Wiley & Sons, 1988), p. 83, Figure 6.1. Reproduced by permission of the author.

indicate that portfolio planning and other general planning techniques help managers strengthen their planning process and solve the problems of managing diversified industrial companies. However, the results also indicate that analytical techniques alone do not result in success. Management must blend these analyses with managerial judgement to deal with the reality of the existing situation.

There are other tools that aid strategic market planning besides those examined here. For example, for many years marketing planners have used the product life cycle concept discussed in Chapters 8 and 10. Many firms have their own approaches to planning that incorporate, to varying degrees, some of the approaches discussed here. All strategic planning approaches have some similarity in that several of the components of strategic market planning outlined in Figure 22.3 (especially market/product relationships) are related to a plan of action for reaching objectives.

Developing Competitive Strategies for Marketing

After analysing business operations and business performance, the next step in strategic market planning is to determine future business directions and develop marketing strategies. A business may choose one or more competitive strategies, including intense growth, diversified growth and integrated growth. Figure 22.11 shows these competitive strategies on a product-market matrix. This matrix can help in determining growth that can be implemented through marketing strategies.

Intense Growth

Intense growth Growth that occurs when current products and current markets have the potential for increasing sales

Market penetration A strategy of increasing sales of current products in current markets

Market development A strategy of increasing sales of current products in new markets

Intense growth can take place when current products and current markets have the potential for increasing sales. There are three main strategies for intense growth: market penetration, market development and product development.

Market penetration is a strategy of increasing sales in current markets with current products. For example, Coca-Cola and PepsiCo try to achieve increased market share through aggressive advertising.

Market development is a strategy of increasing sales of current products in new markets. For example, a European aircraft manufacturer was able to enter the US market by offering Eastern Airlines financing that Boeing could not match. Evian devised a new use for its mineral water by developing its "Brumisateur", an atomiser spray for the skin.

Product development A strategy of increasing sales by improving present products or developing new products for current markets

Product development is a strategy of increasing sales by improving present products or developing new products for current markets. PepsiCo and Coca-Cola both have new container sizes, low calorie/low sugar versions and vending machine services.

Diversified Growth

Diversified growth Growth that occurs when new products are developed to be sold in new markets

Diversified growth occurs when new products are developed to be sold in new markets. Firms have become increasingly diversified since the 1960s. Diversification offers some advantages over single business firms, because it allows firms to spread their risk across a number of markets. More important, it allows firms to make better and wider use of their management, technical and financial resources. For example, marketing expertise can be used across businesses, which may also share advertising themes, distribution channels, warehouse facilities or even sales forces.[28] The three forms of diversification are horizontal, concentric and conglomerate.

Horizontal diversification A process that occurs when new products not technologically related to current products are introduced into current markets

Horizontal diversification results when new products that are not technologically related to current products are introduced to current markets. Sony, for example, has diversified from electronics to film production through its purchase of Columbia Pictures. The purchase gave Sony a library of 2,700 films, including *Ghostbusters 2* and *When Harry Met Sally*, as well as 23,000 television episodes, which it may use to help establish its new line of 8mm videos.[29]

Concentric diversification A process that occurs when new products related to current products are introduced into new markets

In **concentric diversification**, the marketing and technology of new products are related to current products, but the new ones are introduced into new markets. For instance, Dow Chemical is diversifying into agricultural chemicals and pharmaceuticals through joint ventures in those industries.[30]

Conglomerate diversification A process that occurs when new products unrelated to current technology, products or markets are introduced into new markets

Conglomerate diversification occurs when new products are unrelated to current technology, products or markets and are introduced to markets new to the firm. For example, Bass, the British brewer, acquired the American Holiday Inn hotel chain, and Laura Ashley, the UK clothing and furnishings company, has moved into the fragrance market with Laura Ashley No. 1.

Integrated Growth

Integrated growth Growth that occurs in three possible directions: forwards, backwards or horizontally

Integrated growth can occur in the same industry that the firm is in and in three possible directions: forwards, backwards or horizontally. A company growing through forward integration takes ownership or increased control of its distribution system. For example, a shoe manufacturer might start selling its products through wholly owned retail outlets.

In backward integration, a firm takes ownership or increased control of its supply systems. A newspaper company that buys a paper mill is integrating backwards. Horizontal integration occurs when a firm takes ownership or control of some of its competitors. For example, prior to its financial collapse, Polly Peck International, the British/Cypriot fruit grower and distributor, purchased Del Monte's fresh fruit division.[31]

Competitive position An organisation's role in the competitive marketplace, which influences its marketing strategies and tactics

In developing strategies, an organisation must consider the competitive positions in the marketplace and formulate marketing strategies and tactics accordingly. Some authors have adopted warfare analogies to describe the strategic options for competing in a market.[32] This chapter now examines the concept of **competitive positions**—as distinct from product or brand positionings, discussed in Chapter 7—and concludes with an overview of the principal warfare strategies.[33]

Competitive Positions and Warfare

Market leader The single player enjoying the largest individual share in the market

In the world of market shares, there has to be one—and only one—**market leader:** the player enjoying individually the largest slice of the market. In some industrial markets, a market leader can have a majority of industry sales, particularly when patent protection or technical innovation gives it an advantage over competitors. In most markets, however, the market leader may have only 10 to 20 per cent of the market's sales. The market leader has the highest market share and retains its competitive position by expanding the total market or expanding market share at the expense of rivals, while protecting or defending current market share by retaining its customer base. In this context, the market leader perhaps has the most difficult task, that of finding strategies to increase market size and market share, as well as maintaining strategies to defend its current share.

Market challenger A non-market leader that aggressively tries to capture market share from its rivals

Behind the market leader are competing companies, which are market challengers, market followers or market nichers. **Market challengers** are non-market leaders that aggressively attack rivals, including the market leader, to take more market share. In most instances, these players are number two, three and perhaps four in a market. It is important to remember, though, that to qualify as challengers these companies must be proactive and aggressive in their sales and marketing rather than passively reinforcing the existing hierarchy. It is also possible for a relative "minnow" to be a challenger; a company with 1 per cent of the market two years ago and 4.5 per cent this year—a fast mover—is certainly one to monitor.

Market follower A low share competitor without the resources, market position, research and development, or commitment to challenge for extra sales and market share

Market followers are low share competitors without resources, market position, research and development, or commitment to challenge for extra sales and market share. These companies tend to be the "plodders" or "me-toos" in a market, whose raison d'être is to do as before and survive. In boom times these players can latch onto the success of their larger rivals, but in recession—or when faced with rivals' product innovation—they often struggle for business. Most markets also contain **market nichers:** companies that specialise by focusing on only a very narrow range of products (Sock Shop or Saab), or on a select band of consumers (Body Shop or Porsche). Nichers survive by finding a safe, small, profitable market segment—often apparently too small to attract the market leaders and challengers. Nichers specialise and can genuinely gear up a marketing mix that exactly matches their target customers' needs. They are vulnerable to market down turns, the entry of rival nichers and the sudden attention of the major players in the marketplace.

Market nicher A company that specialises by focusing on a very narrow range of products or on a select band of consumers

Defensive warfare A policy of striking a balance between waiting for market developments or competitor activity and proactively parrying competitors' actions

A market leader must defend its position, while simultaneously seeking more market share. Only a market leader should consider **defensive warfare.** Strong defence involves striking a balance between waiting for market developments or competitor activity and proactively parrying competitors' thrusts. As market leader, the company must remember that a false sense of security and passive inactivity lead to disaster; the best defensive strategy is the courage to attack; and strong moves by competitors should always be blocked, never ignored. To defend its market share, a market leader must treat existing customers well and attentively and never take them for granted. The marketing mix must be continually up-dated and target customers' needs regularly considered. New markets, products and opportunities should always be sought and evaluated. Occasionally, if faced by a strong challenger in a small or declining market, a market leader should consider divesting and concentrating resources in its other markets.

A challenger has to attack for market share, but on what basis? The leader, and perhaps other challengers, will be strong and rich in resources. A challenger's attack must be well thought out and not suicidal in terms of the company's medium term future. In **offensive warfare**, the main consideration is the market leader's strength: where are there any chinks in the leader's armour? A challenger must identify a weakness in the leader's marketing mix and develop a genuine corresponding strength. With such a differential advantage or competitive edge, the challenger's resources may well be sufficient to steal ground successfully from the leader. Any attack, however, should be on a narrow front, where the challenger is perceived by the target customers to have an advantage and where resources can be focused. If no real weakness in the market leader exists, a challenger may attack head-on. Such an attack can be successful only if there are numerous, very weak market followers, if the leader is slow to react and if a price cutting war does not result; in the latter situation, the leader's resource base may kill off the challenger's attack.

Followers are vulnerable, but careful monitoring of market, environmental and competitive trends can help ensure their survival. They must serve exactly only a few market segments, specialising rather than diversifying in terms of products and markets and making prudent use of what research and development resources are available. Nichers must watch for signs of competitor threats and possible changes in target segment customers' needs; and they may need to consider product development and, ultimately, diversification. Their marketing mixes must be tailored exactly to meet the expectations of their target segment.

All organisations should know, for all their markets and target segments, which companies occupy these competitive positions. And they must alter their strategies and marketing programmes accordingly. Organisations should also review their rivals' marketing strategies and marketing programmes; many companies are surprisingly predictable. Response to rivals' pricing policies, frequency of new product launches, entry into new markets and timing of promotional campaigns, for example, can often be accurately anticipated. In this way thorough **competitor scanning**—the monitoring of competitive positions and competitors' strategies—helps to establish more realistic marketing goals, develop successful strategies and programmes, and pre-empt nasty shocks caused by competitors' actions. It is essential to understand competitors' strategies, their strengths and weaknesses, and any differential advantages they hold, which must be combatted.[34]

Offensive warfare A policy whereby challengers aggressively seek market share by identifying any weakness in the leader's marketing mix and developing a corresponding strength

Competitor scanning The monitoring of competitive positions and competitors' strengths

- - - - - - - - - - - - - - - - - - -

Summary

● *Marketing strategy* is a plan of action based on thorough analyses of market opportunities, trends in the marketing environment, customers, competitors, organisational goals, capabilities and resources. A marketing strategy aims to target customer segments of most benefit to an organisation in a manner that provides a differential advantage over competitors and matches the organisation's corporate goals.

● A *strategic market plan* is an outline of the methods and resources required to achieve the organisation's goals within a specific target market; it takes into account all the functional areas of a business unit that must be co-ordinated. A *strategic business unit (SBU)* is a division, product line, or other profit centre within the parent company and is used to define areas for consideration in a specific strategic market plan. The process of *strategic market planning* yields a marketing strategy that is the framework for a marketing plan. A *marketing plan* (see Chapter 23) includes the framework and entire set of activities to be performed; it is the written document or blueprint for implementing and controlling an organisation's marketing activities.

- Through the process of strategic market planning, an organisation can develop marketing strategies that, when properly implemented and controlled, will contribute to achieving the organisation's overall goals. The set of marketing strategies that are implemented and used at the same time is referred to as the organisation's *marketing programme*. Environmental forces are important in—and profoundly affect—the strategic market planning process. These forces imply opportunities and threats that influence an organisation's overall goals.

- A firm's organisational goals should be derived from its *mission,* that is, the broad tasks the organisation wants to achieve. These goals should guide planning efforts.

- An organisation should strive for a *differential advantage* (competitive edge) in its markets. Marketing programmes and the marketing mix should emphasise desirable attributes of a company's marketing mix that its target customers consider unmatched by competitors.

- There are three major considerations in assessing opportunities and resources: (1) evaluating marketing opportunities, (2) monitoring environmental forces and (3) understanding the firm's capabilities. A *marketing opportunity,* or *strategic window,* opens when the right combination of circumstances occurs at the right time, allowing an organisation to take action towards a target market. An opportunity offers a favourable chance for the company to generate sales from markets. *Market requirements* relate to the customers' needs or desired benefits. The market requirements are satisfied by components of the marketing mix that provide buyers with these benefits. *Environmental scanning* is a search for information about events and relationships in a company's outside environment; such information aids marketers in planning. A firm's *capabilities* relate to distinctive competencies that it has developed to do something well and efficiently. A firm is likely to enjoy a differential advantage in an area in which its competencies and *marketing assets* out-do those of its potential competition.

- *Corporate strategy* determines the means for utilising resources in the areas of production, finance, research and development, personnel and marketing to reach the organisation's goals.

- A number of tools have been developed to aid marketing managers in their planning efforts, including the Boston Consulting Group (BCG) *product portfolio analysis,* the market attractiveness-business position model, the Profit Impact on Marketing Strategy (PIMS) and the ABC sales: contribution analysis. The BCG approach is based on the philosophy that a product's market growth rate and its market share are key factors influencing marketing strategy. All the firm's products are integrated into a single, overall matrix—including *stars, cash cows, dogs* and *problem children*—and evaluated to determine appropriate strategies for individual SBUs and the overall portfolio strategies.

- The *market attractiveness-business position model* is a two dimensional matrix. The market attractiveness dimension includes all the sources of strength and resources that relate to the market; competition, industry sales and the cost of competing are among the sources. The business position axis measures sales, relative market share, research and development, and other factors that relate to building a market share for a product.

- The *Profit Impact on Marketing Strategy (PIMS)* research programme has developed a databank of confidential information on the successes, failures and marginal products of more than 3,000 strategic business units of the 200 members of the Strategic Planning Institute. The unit of observation in PIMS is an SBU. The results of PIMS include diagnostic and prescriptive information to assist in analysing marketing performance and formulating marketing strategies. The analysis focuses on options, problems, resources and opportunities. The *ABC sales: contribution analysis* examines the financial worth to a company of its products, product groups or customers.

- Tools for strategic market planning are used only to diagnose problem areas or recognise opportunities. They are supplements to, not substitutes for, the marketing manager's own judgement. The real test of each approach, or any integrated approach, is how well it helps management diagnose the firm's strengths and weaknesses and prescribe strategic actions for maintaining or improving performance.

- Competitive strategies that can be implemented through marketing include *intense growth, diversified growth* and *integrated growth.* Intense growth includes *market penetration, market development* or *product development.* Diversified growth includes *horizontal, concentric* and *conglomerate diversification.* Integrated growth includes forwards, backwards and horizontal integration.

● In developing strategies, an organisation must consider the *competitive positions* in the marketplace. The *market leader* must defend its position and seek new sales opportunities. Attack may prove the best form of defence. *Market challengers* must aggressively seek market share gains but carefully select the basis on which to attack: a chink in the leader's armour or a quick response to changing consumer needs. *Market followers* are the "also-rans", prone to be squeezed in recession or in response to challengers' aggression. *Market nichers* specialise in terms of product and customer segment. They can very successfully tailor their marketing to their customers' needs but are vulnerable to competitors' entry into their target segments. To compete successfully, any organisation needs to consider the principles of *offensive* and *defensive warfare* and to understand its competitors' strategies through *competitor scanning*.

Important Terms

Marketing strategy	Corporate strategy	Product development
Strategic market plan	Product portfolio analysis	Diversified growth
Strategic business unit (SBU)	Stars	Horizontal diversification
Strategic market planning	Cash cows	Concentric diversification
Marketing plan	Dogs	Conglomerate diversification
Marketing programme	Problem children	Integrated growth
Mission	Market attractiveness-business	Competitive position
Differential advantage	position model	Market leader
Marketing opportunity	Profit Impact on Marketing	Market challenger
Strategic window	Strategy (PIMS)	Market follower
Market requirements	ABC sales: contribution analysis	Market nicher
Environmental scanning	Intense growth	Defensive warfare
Capabilities	Market penetration	Offensive warfare
Marketing assets	Market development	Competitor scanning

Discussion and Review Questions

1. Why should an organisation develop a marketing strategy? What is the difference between strategic market planning and the strategy itself?

2. Identify the major components of strategic market planning and explain how they are interrelated.

3. In what ways do environmental forces affect strategic market planning? Give some specific examples.

4. What are some of the issues that must be considered in analysing a firm's opportunities and resources? How do these issues affect marketing objectives and marketing strategy?

5. Why is marketing opportunity analysis necessary? What are the determinants of marketing opportunity?

6. In relation to resource constraints, how can environmental scanning affect a company's long term strategic market planning? Consider product costs and benefits affected by the environment.

7. What are the major considerations in developing the product portfolio grid? Define and explain the four basic types of products suggested by the Boston Consulting Group.

8. When should marketers consider using PIMS for strategic market planning?

9. Why do you think more firms are diversifying? Give some examples of diversified firms.

10. How can a market leader best defend its competitive position?

11. What are the strengths of a market nicher? In what way is a nicher vulnerable?

12. Why should companies attempt to understand the strategies of their competitors? Explain your views.

Recommended Readings

D. A. Aaker, *Strategic Marketing Management* (New York: Wiley, 1992).

J. O'Shaughnessy, *Competitive Marketing: A Strategic Approach* (London: Unwin-Hyman, 1995).

D. Littler and D. Wilson, eds, *Marketing Strategy* (Oxford: Butterworth-Heinemann, 1995).

M. E. Porter, *Competitive Advantage: Creating and Sustaining Superior Performance* (New York: Free Press, 1985).

J. Saunders, "Marketing and Competitive Success", in *The Marketing Book*, M. J. Baker, ed. (Oxford: Butterworth-Heinemann, 1994).

•••••••••••••••••

Cases

22.1   Ireland: Marketing a Country

During the 1960s and 1970s, Ireland's economy lagged behind those of its European neighbours. The Irish government realised it needed to create more employment opportunities in industries of the future in order to establish a more affluent, outward looking basis to the country's economy. Today Ireland has a trade surplus in excess of 12.6 per cent of GNP, a balance of payments surplus equivalent to 6.2 per cent of GNP and one of the lowest inflation rates in Europe. Membership in the EU has brought significant benefits to the country, including grants for infrastructure enhancements and improved international links. Over 1,000 international companies have been encouraged to invest in factories, distribution centres or office complexes.

From its previous dependence on agriculture, the economy has become far more balanced. Industry accounts for 35 per cent of GDP; distribution, transport and communication for 18 per cent; services for 31 per cent; and agriculture for just 10 per cent. Although not solely responsible for this change, the Industrial Development Authority (IDA) has figured prominently in Ireland's economic transformation. Established to promote industrial development, the IDA has encouraged overseas companies to locate in Ireland, creating close to 100,000 jobs by 1996, an incredible 10,000 per annum; 400 US companies alone have settled on an Irish base as a gateway into the huge EU market of over 360 million consumers. As many as 180 German companies have set up in Ireland attracted by its skilled workforce, tax base and culture. Household names including IBM, Microsoft, Lotus, Norwich Union, Siemens, CIGNA, McGraw-Hill, Massachusetts Mutual, Ericsson, Philips, Fujitsu, Northern Telecom, Pratt & Whitney, Merck Sharp & Dohme, Braun, Coca-Cola and Nestlé are important investors and employers.

The IDA has succeeded not by good luck but through the development of an evolving business strategy. First, it identified specific sectors of economic activity for international growth. Ireland wanted to attract the growth companies of the future, not yesteryear. Financial services, electronics, high tech engineering, consumer products, branded food and drinks, and health care were earmarked to lead the economy into the twenty-first century. The US, Pacific, Asia, Britain, Germany, Benelux and Scandinavia were home to these growth industries, so the IDA set up a network of 20 offices in these territories to push the Irish message.

Having targeted the growth industries, the IDA knew it had to offer benefits in order to attract any interest in locating and investing in Ireland. Research revealed several negative perceptions of the country and its people as impoverished, rural, agricultural and poorly educated. The facts paint a far different picture, and through glossy printed publicity, seminars, press involvement and various road shows, IDA personnel, politicians and leading Irish industrialists sought to convey the real story.

The message was carefully honed to reflect the target companies' concerns and to offer tangible rewards for investing in Ireland:

- A young, English speaking, highly educated workforce superior to most in Europe.

- A 10 per cent corporate tax rate up to the year 2010 and freedom to repatriate profits.

- A state of the art digital and satellite telecommunications system.

- Generous capital, employment, research and development, and training grants.
- A stable currency and low inflation rate.
- Duty free access to the EU market.
- Return on investment (29.9 per cent) more than three times the EU (9.4 per cent) and world (8.6 per cent) averages.
- Most European cities within two hours' flying time.
- A vigorous sub-contracting and component supply industry.
- A unique, historic culture and quality of life with superb recreational and leisure facilities.

The pliable, capable, young workforce has been a significant attraction, as has the cultural and recreational base. The stable economy and hefty financial incentives for many companies simply helped close the deal for re-location. With extensions to Shannon International Airport, the creation of the associated duty free zone trading estate—the first in the world—significant investment from both the private and public sectors and the recent development of the superb waterfront financial services centre in Dublin, the Irish strategy has worked.

An opportunity existed to create a rationale for overseas companies to put Ireland at the top of their location and investment lists. Advantages were created and existing benefits reinforced to establish a clear basis for companies to choose Ireland. Careful targeting of industries and companies, supported by comprehensive promotion, led to the establishment of operations in Ireland by over 1,000 companies. The IDA and its partner organisations have successfully marketed a country.

Sources: Irish Embassy, London; Industrial Development Authority (IDA); IDA promotional material: "Dublin: the international financial services centre", "Ireland: put yourself in our hands in the 90s"; Shannon Development promotional literature; "Facts about Ireland", IDA, 1995 and 1996.

Questions for Discussion

1. Why was targeting central to the IDA strategy?
2. What problems had to be overcome to attract overseas investors to locate in Ireland?
3. What benefits were offered by the IDA? How did this varied package communicate the Irish message?

22.2 Marks & Spencer: Maintaining Competitive Position—Mail Order and Electronic Shopping Next?

The Marks & Spencer story began in 1884 when Russian refugee Michael Marks set up a haberdashery market stall in the northern English city of Leeds. Ten years later, the empire had expanded to 10 stalls and Marks was joined by Tom Spencer. Today, with close to 750 stores in Europe, the US, Canada and the Far East and profits of more than £800 million, Marks & Spencer has become truly international.

The company's aim of providing quality, value and service, established early on by Michael Marks and Tom Spencer, is still its goal today. The aim has been expanded to form a set of key company principles (see table) which management believes will help to ensure the company's continued success. Through its range of clothing, foods and homeware, Marks & Spencer has a powerful hold on the retailing sector. With 17 per cent of the UK clothing market and 5 per cent of food sales, the company works hard to maintain its competitive position.

Management at Marks & Spencer is acutely aware of the importance of a satisfied and brand loyal customer base. Keeping customers happy means staying in touch with, and adapting quickly to, new trends. The clothing side of the company's business accounts for approaching half of total turnover. To retain its share of this highly competitive market, Marks & Spencer has developed close links with key manufacturers, working together with them to ensure that seasonal sales patterns are reflected in the products in the stores. The company splits its clothing products into "classic" goods—which are not highly susceptible to sudden fashion fluctuations—and fashion goods—which enjoy a short life cycle and become quickly out-moded. This categorisation helps the company match customer desires with appropriate merchandise.

Marks & Spencer does not rely just on its clothing products to maintain its strong market position. The company's range of quality food is an increasingly important aspect of the business. With the 40 per cent share of turnover taken by this range looking set to increase, the company is continually seeking innovative recipes—both convenience and cordon bleu—in order to appeal to customers' taste buds.

Here, too, ensuring quality products and customer satisfaction remains the focus. The handling of chilled foods needs to be undertaken with particular care; and Marks & Spencer has installed systems to ensure that it is. For example, the transport of produce from the point of manufacture to stores—and ultimately to the customer—is especially critical. Fleets of refrigerated lorries ensure the early arrival of produce at stores, where staff move quickly to transfer the food to cold rooms and into shop floor fridges. The Marks & Spencer commitment to quality does not end there. Comprehensive customer instructions are printed on the packs to ensure that produce is stored and used correctly in the home.

Marks & Spencer, currently enjoying a strong competitive position in the UK retailing sector as market leader in terms of market share, profitability and customer loyalty, considers its customers the key to continued success. Monitoring customer needs, responding quickly to them and maintaining standards of quality, service and value for money— while keeping a careful eye on the competition—are all central to keeping the customers happy.

The company certainly has no plans to ease up. An additional 20 stores will soon be open in Spain, with 10 more in Asia-Pacific following the firm's successful entry into Hong Kong; and significant expansion is planned for France and Benelux. Last year's sales in Continental Europe rose by 20 per cent. To keep abreast of consumer trends and technological advances, Marks & Spencer is reportedly now set to launch into mail order and electronic shopping.

SOURCES: *Marks & Spencer Company Facts*, 1992, Marks & Spencer plc, Baker Street, London; *Marks & Spencer Annual Report*, 1993–1996; *A Company of Values*, Marks & Spencer; *Bricks and Mortar*, Marks & Spencer; *Food for Thought*, Marks & Spencer; *Spinning a Yarn*, Marks & Spencer; "Stop press", *Marketing*, 27 July 1995, p. 2; "All sorts of success", *Marketing*, 25 May 1995, p. 8; "Marks & Spencer", *Business Europe*, 6 March 1995, p. 7; John Parry, "Spain", *European Retail*, 22 November 1994, p. 3.

Questions for Discussion

1. With what types of stores does Marks & Spencer compete?
2. Does Marks & Spencer have a differential advantage? If so, what is it?
3. If you were a new clothing retailer selling a full range of family clothes, how would you position your products against Marks & Spencer? What competitive position would your company be likely to occupy in the market?

23

MARKETING PLANNING AND ASSESSING SALES POTENTIAL

"The overall purpose of marketing planning and its principal focus is the identification and creation of sustainable competitive advantage."

Malcolm McDonald
Cranfield University School of Management

OBJECTIVES

- To understand the marketing planning process
- To understand the relationship between marketing analyses, marketing strategy and marketing programmes
- To examine the role of the SWOT analysis in marketing planning
- To gain an overview of the marketing plan
- To gain an understanding of sales potential
- To become familiar with sales forecasting methods
- To become aware of the major components of a marketing audit

Throughout the 1980s, the retail developers could do no wrong. It seemed that most towns and cities at some point woke up to new shopping centres and office developments. Retailers demanded more sites in the main shopping areas, so the developers used any available land or building opportunity to deliver more retail space. Once this was constructed, it was not unusual for there to be waiting lists of eager retailers for each of the empty units. The developers simply had to persuade the municipal planning authorities to grant planning permission to build and then entice one of the leading magnet retail groups—Marks & Spencer or a department store such as Debenhams—to take an anchor unit to guarantee pedestrian footfall as an inducement to other tenant retailers. Burton group, one of the UK's leading retail groups, went one stage further, establishing the Burton Property Trust to act as a property developer and commissioning five major shopping centre developments. Retailers such as British Shoe Corporation had site assessors touring the streets, responding within hours to a letting agent's notification of a vacant unit. If a speedy

A manager of a major development in the Prudential's portfolio of shopping centres is no longer responsible only for signing up tenants and dealing with legal issues of leases, nor just for instigating security arrangements, cleaning contracts and setting car parking charges. Such managers now have to analyse the catchment population of the town centre; types of people; where they come from; how frequently they come; what their spending power is; and what their likes, tastes and needs are. Where else do they shop? Why there? What are the underlying trends and patterns of shopping? Where are the competitive shopping centres? What do they offer? What additional amenities? How do such centres promote themselves? What is their brand proposition and positioning? The Prudential's managers plan for their shopping centre as if they were developing a range of Ford cars. While short term needs must be addressed, so must the longer term requirements of underlying trends and evolving customer expectations. These will have ramifications for the optimum tenant mix, the selection of retailers present, relationships with the municipal authorities, the provision of amenities and car parking. Indeed, modifications will be required in terms of refurbishment, access and tenant mix that require many years of careful planning and budgeting. In such cases, the formality of marketing planning acts as a welcome framework and guiding managerial process. ■

decision was not forthcoming, the shoe retailer knew a rival multiple retailer would sign up the site.

Today a different story prevails in most towns. There is far more shop space than there are retailers able and willing to pay the required rents and agree to the lengthy leases. The developers must now market their centres, malls and precincts. Some have opted for the "any tenant" approach simply to guarantee lease income, leading to a confused mix and style of retail units co-existing with one another: up-market fashion adjacent to an "Anything for a £" discounter, or a department store next to an impromptu budget market. The result in such cases is often a dissatisfied mix of tenants and alienated shoppers attempting to understand just who are the targets of the shopping centre development and what the marketing proposition is. For major insurance companies such as the Prudential, which owns and manages many of Europe's leading shopping centres, a need has arisen for more prudent business planning and marketing expertise.

Sources: "UK steers retailing back to centre of city", ENR, 13 November 1995, pp. 22–23; John Fernie, "The coming of the fourth-wave", International Journal of Retail & Distribution Management, 23 (1), 1995, pp. 4–11; Jonathan Duckworth, centre manager, West Orchards Shopping Centre, 1996.

Manipulation of the marketing mix to match target market needs and expectations constitutes a daily activity for most marketing personnel. However, as explained in the previous chapter, fundamental strategic decisions need to be addressed before the marketing mix(es) are formulated. To expedite this process and link the strategic decision-making to the development of actionable marketing programmes, many organisations turn to formal marketing planning. Some companies conduct a marketing audit as a preliminary analysis to gain a realistic understanding of the organisation, its personnel and its market. Like all business activities, marketing needs to have goals; often these are sales targets and market share objectives. To set the right goals, marketers must be able to forecast future sales and market size trends. Even property development companies have to forecast demand and develop marketing plans for their retail shopping centres. This chapter begins with a discussion of the marketing planning process, including the SWOT analysis. It then examines in detail forecasting and techniques for predicting sales.

Marketing planning is a systematic process involving the assessment of marketing opportunities and resources, the determination of marketing objectives and the development of a plan for implementation and control. A sales forecast is an estimation of the amount of a service or product that an organisation expects to sell during a specific period at a specified level of marketing activities. Market potential is a prediction of industrywide market size, everything else being equal, over a specified time period. The marketing audit, where applied, is a systematic examination of the objectives, strategies, organisation and performance of a company's marketing unit.

● ● ● ● ● ● ● ● ● ● ● ● ● ● ● ● ● ● ●

Marketing Planning

Marketing planning A systematic process of assessing marketing opportunities and resources, determining marketing objectives and developing a thorough plan for implementation and control

Marketing plan A document or blueprint detailing requirements for a company's marketing activity

Marketing planning cycle A circular process that runs in two directions, with planning running one way and feedback the other

Short range plans Plans that cover a period of one year or less

Medium range plans Plans that usually cover two to five years

Long range plans Plans that extend beyond five years

Marketing planning is a systematic process that involves assessing marketing opportunities and resources, determining marketing objectives and developing a thorough plan for implementation and control. A core output of marketing planning is the **marketing plan,** a document or blueprint that details requirements for a company's marketing activity. The marketing planning process involves analysing the marketplace, modifying the recommended marketing strategy accordingly and developing detailed marketing mix programmes designed to implement the specified marketing strategy.

Figure 23.1 illustrates the **marketing planning cycle.** Note that marketing planning is a circular process. As the dotted feedback lines in the figure indicate, planning is not one-way. Feedback is used to co-ordinate and synchronise all the stages of the planning cycle.

The duration of marketing plans varies. Plans that cover a period of one year or less are called **short range plans. Medium range plans** are usually for two to five years. Marketing plans that extend beyond five years are generally viewed as **long range plans.** These plans can sometimes cover a period as long as 20 years. Marketing managers may have short, medium and long range plans all at the same time. Long range plans are relatively rare. However, as the marketing environment continues to change and business decisions become more complex, profitability and survival will depend more and more on the development of long range plans.[1] Most marketing plans are revised annually with a detailed three years' perspective.[2] Organisations choose to up-date fully and revise their marketing plans, modifying their marketing programmes and changing the detail of their marketing mix(es) as a result. Overall strategic market planning as described in the previous chapter is unlikely to face annual changes of such magnitude, although strategy modifications will always be needed to respond to changes in customer needs, the marketing environment and competitors' activities.

The extent to which marketing managers develop and use plans also varies. Although planning provides numerous benefits, some managers do not use formal

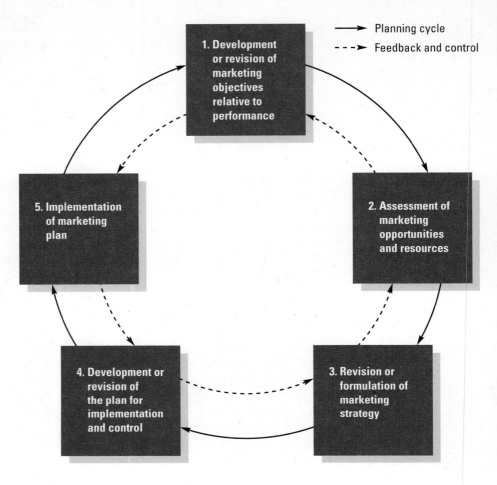

Figure 23.1

The marketing planning cycle

→ Planning cycle

---→ Feedback and control

1. Development or revision of marketing objectives relative to performance

2. Assessment of marketing opportunities and resources

3. Revision or formulation of marketing strategy

4. Development or revision of the plan for implementation and control

5. Implementation of marketing plan

marketing plans because they spend almost all their time dealing with daily problems, many of which would be eliminated by adequate planning. However, planning is becoming more important to marketing managers, who realise that planning is necessary to develop, co-ordinate and control marketing activities effectively and efficiently.[3] When formulating a marketing plan, a new enterprise or a firm with a new product does not have current performance to evaluate or an existing plan to revise. Therefore, its marketing planning centres on analysing available resources and options to assess opportunities. Managers can then develop marketing objectives and a strategy. In addition, many firms recognise the need to include information systems in their plans so that they can have continuous feedback and keep their marketing activities orientated towards objectives. One research study, which examined 207 different companies, found that those that had maintained or increased their planning departments during the past five years and increased their allocation of resources to planning activities out-performed those whose planning departments had become smaller.[4] Sound marketing planning enabled Citroën to establish its Xantia range in the fleet market: the company's first significant success in this highly competitive segment (see Figure 23.2).

To illustrate the marketing planning process, consider the decisions that went into the planning in the United States of the national newspaper *USA Today*. Table

Figure 23.2 The importance of marketing planning. Shrewd marketing planning has enabled Citroën's Xantia to compete effectively in the fleet car market.

SOURCE: Courtesy of Citroën/Euro/RSCG.

23.1 lists several of the more important marketing decisions. Of course, to reach the objective, a detailed course of action was communicated throughout the organisation. In short, specific marketing plans should do the following:

1. Specify expected results so that the organisation can anticipate what its situation will be at the end of the current planning period.
2. Identify the resources needed to carry out the planned activities so that a budget can be developed.
3. Describe in sufficient detail the activities that are to take place so that responsibilities for implementation can be assigned.
4. Provide for the monitoring of activities and the results so that control can be exerted.[5]
5. Lead to the implementation of the organisation's marketing strategy.
6. Be in line with customer needs and market developments.
7. Emphasise any differential advantage or business strength over rivals.

Objective: Achieve 1 million in circulation by reaching an up-market segment, primarily of males who hold professional and managerial positions and who made at least one trip of 200 miles or more within the last year.

Opportunity: Paper tends to be a second newspaper purchase for readers. *USA Today* is not in competition directly with local papers, and it is not positioned against other national newspapers/magazines.

Market: Circulation within a 200 mile radius of 15 major markets, representing 54 per cent of the US population, including such cities as Chicago, Houston, New York, Los Angeles and Denver.

Product: Superior graphic quality; appeal to the television generation through short news items, a colour weather map and other contemporary features.

Price: Competitive.

Promotion: Pedestal-like vending machines with attention grabbing design and a higher position than competitors to differentiate the paper and bring it closer to eye level. Out-door advertising and some print advertising promotes the paper.

Distribution: News-stands, vending machines in busy locations and direct mail.

Implementation and Control: Personnel with experience in the newspaper business who can assist in developing a systematic approach for implementing the marketing strategy and design, as well as an information system to monitor and control the results.

SOURCE: Kevin Higgins, "*USA Today* nears million reader mark", *Marketing News*, 15 April 1983, pp. 1, 5. Reprinted by permission of the American Marketing Association.

Table 23.1 Planning for the introduction of a national newspaper: *USA Today*

There is a logical and relatively straightforward approach to marketing planning:

1. Analysis of markets and the trading environment.
2. Determination of core target markets.
3. Identification of a differential advantage (competitive edge).
4. Statement of specific goals and desired product or service positioning.
5. Development of marketing mixes to implement plans.
6. Determination of required budgets and allocation of marketing tasks.

Table 23.2 illustrates these aspects of the marketing planning process in more detail.

Obviously, the marketing plan document needs to be carefully written to attain these objectives. The next section of this chapter takes a closer look at the marketing plan itself.

• • • • • • • • • • • • • • • • •

The Marketing Plan

The marketing plan is the written document or blueprint governing all of a firm's marketing activities, including the implementation and control of those activities.[6] A marketing plan serves a number of purposes:

Analysis
Marketing opportunities/trends
Customers' needs and perceptions: market segmentation and brand positioning
The marketing environment and trends
Competition and competitors' strategies
Company's Strengths, Weaknesses, Opportunities and Threats (SWOT)
Strategy
Determination of core target markets; basis for competing/differential advantage;
    desired product positioning; marketing objectives and sales targets
Implementation
Specification of sales targets and expected results
Specification of plans for marketing mix programmes:
* products
* promotion
* distribution
* service levels
* pricing
Specification of tasks/responsibilities; timing; costs; budgets.
Ongoing work
Monitoring progress

SOURCE: Sally Dibb, Lyndon Simkin and John Bradley, *The Marketing Planning Workbook*
(London: International Thomson Business Press, 1996).

Table 23.2 The core steps of the marketing planning process

1. It offers a "road map" for implementing the firm's strategies and achieving its objectives.
2. It assists in management control and monitoring of implementation of strategy.
3. It informs new participants in the plan of their role and function.
4. It specifies how resources are to be allocated.
5. It stimulates thinking and makes better use of resources.
6. It assigns responsibilities, tasks and timing.
7. It makes participants aware of problems, opportunities and threats.

A company should have a plan for each marketing strategy it develops. Because such plans must be changed as forces in the company and in the environment change, marketing planning is a continuous process.

Organisations use many different formats when devising marketing plans. Plans may be written for strategic business units, product lines, individual products or brands, or specific markets. Most plans share some common ground, however, by including an executive summary; a statement of objectives; background to the market; market analysis and examination of realistic marketing opportunities (a description of environmental forces, customers' needs and market segments and internal capabilities); competitor activity; an outline of marketing strategy target market priorities, differential advantage, brand and product positioning; a statement of expected sales patterns; the detail of marketing mixes required to implement the marketing plan; controls; financial requirements and budgets; and any operational considerations that arise from the marketing plan (see

1. **Management or Executive Summary**
2. **Marketing Objectives**
   a. Company mission statement
   b. Detailed company objectives
   c. Product group goals
3. **Product/Market Background**
   a. Product range and explanation
   b. Market overview and sales summary
4. **Marketing Analyses**
   a. Marketing environment and trends
   b. Customers' needs and segments
   c. Competition and competitors' strategies
   d. Strengths, weaknesses, opportunities, threats analysis
5. **Marketing Strategies**
   a. Core target markets (segments)
   b. Basis for competing/differential advantage
   c. Desired product/brand positioning
6. **Statement of Expected Sales Forecasts and Results**
7. **Marketing Programmes for Implementation**
   a. Marketing mixes
   b. Tasks and responsibilities
8. **Controls and Evaluation: Monitoring of Performance**
9. **Financial Implications/Required Budgets**
   a. Delineation of costs
   b. Expected returns on investment for implementing the marketing plan
10. **Operational Considerations**
    a. Personnel and internal communications
    b. Research and development/production needs
    c. Marketing information system
11. **Appendices**
    a. SWOT analysis details
    b. Background data and information
    c. Marketing research findings

SOURCE: Adapted from Sally Dibb and Lyndon Simkin, *The Marketing Casebook* (London: Routledge, 1994).

Table 23.3 Parts of a marketing plan

Table 23.3). The following sections consider the major parts of a typical marketing plan, as well as the purpose that each part serves.

Management or Executive Summary

The *management summary,* or *executive summary* (often only one or two pages) should be a concise overview of the entire report, including key aims, overall strategies, fundamental conclusions and salient points regarding the suggested marketing programmes (mixes). Not many people read an entire report, tending to dip in here and there, so the management summary should be comprehensive and clear.

Marketing Objectives

Marketing objective A statement of what is to be accomplished through marketing activities

Objectives are for the benefit of the reader, to give perspective to the report. Aims and objectives should be stated briefly but should include reference to the organisation's mission statement (corporate goals), objectives and any fundamental desires for core product groups or brands. This section describes the objectives underlying the plan. A **marketing objective** is a statement of what is to be accomplished through marketing activities. It specifies the results expected from marketing efforts. A marketing objective should be expressed in clear, simple terms so that all marketing personnel understand exactly what they are trying to achieve. It should be written in such a way that its accomplishment can be measured accurately. If a company has an objective of increasing its market share by 12 per cent, the firm should be able to measure changes in its market share accurately. A marketing objective should also indicate the time frame for accomplishing the objective. For example, a company that sets an objective of introducing three new products should state the time period in which this is to be done.

Objectives may be stated in terms of degree of product introduction or innovation, sales volume, profitability per unit or gains in market share. They must also be consistent with the company's overall organisational goals.

Product/Market Background

Product/market background is a necessary section. Not everyone will be fully familiar with the products and their markets. This section "scene sets", helping the readers—for example, a chief executive or advertising manager—to understand the marketing plan.

Marketing Analysis

The *analysis* section is the heart of the marketing planning exercise: if incomplete or highly subjective, the recommendations are likely to be based on an inaccurate view of the market and the company's potential. This section gives a sound foundation to the recommendations and marketing programmes. It includes analyses of the marketing environment, market trends, customers, competitors, competitive positions and competitors' strategies. In Figure 23.3, such analyses helped Kellogg's determine a successful positioning strategy.

The marketing environment section of the marketing plan describes the current state of the marketing environment, including the legal, political, regulatory, technological, competitive, social and economic forces, as well as ethical considerations. It also makes predictions about future directions of those forces.

For example, the retailer Safeway was among the first to respond to consumer concern about the use of artificial fertilisers and pesticides. It offered its customers a choice of either regular fruit and vegetables or organically grown produce at a higher price.

As mentioned in Chapter 2, environmental forces can hamper an organisation in achieving its objectives. This section of the plan also describes the possible impact of these forces on the implementation of the marketing plan. Most marketing plans include extensive analyses of competitive, legal and regulatory forces, perhaps even creating separate sections for these influential forces of the marketing environment. It is important to note here that, because the forces of the marketing environment are dynamic, marketing plans should be reviewed and modified periodically to adjust to change.

Marketing exists to enable an organisation to meet customers' needs properly. This is particularly true in the marketing planning process. The views, needs and expectations of current and potential customers are important as a basis for formal marketing planning. Without such an understanding and analysis of likely changes in customer requirements, it is impossible to safely target those markets

Figure 23.3

Marketing analyses

With careful marketing planning, Kellogg's has established a worthy position in all of its markets.

Source: Courtesy of Kellogg Company.

of most benefit to the organisation's fortunes. It is also impossible to specify a correct marketing mix (or mixes).

The analysis of the marketing environment includes competitive forces and trends. As explained in the previous chapter, however, a meaningful marketing plan and associated programmes for implementation necessitate a prior comprehensive analysis of an organisation's competitive position in its markets and territories, together with an understanding of rival organisation's marketing strategies.

Situation or SWOT Analyses

SWOT analysis Analysis that determines a company's position by examining four factors: Strengths, Weaknesses, Opportunities and Threats

The *SWOT* or a *situational* analysis is an important foundation for any marketing plan, helping to produce realistic and meaningful recommendations. The section in the main body of the report should be kept to a concise overview, with detailed market-by-market or country-by-country SWOTS—and their full explanations—kept to the appendices. Many marketers conduct a **SWOT analysis:** Strengths, Weaknesses, Opportunities, Threats. The first half of this analysis— strengths and weaknesses—examines the company's position, or that of its product, vis-à-vis customers, competitor activity, environmental trends and company resources. The second half of the SWOT takes this review further to examine the opportunities and threats identified and to make recommendations that feed into marketing strategy and the marketing mix. The result of the SWOT analysis should be a thorough understanding of the organisation's status and its standing in its markets.

Marketing Strategies

Strategies should be self-evident if the analyses have been objective and thorough: which target markets are most beneficial to the company, what is to be the differential advantage or competitive edge in these markets and what is the desired product or brand positioning. This strategy statement must be realistic and detailed enough to act upon.

This section of the marketing plan provides a broad overview of the plan for achieving the marketing objectives and, ultimately, the organisational goals. Marketing strategy focuses on defining a target market and developing a marketing mix to gain long run competitive and consumer advantages. There is a degree of overlap between corporate strategy and marketing strategy. Marketing strategy is unique in that it has the responsibility to assess buyer needs and the firm's potential for gaining competitive advantage, both of which ultimately must guide the corporate mission.[7] In other words, marketing strategy guides the firm's direction in relationships between customers and competitors. The bottom line is that a marketing strategy must be consistent with consumer needs, perceptions and beliefs. Thus this section should describe the firm's intended target market and how product, people, promotion, place (distribution) and price will be used to develop a product or brand positioning that will satisfy the needs of members of the target market.

Generic strategies
Strategies that help firms achieve industry success, including cost leadership, differentiation and focus

Michael Porter[8] describes three **generic strategies,** which he maintains help firms to achieve industry success (see Figure 23.4). The first is *cost leadership,* in which low cost producers exploit experience curve effects to achieve market penetration. The key is the development of a low cost structure allowing high returns even when competition is intense. Amstrad and Texas Instruments have both successfully operated as cost leaders. *Differentiation,* the second generic strategy, involves firms developing a product or service that is unique or superior in some way. Products with this quality, whether in terms of features, image or design, often have higher than average prices. Sony stereos and Raleigh bicycles are both examples of products for which a high price can be demanded. Indeed, the price of items like these is part of the products' character and ethos. The final generic strategy is *focus.* Here companies concentrate their efforts on particular segments

Figure 23.4

Generic routes to competitive advantage

Source: *Based on M. E. Porter,* Competitve Strategy: Techniques for Analysing Industries and Competitors *(New York: Free Press, 1980).* From Distance Learning MBA Notes, *Warwick Business School, 1987.*

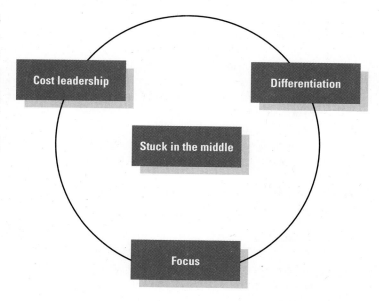

Denmark's Carlsberg Capitalises on Regional Brands

In 1992 there was a revolution in the UK brewing industry as Allied Domecq's Allied Breweries, responsible for such established beer brands as Tetley's Bitter, Castlemaine XXXX and Skol, merged with Carlsberg A/S to form Carlsberg-Tetley. Carlsberg A/S was formed in 1970 with the merger of the Tuborg and Carlsberg breweries, has a turnover of over 15 billion Dkr, employs over 15,000 people and brews in more than 40 countries. With six major breweries around the country, the new Carlsberg-Tetley joint venture certainly had the production capacity to take on the industry to try to become the number one player in the UK. Castlemaine had already become a leading lager brand and with Carlsberg—second only to the Dutch Heineken—the portfolio was even stronger. Indeed, only four beer brands can genuinely claim pan-European coverage: Heineken, Carlsberg, Stella Artois and Guinness.

Unlike rival Whitbread, which now focuses on the leisure industry by operating hotels, entertainment centres and numerous restaurant chains in addition to its beer brands, Carlsberg-Tetley sees itself primarily as a brewer. It has an impressive estate of pubs and inns, plus a wide range of trade and wholesale customers. New product development, an integral aspect of the company's strategy, includes Carlsberg Ice Beer and draught Tetley's Bitter in a can, as well as the revival of the Samuel Allsopp Brewery Company in Burton, which produces small quantities of high quality, speciality beers. The brands are heavily promoted, with sponsorship playing a key role in the promotional mix. Tetley sponsors the England cricket team; Carlsberg has supported Liverpool FC since 1992 and in 1996 co-sponsored the European Football Championships. Carlsberg also is a leading supporter of the Phoenix, Monsters of Rock and Reading music festivals. Skol's Golden Cue has been the premier amateur pool tournament for several years. Various Rugby League and Rugby Union clubs benefit from sponsorship by Carlsberg-Tetley's regional brands.

The regional nature of the company is its core strength and also its key weakness. Rivals Scottish Courage—formed from the merger of Scottish &

of the market. In some instances this is because there are insufficient resources to compete on a larger scale. Focus allows companies like Rolex watches and Porsche in the car market to service particular sub-groups of customers. Although focusing has its attractions in terms of gearing the marketing mix to a quite specific and narrow customer target, the associated risks are high. The danger is that, if attacked head-on, such highly specialised companies may find it difficult to develop alternative competencies. Porter warns against firms becoming "stuck in the middle" of the three strategies. If this happens, he argues, customers may not have a good reason for purchasing a company's products or services.

Expected Results Having highlighted the strategic thrust and intention, it is important to explain the *expected results* and sales volumes to show why the strategies should be followed. These forecasts should be quantified—typically as expected units of sales and possible market shares.

Marketing Programmes for Implementation *Marketing programme recommendations* are the culmination of the various analyses and statements of strategies: exactly what needs to be done, how and why. This is the detailed presentation of the proposed marketing mixes to achieve

Newcastle with Courage—Bass, Whitbread and Guinness have all endeavoured to move away from historical regional markets, with local brands brewed in traditional brewery centres serving only an immediate geographic territory. Whitbread's Boddington's, Heineken and Murphy's are available throughout the UK and beyond. For Carlsberg-Tetley, its regional breweries all produce brands with local heritage and long standing sales records in their own hinterlands: Wrexham Lager in Wrexham; Burton Ale and Ansell's at the Inde Coope site in Burton; Tetley's in Leeds; Walker's and Greenall's in Warrington; Archibald Arrol's and Calder's in Alloa. Several of these breweries now also produce and bottle the truly national brands: Carlsberg, Castlemaine XXXX, Skol, Tuborg and Tetley's.

In Northampton, where it has brewed to its Danish standards since 1972, Carlsberg now produces the complete mix of lagers in the Carlsberg-Tetley line-up: Carlsberg Pilsner, Carlsberg Export, Carlsberg Special Brew, Tuborg Gold, Skol and—for both the British and Danish markets—Carlsberg

Ice. With this relative newcomer, the company has pooled the might of its resources: Carlsberg Ice is produced in Northampton, iced in Wrexham and bottled in Burton.

Carlsberg-Tetley's desire is to retain the traditional regional strengths and extensive distribution based on decades of brewing in the various major brewery centres, while emulating direct rivals such as Whitbread by creating national brands with full marketing and promotional support. This balancing act and support of such an extensive portfolio of well known and regional brands cannot be undertaken without very shrewd marketing planning and prudent use of resources.

SOURCES: The Corporate Communications Office, Carlsberg-Tetley; Tom Wright, "New view at Carlsberg-Tetley", *Campaign*, 15 December 1995, p. 14; "Carlsberg-Tetley creates NPD team to launch 'new age' alcoholic drinks", *Marketing Week*, 27 October 1995, p. 8; George Pitcher, "Breaking the charmed circle", *Marketing Week*, 4 August 1995, p. 25; Emma Hall, "Carlsberg sets off £10 million ad overhaul", *Campaign*, 14 July 1995, p. 1; David Benady and Tom O'Sullivan, "Danes force pace of change at Carlsberg", *Marketing Week*, 7 July 1995, p. 20.

the goals and implement the strategies. In Marketing Insight 23.1, Carlsberg-Tetley has programmes for each of its main brands.

Each market segment to be targeted may require its own, tailor made marketing mix. This section of the marketing plan is of paramount importance, as it gives the specific details of the marketing activity required to implement the marketing plan and to achieve the organisation's strategic goals. Each element of the marketing mix should be discussed in turn, with specific recommendations explained in sufficient detail to enable managers to put them into action. Product, people, pricing, place (distribution) and promotion must all be addressed. Associated tasks should be allocated to personnel and responsibilities for action clearly identified. This is the core output of marketing planning: the detailed plan of action for the business's marketing programmes.

Controls and Evaluation It is essential that *controls* be established along with measures to assess the ongoing implementation of the marketing plan. This section details how the results of the plan will be measured. For example, the results of an advertising campaign designed to increase market share may be measured in terms of increases in sales volume or improved brand recognition and acceptance by consumers. Next, a schedule for comparing the results achieved with the objectives set forth in the marketing plan is developed. Finally, guidelines may be offered outlining who is responsible for monitoring the programme and taking remedial action. Financial measures such as sales volumes, profitability and market shares will be included. "Softer" issues such as brand awareness and customer satisfaction should also be monitored.[9]

Financial Implications/Required Budgets

The full picture may not be known, but an indication of required resources and the *financial implications* must be given. The financial projections and budgets section outlines the returns expected through implementation of the plan. The costs incurred will be weighed against expected revenues. A budget must be prepared to allocate resources in order to accomplish marketing objectives. It should contain estimates of the costs of implementing the plan, including the costs of advertising, sales force training and compensation, development of distribution channels and marketing research.

Operational Considerations

These strategies and marketing programmes may have ramifications for other product groups, sectors or territories, for research and development, for engineering and so on. The *operational implications* must be highlighted, but too much detail may be inappropriate and politically sensitive within the organisation.

Appendices

The main body of the report should be as concise as possible. The document must, though, tell the full story and include evidence and statistics that support the strategies and marketing programmes being recommended. The use of *appendices*—so long as they are fully cross-referenced in the main body of the report—helps to keep the report concise and well focused.

• • • • • • • • • • • • • • • • • •

Forecasting in Marketing

Unfortunately, many organisations' sales and marketing activities are reactions to changes in the marketplace, particularly the actions of competitors, rather than planned and carefully orchestrated activities that anticipate consumer needs and expectations. In such reactive organisations, predictions of future changes in market size and potential tend to be rudimentary or non-existent. Estimations of their own likely sales are often based only on the hunches of managers or on the status quo. The forecasting of market potential and expected sales is problematic but must be undertaken thoroughly and with as much objectivity as marketing intelligence and information permit. This section focuses on market and sales potential and on forecasting techniques.

Market and Sales Potentials

Market potential The total amount of a product that customers will purchase within a specified period of time at a specific level of industry wide marketing activity

Market potential is the total amount of a product that customers will purchase within a specified period at a specific level of industry wide marketing activity. Market potential can be stated in terms of monetary value or units and can refer to a total market or to a market segment. As shown in Figure 23.5, market potential depends on economic, social and other marketing environment factors. Marketing Insight 23.2 discusses the expansion of theme park Alton Towers into new markets: forecasts were required first to help determine market potential.

Figure 23.5

The relationship between market potential, sales potential and sales forecast

SOURCE: *Based on M. E. Porter, Competitve Strategy: Techniques for Analysing Industries and Competitors (New York: Free Press, 1980). From Distance Learning MBA Notes, Warwick Business School, 1987.*

Market potential
- Based on economic, social, and other environmental variables underlying the total demand for a product

Sales potential
- Appraisal of past performance, resources, and future efforts of a firm and projection of the firm's share of sales in the industry

Sales forecast
- Expected sales for future time periods based on a specified level of marketing effort

When analysing market potential, it is important to specify a time frame and to indicate the relevant level of industry marketing activities. One airline determined that in one year 3,300,000 customers travelled to Europe on its aircraft—more customers than any other airline had. Based on this finding, its marketers were able to estimate the market potential for European travel in the following year, taking into account other environmental factors.

Note that marketers have to assume a certain general level of marketing effort in the industry when they estimate market potential. The specific level of marketing effort certainly varies from one firm to another, but the sum of all firms' marketing activities equals industry marketing efforts. A marketing manager must also consider whether and to what extent industry marketing efforts will change. For instance, in estimating the market potential for the spreadsheet software industry, Microsoft must consider changes in marketing efforts by Lotus and other software producers. If marketing managers at Microsoft know that Lotus is planning to introduce a new version of the Lotus 1-2-3 spreadsheet product with a new advertising campaign, this fact will contribute to Microsoft's estimate of the market potential for computer software.

Sales potential is the maximum percentage of market potential that an individual company within an industry can expect to obtain for a specific product or service (see Figure 23.5). Several general factors influence a company's sales potential. First, the market potential places absolute limits on the size of the company's sales potential. Second, the magnitude of industry wide marketing activities has an indirect but definite impact on the company's sales potential. Those activities have a direct bearing on the size of the market potential. When Pizza Hut advertises home delivered pizza, for example, it indirectly promotes pizza in general; its advertisements may, in fact, help sell competitors' home delivered pizza. Third, the intensity and effectiveness of a company's marketing activities relative to those of its competitors affect the size of the company's sales potential. If a company is spending twice as much as any of its competitors on marketing efforts and

Sales potential The maximum percentage of market potential that an individual company can obtain for a specific product or service

Planning for More Than a Day Out—Alton Towers

The theme park is a leisure park consisting of rides and attractions built around a central theme or themes. Walt Disney created the concept in the United States, and the Disney Corporation has since taken the concept to Japan and now to France. The UK theme park industry really took off in the early 1980s. By 1989, 9.5 million visitors had spent £105 million. Current figures estimate that by 2000, 16 million visitors will have spent £250 million in the UK, although the opening of the Paris Disney World and of the Channel Tunnel may have some bearing on these figures. The top five theme parks in the UK are listed below:

	Visitors (millions)
Alton Towers	12.4
Chessington World of Adventure	1.3
Thorpe Park	1.3
Frontierland	1.3
The American Adventure	0.7

Not only do theme parks compete with one another, though geographically many cater for purely local markets, they also compete with a whole range of day trip activities (see table in right column).

Despite the 1990–1993 economic down turn in the UK and the crises in the Middle East and eastern Europe, all economic indicators point to an increase in leisure time and in discretionary income. Alton Towers aims to maintain its market leadership. It continually invests in new rides and facilities and has just opened a £20 million holiday village next to the park (for the leisure and business

	Per Cent of Day Trippers
Museums and galleries	33.0
Historic properties	22.5
Wildlife attractions	10.0
Theme parks	5.5
Gardens	4.0
Other (seaside resorts, holiday centres, etc.)	25.0

conference markets). The strategy is to attract new visitors in the UK and from Continental Europe, while encouraging repeat visits from current users. Key targets are young adults aged 15 to 24, families with children, school parties and, increasingly, the corporate sector for sales incentive schemes and corporate events (AGMs, product launches, sales force parties and so on). Each segment has its own marketing mix and strategy: separate price policies, promotional tactics and even product offerings. From being a day tripper, family orientated park, Alton Towers has monitored demographic changes and competitor activity and is planning to cater for its key segments' differing needs well into the next century, with more hotels, entertainment, under cover rides, events and improved access. No changes to the site are made without researching visitors' needs and market trends or thorough marketing planning.

Sources: British Tourist Authority, 1996; "Visits to tourist attractions", Alton Towers' promotional material, 1996; "CCSB names its Nemesis after roller coaster", *Marketing,* 10 March 1994, p. 6; "Santa's thoughtful sackful", *Professional Engineering,* 7 (21), 1994, p. 9.

if every unit of currency spent is more effective in generating sales, the firm's sales potential will be quite high compared with that of its competitors.

There are two general approaches to measuring sales potential: break down and build up. In the **break down approach,** the marketing manager first develops a general economic forecast for a specific time period. Next, market potential is estimated on the basis of this economic forecast. The company's sales potential is then derived from the general economic forecast and the estimate of market potential.

In the **build up approach,** an analyst begins by estimating how much of a product a potential buyer in a specific geographic area, such as a sales territory, will purchase in a given period. Then the analyst multiplies that amount by the total number of potential buyers in that area. The analyst performs the same calculation for each geographic area in which the firm sells products and then adds the totals for each area to calculate the market potential. To determine the sales potential, the analyst must estimate, by specific levels of marketing activities, the proportion of the total market potential that the company can obtain.

For example, the marketing manager of a regional paper company with three competitors might estimate the company's sales potential for bulk gift wrapping paper using the build up approach. The manager might determine that each of the 66 paper buyers in a single sales territory purchases an average of 10 rolls annually. For that sales territory, then, the market potential is 660 rolls annually. The analyst follows the same procedure for each of the firm's other nine sales territories and then totals the sales potential for each sales territory (see Table 23.4). Assuming that this total market potential is 18,255 rolls of paper (the quantity expected to be sold by all four paper companies), the marketing manager would estimate the company's sales potential by ascertaining that it could sell about 33 per cent of the estimated 18,255 rolls at a certain level of marketing effort. The marketing manager might develop several sales potentials, based on several levels of marketing effort.

Break down approach An approach that derives a company's sales potential from the general economic forecast and the estimate of market potential

Build up approach An approach that measures the sales potential for a product by first calculating its market potential and then estimating what proportion of that potential the company can expect to obtain

Territory	Number of Potential Customers	Estimated Purchases	Total
1	66	10 rolls	660 rolls
2	62	10	620
3	55	5	275
4	28	25	700
5	119	5	595
6	50	20	1,000
7	46	10	460
8	34	15	510
9	63	10	630
10	55	10	550
		Total company sales potential	6,000 rolls

Table 23.4 The sales potential calculations for bulk wrapping paper
(Market potential: 18,255 rolls)

Whether marketers use the break down or the build up approach, they depend heavily on sales estimates. To gain a clearer idea of how these estimates are derived, it is essential to understand sales forecasting.

Developing Sales Forecasts

Sales forecast The amount of a product that the company actually expects to sell during a specific period at a specific level of marketing activities

A **sales forecast** is the amount of a product that the company actually expects to sell during a specific period at a specified level of marketing activities (see Figure 23.5). The sales forecast differs from the sales potential: it concentrates on what the actual sales will be at a certain level of marketing effort, whereas the sales potential assesses what sales are possible at various levels of marketing activities, based on certain environmental conditions. Businesses use the sales forecast for planning, organising, implementing and controlling their activities. The success of numerous activities depends on the accuracy of this forecast. Forecasts help to estimate market attractiveness, monitor performances, allocate resources effectively and efficiently, and gear up production to meet demand. Excess stocks are wasteful and cost money; but production set too low leads to missed sales, and perhaps customer or distributor unease.[10]

A sales forecast must be time specific. Sales projections can be short (one year or less), medium (one to five years) or long (longer than five years). The length of time chosen for the sales forecast depends on the purpose and uses of the forecast, the stability of the market, and the firm's objectives and resources.

To forecast sales, a marketer can choose from a number of forecasting methods. Some of them are arbitrary; others are more scientific, complex and time consuming. A firm's choice of method or methods depends on the costs involved, the type of product, the characteristics of the market, the time span of the forecast, the purposes of the forecast, the stability of the historical sales data, the availability of required information, and the forecasters' expertise and experience.[11] The common forecasting techniques fall into five categories: executive judgement, surveys, time series analysis, correlation methods and market tests.[12]

Executive judgement A way of forecasting sales based on the intuition of one or more executives

Executive Judgement   At times, a company forecasts sales chiefly on the basis of **executive judgement,** which is the intuition of one or more executives. This approach is highly unscientific but expedient and inexpensive. Executive judgement may work reasonably well when product demand is relatively stable and the forecaster has years of market related experience. However, because intuition is swayed most heavily by recent experience, the forecast may be overly optimistic or overly pessimistic. Another drawback to intuition is that the forecaster has only past experience as a guide for deciding where to go in the future.

Surveys A method of questioning customers, sales personnel or experts about their expectations concerning future purchases

Customer forecasting survey A method of asking customers what types and quantities of products they intend to buy during a specific period

Surveys   A second way to forecast sales is to use **surveys,** questioning customers, sales personnel or experts regarding their expectations about future purchases.

Through a **customer forecasting survey,** marketers can ask customers what types and quantities of products they intend to buy during a specific period. This approach may be useful to a business that has relatively few customers. For example, a computer chip producer that markets to less than a hundred computer manufacturers could conduct a customer survey. PepsiCo, though, has millions of customers and cannot feasibly use a customer survey to forecast future sales, unless its sampling is known to reflect the entire market, which is hard to verify.

Customer surveys have several drawbacks. Customers must be able and willing to make accurate estimates of future product requirements. Although industrial buyers can sometimes estimate their anticipated purchases accurately from historical buying data and their own sales forecasts, many cannot make such estimates. In addition, for a variety of reasons, customers may not want to take part in a survey. Occasionally, a few respondents give answers that they know are incorrect, making survey results inaccurate. Moreover, customer surveys reflect buying intentions, not actual purchases. Customers' intentions may not be well formulated, and even when potential purchasers have definite buying intentions, they do not necessarily follow through with them. Finally, customer surveys consume much time and money.

In a **sales force forecasting survey**, members of the firm's sales force are asked to estimate the anticipated sales in their territories for a specified period of time. The forecaster combines these territorial estimates to arrive at a tentative forecast.

A marketer may survey the sales staff for several reasons. The most important one is that the sales staff are closer to customers on a daily basis than other company personnel; therefore they should know more about customers' future product needs. Moreover, when sales representatives assist in developing the forecast, they are more likely to work towards its achievement. Another advantage of this method is that forecasts can be prepared for single territories, for divisions consisting of several territories, for regions made up of multiple divisions and then for the total geographic market. Thus the method readily provides sales forecasts from the smallest geographic sales unit to the largest.

Despite these benefits, a sales force survey has certain limitations. Salespeople can be too optimistic or pessimistic because of recent experiences. In addition, salespeople tend to underestimate the sales potential in their territories when they believe that their sales goals will be determined by their forecasts. They also dislike paperwork because it takes up the time that could be spent selling. If the preparation of a territorial sales forecast is time consuming, the sales staff may not do the job adequately.

Nonetheless, sales force surveys can be effective under certain conditions. If, for instance, the salespeople as a group are accurate—or at least consistent—estimators, the over estimates and under estimates should balance each other out. If the aggregate forecast is consistently over or under actual sales, then the marketer who develops the final forecast can make the necessary adjustments. Assuming that the survey is well administered, the sales force can have the satisfaction of helping to establish reasonable sales goals. It can also be assured that its forecasts are not being used to set sales quotas.

The **Delphi method** is very popular: managers' and sales personnel's views are validated centrally, and the resulting forecasts are returned to those involved for further comment. Participants—such as field managers—make separate, individual forecasts. A central analyst independently aggregates and modifies their forecasts. This revised forecast is returned to the separate participants, who can then amend their forecasts in the context of the consolidated picture. The central analyst then collates the up-dated forecasts to produce the company's overall final forecast. The Delphi technique avoids many weighting and judgemental problems; the median of the group's overall response will tend to be more accurate; and the approach is useful for short, medium and long term forecasts, as well as for new product development, for which there is no historical information on which to base a forecast.

When a company wants an **expert forecasting survey**, it hires experts to help prepare the sales forecast. These experts are usually economists, management consultants, advertising executives, academics or other people outside the firm who have solid experience in a specific market. Drawing on this experience and their analyses of available information about the company and the market, the experts

Sales force forecasting survey A method of asking members of a firm's sales force to estimate the anticipated sales in their territories for a specified period of time

Delphi method A centralised forecasting method that takes into account the views of managers, sales personnel and individual participants; aggregates them; and modifies them

Expert forecasting survey A survey prepared by outside experts such as economists, management consultants, advertising executives or academics prepare and present their forecasts or answer questions regarding a forecast. Using experts is expedient and relatively inexpensive. However, because they work outside the firm, experts may not be as motivated as company personnel to do an effective job.

Time Series Analysis The technique by which the forecaster, using the firm's historical sales data, tries to discover a pattern or patterns in the firm's sales over time is called **time series analysis.** If a pattern is found, it can be used to forecast sales. This forecasting method assumes that the past sales pattern will continue in the future. The accuracy, and thus the usefulness, of time series analysis hinges on the validity of this assumption.

In a time series analysis, a forecaster usually performs four types of analysis: trend, cycle, seasonal and random factor.[13] **Trend analysis** focuses on aggregate sales data, such as a company's annual sales figure, over a period of many years to determine whether annual sales are generally rising, falling or staying about the same. Through **cycle analysis,** a forecaster analyses sales figures (often monthly sales data) over a period of three to five years to ascertain whether sales fluctuate in a consistent, periodic manner. When performing **seasonal analysis,** the analyst studies daily, weekly or monthly sales figures to evaluate the degree to which seasonal factors, such as climate and holiday activities, influence the firm's sales. **Random factor analysis** is an attempt to attribute erratic sales variations to random, non-recurring events, such as a regional power failure, a natural disaster or political unrest in a foreign market. After performing each of these analyses, the forecaster combines the results to develop the sales forecast.

Time series analysis is an effective forecasting method for products with reasonably stable demand, but it is not useful for products with highly erratic demand. Seagram, the importer and producer of spirits and wines, uses several types of time series analysis for forecasting and has found them quite accurate. For example, Seagram's forecasts of industry sales volume have proved correct within ± 1.5 per cent, and the firm's sales forecasts have been accurate within ± 2 per cent.[14] Time series analysis is not always so dependable.

Correlation Methods Like time series analysis, correlation methods are based on historical sales data. When using **correlation methods,**[15] the forecaster attempts to find a relationship between past sales and one or more variables such as population, per capita income or gross national product. To determine whether a correlation exists, the forecaster analyses the statistical relationship between changes in past sales and changes in one or more variables—a technique known as regression analysis.[16] The object of regression analysis is a mathematical formula that accurately describes a relationship between the firm's sales and one or more variables; however, the formula indicates only an association, not a causal relationship. Once an accurate formula has been established, the analyst plugs the necessary information into the formula to derive the sales forecast.

Correlation methods are useful when a precise relationship can be established. However, a forecaster seldom finds a perfect correlation. Furthermore, this method can be used only when the available historical sales data are extensive. Ordinarily, then, correlation techniques are futile for forecasting the sales of new products, or in markets where changes are frequent and extensive.

Market Tests Conducting a **market test** involves making a product available to buyers in one or more test areas and measuring purchases and consumer responses

---

Time series analysis A forecasting technique that uses a firm's historical sales data to discover a pattern or patterns in the firm's sales over time

Trend analysis Analysis that focuses on aggregate sales data over a period of many years to determine whether annual sales are generally rising, falling or constant

Cycle analysis A forecasting technique that analyses a firm's sales figures over a period of three to five years to ascertain whether sales fluctuate in a consistent, periodic manner

Seasonal analysis The study of daily, weekly or monthly sales figures to evaluate the degree to which seasonal factors influence the firm's sales

Random factor analysis An attempt to attribute erratic sales variations to random, non-recurring events

Correlation methods Attempts to find a relationship between past sales and one or more variables such as population, per capita income or gross national product

Market test An experiment in which a product is made available to buyers in one or more test areas, after which purchases and consumer responses to its distribution, promotion and price are measured to distribution, promotion and price. Even though test areas are often cities with populations of 200,000 to 500,000, test sites can be larger metropolitan areas or towns with populations of 50,000 to 200,000, or ITV regions. A market test provides information about consumers' actual purchases rather than about their intended purchases. In addition, purchase volume can be evaluated in relation to the intensity of other marketing activities—advertising, in-store promotions, pricing, packaging, distribution and the like. On the basis of customer response in test areas, forecasters can estimate product sales for larger geographic units. For example, Cadbury's Wispa first appeared in the Tyne Tees area of North East England. Sales showed management that the company had to build more production capacity to cope with a national roll out of the brand and full launch.

Because it does not require historical sales data, a market test is an effective tool for forecasting the sales of new products or the sales of existing products in new geographic areas. The test gives the forecaster information about customers' real actions rather than intended or estimated behaviour. A market test also gives a marketer an opportunity to test various elements of the marketing mix. But these tests are often time consuming and expensive. In addition, a marketer cannot be certain that the consumer response during a market test represents the total market response or that such a response will continue in the future.

Using Multiple Forecasting Methods

Although some businesses depend on a single sales forecasting method, most firms use several techniques. A company is sometimes forced to use several methods when it markets diverse product lines, but even for a single product line several forecasts may be needed, especially when the product is sold in different market segments. Thus a producer of car tyres may rely on one technique to forecast tyre sales for new cars and on another to forecast the sales of replacement tyres. Variation in the length of the needed forecasts may call for several forecast methods. A firm that employs one method for a short range forecast may find it inappropriate for long range forecasting. Sometimes a marketer verifies the results of one method by using one or several other methods and comparing results.[17]

• • • • • • • • • • • • • • • • • • •

The Marketing Audit

Marketing audit A systematic examination of the marketing group's objectives, strategies, organisation and performance

A **marketing audit** is a systematic examination of the marketing group's objectives, strategies, organisation and performance. Its primary purpose is to identify weaknesses in ongoing marketing operations and plan the necessary improvements to correct these weaknesses. The marketing audit does not concern itself with the firm's marketing position; that is the purpose of the firm's marketing plan. Rather, the marketing audit evaluates how effectively the marketing organisation performed its assigned functions.[18]

Like an accounting or financial audit, a marketing audit should be conducted regularly instead of just when performance control mechanisms show that the system is out of control. The marketing audit is not a control process to be used only during a crisis, although a business in trouble may use it to isolate problems and generate solutions.

A marketing audit may be specific and focus on one or a few marketing activities, or it may be comprehensive and encompass all of a company's marketing activities. Table 23.5 lists many possible dimensions of a marketing audit. An audit might deal with only a few of these areas, or it might include them all. Its

Part I. The Marketing Environment Audit

Macroenvironment

A. Economic-Demographic
1. What does the company expect in the way of inflation, material shortages, unemployment and credit availability in the short run, intermediate run and long run?
2. What effect will forecast trends in the size, age distribution and regional distribution of population have on the business?

B. Technological
1. What major changes are occurring in product technology? In process technology?
2. What are the major generic substitutes that might replace this product?

C. Political-Legal
1. What laws are being proposed that may affect marketing strategy and tactics?
2. What national and local government actions should be watched? What is happening with pollution control, equal opportunity employment, product safety, advertising, price controls and so on that is relevant to marketing planning?

D. Cultural
1. What attitude is the public taking towards business and the types of product produced by the company?
2. What changes in consumer lifestyles and values have a bearing on the company's target markets and marketing methods?

E. Ecological
1. Will the cost and availability of natural resources directly affect the company?
2. Are there public concerns about the company's role in pollution and conservation? If so, what is the company's reaction?

Task Environment

A. Markets
1. What is happening to market size, growth, geographical distribution and profits?
2. What are the major market segments and their expected rates of growth? Which are high opportunity and low opportunity segments?

B. Customers
1. How do current customers and prospects judge the company and its competitors on reputation, product quality, service, sales force and price?
2. How do different classes of customers make their buying decisions?
3. What evolving needs and satisfactions are the buyers in this market seeking?

C. Competitors
1. Who are the major competitors? What are the objectives and strategy of each major competitor? What are their strengths and weaknesses? What are the sizes and trends in market shares?
2. What trends can be foreseen in future competition and substitutes for this product?

D. Distribution and Dealers
1. What are the main trade channels bringing products to customers?
2. What are the efficiency levels and growth potentials of the different trade channels?

E. Suppliers
1. What is the outlook for the availability of key resources used in production?
2. What trends are occurring among suppliers in their patterns of selling?

F. Facilitators and Marketing Firms
1. What is the outlook for the cost and availability of transport services?
2. What is the outlook for the cost and availability of warehousing facilities?
3. What is the outlook for the cost and availability of financial resources?
4. How effectively is the advertising agency performing? What trends are occurring in advertising agency services?

G. Publics
1. Where are the opportunity areas or problems for the company?
2. How effectively is the company dealing with publics?

Part II. Marketing Strategy Audit

A. Business Mission
1. Is the business mission clearly focused with marketing terms and is it attainable?

(Continues)

Table 23.5 Dimensions of a marketing audit

B. Marketing Objectives and Goals

1. Are the corporate objectives clearly stated? Do they lead logically to the marketing objectives?
2. Are the marketing objectives stated clearly enough to guide marketing planning and subsequent performance measurement?
3. Are the marketing objectives appropriate, given the company's competitive position, resources and opportunities? Is the appropriate strategic objective to build, hold, harvest or terminate this business?

C. Strategy

1. What is the core marketing strategy for achieving the objectives? Is it sound?
2. Are the resources budgeted to accomplish the marketing objectives inadequate, adequate or excessive?
3. Are the marketing resources allocated optimally to prime market segment, territories and products?
4. Are the marketing resources allocated optimally to the major elements of the marketing mix, i.e. product quality, service, sales force, advertising, promotion and distribution?

Part III. Marketing Organisation Audit

A. Formal Structure

1. Is there a high level marketing manager with adequate authority and responsibility over those company activities that affect customer satisfaction?
2. Are the marketing responsibilities optimally structured along functional, product, end use and territorial lines?

B. Functional Efficiency

1. Are there good communications and working relations between marketing and sales?
2. Is the product management system working effectively? Are the product managers able to plan profits or only sales volume?
3. Are there any groups in marketing that need more training, motivation, supervision or evaluation?

C. Interface Efficiency

1. Are there any problems between marketing and manufacturing, research and development, purchasing, finance, accounting and legal departments that need attention?

Part IV. Marketing Systems Audit

A. Marketing Information System

1. Is the marketing intelligence system producing accurate, sufficient and timely information about developments in the marketplace?
2. Is marketing research being adequately used by company decision-makers?

B. Marketing Planning System

1. Is the marketing planning system well conceived and effective?
2. Is sales forecasting and measurement of market potential soundly carried out?
3. Are sales quotas set on a proper basis?

C. Marketing Control System

1. Are the control procedures (monthly, quarterly, etc.) adequate to ensure that the annual plan's objectives are being achieved?
2. Is provision made to analyse periodically the profitability of different products, markets, territories and channels of distribution?
3. Is provision made to examine and validate periodically various marketing costs?

D. New Product Development System

1. Is the company well organised to gather, generate and screen new product ideas?
2. Does the company do adequate concept research and business analysis before investing heavily in a new idea?
3. Does the company carry out adequate product and market testing before launching a new product?

Part V. Marketing-Productivity Audit

A. Profitability Analysis

1. What is the profitability of the company's different products, served markets, territories and channels of distribution?
2. Should the company enter, expand, contract or withdraw from any business segments, and what would be the short and long run profit consequences?

B. Cost Effective Analysis

1. Do any marketing activities seem to have excessive costs? Are these costs valid? Can cost reducing steps be taken?

(Continues)

Table 23.5 Dimensions of a marketing audit (cont.)

Part VI.   Marketing Function Audits

A. Products

1. What are the product line objectives? Are these objectives sound? Is the current product line meeting these objectives?
2. Are there particular products that should be phased out?
3. Are there new products that are worth adding?
4. Are any products able to benefit from quality, feature or style improvements?

B. Price

1. What are the pricing objectives, policies, strategies and procedures? Are prices set on sound cost, demand and competitive criteria?
2. Do the customers see the company's prices as being in or out of line with the perceived value of its products?
3. Does the company use price promotions effectively?

C. Distribution

1. What are the distribution objectives and strategies?
2. Is there adequate market coverage and service?
3. How effective are the following channel members: distributors, manufacturers' reps, brokers, agents and so on?
4. Should the company consider changing its distribution channels?

D. Advertising, Sales Promotion and Publicity

1. What are the organisation's advertising objectives? Are they sound?

2. Is the right amount being spent on advertising? How is the budget determined?
3. Are the ad themes and copy effective? What do customers and the public think about the advertising?
4. Are the advertising media well chosen?
5. Is the internal advertising staff adequate?
6. Is the sales promotion budget adequate? Is there effective and sufficient use of sales promotion tools, such as samples, coupons, displays and sales contests?
7. Is the publicity budget adequate? Is the public relations staff competent and creative?

E. Sales Force

1. What are the organisation's sales force objectives?
2. Is the sales force large enough to accomplish the company's objectives?
3. Is the sales force organised along the proper principle(s) of specialisation (territory, market, product)? Are there enough (or too many) sales managers to guide the field sales reps?
4. Does the sales compensation level and structure provide adequate incentive and reward?
5. Does the sales force show high morale, ability and effort?
6. Are the procedures for setting quotas and evaluating performance adequate?
7. How does the company's sales force compare with the sales forces of competitors?

SOURCE: Philip Kotler, *Marketing Management: Analysis, Planning, and Control*, 6th edn. (Englewood Cliffs, N.J.: Prentice-Hall, 1988), pp. 748-751. Used by permission.

Table 23.5 Dimensions of a marketing audit (cont.)

scope depends on the costs involved, the target markets served, the structure of the marketing mix and environmental conditions. The results of the audit can be used to re-allocate marketing effort and to re-examine marketing opportunities. For example, after the rise in consumer interest in buying unleaded petrol during the 1980s, the oil companies realised that many customers were still using leaded fuel, because the engine performance of their cars was better. Launching the new "super" unleaded brands late in the 1980s helped to counter these problems.

The marketing audit should aid evaluation by doing the following:

1. Describing current activities and results to sales, costs, prices, profits and other performance feedback.
2. Gathering information about customers, competition and environmental developments that may affect the marketing strategy.

3. Exploring opportunities and alternatives for improving the marketing strategy.
4. Providing an overall database to be used in evaluating the attainment of organisational goals and marketing objectives.

Marketing audits can be performed internally or externally. An internal auditor may be a top level marketing executive, a company wide auditing committee or a manager from another office or of another function. Although it is more expensive, an audit by outside consultants is usually more effective; external auditors have more objectivity, more time for the audit and greater experience.

There is no single set of procedures for all marketing audits. However, firms should adhere to several general guidelines. Audits are often based on a series of questionnaires administered to the firm's personnel. These questionnaires should be developed carefully to ensure that the audit focuses on the right issues. Auditors should develop and follow a step-by-step plan to guarantee that the audit is systematic. When interviewing company personnel, the auditors should strive to talk to a diverse group of people from many parts of the company. The auditor should become familiar with the product line, meet staff from headquarters, visit field organisations, interview customers, interview competitors and analyse information for a report on the marketing environment.[19] The audit framework and associated questionnaires should remain consistent over time, so that improvements and problems can be noted between audits.

To achieve adequate support, the auditors normally focus first on the firm's top management and then move down through the organisational hierarchy. The auditor looks for different points of view within various departments of the organisation or a mismatch between the customers' and the company's perception of the product as signs of trouble in an organisation.[20] The results of the audit should be reported in a comprehensive written document, which should include recommendations that will increase marketing productivity and determine the company's general direction.

The marketing audit lets an organisation change tactics or alter day-to-day activities as problems arise. For example, marketing auditors often wonder whether a change in budgeted sales activity is caused by general market conditions or is due to a change in the firm's market share.

Although the concept of auditing implies an official examination of marketing activities, many organisations audit their marketing activities informally. Any attempt to verify operating results and to compare them with standards can be considered an auditing activity. Many smaller firms probably would not use the word *audit,* but they do perform auditing activities.

Several problems may arise in an audit of marketing activities. Marketing audits can be expensive in time and money. Selecting the auditors may be difficult because objective, qualified personnel may not be available. Marketing audits can also be extremely disruptive because employees sometimes fear comprehensive evaluations, especially by outsiders. The benefits, though, are significant. The audit reveals successes and also problem areas that need to be addressed.

●●●●●●●●●●●●●●●●●

Summary

● A strategic market plan is an outline of the methods and resources required to achieve the organisation's goals within a specific target market; it takes into account all the functional areas of a business unit that must be co-ordinated. The process of strategic market planning (see Chapter 22) yields a marketing strategy that is the framework for a marketing plan. A marketing plan includes the framework and entire set of activities to be performed; it is the written document or blueprint for implementing and controlling an organisation's marketing activities.

● *Market planning* is a systematic process that involves assessing marketing opportunities and resources, determining marketing objectives and developing a full plan for implementation and control. A core output of marketing planning is the *marketing plan* document or blueprint containing the details of a company's marketing activity. The marketing planning process involves (1) analysing the marketplace, (2) modifying the recommended marketing strategy accordingly and (3) developing detailed marketing mix programmes designed to implement the specified strategy.

● The elements analysed include the marketing environment and market trends, customers, competitors and competitive strategies, plus the company's capabilities to respond to marketing opportunities. A *SWOT analysis* is a common component of most businesses' marketing plans. The strategy recommendations within the marketing plan examine target market priorities, the basis for competing and differential advantage, desired brand and product positionings, *marketing objectives* and sales expectations. It is important to have a clearly defined *generic strategy:* a cost emphasis, focus or differentiation. The marketing programmes implement the recommended marketing strategy. They include not only all the ingredients of the marketing mix but also the allocation of schedules, responsibilities, personnel and budgets, plus the monitoring of ongoing performance. In this context, marketing planning acts as a bridge between marketing analysis, marketing strategy and marketing management.

The *marketing planning cycle* is a never ending process of revision and modification. Most companies up-date their plans annually, typically with a three year focus. There are *short, medium* and *long range plans* available, however.

● Whether using a total market or a market segmentation approach, a marketer must be able to measure the sales potential of the target market or markets. *Market potential* is the total amount of a product that customers will purchase within a specific period at a specific level of industry wide marketing activity. *Sales potential* is the maximum percentage of market potential that an individual firm within an industry can expect to obtain for a specific product. There are two general approaches to measuring sales potential: *break down* and *build up*. A *sales forecast* is the amount of a product that the company actually expects to sell during a specific period of time and at a specified level of marketing activities. Several methods are used to forecast sales: *executive judgement, surveys* (*customer, sales force* and *expert forecasting surveys,* including the *Delphi method*), *time series analysis* (*trend analysis, cycle analysis, seasonal analysis, random factor analysis*), *correlation methods* and *market tests*. Although some businesses may rely on a single sales forecasting method, most organisations employ several different techniques.

● To control marketing strategies, it is sometimes necessary to audit marketing activities. A *marketing audit* is a systematic examination of the marketing group's objectives, strategies, organisation and performance. A marketing audit attempts to identify what a marketing unit is doing, to evaluate the effectiveness of these activities and to recommend future marketing activities.

● ● ● ● ● ● ● ● ● ● ● ● ● ● ● ● ● ●

Important Terms

Marketing planning	Sales potential	Expert forecasting survey
Marketing plan	Break down approach	Time series analysis
Marketing planning cycle	Build up approach	Trend analysis
Short range plans	Sales forecast	Cycle analysis
Medium range plans	Executive judgement	Seasonal analysis
Long range plans	Surveys	Random factor analysis
Marketing objective	Customer forecasting survey	Correlation methods
SWOT analysis	Sales force forecasting survey	Market test
Generic strategies	Delphi method	Marketing audit
Market potential		

Discussion and Review Questions

1. What is marketing planning? How does it help companies better target their marketplaces?
2. In what ways do marketing environmental forces affect marketing planning? Give some examples.
3. What is a SWOT analysis? How does it lead to an understanding of realistic market opportunities?
4. What issues *must* be thoroughly analysed during marketing planning prior to the formulation of a marketing programme?
5. Why is it important to determine a differential advantage?
6. Porter's generic strategies warn against being "stuck in the middle". Why?
7. Why is a marketer concerned about sales potential when trying to find a target market?
8. What is a sales forecast, and why is it important?
9. What is the Delphi method to forecasting? Why is it a popular tool?
10. Why would a company use a marketing audit?

Recommended Readings

S. Dibb, L. Simkin and J. Bradley, *The Marketing Planning Workbook* (London: International Thomson Business Press, 1996).

M. McDonald, *Marketing Plans: How to Prepare Them: How to Use Them* (Oxford: Butterworth-Heinemann, 1995).

J. Saunders, ed. "Exploring marketing planning", special issues, *Journal of Marketing Management*, vol. 12, nos. 1–3, 1996).

L. Simkin, "Addressing organisational pre-requisites in marketing planning", *Marketing Intelligence and Planning*, vol. 14, no. 5, 1996, pp. 39–46.

L. Simkin, "People and processes in marketing planning: the benefits of controlling implementation", *Journal of Marketing Management*, vol. 12, no. 5, 1996, pp. 375–390.

Cases

23.1 Cellular Phones—The Market Takes Off for Challenger Orange

When Rover Cars launched its new 800 series in 1986 the company offered buyers of its flagship £20,000 Vitesse or Stirling models either a cash discount or a free fixed car phone worth over £600. To many consumers, possessing such a gimmicky gadget was unappealing and unnecessary—very few people had such "showy" items. Today in the UK there are over 5 million users of mobile phones. The initial take-up was by business people and sales representatives who needed to be in regular contact with their secretaries and colleagues. The second wave came from trades people often away from their own phones—plumbers, decorators, service engineers—who needed to return calls quickly in order to win new business. Currently, major promotional campaigns are targeting the "potentially vulnerable": single mothers, those in the caring sector

who travel around late at night to unfamiliar addresses and lone women travellers. With ever more flexible tariffs, the appeal of mobile phones has broadened dramatically. Technology improvements have simultaneously enabled better reception of signals, wider geographical coverage and even the ability to take a mobile phone out of the country and still make and receive calls—witness the BA departure lounge at Charles de Gaulle Airport in Paris at 5:00 P.M. each day!

Globally, 9 million new subscribers to mobile telephones are now being added every six months, making it the fastest growing sector within the rapidly growing telecommunications industry. It is estimated that 40 per cent of all mobile phones worldwide are connected to cellular networks delivered by Sweden's Ericsson. In the UK, four organisations dominate the cellular telephone industry: Cellnet, One-2-One, Orange and Vodaphone. Currently One-2-One and Orange have just over half a million subscribers each, with Cellnet and leader Vodaphone topping the 2 million mark. It is predicted that the market will grow from its 5.5 million subscribers to around 19 million by the year 2004, with One-2-One having 15 per cent of the market, Orange 25 per cent, and Cellnet and Vodaphone 30 per cent each. In Sweden, where there is the highest penetration of mobile phones (11 per cent of the population, compared with 8.5 per cent in the UK) there are no signs of saturation, and an incredible 90 per cent penetration is expected by the year 2000.

Orange, the newcomer, is a joint venture between Hutchison Telecom and British Aerospace. It is successfully challenging Cellnet and Vodaphone based on a clearly developed marketing strategy with a long term focus:

- access to adequate start up financial resources (£950m) provided by its parent companies, with no initial expectation of any trading revenues until the network infrastructure was created
- good relations with suppliers: a £1.2 billion debt financing programme from Orange's bankers to facilitate the building of a network and dedicated terminals for Orange provided by Ericsson and Nokia
- a long term perspective with no profit targets in the first five years of operation: no short term "City" view forcing cost cutting and price driven sales drives
- the development of distinctive branding through an innovative and eye catching £10 million launch mass media advertising campaign, creating a significant and almost immediate lead in brand awareness over rivals Cellnet and Vodaphone
- lower entry prices for terminals and services compared with key competitors

- adoption of superior product technology based on the PCN standard, allowing greater channel capacity and transmission quality
- innovative service packages, with bespoke and creative billing options

Cellnet and Vodaphone had been the Coca-Cola and PepsiCo of the cellular phone market. Virgin Cola has established a significant market presence in only a year of operation in the cola wars, but in the cellular phone market a new entrant, Orange, has not only established a foothold but, through carefully constructed marketing programmes and well defined strategy, is challenging for market leadership. In 1996 Orange successfully floated on the stock market as an independent company with a capitalisation approaching £2.8 billion. A differential advantage through technology and service packages, clear customer targeting and novel branding have given Orange a healthy start in a highly competitive marketplace. Instead of Cellnet and Vodaphone, the real threat to Orange may well prove to be the much vaunted new technologies with which global operators will set up satellite networks around the earth to offer truly mobile phones based on a whole new technology.

SOURCE: R. Olins, "Mobile phone war hots up", *Sunday Times,* 19 November 1995; T. Jackson, "New kids on the telephony block", *Financial Times,* 15 May 1995; T. Grey and C. Price, "Orange aims to float in March", *Financial Times,* 12 January 1996; Andrew Pickford, Combitech Traffic Systems; Russ Jones, BIP.

Questions for Discussion

1. How has targeting specific groups of customers led to the growth of this market?
2. What must Orange do to create a differential advantage over its rivals?
3. How will marketing planning help Cellnet or Vodaphone to fight off Orange?

23.2 Binney & Smith Brightens Marketing Strategy for Crayola Crayons

While Nintendo games and MTV music videos have captured children's attention, Crayola Crayons have languished on store shelves. Now Binney & Smith, a division of Hallmark Cards, is fighting back with a new marketing strategy for the venerable crayon. The company launched a huge MTV-style campaign, which targets children rather than parents.

Traditionally Binney & Smith targeted Crayola Crayons at parents, using educational themes. But after recognising that children's purchasing power and influence on family purchases have increased in recent years, the company decided to change the crayon's image as an old fashioned toy to an exciting way for kids and teens to express themselves. To this end, the company developed new advertisements featuring rock music, "hip" kids and soaring colours for showing during television programmes seen by children. In-store videos provided to toy stores and retailers of children's clothing followed up the theme.

After marketing research indicated that children prefer brighter colours, the company decided to retire blue grey, green blue, lemon yellow, maize, orange red, orange yellow, raw umber and violet blue to the Crayola Hall of Fame and to replace them with the more vivid cerulean, dandelion, fuchsia, jungle green, royal purple, teal blue, vivid tangerine and wild strawberry. This decision was controversial, however. The company was inundated with phone calls, letters and petitions from people who missed the old colours. Protesters marched on the company, carrying placards with slogans like "We hate the new 8!" and "They call it a retirement, I call it a burial." RUMPS, the Raw Umber and Maize Preservation Society, finally got its way. In late 1991 the company issued a commemorative tin containing the 64 crayon box and a special pack of the eight colours dropped one year earlier. Even though kids liked the new colours, parents liked the old eight colours. The company issued a statement saying that the old colours were revived partly because the company is in the business of providing what the consumer wants.

Along with new advertisements and colours, the company introduced ColourWorks, a line of erasable crayon sticks and retractable coloured pencils and pens. In 1991 the company brought out Silver Swirls, crayons that have twirls of silver mixed in with the wax colours. Pictures coloured with Silver Swirls can be buffed to a high sheen with tissue. The new line was not only tested by children but also named by them. The company has licensed its brand to Concord Cameras for a range of brightly coloured single use cameras aimed at children under 12. Several software companies have recognised the Crayola brand appeal: Micrografx offers the Crayola Amazing Art Adventure and the Crayola Art Studio—software games that encourage art and design a long way from the traditional wax crayon. Clearly, the Crayola brand is still very popular with children, parents and toy stores.

Despite its new focus on children, Binney & Smith did not forget who actually holds the purse strings; the company continues to target parents with advertisements in women's and parents' magazines. The company hopes that its new strategy will lead more children to reach for Crayola Crayons instead of the Nintendo joystick.

So far, the revised strategy for Crayola seems to be working. Sales are up; shelf space in toy stores could not be better, despite stiff competition from a host of rival products and toys; and deals with airlines, fast food outlets and restaurant chains to provide "time filler" packs for children have boosted brand awareness.

SOURCES: Ellen Neuborne, "Crayola crayons have old colors back", *USA Today*, 2 October 1991, p. 2B; Ken Riddle, "Crayola draws brighter lines in the market", *Marketing*, 21 January 1991, p. 4; Beefeater Restaurants, 1993; Toys "R" Us, Leicester, 1996; Loretta Roach, "Single use explosion", *Discount Merchandiser*, September 1995, pp. 28–30; Robyn Parets, "Children's edutainment titles vie for shelf space", *Discount Store News*, 19 June 1995, pp. C6–C9; Binney & Smith UK, 1996.

Questions for Discussion

1. Why did Binney & Smith have to up-date its marketing of Crayola and change its strategy?
2. What are Crayola's target audiences? Why did the company need to approach them differently?
3. Why has the company negotiated with airlines and restaurants to offer give-aways?

IMPLEMENTING STRATEGIES AND MEASURING PERFORMANCE

"The real strategic problem in marketing is not strategy, it is managing implementation and change."

Nigel Piercy
Cardiff Business School

OBJECTIVES

- To understand how the marketing unit fits into a company's organisational structure
- To become familiar with the ways of organising a marketing unit
- To examine several issues relating to the implementation of marketing strategies
- To understand the control processes used in managing marketing strategies
- To learn how cost and sales analyses can be used to evaluate the performance of marketing strategies

To the purist camera buff or photographic enthusiast, the growth in single use cameras is an unwelcome phenomenon. By the mid-1990s, over one million single use, "point and shoot", cheap and relatively disposable cameras were being sold each year. 3M introduced its second generation, Slimline. Kodak continued to introduce more and more single use cameras: the Kodak Wedding camera is tipped to be the largest growing member of the Kodak range, and by specifically targeting such a large market—weddings—the company expects the overall market to more than double in size. The Kodak Fun Saver Pocket cameras are even smaller and cheaper, aimed at children. Concord Camera has gone one further. Licensing the Crayola brand name—famous for crayons and colouring pens—from Hallmark, Concord's single use cameras are very colourfully decorated and are designed to appeal to children under 12. Kalimar has linked up with the Barbie doll, producing Barbie-branded single use cameras aimed at girls aged 5 to 15. Japanese giant Fuji is also active in the single use market, with its Quick Snap range aimed at the holiday season and tourists.

For the manufacturers, the purpose of the single use camera is to encourage people hesitant to use cameras or those unlikely to purchase an expensive Pentax or Ricoh model to enter the market. By targeting youngsters, the camera and film manufacturers are investing in the potential heavy users of the future—the next generation of snap-happy consumers, who make up the bulk of film sales and income from film processing. Companies such as 3M and Kodak have devoted a great deal of time, thought and resources to developing all facets of the photographic market.

It is important for companies to have developed shrewd target market strategies such as those deployed in the Crayola or Barbie tie-ins, and it is essential for them to have clearly identified a customer need and to be able to satisfy it. In marketing terms, however, that is not the complete picture. 3M and Kodak have not only developed carefully honed customer propositions and marketing strategies. In addition, they have devoted a great deal of time and resources to managing the implementation of their determined marketing strategies, recognising that without thorough and careful planning inside their businesses, it is unlikely that their chosen marketing strategies will ever be effectively or successfully actioned.

In many cases markets have been analysed, strategies developed and marketing mix programmes formulated—only to be made redundant by inadequate internal resources, ineffective managerial processes, poor communications, low morale or poor understanding. Implementation is just as important as marketing strategy. Implementation must itself be well planned, carefully controlled and effectively managed to ensure that a business's recommended strategy is put into practice and to facilitate the smooth instigation of the required marketing mix programmes. Both Kodak and 3M expend a significant amount of effort managing the implementation of their marketing activities. ■

SOURCES: Loretta Roach, "Single use explosion", *Discount Merchandiser,* September 1995, pp. 28–30; Boots UK, 1996; Kodak UK, 1996; Pete Hisey, "Photo industry focuses on kids", *Discount Store News,* 20 March 1995, p. 47; Childrensworld store catalogue, 1996.

T his chapter focuses first on the marketing unit's position in the organisation and the ways the unit itself can be organised. It goes on to examine several issues regarding the implementation of marketing strategies, particularly *internal marketing* and *total quality management.* The next section considers the basic components of the process of control. Finally, the chapter discusses the use of cost and sales analyses to evaluate the effectiveness of marketing strategies and to measure the firm's performance.

● ● ● ● ● ● ● ● ● ● ● ● ● ● ● ● ● ●

Organising Marketing Activities

The structure and relationships of a marketing unit, including lines of authority and responsibility that connect and co-ordinate individuals, strongly affect marketing activities. This section first looks at the place of marketing within an organisation and examines the major alternatives available for organising a marketing unit. Then it shows how marketing activities can be structured to fit into an organisation so as to contribute to the accomplishment of overall objectives.

The Place of Marketing in an Organisation

Because the marketing environment is so dynamic, the position of the marketing unit within the organisation has risen during the past 25 years. Companies that truly adopt the marketing concept develop a distinct organisational culture— a culture based on a shared set of beliefs that make the customers' needs the pivotal point of a company's decisions about strategy and operations.[1] Instead of developing products in a vacuum and then trying to persuade consumers to buy them, companies using the marketing concept begin with an orientation towards their customers' needs and desires. If the marketing concept serves as a guiding philosophy, the marketing unit will be closely co-ordinated with other functional areas, such as production, finance and personnel. Figure 24.1 shows the organisation of a marketing unit by types of customers. This form of internal organisation works well for organisations having several groups of customers whose needs differ significantly.

Marketing must interact with other functional departments in a number of key areas. It needs to work with manufacturing in determining the volume and variety of the company's products. Those in charge of production rely on marketers for accurate sales forecasts. Research and development departments depend heavily on information gathered by marketers about product features and benefits desired by consumers, as well as details of complaints concerning current products. Decisions made by the physical distribution department hinge on information about the urgency of delivery schedules and cost/service trade-offs.[2] For example, at Honda, all departments have worked together for a long time, whereas at Chrysler the manufacturing group was not even on the product design committee until 1981. With rapid market segmentation forcing companies to design cars even faster than in the past, co-ordination between engineering, production, marketing and finance is essential.[3]

Marketing orientated organisation A company that concentrates on discovering what buyers want and providing it in a way that lets the company achieve its objectives

A **marketing orientated organisation** concentrates on discovering what buyers want and providing it in a way that lets the company achieve its objectives. Such a company has an organisational culture that effectively and efficiently produces a sustainable competitive advantage. It focuses on customer analysis, competitor analysis and the integration of the firm's resources to provide customer value and satisfaction, as well as long term profits.[4] As Figure 24.2 shows, the marketing director's position is at the same level as those of the financial, production and personnel directors. Thus the marketing director takes part in top level decision-making. Note, too, that the marketing director is responsible for a variety of activities. Some of them—sales forecasting and supervision and product planning—would be under the jurisdiction of other functional managers in production or sales orientated firms.

Both the links between marketing and other functional areas (such as production, finance and personnel) and the importance of marketing to management evolve from the organisation's basic orientation. Marketing encompasses the greatest number of business functions and occupies an important position when a company is marketing orientated; it has a limited role when the company views the role of marketing as simply selling products that it makes. However, a marketing orientation is not achieved simply by re-drawing the organisational chart; management must also adopt and use the marketing orientation as a management philosophy.

Centralised organisation A company in which top level managers delegate very little authority to the lower levels of the organisation

Centralisation Versus Decentralisation

The organisational structure that a company uses to connect and co-ordinate various activities affects its success. Basic decisions relate to how various participants in the company will work together to make important decisions, as well as to co-ordinate, implement and control activities. Top managers create corporate strategies and co-ordinate lower levels. A **centralised organisation** is one in which the top level managers delegate very little authority to lower levels of the organisation. In a **decentralised organisation**, decision-making authority is delegated as far down the chain of command as possible. The decision to centralise or decentralise directly affects marketing in the organisation.

Decentralised organisation A company in which authority is delegated as far down the chain of command as possible

Figure 24.1
Organising the marketing
unit

Note: In some organisations, each marketing manager would have responsibility for a product group rather than a customer group, and would be termed a product manager.

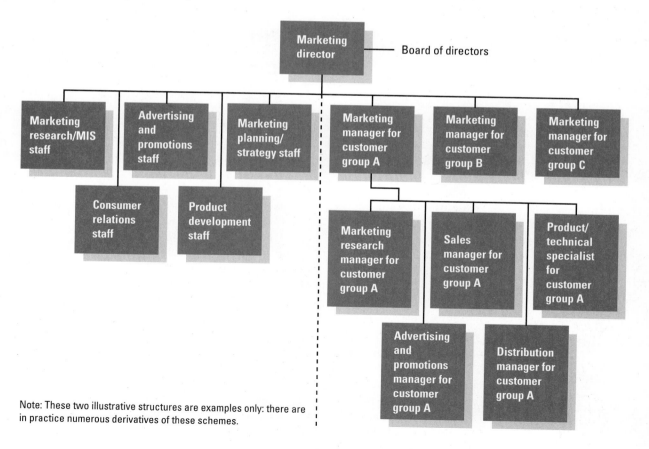

Note: These two illustrative structures are examples only: there are in practice numerous derivatives of these schemes.

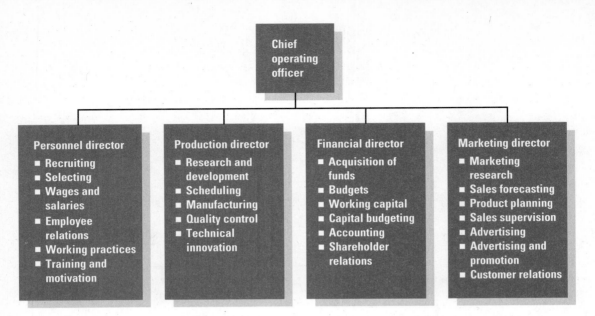

Figure 24.2 Organisational chart of a marketing orientated company

In a centralised organisation, major marketing decisions originate with top management and are transmitted to lower levels of management. A decentralised structure gives marketing managers more opportunity for making key strategic decisions. IBM has adopted a decentralised management structure so that its marketing managers have a chance to customise strategies for customers. On the other hand, Hewlett-Packard and 3M have become more centralised by consolidating functions or eliminating divisional managers.[5] Although decentralising may foster innovation and a greater responsiveness to customers, a decentralised company may be inefficient or appear to have a blurred marketing strategy when dealing with larger customers. A centralised organisation avoids confusion among the marketing staff, vagueness in marketing strategy and autonomous decision-makers who are out of control. Of course, over centralised companies often become dependent on top management and respond too slowly to be able to solve problems or seize new opportunities. Obviously, finding the right degree of centralisation for a particular company is a difficult balancing act.

While many highly centralised organisations are quite successful, the overall trend is for companies to decentralise. This trend is partly caused by the need for organisations to remain very flexible, given the ever changing marketing environment. For some companies, the need to adapt to changing customer needs is of critical importance. These organisations often use an extreme form of decentralisation: **empowerment**. This involves giving front line employees the authority and responsibility to make marketing decisions without seeking the approval of their supervisors.[6] The following examples illustrate empowerment:

Empowerment Letting front line employees make marketing decisions without seeking approval from supervisors

- A car salesperson is allowed to negotiate the price or financing arrangement with a customer without speaking with the sales manager.
- A retail sales assistant decides, without seeking the approval of a manager, whether to refund customers' money on products they return.
- A receptionist at a hotel gives one night's free accommodation to a dissatisfied guest who complains about poor service.

- A retail store manager is permitted to lower prices on merchandise in order to match a competitor without asking the regional manager.

Although employees at any level in an organisation can be empowered to make decisions, empowerment is used most often at the front line, where employees interact daily with customers. Service and retail marketers practise empowerment quite extensively because of the interactive nature of these businesses. However, empowerment can work in a manufacturing organisation as well.

One of the characteristics of empowerment is that employees can perform their jobs the way they see fit, as long as their methods and outcomes are consistent with the mission of the organisation.[7] However, the effectiveness of empowerment is tied to the organisation's culture. Empowerment works best when the corporate culture is guided by a sense of shared direction, which ensures that employees make the right decisions.[8] Obviously, creating this type of culture does not happen overnight. The corporate vision must be communicated to employees so that they understand how their job affects the vision. Employees must also be trained and persuaded to accept the corporate vision and to become a part of the organisation's culture.[9]

Major Alternatives for Organising the Marketing Unit

How effectively a firm's marketing management can plan and implement marketing strategies depends on how the marketing unit is organised. Effective organisational planning can give the firm a competitive advantage. The organisational structure of a marketing department establishes the authority relationships between marketing personnel and specifies who is responsible for making certain decisions and performing particular activities. This internal structure is the vehicle for directing marketing activities.

In organising a marketing unit, managers divide the work into specific activities and delegate responsibility and authority for those activities to people in various positions within the unit. These positions include, for example, the sales manager, the research manager and the advertising manager.

No single approach to organising a marketing unit works equally well in all businesses. A marketing unit can be organised according to (1) functions, (2) products, (3) regions or (4) types of customer. The best approach or approaches depend on the number and diversity of the firm's products, the characteristics and needs of the people in the target market and many other factors.

Firms often use some combination of organisation by functions, products, regions or customer types. Product features may dictate that the marketing unit be structured by products, whereas customers' characteristics require that it be organised by geographical region or by type of customer. Construction equipment leader JCB has organised by product types (crawler excavators, backhoe diggers, compact equipment and so on), but many financial institutions organise by customers, because personal banking needs differ from commercial ones. By using more than one type of organisation, a flexible marketing unit can develop and implement marketing plans to match customers' needs precisely. To develop organisational plans that give a firm a competitive advantage, four issues should be considered:

1. Which jobs or levels of jobs need to be added, deleted or modified? For example, if new products are important to the success of the firm, marketers with strong product development skills should be added to the organisation.
2. How should reporting relationships be structured to create a competitive advantage? This question is discussed further in the following descriptions of organisational structure.

3. To whom should the primary responsibility for accomplishing work be assigned? Identifying primary responsibility explicitly is critical for effective performance appraisal and reward systems.
4. Should any committees or task forces be organised?[10]

Organising by Functions   Some marketing departments adopt a structure known as **organising by functions,** such as marketing research, product development, distribution, sales, advertising and customer relations. The personnel who direct these functions report directly to the top level marketing executive. This structure is fairly common because it works well for some businesses with centralised marketing operations, such as Ford and General Motors. In more decentralised firms, such as some retailers or giants Procter & Gamble and Unilever, functional organisation can raise severe co-ordination problems. The functional approach may, however, suit a large, centralised company whose products and customers are neither numerous nor diverse.

Organising by Products   An organisation that produces and markets diverse products may find the functional approach inadequate. The decisions and problems related to a single marketing function for one product may be quite different from those related to the same marketing function for another product. As a result, businesses that produce diverse products sometimes organise their marketing units according to product groups. **Organising by products** gives a firm the flexibility to develop special marketing mixes for different products.

The product management system, which was introduced by Procter & Gamble, operates in about 85 per cent of firms in the consumer packaged goods industry. In this structure, the product manager oversees all activities related to his or her assigned product. He or she develops product plans, sees that they are implemented, monitors the results and takes corrective action as necessary. The product manager is also responsible for acting as a liaison between the firm and its marketing environment, transmitting essential information about the environment to the company.[11] The product manager may also draw on the resources of specialised staff in the company.

Organising by Regions   A large company that markets products nationally (or internationally) may adopt a structure for its marketing activities known as **organising by regions.** Managers of marketing functions for each region report to their regional marketing manager; all the regional marketing managers report directly to the executive marketing manager. Companies often adopt this regional structure to put more senior management personnel into the field, get closer to customers and enable the company to respond more quickly and efficiently to the regional competitors. This form of organisation is especially effective for a firm whose customers' characteristics and needs vary greatly from one region to another.

A firm with marketing managers for each separate region has a complete marketing staff at its headquarters to provide assistance and guidance to regional marketing managers. The major UK brewers have national headquarters and marketing centres, often in London, but regional brands, each with their own marketing department, in major provincial conurbations. The regional office controls the marketing and promotion of its brand within guidelines specified by head office. However, not all firms organised by regions maintain a full marketing staff at their head offices. Firms that try to penetrate the national market intensively sometimes divide regions into sub-regions.

Organising by type of customer A way of structuring a marketing department suitable for a firm that has several groups of customers with very different needs and problems

Organising by Type of Customer Sometimes the marketing unit opts for **organising by type of customer.** This form of internal organisation works well for a firm that has several groups of customers whose needs and problems differ significantly. For example, Bic may sell pens to large retail stores, wholesalers and institutions. Retailers may want more rapid delivery of small shipments and more personal selling by the producer than do either wholesalers or institutional buyers. Because the marketing decisions and activities required for these two groups of customers differ considerably, the company may find it efficient to organise its marketing unit by type of customer.

In an organisation with a marketing department broken down by customer group, the marketing manager for each group reports to the top level marketing executive and directs most marketing activities for that group. A marketing manager controls all activities needed to market products to a specific customer group.

The planning and organising functions provide purpose, direction and structure for marketing activities. However, until marketing managers implement the marketing plan, exchanges cannot occur. In fact, organisers of marketing activities can become excessively concerned with planning strategy while neglecting implementation. Before John Harvey-Jones joined ICI, some analysts believed that its management's preoccupation with procedures and plans caused the company's business to suffer. Obviously, implementation of plans is important to the success of any organisation as described for Lego in Marketing Insight 24.1.[12] Proper implementation of a marketing plan depends on internal marketing to employees, the motivation of personnel who perform marketing activities, effective communication within the marketing organisation and the co-ordination of marketing activities. In Figure 24.3, Aerospatiale promotes its teamwork philosophy in business with other countries and internally.

· · · · · · · · · · · · · · · · · ·

The Marketing Implementation Process

Marketing implementation A process that involves activities to put marketing strategies into action

Marketing implementation is the "how?" of marketing strategy; it involves activities directed at putting marketing strategies into action. Although implementation is often neglected in favour of strategic planning, the implementation process itself can determine whether a marketing strategy is successful. In short, good marketing strategy combined with bad marketing implementation is a guaranteed recipe for failure.

An important aspect of the implementation process is understanding that marketing strategies almost always turn out differently than expected. In essence, all organisations have two types of strategy: intended strategy and realised strategy.[13] **Intended strategy** is the strategy that the organisation decided on during the planning phase and wants to use. **Realised strategy,** on the other hand, is the strategy that actually takes place; it comes about during the process of implementing the intended strategy. The realised strategy is not necessarily any better than the intended strategy, though it is often worse.

Intended strategy The strategy on which the company decides during the planning phase

Realised strategy The strategy that actually takes place

Problems in Implementing Marketing Activities

Why do marketing strategies sometimes turn out differently than expected? The most common reason is that managers fail to realise that marketing implementation is just as important as marketing strategy. Both strategy and implementation are important to strategic market planning. The relationship between strategic planning and implementation creates a number of problems for managers when

Lego Builds on a Theme

Plagued by poor publicity and inclement weather, Disney's Paris theme park, the best known theme park to open in Europe, is now striving to break into the black. Meanwhile, Europe's latest theme park has opened in the historic city of Windsor on the site of the now bankrupt and defunct Windsor Safari Park. The tigers and chimps have long since gone to other animal collections around the country, but tourists are still heading for the site. In addition to the Tussaud's wax display, Windsor Castle, the River Thames and racing, the great attraction at Windsor now is the famous multi-coloured children's building blocks sold worldwide by Denmark's Lego.

Since its launch in 1949, Lego has grown to a company with sales topping DKK 6 billion. The core product remains the ubiquitous little brick, popular with children all over the world aged 2 to 12. To keep pace with rivals' copy-cat products, plus the plethora of other types of toys, ranging from Nintendo to Barbie, the company must continually appraise children's tastes and up-date its products accordingly. It has done this by launching toddlers' Lego — larger bricks — and Techno kits of robots and spaceships aimed at older children, plus a host of related products from play tables to dressing-up accessories. The theme parks are quite different, being profit centres in their own right, but they are very deliberately related to Lego's core product.

The 150 acre Windsor park focuses on family entertainment and on the use of Lego bricks — both for children to play with by creating monster designs and as the camouflage enveloping the park's buildings and rides. A major theme is the use of giant Lego bricks to re-create famous buildings, such as London's Big Ben, and events and personalities from stage and screen. The intention is to establish an oasis of tranquility for children in an

they plan implementation activities. Three of the most important problems are as follows:[14]

- *Marketing strategy and implementation are related.* Companies that experience this problem typically assume that strategic planning always comes first, followed by implementation. In reality, marketing strategies and implementation activities should be developed simultaneously. The content of the marketing strategy determines how it will be implemented. Likewise, implementation activities may require that changes be made in the marketing strategy. Thus it is important for marketing managers to understand that strategy and implementation are really two sides of the same coin.
- *Marketing strategy and implementation are constantly evolving.* This second problem refers to how strategy and implementation are both affected by the marketing environment. Since the environment is constantly changing, both marketing strategy and implementation must remain flexible enough to adapt. The relationship between strategy and implementation is never fixed; it is always evolving to accommodate changes in customer needs, government regulation or competition.
- *The responsibility for marketing strategy and implementation are separated.* This problem is often the biggest obstacle in implementing marketing strategies.

increasingly rowdy and violent society, building on Lego's hallmark belief that children's innocence should be nurtured and cherished. The Lego company, privately owned by the Kristiansen family, opened its first theme park in 1968 outside Copenhagen. Its 15 million Lego bricks on only 25 acres form Denmark's largest tourist attraction, drawing over 1.3 million visitors each year. Now the Americans are to have a $100 million Legoland in California, destined to receive 1.8 million visitors each year.

It remains to be seen whether the high tech computer games arenas springing up in major cities and the white knuckle ride theme parks such as Alton Towers and The American Adventure do not pose too great a threat to the more laid back Legoland. The creators of this latest theme park are operating in the belief that children can still be drawn into a world of make-believe, along with

their parents. Certainly the continued success in Toys "R" Us and stores around the world of Lego's building bricks indicates that the company has a concept still much in demand with today's children. The company takes this family orientation most seriously, as employees in Legoland will testify. It aims to allow children to enjoy themselves safely in a world untouched by society's troubles. Legoland's staff are thoroughly vetted and trained to ensure that they have the right skills and motivation to make their customers' experiences enjoyable, safe and memorable.

SOURCES: Legoland UK; Charles Darwent, "Lego's billion-dollar brickworks", *Management Today*, September 1995, pp. 64–68; Richard Morais, "Babes in toyland?", *Forbes*, 3 January 1994, pp. 70–71; "A faint squeak from Euro-Mickey", *The Economist*, 29 July 1995, p. 56; Jeff Ferry and Richard Hooper, "The great game of infant-motion", *Director*, September 1995, pp. 30–38.

Typically, marketing strategies are developed by the top managers in an organisation. However, the responsibility for implementing those strategies rests at the front line of the organisation. This separation can impair implementation in two ways (see Figure 24.4). First, because top managers are separated from the front line, where the company interacts daily with customers, they may not grasp the unique problems associated with implementing marketing activities. Second, people, not organisations, implement strategies. Front line managers and employees are often responsible for implementing strategies, even though they had no voice in developing them. Consequently, these front line employees may lack motivation and commitment.[15]

Components of Marketing Implementation

The marketing implementation process has several components, all of which must mesh if the implementation is to succeed. These components are shown in Figure 24.5. The systems component refers to work processes, procedures and the way in which information is structured—elements ensuring that the organisation's day-to-day activities are carried out. Typical organisational systems include marketing information systems, strategic planning systems, budgeting and accounting systems, manufacturing and quality control systems, and performance measurement systems.

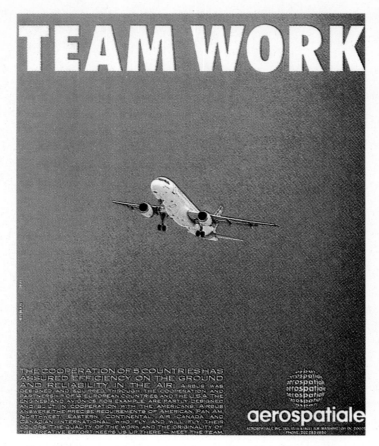

Figure 24.3 Implementing plans involves co-operation. Aerospatiale's teamwork message supports the idea that co-operation is needed to implement marketing strategies.

Source: Courtesy of Aerospatiale.

The people component in Figure 24.5 refers to the importance of employees in the implementation process. It includes such factors as the quality, diversity and skills of the workforce within the organisation and also covers the human resources function. Issues like employee recruitment, selection and training have great bearing on the implementation of marketing activities.[16] Closely linked to the people component is leadership, or the art of managing people. It involves such issues as employee motivation, communication and reward policies.

At the centre of marketing implementation are shared goals; they draw the entire organisation together into a single, functioning unit. These goals may be simple statements of the company's objectives.

On the other hand, the goals may be detailed mission statements, outlining corporate philosophy and direction. Shared goals appear in the centre of Figure 24.5 because they hold all the other components together to ensure successful marketing implementation.[17] Without shared goals to hold the organisation together, different parts of the organisation might work toward different goals or objectives, thus limiting the success of the entire organisation.

Figure 24.4

The separation of strategic
planning and marketing
implementation

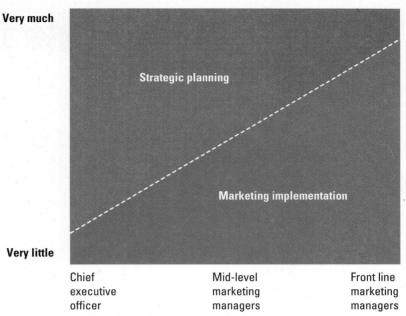

Very much

Strategic planning

Marketing implementation

Very little

| Chief executive officer | Mid-level marketing managers | Front line marketing managers |

• • • • • • • • • • • • • • • • • •

Approaches to Marketing Implementation

Once they grasp the problems and recognise the components of marketing implementation, marketing managers can decide on an approach for implementing marketing activities. Just as organisations can achieve their goals by using different marketing strategies, they can also implement their marketing strategies by using different approaches. This section discusses two general approaches to marketing implementation: internal marketing and total quality management. Both approaches represent mindsets that marketing managers can adopt when organising and planning marketing activities. These approaches are not mutually exclusive; indeed, many companies adopt both when designing marketing activities.

Internal Marketing

Internal marketing Co-ordinating internal exchanges between a firm and its employees to achieve successful external exchanges between the company and its customers

Marketing activities cannot be effectively implemented without the cooperation of employees. Employees are the essential ingredient in increasing productivity, providing customer service and beating the competition. Thus, in addition to marketing activities targeted at external customers, firms use internal marketing to attract, motivate and retain qualified internal customers (employees) by designing internal products (jobs) that satisfy employees' wants and needs. **Internal marketing,** a management philosophy, refers to the co-ordination of internal exchanges between the organisation and its employees to better achieve successful external exchanges between the organisation and its customers.[18] Generally speaking, internal marketing refers to the managerial actions necessary to make all members of the marketing organisation understand and accept their respective roles in implementing the marketing strategy. This means that all of them, from

Figure 24.5

Elements of marketing implementation

Source: Lawrence R. Jauch and William F. Glueck, Strategic Management and Business Policy, *3rd edn. Copyright © 1988 by McGraw-Hill, Inc. Used with permission of the McGraw-Hill Companies.*

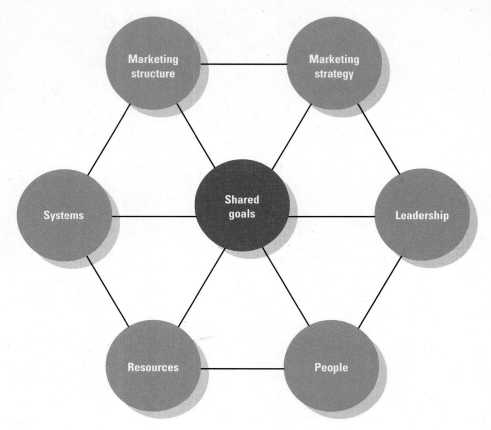

the chairperson of the company to the hourly workers on the shop floor, must understand the role they play in carrying out their jobs and implementing the marketing strategy. Everyone must do his or her part to ensure that customers are satisfied. All personnel within the firm, both marketers and those who perform other functions, must recognise the tenet of customer orientation and service that underlies the marketing concept.

In the internal marketing approach, every employee has two groups of customers: external and internal. **External customers** are the individuals who patronise a business—a familiar definition of customers. The employees who work for the company are **internal customers.** In a supermarket, the manager has a group of external customers whose needs must be met in order for the company to be successful. This same manager also has a group of internal customers, the employees, whose needs must be met as well. For implementation to be successful, the manager must serve the needs of both customer groups. If the internal customers are not dealt with properly, then it is likely that the external customers will not be completely satisfied.

Like external marketing activities, internal marketing may involve market segmentation, product development, research, distribution, and even public relations and sales promotion.[19] The internal marketing framework is shown in Figure 24.6. As in external marketing, the marketing mix is used in the internal marketing approach to satisfy the needs of employees. For example, an organisation may

External customers
Individuals who patronise a business

Internal customers A company's employees

Figure 24.6

The internal marketing
framework

*Source: Adapted from Nigel F.
Piercy,* Market-Led Strategic
Change, *copyright © 1992,
Butterworth-Heinemann Ltd., p.
371. Used with permission.*

sponsor sales competitions to encourage sales personnel to boost their selling efforts. Some companies encourage employees to work for their companies' customers for a period of time, often while continuing to receive their regular salaries. This helps the employees (and ultimately the company) to understand better customers' needs and problems, lets them learn valuable new skills and heightens their enthusiasm for their regular jobs. In addition, many companies use planning sessions, workshops, letters, formal reports and personal conversations as tools of internal distribution to ensure that employees understand the corporate mission, the organisation's goals and the marketing strategy. The ultimate result is more satisfied employees and improved customer relations.

Total Quality Management

Total quality management (TQM) Co-ordinated efforts directed at improving all aspects of a business—from product and service quality to customer and employee satisfaction

A primary concern today in some organisations is total quality management. Major reasons for this concern about quality are competition, more demanding customers and poorer profit performance due to reduced market shares and higher costs. **Total quality management (TQM)** is the co-ordination of efforts directed at improving customer satisfaction, increasing employee participation and empowerment, forming and strengthening supplier partnerships, and facilitating an organisational culture of continuous quality improvement. Customer satisfaction can be improved through higher quality products and better customer service, such as reduced delivery times, faster responses to customer inquiries and treatment of customers that shows caring on the company's part.

As a management philosophy, TQM relies heavily on the talents of employees to continually improve the quality of the organisation's goods and services. The TQM philosophy is founded on three basic principles:[20]

- *Empowered employees.* Ultimately, TQM succeeds or fails because of the efforts of the organisation's employees. Thus employee recruitment, selection and training are critical to the success of marketing implementation. As discussed earlier in the chapter, empowerment means giving employees the authority to make decisions in order to satisfy customer needs. However, empowering employees is successful only if the organisation is guided by an overall corporate vision, shared goals and a culture that supports the TQM effort.[21] Such a system cannot spring up overnight. A great deal of time, effort and patience are needed to develop and sustain a quality orientated culture in an organisation. Three years of training workshops and evolution were required at JCB before TQM became firmly established as a managerial philosophy.
- *Continuous quality improvement.* The continuous improvement of an organisation's products and services is built around the notion that quality is free: not having high quality goods and services can be very expensive, especially in terms of dissatisfied customers.[22] The continuous improvement of quality also means more than simple quality control, or the screening out of bad products during production. Rather, continuous improvement means building in quality from the very beginning—totally redesigning the product if necessary. Continuous improvement is a slow, long term process of creating small improvements in quality. Companies that adopt TQM realise that the major advancements in quality occur because of an accumulation of these small improvements over time.

Benchmarking The process of comparing the quality of a firm's goods, services or processes with that of its best performing competitors

A primary tool of the continuous improvement process is **benchmarking,** or the measurement and evaluation of the quality of an organisation's goods, services or processes as compared with the best performing companies in the industry.[23] Benchmarking lets an organisation know where it stands competitively in its industry, thus giving the company a goal to aim for over time. This goal is usually to be the best in the industry.

- *Quality improvement teams.* The idea behind the team approach is to get the best and brightest people from a wide variety of perspectives working on a quality improvement issue simultaneously. Team members are usually selected from a cross-section of jobs within the organisation, as well as from among suppliers and customers. Customers are included in the quality improvement team because they are in the best position to know what they and other customers want from the company. Suppliers, too, understand the market.

Total quality management can provide several benefits. Overall financial benefits include lower operating costs, a higher return on sales and investment, and an improved ability to use premium pricing rather than competitive pricing. Additional benefits include faster development of innovations, improved access to global markets, higher levels of customer retention and an enhanced reputation.[24] Despite these advantages, only a handful of companies use the TQM approach, although the numbers are growing. The reason is that putting the TQM philosophy into practice requires a great deal of time, effort, money and patience on the part of the organisation. However, companies with the resources necessary to implement TQM gain an effective means of achieving major competitive advantages in their respective industries.

Although many factors can influence the effectiveness of the internal marketing and total quality management approaches, two issues are crucial. First, top management must be totally committed to internal marketing or TQM and must make either one or both of the approaches their top priority. Committed top managers serve as role models for other managers and employees.[25] It is naive for managers to expect employees to be committed to an approach when top managers are not. Second, management must co-ordinate the specific elements of these approaches to ensure that they work in harmony with each other. Over emphasising one aspect of internal marketing or TQM can be detrimental to the other components, thus limiting the success of the overall programme.

● ● ● ● ● ● ● ● ● ● ● ● ● ● ● ● ● ● ●

Implementing Marketing Activities

Motivating Marketing Personnel

An important element in implementing the marketing plan, and in internal marketing, is motivating marketing personnel to perform effectively. People work to satisfy physical, psychological and social needs. To motivate marketing personnel, managers must discover their employees' needs and then develop motivational methods that help them satisfy those needs. It is crucial that the plan for motivating employees be fair, ethical and well understood by them. Additionally, rewards to employees must be tied to organisational goals. In general, to improve employee motivation, companies need to find out what workers think, how they feel and what they want. Some of this information can be obtained from an employee attitude survey. A business organisation can motivate its workers by directly linking pay with performance, informing workers how their performance affects department and corporate results, following through with appropriate compensation, promoting or implementing a flexible benefits programme and adopting a participative management approach.[26]

Consider the following example. Suppose a salesperson can sell product A or B to a particular customer, but not both products. Product A sells for £200,000 and contributes £20,000 to the company's profit margin. Product B sells for £60,000 and has a contribution margin of £40,000. If the salesperson receives a commission of 3 per cent of sales, he or she would obviously prefer to sell product A, even though the sale of product B contributes more to the company's profits. If the salesperson's commission was based on contribution margin instead of sales and the firm's goal was to maximise profits, both the firm and the salesperson would benefit more from the sale of product B.[27] By tying rewards to organisational goals, the company encourages behaviour that meets organisational goals.

Besides tying rewards to organisational goals, managers must motivate individuals by using different motivational tools, based on each individual's value system. For example, some employees value recognition more than a slight pay increase. Managers can reward employees with money, plus additional fringe benefits, prestige or recognition, or even non-financial rewards such as job autonomy, skill variety, task significance and increased feedback. A survey of Fortune 1000 companies found that "the majority of organisations feel that they get more for their money through non-cash awards, if given in addition to a basic compensation plan".

Communicating Within the Marketing Unit

With good communication, marketing managers can motivate personnel and co-ordinate their efforts. Marketing managers must be able to communicate with the firm's high level management to ensure that marketing activities are consistent with the company's overall goals. Communication with top level executives keeps marketing managers aware of the company's overall plans and achievements. It also guides what the marketing unit is to do and how its activities are to be integrated with those of other departments—such as finance, production or personnel—with whose management the marketing manager must also communicate to co-ordinate marketing efforts. For example, marketing personnel must work with the production staff to help design products that customers want. To direct marketing activities, marketing managers must communicate with marketing personnel at the operations level, such as sales and advertising personnel, researchers, wholesalers, retailers and package designers.

To facilitate communication, marketing managers should establish an information system within the marketing unit. The marketing information system (discussed in Chapter 6) should allow for easy communication among marketing managers, sales managers and sales personnel. Marketers need an information system to support a variety of activities, such as planning, budgeting, sales analyses, performance evaluations and the preparation of reports. An information system should also expedite communications with other departments in the organisation and minimise destructive competition between departments for organisational resources.

Co-ordinating Marketing Activities

Because of job specialisation and differences related to marketing activities, marketing managers must synchronise individuals' actions to achieve marketing objectives. In addition, they must work closely with managers in research and development, production, finance, accounting and personnel to see that marketing activities mesh with other functions of the firm. In Figure 24.7, Sony's advertisement is the outward indication of a highly co-ordinated and carefully planned strategy. Marketing managers must co-ordinate the activities of marketing staff within the firm and integrate those activities with the marketing efforts of external organisations—advertising agencies, resellers (wholesalers, retailers and dealers), researchers and shippers, among others. Marketing managers can improve co-ordination by using internal marketing activities to make each employee aware of how his or her job relates to others and how his or her actions contribute to the achievement of marketing plans.

· · · · · · · · · · · · · · · · · ·

Controlling Marketing Activities

Marketing control process
One that establishes performance standards, evaluates actual performance and reduces the differences between desired and actual performance

To achieve marketing objectives as well as general organisational objectives, marketing managers must effectively control marketing efforts. The **marketing control process** consists of establishing performance standards, evaluating actual performance by comparing it with established standards and reducing the differences between desired and actual performance. This process helped Xerox to recover ground lost to competitors. Dunkin' Donuts has developed a programme to ensure consistency throughout its franchises. Dunkin' Donuts controls the quality of operations in its franchised units by having franchisees attend Dunkin' Donuts University. Owners and managers of Dunkin' Donuts are required to take a six week training course, covering everything from customer relations and marketing to production, including a test of making 140 dozen doughnuts in eight hours. As part of the test, an instructor randomly selects 6 of the 1,680 doughnuts made, to ascertain that they weigh around 350 grammes (12 ounces) and measure just under 20 centimetres (8 inches) when stacked. The Dunkin' Donuts University was opened to guarantee uniformity in all aspects of the business operations throughout the 1,700 franchise units.[28] The Coca-Cola Company's efforts

Figure 24.7 Co-ordinating marketing activities. Sony's worldwide success hinges on thorough marketing planning and comprehensive implementation of strategies across national borders.

Source: Courtesy of Sony Europa.

to implement and control its marketing strategy are discussed in Marketing Insight 24.2.

Although the control function is a fundamental management activity, it has received little attention in marketing. There are both formal and informal control systems in organisations. The formal marketing control process involves performance standards, evaluation of actual performance and corrective action to remedy shortfalls (see Figure 24.8). The informal control process, however, involves self-control, social or group control, and cultural control through acceptance of a firm's value system. Which type of control system dominates depends on the environmental context of the firm.[29] These steps in the control process and the major problems they involve are discussed in the next sections.

Performance standard An expected level of performance against which actual performance can be compared

Establishing Performance Standards

Planning and controlling are closely linked because plans include statements about what is to be accomplished. For purposes of control, these statements function as performance standards. A **performance standard** is an expected level of performance against which actual performance can be compared. Examples of

Coca-Cola Manages Its Implementation

Coca-Cola may seem as American as apple pie, but the Coca-Cola name is one of the most recognised brands in the world. The company sells roughly 47 per cent of all the soft drinks consumed globally, more than twice as much as PepsiCo, its nearest rival. And foreign markets provide 80 per cent of Coke's operating earnings. Amazing as it may seem, more Coca-Cola is sold in Japan each year than in the United States.

Coke's international success did not happen overnight. When most American companies were only thinking about global marketing strategies, Coke was implementing them. First, Coke carefully guided and set standards for its overseas bottling partners. To maintain control of its overseas bottlers, Coke generally invested in them, spending more than £1.5 billion in joint bottling ventures worldwide in the 1980s. If bottlers fail to perform as expected, Coke reviews their contracts and takes corrective action, sometimes resulting in ownership of its own bottling plants. When French bottler Pernod Richard S.A. disagreed with Coke over how to revive slow soft drink sales in France, the company took control to solve the problem.

As the barriers in eastern Europe fell, Coca-Cola was quick to enter, buying and modernising bottling plants. In former East Germany, over 180 antiquated bottlers were consolidated into 30 efficient, state-of-the-art plants, with new distribution centres and a fleet of western European vehicles to ensure reliability of supply. Sugar suppliers and glass manufacturers close to Coca-Cola's existing German operation were encouraged to set up modern operations in the east to supply Coca-Cola's needs. Coca-Cola's strategy of remaining the market leader required careful and extensive control over the implementation and execution of its plans.

The second part of Coke's international strategy consists of aggressive advertising, packaging and marketing to foreign consumers. Sometimes being "The Real Thing" isn't enough to ensure success. In many countries, such as Indonesia, Coke attempted to change consumer tastes by incorporating local tastes into the Coca-Cola formula. Thus, by buying strawberry, pineapple and banana flavoured soft drinks, Indonesians became accustomed to carbonated beverages.

By aggressively marketing to foreign consumers, Coke created markets with a high probability of success. It is this high probability of success that allows Coke to be firm but fair with its bottlers. At times, Coke's international bottlers may feel pressure to achieve the company's high standards. However, the dominance of the Coca-Cola brand in most foreign markets all but guarantees success for Coke and its bottlers. Until its competitors move to adopt global marketing strategies, Coca-Cola will remain not just "The Real Thing" but "The Only Thing" in many foreign markets. For Coca-Cola, control is fundamental to any successes.

Sources: "How Coke markets to the world", *Journal of Business Strategy,* September–October 1988, pp. 4–7; Michael J. McCarthy, "The real thing: as a global marketer, Coke excels by being tough and consistent", *Wall Street Journal,* 19 December 1989, pp. A1, A6; "Coke director brands Pepsi Challenge a flop", *Marketing Week,* 11 August 1995, p. 5; "Coca-Cola rejigs European set-up as Hughes quits", *Marketing,* 20 October 1994, p. 1.

performance standards might be the reduction of customers' complaints by 20 per cent, a monthly sales quota of £150,000 or a 10 per cent increase per month in new customer accounts. Performance standards are also given in the form of budget accounts; that is, marketers are expected to achieve a certain objective without spending more than a given amount of resources. As stated earlier, performance standards should be tied to organisational goals. Performance standards can relate to product quality.

Figure 24.8
The marketing control process

4. Corrective action, if necessary

1. Development or adjustment of marketing objectives

Information Control Processes

3. Evaluation of actual performance relative to established standards

2. Establishment of performance standards

Evaluating Actual Performance

To compare actual performance with performance standards, marketing managers must know what marketers within the company are doing and must have information about the activities of external organisations that provide the firm with marketing assistance. (Specific methods for assessing actual performance are discussed later in this chapter.) Information is required about the activities of marketing personnel at the operations level and at various marketing management levels. Most businesses obtain marketing assistance from one or more external individuals or organisations, such as advertising agencies, middlemen, marketing research firms and consultants. To maximise benefits from external sources, a firm's marketing control process must monitor their activities. Although it may be difficult to obtain the necessary information, it is impossible to measure actual performance without it.

Records of actual performance are compared with performance standards to determine whether and how much of a discrepancy exists. For example, a salesperson's actual sales are compared with his or her sales quota. If there is a significant negative discrepancy, the sales manager takes corrective action.

Taking Corrective Action

Marketing managers have several options for reducing a discrepancy between established performance standards and actual performance. They can take steps to improve actual performance, can reduce or totally change the performance standard or do both. Changes in actual performance may require the marketing manager to use better methods of motivating marketing personnel or find more effective techniques for co-ordinating marketing efforts.

Sometimes performance standards are unrealistic when they are written. In other cases, changes in the marketing environment make them unrealistic. For example, a company's annual sales goal may become unrealistic if several aggressive competitors enter the firm's market. In fact, changes in the marketing environment may force managers to change their marketing strategy completely.

Requirements for an Effective Control Process

A marketing manager should consider several requirements in creating and maintaining effective control processes.[30] Effective control hinges on the quantity and quality of information available to the marketing manager and the speed at which it is received. The control process should be designed so that the flow of information is rapid enough to allow the marketing manager to detect quickly differences between actual and planned levels of performance. A single control procedure is not suitable for all types of marketing activities, and internal and environmental changes affect an organisation's activities. Therefore, control procedures should be flexible enough to adjust to both varied activities and changes in the organisation's situation. For the control process to be usable, its costs must be low relative to the costs that would arise if controls were lacking. Finally, the control process should be designed so that both managers and subordinates can understand it and its requirements.

Problems in Controlling Marketing Activities

When marketing managers attempt to control marketing activities, they frequently run into several problems. Often the information required to control marketing activities is unavailable or is available only at a high cost. Even though marketing controls should be flexible enough to allow for environmental changes, the frequency, intensity and unpredictability of such changes may hamper effective control. In addition, the time lag between marketing activities and their effects limits a marketing manager's ability to measure the effectiveness of marketing activities.

Consider the problems of demand fluctuation in the video games industry. By failing to control the number of video game products offered, Nintendo, Atari and Sega glutted the market with so many video game titles that consumers were confused and disappointed with the numerous look-alike products. Companies are avoiding past mistakes by carefully analysing the success of video games and deleting older games that are no longer profitable. For example, Nintendo withdrew 18 of its 36 games to make room for new product introductions. This careful analysis and control of product offerings has helped home video games make a comeback from being a spectacular but short lived fad of the early 1980s.[31] It is estimated that one out of two homes will have either a Nintendo, Sega or Sony system by the end of the decade.

Because marketing and other business activities overlap, marketing managers cannot determine the precise cost of marketing activities. Without an accurate measure of marketing costs, it is difficult to know if the effects of marketing activities are worth their expense. Finally, marketing control may be difficult because it is very hard to develop exact performance standards for marketing personnel.

• • • • • • • • • • • • • • • • • • •

Methods of Evaluating Performance

There are specific methods for assessing and improving the effectiveness of a marketing strategy. A marketer should state in the marketing plan what a marketing strategy is supposed to accomplish. These statements should set forth performance standards, which are usually stated in terms of profits, sales or costs. Actual performance must be measured in similar terms so that comparisons are possible. This section describes sales analysis and cost analysis, two general ways of evaluating the actual performance of marketing strategies. "Softer" measures such as brand awareness and customer satisfaction levels are also important, as detailed in the previous chapter, and can be tracked through qualitative marketing research.

Sales Analysis

Sales analysis The use of sales figures to evaluate a firm's current performance

Sales analysis uses sales figures to evaluate a firm's current performance. It is probably the most common method of evaluation, because sales data partially reflect the target market's reactions to a marketing mix and are often readily available, at least in aggregate form.

Marketers use current sales data to monitor the impact of current marketing efforts. However, that information alone is not enough. To provide useful analyses, current sales data must be compared with forecast sales, industry sales, specific competitors' sales or the costs incurred to achieve the sales volume. For example, knowing that a store attained a £600,000 sales volume this year does not tell management whether its marketing strategy has been successful. However, if managers know that expected sales were £550,000, they are then in a better position to determine the effectiveness of the firm's marketing efforts. In addition, if they know that the marketing costs needed to achieve the £600,000 volume were 12 per cent less than budgeted, they are in an even better position to analyse their marketing strategy precisely.

Sales measurements Data regarding sales transactions that are used to analyse performance

Sales Measurements Although there are several types of **sales measurements,** the basic unit of measurement is the sales transaction. A sales transaction results in a customer order for a specified quantity of an organisation's product sold under specified terms by a particular salesperson or sales group on a certain date. Many organisations record these bits of information about their transactions. With such a record, a company can analyse sales in terms of cash volume or market share.

Firms frequently use cash volume sales analysis because currency is a common denominator of sales, costs and profits. However, price increases and decreases affect total sales figures. For example, if a company increased its prices by 10 per cent this year and its sales volume is 10 per cent greater than last year, it has not experienced any increase in unit sales. A marketing manager who uses cash volume analysis should factor out the effects of price changes.

A firm's market share is the firm's sales of a product stated as a percentage of industry sales of that product. For example, KP, Golden Wonder, Smiths and Walkers account for around 70 per cent of the UK savoury snacks market. In the carbonated drinks sector, Coca-Cola has a leading 16 per cent share by volume.[32] Market share analysis lets a company compare its marketing strategy with competitors' strategies. The primary reason for using market share analysis is to estimate whether sales changes have resulted from the firm's marketing strategy or from uncontrollable environmental forces. When a company's sales volume declines but its share of the market stays the same, the marketer can assume that industry sales declined (because of some uncontrollable factors) and that this decline was reflected in the firm's sales. However, if a company experiences a decline in both sales and market share, it should consider the possibility that its marketing strategy is not effective.

Even though market share analysis can be helpful in evaluating the performance of a marketing strategy, the user must interpret results cautiously. When attributing a sales decline to uncontrollable factors, a marketer must keep in mind that such factors do not affect all firms in the industry equally. Not all firms in an industry have the same objectives, and some change their objectives from one year to the next. Changes in the objectives of one company can affect the market shares of one or all companies in that industry. For example, if a competitor significantly increases promotional efforts or drastically reduces prices to increase market share, a company could lose market share despite a well designed marketing strategy. Within an industry, the entrance of new firms or the demise of established ones also affects a specific firm's market share, and market share analysts should attempt to account for these effects. Kentucky Fried Chicken (KFC), for example, probably re-evaluated its marketing strategies when McDonald's introduced its own fried chicken product.

Whether it is based on sales volume or market share, sales analysis can be performed on aggregate sales figures or on disaggregated data. Aggregate sales analysis provides an overview of current sales. Although helpful, aggregate sales analysis is often insufficient, because it does not bring to light sales variations within the aggregate. It is not uncommon for a marketer to find that a large proportion of aggregate sales comes from a small number of products, geographic areas or customers. This is sometimes called the "iceberg principle" because only a small part of an iceberg is visible above the water. To find such disparities, total sales figures are usually broken down by geographic unit, salesperson, product, customer type or a combination of these categories.

In sales analysis by geographic unit, sales data can be classified by city, county, region, country or any other geographic designation for which a marketer collects sales information. Actual sales in a geographic unit can be compared with sales in a similar geographic unit, with last year's sales or with an estimated market potential for the area. For example, if a firm finds that 18 per cent of its sales are coming from an area that represents only 8 per cent of the potential sales for the product, then it can be assumed that the marketing strategy is successful in that geographic unit.

Because of the cost associated with hiring and maintaining a sales force, businesses commonly analyse sales by salesperson to determine the contribution each member of the sales force makes. Performance standards for each salesperson are often set in terms of sales quotas for a given time period. Evaluation of actual performance is accomplished by comparing a salesperson's current sales with a pre-established quota or some other standard, such as the previous period's sales. If actual sales meet or exceed the standard and the sales representative has not incurred costs above those budgeted, that person's efforts are acceptable.

Sales analysis is often performed according to product group or specific product item. Marketers break down their aggregate sales figures by product to determine the proportion that each contributed to total sales. Columbia Pictures, for example, might break down its total sales figures by box office figures for each film produced. A firm usually sets a sales volume objective—and sometimes a market share objective—for each product item or product group, and sales analysis by product is the only way to measure such objectives. A marketer can compare the breakdown of current sales by product with those of previous years. In addition, within industries for which sales data by product are available, a firm's sales by product type can be compared with industry averages. To gain an accurate picture of where sales of specific products are occurring, marketers sometimes combine sales analysis by product with sales analysis by geographic area or salesperson.

Analyses based on customers are usually broken down by type of customer. Customers can be classified by the way they use a firm's products, their distribution level (producer, wholesaler, retailer), their size, the size of orders or other characteristics. Sales analysis by customer type lets a firm ascertain whether its marketing resources are allocated in a way that achieves the greatest productivity. For example, sales analysis by type of customer may reveal that 60 per cent of the sales force is serving a group that makes only 15 per cent of total sales.

A considerable amount of information is needed for sales analyses, especially if disaggregated analyses are desired. The marketer must develop an operational system for collecting sales information; obviously, the effectiveness of the system for collecting sales information largely determines the ability of a company to develop useful sales analyses.

Marketing Cost Analysis

Marketing cost analysis
The break down and classification of costs to determine which are associated with specific marketing activities

Although sales analysis is critical for evaluating the effectiveness of a marketing strategy, it gives only part of the picture. A marketing strategy that successfully generates sales may also be extremely costly. To obtain a complete picture, a firm must know the marketing costs associated with using a given strategy to achieve a certain sales level. **Marketing cost analysis** breaks down and classifies costs to determine which are associated with specific marketing activities. By comparing costs of previous marketing activities with results generated, a marketer can better allocate the firm's marketing resources in the future. Marketing cost analysis lets a company evaluate the effectiveness of an ongoing or recent marketing strategy by comparing sales achieved and costs incurred. By pin-pointing exactly where a company is experiencing high costs, this form of analysis can help isolate profitable or unprofitable customer segments, products or geographic areas.

For example, the market share of Komatsu, a Japanese construction equipment manufacturer, began to decline in the United States when prices increased because of the high yen value. Komatsu responded by developing an equal joint venture with Dresser Industries, making it the second largest company in this industry. The joint venture with Dresser allowed Komatsu to shift a large amount of its final assembly to the United States, to Dresser plants that had been running at 50 per cent capacity. By using Dresser's unused capacity and existing US plants, Komatsu avoided the start up costs of new construction and gained an immediate manufacturing presence in the United States.[33] This cost control tactic should enable Komatsu to use price more effectively as a marketing variable to compete with industry leader Caterpillar Tractor Co.

In some organisations, personnel in other functional areas—such as production or accounting—see marketers as primarily concerned with generating sales, regardless of the costs incurred. By conducting cost analyses, marketers can counter this criticism and put themselves in a better position to demonstrate how marketing activities contribute to generating profits. Even though hiring a sports figure such as Monica Seles is costly, in many sectors sales goals cannot be reached without large expenditures for promotion. Many advertisers believe that using celebrities helps to increase sales. Research shows that the public are good at identifying which personalities are linked to advertised brands. Ultimately, cost analysis should show if promotion costs are effective in increasing sales.

The task of determining marketing costs is often complex and difficult. Simply ascertaining the costs associated with marketing a product is rarely adequate. Marketers must usually determine the marketing costs of serving specific geographical areas, market segments or even specific customers.

A first step in determining the costs is to examine accounting records. Most accounting systems classify costs into **natural accounts**—such as rent, salaries, office supplies and utilities—which are based on how the money was actually spent. Unfortunately, many natural accounts do not help explain what marketing functions were performed through the expenditure of those funds. It does little good, for example, to know that £80,000 is spent for rent each year. The analyst has no way of knowing whether the money is spent for the rental of production, storage or sales facilities. Therefore, marketing cost analysis usually requires some of the costs in natural accounts to be reclassified into **marketing function accounts**, which indicate the function performed through the expenditure of funds. Common marketing function accounts are transport, storage, order processing, selling, advertising, sales promotion, marketing research and customer credit.

Natural accounts can be reclassified into marketing function accounts as shown in the simplified example in Table 24.1. Note that a few natural accounts, such as advertising, can be reclassified easily into functional accounts because they do not have to be split across several accounts. For most of the natural accounts, however, marketers must develop criteria for assigning them to the various functional accounts. For example, the number of square metres of floor space used was the criterion for dividing the rental costs in Table 24.1 into functional accounts. In some instances, a specific marketing cost is incurred to perform several functions. A packaging cost, for example, could be considered a production function, a distribution function, a promotional function or all three. The marketing cost analyst must reclassify such costs across multiple functions.

Three broad categories are used in marketing cost analysis: direct costs, traceable common costs and non-traceable common costs. **Direct costs** are directly attributable to the performance of marketing functions. For example, sales force

Profit and Loss Statement

Expenses (natural accounts)		Advertising	Personal Selling	Transport	Storage	Marketing Research	Non-Marketing
Sales	£250,000						
Cost of goods sold	45,000						
Gross profit	205,000						
Rent	£ 14,000		£ 7,000		£6,000		£ 1,000
Salaries	72,000	£12,000	32,000	£7,000		£1,000	20,000
Supplies	4,000	1,500	1,000			1,000	500
Advertising	16,000	16,000					
Freight	4,000			2,000			2,000
Taxes	2,000				200		1,800
Insurance	1,000				600		400
Interest	3,000						3,000
Bad debts	6,000						6,000
Total	£122,000	£29,500	£40,000	£9,000	£6,800	£2,000	£34,700
Net profit	£ 83,000						

Table 24.1 Reclassification of natural accounts into functional accounts

Traceable common costs
Costs that can be allocated indirectly, using one or several criteria, to the functions they support

Non-traceable common costs
Costs that cannot be assigned according to any logical criteria

Full cost approach
An approach in which cost analysis includes direct costs, traceable common costs and non-traceable common costs

Direct cost approach   An approach that includes only direct costs and traceable common costs

salaries might be allocated to the cost of selling a specific product item, selling in a specific geographic area or selling to a particular customer. **Traceable common costs** can be allocated indirectly, using one or several criteria, to the functions that they support. For example, if the firm spends £80,000 annually to rent space for production, storage and selling, the rental costs of storage could be determined on the basis of cost per square metre used for storage. **Non-traceable common costs** cannot be assigned according to any logical criteria and thus are assignable only on an arbitrary basis. Interest, taxes and the salaries of top management are non-traceable common costs.

The manner of dealing with these three categories of costs depends on whether the analyst uses a full cost or a direct cost approach. When a **full cost approach** is used, cost analysis includes direct costs, traceable common costs and non-traceable common costs. Proponents of this approach claim that if an accurate profit picture is desired, all costs must be included in the analysis. However, opponents point out that full costing does not yield actual costs, because non-traceable common costs are determined by arbitrary criteria. With different criteria, the full costing approach yields different results. A cost-conscious operating unit can be discouraged if numerous costs are assigned to it arbitrarily. To eliminate such problems, the **direct cost approach,** which includes direct costs and traceable common costs but not non-traceable common costs, is used. Opponents say that this approach is not accurate, because it omits one cost category.

Marketers can use several methods to analyse costs. The methods vary in their precision. This section examines three cost analysis methods—analysis of natural accounts; analysis of functional accounts; and cost analysis by product, geographic area or customer.

Marketers can sometimes determine marketing costs by performing an analysis of natural accounts. The precision of this method depends on how detailed the firm's accounts are. For example, if accounting records contain separate accounts for production wages, sales force wages and executive salaries, the analysis can be more precise than if all wages and salaries are lumped into a single account. An analysis of natural accounts is more meaningful, and thus more useful, when current cost data can be compared with those of previous periods or with average cost figures for the entire industry. Cost analysis of natural accounts frequently treats costs as percentages of sales. The periodic use of cost-to-sales ratios lets a marketer ascertain cost fluctuations quickly.

As indicated earlier, the analysis of natural accounts may not shed much light on the cost of marketing activities. In such cases, natural accounts must be reclassified into marketing function accounts for analysis. Whether certain natural accounts are reclassified into functional accounts and what criteria are used to reclassify them will depend to some degree on whether the analyst is using direct costing or full costing. After natural accounts have been reclassified into functional accounts, the cost of each function is determined by adding together the costs in each functional account. Once the costs of these marketing functions have been determined, the analyst is ready to compare the resulting figures with budgeted costs, sales analysis data, cost data from earlier operating periods or perhaps average industry cost figures, if these are available.

Although marketers usually obtain a more detailed picture of marketing costs by analysing functional accounts than by analysing natural accounts, some firms need an even more precise cost analysis. The need is especially great if the firms sell several types of products, sell in multiple geographic areas or sell to a wide

Functional Accounts		Product Groups		
		A	B	C
Advertising	£29,500	£14,000	£ 8,000	£ 7,500
Personal selling	40,000	18,000	10,000	12,000
Transport	9,000	5,000	2,000	2,000
Storage	6,800	1,800	2,000	3,000
Marketing research	2,000		1,000	1,000
Total	£87,300	£38,800	£23,000	

Table 24.2 Functional accounts divided into product group costs

variety of customers. Activities vary in marketing different products in specific geographic locations to certain customer groups. Therefore, the costs of these activities also vary. By analysing the functional costs of specific product groups, geographic areas or customer groups, a marketer can find out which of these marketing entities are the most cost effective to serve. In Table 24.2, the functional costs derived in Table 24.1 are allocated to specific product categories.

A similar type of analysis could be performed for geographic areas or for specific customer groups. The criteria used to allocate the functional accounts must be developed so as to yield results that are as accurate as possible. Use of faulty criteria is likely to yield inaccurate cost estimates, which in turn lead to less effective control of marketing strategies. Marketers determine the marketing costs for various product categories, geographic areas or customer groups and then compare them with sales. This analysis lets them evaluate the effectiveness of the firm's marketing strategy or strategies.

• • • • • • • • • • • • • • • • • •

Summary

● In a *marketing orientated organisation,* the focus is on finding out what buyers want and providing it in a way that lets the organisation achieve its objectives. The organisation of marketing activities involves the development of an internal structure for the marketing unit. The internal structure is the key to directing marketing activities. A *centralised organisation* is one in which the top level managers delegate very little authority to lower levels of the firm. In a *decentralised organisation,* decision-making authority is delegated as far down the chain of command as possible. An extreme form of decentralisation is *empowerment,* where front line employees are given the authority and responsibility to make marketing decisions without seeking the approval of their supervisors. The marketing unit can be *organised by* (1) *functions,* (2) *products,* (3) *regions* or (4) *types of customer.* An organisation may use only one approach or a combination.

● *Marketing implementation* is an important part of the marketing management process. To help ensure effective implementation, marketing managers must consider why the intended marketing strategies do not always turn out as expected. *Realised strategies* often differ from the *intended strategies* because of the three problems of implementation: that marketing strategy and implementation are related, that they are constantly evolving and that the responsibility for them is separated. Marketing managers must also consider other vital components of implementation—resources, systems, people, leadership and shared goals—to ensure the proper implementation of marketing strategies.

● Organisations have two major approaches to marketing implementation: *internal marketing* and *total quality management (TQM)*. Internal marketing is a management philosophy that refers to the coordination of internal exchanges between the organisation and its employees to better achieve successful external exchanges between the organisation and its customers. In this approach, all employees have both *external* and *internal customers*. For implementation to be successful, employees must serve the needs of both customer groups. The TQM approach relies heavily on the talents of employees to continually improve the quality of the organisation's goods and services. The three essentials of the TQM philosophy are empowered employees, continuous quality improvement and the use of quality improvement teams. One of TQM's primary tools is *benchmarking*, or measuring and evaluating the quality of an organisation's goods, services or processes in relation to the best performing companies in the industry. Putting the TQM philosophy into practice requires a great deal of organisational resources. For internal marketing or TQM to be successful, top management must be totally committed and the specific elements of either program must be co-ordinated to ensure that they work in harmony with each other.

● Implementation is an important part of the marketing management process. Proper implementation of a marketing plan depends on internal marketing to employees, the motivation of personnel who perform marketing activities, effective communication within the marketing organisation and the co-ordination of marketing activities. A company's communication system must allow the marketing manager to communicate with high level management, with managers of other functional areas in the firm and with personnel involved in marketing activities both inside and outside the organisation. Finally, marketing managers must co-ordinate the activities of marketing personnel and integrate these activities with those in other areas of the company and with the marketing efforts of personnel in external organisations.

● The *marketing control process* consists of establishing performance standards, evaluating actual performance by comparing it with established standards and reducing the difference between desired and actual performance. *Performance standards,* which are established in the planning process, are expected levels of performance with which actual performance can be compared. In evaluating actual performance, marketing managers must know what marketers within the firm are doing and must have information about the activities of external organisations that provide the firm with marketing assistance. Then actual performance is compared with performance standards. Marketers must determine whether a discrepancy exists and, if so, whether it requires corrective action, such as changing the performance standards or improving actual performance.

● To maintain effective marketing control, an organisation needs to develop a comprehensive control process that evaluates its marketing operations at a given time. The control of marketing activities is not a simple task. Problems encountered include environmental changes, time lags between marketing activities and their effects, and difficulty in determining the costs of marketing activities. In addition to these, it may be hard to develop performance standards.

● Control of marketing strategy can be achieved through *sales* and *marketing cost analyses. Sales measurements* are usually analysed in terms of either cash volume or market share. For a sales analysis to be effective, it must compare current sales performance with forecast company sales, industry sales, specific competitors' sales or the costs incurred to generate the current sales volume. A sales analysis can be performed on the firm's total sales, or the total sales can be disaggregated and analysed by product, geographic area or customer group.

● Marketing cost analysis involves an examination of accounts records and, frequently, a reclassification of *natural accounts* into *marketing function accounts*. Three broad categories are used in marketing cost analysis: *direct costs, traceable common costs* and *non-traceable common costs*. Such an analysis is often difficult, because there may be no logical, clear cut way to allocate natural accounts into functional accounts. The analyst may choose either a *direct cost* approach or *full cost* approach. Cost analysis can focus on (1) an aggregate cost analysis of natural accounts or functional accounts or (2) an analysis of functional accounts for products, geographic areas or customer groups.

Important Terms

Marketing orientated
  organisation
Centralised organisation
Decentralised organisation
Empowerment
Organising by functions
Organising by products
Organising by regions
Organising by type of customer
Marketing implementation

Intended strategy
Realised strategy
Internal marketing
External customers
Internal customers
Total quality management
  (TQM)
Benchmarking
Marketing control process
Performance standard

Sales analysis
Sales measurements
Marketing cost analysis
Natural accounts
Marketing function accounts
Direct costs
Traceable common costs
Non-traceable common costs
Full cost approach
Direct cost approach

Discussion and Review Questions

1. What determines the place of marketing within an organisation? Which type of organisation is best suited to the marketing concept? Why?
2. What factors can be used to organise the internal aspects of a marketing unit? Discuss the benefits of each type of organisation.
3. Why might an organisation use multiple bases for organising its marketing unit?
4. What is internal marketing? Why is it important in implementing marketing strategies?
5. Total quality management is a growing force in many businesses. What is TQM? How can it help to implement marketing strategies effectively?

6. Why is motivation of marketing personnel important in implementing marketing plans?
7. How does communication help in implementing marketing plans?
8. What are the major steps of the marketing control process?
9. List and discuss the five requirements for an effective control process.
10. Discuss the major problems in controlling marketing activities.
11. What is a sales analysis? What makes it an effective control tool?
12. Identify and describe three cost analysis methods. Compare and contrast direct costing and full costing.

Recommended Readings

S. Dibb, L. Simkin and J. Bradley, *The Marketing Planning Workbook* (London: International Thomson Business Press, 1996).

N. Piercy, *Market-Led Strategic Change* (Oxford: Butterworth-Heinemann, 1992).

L. Simkin, "People and processes in marketing planning: the benefits of controlling implementation",

Journal of Marketing Management, vol. 12, no. 5, 1996, pp. 375–390.

F. V. Cespedes, *Organising and Implementing the Marketing Effort* (Reading Mass.: Addison-Wesley, 1991).

W. D. Giles, "Making strategy work", *Long Range Planning,* vol. 24, no. 4, 1991, pp. 75–91.

Cases

24.1   Mercury Implements Service!

Recent research by Michael Treacy and Fred Wiersma examined why many small companies can

launch and compete effectively with established market leaders and giant conglomerates. Along with other issues, a key conclusion was that many large companies "just don't seem to know how to please". In today's consumer society customers know what they want, tend to want more and more attributes, and are not as prepared to accept dissatisfaction as perhaps they once were. This reality presents a dilemma for companies operating in the 1990s: they must reduce operating costs but simultaneously improve customer satisfaction. The latter invariably costs money, demanding increased staff training and numbers of specialist personnel, as well as guarantees and customer charters to be honoured and meaningful complaints procedures and refund policies.

In the cut-throat telecommunications market, Mercury's One 2 One mobile phone offensive owes as much to its customer service planning as to the company's need to compete with BT and the leaders in cellular phones: Cellnet, Orange and Vodaphone. Coba Group, which advised Mercury on the marketing for its One 2 One mobile phone network, sought to understand the relationship between the mobile phone operators, network hosts and their customers. Coba identified over 80 transactions that customers carry out with a supplying company, either when they adopt a service or as ongoing users. Coba categorised these transactions in terms of those that benefited both the customer and the supplier, those that helped only one or the other, and those that neither the customer nor the supplier felt were beneficial.

One fundamental implication for Mercury's One 2 One was the role of its earlier sales drives, which offered free call bundles targeted at separate segments in the mobile phone market. Out went Mercury's PersonalCall, StandardCall and Business-Call tariffs, to be replaced by Bronze, Silver and Gold Services. These medal colour service packages gave customers flexibility in their choice of price and service selection. The registration transaction for new customers has also been redesigned. This process is no longer a back office function; the point of registration is up front, typically carried out face-to-face with customers. Tariff, credit and payment options can thus be discussed and mutually agreed on, while same day connection to the network and instant customer connection can still be offered. Understanding customers and their expectations of mobile phone operators has been fundamental to Mercury's re-launch.

The initial take-up for the cellular phone market was by business users, notably travelling sales representatives and tradespeople. This was the market that Mercury first attempted to research and serve. The business user has specific service, usage and price expectations, which are very different from those of the residential or private user. When Mercury first realised the growth potential for the mass market, particularly residential customers, the company knew little of such target customers' needs and expectations. Service levels had to be improved and prices minimised. Previously, the relationship Mercury's personnel enjoyed with customers was strictly orientated to selling or fault solving. Coba and Mercury's focus is to maximise the value of Mercury's relationships with its customers, based on a thorough understanding of customers' needs and relationships with their mobile phone supplier. Such expectations tend to focus more on service, which in a commodity business such as telecoms is an aspect on which to build brand values, competitive advantage and, ultimately, satisfied customers. As for the gas, electricity and water markets—the utilities—in telecoms the customer perception is that prices will continue to drop, while customer service will increase in quality and frequency. For Mercury, this proposition has now formed the heart of the One 2 One business strategy and its advertising through London agency Bartle Bogle Hegarty. Mercury had to alter its operations and working practices before the One 2 One marketing strategy could be successfully implemented. The implementation process itself required a significant level of planning and careful execution.

SOURCES: Roger Trapp, "The vital art of giving customers what they want", *Independent on Sunday*, 2 July 1995, p. IB11; Meg Carter, "Mercury gets the service message", *Independent on Sunday*, 1 October 1995, p. IB8; R. Olins, "Mobile phone war hots up", *The Sunday Times*, 19 November 1995; T. Jackson, "New kids on the telephony block", *Financial Times*, 15 May 1995; Michael Treacy and Fred Wiersma, *The Discipline of Market Leaders* (New York: HarperCollins, 1995).

Questions for Discussion

1. Mercury altered its operation. Why? How did these changes affect its personnel?
2. Why will Mercury need to monitor carefully the implementation of its modified practices?
3. Why is it so important for Mercury to monitor the quality of the service provided?

During the 1970s, watches took a technological leap forward from wind-up spring mechanisms to quartz crystals, batteries and digital displays. The Timex Corporation, however, lagged behind other manufacturers in making the changes. When the Swiss made Swatch invaded department stores and convinced customers that their watches were not just time telling devices but fashion statements, Timex was not ready to offer any competition. At Timex, reliability had always been the number one priority, certainly not style and fashion. For years, Timex's sales suffered because of a drab image, especially in contrast with the colourful Swatch.

Then came the 1990s, the decade of value. As value takes precedence over status, more price-conscious consumers are attracted by quality at moderate prices than by designer labels. Timex is taking advantage of this trend to revive its 41 year old brand, the old reliable Timex watch. By blending its "value pricing" message with some trendy new designs and diversifying its product for specific niche markets, Timex is making a comeback.

Consumers can still buy an unadorned Timex watch for about £5, and analysts say that these simple styles with easy to read faces are the company's best sellers. To compete in a crowded market, however, Timex is developing stylish special collections for two separate adult divisions, dress watches and sports watches, as well as expanding its children's unit. The company has even set up studios in France and the United States to design Timex renditions of colourful creative watches. In the adult fashion arena, Timex offers women its Images line with neon accented hands, floral patterned watch bands, and over-sized faces, and men the Carriage III collection. For those with poor vision, Timex created the Easy Reader with large clear numbers. Sports watch buyers can choose from models with names like Surf, Brave Wave and Magnum that are shock and water resistant and offer features like compasses, pedometers, chronographs and thermometers. After soliciting educators' advice, the company came up with its Gizmoz watches to help children aged 5 to 9 tell time. Colourful designs are on the band instead of the face, which displays all of the numbers and colour codes hour and minute hands. For example, black faced watches have white hours and hour hands but green minutes and minute hands. There is even a Lefty Gizmoz available. To appeal to parents, whose money really buys the Gizmoz watches, Timex offers a kids' loss protection plan that replaces a watch for only half the purchase price.

Timex's advertising strategy is to appeal to niche markets by reviving its traditional "durable yet inexpensive" positioning and revitalising its powerful brand identity. The famous Timex theme, "It Takes a Licking and Keeps On Ticking", takes a humorous bent in television spots where Sumo wrestlers wear Timex watches strapped to their middles as they grapple on the mat and rock musicians use Timex watches to strum their guitars. In a recent print advertising campaign, the firm featured real people who, like the Timex watches they wear, have been through rough experiences but survived to tell the tale. On television talk shows, company executives introduced the Timex *Why Pay More* magazine, featuring Timex watches as part of fashion outfits selling for under £50.

With watch sales in most countries declining, most watchmakers are concerned. At Timex, however, executives are celebrating sales and market share increases. The company now controls a larger segment of the market than its four biggest competitors combined. Timex is happy to be shedding its dowdy and boring image. Rising young professional people don't have to put their wrists behind their backs to hide a Timex any more, or announce loudly to colleagues that they are only wearing a Timex while their Rolex is being repaired. Marketing executives have carefully monitored the introduction of this strategy to (1) ensure that early signs of success or failure could be acted upon and (2) modify marketing programmes continually in order to enhance the impact of Timex's new approach. Sales and financial performance are evaluated regularly: so far they reveal a success story. Changing fashions and aggressive competitors such as Swatch caught Timex out once before. The company does not intend to be left behind again, despite its industrial relations problems in Europe.

Timex's European advertising budget is now close to £6 million, through McCann-Erickson. A major £2.2 million blitz in the UK pushed the company's new Indiglo night-light technology before the rest of the watch industry developed rival technology. This campaign, too, was carefully monitored and rivals' reactions assessed. Continual benchmarking of Timex's fortunes is helping the company compete effectively and with great success.

SOURCES: Cara Appelbaum, "High time for Timex", *Adweek's Marketing Week*, 29 July 1991, p. 24; BBC/ITN News Broadcasts, Spring 1993; "Timex races for Indiglo profits", *Marketing*, 31 March 1994, p. 3; "Briefs", *Marketing*, 6 January 1994, p. 6; "Rzed opens shop with Timex infomercial", *Campaign*, 19 May 1995, p. 8.

Questions for Discussion

1. Which environmental forces are likely to be of greatest interest to marketing managers at Timex?
2. Identify the target markets towards which Timex is aiming its products.
3. Why must Timex continually assess its performance and the impact of its marketing?

25 MARKETING ETHICS AND SOCIAL RESPONSIBILITY

"Virtues such as honesty are not self-evident when applied to complex marketing decisions."

O. C. Ferrell
University of Memphis

OBJECTIVES

- To define and understand the importance of marketing ethics
- To recognise factors that influence ethical or unethical decisions
- To discuss some important ethical issues in marketing
- To identify ways to improve ethical decisions in marketing
- To understand the concept of social responsibility
- To explore several important issues of social responsibility
- To describe strategies for dealing with social dilemmas

Alcoholic soft drinks took the UK market by storm in the summer of 1995. In a recent survey of 18 to 24 year olds, 84 per cent of those questioned were aware of the new sector. With names like Hooper's Hooch (Bass), Lemonheads (Carlsberg-Tetley) and Two Dogs (Merrydown), the so called alcopops provided a welcome boost for the brewers and cider makers. Early entrants into the market were quickly followed by a host of others. Even supermarket giant Sainsbury's has joined the foray with its sub-brand Piranha.

However, before long the drinks industry was being resoundingly attacked by consumer pressure groups and politicians who claimed that the packaging and marketing of the drinks was appealing too strongly to under age drinkers. Such was the visibility and success of the campaign that the manufacturers moved quickly to re-package and re-name the brands. The brewer Whitbread, just one of the companies that have elected to modify their branding of alcopops, now openly states its intention not to tempt under age drinkers. As it launched its new range of Shott's Alcoholic

As individual manufacturers move to respond to the concern expressed by the public, the brewers' and cider makers' industry body, the Portman Group, which promotes "sensible drinking", has drawn up a code of conduct to guide marketing activity in the sector. The underlying rationale for the code is in line with the Advertising Standards Authority's recommendation that drinks should not be advertised to appeal to children. Initial feedback from the Portman Group is that the marketing of the drinks should not lead a "reasonable" individual to say that they are targeted at children. The good news for the consumer in all this is that public pressure counts and can persuade businesses to heed their ethical and social responsibilities. ∎

Seltzers aimed at adult drinkers, the company shied away from names Lemonade Bomb and Cream Soda Blast because of their association with soft drinks aimed at children. Instead the company went to market with brand names Lemon Jag, Soda Heist and Cranberry Charge. The company also chose not to market the new range in cans, so often associated with soft drinks. Instead, Shott's Alcoholic Seltzers appeared in 330 ml bottles.

SOURCES: David Benady, "Soft targets", *Marketing Week,* 19 January 1996; David Benady, "Whitbread rejigs alcopop launch for 'adult' appeal", *Marketing Week,* 9 February 1996; Julien Lee, "Sainsbury sinks teeth into 'soft booze' market", *Marketing,* 16 November 1995; Harriet Marsh, "'Soft booze' focuses spend below-the-line", *Marketing,* 23 November 1995; Sharon Marshall, "Will Cott strike gold with cola?", *Marketing,* 25 January 1996; Ros Snowdon, "New 'alcopops' avoid under-18s", *Marketing,* 8 February 1996.

Marketers need to be aware of the ethical and social responsibility issues that may arise out of the marketing of their products and services. The manufacturers of so called alcoholic soft drinks have attracted a considerable degree of media and public criticism from those who feel that the best interests of young consumers were not receiving sufficient attention. The issue of ethics in marketing is evolving and set to increase in prominence.

The debate over the marketing of alcoholic soft drinks illustrates that all marketing activities can be judged as morally right or wrong by society, consumers, interest groups, competitors and others. Although most marketers operate within the limits of the law, some do engage in activities that are not considered acceptable by other marketers, consumers and society in general. A number of recently publicised incidents in marketing, such as deceptive or objectionable advertising, misleading packaging, questionable selling practices, manipulation, corruption and pollution, have raised questions as to whether specific marketing practices are acceptable and beneficial to society. The limits of acceptable marketing practices and the obligations marketers have to society are issues of marketing ethics and social responsibility.

This chapter gives an overview of the role of ethics and social responsibility in marketing decision-making. The chapter first defines marketing ethics and discusses the factors that influence ethical decision-making in marketing. Next it outlines some specific ethical issues in marketing and explores ways to improve ethics in marketing decisions. The chapter then focuses on the issue of social responsibility as its core theme, looking at the impact of marketing decisions on society and developing some strategies for dealing with social responsibility dilemmas. The chapter closes by comparing and contrasting the concepts of marketing ethics and social responsibility.

• • • • • • • • • • • • • • • • • • •

The Nature of Marketing Ethics

Despite the importance of ethics in marketing decisions, no one has yet developed a universally accepted approach for dealing with this controversial and often misunderstood concept. However, marketing personnel need to examine the issue of marketing ethics to help them make marketing decisions that are acceptable and beneficial to society. This is not always easy, as well intentioned marketing managers are frequently pushed in the wrong direction by organisational pressures.[1] This section considers the meaning of marketing ethics.

Marketing Ethics Defined

Marketing ethics Moral principles that define right and wrong behaviour in marketing

Ethics relate to moral evaluations of decisions and actions as right or wrong on the basis of commonly accepted principles of behaviour. **Marketing ethics** are moral principles that define right and wrong behaviour in marketing. The most basic ethical issues have been formalised through laws and regulations to conform to the standards of society. At the very least, marketers are expected to obey these laws and regulations. However, it is important to realise that marketing ethics go beyond legal issues; ethical marketing decisions foster mutual trust among individuals and in marketing relationships.

Ethics are individually defined and may vary from one person to another. Some companies, such as Levi Strauss, have been taking more initiative in this area in the belief that consumers are looking more and more to the company behind the product.[2] Although individual marketers often act in their own self-interest, there must be standards of acceptable behaviour to guide all marketing decisions. Marketers need to operate in accordance with sound moral principles based on ideals such as fairness, justice and trust.[3] Consumers generally regard unethical marketing activities—for instance, deceptive advertising, misleading selling tactics, price fixing and the deliberate marketing of harmful products—as unacceptable and often refuse to do business with marketers that engage in such practices. Thus when marketers deviate from accepted moral principles to further their own interests at the expense of others, continued marketing exchanges become difficult, if not impossible.[4]

Marketing Ethics Are Controversial

Few topics in marketing are more controversial than ethics. Most people can make a judgement as to whether they believe a particular marketing decision to be right or wrong, ethical or unethical, but their ideas depend on the nature of the organisation, their experiences in life and their personal values. Many marketers have such strong convictions about what is morally right or wrong that they deeply resent discussions of alternative ways to make ethical decisions.

Regardless of how a person or an organisation views the acceptability of a particular activity, if society judges that activity to be wrong or unethical, then this view directly affects the organisation's ability to achieve its goals. Although not all activities deemed unethical by society may be illegal, consumer protests against a particular activity may result in legislation that restricts or bans it. When an organisation engages in unethical marketing activities, it may not only lose sales as dissatisfied consumers refuse to deal with it, it may also face lawsuits, fines and even prison for its executives. Manufacturer Hoover ran a now infamous sales promotion in late 1992 offering free flights to anyone purchasing a Hoover product valued over £100. Thousands of consumers purchased Hoover vacuum cleaners and washing machines expressly to take advantage of this offer, but many hundreds were disappointed. The offer was flawed: some of Hoover's agents acted unscrupulously; few people were offered their choice of holiday destination; the BBC programme *Watchdog* showed agents deliberately obstructing consumers attempting to take up the offer. Hoover had not broken any laws but was deemed by the media and consumers to have behaved unethically.[5] Several years have passed, yet many consumers are still suspicious of this form of promotion. Such an example illustrates the importance of understanding marketing ethics and recognising ethical issues.

Because marketing ethics are so controversial, it is important to state that it is not the purpose of this chapter to question anyone's personal ethical beliefs and convictions. Nor is it the purpose of this chapter to examine the behaviour of consumers, although consumers, too, may be unethical (engaging, for instance, in coupon fraud, shoplifting and other abuses). Instead, its goal is to highlight the importance of ethical issues and ethical decision-making in marketing. Understanding the impact of ethical decisions in marketing can help people to recognise and resolve ethical issues within an organisation.

● ● ● ● ● ● ● ● ● ● ● ● ● ● ● ● ● ●

Understanding the Ethical Decision-Making Process

To grasp the significance of ethics in marketing decision-making, it is necessary to examine the factors that influence the ethical decision-making process. Individual factors, organisational relationships and opportunity are three factors that interact to determine ethical decisions in marketing (see Figure 25.1).

Individual Factors

Moral philosophies Principles or rules that individuals use to determine the appropriate way to behave

Moral philosophies are principles or rules that individuals use to determine appropriate behaviour. They provide guidelines for resolving conflicts and ensuring mutual benefit for all members of society.[6] People learn these principles and rules through socialisation by family members, social groups, religion and formal education. Each moral philosophy has its own concept of rightness or "ethicalness" and rules for behaviour. Here two distinct moral philosophies are discussed: utilitarianism and ethical formalism.

Utilitarianism A moral philosophy concerned with maximising the greatest good for the greatest number of people

Utilitarianism **Utilitarianism** is a moral philosophy concerned with maximising the greatest good for the greatest number of people. Utilitarians judge an action on the basis of the consequences for all the people affected by the action. In other words, in a situation with an ethical component, utilitarians compare all possible options and select the one that promises the best results. Under utilitarianism, then, it would be unethical to act in a way that leads to personal gain at the expense of society in general. Consider the following example of an organisation adopting a utilitarian philosophy. In 1990, the offices of Delta Air Lines in Ireland received a telephone threat from terrorists that one of its transatlantic flights

Figure 25.1

Factors that influence the
ethical decision-making
process

would be bombed. Delta decided to publicise the threat and announced that it would allow customers holding tickets on its transatlantic flights to transfer them to other airlines without penalty.[7] When Pan Am received a bomb threat in 1988, it did not notify the public; the subsequent loss of more than 200 lives in the terrorist bombing of Pan Am Flight 103 over Lockerbie and the negative publicity directed at Pan Am damaged the firm. Thus, after weighing the possible loss of life and the negative publicity surrounding a terrorist bombing or crash against the loss of revenue and profits, Delta executives probably concluded that publicising the bomb threat and letting passengers decide whether to fly on Delta would be best for consumers and for the company.

Ethical formalism A system of specific rules for behaviour based on whether an action can be taken consistently as a general rule without concern for alternative results

Ethical Formalism Other moral philosophies focus on the intentions associated with a particular behaviour and on the rights of the individual. **Ethical formalism** develops specific rules for behaviour by determining whether an action can be taken consistently as a general rule without concern for alternative results.[8] Behaviour is judged on the basis of whether it infringes individual rights or universal rules. The Golden Rule—do unto others as you would have them do unto you—exemplifies ethical formalism. In marketing, ethical formalism is consistent with the idea of consumer choice. For example, consumers have a right to know about possible defects in a car or other products that involve safety.[9]

Applying Moral Philosophies to Marketing Decision-Making Traditionally, it has been assumed that personal moral philosophies remain constant in both work and non-work situations. However, research has shown that most business people use one moral philosophy at work and a completely different one outside work.[10] Furthermore, marketers may sometimes change their value structure or moral philosophy when making decisions.[11]

Another study found that although personal moral philosophies and values enter into ethical decisions in business, they are not the central component that guides the decisions, actions and policies of an organisation.[12] This finding may explain why individuals switch moral philosophies between home and work and why personal values make up only one part of an organisation's total value system.

Some marketers use the logic that anything is fair that defeats the competition and increases profits. They have used warfare concepts such as "guerrilla warfare", "pre-emptive first strikes" and "counter attacks" to justify questionable and possibly unethical actions. A distinction should be made between competitors and enemies. Competitors are rivals vying for customers and markets according to socially accepted rules, whereas enemies at war seek total conquest and, in some cases, elimination of the enemy. Given the destructive nature of warfare, the "marketing as warfare" comparison raises ethical concerns.[13]

Others view marketing as a game, like football or boxing, in which ordinary rules and morality do not apply. For example, what if a boxer decided it was wrong to try to injure another person or a rugby player was afraid of hurting another player when he made contact? Sports have rules and referees to regulate the game to ensure safety and equality. However, because customers in marketing exchanges are not economically self-sufficient, they cannot choose to withdraw from the marketing "game". This means that marketing ethics must make clear what rules apply in the marketing "game" and that the rules developed must be appropriate to the non-voluntary character of participation in the game. Most members of society hold that moral principles and standards of acceptable behaviour should guide decisions related to the welfare of customers.[14]

Ethical behaviour may be a function of two different dimensions of an organisation's value structure: the organisation's values and traditions, or corporate culture, and the personal moral philosophies of the organisation's individual members. An employee assumes some measure of moral responsibility by agreeing to abide by an organisation's rules and standard operating procedures. When a marketer decides to behave unethically or even illegally, it may be that competitive pressures and organisational rewards provided the incentive.

Organisational Relationships

Organisational culture A set of values or beliefs, goals, norms and rituals that members of an organisation share

People's personal moral philosophies and ethical behaviour are learned not only from society in general but also from members of their social groups and their **organisational culture**. A corporate or organisational culture can be defined as a set of values, beliefs, goals, norms and rituals that members or employees of an organisation share.[15] Relationships with employees, co-workers, or superiors create ethical problems. Employees must balance the need to maintain confidences, meet obligations and handle responsibilities. Sometimes these needs conflict and lead to ethical dilemmas. For example, a salesperson may be asked to lie to a customer over the phone. Likewise, an employee who sees another employee cheating a customer must decide whether to report the incident.

Marketing managers must carefully balance their duties to the owners or shareholders who employed them to carry out the organisation's objectives and to the employees who look to them for guidance and direction. In addition, managers must also comply with society's wishes and ethical evaluations. Striking an ethical balance between these areas, then, is a difficult task for today's marketing decision-makers.

The role of top management is extremely important in developing the culture of an organisation. Most experts agree that the chief executive officer or the director in charge of marketing sets the ethical tone for the entire marketing organisation. Lower level managers take their cues from top management, yet they, too, impose some of their personal values on the company. This interaction between corporate culture and executive leadership helps determine the ethical value system of the firm.

Powerful superiors can affect employees' activities and directly influence behaviour by putting into practice the company's standards of ethics. Young marketers in particular indicate that they often go along with their superiors to demonstrate loyalty in matters related to judgements of morality. A manager in a position of authority can exert strong pressure to ensure compliance on ethically related issues. In organisations where ethical standards are vague and supervision by superiors is limited, peers may provide guidance in an ethical decision.

The role of peers in the decision-making process depends on the person's ratio of exposure to unethical behaviour to exposure to ethical behaviour. The more people are exposed to unethical activity in the organisational environment, the more likely they are to behave unethically themselves.[16] Employees experience conflict between what is expected of them as workers and managers and what they expect of themselves based on their own personal ethical standards.

Opportunity

Opportunity A favourable set of conditions that limit barriers or provide rewards

Opportunity provides another pressure that may determine whether a person will behave ethically. **Opportunity** is a favourable set of conditions that limit barriers or provide rewards. Rewards may be internal or external. Internal rewards are the feelings of goodness and worth a person experiences after carrying out an altruistic action. External rewards are what a person expects to receive from others in terms of values generated and provided on an exchange basis. External rewards are often received from peers and top management in the form of praise, promotions and pay raises.

If a marketer takes advantage of an opportunity to act unethically and is rewarded or suffers no penalty, he or she may repeat such acts as other opportunities arise. For example, a salesperson who receives a pay rise after using a deceptive sales presentation to increase sales is being rewarded for this behaviour and so will probably continue it. Indeed, opportunity to engage in unethical conduct is often a better predictor of unethical activities than personal values.[17]

Besides rewards and the absence of punishment, other elements in the business environment help to create opportunities. Professional codes of ethics and a company policy on ethics also influence opportunity by prescribing what behaviours are acceptable. The larger the rewards and the lesser the punishment for unethical behaviour, the greater the probability that unethical behaviour will be practised.

● ● ● ● ● ● ● ● ● ● ● ● ● ● ● ● ● ● ●

Ethical Issues in Marketing

Ethical issue An identifiable problem, situation or opportunity requiring an individual or organisation to choose from among several actions that must be evaluated as right or wrong, ethical or unethical

An individual will make an ethical decision only when he or she recognises that a particular issue or situation has an ethical or moral component. Thus developing awareness of ethical issues is important in understanding marketing ethics. An **ethical issue** is an identifiable problem, situation or opportunity requiring an individual or organisation to choose from among several actions that must be evaluated as right or wrong, ethical or unethical. Any time an activity causes consumers to feel deceived, manipulated or cheated, a marketing ethical issue exists, regardless of the legality of that activity.

Ethical issues typically arise because of conflicts between individuals' personal moral philosophies and the marketing strategies, policies and organisational environment in which they work. Ethical issues may stem from conflicts between a marketer's attempts to achieve organisational objectives and customers' desires for safe, fair and reliable products. For example, a London baker took Barclays Bank plc to court, claiming that the bank had failed to pass on interest rate cuts, thus causing him to pay back too much on a commercial loan. Barclays defended its position by saying that it was not obliged to review repayments when base rates were cut. The court ruled in the baker's favour, opening the way for a host of copy-cat claims from other small businesses dissatisfied with their banks. Similarly, organisational objectives that call for increased profits or market share may pressure marketers to steal competitors' secrets, knowingly put an unsafe product on the market or engage in some other questionable activity. For example, in South Korea, Lucky Goldstar Group markets a detergent packaged in an orange box with a whirlpool design just like Procter & Gamble's Tide brand. The product is called Tie, and Procter & Gamble does not make it or license it to Goldstar.[18] Obviously, the attempt to develop a Tide look-alike without Procter & Gamble's permission creates an ethical issue.

Regardless of the reasons behind specific ethical issues, once the issues are identified, marketers and organisations must decide how to deal with them. In marketing many different ethical issues arise, and although it is not possible to review them all here, the following examination of some key issues provides some direction and should lead to an understanding of the ethical problems that marketers must confront.

Product Issues

Product related ethical issues generally arise when marketers fail to disclose risks associated with the product or information about its function, value or use. Competitive pressures can also create product related ethical issues. As competition intensifies and profit margins diminish, there may be pressures to substitute inferior materials or product components so as to reduce costs. An ethical issue arises when marketers fail to inform customers about changes in product quality; this failure is a form of dishonesty about the nature of the product. Consider the following example. Lever Brothers launched a new version of its Persil brand of washing powder. Known as Persil Power, the detergent claimed to have particularly outstanding cleaning ability. When Lever's senior managers launched Persil Power, they strongly believed that the accelerator (special ingredient) the product contained would give them a competitive advantage over rival detergents. Yet concerns were soon being expressed that the product was causing clothes to rot. Consumer concern was evidenced by a slump in the brand's market share. Before long, supermarket Tesco responded to the concerns by removing Persil Power from its shelves. Rival Procter & Gamble was quick to take advantage of the bad publicity, beginning its own black propaganda game aimed at further undermining Lever's position. Meanwhile, Lever Brothers failed to respond decisively to the criticisms. For a while the company stood by Persil Power, claiming that the problems were exaggerated. Ultimately though, it was forced to pull the brand, replacing it with New Generation Persil, backed up with a fresh advertising campaign.[19] Many companies, of course, take care to emphasise product safety concerns in their advertising. Such messages send a signal to all employees in the organisation, as well as to customers, concerning a firm's ethical standards.

Promotion Issues

The communication process provides a variety of situations that can create ethical issues: for instance, false and misleading advertising and manipulative or deceptive sales promotions, tactics or publicity efforts. This [...] some ethical issues associated with advertising and personal se[...]

Advertising Unethical actions in advertising can destroy the tr[...] in an organisation. Sometimes adverts are questioned because t[...]

competitor. For example, after McDonald's introduced a chicken product in some regions of the US, Kentucky Fried Chicken used television advertisements featuring a clown named Mr. R. McDonald being questioned by a congressional committee. In one advert, when asked what McDonald's has that Kentucky Fried Chicken does not, Mr. McDonald replies, "Toys … lots of toys". The CBS television network refused to broadcast the advert, saying, "We felt the commercial was unfairly denigrating to the corporate image of McDonald's". Although both the NBC and ABC networks showed the advertisements, CBS considered them ethically questionable.[20]

Abuses in advertising can range from exaggerated claims and concealed facts to outright lying. Exaggerated claims cannot be substantiated; for example, claims that a certain age reversing skin lotion is superior to any other on the market often cannot be verified by consumers or experts. Concealed facts are material facts deliberately omitted from a message. Perrier's packaging implies that the bubbles in its mineral water are natural and are bottled at the source. Many consumers still believe that the bubbles in their mineral water are natural, yet many products have these bubbles added during the bottling process. When consumers learn that promotion messages are untrue, they may feel cheated and refuse to buy the product again; they may also complain to government or other regulatory bodies. Consequently, marketers should take care to provide all the important facts and avoid making claims that cannot be supported. For a while Sainsbury's refused to stock brand leader Perrier because it considered the labelling misleading to consumers.

Another form of advertising abuse involves ambiguous statement—statements using words so weak that the viewer, reader or listener must infer advertisers' intended messages. These "weasel" words are inherently vague and enable the advertiser to deny any intent to deceive. For example, one common "weasel" word is *help*, as in "helps prevent", "helps fight", or "helps make you feel".[21] Such advertising practices are questionable if they deceive the consumer outright. Although some marketers view such statements as acceptable, others do not. Thus vague messages remain an ethical issue in advertising.

Personal Selling A common problem in personal selling is judging what types of sales activities are acceptable. Consumers may perceive salespeople as unethical because of the common belief that sales personnel often pressure customers to purchase products they neither need nor want. Nevertheless, the sales forces of most firms, such as IBM and Procter & Gamble, are well educated, well trained and professional; they know that they must act ethically or risk losing valuable customers and sales. Although most salespeople are ethical, some do engage in questionable actions. For example, some use very aggressive and manipulative tactics to sell almost worthless gemstones, holidays or other products over the phone. Even though these salespeople may be fined for their activities, their unethical and often illegal actions contribute to consumers' mistrust of telephone selling and personal selling in general.

At one time or another, most salespeople face an ethical conflict in their jobs. For example, a salesperson may have to decide whether to tell a customer the truth and risk losing the customer's business, or somehow mislead the customer to appease him or her and ensure a sale. Failure to train salespeople adequately in how to deal with such situations leaves them unprepared to cope with ethical issues when they arise and may result in high levels of job frustration, anxiety and stress for the personnel concerned.

Pen and pencil set (with company logo)
Five year supply of notepads (with company logo)
Dinner at a four star French restaurant
Box of grapefruit shipped to your house each Christmas
Season tickets to sport of your choice
Weekend break
Three day, all expenses paid golfing holiday
Trip to a ski resort
Lavish trip to an exotic foreign resort
£1,000 in cash
Free PC and software

SOURCE: Adapted from E. J. Muller, "Traffigraft: is accepting a gift from a vendor a breach of ethics? To some people, it's just a perk. To others, it's poison", *Distribution*, January 1990, p. 38. © Distribution Magazine. Reprinted with permission.

Table 25.1 Which of these gifts could be considered a bribe?

Frequently, the problem of ethics has a snowball effect. Once a salesperson has deceived a customer, it becomes increasingly difficult to tell the truth later. If the customer learns of the deception, the sales representative will lose all credibility in the eyes of the customer, as well as that customer's associates and friends. The way in which a salesperson deals with an ethical issue can therefore have far reaching consequences for both the individual and the firm.

Bribery in Selling Situations   When payments, gifts or special favours are granted to obtain a sale or for some other reason, there is always some question of bribery. This important ethical issue is further complicated by the fact that in some countries the use of bribes is accepted business practice. A bribe is anything given to influence improperly the outcome of a decision. Even when a bribe is offered to benefit the organisation, it is usually considered unethical, and it hurts the organisation in the long run by jeopardising trust and fairness. Table 25.1 lists some possible gifts that could be offered by a salesperson in an attempt to gain sales. Clearly, defining a bribe is often a matter of personal values and judgement. Bribery is pernicious, for it stifles fair competition among businesses and limits consumer choice.

Pricing Issues   Price fixing, predatory pricing and failure to disclose the full price associated with a purchase are typical ethical issues. The emotional and subjective nature of price creates many situations in which misunderstandings between the seller and buyer cause ethical problems. Marketers have the right to price their products so that they earn a reasonable profit, but ethical issues may crop up when a company seeks to earn high profits at the expense of its customers. When Richard Branson launched Virgin Cola, he supported its relatively low price by arguing that consumers were effectively paying a brand tax on leading cola brands.

Distribution Issues   Ethical issues in distribution involve relationships between producers and marketing middlemen. Marketing middlemen, or intermediaries (wholesalers, retailers and dealers), facilitate the flow of products from the producer to the ultimate consumer. Each intermediary performs a different role and accepts certain rights, responsibilities and rewards associated with that role. For example, producers can expect retailers to honour payment agreements and keep them informed of inventory needs. Failure to make payments in a timely manner may be considered an ethical issue.

The numerous relationships between marketing intermediaries present many opportunities for conflicts and disputes, some of which may be related to ethical or unethical behaviour. Manipulating a product's availability for purposes of exploitation and using coercion to force intermediaries to behave in a specific manner are particularly serious ethical issues in the distribution sphere. For example, a powerful manufacturer can exert undue influence over an intermediary's choice of whether to handle a product or how to handle it.

Other ethical issues in distribution relate to some stores' refusal to deal with some types of middlemen. A number of conflicts are developing in the distribution of microcomputer software. Many software only stores are bypassing wholesalers and establishing direct relationships with software producers. Some dishonest stores are "hacking", or making unauthorised copies of software, preventing the producers from getting their due compensation. These occurrences have spawned suspicion and general ethical conflict in the distribution of software.[22]

Some controversy also surrounds retailers such as Tesco or Marks & Spencer, which often insist on doing business directly with a producer rather than using an intermediary. Marks & Spencer has been accused of threatening to buy from other producers if firms refuse to sell to it directly. Similar buy direct policies are in effect at B&Q, the largest UK retailer of do-it-yourself building supplies, and at Do It All, the home improvement chain. These retailers, which emphasise low prices, maintain that bypassing intermediaries cuts costs and does not involve any ethical issues. However, some small companies cannot afford to maintain their own sales forces and must rely on intermediaries to sell their products to retailers. The refusal of Tesco or B&Q and others to deal with intermediaries effectively shuts these smaller companies out of the market because they cannot compete with companies that have their own sales forces.

. . . .

Improving Ethical Decisions in Marketing

Unethical behaviour generally arises because of unethical personnel or problems with the organisation's ethical standards. One way to view an organisation's ethical standards is by considering a "bad apple—bad barrel" analogy. Some people always act in their own self-interest regardless of organisational goals or accepted moral standards; they are sometimes called "bad apples". To eliminate unethical behaviour, an organisation must rid itself of these bad apples, or unethical people. It can attain this goal through screening techniques and through enforcement of ethics codes.[23] However, organisations also sometimes become "bad barrels"— not because the individuals within them are bad, but because the pressures to survive and succeed create conditions that reward unethical behaviour. A way of resolving the problem of the bad barrel is to redesign the organisation's image and culture so that it conforms to industry and societal norms of ethical behaviour.[24]

By making marketers aware of ethical issues and potential areas of conflict, it is possible to eliminate or defuse some of the ethical pressures that occur in daily marketing activities. Awareness of and sensitivity towards ethical issues can eliminate the risk of making unethical decisions. Marketing Insight 25.1 (on page 752) illustrates how one retailer, Body Shop, has promoted ethics and social responsibility issues. Ethical values must be built into the organisational culture and marketing strategy by establishing codes of ethics and by controlling unethical behaviour when it occurs.[25]

Codes of Ethics

Codes of ethics Formalised rules and standards that describe what the company expects of its employees

It is difficult for employees to determine whether behaviour within an organisation is acceptable if the organisation does not have uniform policies and standards. Without standards of behaviour, employees will generally make decisions based on their observations of how their peers and managers behave. **Codes of ethics** are formalised rules and standards that describe what the company expects of its employees. Codes of ethics encourage ethical behaviour by minimising opportunities for unethical behaviour: the company's employees know both what is expected of them and what the punishment is for violating the rules. Codes of ethics also help marketers deal with ethical issues or dilemmas that develop in daily operations by prescribing or limiting certain activities. They do this by providing general guidelines for achieving organisational goals and objectives in a morally acceptable manner. Top management should also provide leadership and guidelines in implementing the codes.

Table 25.2 presents the American Marketing Association's Code of Ethics. The code does not cover every ethical issue, but it is a useful overview of what marketers believe are sound moral principles for guiding marketing activities. This code could be used to help structure an organisation's code of ethics.

Controlling Unethical Behaviour

Ethical behaviour in marketing must be based on a strong moral foundation, including personal moral development and an organisational structure that encourages and rewards ethical action. The impact of competitive pressures on ethical behaviour must be understood. The idea that marketing ethics are learned at home, at school and in family relationships does not recognise the impact of opportunity and the organisation on the ethics of decision-makers.

If a company is to maintain ethical behaviour, its policies, rules and standards must be worked into its control system. If the number of employees making ethical decisions on a regular basis is not satisfactory, then the company must take corrective action through enforcement of its code of ethics. If codes are mere window dressing and do not relate to what is expected or to what is rewarded in the corporate culture, then they serve no purpose except to give an illusion of concern about ethical behaviour.

• • • • • • • • • • • • • • • • • •

The Nature of Social Responsibility

Social responsibility An organisation's obligation to maximise its positive impact and minimise its negative impact on society

The concepts of ethics and social responsibility are often used interchangeably, although each has a distinct meaning. **Social responsibility** in marketing refers to an organisation's obligation to maximise its positive impact and minimise its negative impact on society. Whereas ethics relate to individual decisions, social responsibility concerns the impact of an organisation's decisions on society.

For example, the launch of the UK National Lottery (see Case 25.1) has attracted considerable national interest, with top prizes of many millions of

Members of the American Marketing Association (AMA) are committed to ethical professional conduct. They have joined together in subscribing to this Code of Ethics embracing the following topics:

Responsibilities of the Marketer

Marketers must accept responsibility for the consequences of their activities and make every effort to ensure that their decisions, recommendations and actions function to identify, serve and satisfy all relevant publics: consumers, organisations and society. Marketers' professional conduct must be guided by:

1. The basic rule of professional ethics: not knowingly to do harm;
2. The adherence to all applicable laws and regulations;
3. The accurate representation of their education, training and experience; and
4. The active support, practice and promotion of this Code of Ethics.

Honesty and Fairness

Marketers shall uphold and advance the integrity, honour and dignity of the marketing profession by:

1. Being honest in serving consumers, clients, employees, suppliers, distributors and the public;
2. Not knowingly participating in conflict of interest without prior notice to all parties involved; and
3. Establishing equitable fee schedules including the payment or receipt of usual, customary } and/or legal compensation for marketing exchanges.

Rights and Duties of Parties

Participants in the marketing exchange process should be able to expect that:

1. Products and services offered are safe and fit for their intended uses;
2. Communications about offered products and services are not deceptive;
3. All parties intend to discharge their obligations, financial and otherwise, in good faith; and

4. Appropriate internal methods exist for equitable adjustment and/or redress of grievances concerning purchases.

It is understood that the above would include, *but is not limited to,* the following responsibilities of the marketer:

In the Area of Product Development Management:

Disclosure of all substantial risks associated with product or service usage

Identification of any product component substitution that might materially change the product or impact on the buyer's purchase decision

Identification of extra cost added features

In the area of promotions:

Avoidance of false and misleading advertising

Rejection of high pressure manipulations, or misleading sales tactics

Avoidance of sales promotions that use deception or manipulation

In the Area of Distribution:

Not manipulating the availability of a product for purpose of exploitation

Not using coercion in the marketing channel

Not exerting undue influence over the resellers' choice to handle a product

In the Area of Pricing:

Not engaging in price fixing

Not practicing predatory pricing

Disclosing the full price associated with any purchase

In the Area of Marketing Research:

Prohibiting selling or fund raising under the guise of conducting research

Maintaining research integrity by avoiding misrepresentation and omission of pertinent research data

Treating outside clients and suppliers fairly

Organisational Relationships

Marketers should be aware of how their behaviour may influence or impact on the behaviour of others in organisational relationships. They should not

(Continues)

Table 25.2 The American Marketing Association's Code of Ethics encourage or apply coercion to obtain unethical behaviour in their relationships with others, such as employees, suppliers or customers.

1. Apply confidentiality and anonymity in professional relationships with regard to privileged information.
2. Meet their obligations and responsibilities in contracts and mutual agreements in a timely manner.
3. Avoid taking the work of others, in whole, or in part, and representing this work as their own or

directly benefiting from it without compensation or consent of the originator or owner.

4. Avoid manipulation to take advantage of situations to maximise personal welfare in a way that unfairly deprives or damages the organisation or others.

Any AMA members found to be in violation of any provision of this Code of Ethics may have his or her Association membership suspended or revoked.

NOTE: A similar code has yet to be produced in the EU.
SOURCE: Reprinted by permission of the American Marketing Association.

Table 25.2 The American Marketing Association's Code of Ethics (cont.)

pounds on offer. As lottery players become obsessed with the idea of winning a fortune, politicians, community leaders and the clergy are becoming concerned about the possible effects of this new gambling fever on family budgets. While interest groups are divided over a possible solution to this problem, some believe that Camelot, the company that organises the National Lottery, should cut the value of top prizes.[26] Social responsibility, then, can be viewed as a contract with society, whereas ethics relate to carefully thought out rules of moral values that guide individual and group decision-making.

Impact of Social Responsibility on Marketing

Marketing managers try to determine what accepted relationships, obligations and duties exist between the marketing organisation and society. Increasingly, businesses are recognising that the long term value of conducting business in a socially responsible manner far outweighs short term costs.[27] To preserve socially responsible behaviour while achieving organisational goals, organisations must monitor changes and trends in society's values. For example, retailers around the world are responding to public concerns about the conditions in which animals are reared and are putting pressure on producers to develop more humane farming methods. Control procedures are needed to ensure that organisations act appropriately, and the organisation's top management must assume some responsibility for its employees' conduct by establishing and enforcing policies.

Being socially responsible may be a noble and necessary endeavour, but it is not a simple one. To be socially responsible, marketers must confront certain major issues. Robertson's had, for four decades, used its black Golliwog brand mark on its market leading jams. Racial tension and increasingly vocal ethnic groups persuaded the company to minimise this potentially offensive symbol. Marketers therefore must determine what society wants and then predict the long term effects of their decisions, often by turning to experts such as lawyers, doctors and scientists. Even here there can be problems, as experts may disagree with one another.

Forty years ago, for example, tobacco marketers promoted cigarettes as being good for health. Now, years after the discovery that cigarette smoking is

The Body Shop Promotes Ethics and Social Responsibility Worldwide

In 1976, Anita Roddick, then a 33 year old house-wife, opened a store in Brighton to sell natural body lotions. Since then, sales and profits of the Body Shop's retail chain have grown an average of 50 per cent a year. By 1992, the company had 730 Body Shop stores (94 per cent franchised) in 41 countries, with pre-tax profits of £28 million on sales of £147.5 million. A new shop opens every two to three days. There are now over 520 outside the UK. Annual return to investors has averaged 97 per cent over the past five years. Much of the Body Shop's success can be attributed to a combination of smart retailing practices and a strong sense of ethics and social responsibility.

The Body Shop stores sell wholly natural cosmetics made from high quality, biodegradable ingredients packaged in recyclable containers. Its products are not developed in laboratories or tested on animals like those of many other cosmetic companies. Each store is designed to be self-service, and the sales staff, while very knowledgeable about Body Shop products, provide information and do not force sales. To educate consumers about how its products are made and where their ingredients come from, the company uses bright graphics, videos and a sense of style and humour.

What drives Body Shop's socially responsible activities is Roddick's firm belief that companies must be concerned with more than profits, that they must be accountable for their actions and how they affect the environment, just as people are responsible for themselves and their neighbours. This philosophy is further emphasised by the Body Shop's support of such causes as saving endangered whales and vanishing rain forests. All of these issues surround customers in the form of banners, pamphlets, T-shirts and posters emphasising the importance of social issues.

Unlike many other companies that expand operations into various global markets to generate profits but give little or nothing back to the local community, Body Shop's goal is to spread its message of social responsibility and political activism. Roddick spends up to five months per year travelling throughout the developing world in search of trade opportunities that will benefit both the local and the global community. Body Shop does not merely open retail outlets; it organises trade exhibitions and sponsors programmes that boost local economies. For example, the company's Trade Not Aid programme, which attempts to find business opportunities both for and with citizens of the world's nations, has led to agreements with a soap-making factory in a slum in Glasgow, Scotland, an oil processing facility in Brazil and a paper making factory in Nepal.

The Body Shop's unusual approach has helped create a passion in its employees and customers. The company maintains a school in London to teach employees about its products and the value of social consciousness. Additionally, employees are required to put in one hour of paid company time each week towards a community project. By instigating a philosophy of social responsibility, Roddick believes that her employees will be motivated by feeling good about what they are doing.

SOURCES: "Anita Roddick: changing the whole bloody world", *Business Ethics*, September–October 1992, pp. 27–29; Rahul Jacob, "Body Shop International: what selling will be like in the '90's", *Fortune*, 13 January 1992, pp. 63–64; Bo Burlingham, "This woman has changed business forever", *Inc.*, June 1990, pp. 34–48; The Body Shop 1990 Annual Report; 1989 Annual Report; Bernice Huxtable, "Body care firm joins rainforest campaign, *Calgary Herald*, 11 July 1989, p. E5; Dan Parle, "Back to nature", *Business Journal*, January–February 1989, pp. 24–29; 1992 Annual Report.

linked to cancer and other medical problems, society's attitude towards smoking has changed, and marketers are confronted with new social responsibilities, such as providing a smoke free atmosphere for customers. Major airlines now operate only non-smoking flights on certain routes, and most major hotel chains reserve at least some of their rooms for non-smokers. Most other businesses within the food, travel and entertainment industries also provide smoke free areas.

Because society is made up of many diverse groups, finding out what society as a whole wants is difficult, if not impossible. In trying to satisfy the desires of one group, marketers may dissatisfy others. Moreover, there are costs associated with many of society's demands. For example, society wants a cleaner environment and the preservation of wildlife and habitats, but it also wants low priced petrol and heating oil. Shell has recently suffered a spate of bad publicity and negative consumer response following allegations about its environmental record in Nigeria (see Marketing Insight 25.2). Thus companies that market petrol and oil must carefully balance the costs of providing low priced products against the costs of manufacturing and packaging their products in an environmentally responsible manner. Such a balance is difficult to achieve to the satisfaction of all members of society. Marketers must also evaluate the extent to which members of society are willing to pay for what they want. For instance, consumers may want more information about a product yet be unwilling to pay the costs the firm incurs in providing the data. Thus marketers who want to make socially responsible decisions may find the task difficult.

Social Responsibility Issues

Although social responsibility may seem to be an abstract ideal, managers make decisions related to social responsibility on a daily basis. To be successful, a business must determine what customers, government inspectors, competitors and society in general want or expect in terms of social responsibility. The success of international retailer Body Shop has been attributed to the company's awareness of the green movement and demonstration of social responsibility. Table 25.3 summarises several major categories of social responsibility issues, which include the consumer movement, community relations and "green" marketing.

Consumer Issues   One of the most significant social responsibility issues in marketing is the consumer movement, which Chapter 2 defines as the efforts of independent individuals, groups and organisations to protect the rights of consumers. A number of interest groups and individuals have taken actions such as lobbying government officials and agencies, letter writing campaigns, placing advertisements and boycotting companies they consider irresponsible.

David Tench, one of the best known consumer activists in the UK, continues to crusade for consumer rights. Consumer activism on the part of Tench and others has resulted in legislation requiring various safety features in cars: seat belts, padded dashboards, stronger door catches, headrests, shatterproof windscreens and collapsible steering columns. Activists' efforts have furthered the passage of several consumer protection laws, such as the Trade Descriptions Act 1968, the Consumer Protection Act 1987, the Fair Trading Act 1973, the Food Act 1984 and the Weights and Measures Act 1985.

Community Relations   Social responsibility also extends to marketers' roles as community members. Individual communities expect marketers to contribute to the satisfaction and growth of their communities. Thus many marketers view

Social Responsibility: Shell's Onslaught

Oil company Shell is facing an onslaught of public criticism following the execution of campaigner and author Ken Saro-Wiwa and eight others in Nigeria. The public outcry has focused on two charges against Shell: causing environmental damage, and complicity in the Nigerian government's oppression of the Ogoni people. Concerned groups argue that Shell's economic involvement in the country, where it has been operating for over 50 years, inevitably means that it is politically involved too. While Shell continues to insist that it would have been inappropriate to have intervened in the case of Ken Saro-Wiwa, the company's decision to announce a $4 billion liquefied natural gas project within days of the executions added fuel to consumers' concerns. The situation in which Shell finds itself has important implications for many other multinationals globally, as consumers increasingly demand that such companies accept ethical and social responsibility for their business actions.

Shell has come under attack from a range of pressure groups such as Amnesty International, Friends of the Earth and Greenpeace. In particular, the company has been accused of environmental double standards. In the words of environmental campaigner Jonathan Porritt, "Global companies such as Shell can no longer have it both ways. They cannot on the one hand support a very good environmental record in European markets and on the other wreak environmental devastation in other parts of the world". These concerns are echoed by Friends of the Earth executive director Charles Secrett, who accuses Shell executives of only being ". . . concerned about their responsibilities to shareholders and the bottom line. Shell must take its social and environmental responsibilities seriously. Until it does that it will always face difficulties". Meanwhile, the green retailer Body Shop, which has supported the Ogoni cause for more than two years, has entered the fray by running a newspaper advertisement directly criticising Shell's involvement in Nigeria. In only its third above-the-line promotion ever, Body Shop's spoiler advertisement features the words, "Dear Shell, This is the truth and it stinks". The retailer then goes on to exhort consumers to boycott Shell products.

Amidst the flood of accusations, Shell has used newspaper advertisements to try to defuse the crisis, arguing that its investment in Nigeria has led to the creation of thousands of jobs. While the company accepts that there have been environmental difficulties, it insists that it has taken responsibility for some of these problems. As 21 other members of the Ogoni people awaited trial in Nigeria on charges similar to those of which Ken Saro-Wiwa was convicted, it seemed likely that the debate would continue. As consumers around Europe continue to protest, publicise and lobby against Shell, the company has a difficult task ahead. It is possible that ultimately it may be political rather than consumer pressure that threatens Shell the most. The Commonwealth countries, accused in some quarters of passivity in the Saro-Wiwa affair, have now acted to expel Nigeria until it puts its house in order. Pressure is also mounting on governments for an oil embargo, which may force Shell out of Nigeria altogether.

SOURCES: Tom O'Sullivan, "Shell needs more than slick solution", *Marketing Week,* 24 November 1995; This Week, "Body Shop joins Shell row with spoiler ad", *Marketing,* 23 November 1995.

Issue	Description	Major Societal Concerns
Consumer movement	Activities undertaken by independent individuals, groups and organisations to protect their rights as consumers	The right to safety The right to be informed The right to choose The right to be heard
Community relations	Society anxious to have marketers contribute to its well-being, wishing to know what businesses do to help solve social problems Communities demanding that firms listen to their grievances and ideas	Equality issues Disadvantaged members of society Safety and health Education and general welfare
Green products and production	Consumers insisting not only on the quality of life but also on a healthy environment so that they can maintain a high standard of living during their lifetimes	Conservation Water pollution Air pollution Land pollution

Table 25.3 Social responsibility issues

social responsibility as including contributions of resources (money, products, time) to community causes such as education, the arts, recreation, disadvantaged members of the community and others. McDonald's, Shell, Ogilvy & Mather and Hewlett Packard all have programmes that contribute funds, equipment and personnel to educational reform. Similarly, IBM donates or reduces the price of computer equipment to educational institutions, while supermarket chain Tesco has a scheme that allows shoppers to collect vouchers enabling their local schools to obtain computer equipment. All these efforts, of course, have a positive impact on local communities, but they also indirectly help the organisations in the form of goodwill, publicity and exposure to potential future customers. Thus, although social responsibility is certainly a positive concept, most organisations do not embrace it without the expectation of some indirect long term benefit.

Green marketing The specific development, pricing, promotion and distribution of products that do not harm the environment

Green Marketing **Green marketing** refers to the specific development, pricing, promotion and distribution of products that do not harm the environment. An independent coalition of environmentalists, scientists and marketers is one group involved in evaluating products to assess their environmental impact, determining marketers' commitment to the environment and producing *The Green Guide*. For consumers this has been a confusing time, as they are faced by an array of products making a variety of environmental claims. Recently the confusion has been somewhat alleviated by the promotion of two standard labels throughout Europe. Both labels have government backing. The ecolabel is awarded to products that

Figure 25.2

Ethics in marketing

The UK government is supporting a new labelling initiative to reduce consumer confusion over environmental claims.

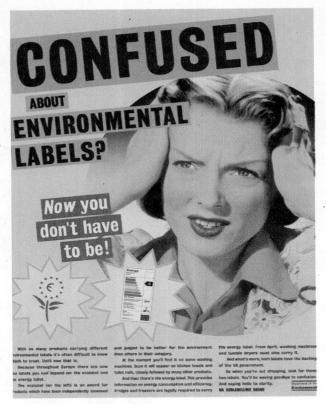

Source: Department of the Environment.

have been judged by independent assessors as better for the environment than the norm in their respective product groups. The energy label, which most white goods will soon be required to carry, provides information about energy consumption and efficiency. The advertisement in Figure 25.2 shows how the UK Ecolabelling Board (Department of the Environment) is informing consumers about the two new labels.

As discussed in Chapter 2, perhaps one of the most fundamental changes in the 1990s facing marketers and consumers alike is the tremendous growth of the **green movement**. Increased environmental awareness has led to changes in production methods—from product design, materials and packaging to promotion and selling messages, and even product disposal. Figure 25.3 illustrates a Dutch campaign for ecologically safe paints, recruiting support from consumers and industry.

Green movement   A movement of consumers committed to increasing environmental awareness and bringing about changes in production, marketing and consumption

Strategies for Dealing with Social Responsibility Issues

There are four basic strategies for systematically dealing with social responsibility issues: (1) reaction, (2) defence, (3) accommodation and (4) proaction.

Reaction strategy   A business's decision to allow a condition or potential problem to go unresolved until the public learns about it

Reaction Strategy   A business adopting a **reaction strategy** allows a condition or potential problem to go unresolved until the public learns about it. The situation may be known to management (like one car maker's problems with fuel tank combustibility) or it may be unknown (like Ford's recent problems with seat belts in the Fiesta). In either case, the business denies responsibility but tries to resolve the

Figure 25.3

Social responsibility

In the Netherlands, the campaign for ecologically safe paints is gathering support from consumers and from industry.

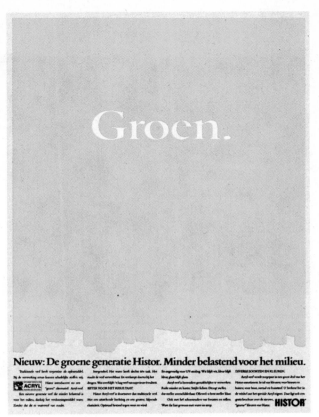

Groen.

Nieuw: De groene generatie Histor. Minder belastend voor het milieu.

SOURCE: *Company: Sigma Coatings; Brand: Histor; Agency: KKBR, Amsterdam; Art: Rob Sluijs; Copy: Ton Drupper.*

problem, deal with its consequences and continue doing business as usual to minimise the negative impact.

Defence strategy A business's decision to try to minimise or avoid additional obligations linked to a problem or problems

Defence Strategy A business using a **defence strategy** tries to minimise or avoid additional obligations linked to a problem or problems. Commonly used defence tactics include legal manoeuvering and seeking the support of trade unions that embrace the company's way of doing business and that support the industry. Businesses often lobby to avoid government action or regulation. For example, the direct mail industry lobbied against an increase in bulk postal rates because it knew it would have to pass on these increases to its clients, advertisers and advertising agencies. Sizeable increases in postal rates could put it at a competitive disadvantage in relation to print media, such as newspaper inserts, which are not carried by mail. Thus the industry took a defensive position to protect its own and its clients' interests.

Accommodation strategy A business's decision to take responsibility for its actions when it is encouraged by special interest groups or threatened by government intervention

Accommodation Strategy A business using an **accommodation strategy** assumes responsibility for its actions. A business might adopt the accommodation strategy when special interest groups are encouraging a particular action or when the business perceives that if it fails to react, the government will pass a law to ensure compliance. Figure 25.4 illustrates how Sunlight aims to address an ecological problem. New EU regulations have set targets for recycling refuse. Many

Figure 25.4 Developing products that solve ecological problems. Sunlight is adopting an accommodation strategy.

SOURCE: Courtesy McCann Erickson/Zurich.

organisations have become involved in initiatives to aid recycling, because they believe that action may be taken against them if they do nothing.

For example, McDonald's developed a nutrition orientated advertising campaign to appease dietitians and nutritionists who had urged that accurate nutritional information should be provided on all fast food products. However, instead of soothing the interest groups, the McDonald's campaign antagonised them. The groups claimed that its portrayal of McDonald's food as healthy was inaccurate. A McDLT, chips and milkshake contain 1,283 calories, approximately 60 per cent of the entire recommended daily calorie intake for an adult woman. In addition, that meal contains 15 teaspoons of fat, 10 teaspoons of sugar, no fibre, and approximately 70 per cent of the recommended daily allowance of salt. In the US, dietitians and nutritionists petitioned the Food and Drug Administration in the hope that the agency would require nutritional labelling on products to alert consumers to high levels of fat, sodium, and sugar and low levels of starch and fibre.[28] McDonald's chose to take an accommodation strategy to curtail lobbying against nutritional information disclosure when it probably should have adopted a proactive strategy.

Proactive strategy A business's decision to take responsibility for its actions and respond to accusations made against it without outside pressure or the threat of government intervention

Proactive Strategy A business that uses a **proactive strategy** assumes responsibility for its actions and responds to accusations made against it without outside pressure or the threat of government intervention. A proactive strategy requires management, of its own free will, to support an action or cause. For example, in response to the increasing concerns about green issues in Europe, BMW is setting up plants throughout Europe to recycle its cars when they reach the end of their road life.[29]

. . . .

Social Responsibility and Marketing Ethics

Although the concepts of marketing ethics and social responsibility are often used interchangeably, it is important to remember that ethics relate to individual moral evaluations—judgements about what is right or wrong in a particular decision-making situation. Social responsibility is the obligation of an organisation to maximise its positive impact and minimise its negative impact on society. Thus social responsibility deals with the total effect of marketing decisions on society. These two concepts work together; a company that supports both socially acceptable moral philosophies and individuals who act ethically is likely to make decisions that have a positive impact on society.

One way to evaluate whether a specific behaviour is ethical and socially responsible is to ask other people in an organisation if they approve of it. For social responsibility issues, contact with concerned consumer groups and industry or government regulatory groups may be helpful. Checking to see if there is a specific company policy about the activity may also resolve the issue. If other people in the organisation approve of the activity and it is legal and customary within the industry, the chances are that the activity is acceptable from both an ethical and social responsibility perspective.

A rule of thumb for ethical and social responsibility issues is that if they can withstand open discussion and result in agreements or limited debate, an acceptable solution may exist. Still, even after a final decision is reached, different viewpoints on the issue may remain. Openness is not the complete solution to the ethics problem; but it does create trust and facilitate learning relationships.[30]

. . . .

Summary

● *Marketing ethics* are moral principles that define right and wrong behaviour in marketing. Most marketing decisions can be judged as ethical or unethical. Ethics are a very important concern in marketing decisions, yet they may be one of the most misunderstood and controversial concepts in marketing.

● Personal *moral philosophies*, organisational factors and opportunity are three important components of ethical decision-making. Moral philosophies are principles or rules that individuals use to determine the right way to behave. They provide guidelines for resolving conflicts and ensuring mutual benefit for all members of society. *Utilitarianism* is concerned with maximising the greatest good for the greatest number of people. *Ethical formalism* philosophies, on the other hand, focus on general rules for guiding behaviour and on the rights of the individual. Organisational relationships with employees or superiors create ethical problems such as maintaining confidentiality in personal relations; meeting obligations, responsibilities and mutual agreements; and avoiding undue pressure that may force others to behave unethically. *Organisational culture* is the set of values, beliefs, goals, norms and rituals that members of an organisation share. *Opportunity*—a favourable set of conditions that limit barriers or provide internal or external rewards—to engage in unethical behaviour provides another pressure that may determine whether a person behaves ethically. If an individual uses an opportunity afforded him or her to act unethically and escapes punishment or even gains a reward, that person is more likely to repeat such acts when circumstances favour them.

● An *ethical issue* is an identifiable problem, situation or opportunity requiring an individual or organisation to choose from alternatives that must be evaluated as right or wrong. Ethical issues typically arise because of conflicts between individuals' personal moral philosophies and the marketing strategies, policies and organisational environment in which they work. Product related ethical issues may develop when marketers fail to disclose risks associated with the product or information that relates to understanding the function, value or use of the product. Competitive pressures can also create product related ethical issues. The promotion process provides situations that can result in ethical issues, such as false and misleading advertising and deceptive sales tactics. Sales promotions and publicity that use deception or manipulation also create significant ethical issues. Bribery may be an ethical issue in some selling situations. The emotional and subjective nature of price creates conditions in which misunderstandings between the seller and buyer lead to ethical problems. Ethical issues in distribution relate to relationships and conflicts among producers and marketing middlemen.

● *Codes of ethics,* which formalise what an organisation expects of its employees, minimise the opportunity for unethical behaviour because they provide rules to guide conduct and punishments for violating the rules. If the number of employees making ethical decisions on a regular basis is not satisfactory, the company needs to determine why and

to take corrective action through enforcement. Enforcement of standards is what makes codes of ethics effective.

● *Social responsibility* in marketing refers to an organisation's obligation to maximise its positive impact and minimise its negative impact on society. Marketing managers try to determine what accepted relationship, obligations and duties exist between the business organisation and society.

● To be successful, a business must determine what customers, government officials, competitors and society in general want or expect in terms of social responsibility. Major categories of social responsibility issues include the consumer movement, community relations and green marketing. The consumer movement refers to the activities of independent individuals, groups and organisations in trying to protect the rights of consumers. Communities expect marketers to contribute to the satisfaction and growth of their communities. *Green marketing* refers to the specific development, pricing, promotion and distribution of products that do not harm the environment. The *green movement* is leading to tremendous changes in the 1990s for consumers, manufacturers and workers alike.

● Four basic strategies for dealing with social responsibility issues are reaction, defence, accommodation and proaction. A business adopting a *reaction strategy* allows a condition or potential problem to go unresolved until the public learns about it. A business using the *defence strategy* tries to minimise or avoid additional obligations associated with a problem or problems. By using the *accommodation strategy,* a business assumes responsibility for its action. A business that uses the *proactive strategy* assumes responsibility for its actions and responds to accusations made against it without outside pressure or the threat of government intervention.

● The concepts of marketing ethics and social responsibility work together because a company that has a corporate culture built on socially acceptable moral philosophies will generally make decisions that have a positive impact on society. If other people in the company approve of an activity and it is legal and customary within the industry, chances are the activity is ethical and socially responsible.

Important Terms

Marketing ethics
Moral philosophies
Utilitarianism
Ethical formalism
Organisational culture

Opportunity
Ethical issue
Codes of ethics
Social responsibility
Green marketing

Green movement
Reaction strategy
Defence strategy
Accommodation strategy
Proactive strategy

Discussion and Review Questions

1. Why are ethics an important consideration in marketing decisions?
2. How do the factors that influence ethical or unethical decisions interact?
3. What ethical conflicts could arise if a firm's employees chose to fly only on certain airlines in order to accrue personal frequent flier miles?
4. Is the view of marketing as warfare, based on seeing competitors as the enemy, a matter for ethical concern?
5. What are some of the areas that result in major ethical issues in marketing?
6. How can ethical decisions in marketing be improved?
7. How can people with different personal values join together to make ethical decisions in an organisation?
8. Explain the difference between ethics and social responsibility and give some examples of each.
9. What are major social responsibility issues?
10. Describe strategies for dealing with social responsibility issues.
11. How do you determine when a gift or payment is a bribe in marketing?

Recommended Readings

W. W. Manley, II, *The Handbook of Good Business Practice* (London and New York: Routledge, 1992).

G. R. Laczniak and P. E. Murphy, *Ethical Marketing Decisions: The Higher Road* (Boston: Allyn and Bacon, 1993).

O. C. Ferrell and J. Fraedrich, *Business Ethics*, 3rd edn (Boston: Houghton Mifflin, 1997).

T. Donaldson, *The Ethics of International Business* (New York: Oxford University Press, 1989).

C. N. Smith, "Marketing strategies for the ethics era", *Sloan Management Review,* vol. 36, no. 4, 1995, pp. 85–97.

Cases

25.1   The UK National Lottery Goes Live: But Who Are the Losers?

At the end of 1994 the UK National Lottery was launched with a massive advertising campaign. The principle was simple: for a £1 stake choose a permutation of 6 numbers out of 49; then tune into *The National Lottery Live* television programme on Saturday night to watch the draw. With a share of the proceeds to go to a wide range of worthy causes and winners of the top prize set to enjoy a share of around £8 million, it wasn't long before the nation was gripped with lottery fever. Despite the over-

The First Year of the National Lottery

November 1994	The UK National Lottery is launched.
December 1994	The anonymity of a £17.8 million winner is revealed by the press.
February 1995	Retailer Superdrug drops the lottery from three of its stores because of the inconvenience it causes.
March 1995	National Lottery Instants (instant win scratch cards) are launched, with £30m of tickets sold in the first week alone. Also in March, research shows that more than 80 per cent of tabloid newspaper readers are playing the lottery.
April 1995	Littlewoods Pools, which for many years has run a gambling game based on football match results, responds to the lottery by launching its first ever advertising campaign.
May 1995	NHS Loto, another lottery game, announces its intention to compete with Camelot.
June 1995	Retailer Superdrug drops all lottery machines from its stores, blaming the disruption they cause.
July 1995	Figures reveal that attendance at bingo clubs has fallen by one-fifth. In a spate of bad publicity, Camelot is accused of trying to drive other charity lotteries out of business.
September 1995	Figures published by the Central Statistical Office indicate that the National Lottery has added almost 10 per cent to the average household spend on leisure.
October 1995	The National Lottery comes in for criticism from the Church, charities and politicians.

whelming odds of 14 million to one, it seemed as if all lottery players had already thought out how they might spend their winnings. With three billion tickets sold during the first year of operation, £1.4 billion in prize money and 119 millionaires created, the contribution to worthwhile causes has been high. With 81 per cent of the population playing the game, figures show that the UK National Lottery has achieved a higher percentage of regular players than any other lottery launched in the last 20 years.

Four months after the launch, National Lottery instant win scratch cards started to appear in retail outlets. Now lottery players were being offered a new way to win. With top prizes of £50,000 on some cards, consumers were soon enjoying the latest version of lottery fever. Before long Camelot, the company organising the lottery, was selling a massive 27 million scratch cards each week.

Amidst the consumer interest generated by the lottery, it soon became clear that this new leisure pastime was resulting in subtle changes in consumer behaviour. Estimates indicate that the lottery has resulted in an extra 12 million visits to the shops each week. Some of the biggest beneficiaries have been the retail outlets with lottery terminals, where sales have increased by an estimated 20 per cent. The lottery has also led to increased sales promotional activity, with the launch of a host of copy-cat "instant win" promotional cards. Suddenly consumers have become obsessed with the prospect of instant riches, creating a significant boost to the buoyant sales promotion sector. Two high street banks have already launched scratch cards targeting students, while beer brands Foster's, Holsten Pils and Miller Pilsner are also being promoted with a scratch card offering free beer for a year. Holiday company Thomas Cook has used the technique to offer extra traveller's cheques.

Yet despite the interest they have generated, the National Lottery and the instant win scratch cards have also attracted considerable and continued criticism. Some of the critics are dissatisfied with the percentage of takings allocated to good causes, pointing to high profits for lottery organiser Camelot. Others argue that the allocation of funds is inappropriate. Meanwhile, religious groups have expressed anxiety about the avarice that has been exposed by the nation's new obsession. Others are concerned about exactly where the millions being spent on lottery tickets are coming from, worrying that the poorest in society may be over-extending themselves by investing their limited income in the lottery dream. Research by the Henley Centre suggests that the spending comes from the following sources: 0.5 per cent from disposable income, 1 per cent from discretionary spending and a further 5 per cent from savings. Perhaps more significant, shopping trips to buy the lottery tickets are also leading to an increase in the purchase of impulse products, such as sweets, soft drinks and newspapers.

As Camelot continues to publicise the good causes that are enjoying the benefits of lottery money, some charities are feeling the effects of consumers' changing behaviour. Estimates one year on from the launch indicate that there has been a £61 million fall in donations to charity since the lottery began. Particularly hard hit have been the medical research and overseas charities. Now these charities are fighting back with a host of innovative money raising initiatives. While some organisations, such as the National Health Service, have launched their own lottery scratch cards, others are looking in other directions. Charity Flowers Direct is one such initiative. Launched by four major charities—Age Concern, the British Heart Foundation, Help the Aged and the Imperial Cancer Research Fund—this flowers-by-post gift service aims to offer the public a combination of a quality service and the opportunity to contribute to charity. In many respects the initiative is a natural progression from the sale of charity Christmas cards.

Meanwhile, the International Red Cross has launched another initiative to raise new funds,

HelpAd. This corporate fund raising programme is designed to raise money from marketing and advertising spend. Companies that sign up for the initiative will be entitled to carry the charity's logo on their packaging. There will be a pro rata charge for every 1,000 advertisements or branded packs. For those companies like SmithKline Beecham, Pizza Hut, Grand Metropolitan, Body Shop and Tesco, which have already joined the scheme, the benefits in terms of public image are obvious. For the International Red Cross, the scheme offers a new way of raising a shortfall in financing. For senior managers at Camelot, the continuing concerns about the effects of changing consumer spending patterns are putting the company in a defensive position that requires careful handling. The interest the lottery has generated is in turn emphasising certain ethical and social responsibility issues with which the company must deal.

SOURCES: Meg Carter, "Charities opt for brand aid", *Independent on Sunday,* 17 September 1995; David Benady, "Camelot accused of new 'dirty tricks'", *Marketing Week,* 19 January 1996; David Benady, "Winning streak", *Marketing Week,* 3 November 1996; David Teather, "A winning solution", *Marketing,* 23 November 1996.

Questions for Discussion

1. What important ethical issues are involved in this case?
2. What are the social responsibility issues that arise from marketing National Lottery tickets that may lead consumers to spend money in ways they cannot afford?
3. How might Camelot improve its ethical climate to assuage its critics?

25.2 McDonald's Social Responsibility

The McDonald's Corporation is the largest food service organisation in the world. McDonald's competes on the basis of price and value by offering quality food products with speed and convenience in reliable, clean restaurants. Its brand is one of the most advertised in the world, and the company spends millions of pounds a year on marketing.

Customer satisfaction is the cornerstone of the McDonald's marketing strategy. The company wants to make every customer contact an enjoyable

experience by serving quality food at affordable prices and providing fast, accurate, friendly service. Most people reading this case have had the McDonald's experience many times.

The philosophy of Ray Kroc, McDonald's founder, was that McDonald's and its franchises should put something back into the communities in which they do business. In addition, McDonald's believes that being a good corporate citizen means treating people with fairness and integrity and sharing success in the communities where the company operates. This philosophy is implemented in many different ways throughout the McDonald's corporation.

Quality education is a priority for most countries, and McDonald's is committed to making a contribution, whether it's in the US, the UK, France, Switzerland or South East Asia. Many young people who work in McDonald's stores are taught the importance of responsibility, self-discipline and good work habits. McDonald's works with parents, educators and students and believes in supporting education through various programmes that encourage and recognise scholastic achievement. The company allows school fund raising and charitable activities such as car washing days on its sites; it sponsors computer equipment; and it encourages school children to continue into higher education.

McDonald's is concerned about affirmative action and equal opportunity. The company attempts to attract minorities, women, disabled and older people and develop their potential without regard to race, sex, religion, ethnicity, educational or cultural background. McJobs is an employment programme established to assist mentally and physically challenged individuals to develop their skills and confidence to succeed. The McMasters programme attempts to recruit, train and retain some of McDonald's most valued employees—people aged 55 and over.

As a responsible corporate citizen, McDonald's is committed to protecting the environment. The company has many ongoing efforts to manage solid waste, conserve and protect natural resources, and promote sound environmental practices. Although many studies indicated that foam packaging is environmentally sound, McDonald's phased out this packaging in 1990 because of customer feedback. There are programmes within the McDonald's organisation to reduce the weight and volume of packaging, to recycle, to implement re-usable materials whenever feasible and to purchase a minimum of £65 million worth a year of recycled materials for use in the construction, equipping and operations of restaurants. In addition, McDonald's refuses to purchase beef from companies that destroy tropical rain forests to create cattle grazing lands. This policy is strictly enforced and closely monitored.

Part of the philosophy of giving something back to the communities is dedicated to helping children

achieve their fullest potential. Since its founding in 1984 in memory of Ray Kroc, Ronald McDonald Children's Charities (RMCC) has funded thousands of grants totalling tens of millions of pounds to help support programmes in the areas of health care and medical research, specially designed rehabilitation facilities and special youth education programmes.

The Ronald McDonald House programme is the cornerstone of RMCC, providing a "home away from home" for families of seriously ill children being treated at nearby hospitals. The first Ronald McDonald House was developed over 20 years ago in Philadelphia, Pennsylvania, when the NFL's Philadelphia Eagles, a children's hospital and owner/operators of McDonald's restaurants decided to establish a place where parents of sick children could be with others who understood their situation and could provide emotional support.

In 1991, the 150th Ronald McDonald House was opened. Houses are now appearing outside America: London's first won praise from all quarters. In total, more than 2,500 bedrooms serve some 4,000 family members each night. Each house is located close to a major medical facility.

Each Ronald McDonald House is run by a local non-profit organisation composed of members of the medical community, McDonald's owner/operators, businesses and civic organisations, and parent volunteers. More than 12,000 volunteers provide the backbone of the programme, helping with all aspects of House operations, including fund raising, renovation, programme development and services to families. Families staying at Ronald McDonald Houses are asked to make a small donation per day. If that is not possible, their stay is free.

McDonald's attempts to contribute to all aspects of community life by supporting education, pursuing equal opportunity and affirmative action in employment practices, operating Ronald McDonald Children's Charities and promoting sound environmental practices. All of these activities combined demonstrate a commitment to putting something back into the communities that spend so much of their disposable income at McDonald's restaurants. Few companies can compete with the high level of commitment McDonald's has made to communities.

SOURCES: McDonald's 1990 annual report; *Ronald McDonald House Fact Sheet*, Ronald McDonald Children's Charities, Kroc Drive, Oakbrook, Ill.; *Ronald McDonald House Backgrounder*, Ronald McDonald Children's Charities; *Ronald McDonald*

House World, a newsletter published for the Ronald McDonald House family, Winter 1991; "Ronald McDonald's Children's Charities" video cassette; McDonald's in-store leaflets; McDonald's, London.

Questions for Discussion

1. Why, in your opinion, has McDonald's selected Ronald McDonald Children's Charities as one of its most visible attempts to implement social responsibility?

2. Why are environmental, educational and equal opportunity/affirmative action issues so important to the long term success of McDonald's?

3. Currently, 65 per cent of all future McDonald's owner/operators in training are minorities and women. What impact will this have on McDonald's operations in the future

Chapter 1 explained that in order to take advantage of any identified marketing opportunities, an organisation must first develop a marketing strategy and then create marketing mix programmes to help implement the recommended strategy. Parts I and II of *Marketing: Concepts and Strategies* examined marketing opportunity analysis. Chapter 7 detailed the principal part of a marketing strategy: target market selection. Part VIII has taken these concepts further, examining in more detail the nature of marketing strategy, implementation and control. In addition, the important issues of ethics and social responsibility have been highlighted.

Readers should be confident that they are now able to:

Describe the key aspects of marketing strategy and competitive forces

• What is marketing strategy? • How can product portfolio analysis, the market attractiveness–business position model, PIMS and ABC sales: contribution analysis assist in the development of marketing strategy? • Why is it important to understand competitors' strategies? • What are competitive positions?

Explain the process of marketing planning and assessing sales potential

• What is the process of marketing planning? • Why is marketing planning useful? • What is the link between marketing analysis, marketing strategy and marketing programmes? • How does the SWOT analysis assist in marketing planning? • What are the components of a marketing plan? • What is meant by assessing sales potential? • What are the principal sales forecasting techniques? • What is the marketing audit?

Understand the issues relating to implementing strategies and measuring performance

• How does the marketing unit fit into a company's organisational structure? • How can the marketing function be organised? • What issues must be considered when implementing marketing strategies? • What are the principal control processes? • How can cost and sales analyses help evaluate marketing performance?

Discuss the relevance of ethics and social responsibility in marketing

• What is meant by ethics in marketing? • Why is it an important concept in marketing? • What factors influence ethical and unethical decisions? • What are the

Marketing Opportunity Analysis	Chapters
• The marketing environment	2
• Marketing in international markets	3
• Consumer markets and buyer behaviour	4
• Business-to-business markets and buyer behaviour	5
• Marketing research and information systems	6

Target Market Selection	Chapters
• Market segmentation and prioritisation	7, 22
• Product and brand positioning	7, 22
• Competitive advantage	7, 22

Marketing Mix Development	Chapters
• Product, branding, packaging and service decisions	8–11
• Distribution (place and channel) decisions	12–15
• Promotion decisions	16–18
• Pricing decisions	19, 20
• Supplementary decisions	3, 21, 24, 25

Marketing Management	Chapters
• Strategic marketing and competitive strategy	22, 23
• Marketing planning and sales forecasting	23
• Implementing strategies and measuring performance	24
• Marketing ethics and social responsibility	25

main ethical issues facing marketers? • How can ethical decision-making be improved? • What is meant by social responsibility? • What are the important social responsibility issues facing marketers? • What strategies exist for dealing with social dilemmas?

APPENDIX

A   CASE STUDY ANALYSIS

This appendix considers how to tackle case study analysis and presents four case studies complete with questions for either classroom discussion or self-tuition. The cases are Colgate-Palmolive, Electrolux, Aer Lingus and Avis.

• • • • • • • • • • • • • • • • • •

How to Tackle Case Study Analysis*

At undergraduate, postgraduate and practitioner level, the case study is a well accepted and widely used learning tool. The popularity of case studies in marketing management education is primarily linked to the technique's ability to bridge the gap between marketing theory and practical situations, thus allowing students to apply the concepts they have learned. Success in providing case study solutions, as in real life, is largely determined by the nature and quality of the analysis carried out. Learning how to make decisions about case studies in a logical, objective and structured way is essential. Such decisions must take into consideration all relevant aspects of the marketing and competitive environment, together with an appreciation of the company's resources. Developing the necessary decision-making and analytical skills promotes an understanding of different corporate structures and philosophies and of the implementation of a range of marketing tools. In addition, the learning process allows the risks and problems associated with managerial decision-making to be experienced first hand.

A popular approach to case study learning is to work in seminar or syndicate groups, which helps develop group as well as individual skills—a very positive contribution, given the extent to which managers in real business situations must work in teams. Developing group skills takes time as individuals learn to cope with the differing opinions and views of colleagues. However, this model closely emulates actual work situations in which a working consensus must be reached. Although preparing cases on an individual basis may appear simpler than taking a range of disparate group views into consideration, a more limited range of

---

*This overview is an abridged version of the guidance offered in Sally Dibb and Lyndon Simkin, *The Marketing Casebook: Cases and Concepts* (International Thomson Business Press: London, 1994).

767

alternatives may be developed. Nevertheless, tackling cases individually also builds up analytical and decision-making skills.

This appendix is divided into three parts. The first considers the fundamentals of situation analysis, which should be undertaken to give a general overview of the key case issues *prior* to the stages outlined above (see Chapter 23 for a detailed discussion). The second part reviews the five stages of case study analysis, and the third examines the presentation of case findings.

• • • • • • • • • • • • • • • • • • •

Situation Analysis

The areas requiring attention are company position (financial, structure, marketing), market analysis, external environment, threats and opportunities, and competitors.

Company's Internal Position

An appreciation of the company's internal position, drawing attention to particular capabilities and resources, is vital. This analysis should take into consideration company structure, the financial situation and marketing.

Company Structure The structure of organisations influences operational and managerial decisions. By answering the following questions, students can develop an appropriate overview of company characteristics. This understanding should be used as a basis for assessing how realistic are the various case solutions eventually recommended.

- Is the organisational structure hierarchical or flat?
- Where does the balance of power lie?
- What is the company's mission statement?
- Does the company have particular philosophies?
- What are the key characteristics of the company?
- Is managerial activity delineated by function?
- Who are the key decision-makers for each functional area?
- How do the lines of communication operate?
- What formal and informal decision-making structures operate?

Company Financial Situation Various techniques can be used to assess the financial position of the company. An overview of the financial health of the company can be achieved from the balance sheet and income statement. Comparing current figures with those from earlier trading periods is especially informative because it allows changes over time to be mapped.

Financial ratios are calculated using information from the basic balance sheet and income statement (see Table A.1 below). These ratios can be used to achieve greater financial insight into an organisation and can be compared with ratios from competing organisations to allow a better understanding of the company's relative position. Sometimes a break even analysis is also useful (see Chapter 20).

When using financial ratios it is important to be aware of the following points. First, ratios represent a snap-shot of a company's financial state at a particular point in time. When comparing the results from more than one ratio, therefore, it is necessary to ensure that the figures applied are from the same time period and calculated according to similar accounting conventions. Second, the way in which ratios are interpreted and used is more important than the figures in isolation. To understand the significance of a particular ratio, it is essential to understand all of the internal and external factors responsible for the financial position reflected in the figures. Once the financial analysis is complete, it is necessary to pull together the different strands of the overall financial picture and identify which issues are likely to have an impact upon the recommended case solutions.

Company Marketing Organisation Evaluating how the company handles its marketing should systematically cover all aspects of the marketing strategy and

a. Profitability ratios

These ratios measure financial and operating efficiency by assessing the organisation's ability to generate profit from revenue and money invested.

Name of Ratio	Calculated
1. Gross profit margin This shows the total margin available to meet operating expenses and generate a profit.	$\dfrac{\text{Sales} - \text{Cost of goods sold}}{\text{Sales}}$
2. Net profit margin Sometimes called return on sales, this ratio shows after tax profit per £ (pound) spent.	$\dfrac{\text{Profit after taxes}}{\text{Sales}}$
3. Return on assets This ratio measures the company's return on total investment.	$\dfrac{\text{Profit after taxes}}{\text{Total assets}}$
4. Return on net worth Also referred to as return on stockholders' equity, this ratio gives a measure of the rate of return on shareholders' equity.	$\dfrac{\text{Profit after taxes}}{\text{Total shareholders' equity}}$

b. Liquidity ratios

These ratios are used to demonstrate the company's ability to meet current liabilities and to ensure solvency.

Name of Ratio	Calculated
1. Current ratio This demonstrates the company's ability to satisfy short term liabilities.	$\dfrac{\text{Current assets}}{\text{Current liabilities}}$
2. Quick ratio Also referred to as the acid test ratio, this demonstrates the company's ability to meet current liabilities, in the period in which they are due, without resorting to the sale of stock.	$\dfrac{\text{Current assets} - \text{Inventory}}{\text{Current liabilities}}$
3. Inventory to net working capital This indicates the degree to which company working capital is tied up in stock.	$\dfrac{\text{Inventory}}{\text{Current assets} - \text{Current liabilities}}$

(*Continues*)

Table A.1 Key financial ratios

c. Leverage ratios

This group of ratios helps in the assessment of the company's responsiveness to debt and ability to meet repayments as scheduled.

Name of Ratio	Calculated
1. Debt to assets ratio	$\dfrac{\text{Total liabilities}}{\text{Total assets}}$
This indicates the extent to which borrowed funds have been employed to finance the company's operations.	
2. Debt to equity ratio	$\dfrac{\text{Total liabilities}}{\text{Total shareholders' equity}}$
This shows the balance of equity provided by the owners, and funds provided by creditors.	
3. Long term debt to equity ratio	$\dfrac{\text{Long term liabilities}}{\text{Total shareholders' equity}}$
This ratio allows the balance between owners' equity and liabilities to be viewed in context of the company's overall capital structure.	

d. Activity Ratios

These ratios can show how effectively the firm generates sales and profit from assets.

Name of Ratio	Calculated
1. Total assets turnover	$\dfrac{\text{Sales}}{\text{Total assets}}$
This ratio, which signals the level of sales productivity and utilisation of total assets, can be compared with the industry average to show whether the volume of business generated justifies the level of asset investment.	
2. Fixed assets turnover	$\dfrac{\text{Sales}}{\text{Fixed assets}}$
This measures both sales productivity and utilisation of equipment and plant.	
3. Inventory turnover	$\dfrac{\text{Sales}}{\text{Inventory}}$
This measure of inventory turnover can be compared with the industry norm to show whether the company carries too large or small an inventory.	

Table A.1 Key financial ratios (cont.)

programmes: marketing research processes and marketing information systems, maintenance of the product portfolio (including new product development), pricing strategies, distribution policy (including the policing and management of distributors), all aspects of marketing communications, personnel, customer and after sales service.

Market Analysis Understanding market structure and customer requirements is a fundamental stage in any case analysis. The following key questions should be addressed:

Market Structure

- What is the market size?
- What are the trends in market size—is it increasing or decreasing? How quickly?

- How is the market structured? What evidence is there of segments?
- Which segment(s) or customer group(s) is the company targeting?

Customers

- Who are the customers?
- What are the customers like?
- For what purpose do they buy the product/service? What are their needs?
- What features do they look for in the product/service?
- What is the buying process?
- Who and what factors influence them as they buy?
- How do they feel about the product/service?
- How do they feel about alternative suppliers?

It is necessary to assess how effectively the company is reaching its target customers and whether it is geared for expected changes in customer needs and/or market structure. This analysis will have an impact on the solution(s) selected.

External Environment

A wide range of factors from the external marketing environment have an impact on the well-being of an organisation. These include economic, political, social, cultural, technological, legal and regulatory issues, as discussed in Chapter 2. Monitoring these factors is important, because changes can have a major impact on a firm's business dealings. Recognising the significance of such changes early on can help companies to maximise the positive benefits and minimise the detrimental effects. Early warning of the effects of environmental factors can be achieved by assessing the potential opportunities/threats presented by changes. In case study analysis, as in real life, it is often necessary to extrapolate trends and make predictions regarding the level of future change. It is helpful to remember that most potential threats can also be viewed as opportunities should an organisation have the resources and interest to pursue them.

Competition

Understanding the competitive structure of markets helps companies put their marketing options into perspective (see Chapters 2 and 22). From the customers' viewpoint, buying decisions are based on the strengths and weaknesses of a particular player relative to other available choices. Questions to be considered in relation to the competitive situation include the following:

- Who are the key players?
- How is market share divided amongst competing organisations?
- What competitive positions do the players occupy; who is market leader; which companies are challengers, followers and nichers?
- How aggressive are the competing organisations and what are the trends? Is it possible to identify fast movers?
- On what basis are key competitors competing? What are their differential advantages—are these sustainable and how are they supported with marketing programmes?

Understanding the answers to these questions allows the case analyst to appreciate fully the relative competitive strengths and weaknesses of the company and to assess whether or not different case solutions are realistic. It may also be possible to use this information to predict how key competitors are likely to respond to different case solutions.

The Case Study Process

After the situational analysis has been conducted, a clear view of the problems/key issues set out in the case study must be developed. Although the use of specific case questions will affect exactly where the key areas lie, the company and other analyses undertaken will usually have revealed a range of problem areas that need to be addressed. Any specific questions can be tackled once these problem areas have been identified. *One* way to make this assessment of the case material and the core issues is to carry out a marketing audit. The marketing audit offers a systematic way of considering all aspects of the company's marketing set-up, within a predetermined structure (see Chapter 24 for a full explanation). For example, it covers the marketing environment, marketing strategy, marketing organisation, marketing systems and marketing programmes. Carrying out a marketing audit should aid the analysis by:

- describing current activities and results: sales, costs, profits, prices, etc.
- gathering data about customers, competitors and relevant environmental developments
- exploring opportunities for improving marketing strategies
- providing an overall database to be used in developing marketing strategies and programmes for implementation.

Not all cases require or have sufficient information for a formal audit. The initial situation analysis may well give adequate focus and understanding. In more complex cases covering dynamic and competitive markets, the marketing audit can assist in sifting through the market and company data to identify more thoroughly the most pertinent issues.

When developing a list of problem areas, it is necessary to distinguish clearly between symptoms of problems and the problems themselves. Symptoms are defined as the outward signs of an underlying problem or problems. For instance, symptoms might include falling sales, declining profits and shrinking market share. The problem may be poor understanding of customers, signalling a need for closer links with customers and regular feedback from the marketplace.

The identification of symptoms and problems should start with the biggest problem(s). The associated symptoms can then be pin-pointed and listed. Minor difficulties, whether or not related to the major problems, should be dealt with after the main problem(s) have been determined. It is helpful to signal whether the problems are affecting the company's position in the short, medium or long term.

Selecting an appropriate case solution is an iterative process that should start by generating a number of alternatives. Each potential solution must relate to the case's key problem area(s) and offer a realistic way of solving it. It is not a good idea to spend time reviewing too many similar solutions. Detailed fine tuning can be carried out at a later stage, once a selection has been made. In some circumstances it is helpful to frame the generation of alternatives around the following questions:

- Where is the company now?
- How did it get to its current position?
- Where does it want to go/what does it want to achieve?
- How can it achieve what it wants and move where it wants to go?

An understanding of the organisation's current position should already have been achieved through the situation analysis, but explicitly framing the first two questions helps ensure that these issues from the earlier analysis are not overlooked. At this stage it ought to be possible to exclude the more unrealistic solutions, so that the more likely options can be analysed further.

Analyse Alternative Solutions

The next step is a critical evaluation of the proposed solutions. This should involve a formal assessment of the advantages and disadvantages of every alternative. Each proposal should be considered within the context of the company, market, competitor and environmental analyses that have already been carried out. Conducting "What if ... ?" analyses—in which attempts are made to predict the likely outcome(s) of alternative solutions—can be useful. It is also helpful to list each advantage and disadvantage formally, if possible, ranking the relative importance of each. This ranking should help identify the best solution.

Recommend the "Best" Alternative

Provided that the case analysis has been thorough, deciding on the best solution should not be too complex. Whichever option is selected, the environmental, competitor and market analyses must be double checked to ensure that the chosen solution is consistent with prevailing market conditions. It is rarely possible to identify a course of action that is ideal in all respects, so it is helpful to consider both the acceptability of the various options and the associated risks. Limited data availability and/or ambiguous market conditions may create problems. However, it should be remembered that managers must often make definitive decisions when only limited information is available.

Once a decision has been made, arguments should be prepared supporting the choice(s). In some circumstances, part of the recommendations may be based on the success of initial actions. Some flexibility will be required in responding to the differing circumstances that may arise.

Implement the Chosen Solution

Ensuring that the recommended plans and marketing programmes can be implemented is as fundamental to case study learning as the analyses and choice of the best solution. Consideration should be given to the following issues.

- At which target groups is the solution aimed?
- How will the company's offering be positioned?
- Exactly how will the solution be implemented?

Marketing mix proposals (product, people, price, promotion and distribution):

- What processes will need to be set up to ensure that implementation occurs?
- Which departments/individuals will take responsibility for the day-to-day implementation?
- When will the solution be implemented?
- What are the likely cost implications of implementing the solution?
- What are the expected benefits of implementing the solution (revenues, cash flow, competitive position, customer perceptions, etc.)?

In real situations, implementation may be affected by a range of interacting factors and unforeseen circumstances. For this reason, it is helpful to recommend a contingency plan, to be followed in the event that the initial recommendations are unsuccessful.

Presenting the Case Study Findings

Various formats can be used to report the findings of case study analysis, among them an informal discussion, a structured presentation or a written report. Learning how to present case solutions, like the analysis itself, takes time. While there is a strong personal element in presentational style, the following guidelines are intended to help develop effectiveness in this area. Marketers must be able to make professional presentations and write good reports.

Formal Presentations

Case study presentations can become turgid, clumsy and monotonous, but with care and imagination they can be easily transformed into a lively and interesting forum for debate. The following simple suggestions should assist in this process:

- Keep repetition of the basic case facts to a minimum. After all, other students will probably have read the case study anyway.
- Try to maintain eye contact with the audience. This can be achieved by not addressing the overhead projector screen/overhead projector/board.
- Avoid the use of fully scripted notes. Prompt cards inserted between overhead transparencies or "key word" notes made on paper copies of the transparencies can be helpful.
- Keep visual materials as simple as possible. An audience will have difficulty taking in highly complex tables or slides that are covered in text. Clever use of colour and diagrams can make visual aids easier to follow. Presentation slides or transparencies must *never* be too "wordy" or detailed.
- Use lively material, add the occasional touch of humour and try to involve the audience. Try to vary the presentation format: do not always opt for the formal style of the frontal lecture.
- Avoid using too much material for the presentation time allocated.
- Do not use too many presenters: hand-over time is wasteful and boring for the audience.
- Rehearse! Never be surprised by your own material. Think through in advance the points to be made at each stage of the presentation. Also check any electrical equipment and know how to use it.
- Introduce the presentation, its aims and presenters. Conclude with a brief summary of key points.

Writing Reports

The most appropriate structure for writing up a case analysis will depend on the student's or tutor's objectives as well as on individual style and any organisation constraints regarding format. Report writing is a skill that takes practice to develop properly but offers considerable rewards when mastered. The purpose of the case study report is to present analyses and recommendations, demonstrating a full and thorough understanding of the situation. The emphasis should be on reasoned argument that supports the key recommendations rather than a mere reiteration of the information presented in the case.

Much has been written about report structure, which is an area of concern for student and tutor alike. Too often reports are submitted with imperceptible structure, verbose paragraphs and no sense of direction or clear recommendations. Although there is no standard report format that can be applied in all circumstances, certain generalisations are possible. Essentially, the report should contain the following:

Background to the Case Study This should give a simple overview of the company/industry and may include an indication of the nature of the market.

Understanding of the Underlying Problem(s) This will probably focus on the areas highlighted by the tutor or in case questions. The problem should be briefly stated at this stage.

Analysis of Case Study Material The analysis part of the case study will involve the most extensive and detailed discussion. It is here that the student reports on the company and market analyses undertaken. The length of this part of the report will probably require a series of sub-headings to add structure and clarity to the discussion.

Recommendations with Justifications The recommendations represent the outcomes of the case study analysis and should emerge naturally out of the discussion section of the report. The report itself should already have *told the story*, leaving no surprises about the recommended course of action.

Every report is different, but the following simple checklist of section headings may be helpful to consider when structuring the final document.

  I. Executive/management summary
  II. Introduction (including objectives)
  III. Background to the problem
  IV. Analysis (divided into relevant sections)
  V. Conclusions and recommendations
  VI. Bibliography/references
  VII. Appendices (supporting data and facts)

Points to Remember

- The executive summary should provide a succinct, one or two page account of the entire report. It should explain the background to the case, discuss the key issues and themes, report on the analysis and list the recommendations.
- The report should be as user-friendly as possible, with page numbers, a table of contents, numbered sections and sub-headings. References should be sourced within the main body of the report and then listed in full in the bibliography. Diagrams and tables should also be properly labelled and referenced.
- The writing style should be as clear as possible, free of long sentences and jargon. If jargon is unavoidable, a glossary should explain terms not in common usage.
- Arguments should be supported with appropriate sources (references, statistics, quotes, examples, comparisons, etc.) as available to add credibility to the discussion.
- Data from the case should be used with care and, if possible, interpreted; this may involve extrapolating trends or making predictions regarding the likely outcome of certain activities. Only data relevant to the point being made should be included.
- Any relevant material that would clutter the main body of the document should be placed in appendices. Each appendix should be referred to within the main body of the report and listed in the table of contents.

CASE A.1

The Global Adventures of Colgate-Palmolive

Founded in 1806 by William Colgate, New York based Colgate-Palmolive Co, is genuinely a multinational enterprise, deriving nearly two-thirds of its business from international sales. Having marketed its products in some regions of the world for over 75 years, the company sells its well known brands, such as Colgate (toothpaste), Palmolive (dishwashing liquid), Ajax (cleanser), Irish Spring (soap), Fab (detergent) and Mennen Speed Stick (deodorant), in more than 150 countries in all corners of the globe. In the early 1990s, four areas of particular international interest to the Colgate-Palmolive Company were geographical expansions in the former East Germany, Poland and Mexico, and ongoing association with the Operation Smile programme.

Successful Expansion into the Former East Germany

Once the dust from the fall of the Berlin Wall had settled and East and West Germany were united under a common currency, the shelves of retail outlets in the former East Germany were transformed virtually overnight from small and drab displays of poor quality products into bright, Western-style assortments of high quality goods from around the world. Colgate-Palmolive was one of the first companies to realise success in the new market, both because it was positioned for easy entry—it had operations in neighbouring countries—and because consumers in the former communist nation were eager to try the company's products, which they had seen on West German television but previously had been unable to cross the border to buy. After less than three years in the region, the company was doing 35 per cent of its total German toothpaste business on the eastern side of the crumbled Berlin Wall, even though the region accounted for only 25 per cent of the total German population.

This early success occurred even though Colgate-Palmolive had some initial problems in expanding into the newly liberated country. For example, besides the financial and political risk involved in investing in the region, hiring a sales force was something of a dilemma. Sales had been a non-existent and unnecessary profession under communist rule; goods were merely produced and then distributed by the all-powerful central government. To overcome this difficulty, Colgate-Palmolive initially brought in experienced West German salespeople but eventually established sales training programmes in the region to teach the "new profession" to local citizens.

The Use of a Joint Venture Approach in Poland

By far the largest potential market in eastern Europe, with a population of 38 million prospective consumers, Poland became a primary target for Colgate-Palmolive when the country began moving to a free market economy in 1990. As soon as the Polish borders opened up to the ways of the Western world, Colgate-Palmolive products were readily available at a range of retail outlets. Open air street markets were also filled with products brought in by individuals from neighbouring countries. Like consumers in the former East Germany, Polish consumers almost overnight saw radical changes in the types and quality of products available to them.

To promote long term growth in the Polish market, Colgate-Palmolive entered into a joint venture agreement with a local entrepreneur experienced in consumer product sales and distribution. Initially, the company planned to offer only a limited line of its top products—Colgate toothpaste, Palmolive soap and shampoo, and Ajax scouring powder—through the joint venture partner, which was entrusted with the responsibilities of manufacturing and marketing the goods. For its manufacturing facilities, Colgate-Palmolive worked with its joint venture partner to buy a partially completed complex, which was then renovated into a highly modern production facility. To make this joint operating arrangement run smoothly, Colgate-Palmolive appointed a native Pole general manager for the region. The new general manager had previously served the company in a variety of senior marketing management positions in both Belgium and France.

The Revolutionary Use of Video Intelligence in Mexico

To better understand Mexico's large and diverse population, particularly in terms of social and cultural differences, Colgate-Palmolive conducted what it termed a "video anthropological study" of the country's rapidly expanding consumer market. This study had two main objectives: to find out, by observing and talking with Mexican consumers, how certain products were actually used, and to gather general information on the lifestyles of these consumers. Colgate-Palmolive was not interested in product use itself, but rather in the *processes* in which its products *could* be used. Five processes were studied: dishwashing, house cleaning, oral care, hair care, and laundry or fabric care.

An independent team of researchers set out across the country, compiling 60 hours of video taped discussions with consumers. The result of this exercise was a series of video tapes covering each of the five main process areas. Initial analysis showed Colgate-Palmolive marketing managers that Mexican consumers' activities diverged significantly along socio-economic lines. For example, those in the higher socio-economic groups did their laundry and took care of fabrics in the same way as many middle class Europeans, using electric appliances and even the service of maids or housekeepers. But less well off Mexican consumers, for whom in-home water was often a luxury, did their washing manually in tubs using washboards or in local streams using rocks, with a variety of soaps to get their clothes clean.

Marketing managers at Colgate-Palmolive learned a great deal from this revolutionary use of video technology. The information directly affected new product development and the creation of advertising themes for existing products in the Mexican market. For example, marketing managers set out to develop new laundry care products that used less water and advertising messages that showed how Colgate-Palmolive products could be used in situations where little water was available. As a result of these efforts, new laundry pre-soak and spray stain removers were developed specifically for the Mexican market.

Operation Smile

Operation Smile is a volunteer organisation of doctors, dentists and corporate sponsors that travels all over the world, performing reconstructive surgery on children who suffer from cleft palates or cleft lips—facial deformities of the mouth and nasal region. Although these disorders are fairly common and corrective surgery is not considered complicated by Western medical standards, for many children in developing or Third World nations such surgery is either unaffordable or unavailable in their immediate geographic areas. In these cases, Operation Smile goes to the patient and performs the surgery free of charge. Since its inception in 1982, Operation Smile has performed reconstructive surgery or specialised dental treatment on well over 5,000 children. In addition, local doctors have been taught how to perform these corrective procedures, so that they can be done on a regular basis in their particular region.

Colgate-Palmolive has joined forces with Operation Smile in several of the developing countries in which it currently operates or hopes to in the future. In Panama, for example, the company organised and funded a public relations campaign featuring a series of "before and after" photo displays to inform parents in isolated rural regions that cleft lips or palates were in fact treatable. Then the company urged these parents to bring their children to local facilities to have the corrective work done free of charge. In addition, Colgate-Palmolive organised fund raising efforts in the local business community to offset the cost of the services provided. In Panama, the company has been at least partly responsible for the treatment of nearly 200 children.

Colgate-Palmolive's affiliation with Operation Smile not only encompasses organising and funding corrective surgery but also includes extensive oral education programmes for children in many less developed nations. For example, in Kenya the company is well known for its education programmes offered in conjunction with various community organisations in rural areas. The company also stocks the Operation Smile facilities with free toothpaste, soap and other supplies. All in all, Colgate-Palmolive's association with Operation Smile gives it a foundation for future investment and a unique opportunity to link its corporate goals with those of a well known and well regarded global charitable organisation.

International Growth

Colgate-Palmolive's Operation Smile activities and its initiatives in Mexico, Poland and the former East Germany form an integral part of its extensive international marketing programme. The company's aggressive concurrent development and introduction of new products in numerous other countries around the world clearly signals its intention to maintain its international focus. As further evidence of the company's strong commitment to the continuing global expansion, in 1992 Colgate-Palmolive became the first Western company to manufacture toothpaste in China, where a market of 4.2 billion potential customers proved eager for the high quality consumer products that Colgate-Palmolive could provide. These efforts, coupled with others, such as its revolutionary use of video intelligence gathering techniques in Mexico and its association with the Operation Smile programme, ensure that Colgate-Palmolive will continue to serve as a model for other companies hoping to succeed as multinational marketers in the dynamic global marketplace.

SOURCES: Gary Hoover, Alta Campbell and Patrick J. Spain, eds, *Hoover's Handbook of American Business 1993* (Austin, Tex.: Reference Press, 1993), p. 204; Colgate-Palmolive Co., *1992 Annual Report*; and Colgate-Palmolive Co., corporate videos, 1990–1992.

Questions for Discussion

1. Discuss how Colgate-Palmolive has responded to changing social, economic and political forces in the former East Germany. Why should firms use caution when expanding into such regions?
2. What kinds of useful information did Colgate-Palmolive gain from its video anthropological study in Mexico? Why is such knowledge especially important for a company entering international markets?
3. What factors might have played a role in Colgate-Palmolive's decision to enter into a joint venture agreement in the Polish market? Discuss the possible rationale for the company's decision to initially market only a limited number of its products in Poland.

●●●●●●●●●●●●●●●●●●

CASE A.2

Sweden's Electrolux Defends Europe from Whirlpool's Customer Orientated Attack

Relatively recently, US white goods giant Whirlpool was a minor player in the European market for dishwashers, cookers, fridge/freezers and washing machines. In the mid-1980s, following a period of mixed fortunes, Whirlpool decided to re-focus on the white goods market with the stated aim of becoming the world's number one manufacturer. In 1989 the company formed a joint venture with Philips of the Netherlands. Other joint ventures followed, along with consolidation by continent: the North American Appliance Group brought together Whirlpool's operations in the US, Canada and Mexico; a new Asian strategy centred on rejuvenated regional headquarters based in Tokyo. In much of the world, however, the white goods market bottomed out, with most major manufacturers reporting sluggish sales and deteriorating profits.

American Rivals Targeted Europe

Arch American rivals Whirlpool and Maytag Corporation targeted the expanding European Union with an eye on the associated benefits of growing trade opportunities with the former Eastern Bloc. In 1989 Maytag bought Britain's Hoover for around £200 million; Whirlpool paid £600 million for the appliance division of Philips, adding a further £312 million for re-tooling and upgrading Philips' plants. The Americans have experienced mixed fortunes in Europe. In 1995, following promotional gaffes—problems with promotional offers of free flights caused consumer uproar, adverse media publicity and declining sales—Maytag sold off its European operations, including Hoover, to an Italian business, accepting a loss of £85 million. Whirlpool, though, has decided to battle on, even though its European sales of around £1.56 billion—30 per cent of its global total sales—have remained flat since 1990. The European division is blamed for a fall in Whirlpool's earnings per share from £2.75 to £1.75 in 1994. To reverse this decline, the company has been highly active.

Pan-European Whirlpool

National designers and researchers have been merged into pan-European teams that work much more closely with Whirlpool's US designers. New products now use common "platforms" enabling different models to be built on the same underlying chassis, with associated development and production economies. Customer service centres, typical of most North American original equipment manufacturers but not the norm in Europe, were established in Germany, the UK, Belgium, Holland and Austria, with plans laid for more Customer Assistance Centres elsewhere, subject to sales levels. The European market is characterised by strong regional and cultural differences. Retail groups with national coverage, such as Currys or Comet, are prevalent in the UK, Benelux, France and Germany, but around the Mediterranean and in eastern Europe, buying groups and independent retailers still dominate. Not all retailers offer the Mastercare warranty support of the Dixons group; in most countries, the onus of after market service still falls on manufacturers' agents. In England, consumers prefer front loading washing machines, whereas their counterparts in France insist on top loading models. In Italy or Portugal, spin speeds are much lower than in Germany, reflecting the general warmth of the climate and preference for drying clothes outdoors. To accommodate these variations, Whirlpool's sales arm accordingly operates 19 sales teams, with 650 representatives liaising with over 40,000 trade partners: retailers, wholesalers and buying groups.

The sales and marketing activities are not set up by country, instead following trade channels and market segments. The marketing strategy centres on building long term relationships with retailers, wholesalers and buying groups, ensuring value added relationships that bring significant financial reward to both Whirlpool and its distributors. The service offer also varies quite distinctly between the various market segments served, with a stated pol-icy of attempting to create a differential advantage through the augmented product: customer service and warranties. This has led to a significant investment in dealer education, electronic data interchange, trade marketing, after sales service, and dealer and strategic trade partnerships.

The Philips-Whirlpool joint venture centred on a strategy of gaining market penetration by building up customer and dealer service levels and by concentrating on the augmented product, as detailed in Figure A2.1. This increased service level guaranteed a replacement machine if product failure occurred in the first 12 months of use, regardless of where in Europe the machine was purchased. Customer care hotlines were established, and customers were offered a 10 year spare part guarantee based on a once only premium payment. If service engineers failed to arrive within two working days, the customer was entitled to a full refund. Dealers' needs were also given priority; Whirlpool Financial Corporation offered a range of financial services to retailers, including extended payment terms and financing of display stock and store inventory. The new look, wholly owned Whirlpool operation in Europe is continuing this service led, customer focused strategy.

As a result, Whirlpool now occupies the number three slot in Europe, with 13 per cent of the market. The company is instigating a new branding initiative, transferring the brand heritage and credentials from its American heartland across Europe, supported by a major pan-European advertising drive. The "Fantastic World" campaign aims to establish both the Whirlpool brand identity and key features of a massive programme of new product development and enhancement. In 1995 the new range of faster dryers and washing machines with wider doors and easier access appeared. These new products reflected the findings of a major programme of marketing research, which examined user behaviour and requirements. By the end of 1996, over 60 per cent of sales stemmed from these new products. The strategy is to provide more value without any proportional price increase. New energy efficient refrigerators and dishwashers also reflect growing consumer concerns about the earth's renewable resources and atmospheric pollution. In a highly competitive marketplace, Whirlpool has demonstrated a commitment to its European ambitions.

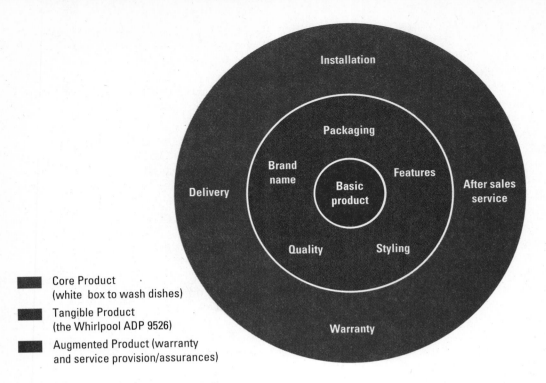

Core Product
(white box to wash dishes)

Tangible Product
(the Whirlpool ADP 9526)

Augmented Product (warranty
and service provision/assurances)

Figure A2.1 The augmented product of Whirlpool

Electrolux Attains Global Leadership

For leading rival Electrolux, the Swedish company with most to lose to Whirlpool's European advance, these activities have proved unwelcome but inevitable. Electrolux is Europe's market leader, Bosch-Siemens and Whirlpool the leading challengers. Electrolux has not been idle. In 1995 it publicly re-affirmed its intention to become the world's dominant manufacturer of white goods, setting up a new Asian operation in Singapore and extending its hold over Brazil. It has invested over £65 million in establishing capabilities in the emerging markets of India and China. The global market is still highly fragmented, though, with Japanese suppliers controlling the Asia Pacific market, US giants General Electric and Whirlpool dominating the Americas and the European operations of Sweden's Electrolux and Germany's Bosch-Siemens leading a plethora of national brands in Europe.

In Europe, to fight back against the inroads of Whirlpool, Electrolux is adopting a three-pronged strategy:

- Multi-branding in existing national markets
- Establishing operations in eastern Europe
- Increasing attention to customer service

First, existing markets are being defended by multi-branding: well known names such as Electrolux, Zanussi (Italian based but Electrolux owned) and newly acquired AEG of Germany are marketed alongside a large number of national brands bought up by the Swedish giant over the years. These rival ranges offer a mix of price, feature, distribution and brand value ingredients, which together provide Electrolux with a formidable range of marketing options.

Second, the opening up of trade opportunities in the once communist Eastern Bloc has proved highly attractive. Refrigerators are assembled in Hungary, portable refrigerators in the Czech Republic and washing machines in Poland. Third, Electrolux's marketers have paid special attention to after market, after sales support and warranties as they seek an edge over ever more combative rivals.

Global Economies and Multi-Branding

Electrolux firmly believes that success in the future will depend on global product development to share information on technology, developments, manufacturing material management, component development and purchasing, combined with regional marketing activity that reflects local consumer needs and brand positionings. While local brands are expected to dominate the ethnocentric North American market, a mix of multinational and local brands will continue to dominate in Europe. In this respect Electrolux believes it has a clear advantage over the US-originated single brand Whirlpool. To consumers across Europe, AEG occupies a high price, high quality, premium position; Zanussi a lower to middle value position (except in the UK, where its famous "Appliance of Science" long standing advertising has established its reputation for technically advanced products); and the name Electrolux is safe, reliable and upper middle market position. Given the plethora of national brands occupying a diversity of niche positions, Electrolux feels it is well placed to provide (1) a highly desirable selection of brand names for customers and dealers seeking the reassurance of internationally recognised brands, (2) Zanussi products or locally produced products for consumers buying on the basis of value for money, and (3) AEG products for consumers prepared to pay more for better features and reliability.

There is no doubt that Electrolux is not prepared to sit back on its 23 per cent of the European market. Acquisition of AEG narrowly placed it in the lead worldwide over Whirlpool. The US rival's inroads on Europe, carefully planned and marketing led, offer an impressive level of customer service. Through a mixture of new product development, new market entry, brand development and customer care, Electrolux intends not only to keep Whirlpool at bay but also to cement its position as the global market leader.

SOURCES: Marcia Berss, "Whirlpool's bloody nose", *Forbes*, 11 March 1996, pp. 90–92; Joe Jancsurak, "Holistic strategy pays off", *Appliance Manufacturer*, February 1996, pp. W3–W18; Patrick Oster and John Rossant, "Call it Worldpool", *Business Week*, 28 November, 1994, pp. 98–99; "Dedication to majors", *Appliance Manufacturer*, May 1994, pp. W4–W10; Neal McGrath, "New broom sweeps into Asia", *Asian Business*, March 1996, p. 22; "Electrolux to assemble washing machines", *Finance East Europe*, 6 October 1995, p. 10; Joe Jancsurak, "Global trends for 1995–2005", *Appliance Manufacturer*, June 1995, pp. A3–A6; Joe Jancsurak, "Big plans for Europe's big three", *Appliance Manufacturer*, April 1995, pp. 26–30; Sally Dibb and Lyndon Simkin, *The Marketing Casebook: Cases and Concepts* (London: Routledge, 1994).

Questions for Discussion

1. In venturing into eastern Europe, what aspects of the marketing environment must the leading white goods manufacturers consider? Discuss.
2. Why has Whirlpool adopted a customer service orientated strategy based on the augmented product? Why might some customers prefer such a service led product offering? Explain which customers.
3. Whirlpool and Electrolux have adopted very different branding strategies in their head to head global battle. Why? What are the relative advantages and disadvantages of the two companies' respective approaches? Discuss.

• • • • • • • • • • • • • • • • • •

CASE A.3

Competing on Nationalistic Fervour and Improving Customer Service—Aer Lingus

The airline industry is unusual: its strategic importance and exacting safety and technical requirements make it highly regulated. People skills, whether those of pilots, ground crews or cabin staff, are specialised and expensive. The cost of leasing or buying aircraft is very high. Routes are highly sought after, particularly into the major international hubs such as London, Amsterdam or Paris. The much vaunted freedom of the skies policy, central to the harmonisation of European deregulation and the creation of the European Union, has yet to materialise, with major carriers still defending relative monopoly conditions on certain routes. Few airlines are as profitable as British Airways, yet every government strives to have a "national" carrier of which its population can be proud. Most states in the EU have a host of smaller airlines attempting to emulate Air France, British Airways, KLM and Lufthansa.

Ireland's Growth

The situation in Ireland is no different, except that the country has recently enjoyed tremendous success in economic growth and in attracting investment from an impressive and diverse list of international corporations that includes Dell, IBM, Siemens, CIGNA, McGraw-Hill, ABN AMRO, Chase Manhattan, Deutsche Bank, General Electric, Grand Metropolitan, Sumitomo, Ericsson, Hitachi, Sandoz, Schering-Plough, Fruit of the Loom, Glen Dimplex, Krups, Heineken, Nestlé and the ubiquitous Coca-Cola. As a result, good communications are crucial. For the government and people of Ireland as well as the expanding international business community, air travel has increasingly become a necessity. The Shannon duty free zone and continued prosperity of Dublin have added to the volume of freight traffic heading to Ireland. For the quasi state airline Aer Lingus, these growing demands have provided a welcome boost to business; they are also the reason more and more rival airlines are seeking slots for flights into Dublin.

Complex Competitive Situation

The highly competitive airline industry is characterised by four strategic groups:

- Global carriers with truly global networks, such as American Airlines, British Airways, KLM, Qantas and United.
- Medium size international carriers, with significant international routes but less global reach, such as Cathay Pacific, SAS and Virgin.
- Regional carriers focused on regional networks and destinations, such as British Midland, Iberia and Swissair.
- Local carriers serving domestic short hop, intercity destinations such as Deutsche BA, Loganair and TAT.

In addition, there are numerous charter operators, such as Air 2000 or Caledonian, plus businesses dealing only with air freight and couriers. Aer Lingus is a regional carrier with a few key international routes emanating from Dublin, an impressive network with most major British regional airports and a growing selection of European destinations. As such the company competes with rivals in all four strategic groups, contending with the Club branding and high service levels offered by British Airways, the cut price deals of Ryanair and the high promotional spends of most major European airlines. In addition, Ireland's proximity to the Welsh coast forces Aer Lingus to consider the ferry operators as competitors for much business to and from the UK.

High Expectations

A lot is expected of Aer Lingus, until recently Ireland's official national carrier. In terms of sales, it is Ireland's thirteenth largest company, and by number of employees (12,000) it is ranked third. Now standing on its own commercial platform, the company has a monumental mission. According to marketing director Maurice Coleman, it is tough for the airline because "we have to compete with several of the really big players on the transatlantic routes, the large airlines in the European Union as well as the smaller, 'no frills' operators within certain UK and Irish domestic routes. So while we have to be commercially competitive with other major carriers in different segments of the free market, back home in Ireland and as a major employer, people expect us to take an accommodating attitude to labour relations, work practices and to provide long term employment".

The official, publicly stated mission statement is equally demanding:

> The Aer Lingus mission is to be a strong niche airline, primarily carrying passengers and freight into and out of Ireland, capable of sustained profitability through commercially viable products and practices and a keen customer focus, delivered by committed and well motivated staff. It will strive to attain a position in which its subsidiaries are profitable and viable within themselves, are strategic to the core airline business and the ownership of which enhances the achievability of the airline's objectives.

For the core business, the airline, there is stiff and varied competition. On its transatlantic routes,

American Airlines, British Airways, Delta, KLM, Northwest and Singapore offer premium service competition, while Virgin and Air India provide value for money rivalry. Principal competition on its European routes stems from the trimmer regional carriers—notably Air UK, British Midlands, Maersk Air and SAS. On the London and UK provincial routes, BA's stronger franchises, especially CityFlyer Express and Maersk Air, provide competition, while Virgin's Dublin based CityJet and its major challenger Ryanair provide significant competition. Nevertheless, Aer Lingus believes it holds a successful operating niche, helped by its distinct national identity, which appeals strongly to the Irish both at home and abroad. Indeed, the 1993 financial loss of £34 million was turned round a year later into an operating profit of £35 million. The current financial situation is just as volatile, although there is an operating profit, as indicated in the financial statements on pages 784–785.

Irish Nationalism

The essence of the successful niche central to Aer Lingus's marketing is Irish nationalism. Its transatlantic routes, where it has no other Irish based rivals, are its most profitable. To feed this route, Aer Lingus operates Dublin as a hub for all its domestic, London, other UK and European flights. These flights operate on co-ordinated timetables with the US flights to offer passengers "seamless" travel. There are believed to be over 44 million Americans of Irish ancestry. Henry Ford, John Paul Getty, Gene Kelly, Gregory Peck, the Kennedys, Ronald Reagan and Bill Clinton are just some of the more famous examples. Accordingly, there are US Immigration and Naturalisation Service clearing facilities in Dublin and Shannon airports, offering users of the Aer Lingus Dublin hub destined for Boston and New York significant time savings.

The transatlantic route is at the forefront of Aer Lingus's development programme and marketing initiatives. The highly profitable business class has 52 inch pitch sleeperettes instead of the standard 42 inch pitch business class seats found in most airlines; coupled with multi-channel personal videos, loyalty programmes for frequent fliers and luxury lounges at airports, these have given Aer Lingus an edge over rivals on its transatlantic lifeline. Because business class passengers generate up to five times as much

profit as tourist class passengers, Premier class accommodation has recently been expanded from 24 to 36 seats. In the economy cabin section, price competition with rivals has reached a peak, but by removing in-flight entertainment and reducing refreshments, Aer Lingus Ireland Vacations has been able to undercut rivals' discount deals. Regular fliers, chambers of commerce and Ireland's Air Transport Users' Committee have welcomed the attention being devoted to the Premier class; "best executive class on transatlantic routes", "best transatlantic airline", "best Ireland/UK airline", "best Ireland/Europe airline" are just some of the accolades. High take-up of the "no frills" economy service and Aer Lingus Ireland Vacations indicates that those passengers, too, are satisfied with Aer Lingus's efforts.

While pricing is often critical in the airline wars, operators such as British Airways and Singapore Airlines are perpetually seeking to create a differential advantage through improvements in customer service and customer handling: larger and more comfortable seats, better trained cabin crew, superior entertainment and food, faster check-ins, in-flight faxes and phones, limousine pick up and delivery, smart airport lounges, exercise facilities, and more pleasant staff. The challenge has not gone unnoticed by Aer Lingus. Chairman Gary McGann is on record as stating that "Aer Lingus is in the service business, not a supplier of seats on aircraft—a traditional focus of many airlines—but as a supplier of a total travel experience. To compete successfully, Aer Lingus must increase its already strong focus on service and quality. The Aer Lingus brand is strong and can only be developed further through the provision of ever improved levels of customer satisfaction".

A Future of Customer Service

This reflects the view expressed in some quarters that the company will have difficulty moving away from the transatlantic economy market to compete purely on the basis of low price against operators such as Ryanair. Aer Lingus's cost base, culture and role in the Irish transport and communications system do not lend themselves to operating entirely as a price driven "no frills" airline along the lines of EasyJet. Away from premium (business) class, Aer Lingus will have difficulty developing a competitive

a. Aer Lingus Group Plc, Consolidated Profit and Loss Account for the year ended 31 December 1995

		Year ended 31 December 1995 IR£000	Twenty one month period ended 31 December 1994 IR£000
Turnover	- continuing operations	705,664	1,190,959
	- discontinued operations	89,738	289,523
		795,402	1,480,482
Cost of sales	- operating	(552,677)	(1,077,197)
	- exceptional items	(102)	(33,052)
		(552,779)	(1,110,249)
Gross Profit		242,623	370,233
Other operating expenses	- operating	(189,578)	(331,778)
	- exceptional items	—	(3,620)
	- employee participation	(3,280)	—
		(192,858)	(335,398)
Operating Profit	- continuing operations	36,757	7,841
	- discontinued operations	13,008	26,994
		49,765	34,835
Profit on sale of fixed assets in continuing operations		3,917	—
Cost of rationalisation and restructuring of continuing operations		—	(65,879)
Losses and provisions for losses on the sale or termination of operations, net		(15,537)	(36,703)
Profit (Loss) on Ordinary Activities before Interest		38,145	(67,747)
Income from financial assets and similar income		13,218	12,921
Interest payable and similar charges		(33,566)	(73,974)
Profit (Loss) on Ordinary Activities before Taxation		17,797	(128,800)
Tax on profit or loss on ordinary activities		(2,485)	(315)
Profit (Loss) on Ordinary Activities after Taxation		15,312	(129,115)
Minority interests		(253)	(757)
Profit (Loss) for the Year		15,059	(129,872)
Profit and Loss Account, Start of Year		(147,766)	(43,097)
Retained Profit (Loss) for the year		15,059	(129,872)
Transfers from revaluation reserve		44,504	—
Goodwill previously written off to reserves		—	18,608
Other movements, principally currency translation adjustments		(232)	6,595
Profit and Loss Account, End of Year		(88,435)	(147,766)
Profit (Loss) per Share (Pence)		7.7p	(115.1p)

B. Cahill, CHAIRMAN   **M. Rafferty,** DIRECTOR   Approved by the Board of Directors on 14 March 1996.

b. Aer Lingus Group Plc, Consolidated Balance Sheet, as at 31 December 1995

	1995 IR£000	1994 IR£000
Fixed Assets		
Intangible assets	1,971	2,684
Tangible assets	362,868	676,218
Financial assets	3,469	4,283
	368,308	683,185
Current Assets		
Stocks	26,254	27,996
Debtors	97,179	97,021
Investments	7,873	627
Cash at bank and in hand	376,537	174,558
	507,843	300,202
Creditors: Amounts falling due within one year	(268,117)	(259,705)
Net Current Assets	239,726	40,497
Total Assets less Current Liabilities	608,034	723,682
Creditors: Amounts falling due after more than one year	(317,723)	(462,187)
Investment Grants	(6,453)	(11,732)
Provisions for Liabilities and Charges	(124,745)	(146,319)
Net Assets	159,113	103,444
Capital and Reserves		
Called-up share capital	243,610	193,610
Revaluation reserve	2,807	48,498
Profit and loss account	(88,435)	(147,766)
Shareholders' funds	157,982	94,342
Minority Interests	1,131	9,102
	159,113	103,444

B. Cahill, CHAIRMAN   **M. Rafferty,** DIRECTOR   Approved by the Board of Directors on 14 March 1996.

advantage as it is likely not to match discount operators' pricing. In the premium business sector, Aer Lingus believes it genuinely has an edge over its rivals, helped by its nationalistic profile and existing reputation for providing a good level of customer service. This may be true for the transatlantic market, where so many travellers are of Irish heritage, but perhaps less so on European and UK routes. In such a competitive and harsh marketplace, Aer Lingus cannot afford to be stuck in the middle. The future seems clear: the focus must be to enhance customer service levels, particularly in Aer Lingus's premium class. Rivals, though, will not stand still, and on most routes, Aer Lingus is still a relatively small operator. The future is not without its challenges. Understanding and serving customer requirements in a manner that takes account of rivals' strategies will be important in both the business class and the economy segments of this market.

SOURCES: Aer Lingus Annual Reports; Maurice Coleman, Aer Lingus, 1995; Jimmy Ang; The Industrial Development Agency, Dublin.

1. The culture of its target market is particularly important to Aer Lingus. Why? Explain how the airline can use this situation to its advantage.
2. Aer Lingus's competitive situation is complex. Why is this such a problem for its economy class business? Discuss the implications of this situation.

3. Discuss the importance of customer service in developing a differential advantage in the airline business.
4. How best should Aer Lingus promote its premium class?

● ● ● ● ● ● ● ● ● ● ● ● ● ● ● ● ● ● ● ●

CASE A.4

The Competitive Environment of Avis Rent-A-Car

Avis is the largest car rental company in the world. Currently operating in around 140 different countries, with 4,800 outlets, the company prides itself in its strong brand name and global network. Avis has a particularly strong presence in Europe, with more than 2,200 outlets in over 40 countries. In the UK, where the company has a 15 per cent market share, customers can visit any one of almost 200 Avis outlets. Avis is owned jointly by Belgian car dealer D'Ieteren (which owns 65 per cent of the equity), General Motors (27 per cent equity) and Avis Inc. (8 per cent equity).

Avis's size plays an important role in the company's success. In particular, its position as the largest company in its sector buys a strong bargaining position with the car manufacturers. Avis UK, for example, has a fleet of 20,000 cars. By changing these vehicles two or three times a year, the company may buy up to 60,000 cars per annum. In 1994 the company bought around 35,000 cars for its UK fleet (£400 million at showroom prices), half of them from UK manufacturers. This is obviously a significant proportion of the 2 million or so new cars registered each year in the UK, which gives the company a great deal of buying power. In order to maintain its power in relationships and ensure competitiveness from its suppliers, Avis will sometimes switch to different manufacturers. Avis is able to use the power it has built up to negotiate good buying terms, sometimes up to 50 per cent off list prices. In addition, the company often negotiates generous "sell back" terms when the vehicles are replaced. This arrangement is also in the interests of the car manufacturers, who wish to maintain a degree of control over the sale of "nearly new" vehicles and enjoy the benefits of market share publicity. The

scale economies Avis is able to achieve as a result of its size further enable the company to secure attractive credit terms from financial institutions.

The Car Rental Business

The companies operating in the car rental business can be divided into three groups:

- companies such as Avis, Budget, Europcar Interrent and Hertz, which operate internationally under a strong global brand
- operators using a national or international brand name such as Europcar, United Kenning and U-Drive, including some manufacturers' dealers such as Ford Rent-A-Car and Vauxhall Rental, which hire out "nearly new" fleet cars
- local chains and franchises, such as Salford Van Hire and Practical Car and Van Rental, as well as hundreds of independent operators, typically targeting more price sensitive customers and trading from one or two outlets.

Rivalry among competing car rental companies is intense. Perhaps the major difficulty operators face is that, to many renters, one car is much like another. Once rental companies have attempted to differentiate themselves on the basis of car age and make, which anyway may be unimportant to the renter, there are few tools left to use in the battle for customers. Not surprisingly, many operators are also reluctant to engage in a price war, despite the price sensitivity of renters. Perhaps then, as Table A4.1 shows, the fact that the largest operators are close together in terms of market share should come as no surprise.

Car Rental Company	1991 £m	1991 %	1994 (estimate) £m	1994 (estimate) %
Avis	68	14	77	15
Eurodollar	50	10	73	14
Hertz	38	8	47	10
Europcar Interrent	42	9	43	9
Budget Rent A Car	47	10	43	9
Others	225	49	217	43
Total	470	100	500	100

SOURCE: Central Statistical Office/Mintel, April 1995.

Table A4.1: Market share of the UK car rental sector

The breakdown of business and private users for the rental business is shown in Table A4.2.

Type of Renter	1990 £m	1990 %	1992 £m	1992 %	1994 £m	1994 %
Private hire	195	36	160	38	182	36
Business hire	350	64	260	62	318	64
Total	545	100	420	100	500	100

SOURCE: Central Statistical Office/Mintel, April 1995.

Table A4.2: UK private and business usage of car rental

Developing a Differential Advantage

Developing a differential advantage in this market is difficult. Even company size is no guarantee that Avis will be able to sustain its current position. While the company is the world's largest car rental company, leading rivals Eurodollar and Hertz, with networks which come close to rivalling Avis, are never far behind. The largest car rental chains all renew their cars every four to six months, so it is not possible for Avis to differentiate its offering on the basis of the age or make of its vehicles. The company, like many others in the industry, is also reluctant to use price as a potential differentiator. However, customer sensitivity to the cost of car hire compels Avis to use this tool to some degree. For example, in January 1995 the industry was rocked by Hertz's commitment to offer car rental terms of £1 less than any comparable rates. The offer was backed up by the Hertz Price Promise programme.

Not surprisingly, in what is essentially a service business, Avis devotes considerable resources to providing efficient and friendly customer service. In 1993–94 the company invested more than £3.5 million upgrading its UK "front desk" facilities and customer service points. This process included the installation of hand-held computer terminals, designed to ease the vehicle check-out process, at 10 UK airport locations.

Avis's emphasis on computer technology is an area in which the business has developed considerable strength and is now an important factor in its success. Increasing computer technology is seen as a way of reducing operating costs and generating increases in volume. As a result of its commitment to computer technology, Avis has invested £750 million, spread over two decades, in the company's own car rental computerised reservation system (CRS). Research in the car rental business indicates that some 20 per cent of vehicle reservations are now booked through CRS. Figures from the US suggest that this figure is likely to rise further. The Avis CRS, known as Wizard, directly links nearly 15,000 terminals around the world, as well as interfacing with the airlines' computerised reservation systems. These links allow easier booking: customers can reserve a vehicle anywhere in the world from any one of the terminals available. In addition, the CRS offers more efficient check-in and check-out, easier tracking of vehicles and better price management. The airline computer reservations systems with which Avis is linked have special car rental reservation systems. There are four key systems:

- Amadeus: jointly owned by Amadeus, Air France, Iberia Airlines and Lufthansa. Amadeus Cars, the car rental facility was launched in 1992 and serves 9 to 15 major car rental companies.
- Galileo: jointly owned by 12 airlines including United Airlines, USAir, British Airways, Swissair and Alitalia. CarMaster, the car rental module, was launched in 1989 and serves 50 car rental companies.
- Worldspan: jointly owned by Delta Airlines, Northwest Airlines and TWA. Car Select, the car rental facility, was launched in 1991 and serves 40 car rental firms, including Alamo, Avis and Hertz.

- Sabre: wholly owned by American Airlines. CARS (Car Availability and Rate System) is the car reservation module.

Avis is not the only car rental company to invest in a CRS. Key rival Hertz has its own CRS system, which it uses to compare competitors' prices worldwide. Meanwhile, Europcar has invested nearly £300 million in its Greenway reservation system, which is also linked to travel agents' CRS terminals. For Budget, the experience of trying to develop a joint CRS with Marriott and Hilton Hotels has not been a happy one. After investing over £65 million in the system, the partners are now suing the provider, a subsidiary of AMR Corp., for non-delivery. In order to fill its CRS gap, Budget has now signed up as a Wizard CRS user with WizCom (Avis's wholly owned subsidiary, which developed Wizard).

In addition to its strengths in computer technology, the company has a number of other important strengths that play an important role in establishing its position in the market, for example:

- the Avis global brand name, which gives the company a high level of buying power in its relationships with suppliers
- an extensive worldwide network of outlets, which allows customers easy access and makes it easier to build customer loyalty
- a high proportion of company owned (rather than franchised) outlets, which gives it a high level of control over standards.

Targeting the Business User

As it seeks to develop its strong position, Avis's primary focus is on the business and corporate renters. This focus is not surprising given the company's particularly strong market share of the airport and city centre business, where much of the corporate business is generated. For example, EIU figures show that in the UK Avis enjoys a 30 per cent share of the airport segment, compared with 15 per cent of the market as a whole. Targeting the corporate customer is one particular area where Wizard can help the company by providing efficient, hassle free service. The company also uses its CRS technology to identify and target business and other frequent customers with a range of special offerings, for example:

Wizard Card This card offers corporate customers and frequent renters guaranteed preferential rates and discounts.

Avis Express This service guarantees a dedicated check-in booth for users, no queues and form free rental. Described by the company as "the world's fastest car rental service", Avis Express is open to all Avis Wizard Card holders. Avis lists the benefits of this service as speed, efficiency, priority, availability and extra value (20 per cent discount off standard airport rates).

Avis Local Described by the company as an Avis Best Deal Promise, this service saves renters shopping around by guaranteeing the best value from the renters' local station. Additional discounts and benefits are available to Avis Club members.

Among other current initiatives is a partnership with Air UK. The Air UK and Avis deal offers Air UK customers special car rental rates and simple reservations available from all Air UK destinations. Aimed at private and business travellers, the promotion stresses the combination of convenience and quality at competitive prices.

These are just some of the marketing tools Avis is now using in its continuing efforts to maintain leadership in the car rental sector. Staying ahead will not be an easy task in a market characterised by intense competitiveness and price sensitive customers. In such an environment, Avis will continue to build upon its key strengths, so that it can live up to its positioning statement: "We try harder".

SOURCES: Jimmy Ang; "Car hire retail business", *Economic Intelligence Unit*, July 1995; "Hertz keeps its promise with £1 million", *Marketing Week*, 3 February 1995, p. 8; "The supply structure", *Car and Van Hire*, Mintel Marketing Intelligence, April 1995; "Market factors", *Car and Van Hire*, Mintel Marketing Intelligence, April 1995; "The European car rental market", *The European Car Rental Industry Research Establishment*, 1993/1994, pp. 53–56; P. Lilley, "Europcar claims it has high-tech edge", *Travel Trade Gazette Europa*, 8 September 1994, p. 14; V. Houlder, "Technology—electronic librarians", *Financial Times*, 21 April 1995, p. 21; "WizCom to provide Budget with advanced computer reservation system", *PR Newswire*, 3 May 1995; "Competitor analysis", *Vehicle Leasing and Hire*, 1995, p. 58; Avis Wizard Card and Avis Express promotional leaflets.

Questions for Discussion

1. What are Avis Rent-A-Car's competitive strengths? How does the company exploit these strengths to develop a differential advantage?
2. How is the car rental market segmented?
3. Avis Rent-A-Car has a mix of business and non-business customers. Why does the company emphasise the business renter? How might the "buying" process differ between business and non-business customers?

B REVISION TIPS

Each tutor and examination will have specific requirements and ground rules. The views expressed in this appendix should not be allowed to over-rule any guidance given by students' own tutors and examination invigilators.

The Paper

Contrary to popular belief, tutors do not generally set examination papers in order to catch students out with trick questions or by referring questions to topics not covered in lectures or course texts. Examinations are based on the syllabuses set and the concepts presented in lectures and course readings. A great deal of benefit will be gained from attending lectures and hearing tutors' views about key concepts. There is no substitute for painstaking, thorough revision, commenced well before examinations are due to be taken. There is probably little point in spending time trying to "question spot" by looking at papers from previous years. The syllabus in the current year is not necessarily the same as in previous years, and tutors may not even refer to earlier papers when designing current examinations. This means that there is rarely a pattern in the topics which are chosen.

Coping with Examination Conditions

Very few people enjoy taking examinations. MBA and master's degree students may not have sat an examination for a long time. Not surprisingly for many undergraduates and postgraduate students, examinations are stressful. Although there are no easy ways to eliminate this problem, steps can be taken in the examination itself to make the experience less traumatic.

- Manage time as effectively as possible. The format of the examination will specify the number of questions to be answered. There is no point in answering too many questions, as credit will not be awarded for the "extra" answers. Failure to answer enough questions, on the other hand, *undoubtedly* will result in low marks being awarded for the paper. Poor time management is generally the main reason for poor examination performance (assuming a reasonable level of revision has been undertaken!). Leave a few minutes at the end to check back through answers.

- Read the questions properly and then answer the question actually set. Remember that the questions are there to help lead students to provide the answer that tutors are seeking. It is good practice to read each question *at least twice* to check that what is required is completely clear. There are two types of problems with answers that do not tackle the question that has been set. (1) Total misunderstanding of what is required. This is extremely rare. The papers are carefully checked by the staff teaching the courses, and often by an external examiner, to minimise the chance of any ambiguities. (2) Latching onto one key word or theme in a question. Sometimes individuals spot a particular word or phrase in a question and then tell their tutors absolutely everything they know about this particular topic. In some cases they do not, however, discuss the issue in relation to the question asked! Once again, the more carefully the question is read before starting to answer it, the less likely this problem is to arise.

• • • • • • • • • • • • • • • • • • • •

Format of Answers

It is important to give some thought to how ideas can best be presented in the examination. The following suggestions should help:

- Use examples to illustrate answers. Marketing is a practical subject, so it is important to demonstrate understanding of how the theoretical concepts work by referring to examples. Some questions may specifically state a named example (product, brand or company), which must be referred to in the answer. In such questions, it is essential that answers do use this named example and that the pertinent theoretical concepts are related to it. Some questions may ask students to illustrate their answers using examples of their choice. The tutors' aim in asking such questions is to require students to demonstrate their genuine understanding of the concepts taught in a course.
- It is a good idea to prepare some examples in advance of the examination. It is much easier to think about possible examples away from the pressure of the examination itself, and doing so should also save precious time. Take a break from the pain of revision and wander around the supermarket: it is surprising what can be learned there about new products and brands and how they are marketed. Spend some time watching television advertisements or browsing through magazines for example ideas. Magazines aimed at the marketing profession, such as *Marketing, Marketing Week* or *Campaign,* all have lively, interesting articles and also present up-dates on new and existing products and marketing campaigns. Copies of these magazines are available in most libraries or by order from newsagents.
- Think about the structure of answers. At the very least, make sure that each answer starts with a "scene setting" introduction and finishes with some kind of conclusion or summary. A summary helps to check that the question really has been addressed and reminds tutors of an answer's key points.
- Try to avoid the "wallpaper syndrome"—pages and pages of script completely uninterrupted by new paragraphs, headings, figures, etc. Make sure that each

- Be sensible about diagrams. Diagrams are often a useful tool to use in answers. They can illustrate points or models in a concise and easy to follow manner. However, do not spend too long drawing them! A simple sketch is worth as many marks as a perfectly drawn and multi-coloured piece of artwork. Also, remember that the diagrams used must still be briefly explained in the text: they cannot entirely take the place of written analysis.

Commonly Asked Students' Questions

1. *How long should my answer be?*

   This is really impossible to answer. As might be expected, the quantity and quality of answers are not necessarily correlated. The variation in handwriting size also makes this impossible to judge. A typical essay answer, in say 45 minutes, for someone with average handwriting might vary from between three to six pages!

2. *What should I do if I run out of time?*

   First of all, please do not! If, despite best efforts to manage time, this problem arises and the end of the examination is approaching fast, complete as much of the rest of the paper as possible in brief note form. This is probably not going to score as many marks as a more considered and reasoned explanation, but at least it will show the areas that would have been covered.

3. *I don't have time to revise all of the topics, so which ones should I leave out?*

   Unfortunately, there is no easy answer to this one! Of course everyone has to undertake revision as efficiently as possible, but the laws of probability dictate that the more topics cut out of revision, the greater the risk that too few will be known well enough to answer the tutors' selections of questions.

4. *Should I use essay or report format?*

   Most tutors do not mind which format is adopted as long as the answer is legible, well structured and clearly addresses the question as set. Some examination papers may specify a required format in the opening instructions. Always read and understand an examination paper's covering instructions. You must adhere to these requirements and your own tutors' guidance. Remember that tutors may be marking many examination scripts, so produce clear answers that are unambiguous and easy to read.

CAREERS IN MARKETING

Although jobs in marketing are numerous and varied, not everyone will find a career in marketing satisfying. The work associated with a particular career should be enjoyable and stimulating. Because you will spend almost 40 per cent of your waking hours at work, you should not allow such factors as economic conditions or status to over ride your personal goals as you select a life long career. Too often, people do not weigh these factors realistically. You should give considerable thought to your choice of career, and you should adopt a well planned, systematic approach to finding a position that meets your personal and career objectives.

After determining your objectives, you should identify the organisations that are likely to offer desirable opportunities. Learn as much as possible about these organisations before setting up employment interviews; job recruiters are impressed with applicants who have done their homework.

When making initial contact with potential employers by mail, enclose a brief, clearly written letter of introduction. After an initial interview, you should send a brief letter of thanks to the interviewer. The job of getting the right job is important, and you owe it to yourself to take this process seriously.

The Résumé or Curriculum Vitae

The résumé or curriculum vitae (CV) is one of the keys to being considered for a good job. Because it states your qualifications, experiences, education and career goals, the résumé is a chance for a potential employer to assess your compatibility with the job requirements. For the employer's and individual's benefit, the résumé should be accurate and current.

To be effective, the résumé can be targeted towards a specific position, as Figure C.1 shows. This document is only one example of an acceptable résumé. The job target section is specific and leads directly to the applicant's qualifications for the job. Capabilities show what the applicant can do and that the person has an understanding of the job's requirements. Skills and strengths as they relate to

Figure C.1

A résumé targeted towards
a specific position

LORRAINE WHEELER
35 EAST PARK ROAD
REEDLEY
LEEDS, L517 9NP
(0532) 482111

EDUCATION: B.Sc. Honours, The Best University, 1984, Marketing

DATE OF BIRTH: 2/8/59

POSITION DESIRED: PRODUCT MANAGER WITH AN INTERNATIONAL FIRM PROVIDING
FUTURE CAREER DEVELOPMENT AT THE EXECUTIVE LEVEL.

QUALIFICATIONS:

* communicates well with individuals to achieve a common goal

* handles tasks efficiently and in a timely manner

* knowledge of advertising, sales, management, marketing research, packaging, pricing,
distribution, and warehousing

* co-ordinates many activities at one time

* receives and carries out assigned tasks or directives

* writes complete status or research reports

EXPERIENCE:

* Assistant Editor on student newspaper

* Treasurer of the hockey club

* Student Researcher with Dr. Steven Who, Lecturer of Marketing, The Best University

* Achieved 2.1 degree

WORK RECORD:

1984 – Present	Wiggins & Co.
	* Junior Advertising Account Executive
1981 – 1983	The Place
	* Retail sales and consumer relations
1979 – 1981	Do All Builders
	* Labourer (part time/holidays)

EDUCATION:

| 1981 – 1984 | B. Sc. Management Science, The Best University, London. 2.1 Honours awarded. Dissertation topic: the marketing of charities. |
| 1978 – 1980 | Middlethorn Sixth Form College, Dullsville. A levels: English (A); Economics (B); General Studies (A). |

the specific job should be highlighted. The achievement section indicates success at accomplishing tasks or goals within the job market and at school/college. The work experience section includes educational background, which adds credibility to the résumé but is not the major area of focus; it is the applicant's ability to function successfully in a specific job that receives the major emphasis.

Common suggestions for improving résumés include deleting useless information, improving organisation, using professional printing and typing, listing duties (not accomplishments), maintaining grammatical perfection and avoiding an excessively elaborate or fancy format.[1] One of the biggest problems in résumés, according to a survey of personnel experts, is distortions and lies; 36 per cent of the experts thought that this was a major problem.[2] People lie most often about previous salaries and tasks performed in former jobs. Present career/education details in reverse order, since your most recent exploits are of most interest to potential employers. A good CV or résumé is essential.

The Interview

Most job searches involve interviews. The Davis Company, a leading firm of careers consultants, offers the following tips for candidates being interviewed:

- Work out what are your essential and desirable criteria for the new job. Do not lose sight of these during the interview.
- Prepare well. Find out about the company's products/services and the person who is interviewing you.
- Do not be late.
- Be smart, clean and presentable. Do not look glum.
- Be comfortable in your seat.
- Answer the questions asked. Do not ramble.
- If you are not sure of the question, ask for clarification.
- Keep focused on the current question. Do not be phased by interruptions.
- Ask questions. Show interest and enthusiasm for the business.
- Listen carefully.
- Maintain eye contact, but do not stare. Do not appear furtive.
- Be positive and up-beat.
- Do not discuss politics or contentious issues.
- Do not make—or appear to make—instant judgements.
- Do not criticise strongly your current employer or college.
- Ask if there are any other questions they need to ask you.
- Clarify the rest of the interview/recruitment procedure.
- Do not be afraid to ask for the job!
- Jot down the essential points of the interview afterwards—you will only remember subsequently a tiny part of what was said.
- Go for it!

Types of Marketing Careers

A separate volume of *Marketing: Concepts and Strategies* would be needed to describe fully the multitude of marketing career options. Table C.1 presents the typical hierarchy within marketing, which commences with the junior marketing assistant, progresses to the marketing director (who may or may not have a seat on the board) and finally reaches the senior directors of the business. The choice initially relates more to the sphere of activity. An opportunity may arise in a marketing services operation such as a management consultancy, direct mail house or marketing research agency; or with a manufacturer, wholesaler, retailer or dealer; in the public sector, service sector or not-for-profit sector; or with a consumer, services or business-to-business marketer. The following list indicates some of the wide selection of options:

- Marketing research—agency or in-house
- Selling—retail, wholesale, dealer or for a manufacturer
- Promotion—advertising, public relations, sales promotion, sponsorship, direct mail: creative, planning or strategy

	Predominant Sex	Age	Education	Work Experience	Perks
Marketing Assistant (£13,000)	F	25.7	degree	less than 2 years	none
Marketing Executive (£16,000)	F	28	degree	3–5 years	contributory pension
Product Brand Manager (£19,000)	F/M	28.6	degree	3–5 years	company car, medical insurance, contributory pension scheme
Group Product Manager (£26,000)	M	32.8	degree	6–10 years	company car, car running costs, medical insurance, contributory pension
Marketing Manager (£29,000)	M	35	degree	6–15 years	company car, car running costs, medical insurance, contributory pension
Marketing Director (£45,000)	M	30	degree	11 + years	company car, car running costs, medical insurance, contributory pension
Proprietor (£36,300)	M	44.7	degree	21 + years	company car, car running costs
Managing Director/ Deputy Managing Director (£65,000)	M	43	degree	21 + years	company car, car running costs, car telephone, medical insurance, contributory pension
Chairman/Chief Executive (£95,000)	M	43.5	degree	21 + years	company car, car running costs, medical insurance, contributory pension

SOURCE: "The *Marketing* Salary Survey", *Marketing*, 17 January 1991, pp. 19–22, revised in 1996.

Table C.1 A career in marketing

- Telemarketing, telesales, direct marketing
- Business-to-business buying
- Distribution management
- Product management/brand management
- Retail management

Each of these facets of marketing has been explored in *Marketing: Concepts and Strategies*. Careers consultants will be able to explain the opportunities currently available in more detail. The classified sections of the weekly trade magazines, such as *Marketing* or *Marketing Week,* provide a good indication of where there are openings and on what terms.

Good luck in your search for a career in marketing! We hope that *Marketing: Concepts and Strategies* has increased your understanding of and interest in the world of marketing.

NOTES

Chapter 1

1. Jim Lynch in *Effective Industrial Marketing*, Norman Hart, ed. (London: Kogan Page, 1994).
2. Sally Dibb, Lyndon Simkin and John Bradley, *The Marketing Planning Workbook* (London: Routledge/International Thomson Business Publishing, 1996).
3. Philip Kotler, *Marketing Management: Analysis, Planning, Implementation, and Control,* 6th edn. (Englewood Cliffs, N.J.: Prentice-Hall, 1988), p. 6.
4. O.C. Ferrell and George Lucas, "An evaluation of progress in the development of a definition of marketing", *Journal of the Academy of Marketing Science,* Fall 1987.
5. Gene R. Laczniak and Robert F. Lusch, "Environment and strategy in 1995: a survey of high-level executives", *Journal of Consumer Marketing,* Spring 1986, p. 28.
6. Sally Dibb and Lyndon Simkin, *The Marketing Segmentation Workbook* (London: Routledge/International Thomson Business Publishing, 1996).

Chapter 2

1. Philip Kotler, "Megamarketing", *Harvard Business Review,* March–April 1986, pp. 117–124.
2. *Britain 1990: An Official Handbook* (London: Central Office of Information, 1990).
3. Joseph Plummer, "The concept of application of life style segmentation", *Journal of Marketing,* January 1974, p. 34.
4. *The IBA Code of Advertising Standards and Practice* (London: Independent Broadcasting Authority, December 1977), p. 3. (The IBA is now the ITC.)
5. Brian Bremner, "A new sales pitch: the environment", *Business Week,* 24 July 1989, p. 50.
6. Robin Knight, with Eleni Dimmler, "The greening of Europe's industries", *U.S. News & World Report,* 5 June 1989, pp. 45–46.
7. Reprinted by permission from Herbert Simon, "Technology and environment", *Management Science,* 19(10), June 1973. Copyright 1973, The Institute of Management Sciences.
8. Wroe Alderson, *Dynamic Marketing Behavior* (Homewood, Ill.: Irwin, 1965), pp. 195–197.

Chapter 3

1. Vern Terpstra, *International Marketing,* 4th edn (Hinsdale, Ill.: Dryden Press, 1987), p. 4.
2. Theodore Levitt, "The globalisation of markets", *Harvard Business Review,* May–June 1983, p. 92.
3. Ibid.
4. Subhash C. Jain, "Standardisation of international marketing strategy: some research hypotheses", *Journal of Marketing,* January 1989, pp. 70–79.
5. "Global brands need local ad flavor", *Advertising Age,* 3 September 1984, p. 26.

6. Vern Terpstra, "Critical mass and international marketing strategy", *Journal of the Academy of Marketing Science,* Summer 1983, pp. 269–282.
7. C. Min Han, "Country image: halo or summary construct?", *Journal of Marketing Research,* May 1989, pp. 222–229.
8. Nigel G. G. Campbell, John L. Graham, Alain Jolibert and Hans Gunther Meissner, "Marketing negotiations in France, Germany, the United Kingdom, and the United States", *Journal of Marketing,* April 1988, pp. 49–62.
9. Brian Oliver, "UK soccer advertising in trouble", *Advertising Age,* 8 July 1985, p. 36.
10. Laurel Wentz, "Local laws keep international marketers hopping", *Advertising Age,* 11 July 1985, p. 20.
11. Lee Smith, "Japan wants to make friends", *Fortune,* 2 September 1985, p. 84.
12. Jean-Pierre Jeannet and Hubert D. Hennessey, *Global Marketing Strategies* (Boston: Houghton Mifflin, 1995), p. 60.
13. *Europe in Figures,* 4th edn (Brussels: Eurostat, 1995).
14. Sandra Vandermerwe and Marc-André L'Huillier, "Euroconsumers in 1992", *Business Horizons,* January–February 1989, pp. 34–40.
15. Eric G. Friberg, "1992: moves Europeans are making", *Harvard Business Review,* May–June 1989, p. 89.
16. Warren J. Keegan, *Global Marketing Management,* (Englewood Cliffs, N.J.: Prentice-Hall, 1995), pp. 285–286.
17. Carla Rapaport, "Why Japan keeps on winning", *Fortune,* 15 July 1991, p. 76.
18. Leslie Helm, with Laxmi Nakarmi, Jang Jung Soo, William J. Holstein and Edith Terry, "The Koreans are Coming", *Business Week,* 25 December 1985, pp. 46–52.
19. Dori Jones Yang, with Dirk Bennett and Bill Javerski, "The other China is starting to soar", *Business Weekly,* 6 November 1989, pp. 60–62.
20. Louis Kraar, "Asia's rising export powers", *Fortune,* Special Pacific Rim 1989 issue, pp. 43–50.
21. George Paine, "US-ASEAN dialogue in Bangkok will review economic issues", *Business America,* 21 May 1990, pp. 2–3.
22. Michael Vatiloptos, "Sense of purpose—new challenges lead member states to examine role", *Far Eastern Economic Review,* vol. 152, no. 25, 20 June 1991, pp. 24–25; "Trade rivalries calmed by pacific message", *Financial Times,* 2 August 1993, p. 13.
23. Jean-Pierre Jeannet and Hubert D. Hennessey, *Global Marketing Strategies* (Boston: Houghton Mifflin, 1995), p. 173.
24. Allan C. Reddy, "The role of marketing in the economic development of eastern European countries", *Journal of Applied Business Research,* vol. 7, no. 3, Summer 1991, pp. 106–107.
25. John A. Quelch, Erich Joachimsthaler and Jose Luis Nueno, "After the wall: marketing guidelines for eastern

Europe", *Sloan Management Review,* Winter 1991, pp. 90–91.

26. *The World Bank Atlas,* 1994, data for 1992.

27. "Rising in Russia", *Fortune,* 24 January 1996, pp. 93, 95.

28. Jean-Pierre Jeannet and Hubert D. Hennessey, *Global Marketing Strategies* (Boston: Houghton Mifflin, 1995), p. 170.

29. Peter Gumbel, "Soviet reformers urge bold push to liberalise faltering economy", *Wall Street Journal,* 27 October 1989, p. A9.

30. Paul Meller, "Back to the USSR", *Marketing,* 9 August 1990, pp. 22–23.

31. John Templeman, Thane Peterson, Gail E. Schares and Jonathan Kapstein, "The shape of Europe to come", *Business Week,* 27 November 1989, pp. 60–64.

32. John A. Quelch, "How to build a product licensing program", *Harvard Business Review,* May–June 1985, pp. 186–187.

33. Frank Bradley, *International Marketing Strategy* (London: Prentice Hall, 1995), p. 393.

34. J. Adams and M. Mendelsohn, "Recent developments in franchising", *Journal of Business Law,* 1986, pp. 206–219.

35. P. Stern and J. Stanworth, "The development of franchising in Britain", *National Westminster Quarterly Review,* May 1988, pp. 38–48; D. Ayling, "Franchising has its dark side", *Accountancy,* 99, 1987, pp. 113–117.

36. Andrew Kupfer, "How to be a global manager", *Fortune,* 14 March 1988, pp. 52–58.

37. Kathryn Rudie Harrigan, "Joint ventures and competitive advantage", *Strategic Management Journal,* May 1988, pp. 141–158.

38. A. Dunlap Smith, "Europe's truckmakers face survival of the biggest", *Business Week,* 6 November 1989, p. 68.

39. J. Killing, "How to make a global joint venture work", *Harvard Business Review,* vol. 60, 1982, pp. 120–127.

40. Kathryn R. Harrigan, "Joint ventures and competitive strategy", *Strategic Management Journal,* vol. 9, no. 2, 1988, pp. 141–158.

41. S. C. Jain, "Some perspectives on international strategic alliances", in *Advances in International Marketing* (New York: JAI Press, 1987), pp. 103–120.

42. "More companies prefer liaisons to marriage", *Wall Street Journal,* 12 April 1988, p. 35.

43. Thomas Gross and John Neuman, "Strategic alliances vital in global marketing", *Marketing News,* June 1989, pp. 1–2.

44. Margaret H. Cunningham, "Marketing's new frontier: international strategic alliances", working paper, Queens University (Ontario), 1990.

45. Stephen Young, James Hamill, Colin Wheeler and J. Richard Davies, *International Market Entry and Development. Strategies and Management* (Englewood Cliffs, N.J.: Prentice-Hall, 1989).

Chapter 4

1. James F. Engel, Roger D. Blackwell and Paul W. Miniard, *Consumer Behavior,* 7th edn (Hinsdale, Ill.: Dryden Press, 1993), p. 4.

2. John A. Howard and Jagdish N. Sheth, *The Theory of Buyer Behavior* (New York: Wiley, 1969), pp. 27–28.

3. G. Foxall, "Consumer decision-making", in *The Marketing Book,* 3rd edn M. Baker, ed. (London: Heinemann/ Chartered Institute of Marketing, 1995).

4. Paul M. Herr, Frank R. Kardes and John Kim, "Effects of word-of-mouth and product-attribute information on persuasion: an accessibility-diagnosticity perspective", *Journal of Consumer Research,* March 1991, pp. 454–462.

5. Kevin L. Keller and Richard Staelin, "Effects of quality and quantity of information on decision effectiveness", *Journal of Consumer Research,* September 1987, pp. 200–213.

6. Gabriel Biehal and Dipankar Chakravarti, "Consumers' use of memory and external information in choice: macro and micro perspectives", *Journal of Consumer Research,* March 1986, pp. 382–405.

7. Bobby J. Calder and Brian Sternthal, "Television commercial wearout: an information processing view", *Journal of Marketing Research,* May 1980, pp. 173–186.

8. Michael J. Houston, Terry L. Childers and Susan E. Heckler, "Picture-word consistency and the elaborative processing of advertisements", *Journal of Marketing Research,* November 1987, pp. 359–369.

9. James R. Bettman and Mita Sujan, "Effects of framing on evaluation of comparable and noncomparable alternatives by expert and novice consumers", *Journal of Consumer Research,* September 1987, pp. 141–154.

10. Robert A. Westbrook, "Product/consumption-based affective responses and postpurchase processes", *Journal of Marketing Research,* August 1987, pp. 258–270.

11. Patricia Sellers, "The ABC's of marketing to kids", *Fortune,* 8 May 1989, p. 115.

12. Judith Waldrop, "Inside America's households", *American Demographics,* March 1989, pp. 20–27.

13. Houston, Childers and Heckler, pp. 359–369.

14. Thomas S. Robertson and Hubert Gatignon, "Competitive effects on technology diffusion", *Journal of Marketing,* July 1986, pp. 1–12.

15. Robertson and Gatignon, pp. 1–12.

16. Al Ries and Jack Trout, *Positioning the Battle for Your Mind* (New York: McGraw-Hill Book Co., 1986).

17. James R. Bettman, *An Information Processing Theory of Consumer Choice* (Reading, Mass.: Addison-Wesley, 1979), pp. 18–24.

18. David Aaker and Douglas Stayman, "Implementing the concept of transformational advertising", *Psychology and Marketing,* May and June 1992, pp. 237–253.

19. Joseph W. Alba and J. Wesley Hutchinson, "Dimensions of consumer expertise", *Journal of Consumer Research,* March 1987, pp. 411–454.

20. Akshay R. Rao and Kent B. Monroe, "The moderating effect of prior knowledge on cue utilization in product evaluations", *Journal of Consumer Research,* September 1988, pp. 253–264.

21. Ibid.

22. John L. Lastovika and Erich A. Joachimsthaler, "Improving the detection of personality-behavior relationships in consumer research", *Journal of Consumer Research,* March 1988, pp. 583–587.

23. Martha T. Moore, "Spring break: brand names chase sales", *USA Today,* 17 March 1989, p. B1.

24. Henry Assael, *Consumer Behavior and Marketing Action,* 4th edn (Boston: Kent Publishing, 1992), p. 369.

25. Leonard L. Berry, "The time-sharing consumer", *Journal of Retailing,* Winter 1979, p. 69.
26. Mona Doyle, "The metamorphosis of the consumer", *Marketing Communications,* April 1989, pp. 18–22.

Chapter 5

1. Gregory D. Utah and Monroe M. Bird, "Changes in industrial buying: implications for industrial marketers", *Industrial Marketing Management,* 9, May 1980, pp. 117–121. Reed Moyer, "Reciprocity: retrospect and prospect", *Journal of Marketing,* October 1970, pp. 47–54.
2. P. Green, P. Robinson and Y. Wind, "The determinant of vendor selection. The evaluation function approach", *Journal of Purchasing,* August 1968.
3. John I. Coppett, "Auditing your customer service activities", *Industrial Marketing Management,* November 1988, pp. 277–284.
4. Thomas L. Powers, "Identify and fulfill customer service expectations", *Industrial Marketing Management,* November 1988, pp. 273–276.
5. Mary Jo Bitner, Bernard H. Booms and Mary Stanfield Tetreault, "The service encounter: diagnosing favorable and unfavorable incidents", *Journal of Marketing,* 54, January 1990, pp. 71–84.
6. Jim Shaw, Joe Giglierano and Jeff Kallis, "Marketing complex technical products: the importance of intangible attributes", *Industrial Marketing Management,* 18, 1989, pp. 45–53.
7. Frederick E. Webster, Jr. and Yoram Wind, *Organizational Buying Behavior* (Englewood Cliffs, N.J.: Prentice-Hall, 1972), pp. 78–80.
8. E. Gummesson, "The new marketing: developing long-term interactive relationships", *Long Range Planning,* vol. 20, issue 3, 1987, pp. 10–20.
9. H. Hakansson, *International Marketing and Purchasing of Industrial Goods* (Chichester: Wiley, 1982).
10. M. Christopher, A. Payne and D. Ballantyne, *Relationship Marketing* (Oxford: Butterworth-Heinemann, 1991).
11. Tony Cram, *The Power of Relationship Marketing,* (London: Pitman Publishing, 1994).
12. Regis McKenna, *Relationship Marketing* (Reading, Mass.: Addison-Wesley, 1991).
13. Nigel C. G. Campbell, John L. Graham, Alan Jolibert and Hans Gunthe Meissner, "Marketing negotiations in France, Germany, the United Kingdom and the United States", *Journal of Marketing,* 52, April 1988, pp. 49–62.
14. J. Carlos Jarrillo and Howard H. Stevenson, "Co-operative strategies: the payoffs and the pitfalls", *Long Range Planning,* February 1991, pp. 64–70.
15. Robert W. Haas, *Industrial Marketing Management* (New York: Petrocelli Charter, 1976), pp. 37–48.
16. *Standard Industrial Classification Revision* (London: Central Statistical Office, 1979).
17. Peter Doyle and John Saunders, "Market segmentation and positioning in specialized industrial markets", *Journal of Marketing,* Spring 1985, p. 25.

Chapter 6

1. David Birks, chapter 10 in *The Marketing Book,* M. Baker, ed. (Oxford Butterworth-Heinemann, 1994).
2. "Research" is accredited by The Market Research Society (Great Britain). Reprinted by permission.
3. Sally Dibb and Lyndon Simkin, *The Marketing Casebook* (London: Routledge, 1994).
4. Andrea Dunham, "Information systems are the key to managing future business needs", *Marketing News,* 23 May 1986, p. 11.
5. R. Birn, *The Effective Use of Market Research* (London: Kogan Page, 1990).
6. P. M. Chisnall, *Marketing Research* (London: McGraw-Hill, 1992).
7. Johny K. Johansson and Ikujiro Nonaha, "Market research the Japanese way", *Harvard Business Review,* May–June 1987, pp. 16–22.
8. Raymond E. Taylor, "Using the Delphi method to define marketing problems", *Business,* October–December 1984, p. 17.
9. Donald Tull and Del Hawkins, *Marketing Research* (New York: Macmillan, 1990).
10. Ronald L. Vaughn, "Demographic data banks: a new management resource", *Business Horizons,* November–December 1984, pp. 38–42. See also chapter 5.
11. Gary Levin, "IRI says data can now link ads to sales", *Advertising Age,* 26 January 1987, pp. 3, 74.
12. Based on a survey conducted by Market Facts, Inc., 28 April 1983.
13. Peter Jackson, Adsearch, Richmond.
14. Martha Farnsworth Riche, "Who says yes?", *American Demographics,* February 1987, p. 8; George Gallup, Jr, "Survey research: current problems and future opportunities", *Journal of Consumer Marketing,* Winter 1988, pp. 27–29.
15. Jeffrey S. Conant, Denise T. Smart and Bruce J. Walker, "Main survey facilitation techniques: an assessment and proposal regarding reporting practices" (working paper, Texas A&M University, 1990).
16. Riche, p. 8.
17. Diane K. Bowers, "Telephone legislation", *Marketing Research,* March 1989, p. 47.
18. Stephen M. Billing, "Go slow, be wary when considering switch to computer assisted interviewing system", *Marketing News,* 26 November 1982, secl. 2. p. 2.
19. Tull and Hawkins.
20. Alan J. Bush and A. Parasuraman, "Mall intercept versus telephone interviewing environment", *Journal of Advertising Research,* April–May 1985, p. 42.
21. Alan J. Bush and Joseph F. Hair, Jr, "An assessment of the mall intercept as a data collecting method", *Journal of Marketing Research,* May 1985, p. 162.
22. Jeff Wiss, "Meet MAX: computerized survey taker", *Marketing News,* 22 May 1989, p. 16.
23. Yorkshire Television's *The Marketing Mix* series.
24. Hal Sokolow, "In-depth interviews increasing in importance", *Marketing News,* 13 September 1985, p. 26.
25. Norman Hart and John Stapleton, *Glossary of Marketing Terms* (Oxford: Butterworth-Heinemann), 1981.

26. Pauline Bickerton, Matthew Bickerton and Upkar Pardes, *Cybermarketing* (Oxford: Butterworth-Heinemann, 1996).
27. Tull and Hawkins.
28. Michael J. Olivette, "Marketing research in the electric utility industry", *Marketing News*, 2 January 1987, p. 13.
29. Hanjoon Lee, Frank Acits and Ralph L. Day, "Evaluation and use of marketing research by decision makers: a behavioral simulation", *Journal of Marketing Research*, May 1987, p. 187.
30. Lynn Colemar, "It's selling disguised as research", *Marketing News*, 4 January 1988, p. 1.
31. O. C. Ferrell and Steven J. Skinner, "Ethical behavior and bureaucratic structure in marketing research organizations", *Journal of Marketing Research*, February 1988, pp. 103–104.
32. Brandt Allen, "Make information services pay its way", *Harvard Business Review*, January–February 1987, p. 57.

Chapter 7

1. R. Frank and Y. Wind, *Market Segmentation* (Englewood Cliffs, N.J.: Prentice-Hall, 1972).
2. Yoram Wind, "Issues and advances in segmentation research", *Journal of Marketing Research*, August 1978, pp. 317–327.
3. Donald K. Clifford, Jr and Richard E. Cavanagh, *The Winning Performance: How America's High-Growth Companies Succeed* (New York: Bantam Books, 1985), p. 53.
4. Joseph G. Albonetti and Luis V. Dominguez, "Major influences on consumer goods marketers' decision to target US Hispanics", *Journal of Advertising Research*, February–March 1989, pp. 9–11.
5. John L. Lastovicka and Erich A. Joachimsthaler, "Improving the detection of personality-behavior relationships in consumer research", *Journal of Consumer Research*, March 1988, pp. 583–587.
6. Joseph T. Plummer, "The concept and application of life style segmentation", *Journal of Marketing*, January 1974, p. 33.
7. James F. Engel, Roger D. Blackwell and Paul W. Miniard, *Consumer Behavior* (Orlando, Fla.: Dryden Press, 1990), pp. 348–349.
8. Russell I. Haley, "Benefit segmentation: a decision-oriented research tool", *Journal of Marketing*, July 1968, pp. 30–35.
9. Yoram Wind and Richard Cardoza, "Industrial market segmentation", *Industrial Marketing Management*, vol. 3, 1974, pp. 153–166.
10. T. P. Beane and D. M. Ennis, "Market segmentation: a review", *European Journal of Marketing*, vol. 21 (5), 1987, pp. 20–42.
11. Thomas Bonomo and B. P. Shapiro, *Segmenting the Industrial Market* (Lexington, Mass.: Lexington Books, 1983).
12. Donald F. Blumberg, "Developing service as a line of business", *Management Review*, vol. 76, February 1987, p. 61.
13. Y. Wind, "Going to market: new twist for some old tricks", *Wharton Magazine*, 4, 1980.
14. T. Harrison, *A Handbook of Advertising Techniques* (London: Kogan Page, 1987), p. 7.

15. A. Ries and J. Trout, *Positioning: The Battle for Your Mind* (New York: McGraw-Hill, 1981); Jack Trout with Steve Rivkin, *The New Positioning: The Latest on the World's #1 Business Strategy* (New York: McGraw Hill, 1996).
16. Peter Doyle, John Saunders and Veronica Wong, "A comparative study of Japanese marketing strategies in the British market", *Journal of International Business Studies*, 17 (1), 1986.
17. Graham Hooley and John Saunders, *Competitive Positioning* (London: Prentice-Hall, 1993).
18. Sally Dibb, Lyndon Simkin and John Bradley, *The Marketing Planning Workbook* (London: ITPB/Routledge, 1996).
19. Sally Dibb and Lyndon Simkin, *The Market Segmentation Workbook* (London: ITPB/Routledge, 1996).
20. Philip Kotler, *Marketing Management: Analysis, Planning, and Control*, 6th ed. (Englewood Cliffs, N.J., Prentice-Hall, 1988), p. 257.

Chapter 8

1. Part of this definition is adapted from James D. Scott, Martin R. Warshaw and James R. Taylor, *Introduction to Marketing Management*, 5th edn (Homewood, Ill.: Irwin, 1985), p. 215.
2. Theodore Levitt, "Marketing intangible products and product intangibles", *Harvard Business Review*, May–June 1981, pp. 94–102.
3. Robert W. Haas, *Industrial Marketing Management*, 3rd edn (Boston: Kent Publishing, 1986), pp. 15–25.
4. M. J. Thomas, "Product development management", in *The Marketing Book*, M. Baker, ed. (London: Heinemann/The Chartered Institute of Marketing, 1987).
5. "New product failure: a self-fulfilling prophecy?" *Marketing Communications*, April 1989, p. 27.
6. Levitt, "Marketing intangible products and product intangibles", p. 96.
7. Christopher W. L. Hart, "The power of unconditional service guarantees", *Harvard Business Review*, July–August 1988, pp. 54–62.
8. Peter Doyle, *Marketing Management and Strategy* (London: Prentice-Hall, 1994).

Chapter 9

1. Peter D. Bennett, ed., *Dictionary of Marketing Terms* (Chicago: American Marketing Association, 1988), p. 18.
2. James U. McNeal and Linda Zeren, "Brand name selection for consumer products", *MSU Business Topics*, Spring 1981, p. 35.
3. Peter Doyle, "Building successful brands: the strategic options", *The Journal of Consumer Marketing*, vol. 7, no. 2, 1993, pp. 5–20.
4. Henry Assael, *Consumer Behaviour and Marketing Action*, 4th edn (Boston: PWS-Kent, 1992).
5. Ronald Alsop, "Brand loyalty is rarely blind loyalty; rise in coupons, choices blamed for '80s erosion", *Wall Street Journal*, 19 October 1989, pp. B1, B6.
6. Chip Walker, "What's in a name?" *American Demographics*, February 1991, pp. 54–57.
7. Alan Miller, "Gains share in dollars and units during 1990

third quarter", *Private Label,* January–February 1991, pp. 85–89.

8. Judann Dagnoli, "New study blasts private labels," *Advertising Age,* 19 June 1989, p. 34.

9. "No brand like an old brand", *Forbes,* 11 June 1990, p. 180.

10. Leonard L. Berry, Edwin E. Lefkowith and Terry Clark, "In services, what's in a name?" *Harvard Business Review,* September–October 1988, pp. 2–4.

11. Dorothy Cohen, "Trademark Strategy", *Journal of Marketing,* January 1986, p. 63.

12. "Trademark Stylesheet", U.S. Trademark Association, no. 1A.

13. Ronald F. Bush, Peter H. Bloch and Scott Dawson, "Remedies for product counterfeiting", *Business Horizons,* January–February 1989, pp. 59–65; Peter Engardio, with Todd Vogel and Dinah Lee, "Companies are knocking off the knockoff outfits", *Business Week,* 26 September 1988, pp. 86–88; and Michael Harvey, "A new way to combat product counterfeiting", *Business Horizons,* July–August 1988, pp. 19–28.

14. Peter Doyle, *Marketing Management and Strategy* (London: Prentice-Hall, 1994) and chapter 20 in M. Baker, ed., *The Marketing Book* (Oxford: Butterworth-Heinemann, 1995).

15. Fred W. Morgan, "Tampered goods: legal developments and marketing guidelines" *Journal of Marketing,* April 1988, pp. 86–96.

16. Ibid.

17. James U. McNeal, *Consumer Behaviour: An Integrative Approach* (Boston: Little, Brown, 1982), pp. 221–222.

18. "Not in my backyard", CNN Special Report, Cable News Network, 19 December 1988.

19. Alecia Swasy, "Ecology and buyer wants don't jibe", *Wall Street Journal,* 23 August 1989, p. B1.

20. Laura Bird, "Romancing the package", *Adweek's Marketing Week,* 21 January 1991, p. 11.

21. CGM, *Marketing Guide 14: 3D Packaging Design,* Haymarket Publishing Services Ltd, 1992.

Chapter 10

1. Roger C. Bennet and Robert G. Cooper, "The product life cycle trap", *Business Horizons,* September–October 1984, pp. 7–16.

2. "Product development: where planning and marketing meet," *Journal of Business Strategy,* September–October 1990, pp. 13–16.

3. Peter F. Drucker, "The discipline of innovation", *Harvard Business Review,* May–June 1985, pp. 67–68.

4. Lawrence Ingrassia, "By improving scotch paper, 3M gets new product winner", *Wall Street Journal,* 31 March 1983, p. 27.

5. Jonathan B. Levine, "Keeping new ideas kicking around", *Business Week,* Innovation 1989 issue, p. 128.

6. Joseph Weber, "Going over the lab wall in search of new ideas", *Business Week,* Innovation 1989 issue, p. 132.

7. Joshua Hyatt, "Ask and you shall receive", *Inc.,* September 1989, pp. 90–101.

8. "Winging it at McDonald's", *USA Today,* 5 September 1989, p. 1B.

9. Eleanor Johnson Tracy, "Testing time for test marketing", *Fortune,* 29 October 1984, pp. 75–76.

10. Cyndee Miller, "Little relief seen for new product failure rate," *Marketing News,* 21 June 1993, p. 5.

11. Adapted from Everett M. Rogers, *Diffusion of Innovations* (New York: Macmillan, 1962), pp. 81–86.

12. Graham J. Hooley and John Saunders, *Competitive Positioning: The Key to Market Success* (Englewood Cliffs, N.J.: Prentice-Hall, 1993).

13. F. Stewart DeBruicker and Gregory L. Summe, "Make sure your customers keep coming back", *Harvard Business Review,* January–February 1985, pp. 92–98.

14. Geoffrey L. Gordon, Roger J. Calantone and Anthony di Benedetto, "Mature markets and revitalization strategies: an American fable", *Business Horizons,* May–June 1991, p. 42.

15. Kim B. Clark and Takahiro Fujimoto, "The power of product integrity," *Harvard Business Review,* November–December 1990, pp. 108–118.

16. Lynn W. Phillips, Dae R. Chang and Robert D. Buzzell, "Product quality, cost position and business performance: a test of some key hypotheses", *Journal of Marketing,* Spring 1983, pp. 26–43.

17. Douglas M. Lambert and Jay U. Sterling, "Identifying and eliminating weak products", *Business,* July–September 1988, pp. 3–10.

Chapter 11

1. Leonard L. Berry, "Services marketing is different", *Business Horizons,* May–June 1980, pp. 24–29.

2. David Pottruck, "Building company loyalty and retention through direct marketing", *Journal of Services Marketing,* Autumn 1987, p. 56.

3. Donald Cowell, *The Marketing of Services* (London: Heinemann, 1984).

4. Valarie A. Zeithaml, A. Parasuraman and Leonard L. Berry, "Problems and strategies in services marketing", *Journal of Marketing,* Spring 1985, pp. 33–46.

5. John E. G. Bateson, "Why we need service marketing", in O. C. Ferrell, S. W. Brown and C. W. Lamb, Jr, eds, *Conceptual and Theoretical Development in Marketing* (Chicago: American Marketing Association, 1979), pp. 131–146.

6. Valarie A. Zeithaml, "How consumer evaluation processes differ between goods and services", in James H. Donnelly and William R. George, eds, *Marketing of Services* (Chicago: American Marketing Association, 1981), pp. 186–190.

7. Leonard L. Berry, Valarie A. Zeithaml and A. Parasuraman, "Responding to demand fluctuations: key challenge for service businesses", in Russell Belk et al., eds, *AMA Educators' Proceedings* (Chicago: American Marketing Association, 1984), pp. 231–234.

8. Brian Moores, *Are They Being Served?* (Oxford: Philip Allan, 1986).

9. Christopher H. Lovelock, "Classifying services to gain strategic marketing insights", *Journal of Marketing,* Summer 1983, p. 15.

10. Christopher H. Lovelock, *Services Marketing* (Englewood Cliffs, N.J.: Prentice-Hall, 1984), pp. 46–64.

11. Yoram Wind, "Financial services: increasing your marketing productivity and profitability", *Journal of Services Marketing*, Fall 1987, p. 8.
12. Lovelock, *Services Marketing*, pp. 279–289.
13. Ibid.
14. Berry, Zeithaml and Parasuraman, pp. 231–234.
15. James L. Heskett, "Lessons in the Service Sector", *Harvard Business Review*, March/April 1987, pp. 118–126.
16. Leonard L. Berry, "Big ideas in services marketing", *Journal of Services Marketing*, Fall 1987, pp. 5–9.
17. J. Whyte, "Organisation, person and idea marketing as exchange", *Quarterly Review of Marketing*, January 1985, pp. 25–30.
18. John Garrison, "Telethons—the positive story", *Fund Raising Management*, November 1987, pp. 48–52.
19. Philip Kotler, *Marketing for Non-profit Organisations*, 2nd. edn (Englewood Cliffs, N.J.: Prentice-Hall, 1982), p. 37.
20. Ibid.
21. Meryl Davids, "Doing well by doing good", *Public Relations Journal*, July 1987, pp. 17–21.
22. Leyland F. Pitt and Russell Abratt, "Pricing in non-profit organisations—a framework and conceptual overview", *Quarterly Review of Marketing*, Spring–Summer 1987, pp. 13–15.
23. Kelly Walker, "Not-for-profit profits", *Forbes*, 10 September 1984, p. 165.

Chapter 12

1. Wroe Alderson, *Marketing Behavior and Executive Action* (Homewood, Ill.: Irwin, 1957), pp. 201–211.
2. James D. Hlavacek and Tommy J. McCuistion, "Industrial distributors: when, who, and how?" *Harvard Business Review*, March–April 1983, p. 97.
3. Jordan D. Lewis, "Using alliances to build market power", *Planning Review*, September–October 1990, pp. 4–9, 48.
4. Leo Aspinwall, "The marketing characteristics of goods", in *Four Marketing Theories* (Boulder: University of Colorado Press, 1961), pp. 27–32.
5. Allan J. Magrath, "Differentiating yourself via distribution", *Sales & Marketing Management*, March 1991, pp. 50–57.
6. David W. Cravens, Thomas N. Ingram and Raymond W. LaForge, "Evaluating multiple sales channel strategies", *Journal of Business and Industrial Marketing*, Summer–Fall 1991, pp. 3–4.
7. Bert Rosenbloom, *Marketing Channels: A Management View* (Hinsdale, Ill.: Dryden, 1987), p. 160.
8. Ibid., p. 161.
9. Donald J. Bowersox and M. Bixby Cooper, *Strategic Marketing Channel Management* (New York: McGraw-Hill, 1992), pp. 177–178.
10. Wroe Alderson, *Dynamic Marketing Behavior* (Homewood, Ill.: Irwin, 1965), p. 239.
11. Steven J. Skinner, Julie B. Gassenheimer and Scott W. Kelley, "Cooperation in supplier-dealer relations", *Journal of Retailing*, Summer 1992, pp. 174–193; H. Hakansson, *International Marketing and Purchasing of Industrial Goods* (Wiley: Chicester, 1982).

12. Jakki Mohr and John R. Nevin, "Communication strategies in marketing channels: a theoretical perspective", *Journal of Marketing*, October 1990, pp. 36–51.
13. Lanny J. Ryan, Gaye C. Dawson and Thomas Galek, "New distribution channels for microcomputer software", *Business*, October–December 1985, pp. 21–22.
14. Adel I. El-Ansary, "Perspectives on channel system performance", in *Contemporary Issues in Marketing Channels*, ed. Robert F. Lusch and Paul H. Zinszer (Norman: University of Oklahoma Press, 1979), p. 50.
15. Kenneth G. Hardy and Allan J. Magrath, "Ten ways for manufacturers to improve distribution management", *Business Horizons*, November–December 1988, p. 68.
16. Ronald D. Michman and Stanley D. Sibley, *Marketing Channels and Strategies* (Columbus, Ohio: Grid Publishing, 1980), pp. 412–417.
17. Janet E. Keith, Donald W. Jackson and Lawrence A. Crosby, "Effect of alternative types of influence strategies under different dependence structures," *Journal of Marketing*, July 1990, pp. 30–41.
18. John F. Gaski and John R. Nevin, "The differential effects of exercised and unexercised power sources in a marketing channel", *Journal of Marketing Research*, July 1985, p. 139.
19. Rosenbloom, *Marketing Channels*, p. 98.
20. Ibid, pp. 96–97.

Chapter 13

1. Clarence Casson, "1988 wholesaler giants; making all the right moves", Building Supply Home Centers, September 1988, p. 56.
2. Rajesh Tyagi and Chandrasekhar Das, "Manufacturer and warehouse selection for stable relationships in dynamic wholesaling and location problems", *International Journal of Physical Distribution and Logistics Management*, 25 (6) 1995, pp. 54–72.
3. Rebecca Rolfes, "Wholesaling without borders", *Medical Marketing & Media*, February 1991, pp. 74–76.
4. Bert Rosenbloom, *Marketing Channels: A Management View* (Hinsdale, Ill.: Dryden Press, 1987), p. 63.
5. *US Census of Wholesale Trade*, May 1985, p. 207.
6. Rosenbloom, p. 34.
7. Ibid., p. 63.
8. Arthur Meidan and Anne Tomes, "Cash and carry customers' shopping habits and supplier choice criteria", *International Journal of Retail & Distribution Management*, 19 May 1991, pp. 29–36.
9. Elizabeth Jane Moore, "Grocery distribution in the UK: recent changes and future prospects", *International Journal of Retail & Distribution Management*, 19 July 1991, pp. 18–24.
10. "Drop-shipping grows to save depot costs", *Supermarket News*, 1 April 1985, pp. 1, 17.
11. *US Census of Wholesale Trade*, May 1985, p. 207.
12. Rosenbloom, p. 61.
13. Ibid.
14. Ibid., p. 62.
15. Thomas V. Bonoma, "Get more out of your trade shows", *Harvard Business Review*, January–February 1983, pp. 75–83.

16. Rosenbloom, p. 185.
17. "Trade shows—part 1; a major sales and marketing tool", *Small Business Report,* June 1988, pp. 34–39.
18. Rosenbloom, p. 185.
19. Richard K. Swandby and Jonathan M. Cox, "Trade show trends: exhibiting growth paces economic strengths", *Business Marketing,* May 1985, p. 50.
20. "Why Cargo Club was off target", *Marketing,* 23 March 1995, p. 3.
21. Joseph Weber, "Mom and Pop move out of wholesaling", *Business Week,* 9 January 1989, p. 91.
22. Ibid.

Chapter 14

1. H. Carter, *The Study of Urban Geography* (London: Edward Arnold, 1972), pp. 205–247.
2. J. A. Dawson, *Shopping Centre Development* (Harlow: Longman, 1983), Chapter 2.
3. Ibid.
4. Russell Schiller, "Out of town exodus", in *The Changing Face of British Retailing* (London: Newman Books, 1987), pp. 64–73.
5. Kenneth C. Schneider, "Telemarketing as a promotional tool—its effects and side effects", *Journal of Consumer Marketing,* Winter 1985, pp. 29–39.
6. Joel Dreyfuss, "Reach out and sell something", *Fortune,* 26 November 1984, pp. 127–128.
7. "V/T census of the industry issue—1988", *Vending Times,* 1988, p. 49. Reprinted by permission.
8. Ronald Alsop, "Food giants take to mails to push fancy product lines", *Wall Street Journal,* 28 February 1985, p. 85.
9. Keynote Publications, 1989.
10. Al Urbanski, "The franchise option", *Sales & Marketing Management,* February 1988, pp. 28–33.
11. Jim Forward and Christina Fulop, "Large established firms' entry into franchising", *Retail, Distribution and Consumer Research,* 6 (1), 1996, pp. 34–52.
12. Statistical Abstract of the US, 1989, p. 760.
13. C. H. Anderson, *Retailing* (St. Paul, Minn.: West, 1993).
14. R. L. Davies and D. S. Rogers, *Store Location and Store Assessment Research* (Chichester: Wiley, 1984).
15. R. L. Davies, *Marketing Geography* (London: Methuen, 1976).
16. L. Simkin, "SLAM: store location assessment model—theory and practice", *OMEGA,* 17 (1), 1989, pp. 53–58; Lyndon Simkin, "Tackling barriers to effective implementation of modelling in retail marketing applications", *Retail, Distribution and Consumer Research,* 6 (3), 1996, pp. 225–241.
17. Ruth Schmidt, Rupert Segal and Christy Cartwright, "Two-stop shopping or polarisation", *International Journal of Retail and Distribution Management,* 22 (1), 1994, pp. 12–19.
18. C. Glenn Walters and Blaise J. Bergiel, *Marketing Channels,* 2nd edn (Glenview, Ill.: Scott, Foresman, 1982), p. 205.
19. J. R. Maier and L. Simkin, "Prioritising stock phasing for multiple retailers", *OMEGA,* 18 (1), 1988, pp. 33–40.
20. D. Cook and R. D. Walters, *Retail Marketing* (London: Prentice-Hall, 1991).

21. George H. Lucas, Jr., and Larry G. Gresham, "How to position for retail success", *Business,* April–June 1988, pp. 3–13.
22. G. J. Davies and J. M. Brooks, *Positioning Strategy in Retailing* (London: Paul Chapman, 1989).
23. Leslie Wayne, "Rewriting the rules of retailing", *The New York Times,* 15 October 1989, p. F6.
24. Terence Conran, "The retail image", in *The Retail Report* (London: Healey & Baker, 1985).
25. Francine Schwadel, "Little touches spur Wal-Mart's rise; shoppers react to logo, decor, employee vests", *Wall Street Journal,* 22 September 1989, p. B1.
26. Peter McGoldrick, *Retail Marketing* (London: McGraw-Hill, 1990).
27. Stanley C. Hollander, "The wheel of retailing", *Journal of Marketing,* July 1960, p. 37.
28. W. S. Howe, "UK retailer vertical power, market competition and consumer welfare", *International Journal of Retail and Distribution Management,* 18 (2), 1990, pp. 16–25.
29. Lynne Richardson, John Swan and James Hulton, "The effects of the presence and use of channel power sources on distributor satisfaction", *Retail, Distribution and Consumer Research,* 5 (2), 1995, pp. 185–202.
30. K. K. Tse, "Marks & Spencer: a manufacturer without factories", *International Trends in Retailing,* 6 (2), 1989, pp. 23–36.
31. R. M. Grant, "Manufacturer-retailer relations: the shifting balance of power", in Gerry Johnson, *Business Strategy and Retailing* (Chichester: Wiley, 1987), pp. 43–58.
32. Gerry Johnson, *Business Strategy and Retailing* (Chichester: Wiley, 1987).
33. Lynd Morley, "Mapping the future", *Retail Technology,* 2(7), 1988, pp. 40–2.
34. Tony Rudd, "Trends in physical distribution", in *The Changing Face of British Retailing* (London: Newman Books, 1987), pp. 84–93.
35. C. Doherty, J. R. Maier and L. Simkin, "DPP decision support in retail merchandising", *OMEGA* 21 (1), 1993, pp. 25–33.
36. Nicholas Alexander, "Expansion within the single European market: a motivational structure", *Retail, Distribution and Consumer Research,* 5 (4), 1999, pp. 488–504.
37. Terry Robinson and Colin M. Clarke-Hill, "International alliances in European retailing", *Retail, Distribution and Consumer Research,* 5 (2), 1995, pp. 167–184.

Chapter 15

1. Carl M. Guelzo, *Introduction to Logistics Management* (Englewood Cliffs, N.J.: Prentice-Hall, 1986), p. 32.
2. John T. Mentzer, Roger Gomes and Robert E. Krapfel, Jr., "Physical distribution service: a fundamental marketing concept?", *Journal of the Academy of Marketing Science,* Winter 1989, p. 59.
3. Lloyd M. Rinehart, M. Bixby Cooper and George D. Wagenheim, "Furthering the integration of marketing and logistics through customer service in the channel", *Journal of the Academy of Marketing Science,* Winter 1989, p. 67.
4. Charles A. Taff, *Management of Physical Distribution and Transportation* (Homewood, Ill.: Irwin, 1984), p. 250.

5. Judith Graham, "IKEA furnishing its US identity", *Advertising Age,* 14 September 1989, p. 79; and Jonathan Reynolds, "IKEA: a competitive company with style", *Retail & Distribution Management (UK),* May/June 1988, pp. 32–34.
6. Rinehart, Cooper and Wagenheim, p. 67.
7. Guelzo, pp. 35–36.
8. Taff, p. 240.
9. Carol Doherty, Jens Maier and Lyndon Simkin, "DPP modelling in retail marketing: an application", *OMEGA,* 20 (3), 1992, pp. 25–33.
10. Guelzo, p. 102.
11. Adapted from John F. Magee, *Physical Distribution Systems* (New York: McGraw-Hill, Inc., 1967). Reprinted by permission of the author.
12. James C. Johnson and Donald F. Wood, *Contemporary Physical Distribution & Logistics,* 2nd edn (Tulsa, Okla.: Penn Well Publishing Company, 1982), p. 356.
13. Guelzo, p. 102.
14. The EOQ formula for the optimal order quantity is EOQ = 2DR/I, where EOQ = optimum average order size, D = total demand, R = cost of processing an order and I = cost of maintaining one unit of inventory per year. For a more complete description of EOQ methods and terminology, see Frank S. McLaughlin and Robert C. Pickardt, *Quantitative Techniques for Management Decisions* (Boston: Houghton Mifflin, 1978), pp. 104–119.
15. "Watch for these red flags", *Traffic Management,* January 1983, p. 8.
16. David N. Burt, "Managing suppliers up to speed", *Harvard Business Review,* July–August 1989, p. 128.
17. Ibid., p. 129.
18. Peter D. Bennett, ed., *Dictionary of Marketing Terms* (Chicago: American Marketing Association, 1988), p. 204.
19. Guelzo, pp. 50–52.
20. John Gattorna, *Handbook of Physical Distribution Management* (Aldershot: Gower Publishing Co. Ltd, 1983), pp. 263–266.
21. Donald F. Wood and James C. Johnson, *Contemporary Transportation* (Tulsa, Okla.: Petroleum Publishing, 1980), p. 289.
22. Taff, p. 126.
23. Guelzo, p. 53.
24. John J. Coyle, Edward Bardi and C. John Langley, Jr., *The Management of Business Logistics* (St. Paul, Minn.: West, 1988), pp. 327–329.
25. Thomas A. Foster and Joseph V. Barks, "Here comes the best", *Distribution,* September 1984, p. 25.
26. Allen R. Wastler, "Intermodal leaders ponder riddle of winning more freight", *Traffic World,* 19 June 1989, pp. 14–15.

Chapter 16

1. Richard W. Pollay, "On the value of reflections on the values in 'The distorted mirror'", *Journal of Marketing,* July 1987, pp. 104–109.
2. Morris B. Holbrook, "Mirror, mirror, on the wall, what's unfair in the reflections on advertising", *Journal of Marketing,* July 1987, pp. 95–103.

3. Richard N. Farmer, "Would you want your granddaughter to marry a Taiwanese marketing man?" *Journal of Marketing,* October 1987, pp. 111–116.
4. Colin Coulson-Thomas, *Marketing Communications* (London: Heinemann, 1986).
5. P. "Rajan" Varadarajan and Anil Menon, "Cause-related marketing: a coalignment of marketing strategy and corporate philanthropy", *Journal of Marketing,* July 1988, pp. 58–74.
6. James Engel, Martin Warshaw and Thomas Kinnear, *Promotional Strategy: Managing the Marketing Communications Process* (Boston: Irwin, 1994).
7. John Rossiter and Larry Percy, *Advertising and Promotion Management* (New York: McGraw-Hill, 1987).
8. In case you do not read Chinese, this says, "In the factory we make cosmetics, and in the store we sell hope". Prepared by Chih Kang Wang.
9. Terence A. Shimp and M. Wayne Delozier, *Promotion Management and Marketing Communication* (Hinsdale, Ill.: Dryden Press, 1986), pp. 25–26.
10. Carlos E. Garcia, "Hispanic market is accessible if research is designed correctly", *Marketing News,* 4 January 1988, p. 46.
11. David Jones, "Setting promotional goals: a communications' relationship model", *Journal of Consumer Marketing,* 11 (1), 1994, pp. 38–49.
12. Adapted from Everett M. Rogers, *Diffusion of Innovations* (New York: Free Press, 1962), pp. 81–86, 98–102.
13. Lawrence J. Marks and Michael A. Kamins, "Product sampling and advertising sequence, belief strength, confidence and attitudes", *Journal of Marketing Research,* August 1988, pp. 266–281.
14. Rogers, pp. 247–250.
15. Rossiter and Percy.
16. M. Flandin, E. Martin and L. Simkin, "Advertising effectiveness research: a survey of agencies, clients and conflicts", *International Journal of Advertising,* 11 March 1992, pp. 203–214.
17. Todd Hunt and James Grunig, *Public Relations Techniques* (Fort Worth: Harcourt Brace, 1994).
18. Sally Dibb, Lyndon Simkin and Adam Vancini, "Competition, strategy, technology and people: the challenges facing PR", *International Journal of Advertising,* 15 (2), 1996, pp. 116–127.
19. This definition is adapted from John F. Luick and William L. Ziegler, *Sales Promotion and Modern Merchandising* (New York: McGraw-Hill, 1968), p. 4.
20. Roger A. Kerin and William L. Cron, "Assessing trade show functions and performance: an exploratory study", *Journal of Marketing,* July 1987, pp. 87–94.
21. Marcy Magiera, "Holy Batvideo! Christmas already?" *Advertising Age,* 11 September 1989, p. 6.
22. *Marketing Week,* 5 July 1996, p. 13.
23. Alvin A. Achenbaum and F. Kent Mitchel, "Pulling away from push marketing", *Harvard Business Review,* May–June 1987, p. 38.

Chapter 17

1. S. Dibb, L. Simkin and R. Yuen, "Pan-European advertising: think Europe—act local", *International Journal of Advertising,* 13 (2), 1994, pp. 125–136.

2. *Students' Briefs* (London: The Advertising Association, 1988).

3. *CBS This Morning*, CBS (TV), 11 April 1990.

4. Scott Hume, "Pizza Hut is frosted; new ad takes slap at McDonald's test product", *Advertising Age,* 18 September 1989, p. 4.

5. Torin Douglas, *The Complete Guide to Advertising* (London: Macmillan, 1985).

6. Peter Jackson, Adsearch, Richmond-upon-Thames.

7. *Campaign,* 19 July 1996, p. 1.

8. Laurie Freeman, "P&G to unveil refill package", *Advertising Age,* 6 November 1989, pp. 1, 69.

9. Pauline Bickerton, Matthew Bickerton and Upkor Pardesi, *Cybermarketing* (Oxford: Butterworth-Heinemann, 1996).

10. James E. Littlefield and C. A. Kirkpatrick, *Advertising Mass Communication in Marketing* (Boston: Houghton Mifflin, 1970), p. 178.

11. S. Watson Dunn and Arnold M. Barban, *Advertising: Its Role in Modern Marketing,* 6th edn (Hinsdale, Ill.: Dryden Press, 1986), p. 493.

12. Patrick Quinn, *Low Budget Advertising* (London: Heinemann, 1988).

13. M. Flandin, E. Martin and L. Simkin, "Advertising effectiveness research: a survey of agencies, clients and conflicts", *International Journal of Advertising*, 11 (3), 1992, pp. 203–214.

14. Ronald Alsop, "TV ads that are likeable get plus ratings for persuasiveness", *Wall Street Journal,* 20 February 1986, p. 21.

15. Marvin E. Goldberg and Gerald J. Gorn, "Happy and sad TV programmes: how they affect reactions to commercials", *Journal of Consumer Research,* December 1987, pp. 387–403.

16. *Marketing,* 24 May 1990, p. 5.

17. *Public Relations Practice—Its Role and Parameters* (London: The Institute of Public Relations, 1984).

18. The Advertising Association, London, 1990; *The Independent,* 12 August 1990; Robin Cobb, "The art of gentle persuasion", *Marketing,* 6 September 1990, pp. 25–26; Bill Britt, "PR leads from front as buy-up battles rage", *Marketing,* 1 February 1990, p. 13; P. J. Kitchen and T. Proctor, "The increasing importance of public relations in fast moving consumer goods firms", *Journal of Marketing Management,* 7 (4), 1991, pp. 357–370.

19. David Wragg, *Public Relations for Sales and Marketing Management* (London: Kogan Page, 1987).

20. J. White, *How to Understand and Manage Public Relations* (London: Business Books, 1991).

21. Frank Jefkins, *Public Relations Techniques* (London: Heinemann, 1988).

22. S. Dibb, L. Simkin and A. Vancini, "Competition, strategy, technology and people: the challenges facing PR", *International Journal of Advertising,* 15 (2), 1996, pp. 116–127.

23. BBC and ITN news broadcasts, February and March 1993.

24. Marc G. Weinberger and Jean B. Romeo, "The impact of negative product news", *Business Horizons,* January–February 1989, p. 44.

25. Dibb, Simkin and Yuen.

26. M. Flandin, E. Martin and L. Simkin, "Advertising effectiveness research: a survey of agencies, clients and conflicts", *International Journal of Advertising*, 11 (3), 1992, pp. 203–214.

27. John Wringe, managing director of Cogent, talking to IB365 students at Warwick Business School, 1996.

28. Dibb, Simkin and Vancini.

29. S. Sleight, *Sponsorship: What It Is and How to Use It* (Maidenhead: McGraw-Hill, 1989).

30. M. G. Crowley, "Prioritising the sponsorship audience," *European Journal of Marketing,* 25, 1991, pp. 11–21.

Chapter 18

1. Marketing, 28 June 1990, p. 13.

2. Julian Cummins, *Sales Promotion* (London: Kogan Page, 1989).

3. Myron Gable and B. J. Reed, "The current status of women in professional selling", *Journal of Personal Selling & Sales Management,* May 1987, pp. 33–39.

4. William A. Weeks and Darrel D. Muehing, "Students' perceptions of personal selling", *Industrial Marketing Management,* May 1987, pp. 145–151.

5. Geoff Lancaster and David Jobber, *Selling and Sales Management* (London: Pitman, 1994).

6. "Getting ahead and staying ahead as the competition heats up", *Agency Sales Magazine,* June 1987, pp. 38–42.

7. Chris de Winter, *Telephone Selling* (London: Heinemann, 1988).

8. Thomas W. Leigh and Patrick F. McGraw, "Mapping the procedural knowledge of industrial sales personnel: a script-theoretic investigation", *Journal of Marketing,* January 1989, pp. 16–34.

9. Thayer C. Taylor, "Xerox: who says you can't be big and fast?" *Sales & Marketing Management,* November 1987, pp. 62–65.

10. Leigh and McGraw, pp. 16–34.

11. John Nemec, "Do you have grand finales?" *American Salesman,* June 1987, pp. 3–6.

12. William C. Moncrief, "Five types of industrial sales jobs", *Industrial Marketing Management,* 17, 1988, p. 164.

13. A. J. Magrath, "Are you overdoing 'lean and mean'?", *Sales & Marketing Management,* January 1988, pp. 46–53.

14. Tony Adams, *Successful Sales Management* (London: Heinemann, 1988).

15. Coleman, pp. 6, 21.

16. Patrick C. Fleenor, "Selling and sales management in action: assessment centre selection of sales representatives," *Journal of Personal Selling & Sales Management,* May 1987, pp. 57–59.

17. René Y. Darmon, "The impact of incentive compensation on the salesperson's work habits: an economic model", *Journal of Personal Selling & Sales Management,* May 1987, pp. 21–32.

18. Aimee Stern, "Commissions catch on at department stores", *Adweek's Marketing Week,* 1 February 1988, p. 5.

19. Terese Hudson, "Holding meetings sharpens employees' sales skills", *Savings Institutions,* July 1987, pp. 109–111.

20. Dan Woog, "Taking sales high tech", *High Tech Marketing,* May 1987, pp. 17–22.

21. Sandra Hile Hart, William C. Moncrief and A. Parasuraman, "An empirical investigation of salespeople's performance, effort and selling method during a sales

contest", *Journal of the Academy of Marketing Science,* Winter 1989, pp. 29–39.

22. Robert Martinott, "The traveling salesman goes high tech", *Chemical Week,* 10 June 1987, pp. 22–24.

23. John F. Luick and William L. Ziegler, *Sales Promotion and Modern Merchandising* (New York: McGraw-Hill, 1968), and Don E. Schultz and William A. Robinson, *Sales Promotion Management* (Chicago: Crain Books, 1982).

24. Thomas McCann, "Promotions will gain more clout in the '90s," *Marketing News,* 6 November 1989, pp. 4, 24.

25. Cummins, p. 14.

26. "Factfile," *Marketing,* 12 July 1990, p. 18.

27. P. R. Smith, *Marketing Communication: An Integrated Approach* (London: Kogan Page, 1993).

28. K. Peattie and S. Peattie, "Sales promotion: playing to win?" *Journal of Marketing Management,* 9, 1993, pp. 225–269.

29. W. E. Phillips and Bill Robinson, "Continued sales (price) promotion destroys brands: yes; no", *Marketing News,* 16 January 1989, pp. 4, 8.

30. Cummins, p. 14.

31. Emin Babakus, Peter Tat and William Cunningham, "Coupon redemption: a motivational perspective", *Journal of Consumer Marketing,* Spring 1988, p. 40.

32. Donna Campanella, "Sales promotion: couponmania", *Marketing and Media Decisions,* June 1987, pp. 118–122.

33. Alison Fahey, "Coupon war fallout", *Advertising Age,* 4 September 1989, p. 2.

34. Campanella, pp. 118–122.

35. Ibid.

36. Joe Agnew, "P-O-P [P-O-S] displays are becoming a matter of consumer convenience", *Marketing News,* 9 October 1987, p. 14.

37. Ibid., p. 16.

38. Alison Fahey, "Study shows retailers rely on P-O-P [P-O-S]", *Advertising Age,* 27 November 1989, p. 83.

39. "Sampling accelerates adoption of new products", *Marketing News,* 11 September 1987, p. 21.

40. Peter Tat, William A. Cunningham and Emin Babakus, "Consumer perceptions of rebates", *Journal of Advertising Research,* August–September 1988, p. 48.

41. Gerrie Anthea, "Sales promotion putting up the premium", *Marketing,* 16 April 1987.

42. Steven W. Colford, "Marriott sets largest promo", *Advertising Age,* 2 October 1989, p. 58.

43. Eileen Norris, "Everyone will grab at a chance to win", *Advertising Age,* 22 August 1983, p. M10.

44. Ed Crimmins, "A co-op myth: it is a tragedy that stores don't spend all their accruals", *Sales & Marketing Management,* 7 February 1983, pp. 72–73.

45. Gillian Upton, "Sales promotion: getting results Barbados style", *Marketing,* 16 April 1987, pp. 37–40.

46. D. Bird, *Commonsense Direct Marketing* (London: Kogan Page, 1989).

47. B. North, "Consumer companies take direct stance", *Marketing,* 20 May 1993, pp. 24–25.

Chapter 19

1. Stephen J. Hoch, Xavier Dreze and Mary Park, "EDLP—hi-lo, and margin arithmetic", *Journal of Marketing,* 58 (4), 1994, pp. 16–22; Allan Mitchell, "Two sides of the same argument", *Marketing Week,* 16 February 1996, pp. 26–27.

2. Michael J. O'Connor, "What is the logic of a price war?", Arthur Andersen & Company, *International Trends in Retailing,* Spring 1986.

3. Saeed Samier, "Pricing in marketing strategies of U.S. and foreign based companies," *Journal of Business Research,* 1987, pp. 15–23.

4. Robert P. Ford, "Pricing operating services, *Bankers Magazine,* May–June 1987.

5. George S. Day and Liam Fahey, "Valuing market strategies", *Journal of Marketing,* July 1988, pp. 45–57.

6. David Landis, "It's cutting prices to win lost ground", *USA Today,* 4 October 1989, pp. 1B, 2B.

7. JCB company literature, 1992.

8. *What Car?,* February 1996.

9. J. Winkler, "Pricing", M. Baker, ed., in *The Marketing Book* (London: Heinemann, 1987).

10. Joseph P. Guiltinan, "The price-bundling of services: a normative framework", *Journal of Marketing,* April 1987, pp. 74–85.

11. Susan M. Petroshius and Kent B. Monroe, "Effect of product-line pricing characterics on product evaluations", *Journal of Consumer Research,* March 1988, pp. 511–519.

12. Valerie A. Zeithaml, "Consumer perceptions of price, quality and value: a means-end model and synthesis of evidence", *Journal of Marketing,* July 1988, pp. 2–22.

13. Andrew T. Chalk and John A. Steiber, "Managing the airlines in the 1990's", *Journal of Business Strategy,* Winter 1987, pp. 87–91.

14. James B. Wilcox, Roy D. Howell, Paul Kuzdrall and Robert Britney, "Price quantity discounts: some implications for buyers and sellers", *Journal of Marketing,* July 1987, pp. 60–61.

15. Robert G. Eccles, "Control with fairness in transfer pricing", *Harvard Business Review,* November–December 1983, pp. 149–161.

16. Michael H. Morris, "Separate prices as a marketing tool", *Industrial Marketing Management,* 16, 1987, pp. 79–86.

Chapter 20

1. Reprinted from Peter D. Bennett, ed., *Dictionary of Marketing Terms* (American Marketing Association, 1988), p. 54. Used by permission.

2. Bennett, p. 150. Reprinted by permission.

3. Kent B. Monroe, "Effect of product line pricing characteristics on product evaluation", *Journal of Consumer Research,* March 1987, p. 518.

4. Marylin Chase, "Burroughs-Wellcome cuts price of AZT under pressure from AIDS activists", *Wall Street Journal,* 19 September 1989, p. A3.

5. Amanda Richards, "P&G price cuts to hit own label", *Marketing,* 15 February 1996, p. 1; "P&G censures press over memo coverage", *Marketing Week,* 23 February 1996, pp. 8–9; Allan Mitchell, "Two sides of the same argument", *Marketing Week,* 16 February 1996, pp. 26–27; Stephen Hoch, Xavier Dreze and Mary Purk, "EDLP—hi-lo, and margin arithmetic", *Journal of Marketing,* 58 (4), 1994, pp. 16–27.

6. National Federation of Consumer Groups, *A Handbook of Consumer Law, Which?* Books (London, 1989).

7. Daewoo; *The Evening Telegraph*, 1 March 1996, p. 30.

8. "Frantic cheap phone buy-up reveals a lot about Japanese marketing", *Ann Arbor News* (Ann Arbor, Mich.), 14 February 1988, p. C9.

Chapter 21

1. Peter Doyle and John Saunders, "Market segmentation and positioning in specialised industrial markets", *Journal of Marketing*, Spring 1995, p. 25.

2. Erin Anderson and Anne T. Coughlan, "International market entry and expansion via independent or integrated channels of distribution", *Journal of Marketing*, January 1987, pp. 71–82.

3. Hiram C. Barksdale, Jr., Terry E. Powell and Ernestine Hargrove, "Complaint voicing by industrial buyers", *Industrial Marketing Management*, May 1984, pp. 93–99.

4. James D. Hlavacek and Tommy J. McCuiston, "Industrial distributors: when, who, and how?" *Harvard Business Review*, March–April 1983, p. 97.

5. Gary L. Frazier, Robert E. Spekman and Charles R. O'Neal, "Just-in-time exchange relationships in industrial markets", *Journal of Marketing*, October 1988, pp. 52–67.

6. Daniel H. McQuiston, "Novelty, complexity and importance as casual determinants of industrial buyer behavior", *Journal of Marketing*, April 1989, pp. 66–79.

7. Laboratory of Advertising Performance (LAP) report 8052.3, McGraw-Hill Research.

8. Steve Sulerno, "The close of the new salesmanship", *PSA*, April 1985, p. 63.

9. "Aircraft industry emerging from engineering dominance", *Marketing News*, 2 August 1985, p. 7.

10. Roger A. Kerin and William L. Cron, "Assessing trade show functions and performance: an exploratory study", *Journal of Marketing*, July 1987, pp. 87–94.

11. John C. Narver and Stanley F. Slater, "Creating a market-oriented business", *The Channel of Communications*, Summer 1989, pp. 5–8.

12. Robert Jacobson and David A. Aaker, "The strategic role of product quality", *Journal of Marketing*, October 1987, pp. 31–44.

13. Douglas G. Brooks, "Bidding for the sake of follow-on contracts", *Journal of Marketing*, January 1978, p. 35.

14. Don Cowell, *The Marketing of Services* (Oxford: Butterworth-Heinemann, 1994).

15. Christopher Lovelock, *Managing Services* (Englewood Cliffs, N.J.: Prentice-Hall, 1992).

16. G. Lynn Shostack, "Breaking free from product marketing", *Journal of Marketing*, April 1977, pp. 73–80.

17. Sak Onkvisit and John J. Shaw, "Service marketing: image, branding, and competition", *Business Horizons*, January–February 1989, p. 16.

18. Tom Peters, "More expensive, but worth it", *U.S. News & World Report*, 3 February 1986, p. 54.

19. Valarie A. Zeithaml, "Consumer perceptions of price, quality, and value: a means-end model and synthesis of evidence", *Journal of Marketing*, July 1988, pp. 2–22.

20. Leonard L. Berry, "8 keys to top service at financial institutions", *American Banker*, August 1987.

21. A. Parasuraman, Valarie A. Zeithaml and Leonard L. Berry, "SERVQUAL: a multiple item scale for measuring consumer perceptions of service quality", *Journal of Retailing*, Spring 1988, pp. 12–40.

22. Stephen W. Brown and Teresa A. Swartz, "A gap analysis of professional service quality", *Journal of Marketing*, April 1989, pp. 92–98.

23. Ibid.

24. G. Lynn Shostack, "Service positioning through structural change", *Journal of Marketing*, January 1987, pp. 34–43.

25. William R. George and Leonard L. Berry, "Guidelines for the advertising of services", *Business Horizons*, July–August 1981, pp. 52–56.

26. Sally Dibb and Lyndon Simkin. "The strength of branding and positioning in services", *International Journal of Service Industry Management*, 4 (1), 1993, pp. 25–33.

27. Sally Dibb and Lyndon Simkin, "Strategy and tactics: marketing leisure facilities", *The Service Industries Journal*, 13 (3), 1993, pp. 110–124; Dibb and Simkin, "The strength of branding and positioning in services", pp. 25–35.

28. James L. Heskett, "Lessons in the Service Sector", *Harvard Business Review*, March/April 1987, pp. 118–127.

29. George and Berry, pp. 55–70.

30. William R. George and J. Patrick Kelly. "The promotion and selling of services", *Business*, July–September 1983, pp. 14–20.

31. John M. Rathmell, *Marketing in the Services Sector* (Cambridge, Mass.: Winthrop, 1974), p. 100.

32. George and Kelly, pp. 14–20; George and Berry, pp. 55–70.

33. Doris C. Van Doren and Louise W. Smith, "Marketing in the restructured professional services field", *Journal of Services Marketing*, Summer 1987, pp. 69–70.

34. James B. Ayers, "Lessons from industry for healthcare", *Administrative Radiology*, July 1987, p. 53.

35. Joseph R. Guiltinan, "The price bundling of services: a normative framework", *Journal of Marketing*, April 1987, p. 74.

36. James H. Donnelly, Jr., "Marketing intermediaries in channels of distribution for services", *Journal of Marketing*, January, 1976, pp. 55–70.

37. Ibid.

38. Nigel A. L. Brooks, "Strategic issues for financial services marketing", *Journal of Services Marketing*, Summer 1987, p. 65.

39. Dibb and Simkin, "Strategy and tactics", pp. 110–124.

40. Adrian Payne, *The Essence of Services Marketing* (Hemel Hempstead: Prentice-Hall, 1993).

41. Warren J. Keegan, *Global Marketing Management*, 4th edn (Englewood Cliffs, N.J.: Prentice-Hall, 1989), pp. 378–382.

42. Colin Egan, De Montfort University.

43. Kamran Kashani, "Beware the pitfalls of global marketing", *Harvard Business Review*, September–October 1989, pp. 93–94.

44. Allecia Swasy, "After early stumbles, P&G is making inroads overseas", *Wall Street Journal*, 6 February 1989, p. B1.

45. Douglass G. Norvell and Robert Morey, "Ethnodomination in the channels of distribution of Third World nations", *Journal of the Academy of Marketing Science,* Summer 1983, pp. 204–235.
46. Erin Anderson and Anne T. Coughlan, "International market entry and expansion via independent or integrated channels of distribution", *Journal of Marketing,* January 1987, pp. 71–82.
47. David Jobber, *Principles and Practice of Marketing* (London: McGraw-Hill, 1995).
48. Sally Dibb, Lyndon Simkin and John Bradley, *The Marketing Planning Workbook* (London: Routledge, 1996).

Chapter 22

1. B. A. Weitz and R. Wensley, *Readings in Strategic Marketing* (Chicago: Dryden, 1988).
2. Sally Dibb, Lyndon Simkin and John Bradley, *The Marketing Planning Workbook* (London: Routledge, 1996).
3. Derek F. Abell and John S. Hammond, *Strategic Market Planning* (Englewood Cliffs, N.J.: Prentice-Hall, 1979), p. 10.
4. P. Rajan Varadarajan, Terry Clark and William Pride, "Determining your company's destiny", working paper, Texas A&M University, 1990.
5. J. Paul Peter and James H. Donnelly, Jr., *A Preface to Marketing Management,* 5th edn (Homewood, Ill.: Irwin, 1991), p. 9.
6. Adapted from Peter and Donnelly, *A Preface to Marketing Management,* pp. 8–12.
7. David A. Aaker, *Strategic Market Management,* 2nd edn (New York: Wiley, 1988), p. 35.
8. John Saunders, "Marketing and competitive success", Michael J. Baker, ed., in *The Marketing Book* (London: Heinemann, 1987), pp. 10–28.
9. Zachary Schiller, with Russell Mitchell, Wendy Zellner, Lois Therrien, Andrea Rothman and Walecia Konrad, "The great American health pitch", *Business Week,* 9 October 1989, p. 116.
10. Derek F. Abell, "Strategic windows", *Journal of Marketing,* July 1978, p. 21.
11. Abell and Hammond, p. 213.
12. Liam Fahey, William K. King and Vodake K. Naraganan, "Environmental scanning and forecasting in strategic planning—the state of the art", *Long Range Planning,* February 1981, p. 38.
13. David M. Georgaff and Robert G. Mundick, "Managers' guide to forecasting", *Harvard Business Review,* January–February 1986, p. 120.
14. "Energy efficient house design", *House Builder Magazine,* September 1986.
15. "The 'bumpy road to clean fuels'", *U.S. News & World Report,* 26 June 1989, pp. 10–11.
16. Ibid.
17. Philip Kotler, "Strategic planning and the marketing process", *Business,* May–June 1980, pp. 6–7.
18. Nigel Piercy, *Market-Led Strategic Change* (Oxford: Butterworth-Heinemann Ltd, 1992).

19. Joseph P. Guiltinan and Gordon W. Paul, *Marketing Management: Strategies and Programmes* (New York: McGraw-Hill, 1982), p. 31.
20. George S. Day, "Diagnosing the Product Portfolio", *Journal of Marketing,* April 1977, pp. 30–31.
21. Sally Dibb and Lyndon Simkin, *The Market Segmentation Workbook* (London: Routledge, 1996).
22. Robert Jacobson, "Distinguishing among competing theories of the market share effect", *Journal of Marketing,* October 1988, pp. 68–80.
23. George S. Day, *Analysis for Strategic Market Decisions* (St. Paul, Minn.: West, 1986), pp. 117–118.
24. Robert D. Buzzell and Bradley T. Gale, *The PIMS Principles: Linking Strategy to Performance* (New York: Free Press, 1987).
25. Day, *Analysis for Strategic Market Decisions,* p. 10.
26. David W. Cravens, "Strategic marketing's new challenge", *Business Horizons,* March–April 1983, p. 19.
27. Yoram Wind, Vijay Majahan and Donald J. Swire, "An empirical comparison of standardised portfolio models", *Journal of Marketing,* Spring 1983, pp. 89–99.
28. Roger A. Kerin, Vijay Majahan and P. Rajan Varadarajan, *Contemporary Perspectives on Strategic Marketing Planning* (Boston: Allyn & Bacon, 1990).
29. Ronald Grover, "When Columbia met Sony … a love story", *Business Week,* 9 October 1989, pp. 44–45.
30. David Woodruff, "Has Dow Chemical found the right formula?" *Business Week,* 7 August 1989, pp. 62, 64.
31. Mark Maremont, with Judith H. Dobrzynski, "Meet Asil Nadir, the billion-dollar fruit king", *Business Week,* 18 September 1989, p. 32.
32. Graham Hooley and John Saunders, *Competitive Positioning: The Key to Market Success* (London: Prentice-Hall, 1993).
33. Al Ries and Jack Trout, *Marketing Warfare* (New York: McGraw-Hill, 1986); John Saunders, "Marketing and competitive success", in Michael Baker, ed., *The Marketing Book* (London: Heinemann, 1987).
34. Peter Doyle, *Marketing Management and Strategy* (London: Prentice-Hall, 1994).

Chapter 23

1. Ronald D. Michman, "Linking futuristics with marketing planning, forecasting, and strategy", *Journal of Consumer Marketing,* Summer 1984, pp. 17, 23.
2. Sally Dibb, Lyndon Simkin and John Bradley, *The Marketing Planning Workbook* (London: Routledge, 1996).
3. Lyndon Simkin, "People and processes in marketing planning: the benefits of controlling implementation in marketing planning", *Journal of Marketing Management,* vol. 12, no. 5, 1996, pp. 375–390.
4. Vasudevan Ramanujam and N. Venkatraman, "Planning and performance: a new look at an old question", *Business Horizons,* May–June 1987, pp. 19–25.
5. David J. Luck, O. C. Ferrell and George Lucas, *Marketing Strategy and Plans,* 3rd edn (Englewood Cliffs, N.J.: Prentice-Hall, 1989), p. 328.
6. Malcolm McDonald, *Marketing Plans: How to Prepare Them, How to Use Them* (Oxford: Butterworth Heinemann, 1989).

7. Yoram Wind and Thomas S. Robertson, "Marketing strategy: new directions for theory and research", *Journal of Marketing,* Spring 1983, p. 12.

8. M. E. Porter, *Competitive Strategy: Techniques for Analysing Industries and Competitors* (New York: Free Press, 1980).

9. Lyndon Simkin, "Addressing organisational pre-requisites in marketing planning programmes", *Marketing Intelligence and Planning,* vol. 14, no. 5, 1996, pp. 39–46.

10. Sally Dibb and Lyndon Simkin, *The Marketing Casebook* (London: Routledge, 1994).

11. David Hurwood, Elliot S. Grossman and Earl Bailey, *Sales Forecasting* (New York: Conference Board, 1978), p. 2.

12. D. S. Tull and D. I. Hawkins, *Marketing Research* (New York: Macmillan, 1990).

13. Kenneth E. Marino, *Forecasting Sales and Planning Profits* (Chicago: Probus Publishing, 1986), p. 155.

14. Hurwood, Grossman and Bailey, p. 61.

15. G. L. Lilien and P. Kotler, *Marketing Decision-Making* (New York: Harper & Row, 1983).

16. P. Naert and P. Leeflang, *Building Implementable Marketing Models* (Leiden: Martinus Nijhoff, 1978).

17. *Accurate Business Forecasting* (Boston's *Harvard Business Review* Booklet, 1991).

18. William A. Band, "A marketing audit provides an opportunity for improvement", *Sales & Marketing Management in Canada,* March 1984, pp. 24–26.

19. Ely S. Lurin, "Audit determines the weak link in marketing chain", *Marketing News,* 12 September 1986, pp. 35–37.

20. Ibid.

Chapter 24

1. Rohit Despande and Frederick E. Webster, Jr., "Organisational culture and marketing: defining the research agenda", *Journal of Marketing,* January 1989, pp. 3–15.

2. Michael D. Hutt and Thomas W. Speh, "The marketing strategy centre: diagnosing the industrial marketer's interdisciplinary role", *Journal of Marketing,* Fall 1984, pp. 16–53.

3. John Bussy, "Manufacturers strive to slice time needed to develop products", *Wall Street Journal,* 23 February 1988, p. 18.

4. John C. Narver and Stanley F. Slater, "Creating a market orientated business", *The Channel of Communications,* Summer 1989, pp. 5–8.

5. Larry Reibstein, "IBM's plan to decentralise may set a trend—but imitation has a price", *Wall Street Journal,* 19 February 1988, p. 17.

6. Kenneth W. Thomas and Betty A. Velthouse, "Cognitive elements of empowerment: an 'interpretive' model of intrinsic task motivation", *Academy of Management Review,* October 1990, pp. 666–681.

7. O. C. Ferrell, George H. Lucas and David J. Luck, *Strategic Marketing Management: Text and Cases* (Cincinnati: South-Western, 1994), pp. 193–194.

8. Michael D. Hartline and O. C. Ferrell, "Service quality implementation: the effects of organizational socialization and managerial actions on the behaviors of customer-contact employees", *Marketing Science Institute Working Paper Series,* Report no. 93–122 (Cambridge, Mass.: Marketing Science Institute, 1993), pp. 36–48.

9. Ibid., pp. 36–40.

10. Dave Ulrich, "Strategic human resources planning: why and how?", *Human Resources Planning,* 10, no. 1, 1987, pp. 25–57.

11. Steven Lysonski, "A boundary theory investigation of the product manager's role", *Journal of Marketing,* Winter 1985, pp. 26–40.

12. Richard Gibson and Robert Johnson, "Why Pillsbury's chief from the 70's is again taking firm's helm", *Wall Street Journal,* 1 March 1988, p. 25.

13. Based on Orville C. Walker, Jr. and Robert W. Ruekert, "Marketing's role in the implementation of business strategies: a critical review and conceptual framework", *Journal of Marketing,* July 1987, pp. 15–33.

14. Robert Howard, "Values make the company: an interview with Robert Haas", *Harvard Business Review,* September–October 1990, pp. 132–144.

15. Ferrell, Lucas and Luck, *Strategic Marketing Management,* pp. 190–200.

16. Myron Glassman and Bruce McAfee, "Integrating the personnel and marketing functions: the challenge of the 1990s", *Business Horizons,* May–June 1992, pp. 52–59.

17. Ferrell, Lucas and Luck, *Strategic Marketing Management,* pp. 190–200.

18. Adapted from Nigel F. Piercy, *Market-Led Strategic Change* (Stoneham, Mass.: Butterworth-Heinemann, 1992), pp. 370–375.

19. Sybil F. Stershic, "Internal marketing campaign reinforces service goals", *Marketing News,* 31 July 1989, p. 11.

20. Adapted from Joseph R. Jablonski, *Implementing Total Quality Management* (Albuquerque, N. Mex.: Technical Management Consortium, 1990).

21. Hartline and Ferrell, "Service quality implementation", pp. 36–40.

22. Philip B. Crosby, *Quality is Free—The Art of Making Quality Certain* (New York: McGraw-Hill, 1979), pp. 9–10.

23. N. Piercy, *Market-Led Strategic Change* (Oxford: Butterworth-Heinemann, 1992).

24. Fred Steingraber, "Total quality management: a new look at a basic issue", *Vital Speeches of the Day,* May 1990, pp. 415–416.

25. Hartline and Ferrell, "Service Quality Implementation," pp. 36–48.

26. David C. Jones, "Motivation the catalyst in profit formula", *National Underwriter,* 13 July 1987, pp. 10, 13.

27. Jerry McAdams, "Rewarding sales and marketing performance", *Management Review,* April 1987, p. 36.

28. "Higher education in doughnuts", *Ann Arbor News,* 9 March 1988, p. B7.

29. Bernard J. Jaworski, "Toward a theory of marketing control: environmental context, control types, and consequences", *Journal of Marketing,* July 1988, pp. 23–39.

30. See Theo Haimann, William G. Scott and Patrick E. Connor, *Management,* 5th edn (Boston: Houghton Mifflin, 1985), pp. 478–492.

31. Jeffrey A. Tannenbaum, "Video games revive—and makers hope this time the fad will last", *Wall Street Journal,* 8 March 1988, p. 35.

32. "Carbonates and concentrates", *Marketing Intelligence,* January 1990, pp. 2.10–2.17.

33. Kevin Kelly and Neil Gross, "A weakened Komatsu tries to come back swinging", Business Week, 22 February 1988, p. 48.

Chapter 25

1. Andrew Stark, *Harvard Business Review,* May–June 1993, p. 38.

2. Jim Impoco, "Working for Mr. Clean Jeans", *U.S. News & World Report,* 2 August 1993, p. 50.

3. Donald P. Robin and R. Eric Reidenbach, "Social responsibility, ethics in marketing strategy, closing the gap between concept and application", *Journal of Marketing,* January 1987, pp. 44–58.

4. Vernon R. Loucks, Jr., "A CEO looks at ethics", *Business Horizons,* March–April 1987, p. 4.

5. Clare Sambrook, "Do free flights really build brands?" *Marketing,* 15 October 1992, p. 11.

6. O. C. Ferrell and John Fraedrich, *Business Ethics* (Boston: Houghton Mifflin, 1994), p. 52.

7. *CNN Worldday,* Cable News Network (TV), 5 January 1990.

8. F. Neil Brady, *Ethical Managing: Rules and Results* (New York: Macmillan, 1990), pp. 4–6.

9. Ibid.

10. John Fraedrich, Philosophy type interaction in the ethical decision making process of retailers", Ph.D. dissertation, Texas A&M University, 1988.

11. John Fraedrich and O. C. Ferrell, "Cognitive consistency of marketing managers in ethical situations," *Journal of the Academy of Marketing Science,* 1992, pp. 245–252.

12. William C. Frederick and James Weber, "The value of corporate managers and their critics: an empirical description and normative implications", in William C. Frederick and Lee E. Preston, eds., *Research in Corporate Social Performance and Social Responsibility* (Greenwich, Conn.: JAI Press, 1987), pp. 149–150.

13. Charles L. Tomkovick, "Time for a cease-fire with strategic marketing warfare", in Peter J. Gordon and Bert J. Kellerman, eds., *Advances in Marketing* (Southwest Marketing Association, 1990), p. 212.

14. Eric H. Beversluis, "Is there 'no such thing as business ethics'?", *Journal of Business Ethics,* no. 6, 1987, pp. 81–88.

15. Ferrell and Fraedrich, *Business Ethics,* pp. 113–114.

16. O. C. Ferrell, Larry G. Gresham and John Fraedrich, "A synthesis of ethical decision models for marketing", *Journal of Macromarketing,* Fall 1989, pp. 58–59.

17. Ferrell and Gresham, p. 92.

18. Damon Darlin, "Where trademarks are up for grabs", *Wall Street Journal,* 5 December 1989, p. B1.

19. "Persil Power trouble shooter nets Rockitt global group director role", *Marketing Week,* 17 May 1996, p. 10; Julian Lee and Claire Murphy, "P&G and Sears to fight Persil", *Marketing,* 2 May 1996, p. 1; Claire Cozens, "Unilever braced for price war with P&G", *Corporate Finance,* March 1996, pp. 9–11; Harriet Green, "Persil opts for change of direction", *Campaign,* 31 May 1996, p. 7.

20. Scott Hume, "Squawk over KFC ads—company challenges Y&R with new strategy", *Advertising Age,* 15 January 1990, p. 16.

21. Archie B. Carroll, *Business and Society: Ethics and Stakeholder Management* (Cincinnati: South-Western Publishing, 1989), pp. 228–230.

22. Lanny J. Ryan, Gay C. Dawson and Thomas Galek, "New distribution channels for microcomputer software", *Business,* October–December 1985, pp. 21–22.

23. Linda K. Trevino and Stuart Youngblood, "Bad apples in bad barrels: a causal analysis of ethical decision making behaviour", *Journal of Applied Psychology,* 75 (4), 1990, pp. 378–385.

24. Ibid.

25. Robin and Reidenbach, pp. 44–58.

26. Carroll, *Business and Society,* p. 45.

27. Margaret A. Stroup, Ralph L. Newbert and Jerry W. Anderson, Jr., "Doing good, doing better: two views of social responsibility", *Business Horizons,* March–April 1987, p. 23.

28. "McD ads draw protests from nutritional experts", *Nation's Restaurant News,* 22 June 1987, p. 26.

29. John Eisenhammer, "Where cars will go when they die", *Independent on Sunday,* 21 February 1993, pp. 24–25.

30. Sir Adrian Cadbury, "Ethical managers make their own rules", *Harvard Business Review,* September–October 1987, p. 33.

Appendix C

1. T. Jackson, "Writing the targeted résumé", *Business Week's Guide to Careers,* Spring 1983, pp. 26–27.

2. Burke Marketing Research for Robert Hall Inc. Reported in *USA Today,* 2 October 1987, p. B1.

Excel cars, 84
Excel Logistics, 450, 451
Executive Shuttle, 519
Explorer cars, 236, 307
Exxon, 443

Fab detergent, 776
FADS Homestyle, 405 (table)
Fage, 484 (table)
Fahey, Alison, 805n
Fahey, Liam, 805n, 807n
Fairly, Peter, 162n, 663n
Fairy Liquid detergent, 264, 559
Faith, Nicholas, 653n
"Falling and Laughing" (record), 458
Family Album, 426 (table)
Family Choice brand, 266, 389
Fannie May Candy Shops, 414
Fanta soft drink, 309 (table), 310
Fanuc, 90 (table)
Farmer, Richard N., 803n
Farquhar, Caroline, 259n, 317n, 367n, 585n
Farrell, Greg, 429n
Fasa Renault, 484 (table)
Fashion Extra, 426 (table)
Fast Track, 312
Faulds Advertising, 504 (table)
Favourite Chicken, 272
FDB, 401 (table), 484 (table)
FDS Market Research Group Ltd., 184 (table)
FedEx, 46, 383 (illus.), 553
Fernie, John, 368, 678n
Ferranti, 138
Ferrari, 513
Ferrell, O.C., 345 (table), 717 (illus.), 738, 796n, 799n, 800n, 807n, 808n, 809n
Ferrero, 484 (table)
Ferry, Jeff, 715n
Fiat, 84, 90 (table), 236, 307, 484 (table)
Fiat Auto Portuguesa, 484 (table)
Fiat SpA, 92 (table)
Fiesta cars, 22, 307, 756
Fill and Save card, 341
Film Finder, 529
Fima Indústria Alimentar, 484 (table)
Financial Times, 73 (table)
Fina Oil, 553
Findus Lean Cuisine, 268
Fine Art, 426 (table)
Fine Fare, 399, 563
Firstchoice, 336

First Direct, 274, 631
Firstdirect, 365
Fisher, Liz, 336n
Fitzgerald, Michael, 643n
Fitzwilton group, 388
Five Star Europe Service, 119
Flandin, M., 803n, 804n
Flash, 269
Fleenor, Patrick C., 804n
Flint, Jerry, 96n
Fluppy Dogs, 260
Foamex, 90 (table)
Forbuoys, 400 (table)
Ford, David, 133
Ford, Henry, 16, 783
Ford, Robert P., 805n
Ford España, 484 (table)
Ford Motor Company, 11, 22, 91, 108, 167, 235, 265, 271, 307, 308, 409, 439, 486, 494 (table), 568, 658, 712, 756
Ford Rent-A-Car, 786
Forest of Arden golf course, 240
Formule group, 607
Formule 1 hotels, 607
Forte bookshops, 390, 391
Forte hotels, 606
Fortnum & Mason, 416
Fortune, 175, 643
Forward, Jim, 802n
Forward Trust Group, 515
Foster, Thomas A., 803n
Foster, Wenche Marshall, 519
Fosters, 405 (table)
Foster's beer, 170, 762
Fox, Harriet, 436n
Fox, Harriot, 14n
Foxall, G., 101, 797n
Fraedrich, John, 809n
France Telecom, 92 (table)
Franchise Exhibition, 412–413
Francis, John, 519n
Frank, R., 799n
Fraser, Ian, 376n
Frazier, Gary L., 806n
Frederick, William C., 809n
Freeman, Laurie, 804n
Freemans, 405 (table), 410, 425, 426 (table), 427, 657
Freiday, Bob, 450n
Frey, Albert Wesley, 508 (table)
Friberg, Eric G., 796n
Friends of the Earth, 754
Friskies cat food, 117, 117 (illus.)
Frontera cars, 6
Frontierland theme park, 692
Frosties cereal, 11

Fruitinni, 275
Fruit of the Loom, 96, 782
Fruitopia soft drink, 310
Fry, Andy, 14n, 97n, 358n, 369n
Fuji, 706
Fujifilm, 456
Fujimoto, Takahiro, 800n
Fujitsu, 90 (table), 674
Fuld, Leonard M., 73 (table)
Fulop, Christina, 802n

GA, 529
Gable, Myron, 804n
Gabor, Andrea, 260n
Gain detergent, 251 (illus.)
Galaxy cars, 236
Gala Yuzawa ski resort, 76
Gale, Bradley T., 807n
Galek, Thomas, 801n, 809n
Galeries Lafayette, 403 (table)
Galileo reservation system, 787
Gallaher, 400 (table)
Gallaher Tobacco, 494 (table)
Gallup, 184 (table), 503
Galway Irish Crystal, 563
Garcia, Carlos E., 803n
Garden Court hotels, 606
Garfield, 272
Garfield, Bob, 479n, 489n
Garfunkels, 390
Garrison, John, 801n
Gaski, John F., 801n
Gassenheimer, Julie B., 801n
Gateshead's Metro Centre shopping mall, 396, 397 (illus.)
Gateway, 195, 424
Gatignon, Hubert, 797n
Gattorna, John, 803n
Gatwick Airport, 226, 226 (illus.), 311–312, 390
GEC, 138
GEC Large Machines, 245
Gelb, Betsy D., 324 (table)
General Electric, 63, 64, 90 (table), 660, 780, 782
General Electric Information Services, 436
General Foods, 410
General Motors, 6, 90 (table), 91, 235, 270, 566, 635, 655, 712, 786
Georgaff, David M., 807n
George, 266, 418
George, William R., 800n, 806n
Getty, John Paul, 783
GFK, 195
GfK Great Britain Ltd., 184 (table)

GGK, 653
Ghia Saetta cars, 308
Ghostbusters 2 (film), 669
GIB Group, 401 *(table)*, 403 *(table)*, 484 *(table)*
Gibson, Barry, 391
Gibson, Richard, 808*n*
Giglierano, Joe, 798*n*
Gilgrist, Andy, 278*n*
Gillette, 255, 290, 504 *(table)*
Givenchy perfume, 579, 580
Gizmoz watches, 736
Glaskowsky, J. Nicholas, 443 *(table)*
Glassman, Myron, 808*n*
Gleem toothpaste, 251 *(illus.)*
Glen Dimplex, 782
Glueck, William F., 718 *(illus.)*
GM/Vauxhall, 6
Goes, Frankie, 458
Gofton, Ken, 326*n*, 341*n*, 388*n*
Goldberg, Marvin E., 804*n*
The Golden Girls (television programme), 260
Golden Wonder, 727
Golf cars, 566, 568
Golliwog, 751
Gomes, Roger, 802*n*
Gordon, Geoffrey L., 800*n*
Gordon, Peter J., 809*n*
Gordons gin, 112
Gordon Simmons Research Group Ltd., 184 *(table)*
Gorham, 584
Gorn, Gerald J., 804*n*
Götberg, Göran, 88 *(illus.)*
Graham, John L., 796*n*, 798*n*
Graham, Judith, 803*n*
Granada Lodges, 606
Granada Scorpio cars, 568
Granary, 390
Grand Dick wine, 632–633
Grand Metropolitan, 20, 479, 782
Grand Slam tour, 512
Grant, R.M., 802*n*
Grattan, 410, 425, 426 *(table)*, 427
Gray, Robert, 585*n*
Great Universal Stores, 425, 426 *(table)*
Green, Gunella, 88 *(illus.)*
Green, Harriet, 489*n*, 653*n*, 809*n*
Green, P., 798*n*
Greenall's beer, 689
Greenbaum, Thomas L., 197*n*
Green Giant, 266

The Green Guide, 755
Greenley, Ken, 236
Greenpeace, 325, 754
Green Shield stamps, 521, 542
Greenway reservation system, 788
Gresham, Larry G., 802*n*, 809*n*
Grey, T., 64*n*, 704*n*
Grey Advertising, 504 *(table)*
Griffiths, John, 616*n*
Gross, Neil, 809*n*
Gross, Thomas, 797*n*
Grossman, Elliot S., 808*n*
Groupe Delhaize le Lion, 403 *(table)*
Grove, Andy, 152
Grover, Ronald, 261*n*, 292 *(table)*, 807*n*
Grunig, James, 803*n*
GS, 401 *(table)*
Gucci, 76, 564
Guelzo, Carl M., 802*n*, 803*n*
Guiltinan, Joseph P., 805*n*, 806*n*, 807*n*
Guinness beer, 241, 688, 689
Gumbel, Peter, 797*n*
Gummesson, E., 798*n*
GUS, 410, 426 *(table)*, 427, 550
Gustafsson, Karl Erik, 88 *(illus.)*
Guttman, Robert J., 429*n*
Gwin, Peter, 643*n*

Häagen-Dazs, 20, 390, 479–480
Haas, Robert W., 798*n*, 799*n*
Habitat, 29, 402
Haimann, Theo, 808*n*
Hair, Joseph F., Jr., 798*n*
Hakansson, H., 798*n*
Hakon, 401 *(table)*
Haley, Russell I., 799*n*
Halfords, 358, 369, 405 *(table)*
The Halifax, 512
Hall, Emma, 30*n*, 263*n*, 288*n*, 689*n*
Hall, Trish, 608*n*
Hallmark Cards, 360, 704, 706
Hamill, J., 90 *(table)*, 797*n*
Hamilton, Douglas, 568*n*
Hamilton International (UK) Ltd., 161*n*
Hammicks, 405 *(table)*
Hammond, John S., 662 *(illus.)*, 807*n*
Han, C. Min, 796*n*
Hanes, 410
Hanks, Tom, 294
Hanson, 352
Hanson, Gayle, 76*n*

Hanson Trust, 485
Happy Eater restaurants, 606
Happy Shopper brand, 266, 389
Hardy, Kenneth G., 801*n*
Hargrove, Ernestine, 806*n*
Harley-Davidson, 273
Harrigan, Kathryn Rudie, 797*n*
Harris, C., 132*n*
Harris, Jim, 642
Harrison, T., 799*n*
The Harris Research Centre, 184 *(table)*
Harrods, 390, 391, 580
Harrods Holdings, 400 *(table)*
Hart, Christopher W.L., 799*n*
Hart, Norman, 481, 796*n*, 798*n*
Hart, Sandra Hile, 804*n*
Hart, Susan, 240
Hartley, Robert F., 415 *(illus.)*, 419 *(illus.)*
Hartline, Michael D., 808*n*
Harvard Business Review, 667
Harvest, 176 *(table)*
Harvey, Michael, 800*n*
Harvey-Jones, John, 713
Hasell, Nick, 648*n*
Haslam, Colin, 358*n*
Hatfield, Stefano, 470*n*
Hawkins, Del, 798*n*, 799*n*
Hawkins, D.I., 808*n*
Hawkins, Steve L., 260*n*
Haynes, Walter, 308
Head & Shoulders shampoo, 251 *(illus.)*, 269
Healds Day & Nite, 420 *(table)*
Heathrow Airport, 311, 312, 390, 391, 450
Heckler, Susan E., 797*n*
Heineken, 44, 240, 258–259, 366, 471, 511, 688, 689, 782
Heineken Nederland, 484 *(table)*
Heinz, 14, 23, 208, 208 *(illus.)*, 271, 273 *(illus.)*, 276, 277, 282, 303, 388, 430, 485 *(table)*, 581–582
Heller, Robert, 434*n*
Hellmann's mayonnaise, 104, 106 *(illus.)*
Helm, Leslie, 554*n*, 796*n*
HelpAd, 763
Help the Aged, 763
Henkel, 247, 247 *(illus.)*
Henkel Austria, 484 *(table)*
Henkel Iberica, 484 *(table)*
Henkel Waschmittel GMbH, 484 *(table)*
Henley, James R., 96*n*

total quality management and, 719–721

Quality improvement teams, 720

Quality modifications, 300, 300–301

Quality of life, 41–45

Quantitative research, 166

Quantity discounts, 573

Questionnaires, 187, 187–189

Quotas, 79

Quota sampling, 181

Racial stereotyping, 212

Rack jobbers, 375

Railways, as transport mode, 441

Random factor analysis, 696

Random sampling, 180

Ratchet effect, 538

Raw materials, 245

Reaction strategy, 756, 756–757

Realised strategy, 713

Re-buy purchases, 145

Receiver, 459

Recessions, 48

Reciprocity, 140

Recognition test, 503

Recovery, 49

Recruitment, of sales personnel, 531–532

Reference groups, 123
in buying decision process, 123–124

Refusal to deal, 362

Regional issues, 498

Regulation, 38–41
deregulation and, 41, 42, 352
by local government, 39–40
by national government, 38–39
non-governmental, 40–41
pricing decisions and, 572

Reinforcement advertising, 489

Relationship(s), 625
building, in marketing channels, 359
organisational, ethical decision-making and, 743–744

Relationship management, 149

Relationship marketing, 148, 148–149, 149 *(illus.)*

Reliability, 177, 444

Reminder advertising, 489

Re-order point, 438

Replenishment costs, 437–438

Reports, of research findings, 190–191

Reputable partnerships, 515

Research, *see* Marketing research

Reseller markets, 137, 137–138

Resource allocation, 204

Restricted sales territories, 362

Restrictive Trade Practices Act (1976), 37

Résumés, 792–793, 794 *(illus.)*

Retailers, 137, 137–138, 392
wholesaler services to, 371–372

Retailing, 390–423, 392
categories of, 407
franchising and, 410–412
locations for, 392–396
nature of, 392, 393–394 *(table)*
non-store, 407–410, 408 *(table)*
store types in, 397–407
strategic issues in, 412–422
trends in, 418–422
wheel of, 418

Retail parks, 396, 397 *(illus.)*

Retail positioning, 415, 415–416

Retail technology, 419, 420–421 *(table),* 421

Return on investment, as pricing objective, 566

Revision, 789–791

Roles, 123
in buying decision process, 123

Routine response behaviour, 103

Run out, 305

Safety stock, 438

Sales, advertising to reduce fluctuations in, 490

Sales analysis, 727, 727–729

Sales branches, 381

Sales contests, 546, 546–547

Sales era, 16

Sales force, 529–538
advertising to increase effectiveness of, 488
compensation of, 533–535, 534 *(table)*
motivating, 535
objectives for, 530 *(illus.),* 530–531
performance control and evaluation, 537–538
recruitment and selection of, 531–532
sales territory management and, 535–537
size of, 531
training of, 532–533
types of salespeople and, 526–528

Sales force forecasting surveys, 695

Sales forecasts, 231–232, 694, 694–697

Sales measurements, 727, 727–729

Sales offices, 381

Sales potential, 691, 691, 693–694

Sales promotion, 471, 538, 538–547
consumer methods for, 540–545, 541 *(table)*
nature of, 538, 539 *(illus.)*
opportunities and limitations of, 539
trade methods for, 545–547

Sales territories, 535–537
restricted, 362

Salience, 107

Samples, 180

Sampling, 180, 180–181
as organisational buying method, 143

Scientific decision-making, 168, 168–169, 169 *(table)*

Scrambled merchandising, 417, 417–418

Screening ideas, 292

Search qualities, of services, 315

Search stage of consumer buying decision process, 105–107

Seasonal analysis, 696

Seasonal discounts, 573

Secondary data, 173
collection of, 174–175, 176 *(table),* 177

Secondary use packaging, 279

Security, 444

Segmentation, *see* Market segmentation; Segmentation variables (bases)

Segmentation variables (bases), 206, 206–223
for consumer markets, 207 *(table),* 207–217
for organisational markets, 218–222, 219 *(table)*
product related behavioural characteristics and, 217–218
single versus multiple, 222 *(illus.),* 222–223, 223 *(illus.)*

Selection, of sales personnel, 531–532

Selective distortion, 115

Selective distribution, 354

Selective exposure, 114, 114–115

Selective retention, 115

Self-concept, 116